# HARLEM RENAISSANCE

*A Gale Critical Companion*

# HARLEM RENAISSANCE

*A Gale Critical Companion*

**Volume 1: Topics**

*Foreword by* Trudier Harris-Lopez, Ph.D.
*University of North Carolina at Chapel Hill*

Janet Witalec, Project Editor

GALE®

THOMSON

GALE

Detroit • New York • San Diego • San Francisco • Cleveland • New Haven, Conn. • Waterville, Maine • London • Munich

# Harlem Renaissance, Vol. 1

**Project Editor**
Janet Witalec

**Editorial**
Tom Burns, Kathy D. Darrow, Lisa Gellert, Madeline S. Harris, Edna M. Hedblad, Michelle Kazensky, Jelena Krstović, Allison Marion, Ellen McGeagh, Jessica Menzo, Thomas J. Schoenberg, Lawrence J. Trudeau, Russel Whitaker

**Research**
Nicodemus Ford, Sarah Genik, Tamara C. Nott, Tracie A. Richardson

**Permissions**
Kim Davis, Susan Rudolph

**Imaging and Multimedia**
Leitha Etheridge-Sims, Lezlie Light, Christine O'Bryan, Kelly A. Quin

**Product Design**
Pamela Galbreath, Michael Logusz

**Composition and Electronic Capture**
Carolyn Roney

**Manufacturing**
Stacy L. Melson

**LIBRARY OF CONGRESS CATALOGING-IN-PUBLICATION DATA**

The Harlem Renaissance : a Gale critical companion / Janet Witalec, project editor.
        p. cm. -- (Gale critical companion collection)
Includes bibliographical references and index.
ISBN 0-7876-6618-1 (set hardcover) -- ISBN 0-7876-6619-X (v. 1) --
ISBN 0-7876-6620-3 (v. 2) -- ISBN 0-7876-6621-1 (v. 3)
    1.    American literature--African American authors--History and criticism--Handbooks, manuals, etc.   2. American literature--New York (State)--New York--History and criticism--Handbooks, manuals, etc. 3. American literature--20th century--History and criticism--Handbooks, manuals, etc. 4. Harlem (New York, N.Y.)--Intellectual life--20th century--Handbooks, manuals, etc. 5. African Americans--Intellectual life--Handbooks, manuals, etc.   6. African Americans in literature--Handbooks, manuals, etc.    7. Harlem Renaissance--Handbooks, manuals, etc. I.   Witalec, Janet, 1965- II. Series.
PS153.N5 H245 2003
810.9'89607307471--dc21
                                                    2002010076

Printed in the United States of America
10 9 8 7 6 5 4 3 2 1

# VOLUME 2

# VOLUME 3

In 1950, Alain Locke offered several reflective comments on the significance of the Harlem Renaissance. He considered it a movement that never surpassed the "gawky" and "pimply" stage of adolescence, one that had essentially failed in its attempt to achieve universal, objective approaches in its creations. Overall, he concluded that perhaps he and others had "expected too much of the Negro Renaissance" (*Phylon* 11 : 391). Locke, who had been one of the key supporters of and inspirational figures in the lives of several of the writers who came to prominence during that period, was perhaps more critical of what the movement had achieved than his contemporaries during the Renaissance or in the 1950s. He was certainly more disparaging than literary evaluations have proven to be in the past five decades. The period of the 1920s has become one of the most written about in African American literary history and one in which numerous scholars specialize. And not undeservedly so. By most standards of measurement, especially ones that might take into consideration a before and after effect, the Harlem Renaissance, or the New Negro Movement as some prefer to call it, is arguably *the* defining moment in African American literary creativity.

That moment occurred because of the confluence of historical and social forces. The devastation the boll weevil wrought on southern crops and the ensuing economic chaos led many Blacks to migrate from the South to northern cities as a part of what became known as the Great Migration, a mass movement that noted artist Jacob Lawrence captures vividly and colorfully in his Migration Series. Economic opportunity the North represented was appealing not only because of the decline in the southern farm economy but because the mythical presentations by relatives of Black people who had migrated north made it equally glamorous. The legendary promise of the North and particularly New York City, as Rudolph Fisher depicts in "The City of Refuge" (1925) and about which Langston Hughes rhapsodizes in several poems as well as his autobiographies, drew Black people from the southern United States, the Caribbean, and Africa. Harlem thus more than tripled its Black population between 1900 and 1930. Word of mouth was powerful, but determined efforts to gather a critical mass of young Black creative artists were also factors in bringing about the literary production known as the Harlem Renaissance. Charles Spurgeon Johnson, who became editor of *Opportunity*, the official organ of the National Urban League, directed his secretary, Ethel Nance, to write to aspiring young writers and artists and encourage their migration to New York. While many responded eagerly, it was only with repeated coaxing that Aaron Douglas, who became the foremost artist of the period, was persuaded to leave his position as an art teacher in Kansas and head to

New York. Of the writers who are now prominently identified with the movement, Hughes came from Kansas and Ohio, Zora Neale Hurston from Florida, Wallace Thurman from Idaho, Claude McKay from Jamaica, Eric Walrond from British Guiana, Jean Toomer from Washington, D.C., Dorothy West from Boston, and Countee Cullen from Kentucky (although he always claimed New York as his point of origin).

From its beginnings, therefore, the Harlem Renaissance was spawned by a mixture of happenstance and deliberate planning. This was the first time in African American literary history that editors and writers saw the possibilities of collaborative creative efforts—or at least creative efforts expended in the midst of others who were also about literary production. Such concerted effort distinguished the 1920s from what had gone before, distinguished the New Negro with a self-directed cultural purpose from the Old Negro who was often driven by circumstance. Awareness of themselves as artists in a variety of media was one of the distinguishing characteristics of the editors, writers, visual artists, and musicians who became the most well-known figures of the Harlem Renaissance and about whom Hughes wrote in his first autobiography, *The Big Sea* (1940), and whom Thurman fictionalized in *Infants of the Spring* (1932).

The movement thus marks the period in African American literary development during which Black writers could *claim* their creativity in ways that were not previously available to them. The tradition of slave—or *freedom*—narratives was the most productive group effort prior to the Harlem Renaissance (the grouping, however, was not something the writers themselves orchestrated); the productivity was frequently cast in a white envelope/Black message mold. Abolitionists and other persons who identified potential writers as well as those who published their works often had their own agendas for what Black narrators could or should put forth in their own so-called individualized works. Black writers did not control the means of production of their words or the editorial prerogatives that sometimes shaped their final form. Black literary dependency on white cultural philanthropy was the order of the day. While it would be rash to suggest that such limitations completely disappeared during the 1920s, it is nonetheless reasonable to argue that persons of African descent had a stronger say in what they published, where, and under what circumstances. Of course we are familiar with the stories of how Carl Van Vechten, guru and midwife extraordinaire of the Renaissance, read, revised, and suggested further revisions to *The Weary Blues* (1926), Hughes's first volume of poetry. And the tales of Mrs. Charlotte Osgood Mason's attempts to interfere in the creativity of Hughes and Hurston are equally well known. More to the point, however, are the instances in which African American writers were mostly in charge of what they produced and the manner of its production.

Two significant outlets for "in charge" production were *Opportunity* magazine and its counterpart, the *Crisis,* the official publication of the National Association for the Advancement of Colored People (NAACP). The latter was developed by the eminent W. E. B. Du Bois, who served as general editor; Jessie Fauset served as literary editor, a position from which she would encourage many of the younger writers. For these two publications, Black writers did not go, hat in hand, to white editors requesting publication of their work. As African Americans, both Charles S. Johnson and Du Bois were acutely aware of the need for as much African American control of publishing outlets as possible. This position, combined with their general notions of mission and service, led both editors to sponsor contests to encourage Black writing even as they regularly published what came to them voluntarily. By establishing the outlets for publication, determining the criteria, and passing judgment on the works, these editors and their staffs moved dramatically away from the censorship that had defined cross-racial publication by writers such as Paul Laurence Dunbar and Charles W. Chesnutt prior to this period. Again, an assessment of the Harlem Renaissance in this area is not to suggest that all was sweetness and light, for both Johnson and Du Bois had rather specific notions of what they believed should be published. The point is that African Americans, whatever their criteria, were making the decisions that they had not previously made except for newspapers, white-owned/Black-edited small magazines (*Voice of the Negro*), and denominational outlets (the *Christian Recorder,* the *A.M.E. Church Review*).

The claiming of creativity was even history-making in the anthologies that appeared during this period. Two of the most important were *The Book of American Negro Poetry,* edited and published by James Weldon Johnson in 1922, and *The New Negro,* edited and published by Alain Locke in 1925 (expanded from a special issue of *Survey Graphic*). Black writers had appeared in yearbooks such as William Stanley Braithwaite's *Anthology of Magazine Verse* (beginning in 1913), but Johnson's and Locke's were volumes devoted almost exclusively to African American writers. Johnson was careful to include as many up-and-coming poets as he could locate, and he expanded his original inclusions when the volume was revised and republished in 1931. Locke's volume, of course, served as the defining statement for the Renaissance, just as Hughes's "The Negro Artist and the Racial Mountain" (1926) served as the defining manifesto for younger Black writers. Locke wanted to assure his readers that the Old Negro was dead, that this was an age of unparalleled creativity by African American writers. While it has become clear that Locke, even in his seeming expansiveness, gave preferential treatment to certain kinds of writers and subjects, it is nonetheless more significant that he was doing the choosing, that an African American scholar, researcher, and writer was in charge of shaping a volume that showcased the richness of African American cultural creativity. The bountifulness of that creativity could not be constrained by the mind that offered it for public consumption. Thus the legacy of the Renaissance was measurable from even that single volume of claimed creativity.

An even more proper appreciation of the claiming of African American creativity during the Harlem Renaissance might begin in the middle of the 1920s, with the publication of the little magazine called *Fire!!* (1926). The work of Hughes, Hurston, Thurman, Richard Bruce Nugent, Gwendolyn Bennett, and a few others, it represented the efforts of younger African American writers to claim their creativity from their elders, all members of Du Bois's "talented tenth" of well-educated Blacks with leadership potential (and often "high yaller"), as well as from potential white exploiters. *Fire!!* was in bas relief against the backdrop of prevailing elder wisdom represented by the likes of Du Bois, James Weldon Johnson, and Braithwaite, all of whom espoused best-foot-forward, universalized portrayals of Black experience that could serve to bridge the gaps between Blacks and whites. *Fire!!* represented the first time a group of young African American writers consciously sought to define themselves against a larger tradition, which means that it was the first time that there were measurable *layerings* of African American literary creativity. When Nugent and Thurman flipped a coin to see who would write a story on prostitution and who on drugs, they were claiming their creativity as young writers breaking away from their elders: "If black people are pleased, it doesn't matter."

The fact that *Fire!!* exists would be reason enough to label the 1920s a noteworthy period of African American creativity. Here were several young Black writers bent upon cultural produc-

tion at a time when it was not yet historically established that they indeed had a culture. That independence of spirit is no less remarkable than that exhibited by Frederick Douglass and others who escaped from slavery in the South and went on to produce narratives about their experiences. The difference is one of orchestration, not one of kind. Whereas Douglass was manipulated—though his genius nonetheless showed through that manipulation—these young writers made their own decisions about who and what to publish. They may have failed to sustain the magazine, but what they sought to accomplish is the guiding motivation for scholarly focus on the Harlem Renaissance: the documentation of African American creative genius as widespread, diverse, and ever evolving.

A careful look at Johnson's *Book of Negro Poetry* will reveal that several of the figures Johnson singled out for greatness did not make it. Of those who did, Countee Cullen, Langston Hughes, and Claude McKay have garnered critical attention worthy of their talent, and that attention continues. In 2002, when the Academy of American Poets conducted a survey to determine who was the most well-known American poet, Langston Hughes won by a landslide. It would have been difficult in the 1920s, however, for literary observers to conclude that Hughes's reputation would exceed Cullen's, for Cullen was the darling of critics and critical readers. His imitation of Keatsian poetic forms undoubtedly informed those judgments, whereas Hughes's focus on the Black masses was a bit more to the left than some elitists in the "talented tenth" tradition might have wished. Ensuing decades, especially the Black-centered 1960s, coupled with Hughes's own longevity and interaction with later writers, probably influenced ultimate scholarly and popular preference for Hughes.

Hughes and McKay, whose strong emotional sentiments overshadowed his Shakespearean sonnets, make clear the importance of audience as an ongoing, shaping force in Harlem Renaissance successes. The increase in Black audiences during the 1920s, which found their parallels in the 1960s, spurred acceptance by some of sentiments that were slightly more militant than many of Cullen's sugar-coated creations. Publication in outlets aimed primarily at Black people during the 1920s was a marked contrast to the outlets in which Dunbar and Chesnutt had published their early works, such as the *Atlantic Monthly*. Talented poets such as Hughes and McKay, along with a host of other writers during the 1920s, thus facilitated the institutionalization of African American literary arts within Black communities.

The anthologies, volumes of poetry, novels, dramas, and newspaper columns that the Harlem Renaissance has yielded make the claim more than anything else for the period having been substantive and of greater import than Locke allowed. We can certainly measure individual accomplishment, as with Hughes's focus on the blues as a source for literary creativity in *The Weary Blues,* or Jean Toomer's experimentation in *Cane* (1923), or Hurston's concern with colorphobia in *Color Struck* (1926). Of greater import is the stage-setting or path-breaking that these accomplishments pointed toward. *Fire!!* easily leads to *Black World/Negro Digest* and on to *Callaloo. Cane* anticipates works such as Ntozake Shange's *Sassafras, Cypress and Indigo* (1982), Alice Walker's *The Color Purple* (1982), and practically all of Toni Morrison's novels. Hurston is godmother to a host of African American women writers, including Walker, Tina McElroy Ansa, and Gloria Naylor. Thus institution-building and midwifing a literary tradition were functions Harlem Renaissance writers served for ensuing generations as assuredly as Alain Locke and Jessie Fauset midwifed them.

Godmothering, however, is not always altruistic, as was the case with Mrs. Mason's impact on Hurston as well as on Hughes. The issue of patronage for African American writers remains a central concern in the twenty-first century. What does a writer owe to the providers of fellowships and leisure time to write? At what point does a writer who receives such aid give up his or her autonomy to his or her work? The issue is relevant not only to isolated writers trying to find the funds for a semester's leave from teaching, but also to the choreographer or the dramatist or the musician whose creative space can be provided by funders who may or may not be sympathetic to the total direction of the project. The Harlem Renaissance gave us models for thinking through these crucial issues and for weighing the shackles as well as the opportunities of patronage across racial lines.

That continues to be a source of exploration in contemporary scholars' understanding of the factors that influenced how successful some of the most important writers of the Harlem Renaissance were —or were not—in claiming their creativity.

In the early years of the twenty-first century, the Harlem Renaissance is a scholarly industry. It became institutionalized with the advent of Black studies courses and programs in American academies in the 1960s and 1970s. No scholar of African American literary studies could be taken seriously without in-depth knowledge of the Harlem Renaissance. No doctoral candidate studying for written and oral examinations could expect to be taken seriously without detailed knowledge of the Harlem Renaissance. In contrast to the 1960s, when a single survey course might have sufficed to introduce students to African American literature, today there are two and three courses designed to provide that coverage. Specialized courses focusing exclusively on the Harlem Renaissance are offered routinely. Equally as significant, graduate students in African American literary studies remain engrossed enough by the Renaissance to select writers and topics relevant to it for the subjects of their masters theses and doctoral dissertations. Their interest, in turn, has been guided in large part by the numerous scholarly studies of the Harlem Renaissance that have been published in the past thirty years. In striking contrast to Alain Locke's assessment, the Harlem Renaissance is alive and well in every college and university in the United States where students explore the multi-faceted meanings and ramifications of the literature, its producers, and its production. These three volumes are welcome additions to those ongoing dialogues and will undoubtedly provide invaluable insights that will continue to illustrate the undying significance of the Harlem Renaissance.

*—Trudier Harris-Lopez, Ph.D.*
*J. Carlyle Sitterson Professor of English*
*University of North Carolina at Chapel Hill*

## The Gale Critical Companion Collection

In response to a growing demand for relevant criticism and interpretation of perennial topics and important literary movements throughout history, the Gale Critical Companion Collection (GCCC) was designed to meet the research needs of upper high school and undergraduate students. Each edition of GCCC focuses on a different literary movement or topic of broad interest to students of literature, history, multicultural studies, humanities, foreign language studies, and other subject areas. Topics covered are based on feedback from a standing advisory board consisting of reference librarians and subject specialists from public, academic, and school library systems.

The GCCC is designed to complement Gale's existing Literary Criticism Series (LCS) , which includes such award-winning and distinguished titles as *Nineteenth-Century Literature Criticism* (NCLC), *Twentieth-Century Literary Criticism* (TCLC), and *Contemporary Literary Criticism* (CLC). Like the LCS titles, the GCCC editions provide selected reprinted essays that offer an inclusive range of critical and scholarly response to authors and topics widely studied in high school and undergraduate classes; however, the GCCC also includes primary source documents, chronologies, sidebars, supplemental photographs, and other material not included in the LCS products. The graphic and supplemental material is designed to extend the usefulness of the critical essays and provide students with historical and cultural context on a topic or author's work. GCCC titles will benefit larger institutions with ongoing subscriptions to Gale's LCS products as well as smaller libraries and school systems with less extensive reference collections. Each edition of the GCCC is created as a stand- alone set providing a wealth of information on the topic or movement. Importantly, the overlap between the GCCC and LCS titles is 15% or less, ensuring that LCS subscribers will not duplicate resources in their collection.

Editions within the GCCC are either single-volume or multi-volume sets, depending on the nature and scope of the topic being covered. Topic entries and author entries are treated separately, with entries on related topics appearing first, followed by author entries in an A-Z arrangement. Each volume is approximately 500 pages in length and includes approximately 50 images and side-bar graphics. These sidebars include summaries of important historical events, newspaper clippings, brief biographies of important non-literary figures, complete poems or passages of fiction written by the author, descriptions of events in the related arts (music, visual arts, and dance), and so on.

The reprinted essays in each GCCC edition explicate the major themes and literary techniques of the authors and literary works. It is important to note that approximately 85% of the essays reprinted in GCCC editions are full-text, meaning that they are reprinted in their entirety, including footnotes and lists of abbreviations. Essays are selected based on their coverage of the seminal works and themes of an author, and based on the importance of those essays to an appreciation of the author's contribution to the movement and to literature in general. Gale's editors select those essays of most value to upper high school and undergraduate students, avoiding narrow and highly pedantic interpretations of individual works or of an author's canon.

### Scope of Harlem Renaissance

*Harlem Renaissance,* the inaugural set in the Gale Critical Companion Collection, consists of three volumes. Each volume includes a detailed table of contents, a foreword on the Harlem Renaissance written by noted scholar Trudier Harris-Lopez, and a descriptive chronology of key events of the movement. The main body of volume 1 consists of entries on five topics relevant to the Harlem Renaissance, including 1) Overviews and General Studies; 2) Social, Economic, and Political Factors that Influenced the Harlem Renaissance; 3) Publishing and Periodicals during the Harlem Renaissance; 4) Performing Arts during the Harlem Renaissance; and 5) Visual Arts during the Harlem Renaissance. Volumes 2 and 3 include entries on thirty-three authors and literary figures associated with the movement, including such notables as Countee Cullen, W. E. B. Du Bois, Jessie Redmon Fauset, Langston Hughes, Zora Neale Hurston, Claude McKay, and Jean Toomer, as well as entries on individuals who have garnered less attention, but whose contributions to the Harlem Renaissance are noteworthy, such as Alice Dunbar-Nelson, Angelina Weld Grimké, Georgia Douglas Johnson, Richard Bruce Nugent, and Willis Richardson.

### Organization of the Harlem Renaissance

A *Harlem Renaissance* topic entry consists of the following elements:

- The **Introduction** defines the subject of the entry and provides social and historical information important to understanding the criticism.
- The list of **Representative Works** identifies writings and works by authors and figures associated with the subject. The list is divided into alphabetical sections by name; works listed under each name appear in chronological order. The genre and publication date of each work is given. Unless otherwise indicated, dramas are dated by first performance, not first publication.

- Entries generally begin with a section of **Primary Sources,** which includes essays, speeches, social history, newspaper accounts and other materials that were produced during the time of the Harlem Renaissance.
- Reprinted **Criticism** in topic entries is arranged thematically. Topic entries commonly begin with general surveys of the subject or essays providing historical or background information, followed by essays that develop particular aspects of the topic. For example, the Publishing and Periodicals topic entry in volume 1 of *Harlem Renaissance* begins with a section providing an overview of the topic. This is followed by three other sections: African American Writers and Mainstream Publishers; Anthologies: *The New Negro* and Others; and African American Periodicals and the Harlem Renaissance. Each section has a separate title heading and is identified with a page number in the table of contents. The critic's name and the date of composition or publication of the critical work are given at the beginning of each piece of criticism. Unsigned criticism is preceded by the title of the source in which it appeared. Footnotes are reprinted at the end of each essay or excerpt. In the case of excerpted criticism, only those footnotes that pertain to the excerpted texts are included.
- A complete **Bibliographical Citation** of the original essay or book precedes each piece of criticism.
- Critical essays are prefaced by brief **Annotations** explicating each piece. Unless the descriptor "excerpt" is used in the annotation, the essay is being reprinted in its entirety.
- An annotated bibliography of **Further Reading** appears at the end of each entry and suggests resources for additional study. In some cases, significant essays for which the editors could not obtain reprint rights are included here.

A *Harlem Renaissance* author entry consists of the following elements:

- The **Author Heading** cites the name under which the author most commonly wrote, followed by birth and death dates. Also located here are any name variations under which an author wrote. If the author wrote consistently under a pseudonym, the pseudonym will be listed in the author heading and the author's actual name given in parentheses on the first line of the biographical and critical information. Uncertain birth or death dates are indicated by question marks.

- A **Portrait of the Author** is included when available.

- The **Introduction** contains background information that introduces the reader to the author that is the subject of the entry.

- The list of **Principal Works** is ordered chronologically by date of first publication and lists the most important works by the author. The genre and publication date of each work is given. Unless otherwise indicated, dramas are dated by first performance, not first publication.

- Author entries are arranged into three sections: **Primary Sources, General Commentary,** and **Title Commentary.** The Primary Sources section includes letters, poems, short stories, journal entries, and essays written by the featured author. General Commentary includes overviews of the author's career and general studies; Title Commentary includes in-depth analyses of seminal works by the author. Within the Title Commentary section, the reprinted criticism is further organized by title, then by date of publication. The critic's name and the date of composition or publication of the critical work are given at the beginning of each piece of criticism. Unsigned criticism is preceded by the title of the source in which it appeared. All titles by the author featured in the text are printed in boldface type. However, not all boldfaced titles are included in the author and subject indexes; only substantial discussions of works are indexed. Footnotes are reprinted at the end of each essay or excerpt. In the case of excerpted criticism, only those footnotes that pertain to the excerpted texts are included.

- A complete **Bibliographical Citation** of the original essay or book precedes each piece of criticism.

- Critical essays are prefaced by brief **Annotations** explicating each piece. Unless the descriptor "excerpt" is used in the annotation, the essay is being reprinted in its entirety.

- An annotated bibliography of **Further Reading** appears at the end of each entry and suggests resources for additional study. In some cases, significant essays for which the editors could not obtain reprint rights are included here. A list of **Other Sources from Gale** follows the further reading section and provides references to other biographical and critical sources on the author in series published by Gale.

## *Indexes*

The **Author Index** lists all of the authors featured in the *Harlem Renaissance* set, with references to the main author entries in volumes 2 and 3 as well as commentary on the featured author in other author entries and in the topic volume. Page references to substantial discussions of the authors appear in boldface. The Author Index also includes birth and death dates and cross references between pseudonyms and actual names, and cross references to other Gale series in which the authors have appeared. A complete list of these sources is found facing the first page of the Author Index.

The **Title Index** alphabetically lists the titles of works written by the authors featured in volumes 2 and 3 and provides page numbers or page ranges where commentary on these titles can be found. Page references to substantial discussions of the titles appear in boldface. English translations of foreign titles and variations of titles are cross-referenced to the title under which a work was originally published. Titles of novels, dramas, nonfiction books, and poetry, short story, or essay collections are printed in italics, while individual poems, short stories, and essays are printed in body type within quotation marks.

The **Subject Index** includes the authors and titles that appear in the Author Index and the Title Index as well as the names of other authors and figures that are discussed in the set. The Subject Index also lists hundreds of literary terms and topics covered in the criticism. The index provides page numbers or page ranges where subjects are discussed and is fully cross referenced.

## *Citing* Harlem Renaissance

When writing papers, students who quote directly from the *Harlem Renaissance* set may use the following general format to footnote reprinted criticism. The first example pertains to material drawn from periodicals, the second to material reprinted from books.

Alvarez, Joseph A., "The Lonesome Boy Theme as Emblem for Arna Bontemps's Children's Literature," *African American Review* 32, no. 1 (spring 1998): 23-31; reprinted in *Harlem Renaissance: A Gale Critical Companion,* vol. 2, ed. Janet Witalec (Farmington Hills, Mich: The Gale Group, 2003), 72-8.

Helbling, Mark, introduction to *The Harlem Renaissance: The One and the Many* (Westport, Conn.: Greenwood Press, 1999), 1-18; reprinted in *Harlem Renaissance: A Gale Critical Companion,* vol. 1, ed. Janet Witalec (Farmington Hills, Mich: The Gale Group, 2003), 27-38.

## Harlem Renaissance *Advisory Board*

The members of the *Harlem Renaissance* Advisory Board—reference librarians and subject specialists from public, academic, and school library systems—offered a variety of informed perspectives on both the presentation and content of the *Harlem Renaissance* set. Advisory board members assessed and defined such quality issues as the relevance, currency, and usefulness of the author coverage, critical content, and topics included in our product; evaluated the layout, presentation, and general quality of our product; provided feedback on the criteria used for selecting authors and topics covered in our product; identified any gaps in our coverage of authors or topics, recommending authors or topics for inclusion; and analyzed the appropriateness of our content and presentation for various user audiences, such as high school students, undergraduates, graduate students, librarians, and educators. We wish to thank the advisors for their advice during the development of *Harlem Renaissance*.

### *Suggestions are Welcome*

Readers who wish to suggest new features, topics, or authors to appear in future volumes of the Gale Critical Companion Collection, or who have other suggestions or comments are cordially invited to call, write, or fax the Project Editor:

Project Editor, Gale Critical Companion
    Collection
The Gale Group
27500 Drake Road
Farmington Hills, MI 48331-3535
1-800-347-4253 (GALE)
Fax: 248-699-8054

The editors wish to thank the copyright holders of the criticism included in this volume and the permissions managers of many book and magazine publishing companies for assisting us in securing reproduction rights. We are also grateful to the staffs of the Detroit Public Library, the Library of Congress, the University of Detroit Mercy Library, Wayne State University Purdy/Kresge Library Complex, and the University of Michigan Libraries for making their resources available to us. Following is a list of the copyright holders who have granted us permission to reproduce material in this edition of *Harlem Renaissance*. Every effort has been made to trace copyright, but if omissions have been made, please let us know.

### *Copyrighted material in* Harlem Renaissance *was reproduced from the following periodicals:*

*African American Review,* v. 26, Fall, 1992; v. 27, Fall, 1993; v. 31, Autumn, 1997. All reproduced by permission of the *African American Review,* formerly the *Black American Literature Forum.*/v. 32, Spring, 1998 for "The Lonesome Boy Theme as Emblem for Arna Bontemps' Children's Literature," by Joseph A. Alvarez. Copyright © 1998 by the author. Reproduced by permission of the publisher and the author./v. 32, Winter, 1998 for "Countee Cullen's *Medea,*" by Lillian Corti. Reproduced by permission of the author./v. 32, Winter,

1998 for "The World Would Do Better to Ask Why Is Frimbo Sherlock Holmes?: Investigating Liminality in Rudolph Fisher's *The Conjure-Man Dies,*" by Adrienne Johnson Gosselin. Reproduced by permission of the author./v. 33, Fall, 1999 for "And Yet They Paused and A Bill to be Passed: Newly Recovered Lynching Dramas by Georgia Douglas Johnson," by Judith Stephens. Reproduced by permission of the author.—*Afro-Americans in New York Life and History,* v. 10, 1986. Reproduced by permission.—*American Drama,* v. 5, 1996. Reproduced by permission.—*American Literary History,* v. 3, 1991 for "Community and Cultural Crisis: The 'Transfiguring Imagination' of Alain Locke," by Everett Akam. Reproduced by permission of Oxford University Press and the author.—*American Literature,* v. 43, March, 1971; v. 44, 1972; v. 47, 1975; v. 51, March, 1979. Copyright © 1971, 1972, 1975, 1979 by Duke University Press, Durham, NC. All reproduced by permission.—*American Quarterly,* v. 17, Summer, 1965; v. 32, Winter, 1980; v. 48, March, 1996; v. 50, September, 1998; v. 51, 1999. © The Johns Hopkins University Press. All reproduced by permission.—*American Studies,* v. 18, Spring, 1977 for "Combatting Racism with Art: Charles S. Johnson and the Harlem Renaissance," by Ralph L. Pearson. Copyright Mid-America American Studies Association Reproduced by permission.—*ANQ: A Quarterly Journal of Short Ar-*

*ticles, Notes, and Reviews,* v. 8, Summer, 1995. Copyright © 1985 Helen Dwight Reid Educational Foundation. Reproduced with permission of the Helen Dwight Reid Educational Foundation, published by Heldref Publications, 1319 18th Street, NW, Washington, DC 20036-1802.—*Arizona Quarterly,* v. 39, Fall, 1983 for "Jean Toomer's *Cane*: The Search for Identity through Form," by Alan Golding. Copyright © 1983 by the Regents of the University of Arizona. Reproduced by permission of the publisher and the author.—*Black American Literature Forum,* v. 12, Autumn, 1978; v. 14, 1980; v. 19, 1985; v. 21, Fall, 1987; v. 21, Spring-Summer, 1987. All reproduced by permission of the *Black American Literature Forum,* currently the *African American Review.*—*Black World,* v. 20, November, 1970 for "Alain Locke," by Richard A. Long. Reproduced by permission of the author./v. 20, November, 1970 for "Voice for the Jazz Age, Great Migration, or Black Bourgeoisie," by Faith Berry. Reproduced by permission of the Gail Berry for the author./v. 21, April, 1972 for "Alain Locke & Black Drama," by Samuel A. Hay. Reproduced by permission of the author./v. 25, February, 1976 for "Renaissance 'Renegade'? Wallace Thurman," by Huel D. Perkins. Reproduced by permission of the author./v. 25, February, 1976 for "The Genesis of Locke's *The New Negro,*" by Richard A. Long. Reproduced by permission of the author./v. 25, February, 1976 for "Toward a Sociological Analysis of the Renaissance: Why Harlem?" by Jabulani Kamau Makalani. Reproduced by permission of the author.—*Callaloo,* v. 9, 1986; v. 21, Fall, 1998. Both reproduced by permission.—*CLA Journal,* v. 15, March, 1972; v. 16, March, 1973; v. 16, June, 1973; v. 17, September, 1973; v. 18, 1974; v. 19, 1976; v. 26, December, 1982; v. 29, September, 1985; v. 32, December, 1988; v. 32, March, 1989; v. 32, June, 1989; v. 34, March, 1991; v. 35, June, 1992; v. 37, March, 1994; v. 38, September, 1994; v. 39, December, 1995; v. 41, June, 1998; v. 42 September 1998; 42, June 1999. Copyright, 1972, 1973, 1974, 1976, 1982, 1985, 1988, 1989, 1991, 1992, 1994, 1995, 1998, 1999 by The College Language Association. All reproduced by permission.—*The Crisis,* v. 76, March, 1969; v. 78, July, 1971; v. 90, June/July, 1983. All reproduced by permission.—*Federal Writers' Project,* August 23, 1938; December 1, 1938; January 17, 1939; January 19, 1939; April 19, 1939. All courtesy of The Library of Congress. All reproduced by permission.—*Georgia Historical Quarterly,* v. 80, Winter, 1996. Courtesy of the Georgia Historical Society. Reproduced by permis-

sion.—*Georgia Review,* v. 5, Fall, 1951, renewed 1979 by the *Georgia Review.* Reproduced by permission.—*International Review of African American Art,* v. 4, 1995. Reproduced by permission.—*Journal of Black Studies,* v. 12, September, 1981. Copyright © 1981 by Sage Publications, Inc. Reproduced by permissions of Sage Publications, Inc.—*Journal of Negro History,* v. 52, 1967; v. 57, 1972. Both reproduced by permission.—*Langston Hughes Review,* v. 1, Fall, 1982. Reproduced by permission.—*Legacy: A Journal of American Women Writers,* v. 18, 2001. Reproduced by permission.—*Markham Review,* v. 5, Summer, 1976. Reproduced by permission.—*The Massachusetts Review,* v. 24, Autumn, 1983; v. 28, Winter, 1987. © 1983, 1987. Both reproduced from The Massachusetts Review, Inc. by permission.—*The Modern Schoolmen,* v. 74, May, 1997. Reproduced by permission.—*MELUS,* v. 23, 1998. Copyright, MELUS: The Society for the Study of Multi-Ethnic Literature of the United States, 1998. Reproduced by permission.—*The Midwest Quarterly,* v. 24, Winter, 1983. Reproduced by permission.—*Narrative,* v. 7, May, 1999. Reproduced by permission.—*Negro American Literature Forum,* v. 14, January, 1965; v. 6, Summer, 1972. Both reproduced by permission of the *African American Review.*/v. 5, Spring, 1971 for "The Vagabond Motif in the Writings of Claude McKay," by Mary Conroy. Copyright © 1971 by the author. Reproduced by permission of the publisher and the author./v. 10, 1976 for "Carl Van Vechten and the Harlem Renaissance" by Mark Helbling. Reproduced by permission of the author.—*New England Quarterly,* v. 74, March, 2001 for "Encouraging Verse: William S. Braithwaite and the Poetics of Race," by Lisa Szefel. Copyright held by *The New England Quarterly.* Reproduced by permission of the publisher and the author.—*New Orleans Review,* v. 15, 1989. Copyright © 1989 by Loyola University. Reproduced by permission.—*New York Herald Tribune Books,* January 10, 1926. Reproduced by permission.—*The New York Times,* February 29, 1932. Copyright 1932 by The New York Times Company. Reproduced by permission.—*The New York Times Book Review,* August 21, 1927; March 4, 1945; Copyright © 1945, renewed 1972 by The New York Times Company; September 20, 1992 Copyright © 1992 by The New York Times Company; January 3, 1999. Copyright © 1999 by The New York Times Company. All reproduced by permission.—*The New Yorker,* v. 74, September 27, 1998 for "Beyond the Color Line," by Henry Louis Gates, Jr. © 1998 by the author. All rights reserved. Reproduced by permission of the author.—*Novel,* v. 30, Winter, 1997. Copyright NOVEL Corp. © 1997 Reproduced with permission.—*Pacific Coast Philology,* v. 15, December, 1980. Reproduced by permission.—*Phylon: The Atlanta University of Race and Culture,* v.6, 1945; v. 9, 1948; v. 11, 1950; v. 17, 1956; v. 18, 1957; v. 21, 1960;v. 25, 1964; v. 32, 1971; v. 39, 1978; v. 40, 1979; v. 57, 1996. Copyright 1945, 1948, 1950, 1956, 1957, 1960, 1964, 1971, 1978, 1979, 1996 by Atlanta University. All reproduced by permission.—*PMLA,* v. 105, January, 1990. Copyright © 1990 by the Modern Language Association of America. Reproduced by permission of the Modern Language Association of America.—*Poetry,* v. 24, February, 1930. Reproduced by permission.—*South Carolina Review,* v. 2, May, 1970. Reproduced by permission.—*Studies in American Fiction,* v. 19, Spring, 1991. Copyright © 1991 Northeastern University. Reproduced by permission.—*Studies in Black Literature,* v. 3, Summer, 1972; v. 5, Winter, 1974. Copyright 1972, 1974 by the editor. Both reproduced by permission.—*Studies in Short Fiction,* v. 2, 1965. Reproduced by permission.—*Studies in the Literary Imagination,* v. 7, Fall, 1974. Reproduced by permission.—*Susquehanna University Studies,* v. 7, June, 1963. Reproduced by permission.—*Theatre Annual,* 1985. Reproduced by permission.—*Virginia Cavalcade,* v. 27, 1978. Reproduced by permission.—*Western American Literature,* v. 6, Spring, 1971. Copyright 1971, by the Western American Literature Association. Reproduced by permission.—*Western Journal of Black Studies,* v. 22, 1998. Reproduced by permission.

## Copyrighted material in Harlem Renaissance *was reproduced from the following books:*

Anderson, Paul A. From "'My Lord, What a Morning': The 'Sorrow Songs' in Harlem Renaissance Thought," in *Symbolic Loss: The Ambiguity of Mourning and Memory at Century's End.* Edited by Peter Homans. University Press of Virginia, 2000. Copyright © 2000 by University Press of Virginia. All rights reserved. Reproduced by permission.—Baker, Houston A., Jr. From *Modernism and the Harlem Renaissance.* University of Chicago Press, 1987. Copyright © 1987 by University of Chicago Press. All rights reserved. Reproduced by permission.—Balshaw, Maria. From *Looking for Harlem: Urban Aesthetics in African American Literature.* Pluto Press, 2000. Copyright © 2000 by Pluto Press. All rights reserved. Reproduced by permission.—Barfoot, C. C., et al. From "The New Negro in Context," in *Wallace Thurman's Harlem Renaissance.* Editions Rodopi B.V., 1994. Copyright © 1994 by Editions Rodopi B.V. All rights reserved. Reproduced by permission.—Barksdale, Richard K. From "Langston Hughes and the Blues He Couldn't Lose," in *The Harlem Renaissance: Revaluations.* Edited by Amritjit Singh, William S. Shiver, and Stanley Brodwin. Garland Publishing, Inc., 1989. © 1989 Amritjit Singh, William S. Shiver, and Stanley Brodwin. All rights reserved. Reproduced by permission of the editors.—Bearden, Romare and Harry Henderson. From *A History of African-American Artists From 1792 to the Present.* Pantheon Books, 1993. Copyright © 1993 by Pantheon Books. All rights reserved. Reproduced by permission.—Bone, Robert. From *The Negro Novel in America.* Yale University Press, 1958. Copyright © 1958 by Yale University Press. Revised edition © 1965 by Yale University. Copyright © renewed 1985 by Robert Bone. Reproduced by permission of the author.—Bontemps, Arna. From *Personals.* P. Breman, 1973. Reproduced by permission of Harold Ober Associates, Inc. for the Literary Estate of Arna Bontemps.—Booker, Peter. From "Modernism Deferred: Langston Hughes, Harlem and Jazz Montage," in *Locations of Liberty Modernism: Region and Nation in British and American Modernist Poetry.* Edited by Alex Davis and Lee M. Jenkins. Cambridge University Press, 2000. Copyright © 2000 by Cambridge University Press. All rights reserved. Reprinted with permission of Cambridge University Press and the author.—Brown-Guillory, Elizabeth. From "Disrupted Motherlines: Mothers and Daughters in a Genderized, Sexualized, and Racialized World," in *Women of Color: Mother-Daughter Relationships in 20th-Century Literature.* Edited by Elizabeth Brown-Guillory. University of Texas Press, 1996. Copyright © 1996 by University of Texas Press. All rights reserved. Reproduced by permission.—Byrd, Rudolph P. From "Jean Toomer and the Writers of the Harlem Renaissance: Was He There with Them?" in *The Harlem Renaissance: Revaluations.* Edited by Amritjit Singh, William S. Shiver, and Stanley Brodwin. Garland Publishing, Inc., 1989. © 1989 Amritjit Singh, William S. Shiver, and Stanley Brodwin. All rights reserved. Reproduced by permission of the editors.—Champion, Laurie. From "Dorothy West (1907-1998)," in *American Women Writers, 1900-1945: A Bio- Bibliographical Critical Sourcebook.* Edited by Laurie Champion. Greenwood Press, 2000. Copyright © 2000 by Greenwood Press, Greenwood Publishing Group, Inc., Westport, CT. All

ACKNOWLEDGMENTS

rights reserved. Reproduced by permission of Greenwood Publishing Group, Inc., Westport, CT.—Clum, John M. From *Ridgely Torrence.* Twayne Publishers, 1972. Copyright © 1972 by Twayne Publishers. All rights reserved. The Gale Group.—Coleman, Leon. From *Carl Van Vechten and the Harlem Renaissance: A Critical Assessment.* Garland Publishing, Inc., 1989. Copyright © 1989 by Garland Publishing, Inc. All rights reserved. Reproduced by permission.—Collier, Eugenia. From "Message to the Generations: The Mythic Hero in Sterling Brown's Poetry," in *The Furious Flowering of African American Poetry.* Edited by Joanne V. Gabbin. University of Virginia, 1999. Copyright © 1999 by University of Virginia. All rights reserved. Reproduced by permission.—Cripps, Thomas. From "Introduction: A Monument to Lost Innocence," in *The Green Pastures.* Edited by Thomas Cripps. University of Wisconsin Press, 1979. Copyright © 1979 The Board of Regents of the University of Wisconsin System. All rights reserved. Reproduced by permission.—Cullen, Countee. From *Caroling Dusk: An Anthology of Verse by Negro Poets.* Edited by Countee Cullen. Harper & Row, 1974. Copyright © 1974 by Harper & Row. All rights reserved. Reproduced by permission of Thompson and Thompson for the Estate of Countee Cullen.—Cullen, Countee. From *Copper Sun.* Harper, 1927. Copyright 1927 by Harper. Renewed 1954 by Ida M. Cullen. All rights reserved. Reproduced by permission of Thompson and Thompson for the Estate of Countee Cullen.—Davis, Thadious M. From "Nella Larsen's Harlem Aesthetic," in *The Harlem Renaissance: Revaluations.* Edited by Amritjit Singh, William S. Shiver, and Stanley Brodwin. Garland Publishing, Inc., 1989. © 1989 Amritjit Singh, William S. Shiver, and Stanley Brodwin. All rights reserved. Reproduced by permission of the editors.—Douglas, Aaron with L. M. Collins. From "Aaron Douglas Chats about the Harlem Renaissance," in *The Portable Harlem Renaissance Reader.* Edited by David Levering Lewis. Viking, 1994. Copyright © 1994 by Viking. All rights reserved. Reproduced by permission.—Doyle, Don H. From the introduction to *Mamba's Daughters: A Novel of Charleston,* by DuBose Heyward. University of South Carolina Press, 1995. Copyright © 1995 by University of South Carolina Press. All rights reserved. Reproduced by permission.—Driskell, David. *From Harlem Renaissance: Art of Black America.* Harry N. Abrams, Inc., 1987. Copyright © 1987 by Harry N. Abrams, Inc. All rights reserved. Reproduced by permission.—Du Bois, W. E. B. "Editing The Crisis," in *Black Titan: W. E. B. Du Bois: An Anthology by the Editors of "Freedomways."* Edited by John Henrik Clarke, et al. Beacon Press, 1970. Copyright © 1970 by Beacon Press. All rights reserved. Reproduced by permission.—Durham, Frank. From *DuBose Heyward: The Man Who Wrote Porgy.* University of South Carolina Press, 1954. Copyright © 1954 by University of South Carolina Press. Renewed 1982 by Kathleen C. Durham. All rights reserved. Reproduced by permission.—Early, Gerald. From *My Soul's High Song.* Doubleday, 1991. Copyright © 1991 by Doubleday. All rights reserved. Reproduced by permission.—Ellington, Duke. From *Music is My Mistress.* Doubleday, 1973. Copyright © 1973 by Doubleday. All rights reserved. Reproduced by permission.—Fabre, Michel. From *From Harlem to Paris: Black American Writers in France, 1840-1980.* University of Illinois Press, 1991. Copyright 1991 by Board of Trustees. Used with permission of the University of Illinois Press.—Flamming, Douglas. From "A Westerner in Search of 'Negroness': Region and Race in the Writing of Arna Bontemps," in *Over the Edge: Remapping the American West.* Edited by Valerie J. Matsumoto and Blake Allmendinger. University of California Press, 1999. Copyright © 1999 by University of California Press. All rights reserved. Reproduced by permission.—Flynn, Joyce. From the introduction to *Frye Street & Environs: The Collected Works of Marita Bonner.* Edited by Joyce Flynn and Joyce Occomy Stricklin. Beacon Press, 1987. Copyright © 1987 by Beacon Press. All rights reserved. Reproduced by permission.—Garber, Eric. From "Richard Bruce Nugent," in *Dictionary of Literary Biography, Volume 51: Afro-American Writers from the Harlem Renaissance to 1940.* Edited by Trudier Harris and Thadious M. Davis. Gale Research, Inc., 1987. Copyright © 1987 by Gale Research, Inc. All rights reserved.—Govan, Sandra Y. From "A Blend of Voices: Composite Narrative Strategies in Biographical Reconstruction," in *Recovered Writers/Recovered Texts: Race, Class, and Gender in Black Women's Literature.* Edited by Dolan Hubbard. University of Tennessee Press, 1997. Copyright © 1997 by University of Tennessee Press. All rights reserved. Reproduced by permission.—Gray, Christine Rauchfuss. From *Willis Richardson: Forgotten Pioneer of African-American Drama.* Greenwood Press, 1999. Copyright © 1999 by Greenwood Press. All rights reserved. Reproduced by permission of Greenwood Publishing Group, Inc., Westport, CT.—Greene, J. Lee. From "Anne Spencer," in *Dictionary of Literary Biography, Volume 51: Afro-American Writers from the Harlem Renaissance to 1940.* Edited by Trudier Harris and Thadious M. Davis. Gale Research, Inc., 1987. Copyright © 1987 by Gale Research, Inc. All rights reserved.—Greene, J. Lee. From *Time's Unfading Garden: Anne Spencer's Life and Poetry.* Louisiana State University, 1977. Copyright © 1977 by Louisiana State University. All rights reserved. Reproduced by permission of the author.—Hayden, Robert. From the preface to *The New Negro.* Edited by Alain Locke. Atheneum, 1968. Copyright © 1968 by Atheneum. All rights reserved. Reproduced by permission.—Helbling, Mark. From the introduction to *The Harlem Renaissance: The One and the Many.* Greenwood Press, 1999. Copyright © 1999 by Greenwood Press, Inc., Westport, CT. All rights reserved. Reproduced by permission of Greenwood Publishing Group, Inc., Westport, CT.—Hemenway, Robert E. From "Zora Neale Hurston and the Eatonville Anthropology," in *Harlem Renaissance Remembered.* Edited by Arna Bontemps. Dodd, Mead, 1972. Copyright © 1972 by Dodd, Mead. All rights reserved. Reproduced by permission.—Henderson, Mae Gwendolyn. From "Portrait of Wallace Thurman," in *The Harlem Renaissance Remembered.* Edited by Arna Bontemps. Dodd, Mead & Company, 1972. Copyright © 1972 by Dodd, Mead & Company. All rights reserved. Reproduced by permission.—Herron, Carolivia. From the introduction to *Selected Works of Angelina Weld Grimké.* Edited by Carolivia Herron. Oxford University Press, 1991. Copyright © 1991 by Oxford University Press. All rights reserved. Reproduced by permission.—Hill, Robert A. From the introduction to *Marcus Garvey: Life and Lessons.* University of California Press, 1987. Copyright © 1987 by University of California Press. All rights reserved. Reproduced by permission.—Howard, Elizabeth F. From "Arna Bontemps," in *The Scribner Writers Series.* Gale Group, 2002. Copyright © 2002 by Gale Group. All rights reserved.—Huggins, Nathan Irvin. From "Alain Locke: Aesthetic Value-System and Afro-American Art," in *Revelation: American History, American Myths.* Edited by Brenda Smith Huggins. Oxford University Press, 1995. Copyright © 1995 by Oxford University Press. All rights reserved. Reproduced by permission.—Hughes, Langston. From "The Negro and the Racial Mountain," in *African American Literary Criticism.* Edited by Hazel Arnett Ervin. Twayne Publishers, 1999. Copyright © 1999 by Twayne Publishers. All rights reserved. Reproduced by permission of Harold Ober Associates for the Estate of Langston Hughes.—Hull, Gloria T. From "Black Women Poets from Wheatley to Walker," in *Sturdy Black Bridges: Visions of Black Women in Literature.* Edited by Roseann P. Bell, Bettye J. Parker, and Beverly Guy-Sheftall. Anchor Books, 1979. Copyright © 1979 by Anchor Books. All rights reserved. Reproduced by permission of the author.—Hull, Gloria T. From the introduction to *Give Us Each Day: The Diary of Alice Dunbar-Nelson.* W.W. Norton, 1984. Copyright © 1984 by W.W. Norton. All rights reserved. Reproduced by permission of the author.—Hurston, Zora Neale. From "What White Publishers Won't Print," in *I Love Myself When I Am Laughing … And Then again When I Am Looking Mean and Impressive: A Zora Neale Hurston Reader.* Edited by Alice Walker. The Feminist Press, 1979. Copyright © 1979 by The Feminist Press. All rights reserved. Reproduced by permission of the Victoria Sanders Literary Agency for the Estate of Zora Neale Hurston.—Hutchinson, George. *The Harlem Renaissance in Black and White.* The Belknap Press of Harvard University Press, 1995. Copyright © 1995 by The Belknap Press of Harvard University Press. Reprinted by permission of the publisher.—Hutson, Jean Blackwell. From *Black Bibliophiles and Collectors: Preservers of Black History.* Howard University Press, 1990. Copyright © 1990 by Howard University Press. All rights reserved. Reproduced by permission.—Ikonne, Chidi. From *From Du Bois to Van Vechten: The Early New Negro Literature, 1903-1926.* Greenwood Press, 1981. Copyright © 1981 by Greenwood Press. All rights reserved. Reproduced by permission of Greenwood Publishing Group, Inc., Westport, CT.—Jimoh, A. Yemisi. From "Dorothy West (1907-1998)," in *Contemporary African American Novelists: A Bio-Bibliographical Critical Sourcebook.* Edited by Emmanuel S. Nelson. Greenwood Press, 1999. Copyright © 1999 by Greenwood Press. All rights reserved. Reproduced by permission of Greenwood Publishing Group, Inc., Westport, CT.—Johnson, Abby Arthur and Ronald Maberry Johnson. From *Propaganda and Aesthetics: The Literary Politics of Afro-American Magazines in the Twentieth Century.* University of Massachusetts Press, 1979. Copyright © 1979 by University of Massachusetts Press. All rights reserved. Reproduced by permission.—Johnson, Charles S. From "The Negro Renaissance and Its Significance," in *The Portable Harlem Renaissance Reader.* Edited by David Levering Lewis. Viking, 1994. Copyright © 1994 by Viking. All rights reserved. Reproduced by permission.—Johnson, Eloise. From *Rediscovering the Harlem Renaissance: The Politics of Exclusion.* Garland Publishing, Inc., 1997. Copyright © 1997 by Garland Publishing, Inc. All rights reserved. Reproduced by permission.—Kellner, Bruce. From "Carl Van Vechten's Black Renaissance," in *The Harlem Renaissance: Revalua-*

ACKNOWLEDGMENTS

*tions.* Edited by Amritjit Singh, William S. Shiver, and Stanley Brodwin. Garland Publishing, Inc., 1989. © 1989 Amritjit Singh, William S. Shiver, and Stanley Brodwin. All rights reserved. Reproduced by permission of the editors.—Kostelanetz, Richard. From *Politics in the African American Novel: James Weldon Johnson, W. E. B. Du Bois, Richard Wright, and Ralph Ellison.* Greenwood Press, 1991. Copyright © 1991 by Greenwood Press. All rights reserved. Reproduced by permission of Greenwood Publishing Group, Inc., Westport, CT.—Lang, Robert. From "'The Birth of a Nation': History, Ideology, Narrative Form" in *The Birth of a Nation: D.W. Griffith, Director.* Edited by Robert Lang. Rutgers University Press, 1994. Copyright © 1994 by Rutgers University Press. All rights reserved. Reproduced by permission.—LeSeur, Geta. From "Claude McKay's Marxism," in *The Harlem Renaissance: Revaluations.* Edited by Amritjit Singh, William S. Shiver, and Stanley Brodwin. Garland Publishing, Inc., 1989. © 1989 Amritjit Singh, William S. Shiver, and Stanley Brodwin. All rights reserved. Reproduced by permission of the editors.—Lewis, David Levering. From the introduction to *The Portable Harlem Renaissance Reader.* Edited by David Levering Lewis. Viking, 1994. Copyright © 1994 by Viking. All rights reserved. Reproduced by permission of Brandt & Hochman for the editor.—Locke, Alain. From "Art or Propaganda," in *The Critical Temper of Alain Locke: A Selection of His Essays on Art and Culture.* Edited by Jeffrey C. Stewart. Garland Publishing, Inc., 1983. Copyright © 1983 by Garland Publishing, Inc. All rights reserved. Reproduced by permission.—Locke, Alain. From "The Negro Takes His Place in American Art," in *The Portable Harlem Renaissance Reader.* Edited by David Levering Lewis. Viking, 1994. Copyright © 1994 by Viking. All rights reserved. Publisher, 1994. © info from verso. Reproduced by permission of the author.—Lutz, Tom. From "Claude McKay: Music, Sexuality, and Literary Cosmopolitanism," in *Black Orpheus: Music in African American Fiction from the Harlem Renaissance to Toni Morrison.* Edited by Saadi A. Simawe. Garland Publishing, Inc., 2000. Copyright © 2000 by Garland Publishing, Inc. All rights reserved. Reproduced by permission.—Martin, Tony. From *Literary Garveyism: Garvey, Black Arts, and the Harlem Renaissance.* Majority Press, 1983. Copyright © 1983 by Majority Press. All rights reserved. Reproduced by permission.—McDonald, C. Ann. From "James Weldon Johnson," in *American Women Writers, 1900-1945: A Bio-Bibliographical Critical Sourcebook.* Edited by Laurie Champion. Greenwood Press, 2000. Copyright ©

2000. Reproduced by permission of Greenwood Publishing Group, Inc., Westport, CT.—McKay, Nellie. From "Jean Toomer in his Time: An Introduction," in *Jean Toomer: A Critical Evaluation.* Edited by Therman B. O'Daniel. Howard University Press, 1988. Copyright © 1988 by Howard University Press. All rights reserved. Reproduced by permission.—McLaren, Joseph M. From "Early Recognitions: Duke Ellington and Langston Hughes in New York, 1920-1930," in *The Harlem Renaissance: Revaluations.* Edited by Amritjit Singh, William S. Shiver, and Stanley Brodwin. Garland Publishing, Inc., 1989. © 1989 Amritjit Singh, William S. Shiver, and Stanley Brodwin. All rights reserved. Reproduced by permission of the editors.—Meche, Jude R. From "Marita Bonner," in *Dictionary of Literary Biography, Volume 228: Twentieth-Century American Dramatists.* Edited by Christopher J. Wheatley. The Gale Group, 2000. Copyright © 2000 by The Gale Group. Reproduced by permission.—Miller, Nina. From "'Our Younger Negro (Women) Artists': Gwendolyn Bennett and Helene Johnson," in *Making Love Modern: The Intimate Public Worlds of New York's Literary Women.* Oxford University Press, 1998. Copyright © 1998 by Oxford University Press. All rights reserved. Reproduced by permission.—Miller, R. Baxter. From "'Some Mark to Make': the Lyrical Imagination of Langston Hughes," in *Critical Essays on Langston Hughes.* G.K. Hall, 1986. Copyright © 1986 by G.K. Hall. All rights reserved. The Gale Group.—Mitchell, Verner D. From the introduction to *This Waiting for Love: Helene Johnson, Poet of the Harlem Renaissance.* University of Massachusetts Press, 2000. Copyright © 2000 by University of Massachusetts Press. All rights reserved. Reproduced by permission.—Parascandola, Louis J. From *An Eric Walrond Reader.* Wayne State University Press, 1998. Copyright © 1998 by Wayne State University Press. All rights reserved. Reproduced by permission.—Peplow, Michael W. From *George S. Schuyler.* Twayne Publishers, 1980. Copyright © 1980 by Twayne Publishers. The Gale Group.—Perry, Patsy B. From "Willis Richardson," in *Dictionary of Literary Biography, Volume 51: Afro-Ameican Writers from the Harlem Renaissance to 1940.* Edited by Trudier Harris and Thadious M. Davis. The Gale Group, 1987. Copyright © 1987 Gale Research Company.—Rampersad, Arnold. From "Langston Hughes and Approaches to Modernism in the Harlem Renaissance," in *The Harlem Renaissance: Revaluations.* Edited by Amritjit Singh, William S. Shiver, and Stanley Brodwin. Garland Publishing, Inc., 1989. © 1989 Amritjit Singh, William S. Shiver, and Stanley

Brodwin. All rights reserved. Reproduced by permission of the editors.—Robinson, William H. From *Black New England Letters: The Uses of Writings in Black New England.* Trustees of the Public Library of the City of Boston, 1977. Copyright © 1977 by Trustees of the Public Library of the City of Boston. All rights reserved. Reproduced by permission.—Sanders, Mark A. From "The Ballad, the Hero, and the Ride: A Reading of Sterling Brown's 'The Last Ride of Wild Bill,'" in *The Furious Flowering of African American Poetry.* Edited by Joanne V. Gabbin. University of Virginia, 1999. Copyright © 1999 by University of Virginia. All rights reserved. Reproduced by permission.—Sinnette, Elinor Des Verney. From *Arthur Alfonso Schomburg: Black Bibliophile & Collector.* The New York Public Library & Wayne State University Press, 1989. Copyright © 1989 by The New York Public Library & Wayne State University Press. All rights reserved. Reproduced by permission of the author.—Slavick, William H. From "Going to School to DuBose Heyward," in *The Harlem Renaissance Re-Examined.* Edited by Victor A. Kramer. AMS, 1987. Copyright © 1987 by AMS. All rights reserved. Reproduced by permission.—Slavick, William H. From *DuBose Heyward.* Twayne Publishers, 1981. Copyright © 1981 by Twayne Publishers. The Gale Group.—Stewart, Jeffrey C. From *Rhapsodies in Black: Art of the Harlem Renaissance.* University of California Press, 1997. Copyright © 1997 by University of California Press. All rights reserved. Reproduced by permission.—Stoff, Michael B. From "Claude McKay and the Cult of Primitivism," in *The Harlem Renaissance Remembered.* Edited by Arna Bontemps. Dodd, Mead & Company, 1972. Copyright © 1972 by Dodd, Mead & Company. All rights reserved. Reproduced by permission.—Sundquist, Eric J. From the introduction to *The Oxford W. E. B. Du Bois Reader.* Oxford University Press, 1996. Copyright © 1996 by Oxford University Press. All rights reserved. Reproduced by permission.—Tate, Claudia. From *The Selected Works of Georgia Douglas Johnson.* G.K. Hall & Co., 1997. Copyright © 1997 by G.K. Hall & Co. All rights reserved. The Gale Group.—Tracy, Steven C. From "To the Tune of Those Weary Blues," in *Langston Hughes: Critical Perspectives Past and Present.* Edited by Henry Louis Gates, Jr., and K.A. Appiah. Amistad Press, 1993. Copyright © 1993 by Amistad Press. Reproduced by permission of Henry Louis Gates, Jr.—Turner, Deborah. From *Gay and Lesbian Literature,* Volume 2. St. James Press, 1998. Copyright © 1998 by St. James Press. All rights reserved. The Gale Group.—Tuttleton, James W. From "Countee Cullen at

'The Heights,'" in *The Harlem Renaissance: Revaluations.* Edited by Amritjit Singh, William S. Shiver, and Stanley Brodwin. Garland Publishing, Inc., 1989. © 1989 Amritjit Singh, William S. Shiver, and Stanley Brodwin. All rights reserved. Reproduced by permission of the editors.—Tyler, Bruce M. From *From Harlem to Hollywood: The Struggle for Racial and Cultural Democracy, 1920-1943.* Garland Publishing, Inc., 1992. Copyright © 1992 by Garland Publishing, Inc. All rights reserved. Reproduced by permission.—van Notten, Eleanor. From *Wallace Thurman's Harlem Renaissance.* Rodopi, 1994. Copyright © 1994 by Rodopi. All rights reserved. Reproduced by permission.—Walden, Daniel. From "'The Canker Galls ... ,' or, the Short Promising Life of Wallace Thurman," in *The Harlem Renaissance Re-Examined.* Edited by Victor A. Kramer. AMS Press, 1987. Copyright © 1987 by AMS Press. All rights reserved. Reproduced by permission.—Walker, Alice. From "Dedication," in *I Love Myself When I am Laughing ... And Then again When I am Looking Mean and Impressive: A Zora Neale Hurston Reader.* Edited by Alice Walker. The Feminist Press, 1979. Copyright © 1979 by The Feminist Press. All rights reserved. Reproduced by permission.—Wall, Cheryl A. From "Zora Neal Hurston: Changing Her Own Words," in *American Novelists Revisited: Essays in Feminist Criticism.* Edited by Friz Fleischmann. G.K. Hall, 1982. Copyright © 1982 by G.K. Hall. All rights reserved. Reproduced by permission.—Wall, Cheryl A. From "Whose Sweet Angel Child? Blues Women, Langston Hughes, and Writing during the Harlem Renaissance," in *Langston Hughes: The Man, His Art, and His Continuing Influence.* Edited by C. James Trotman. Garland Publishing, Inc., 1995. Copyright © 1995 by Garland Publishing, Inc. All rights reserved. Reproduced by permission.—Wall, Cheryl A. From the foreword to *This Waiting for Love: Helene Johnson, Poet of the Harlem Renaissance.* Edited by Verner D. Mitchell. University of Massachusetts Press, 2000. Copyright © 2000 by University of Massachusetts Press. All rights reserved. Reproduced by permission.—Wall, Cheryl A. From *Women of the Harlem Renaissance.* Indiana University Press, 1995. Copyright © 1995 by Indiana University Press. All rights reserved. Reproduced by permission.—Washington, Mary Helen. From "'I Love the Way Janie Crawford Left Her Husbands': Hurston's Emergent Female Hero," in *Zora Neale Hurston: Critical Perspectives Past and Present.* Edited by Henry Louis Gates, Jr. and K.A. Appiah. Amistad Press, 1993. Copyright © 1993 by Amistad Press. Reproduced by permission of Henry Louis Gates, Jr.—

ACKNOWLEDGMENTS

Washington, Sarah M. From "Frank S. Horne," in *Dictionary of Literary Biography, Volume 51: Afro- American Writers from the Harlem Renaissance to 1940.* Edited by Trudier Harris. Gale Research, Inc., 1987. Copyright © 1987 by Gale Research, Inc. All rights reserved. Reproduced by permission.—Willis-Braithwaite, Deborah. From *James Van DerZee: Photographer 1886-1983.* Harry N. Abrams, Inc., 1987. Copyright © 1987 by Harry N. Abrams, Inc. All rights reserved. Reproduced by permission.—Wintz, Cary D. From "Booker T. Washington, W. E. B. Du Bois, and the 'New Negro' in Black America," in *Black Culture and the Harlem Renaissance.* Rice University Press, 1988. Copyright © 1996 by Texas A&M University Press. Reproduced by permission.—Wolseley, Roland E. From *The Black Press, U.S.A.* Iowa State University Press, 1990. Copyright © 1990 by Iowa State University Press. All rights reserved. Reproduced by permission. Copyright to all editions of the Black Press, U.S.A. is owned by Alice A. Tait.—Woodson, Jon. From *To Make a New Race: Gurdjieff, Toomer, and the Harlem Renaissance.* University of Mississippi Press, 1999. Copyright © 1998 by University of Mississippi Press. All rights reserved. Reproduced by permission.—Zamir, Shamoon. From *Dark Voices: W. E. B. Du Bois and American Thought, 1888-1903.* University of Chicago Press, 1995. Copyright © 1995 by University of Chicago Press. All rights reserved. Reproduced by permission.

### *Photographs and illustrations in* Harlem Renaissance *were received from the following sources:*

African American soldiers of the 368 Infantry, photograph. Corbis. Reproduced by permission.—Apollo Theater marquee, "See You Soon," photograph. AP/Wide World Photos. Reproduced by permission.—"Aspects of Negro Life: The Negro in an African Setting," painting by Aaron Douglas, photograph by Manu Sassoonian. Schomburg Center for Research in Black Culture, The New York Public Library, Art Resource, NY. Reproduced by permission.—"Ethiopia Awakening," sculpture by Meta Warrick Fuller, photograph. Schomburg Center for Research in Black Culture, The New York Public Library/Art Resource, NY. Reproduced by permission. Bailey, Pearl, photograph by Carl Van Vechten. Reproduced by permission of the Estate of Carl Van Vechten.—Baker, Josephine, in a scene from the 1934 film Zou Zou, directed by Marc Allegret, photograph. The Kobal Collection. Reproduced by permission.—Bennett, Gwendolyn, photograph. Reproduced by permission of Helaine Victoria Press and

the Moorland-Spingarn Research Center, Howard University.—Black Cross nurses, parading down a street in Harlem during the opening of the Universal Negro Improvement Association convention, photograph. © Underwood & Underwood/Corbis. Reproduced by permission.—Bonner, Marita, sitting with her husband, William Occomy, photograph. Radcliffe Archives, Radcliffe Institute, Harvard University. Reproduced by permission.— Bontemps, Arna, photograph. Fisk University Library. Reproduced by permission.—Braithwaite, William Stanley, photograph. Fisk University Library. Reproduced by permission.—Brown, Sterling, photograph. Fisk University Library. Reproduced by permission.—Calloway, Cab, photograph by Carl Van Vechten. The Estate of Carl Van Vechten. Reproduced by permission.— Circular diagram showing difference between speech and silence (Figure A), compared with circular diagram showing the linearity of silence and speech by marking the trajectory as a circuit (Figure B). The Gale Group.—Cotton Club, Harlem, New York City, ca. 1920-1940, photograph. Corbis Corporation. Reproduced by permission.—Cover from *Black Thunder,* by Arna Bontemps. Beacon Press, 1992. Copyright 1936 by The Macmillan Company, renewed 1963 by Arna Bontemps. Reproduced by permission.—Cover from *The Crisis: A Record of the Darker Races,* edited by W. E. B. Du Bois, 1910, print.—Cover of the program for DuBose Heyward and Ira Gershwin's libretto *Porgy and Bess,* photograph. Hulton/Archive. Reproduced by permission.—Cullen, Countee, photograph. The Bettmann Archive/Corbis-Bettmann. Reproduced by permission.— Diagram showing the word fixed in the middle of a diagrammatically circumscribed cross becoming a vehicle for the attempted transcendence of silent difference and the aspiration to silent non-difference. The Gale Group.—Douglas, Aaron (oil on canvas painting), photograph. Gibbs Museum of Art/CAA. Reproduced by permission.—Du Bois, W. E. B., photograph. Fisk University Library. Reproduced by permission.—Du Bois, W. E. B. (top right), and others working in the offices of the NAACP's *Crisis* magazine, photograph. © Underwood & Underwood/Corbis. Reproduced by permission.—Ellington, Duke, and Louis Armstrong (performing), 1946, photograph. AP/Wide World Photos Inc. Reproduced by permission.— Exterior view of Abyssinian Baptist Church, New York City, c. 1923, photograph. Corbis Corporation. Reproduced by permission.—Exterior view of Lafayette Theatre in Harlem, 7th Avenue between 131st and 132nd Streets, photograph. Corbis. Reproduced by permission.—"Ezekiel Saw the

Wheels," painting by William H. Johnson. The Library of Congress.—Fauset, Jesse Redmon, photograph. The Library of Congress.—Fauset, Jessie, Langston Hughes and Zora Neale Hurston, photograph. Schomburg Center for Research in Black Culture, The New York Public Library/Art Resource, NY. Reproduced by permission.—Fisher, Rudolph, photograph. The Beinecke Rare Book and Manuscript Library. Reproduced by permission.—Frontispiece, caricature drawing by Miguel Covarrubias, from "Keep A-Inchin' along," written by Carl Van Vechten, (left to right), Carl Van Vechten, Fania Marinoff, and Taylor Gordon. Special Collections Library, University of Michigan. Reproduced by permission.—Garvey, Marcus (center), handcuffed to a deputy after he is escorted from a courtroom after being sentenced to five years in Atlanta Penitentiary for mail fraud, photograph. © Bettmann/Corbis. Reproduced by permission.—Garvey, Marcus, photograph. Consulate General of Jamaica. Reproduced by permission.—Garvey, Marcus, standing in front of a UNIA club in New York, photograph. Hulton/Archive. Reproduced by permission.—Grimké, Angelina Weld, photograph. Reproduced by permission of Helaine Victoria Press and the Moorland-Spingarn Research Center, Howard University.—Harlem bookstore known as the "House of Common Sense and the Home of Proper Propaganda" hosting the registration for the Back-to-Africa movement, photograph. © Bettmann/Corbis. Reproduced by permission.—Heyward, DuBose, photograph. The Library of Congress.—Horne, Frank, photograph. AP/Wide World Photos. Reproduced by permission.—Hughes, Langston, photograph. The Bettmann Archive/Newsphotos, Inc./Corbis-Bettmann. Reproduced by permission.—Hurston, Zora Neale, photograph. Yale Collection of American Literature, Beinecke Rare Book and Manuscript Library. Reproduced by permission of Carl Van Vechten Papers.—Jacket of *The Souls of Black Folk*, by W. E. B. Du Bois. Random House, 1996. Jacket portrait courtesy of the Bettman Archive.—The January, 1991 PLAYBILL for Langston Hughes and Zora Neale Hurston's *Mule Bone*, directed by Michael Schultz by the Ethel Barrymore Theatre, at Lincoln Center Theater, some men and one woman are sitting on a porch listening to a man playing a guitar, photograph. PLAYBILL ® is a registered trademark of Playbill Incorporated, N.Y.C. All rights reserved. Reproduced by permission.—Johnson, Charles S., photograph. Fisk University Library. Reproduced by permission.—Johnson, William H., self portrait painting. The Library of Congress.—Johnson, James Weldon,

photograph. The Library of Congress.—Larsen, Nella (1891-1964), photograph. The Beinecke Rare Book and Manuscript Library. Reproduced by permission.—Larsen, Nella (shaking hands, four men to her left), photograph. UPI/Corbis-Bettmann. Reproduced by permission.—Leibowitz, Sam, Patterson, Heywood (Scottsboro boys), phototgraph. UPI/Corbis-Bettmann. Reproduced by permission.—Locke, Dr. Alain, photograph. The Library of Congress.—McKay, Claude, photograph. The Granger Collection, New York. Reproduced by permission.—Members of the NAACP New York City Youth Council holding signs and picketing for anti-lynching legislation in front of the Strand Theatre in Times Square, photograph. Courtesy of The Library of Congress. Reproduced by permission.—NAACP anti-lynching poster, photograph. Archive Photos. Reproduced by permission.—Nelson, Alice Ruth Moore Dunbar, photograph. Reproduced by permission of Helaine Victoria Press and the Ohio Historical Society.—Original typewritten manuscript from *Harlem/Good Morning, Daddy,* written by Langston Hughes. Reproduced by permission of Harold Ober Associates Incorporated for the Estate of Langston Hughes.—Parade of men, opening of the annual convention of the Provisional Republic of Africa in Harlem, carrying banners and a paintng of the "Ethiopian Christ," banner above street: "Summer Chatauqua of the Abyssinian Baptist Church," New York, photograph by George Rinhart. Corbis Corporation. Reproduced by permission.—Pedestrians walking on East 112th Street in Harlem, New York, photograph. © Bettmann/Corbis. Reproduced by permission.—Rex, Ingram, photograph. The Kobal Collection. Reproduced by permission.—Robeson, Paul, as Brutus Jones, throwing his hands up, surrounded by ghosts, scene from the 1933 film *The Emperor Jones,* photograph. ©Underwood & Underwood/Corbis. Reproduced by permission.—Robinson, Bill (with Shirley Temple), photograph. AP/Wide World Photos. Reproduced by permission.—Scene from the movie *Birth of A Nation,* 1915, photograph. The Kobal Collection. Reproduced by permission.—Schuyler, George S., photograph by Carl Van Vechten. Reproduced by permission of the Estate of Carl Van Vechten.—Smith, Bessie, photograph. New York Public Library.—Spencer, Anne, photograph. Reproduced by permission of Helaine Victoria Press and the Literary Estate of Anne Spencer.—Thurman, Wallace, photograph. Reproduced by permission of the Beinecke Rare Book and Manuscript Library.—Title page from *Anthology of Magazine Verse for 1920,* edited by William Stanley Braithwaite, all text. Courtesy of

ACKNOWLEDGMENTS

the Graduate Library, University of Michigan. Reproduced by permission.—Title page from *The Book of American Negro Poetry,* written by James Weldon Johnson, all text. Courtesy of the Graduate Library, University of Michigan. Reproduced by permission.—Title page from *Caroling Dusk,* edited by Countee Cullen, all text. Special Collections Library, University of Michigan. Reproduced by permission.—Title page from *Frye Street & Environs: The Collected Works of Marita Bonner,* by Joyce Flynn and Joyce Occomy Stricklin. Copyright © 1987 by Joyce Flynn and Joyce Occomy Stricklin. Reproduced by permission of Beacon Press, Boston.—Title page from *The Weary Blues,* written by Langston Hughes. Special Collections Library, University of Michigan. Reproduced by permission.—Toomer, Jean (foreground), sitting in front of typewriter while his wife, Marjory Latimer, stands next to him looking over his shoulder, photograph. © Bettmann/Corbis. Reproduced by permission.—Toomer, Jean, photograph. Beinecke Library, Yale University. Reproduced by permission.—Two women walking with two girls, photograph. Corbis. Reproduced by permission.—Unemployed black men talking together, 1935, Lennox Avenue, Harlem, photograph. Corbis-Bettmann. Reproduced by permission.—VanDerZee, James, photograph. AP/Wide World Photos. Reproduced by permission.—Van Vechten, Carl, photograph. AP/Wide World Photos. Reproduced by permission.—View of Lenox Avenue in Harlem, photograph. Corbis. Reproduced by permission.—Walrond, Eric, a drawing. Winold Reiss Collecection/Fisk University Library. Reproduced by permission.—West, Dorothy, Martha's Vineyard, Massachusetts, 1995, photograph. AP/Wide World Photos. Reproduced by permission.—White, Walter, photograph. Library of Congress.

= historical event

■ = literary event

## 1890

● Between 1890 and 1920, about two million African Americans migrate from the rural southern states to the northern cities, where they hope to find better opportunities and less discrimination.

## 1908

● The Frogs, a group of African American theatrical professionals including George Walker, James Reese Europe, and Bert Williams, is founded.

● Reverend Adam Clayton Powell is named pastor of Harlem's Abyssinian Baptist Church.

## 1909

● The National Negro Committee holds its first meeting. The organization will evolve into the National Association for the Advancement of Colored People (NAACP) the next year.

## 1910

● The NAACP is founded, and prominent Black leader W. E. B. Du Bois becomes editor of the group's monthly magazine, *Crisis,* which publishes its first issue.

● The National Urban League, a merger of the Committee for Improving the Industrial Conditions of Negroes in New York, the Committee on Urban Conditions, and the National League for the Protection of Colored Women is founded under the direction of Dr. George E. Haynes.

## 1912

■ James Weldon Johnson's influential novel *The Autobiography of an Ex-Colored Man* is published.

## 1914

● Madame C. J. Walker, the first African American woman to become a self-made millionaire, moves to New York City with her daughter L'Alelia. The family moves to Harlem in 1916. The founder of a line of hair and cosmetic products for Black women, Madame Walker's fortune will finance her daughter's foray into the nightclub and literary salon business.

## 1917

● Jamaican-born Marcus Garvey arrives in Harlem and founds the Universal Negro Improvement Association (UNIA), an organization that urges Blacks to unite and form their own nation.

- Between 10,000 and 15,000 African Americans join the Silent Protest Parade, marching down Fifth Avenue in complete silence to protest violence against Blacks.
- The politically radical Black publication *The Messenger* is founded.
- Two of Claude McKay's poems, "Invocation" and "The Harlem Dancer," are published in the white literary journal *Seven Arts*.

### 1918

- Garvey's UNIA begins publishing *Negro World*, the organization's weekly newspaper.

### 1919

- The 369th Infantry Regiment, a highly decorated unit made up entirely of African American soldiers, returns from World War I to a heroes' welcome in Harlem.
- During the "Red Summer of Hate," African Americans react angrily to widespread lynchings and other violence directed against them, with race riots occurring in Chicago, Washington, D.C., and two dozen other American cities. The NAACP holds a conference on lynching and publishes *Thirty Years of Lynching in the United States 1889-1918.*
- Jessie Redmon Fauset becomes literary editor of *Crisis*.
- McKay publishes "If We Must Die" in the *Liberator*.

### 1920

- James Weldon Johnson becomes the first African American executive secretary of the NAACP.
- Garvey's UNIA holds the First International Convention of the Negro Peoples of the World in New York
- The NAACP awards the Springarn Medal to W. E. B. Du Bois for "the founding and the calling of the Pan African Congress."
- Acclaimed American playwright Eugene O'Neil's drama *The Emperor Jones* opens at the Provincetown Playhouse with Black actor Charles Gilpin in the lead role.

### 1921

- Harry Pace founds the Black Swan Phonograph Corporation and begins production of the "race records" that will help to bring jazz and blues music to a wider audience.

- The musical revue *Shuffle Along* opens on Broadway, delighting audiences with its high-energy singing and dancing and, many believe, providing the spark that ignites the Harlem Renaissance.
- An exhibition of works by such African American artists as Henry Tanner and Meta Vaux Warrick Fuller is held at Harlem's 135th Street branch of the New York Public Library.
- Langston Hughes's great poem "The Negro Speaks of Rivers" is published in *Crisis*.

### 1922

- Marian Anderson performs at New York's Town Hall, launching her career as a classical singer.
- Warrick Fuller's sculpture *Ethiopia Awakening* is shown at the "Making of America" exhibition in New York.
- The first major book of the Harlem Renaissance appears when Claude McKay's novel *Harlem Shadows* is published by Harcourt, Brace.
- James Weldon Johnson's *The Book of American Negro Poetry* is published by Harcourt, Brace.

### 1923

- Bessie Smith records "Downhearted Blues" and "Gulf Coast Blues," soon becoming the most famous blues singer in both the northern and southern states.
- Roland Hayes makes his New York debut, singing a program of classical music as well as African American spirituals.
- Marcus Garvey is arrested for mail fraud and imprisoned for three months.
- Joe "King" Oliver's Creole Jazz Band makes a series of thirty- seven recordings with trumpet player Louis Armstrong.
- Pianist, composer, and band leader Duke Ellington arrives in New York with his band, the Washingtonians.
- Louis Armstrong joins Fletcher Henderson's orchestra, which— performing at the famed Roseland Ballroom— becomes the most popular dance band in New York.
- Kansas City-born artist Aaron Douglas arrives in New York and begins developing a new style that will make him the official artist of the Harlem Renaissance.

- Harlem's largest and most famous cabaret, the Cotton Club, opens.
- Josephine Baker appears in *Chocolate Dandies* on Broadway.
- Roland Hayes performs at Carnegie Hall.
- The Harlem Renaissance Basketball Club is formed to provide Black athletes who have been unable to play on white teams with a league of their own.
- The National Urban League establishes *Opportunity* magazine, which will not only publish the work of Harlem Renaissance writers and artists but will help to support them through an annual contest.
- The National Ethiopian Art Players produce Willis Richardson's *The Chip Woman's Fortune,* the first drama by a Black playwright to appear on the Broadway stage.
- Jean Toomer's innovative novel *Cane* is published and Toomer is hailed as one of the most promising young authors of the Harlem Renaissance.
- The Ethiopian Art Players perform Eugene O'Neill's play *All God's Chillun Got Wings* in Washington, D.C., while in Cleveland the Gilpin Players at Karamu Theatre present *In Abraham's Bosom* by Paul Green.
- Poems by Harlem Renaissance star Countee Cullen appear in four major white publications.

## 1924

- James VanDerZee begins a series of photographs chronicling Marcus Garvey and the activities of UNIA.
- Filmmaker Oscar Micheaux completes *Birthright* and *Body and Soul,* the latter starring Paul Robeson.
- At the Civic Club dinner hosted by *Opportunity*'s Charles S. Johnson, promising young writers meet the influential editors and publishers who can boost their careers.
- *The Fire in the Flint,* a novel by NAACP leader Walter White, is published.
- The publication of Jessie Redmon Fauset's *There Is Confusion* marks the first Harlem Renaissance book by a woman writer.

## 1925

- The exciting new musical form known as jazz is showcased in the "First American Jazz Concert" at Aeolian Hall in New York.

- Small's Paradise nightclub opens in Harlem; the club will prove to be a one of the city's most popular jazz destinations.
- Marcus Garvey is convicted of mail fraud and imprisoned in the Atlanta Penitentiary.
- Marian Anderson wins a singing competition sponsored by the New York Philharmonic Orchestra.
- Artist Sargent Johnson exhibits his paintings at the San Francisco Art Association, and Archibald Motley wins a medal from the Art Institute of Chicago for his painting "A Mulatress."
- James Weldon Johnson is awarded the NAACP's Springarn Medal for his work as an author, diplomat, and leader.
- *Survey Graphic* magazine publishes *Harlem: The Mecca of the New Negro,* an issue devoted entirely to the work of Harlem Renaissance writers and artists.
- Zora Neale Hurston publishes her short story "Spunk" in *Opportunity*.
- Countee Cullen's first volume of poetry, *Color,* is published.
- Wallace Thurman moves from Los Angeles to New York and soon becomes a leader of the younger generation of Harlem Renaissance writers and artists.
- Zora Neale Hurston enters Barnard College on a scholarship, studying anthropology.
- Well-known white poet Vachel Lindsay reads the poems of the Langston Hughes, then working as a restaurant busboy, to the audience at his own poetry reading, announcing that he has discovered a bright new talent.
- The *New Negro* anthology, edited by Alain Locke, introduces the work and ideas of the Harlem Renaissance.

## 1926

- W.C. Handy's *Blues: An Anthology* is published, bringing wider attention to this unique African American musical form.
- Another jazz hotspot, the Savoy Ballroom, opens in Harlem with Fletcher Henderson and his orchestra established as the house band.
- The Harmon Foundation holds its first annual art exhibition of works by African American artists, and Palmer Hayden and Hale Woodruff win top awards.

- The Carnegie Corporation buys Arthur Schomburg's African American collection and donates it to the newly established Negro Reference Library at the Harlem branch of the New York Public Library.

- The NAACP-sponsored theatrical group the Krigwa Players stages three plays.

- White author Carl Van Vechten's controversial novel *Nigger Heaven* is published.

- Langston Hughes's first volume of poetry, *The Weary Blues,* is published.

- *Crisis* awards its first prizes in literature and art. Winnners include Arna Bontemps, Countee Cullen, Aaron Douglas, and Hale Woodruff.

- A daring new (but short-lived) literary journal called *Fire!!* is launched by Langston Hughes, Wallace Thurman, Zora Neale Hurston, Aaron Douglas, and Richard Bruce Nugent, with artwork by Douglas and Nugent.

## 1927

- Duke Ellington begins a three-year stint at the Cotton Club, gaining fame and praise for his innovative style and compositions.

- Ordered to leave the United States, Marcus Garvey returns to Jamaica.

- Wealthy African American L'Alelia Walker, whose mother founded a successful Black hair and skin care business, opens a nightclub and literary salon called the Dark Tower.

- *Caroling Dusk: An Anthology of Verse by Negro Poets,* edited by Countee Cullen, is published by Harper.

- Charles S. Johnson publishes *Ebony and Topaz: A Collectanea,* an anthology of writings that originally appeared in *Opportunity.*

- Dorothy and DuBose Heyward's *Porgy,* a musical play with Black characters and themes, opens on Broadway; the work is adapted from DuBose's novel of the same name.

- James Weldon Johnson's *God's Trombones,* a book of poems modeled after sermons by Black preachers and illustrated by Aaron Douglas, is published.

- Several young Harlem Renaissance writers and artists—notably Zora Neale Hurston and Langston Hughes— accept money and other help from wealthy patron Charlotte Osgood Mason, who insists that those under her patronage call her "Godmother."

- Langston Hughes's second poetry collection, *Fine Clothes to the Jew,* features blues rhythms and Harlem-inspired imagery.

## 1928

- Palmer Hayden's work is featured in a one-man exhibition at a Paris art gallery, and Archibald Motley exhibits his paintings at the New Galleries in New York

- Aaron Douglas is awarded a fellowship to study at the Barnes Foundation in Pennsylvania.

- A number of important Harlem Renaissance works are published, including Rudolph Fisher's *Walls of Jericho,* Nella Larsen's *Quicksand,* Jessie Redmon Fauset's *Plum Bun,* W. E. B. Du Bois's *Dark Princess,* and Claude McKay's *Home to Harlem* (which becomes the first bestseller by a Black author).

- Poet Countee Cullen marries Yolande Du Bois, daughter of the great Black leader, in an extravagant wedding that is one of the most memorable social events of the Harlem Renaissance.

- Wallace Thurman edits another literary journal, *Harlem,* that is—like its predecessor, *Fire!!*— destined to appear only once.

## 1929

- The Harmon Foundation sponsors the exhibition *Paintings and Sculptures by American Negro Artists* at the National Gallery in Washington, D.C.

- The Negro Experimental Theater is founded.

- Films showcasing African American musicians debut, including *Black and Tan,* featuring Duke Ellington and his orchestra, and *St. Louis Blues,* which features Bessie Smith.

- The Broadway show *Ain't Misbehavin'* features music by piano player Fats Waller.

- The stock market crashes, ending the Jazz Age and ushering in the Great Depression.

- Wallace Thurman's play *Harlem,* written with William Jourdan Rapp, opens on Broadway, becoming the most successful such production by a Black author.

- Novels by Wallace Thurman (*The Blacker the Berry*) and Claude McKay (*Banjo*) are published, as is Countee Cullen's *The Black Christ and Other Poems.*

## 1930

- Aaron Douglas is commissioned to create a series of murals for the campus library at Fisk University in Nashville.

- James V. Herring creates the Howard University Gallery of Art. It is the first gallery in the United States to be autonomously curated and directed by African Americans.

- Marc Connelly's play *The Green Pastures,* notable for its African American characters and content, opens to great acclaim on Broadway.

- Langston Hughes's novel *Not without Laughter* is published.

- James Weldon Johnson's historical account of Harlem, *Black Manhattan,* is published by Knopf.

- Willis Richardson's *Plays and Pageants from the Life of the Negro* is published by Associated Publishers.

## 1931

- Artist August Savage opens the Savage School of Arts and Crafts in Harlem. It is the first of several art schools she will open in Harlem.

## 1932

- Louis Armstrong stars in the musical film short *A Rhapsody in Black and Blue.*

## 1933

- A number of Harlem Renaissance writers and artists find employment with the Works Project Administration (WPA), a government-sponsored program designed to put Americans back to work.

- Aaron Douglas paints murals for the YMCA in Harlem.

- The film adaptation of Eugene O'Neill's *The Emperor Jones,* starring Paul Robeson, is released. The screenplay is written by DuBose Heyward.

## 1934

- Aaron Douglas is commissioned to create a series of murals, which will be entitled *Aspects of Negro Life,* for the 135th Street (Harlem) branch of the New York Public Library.

- The NAACP and the American Fund for Public Service plan a coordinated legal campaign, directed by Howard University Law School vice-dean Charles H. Houston, against segregation and discrimination.

- Oscar Michaux releases his film *Harlem After Midnight.*

- Wallace Thurman's death in the charity ward of a New York hospital stuns and sobers his Harlem Renaissance friends.

- Zora Neale Hurston's first novel, *Jonah's Gourd Wine,* is published by Lippincott.

- Nancy Cunard, a British socialite, assembles and edits the *Negro Anthology,* a sprawling 855 page work that features photographs and scores for African music as well as articles on ethnography, linguistics, poetry, and political commentary. Contributors include Sterling Brown, Langston Hughes, and Zora Neale Hurston.

## 1935

- Harlem is the scene of a major riot sparked by anger over discrimination by white-owned businesses.

- The exhibition *African Negro Art* opens at the Museum of Modern Art in New York City.

- Carl Van Vechten debuts his first collection of photographs in *The Leica Exhibition* at the Bergdorf Goodman in New York City.

- Lippincott publishes Hurston's ethnographic study *Mules and Men,* with illustrations by Miguel Covarrubias.

## 1936

- African American actors Paul Robeson and Hattie McDaniel appear in director James Whales's film adaptation of Kern and Hammerstein's musical *Show Boat.*

## 1937

- *Their Eyes Were Watching God* by Zora Neale Hurston is published by Lippincott.

# OVERVIEWS AND GENERAL STUDIES OF THE HARLEM RENAISSANCE

Acultural movement of the 1920s and early 1930s, the Harlem Renaissance refers to a period of race consciousness and solidarity among African American and Caribbean American artists, writers, and musicians centered in the Harlem section of New York City. Black art and literature flourished during this period, fueled by new opportunities for publication and widespread distribution as the aesthetic associated with the "New Negro" gained recognition outside the Black community. The movement began to unravel with the onset of the Great Depression in the 1930s, and even the major figures of the Harlem Renaissance fell out of vogue until they were rediscovered and their works were reprinted and exhibited during the Black Arts movement of the 1960s.

Two of the most important factors contributing to the creative phenomenon known as the Harlem Renaissance were World War I and the great migration of Blacks from the rural South to the industrial North during the war years and continuing throughout the 1920s. Many African Americans supported the war effort enthusiastically by serving in the armed forces or by filling jobs vacated by white soldiers in cities like New York, Detroit, Chicago, and Philadelphia. After the war they were hopeful that their patriotism would earn them a greater measure of equality, but their expectations were thwarted by the 1919 race riots in both the North and the South and by a record number of lynchings that same year. A new racial pride and a sense of community among Blacks emerged during this period and its center was Harlem, the birthplace of the "New Negro," who refused to accept either the plantation mentality of the South or the ghetto mentality of the North.

The Black literary journals *Crisis* and *Opportunity* provided a forum for the young writers of the Harlem Renaissance, publishing their poetry, stories, essays, and reviews. *Crisis,* associated with W. E. B. Du Bois and the National Association for the Advancement of Colored People (NAACP), was the more militant of the two, and was eventually overshadowed by *Opportunity,* the organ of the National Urban League, which advocated cooperation between the races, job opportunities for Blacks, and the adopting of middle-class morality and manners by the newly arrived Southern Blacks. *Opportunity*'s editor, Charles S. Johnson, provided encouragement and support for the young writers of the movement and held literary contests to reward their best work. Johnson, together with Robert E. Park and Alain Locke, helped articulate the principles of the New Negro aesthetic, which celebrated idealism, racial pride, and Black nationalism. According to George Hutchinson (1995), Johnson advocated a "self-expressive" literature that "would not be burdened with 'propaganda' of the 'best foot forward' sort but instead attempt to exemplify in its very form the cultural meanings (that is, the 'experience,' in pragmatist terms) of a people." African American writers were encouraged to establish their own literary tradition, independent of white critical standards.

Despite these efforts, white critical standards were nonetheless brought to bear on Black literature, since publishing opportunities (aside from those afforded by the Black literary journals) and patronage were almost exclusively controlled by whites, who were often attracted to what they considered the "primitive" and "exotic" elements of African American culture. Critics have studied the relationships between Black writers of the 1920s and their white publishers, patrons, and friends, concluding that white involvement was essential to the success of the Harlem Renaissance since Black writers lacked means and connections. But that involvement was often a source of friction between white editors, who offered advice on both style and content, and Black authors, who wanted to choose their own projects. Even more rancorous could be the relationship between white patron and Black writer. Charlotte Osgood Mason, perhaps the most famous patron of the Harlem Renaissance writers—among them Langston Hughes and Zora Neal Hurston—was fascinated with primitivism, and considered African Americans to be innately connected to the rhythms and spirituality of Africa. When their work did not focus on "the primitive nature of black life" according to her expectations, Mason withdrew her support, as she did when Hughes began producing political poetry.

Cheryl A. Wall (1995) has explored the unique problems of women during the Harlem Renaissance by contrasting Locke's optimistic vision of racial identity in *The New Negro* (1925) with Marita Bonner's essay of the same year, "On Being Young—A Woman—and Colored." Where Locke presented images of pride, confidence, and progressive change, Bonner's essay involves images of paralysis, of "stasis and claustrophobia." The lives of Black women were constrained not only by the racist white culture, but also by other Blacks who feared whites' perception of Black women as not quite respectable; traveling alone, for example, would "offend propriety," so that even an educated woman like Bonner was unable to move freely from Washington, D.C., to New York.

Although women contributed significantly to the Black journals and literary anthologies associated with the Harlem Renaissance, they were often discouraged from pursuing the issue of gender bias in the name of racial solidarity. Wall claims that "the heightened race consciousness of the period made issues of sexism more difficult to raise . . . Amid the effort to forge a revised racial identity, a woman who persisted in raising such concerns might see them dismissed as irrelevant or trivial; she might herself be perceived as disloyal to the race."

The economic hard times of the Great Depression effectively ended the Harlem Renaissance as a cohesive cultural movement, although many writers, both male and female, continued to publish throughout the 1930s. By 1941, Wall reports, *The Negro Caravan,* the comprehensive anthology of Black writing that was instrumental in establishing the canon of African American literature, devalued much of the work of the women of the Harlem Renaissance. Feminism and the Black Arts movement of the 1960s, however, brought about a revival of interest in the work of artists, writers, and musicians of the period and in recent years many of the works of even minor figures associated with the movement have been reprinted, or in some cases, published in collections for the first time.

## REPRESENTATIVE WORKS

**Marita Bonner**
"On Being Young—A Woman—And Colored" [published in journal *The Crisis*] (essay) 1925

*The Purple Flower* [published in journal *The Crisis*] (play) 1928

**Arna Bontemps**
*Black Thunder* (novel) 1936

**Sterling Allen Brown**
*Southern Road* (poetry) 1932

**Countee Cullen**
*Color* (poetry) 1925

*The Ballad of the Brown Girl* (poetry) 1927

*Caroling Dusk: An Anthology of Verse by Negro Poets* [editor] (poetry anthology) 1927

*Copper Sun* (poetry) 1927

*The Black Christ and Other Poems* (poetry) 1929

*One Way to Heaven* (novel) 1932

**W. E. B. Du Bois**
*The Souls of Black Folk* (fiction, nonfiction, and folklore) 1903

*Darkwater: Voices from Within the Veil* (poetry, nonfiction, and autobiography) 1920

*The Gift of Black Folk: The Negroes in the Making of America* (nonfiction) 1924

*Dark Princess* (novel) 1928

## Jessie Fauset

*There Is Confusion* (novel) 1924

*Plum Bun* (novel) 1929

*The Chinaberry Tree* (novel) 1931

*Comedy: American Style* (novel) 1933

## Rudolph Fisher

*The Walls of Jericho* (novel) 1928

*The Conjure-Man Dies: A Mystery Tale of Dark Harlem* (novel) 1932

## Angelina Weld Grimké

*Rachel* (play) 1916

## DuBose Heyward

*Porgy* (novel) 1925

## Langston Hughes

*The Weary Blues* (poetry) 1926

*Fine Clothes to the Jew* (poetry) 1927

*Not Without Laughter* (novel) 1930

*The Ways of White Folks* (short stories) 1934

## Zora Neale Hurston

*Jonah's Gourd Vine* (novel) 1934

*Mules and Men* (folklore) 1935

*Their Eyes Were Watching God* (novel) 1937

## Georgia Douglas Johnson

*Bronze: A Book of Verse* (poetry) 1922

*An Autumn Love Cycle* (poetry) 1928

## James Weldon Johnson

*The Autobiography of an Ex-Colored Man* (novel) 1912; re-released 1927

*The Book of American Negro Poetry* [editor] (poetry anthology) 1922; revised 1931

## Nella Larsen

*Quicksand* (novel) 1928

*Passing* (novel) 1929

## Alain Locke

*The New Negro: An Interpretation* [editor] (poetry, fiction, drama, essays) 1925

## Claude McKay

*Harlem Shadows* (poetry) 1922

*Home to Harlem* (novel) 1928

## Willis Richardson

*The Chip Woman's Fortune* (play) 1923

## George Samuel Schuyler

*Black No More: Being an Account of the Strange and Wonderful Workings of Science in the Land of the Free, A.D. 1933-1940* (novel) 1931

## Wallace Thurman

*The Blacker the Berry* (novel) 1929

*Infants of the Spring* (novel) 1932

## Jean Toomer

*Cane* (stories and poems) 1923

## Carl Van Vechten

*Nigger Heaven* (novel) 1926

## Eric Walrond

*Tropic Death* (short stories) 1926

## Walter White

*The Fire in the Flint* (novel) 1924

*Flight* (novel) 1928

# PRIMARY SOURCES

## NEW YORK HERALD (ESSAY DATE 1905)

**SOURCE:** "Negroes Move into Harlem." *New York Herald* (December 24, 1905).

*This short piece foretells the cultural and social expansion that will ultimately result in the Harlem Renaissance.*

An untoward circumstance has been injected into the private-dwelling market in the vicinity of 133rd and 134th Streets. During the last three years the flats in 134th Street between Lenox and Seventh Avenues, that were occupied entirely by white folks, have been captured for occupancy by a Negro population. Its presence there has tended also to lend much color to conditions in 133rd and 135th Streets between Lenox and Seventh Avenues.

One Hundred and Thirty-third Street still shows some signs of resistance to the blending of colors in that street, but between Lenox and Seventh Avenues has practically succumbed to the ingress of colored tenants. Nearly all the old dwellings in 134th Street to midway in the block west from Seventh Avenue are occupied by colored tenants, and real estate brokers predict that it is only a matter of time when the entire block, to Eighth Avenue, will be a stronghold of the Negro population.

As a result of the extension of this African colony dwellings in 133rd Street between Seventh and Eighth Avenues, and in 132nd Street from Lenox to Eighth Avenues, have depreciated from fifteen to twenty per cent in value, especially in the sides of those streets nearest to 134th Street. The cause of the colored influx is inexplicable.

## NEW YORK WORLD (ESSAY DATE 1917)

**SOURCE:** "118,000 Negroes Move from the South." *New York World* (November 5, 1917).

*This article chronicles the continued migration of African Americans to northern cities, particularly to areas of cultural flowering and social freedom such as Harlem.*

Since the first of last April, 118,000 Negroes have gone from the South to West Virginia, Pennsylvania, New York, New Jersey, Ohio, Indiana, Missouri, Illinois, Michigan and Connecticut to accept work. They went to take places vacated by thousands of unskilled foreign laborers who returned to Europe after the outbreak of the Great War. This Negro migration to the North, East and West has recently assumed such gigantic proportions that it threatens the very existence of some of the leading industries of Georgia, Florida, Tennessee and Alabama, which have borne the burden of the exodus. The World correspondent, after interviewing hundreds of Negroes, and white people in this section of the country, has found the chief reasons for the tremendous flow of colored citizens to the North to be

1. The natural desire to get a promised increase of wages, accompanied by a free ride to the new field of labor.

2. To gratify a natural impulse to travel, and see the country.

3. To better the condition of the Negro by a freer use of schools and other advantages offered in the North, East and West.

4. The desire of some Negroes to escape the persecution of thoughtless and irresponsible white people who mistreat them.

5. To see the fulfillment of a dream to be on a social equality with white people.

6. The Negro who is educated wants to go where he can vote and take part in running the Government.

The dominant reason for the migration is more money. The alluring tales of the labor agent have made the Southern Negro long for the North. He is in a state of unrest. Every sane Negro in the states of Florida, Georgia, Alabama and Tennessee has heard of the "recruiting man" from the North who has come South to take the Negro to his "real friends."

Great excitement prevails in the entire cotton belt. Crops are short and many Negroes will be idle until spring unless they leave the cotton plantations. The boll weevil and floods destroyed thousands of acres of cotton on the Mississippi this year and left hundreds of Negro families penniless. That is why the call for labor met such a ready response in some regions. The following figures, showing the number of Negroes leaving the various States, indicate the extent of the transfer of labor from the South to other sections of the country: from Alabama, 60,000; from Tennessee, 22,000; from Florida, 12,000; from Georgia, 10,000; from Virginia, 3,000; from North Carolina, 2,000; from Kentucky, 3,000; from South Carolina, 2,000; from Arkansas, 2,000; from Mississippi, 2,000.

It is estimated that ninety-five per cent of the Negroes who have left the South in this movement are men. The demand is for laborers for freight and section-hand work on railroads, miners for coal and iron mines, and unskilled workmen for general outside work at industrial plants throughout the Middle West and North. Most of the black men are now doing the heavy work done by Italians, Montenegrins, Roumanians, Greeks and other foreigners before the European war broke out. The reports of the Bureau of Immigration of the Department of Labor show that during the fiscal years of 1915 and 1916, 169,300 Italians returned to Italy; 2,170 Bulgarians, Serbs and Montenegrins; 3,622 Germans; 18,500 subjects of Great Britain; 8,096 Frenchment; 1,400 Roumanians; 1,000 Russians and 1,600 Japs to their native countries.

Last spring, when the business of the railroads and the mines began to prosper as they had not done before in years, the demand for unskilled labor increased rapidly. The freight congestion in and about New York caused a pressing demand for truck hands. In former years the railroads had called on Europe and Asia for extra supplies. Labor agents and steamship companies cooperated to fill orders for thousands of men for rough work. This year, when they could not get people from the war zone, they returned to the South. The present movement of colored labor from the cotton States of the South to the great industrial centers of the North, East and West was started by the Erie and Pennsylvania Railroads in a legitimate way. The agents of these roads commenced their efforts to increase their operating forces by appealing to the Federal Department of Labor's distribution office, connected with the division of information. The roads took advantage of Secretary Wilson's plan to land the "jobless man" in the "manless job." The first call was made on Florida and Georgia. It was made known at Jacksonville and Savannah that these two great roads would pay 22 cents an hour, seven days a week, and use the men overtime. It was announced that bunkhouses made from boxcars, or railroad hotels, would be provided for the Negroes, and that food would be sold to them at the rate of $2 a week.

It was stated that an able-bodied hard-working Negro man could earn from $70 to $85 a month, laboring for the Erie or Pennsylvania Roads. This appeal started the ball going; the news of the desire for labor spread throughout both States. But the final inducement that reached all of the idle Negroes, and most of the busy ones, was the offer of a "free ride" or a ride on "credit." When it became known that the railroads would not only provide jobs at good wages but would haul the Negroes free, the entire colored population of Georgia and Florida became excited. Farm hands who had driven their employers' teams into towns left their wagons in the streets, and caught outgoing labor trains. Sawmills that had a full corps of laborers when they stopped for the noon hour were deserted without notice, and when the operators investigated they found that their "hands" had gone "North" without a moment's notice. Every industry was affected. A half-dozen doctors in Jacksonville lost their drivers the first day of the "free ride" call.

The conditions in Georgia and Florida were duplicated in Alabama and Tennessee. Soon the movement spread to other States and is still spreading. Many of the first Negroes to migrate have written back and told of the glorious land beyond the Mason Dixon line. John Suggs, a Florida Negro who was sojourning in Georgia when the labor agent got him, wrote back to a brother from Wheeling, West Virginia: "Tim: Get on the first train West Virginia. We come here to work in the mines. We get 25 cents an hour, and gin and whiskey flow like water. I am going with a lot of Georgia Negroes to Pittsburgh Sunday. It don't cost much and I may not come back here. In Pittsburgh the coal and iron men are paying $2.50, $3 and $3.50 a day. And here the people don't call you 'nigger' but 'mister.'" Every community from which the first batches of Negro went is receiving similar letters and appeals. The laborers who went before and are doing well write back to their kith and kin. The higher wages of the North, East and West are being advertised in every Negro home of Florida, Georgia, Alabama and Tennessee.

This Negro movement [was] well under way before the people of the South realized [what] it meant. Jacksonville, Birmingham and Savannah began [to] protest. The Department of Labor soon stopped its efforts to get the "manless job" of the North, East and West, and a "jobless man" from Florida, Georgia or Alabama. Senators Fletcher and Bryan took the matter up with Assistant Secretary Post of the Department of Labor. The Government agent at Jackson was instructed to desist. The city of Jacksonville passed an ordinance taxing all labor agents operating inside the crop limits. The efforts to hold Negroes served to advertise the movement, and some of the labor agents had "labor specials" stop just outside of the city limits and pick up the men who wanted to go "North." Negro preachers and Negro women were paid to urge the men to go North and get better wages. Pictures showing the homes of Negro men with white wives in Chicago and other Western communities were stealthily exhibited. The prospective recruit was told that in the North, East and West his children would go to school with white children and have ten months of school training each year. He was told that he could go to the "white" moving picture shows, and that he could sit anywhere in a streetcar or railroad train, as there are no "Jim Crow" laws outside of the South. All the seductive arguments known to cunning man have been used in Georgia and the neighboring states.

## ALAIN LOCKE (ESSAY DATE 1925)

**SOURCE:** Locke, Alain. "The New Negro." In *Black Literature in America,* edited by Houston A. Baker, Jr., pp. 144-53. New York: McGraw-Hill, 1971.

*In the following excerpt, originally published in 1925, Locke discusses how the New Negro differs from earlier generations of Blacks.*

In the last decade something beyond the watch and guard of statistics has happened in the life of the American Negro and the three norns who have traditionally presided over the Negro problem have a changeling in their laps. The Sociologist, the Philanthropist, the Race-leader are not unaware of the New Negro, but they are at a loss to account for him. He simply cannot be swathed in their formulæ. For the younger generation is vibrant with a new psychology; the new spirit is awake in the masses, and under the very eyes of the professional observers is transforming what has been a perennial problem into the progressive phases of contemporary Negro life.

Could such a metamorphosis have taken place as suddenly as it has appeared to? The answer is no; not because the New Negro is not here, but because the Old Negro had long become more of a myth than a man. The Old Negro, we must remember, was a creature of moral debate and historical controversy. His has been a stock figure perpetuated as an historical fiction partly in innocent sentimentalism, partly in deliberate reactionism. The Negro himself has contributed his share to this through a sort of protective social mimicry forced upon him by the adverse circumstances of dependence. So for generations in the mind of America, the Negro has been more of a formula than a human being—a something to be argued about, condemned or defended, to be "kept down," or "in his place," or "helped up," to be worried with or worried over, harassed or patronized, a social bogey or a social burden. The thinking Negro even has been induced to share this same general attitude, to focus his attention on controversial issues, to see himself in the distorted perspective of a social problem. His shadow, so to speak, has been more real to him than his personality. Through having had to appeal from the unjust stereotypes of his oppressors and traducers to those of his liberators, friends and benefactors he has had to subscribe to the traditional positions from which his case has been viewed. Little true social or self-understanding has or could come from such a situation.

But while the minds of most of us, black and white, have thus burrowed in the trenches of the Civil War and Reconstruction, the actual march of development has simply flanked these positions, necessitating a sudden reorientation of view. We have not been watching in the right direction; set North and South on a sectional axis, we have not noticed the East till the sun has us blinking.

Recall how suddenly the Negro spirituals revealed themselves; suppressed for generations under the stereotypes of Wesleyan hymn harmony, secretive, half-ashamed, until the courage of being natural brought them out—and behold, there was folk-music. Similarly the mind of the Negro seems suddenly to have slipped from under the tyranny of social intimidation and to be shaking off the psychology of imitation and implied inferiority. By shedding the old chrysalis of the Negro problem we are achieving something like a spiritual emancipation. Until recently, lacking self-understanding, we have been almost as much of a problem to ourselves as we still are to others. But the decade that found us with a problem has left us with only a task. The multitude perhaps feels as yet only a strange relief and a new vague urge, but the thinking few know that in the reaction the vital inner grip of prejudice has been broken.

With this renewed self-respect and self-dependence, the life of the Negro community is bound to enter a new dynamic phase, the buoyancy from within compensating for whatever pressure there may be of conditions from without. The migrant masses, shifting from countryside to city, hurdle several generations of experience at a leap, but more important, the same thing happens spiritually in the life-attitudes and self-expression of the Young Negro, in his poetry, his art, his education and his new outlook, with the additional advantage, of course, of the poise and greater certainty of knowing what it is all about. From this comes the promise and warrant of a new leadership. As one of them has discerningly put it:

> We have tomorrow
> Bright before us
> Like a flame.
>
> Yesterday, a night-gone thing
> A sun-down name.
>
> And dawn today
> Broad arch above the road we came.
> We march!

This is what, even more than any "most creditable record of fifty years of freedom," requires that the Negro of to-day be seen through other than the dusty spectacles of past controversy. The day of "aunties," "uncles" and "mammies" is equally gone. Uncle Tom and Sambo have passed on, and even the "Colonel" and "George" play barnstorm rôles from which they escape with relief when the public spotlight is off. The popular melodrama has about played itself out, and it is time to scrap the fictions, garret the bogeys and settle down to a realistic facing of facts.

First we must observe some of the changes which since the traditional lines of opinion were drawn have rendered these quite obsolete. A main change has been, of course, that shifting of the Negro population which has made the Negro problem no longer exclusively or even predominantly Southern. Why should our minds remain sectionalized, when the problem itself no longer is? Then the trend of migration has not only been toward the North and the Central Midwest, but city-ward and to the great centers of industry—the problems of adjustment are new, practical, local and not peculiarly racial. Rather they are an integral part of the large industrial and social problems of our present-day democracy. And finally, with the Negro rapidly in process of class differentiation, if it ever was warrantable to regard and treat the Negro *en masse* it is becoming with every day less possible, more unjust and more ridiculous.

In the very process of being transplanted, the Negro is becoming transformed.

The tide of Negro migration, northward and city-ward, is not to be fully explained as a blind flood started by the demands of war industry coupled with the shutting off of foreign migration, or by the pressure of poor crops coupled with increased social terrorism in certain sections of the South and Southwest. Neither labor demand, the bollweevil nor the Ku Klux Klan is a basic factor, however contributory any or all of them may have been. The wash and rush of this human tide on the beach line of the northern city centers is to be explained primarily in terms of a new vision of opportunity, of social and economic freedom, of a spirit to seize, even in the face of an extortionate and heavy toll, a chance for the improvement of conditions. With each successive wave of it, the movement of the Negro becomes more and more a mass movement toward the larger and the more democratic chance—in the Negro's case a deliberate flight not only from countryside to city, but from medieval America to modern.

Take Harlem as an instance of this. Here in Manhattan is not merely the largest Negro community in the world, but the first concentration in history of so many diverse elements of Negro life. It has attracted the African, the West Indian, the Negro American; has brought together the Negro of the North and the Negro of the South; the man from the city and the man from the town and village; the peasant, the student, the business man, the professional man, artist, poet, musician, adventurer and worker, preacher and criminal, exploiter and social outcast. Each group has come with its own separate motives and for its own special ends, but their greatest experience has been the finding of one another. Proscription and prejudice have thrown these dissimilar elements into a common area of contact and interaction. Within this area, race sympathy and unity have determined a further fusing of sentiment and experience. So what began in terms of segregation becomes more and more, as its elements mix and react, the laboratory of a great race-welding. Hitherto, it must be admitted that American Negroes have been a race more in name than in fact, or to be exact, more in sentiment than in experience. The chief bond between them has been that of a common condition rather than a common consciousness; a problem in common rather than a life in common. In Harlem, Negro life is seizing upon its first chances for group expression and self-determination. It is—or promises at least to be—a race capital. That is why our comparison is taken with those nascent centers of folk-expression and self-determination which are playing a creative part in the world to-day. Without pretense to their political significance, Harlem has the same rôle to play for the New Negro as Dublin has had for the New Ireland or Prague for the New Czechoslovakia.

Harlem, I grant you, isn't typical—but it is significant, it is prophetic. No sane observer, however sympathetic to the new trend, would contend that the great masses are articulate as yet, but they stir, they move, they are more than physically restless. The challenge of the new intellectuals among them is clear enough—the "race radicals" and realists who have broken with the old epoch of philanthropic guidance, sentimental appeal and protest. But are we after all only reading into the stirrings of a sleeping giant the dreams of an agitator? The answer is in the migrating peasant. It is the "man farthest down" who is most active in getting up. One of the most characteristic symptoms of this is the professional man, himself migrating to recapture his constituency after a vain effort to maintain in some Southern corner what for years back seemed an established living and clientele. The clergyman following his errant flock, the physician or lawyer trailing his clients, supply the true clues. In a real sense it is the rank and file who are leading, and the leaders who are following. A transformed and transforming psychology permeates the masses.

When the racial leaders of twenty years ago spoke of developing race-pride and stimulating race-consciousness, and of the desirability of race solidarity, they could not in any accurate degree have anticipated the abrupt feeling that has surged up and now pervades the awakened centers. Some of the recognized Negro leaders and a powerful section of white opinion identified with "race work" of the older order have indeed attempted to discount this feeling as a "passing phase," an attack of "race nerves" so to speak, an "aftermath of the war," and the like. It has not abated, however, if we are to gauge by the present tone and temper of the Negro press, or by the shift in popular support from the officially recognized and orthodox spokesmen to those of the independent, popular, and often radical type who are unmistakable symptoms of a new order. It is a social disservice to blunt the fact that the Negro of the Northern centers has reached a stage where tutelage, even of the most interested and well-intentioned sort, must give place to new relationships, where positive self-direction must be reckoned with in ever increasing measure. The American mind must reckon with a fundamentally changed Negro.

The Negro too, for his part, has idols of the tribe to smash. If on the one hand the white man has erred in making the Negro appear to be that which would excuse or extenuate his treatment of him, the Negro, in turn, has too often unnecessarily excused himself because of the way he has been treated. The intelligent Negro of to-day is resolved not to make discrimination an extenuation for his shortcomings in performance, individual or collective; he is trying to hold himself at par, neither inflated by sentimental allowances nor depreciated by current social discounts. For this he must know himself and be known for precisely what he is, and for that reason he welcomes the new scientific rather than the old sentimental interest. Sentimental interest in the Negro has ebbed. We used to lament this as the falling off of our friends; now we rejoice and pray to be delivered both from self-pity and condescension. The mind of each racial group has had a bitter weaning, apathy or hatred on one side matching disillusionment or resentment on the other; but they face each other to-day with the possibility at least of entirely new mutual attitudes.

It does not follow that if the Negro were better known, he would be better liked or better treated. But mutual understanding is basic for any subsequent coöperation and adjustment. The effort toward this will at least have the effect of remedying in large part what has been the most unsatisfactory feature of our present stage of race relationships in America, namely the fact that the more intelligent and representative elements of the two race groups have at so many points got quite out of vital touch with one another.

The fiction is that the life of the races is separate, and increasingly so. The fact is that they have touched too closely at the unfavorable and too lightly at the favorable levels.

While inter-racial councils have sprung up in the South, drawing on forward elements of both races, in the Northern cities manual laborers may brush elbows in their everyday work, but the community and business leaders have experienced no such interplay or far too little of it. These segments must achieve contact or the race situation in America becomes desperate. Fortunately this is happening. There is a growing realization that in social effort the co-operative basis must supplant long-distance philanthropy, and that the only safeguard for mass relations in the future must be provided in the carefully maintained contacts of the enlightened minorities of both race groups. In the intellectual realm a renewed and keen curiosity is replacing the recent apathy; the Negro is being carefully studied, not just talked about and discussed. In art and letters, instead of being wholly caricatured, he is being seriously portrayed and painted.

To all of this the New Negro is keenly responsive as an augury of a new democracy in American culture. He is contributing his share to the new social understanding. But the desire to be understood would never in itself have been sufficient to have opened so completely the protectively closed portals of the thinking Negro's mind. There is still too much possibility of being snubbed or patronized for that. It was rather the necessity for fuller, truer self-expression, the realization of the unwisdom of allowing social discrimination to segregate him mentally, and a counter-attitude to cramp and fetter his own living—and so the "spite-wall" that the intellectuals built over the "color-line" has happily been taken down. Much of this reopening of intellectual contacts has centered in New York and has been richly fruitful not merely in the enlarging of personal experience, but in the definite enrichment of American art and letters and in the clarifying of our common vision of the social tasks ahead.

The particular significance in the re-establishment of contact between the more advanced and representative classes is that it promises to offset some of the unfavorable reactions of the past, or at least to re-surface race contacts somewhat for the future. Subtly the conditions that are molding a New Negro are molding a new American attitude.

However, this new phase of things is delicate; it will call for less charity but more justice; less help, but infinitely closer understanding. This is indeed a critical stage of race relationships because of the likelihood, if the new temper is not understood, of engendering sharp group antagonism and a second crop of more calculated prejudice. In some quarters, it has already done so. Having weaned the Negro, public opinion cannot continue to paternalize. The Negro to-day is inevitably moving forward under the control largely of his own objectives. What are these objectives? Those of his outer life are happily already well and finally formulated, for they are none other than the ideals of American institutions and democracy. Those of his inner life are yet in process of formation, for the new psychology at present is more of a consensus of feeling than of opinion, of attitude rather than of program. Still some points seem to have crystallized.

Up to the present one may adequately describe the Negro's "inner objectives" as an attempt to repair a damaged group psychology and reshape a warped social perspective. Their realization has required a new mentality for the American Negro. And as it matures we begin to see its effects; at first, negative, iconoclastic, and then positive and constructive. In this new group psychology we note the lapse of sentimental appeal, then the development of a more positive self-respect and self-reliance; the repudiation of social dependence, and then the gradual recovery from hyper-sensitiveness and "touchy" nerves, the repudiation of the double standard of judgment with its special philanthropic allowances and then the sturdier desire for objective and scientific appraisal; and finally the rise from social disillusionment to race pride, from the sense of social debt to the responsibilities of social contribution, and offsetting the necessary working and commonsense acceptance of restricted conditions, the belief in ultimate esteem and recognition. Therefore the Negro to-day wishes to be known for what he is, even in his faults and shortcomings, and scorns a craven and precarious survival at the price of seeming to be what he is not. He resents being spoken of as a social ward or minor, even by his own, and to being regarded a chronic patient for the sociological clinic, the sick man of American Democracy. For the same reasons, he himself is through with those social nostrums and panaceas, the so-called "solutions" of his "problem," with which he and the country have been so liberally dosed in the past. Religion, freedom, education, money—in turn, he has ardently hoped for and peculiarly trusted these things; he still believes in them, but not in blind trust that they alone will solve his life-problem.

Each generation, however, will have its creed, and that of the present is the belief in the efficacy of collective effort, in race co-operation. This deep feeling of race is at present the mainspring of Negro life. It seems to be the outcome of the reaction to proscription and prejudice; an attempt, fairly successful on the whole, to convert a defensive into an offensive position, a handicap into an incentive. It is radical in tone, but not in purpose and only the most stupid forms of opposition, misunderstanding or persecution could make it otherwise. Of course, the thinking Negro has shifted a little toward the left with the world-trend, and there is an increasing group who affiliate with radical and liberal movements. But fundamentally for the present the Negro is radical on race matters, conservative on others, in other words, a "forced radical," a social protestant rather than a genuine radical. Yet under further pressure and injustice iconoclastic thought and motives will inevitably increase. Harlem's quixotic radicalisms call for their ounce of democracy to-day lest to-morrow they be beyond cure.

The Negro mind reaches out as yet to nothing but American wants, American ideas. But this forced attempt to build his Americanism on race values is a unique social experiment, and its ultimate success is impossible except through the fullest sharing of American culture and institutions. There should be no delusion about this. American nerves in sections unstrung with race hysteria are often fed the opiate that the trend of Negro advance is wholly separatist, and that the effect of its operation will be to encyst the Negro as a benign foreign body in the body politic. This cannot be—even if it were desirable. The racialism of the Negro is no limitation or reservation with respect to American life; it is only a constructive effort to build the obstructions in the stream of his progress into an efficient dam of social energy and power. Democracy itself is obstructed and stagnated to the extent that any of its channels are closed. Indeed they cannot be selectively closed. So the choice is not between one way for the Negro and another way for the rest, but between American institutions frustrated on the one hand and American ideals progressively fulfilled and realized on the other.

There is, of course, a warrantably comfortable feeling in being on the right side of the country's professed ideals. We realize that we cannot be undone without America's undoing. It is within the gamut of this attitude that the thinking Negro faces America, but with variations of mood that are if anything more significant than the attitude itself. Sometimes we have it taken with the defiant ironic challenge of McKay:

> Mine is the future grinding down to-day
> Like a great landslip moving to the sea,
> Bearing its freight of débris far away
> Where the green hungry waters restlessly
> Heave mammoth pyramids, and break and roar
> Their eerie challenge to the crumbling shore.

Sometimes, perhaps more frequently as yet, it is taken in the fervent and almost filial appeal and counsel of Weldon Johnson's:

> O Southland, dear Southland!
> Then why do you still cling
> To an idle age and a musty page,
> To a dead and useless thing?

But between defiance and appeal, midway almost between cynicism and hope, the prevailing mind stands in the mood of the same author's *To America,* an attitude of sober query and stoical challenge:

> How would you have us, as we are?
>     Or sinking 'neath the load we bear,
> Our eyes fixed forward on a star,
>     Or gazing empty at despair?
>
> Rising or falling? Men or things?
>     With dragging pace or footsteps fleet?
> Strong, willing sinews in your wings,
>     Or tightening chains about your feet?

More and more, however, an intelligent realization of the great discrepancy between the American social creed and the American social practice forces upon the Negro the taking of the moral advantage that is his. Only the steadying and sobering effect of a truly characteristic gentleness of spirit prevents the rapid rise of a definite cynicism and counter-hate and a defiant superiority feeling. Human as this reaction would be, the majority still deprecate its advent, and would gladly see it forestalled by the speedy amelioration of its causes. We wish our race pride to be a healthier, more positive achievement than a feeling based upon a realization of the shortcomings of others. But all paths toward the attainment of a sound social attitude have been difficult; only a relatively few enlightened minds have been able as the phrase puts it "to rise above" prejudice. The ordinary man has had until recently only a hard choice between the alternatives of supine and humiliating submission and stimulating but hurtful counter-prejudice. Fortunately from some inner, desperate resourcefulness has recently sprung up the simple expedient of fighting prejudice by mental passive resistance, in other words by trying to ignore it. For the few, this manna may perhaps be effective, but the masses cannot thrive upon it.

Fortunately there are constructive channels opening out into which the balked social feelings of the American Negro can flow freely.

Without them there would be much more pressure and danger than there is. These compensating interests are racial but in a new and enlarged way. One is the consciousness of acting as the advance-guard of the African peoples in their contact with Twentieth Century civilization; the other, the sense of a mission of rehabilitating the race in world esteem from that loss of prestige for which the fate and conditions of slavery have so largely been responsible. Harlem, as we shall see, is the center of both these movements; she is the home of the Negro's "Zionism." The pulse of the Negro world has begun to beat in Harlem. A Negro newspaper carrying news material in English, French and Spanish, gathered from all quarters of America, the West Indies and Africa has maintained itself in Harlem for over five years. Two important magazines, both edited from New York, maintain their news and circulation consistently on a cosmopolitan scale. Under American auspices and backing, three pan-African congresses have been held abroad for the discussion of common interests, colonial questions and the future co-operative development of Africa. In terms of the race question as a world problem, the Negro mind has leapt, so to speak, upon the parapets of prejudice and extended its cramped horizons. In so doing it has linked up with the growing group consciousness of the dark-peoples and is gradually learning their common interests. As one of our writers has recently put it: "It is imperative that we understand the white world in its rela-

tions to the non-white world." As with the Jew, persecution is making the Negro international.

As a world phenomenon this wider race consciousness is a different thing from the much asserted rising tide of color. Its inevitable causes are not of our making. The consequences are not necessarily damaging to the best interests of civilization. Whether it actually brings into being new Armadas of conflict or argosies of cultural exchange and enlightenment can only be decided by the attitude of the dominant races in an era of critical change. With the American Negro, his new internationalism is primarily an effort to recapture contact with the scattered peoples of African derivation. Garveyism may be a transient, if spectacular, phenomenon, but the possible rôle of the American Negro in the future development of Africa is one of the most constructive and universally helpful missions that any modern people can lay claim to.

Constructive participation in such causes cannot help giving the Negro valuable group incentives, as well as increased prestigé at home and abroad. Our greatest rehabilitation may possibly come through such channels, but for the present, more immediate hope rests in the revaluation by white and black alike of the Negro in terms of his artistic endowments and cultural contributions, past and prospective. It must be increasingly recognized that the Negro has already made very substantial contributions, not only in his folk-art, music especially, which has always found appreciation, but in larger, though humbler and less acknowledged ways. For generations the Negro has been the peasant matrix of that section of America which has most undervalued him, and here he has contributed not only materially in labor and in social patience, but spiritually as well. The South has unconsciously absorbed the gift of his folk-temperament. In less than half a generation it will be easier to recognize this, but the fact remains that a leaven of humor, sentiment, imagination and tropic nonchalance has gone into the making of the South from a humble, unacknowledged source. A second crop of the Negro's gifts promises still more largely. He now becomes a conscious contributor and lays aside the status of a beneficiary and ward for that of a collaborator and participant in American civilization. The great social gain in this is the releasing of our talented group from the arid fields of controversy and debate to the productive fields of creative expression. The especially cultural recognition they win should in turn prove the key to that revaluation of the Negro which must precede or accompany any considerable further betterment of race relationships. But whatever the general effect, the present generation will have added the motives of self-expression and spiritual development to the old and still unfinished task of making material headway and progress. No one who understandingly faces the situation with its substantial accomplishment or views the new scene with its still more abundant promise can be entirely without hope. And certainly, if in our lifetime the Negro should not be able to celebrate his full initiation into American democracy, he can at least, on the warrant of these things, celebrate the attainment of a significant and satisfying new phase of group development, and with it a spiritual Coming of Age.

## MARCUS GARVEY (ESSAY DATE 1928)

SOURCE: Garvey, Marcus. "*Home to Harlem*: An Insult to the Race." In *Voices of a Black Nation: Political Journalism in the Harlem Renaissance,* edited by Theodore G. Vincent, pp. 357-59. Trenton: Africa World Press, 1990.

*In the following essay, originally published in 1928, Garvey criticizes the writings of McKay, Du Bois, and others as "literary prostitution."*

Fellowmen of the Negro Race, Greeting:

It is my duty to bring to your attention this week a grave evil that afflicts us as a people at this time. Our race, within recent years, has developed a new group of writers who have been prostituting their intelligence, under the direction of the white man, to bring out and show up the worse traits of our people. Several of these writers are American and West Indian Negroes. They have been writing books, novels and poems, under the advice of white publishers, to portray to the world the looseness, laxity and immorality that are peculiar to our group, for the purpose of these publishers circulating the libel against us among the white peoples of the world, to further hold us up to ridicule and contempt and universal prejudice.

### McKay's Home to Harlem

Several of these books have been published in America recently, the last of which is Claude McKay's "Home to Harlem," published by Harper Bros. of New York. This book . . . is a damnable libel against the Negro. . . . Claude McKay, the Jamaican Negro, is not singular in the authorship of such books, W. E. B. DuBois, of America; Walter White, Weldon Johnson, Eric Walrond, of British Guiana, and others, have written similar books, while we have had recently a large number of sappy poems from the rising poets.

### White Publishers Use Negroes

The white people have these Negroes to write [this] kind of stuff . . . so that the Negro can still be regarded as a monkey or some imbecilic creature. Whenever authors of the Negro race write good literature for publication the white publishers refuse to publish it, but wherever the Negro is sufficiently known to attract attention he is advised to write in the way that the white man wants. That is just what has happened to Claude McKay. The time has come for us to boycott such Negro authors whom we may fairly designate as "literary prostitutes." We must make them understand that we are not going to stand for their insults indulged in to suit prejudiced white people who desire to hold the Negro up to contempt and ridicule. We must encourage our own black authors who have character, who are loyal to their race, who feel proud to be black, and in every way let them feel that we appreciate their efforts to advance our race through healthy and decent literature.

### Writers to Fight Negro Cause

We want writers who will fight [for] the Negro's cause, as H. G. Wells of the white race fights for the cause of the Anglo-Saxon group. Let us imagine Wells prostituting his intelligence and ability as an author to suit Negro publishers, as against the morals or interest of the Anglo-Saxon race. It is impossible. Yet there are many Negro writers who prostituted their intelligence to do the most damaging harm to the morals and reputations of the black race. . . .

The preceding bore the following headlines: "'Home to Harlem' . . . Should Earn Wholesale Condemnation/Marcus Garvey, Foremost Negro Leader, Condemns Harmful Trend of Books of a New Group of Race Writers/Says Jamaican Negro's Latest Offering Is an Insult to Black Race/Sappy Poems and Pernicious Novels Written by 'Literary Prostitutes' to Suit White Publishers/Halt Must Be Called on Libelous Writers So That Negro Race May Develop Helpful Authors."

## FRANK BYRD (DOCUMENT DATE 1939)

SOURCE: "Negro Folk Arts—Mae Berkeley." Federal Writers' Project (January 19, 1939).

*The following article, part of the Works Projects Administration's Federal Writers' Project, examines the burgeoning interest in African folklore and art through a portrait of Mae Berkeley, a street vendor trafficking in African "curios" and small artworks.*

Mae Berkeley is probably the most unique merchant in the Park Avenue Market. She is not a licensed peddler and, unlike many of those who are, she does not work at her stand everyday. On the contrary, she puts in her appearance only on those days when she feels particularly good or when the weather is bright and inviting. She is a vendor of native African curios done in clay, brass, wood, straw, ivory and other materials available to the primitive tribes of the African jungles.

How Mae, who lives at 222 West 121 Street, began selling these pieces of native handiwork in the market-place is a surprising story; for Mae herself is not African. She is a product of Trinidad in the British West Indies. She has . . . always . . . been tremendously interested, however, in Negro folklore and art, and as a consequence of this, she has sought in almost every direction for additional information concerning every branch of Negro art. Feeling that she could attain a wider and more authentic knowledge by studying the most primitive forms, she naturally turned to the African.

Her first step was to widen her acquaintance among Africans in New York. Her search for them led to the discovery of the Native African Union at 254 West 135 Street. Here she met all or practically all of those who make their homes in Harlem. She also learned that a troupe of native African Ballet Dancers were staging periodic dance recitals at Town Hall, Roerich Hall and, occasionally, in Harlem. Through some of her newly found friends, she was able to study and dance with this group, having already achieved a fair reputation as a dancer in Harlem and Greenwich Village Night Clubs. Her dancing led to more friendly relations and she soon began to inquire as to the possibility of importing native handicraft from the various tribes represented by the group. The idea met with approval and it was not long before she was receiving regular shipments of curios, war-implements etc. from both the South and West Coasts of Africa.

When Mae received her first shipment of goods, she was dancing in a little night club in the Village called the . . . Rubiyat. . . . She received permission from the management to sell her things there. Her sales were far more numerous than she expected. It was not long before she had placed parts of her shipment in curio-shops in West fourth and eighth streets. They attracted much attention. Mae decided to branch out to Harlem. She began with free exhibits in the public library and in the homes of various club-women. This gave her the necessary publicity. She let it

become known that . . . they . . . could be found either in the Eighth or Park Avenue markets or at the Native African Union.

Mae's sales have increased greatly in the past two years.

If it were not for her dancing which takes so much of her time, she would probably make a regular, paying business of this hobby. Instead, she devotes only a comparatively small part of her spare time to it. She [does?], however, exhibit her own private collection at all dance recitals of the Group. When asked why she does not open a regular shop or place a helper on each of her stands in both Harlem Markets, she replies:

"Some day, perhaps, I will. Now, I am much too busy with my dancing. Besides, I don't just want to sell them. I want my people (Negroes) to learn of the value of their native art."

# OVERVIEWS

## DAVID LEVERING LEWIS (ESSAY DATE 1994)

**SOURCE:** Lewis, David Levering. Introduction to *The Portable Harlem Renaissance Reader,* edited by David Levering Lewis, pp. xv-xliii. New York: Viking, 1994.

*In the following essay, Lewis provides an overview of the cultural context of the Harlem Renaissance.*

The Harlem Renaissance was a somewhat forced phenomenon, a cultural nationalism of the parlor, institutionally encouraged and directed by leaders of the national civil rights establishment for the paramount purpose of improving race relations in a time of extreme national backlash, caused in large part by economic gains won by Afro-Americans during the Great War. W. E. B. Du Bois labeled this mobilizing elite the "Talented Tenth" in a seminal 1903 essay. He fleshed out the concept that same year in "The Advance Guard of the Race," a piece in *Booklover's Magazine* in which he identified the poet Paul Laurence Dunbar, the novelist Charles W. Chesnutt, and the painter Henry O. Tanner, among a small number of other well-educated professionals, as representatives of this class. The Talented Tenth formulated and propagated a new ideology of racial assertiveness that was to be embraced by the physicians, dentists, educators, preachers, businesspeople, lawyers, and morticians who comprised the bulk of the African American affluent and influential—some ten thousand men and women out of a total population in 1920 of more than ten million. (In 1917, traditionally cited as the natal year of the Harlem Renaissance, there were 2,132 African Americans in colleges and universities, probably no more than fifty of them attending "white" institutions.)

It was, then, the minuscule vanguard of a minority—a fraction of 0.1 percent of the racial total—that jump-started the New Negro Arts Movement, using as its vehicles the National Association for the Advancement of Colored People (NAACP) and the National Urban League (NUL), and their respective publications, *The Crisis* and *Opportunity* magazine. The Harlem Renaissance was not, as some students have maintained, all-inclusive of the early twentieth-century African American urban experience. Not everything that happened between 1917 and 1935 was a Renaissance happening. The potent mass movement founded and led by the charismatic Marcus Garvey was to the Renaissance what nineteenth-century populism was to progressive reform: a parallel but socially different force related primarily through dialectical confrontation. Equally different from the institutional ethos and purpose of the Renaissance was the Black Church. If the leading intellectual of the race, Du Bois, publicly denigrated the personnel and preachings of the Black Church, his animadversions were merely more forthright than those of other New Negro notables James Weldon Johnson, Charles S. Johnson, Jessie Redmon Fauset, Alain Locke, and Walter Francis White. An occasional minister (such as the father of poet Countee Cullen) or exceptional Garveyites (such as Yale-Harvard man William H. Ferris) might move in both worlds, but black evangelism and its cultist manifestations, such as Black Zionism, represented emotional and cultural retrogression in the eyes of the principal actors in the Renaissance.

When Du Bois wrote a few years after the beginning of the New Negro movement in arts and letters that "until the art of the black folk compels recognition they will not be rated as human," he, like most of his Renaissance peers, fully intended to exclude the blues of Bessie Smith and the jazz of "King" Oliver. Spirituals sung like *Lieder* by the disciplined Hall Johnson Choir—and, better yet, *Lieder* sung by conservatory-trained Roland Hayes, 1924 recipient of the NAACP's prestigious Spingarn Medal—were deemed appropriate musical forms to present to mainstream America. The deans of the Renaissance were entirely content to leave discovery and celebration of Bessie, Clara, Trixie, and various other blues-singing Smiths to white music critic Carl Van Vechten's effusions in *Vanity Fair*. When the visiting Russian film director Sergei Eisenstein enthused about new black musicals, Charles S. Johnson and Alain Locke expressed mild consternation in their interview in *Opportunity* magazine. As board members of the Pace Phonograph Company, Du Bois, James Weldon Johnson, and others banned "funky" artists from the Black Swan list of recordings, thereby contributing to the demise of the African American-owned firm. But the wild Broadway success of Miller and Lyles's musical *Shuffle Along* (which helped to popularize the Charleston) or Florence Mills's *Blackbirds* revue flouted such artistic fastidiousness. The very centrality of music in black life, as well as of black musical stereotypes in white minds, caused popular musical forms to impinge inescapably on Renaissance high culture. Eventually, the Renaissance deans made a virtue out of necessity; they applauded the concert-hall ragtime of "Big Jim" Europe and the "educated" jazz of Atlanta University graduate and big-band leader Fletcher Henderson, and took to hiring Duke Ellington or Cab Calloway as drawing cards for fund-raising socials. Still, their relationship to music remained beset by paradox. New York ragtime, with its "Jelly Roll" Morton strides and Joplinesque elegance, had as much in common with Chicago jazz as Mozart did with "Fats" Waller.

Although the emergence of the Harlem Renaissance seems much more sudden and dramatic in retrospect than the historic reality, its institutional elaboration was, in fact, relatively quick. Because so little fiction or poetry had been produced by African Americans in the years immediately prior to the Harlem Renaissance, the appearance of a dozen or more poets and novelists and essayists seemed all the more striking and improbable. Death from tuberculosis had silenced poet-novelist Dunbar in 1906, and poor royalties had done the same for novelist Chesnutt after publication the previous year of *The Colonel's Dream*. Since then, no more than five African Americans had published significant works of fiction and verse. There had been *Pointing the Way* in 1908, a flawed, fascinating civil rights novel by the Baptist preacher Sutton Griggs. Three years later, Du Bois's sweeping sociological allegory *The Quest of the Silver Fleece* appeared. The following year came James Weldon Johnson's well-crafted *The Autobiography of an Ex-Colored Man,* but the author felt compelled to disguise his racial identity. A ten-year silence fell afterward, finally to be broken in 1922 by Claude McKay's *Harlem Shadows,* the first book of poetry since Dunbar.

Altogether, the Harlem Renaissance evolved through three stages. The first phase, ending in 1923 with the publication of Jean Toomer's unique prose poem *Cane,* was deeply influenced by white artists and writers—Bohemians and Revolutionaries—fascinated for a variety of reasons with the life of black people. The second phase, from early 1924 to mid-1926, was presided over by the Civil Rights Establishment of the NUL and the NAACP, a period of interracial collaboration between Zora Neale Hurston's "Negrotarian" whites and the African American Talented Tenth. The last phase, from mid-1926 to the Harlem Riot of March 1935, was increasingly dominated by the African American artists themselves—the "Niggerati," in Hurston's pungent phrase. The movement, then, was above all literary and self-consciously an enterprise of high culture well into its middle years. When Charles S. Johnson, new editor of *Opportunity,* sent invitations to some dozen young and mostly unknown African American poets and writers to attend a celebration at Manhattan's Civic Club of the sudden outpouring of "Negro" writing, on March 21, 1924, the Renaissance shifted into high gear. "A group of the younger writers, which includes Eric Walrond, Jessie Fauset, Gwendolyn Bennett, Countee Cullen, Langston Hughes, Alain Locke, and some others," would be present, Johnson promised each invitee. All told, in addition to the "younger writers," some fifty persons were expected: "Eugene O'Neill, H. L. Mencken, Oswald Garrison Villard, Mary Johnston, Zona Gale, Robert Morss Lovett, Carl Van Doren, Ridgely Torrence, and about twenty more of this type. I think you might find this group interesting enough to draw you away for a few hours from your work on your next book," Johnson wrote almost coyly to the recently published Jean Toomer.

Although both Toomer and Langston Hughes were absent in Europe, approximately 110 celebrants and honorees assembled that evening; included among them were Du Bois, James Weldon Johnson, and the young NAACP officer Walter Francis White, whose energies as a literary entrepreneur would soon excel even Charles Johnson's. Locke, a professor of philosophy at Howard University and the first African American Rhodes scholar, served as Civic Club master of ceremonies. Fauset, the literary editor of *The Crisis* and a Phi Beta Kappa graduate of Cornell University, enjoyed the distinction of having written the second fictional work and first novel of the Renaissance, *There Is Confusion,* just released by Horace Liveright. Liveright, who was present, rose

to praise Fauset as well as Toomer, whose prose poem *Cane* his firm had published in 1923. Speeches followed pell mell—Du Bois, James Weldon Johnson, Fauset. White called attention to the next Renaissance novel—his own, *The Fire in the Flint,* shortly forthcoming from Knopf. Albert Barnes, the crusty Philadelphia pharmaceutical millionaire and art collector, described the decisive impact of African art on modern art. Poets and poems were commended—Hughes, Cullen, and Georgia Douglas Johnson of Washington, D.C., with Gwendolyn Bennett's stilted yet appropriate "To Usward" punctuating the evening: "We claim no part with racial dearth, / We want to sing the songs of birth!" Charles Johnson wrote the vastly competent Ethel Ray Nance, his future secretary, of his enormous gratification that Paul Kellogg, editor of the influential *Survey Graphic,* had proposed that evening to place a special number of his magazine "at the service of representatives of the group."

Two compelling messages emerged from the Civic Club gathering: Du Bois's that the literature of apology and the denial to his generation of its authentic voice were now ending; Van Doren's that African American artists were developing at a uniquely propitious moment. They were "in a remarkable strategic position with reference to the new literary age which seems to be impending," Van Doren predicted. "What American literature decidedly needs at this moment," he continued, "is color, music, gusto, the free expression of gay or desperate moods. If the Negroes are not in a position to contribute these items," Van Doren could not imagine who else could. The African American had indisputably moved to the center of Mainstream imagination with the end of the Great War, a development nurtured in the chrysalis of the Lost Generation—Greenwich Village Bohemia. Ready conversance with the essentials of Freud and Marx became the measure of serious conversation in MacDougal Street coffeehouses, Albert Boni's Washington Square Book Shop, or the Hotel Brevoort's restaurant, where Floyd Dell, Robert Minor, Matthew Josephson, Max Eastman, and other *enragés* denounced the social system, the Great War to which it had ineluctably led, and the soul-dead world created in its aftermath, with McKay and Toomer, two of the Renaissance's first stars, participating. The first issue of Randolph Bourne's *Seven Arts* (November 1916)—which featured, among others of the "Lyrical Left," Waldo Frank, James Oppenheim, Robert Frost, Paul Rosenfeld, Van Wyck Brooks, and the French intellectual Romain Rolland—

professed contempt for "the people who actually run things" in America. Waldo Frank, Toomer's bosom friend and literary mentor, foresaw a revolutionary new America emerging "out of our terrifying welter or steel and scarlet." The Marxist radicals (John Reed, Floyd Dell, Helen Keller, Max Eastman) associated with *Masses* and its successor magazine, *Liberator,* edited by Max and Crystal Eastman, were theoretically much more oriented to politics. The inaugural March 1918 issue of *Liberator* announced that they would "fight for the ownership and control of industry by the workers."

Among the Lyrical Left writers gathered around *Broom, S4N,* and *Seven Arts,* and the political radicals associated with *Liberator,* there was a shared reaction against the ruling Anglo-Saxon cultural paradigm. Bourne's concept of a "transnational" America, democratically respectful of its ethnic, racial, and religious constituents, complemented Du Bois's earlier concept of divided racial identity in *The Souls of Black Folk.* From such conceptions, the Village's discovery of Harlem followed both logically and, more compellingly, psychologically, for if the factory, campus, office, and corporation were dehumanizing, stultifying, or predatory, the African American, largely excluded because of race from all of the above, was a perfect symbol of cultural innocence and regeneration. He was perceived as an integral, indispensable part of the hoped-for design, somehow destined to aid in the reclamation of a diseased, dessicated civilization.

Public annunciation of the rediscovered Negro came in the fall of 1917 with Emily Hapgood's production at the old Garden Street Theatre of three one-act plays by her husband, Ridgely Torrence. *The Rider of Dreams, Simon the Cyrenian,* and *Granny Maumee* were considered daring because the casts were black and the parts were dignified. The drama critic from *Theatre Magazine* enthused of one lead player that "nobody who saw Opal Cooper—and heard him as the dreamer, Madison Sparrow—will ever forget the lift his performance gave." Du Bois commended the playwright by letter, and James Weldon Johnson excitedly wrote his friend, the African American literary critic Benjamin Brawley, that *The Smart Set*'s Jean Nathan "spoke most highly about the work of these colored performers." From this watershed flowed a number of dramatic productions, musicals, and several successful novels by whites—yet also, with great significance, *Shuffle Along,* a cathartic musical by the African Americans Aubry Lyles and Flournoy Miller. Theodore Dreiser

Harlem street scene.

grappled with the explosive subject of lynching in his 1918 short story "Nigger Jeff." Two years later, the magnetic African American actor Charles Gilpin energized O'Neill's *Emperor Jones* in the 150-seat theater in a MacDougal Street brownstone taken over by the Provincetown Players.

The year 1921 brought *Shuffle Along* to the 63rd Street Theatre, with music, lyrics, choreography, cast, and production uniquely in African American hands, and composer Eubie Blake's "I'm Just Wild About Harry" and "Love Will Find a Way" entered the list of all-time favorites. Mary Hoyt Wiborg's *Taboo* was produced that year, with a green Paul Robeson making his theatrical debut. Clement Wood's 1922 sociological novel *Nigger* sympathetically tracked a beleaguered African American family from slavery through the Great War into urban adversity. *Emperor Jones* (revived in 1922 with Robeson in the lead part) showed civilization's pretentions being mocked by forces from the dark subconscious. That same year T. S. Stribling's *Birthright* appeared, a novel remarkable for its effort to portray an African American male protagonist of superior education (a Harvard-educated physician) martyred for his ideals after returning to the South. "Jean Le

HARLEM RENAISSANCE: A GALE CRITICAL COMPANION, VOL. 1

15

Negre," the black character in e. e. cummings's *The Enormous Room* (1922), was another Noble Savage paradigm observed through a Freudian prism.

But Village artists and intellectuals were aware and unhappy that they were theorizing about Afro-America and spinning out African American fictional characters in a vacuum—that they knew almost nothing firsthand about these subjects. Sherwood Anderson's June 1922 letter to H. L. Mencken spoke for much of the Lost Generation: "Damn it, man, if I could really get inside the niggers and write about them with some intelligence, I'd be willing to be hanged later and perhaps would be." Anderson's prayers were answered almost immediately when he chanced to read a Jean Toomer short story in *Double-Dealer* magazine. With the novelist's assistance, Toomer's stories began to appear in the magazines of the Lyrical Left and the Marxists, in *Dial, S4N, Broom,* and *Liberator.* Anderson's 1925 novel *Dark Laughter* bore unmistakable signs of indebtedness to Toomer, whose work, Anderson readily admitted, had given him a true insight into the cultural energies that could be harnessed to pull America back from the abyss of fatal materialism. Celebrity in the Village brought Toomer into Waldo Frank's circle, and with it criticism from Toomer about the omission of African Americans from Frank's sprawling work *Our America.* After a trip with Toomer to South Carolina in the fall of 1922, Frank published *Holiday* the following year, a somewhat overwrought treatment of the struggle between the two races in the South, "each of which . . . needs what the other possesses."

Claude McKay, whose volume of poetry *Harlem Shadows* (1922) made him a Village celebrity (he lived in Gay Street, then entirely inhabited by nonwhites), found his niche among the *Liberator* group, where he soon became co-editor of the magazine with Michael Gold. The Eastmans saw the Jamaican poet as the kind of writer who would deepen the magazine's proletarian voice. McKay increased the circulation of *Liberator* to sixty thousand, published the first poetry of e. e. cummings (over Gold's objections), introduced Garvey's Universal Negro Improvement Association (UNIA), and generally treated the readership to experimentation that had little to do with proletarian literature. "It was much easier to talk about real proletarians writing masterpieces than to find such masterpieces," McKay told the Eastmans and the exasperated hard-line Marxist Gold. Soon all manner of Harlem radicals began meeting, at McKay's invitation, in West 13th Street, while the

Eastmans fretted about Justice Department surveillance. Richard B. Moore, Cyril Briggs, Otto Huiswood; Grace Campbell, W. A. Domingo, inter alia, represented Harlem movements ranging from Garvey's UNIA and Briggs's African Blood Brotherhood to the CPUSA with Huiswood and Campbell. McKay also attempted to bring the Village to Harlem, in one memorable sortie taking Eastman and another Villager to Ned's, his favorite Harlem cabaret. Ned, notoriously anti-white, expelled them.

This was part of the background to the Talented Tenth's abrupt, enthusiastic, and programmatic embrace of arts and letters after the First World War. With white Broadway audiences flocking to O'Neill plays and shrieking with delight at *Liza, Runnin' Wild,* and other imitations of *Shuffle Along,* Charles Johnson and James Weldon Johnson, Du Bois, Fauset, White, Locke, and others saw a unique opportunity to tap into the American mainstream. Harlem, the Negro Capital of the World, filled up with successful bootleggers and racketeers, political and religious charlatans, cults of exotic character ("Black Jews"), street-corner pundits and health practitioners (Hubert Harrison, "Black Herman"), beauty culturists and distinguished professionals (Madame C. J. Walker, Louis T. Wright), religious and civil rights notables (Reverends Cullen and Powell, Du Bois, Johnson, White), and hard-pressed, hard-working families determined to make decent lives for their children. Memories of the nightspots in "The Jungle" (133rd Street), of Bill "Bojangles" Robinson demonstrating his footwork on Lenox Avenue, of raucous shows at the Lafayette that gave Florenz Ziegfeld some of his ideas, of the Tree of Hope outside Connie's Inn where musicians gathered as at a labor exchange, have been vividly set down by Arthur P. Davis, Regina Andrews, Arna Bontemps, and Langston Hughes.

If they were adroit, African American civil rights officials and intellectuals believed they stood a fair chance of succeeding in reshaping the images and repackaging the messages out of which Mainstream racial behavior emerged. Bohemia and the Lost Generation suggested to the Talented Tenth the new approach to the old problem of race relations, but their shared premise about art and society obscured the diametrically opposite conclusions white and black intellectuals and artists drew from them. Harold Stearns's Lost Generation *revoltés* were lost in the sense that they professed to have no wish to find themselves in a materialistic, mammon-mad, homogenizing America. Locke's New Negroes very much wanted full acceptance by Mainstream America, even if some, like Du Bois, McKay, and the future *enfant terrible* of the Renaissance, Wallace Thurman, might have immediately exercised the privilege of rejecting it. For the whites, art was the means to change society before they would accept it. For the blacks, art was the means to change society in order to be accepted into it. For this reason, many of the Harlem intellectuals found the white vogue in Afro-Americana troubling, although they usually feigned enthusiasm about the new dramatic and literary themes. Despite the insensitivity, burlesquing, and calumny, however, the Talented Tenth convinced itself that the civil rights dividends were potentially greater than the liabilities. Benjamin Brawley put this potential straightforwardly to James Weldon Johnson: "We have a tremendous opportunity to boost the NAACP, letters, and art, and anything else that calls attention to our development along the higher lines."

Brawley knew that he was preaching to the converted. Johnson's preface to his best-selling anthology *The Book of American Negro Poetry* (1922) proclaimed that nothing could "do more to change the mental attitude and raise his status than a demonstration of intellectual parity by the Negro through his production of literature and art." Putting T. S. Stribling's *Birthright* down, an impressed Jessie Fauset nevertheless felt that she and her peers could do better. "We reasoned," she recalled later, "'Here is an audience waiting to hear the truth about us. Let us who are better qualified to present that truth than any white writer, try to do so.'" The result was *There Is Confusion,* her novel about genteel life among Philadelphia's aristocrats of color. Similarly troubled by *Birthright* and other two-dimensional or symbolically gross representations of African American life, Walter White complained loudly to H. L. Mencken, who finally silenced him with the challenge "Why don't you do the right kind of novel? You could do it, and it would create a sensation." White did. And the sensation turned out to be *The Fire in the Flint* (1924), the second novel of the Renaissance, which he wrote in less than a month in a borrowed country house in the Berkshires. Meanwhile, Langston Hughes, whose genius (like that of Toomer's) had been immediately recognized by Fauset, published several poems in *The Crisis* that would later appear in the collection *The Weary Blues.* The euphonious "The Negro Speaks of Rivers" (dedicated to Du Bois) ran in *The Crisis* in 1921. With the appearance of McKay's *Harlem Shadows* and Toomer's *Cane* the next year, 1923, the African American officers of the NAACP and the NUL saw how a theory could be put into action. The young New York University prodigy Countee Cullen, already published in *The Crisis* and *Opportunity,* had his Mainstream breakthrough in 1923 in *Harper's* and *Century* magazines. Two years later, with Carl Sandburg as one of the three judges, Cullen won the prestigious Witter Bynner poetry prize. Meanwhile, Paul Kellogg's *Survey Graphic* project moved apace under the editorship of Locke.

Two preconditions made this unprecedented mobilization of talent and group support in the service of a racial arts-and-letters movement more than a conceit in the minds of a handful of leaders: demography and repression. The Great Black Migration from the rural South to the industrial North produced the metropolitan dynamism undergirding the Renaissance. The Red Summer of 1919, a period of socialist agitation and conservative backlash following the Russian Revolution, produced the trauma that led to the cultural sublimation of civil rights. In pressure-cooker fashion, the increase in its African American population caused Harlem to pulsate as it pushed its racial boundaries south below 135th Street to Central Park and north beyond 139th ("Strivers' Row"). In the first flush of Harlem's realization and of general African American exuberance, the Red Summer of 1919 had a cruelly decompressing impact upon Harlem and Afro-America in general. Charleston, South Carolina, erupted in riot in May, followed by Longview, Texas, in July, and Washington, D.C., later in the month. Chicago exploded on July 27. Lynchings of returning African American soldiers and expulsion of African American workers from unions abounded. In the North, the white working classes struck out against perceived and manipulated threats to job security and unionism from blacks streaming north. In Helena, Arkansas, where a pogrom was unleashed against black farmers organizing a cotton cooperative, and outside Atlanta, where the Ku Klux Klan was reconstituted, the message of the white South to African Americans was that the racial *status quo ante bellum* was on again with a vengeance. Twenty-six race riots in towns, cities, and counties swept across the nation all the way to Nebraska. The "race problem" became definitively an American dilemma in the summer of 1919, and no longer a remote complexity in the exotic South.

The term "New Negro" entered the vocabulary in reaction to the Red Summer, along with McKay's poetic catechism—"Like men we'll face the murderous, cowardly pack / Pressed to the wall, dying, but fighting back!" There was a groundswell of support for Marcus Garvey's UNIA. Until his 1924 imprisonment for mail fraud, the Jamaican immigrant's message of African Zionism, anti-integrationism, working-class assertiveness, and Bookerite business enterprise increasingly threatened the hegemony of the Talented Tenth and its major organizations, the NAACP and NUL, among people of color in America (much of Garvey's support came from the West Indians). "Garvey," wrote Mary White Ovington, one of the NAACP's white founders, "was the first Negro in the United States to capture the imagination of the masses." *The Negro World,* Garvey's multilingual newspaper, circulated throughout Latin America and the African empires of Britain and France. Locke spoke for the alarmed "respectable" civil rights leadership when he wrote, in his introductory remarks to the special issue of *Survey Graphic,* that, although "the thinking Negro has shifted a little to the left with the world trend," black separatism (Locke clearly had Garveyism in mind) "cannot be—even if it were desirable." Although the movement was its own worst enemy, the Talented Tenth was pleased to help the Justice Department speed its demise.

No less an apostle of high culture than Du Bois, initially a Renaissance enthusiast, vividly expressed the farfetched nature of the arts-and-letters movement as early as 1926: "How is it that an organization of this kind [the NAACP] can turn aside to talk about art? After all, what have we who are slaves and black to do with art?" It was the brilliant insight of the men and women associated with the NAACP and NUL that, although the road to the ballot box, the union hall, the decent neighborhood, and the office was blocked, there were two untried paths that had not been barred, in large part because of their very implausibility, as well as irrelevancy to most Americans: arts and letters. They saw the small cracks in the wall of racism that could, they anticipated, be widened through the production of exemplary racial images in collaboration with liberal white philanthropy, the robust culture industry primarily located in New York, and artists from white Bohemia (like themselves marginal and in tension with the status quo). If, in retrospect, then, the New Negro Arts Movement has been interpreted as a natural phase in the cultural evolution of another American group, as a band in the literary continuum running from New England, Knickerbocker New York, Hoosier Indiana, to the Village's Bohemia, to East Side Yiddish drama and fiction, and then on to the Southern Agrarians, such an

interpretation sacrifices causation to appearance. Instead, the Renaissance represented much less an evolutionary part of a common experience than it did a generation-skipping phenomenon in which a vanguard of the Talented Tenth elite recruited, organized, subventioned, and guided an unevenly endowed cohort of artists and writers to make statements that advanced a certain conception of the race, a cohort of men and women most of whom would never have imagined the possibility of artistic and literary careers.

Toomer, McKay, Hughes, and Cullen possessed the rare ability combined with personal eccentricity that defined the artist, but the Renaissance not only needed more like them but a large cast of supporters and extras. American dropouts heading for seminars in garrets and cafés in Paris were invariably white and descended from an older gentry displaced by new moneyed elites. Charles Johnson and his allies were able to make the critical Renaissance mass possible. Johnson assembled files on prospective recruits throughout the country, going so far as to cajole Aaron Douglas, the artist from Kansas, and others into coming to Harlem, where a network manned by his secretary, Ethel Ray Nance, and her friends Regina Anderson and Louella Tucker (assisted by gifted Trinidadian short-story writer Eric Walrond) looked after them until a salary or a fellowship was secured. White, the very self-important assistant secretary of the NAACP, urged Paul Robeson to abandon law for an acting career, encouraged Nella Larsen to follow his own example as a novelist, and passed the hat for artist Hale Woodruff. Fauset continued to discover and publish short stories and verse, such as those of Wallace Thurman and Arna Bontemps. Shortly after the Civic Club evening, both the NAACP and the NUL announced the creation of annual awards ceremonies bearing the titles of their respective publications, *Crisis* and *Opportunity.*

The award of the first *Opportunity* prizes came in May 1925 in an elaborate ceremony at the Fifth Avenue Restaurant with some three hundred participants. Twenty-four distinguished judges (among them Carl Van Doren, Zona Gale, Eugene O'Neill, James Weldon Johnson, and Van Wyck Brooks) had ruled on the worthiness of entries in five categories. The awards ceremony was interracial, but white capital and influence were crucial to success, and the white presence, in the beginning, was pervasive, setting the outer boundaries for what was creatively normative. Money to start the *Crisis* prizes had come from Amy Spingarn, an accomplished artist and poet, and wife of Joel Spingarn, chairman of the NAACP's board of directors. The wife of the influential attorney, Fisk University trustee, and Urban League Board chairman, L. Hollingsworth Wood, had made a similar contribution to initiate the *Opportunity* prizes. These were the whites Zora Neal Hurston, one of the first *Opportunity* prizewinners, memorably dubbed "Negrotarians." There were several categories: Political Negrotarians like progressive journalist Ray Stannard Baker, and maverick socialist types associated with *Modern Quarterly* (V. F. Calverton, Max Eastman, Lewis Mumford, Scott Nearing); salon Negrotarians like Robert Chanler, Charles Studin, Carl and Fania (Marinoff) Van Vechten, and Eleanor Wylie, for whom the Harlem artists were more exotics than talents. They were kindred spirits to Lost Generation Negrotarians, drawn to Harlem on their way to Paris by a need for personal nourishment and confirmation of a vision of cultural health, in which their romantic or revolutionary perceptions of African American vitality played a key role—Anderson, O'Neill, Georgia O'Keefe, Zona Gale, Waldo Frank, Louise Bryant, Sinclair Lewis, Hart Crane. The commercial Negrotarians like the Knopfs, the Gershwins, Rowena Jelliffe, Horace Liveright, V. F. Calverton, and Sol Hurok scouted and mined Afro-American like prospectors.

The May 1925 *Opportunity* gala showcased the steadily augmenting talent in the Renaissance—what Hurston characterized as the "Niggerati." Two laureates, Cullen and Hughes, had already won notice beyond Harlem. The latter had engineered "discovery" as a Washington, D.C., bellhop by placing dinner and three poems on Vachel Lindsay's hotel table. Some prizewinners were barely to be heard from again: Joseph Cotter, G. D. Lipscomb, Warren MacDonald, Fidelia Ripley. Others, like John Matheus (first prize in the short-story category) and Frank Horne (honorable mention in short-story writing), fell short of first-rank standing in the Renaissance. Most of those whose talent had staying power were introduced that night: E. Franklin Frazier, who won the first prize for an essay on social equality; Sterling Brown, who took second prize for an essay on the singer Roland Hayes; Hurston, awarded second prize for a short story, "Spunk"; and Eric Walrond, third-prize winner for his short story "Voodoo's Revenge." James Weldon Johnson read the poem that took first prize, "The Weary Blues," Langston Hughes's turning-point poem, combining the gift of a superior artist and the enduring, music-encased spirit of the black migrant. Comments from Negrotarian judges ranged from O'Neill's

## ON THE SUBJECT OF...

### THE HARLEM RENAISSANCE

The one period in black letters that stands out above all others is the one commonly referred to as the Harlem Renaissance. Not easily reducible to exact dates, the Harlem Renaissance is defined as that flowering of Afro-American creativity beginning around World War I and extending into the early days of the 1930s. Coming from Florida and Idaho, California and Jamaica, Missouri and Ohio, Boston and Washington, D.C., black artists and writers flocked into Harlem, making it the race capital of the world; they arrived there to begin a decade of self-concious striving to change popular perceptions of their people. Langston Hughes, Countee Cullen, Claude McKay, Zora Neale Hurston, Nella Larsen, Jessie Fauset, and many others worked to claim a place for themselves in a literary history that had narrow meaning before their contributions in the 1920s.

**SOURCE:** Trudier Harris, from the *Dictionary of Literary Biography* 51: *Afro-American Writers from the Harlem Renaissance to 1940,* Gale Research, 1987, p. xi.

advice to "be yourselves," to novelist Edna Worthley Underwood's exultant anticipation of a "new epoch in American letters," and Clement Wood's judgment that the general standard "was higher than such contests usually bring out."

The measures of Charles S. Johnson's success were the announcement of a second *Opportunity* contest to be underwritten by Harlem "businessman" (and numbers king) Caspar Holstein, former *Times* music critic Carl Van Vechten's enthusiasm over Hughes and subsequent arranging of a contract with Knopf for Hughes's first volume of poetry, and, one week after the awards ceremony, a prediction by the New York *Herald Tribune* that the country was "on the edge, if not already in the midst of, what might not improperly be called a Negro renaissance"—thereby giving the movement its name. Priming the public for the Fifth Avenue Restaurant occasion, the special edition of *Survey Graphic,* "Harlem: Mecca of the New Negro," edited by Locke, had reached an unprecedented 42,000 readers in March 1926. The ideology of cultural nationalism at the heart of the Renaissance was crisply delineated in Locke's opening essay, "Harlem," stating that, "without pretense to their political significance, Harlem has the same role to play for the New Negro as Dublin has had for the New Ireland or Prague for the New Czechoslovakia." A vast racial formation was under way in the relocation of the peasant masses ("they stir, they move, they are more than physically restless"), the editor announced. "The challenge of the new intellectuals among them is clear enough." The migrating peasants from the South were the soil out of which all success must come, but soil must be tilled, and the Howard University philosopher reserved that task exclusively for the Talented Tenth in liaison with its Mainstream analogues—in the "carefully maintained contacts of the enlightened minorities of both race groups." There was little amiss about America that interracial elitism could not set right, Locke and the others believed. Despite historic discrimination and the Red Summer, the Rhodes scholar assured readers that the increasing radicalism among African Americans was superficial. At year's end, Albert and Charles Boni published Locke's *The New Negro,* an expanded and polished edition of the poetry and prose from the *Opportunity* contest and the special *Survey Graphic.*

The course of American letters was unchanged by the offerings in *The New Negro.* Still, it carried several memorable works, such as the short story "The South Lingers On" by Brown University and Howard Medical School graduate Rudolph Fisher; the acid poem "White House(s)" and the euphonic "The Tropics in New York" by McKay, now in European self-exile; and several poetic vignettes from Toomer's *Cane.* Hughes's "Jazzonia," previously published in *The Crisis,* was so poignant as to be almost tactile as it described "six long-headed jazzers" playing while a dancing woman "lifts high a dress of silken gold." In "Heritage," a poem previously unpublished, Cullen outdid himself in his grandest (if not his best) effort with its famous refrain, "What is Africa to me." The book carried the distinctive silhouette drawings and Egyptian-influenced motifs by Aaron Douglas, whose work was to become the artistic signature of the Renaissance. With thirty-four African American contributors (four were white), Locke's work included most of the Renaissance regulars. The notable omissions from *The New Negro* were Asa Randolph, George Schuyler,

and Wallace Thurman. These were the gifted men and women who were to show by example what the potential of some African Americans could be and who proposed to lead their people into an era of opportunity and justice.

By virtue of their symbolic achievements and their adroit collaboration with the philanthropic and reform-minded Mainstream, their augmenting influence would ameliorate the socioeconomic conditions of their race over time and from the top downward. Slowly but surely, they would promote an era of opportunity and justice. It was a Talented Tenth conceit, Schuyler snorted in Asa Randolph's *Messenger* magazine, worthy of a "high priest of the intellectual snobbocracy," and he awarded Locke the magazine's "elegantly embossed and beautifully lacquered dill pickle." Yet it seemed to work, for although the objective conditions confronting most African Americans in Harlem and elsewhere were deteriorating, optimism remained high. Harlem recoiled from Garveyism and socialism to applaud Phi Beta Kappa poets, university-trained painters, concertizing musicians, and novel-writing officers of civil rights organizations. "Everywhere we heard the sighs of wonder, amazement and sometimes admiration when it was whispered or announced that here was one of the 'New Negroes,'" Bontemps recalled.

By summer of 1926, Renaissance titles included *Cane* (1923), *There Is Confusion* (1924), *Fire in the Flint* (1924), *Flight* (1926), McKay's *Harlem Shadows* (1922), Cullen's *Color* poetry volume (1924), and *The Weary Blues* volume of poetry (1926). The second *Opportunity* awards banquet, April 1926, was another artistic and interracial success. Playwright Joseph Cotter was honored again, as was Hurston, for a short story. Bontemps, a California-educated poet struggling in Harlem, won first prize for "Golgotha Is a Mountain," and Dorothy West, a Bostonian aspiring to make a name in fiction, made her debut, as did essayist Arthur Fauset, Jessie's able brother. The William E. Harmon Foundation transferred its attention at the beginning of 1926 from student loans and blind children to the Renaissance, announcing seven annual prizes for literature, music, fine arts, industry, science, education, and race relations, with George Edmund Haynes, African American official in the Federal Council of Churches, and Locke as chief advisors. That same year, the publishers Boni & Liveright offered a thousand-dollar prize for the "best novel on Negro life" by an African American. Casper Holstein contributed one thousand dollars that year to endow *Opportu-*

*nity* prizes. Van Vechten made a smaller contribution to the same cause. Amy Spingarn provided six hundred dollars toward the *Crisis* awards. Otto Kanh underwrote two years in France for the young artist Hale Woodruff. There were Louis Rodman Wanamaker prizes in music composition.

The third *Opportunity* awards dinner was a vintage one for poetry, with entries by Bontemps, Sterling Brown, Hughes, Helene Johnson, and Jonathan H. Brooks. In praising their general high quality, the white literary critic Robert T. Kerlin added the revealing comment that their effect would be "hostile to lynching and to jim-crowing." Eric Walrond's lush, impressionistic collection of short stories *Tropic Death* appeared from Boni & Liveright at the end of 1926, the most probing exploration of the psychology of cultural underdevelopment since Toomer's *Cane.* If *Cane* recaptured in a string of glowing vignettes (most of them about women) the sunset beauty and agony of a preindustrial culture, *Tropic Death* did much the same for the Antilles. Hughes's second volume of poetry, *Fine Clothes to the Jew* (1927), spiritedly portrayed the city life of ordinary men and women who had traded the hard-scrabble of farming for the hardscrabble of domestic work and odd jobs. Hughes scanned the low-down pursuits of "Bad Man," "Ruby Brown," and "Beale Street" and shocked Brawley and other Talented Tenth elders with the bawdy "Red Silk Stockings." "Put on yo red silk stockings, /Black gal," it began, urging the protagonist to show herself to white boys. It ended wickedly with "An' tomorrow's chile'll / Be a high yaller."

A veritable Ministry of Culture now presided over Afro-America. McKay, viewing the scene from abroad, spoke derisively of the artistic and literary autocracy of "that NAACP crowd." The Ministry mounted a movable feast to which the anointed were invited, sometimes to Walter and Gladys White's apartment at 409 Edgecombe Avenue, where they might share cocktails with Sinclair Lewis or Mencken; often (after 1928) to the famous 136th Street "Dark Tower" salon maintained by beauty culture heiress A'Lelia Walker, where guests might include Sir Osbert Sitwell, the Crown Prince of Sweden, or Lady Mountbatten; and very frequently to the home of Carl and Fania Van Vechten, to imbibe the host's sidecars and listen to Robeson sing or Jim Johnson recite from "God's Trombones" or George Gershwin play the piano. Meanwhile, Harlem's appeal to white rev-

ellers inspired the young physician Rudolph Fisher to write "The Caucasian Storms Harlem," a satiric piece in the August 1927 *American Mercury.*

The third phase of the Harlem Renaissance began even as the second had only just gotten under way. The second phase (1924 to mid-1926) was dominated by the officialdom of the two major civil rights organizations, with its ideology of civil rights advancement of African Americans through the creation and mobilization of an artistic-literary movement. Its essence was summed up in blunt declarations by Du Bois that he didn't care "a damn for any art that is not used for propaganda" or in exalted formulations by Locke that the New Negro was "an augury of a new democracy in American culture." The third phase of the Renaissance, from mid-1926 to the end of 1934, was marked by rebellion against the Civil Rights Establishment on the part of many of the artists and writers whom that Establishment had assembled and promoted. Three publications during 1926 formed a watershed between the genteel and the demotic Renaissance. Hughes's "The Negro Artist and the Racial Mountain," which appeared in the June 1926 issue of *The Nation,* served as manifesto of the breakaway from the arts-and-letters party line. Van Vechten's *Nigger Heaven,* released by Knopf that August, drove much of literate Afro-America into a dichotomy of approval and apoplexy over "authentic" versus "proper" cultural expression. Wallace Thurman's *Fire!!,* available in November, assembled the rebels for a major assault against the Civil Rights Ministry of Culture.

Hughes's turning-point essay had been provoked by Schuyler's essay in *The Nation,* "The Negro-Art Hokum," ridiculing "eager apostles from Greenwich Village, Harlem, and environs" who made claims for a special African American artistic vision distinct from that of white Americans. "The Aframerican is merely a lamp-blacked Anglo-Saxon," Schuyler had sneered. In a famous peroration, Hughes answered that he and his fellow artists intended to express their "individual dark-skinned selves without fear or shame. If white people are pleased we are glad. . . . If colored people are pleased we are glad. If they are not, their displeasure doesn't matter either." There was considerable African American displeasure; and it was complex. Much of the condemnation of the license for expression Hughes, Thurman, Hurston, and other artists arrogated to themselves was generational or puritanical, and usually both. "Vulgarity has been mistaken for art," Brawley spluttered after leafing the pages of the new magazine *Fire!!,* which contained among other shockers Richard Bruce Nugent's extravagantly homoerotic short story "Smoke, Lillies and Jade!" Du Bois was said to be deeply aggrieved.

But much of the condemnation stemmed from racial sensitivity, from sheer mortification at seeing uneducated, crude, and scrappy black men and women depicted without tinsel and soap. Thurman and associate editors John Davis, Aaron Douglas, Gwendolyn Bennett, Arthur Huff Fauset, Hughes, Hurston, and Nugent took the Renaissance out of the parlor, the editorial office, and the banquet room. With African motifs by Douglas and Nordic-featured African Americans with exaggeratedly kinky hair by Nugent; poems to an elevator boy by Hughes; a taste for the jungle by Edward Silvera; short stories about prostitution ("Cordelia the Crude") by Thurman, gender conflict between black men and women at the bottom of the economy ("Sweat") by Hurston, and a burly boxer's hatred of white people ("Wedding Day") by Gwendolyn Bennett; a short play about pigment complexes within the race (*Color Struck*) by Hurston—the focus shifted to Locke's "peasant matrix," to the sorrows and joys of those outside the Talented Tenth. "Let the blare of Negro jazz bands and the bellowing voice of Bessie Smith . . . penetrate the closed ears of the colored near-intellectuals," Hughes exhorted in "The Negro Artists and the Racial Mountain."

Carl Van Vechten's influence decidedly complicated the reactions of otherwise worldly critics like Du Bois, Fauset, Locke, and Cullen. While the novel's title alone enraged many harlemites who felt their trust and hospitality betrayed, the deeper objections of the sophisticated to *Nigger Heaven* lay in its message that the Talented Tenth's preoccupation with cultural improvement was a misguided affectation that would cost the race its vitality. It was the "archaic Negroes" who were at ease in their skins and capable of action, Van Vechten's characters demonstrated. Significantly, although Du Bois and Fauset found themselves in the majority among the Renaissance leadership (ordinary Harlemites burned Van Vechten in effigy at 135th Street and Lenox Avenue), Charles Johnson, James Weldon Johnson, Schuyler, White, and Hughes praised the novel's sociological verve and veracity and the service they believed it rendered to race relations.

The younger artists embraced Van Vechten's fiction as a worthy model because of its ribald iconoclasm and iteration that the future of Afri-

can American arts and letters lay in the culture of the working poor and even of the underclass—in bottom-up drama, fiction, music, and poetry, and painting. Regularly convening at the notorious "267 House," the brownstone an indulgent landlady provided Thurman rent-free on 136th Street (alternately known as "Niggerati Manor"), the group that came to produce *Fire!!* saw art not as politics by other means—civil rights between covers or from a stage or an easel—but as an expression of the intrinsic conditions most men and women of African descent were experiencing. They spoke of the need "for a truly Negroid note," for empathy with "those elements within the race which are still too potent for easy assimilation," and they openly mocked the premise of the Civil Rights Establishment that (as a Hughes character says in *The Ways of White Folks*) "art would break down color lines, art would save the race and prevent lynchings! Bunk!" Finally, like creative agents in society from time immemorial, they were impelled to insult their patrons and to defy conventions.

To put the Renaissance back on track, Du Bois sponsored a symposium in late 1926, "The Criteria of Negro Art," inviting a spectrum of views about the appropriate course the arts should take. His unhappiness was readily apparent, both with the overly literary tendencies of Locke and with the bottom-up school of Hughes and Thurman. The great danger was that politics were dropping out of the Renaissance, that the movement was turning into an evasion, sedulously encouraged by certain whites. "They are whispering, 'Here is a way out. Here is the real solution to the color problem. The recognition accorded Cullen, Hughes, Fauset, White and others shows there is no real color line,'" Du Bois charged. He then announced that *Crisis* literary prizes would henceforth be reserved for works encouraging "general knowledge of banking and insurance in modern life and specific knowledge of what American Negroes are doing in these fields." Walter White's own effort to sustain the civil-rights-by-copyright strategy was the ambitious novel *Flight,* edited by his friend Sinclair Lewis and released by Knopf in 1926. Kind critics found White's novel (a tale of near-white African Americans of unusual culture and professional accomplishment who prove their moral superiority to their oppressors) somewhat flat. The reissue the following year of *The Autobiography of an Ex-Colored Man* (with Johnson's authorship finally acknowledged) and publication of a volume of Cullen poetry, *Copper*

*Sun,* continued the tradition of genteel, exemplary letters. In a further effort to restore direction, Du Bois's *Dark Princess* appeared in 1928 from Harcourt, Brace, a large, serious novel in which the "problem of the twentieth century" is taken in charge by a Talented Tenth International whose prime mover is a princess from India. But the momentum stayed firmly with the rebels.

Although Thurman's magazine died after one issue, respectable Afro-America was unable to ignore the novel that embodied the values of the Niggerati—the first Renaissance best-seller by a black author—McKay's *Home to Harlem,* released by Harper & Brothers in spring 1928. Its milieu is wholly plebeian. The protagonist, Jake, is a Lenox Avenue Noble Savage who demonstrates (in marked contrast to the book-reading Ray) the superiority of the Negro mind uncorrupted by European learning. *Home to Harlem* finally shattered the enforced literary code of the Civil Rights Establishment. Du Bois confessed to feeling "distinctly like needing a bath" after reading McKay's novel about the "debauched tenth." Rudolph Fisher's *The Walls of Jericho,* appearing that year from Knopf, was a brilliant, deftly executed satire which upset Du Bois as much as it heartened Thurman. Fisher, a successful Harlem physician with solid Talented Tenth family credentials, satirized the NAACP, the Negrotarians, Harlem high society, and easily recognized Renaissance notables, while entering convincingly into the world of the working classes, organized crime, and romance across classes.

Charles Johnson, preparing to leave the editorship of *Opportunity* for a professorship in sociology at Fisk University, now encouraged the young rebels. Renaissance artists were "now less self-conscious, less interested in proving that they are just like white people. . . . Relief from the stifling consciousness of being a problem has brought a certain superiority" to the Harlem Renaissance, Johnson asserted. Meanwhile, McKay's and Fisher's fiction inspired the Niggerati to publish an improved version of *Fire!!.* The magazine, *Harlem,* appeared in November 1928. Editor Thurman announced portentously, "The time has now come when the Negro artist can be his true self and pander to the stupidities of no one, either white or black." While Brawley, Du Bois, and Fauset continued to grimace, *Harlem* benefitted from significant defections. It won the collaboration of Locke and White, and lasted two issues. Roy de Coverly, George W. Little, and Schuyler signed on, and Hughes contributed one of the finest

short stories, based on his travels down the West Coast of Africa—"Luani of the Jungles," a polished genre piece on the seductions of the civilized and the primitive.

The other Renaissance novel that year from Knopf, Nella Larsen's *Quicksand,* achieved the distinction of being praised by Du Bois, Locke, and Hughes. Larsen claimed to have been the daughter of a Danish mother and an African American father from the Danish Virgin Islands. In fact, her father was probably a chauffeur who lived in New York; and Larsen was probably born in New York, rather than in Chicago as she claimed. Trained in the sciences at Fisk, she never pursued further studies, as has been reported, at the University of Copenhagen. She would remain something of a mystery woman, helped in her career by Van Vechten and White but somehow always receding, and finally disappearing altogether from the Harlem scene. *Quicksand* was a triumph of vivid yet economic writing and rich allegory. Its very modern heroine experiences misfortunes and ultimate destruction from causes that are both racial and individual. She is not a tragic mulatto but a mulatto who is tragic for reasons that are both sociological and existential. Helga Crane, Larsen's protagonist, was the Virginia Slim of Renaissance fiction. If there were reviews (*Crisis, New Republic, New York Times*) that were as laudatory about Fauset's *Plum Bun,* also a 1928 release, they were primarily due to the novel's engrossing reconstruction of rarefied, upper-class African American life in Philadelphia, rather than to special literary merit. Angela Murray (Angele, in her white persona), the heroine of Fauset's second novel, was the Gibson Girl of Renaissance fiction. *Plum Bun* continued the second phase of the Renaissance, as did Cullen's second volume of poetry, published in 1929, *The Black Christ.* Ostensibly about a lynching, the lengthy title poem lost its way in mysticism, paganism, and religious remorse. The volume also lost the sympathies of most reviewers.

Thurman's *The Blacker the Berry,* published by Macaulay in early 1929, although talky and awkward in spots (Thurman had hoped to write the Great African American Novel), was a breakthrough novel. The reviewer for the Chicago *Defender* enthused, "Here at last is the book for which I have been waiting, and for which you have been waiting." Hughes praised it as a "gorgeous book," mischieveously writing Thurman that it would embarrass those who bestowed the "seal-of-high-and-holy approval of Harmon awards." The Ministry of Culture found the novel distinctly distasteful, *Opportunity* judging *The Blacker the Berry* to be fatally flawed by "immaturity and gaucherie." For the first time in African American fiction, color prejudice within the race was the central theme of a novel. Emma Lou, its heroine (like the author very dark and conventionally unattractive), is obsessed with respectability as well as tortured by her pigment, for Thurman makes the point on every page that Afro-America's aesthetic and spiritual center resides in the unaffected, unblended, noisome common folk and the liberated, unconventional artists. With the unprecedented Broadway success of *Harlem,* Thurman's sensationalized romp through the underside of Harlem, the triumph of Niggerati aesthetics over Civil Rights arts and letters was impressively confirmed. Another equally sharp smell of reality irritated Establishment nostrils that same year, with the publication of McKay's second novel, *Banjo,* appearing only weeks after *The Blacker the Berry.* "The Negroes are writing against themselves," lamented the reviewer for the *Amsterdam News.* Set among the human flotsam and jetsam of Marseilles and West Africa, the message of McKay's novel was again that European civilization was inimical to Africans everywhere.

The stock market collapsed, but reverberations from the Harlem Renaissance seemed stronger than ever. Larsen's second novel, *Passing,* appeared. Its theme, like Fauset's, was the burden of mixed racial ancestry. But, although *Passing* was less successful than *Quicksand,* Larsen's novel again evaded the trap of writing another tragic-mulatto novel by opposing the richness of African American life to the material advantages afforded by the option of "passing." In February 1930, Marc Connelly's dramatization of Roark Bradford's book of short stories opened on Broadway as *The Green Pastures.* The Hall Johnson Choir sang in it, Richard Harrison played "De Lawd," and scores of Harlemites found parts during 557 performances at the Mansfield Theatre, and then on tour across the country. The demanding young critic and Howard University professor of English Sterling Brown pronounced the play a "miracle." After *The Green Pastures* came *Not Without Laughter,* Hughes's glowing novel from Knopf. Financed by Charlotte Osgood Mason (the often tyrannical bestower of artistic largesse nicknamed "Godmother") and Amy Spingarn, Hughes had resumed his college education at Lincoln University and completed *Not Without Laughter* his senior year. The beleaguered family at the center of

the novel represents Afro-America in transition in white America. Hughes's young male protagonist learns that proving his equality means affirming his distinctive racial qualities. Not only Locke admired *Not Without Laughter;* the *New Masses* reviewer embraced it as "our novel." The Ministry of Culture decreed Hughes worthy of the Harmon gold medal for 1930. The year ended with Schuyler's ribald, sprawling satire *Black No More,* an unsparing demolition of every personality and institution in Afro-America. Little wonder that Locke titled his retrospective piece in the February 1931 *Opportunity* "The Year of Grace."

Depression notwithstanding, the health of the Renaissance appeared to be more robust than ever. The first Rosenwald fellowships for African Americans had been secured largely due to James Weldon Johnson's influence the previous year. Since 1928, advised by Locke, the Harmon Foundation had mounted an annual traveling exhibition of drawings, paintings, and sculpture by African Americans. The 1930 participants introduced the generally unsuspected talent and genius of Palmer Hayden, William H. Johnson, Archibald Motley, Jr., James A. Porter, and Laura Wheeler Waring in painting. Sargent Johnson, Elizabeth Prophet, and Augusta Savage were the outstanding sculptors of the show. Both Aaron Douglas and Romare Bearden came to feel that the standards of the foundation were somewhat indulgent and, therefore, injurious to many young artists, which was undoubtedly true even though the 1931 Harmon Travelling Exhibition of the Work of Negro Artists was seen by more than 150,000 people.

Superficially, Harlem itself appeared to be in fair health well into 1931. James Weldon Johnson's celebration of the community's strengths, *Black Manhattan,* was published near the end of 1930. "Harlem is still in the process of making," the book proclaimed, and the author's confidence in the power of the "recent literary and artistic emergence" to ameliorate race relations was unshaken. In Johnson's Harlem, redcaps and cooks cheered when Renaissance talents won Guggenheim and Rosenwald fellowships; they rushed to newsstands whenever the *American Mercury* or *New Republic* mentioned activities above Central Park. It was much too easy for Talented Tenth notables like Johnson, White, and Locke not to notice in the second year of the Great Depression that, for the great majority of the population, Harlem was in the process of unmaking. Still, there was a definite prefiguration of Harlem's mortality when A'Lelia Walker suddenly died in

August 1931, a doleful occurrence shortly followed by the sale of Villa Lewaro, her Hudson mansion, at public auction. By the end of 1929, African Americans lived in the five-hundred block of Edgecombe Avenue, known as "Sugar Hill." The famous "409" overlooking the Polo Grounds was home at one time or another to the Du Boises, the Fishers, and the Whites. Below Sugar Hill was the five-acre Rockefeller-financed Dunbar Apartments complex, its 511 units fully occupied in mid-1928. The Dunbar eventually became home for the Du Boises, E. Simms Campbell (illustrator and cartoonist), Fletcher Henderson, the A. Philip Randolphs, Leigh Whipper (actor), and (briefly) Paul and Essie Robeson. The complex published its own weekly bulletin, the *Dunbar News,* an even more valuable record of Talented Tenth activities during the Renaissance than the *Inter-State Tattler.*

The 1931 *Report on Negro Housing,* presented to President Hoover, was a document starkly in contrast to the optimism found in *Black Manhattan.* Nearly 50 percent of Harlem's families would be unemployed by the end of 1932. The syphilis rate was nine times higher than white Manhattan's; the tuberculosis rate was five times greater; pneumonia and typhoid were twice that of whites. Two African American mothers and two babies died for every white mother and child. Harlem General Hospital, the single public facility, served 200,000 African Americans with 273 beds. A Harlem family paid twice as much of their income for rent as a white family. Meanwhile, median family income in Harlem dropped 43.6 percent by 1932. The ending of Prohibition would devastate scores of marginal speakeasies, as well as prove fatal to theaters like the Lafayette. Connie's Inn would eventually migrate downtown. Until then, however, the clubs in "The Jungle" (133rd Street)—Bamville, Connor's, Clam House, Nest Club—and elsewhere (Pod's and Jerry's, Smalls' Paradise) continued to do a land-office business. With the repeal of the Eighteenth Amendment, honorary Harlemites like Van Vechten sobered up and turned to other pursuits. Locke's letters to Charlotte Osgood Mason turned increasingly pessimistic in the winter of 1931. In June 1932, he perked up a bit to praise the choral ballet presented at the Eastman School of Music—*Sahdji,* with music by William Grant Still and scenario by Nugent, but most of Locke's news was distinctly downbeat. The writing partnership of two of his protégés, Hughes and Hurston, their material needs underwritten in a New Jersey township by "Godmother" Charlotte Mason, col-

lapsed in acrimonious dispute. Each claimed principal authorship of the only dramatic comedy written during the Renaissance, *Mule Bone,* a three-act folk play unperformed (as a result of the dispute) until 1991. Locke took the side of Hurston, undermining the tie of affection between Godmother and Hughes and effectively ending his relationship with the latter. The part played in this controversy by their brilliant secretary, Louise Thompson, the strong-willed, estranged wife of Wallace Thurman, remains murky, but it seems clear that Thompson's Marxism had a deep influence on Hughes in the aftermath of his painful breakup with Godmother, Locke, and Hurston.

In any case, beginning with "Advertisement for the Waldorf-Astoria" published in the December 1931 *New Masses,* Hughes's poetry became markedly political. "Elderly Race Leaders" and "Goodbye Christ," as well as the play "Scottsboro, Limited," were irreverent, staccato offerings to the coming triumph of the proletariat. The poet's departure in June 1932 for Moscow, along with Louise Thompson, Mollie Lewis, Henry Moon, Loren Miller, Theodore Poston, and thirteen others, ostensibly to act in a Soviet film about American race relations, *Black and White,* symbolized the shift in patronage and accompanying politicization of Renaissance artists. *One Way to Heaven,* Cullen's first novel, badly flawed and clearly influenced by *Nigger Heaven,* appeared in 1932, but it seemed already a baroque anachronism with its knife-wielding Lotharios and elaborately educated types. An impatient Du Bois, already deeply alienated from the Renaissance, called for a second Amenia Conference to radicalize the movement's ideology and renew its personnel. Jessie Fauset remained oblivious to the profound artistic and political changes under way. Her final novel, *Comedy: American Style* (1933), was technically much the same as *Plum Bun.* Her subject, once again, was skin pigment and the neuroses of those who had just enough of it to spend their lives obsessed by it. James Weldon Johnson's autobiography, *Along This Way,* an elegantly written review of his sui generis public career as archetypal renaissance man in both meanings of the word, was the publishing event of the year. McKay's final novel also appeared that year. He worried familiar themes, but *Banana Bottom* represented a philosophical advance over *Home to Harlem* and *Banjo* in its reconciliation through the protagonist, Bita Plant, of the previously destructive tension in McKay between the natural and the artificial—soul and civilization.

The Lafayette Theatre in Harlem.

The publication at the beginning of 1932 of Thurman's last novel, *Infants of the Spring,* had already announced the end of the Harlem Renaissance. The action of Thurman's novel is in the ideas of the characters, in their incessant talk about themselves, Booker T. Washington, Du Bois, racism, and the destiny of the race. Its prose is generally disappointing, but the ending is conceptually poignant. Paul Arbian (Richard Bruce Nugent) commits suicide in a full tub of water, which splashes over and obliterates the pages of Arbian's unfinished novel on the bathroom floor. A still legible page, however, contains this paragraph, which was, in effect, an epitaph:

> He had drawn a distorted, inky black skyscraper, modeled after Niggerati Manor, and on which were focused an array of blindingly white beams of light. The foundation of this building was composed of crumbling stone. At first glance it could be ascertained that the skyscraper would soon crumple and fall, leaving the dominating white lights in full possession of the sky.

The literary energies of the Renaissance finally slumped. McKay returned to Harlem in February 1934 after a twelve-year so-journ abroad, but his creative powers were spent. The last novel of the movement, Hurston's beautifully written *Jonah's Gourd Vine,* went on sale in May 1934. Charles Johnson, James Weldon Johnson, and Locke applauded Hurston's allegorical story of her immediate family (especially her father) and the mores of an African American town in Florida called Eatonville. Fisher and Thurman could have been expected to continue to write, but their fates were sealed by professional carelessness. Thurman died a few days before Christmas 1934, soon after his return from an abortive Hollywood film project. Ignoring his physician's strictures, he hemorrhaged after drinking to excess while hosting a party in the infamous house at 267 West 136th Street. Four days later, Fisher expired from intestinal cancer caused by repeated exposure to his own X-ray equipment.

Locke's *New Negro* anthology had been crucial to the formation of the Renaissance. As the movement ran down, another anthology, English heiress Nancy Cunard's *Negro,* far more massive in scope, recharged the Renaissance for a brief period, enlisting the contributions of most of the principals (though McKay and Walrond refused, and Toomer no longer acknowledged his African American roots), and captured its essence in the manner of expert taxidermy. A grieving Locke wrote Charlotte Mason from Howard University, "It is hard to see the collapse of things you have labored to raise on a sound base."

Arthur Fauset, Jessie's perceptive brother, attempted to explain the collapse to Locke and the readers of *Opportunity* at the beginning of 1934. He foresaw "a socio-political-economic setback from which it may take decades to recover." The Renaissance had left the race unprepared, Fauset charged, because of its unrealistic belief "that social and economic recognition will be inevitable when once the race has produced a sufficiently large number of persons who have properly qualified themselves in the arts." Du Bois had not only turned his back on the movement, he had left the NAACP and Harlem for a university professorship in Atlanta after an enormous row over civil rights policy. Marxism had begun to exercise a decided appeal for him, but as the 1933 essay "Marxism and the Negro Problem" had made abundantly clear, Du Bois ruled out collaboration with American Marxists because they were much too racist. James Weldon Johnson's philosophical *tour d'horizon* appearing in 1934, *Negro Americans, What Now?,* asked precisely the question of the decade. Most Harlemites were certain that the riot exploding on the evening of March 19, 1935, taking three lives and costing two million dollars in property damage, was not an answer. By then, the Works Progress Administration (WPA) had become the major patron of African American artists and writers. Writers William Attaway, Ralph Ellison, Margaret Walker, Richard Wright, and Frank Yerby would emerge under its aegis, as would painters Romare Bearden, Jacob Lawrence, Charles Sebree, Lois Maillou Jones, and Charles White. The Communist Party was another patron, notably for Richard Wright, whose 1937 essay "Blueprint for Negro Writing" would materially contribute to the premise of Hughes's "The Negro Artist and the Racial Mountain." For thousands of ordinary Harlemites who had looked to Garvey's UNIA for inspiration, then to the Renaissance, there was now Father Divine and his "heavens."

In the ensuing years, much was renounced, more was lost or forgotten, yet the Renaissance, however artificial and overreaching, left a positive mark. Locke's *New Negro* anthology featured thirty of the movement's thirty-five stars. They and a small number of less gifted collaborators generated twenty-six novels, ten volumes of poetry, five Broadway plays, countless essays and short stories, three performed ballets and concerti, and a considerable output of canvas and sculpture. If the achievement was less than the titanic expectations of the Ministry of Culture, it was an arts-and-letters legacy, nevertheless, of which a beleaguered and belittled Afro-America could be proud, and by which it could be sustained. If more by osmosis than conscious attention, Mainstream America was also richer for the color, emotion, humanity, and cautionary vision produced by Harlem during its Golden Age.

"If I had supposed that all Negroes were illiterate brutes, I might be astonished to discover that they can write good third rate poetry, readable and unreadable magazine fiction," wrote one contemporary white Marxist passing flinty judgment upon the Renaissance. Nevertheless there were many white Americans—perhaps the majority—who found the African American artistic and literary ferment of the period wholly unexpected and little short of incredible. If the judgment of the Marxist observer soon became a commonplace, it was because the Harlem Renaissance demonstrated—finally, irrefutably, during slightly more than a decade—the considerable creative capacities of the best and brightest of a disadvantaged racial minority.

## MARK HELBLING (ESSAY DATE 1999)

**SOURCE:** Helbling, Mark. Introduction to *The Harlem Renaissance: The One and the Many,* pp. 1-18. Westport, Conn.: Greenwood Press, 1999.

*In the following introduction, Helbling provides an overview of late twentieth-century critical assessments of the Harlem Renaissance.*

Harlem, the Harlem of the 1920s has never been entirely absent from our minds. But one had to know where to look to keep in touch with that remarkable generation of poets, novelists, playwrights, painters, essayists, and musicians who collectively represent what is now known as the Harlem Renaissance. It has been a difficult search at best; the individuals, let alone their works, had all but vanished from view. In the 1960s, however, the American public began to discover what only a few remembered and a few others had sought to keep alive. In Harold Cruse's, *The Crisis of the Negro Intellectual* (1967), Robert Bone's, *The Negro Novel in America* (1965), and in the explosive response to the photographic exhibit "Harlem on My Mind" held at the Metropolitan Museum of Art (1969), the renaissance centered in Harlem was reborn.

Soon, most of the literature of that time and place was reissued; scholars began to comb overlooked archives and private collections; books and dissertations appeared; conferences blossomed; and universities as well as high schools began to teach the writings of Jean Toomer, Claude McKay, Zora Neale Hurston, Countee Cullen, and Langston Hughes, among others. We stand in their debt, for this scholarship has enriched our understanding, recreating a past that was too quickly neglected and too quickly forgotten. This scholarship, however, was more than the celebration of an earlier generation, for there was also a sense that what took place was flawed in its very inception and thus predetermined to be somewhat inconclusive.

Harold Cruse was one of the first to call attention to the Harlem Renaissance ("something . . . which has not been adequately dealt with in the history books") and to link this outburst of creative energy with what he argued to be the problematic cultural identity of present-day black Americans, a people "left in the limbo of social marginality, alienated and directionless on the landscape of America." Direction should come and should have come from the black intelligentsia, but, in his opinion, there were only aimless and contradictory gestures that trace back to the truncated visions of the 1920s.

> The essentially original and native creative element of the nineteen twenties was the Negro ingredient—as all the whites who were running to Harlem actually knew. But the Harlem intellectuals were so overwhelmed at being "discovered" and courted that they allowed a bona fide cultural movement . . . to degenerate into a pampered and paternalized vogue.[1]

Thus, a unique historic opportunity to forge the cultural and intellectual identity of black Americans was missed. Equally important, Cruse argues, these cultural stirrings mark "a twentieth century harbinger of the African awakening in political and cultural terms."[2] That this clarification failed to take place, however, was the movement's greatest failure and has been the burden subsequent generations have continued to bear.

Elements of Cruse's analysis inform Nathan Huggins's *Harlem Renaissance* (1971). In particular, Huggins sees reenacted on this newly constructed urban stage deeply rooted patterns dictated by those with power and wealth:

> As long as the white norms remained unchallenged, no matter what the Negro's reaction to them, he always needed to return to the white judge to measure his achievement. It would have required a much more profound rejection of white

values than was likely in the 1920s for Negroes to have freed themselves for creating the desired self-generating and self-confident Negro art.[3]

Rather than a bright new beginning, the renaissance was profoundly conservative, best understood as an updated minstrel show staged by whites. However, whereas Cruse challenged his readers to break with the past so as to free the present, Huggins argued that Cruse's understanding of a "bona fide cultural movement" simply perpetuated the past he sought to escape: "as one looks today, there is a similar race promotion and self-conscious search for identity which cannot help but perpetuate the ethnic province. Whatever that provincialism may contribute to identity and sociology, it will constrict the vision, limiting the possibilities of personality."[4]

Cruse had argued that although the reality of America was "a nation dominated by the social power of groups, classes, in-groups, and cliques," the intellectuals of the Harlem Renaissance had looked at their world with individualistic eyes.[5] As a consequence, they remained powerless and marginal, their art imitative and thin. Huggins, however, saw this emphasis on group identity as a form of provincialism, a provincialism that enfeebled artistic expression and marginalized those who stayed within its protective or enforced embrace. For Huggins, "artistic production [was] an extremely personal, individualistic thing, not to be turned on or off by nationalism of any kind."[6] As a consequence, the true "Negro renaissance" awaited those with the courage to explore their deepest individual natures and the confidence to assume their rightful place in the "seamless web" of American society.

Two more recent interpretations traverse what their authors now consider to be well-traveled territory. Although Robert Bone considered the story of the Harlem Renaissance to be a twice-told tale, he offered one more interpretation, "a truly literary interpretation," to supplement the work of Cruse and Huggins. Bone's focus in *Down Home* (1975) was on "two traditional literary modes: pastoral and anti-pastoral," which, he argued, were a natural voice for black writers. With the forms themselves—"the 'deep structures' of Afro-American fiction"—he had no quarrel and found them a perfect vehicle to explore "the antagonism between the self and the objective world."[7] But when he turned to the writers of the Harlem Renaissance, Bone perceived these black writers to have been especially vulnerable to white conceptions of black identity:

The modernist writers who arose in the first three decades of the century introduced a new stereotype into American literature. They abandoned the image of the Negro as contented slave, or as ravisher of white womanhood, replacing these with subtler, if no less racist caricature. In the writings of the Lost Generation, the Negro was depicted as a primitive. This was the image, for better or worse, that was thrust upon the writers of the Harlem Renaissance. Some black authors embraced the new stereotype, others tried to fend it off, or adapt it to their own ends, but all succumbed in one way or another to its seductive power.[8]

As a consequence, true self-understanding was impossible and art inevitably foundered upon the more general failure to replace racial stereotype with human complexity.

Following in the wake of these three scholars, David Levering Lewis felt it was time to move on to other considerations, at least to ask questions that had as yet not been posed:

> Whether the output of the Harlem Renaissance was unevenly outstanding or was truncated by the Depression at the very moment when truly great products would have been offered to publishers who no longer wanted "exotica," or whether, as Alfred Knopf maintains, there was little more worth publishing, is more or less well expatiated in an extensive literature, of which the works of Vernon Loggins, Saunders Redding, Robert Bone, Darwin Turner, Jean Wagner, and Arthur P. Davis, inter alia, are only some of the more distinguished sources.[9]

Successful or not, how, Lewis wondered, did it all take place? Was there, in fact, a structure of support (or control) that made possible what more breathless accounts attributed to the "spirit" of the times? Thus, Lewis provided in *When Harlem Was in Vogue* (1982) a detailed account of six principal figures—Jessie Fauset, Charles S. Johnson, Alain Locke, Walter White, Casper Holstein, and James Weldon Johnson—whose networks of influence, assistance, and ambition helped make possible the work that was achieved: "without the patient assemblage and management by [this] handful of Harlem notables of a substantial white patronage . . . the Harlem cultural scene would have been little more than a larger version of Philadelphia or Washington, places where belle-lettres meant Saturday night adventures in tidy parlors, among mostly tidy-minded literati."[10]

Of the six principal figures Holstein was the least visible, for he controlled organized gambling in Harlem and the money he gave for literary awards had little directly to do with cultivating a white patronage. But for the others outside support was the game to play, and, Lewis argued, they played it well—some perhaps too well. Alain Locke's principal benefactor, for example, was the wealthy Mrs. Charlotte Osgood Mason. Through Locke she met and gave money to Zora Neale Hurston, Aaron Douglas, Arthur Huff Fauset, Hall Johnson, Claude McKay, Richmond Barthé, Langston Hughes, and others.[11] Support, however, did not come without a price, especially to those who did not heed her advice "to slough off white culture" and to tread lightly the "slippery pond of civilization." As Hughes later recalled, once he no longer felt "the rhythms of the primitive surging" Mrs. Mason severed all ties with "her most precious child."[12] For the next few months Hughes was physically and emotionally sick. Although Lewis shifts our attention to the men and women behind the scenes, we are still witness to actors performing roles in scripts written by others. As the title of his book suggests, we look back to a time that was soon to collapse under the weight of the depression and its own artificiality.

There is much to recommend in these several interpretations. For these various critics have sharpened our awareness of the racial dynamics of creative expression and the vulnerability of black artists in the 1920s to the demands, the constraints, and the fantasies of others. How appropriate, then, that Alain Locke himself, looking back from the wreckage of the 1930s helped set the tone for subsequent criticism: "Eleven brief years ago Harlem was full of the thrill and ferment of sudden progress and prosperity; and *Survey Graphic* sounded the tocsin of the emergence of a 'new Negro' and the onset of a 'Negro renaissance.' Today, with that same Harlem prostate in the grip of the depression and throes of social unrest, we confront the sobering facts of a serious relapse and premature setback; indeed, find it hard to believe that the rosy enthusiasm and hopes of 1925 were more than bright illusions or a cruelly deceptive mirage."[13] Now, it seemed, Harlem stood forth for what it really was, "a mass of unemployed stranded in an over-expensive, disease and crime-ridden slum."[14] And Locke was quick to conclude, "there is no cure or saving magic in poetry and art, an emerging generation of talent, or international prestige and interracial recognition, for unemployment or precarious marginal employment."[15] One hears in Locke's disillusionment the future voices of Cruse, Huggins, and Lewis. Rather than a new beginning, as Locke had once prophesied, there was only a frustrating sameness. If Harlem was a vogue, it was a vogue long in the making.

More recently, however, a second generation of critics—Bernard Bell, Henry Louis Gates, Jr., Houston A. Baker, Jr., and Arnold Rampersad—has both drawn upon and modified the work of these pioneering interpretations. In so doing they have significantly altered our understanding of the past and the terms in which we understand that past. In *Modernism and the Harlem Renaissance* (1987), for example, Baker offers an important revision of the critical lens through which the Harlem Renaissance has been viewed. In particular, Baker singles out the interpretations of Huggins and Lewis, both of whom argued for a renaissance more problematic than achieved—"While Huggins adduces provinciality and narrowness as causes for a failed Harlem Renaissance, his contemporary and fellow Afro-American historian David Levering Lewis takes a contrary view. Lewis ascribes Harlem's failings to a tragically wide, ambitious, and delusional striving on the part of renaissance intellectuals."[16] But the real failure, Baker argued, was in the judgment of those unable to see (to hear) what, in fact, had taken place. The renaissance could only be judged to be "provincial," a "failure," a "vogue" if one assumed that "notions of British, Anglo-American, and Irish 'modernism'" were relevant to understanding the "history of Afro-American modernism, especially the discursive history of such modernism."[17] Thus, Baker directly challenged the dominant analytical trope, modernism, which had served in the critical literature to define as well as explain the failure of black writers and intellectuals in the 1920s. Ironically, then, it is not the men and women of the renaissance who failed but the "scholarly" establishment of African Americans who, having failed to transcend the "critical vocabulary and . . . assumptions of a dominating culture," have employed this vocabulary to see failure in others.

Baker not only deconstructs the critical assumptions and vocabulary of past scholarship but makes deconstruction itself what is uniquely modern about the Harlem Renaissance and the consciousness of African Americans—"I suggest that the analysis of discursive strategies that I designate 'the mastery of form' and 'the deformation of mastery' produces more accurate and culturally enriching interpretations of the sound and soundings of Afro-American modernism than do traditional methods."[18] As a consequence, we now see the past from a radically different perspective and encounter familiar individuals playing unfamiliar roles. Booker T. Washington, for example, is no longer the sycophant mouthing "accommodationist" platitudes, but the consummate trickster who had both mastered and subverted the language of the dominant culture. As a consequence, whites were lulled to sleep with the language of the day while Washington's black audience was awakened to healthy doses of ridicule, burlesque, and contempt for those who thought they understood what he had to say. Even more surprising, Washington's *Up from Slavery* now emerges, in Baker's telling, as the defining text and his address at the Negro exhibit of the Atlanta Cotton States and International Exposition the defining moment "that constitutes a primary move in Afro-American discursive modernism."[19]

In shifting the discussion away from the "familiar geography of a familiar Harlem-Renaissance" to what he calls "areas of Afro-American production," Baker situates Locke, Countee Cullen, and Claude McKay in the lengthened perspective of Washington and Washington's contemporaries Charles Chesnutt and Paul Laurence Dunbar. This larger perspective, however, is itself but a bracket of time grounded in the deeper imaginative structures of African American consciousness, the "sounding strategies" or language an enslaved and exploited people have employed to challenge power and to sustain their integrity and identity as a people. But even this voicing, "the common sense of the tribe," is rooted in the "sound and space of an African ancestral past."

In order to redefine and recenter the moral and cultural geography of the Harlem Renaissance, Baker draws upon the writings of Michel Foucault, Jacques Derrida, Roland Barthes, and Mikhail Bakhtin. However, Baker's most profound intellectual and emotional debts are to individuals, writings, and "performances" closer to home. As Baker writes in the preface,

> The orientation of the reflections that follow derives from a family history and, in particular, from reminiscences of the life of my father, Houston A. Baker, Sr., who died in 1983. Reflecting the labors of generations of black men and women in the United States who have been exploited, segregated, physically and verbally abused, denied access to opportunity, and called all manner of untoward names, and who have, nonetheless, forged a mighty identity and forced the white world to stand in awe and, sometimes, to effect powerful imitations of their signal labors—thinking on such indisputable facts of our family history (and on my father as metonym for that history) I suddenly wondered who, precisely, had consigned the Harlem Renaissance to the domain of "failure" and how we, as Afro-American scholars (but more importantly as descendants of a resonant black lineage), could tolerate this consignment.[20]

Not only is Baker's vision intentionally personal, even intimate, but it is a point of view and a self-consciousness that marks a profound shift in the visions of a generation of scholars who have came of age since the climactic years of the 1960s.[21]

Baker's immediate intellectual debt is to John Blassingame whose "sensitive ear to black communal sounds" detected in Booker T. Washington levels of meaning, discursive strategies, both traditional and modern. However, it is to the fertile imagination of Henry Louis Gates, Jr. that Baker is most indebted. In *Modernism and the Harlem Renaissance* he pays special tribute to Gates, whose essay on masking and dialect in African American expression—"Dis and Dat: Dialect and the Descent"—(indeed all of his writings) helped Baker to see language itself as simultaneously the "mastery of form" and "the deformation of mastery." Gates, in turn, in his important work *The Signifying Monkey* distinguished Baker as his "ideal reader," the "critical voice that I trust and respect and to which I address my work." Thus, Baker's *Blues, Ideology, and Afro-American Literature: A Vernacular Theory* both inspired and reassured Gates in his effort to locate within the African and African American expressive traditions a genuinely "black" system of theory and criticism. Taken together, the work of Blassingame, Gates, and Baker reflects in broad outline an important turning point in literary and historical scholarship.

Central to this increasingly conscious, even self-conscious, awareness of the problematics of scholarship itself is the question of language as it functions in scholarly discourse as well as the symbolic world of those one seeks to comprehend. In *Blues, Ideology, and Afro-American Literature,* for example, Baker nicely details these various referential levels and the challenge this self-consciousness now poses:

> The assumption of normative relativity, far from being a call to abandonment or retrenchment in the critical arena, constitutes an invitation to speculative explorations that are aware both of their own partiality and their heuristic transitions from suggestive (sometimes dramatic) images to inscribed concepts. The openness implied by relativity enables, say, the literary critic to re-cognize his endeavors, presupposing from the outset that such labors are not directed toward independent, observable, empirical phenomena but rather toward processes, objects, and events that he or she half-creates (and privileges as "art") through his or her own speculative, inventive energies and interests.[22]

Most important, Baker argues, this "openness" allows for a freedom to imagine the past and the present in radically new ways. Thus, we see a privileging not only of culture, but an African American culture, to contextualize historical experience. In Baker's own words, "if the investigator's efforts are sufficiently charged with blues energy, he is almost certain to remodel elements and events appearing in traditional, Anglo-American space-time in ways that make them "jump" several rings toward blackness and the vernacular."[23] With this shift in emphasis, black Americans emerge as resourceful men and women and not simply pawns in the stream of someone else's history.[24]

Thus, Baker insists, the Harlem Renaissance was not the half realized efforts of imaginative individuals, but a "complex field of sounding strategies" drawn from the collective experience and consciousness of black peoples, "the spirit house and space of black habitation." Freedom not frustration; openness not closure; ingenuity not imitation; assertion not acceptance—"the human will's resistance to tyranny and the human mind's masterful and insistent engagement with forms and deformations"—marked the birth, the rebirth, and the birthright of the Harlem Renaissance. Likewise, in his own scholarship and that of others, we see not only a shift from an "Anglo-American space-time," to what Baker calls "a national racial expressivity," but a linking of this cultural emphasis to the larger universe of African culture.

Freed themselves, these scholars have found in others a freedom and a vitality earlier scholars all but failed to imagine. The "discovery" of the Harlem Renaissance itself mirrors this renaissance of the imagination and serves, in turn, to sustain these imaginative revisions. However, just as Baker's scholarship both nourishes and is nourished by the challenges to intellectual and political authority presently sweeping the world, there remains an inner tension, at least a question, that is not easily resolved and opens onto an understanding of the past, of the Harlem Renaissance, that has yet to be addressed.

In *Modernism and the Harlem Renaissance,* Baker employs the term *"marronage"*—"the bonding together [of fugitives from slavery] to create independent communities of their own"—so as to establish the historical and cultural contours of the Harlem Renaissance. Thus, Baker speaks of the renaissance generally and Alain Locke's *The New Negro* (1925) in particular as the representation of "a unified community of national interests set in

# ON THE SUBJECT OF...

**A COLLECTIVE DEFINITION OF BLACK CULTURE**

Although there were attempts at realistic depiction of Black life before they came on the scene, the writers of the Harlem Renaissance were the first to do this in a systematic manner, as even a cursory look at the period will reveal. . . . Alain Locke's essay entitled "The New Negro," which appeared in his larger "statement," the epoch-making volume of the same name, brought the issues into focus. Afro-Americans had come of age; they could look at themselves for what they were, without false piety and without shame, rejecting the "social nostrums and the panaceas," and realizing that although religion, freedom, and education were important to their cause, they alone were not sufficient. What was needed was group solidarity and collective effort.

**SOURCE:** Stephen E. Henderson, excerpt from "The Forms of Things Unknown," in *Understanding the New Black Poetry: Black Speech and Black Music as Poetic References,* William Morrow and Company, 1972.

direct opposition to the general economic, political, and theological tenets of a racist land."[25] This "inner-objective" ("the founding of a nation of Afro-Americans on the basis of Race") rests upon the bed-rock of "self-in-*marronage*"—"the always already AFRICAN SELF that has its being in community and cultural/racial/tribal interiority."[26] Not only does Baker ground the Harlem Renaissance culturally and racially but in so doing he controls or stabilizes the "deconstructionist activities" of his trickster figures. As a consequence, ambiguity is understood to have purpose, disorder is not without order, and performance springs from conviction. For others, however, for James Clifford and for George Hutchinson, for example, this "always already AFRICAN SELF" is no less problematic than other efforts to authenticate identity and to authenticate the ethnic and cultural boundaries of the Harlem Renaissance.

Although Clifford has little directly to say about the Harlem Renaissance, he traces in *The Predicament of Culture: Twentieth-Century Ethnography, Literature, and Art,* "the formation and breakup of ethnographic authority in twentieth century anthropology."[27] In so doing, he, like Baker, applauds as well as contributes to this "critique of deep-seated Western habits of mind and systems of values." For this helps Clifford to realize his primary goal, "to open space for cultural futures, for the recognition of emergence."[28] However, the predicament Clifford addresses includes not only those whose work is in question, and the work itself, but also those (like himself) who now question this work. For if, "there is no neutral standpoint in the power-laden field of discursive positionings," isn't this equally true for those who counter the "truths" others have fashioned?[29] Thus, Clifford concludes, "if authenticity is relational, there can be no essence except as a political, cultural invention, a local tactic."[30]

Clifford has no final answer for the questions he raises, but he finds in the writing of Aimé Césaire and the "creolized" culture and consciousness of Carribean peoples an analogue and a strategy to apprehend as well as represent both one's cultural identity and modernity itself—"For Césaire culture and identity are inventive and mobile. They need not take root in ancestral plots; they live by pollination, by (historical) transplanting."[31] Airborne inspiration, pollination, and not root-deep certainties nourish his being and his poetics. As a consequence, Clifford suggests that for Césaire the term "*marron*" or "*marronage*" as a noun was insufficient to fully convey his and his peoples inner being. For this reason, Césaire turns noun into verb, coining the new word "*marronner.*" In so doing, he shifts the emphasis from the historical fact of cultural displacement (context) to the creative act of cultural construction (consciousness). As a consequence, the geography of his imagination—West Africa, France, Hispanic America, Brazil, Haiti—now becomes the alembic of imagination itself.

On a more personal note, James Baldwin anticipated the concerns that inform Clifford's reading of Césaire. Many years before Césaire had written the poem "The Verb '*Marronner*'/for René Depestre, Haitian Poet," Baldwin stood riveted by Césaire's electrifying speech given at the "The Conference of Negro-African Writers and Artists" in Paris (1956):

We find ourselves today in a cultural chaos. And this is our role: to liberate the forces which, alone, can organize from this chaos a new synthesis, a synthesis which will deserve the name of culture, a synthesis which will be the reconciliation—*et dépassement*—of the old and the new. We are here to proclaim the right of our people to speak, to let our people, black people, make their entrance on the great stage of history.[32]

Baldwin was thrilled with Césaire's "water tight" case against Europe. But he was also puzzled, even "stirred in a disagreeable way." For in his opinion, "Césaire's speech left out of account one of the great effects of the colonial experience: its creation, precisely, of men like himself."[33] Thus, questions implicit in Baldwin's concern have become, as seen, others concern as we puzzle "conjectural" identities as well as languages and voices no less conjectural. At the same time, Baldwin's question also reaches backward in time to the men and women of the Harlem Renaissance and provides, along with Clifford's response, support for, as well as a critical counterpoint to, the most recent interpretation of the Harlem Renaissance, George Hutchinson's *The Harlem Renaissance in Black and White*.

In *The Harlem Renaissance in Black and White*, Hutchinson challenges all previous interpretations of the Harlem Renaissance, grounding its significance and meaning in the search for an American national identity commonly pursued and contested by white and black intellectuals in the initial decades of the twentieth century. As Hutchinson writes,

> The issue of American national identity was, in any case, the dominant *problematic* structuring the literary field relevant to the Harlem Renaissance. . . . The attempt, overall, came down to an effort to expand the notion of "the people" who compose the American national community, and thus who, in a liberal democratic state, have an acknowledged, socially *legitimated* right to help set the general direction and specific policies of that community—have a moral claim, according to that community's self-understanding, upon the common conscience and the structuring of the social order.[34]

To achieve this perspective, however, to see both the concern for an American national identity and the equally compelling effort to construct a pluralistic vision of American culture, Hutchinson argues that it is first necessary to come to terms with "traditional conceptions of American modernism." For, as he writes, "the limitations and exclusions built into traditional views of modernism have much to do with the problems afflicting understandings of the institutional contexts and intellectual trajectories of the Harlem

Renaissance."[35] Thus, modernism is key to a conceptual understanding of the Harlem Renaissance and key, as well, to the intellectual and institutional dynamics that mark these years—"To enter the history of American modernism by way of an interracial perspective, I believe, can offer a new vision of the period."[36]

To make his case, Hutchinson draws upon Daniel Joseph Singal's "Towards a Definition of American Modernism" to help distinguish European "high" modernism and American "lost generation" modernism from the thought and work of those who, for the most part, remained on American shores. In particular, Hutchinson claims that "the drifting apart of social and personal spheres typical of high modernism is not typical of New Negro writing; nor is it typical of the writing of the socialists, cultural nationalists, and regional realists who responded to their work and with whom they affiliated."[37] On this basis, Hutchinson critiques Baker as well as Huggins (indeed, all interpretations) that employed "high" modernism in one way or another as if it was a relevant concern:

> Indeed, it is still the case that discussions of modernism and the Harlem Renaissance often pit black writers against white writers like Eliot, Pound, and Stein, who inhabited a very different space (literally!) in the modernist landscape, while ignoring or giving little careful attention to the forms of uncanonical, "native" (white) modernism with which the African American renaissance was intimately related.[38]

Thus, Hutchinson opens the way to see the Harlem Renaissance in a new perspective, a perspective that importantly challenges his readers to realize the commonalities that sustain cultural diversity as well as the diversity needed to strengthen what a people have in common.[39]

The challenge "to appreciate a once-acknowledged but long-forgotten and repressed kinship," however, is not the only challenge the renaissance or Hutchinson's argument presents. For the sense of consciousness, even self-consciousness, addressed by both Clifford and Baldwin is no less the legacy of the Harlem Renaissance. As seen, Hutchinson argued that for present-day Americans, white and black, to realize their shared identity, it was first necessary, "to reconceive what 'American modernism' is, and also to begin thinking of American literature less as a tradition (or set of separate traditions) following noble lines of descent than as the continually reforming product of historical fields of action, power, and experience."[40] It is my argument, however, that American modernism was not only (was more than) an imaginative field that evolved from and upon which competing notions of a national American cultural identity were fought. For woven into the very texture of American modernism was both a search for and a questioning of all forms of collective identity.

At issue was the question of identity, often conceptualized as the personality, of the individual. For in the very search for a meaningful structure or a set of relationships for personality to develop there existed a simultaneous questioning of the very grounds that one imagined how personality might be achieved. In other words, American modernism is marked by an inner tension that structured as well as complicated this critical discourse. Hutchinson is right. American modernism is not best defined as "the drifting apart of social and personal spheres." No one argued, for example, as did T. S. Eliot, for an extinction of personality.[41] In contrast to Eliot, Van Wyck Brooks argued that "the essence of art, religion, literature—the essence of personality itself—since the beginning of things" had to be engaged if one was to think seriously about society and social reform.[42] And Alain Locke declared that

> So for generations in the mind of America, the Negro has been more of a formula than a human being. . . . The thinking Negro even has been induced to share this same general attitude . . . to see himself in the distorted perspective of a social problem. His shadow, so to speak has been more real to him than his personality.[43]

However, if a concern for personality was central to the general idea of a cultural renaissance, the link between personal and social spheres was problematic at best.

To help suggest this tension between the individual and forms of collective identity, it is important to briefly address three key intellectual concerns that Hutchinson claims link the Harlem Renaissance and American modernism—cultural pluralism, Boasian anthropology, and philosophical pragmatism.[44]

### Cultural Pluralism

In "William James and Twentieth Century Ethnic Thought," Larry C. Miller explores the degree to which James's pluralistic philosophy might have influenced the emphasis on cultural pluralism and ethnic diversity articulated by Horace Kallen, Robert Park, and W. E. B. Du Bois. Although James's ideas were, as Miller claims, "relevant" to their work, the primary thrust of his own thinking was to link pluralism with individu-

alism and voluntarism.[45] In a somewhat similar vein, John J. Mc Dermott argues in "The Promethean Self and Community in the Philosophy of William James," that James has much to teach us about a "doctrine of community" so long as we understand that the individual and the community (society in general) are for James in an interdependent yet problematic relationship. If the self is a social construct so too is society an individual construct. As Mc Dermott quotes James, "Individuality is founded in feeling; and the recesses of feeling, the darker, blinder strata of character, are the only places in the world in which we catch real fact in the making, and directly perceive how events happen, and how work is actually done."[46] The language is that of James, but the emphasis is not too different from that of Alain Locke in "The Problem of Classification in Theory of Value," Locke's dissertation written at Harvard, and the intellectual groundwork for his critical writings in the 1920s. Finally, John P. Diggins argues in *The Promise of Pragmatism: Modernism and the Crisis of Knowledge and Authority* that James's commitment to "self-sovereignty" not only distinguished his intellectual thought but provoked John Dewey, as well as Charles H. Cooley and George H. Mead, to formulate alternative social philosophies.[47]

### Boasian Anthropology

Franz Boas, whose concepts, Hutchinson claims, "became bedrock assumptions among 'New Negro' authors of virtually every persuasion," was no less challenged to locate the individual within the understanding of culture he did so much to pioneer. Thus, in "The Aims of Anthropological Research," Boas wrote, "The problems of the relation of the individual to his culture, to the society in which he lives have received too little attention. The standardized anthropological data that inform us of customary behavior, give no clue to the reaction of the individual to his culture, nor to an understanding of his influence upon it."[48] Four years later, Boas argued that although "it seems most desirable and worthwhile to understand each culture as a whole and to define its character," he doubted that "it is possible to give a picture of the culture which is at the same time a picture of a personality."[49] In addition to the methodological problem posed by Boas, his students also struggled to find their own personal voice as that voice was shaped, in part, by their theoretical concerns. As Richard Handler has argued, "In my work on the literary endeavors of Boasian anthropologists, I have examined a similar tension [the tension between the quest for self-expression and the desire to recover a viable tradition] in the development of a cultural theory that could accommodate both cultural holism and human individuality."[50]

## Philosophical Pragmatism

In addressing "the central role of aesthetic experience in the achievement of new forms of solidarity and understanding," Hutchinson singled out Van Wyck Brooks and the impact his influential work, *America's Coming of Age,* had on Locke, his classmate at Harvard.[51] As Hutchinson concludes, "Brooks and his cohorts at *The Seven Arts* provided a cluster of terms that helped shape the discourse not only of the 'Little Renaissance' but of the New Negro movement."[52] At the same time, Hutchinson argues that "Locke's incorporation of *The Seven Arts* critics' ideas foreshadowed the development of related positions by younger authors such as Langston Hughes and Jean Toomer."[53] The impact of these terms, however, had a double edge. As Casey Nelson Blake argues in *Beloved Community,* Brooks, along with Randolph Bourne, came to realize that "if culture was immediately equated with community life . . . it would have little to contribute to personalities engaged in reshaping their world" precisely because community itself threatened to obliterate the independence of mind they sought to achieve.[54] As a consequence, it was necessary for "intellectuals [to exploit] the tensions between the two, honing their ideas into a critical discourse of social transformation."[55] Blake goes on to argue that this tension between personality and community was central to the thinking of all the "Young Americans," though it was most fully recognized by Lewis Mumford that "it was precisely that tension that held the greatest promise for a genuine Beloved Community."[56]

Perhaps this emphasis on personality, the place and fulfillment of the individual in tension with the search for a sustaining organic culture, especially marks American modernism. If so it is partly a question of degree. As Charles Taylor argues in *Sources of the Self: The Making of the Modern Identity,* "expressive individuation [is] one of the cornerstones of modern culture."[57] Taylor traces this "inward turning," this retrieval of "experience or interiority," back to European thought in the late eighteenth century.[58] In this context, the intellectual influence of the German philosopher Johann Gottfried Herder deserves special attention.[59] However, tracing lines of influence, a problematic quest at best, is not my particular concern. It is more suggestive to note that in Herder's effort to conceptualize the one and the many one can see the same tensions surface that surface in the Harlem Renaissance. In our own more recent time, one can see this ongoing tension in the thought of those (Kwame Anthony Appiah and Hazel Carby, for example) who are concerned with the creative act of cultural construction.

In "Identity, Authenticity, Survival: Multicultural Societies and Social Reproduction," Appiah asks "What is the relationship between this collective language and the individualist thrust of the modern notion of the self?" His answer is that identity is dialogical, something negotiated, a process both reflective and self-reflective. Thus, he argues, "Too much multi-cultural talk presupposes concepts of collective identity that are remarkably unsubtle in their understandings of the process by which identities, both individual and collective, develop.[60] When he turns his attention to Africa and African writers, Appiah notes a similar tension. Writing of Wole Soyinka, Appiah argues, "This struggle [that of the authorial 'I' with that of the 'we' of oral narration] is as central to Soyinka's situation as it is to that of African writers generally. . . . Once again the 'I' seeks to escape the persistent and engulfing 'we.'"[61]

No less concerned with the boundaries of cultural construction and individual consciousness, Hazel Carby is interested in "The Politics of Fiction, Anthropology and the Folk: Zora Neale Hurston" in Hurston's existential relationship as an intellectual to the various narrative voices she employed to fashion her fine work *Their Eyes Were Watching God:*

> Hurston . . . was concerned with the relationships among the lives and cultures that she reconstructed and her own search for a construction of the self. She lived the contradictions of the various constructions of her social identity and rewrote them in *Their Eyes Were Watching God.* Her anthropological "spyglass" which she trained on the society that produced her, allowed her to return to that society in the guise of being a listener and a reporter. In her fictional return, Hurston represents the tensions inherent in her position as an intellectual—in particular as a writer—in antagonistic relation to her construction of the folk community. It is in this sense that I think Hurston is as concerned with the production of a sense of self as she is with the representation of a folk consciousness through its cultural forms.[62]

When Carby turns her attention more generally to the Harlem Renaissance, she argues in "Quicksands of Representation: Rethinking Black

Cultural Politics" that what we presently would like to believe about the past doesn't hold up under close inspection: "Indeed, the Harlem renaissance is frequently conceived as a unique, intellectually cohesive and homogeneous historical moment, a mythology which has disguised the contradictory impulses of the Harlem intellectuals."[63] For both Carby and Appiah, the "production of a sense of self" is inherently problematic, a challenge rooted in the past yet no less compelling for those who live in the present.

This study is focused on five important individuals of the Harlem Renaissance who struggled to come to terms with the tension between the one and the many—W. E. B. Du Bois, Alain Locke, Claude McKay, Jean Toomer, and Zora Neale Hurston. For Du Bois and Locke, the imaginative construction of a cultural identity was simultaneously an act of self-reflection. For Du Bois this took the form in *The Souls of Black Folk* of a self-conscious narration historically as well as personally grounded, whereas Locke explored in various writings and *The New Negro* the complex sense of culture as both an objective construct and a subjective experience. As for McKay, Toomer, and Hurston, all three struggled with what Hazel Carby has called "the production of a sense of self." Although this meant very different things to each of these writers, all sought to establish the self that challenged the claims others sought to impose.

## Notes

1. Harold Cruse, *The Crisis of the Negro Intellectual* (New York: William Morris and Co., 1967), 21-22.

2. Ibid., 63.

3. Nathan Huggins, *Harlem Renaissance* (New York: Oxford University Press, 1971), 306-7.

4. Ibid., 308.

5. Cruse, *Crisis*, 7.

6. Huggins, *Harlem Renaissance*, 241.

7. Robert Bone, *Down Home* (New York: G. P. Putnam's Sons, 1975), xix

8. Ibid., 125.

9. David Levering Lewis, "The New Negro, 1920-1935," *Prospects* 3 (1997): 251.

10. Ibid., 120-21.

11. See Steven Watson, *The Harlem Renaissance: Hub of African-American Culture, 1920-1930* (New York: Pantheon Books, 1995).

12. David Levering Lewis, *When Harlem Was in Vogue* (New York: Vintage Books, 1982), 257.

13. Alain Locke, "Harlem: Dark Weather-Vane," *Survey Graphic* 25 (August 1936): 457. George Hutchinson makes the following important point—"Contrary to popular belief, publishers did not suddenly lose interest in black authors with the onset of the Depression. None of the publishers that survived stopped publishing the New Negro writers they had picked up in the 1920s. Indeed, one of the strangest charges against the Harlem Renaissance is that, having been buoyed by white fascination for the primitive, it crashed with the stock market in 1929. Simply consulting the standard bibliographies disproves this notion." However, as Hutchinson goes on to argue, there was a distinct shift in intellectual and social focus, a shift that even ridiculed the "Harlem Renaissance interest in recuperating African cultural traditions as well as what came to be regarded as the outmoded racialism of the New Negro intellectual leaders." Hutchinson, *The Harlem Renaissance in Black and White* (Cambridge: Harvard University Press, 1995), 384, 435.

14. Locke, "Harlem," 457.

15. Ibid., 457.

16. Houston A. Baker, Jr., *Modernism and the Harlem Renaissance* (Chicago: University of Chicago Press, 1987), 10.

17. Ibid., xvi.

18. Ibid.

19. Ibid., 17. Thus, Baker grounds "renaissancism in Afro-American culture as a whole" in Washington's famous address and not in the more conventional modernist time line (c. December, 1910) suggested by Virginia Woolf.

20. Ibid., xiv-xv.

21. In his earlier work, *Blues, Ideology and Afro-American Literature*, Baker singled out for special praise the readings of Frederick Jameson, Hayden White, and Marshall Sahlins and linked their critical importance for him with that of Hegel's "Phenomenology of the Spirit." Houston A. Baker, Jr., *Blues, Ideology and Afro-American Literature* (Chicago: The University of Chicago Press, 1984). These names, together with those of the French structuralists and deconstructionists who appeared in *Modernism and the Harlem Renaissance,* reflect that this rethinking of the past is, itself, part of a widespread reconceptualization of intellectual activity that has profoundly altered scholarship in the humanities and the social sciences in the last few decades. The following titles, by name alone, suggest the widespread attention now given to the problematics of intellectual discourse and analysis: *The Invention of Primitive Society: Transformations of an Illusion* (1988), *The Invention of Tradition; The Invention of Culture; The Invention of Africa: Gnosis, Philosophy and the Order of Knowledge* (1990), *The Invention of Ethnicity* (1989).

Invention suggests discovery as well as fabrication, and the most significant discovery is the fact or act of fabrication itself. As Adam Kuper writes in *The Invention of Primitive Society* (London: Routledge, 1988), "The anthropologists took . . . primitive society as their special subject, but in practice primitive society proved to be their own society (as they understood it) seen in a distorting mirror." And, as Marianna Torgovnick writes in *Gone Primitive: Savage Intellects, Modern Lives* (Chicago: University of Chicago Press, 1990), "The real secret of the primitive in this century has often been the same secret as always: the primitive can be—has been, will be (?)—whatever Euro-

Americans want it to be." As these comments suggest, power no less than "problematics" is at issue, for the authority to write about others reflects not only the power of those in authority but serves itself to subordinate those written about to the terms and terminology one employs.

22. Baker, *Blues,* 10.

23. Baker, *Modernism,* 10.

24. One only needs to compare Stanley Elkins, *Slavery—A Problem in American Institutional and Intellectual Life* (1959) with Blassingame's, *The Slave Community—Plantation Life in the Antebellum South* (1972) or Sterling Stuckey's, *Slave Culture* (1986) to see this shift in emphasis, a people once presented as objects or victims now seen as actors affirming their humanity within the constraints that existed.

25. Baker, *Modernism,* 77.

26. Ibid., 114.

27. As Clifford writes, "The development of ethnographic science cannot ultimately be understood in isolation from more general political-epistemological debates about writing and the representation of otherness." Clifford, *The Predicament of Culture: Twentieth-Century Ethnography, Literature, and Art* (Cambridge: Harvard University Press, 1988), 24.

28. Ibid., 15-16.

29. Here Clifford is paraphrasing Jeanne Favret-Saada's argument in *Les mots, la mort, les sorts* (1977), 42. Thus, Clifford asks of Edward Said's *Orientalism,* "if criticism must struggle against the procedures of representation itself, how is it to begin? How, for example, is an oppositional critique of Orientalism to avoid falling into 'Occidentalism'?" Clifford, *Predicament of Culture,* 259.

30. Ibid., 12.

31. Ibid., 15.

32. James Baldwin, "Princes and Powers," in *Nobody Knows My Name* (New York: Dell, 1961), 40.

33. Ibid., 41.

34. Hutchinson, *The Harlem Renaissance,* 13.

35. Ibid., 14.

36. Ibid., 31.

37. Ibid., 119. To support this distinction—"the division between social and personal spheres in 'high' modernism"—Hutchinson calls attention to J. P. Stern's, "The Theme of Consciousness: Thomas Mann," in *Modernism, 1890-1930,* ed. Malcolm Bradbury and James McFarlane (Harmondsworth: Penguin, 1976).

38. Hutchinson, *The Harlem Renaissance,* 14.

39. "The literary renaissance was in part an attempt to augment the value of black culture within the national cultural field . . . it remains a primary concern among all parties to the debate over multiculturalism in the United States today." Ibid., 12-13.

40. Ibid., 447.

41. As Eliot writes, "The progress of an artist is a continual self-sacrifice, a continual extinction of personality." "Tradition and the Individual Talent," in *The Sacred Wood* (London: The Thanet Press, 1928), 53.

42. Van Wyck Brooks, "Highbrow and Lowbrow," in *America's Coming of Age* (New York: Doubleday, 1958), 18.

43. Alain Locke, *The New Negro* (New York: Atheneum, 1968), 3-4.

44. Hutchinson writes, "The Harlem Renaissance was in fact a striking experiment in cultural pluralism, with pervasive connections to philosophical pragmatism and Boasian anthroplogy." Hutchinson, *The Harlem Renaissance,* 90.

45. "For James, individualism, voluntarism, and pluralism were inseparable principles. He believed that each person through an exertion of will added something to the world not knowable before hand to any external or superhuman consciousness and not predictable from the properties of atoms. However small this addition, it sufficed to maintain the dignity of human effort. James also held that when more or less unpredictable individuals accidentally formed stable groups, the average behavior of all members of the group was predictable even though the behavior of each member was not. In arguing for individual freedom, he thus stressed groups to account for scientific laws that were neither implicit in atoms nor in some kind of superhuman consciousness."

Larry C. Miller, "William James and Twentieth Century Ethnic Thought," *American Quarterly* 31, no. 4 (Fall, 1979): 536-37.

46. John J. Mc Dermott, "The Promethean Self and Community in the Philosophy of William James," in *Streams of Experience: Reflections on the History and Philosophy of American Culture* (Amherst: University of Massachusetts Press, 1986), 58.

47. Diggins, for example, writes, "To Dewey James's position seemed to rely on an emotional inwardness that had little reference to either public awareness or the uses of cool, reflective intelligence. . . . What troubled Dewey was James's subjective individualism, which seemed almost oblivious to any social context." *The Promise of Pragmatism: Modernism and the Crisis of Knowledge and Authority* (Chicago: University of Chicago Press, 1994), 140.

48. Franz Boas, "The Aims of Anthropological Research," in *Race, Language, and Culture* (New York: The Free Press, 1966), 260.

49. Franz Boas, ed. *General Anthropology* (Boston: D. C. Heath, 1938), 680-81.

50. Richard Handler, "Ruth Benedict and the Modernist Sensibility," in *Modernist Anthropology: From Field Work to Text,* ed. Marc Manganaro (Princeton: Princeton University Press, 1990), 163.

51. Hutchinson notes that "Locke would later speak of the Negro's coming of age." He also notes that S. P. Fullinwider referred to Locke as "the Van Wyck Brooks of the black Americans," "and briefly compared the Harlem Renaissance with the 'Little Renaissance' of New York in which Brooks figured so prominently." Hutchinson, *The Harlem Renaissance,* 99.

52. Ibid., 100. In his important book, Hutchinson gives attention to John Dewey, Josiah Royce, and William James; Franz Boas; Randolph Bourne, Van Wyck Brooks, Waldo Frank, and Lewis Mumford. A second or middle section gives extended attention to the politics of the many new journals and publishing

OVERVIEWS AND GENERAL STUDIES

houses that flourished in these years—*The New Republic, The Liberator, The Seven Arts, American Mercury, Modern Quarterly, The Crisis, Opportunity,* to name but a few. A third and final section gives an interpretive reading as well as detailed genesis of *The New Negro,* that unprecedented anthology of readings put together by Alain Locke, which appeared in 1925.

53. Ibid., 99.

54. As Blake writes of Randolph Bourne, "The collapse of competitive individualism in an age of large-scale bureaucracies and corporations had led Bourne to develop his own theory of a personality that gained independence and self-knowledge in exchanges with friends. Yet Bourne also seemed to suggest that the independence necessary to the life of irony was finally impossible because there existed no irreducible core of personality free of the pressures of group life." Casey Nelson Blake, *Beloved Community: The Cultural Criticism of Randolph Bourne, Van Wyck Brooks, Waldo Frank, and Lewis Mumford* (Chapel Hill: University of North Carolina Press, 1990), 71.

55. Ibid., 118.

56. Ibid., 264-65.

57. Charles Taylor, *Sources of the Self: The Making of the Modern Identity* (Cambridge: Harvard University Press, 1989), 376.

58. "What we can describe as a new moral culture radiates outward and downward from the upper middle classes of England, America, and (for some facets) France. In making the transition to new societies and strata, it is frequently transformed; so that what we end up with is a family of resembling moral cultures, or certain civilization-wide traits with important variations among nations and social classes. . . . But through all the variations, some common themes are visible. It is a culture that is individualist in the three senses I invoked earlier: it prizes autonomy; it gives an important place to self-exploration, in particular of feeling; and its visions of the good life generally involve personal commitment." Ibid., 305

59. As Taylor writes in "The Politics of Recognition, "This [the principle of originality] is the background understanding to the modern ideal of authenticity, and to the goals of self-fulfillment and self-realization in which the ideal is usually couched. I should note here that Herder applied his conception of originality at two levels, not only to the individual person among other persons, but also to the culture bearing people among other peoples. Just like individuals, a *Volk* should be true to itself, that is, its own culture." Taylor, *Multiculturalism,* ed. Amy Gutman (Princeton, NJ: Princeton University Press, 1994), 31. Also see Ingeborg Solbrig, "Herder and the 'Harlem Renaissance' of Black Culture in America: The Case of the 'Neger-Idyllen,'" in *Herder Today,* ed. Kurt Mueller-Vollmer (Berlin-New York: Walter de Gruyter, 1990), 402-14. Also, Paul Gilroy, *The Black Atlantic: Modernity and Double Consciousness* (Cambridge: Harvard University Press, 1993).

60. Kwame Anthony Appiah, *Multiculturalism,* ed. Amy Gutman (Princeton, NJ: Princeton University Press, 1994), 149-50.

61. Kwame Anthony Appiah, *In My Father's House: Africa in the Philosophy of Culture* (New York: Oxford University Press, 1992), 83.

62. Hazel Carby, "The Politics of Fiction, Anthropology and the Folk: Zora Neale Hurston," in *New Essays On Their Eyes Were Watching God,* ed. Michael Awkward (New York: Cambridge University Press, 1990), 80-81.

63. Hazel Carby, "Quicksands of Representation: Rethinking Black Cultural Politics," in *Reconstructing Womanhood: The Emergence of the Afro-American Novelist* (New York: Oxford University Press, 1987), 163.

# BACKGROUND AND SOURCES OF THE HARLEM RENAISSANCE

## MICHELLE A. STEPHENS (ESSAY DATE 1998)

**SOURCE:** Stephens, Michelle A. "Black Transnationalism and the Politics of National Identity: West Indian Intellectuals in Harlem in the Age of War and Revolution." *American Quarterly* 50, no. 3 (Sept. 1998): 592-608.

*In the following essay, Stephens analyzes the role of Caribbean American intellectuals—Cyril Briggs, Marcus Garvey, and Claude McKay—in the Harlem Renaissance.*

It is at the heart of national consciousness
that international consciousness lives
and grows. And this two-fold emerging
is ultimately only the source of all culture.
                    —Frantz Fanon, "On National Culture"

In 1996, the American Studies Association Conference, entitled "Global Migration, American Cultures, and the State," called for papers addressing the "historical and contemporary significance of transnational and intranational migrations for American society [and its] forms of expressive, material, and popular culture."[1] While migration itself had always been an important theme in the study of American culture, the use of the term *transnational* signaled a new orientation in American studies scholarship. Transnational approaches to migration examined the heterogeneous racial, cultural, and national characteristics of migrants to the United States, and the degree to which they disrupted the integrity of the state as a homogeneous, nationally-imagined community.

As a discourse on *transnationalism* has developed over the past decade, the term has acquired a number of different meanings depending on context and discipline. As one group of social scientists have described, in the humanities:

The term "transnational" is used to signal the fluidity with which ideas, objects, capital, and people now move across borders and boundaries. Scholars of transnational culture speak in the vocabulary of postmodernism and make reference to hybridity, hyperspace, displacement, disjuncture, decentering, and diaspora.[2]

Researchers in the social sciences focus less on the cultural fluidity encouraged by transnationalism, and more on an analysis of the process by which immigrants become "transmigrants," social actors with allegiances, loyalties and networks that go beyond their citizenship in one nation-state. Linda Basch, Nina Glick Schiller, and Cristina Szanton Blanc explore social relations, "how linkages are maintained, renewed, and reconstituted in the context of families, of institutions, of political organizations, of political structures, and of economic investments, business, and finance."[3]

Already, then, transnational studies has developed both a culturalist and structuralist focus. Rather than seeing this as a dichotomy, transnational studies has become a useful site for the interaction of researchers from both the humanities and social sciences. It is precisely the work done by scholars in humanities fields such as cultural and literary studies that has led to a questioning of the bounded meanings of traditional social science categories such as "race," "ethnicity," and "nationality." However, it was also more social scientific approaches such as world-systems theory that first paved the way for an analysis of the economic and political structures of global capitalism that produced "transmigrants" in the first place.[4] At its best, transnational studies offers a new lens or framework for identifying processes, identities, structures, and cultures that criss-cross with those of the nation-building project.

This essay reflects on the emergence of "transnationalism" as an idea in American cultural and intellectual history, by looking at a particular group of transmigrants in America: black intellectuals from the English-speaking Caribbean. The Caribbean American ethnic community has produced some of the most influential figures in American race and cultural politics throughout the twentieth century, figures ranging from Marcus Garvey and Claude McKay through Harry Belafonte, C. L. R. James, Stokeley Carmichael, and Bob Marley, to contemporary writers such as Paule Marshall and Jamaica Kincaid. Yet, despite the continual immigration of Caribbean people to the United States throughout the twentieth century, it is only recently that they have come close to establishing their own group identity as West Indian Americans, a specific American ethnicity in its own right.[5] One reason for this is their own sometimes willed, sometimes imposed, conflation with African Americans due to the shared racial identity of both groups and the "black-and-white" history of race relations in the United States. In addition, Caribbean Americans have

always been seen as maintaining an ambivalent relationship to their American citizenship, and as having a keen loyalty to their islands of origin. Therefore, as Basch, Schiller, and Blanc argue, the Caribbean experience in the United States was seen as a "special case."

However, it is precisely their "specialness" that makes West Indian Americans such an interesting case study in analyzing the impact and meaning of contemporary and historical transnationalism in North American culture. As the Caribbean experience becomes more and more "a growing global pattern that challenge[s] our conceptualizations of migration and 'the immigrant,'" so too does historicizing that experience teach us something new about the very construction and use of hegemonic categories of race, nation and ethnicity throughout the twentieth century.[6]

The one analytic piece that sometimes seems unexplored in this new focus on the transnational is the answer to the historical question, why? Why, historically, do and did transnational structures, processes, ideologies, and subjects emerge in certain places at certain times in the modern twentieth century? Or, to turn the question around, why the need for bounded categories such as "race," "ethnicity" and "nationality" for describing collective social identities? One of my suggestions here is that transnationalism itself is fundamentally a twentieth century phenomenon, finding its origins in very specific historical conditions during the opening decades of this century.

### Trans-National America

Transnationalism is not a new concept in American intellectual thought. As early as 1918, Randolph Bourne wrote an essay entitled "Trans-national America" in which he argued that World War I had revealed the failure of the "melting pot" theory of American national culture.[7] Just as the war awakened a powerful set of national antagonisms in Europe, so did it activate a strong sense of ethnic nationalism and particularism within the United States. Bourne observed that disparate European immigrant groups had simply not melted into a dominant American national culture of Puritan, Anglo-Saxon origin. Rather, the war exposed vigorous nationalistic and cultural movements among various ethnic groups such as Germans, Scandinavians, and Poles. These ethnic nationalisms stubbornly persisted in the United States and were sources of identity which resisted the process of Americanization.

Bourne's focus on the ethnic nationalisms of white immigrants to the United States reflected not only heightened European wartime patriotism, but also a new, transnational focus on the concept of nationalism itself. In the years Bourne was writing, nationalism and the model of the nation-state were quickly becoming *the* international political norms of the twentieth century. As the imperial order declined, European state power sought new political forms and reconstituted itself through new political ideologies. The European imperialist powers offered—through the Treaty of Versailles and the League of Nations in 1919—the principle of democratic, national self-determination as a new model for political organization. The Bolsheviks, on the other hand, called for a proletarian internationalist movement, embodied in the revolutionary Russian state after 1917. The emergence of the nation-state and the drama of social revolution raised one common question: if empire was no longer tenable, what was the best way for a state to represent its people, both imaginatively and politically? Was it through Lenin's internationalist and revolutionary conception of political identity, as not bound by national borders but based on one's class consciousness? Or was it through U.S. President Woodrow Wilson's liberal democratic nation-state, founded on a principle of self-determination that fixed political identity in a specific geographical territory, and constructed peoplehood around shared cultural and linguistic bonds? This historic conflict, over the political organization of the peoples of the modern world, was the most important geopolitical question of this era.

Randolph Bourne was writing at precisely this moment of the emerging of nationalism and internationalism at the beginning of the modern twentieth century. His use of the term "transnational" as a framework for understanding and identifying the impact of European immigration on American society reflected his recognition that these new ethnic nationalisms were part of a larger transnational phenomenon. In his words, America was simply the "intellectual battleground" of a global struggle over the nature and power of the modern, integrated European state.[8]

Bourne's account provides a useful historical starting point for any study of transnationality and America for two reasons. First, he identifies and historically situates a European immigrant transnationalism, their resistance of exclusively "American" identities, in the moment of the Western shift from empire to nationhood. White European ethnics become, in his account, early twentieth century "transmigrants." Second, given the fissure in American nationalism represented by the failure of the "melting pot" theory of American culture, Bourne attempts to imagine and recast the imperial American state in a new image of the nation that "borrows" from the internationalist rhetoric of the Russian revolution. For Bourne the failure of the melting pot, far from being the end of the great American national democratic experiment, meant that it had only just begun. Since the intellectual contradictions of European nationalism were playing themselves out on the ethnic body-politic of America, American nationalism would become by necessity something very different from the nationalisms of twentieth century Europe. In a world which had dreamed of both nationalism and internationalism, Americans would find that they had all unawares been building up the first international nation.[9]

Transnationalism for Bourne then was the attempt to imagine a new America that could somehow incorporate a culture of international identities into a national domestic political framework. However, if, as Bourne described, European ethnics were constructing newly imagined homelands with the rise of European nationalism in the post-World War I era, black Caribbean colonial immigrants were in a somewhat different situation in that they had no easily identifiable national homelands. Caribbean immigrants came to America from diverse colonies whose only bond was, at best, their shared history of colonialism and European exploitation. In his autobiography, *North of Jamaica,* Jamaican poet Louis Simpson described the difficulties of constructing a Caribbean national or ethnic identity in the United States, when one's colonial education "assumed that we would be living in England and no attempt was made to translate what we learned into Jamaican."[10] The result was the development of a "colonial mentality":

> As Jamaicans did not govern themselves they felt inferior in other respects. "Among the legacies of a colonial culture is the habit of thinking of creative sources as somehow remote from itself." This was true of Jamaicans.
>
> They were only a remote branch of England. They were not self-sufficient, and had created no important works. The history of Jamaica was the history of the Europeans who had ruled it.[11]

For Simpson, political questions of self-governance and cultural questions of self-construction had a mutual and reciprocal effect on each other. The lack of political self-determination in the Caribbean and the inculcation of a "colonial mentality" prevented cultural self-determination and self-representation—a sense of "Jamaicanness" or "Caribbeanness." The colonial transmigrant's experience did not match that of Polish, Slovak, or Czech immigrants, who could conceive of themselves as sharing a particular linguistic and cultural heritage which had grown and developed over time, within a single geographical territory. Instead, Caribbeans' experience was one of two acts of displacement, the middle passage from Africa and the journey from the colony to America. Hence early twentieth century Caribbean intellectual immigrants in the United States had uncertain ethnic identities, unimaginable really in national terms.

The challenge of Caribbean ethnicity then was precisely how to represent it. What exactly did it mean to be a transmigrant if "citizenship" was not available to you either in America or in your country of origin? Intellectuals and organizers such as Marcus Garvey and Cyril Briggs, and writers such as Claude McKay, searched for models of black self-determination—"black nationalisms"—in which they could locate and ground ethnic identity. Were black colonial subjects, as transmigrants in the West, now to be included in the new European nationalisms emerging with the decline of empire? If not, could they turn to Africa as an originary homeland? Or should they locate home and nationalism in American citizenship? These questions lay at the heart of Caribbean intellectuals' obsession with transnational frameworks of identity during this period, as they attempted to construct oppositional forms of black nationalism that could reflect the unique condition of the modern black subject.

## Black Transnationals

Precisely because Caribbean immigrants in North America throughout the twentieth century have been living their lives across borders, from early on they found themselves in the basic dilemma of the "transmigrant," "confronted with and engaged in the nation building processes of two or more nation-states."[12] However, due to their very specific racial and colonial history, early twentieth century Caribbean immigrants to America were forced to engage with and imagine alternatives to nationalism as they realized their *exclusion* from the nation building processes of both the United States and their imperial European motherlands. Caribbean American intel-

lectuals and cultural producers therefore became key figures in a series of what I call "black transnational" cultural formations in the United States throughout the twentieth century, formations in which intellectuals struggled to produce, like Bourne, *international* political and cultural conceptions of black collective identity. Three figures in particular, Cyril Briggs, Marcus Garvey, and Claude McKay, were among the first to articulate a transnational vision of blackness in the years between World War I and the Great Depression. I will examine briefly each of their individual solutions to the problem of representing black transnationality, and then close by pointing to some of the theoretical insights gained by a transnational approach to questions of race, ethnicity, and the politics of national identity in America.

As a group, Cyril Briggs, Marcus Garvey, and Claude McKay formed the core of a specifically transnational formation of black intellectuals during the New Negro movement in Harlem of the 1910s through the 1920s. World War I had profound implications for the development of a radical black ethnic consciousness amongst Caribbean American intellectuals. As black intellectuals became increasingly aware that the principle of national self-determination did not apply to them, the underlying imperialism of the League of Nations became more and more apparent. Lenin's internationalist theories of revolution also traveled quickly to the United States. Black radicals in Harlem who had taken up the banner of self-determination used internationalism and revolution to modify and transform black nationalist ideologies.

This was precisely the trajectory of Cyril Briggs, the editor of the Negro journal *The Crusader*. In the pages of his journal Briggs developed over time a framework for black identity, which would effectively wage a critique of American imperialism in the struggle for effective representation of black subjects in the new twentieth century world order. As early as 1917, in an editorial written for the *Amsterdam News* entitled, "'Security of Life' For Poles and Serbs—Why Not Colored Americans?," Briggs made the connection between the larger international context and the status of black Americans.[13] He consistently interrogated Woodrow Wilson's own public statements on self-determination, setting up an effective counter narrative to Wilson's promises which ultimately revealed them for what they were—masks of U.S. imperialism. His challenge to Wilson was particularly significant at the end of the war as the black world looked to the League of Nations for the fair settlement of the question of Africa's right to self-determination and free nationhood.

By January of 1919 all eyes were turned to the Peace Conference in Versailles as a first instance of how blacks would fare in the new nationalist world-order. As Briggs reminded his readers, Wilson had promised the world that as a result of the Peace Conference and the formation of the proposed League of Nations, "New nations are to be formed. Old nations are to be recreated. Tyranny is to die. Subject races are to be freed."[14] But the upshot of the League of Nations peace conference ultimately made clear the contradictions within the Wilsonian principle of national self-determination. The League refused to include anyone but free states as its members. If free statehood was the criteria for membership in this coalition, precisely those peoples who most needed self-determination and international protection from imperialism, black colonial subjects, were excluded. As Briggs ironically concluded, "the League for Some Nations . . . will not tend to inspire the rest of the Little Self-Determiners with any further confidence in the presumably good intentions of the Big Leaguers."[15]

Briggs's disillusionment with the League of Nations and the Wilsonian promise of the nation-state led to his interest in Bolshevik internationalism. The rejuvenation of Briggs's political hopes for black freedom through internationalism inspired his founding of the secret revolutionary army the African Blood Brotherhood (ABB), created as the black arm of the international revolution. By January of 1921, Briggs was attempting to imagine what a "radical revision of the concept of black self-determination, combining the preexisting ideal of racial sovereignty with a revolutionary vision of a communist society" could look like.[16] He found it in his vision of the Federation, a plan that would serve as the ideological "rudder for the Negro Ship of State."[17] As he described it, "there must emerge a federation of all existent Negro organizations, molding all Negro factions into one mighty and irresistible factor, governed and directed by a central body made up of representatives from all major Negro organizations."[18] This federation imagined joining all black organizations to form both a mass social movement and an international form of Negro government.

Briggs's Federation Plan was conceived in a historic meeting of the members of the African Blood Brotherhood in 1921. At this meeting, which included Claude McKay, recently returned to America from England and editor of the white radical journal *The Liberator,* the members of the ABB strategized on how to take their program aboveground to the mass community. The culmination of this meeting was the ABB's decision to use the power and reach of contemporary Marcus Garvey's mass organization, the Universal Negro Improvement Association (UNIA), to mobilize for a real political vision of black representation through federation. Their hope was that, with their instigation, the federation would emerge out of Garvey's annual international conference.

Briggs's concept of Federation was both a new political idea of black representation and a new conception of a federated blackness, an international racial framework that countered the new political identity of the nation state. The Federation Plan is one that later generations of Caribbean American intellectuals would return to when they sought both political and metaphoric ways of imagining black sovereignty.[19] It was not one, however, that Briggs's contemporary Marcus Garvey found appealing. Interpreting the ABB's plan as an attempt to co-opt his organization with this idea of Federation, Garvey expelled the ABB's delegates from the 1921 UNIA convention. However, Briggs's grounding of ethnicity in the international was not that dissimilar, structurally, from Garvey's notions of the black Empire and his actual transnational practise. For while both Briggs and Garvey represented somewhat different creative responses to the situation produced from imperial war and social revolution, Garvey was as fundamentally shaped by the general international realities and imperialist national projects emerging from World War I as Briggs.

Garvey began his career actually more interested in the question of diaspora than in self-determination. As he would describe in his biographical writings, one of his first impressions upon leaving Jamaica in his travels around the world was the great need for steamship communication "among the different branches of the Negro race scattered in Africa, the Americas, and the West Indies":

> Having traveled extensively throughout the world and seriously studying the economical, commercial and industrial needs of our people, I found out that the quickest and easiest way to reach them was by steamship communication. So immediately after I succeeded in forming the Universal Negro Improvement Association in America, I launched the idea of floating ships under the direction of Negroes.[20]

It was this observation that led to his starting the Black Star Line of steamships in 1919. Garvey's steamship ventures were not solely nation-building features of his "Back to Africa" campaign; rather, the Black Star Line was meant to function as an organized transnational network for the creation of a black diaspora based on transnational movement and communication. It was precisely this possibility for international mobilization which led to the UNIA's sponsorship of the yearly International Conference for the Negro.

Garvey's first convention in 1920 represented his attempt to harness the political energy of black transnationalism, fostered by his own sponsorship of diasporic travel and communication, for his vision of black Empire. In essays with titles like "Nothing Must Kill the Empire Urge," Garvey asserted the dominance of Empire as a model for black self-determined identity.[21] The Black Empire embodied a black freedom that originated not in self-determination nor in social revolution, but in imperial political and cultural conquest. For Garvey the black diaspora was itself the product of African imperialism rather than European colonialism. He reconstructed an African homeland which transcended the nation by spreading the blood and culture of the race throughout ancient Europe in imperial conquest.

In the context of the larger European struggle, Garvey's imperial version of self-determined black nationalism was as much an oppositional one as Briggs's, just paradoxically both revolutionary and imperial. His convention was explicitly understood to be the black counter to the League of Nations. The symbolic black nations that had been excluded from the 1919 international peace conference were now sending their delegates to Garvey's UNIA International Convention for the Negro. They arrived wearing their own national costumes and representing an eclectic assortment of nationally-imagined communities, including individual contingents from American cities such as Detroit and Philadelphia. Their power, as spectacularized in their parade of thousands at the end of the convention, lay in their collective representation of black subjects' ability to imagine their own forms of self-determination.

Like Briggs, Garvey recognized that the question of the age, the need for new models of state-construction and political self-governance, required dramatic and spectacular imagination. In the very act of imagining Black Empire, Garvey was taking a dramatic and oppositional leap away from the "colonial mentality" which he had learned as a child. Behind the more fascistic elements of Garvey's imperial model of diaspora also lay a political hope: "not only the inspiration of

the Empire: but its solidarity," as he described it. His philosophy had a powerful international appeal for the delegates to his conference who could find in this counter-vision of black Empire political protection from the divide and conquer strategy embedded in the European nation model. Garvey's imperial fiction was a protective strategy which relied on the combined strength of *all* the members of the racial diaspora. The real historical strength and power of his movement was the transnational network he constructed beyond the reach of the Western national order being constructed during the First World War and exemplified in the League of Nations.

Claude McKay's relationship to both Briggs and Garvey is also best represented by that historic meeting in 1921. Of all three figures he had the greatest understanding of what the coming together of the ABB and the UNIA would have meant for a radical vision and a movement of black self-determination. Later he would credit Garvey's energetic and quick-witted mind, but criticize the latter's inability to understand the significance of modern revolutionary developments for reconceptualizing the relationship between black nationalism and internationalism.[22] McKay began his literary career with a serious and sustained engagement with internationalism and its role in the identity of the modern black subject. He traveled to Moscow about a year after that historic meeting of the ABB, where he attended the Second Congress of the Third Communist International. There he proposed a Communist definition of self-determined blackness which would affix black nationalist sentiment to actual geographic territory in America by identifying the southern black belt of the United States as an oppressed nation.[23] With this proposal, which was to finally pass at the Sixth Congress of the Comintern in 1928, McKay revealed his own desire to find some way to represent the international revolutionary potential of the black masses in a fixed national form.

Unlike Briggs and Garvey, McKay became disillusioned with both nationalism and internationalism. While the war revealed the futility and dangers of nationalism, the impossibility of a proletarian revolution by blacks in America eroded McKay's confidence in internationalism as a political movement. His imagination stifled by the political realities around him, McKay turned to fiction as a way of doing what Bourne had also attempted; imagining the transnational nation. This is precisely what McKay constructed in his novel *Banjo: The Story without a Plot*. This less well known sequel to *Home to Harlem* used the same main character of the West Indian intellectual, Ray, as a guide to take us through a world of denationalized black colonial migrants in the French seaport of Marseilles. This community of aliens used their marginalization in Europe and their very exclusion from the League of Nations as the basis for a transnationally imagined black community. The thrust of the novel is perhaps best captured in McKay's closing image of the seaman from West Africa, Taloufa. This colonial migrant, officially barred from European territory by the categorization "Nationality Doubtful," loses the protection of the imperial nation but gains the freedom to cross borders and the ability to form alliances and friendships with other colonial drifters on grounds other than those of the nation.[24]

### Transnationalism, Race, and Ethnicity

McKay's construction of a transnational community of blacks of "doubtful nationality" is an interesting figure for a racialized, denationalized, Caribbean American ethnicity. Stuart Hall has identified the "new ethnicities" of the late twentieth century as embodying a "slow and contradictory movement from 'nationalism' to 'ethnicity' as a source of identity."[25] This is "part of a new politics," a politics of the diaspora which constructs racial, ethnic and national identity in new, internationalized, sometimes transnational, ways.[26] My understanding of black transnational migrant identity as a "new ethnicity" as early as the 1910s benefits from Hall's insights and sees Caribbean intellectuals' politics of identity in ways which are similar to Fanon's sense of national culture: as the result of a "two-fold emerging" of the international and the national.

However, as Taloufa's actual history as a black colonial points to, "black transnationalism" does not consist solely of fluid border-crossing identities. Rather, it also provides a sharp sense of the *political exclusions* created by western imperialism. The exclusion of black subjects from the originating political conceptions of modernity—nationhood, self-determination, democracy—forced Caribbean intellectuals in the United States in two interdependent directions. On the one hand, this exclusion afforded them a keen critical insight into the nature of modern imperialism. Their "transnationalism" involved their ability to link questions of ethnicity and national identity to American international relations and empire formation. The debates around the meaning of the national at the beginning of this century also

represented attempts on the part of some European empires to delimit the power and reach of others. Cyril Briggs directly implicated the United States in this European tug-of-war: in one mock dialogue between the German "Kaiser" and President Wilson, Briggs demonstrated how Wilson's advocacy of self-determination contradicted, and to some extent hid, American acts of imperialism in the Caribbean such as the invasion of Haiti in 1914.

Secondly, however, "black transnationalism" meant the creative development of new internationalist alternatives to the nationalism of the imperial states. Such alternatives as the idea of the Federation were profoundly influenced by the socialist theories of the Russian revolution. Bourne's essay serves as a necessary starting point in historicizing the appearance of the "transnational" as a concept in American culture, because it situates questions of national and ethnic identity during this period in the political context of World War I and the search for an alternative to empire. The power of a state in relation to other states, and the state's effectivity as a political representative of a "people," were precisely the issues at stake in imperial nationalism on the one hand, and revolutionary internationalism on the other. As the Cold War epitomized, this is also the question that has driven the main political and ideological disputes of this century.[27] Historically throughout the twentieth century, "Third World" denationalized migrants have constructed nationalisms which move between these two political ideologies and identities and borrow from both. Caribbean immigration to and incorporation into American society has taken place under these distinct historical conditions of world war and revolution.

Caribbean intellectuals' immigration to and incorporation into American society during the first three decades of the twentieth century cannot be understood as separate from these distinct political and historical conditions, precisely because they thought about black identity in the terms created by those conditions. For Briggs, Garvey, and McKay, questions of ethnic and racial identity were intricately tied up in questions of political representation, the nature of statehood and citizenship in the modern world order. In an international imperial world that did not recognize black colonial subjects such as McKay's Taloufa as "peoples," for many black intellectuals "ethnic nationalism and internationalism were not mutually exclusive" categories.[28] If national status for locally situated black subjects was the goal, and the European global imperialists were the obstacle, the black struggle for self-determination would have to occur as a transnational one. And if the Bolsheviks could ground revolutionary identity not in the nation but in international proletarian solidarity, black subjects could strengthen their individual nationalist struggles through *international racial* formations, transnational, race-based networks, grounded in political identities as various as Briggs's communist Federation, Garvey's diasporic Empire, and McKay's transnational community. Far from resorting to a disengaged cosmopolitanism or state of exile, these alternatives represented the hope for an engaged, black internationalism that could generate new conceptions of "citizenship," new conceptions of the meaning of a "national community."

Caribbean American intellectuals are also significant in the study of United States culture precisely because they constitute a second transnational America, one which was in the process of formation precisely at the moment that Randolph Bourne was writing. No one knew this better than another contemporary black transnational of this era, W. E. B. DuBois, who created his own Pan-African networks and congresses in the early decades of the century. His famous statement—"The problem of the twentieth century is the problem of the color line"—has often been used domestically by both black and white American intellectuals to describe the fundamental racial tensions at the heart of American national identity. But in an essay written in 1924 for the American quarterly review, *Foreign Affairs,* Du Bois returned to his classic formulation precisely in order to question "how far . . . this prophecy or speculation" could be applied.[29]

In the aftermath of World War I DuBois suggested that, "Most men would agree that our present problem of problems was not the Color problem, but what we call Labor, the problem of allocation of work and income." He then outlined what has since become the core of world-systems theory, the intertwining of race and class when viewed from an internationalist perspective of core-periphery relations. DuBois charged his contemporaries with their inability to see these larger connections:

> Our good will is too often confined to that labor which we see and feel and exercise around us, rather than directed to the periphery of the vast circle, where unseen and inarticulate, the determining factors are at work.

To remedy this, and prove that the "race problem is the other side of the labor problem," DuBois took his own journey through the battlefields of Europe, charting the course of imperialism and also its "dark colonial shadow." Ending back in America, DuBois evoked his own shadow of Bourne's trans-national America:

> a new group of groups is setting its face. Pan-Africanism as a living movement, a tangible accomplishment, is a little and negligible thing. But there are twenty-three millions of Negroes in British West Africa, eighteen millions in French Africa, eleven millions and more in the United States. . . . The main seat of their leadership is today the United States.

When DuBois concluded once again, "And thus again in 1924 as in 1899 I seem to see the problem of the twentieth century as the Problem of the Color Line," he was now speaking to the world.

As we see the return of the notion of the transnational as an analytic category in our own contemporary moment, it is important to examine the *ways* in which this very particular conception of ethnicity and identity emerges when it does. One could argue that the moment of transnationalism is less the transcendence of the national than the very moment of its construction: the real distinction lies in whether the "nation" under construction is understood and represented in domestic or international terms. The melting-pot, the eighties vision of a multicultural America, even Bourne's more nuanced international nation, all become simply metaphors for the domestication of difference when they lack a historical sense that the politics of difference, or race relations, in the United States has always been an international phenomenon. This is precisely the knowledge Caribbean Americans and other black transnationals have brought to bear on the politics of American national identity throughout the twentieth century.

## Notes

1. *American Studies Association Newsletter* 18 (Dec. 1995).

2. Linda Basch, Nina Glick Schiller, and Cristina Szanton Blanc, *Nations Unbound: Transnational Projects, Postcolonial Predicaments and Deterritorialized Nation-States* (Amsterdam, 1994), 27.

3. Ibid., 29.

4. This branch of theory is of course best represented in Immanuel Wallerstein's work, for example, *The Modern World System* (New York, 1974).

5. See Philip Kasinitz, *Caribbean New York: Black Immigrants and the Politics of Race* (Ithaca, N.Y., 1992).

6. Basch et. al., *Nation Unbound.*

7. Randolph Bourne, "Trans-national America," in *Randolph Bourne: The Radical Will: Selected Writings 1911-1918* (Berkeley, Calif., 1992), 248-65.

8. Ibid., 258.

9. Ibid.

10. Louis Simpson, *North of Jamaica,* (New York, 1972), 48.

11. Ibid.

12. Basch et. al., *Nation Unbound.*

13. Robert Hill, "Racial and Radical: Cyril V. Briggs, THE CRUSADER Magazine, and the African Blood Brotherhood, 1918-1922," intro. to *Volume 1: The Crusader: September 1918-August 1919,* (New York, 1987), xiii.

14. *Volume 1: The Crusader,* (Jan. 1919), 153.

15. *Volume 3-6: The Crusader,* (Feb. 1921), 1025.

16. Hill, intro., xxxix.

17. *Volume 3-6: The Crusader,* (Oct. 1921), 1249.

18. Hill, intro., p. xlii and lxiii. This description of the proposed federation was advertised in pamphlets announcing "Plan of Having All Negro Organizations in a Mighty Federation to Make Race a World Power. . . ." [*Negro Congress Bulletin and NewsService,* 1 (6 Aug. 1921)].

19. I am thinking of the West India Federation of the late 1930s and 1940s as one example, with Richard B. Moore, C. L. R. James, Phyllis Shand Allfrey, and Eric Williams as four of its major architects.

20. Robert Hill and Barbara Bair, eds., *Marcus Garvey: Life and Lessons* (Berkeley, Calif., 1987), 53.

21. Ibid., p. 5.

22. Claude McKay, "Garvey as a Negro Moses," in *The Passion of Claude McKay: Selected Poetry and Prose, 1912-1948,* ed. Wayne F. Cooper (New York, 1973).

23. See Pt. 4, "The Magic Pilgrimage," in Claude McKay's autobiography *A Long Way From Home* for a description of his trip to Russia, his motivations for going and his actions and impressions once there.

24. McKay describes Taloufa's dillemma in the last chapter of *Banjo* (New York, 1929), 310-12.

25. Stuart Hall has written on identity in a number of essays including: "Cultural Identity and Diaspora" in *Identity: Community, Culture, Difference,* ed. Jonathan Rutherford (London, 1990); "Minimal Selves" in *Identity Documents; The Real Me: Postmodernism and the Question of Identity* (London, 1988); "Ethnicity: Identity and Difference" in *Radical America* 23 (Oct.-Dec., 1989). The quotation here is taken from "Minimal Selves."

26. Throughout, I am making a distinction between internationalism and transnationalism. I see the one as a movement which aims to bring nations together, the other as a movement which seeks to go beyond the nation form itself.

27. Eric Hobsbawm, *The Age of Extremes: A History of the World, 1914-1991* (New York, 1994). Hobsbawm has described our contemporary moment as part of the "Short Twentieth Century, that is to say of the years from the outbreak of the First World War to the collapse of the U.S.S.R. which, as we can now see in retrospect, forms a coherent historical period that has now ended" (5). That period was fundamentally shaped by the competing nationalist ideologies of American capitalist democracy and the revolutionary internationalism of communist Russia. It is therefore logical that the term "transnational" is appearing once again as the Cold War dichotomies collapse and the nation-state's internal containment strategies disappear to reveal global capital moving beyond the nation with ever more efficacy.

28. Robin D. G. Kelley makes this point in his chapter on black American and Caribbean communists during the 1920s and 1930s, "'Afric's Sons With Banner Red': African American Communists and the Politics of Culture, 1919-1934," in *Race Rebels: Culture, Politics, and the Black Working Class* (New York, 1994), 105.

29. W. E. B. DuBois, "The Negro Mind Reaches Out" in the section "Worlds of Color" in *The New Negro: Voices of the Harlem Renaissance,* ed. Alain Locke (New York, 1992) 385-415.

# LEON COLEMAN (ESSAY DATE 1998)

**SOURCE:** Coleman, Leon. "Background of the Negro Renaissance." In *Carl Van Vechten and the Harlem Renaissance: A Critical Assessment,* pp. 9-28. New York: Garland, 1998.

*In the following excerpt, Coleman discusses the historical, social, and cultural conditions of early twentieth-century America that led to the Harlem Renaissance.*

## The Impact of World War I on African American Life

The soil which nourished the growth of African American literature and art during the decade of the 1920s was fertilized by the seminal influence of World War I upon the lives of black people in America. The first effect of this influence was observable in the establishment of a pattern of large migrations of blacks from the South to the urban areas of the North. Prior to the First World War, the pattern of black migration from the South had been to Kansas and the West in the 1860s and 1870s, with the greatest number migrating to Arkansas during this period.[1] There also had been a small but constant stream of families and individuals moving into the towns and cities of the North and South.

In 1915 Northern industrialists began to feel the effects of the diminishing labor supply caused by the advent of war in Europe, and they sought new sources of labor to replace that lost through the cessation of European immigration. With the entrance of America into the conflict, the demand for labor became imperative. Northern manufacturers' agents scoured the South recruiting Negroes to work in their plants, much to the chagrin of Southern whites who also were suffering from the labor shortage. James Weldon Johnson recalls in *Black Manhattan* that he had "witnessed the sending north from a Southern city in one day a crowd estimated at twenty-five hundred. They were shipped on a train run in three sections, packed in day coaches, with all their baggage and impedimenta."[2]

The strong appeal of higher wages helped to motivate the Negro migrants to forsake the farms, towns and cities that they knew for the relatively unknown lands of the North. Negroes employed in the North received as much as four and a half dollars a day in contrast to the seventy-five cents to a dollar a day wages paid to them in the South.[3] Although the cost of living was higher in the North, there was still an appreciable gain in real wages.

The majority of black workers in industrial plants were hired as unskilled laborers and, in spite of white union opposition to their employment, they even secured a foothold in the Northern iron, steel, and meat packing industries where they were first used as strike breakers. For many of those who left the South, the move northward brought occupational advancement to positions of skilled workmen in industry. Traditionally, Negroes in the North had held, almost exclusively, jobs as domestic servants, laborers, bootblacks, barbers, janitors, cooks, and a variety of similar low-prestige positions. The migration of Negroes to the North was followed by an increase in the proportions of those employed in industry as skilled workers from 2.2 percent of the Northern Negro population in 1910 to 3.1 percent in 1920.[4] While it is true that most of the increase of jobs for Negroes in the North occurred in the non-manufacturing occupations such as those which had been held traditionally, World War I offered a large number of blacks their first opportunity to rise above the level of menial and unskilled labor.

The economic gains to be found in Northern cities were considerable, and there were other less tangible but perhaps equally important advantages awaiting Negroes who migrated. Among these benefits were the greater opportunities for social and cultural advancement. Of primary importance were the educational opportunities available to black children from the South. According to E. Franklin Frazier, "One of the first effects of the migration to northern cities was that it gave Negro children access to a standard American education."[5] The quality of the education offered to the children in the rapidly growing Northern ghettoes may not have equalled that of

their white counterparts, but it was vastly superior to what they would have received in most parts of the South.

An additional cultural advantage was the relative freedom in the North from racial oppression; a condition which contributed to an increase in Negro self-respect. In the South, where the practical application of the dictum that "no Negro had any rights that a white man was bound to respect" was a part of daily living, intimidation and violence, against which he had no legal protection, eroded the African American's image of himself and subordinated him to a position of subservience. Arnold Rose and Caroline Rose state that the "North's chief contribution to the Negro was the regular security, the absence of violence and of the threat of violence that the Southern Negro had constantly to be aware of."[6] They further point out that the Northern whites tended to ignore the Negro outside of an economic relationship—leaving the Negro free to improve his cultural and economic status.[7] Freedom from Southern coercive influences also meant that blacks, for the first time in American history were able to articulate their grievances and to support protest organizations in numbers large enough to be politically significant.

With the exception of a brief decline at the end of World War I, the Northern migrations continued throughout the 1920s. In 1910, approximately nine-tenths of all Negroes in the United States lived in the South. Twenty years later, the number remaining in the South had diminished to 78.7 percent.[8] The urbanization of Negroes proceeded at an even more rapid rate, increasing from 27.4 percent of the total Negro population in 1910 to 43.7 percent in 1930. The Northern cities receiving the greatest numbers of the Negro migrants were New York, Detroit, Chicago, and Philadelphia. By 1920, New York City contained a black community of approximately 152,000 with more than half this number composed of migrants from other states. The ensuing decade would see the population of Harlem alone more than double from 82,248 in 1920 to 203,894 in 1930.[9] It could truly be said that Harlem, an area of less than two square miles, contained more African Americans per square mile than any other spot on earth.

This inundation of Northern cities by Southern blacks necessarily effected changes in the social and economic structures of the existent black communities of the North. Prior to World War I, the urban black community, which was relatively small, contained little differentiation upon which to base social divisions. "Tailors, barbers, waiters, and undertakers mingled with a few physicians, teachers, and businessmen in the Negro upper class of the day."[10] The large-scale urbanization of the Negro population upset this socio-economic relationship, first, by creating a sizable black proletariat which served as a base for increasing numbers of black professionals, and second, by providing the economic basis for a new middle class. Because of the concentration of Negroes in limited areas of Northern cities, the ratio of black professionals such as doctors, lawyers, teachers, ministers, and social workers rose to a higher percentage of the population in the North than in the South, although numerically, the South ranked higher in the number of black people in professional occupations.[11]

African Americans of professional status were among the rank and file of those who journeyed North, as well as many younger Negroes of the upper economic and educational levels. An examination of *Who's Who in Colored America* (1928-1929) reveals that of the Negroes listed, 76.7 percent were born in the South, while only 39.4 percent lived there—a migration of 37.3 percent.[12] There were also many instances of physicians and preachers who followed their patients and congregations northward.

In explaining the rise of the urban Negro middle class, Frazier cites the following conditions as being important: the occupational differentiation of Negroes in response to the new needs of the Negro communities; the access to political power in the North as an aid to the improvement of the Negro's economic and social position; and the increase in the proportion of Negroes engaged in clerical and other white collar positions.[13] Ghetto concentrations of large numbers of blacks also stimulated the growth of black business of the small enterpreneur class.

Economic differentiation was very important in determining class status. Members of the Negro lower class were usually employed as laborers, service workers, and domestics; the middle class was composed of wage earners in skilled and semi-skilled occupations who were often also employed in domestic and service occupations; and the professional class included doctors, lawyers, ministers, and school teachers. In contrast to earlier standards of social stratification in both North and South, which had been based upon such diverse criteria as lightness of skin color, amount of education, degree or respectability, property ownership, and family stability, "the new class distinc-

tions based upon occupation and income first appeared during World War I."[14] The emerging black upper and middle classes were a small minority of the black population, but they were the most articulate segment of it and it was they who provided most of the writers, artists, and concert musicians of the Negro Renaissance. Therefore, it was particularly galling to them when the young Negro Renaissance intellectuals and artists later rebelled against middle-class values.

The chief value of the African American middle class was respectability in moral conduct, as well as in correct public behavior. This genteel tradition had roots extending deep into the period of slavery when the small group of mulattoes, who were commonly house servants of the master and sometimes related to him, attempted to assimilate the manners and morals of their betters and considered themselves superior to the ordinary field hands.

After the Civil War, upward social mobility from lower to middle class was dependent mainly upon education, type of employment, and acceptance of middle-class values. Although World War I increased the opportunities for social advance, the bulk of the Negro population continued to remain in a socially inferior status because of lack of vocational skills, education, and participation in community institutions. The emphasis upon respectability by the middle class was partly a means by which they sought to differentiate themselves from an identification with the lower class, whom they thought to be shiftless and irresponsible.[15]

As the migrations from the South increased the size of Northern ghettoes, the upper and middle classes found themselves trapped within them as white realtors, property owners, and neighborhood associations tried to confine blacks to limited sections of the cities. Unable to separate themselves from the masses by moving from the ghetto, some sought a solution in the establishment of exclusive neighborhoods within the ghetto. In Harlem "a considerable number of doctors, lawyers, actors, musicians and others attempted to establish oases of respectability, but their numbers were not large enough to create an exclusive residential district and they could not escape the flood of common people who surrounded them."[16] A block of Stanford White-designed model houses, acquired en masse in 1920 by affluent African Americans at a price of about two million dollars, is a case in point. Inexorably, the new middle class saw itself identified, in the eyes of whites, with the mass population and measured by its standards. The most scathing criticism that the middle-class spokesmen were to level at the artists of the Harlem Renaissance was that they chose to ignore the portrayal of middle-class gentility and found their inspiration in the life of the black masses.

Besides affecting the social structure of African American life, the war and its aftermath created a new mood among black Americans. At the entrance of America into the War in 1917, the United States government was hardly prepared for the enthusiastic response of African Americans from all walks of life. In fact, the War Department issued an order to halt the recruitment of black volunteers. Negro leaders, especially W. E. B. DuBois, who had been an outspoken critic of the government's handling of Negro problems, called for full support of the war effort, and a Negro bank in Virginia "was awarded first place among the banks of the country in the Third Liberty Loan Drive, having oversubscribed its quota nineteen times."[17] Perhaps the stimulus evoking this patriotic response was the hope that, by whole-heartedly participating in a war for the preservation of democracy, Negroes would have a greater claim to equality of treatment in their own country.

On the battlefield, the colored troops, particularly the 369th and the 370th infantry regiments, acquitted themselves with valor and heroism. Despite incidents of racial disturbance during the war years, the prevailing mood of Negroes at the end of the war was one of optimism. Fenton Johnson, a Chicago poet, writing at the war's end, expresses this new aspiration and hope in a poem titled, "The New Day," which is in part as follows:

> Forget not, O my brothers, how we fought
> In No Man's Land that peace might come again!
> Forget not, O my brothers, how we gave
> Red Blood to save the freedom of the world!
>
> . . . . .
>
> For we have been with thee in No Man's Land
> Through lake of fire and down to Hell itself;
> and now we ask of thee our liberty,
> Our freedom in the land of Stars and Stripes.[18]

The atmosphere of hopeful expectancy which greeted the return of the black soldiers in 1919 was not reciprocated by many white people either in the North or the South. The majority saw in the return of the black troops a "new Negro," coming home from France anxious for social and economic equality. In his study of the Ku Klux Klan, Kenneth T. Jackson maintains that it was the fear

that the Negro would not accept his former station that was partially responsible for the racial strife which occurred in 1919.[19]

Eight months after the Armistice, during the "Red Summer" of 1919, savage race riots erupted in Northern and Southern urban centers, and in the same year more than seventy-five Negroes were lynched, among them black soldiers still in uniform. The bitterness engendered by these occurrences fostered a new attitude of militancy among African Americans, who in some of the riots revealed a determination to defend themselves. Despairing of the hope expressed in Johnson's poem, Claude McKay wrote a sonnet titled, "If We Must Die." Ending with the lines,

> Like men we'll face the murderous, cowardly
>     pack,
> Pressed to the wall, dying, but fighting back!

this poem typifies the new militant spirit. McKay tells of the uneasiness of black railroad men following the end of the war. In travelling from city to city, they felt so threatened by the antagonistic attitude of white men toward them that they remained together, some of them armed, in their quarters between the arrival and departure of their trains. He speaks of the poem as "exploding" out of him during those days. The sonnet's applicability to the Negro temper of the times is indicated in his statement that, although his first book of poetry had been published in 1912, "this is the one poem by which the Negro people acclaimed me a poet."[20]

African American race consciousness, previously stimulated by the mass migrations, was further intensified by the shock of the reverses suffered after the war. The attempts to ameliorate racial conditions took diverse forms, from the Garvey Movement, characterized by Gunnar Myrdal as "the only real mass movement of Negroes," which was directed at the Negro lower class and which advocated a return to Africa, to the rallying of the middle class in support of the N. A. A. C. P., whose house organ, *Crisis,* soared from a circulation of 12,000 in 1912 to 104,000 in 1920.[21]

The social and economic forces released by the First World War were responsible for accelerating the transition of the African Americans from a bystander's role outside the current of American life into that of a more active participant in the mainstream of American culture. The beginning of this process marked a break with the past so dramatic that the old image of the Negro no longer sufficed and was to be replaced by the "New Negro" of the 1920s.

Northern cities were focal points for the expression of Negro protest, defiance, and anger. Negro publications expressed these reactions and sentiments throughout the country, and "Harlem became the center where they were formulated and voiced to the Negroes of America and the world."[22] In stressing the importance of the city environment upon the change in Negro attitudes, Myrdal states:

> The impact of urban living upon the Negro changed his outlook on life. Racial conflicts in the North tended not only to intensify the consciousness of being a Negro but it also gave new meaning to being a Negro. Identification with the Negro race meant being a member of a group with a cause if not a history.[23]

The New Negro, emerging from the crucile of war, awaited the mold that would cast his image in literature and art. The question to be answered in the Twenties was whether the older Negro traditions in the arts were adaptable to this task.

## Traditions in African American Literature, Art and Music before World War I

### POETRY

One of the most important forms of African American creative literary expression has been poetry. From the imitative odes and elegies of the eighteenth-century poets, Jupiter Hammon and Phyliss Wheatley, to the Harlem Renaissance verses of Langston Hughes and Countee Cullen, Negro writers received greater acclaim for their poetry than for their prose fiction. There have been many conjectures offered to explain this fact. Jerome Dowd, a Yale University sociologist writing in 1926, quoted Macaulay's opinion that the minds of backward people are filled with images of the outer world and are more prone to express themselves in poetic imagery, while the minds of highly civilized people are stored with abstract and classified knowledge.[24] Another possible explanation is that the creation of simple verse was less demanding upon early black writers of limited education than the more complex construction of short stories and novels.

Until the latter half of the Twenties, Negro poetry was more readily accepted than Negro fiction by both white and black readers. The fact that even this small audience existed offered a greater opportunity for the publication of poetry in magazines, newspapers, and in collections of verse. This may be one of the chief reasons for the dominance of poetry as a form of literary expression among black writers. Before the 1920s, black authors generally found it difficult to secure publishers for their work because of a lack of widespread interest in African American writing.[25] This was true even of Paul Laurence Dunbar (1872-1906), the first black poet to achieve outstanding literary success.

Born in Dayton, Ohio, Dunbar began to write verse while still in high school. After he graduated two collections of his poetry were privately printed—*Oak and Ivy* in 1893 and *Majors and Minors* in 1895. These poems were favorably reviewed by William Dean Howells in *Harper's Weekly* in 1897, and thus encouraged, Dunbar secured a publisher for his third volume, *Lyrics of Lowly Life,* and undertook writing as a career, becoming the first Negro author to earn a living exclusively by his pen.

Dunbar's merit as a poet consists in his sincere portrayal of rural Negro life through the artful use of dialect. His dialect poetry is touched with gentle humor and pathos, but as a writer of classic English verse, which was his real aspiration, he is most often only sentimental and conventional. His early death at the age of thirty-four cut short a promising career.

William Stanley Braithwaite, the African American editor of the *Anthology of Magazine Verse,* judged the period from the death of Paul Laurence Dunbar in 1906 to the publication of James Weldon Johnson's *Fifty Years and Other Poems* as a desert so far as the production of poetic literature by the American Negro was concerned. His judgment seems metaphorically correct for there was certainly a bareness of poetic innovation and an aridity of style displayed in the writings of black poets during this time. Dunbar's phenomenal success as a writer of Negro dialect poetry, as well as his lesser success in writing sentimental poetry in the genteel style, may well have influenced the poetry of his contemporaries. Or, perhaps, in an attempt to gain an audience, Negro poets may have been guided by the belief that "only by using dialect could they reach the bookbuying public, which was almost wholly a white public."[26]

Most of the African American poets writing between 1907 and 1917, with few exceptions, wrote both genteel and dialect poetry, as though they intended the first style as an assertion of their qualifications as men of letters, and the second style as a necessary condescension to popular taste. The common result was that neither rang true. Lacking the skill of Dunbar in delineating the humor and pathos of black folk life, their dialect poetry usually reveals their cultural distance from the Negro masses and their Romantic poetry often seems imitative and superficial.

The following examples of dialect and genteel poetry are illustrative of the poetic failings of the period. The first, is a stanza of dialect verse from the poem "Way in De Woods, An' Nobody Dah" written by James Corrothers, a native of Michigan, who attended Northwestern University and authored *Selected Poems* (1907) and *The Dream and the Song* (1914):

'Way down in my Southern home—
    'Way in de woods, an' nobody dah—
Dah's de place I longs to roam—
    'Way in de woods, an' nobody dah—
O ma lub wid eyes ob coal,
    Listen 'til ma story's tole;
Owl's a-hootin' in my soul—
    'Way in de woods, an nobody dah!²⁷

Walter E. Hawkins, a native of North Carolina, published *Chords and Discords* which contained the poem "Ask Me Why I Love You" from which the following stanza is taken:

Ask me why I love you, dear,
    And I will ask the rose
Why it loves the dews of Spring
    At the Winter's close;
Why the blossoms' nectared sweets
    Loved by questing bee,—
I will gladly answer you,
    If they answer me.²⁸

Poems protesting the Negro's plight were also written in genteel terms, much in the manner of Dunbar's poem "Sympathy" which expresses the anguish and frustration of being a black poet by stating, "I know what the caged bird feels, Alas!" The problems of being a mulatto were similarly romanticized by Fenton Johnson in "The Mulatto's Song," as illustrated by the following stanza:

Die, you vain but sweet desires!
    Die, you living burning fires!
I am like a Prince of France,—
    Like a prince whose noble sires
Have been robbed of heritage;
    I am phantom derelict,
Drifting on a flaming sea.²⁹

During the pre-war years of the twentieth century, Negro poetry was steeped in a tradition of nineteenth-century gentility, which was incapable of reflecting the rapid social and cultural changes that occurred in Negro life during the post-war years.

Although poetry dominated fiction among black writers, by the year 1920, thirty full length novels by twenty black authors had been published in America. Two of these, *Clotel,* or the *President's Daughter* (1853) by William Wells Brown and *The Garies and Their Friends* by Frank J. Webb, had appeared before the Civil War. It was not until 1886 that the third novel by a black writer was published, but it was followed by eight other novels within a period of four years. Predictably, the novels of the post-Reconstruction period are largely protests against the caste barriers erected by the disenfranchisement and segregation laws which subordinated the Negro in the South to an inferior economic and social status. These authors "wrote as participants in a desperate social struggle, defending themselves as best they could against peonage, lynching. . . .and segregation."³⁰ The result was that their novels are little more than vehicles of propaganda against racial injustice.

In their portrayal of the Negro masses, the post-Reconstruction novelists reveal the middle-class bias that characterized the writing of the Talented Tenth. The term, "Talented Tenth," was coined by W. E. B. DuBois as a descriptive label for that ten percent of the black population who were striving to rise by means of education, thrift, and industry to a secure position above the black masses. It was the fond hope of DuBois that this group would provide inspiration and leadership for those who, through laziness and self-indulgence or through lack of opportunity, remained below. The novelists of the Talented Tenth, believing that educated and refined African Americans had a greater claim to social and economic acceptance by whites on the basis of cultural similarity, depicted their own group as fictional models of irreproachable decorum who shared the "white folks" contempt of the black lower class. Robert Bone describes these authors as "trying to breach caste with class," and contending that "whiteness of appearance and behavior entitled them to special treatment."³¹ This attitude of racial ambivalence remained a part of the class-consciousness of the black middle class during the Twenties and was to continue to influence their concepts as to what was racially acceptable in African American literature.

Like the Negro poet, the Negro novelist of the pre-1920s was an inheritor of the nineteenth-century Romantic and genteel traditions in literature. Unlike the poet, whose subject matter was more nearly congruent with its style, the novelist attempted to express his feelings of protest in an incompatible literary form. Arriving late on the literary scene, the novelists of the Talented Tenth were not conversant with the social realism of Howells and Garland or with the naturalism of Dreiser and Norris, which had not yet achieved dominance over the older stylistic traditions. The limitations of style, therefore, weakened the force of Negro novelists' protests. "Gentility of style may be appropriate enough in a sheltered Victorian world of swooning ladies and gallant gentlemen, but for the purpose of describing a lynching it has its limitations."[32] The expression of social protest was the main reason that the early Negro novelists wrote at all; yet they did not succeed in resolving the enervating contradiction between their subject and their style. The dilemma was resolved by later Negro writers with the abandonment of Romanticism during the 1920s.

Of all the black novelists writing before the war, only Paul Laurence Dunbar and Charles Chesnutt (1858-1932) managed to attract the attention of the white literary world. Dunbar's four novels, *The Uncalled* (1899), *The Love of Landry* (1900), *The Fanatics* (1901) and *The Sport of the Gods* (1902) were designed to entertain and amuse his white readers upon whom he depended for his income and for his literary success. Dunbar generally avoided themes of racial protest, and he has even been accused of pandering to the prejudices of his white audience by caricaturing the minor Negro characters in his novels.[33] Writing with strong pro-agrarian sympathies, he warned Negroes against the dangers of lurking in the urban centers of the North. His last novel, *The Sport of the Gods,* tells the story of the demoralization of the rural blacks when they are confronted with the sinful temptations of New York. Such racial and provincial attitudes were plainly contrary to the developing trend of Negro thought. Accordingly, the novels of Paul Laurence Dunbar represent the end of an old era rather than the beginning of a new one.

Charles Chesnutt, born in Cleveland, Ohio, was a self-educated man. Formally educated only through grade school, he taught himself stenography and law, working for a time as court reporter before being admitted to the Ohio bar in 1887. In the same year, his first short story, "The Goophered Grapevine," was published in the *Atlantic Monthly*. Between 1899 and 1905, Chesnutt published three novels and two collections of short stories. The two volumes of short stories, *The Conjure Woman* (1899) and *The Wife of His Youth,* were published during the same year, and of the two, the former was the greater artistic success.

*The Conjure Woman* contained seven stories based upon Southern Negro folklore, with which Chesnutt had become acquainted while living in North Carolina. These stories portray sympathetically and realistically the dialect, manners, and superstitions of the rural Negro, and are notable for their avoidance of disparaging caricature.

Primarily, a short story writer, Chesnutt never succeeded in mastering the formal complexities of novel writing. He attempted the portrayal of color line problems afflicting mulattoes in *The House Behind the Cedars* (1900), but his characters seem more stereotypical than real. His other two novels, *The Marrow of Tradition* (1901) and *The Colonel's Dream* (1905) are largely polemics against racial oppression constructed in fictional form.

Chesnutt's short stories, rather than his novels, present a new view of the Negro folk in fiction. Conventional though these stories were, owing as they did, something to the tales of Joel Chandler Harris, they still "raised the standards of Negro fiction to a new and higher plane."[34] However, they failed to bridge the gap between pre-war and post-war fiction because they were concerned with depicting Southern rural life, and in the Twenties the prevailing literary winds were Northern.

The novelists of the Talented Tenth did not transmit a viable tradition of Negro letters to the writers of the post-war decade. Hindered from a realistic portrayal of African American life by their own narrow class-consciousness and hampered by an inappropriate literary style, they failed to influence Negro Renaissance writers.[35] Robert Bone affirms that the effect of the war upon Negro life was influential in changing the direction of Negro literature:

> By the beginning of World War I the creative force of the Talented Tenth had been spent. The Victorian tradition, within which the early Negro novel moved and had its being, was disintegrating under the shattering impact of war. . . . The next generation of Negro novelists found that their literary heritage from the early period was largely negative. It taught them only what pitfalls to avoid.[36]

ART

Perhaps the most significant commentary that could be made concerning the tradition of Negro paintings and sculpture before World War I is to be found in the amount of space allotted to the subject in the *American Negro Reference Book*. In comparison with fifty pages devoted to activities of blacks in American sports and twenty-eight pages devoted to a discussion of African American literary contributions, only eight pages were devoted to blacks in the fine arts, and two pages deemed sufficient to discuss African American painters and sculptors before the war. Alain Locke, editor of *The New Negro,* suggested that the earlier Negro artists had lived and prayed like Elijah in a hostile desert while fed by only an occasional raven.

Since colonial times, a few black artists always existed on the periphery of American art. Negro Limners were to be found painting portraits in the eighteenth century, and the first formally trained Negro artist in America, Scipio Moorehead, was painting before the Revolutionary War. He inspired Phyliss Wheatley to write a poem titled, "S. M., A Young African Painter on Seeing His Works."[37]

Before the Civil War, black artists earned money by painting in their spare time, but there were only two widely known black professional artists in the nineteenth century—Edward M. Bannister and Henry O. Tanner. Bannister, born in Nova Scotia in 1828, became a print maker and opened a studio in Boston. Primarily interested in landscapes, his paintings were done in the atelier style of art and were not concerned with themes drawn from African American life. His work was awarded a medal at the Philadelphia Centennial in 1876.[38]

Henry O. Tanner was the more celebrated of the two artists. He achieved an international reputation for a series of religious paintings, some of which were later acquired by art museums in America and abroad. Born in Pittsburg, Ohio in 1859, Tanner studied at the Pennsylvania Academy of Fine Arts and was a student of Thomas Eakins. After graduation, Tanner taught for several years at Clark University in Atlanta, Georgia. Through the generosity of a Bishop Hartzwell, he received funds for study in Paris and later travelled to Palestine, where he was inspired to paint the Biblical scenes that made him famous. He was awarded the Legion of Honor by the French Government, and he became the first Negro to be elected to the National Academy of Design in America.

Tanner's paintings are mostly of white subjects, but he did, on occasion, paint Negroes. One of his most charming genre paintings is called *The Banjo Lesson* (1890). It portrays a rural scene in which a little boy is being taught to play the banjo by his smiling, patient grandfather.[39]

The first important African American sculptor was a woman, Edmonia Lewis, who was also born in the North, at Albany, New York in 1845. She attended classes at Oberlin College in Ohio, and studied sculpture in Boston. She successfully secured commissions for portrait busts, and sales of her work enabled her to go to Rome for further study while still in her early twenties. Lewis executed portrait studies in marble of Charles Sumner, Robert Gould, and many famous abolitionists. She also sculpted figures of Negroes and Indians, although many of these statues show the influence of neo-classicism rather than realism. One such work titled *Forever Free* (1867) depicts a freed slave couple. The man is brandishing his shackles and the woman is kneeling at his side in an attitude of grateful prayer. The features of the faces are broadly generalized and impersonal, the drapery is arranged in togo-like folds, and the man's posture seems to be derived from classical Greek statuary.

What little there was of Negro art before World War I was not widely known among aspiring young black artists of the post-war period. Most histories of American art were silent about the work of African American artists. Only a few American art schools accepted black students in the early years of this century and, without funds to study abroad, they were unable to receive adequate training. It may be said that when the artists of the Negro Renaissance began to paint during the 1920s, they did so almost in the absence of any Negro art tradition from the past.

MUSIC

Before the First World War, most Americans would have credited African Americans with a single contribution to American music—the spirituals. Spirituals had been a part of the ante-bellum slave-music tradition, but when the Civil War ended, spirituals all but disappeared as blacks tried to forget songs that were associated with slavery.[40] A dramatic reawakening of interest in spirituals was accomplished through the extremely successful concert tours of the Fisk Jubilee Singers from 1871 to 1879.

Nine young men and women, students of Fisk School in Nashville, Tennessee, composed the original chorus. Seven of them were former slaves. The tour and the chorus were organized by the school's white treasurer and music teacher, George L. White, to raise money for the institution which was in desperate financial straits. After having a great deal of difficulty in overcoming the reluctance of the group to sing spirituals in public, White led the students to triumphant concert appearances throughout America and Europe, singing spirituals in the original plantation manner before the proverbial "crowned heads of Europe" and for President Grant in America. At the end of their tours they had earned $150,000 and had introduced America and Europe to the spirituals.[41]

As the students had been reluctant to sing the spirituals, so were the Negroes of the middle class reluctant to hear them sung in public. The middle class felt some ambivalence about the spirituals, which they regarded as somewhat primitive and of lower-class origin, but for which they also felt a certain race pride, as constituting a unique African American gift to American culture. Acceptance of the spirituals as an acknowledged part of the Negro cultural heritage would become a matter of controversy in the Twenties as black musicians returned to their folk materials as the basis of creative expression.

Two other musical streams of African American origin flowed from the latter years of the nineteenth century into the twentieth century, although one would not fully emerge from its Southern source until the 1920s. One was ragtime music and the other was jazz. Two Missouri cities, Sedalia and St. Louis, were the centers of ragtime music in the 1890s. Ragtime was a style of syncopation in which the normally weak beats are accented. Originally, ragtime music was a style of piano playing developed by black pianists in the South. The right hand played the syncopation and the left hand played an unsyncopated beat in march time. Negro composers Scott Joplin, James Scott, and Tom Turpin turned out scores of ragtime tunes, which were based more upon European music than upon Negro folk sources.

Introduced to the general public at the world's fairs held at Chicago, Omaha, Buffalo and St. Louis at the turn of the century and popularized by Tin Pan Alley tunesmiths thereafter, ragtime swept the nation and then spread to Europe. During World War I, this music was further popularized in France by the playing of Negro army bands. As quickly as it arose, the ragtime craze subsided and by the end of the war ragtime "as a separate and distinct popular music was finished."[42] Whatever elements of it that continued to survive were merged into the mainstream of jazz.[43]

Since jazz music spans the pre-war and post-war periods, it is necessary to mention it here. The origins of jazz and the influences of jazz are many and are often disputed. For the purpose of this discussion it is sufficient to say that most jazz historians agree that jazz is distinctly an American Negro musical idiom, having its roots in the "blues," Negro "work songs," "hot spirituals," as well as in other sources.[44] This music may have originated in New Orleans where it was widely played as "Dixieland" music at the turn of the century and in the early 1900s.[45] Jazz musicians were slowly making their music heard in the mid-West before the war, as they played on excursion boats that sailed from New Orleans to St. Paul, Minnesota, giving performances along the river shore.

The dispersion of jazz to Northern cities was accelerated by the war-time closing of the extensive New Orleans's Storyville red-light district, where most of the professional jazz musicians made their living, and by the migration of black people to the North. Southern musicians travelled to the Northern urban centers bringing their music to the new black audiences concentrated in the cities, who crowded the cabarets, dance halls, and theaters. Inevitably, Northern musicians, black and white, were influenced by the "hot" or "blue" intonation in the playing and singing of the Southerners. According to legend, Bix Beiderbecke, the famous white cornet player, was so excited when he first heard Bessie Smith sing the blues at a cabaret in Chicago, that he threw a whole week's pay on the floor to keep her singing.

Recordings and then radio broadcasting spread the sound of jazz to millions of Americans in the early Twenties. White musicians performed their versions of the music on the standard record labels of the day, and Negro musicians reached Negro audiences by means of "Race Records" which were often produced by the same companies. Immensely popular, jazz seemed suited to the volatile mood of post-war America, and, through F. Scott Fitzgerald, the music gave its name to the decade of the Twenties—The Jazz Age.

Traditional African American music at the beginning of the 1920s was unmistakably of folk origin and, although subject to artistic interpretation, had to be accepted or rejected for what it was—an expression of folk life. However, in 1920, Negro music was the one area in art which the black musician could claim as being uniquely his own, and in which, if given the opportunity, he could clearly out-distance his white competitors. In literature and painting the standards by which blacks were judged were based upon a cultural background that they had not fully shared and in which they were still serving an apprenticeship.

In Negro music the black artist was an exponent of his own cultural tradition and success was more easily attained. Aside from successful Negro participation in sport, "Negro music and musicians have provided a tradition of success, and until recent years, they have often been the only source of a healthy self-esteem and self-confidence for the total group."[46] Though correct in her evaluation of the role of Negro music, Zelma George is in error when she implies complete acceptance of Negro music by all levels of black society, for this was to be yet another area of contention during the period of the Negro Renaissance.

## Notes

1. Maurice Davie, *Negroes in American Society* (New York, 1949), 90-91 passim.

2. James Weldon Johnson, *Black Manhattan* (New York, 1930), 151.

3. Davie, *Negroes in American Society,* 94. For further discussion of factors contributing to the Great Migration, see Gunnar Myrdal, *An American Dilemma: The Negro Problem and Modern Democracy* (New York, 1944), 191-197.

4. Davie, *Ibid.,* 134.

5. E. Franklin Frazier, "The New Negro Middle Class," in *The Negro Thirty Years Afterward; Papers Contributed to the Sixteenth Annual Spring Conference of the Division of Social Sciences,* eds., Rayford W. Logan, et al. (Washington, D.C., 1955), 27.

6. Arnold Rose and Caroline Rose, *America Divided: Minority Group Relations in the United States* (New York, 1948), 186.

7. *Ibid.*

8. United States Bureau of the Census, Negro Population in the United States 1790-1915 and Negroes in the United States 1920-1932, quoted in Davie, *Negroes in American Society,* 91.

9. E. Franklin Frazier, *The Negro in the United States,* rev. ed., (New York, 1957), 262.

10. Milton Gordon, *Assimilation in American Life: the Role of Race, Religion, and National Origins* (New York, 1964), 167.

11. Davie, *Negroes in American Society,* 115.

12. *Ibid.,* 95.

13. Frazier, "New Negro Middle Class," 27.

14. Frazier, *Negro in the United States,* 283.

15. *Ibid.,* 301-304, *passim.*

16. Claude McKay, *Harlem: Negro Metropolis* (New York, 1940), 27.

17. Benjamin Quarles, *The Negro in the Making of America* (New York, 1964), 187.

18. Fenton Johnson, *Tales of Darkest America* (Chicago, 1920), 35.

19. Kenneth T. Jackson, *The Ku Klux Klan in the City 1915-1930* (New York, 1967), 22.

20. Claude McKay, *A Long Way from Home* (New York, 1937), 31.

21. Langston Hughes, *Fight for Freedom: The Story of the N.A.A.C.P.* (New York, 1962), 25.

22. Johnson, *Black Manhattan,* 257.

23. Myrdal, *An American Dilemma,* 531.

24. Jerome Dowd, *The Negro in American Life* (New York, 1926), 324.

25. Charles W. Chesnutt, "Post-Bellum—Pre-Harlem," *The Colophon* (February 1931), Part V (no pagination).

26. Quarles, *Negro in the Making of America,* 200.

27. Dowd, *Negro in American Life,* 316. Dowd quotes this poem and the two following examples, among others, as illustrations of excellence in Negro poetry.

28. *Ibid.,* 314.

29. *Ibid.,* 317.

30. Robert Bone, *The Negro Novel in America,* rev. ed. (New Haven, 1965), 17.

31. *Ibid.,* 20.

32. *Ibid.,* 27.

33. *Ibid.,* 41. Also Hugh M. Gloster, *Negro Voices in American Fiction* (Chapel Hill, 1948), 56.

34. *Ibid.,* 38. Also, Frazier, *Negro in the United States,* 505.

35. Gloster does not completely concur with this view. Although he feels that World War I was the most influential force in the cultural emancipation of the American Negro, he thinks that Dunbar was influential upon later Negro writers by helping to prepare an audience for their work and that Chesnutt pioneered by suggesting themes which appeared in Negro Renaissance fiction.

36. Bone, *Negro Novel in America,* 49-50.

37. Cedric Dover, *American Negro Art* (Greenwich, 1960), 22.

38. *Ibid.,* 23.

39. *Ibid.,* Plate 90.

40. Lillian Erlich, *What Jazz Is All About* (New York, 1962), 33.

41. *Ibid.*

42. *Ibid.,* 50.

43. Gunther Schuller, *Early Jazz: Its Roots and Musical Development* (New York, 1968), 67, 139-145.

44. Winthrop Sargeant, *Jazz: A History,* rev. ed. (New York, 1964), 45-54. For other discussions of the origins of jazz, see Andre Hodeir, *Jazz: Its Evolution and Essence* (New York, 1956); Marshall Stearns, *The Story of Jazz* (New York, 1956); Schuller, ibid.

45. Sargeant, *Jazz,* 71. There are several schools of thought about just what constitutes Dixieland. Some jazz historians feel that the term may be properly applied only to the style of certain white bands, notably the Original Dixieland Jazz Band and the New Orleans Rhythm Kings, who popularized a New Orleans type of ragtime. Others feel that the tag Dixieland may be

loosely applied to any jazz played in the New Orleans manner—which includes the work of pioneer jazzmen, Negro and white, and their musical heirs of the Dixieland revival.

46. Zelma George, "Negro Music and Musicians." *The American Negro Reference Book,* ed., John P. Davis (Englewood Cliffs, 1966), 731.

# THE NEW NEGRO AESTHETIC

## GILBERT OSOFSKY (ESSAY DATE 1965)

**SOURCE:** Osofsky, Gilbert. "Symbols of the Jazz Age: The New Negro and Harlem Discovered." *American Quarterly* 17, no. 2 (summer 1965): 229-38.

*In the following essay, Osofsky discusses how white people of the 1920s perceived and defined the New Negro.*

American society has anticipated the arrival of a "new Negro" for at least seventy-five years. In the white South of the 1890s, for example, it was common to contrast the former slaves with the first Negro generation born in freedom—to the detriment of the latter. "The good old Negroes," said a southern farmer at the turn of the century, "are a first-rate class of labor. The younger ones [are] discontented and want to be roaming."[1] At about the same time Booker T. Washington surveyed America's racial scene and, contrary to the view of white Southerners, found it good. He related tales of Negro achievement and success since the Civil War which encouraged him to believe that the "Negro of to-day is in every phase of life far advanced over the Negro of thirty years ago." Washington hoped all Negroes would strive to achieve "the new life" and, accordingly, called his book *A New Negro for a New Century.*[2] The racial crises that followed the two world wars of the present century revived the concept. William Pickens, Negro educator and NAACP official, discovered a "New Negro" militancy and racial consciousness in 1916, and others have used the phrase to describe the Negro protest movements of the 1950s and 1960s.[3]

Amid the confusions that have hovered around the meaning of the term "New Negro" is one solid fact: the phrase entered the main stream of American thought in the 1920s, in the Jazz Age. A "New Negro," and his supposed place of residence, Harlem, were discovered by the white world then. Despite the romance and pride traditionally associated with the "Harlem Renaissance," the portrayal of the Negro that developed in the 1920s was *primarily* a product of broader

changes in American society. It would be difficult to find a better example of the confusions, distortions, half-truths and quarter-truths that are the foundations of racial and ethnic stereotypes than the white world's image of the "New Negro" and Harlem in the 1920s.

* * *

The 1920s, as is well known, was a remarkable age in American intellectual history. A cultural rebellion of the first order erupted from beneath the complacency and conservatism that were dominant characteristics of American society and politics then. It was the time when writers, artists, scholars, aesthetes and bohemians became aware of the standardization of life that resulted from mass production and large-scale, efficient industrialization—the "Machine Civilization," that "profound national impulse [that] drives the hundred millions steadily toward uniformity."[4] These intellectuals declared war on tenets of American thought and faith that had remained sacrosanct for three hundred years. As a by-product of their attack on traditional American middle-class values, which were constantly called "Puritanical," literary rebels and others discovered the Negro, America's "outcast," and created a semimythical dreamland which they came to idealize—"storied Harlem."[5]

In some part, this growing national awareness was caused by significant changes within Negro society. There seemed to be a new militancy in the Negro world after World War I—reflected in Harlem's well-known Silent Parade to protest the East St. Louis race riots, in the racial program and consciousness of Marcus Garvey, in A. Philip Randolph's struggling movement to found the Brotherhood of Sleeping Car Porters and Maids, in the numerous little leftist groups active in the Negro ghettos, in the national campaign to promote federal anti-lynching legislation. Yet American society never really took these movements seriously in the 1920s—Garvey was considered a comical figure; an anti-lynching law was never enacted; riots continued; Randolph's union made little headway until the Great Depression; the leftists were ignored or considered crackpots.

The 1920s also saw the rise of a noteworthy group of Negro writers and scholars, and America gave *them* considerable recognition. Some of the novels, plays, poems, books and articles of Countee Cullen, James Weldon Johnson, George S. Schuyler, Claude McKay, Wallace Thurman, Zora Neale Hurston, Jessie Fauset, Rudolph Fisher, Jean Toomer, Charles S. Johnson, E. Franklin Frazier and others were good enough in their own right to justify public acclaim. The poetry of Langston Hughes continues to be widely read. Harlem was the center of this "New Negro Renaissance" and, like an "ebony flute," it lured Negro writers to it: "Harlem was like a great magnet for the Negro intellectual, pulling him from everywhere," wrote Langston Hughes.[6] Claude McKay came to Harlem from Jamaica, after two years at an agricultural college in Kansas; Jean Toomer was from an Alabama plantation; Langston Hughes arrived in 1921 after a sojourn in Mexico. "I can never put on paper the thrill of the underground ride to Harlem," Hughes recalled. "I went up the steps and out into the bright September sunlight. Harlem! I stood there, dropped my bags, took a deep breath and felt happy again."[7] Wherever they wandered in the 1920s, and many went to Paris or Africa for a time, the Negro literati always returned *Home to Harlem* (to use the title of a McKay novel). Little theater, art and political discussion groups flourished in the community. Negro literary and political magazines made their appearance: *Fire, The Messenger, Voice of the Negro, The Negro Champion, Harlem.* The 135th Street library became Harlem's cultural center. "The Schomburg Collection," remembered George S. Schuyler, "used to be a great gathering place for all the people of the Renaissance."[8] In the 1920s one could hear lectures there by such prominent people as Franz Boas, W. E. B. DuBois, Carl Van Doren, James Weldon Johnson, Carter G. Woodson, Kelly Miller, Melville J. Herskovits, R. R. Moton and Arthur A. Schomburg. Harlem became what contemporaries called the "Mecca of the New Negro."[9]

Some observers, Negro and white, looked to this outburst of literary and artistic expression as a significant step in the direction of a more general acceptance of Negroes by American society. Alain Locke, gifted writer and Howard University professor, argued that social equality would result from the recognition of the "New Negro" as an "artist class." ". . . it seems that the interest in the cultural expression of Negro life . . . heralds an almost revolutionary revaluation of the Negro," he wrote in 1927. It was "an augury of a new democracy in American culture."[10] Heywood Broun, well-known journalist and critic, addressed the New York Urban League at a Harlem church. He believed "a supremely great negro artist, [an artist] who could catch the imagination of the world, would do more than any other agency to remove the disabilities against which the negro race now labors. . . . This great artist may come at any time," Broun concluded, and he asked his audi-

ence to remain silent for ten seconds to imagine the coming of the savior-genius.[11] This same theme of a broad cultural acceptance evolving from the recognition of the "New Negro" as "a creator" dominates the writings of James Weldon Johnson in the 1920s. Johnson and others somehow believed that American racism was a process that could be reasoned with; a phenomenon that would crumble when whites recognized Negroes had extraordinary and unique artistic talents. "I am coming to believe," Johnson wrote his close friend Carl Van Vechten, "that nothing can go farther to destroy race prejudice than the recognition of the Negro as a creator and contributor to American civilization."[12] "Harlemites thought the millennium had come," remembered Langston Hughes. "They thought the race problem had at last been solved through Art. . . ."[13]

There was an element of realism in the romantic hopes of Johnson, Broun and Locke. For white Americans to grant that the Negro was capable of making *any* contribution to American culture was in itself a new idea—"that the Negro is a creator as well as creature . . . a giver as well as . . . receiver."[14] A new and more liberal vision of democracy developed among social scientists in the 1920s. Scholars like Robert E. Park, Herbert A. Miller, Franz Boas, Melville J. Herskovits, Charles S. Johnson, Bruno Lasker, E. Franklin Frazier and Horace M. Kallen attacked traditional American attitudes toward assimilation and "Americanization." A more vital and beautiful democracy would arise, they argued, by permitting ethnic groups to maintain their individuality, rather than conceiving them swallowed up (or melted down) in the one dominant American culture. Each group, given freedom of expression and development, would then make valuable contributions to American society. Diversity, cultural pluralism, should be fostered and encouraged, not stifled, they wrote.[15]

A spate of articles and books published in the 1920s seriously analyzed and attempted to understand the Negro's place in the nation. The dozens of volumes about Negroes written by pseudo-scientists and racists at the turn of the century were now replaced by works which attempted to cut through racial stereotypes ("generalized theories about racial qualities") and tried to find some viable program for "interracial cooperation." "The American Negro can no longer be dismissed as an unimportant element in the population of the United States," concluded one man. Bruno Lasker's *And Who Is My Neighbor?* and *All Colors* were among the earliest serious studies of Ameri-

# ON THE SUBJECT OF...

## THE CHANGING FACE OF HARLEM

I remembered one place especially where my own crowd used to hold forth; and, hoping to find some old-timers there still, I sought it out one midnight. The old, familiar plunkety-plunk welcomed me from below as I entered. I descended the same old narrow stairs, came into the same smoke-misty basement, and found myself a chair at one of the ancient white-porcelain, mirror-smooth tables. I drew a deep breath and looked about, seeking familiar faces. "What a lot of 'fays!" I thought, as I noticed the number of white guests. Presently I grew puzzled and began to stare, then I gaped—and gasped. I found myself wondering if this was the right place—if, indeed, this was Harlem at all. I suddenly became aware that, except for the waiters and members of the orchestra, I was the only Negro in the place.

**SOURCE:** Rudolph Fisher, excerpt from "The Caucasian Storms Harlem," in the *American Mercury*, August 1927.

can interracial attitudes.[16] *The Annals* of the American Academy of Political and Social Science printed a thick volume of studies on Negroes by the nation's leading social scientists.[17] *The World Tomorrow*, a fascinating Christian Pacifist journal, devoted two full issues to similar articles in the 1920s.[18] Most of the major periodicals of the decade contained large numbers of serious and important studies of Negro life. The artistic and human value of Negro spirituals, folk songs, folk legends and music was first recognized in the 1920s (many considered them America's most important contribution to world culture); Darius Milhaud, after listening to Negro music in Lenox Avenue cafes, composed pieces which made use of jazz rhythms and instruments; *In Abraham's Bosom,* one of Paul Green's many plays of southern Negro life, won the Pulitzer Prize in 1926; Eugene O'Neill and Robert E. Sherwood constructed plays and novels around Negro characters and themes.[19] As important as this new recognition was, how-

ever, it was a minor trend in American thought. The generation that advocated cultural pluralism was also the generation that saw the revival of the Ku Klux Klan, and permanently restricted foreign immigration to the United States.

Had intellectuals like Johnson and Locke looked more critically at the stereotype of the "New Negro" that developed in the writings of most white commentators of the 1920s, they would have had further cause to question the extent of interracial understanding that existed then. White literary rebels created a "vogue in things Negro," "an enthusiasm for negro life and art" that bordered on being a cult.[20] They saw Negroes not as people but as symbols of everything America was not. The concept of the existence of a "New Negro" and the publicity given to it in the 1920s was primarily the result of this new awareness and interest in Negro society by what one writer called the "New White Man."[21] The generation that discovered "newness" all around itself—New Humanism, New Thought, New Woman, New Psychology, New Masses, New Poetry, New Criticism, and so on—also found a "New Negro"; and the concept became a cultural weapon: "Another Bombshell Fired into the Heart of Bourgeois Culture." "Negro stock is going up," wrote novelist Rudolph Fisher, "and everybody's buying."[22]

In the literature of the 1920s Negroes were conceived as "expressive" ("a singing race") in a society burdened with "unnatural inhibitions"; their lives were "primitive" and "exotic" (these two words appear repeatedly) in a "dull," "weary" and "monotonous" age; they could laugh and love freely in a "land flowing with Socony and Bryan and pristine Rotary purity." Negroes were presented as people who lived an "entire lifetime of laughs and thrills, [of] excitement and fun"—they had an "innate gayety of soul." "Ecstasy," wrote Joseph Wood Krutch in *The Nation*, "seems . . . to be his natural state."[23] The stereotype of the Negro that had existed in American society in the nineteenth century was largely untouched by the new interest in Negro life. It was continued, for example, in such "all-talking melodramas" as "Lucky Sambo," "Hearts in Dixie" and "Hallelujah," and in the new radio hit "Amos and Andy." In the 1920s, however, the ludicrous image of Negro as "darkey" became a subordinate theme, eclipsed by the conception of the Negro as sensuous and rhythmic African. Negroes were still thought to be alienated from traditional American virtues and values, as they had been since colonial times, but this was now considered a great asset. "To Americans," wrote a perceptive contemporary in 1929, "the Negro is not a human being but a concept."[24]

\* \* \*

This was the background against which white America and the world came to know the "New Negro" and Harlem: "with our eyes focused on the Harlem scene we may dramatically glimpse the New Negro."[25] A large Negro community had gathered in Harlem prior to World War I but, aside from small numbers of dedicated social workers, American society seemed willing to overlook its existence. In the 1920s, however, Harlem was made a national symbol—a symbol of the Jazz Age. It was seen as the antithesis of Main Street, Zenith and Gopher Prairie. Whatever seemed thrilling, bizarre or sensuous about Harlem life was made a part of the community's image; whatever was tragic about it, ignored.

Harlem of the Twenties was presented as a "great playground," America's answer to Paris.[26] The institution that best describes this aspect of Harlem's image was the white slumming party: "it became quite a rage . . . to go to night clubs in Harlem," recalled Carl Van Vechten.[27] Cabarets were filled nightly with handsomely dressed white slummers who danced the Charleston, Turkey or Black Bottom, listened to jazz or watched risqué revues. Some night spots, like the Cotton Club (which had "the hottest show in town"), and Connie's Inn (which competed for the honor), catered exclusively to whites. They were, wrote a journalist, dives "where white people from downtown could be entertained by colored girls."[28] If one was looking "to go on a moral vacation," or wished to soften "the asperities of a Puritan conscience," Harlem's cabarets promised to do the job. The following is an advertisement, written especially for "white consumption," and distributed by a man who supplied "Slumming Hostesses" to "inquisitive Nordics" (each card was said to have a suggestive picture on it):[29]

> Here in the world's greatest city it would both amuse and also interest you to see the real inside of the New Negro Race of Harlem. You have heard it discussed, but there are very few who really know. . . . I am in a position to carry you through Harlem as you would go slumming through Chinatown. My guides are honest and have been instructed to give the best service. . . . Your season is not completed with thrills until you have visited Harlem.

"White people," editorialized a Negro journal, "are taking a morbid interest in the night life of [Harlem]."[30]

And the interest continued to grow throughout the decade. Carl Van Vechten's novel of Harlem life, *Nigger Heaven* (1925), sold 100,000 copies "almost immediately," and brought its author a substantial fortune. It was translated into French, Swedish, Russian and Japanese.[31] Van Vechten's book contained some interesting commentaries on the structure and problems of Negro society (the role of the middle class; "passing"; prejudice; color consciousness) but its plot was contrived, sensational and melodramatic; replete with orgies, drugs and seduction; a hodgepodge of *True Confessions* and the front pages of a tabloid. Its characters were unbelievable as people. "The squalor of Negro life, the vice of Negro life," wrote Van Vechten, "offer a wealth of novel, exotic, picturesque materials to the artist."[32] *Nigger Heaven* was "recognized in every quarter . . . as *the* portrayal of contemporary life in Harlem," said its publisher (and it undoubtedly was).[33] The white world looked curiously at the success of Marcus Garvey (whose movement basically reflected a profound Negro desire for racial pride and respect in a society that denied it), and concluded that Negroes "have parades almost every day."[34] White intellectuals and bohemians knew Harlem only through the cabarets, or the famous parties in the salon of the "joy-goddess of Harlem"—A'Lelia Walker's "Dark Tower": "dedicated to the aesthetes, young writers, sculptors, painters—a rendezvous where they may feel at home."[35] Bessie Smith, the great blues singer, toured America with her "Harlem Frolic" company. Josephine Baker ("Josephine of the Jazz Age") wowed them in Harlem as a young chorus girl, and went on to international acclaim in Europe. "From a world of stone with metal decoys / Drab stone streets and drab stone masses / New York's mold for the great middle-classes, Africa passes / With syncopated talking the Congo arouses."[36]

White audiences, like gluttons at a feast, vicariously tasted the "high yallers," "tantalizin tans" and "hot chocolates" that strutted around in the Blackbird Revues, or in such plays as *Lulu Belle* (1926) and *Harlem* (1928)—and made them top box-office successes. (*Black Boy* and *Deep River,* dramas which emphasized a more serious side of Negro life, were failures.)[37] "Ten years ago," wrote one Negro reviewer of *Lulu Belle,* "this play would have been unprofitable. Twenty years ago it would have caused a riot."[38] The following is a handbill

The Cotton Club.

distributed to advertise the play *Harlem* ("A Thrilling Play of the Black Belt"):[39]

> Harlem! . . . The City that Never Sleeps! . . . A Strange, Exotic Island in the Heart of New York! . . . Rent Parties! . . . Number Runners! . . . Chippies! . . . Jazz Love! . . . Primitive Passion!

"How soon this common theme shall reach the nauseating state," remarked a caustic critic, "is not easy to tell."[40]

The Great Depression brought an abrupt end to the dream of a "New Negro" and the image of Harlem as erotic utopia. A nation sobered by bread lines no longer searched for a paradise inhabited by people who danced and loved and laughed for an "entire lifetime." Connie's Inn and other places of white entertainment closed down. Leading figures of the Renaissance: Wallace Thurman, Richard B. Harrison, A'Lelia Walker, Charles S. Gilpin, Florence Mills, Arthur A. Schomburg, died in the late 1920s or 1930s. Most of the Negro literati, though not all, stopped writing or, if they continued to do so, found a less responsive American audience for their works.[41] All the Negro literary magazines folded.

And, as the exotic vision of the 1920s passed, a new image of the Negro and Harlem emerged—a Harlem already known to stolid census-takers, city health officers and social workers. "The rosy enthusiasms and hopes of 1925," wrote Alain Locke ten years later, "were . . . cruelly deceptive mirage[s]." The ghetto was revealed in the 1930s as "a nasty, sordid corner into which black folk are herded"—"*a Harlem that the social worker knew all along but had not been able to dramatize. . . . There is no cure or saving magic in poetry and art for . . . precarious marginal employment, high mortality rates, civic neglect,*" concluded Locke.[42] It was this Harlem, the neighborhood not visible "from the raucous interior of a smoke-filled, jazz-drunken cabaret," the Harlem hidden by the "bright surface . . . of . . . night clubs, cabaret tours and . . . arty magazines," that was devastated by the depression; and has remained a community with an inordinate share of sorrow and deprivation ever since. "The depression brought everybody down a peg or two," wrote Langston Hughes. "And the Negroes had but few pegs to fall." The myth-world of the 1920s had ended.[43]

## Notes

1. *Report of the Industrial Commission on Agriculture and Agricultural Labor* (Washington, D. C., 1901), X, 50, 504, 770.

2. Booker T. Washington, *A New Negro for a New Century* (Chicago, 1900?), pp. 3 and *passim*.

3. William Pickens, *The New Negro* (New York, 1916); *The New Negro,* ed. Mathew H. Ahmann (Notre Dame, Ind., 1961); *The New Negro: Thirty Years Afterward,* ed. Charles S. Johnson (Washington, D. C., 1955).

4. Carl Van Doren, "The Negro Renaissance," *Century Magazine,* CXI (March 1926), 637.

5. Gilbert Seldes, "The Negro's Songs," *Dial,* LXXX (March 1926), 247-51.

6. Langston Hughes, *The Big Sea* (New York, 1940), p. 240.

7. *Ibid.,* p. 81.

8. "The Reminiscences of George S. Schuyler" (Oral History Research Office, Columbia University, 1962), p. 208.

9. Claude McKay, *A Long Way From Home* (New York, 1937), *passim,* and *Home to Harlem* (New York, 1927); "Harlem: Mecca of the New Negro," *Survey,* LIII (March 1, 1925), 629-724; Alain Locke, *The New Negro: An Interpretation* (New York, 1925).

10. Alain Locke and Lothrop Stoddard, "Should the Negro Be Encouraged to Cultural Equality?" *Forum,* LXXVIII (October 1927), 508; Locke, "Enter the New Negro," *Survey,* LIII (March 1, 1925), 631-34; Locke, "Negro Contributions to America," *World Tomorrow,* XII (June 1929), 255-57.

11. *New York Times,* January 26, 1925.

12. James Weldon Johnson to Carl Van Vechten, envelope dated March 6, 1927. James Weldon Johnson Collection of Negro Arts and Letters, Yale University.

13. *The Big Sea,* p. 288.

14. Johnson to Van Vechten, envelope dated March 6, 1927. Johnson Collection.

15. See, for example, Robert W. Bagnall, "The Divine Right of Race," *World Tomorrow,* VI (May 1923), 149; Herbert A. Miller, "Democracy and Diversity," *World Tomorrow,* VII (June 1924), 190-91; Robert E. Park, *The Immigrant Press and Its Control* (New York, 1922); Horace M. Kallen, *Culture and Democracy in the United States: Studies in the Group Psychology of the American Peoples* (New York, 1924).

16. "The Reminiscences of Bruno Lasker" (Oral History Research Office, Columbia University, 1957), p. 242 and chap. ix.

17. *The Annals of the American Academy of Political and Social Sciences,* CXL (November 1928).

18. *World Tomorrow,* VI (May 1923) and IX (April 1926).

19. Laurence Buermeyer, "The Negro Spirituals and American Art," *Opportunity,* IV (May 1926), 158-59, 167; Harry Alan Potamkin, "African Sculpture," *Opportunity,* VI (May 1929), 139-40, 147; James Weldon Johnson to Carl Van Vechten, envelope dated February 16, 1931, Johnson Collection; A. M. Chirgwin, "The Vogue of the Negro Spiritual," *Edinburgh Review,* CCXLVII (January 1928), 57-74; Darius Milhaud, "The Jazz Band and Negro Music," *Living Age,* CCCXXIII (October 18, 1924), 169-73.

20. Langston Hughes, "The Negro Artist and the Racial Mountain," *Nation,* CXXII (June 23, 1926), 693; Charles S. Johnson, "The Balance Sheet: Debits and Credits in Negro-White Relations," *World Tomorrow,* XI (January 1928), 13-16; Ernest Boyd, "Readers and Writers," *Independent,* CXVI (January 16, 1926), 77; George Jean Nathan, "The Wail of the Negro," *American Mercury,* XVIII (September 1929), 114-16; Claude McKay to James Weldon Johnson, April 30, 1928, Johnson Collection.

21. "The New White Man," *World Tomorrow,* X (March 1927), 124-25.

22. Rudolph Fisher, "The Caucasian Storms Harlem," *American Mercury,* XI (May 1927), 396.

23. Eugene Gordon, "The Negro's Inhibitions," *American Mercury,* XIII (February 1928), 159-65; Clement Wood, "Hosea Before the Rotary Club," *World Tomorrow,* VIII (July 1925), 209-10; Herman Keyserling, "What the Negro Means to America," *Atlantic Monthly,* CXLIV (October 1929), 444-47; Joseph Wood Krutch, "Black Ecstasy," *Nation,* CXXV (October 26, 1927), 456-58; George S. Schuyler, "Blessed Are the Sons of Ham," *Nation,* CXXIV (March 23, 1927), 313-15; "Black Voices," *Nation,* CXIX (September 17, 1924), 278.

24. George Chester Morse, "The Fictitious Negro," *Outlook and Independent,* CLII (August 21, 1929), 648.

25. *A Long Way From Home,* p. 322.

26. Beverly Smith, "Harlem—Negro City," *New York Herald Tribune,* February 10, 1930.

27. "The Reminiscences of Carl Van Vechten" (Oral History Research Office, Columbia University, 1960), p. 196.

28. *Crisis,* XXXIX (September 1932), 293; *New York Age,* August 6, 1927. For a survey of Harlem cabarets see Archie Seale, "The Rise of Harlem As An Amusement Center," *Age,* November 2, 1935; and obituary of Moe Gale, owner of the Savoy Ballroom, *New York Times,* September 3, 1964.

29. "The Slumming Hostess," *New York Age,* November 6, 1926.

30. "Giving Harlem A Bad Name," "Is Harlem to be a Chinatown?" "In the Negro Cabarets," "Nordic Invasion of Harlem," *New York Age,* September 5, 1922; October 27, 1923; July 23, August 6, 1927; Committee of Fourteen, *Annual Report for 1928* (New York, 1929), pp. 31-34.

31. "The Reminiscences of Carl Van Vechten," p. 205.

32. Carl Van Vechten, *Nigger Heaven* (New York, 1925), *passim.*

33. "The Negro in Art—A Symposium," *Crisis,* XXXI (March 1926), 219-20; *Crisis,* XXXIV (September 1927), 248.

34. Chester T. Crowell, "The World's Largest Negro City," *Saturday Evening Post,* CXCVIII (August 8, 1925), 9. "The Caucasian Storms Harlem," *American Mercury,* XI (May 1927), 398.

35. "I am to be hostess at the Dark Tower Sunday Night April 21st, and I thought probably you and your friends would like to be present. . . ." A'Lelia Walker to Max Ewing, April 18, 1929. Ewing Collection, Yale University. A'Lelia Walker was the daughter and heir of the wealthy Madame C. J. Walker. Eric D. Walrond, "The Black City," *Messenger,* VI (January 1924), 14. *New York Age,* October 29, 1927.

36. Paul Oliver, *Bessie Smith* (New York, 1959), p. 45. Ermine Kahn, "Lenox Avenue—Saturday Night," *World Tomorrow,* VIII (November 1925), 337.

37. *New York Age,* November 27, 1926.

38. Hubert H. Harrison, "The Significance of Lulu Belle," *Opportunity,* IV (July 1926), 228-29; *Crisis,* XXXII (May 1926), 34; "Black Harlem Dramatized," *Literary Digest,* C (March 16, 1929), 21-24; James Weldon Johnson to Carl Van Vechten, envelope dated April 4, 1930, Johnson Collection.

39. Quoted in Diana N. Lockard, "The Negro on the Stage in the Nineteen Twenties" (Master's thesis, Columbia University, 1960), p. 38.

40. *Outlook and Independent,* CLII (August 21, 1929), 649; Charles S. Johnson, "Public Opinion and the Negro," *Proceedings of National Conference in Social Work, 1923* (Chicago, 1924), 497-502.

41. The most glaring exception to this generalization is Langston Hughes.

42. "Harlem had been too long the nighttime playground of New York. . . ." Alain Locke, "La Guardia and Harlem," manuscript in La Guardia Papers. Locke, "Harlem: Dark Weather-Vane," *Survey Graphic,* XXV (August 1936), 457-62, 493-95. Quotations in the above text are from the manuscript of this article in the La Guardia Papers. Italics mine.

43. Wallace Thurman, "Harlem Facets," *World Tomorrow,* X (November 1927), 466. E. Franklin Frazier, "Negro Harlem: An Ecological Study," *American Journal of Sociology,* XLIII (July 1937), 86. *The Big Sea,* p. 247; George W. Harris, "Harlem Gets a New Jail," *Nation,* CXXXIII (September 9, 1931), 258; "Negro Children in New York," *Nation,* CXXXIV (May 25, 1932), 588.

# HOUSTON A. BAKER, JR. (ESSAY DATE 1987)

**SOURCE:** Baker, Houston A., Jr. "8" and "9" in *Modernism and the Harlem Renaissance,* pp. 71-89. Chicago: University of Chicago Press, 1987.

*In the following excerpt, Baker discusses the role of Alain Locke's* The New Negro *in defining the collective culture of African American life in the Harlem Renaissance.*

A nation's emergence is always predicated on the construction of a field of meaningful sounds. Just as infants babble through a welter of phones to achieve the phonemics of a native language, so conglomerates of human beings seeking national identity engage myriad sounds in order to achieve a vocabulary of *national* possibilities. The codes, statutes, declarations, articles, amendments, and constitution of colonial America constitute, for example, what Sacvan Bercovitch calls a "logoc-

racy." In Bercovitch's reading, the American nation as such is but an edifice and enterprise of distinctive and distinguishing words.

Similarly, efforts of turn-of-the-century black spokespersons provide tactics, strategies, and sounds that mark a field of possibilities for an emergent Afro-American *national* enterprise. This enterprise (which has been an immanent object of African desire since the Jamestown landing of "twenty negres" in 1619) can be fittingly characterized as the establishment of a mode of *sounding* reality that is identifiably and self-consciously black and empowering. Attempting to answer the question, What, then, is the Negro, this new man?—an inquiry that takes effect only through willed faith in black national possibilities and a corresponding willingness to sound such possibilities—turn-of-the-century spokespersons demonstrated amazing capacities. For they had not only to filter the absurd noises of minstrelsy but also, and at the same instant, to recall sounds of African origin in an age characterized by divided aims, betrayed hopes, and open brutalities. What was required was a shrewd combination of formal mastery and deformative creativity.

If we turn to the Harlem Renaissance of the twenties, it is difficult in the presence of a seminal discursive act like Alain Locke's *New Negro* to conceive of that modern, Afro-American, expressive moment as other than an intensely successful act of national self-definition working itself out in a field of possibilities constructed by turn-of-the-century spokespersons. The title of the book, in its first amazing edition, was *The New Negro: An Interpretation.* This title calls to mind the response that Sterling Brown made to Robert Penn Warren's poetic line, "Nigger, your breed ain't metaphysical." Brown's response: "Cracker, your breed ain't exegetical." Exegesis, hermeneutics, the offices of *interpretation* and fitting analysis vis-à-vis Afro-America, according to Locke's title, are now the project of the black spokesperson him- or herself.

Further, *The New Negro's* dedication to "the younger generation" signals a realization of *change* qualified by *traditional* expressive possibilities. The prose of the dedication is immediately followed by the notation and score of an Afro-American spiritual: "O, rise, shine for Thy Light is a' coming." It is possible to assert, I think, that Locke's editorial work constitutes his song of a new generation, his attempt to provide a singing book of (and for) a new era in Afro-American expressive history.

Surely the space between *The Souls of Black Folk* and *The New Negro*—given the bar from "O, rise, shine for Thy Light is a' coming"—can be thought of as bridged by spiritual sound. It is Locke himself who writes most eloquently of the spirituals in his collection:

Thematically rich, in idiom of rhythm and harmony richer still, in potentialities of new musical forms and new technical traditions so deep as to be accessible only to genius, they have the respect of the connoisseur even while still under the sentimental and condescending patronage of the amateur.[1]

His most important gesture in regard to the spirituals, however, was his inclusion at virtually the midpoint of his anthology of two songs in their full notation and text. Thus at the center of *The New Negro* one hears the classical sound of Afro-America. And this sounding gesture of national significance is not isolated in the context of the collection as a whole. For Locke's entire project is rife with graphic gestures that produce an *interpretation* of the Afro-American unlike any that had preceded *The New Negro* in Afro-American discursive history.

We witness, for example, the illustrations of Winold Reiss and Aaron Douglas that exploit African motifs (masks in particular) to serve as "ancestral" and culturally specific leitmotivs. The work of Reiss and Douglas serves in fact as a kind of graphic, African presence qualifying and surrounding all prose, poetry, and drama in the volume. In addition, we see Reiss's magnificent color portraits of figures such as Locke, Paul Robeson, Jean Toomer, Countee Cullen, Claude McKay, as well as his genre studies in color and black and white of figures such as the "Brown Madonna," "Negro Teachers," and the "Negro Librarian." We also behold in Locke's essay on the "ancestral arts" photographs of African masks and statues from Bushongo, Sudan-Niger, the Ivory Coast, Dahomey, and Congo. There are, as well, reproductions of title pages from rare and venerable books by Africans in the New World and transcriptions (including musical notations) of the actual *telling* of Afro-American lore recorded by Arthur Huff Fauset.

If DuBois's *Souls* is a diorama of the folk conceived in terms of a "problem," Locke's *New Negro* is surely something more extensive. It is, I believe, a broadening and enlargement of the field of traditional Afro-American discursive possibilities. The work has, in effect, the character of a panorama's "unlimited" view, summoning concerns not of a problematical "folk" but rather those of a

newly emergent "race" or "nation"—a *national culture.* Locke's effort is no less performative than DuBois's, and it manages to provide a visual, auditory, and, indeed, almost tactile field that offers new national modes of sounding, interpreting, and speaking "the Negro."

This nationalistic mode sounds in the foreword:

The New Negro must be seen in the perspective of a New World, and especially of a New America. Europe seething in a dozen centers with emergent nationalities, Palestine full of a renascent Judaism—these are no more alive with the progressive forces of our era than the quickened centers of the lives of black folk. America seeking a new spiritual expansion and artistic maturity, trying to found an American literature, a national art, and a national music implies a Negro-American culture seeking the same satisfactions and objectives.

[pp. xv-xvi]

The world envisioned by *The New Negro,* then, is not one of southern country districts, nor "darkened ghetto[s] of a segregated race life" (p. xvi). Nor does it remotely resemble the universe of minstrel nonsense.

Indeed, the world projected by Locke's collection is a nation comprised of self-consciously aspiring individuals who view their efforts as coextensive with global strivings for self-determination and national cultural expression. One of the strongest statements of this projection occurs in the work's introduction:

Hitherto, it must be admitted that American Negroes have been a race more in name than in fact, or to be exact, more in sentiment than in experience. The chief bond between them has been that of a common condition rather than a common consciousness; a problem in common rather than a life in common. In Harlem, Negro life is seizing upon its first chances for group expression and self-determination. It is—or promises at least to be—a race capital. That is why our comparison is taken with those nascent centers of folk-expression and self-determination which are playing a creative part in the world today. Without pretense to their political significance, Harlem has the same role to play for the New Negro as Dublin has had for the New Ireland or Prague for the New Czechoslovakia.

[p. 7]

Not a "problem" but a NATION—this is indeed what might be considered the extraordinary departure. In an American era populated by Tom Buchanans in the upper echelon, Theodore Bilbo and Woodrow Wilson in local and national politics, Lothrop Stoddard and William Graham Sumner in scholarship, Octavus Roy Cohen in popular media, and Snopeses everywhere, Locke's discursive act was veritably one of *extreme deforma-*

tion—of what I want to call here (and explain fully in a moment) *radical marronage*. We need but listen to the historian C. Vann Woodward describing the postwar years in order to gain a reasoned perspective on the enormous magnitude of *The New Negro's* flight from the common racialist ground of its era. Woodward writes:

> In the postwar era there were new indications that the Southern Way was spreading as the American Way in race relations. The great migration of Negroes into the residential slum areas and the industrial plants of the big Northern cities increased tension between races. Northern labor was jealous of its status and resentful of the competition of Negroes, who were excluded from unions. Negroes were pushed out of the more desirable jobs in industries that they had succeeded in invading during the manpower shortage of the war years. They were squeezed out of federal employment more and more. Negro postmen began to disappear from the old routes, as Negro policemen did from their old beats. They began to lose their grip upon crafts such as that of the barbers, which had once been a virtual monopoly in the South.[2]

The historian J. Saunders Redding also offers a bleak picture of the black situation during the first three decades of the twentieth century in *They Came in Chains,* noting that some two million blacks fled the South's disfranchisement, lynchings, crop failures, and general miseries in a mere five years during the second decade.[3] It is difficult to conceive of the horribleness of the American scene for black people during the era in which Locke produced his classic collection. But it seems fair to say that patent nonsense and murderous exclusion (lynching statistics rose significantly in an atmosphere of racist, postwar hysteria) were the two most common responses in a United States that adopted Jim Crow, either de facto or de jure, as the law of the land.

I want to suggest that what Locke's declaration of a *nation* amounted to was a gesture commensurate with what Richard Price describes in the introduction to *Maroon Societies* as "marronage on the grand scale."[4] Price defines such marronage as "the banding together [of individual fugitives] to create independent communities of their own, [communities] that struck directly at the foundations of the plantation system, presenting military and economic threats that often taxed the colonists to their very limits" (p. 3). Maroon societies as standard features of the American landscape are noted by Herbert Aptheker in "Maroons Within the Present Limits of the United States":

> An ever-present feature of antebellum southern life was the existence of camps of runaway Negro slaves, often called maroons, when they all but established themselves independently on the frontier. These were seriously annoying, for they were sources of insubordination. They offered havens for fugitives, served as bases for marauding expeditions against nearby plantations and, at times, supplied the nucleus of leadership for planned uprisings.
>
> [Quoted in Price, p. 151]

The most astute image of the maroon comes from Price's introduction where the figure is characterized as a person not only possessed of the skills and knowledge of a "master culture" but also motivated by a firm understanding of African modes of existence (p. 20). Price's image captures my own sense of the overall effect and ambience of Locke's *New Negro* as a discursive project:

> Maroon men [and women] throughout the hemisphere developed extraordinary skills in guerrilla warfare. To the bewilderment of their European enemies, whose rigid and conventional tactics were learned on the open battlefields of Europe, these highly adaptable and mobile warriors took maximum advantage of local environments, striking and withdrawing with great rapidity, making extensive use of ambushes to catch their adversaries in crossfire, fighting only when and where they chose, depending on reliable intelligence networks among nonmaroons (both slave and white settlers), and often communicating by horns.
>
> [pp. 7-8]

The world of *The New Negro* represents a unified community of national interests set in direct opposition to the general economic, political, and theological tenets of a racist land. The work is, in itself, a *communal* project, drawing on resources, talents, sounds, images, rhythms of a marooned society or nation existing on the frontiers or margins of *all* American promise, profit, and modes of production. It thus seeks its inspiration in the very flight, or marronage, to the urban North of millions of black folk.

The Afro-American masses may feel, in Locke's phrase, "only a strange relief and a new vague urge" (p. 4). They may not be "articulate as yet" (p. 7). Moreover, their current condition may compel them to entrust their expressive potential to black spokespersons of a younger generation. Yet Locke is acutely aware that it is the masses—those millions of blacks leaving, departing, engaged in marronage *on a grand scale*—who are at the forefront of what he conceives as a black national emergence: "The clergyman following his errant flock, the physician or lawyer trailing his clients, supply the true clues. In a real sense it is the rank and file who are leading, and the leaders who are following. A transformed and transforming psychology permeates the masses" (p. 7). The "transforming psychology" which Locke extrapolates from the marronage of Afro-American masses has little to do with frightened and unthinking retreat. Rather:

> The wash and rush of this human tide on the beach line of the northern city centers is to be explained primarily in terms of a new vision of opportunity, of social and economic freedom, of a spirit to seize, even in the face of an extortionate and heavy toll, a chance for the improvement of conditions. With each successive wave of it, the movement of the Negro becomes more and more a mass movement toward the larger and the more democratic chance—in the Negro's case a deliberate flight not only from countryside to city, but from medieval America to modern.
>
> [p. 6]

I think one can say without overstatement that Locke's formative propositions in *The New Negro* are essentially deformative in intent. For they remove the Afro-American decisively from "country districts" of the South and cast a black mass movement in terms that sound like the formulations of nineteenth-century Victorian sages. Locke—like a proud Jeremy Bentham or a confident John Stuart Mill—welcomes "Harlem" and its new masses as a sign of an irreversible shift from the medieval to the modern.

Marronage, masses, and modernism come together in a striking, even an aggressive manner in *The New Negro.* For Locke quickly concedes that the *outer* objectives of the life of Afro-America are coextensive with general American ideals. But he also forcefully notes that the *inner* objectives of the Afro-American nation—located in "the very heart of the folk-spirit" (p. xv)—are still in the process of uneasy formation. What these inner objectives constitute is represented, I think, by the drive and force implied by the graphics of the collection with its African masks, and transcribed spirituals, and the energized portrait of a madonna who gives life to succeeding generations as its frontispiece. Simply stated, the inner objective is to found a nation of Afro-Americans on the basis of RACE.

In a world of murderous exclusion, the mass spirit—articulated through the voices of a younger, expressive generation—demands an inversion that converts "a defensive into an offensive position, a handicap into an incentive" (p. 11). In short, the discourse of lordship and bondage, controlled by the master, will be taken up and transmuted—deformed, as it were—by the maroon. "You have confined me to the language of RACE," Locke's mass spirit seems to say, "and I shall convert it into a weapon and creative instrument of massed, *national,* racial will." Relegated by a national white consensus to marginality, a position resonant only with *different* expressive possibilities ("and often communicating by horns"), the *New Negro* seeks community and self-consciously pursues democratic advantage through the medium of race.

Words of Richard Wright's narrator in *Black Boy* come to mind: "I did not embrace insurgency through open choice." Similarly, Locke refers to the New Negro's racial/expressive strategy as "forced"; it is a desperate attempt to build "Americanism" on race values (p. 12). But even with its racialistically compelled character, it is *still* insurgency. And Locke knows that only the articulate elite can channel such racially constrained energies in "constructive" ways. He talks of the threat, the danger, the radicalism of the masses represented by such leadership and following as that of Marcus Garvey. Such radicalism can destroy America if a black talented tenth is not allowed to bring about a revaluation of Afro-American expressive culture and communicate with advanced sectors of the white community. The principal metaphor of *The New Negro*'s introduction heightens dramatically one's sense of the work as a deformative act. For that metaphor is of a dammed, blocked, unjustly constrained black current ready to overflow and flood calm plantations beyond marronage. Only a radical change in American polity can forestall this disaster.

The urban masses have thus entered the Afro-American field of possibilities, carrying both leadership force and energetic potential. While Locke's vision is not of a full merger of a formerly distinctive class and mass in Afro-America, it does suggest that the only worthwhile expressive project available to *class* is a national, racial expressivity that takes form and draws heart *only* from the "awakened" Afro-American mass. Further, it suggests that any Afro-American expressive project must find its ultimate validity in a global community—the world, black masses, as it were—of Africans, both continental, and diasporic. Locke knew that guerrilla warfare is always a function of mass and massive support.

. . . . .

The radically advanced aspect of *The New Negro* is its inscription of Afro-American modernity in mass, urban, national, and international terms. To achieve this inscription the work appropriates sounding strategies brought to resonant potentiality by turn-of-the-century spokespersons. The collection is in a sense a kind of community of accomplished discursive possibilities. Just as Harlem appears in the work as a sign of marronage and deformation, so Durham, described eloquently by the sociologist E. Franklin Frazier, appears as a sign of formal mastery. If Harlem is, indeed, the "progressive Negro community of the American metropolis" (Locke's phrase, p. xvi) and the veritable national seat of Afro-American intellectual and artistic leadership, then Durham is, in Frazier's piquant phrase, the "Capital of the Black Middle Class" (p. 333). Both city names—one northern, the other southern—stand as tangible emblems, as representations of sounding practices that give birth to Afro-American modernity. Taken together, they give locational form to the projections found at the close of Locke's introduction:

> But whatever the general effect, the present generation will have added the motives of self-expression and spiritual development [Harlem] to the old and still unfinished task of making material headway and progress [Durham]. No one who understandingly faces the situation with its substantial accomplishment or views the new scene with its still more abundant promise can be entirely without hope.
>
> [pp. 15-16]

Indeed, Locke's volume itself provides substantial discursive grounds for hope. His compendium virtually collects, organizes, and gives form to the fullest extensions of a field of sounding possibilities; it serves as both the speaking manual *and* the singing book of a pioneering civilization freed from the burden of nonsensically and polemically constrained expression. Both Paul Kellogg in his essay "Negro Pioneers" and Charles S. Johnson in "The New Frontage on American Life" project a vision of Afro-American settlers bringing into existence what a participant in a seminar I recently conducted called a new American "folk hero"—the "New Negro."[5] Kellogg (a white contributor) sounds this pioneering note as follows:

> In the northward movement of the Negroes in the last ten years, we have another folk migration which in human significance can be compared only with this pushing back of the Western frontier in the first half of the last century or with the waves of immigration which have swept in from overseas in the last half. Indeed, though numerically far smaller than either of these, this folk movement is unique. For this time we have a people singing as they come—breaking through to cultural expression and economic freedom together.
>
> [p. 271]

The description of a collective body of people—conjoined in national sentiment and determination—making their way to both the headlands of material success and the peaks of expressive creativity in a single trek is inspiring in the extreme. And what might be called the *institutional* character of their dual achievement (expressive-intellectual as well as material) is projected by Kelly Miller's and Robert R. Moton's respective essays on "Howard: The National Negro University" and "Hampton-Tuskegee: Missioners of the Mass." Like Harlem and Durham, Howard and Hampton-Tuskegee stand as signs of an achieved extension of discursive possibilities first brought forth by DuBois's siting of the *black university* and Washington's delineation of a *black skills center.*

*The New Negro,* like the valued documents from which we grasp iconic images and pictorial myths of a colonial or frontier America, is perhaps our first *national* book, offering not only a description of streams of tendency in our collective lives but also an actual construction within its pages of the sounds, songs, images, and signs of a nation. The collection's combination of phaneric display and formal mastery can come as no surprise to the person who has followed the lines of Afro-American development through an extensive discursive field. For though the enabling conditions for Locke's collection are found in marronage, there is no gainsaying the work's quite canny presentation, utilization, and praise of formal mastery. Witness, for example, the high evaluation of Countee Cullen's poetry, poetry that is meant to imitate with astute fidelity the efforts of British romanticism. Or turn to Claude McKay's "The White House," a poem whose title Locke changed to "White Houses," and you find an English, or modified Shakespearean, sonnet. Again, most of the short fiction and, certainly, the single drama presented in *The New Negro* scarcely escape initial recognition as formally *standard* works.

The present discussion is hardly the place to explore fully the Afro-American cultural dimensions and significances of McKay's or Cullen's *standard* artistic postures. But one can contextualize such efforts by saying that McKay's "sonnet," like Cullen's "ballads," are just as much mastered *masks* as the minstrel manipulations of Booker T. Washington and Charles Chesnutt are. The trick of McKay and Cullen was what one of my colleagues calls the denigration of form—a necessary ("forced," as it were) adoption of the standard that results in an effective *blackening.*[6] Locke was never of the opinion that Western *standards* in art were anything other than adequate goals for high Afro-

American cultural achievement. And the revaluation of the Afro-American based on artistic accomplishment for which he calls mandated, in his view, a willingness on the part of black spokespersons to aspire toward such standards. Hence, one would have to present *recognizably* standard forms and get what black mileage one could out of subtle, or, by contrast, straining (like McKay's rebellious cries) variations and deepenings of these forms. If the younger generation was to proffer "artistic" gifts, such gifts had first to be recognizable as "artistic" by Western, formal standards and not simply as unadorned or primitive *folk* creations.

Now Locke—and, indeed, the entire Harlem movement—has often been criticized severely for its advocacy of the standard. Yet it seems that such criticism proceeds somewhat in ignorance of the full discursive field marking Afro-American national possibilities. For we may not enjoy or find courageous models of derring-do in the masking that characterizes formal mastery, but we certainly cannot minimize its significant and strategic presence in our history. Furthermore, such masking carries subtle resonances and effects that cannot even be perceived (much less evaluated) by the person who begins with the notion that recognizably *standard* form automatically disqualifies a work as an authentic and valuable Afro-American national production. Analysis is in fact foreclosed by a first assumption of failure. Certainly Countee Cullen, for example, served a national need in a time of "forced" institution building and national projection. He gained white American recognition for "Negro poetry" at a moment when there was little encouraging recognition in the United States for *anything* Negro. And Cullen gained such recognition by means of a mastery of form pleasing *to Afro-Americans* as well as Anglo-Americans. It seems inconceivable that, in the first flush of pioneering urbanity and heady self-consciousness, the congregation of Reverend Frederick Cullen's well-attended Salem Methodist Episcopal Church in Harlem would have responded positively if, after the father's announcement of his son's accomplishments as *a poet,* the young Countee had produced sounds such as: "April is the cruellest month, breeding / Lilacs out of the dead land, mixing / Memory and desire, stirring / Dull roots with spring rain." The delivery of such lines would probably have caused consternation akin to the congregation's reaction to John in DuBois's classic story "Of the Coming of John": "Little had they understood of what he said, for he spoke an unknown tongue." Not only was the "tongue" of such collaged allusiveness as Eliot's

*unknown* to a congregation like Reverend Cullen's; it was also unnecessary, unneeded, of little use in a world bent on recognizable (rhyme, meter, form, etc.) artistic "contributions." One has only to peruse the 1913 issue of *Poetry* in which Ezra Pound's famous imagist manifesto appeared to see that "cruellest months" and breeding lilacs were the exception rather than the American rule in Cullen's day.

There is no real need to enter apologetics for *The New Negros'* presentation and use of formal mastery, however, since this strategy takes its significance from the entire sounding field of our nation; it is, moreover, dramatically complemented or even *out-sounded* by the deformative iconography and syllables of the collection. This deformation finds resonance in Jean Toomer's intensely lyrical prose-songs of Southern black women and in Cugo Lewis's rendition of the etiological "T'appin." It takes effect in Jessie Fauset's keen signifying on Joel Chandler Harris and all white spokesmen who would make the Negro merely the "funny man" of American life. It expresses itself in the call for a National Black Theatre (Montgomery Gregory), a National Black University (Kelly Miller), and a National School of Negro Art (Locke). But most important, the deformative rhythms, signs, and images of *The New Negro* find their proper curve in the movement of Locke's collection from a reasoned, if heady, statement of Afro-American national ideals to an impassioned delineation by a venerable and formidable Afro-American scholar of the global significance and mission implicit in the achievement of such ideals.

One might say in fact that *The New Negro*—commencing with the figure of 175,000 men and women of color in Harlem—ends with a vision of the mission of Harlem vis-à-vis a global community of Africans 150 million in number. For the collection concludes with W. E. B. DuBois's "The Negro Mind Reaches Out."

DuBois's work analyzes world colonialism as a function of the bizarre and unfortunate alliance of exploitative capital and derogated labor, suggesting that a murderous white exclusion is the enabling condition for this alliance. Surely, DuBois's is a phaneric voice when he writes:

The attitude of the white laborer toward colored folk is largely a matter of long continued propaganda and gossip. The white laborers can read and write, but beyond this their education and experience are limited and they live in a world of color prejudice. The curious, most childish propaganda dominates us, by which good, earnest, even intelligent men have come by millions to believe almost religiously that white folk are a peculiar and chosen people whose one great accomplishment is civilization and that civilization must be protected from the rest of the world by cheating, stealing, lying, and murder.

[p. 407]

Hope for the future lies in the political reeducation of white workers and in effective leadership for global black masses who suffer the effects of an industrial imperialism unchecked in its greed and brutality. DuBois, of course, designates the seat of leadership for the black masses as the United States:

This hundred and fifty millions of people are gaining slowly an intelligent thoughtful leadership. The main seat of their leadership is to-day the United States. [For] in the United States there are certain unheralded indications of development in the Negro problem. One is the fact that for the first time in America, the American Negro is to-day universally recognized as capable of speaking for himself.

[p. 411]

("And often communicating by horns," "and often communicating by horns . . .") The *sound* of DuBois is a challenge to those celebrated at the beginning of *The New Negro*—the younger generation. The collection is not only a national sounding field but also the sounding of an international mission bestowed by venerability upon youth. The maroon community of "Harlem," conceived as the *modern* capital of those "capable of speaking" for themselves, is thus source (of insubordination)—haven (for fugitives)—base (for marauding expeditions)—and nucleus (of leadership for planned uprisings).

### Notes

1. Alain Locke, ed., *The New Negro* (New York: Atheneum, 1968), p. 200. All citations to essays in this collection refer to this edition and are hereafter marked by page numbers in parentheses.

2. C. Vann Woodward, *The Strange Career of Jim Crow* (New York: Oxford University Press, 1968), p. 115.

3. See J. Saunders Redding, *They Came in Chains* (New York: Lippincott, 1950), p. 235.

4. Richard Price, ed., *Maroon Societies: Rebel Slave Communities in the Americas* (Baltimore: Johns Hopkins University Press, 1979), p. 3. All citations refer to this edition.

5. . . . The observation came from Professor Carolyn Liston.

6. The note on *denigration* comes from my former student, Professor Michael Awkward, who has constructed his own quite provocative model of black discursive practices vis-à-vis Afro-American women writers.

# GEORGE HUTCHINSON (ESSAY DATE 1995)

**SOURCE:** Hutchinson, George. "Toward a New Negro Aesthetic." In *The Harlem Renaissance in Black and White,* pp. 170-208. Cambridge, Mass.: Belknap Press, 1995.

*In the following excerpt, Hutchinson traces the development of the new aesthetic associated with African American literature and the arts during the 1920s and the role played in that development by the journal* Opportunity *and the National Urban League.*

While *Crisis* magazine, driven by Du Bois's disillusionment, faded as the main organ of "New Negro" writing, *Opportunity*'s importance rose. Though its circulation never approached that of *The Crisis,* within a year of its founding it had surpassed the earlier magazine as the premier journal of African American cultural criticism and performance. It provided a legitimizing space for experiments that were losing the confidence of *The Crisis.* The contrasts between the magazines' aesthetic preferences were not unrelated to the contrasts between the organizations to which they "belonged" as well as the differences between their editors. Hence a full understanding of the cultural matrix of the "renaissance" requires a more detailed examination than has previously been offered of the linkage between the institutional and intellectual backgrounds of *Opportunity* and its aesthetic emphases.

## *"Not Alms but Opportunity"*

As Nancy J. Weiss has pointed out, the National Urban League grew out of a "second reform tradition" somewhat different from the "protest tradition" of the NAACP and the Niagara Movement.[1] The Urban League had different methods and a different focus, subordinating the drive for political and civil rights to the need for economic and, to a lesser degree, "moral" progress. Focusing on job opportunities, housing, education, and moral uplift, it also opted for a less militant demeanor. In fact, the Urban Leaguers generally seem to have agreed that the programs of both Du Bois and Washington were crucial to the advancement of blacks in American society and sought to avoid antagonizing either side of the great debate over black social strategy.

The president from the league's beginning in 1911 until 1914 was the Columbia professor E. R. A. Seligman, one of the founders of Greenwich Settlement House and president of Felix Adler's Society for Ethical Culture from 1908 to 1921; Seligman had also participated in the founding of the NAACP and addressed that organization's first conference in 1909. In fact, several people influential in the NAACP, including Mary White

East 112th Street in Harlem.

Ovington and Oswald Garrison Villard, had been closely involved with organizations that folded into each other to form the Urban League. Moreover, one of the founders of the league, George Edmund Haynes, had studied social and political ethics under Felix Adler on his way to becoming a sociologist. The social philosophies and tactics that coalesced in the Urban League have clear ramifications for cultural politics, as the connections between the organization's founders and Ethical Culture, for example, make clear.

The Urban League would emphasize interracial cooperation in the development of a common civilization and the "moral progress" of the nation. The point was not "charity," but the development of "a sounder national democracy," in the words of Ruth Standish Baldwin, the realization of "sound community living."[2] For years National Urban League stationery carried the motto she had written: "Let us work, not as colored people nor as white people for the narrow benefit of any group alone, but *together,* as American citizens, for the common good of our common city, our common country."[3] This basic point

would be reiterated continually in *Opportunity* magazine, side by side with the "literature of the New Negro."

In terms of social activism, the Urban League specifically wanted to avoid duplicating the NAACP's efforts. It would concentrate on opening up employment opportunity and "social services to ease the process of urbanization."[4] Its tactics would also differ. Whereas the NAACP undertook direct action and immediatism, the Urban League tended toward diplomacy and gradualism. As leaders of both organizations agreed, the NAACP would strike and advance the front line, and then the Urban League would hold the ground and solidify positions. Indeed, this distinction between the organizations is well emblemized in the titles of *The Crisis* and *Opportunity.*[5]

In addition to pushing for greater opportunity for urban blacks, however, the Urban League focused on behavioral reformation of black migrants. Anxious that new arrivals would get into the hands of "the wrong class of people," traveler's aid workers would meet incoming trains and direct people to Urban League offices for help in finding lodging and employment. They sponsored "wholesome" activities to attract their charges away from the tempting brothels and saloons. They taught "modern" hygiene, cleanliness, proper dress, tooth-brushing, good manners, punctuality, efficiency, proper deportment. They discouraged "loud-talking" and "boisterous laughter"—virtually any behavior that caused the new city-dwellers to stand out as "different" and thus arouse antagonism or confirm stereotypes that whites held toward blacks in general. All of these efforts contributed to the overall aim of "race adjustment," economic advancement, and intercultural harmony.

A number of apparent paradoxes become evident when one considers the Urban League's ideological positions and tactics in relation to the aesthetic criticism of *Opportunity*. There is, of course, the obvious question of why a social-work organization would interest itself in artistic affairs at all, which I will address in a moment. Why, moreover, would the magazine of an institution that eschewed "sentimental appeal" and "subjective" rhetoric, that insisted upon the patient collection and "objective" communication of social "facts" to combat American racism, become the defender of what W. E. B. Du Bois considered (wrongly, I believe) an "art for art's sake" aesthetic? Even more to the point, however, how is it that an organization that sought to aid the "adjustment" of rural migrants to Northern cities, that helped them gain "decent" employment and encouraged the acquisition of middle-class manners and morals, that worried about moral degradation hurting the image of the race in the North as Southern peasants settled there—that, indeed, explicitly instructed its members to discourage "shiftless" and "inefficient" blacks from migrating to the North—how is it that the organ of *this* group, rather than that of the NAACP or the socialist *Messenger,* became identified with the bohemian wing of the "Negro renaissance," lauded folk plays set in the black South, promoted the urban realism of fiction and poetry focusing on the urban black masses rather than the "best foot forward" school, and became the champion of what was called, in *Modern Quarterly* advertisements for *Opportunity,* a "New Negro aesthetic"?

### Charles S. Johnson and "the Beauty of Familiar Things"

Key to these apparent paradoxes is the intellectual orientation of *Opportunity*'s editor from its inception to 1928, Charles S. Johnson. Several important writers of the Harlem Renaissance later

attested to Johnson's importance. Zora Neale Hurston called him "the root of the so-called Negro Renaissance."[6] Langston Hughes said he "did more to encourage and develop Negro writers during the 1920's than anyone else in America"; along with Jessie Fauset at *The Crisis* and Alain Locke in Washington (Johnson's chosen "dean" of the movement), he "midwifed the so-called New Negro literature into being."[7] Echoing Hughes, Arna Bontemps has written that Johnson was a "nursemaid" of the Harlem Renaissance.[8] Johnson gave New Negro literature pride of place in *Opportunity* and acted as the behind-the-scenes manager of the movement. He was primarily responsible for making *Opportunity,* within months of its founding, the most important medium of the Harlem Renaissance, even as he also used it to publicize the results of social research. Far from being unrelated to each other, these two aspects of the magazine together expressed a carefully considered social philosophy that also shaped Johnson's aesthetic preferences.[9]

Typically Johnson's rationale for promoting the arts is attributed either to a belief that artistic achievement would prove the Negro's fitness for full integration into American democracy or to a recognition of the arts as the one area for black advancement that had not been proscribed; providing high visibility and low vulnerability, an artistic movement could provide the entering wedge for black integration. "Through secrecy and manipulation," David Levering Lewis argues, Johnson would try "to redeem, through art, the standing of his people."[10] According to Lewis, it was all part of a confidence game played on unwitting white liberals, who for various self-interested reasons had become fascinated by Negroes. Much as Houston Baker sees Booker T. Washington as "running a game" on myopic white folks who never had any interest in racial equality, Lewis argues that Johnson was applying Washingtonian methods for the Talented Tenth. While there is a partial truth to this characterization, a careful investigation of Johnson's intellectual matrix, revealed by his autobiographical writings, and of *Opportunity*'s cultural criticism forces a more complex and far less cynical interpretation.

Johnson's manuscripts and educational background provide little support for viewing him as a classic trickster using the blindnesses of a supposed racial opponent to "run a game" on him. He was much more interested in achieving dialogue with the "other." Johnson himself mentions that his intellectual development took its first decisive turn when he was an undergraduate working for a charity organization in Virginia. It dawned on him at this time that "no man can be justly judged until you have looked at the world through his eyes," a lesson that became the "core" of his "social philosophy." This conviction, he writes in his "Spiritual Autobiography," led him in 1917 to the University of Chicago and the "great social philosopher and teacher, Robert E. Park. It was he who linked this deep and moving human concern with science and human understanding, and with the great minds that have struggled with these issues—William James, John Dewey, George Santayana, Josiah Royce, all his friends."[11]

. . . The most distinctive aspect of Park's sociological approach (both theoretically and methodologically) was his emphasis on the subjectivity of social agents. He quoted James often: "The most real thing is a thing that is most keenly felt rather than the thing that is most clearly conceived."[12] Park encouraged his students to enter into the worlds they studied and to strive to understand the values they found there, for he worried that we "miss the point and mistake the inner significance of the lives of those about us unless we share their experience"—and that "experience" is always connected with a long history we can never fully know.[13] He sought a combination of something akin to the Boasian method of ethnology (which, in fact, he much admired) and the "new" journalist's or novelist's skill at portraying personalities and group life. One of his graduate students remembered his "genuine interests" as being in particulars, and journalistic in nature:

> He was more of a journalist, or artist . . . concerned with individuals, pictures of the life of groups—immigrants, denizens of skid row, hoodlums, etc., much as Dreiser, Gorky, et al., were. . . . I remember well his showing me a doctoral thesis written under his direction. . . . It was an intimate account of a small town in the west. He had everything in it about all the characters, both respectable and otherwise. It was exactly the sort of thing that Sherwood Anderson and Dreiser wrote. Park was fascinated by it. This is what he was interested in.[14]

It may be worth pointing out that Midwestern realists like Dreiser and Zona Gale were prominent among judges of the *Opportunity* literary contests that Charles S. Johnson organized in the late 1920s.

The more usable aspects of Park's thinking, in terms of Johnson's program at *Opportunity*, come out in Park's own reflections on the emerging "Negro Renaissance" in 1923, in comments that Johnson quoted in an *Opportunity* editorial, "Negro Life and Its Poets."[15] Approving of Robert Ker-

lin's statement that "a people's poetry . . . affords the most serious subject of study to those who would understand the people—that people's soul, that people's status, that people's potentialities," Park did not note any "primitive and exotic" qualities in the New Negro poetry but rather emphasized its militancy, idealism, black nationalism, and prophetic character:

> In some respects . . . it seems to me the Negro, like all the other disinherited peoples, is more fortunate than the dominant races. He is restless, but he knows what he wants. The issues in his case, at least, are clearly defined. More than that, in this racial struggle, he is daily gaining not merely faith in himself, but new faith in the world. Since he wants nothing except what he is willing to give to every other man on the same terms he feels that the great forces that shape the destinies of peoples are on his side.[16]

Even before Alain Locke's similar observation in *The New Negro*, Park likened the Harlem Renaissance to the nationalist movements of dominated peoples elsewhere in the world, finding the same "natural history" in each, including a linguistic and literary movement, a renaissance—as in Czechoslovakia, Ireland, Finland, Norway, Italy, and the Zionist movement. In Park's view of the cyclical "natural history" of race relations, such nationalistic competition would be followed by accommodation between "national" groups and ultimate integration—first within the United States, and ultimately throughout the world.

Like Park (and Locke), Charles Johnson viewed the "cultural racialism" of the New Negro as integral with the American cultural field as a whole. More than any other group, he insisted, the Negro had been stripped of the ancestral culture upon coming to the "New World"; hence "his" claim to "indigenous" status: "With the exceptions of the Indian and the Appalachian Mountaineer [of Johnson's own natal region], no man in America is so entirely native to the soil. The Negro on the plantation is the only peasant class America has produced, and his is the only native folk culture that America possesses."[17] In fact, as he would state in 1928, the religious expressions of the slave "are no less significant than Puritanism, and the early American farm house, as spiritual and artistic antecedents of contemporary America."[18]

The differences between black and white Americans, Johnson believed, were based not on cultural differences inherited from Africa and Europe but on "physical and racial characteristics" as well as historical experience within the United States—another point on which he was in thorough agreement with Park.[19] In a review of the 1920s he emphasized the rootedness of the new black literature in specifically black historical experience and called the Harlem poets "the legitimate successors of the voices that first sang the Spirituals." He continued: "It is important, therefore, to consider Negro literature, in all its different expressions, as an integral part of a single tradition and as a unique collective experience. Only as these different expressions of the racial life are viewed as parts of a whole is it possible to arrive at any true estimate of the character of the Negro's cultural achievement or his traits."[20] This view differs dramatically from that of, say, William Stanley Braithwaite and the dominant critical stance at *The Crisis*.

One's estimate of the cultural tradition, according to Johnson's formulation, depended upon both the hermeneutic brought to bear on the tradition and the quality of the "expressions of the racial life," and for Johnson this meant a swerve from propaganda and protest. If responsible sociological inquiry required dispassionate methods, so, paradoxically enough, did a truly "self-expressive" fiction. The aesthetic work would not be burdened with "propaganda" of the "best foot forward" sort but instead attempt to exemplify in its very form the cultural meanings (that is, the "experience," in pragmatist terms) of a people. Without giving all the credit (or blame) to Johnson, one can go through virtually all the criticism published in *Opportunity* and find this criterion of judgment to be fundamental.

To look at the cultural orientation of *Opportunity* from this perspective is to see how shallow many critiques of the Harlem Renaissance have been. Shortly after he left New York for Nashville, when the Harlem Renaissance was still (briefly) near its zenith, Johnson quoted Santayana in a chapel talk to students at Fisk: "Whenever beauty is really seen and loved . . . it has a definite embodiment: The eye has precision, the work has style and the object has perfection."[21] What Du Bois took to be an "art for art's sake" doctrine was really a determination to explore "native values" typical of American writers at the time: "The beginning of the 20th century has been marked in America by a conscious movement 'back to the concrete,' which has yielded the new fascination of watching the strangeness and beauty of familiar things. It is America in revolt against the stiff conventionalism of borrowed patterns. The commentators of the present begin the new era in America with such characters as Sandburg and Robinson, apostles of freedom, who have launched the search for beauty in forgotten lives. It is the spirit of the New America."[22] Could the "New Negro" be far behind? "This compulsion exists now for the new generation of Negroes—the compulsion to find a new beauty in their own lives, ideals, and feelings. The new generation of Negro writers and artists have led the way here. The poetry represents this liberated energy. It is beginning the embodiment of new and beautiful life conceptions. It is revising old patterns, investing Negro life with a new charm and dignity, and power. No life for them is without beauty, no beginning too low."[23] Johnson here expresses the Deweyan point that art and life are inseparable, that art serves the enrichment of everyday experience of the common world, and thus ultimately the improvement of that world for enhanced living—art is, in the widest possible sense, "use-full."

The reformation of art serves the reformation of society. Moreover, discovery of the beauty of one's life is the path to freedom: "I am convinced," Johnson told the Fisk students, "that the road to a new freedom for us lies in the discovery of the surrounding beauties of our lives, and in the recognition that beauty itself is a mark of the highest expression of the human spirit."[24] Johnson suspected that his audience would be wondering, What beauty?—precisely because of their adherence to "alien" concepts of beauty rather than those evoked by common experience in the world.

Just as white American writers needed to become comfortable with "different standards of perfection" from the English—as John Macy, chairman of the second *Opportunity* awards meeting, had argued in *The Spirit of American Literature*—so "American Negroes" needed to become self-assured, with different standards from those of "American Caucasians." "It was the dull lack of some idealism here that held America in a suspended cultural animation until it sought freedom through self-criticism and its own native sources of beauty. In the same manner, American Negroes, born into a culture which they did not wholly share, have responded falsely to the dominant pattern. Their expression has been, to borrow a term which Lewis Mumford employs in referring to Americans in relation to Europe, 'sickly and derivative, a mere echo of old notes.'"[25] This argument is not based on foundationalist premises of unchanging racial "essences" but is instead a corollary to the notion of art as experience: "The cultural difference between an Englishman and an American is not so much in the germ plasm as in the accumulated stores of culture which impose for each different standards of perfection. The same condition applies in the cultural differences between [white] Americans and American Negroes."[26] The New Negro authors provided an aesthetic correlative to Booker T. Washington's statement "You can beat me being a white man but I can beat you being a Negro." "In their new representations of Negro life," wrote Johnson, "the Negro writers and artists . . . are doing the same thing for which he found a phrase."[27]

Nonetheless, Johnson contended in the 1930s that there could be no truly separate black culture in the United States: "Those of the younger generation of Negroes, who, by virtue of their competence in the general culture have achieved a measure of cultural emancipation have turned back frankly to discover the beauty and charm of the life of the folk Negro. The result of this emancipation, paradoxically enough, has been to enrich the general culture rather than to develop a distinctive Negro expression."[28] He regarded the aims of the Negro renaissance to be integration, even "assimilation," which would assure the just operation of democratic government. Such assimilation could not occur until the peoples of the United States came to understand their mutual interests and to speak the same language. Johnson argued that people must gradually come to share the same "universe of discourse," for "men must live and work and fight together in order to create that community of interest and sentiment which will enable them to meet the common crises of life with a common will."[29] When cultural differences grow so great that they provoke "racial consciousness" and make full and free discussion of differences impossible, assimilation cannot take place and democracy cannot work. It is crucial to understand that Johnson is talking about an assimilation of separate groups to one another, rather than black culture being "assimilated" to an Anglo norm.

Johnson put this line of reasoning to use by liberally calling upon white writers and critics of the cultural nationalist and regionalist type to review the works of New Negro authors, and by having African Americans review the works of European Americans. Many of the featured critical essays published in *Opportunity* followed this cross-cultural pattern, just as the magazine's literary contests were judged by integrated panels. Was this an example of cynical manipulation on Johnson's part, or a practice in harmony with his expressed convictions?

In an interesting *Opportunity* essay on Booker T. Washington's "social philosophy," Johnson suggests a continuity between the Tuskegee experiment and the "Negro Renaissance." The latter movement would not have been possible, he claims, without Washington's success in precipitating a subjective transformation of a small but important segment of *white* America while simultaneously building up an educational, economic, and social foundation for black self-advancement. "The strategies which he employed consciously or unconsciously, are only now finding their most pronounced effect in the self-concern of Negroes and in the attitudes of white persons with respect to them."[30] Johnson considered Washington's strategy more complex and effective than Du Bois's in bringing about change in the conditions blocking full equality. Furthermore, Washington's "social philosophy" (essentially pragmatist, in Johnson's telling, though developed independently out of the "survival elements" of black culture) was further exemplified in the Negro Renaissance: "The most effective interest of the present is art, and even of this it may be said that it is but an elaboration of Washington's principles of stressing work rather than the rewards of work."[31] Here work is an educative *process* of self-expression, self-development, and social transformation, in which white America "must be untaught the traditions of hundreds of years, and new principles instilled."[32] One sign of Washington's success, Johnson may have believed, was the realistic fiction of the New South by such authors as DuBose Heyward and Julia Peterkin, whose novels were praised extravagantly in the pages of *Opportunity*.[33] American literature of the early twentieth century appeared to be making possible the sort of integrated society Johnson regarded as the nation's only hope.

But Johnson not only recognized the necessity of some sort of national community to help realize the hopes of black Americans; he understood the function of a national press in nourishing the growth of a communal African American consciousness, which was a necessary stage in the development of an integrated America. *Opportunity,* like *The Crisis,* was not only seeking integration through art but also seeking to create a national New Negro community (a process purportedly begun by Booker T. Washington), and Johnson viewed the arts as crucial to that endeavor. A nationally circulated magazine, after all, is a powerful tool for creating a sense of shared life in a world where modernization, migration, and urbanization are shattering older forms of community maintenance (particularly face-to-face interaction) as well as providing opportunities for new types of community. *Opportunity*'s relentless advocacy of a folk drama movement precisely exemplifies its communitarian thrust, invoking the folk past to create a "community of memory" (in Royce's terms), to revitalize a community of expression and a "community of hope" (Royce again) for a continentally scattered *urban* middle-class readership—just as the old "colored aristocracy" of Philadelphia, Washington, and elsewhere was being eclipsed by "New Negro" elites, especially in New York.

### The Spirit and the Folk

Articles on "Negro folk song" exemplify the American cultural nationalist/cultural pluralist and socially conscious nature of *Opportunity*'s advocacy of a black aesthetic. In a feature essay of 1923, for example, John W. Work emphasized the social and historical context of the creation of folk songs, building on Dvořák's oft-cited opinion that "if America ever had a national music, it must be based upon the songs found among the southern Negroes."[34] Devoting himself to the argument that "this music is original with the Negro, and that it is genuinely American," Work proceeds to demonstrate that "the evolution of the pentatonic (African) into the sexatonic (American) scale was contemporaneous with the evolution of the African into the American."[35] The black slaves had created an entirely new scale and new forms of rhythmic syncopation in the process of responding lyrically to their experiences on the North American continent. The result was America's only folk song. Hence, "conditions point to the plain truth that, since the Negro Folk Song is the only American Folk Music that meets the scientific definition of Folk Song, since it is so rich in theme and in the beauty of its melody, since it is so comprehensive, so strikingly original and so strong in its appeal, it is the only natural basis and inspiration for American National Music."[36]

The point was made over and over again—in Newell Niles Puckett's "Race-Pride and Folk-Lore," for example, which tried to liberate the black bourgeoisie from its shame about its connections with the rural "folk"—and notably in Laurence Buermeyer's "The Negro Spirituals and American Art." Buermeyer, associate director of education at the Barnes Foundation and a pragmatist aesthetician, cites the frequent complaint that Americans have no "deeply felt religious experience," that American life suffers from "emotional poverty." As a result, "American art . . . has been in the main a rather feeble and savorless echo of European art, not growing out of the soil of national life, but transplanted from abroad and kept alive in a hot-house."[37] The sole exception is "Negro art," the only American tradition upon which future self-expression can productively build, for such tradition requires "roots that go down into the deeper soil of experience, of common activities inter-related at many points." It must have "primitive" elements in the sense that it is not grafted onto an older stock but rather has an origin *here* (as only Whitman's work, among that of white artists, did), in response to the humble experiences of everyday living.[38] The aesthetics of black experience, rich with emotional response and "deepened" by the need to give meaning to suffering in the encounter with radical evil, had produced an unmatched tradition of native spirituality and artistic expression.

The interest in black folklore, then, was not restricted to its assimilation to the romantic and pastoral, let alone the exotic. In "Self-Portraiture and Social Criticism in Negro Folk-Song," for example, B. A. Botkin featured the ways in which secular folk forms such as the blues responded to historical oppression and the conditions of industrial work. "An inseparable part of the self-portraiture of Negro workaday songs," he writes in his *Opportunity* essay, "is their social criticism. Out of the Negro's sense of self-pity develops an inevitable conviction of social injustice and an indictment of the existing order."[39] Botkin draws attention to the powerful irony directed toward white supervisors (and stereotypes of black workers) in such lines as "White man in starched shirt settin' in shade, / Laziest man that God ever made"—and the development of the trickster motif:

> I steal dat corn
> From de white man's barn,
> Den I slips aroun',
> Tells a yarn,
> An' sells it back again.[40]

Botkin notes not only the different personae and character types (for example, trickster and bad man) but also the formal virtuosity of the songs, which employ parallelism and compression, narrative by elliptical suggestion.

Moreover, these techniques match the modern social context of the songs' creation: "The child-like faith of slave-days is giving way to the worldly cynicism, the disillusionment of freedom, the product of industrial exploitation, migration, and concentration in cities."[41] While a continuity with the spirituals can be found in the note of homelessness, Botkin wants to distinguish the secular songs on the basis of their social reference and contemporaneity. Similarly, in the 1920s Botkin was ahead of his time in stressing the importance of urban folklore, objecting to the antiquarian and pastoral emphases of most "collectors" and their neglect of the contemporary, the modern.[42] This counterweight to nostalgic pastoralism is also evident in *Opportunity*'s appreciation of jazz, which one editorial identified as the preeminent expression of "modern American life," with broad appeal to the "masses" and "artists" alike: "The amusing and yet profoundly significant paradox of the whole situation is that it is the Negroes, who not only can best express the spirit of American life, but who have created the very forms of expression." Through jazz, Negroes have "forged the key to the interpretation of the American spirit."[43]

## African Classicism and American Art

*Opportunity* criticism drew a distinction between respecting black folklore as a basis of American art and extolling the exotically "primitive." This distinction corresponded to the distinction between Franz Boas' interests in classical African civilizations, on the one hand, and the ecstatic, Bergson- and Freud-inspired fantasies of de Zayas and other "high modernists." Here, in fact, is one of the most significant homologies of the Harlem Renaissance; for the interest in a particularized and historicized yet respectful revaluation of African cultures went along with an attitude toward the African American "folk" that resisted their enshrinement as exotic "others," drawing attention to historical experience in America as determinant of a specially "native" American/Negro cultural matrix. In tension with the exotic primitivism that conflated African American with African identity was a more carefully contextualized, historical understanding of both the "folk" and of African peoples. Those who approached the relationship between African and African American cultures from this standpoint argued for study of the African past and engagement with current African struggles as part of a program for the modernist reconstitution of sundered identity and for political solidarity against racist oppression. It was also from this standpoint, specifically through the researches of Boas' students, that the actual historical connections between African and African American cultures began to be appreciated in the 1930s on nonracialist grounds.

The perceived correspondence between the "new" approach to the folk and the historical understanding of Africa is exemplified by the fact that, in the same essay in which he praised the work of Peterkin, Fisher, and McKay, Locke concluded with what he regarded as "the most significant of all recent developments; the new interest in Negro origins. If there is anything that points to a permanent revaluation of the Negro, it is the thorough-going change of attitude which is getting established about Africa and things African" in such books as Blaise Cendrars' anthology of African folklore, *The African Saga*; Captain Canot's *Adventures of an African Slaver*; Mrs. Gollock's *Lives of Eminent Africans* and *Sons of Africa*; Donald Fraser's *The New Africa*; Milton Staffer's symposium, *Thinking With Africa*; and "very notably, I think, J. W. Vandercook's *Black Majesty* [on Le Roi Christophe of Haiti]."[44]

Understanding of African cultures would provide a foundation for the wholesale revaluation of Negro achievement and potential globally, while it would also supply ideas to young artists who wanted to affirm a nonessentialized Negro identity as a psychosocial fact—indeed, a necessity, given the inescapable racialization of identities spread by Western imperialism. "Because of our Europeanized conventions, the key to the proper understanding and appreciation of [African art] will in all probability first come from an appreciation of its influence upon contemporary French art, but we must believe that there still slumbers in the blood something which once stirred will react with peculiar emotional intensity toward it. *If by nothing more mystical than the sense of being ethnically related, some of us will feel its influence at least as keenly as those who have already made it recognized and famous. Nothing is more galvanizing than the sense of a cultural past.*"[45]

Closer knowledge of African art forms—as the Barnes Foundation was advancing—would give incentives for "fresher and bolder forms of artistic expression and a lessening of that timid imitativeness which at present hampers all but our very best artists."[46] Locke cites Alexander Goldenweiser's point that "primitive art has in it both the decorative and the realistic motives, and often as not it is the abstract principles of design and aesthetic form which are the determinants of its stylistic technique and conventions."[47] Locke then takes direct aim at the identification of all things African with the "primitive" and "exotic":

Perhaps the most important effect of interpretations like these is to break down the invidious distinction between art with a capital A for European forms of expression and 'exotic' and 'primitive' art for the art expressions of other peoples. Technically speaking an art is primitive in any phase before it has mastered its idiom of expression, and classic when it has arrived at maturity and before it has begun to decline. Similarly art is exotic with relation only to its relative incommensurability with other cultures; in influencing them at all vitally it ceases to be exotic. From this we can see what misnomers these terms really are when applied to all phases of African art.[48]

Locke would continue to call African American folk forms "primitive" on *this* basis, as would, for example V. F. Calverton, while calling African sculpture "classical."

African American folklore, then, was not "organically" continuous with classical African cultures (a claim Locke would have identified with "scientific" racism) but rather an indigenously American "mixed" cultural tradition still at a relatively early period of development. Modernist African American art would draw from both sources in the process of its own "impure" and "cosmopolitan" development of "cultural racialism." The desire to "recapture" the African heritage and promote pan-African consciousness coexists with pride in African American culture as both "mixed" and uniquely "American"—in fact, with a commitment to American cultural nationalism. Hence, Nathan Huggins' influential formulation is curiously ironic:

> The Negro intellectual's fascination with primitivism was filled with ironies. Contrary to assertions of the soul-community of black folks, the American Negroes had to learn to appreciate the value of African art and culture. Too often they were taught by Europeans for whom Africa had a powerful, but limited, significance. . . . It was liberating for these men who stood squarely on a tradition and who would never wholly abandon it. But when the black American intellectual got the news, he wanted to be able to identify completely with Africa, to find his tradition there. Now that was quite fanciful.[49]

The criticism is ironic because the treatment of Africa in *Opportunity* suggests not so much the "finding" as the self-conscious construction of a tradition borrowing from Africa while holding fast to American ground.

The point I am suggesting here is that the dominant view of the approach of the New Negroes—and their white friends—to African identity and its relationship to African American identity simply does not square with the documentary evidence. It recognizes only one side of a complex dialectical relation and ignores the real significance of Boasian anthropology, pragmatism, literary realism, and historicism to the New Negro

movement—all of which exerted a powerful and salutary counterpressure to the exploitation of "primitive and exotic" projections of the white racial psyche.

The distinction I am drawing was not absolute, of course. Langston Hughes, Eugene O'Neill, Paul Green, Countee Cullen, and others were capable of "exotic primitive" tableaus as well as more disciplined and durable performances, whether of African or African American social reality. Alain Locke's selected authorities on African art—Paul Guillaume and Albert Barnes—produced a discourse mixing arguments for the self-consciousness of African art forms with belief in the sense of rhythm as racially innate; Guillaume even fell for De Gobineau's statement that "the source from which the arts have sprung is concealed in the blood of the blacks."[50] (This idea had greater force in Europe—especially surrealist-inspired Paris—than in the United States in part because of the different anthropological schools on either side of the Atlantic.) The same text could gesture in both directions simultaneously, and supposed "realists" could spout ecstatic attestations to the Negro's "natural" acting ability, sense of rhythm, and so forth. But the primitive and exotic was a focus for neither the white nor the black critics who wrote for *Opportunity* and the other chief journals of the movement—these critics were, in fact, early in recognizing the more neurotic and exploitative offshoots of the "vogue."[51] After the second *Opportunity* awards dinner, for example, Columbia professor Leon Whipple attacked the "profiteers and parasites" in his report for *The Survey*: "This sorry crew are not important in themselves. Next year they will be flittering round the candle of some new fad. But they may misguide the Negro for a time unless he can steel himself in anger or wrap himself in his own guffaws against their flattery, false witness, and bribes. It would be the final tragedy if after exploiting the Negro's body for two centuries we ended by exploiting his heart and soul."[52]

## Modern Measures, Native Sounds

The recognition of the "indigenous" spirituality of black folklore and its significance for "native" American art carried over into the criticism of black poetry in *Opportunity*. Reviews of the work of four quite different poets reveal an emphasis on poetic strategies that witness the indivisibility of spiritual from social experience, and that, for this very reason, make African American poetry crucial to "native" modernism. Thus Joseph Auslander, reviewing James Weldon Johnson's *God's*

*Trombones,* wrote that the volume was "native, necessary, valid. It is novel without being peculiar and beautiful without being orthodox. It belongs to the literature of the spirit. Racial at the root though it is and must be, it coincides, none the less, with our common humanity, towering like poetry, like prayer beyond its origin."[53]

Auslander's comments are important for a number of reasons. It is clear that he is striving self-consciously for terms that appreciate "racial" difference without exoticizing, terms that recognize spirituality without reference to racialist primitivism. In fact, Auslander (who also served as a judge in the *Opportunity* literary contest) locates the source of spirituality in the aesthetics of existence and resistance: "Never servile, though enslaved, the Negro is speaking out in accents that condemn with as keen a bitterness and celebrate with as jubilant a measure as any poets alive."[54] He appreciates the sermons not on pastoral or antiquarian grounds but for the way they show the "Afro-American imagination making new applications of old ecstasies," in such lines as "Put his eye to the telescope of eternity, / And let him look upon the paper walls of time."[55] In short, he views Johnson's use of the "sermon sagas" of his people as expressly modernist: "The Renaissance of American poetry that seemed a feeble and sorry affair at Amy Lowell's death, rests more than ever with the turbulence and candour of our Negro contemporaries."[56] But Auslander disagrees with Johnson's "contention touching dialect." Recognizing the limitations fixed upon the medium by "popular superstition which confines its use to the stage burlesque or sob variety of Negro humour and pathos," he nonetheless argues that "it is better to explode a superstition than to abandon a gold mine."[57]

To some extent, the enthusiasm of poets like Auslander for New Negro poetry was an effect of their reaction against the expatriate modernism of Pound and Eliot, whose high status came at the expense of the "native" cultural nationalists. Thus, in her featured review of Langston Hughes's *Fine Clothes to the Jew,* Margaret Larkin holds up Hughes's work as "a valuable example for all poets of what can be done with simple technique and 'every day' subjects"—in contrast to "the neurotic fantasies of more sophisticated poets."[58] Capturing the "dialect, speech cadence, and character of the people," Hughes writes an accessible, socially engaged poetry that expresses the philosophy of the black working class. Poets looking for "native American rhythms" can learn something from his deft use of the blues. Hughes's

work exerts an important counterforce to the elitist philosophy "that art is the precious possession of the few initiate." Larkin, who did publicity work for New York labor organizations in addition to writing poetry, regards Hughes not as an exotic primitive (she ignores his poems along those lines) but as a poet and prophet of social consciousness.[59]

Indeed, contrary to Du Bois's suspicions, *Opportunity* was certainly no forum of "art for art's sake." In striving to extricate black artists from enclosure in propaganda, it did not counsel the evisceration of the artist's social conscience. Nor did it play to white interest in the primitive. Robert T. Kerlin, in a review of *Cane, The Weary Blues,* and *Color,* wrote: "It is easy enough to conceive of the American Negro outstripping every competitor in every art and in every spiritual quality or achievement"—not because of some natural endowment but because of the wisdom born of suffering in the struggle for freedom. "And wisdom is more precious, according to very good authority, than the choicest residential sections of cities, and Pullman privileges, and theatre seats, and equal educational opportunities. *Though it is only by demanding these that those experiences come whose fruit is wisdom.* And such wisdom always finds embodiment in poetry. It is now doing so."[60] A teacher of Langston Hughes at Lincoln University, Kerlin was not one to rationalize the sublimation through poetry of activism against injustice; he had lost two faculty positions in a row for his public stance against racism and black peonage; and his first book was *The Voice of the Negro, 1919,* a survey of editorials from the black press in the year of the Red Summer, illustrating the new black militancy of the postwar period. His next book would be an important anthology for the rise of the renaissance, *Negro Poets and Their Poems* (1923), published by the African American press Associated Publishers.[61]

The attitude toward the folk heritage as sole reservoir of native "spirituality" also carries over into appreciations of Countee Cullen's poetry. Thus E. Merrill Root praised Cullen's "sensuous rhythms" and "translation of heart's blood into words." Cullen offers tones of revolt, grief, "pantheistic mysticism," and, like A. E. Housman, "the ache and ecstasy of love." What Root most likes is Cullen's hard-won affirmation of life and acceptance of death, both attributes connected with the "sensual mysticism" that suggests he could be the "spiritual leader of a new day" and the greatest of American poets. Cullen is the poet Keats might be, had Keats been born in "this Labrador of the soul which we call America."[62] Again the praise of Cullen carries an implicit (and sometimes explicit) critique of the despairing "wasteland" visions, as Root would have it, that characterize the most prestigious modernist poetry, a poetry that had carried the day against more accessible "native" art.

Joining the staff of *Opportunity* after receiving his master's degree from Harvard, Countee Cullen himself published seventeen columns entitled "The Dark Tower" from December 1926 through 1928, discussing both black and white writers and frequently taking exception to those, like Locke and Hughes, who stressed the importance of race for "Negro poets" and the need for an exploration of new literary forms. The tone was set in his review of *The Weary Blues*. Here Cullen took deliberate aim at Hughes's "jazz" poems, which he regarded as "interlopers in the company of the truly beautiful poems in other sections of the book." To Cullen, these poems create a superficial and transporting excitement, like a religious revival meeting, "but when the storm is over, I wonder if the quiet way of communing is not more spiritual for the God-seeking heart; and in the light of reflection I wonder if jazz poems really belong to that dignified company, that select and austere circle of high literary expression which we call poetry."[63] With views like these (echoing those of William Stanley Braithwaite, whom Cullen had come to know well in Cambridge),[64] it is little wonder that Cullen felt Hughes and others were being misled by white critics encouraging a vernacular approach (to Cullen, stereotypical treatments of black life).

In his "Dark Tower" columns, as Gerald Early and Alan R. Shucard have shown, Cullen consistently resisted "racial" poetics and stressed a "respectable," "representative" middle-class approach, showing how concerned he was about displaying the "embarrassing" aspects of the race to white people: "Negroes should be concerned with making good impressions. . . . Every phase of Negro life should not be the white man's concern. The parlor should be large enough for his entertainment and instruction."[65] However, Cullen was never the "dominant" presence in *Opportunity,* let alone in the Harlem Renaissance.[66] In *Opportunity* he represented the "loyal opposition"—a respected minority view, brought on to the staff perhaps because Charles Johnson wanted to give a forum to all perspectives in the period of Du Bois's crescendo of attacks on the "sewer-dwellers."

## "If There Is to Be One, It Will Be Yours": American Drama

Like *The Crisis, Opportunity* expected drama to be a particularly important genre for African American artists, and it continually exhorted black writers to turn their hands to writing plays. "Negro plays" by white writers were frequently held out as inspiration and challenge. In one of its first issues (April 1923), *Opportunity* ran Esther Fulks Scott's "Negroes as Actors in Serious Plays," which focused particularly on Chicago's All-American Theatre Association, which, as we have seen, became known as the Ethiopian Art Theatre under Raymond O'Neil's direction, with Tennessee Anderson as producer. Initially, Fulks Scott relates, the repertory included a mixture of works, mainly by whites, based on "Negro life" as well as classical subjects. The choice of *Salome*—the first play the group produced—was particularly interesting, since it could be regarded as neither "Negro" nor "all-American," but it gave an opportunity to the black actress Evelyn Preer to reinterpret the notorious title character—to the reviewer's delight—as a virtuous religious fanatic who wanted neither to attract nor to dance for Herod, being in love with a man of her own ethnicity. The infamous dance of Salome was therefore made chaste though intense—a subtle retort to theatrical exploitation of black female sexuality. Hinting at the parallelism between biblical and black American historical experiences, the play also enacted a traditional strategy of African American cultural politics.[67]

*Opportunity*'s reviewer drew special attention to the fact that prior to this production Evelyn Preer had been confined to comic parts with the Chicago Ladies Amateur Minstrels, Oscar Micheaux Film Productions, and the Lafayette Players—all black production companies. Members of the *Salome* cast attested to their own changed views of the possibility of "serious" black drama as a result of their experience with O'Neil and blithely thought such drama could be "an ideal means of fostering racial co-operation"; "the so-called race problem could well be solved thru artistic and cultural avenues, giving each group a common interest," as one actress attested.[68] Strangely, the *Opportunity* critic gives barely a mention of Willis Richardson's *The Chip Woman's Fortune*, which served as curtain-raiser for the *Salome* performance.

The ambiguity in "Negro theatre" is prevalent throughout *Opportunity*'s drama criticism. Was it a theater composed of Negro actors? Producing plays on Negro themes? By Negro playwrights?

There is no question but that the ideal would be to have black-run companies performing plays written by black artists and performed by black actors—but *Opportunity* never accepted the definition of "Negro drama" as drama written by and for Negroes. Part of the problem is that the sort of theater the *Opportunity* critics (or the *Crisis* critics, or the *Messenger* critics) wanted to see developed—so-called legitimate theater—had little support within the black community. Furthermore, they complained that few talented black writers were turning their attention to drama. No wonder, when the most promising "serious" dramatic treatments of "Negro life" were met by hostility or simple disinterest. Montgomery Gregory, himself a playwright and founder of the Howard University Players, approvingly summarized Max Reinhardt's statement that "the chief contribution of America to the drama of tomorrow would be its development of Negro folk-drama. But what has been the attitude of the Negro himself? Unqualified opposition to the utilization of his mass life in fiction, in music, or in drama."[69] Warming to his theme, Gregory went on: "What has this attitude meant? It has robbed the race of its birthright for a mess of pottage. It has damned the possibilities of true artistic expression at its very source," and left the entire field of "Negro" literature in the control of white artists.[70]

Invoking the authority of Max Reinhardt to make his point was a significant move on Gregory's part, for Reinhardt was the rage of New York at the time. (He was also, incidentally, the man under whom Robert Edmond Jones had studied in Berlin before helping form the Provincetown Players and importing Reinhardt's concept of "total theatre" to the United States;[71] Jones made his debut with Ridgely Torrence's *Three Plays for a Negro Theatre* in 1917.) In another article based on an interview with Reinhardt, Alain Locke, cofounder with Gregory of the Howard University Players, quoted the director as saying that if he ever tried to do "anything American" he would build it on the musical comedies of the American Negro. This was not exactly what Locke or Charles S. Johnson (who was also present) wanted to hear, but Reinhardt went on to clarify that what he admired was the black genius for "pantomime," the primitive and crucial element of all drama. Though currently "prostituted to farce" and "trite comedy," the distinctively African American technical mastery of the body was the treasure of American drama.

How, Locke and Johnson inquired, could this technical gift be utilized rather than exploited? How avoid its perversion in the face of the American demand for caricature? "Only you can do it, you yourselves," Reinhardt responded. "You must not even try to link up to the drama of the past, to the European drama. That is why there is no American drama as yet. And if there is to be one, it will be yours."[72] Reinhardt's chief interest was in folk drama, so it is not surprising that this is the direction he thought black American drama should take. It was also, of course, the direction Locke, Johnson, and Montgomery Gregory thought it should take, as opposed to stark "propaganda" and "race pride." Their position on this point, as we have seen from an article Locke wrote for *The Crisis* the year before *Opportunity* came into existence, was the occasion for the founding of the Howard University Players when Locke and Gregory split from the NAACP drama committee.[73] Not surprisingly, *Opportunity* generally criticized the "pitfalls of propaganda and moralizing on the one hand and the snares of a false and hollow race pride on the other hand," in the words of Gregory—clearly taking a swipe at several of the cultural arbiters of the NAACP.[74]

As the months went on, *Opportunity* continued to look in vain for the movement it wanted; the plays it most praised were almost exclusively those written by white playwrights. Charles Johnson even dedicated an editorial to the topic in 1927, lamenting that Negro drama had not kept pace with advances in the other literary arts. This disappointment could not be blamed entirely on a lack of audience; the submissions for the magazine's drama prize were mediocre, showing a lack of attention to effective techniques of play construction—a problem *The Crisis* had also noted. In fact, despite the differences between the aesthetic emphases of the magazines, *Opportunity*'s remarks on drama often echo those of *The Crisis*. "The recent plays of Negro life, which include Ridgely Torrence's *Three Plays for a Negro Theatre*, *The Emperor Jones*, *All God's Chillun*, *The No 'Count Boy*, *The Chip Woman's Fortune*, have all with the exception of the last been written by white playwrights," Johnson lamented.[75] Although Willis Richardson, Eloise Bibb Thompson, Frank Wilson, and Eulalie Spence had shown some promise, on the whole Negro writers had not "sensed the possibilities of Negro drama. . . . They have been too ashamed of the material of their own lives to give it artistic portrayal. The new writers [mostly white] are beginning to see these situations and are clothing them in a new beauty. Herein lies the great future of the Negro in drama."[76]

Johnson, Locke, and Gregory were joined by Edwin D. Johnson a year later. The drama by black playwrights, Edwin Johnson charged in 1928, remained mediocre: "The concrete efforts have little if anything to recommend them." Again, the old problem of racial self-defensiveness appeared as the culprit: "The most serious obstacle that the Negro theatre has is that race-conscious specimen of the literati of color that styles itself dramatic critic."[77] Although a few magazines have well-trained editors, Johnson charged, "the most baldly incompetents show themselves in the Negro weeklies"; their "so-called criticism" is "the sheerest sort of twaddle."[78] While noting that *Porgy* had justly been well received by most black critics, he protested the simplistic condemnation of *Lulu Belle* (a play written by Edward Sheldon); none other than James Weldon Johnson had been roundly denounced merely for coming to the play's defense as "a work of art."[79] The *Opportunity* critic accused the black public of cultural antimodernism, arguing that "Negro drama" did not focus more often on "high" society because modern drama in general had broken from Victorian conventions. Johnson's final judgment on the situation for African American drama was bleak indeed: "With self-conscious critics, weak playwrights, and no clientele seriously interested in the theatre, it seems that our excellent actors of color must feed from the hands of the white playmakers for a long time to come."[80]

Edwin Johnson's complaints were seconded by the playwright Eulalie Spence. Like all the writers for *Opportunity,* Spence (though black herself) held that "Negro drama does not of necessity include the work of the Negro dramatist"; rather, it is drama that strives to portray the life of the Negro. Sadly, Negro dramatists capable of accomplishing such portrayal scarcely existed, wrote Spence. The vehicles for the talents of Gilpin, Robeson, Rose McClendon, and Julius Bledsoe were plays by whites. "Some there are who have shuddered distastefully at these plays; been affronted by Paul Green, degraded by DuBose Heyward, and misunderstood by Eugene O'Neill. But ask the Negro artist if he is grateful to these writers. He will tell you. And ask the Negro dramatist what he feels about it. If he is forward-thinking, he will admit that these writers have been a great inspiration; that they have pointed the way and heralded a new dawn."[81] Like Edwin Johnson, Spence lamented that Negro dramatists

had failed to appreciate the need for study and hard work to gain the technical mastery of play-writing; and, like all the *Opportunity* critics, she warned against the conventional protest play, both because of its tendency to fall into outworn patterns and because it was unpalatable to both white and black audiences. Propaganda plays on Negro subjects were not likely to meet with success when even the propaganda plays of John Galsworthy were failing at the box office.

*Opportunity* repeatedly defended "Negro plays" by white artists that would be interrogated today for their complicity with racist ideology. It defended them not merely because they were an improvement upon the blatant racism of earlier drama, nor because any "positive" attention to black life was better than none, but also because the *Opportunity* critics considered the plays of Ridgely Torrence, Eugene O'Neill, DuBose Heyward, and Paul Green to be models for black playwrights to learn from. When David Levering Lewis suggests that "among themselves Harlem's intellectuals had serious doubts about this new wave of white discovery" and argues that "Harlem intellectuals *pretended* they were enthusiastic about the new dramatic and literary themes," he ignores a wealth of evidence and makes two related mistakes.[82] One is to amalgamate distinctly different responses on the part of different black intellectuals to "Negro writing" by whites; the other is to amalgamate different works by white authors—works distinctly differentiated by black intellectuals of the period—into one category. Perhaps Harlem intellectuals were blind to the more subtle shadings of racist ideology; but certainly several of them were not merely pretending to admire, for example, O'Neill's plays. African Americanists today might want to believe that New Negroes were only feigning admiration for *The Emperor Jones, Porgy,* and *In Abraham's Bosom,* but the evidence suggests otherwise—they were either unabashedly attacking these plays or unabashedly praising them. Specifically, contributors for *Opportunity* were not only glorifying them but incisively attacking their critics—a tactic completely unnecessary to a program of pretended enthusiasm meant to win white patronage.

Paul Robeson's "Reflections on O'Neill's Plays," for example, appeared in the December 1924 issue of the magazine, calling *The Emperor Jones* "undoubtedly one of '*the* great plays'—a true classic of the drama, American or otherwise."[83] Robeson regarded *All God's Chillun* as another great play, despite the "ridiculous critical reaction" accorded it by both white and black critics.

When asked whether in the future he would play more "dignified" roles than those he had played in these productions, he responded: "I honestly believe that perhaps never will I portray a nobler type than 'Jim Harris' or a more heroically tragic figure than 'Brutus Jones, Emperor,' not excepting 'Othello.'"[84] Finally, Robeson came to the point so often made in the pages of *Opportunity*, one even made by Du Bois apropos the reception of O'Neill's plays: "The reactions to these two plays among Negroes but point out one of the most serious drawbacks to the development of a true Negro dramatic literature. We are too self-conscious, too afraid of showing all phases of our life,—especially those phases which are of greatest dramatic value. The great mass of our group discourage any member who has the courage to fight these petty prejudices."[85] In addition to Robeson's essay, *Opportunity* reprinted E. A. Carter's review of *All God's Chillun* from *The American Mercury*, printed James Light's "On Producing O'Neill's Play"—obviously as a lesson in stage production—and assigned Eric Walrond to review the play, which he did in a curiously schizophrenic piece, calling it both "another instance of the supreme triumph of art" and "a dull, morbid play."[86] Other *Opportunity* contributors who came to O'Neill's defense, sooner or later, included Sterling Brown and Rudolph Fisher—two authors famously sensitive to white exploitation.[87]

One could go on. Eulalie Spence regretted a poor production of Torrence's *The Rider of Dreams* and contrasted it with the original presentation by the Hapgood Players in 1917, saying the play "will always take its place in every noteworthy collection of Negro plays."[88] Gwendolyn Bennett found Paul Green's *In Abraham's Bosom* worthy of regard as a "powerful tragedy," while an editorial in the June 1927 issue of the magazine expressed enthusiasm for Green's speech at the recent *Opportunity* dinner and gushed, apropos the play that had won him a Pulitzer Prize, "He was the artist who comprehended his materials; who felt the force of tragedy in the lives he portrayed." No wonder that in his remarks at the *Opportunity* gathering, "he found himself, without a single appeal beyond his own sincerity, strangely akin to his audience. Before them was the new South itself, speaking, but strangest of all, seeming to comprehend and to be understood."[89] Here was a model of Johnson's hope for interracial understanding that would nourish a composite national community.

This is not to say that reviewers in *Opportunity* failed to attack literary exploitation and white thirst for the primitive and exotic; but the works they attacked along these lines were not the works of Torrence, O'Neill, and Green in drama, or of Waldo Frank, Julia Peterkin, and DuBose Heyward in fiction. The works they attacked along these lines were ones we never even hear of today, works of a different order, such as Roark Bradford's *This Side of Jordan*, T. Bower Campbell's *Black Sadie*, Lily Young Cohen's *Lost Spirituals*, Hugh Wiley's *Lily*, Vera Caspary's *The White Girl*, William Seabrook's *Magic Island*, and the stories of Octavus Roy Cohen. Moreover, they did not single out white exploiters; they also lamented inappropriate and "degrading" uses of the spirituals by "Negro revues," black-directed and -produced shows deriving from the black blackface minstrel show tradition.

These were the shows, ironically, that a fairly large black public *would* support. Obviously, something was happening in these shows to which the *Opportunity* critics, in their search for "art theatre," were deaf and blind. At the same time, in proposing "Negro plays" for the "legitimate stage," directors ran into a kind of black resistance *Opportunity* tried to combat. Indeed, when Rowena Woodham Jelliffe first became associated with a "Negro Little Theatre group" in 1920, according to her article of 1928, "both actors and audience were emphatically opposed to Negro plays and thought them highly degrading to their race."[90] The actors all wanted to play heroic leading roles, and none would play a character of "lowly state." They would play a villain only if he was well dressed and not black.[91] The audience demanded comedies, whereas the actors wanted to present serious drama. Gradually they warmed to the idea of presenting a play based on "Negro life," but the majority would only accede to a theater of propaganda. Hence the group—the Gilpin Players of Cleveland—stuck chiefly to European drama in their early years. Finally, in 1924, after an inspirational visit from Charles Gilpin (who was performing *The Emperor Jones* in Cleveland), they tried two "Negro plays"—Ridgely Torrence's *Granny Maumee*, followed by Willis Richardson's *Compromise*. Subsequently, they were happiest doing "Negro plays," and when they moved into their own building they gave it the Swahili name Karamu House and decorated it with African designs. Rowena Jelliffe, the white director, thus saw her aims accomplished: "It has been my fundamental purpose . . . to capture, preserve and develop the dramatic qualities peculiar to the Negro race. I have tried always to avoid the use of the proverbial trick bag of the white theatrical world. We strive to develop a sound dramatic technique which shall strengthen us without subduing us; which shall give us freer mediums through which to make our contributions to the Nation's drama.'"[92]

Jelliffe's personal history deserves a further gloss here.[93] Recent graduate students at the University of Chicago, Rowena and Russell Jelliffe had had ambitions of founding a cultural center on the order of Hull House when they moved to Cleveland in the early teens, and in 1915 they befriended Langston Hughes. He found solace at their home during a particularly lonely period of his adolescence, when he was living alone in a rooming house. He spent countless hours reading at the Jelliffes' during his high school years, and shared his first poems with them at a time when his mother scorned his poetic ambitions. Rowena Jelliffe was probably the first person with whom he shared "When Sue Wears Red," his first "racial" poem. He also became one of the first teachers at the Jelliffes' settlement house and later returned to work with the Gilpin Players. Rowena Jelliffe, as Arnold Rampersad writes, "staged most of [Hughes's] plays in the thirties"—over the objections of middle-class African Americans, who considered them "Awful."[94] The resemblance between his and Rowena Jelliffe's ideas about black drama is, then, more than coincidental.

Jelliffe's reasons for believing in "Negro drama" fit the overall *Opportunity* line, recalling Reinhardt's observations. The chief talent the Negro actor brings to the stage is "his peculiar quality of motorness, his extraordinary body expressiveness," followed by his "sense of rhythm" as evidenced in both movement and diction, and his "vitality." But aside from the actor's distinctive attributes are the dramatic qualities inherent in black vernacular expression. "The picture building quality of Negro dialect, its rhythmic rise and fall, the earthy quality of Negro folk life," are the prime advantages of black drama. Jelliffe concludes that the greatest Negro drama will be written and produced by Negroes themselves, and that its possibilities have yet to be fully explored.[95] And yet by the end of 1928, the majority of "Negro plays" the Gilpin Players had presented were white-authored.[96]

What the gamut of *Opportunity* drama criticism shows us is that interest in "folk drama" was anything but a decisive attempt on the part of black artists to make a clean break from white American modernism. "Native" white modernists, in alliance with those black intellectuals who were followers of the European-American modernist transformation, tried their damnedest, as they saw it, to awaken African Americans to the riches of their folk heritage. Nor were their attempts motivated mainly by the vogue of Freud (who is not mentioned once) or a fascination with the primitive and exotic. Rather, they were motivated by a decisive reinterpretation and reevaluation of the inherent theatrical qualities of black vernacular speech and distinctively black traditions of mime—inverting the values attached to these qualities in the minstrel show to make them vehicles of "classical" tragedy—and by a Herderian romanticization of the folk inspired chiefly by the successes of the Abbey Theatre and the Moscow Art Players in the years immediately preceding the "Negro renaissance." These are the same theater groups that had inspired Edward Sheldon, Ridgely Torrence, George Cram Cook, Susan Glaspell, Floyd Dell, Robert Edmond Jones, and others to fulfill the need for an American "native stage for native plays," to prove that "the finest culture is a possibility of democracy."[97]

## Fictions of Race

I do not mean to suggest that *Opportunity* critics were blind to the stereotypes that could be found in much white "Negro" literature, particularly fiction, and in much European-American criticism of African American writing. Charles S. Johnson felt that even the most "sympathetic" white authors worked at a great disadvantage in treating "Negro themes," as they had "never yet been wholly admitted to the privacy of Negro thots."[98] Yet Johnson clearly felt that African American authors must learn aspects of technical mastery from the examples of white authors, and the works he thought exemplary were those of the native realists; hence the short story judges for the first *Opportunity* literary contest, for example, were Blanche Colton Williams, Carl Van Doren, Zona Gale, Fannie Hurst, Robert Hobart Davis, Dorothy Canfield Fisher, Edna Worthley Underwood, Alain Locke, and Dorothy Scarborough. There was never much question that the great literature about the Negro would be written by African Americans themselves according to aesthetic criteria they would develop, but these criteria could only be formulated gradually; in the meantime, *Opportunity* criticism would define certain parameters of success, more often than not through the criticism of fiction by white authors. *Opportunity* reviewers could be scathing in their denunciation of exploitation by the Irvin Cobbs and Octavus Roy Cohens; and they could provide just critiques of such "well-meaning" efforts as Clement Wood's novel *Nigger*. The criticism of fiction reveals a particularly nuanced reading of contemporary racial writing. Eric Walrond, for example, liked to thumb his nose at the "philistines" and polemicists, in the context of recommending such novels as Ronald Firbank's *Prancing Nigger*, "a work of haunting, compelling beauty."[99] A native of Panama, Walrond finds the novel remarkable for its evocation of the lush beauty of the Caribbean islands, defending the book against the anticipated criticism of those who will find "its content, like its title, . . . a gesture of opprobrium." Apparently to its credit, in the reviewer's eyes, the book makes no overt statement against the British colonial system. Its characters, to Walrond, are absolutely authentic. Most remarkably, the novelist has for once captured the quality of West Indian humor while avoiding minstrel show stereotypes—"It is a delicate, subtle, sophisticated, almost Rabelaisian touch with which 'Prancing Nigger' is consistently shot through. Sometimes it is almost breathtaking."[100] Walrond, an admirer of Van Vechten's preciosity and near-decadence, liked to strike the pose of the apolitical, bohemian aesthete.

Charles S. Johnson, on the other hand, was more sober and politically judgmental. He could appreciate the attempt in Clement Wood's *Nigger* to avoid the "pit falls of over sentimentality one way or the other" while critiquing its attempt to include every form of degrading misfortune in the life of one black family, and its suggestion that the main activity of the African American fraternal lodge was the hatching of rebellions. Lightened by occasional attempts at humor that only rehash old jokes about the Negro, *Nigger* in Johnson's estimation suffers from its author's lack of true intimacy with black life: "His sympathies have carried him a long way, but he could not make his characters live, feel, think and act"—except in frequently stereotypical ways. And yet Johnson ultimately judges the novel "serious, honest, and tremendously impressive—a real tragedy."[101] Apparently he was willing to discount the novel's sins in the interest of promoting it as a "step forward," addressing controversial racial issues in a way that was helping to discredit earlier and even contemporary types of exploitative racist fiction. He even published work by Wood in *Opportunity* and chose him to chair the poetry selection committee for the *Opportunity* awards in literature.

Further evidence of Johnson's taste can be found in his review of Walter White's *The Fire in the Flint,* which he characterizes as the sort of book only an African American could write: "Even the magnificent effort of Clement Wood, despite its earnestness, failed to capture the essense [*sic*] so familiar to Negroes, so incomprehensible to others."[102] Johnson stresses fidelity to the experiences of educated blacks in the South and realistic characterization; in this respect *The Fire in the Flint* is a "trailblazer" like Upton Sinclair's *The Jungle,* "an epoch marker of sociologic interest." When the novel stumbles, it does so through heavy-handed treatment of character types the author cannot allow himself to treat understandingly: "The white mind could be made more intelligible. They are mad men, most of them. Certainly this conduct has some justification in their own minds even if irrational and unsound."[103] Yet as a tragedy breaking the tradition of Southern apologetics, the work marks a new standard—to be followed, Johnson hopes, by realistic fiction of the "lower classes": "There is yet even more poignant tragedy in the lives of the droning millions who are ground down and broken and who are not permitted even the escape of death."[104]

In stark contrast to Johnson's method, but similarly indulgent to white racial fiction, is Eunice Roberta Hunton's rhapsodic review of Waldo Frank's *Holiday,* written in the same overwrought style as the novel itself: "It isn't poetic prose. It is sheer poetry—poetry running riot, an epic too rich in beauty, hate, and tears to be held in the bonds of meter and form; now singing, now wailing itself to its tragic close thru chapters painted clear by an author who has indeed probed America's open sore and dipped his pen in its blood, cleansed somewhat of its putridness by kind understanding."[105] Hunton, a frequent contributor to *Opportunity,* finds *Holiday* brilliant both as art and as social analysis, coming up short only in its hopelessness, its inability to see beyond the division between the races to their violent and passionate interrelationship: "Yes, there is black and white but between there is red, the red of rivers of blood, of red hot iron, of glowing coals and barbarous fires, and too, oh God, the red of flaming passion!"[106] This orgiastic closing exclamation seems oddly blind to the fact that Frank's whole novel focuses upon precisely this suppressed interracial blood-kinship, a focus that seems even to have inspired Hunton's own red vision. Perhaps she wanted a more "positive" denouement.

Waldo Frank's own review of Eric Walrond's *Tropic Death,* beautifully featured on one page of *Opportunity* under the title "In Our American Language," deserves some comment here. Walrond was one of those writers most given to what might be called exoticism, a feature white intellectuals, it has been assumed, always demanded in black fiction. Yet the "exoticism" in *Tropic Death* is exactly what Waldo Frank does not like: "I find here taints of what I might call the *Vanity Fair* school: cleverisms, forcedness, devotions to brash effects for their own sake, which bungling American writers have tried to naturalize from the sophisticated schools of France and England."[107] The "chief feature of interest and importance" in the work, for Frank, is its language—for Walrond is recognizably a modern New World writer, developing a new language like other authors of the Americas, whatever their ethnic ancestry may be: "How can I make clear that the basis of this book—the very substance of its language—relates it to Poe, Melville, Thoreau even—and to their contemporary successors: excludes it radically, moreover, from the noble and long lineage of English literary prose?"[108]

He does not suggest that Walrond should adopt the language of white American writers, only that, like them, he should develop his art as one would labor in native ground with the tools at hand: "Perhaps one of your ancestors was a Caribbean peasant. When he wielded the hoe or the knife, did he not grasp it loose in his brown hand? Do you likewise with your language. . . . I prophecy that forthway a miracle will happen. Your story will open, too. It will achieve overtones, undertones, vistas, dimensions—which in this book it lacks."[109] The review is redolent of Frank's usual mistiness, presumptuousness, and prophetic condescension, but it is virtually the opposite of a counsel to exotic primitivism. And it is quite in line with the overall emphasis in *Opportunity* upon vernacular experimentation with literary language, connected with the drive to realize "native" American life in fiction.

Critics for *Opportunity* repeatedly hailed a decisive change in "Negro portraiture" even while acknowledging the great disadvantages of white writers in this area. The general argument was that mastery of the techniques and social analysis required by fiction would grow slowly; white novelists would provide models initially, and gradually black authors would learn from and finally surpass them in fiction about black life. Sterling Brown's "The New Secession—A Review" makes explicit the hopes raised among New Negro au-

thors by the realist fiction of the New South, and suggests that this fiction provided models of technical experimentation for black writers themselves. Ostensibly a review of Julia Peterkin's *Black April,* Brown's piece ends up being a more general commentary on the "new" Southern white writers' secession from their "Bourbon" predecessors: "Ambrose Gonzales helped start it, DuBose Heyward continued it. And now Julia Peterkin shows herself of their ilk. . . . It is one of the paradoxes of history that this should be so; that North Carolina, with Odum, Johnson, and Paul Green; and that South Carolina with these capable writers; should at last be recognizing in the Negro what Synge has seen in Aran Islanders, Gorki in Russian peasants, and Masefield and Gibson in the lowly folk of England."[110] One of the most influential critics of black stereotypes in the white American literary tradition, Brown finds apparently no primitivism and exoticism in this new realism; what stands out for Brown is the turn to the vernacular and "indigenous."

In this respect Brown claims Peterkin as a model for African American authors. She has shown the truth of Wordsworth's belief in going back to the "soil," as black writers ought to do, "digging our roots deeply therein. . . . If we do decide to try this, there could be few better mentors than Julia Peterkin."[111] Brown differentiates Peterkin's fiction from that of Sherwood Anderson, Carl Van Vechten (whose *Nigger Heaven* he detested), and Walter White, likening it to Toomer's *Cane.* Her limning of the folk is nearly flawless: "Where does she get this uncanny insight into the ways of our folk; their superstitions, their speech, the 'rhythm' of their lives; she of such entirely different beliefs, speech, rhythm."[112] Those elements that Brown does find unlikely are interesting in view of recent fiction by black women integrating folk spirituality and superstition into the lives of college-educated urban heroines: "Joy, who has been away to college comes back and her first words swing into the old Gullah dialect, and her later acts show an ineradicable faith in folklore. To the reviewer it would seem more likely to flaunt some of her newly acquired words as well as her red satin." Moreover, "the coincidence of Zeda's curse and April's gangrene is a bit too fortuitous"—suggesting that the curse really *worked.* After Toni Morrison's *Beloved,* Alice Walker's *The Temple of My Familiar,* and especially Gloria Naylor's *Mama Day,* the grounds of Brown's criticism seem curiously ironic. Again, however, Brown feels the need to defend *Black April* against the objections of black middle-class "philistines" who will accuse Peterkin (as Du Bois was doing) of exploiting old stereotypes: "Those who read into it what is not there, namely propaganda against the Negro, because the characters are not all 'successes'; will alas, have to be of that opinion still. But that Julia Peterkin would consider illegitimacy to be Negroid; betrays scant reading—and insults a writer as sane as she is brilliant."[113] In his "Dark Tower" column for the same issue of *Opportunity*, Countee Cullen likewise praised the volume and upbraided those who had criticized it. But Cullen and Brown may have overestimated black resistance to the book; a report in *Opportunity* two years later noted that Peterkin's next novel, *Scarlet Sister Mary,* was one of the two most popular books at the 135th Street branch of the New York Public Library, the hub of "literary" Harlem.

The criticism in *Opportunity* shows unmistakably that texts interpreted by university professors today as continuous with plantation tradition read as major disruptions of that tradition to New Negro writers of the 1920s, *particularly* to those intent on developing a "Negro aesthetic" from vernacular resources. The new understanding on the part of white writers confirmed Charles Johnson's faith in fiction's potential to undermine the walls of "mutual ignorance and prejudice, hatred and fear" which came between the races in America. Again, it was "native modernism" developing in the wake of the work of black reformers such as Booker T. Washington and W. E. B. Du Bois that Johnson perceived as the impetus behind the new understanding. But this "understanding" should also, according to *Opportunity* critics, be an inspiration to *self*-understanding on the part of African American authors and audiences.

In "Our Literary Audience," for example, Sterling Brown offers no apology for the works of O'Neill, Peterkin, Green, and Heyward on the basis that they had done pretty well for "crackers"; he argues instead that Peterkin's and Heyward's particular uses of dialect in fiction, for example, were expanding the possibilities of black fictional form and technique, breaking out of the conventional limitation to humor and pathos.[114] These writers were helping show the way to a revitalization of the African American cultural tradition by inspiring a new regard for the culture of the "lowly": "But there is more to lowliness than 'lowness.' If we have eyes to see, and willingness to see, we might be able to find in Mamba, an astute heroism, in Hagar a heartbreaking courage, in Porgy, a nobility, and in E. C. L. Adams' Scrip

and Tad, a shrewd, philosophical irony. And all of these qualities we need, just now, to see in our group."[115] Readers who object to these fictional characters, Brown suggests, are "ashamed of being Negroes" and lack "mental bravery"—like many Irish readers of Bernard Shaw—and their shame and timidity threatens to nip in the bud the black literary renaissance as exemplified by Langston Hughes, Jean Toomer, and George Schuyler (not to mention Sterling Brown, whose *Southern Road* would appear two years later). Criticism of these New Negroes' work, in Brown's view, was of a piece with the criticism of Heyward and Peterkin.

Alain Locke thought *Scarlet Sister Mary* destined to become a classic, surpassing "surface realism" to go down "deep to the bone and marrow of life" and to strike "living truth and vital spirituality. It is a tragedy to record that only one or two Negro writers of prose have found the depth of analysis or the penetration of spirit which characterized DuBose Heyward's 'Porgy,' or which characterizes Mrs. Peterkin's 'Scarlet Sister Mary.'"[116] His retrospective review of the literature of 1928 ranked the novel's publication with that of McKay's *Home to Harlem* and Rudolph Fisher's *Walls of Jericho* as one of the "three really important events" of the year. "An appraisal of the outstanding creative achievement in fiction a year ago would not have given us a majority on the Negro side. That in itself reflects a solid gain, . . . for no movement can be a fad from the inside."[117] While he does not base his discriminations on the racial identities of authors, Locke thus recognizes the absolute necessity of a self-determining movement with its own aesthetic and high standards of judgment. The same issue in which Locke lauded *Scarlet Sister Mary* as a classic carried his scathing review of William Seabrook's *Magic Island,* "the product of the intersection of two rapid streams of contemporary interest and taste,—the fad for things Negro and the cult of the primitive."[118]

*Opportunity* critics, while often adhering to the concept of a New Negro aesthetic, lamented that black writers, by the late 1920s, were not being held to the same standards of excellence as white authors; much mediocre work was being unduly praised and too easily accepted for publication.[119] As a result, writers on "Negro themes" were not being forced to do their best and were acceding to facile exploitation of temporary (white folks') fascinations. Eunice Hunton Carter wrote in 1929, "The more quickly the novelty of the Negro theme wears off and publishers and critics begin to exact from Negro writers that same high standard which they do from others, the more quickly may we expect something better from writers like Wallace Thurman who are capable of things infinitely better than they give."[120] To "win a hearing," Alain Locke acknowledged, the "true" Negro artists had had to tolerate exploitation and endure some "forcing" of meager talent—"There is as much spiritual bondage in these things as there ever was material bondage in slavery"—but the time of true critical appraisal was near: "Certainly the Negro artist must point the way when this significant moment comes, and establish the values by which Negro literature and art are to be permanently gauged after the fluctuating experimentalism of the last few years."[121] Locke lamented that the "Negrophile movement" had swelled to a fad by 1929, and looked forward to the inevitable devaluing of "inflated stock" that would make it possible to discriminate between the "fair-weather friends and true supporters, the stock-brokers and the real productive talents"[122]—prophetic metaphors for that fateful year!

Locke (like Theophilus Lewis in *The Messenger* and H. L. Mencken in *American Mercury*) noted that black fiction was developing more slowly than black poetry, "for creative fiction involves one additional factor of cultural maturity,—the art of social analysis and criticism."[123] The statement exemplifies the approach to fiction taken in *Opportunity* generally, an approach largely shaped by early twentieth-century American realism and naturalism in the wake of Dreiser—whose *An American Tragedy,* by the way, was the most popular book at the Harlem branch of the New York Public Library in November 1926, according to an *Opportunity* report.[124] In *Home to Harlem,* Locke found "the peculiar and persistent quality of Negro peasant life transposed to the city and the modern mode, but still vibrant with a clean folkiness of the soil instead of the decadent muck of the city-gutter." Rudolph Fisher's *Walls of Jericho,* on the other hand, would stand "as the answer to the charge that the Negro artist is not yet ripe for social criticism or balanced in social perspective" (a charge Locke implicitly accepted with regard to earlier black fiction generally!).[125] In fact, in the same article Locke criticizes Du Bois's *Dark Princess* for falling "an artistic victim to its own propagandist ambushes."

In contrast, Nella Larsen's *Quicksand* "is truly a social document of importance." While Locke shares Du Bois's admiration for this novel, his interpretation markedly differs from the *Crisis* editor's. Larsen, in Locke's astute reading, departs from typical renditions of the "tragic mulatto"

theme by focusing on "the problem of divided social loyalties and the issues of the conflict of cultures" rather than the "grim tragedy of blood and fateful heredity." In other words, while subverting racial essentialism Larsen explores the force of social constructions of racial identity and the conflicts deriving from the fact that not everyone "belongs" to just one "race."[126] *Quicksand* reveals the contradictions inherent in the binarism of American racial discourse.

Expectations similar to Locke's inform Gwendolyn Bennett's review of *Plum Bun* by Jessie Fauset. Bennett emphasizes the working through of social issues surrounding constructions of personal identity in this novel of passing. The critical way in which these issues affect "mixed-bloods" helps foreground the operation of "race" in American culture generally. And if the thematic importance of the novel derives from its social analysis, its specific texture derives from the author's fidelity to her personal experience of life in particular places. Fauset's strength lies in the precision of her scenes depicting middle-class African American home life in Philadelphia; her weaknesses show in her attempts to produce more "cosmopolitan" scenes in New York.[127] Bennett's evaluation thus reveals again a major division in New Negro fiction, based not on whether one should treat "high" or "low" class life but on attitude and perspective, particularly concerning cross-cultural relationships.

In her review of a decidedly different novel—Claude McKay's *Banjo*—Bennett again stresses the author's intimacy with the experiences and styles of life he successfully depicts. Rather than playing his novel off against those of Jessie Fauset, the reviewer praises it—as she did *Plum Bun*—for its "priceless observations" about aspects of black life in a particular, little-known context. "I wondered as I read the book how the people who will criticize it from a moral standpoint would have written a novel around Marseilles. But I suppose the answer to that is that one should not choose Marseilles for a subject under any circumstances."[128] Bennett does not feel that McKay panders to primitivist delectations: "To him this tale was life as he saw it about him in Marseilles. There is no snigger of wrong emphasis in his discussion of the most taboo subject."[129]

The criticism of critics of "bourgeois" black fiction was undertaken on the same grounds of social "realism" as Bennett's critique of McKay's fiction. Hence, in a review of *Passing* immediately following Bennett's of *Banjo,* Mary Fleming Labaree (a white critic and contributor to the *Saturday*

*Review*) writes: "There is no layer or segment of humanity that is *verboten* to the maker of novels, if he be an honest workman. And the honest reader need not flinch from honest fact or honest interpretation of any phase of life. Yet certain literary somebodies and other literary nobodies would have us believe that only life in the raw or bloody-rare is life at all and worth writing up. The pity of it!—if 'Walls of Jericho' and 'Home to Harlem' perched upon our bookshelves with 'Plum Bun' and 'Passing' nowhere to be seen."[130] Labaree—a good friend of Langston Hughes, who studied the social sciences under her husband at Lincoln[131]—praises Larsen's ability to avoid melodrama while exploding "the stupid Nordic complex and its unlovely sequelae" through subtle, precise development of character and social interaction. Regretting that the novel falls short of "greatness," Labaree hopes Larsen will take her time in her next effort and "give the world its needed epic of racial interaction between thinking members of the American social order belonging to both African and European stocks."[132] Labaree dismisses interest in primitivism and exoticism, looking instead for fidelity to "native" life. This aesthetic preference is connected with a kind of social philosophy. The exploration of otherness in novels of social analysis trains self-understanding and expands the range of human solidarity: "Doctors, lawyers, men of affairs, their wives and daughters are neither less valuable nor less richly human members of society than jazz boys and girls, roustabouts and drunks—though it takes a more gifted, understanding and highly experienced artist to make them breathe and move and speak so that we know them for what they really are, so that we ourselves breathing, moving and speaking with them, come to perceive more clearly what we ourselves really are—of one blood with them and all humanity."[133] The statement epitomizes the criteria for black fiction *Opportunity* generally stressed, whether promoting literature of the "folk" or of the "bourgeoisie." It is of a piece with Charles S. Johnson's personal philosophy.

Of a piece with that philosophy, too (though appearing after Johnson's departure), is Sterling Brown's laudatory review of Langston Hughes's first novel, *Not Without Laughter*: "Tolerant, humane, and wise in the ways of mortals, he has revealed beauty where too many of us, dazzled by false lights, are unable to see it."[134] Brown admires the "simplicity" and accessibility of the story along with its fidelity to social relations and sensitive characterizations, products of Hughes's ability to identify sympathetically with different personalities. The book falters, in fact, only through Hughes's failure to sympathize with the "bourgeois" worshiper of white folks' ways, Tempy; the result is unconvincing caricature in the portrait of this too easily dismissed "type." Lack of sympathy effects the erasure of otherness through caricature as surely as does the *premature*, socially naïve leap to human "universals." It is interesting to note Brown's association of realistic characterization and social awareness with "universality," for here universality signifies not the erasure of difference but a counterforce to its exploitation as the exotic:

> Excepting Tempy, who to the reviewer seems slightly caricatured, all of the characters are completely convincing. There is a universality about them. They have, of course peculiar problems as Negroes. Harriet, for instance, hates all whites, with reason. But they have even more the problems that are universally human. Our author does not exploit either local color, or race. He has selected an interesting family and has told us candidly, unembitteredly, poetically of their joy lightened and sorrow laden life.[135]

By "universality" I take it that Brown is attempting to define human mutuality as against racial essentialism, rather than a category effacing historical particularity. The same "universality" typifies the "laughing to keep from crying" motif of the blues that imbues the entire work with authenticity in its quiet blending of tragedy and comedy—that is, a distinctive aspect of African American expression that is accessible to all who read in "sympathy." Through such fiction, and such reading, is the realm of solidarity expanded, enriched, articulated with ever-increasing precision.

Charles S. Johnson's rationale for the *Opportunity* literary contests reveals the purpose behind his impressive labors in service of a "New Negro aesthetic." In a deliberate statement of that rationale, he stressed the

> extreme usefulness for the cause of inter-racial good-will as well as racial culture and American literature in interpreting the life and longings and emotional experiences of the Negro people to their shrinking and spiritually alien neighbors; of flushing old festers of hate and disgruntlement by becoming triumphantly articulate; of forcing the interest and kindred feeling of the rest of the world by sheer force of the humanness and beauty of one's own story. . . . There is an opportunity now for Negroes themselves to replace their outworn representations in fiction faithfully and incidentally to make themselves better understood.[136]

Johnson added that he particularly wanted the contests "to stimulate and foster a type of writing by Negroes which shakes itself free of deliberate propaganda and protest."[137] What is remarkable about Johnson's work is not only the coherence of his aesthetic, sociological, and philosophical positions, but also his success in bringing diverse artists and critics together into a community of discourse that expressed his vision across a broad array of genres and racial as well as class positions. While he fostered the growth of a "Negro aesthetic" in literature, he did so with the understanding that it was an aspect of the development of an American literature—central, indeed, to the development of such a literature. The Negro aesthetic, moreover, was neither an extension of a *hermetic* tradition nor a growth out of some organic racial truth. African American literature would not tear aside distorting veils to the Real reality but would make a cultural reality out of the beauty of familiar things.

In 1928 Johnson resigned from the Urban League to head the department of social sciences at Fisk—in part, apparently, because of financial difficulties that were forcing the Urban League to reconsider *Opportunity*'s role. After his departure, *Opportunity*'s connection with cultural affairs declined considerably, although Alain Locke would continue to express the critical orientation of *Opportunity* throughout the 1930s and Sterling Brown made some crucial contributions. Together with Du Bois's disaffection with the Harlem Renaissance artists, Johnson's departure from the magazine was a severe loss; yet in the few years of his editorship, *Opportunity* had an impact out of all proportion to its circulation. To put it another way, it achieved a critical mass the force of which can be detected throughout important sectors of the American literary field of the 1920s and 1930s, creating new spaces and shaping new vectors of power for the development of African American culture, for the "Americanization" of the United States.

## Notes

1. Nancy J. Weiss, *The National Urban League, 1910-1940* (New York: Oxford University Press, 1974), 10. The following discussion of the origins of the Urban League derives from Weiss's authoritative study. Unfortunately, Weiss does not devote much attention to *Opportunity*.

2. Ibid., 70.

3. Quoted in ibid., 64.

4. Ibid., 66.

5. Ibid., 67-69.

6. Zora Neale Hurston, *Dust Tracks on a Road* (1942; rpt. Philadelphia: Arno Press, 1969), 175-176.

7. Langston Hughes, *The Big Sea* (1940; rpt. New York: Hill & Wang, 1963), 218.

8. Arna Bontemps, *100 Years of Negro Freedom* (New York: Dodd, Mead, 1961), 229.

9. The best discussion of Johnson so far is Patrick J. Gilpin's "Charles S. Johnson: Entrepreneur of the Harlem Renaissance," in *The Harlem Renaissance Remembered,* ed. Arna Bontemps (New York: Dodd, Mead, 1972), 215-246. However, Gilpin focuses on Johnson's organization of dinners and literary contests rather than showing the connection between his philosophy and the aesthetic criticism in the magazine. Another study focusing on the *Crisis* and *Opportunity* contests is Adell P. Austin's "The *Opportunity* and *Crisis* Literary Contests, 1924-27," *CLA Journal* 32 (1988): 235-246. I have been unable to locate scholarship analyzing in any depth or comprehensiveness the *criticism* Johnson published in *Opportunity,* or any careful study of his philosophy and aesthetics.

10. David Levering Lewis, *When Harlem Was in Vogue* (New York: Knopf, 1981), 90.

11. Charles S. Johnson, "Spiritual Autobiography," box 144, folder 1, Charles S. Johnson Papers, Fisk University Library.

12. Martin Bulmer, *The Chicago School of Sociology: Institutionalization, Diversity, and the Rise of Sociological Research* (Chicago: University of Chicago Press, 1984), 93.

13. Robert E. Park, "Education in Its Relation to the Conflict and Fusion of Cultures" (1918), in Park, *Race and Culture* (Glencoe, Ill.: Free Press, 1950), 266.

14. Leslie A. White, quoted in Fred H. Matthews, *Quest for an American Sociology: Robert E. Park and the Chicago School* (Montreal: McGill-Queen's University Press, 1977), 108.

15. *Opportunity* 1 (1923): 355.

16. Robert E. Park, "Negro Race Consciousness as Reflected in Race Literature" (1923), in *Race and Culture,* 284, 300.

17. Charles S. Johnson, "Social Assimilation Defined," typescript, box 173, folder 25, Charles S. Johnson Papers.

18. Charles S. Johnson, "A Chapel Talk to the Students of Fisk University" (17 October 1928), p. 14, box 158, folder 23, Charles S. Johnson Papers.

19. Johnson, "Social Assimilation Defined." Like the early Du Bois, Park hung on to racialist ideas about the differing "geniuses" of the races. The "innate traits" of a people, Park suspected, led to modifications of traditions "transmitted" to them through contact with others. Cultural "assimilation," it follows, is always incomplete, for the "deep structure" of a culture may remain intact despite extensive borrowing. (His thought on this subject is much like Horace Kallen's initial belief in each race's "psychophysical inheritance" and Du Bois's and Locke's ideas about "temperamental" distinctions between races.) While the external trappings of societies may be quickly exchanged, the sentiments, attitudes, aims, and ideals of a group are very slow to be adopted or transmitted.

Park is perhaps best known to students of African American literature for writing in 1918 that although the "racial temperament" of the Negro had changed as a result of encounters with whites and the influence of slavery, it consists of "a few elementary but distinctive characteristics, determined by physical organizations and transmitted biologically. These characteristics manifest themselves in a genial, sunny, and social disposition, in an interest and attachment to external, physical things rather than to subjective states and objects of introspection; in a disposition for expression rather than enterprise and action" ("Education in Its Relation to the Conflict and Fusion of Cultures," 280). Such temperamental characteristics, one gathers, would determine the Negro's chief contributions to American civilization: "The Negro is, by natural disposition, neither an intellectual nor an idealist, like the Jew; nor a brooding introspective, like the East African; nor a pioneer and frontiersman, like the Anglo-Saxon. He is primarily an artist, loving life for its own sake. His *metier* is expression rather than action. He is, so to speak, the lady among the races" (ibid.). Despite its racism and sexism, this hypothesis (which Park later repudiated) implies the Negro's special "temperamental" advantage for playing the most powerful role in American expressive culture—a belief also held by Alain Locke, W. E. B. Du Bois, and Charles S. Johnson.

20. Johnson, typescript, untitled piece on Negro literature. This is a review, clearly of the 1920s, of ten books concerning the Negro, including Howard Odom's *Rainbow 'Round My Shoulder*. Box 167, folder 30, Charles S. Johnson Papers.

21. Johnson, "A Chapel Talk to the Students of Fisk University," p. 11, 17 October 1928, box 158, folder 23, Charles S. Johnson Papers.

22. Ibid., 14.

23. Ibid., 15.

24. Ibid., 13.

25. Ibid., 12.

26. Ibid.

27. Charles S. Johnson, "The Social Philosophy of Booker T. Washington," *Opportunity* 6 (1928): 105.

28. Charles S. Johnson, "Can There Be a Separate Negro Culture?" Address at the Swarthmore Race Relations Institute (1939), box 158, folder 14, Charles S. Johnson Papers.

29. "Social Assimilation Defined," n.p.

30. "The Social Philosophy of Booker T. Washington," 102.

31. Ibid., 115.

32. Ibid.

33. "Welcome the New South—A Review," *Opportunity* 4 (1926): 374-375.

34. John W. Work, "Negro Folk Song," *Opportunity* 1 (1923): 292.

35. Ibid., 293, 293-294.

36. Ibid., 294.

37. Laurence Buermeyer, "The Negro Spirituals and American Art," *Opportunity* 4 (1926): 158-159.

38. Ibid., 159.

39. B. A. Botkin, "Self-Portraiture and Social Criticism in Negro Folk-Song," *Opportunity* 5 (1927): 41.

40. Ibid.

41. Ibid., 42.

42. Botkin, a professor of English at the University of Oklahoma, would later found *Folk-Say,* a journal focusing on regional and multiethnic folk or folk-derived literature (in which some of Sterling Brown's poems first appeared). During the depression he became folklore editor of the Federal Writers' Project and President of the Joint Committee on Folk Arts of the WPA; upon his accession to the editorship at the Writers' Project, he and Sterling Brown (whom he brought on as his assistant) redesigned the interviewers' questionaires for the collection of ex-slave narratives throughout the South and pushed to have African Americans do the interviewing. See Jerre Mangione, *The Dream and the Deal: The Federal Writers' Project, 1935-1943* (Boston: Little, Brown, 1972), 263-270, 276; and Joanne V. Gabbin, *Sterling A. Brown: Building the Black Aesthetic Tradition* (Westport, Conn.: Greenwood Press, 1985), 75.

43. Unsigned editorial, "Jazz," *Opportunity* 3 (1925): 132-133.

44. Alain Locke, "1928: A Retrospective Review," *Opportunity* 7 (1929): 11.

45. Alain Locke, "A Note on African Art," *Opportunity* 2 (1924): 138. My emphasis.

46. Ibid.

47. Ibid., 136.

48. Ibid.

49. Nathan Irvin Huggins, *Harlem Renaissance* (New York: Oxford University Press, 1971), 187.

50. Paul Guillaume, "African Art at the Barnes Foundation," *Opportunity* 2 (1924): 141. See also the editorial in the same issue of *Opportunity,* "Dr. Barnes," 133.

51. See, for example, the editorial "Some Perils of the 'Renaissance,'" *Opportunity* 5 (1927): 68.

52. Leon Whipple, "Letters and Life," *Survey* 56 (1926): 517.

53. Joseph Auslander, "Sermon Sagas," *Opportunity* 5 (1927): 274.

54. Ibid.

55. Ibid., 275.

56. Ibid., 274.

57. Ibid., 275.

58. Margaret Larkin, "A Poet for the People—A Review," *Opportunity* 5 (1927): 84.

59. Ibid.

60. Robert T. Kerlin, "Singers of New Songs," *Opportunity* 4 (1926): 164. My emphasis.

61. Kerlin was fired in 1921 from Virginia Military Institute for an open letter published in *The Nation* protesting charges brought against Negro "insurrectionists" who had merely sought to defend themselves against armed whites. Hughes took a course called "The Art of

Poetry" from Kerlin (a visiting professor) in the fall of 1926; a year later Kerlin was fired from his faculty position at the nearby West Chester (Pennsylvania) State College for supporting "'the social amalgamation of the races'" after entertaining African Americans at his home. Hughes corresponded with Kerlin and shared drafts of poems with him into the early 1930s. See Robert T. Kerlin, "An Open Letter to the Governor of Arkansas," *Nation* 112 (1921): 847-848; items on Kerlin in *Messenger* 3 (1921): 257; "Robert T. Kerlin" (editorial), *Crisis* 23 (1921): 10; Arnold Rampersad, *The Life of Langston Hughes,* vol. 1 (New York: Oxford University Press, 1986), 135; and Hughes-Kerlin correspondence in the Langston Hughes Papers, James Weldon Johnson Collection, Yale University.

62. E. Merrill Root, "Keats in Labrador," *Opportunity* 5 (1927): 270-271.

63. Countee Cullen, "Poet on Poet," *Opportunity* 4 (1926): 73. A note on the spelling of "Countee": Throughout *The New Negro,* Cullen's first name is spelled with an acute accent over the first "e." In fact, he and his second wife, Ida Mae Cullen, pronounced the name "count-tay." (Ida Mae Cullen, oral history interview by Ann Allen Shockley, 15 July 1970, Fisk University Library.) However, in letters to both Ida and his father, Cullen signs his name without the accent, and the accent does not appear on the title pages of his books. It appears occasionally, but not usually, in his contributions to *Opportunity, American Mercury,* and other magazines. I have followed the usual practice throughout this book by leaving the accent off. Thanks to Rebecca Hankins, acquisitions archivist at Amistad Research Center, for checking Cullen's family correspondence for me.

64. Alan R. Shucard, *Countee Cullen* (Boston: Twayne, 1984), 11. Shucard calls Braithwaite "one of [Cullen's] Harvard mentors" and points out that Cullen even dated one of Braithwaite's daughters. Braithwaite was not, however, on the faculty at Harvard; nor had he been a student at Harvard, contrary to some sources.

65. Countee Cullen, "The Dark Tower," *Opportunity* 6 (1928): 90. For more detailed discussions of Cullen's aesthetics, see Alan R. Shucard, *Countee Cullen;* and Gerald Early, "Introduction," in *My Soul's High Song: The Collected Writings of Countee Cullen* (New York: Anchor Books, 1991), 3-63.

66. Gerald Early's introduction to Cullen's poetry over-emphasizes the poet's role in the Harlem Renaissance, although the treatment of Cullen himself is excellent.

67. Esther Fulks Scott, "Negroes as Actors in Serious Plays," *Opportunity* 1 (1923): 20.

68. Ibid., 21.

69. Montgomery Gregory, review of *Cane, Opportunity* 1 (1923): 374-375.

70. Ibid., 374.

71. Adele Heller, "The New Theatre," in *1915: The Cultural Moment,* ed. Adele Heller and Lois Rudnick (New Brunswick, N.J.: Rutgers University Press, 1991), 221.

72. Alain Locke, "Max Rheinhardt Reads the Negro's Dramatic Horoscope," *Opportunity* 2 (1924): 145, 146.

73. See the discussion in Chapter 5 [in *The Harlem Renaissance in Black and White.* Cambridge, Mass.: Belknap Press, 1995] of *The Crisis*'s drama criticism. Apparently the split came specifically over a performance of Angelina Grimké's *Rachel,* which Locke and Gregory considered too propagandistic. More pointedly than Locke in the *Crisis* article of 1922, Gregory alludes to the argument in "A Chronology of the Negro Theatre," in *Plays of Negro Life,* ed. Montgomery Gregory and Alain Locke (New York: Harper and Brothers, 1927), 412.

74. Gregory, review of *Cane,* 374.

75. Unsigned editorial, "On the Need of Better Plays," *Opportunity* 5 (1927): 5-6.

76. Ibid., 6.

77. Edwin D. Johnson, "The Jewel in Ethiope's Ear," *Opportunity* 6 (1928): 166.

78. Ibid.

79. Ibid.

80. Ibid., 167-168.

81. Eulalie Spence, "A Criticism of the Negro Drama as It Relates to the Negro Dramatist and Artist," *Opportunity* 6 (1928): 180.

82. Lewis, *When Harlem Was in Vogue,* 92. My emphasis.

83. Paul Robeson, "Reflections on O'Neill's Plays," *Opportunity* 2 (1924): 368.

84. Ibid., 369.

85. Ibid.

86. E. A. Carter, *"All God's Chillun Got Wings,"* *Opportunity* 2 (1924): 112-113; James Light, "On Producing O'Neill's Play," *Opportunity* 2 (1924): 113; and Eric Walrond, *"All God's Chillun Got Wings,"* *Opportunity* 2 (1924): 220-221.

87. See Rudolph Fisher, review of *The White Girl* by Vera Caspary, *Opportunity* 7 (1929): 255-256; and Sterling Brown, "Our Literary Audience," *Opportunity* 8 (1930): 42-43.

88. Eulalie Spence, "Negro Art Players in Harlem," *Opportunity* 6 (1928): 381.

89. Unsigned editorial, "Paul Green," *Opportunity* 5 (1927): 159.

90. Rowena Woodham Jelliffe, "The Negro in the Field of Drama," *Opportunity* 6 (1928): 214.

91. Jelliffe, "The Negro in the Field of Drama," 214.

92. Jelliffe, "The Gilpin Players," *Opportunity* 6 (1928): 345.

93. For information on the Jelliffes, I have relied on Arnold Rampersad's *The Life of Langston Hughes,* vol. 1 (New York: Oxford University Press, 1986), 26, 36-39 and passim; and vol. 2 (New York: Oxford University Press, 1987), 16 and passim. Rampersad shows the depth and durability of Hughes's friendship with the Jelliffes, by the 1950s the longest of his life.

94. Ibid., vol. 1, pp. 26, 37; and vol. 2, pp. 16, 39.

95. Jelliffe, "The Negro in the Field of Drama," 214.

96. See playlist in Jelliffe, "The Gilpin Players," 344.

97. George Cram Cook, quoted in Adele Heller, "The New Theatre," 229.

98. Charles S. Johnson, "On Writing About Negroes," *Opportunity* 3 (1925): 228.

99. Eric D. Walrond, "'Prancing Nigger' by Roland [sic] Firbank," *Opportunity* 2 (1924): 219.

100. Ibid.

101. Charles S. Johnson, "*Nigger*—A Novel by Clement Wood," *Opportunity* 1 (1923): 30.

102. Charles S. Johnson, review of *The Fire in the Flint, Opportunity* 2 (1924): 344.

103. Ibid., 345.

104. Ibid.

105. Eunice Roberta Hunton, "'Holiday' by Waldo Frank," *Opportunity* 2 (1924): 59.

106. Ibid.

107. Waldo Frank, "In Our American Language," *Opportunity* 4 (1926): 352.

108. Ibid.

109. Ibid.

110. Sterling A. Brown, "The New Secession—A Review," *Opportunity* 5 (1927): 147.

111. Ibid.

112. Ibid.

113. Ibid.

114. Sterling A. Brown, "Our Literary Audience," *Opportunity* 8 (1930): 44-45.

115. Ibid., 46. See also Brown's review of DuBose Heyward's *Mamba's Daughters, Opportunity* 7 (1929): 161-162.

116. Alain Locke, review of *Scarlet Sister Mary, Opportunity* 7 (1929): 190-191.

117. Locke, "1928," 8.

118. Alain Locke, review of *Magic Island* by William Seabrook, *Opportunity* 7 (1929): 190.

119. Editorial, "A Note on the New Literary Movement," *Opportunity* 4 (1926): 80-81; Locke, "1928," 8-11; Eunice Hunton Carter, review of *The Blacker the Berry*, by Wallace Thurman, *Opportunity* 7 (1929): 162-163.

120. Carter, review of *The Blacker the Berry*, 163.

121. Locke, "1928," 8.

122. Ibid.

123. Ibid., 8-9.

124. Countee Cullen, "The Dark Tower," *Opportunity* 4 (1926): 389.

125. Locke, "1928," 9.

126. Ibid.

127. Gwendolyn Bennett, review of *Plum Bun, Opportunity* 7 (1929): 287.

128. Gwendolyn Bennett, review of *Banjo, Opportunity* 7 (1929): 254-255.

129. Ibid., 254.

130. Mary Fleming Labaree, review of *Passing* by Nella Larsen, *Opportunity* 7 (1929): 255.

131. Rampersad, *Life of Langston Hughes*, vol. 1: 126, 130, 166, 169.

132. Labaree, review of *Passing*, 255.

133. Ibid.

134. Sterling A. Brown, review of *Not Without Laughter, Opportunity* 8 (1930): 280.

135. Ibid.

136. Charles S. Johnson, "An Opportunity for Negro Writers," *Opportunity* 2 (1924): 258.

137. Ibid.

# PATRONS, PROMOTERS, AND THE NEW YORK PUBLIC LIBRARY

## RALPH D. STORY (ESSAY DATE 1989)

**SOURCE:** Story, Ralph D. "Patronage and the Harlem Renaissance: You Get What You Pay for." *College Language Association Journal* 32, no. 3 (March 1989): 284-95.

*In the following essay, Story discusses the relationship between various Harlem Renaissance writers and their literary patron, Charlotte Osgood Mason.*

\* \* \*

*The New Negro is not to me a group of writers centered in Harlem during the second half of the twenties. Most of the writers were not Harlemites; much of the best writing was not about Harlem, which was the show-window, the cashier's till, but no more Negro America than New York is America.*

—Sterling Brown (1955)[1]

*Why was it that the Renaissance of literature, which began among Negroes ten years ago, has never taken real and lasting root? It was because it was a transplanted and exotic thing. It was a literature written for the benefit of white people and at the behest of white readers, and started out privately from the white point of view. It never had a real Negro constituency, and it did not grow out of the inmost heart and frank experiences of Negroes; on such an artificial basis no real literature can grow.*

—W. E. B. Du Bois (1933)[2]

Very few writers have had to confront the issue of patron-artist relations as did Langston Hughes (1902-1967) at the end of the Harlem Renaissance (HR). The preceding commentary of Brown and Du Bois, two of the most eminent black scholars ever, and Hughes' particular case reveal that he was faced with more than just a personal decision. His choice to disassociate himself from his patron, Charlotte Osgood Mason, would also have psychological, cultural, racial,

# ON THE SUBJECT OF...

## CHARLOTTE OSGOOD MASON

Charlotte Osgood Mason was a socially prominent patron of the Negro arts notable for the early support she gave to Zora Neale Hurston. Hurston met Mason in September 1927; they signed a legal contract in December of that year that assured Hurston $200 each month plus the use of a car to travel to the South to begin a serious collection of black folklore. A formal arrangement lasted until the end of March 1931 and continued with irregular payments until September 1932. The major downside of the agreement for Hurston was that the collection was to become the property of Mrs. Mason. When Hurston settled in to write *Their Eyes Were Watching God* in the late fall of 1936, she was distantly removed from Mrs. Mason's money. However, the memory of her dependence on the white woman's dollar and her obvious awareness of the powerful control accepting that money had had on her creative output plays a significant part in the development of the work's thematic journey into Black inferiority.

Referred to as "godmother" by her protégés, Mrs. Mason was a patron for a number of talented, young, Black writers and artists of the Harlem Renaissance—most notably, Langston Hughes, whose relationship with her was also a struggle against censorship and excessive dependence.

and political implications for generations of black writers. Indeed, Hughes, as many other black American writers have discovered, essentially could have threatened his career by severing his ties with this rich white widow who liked to be referred to as "Godmother" by the artists she sponsored. Thus, despite the existence of numerous celebratory critiques of the HR, and despite the glossing over of the role of patronage during the era of the "New Negro," it is impossible to say that the art produced by black Americans between 1920 and 1932 would have ever made it into print without the support of rich whites. Their motives

for providing such support, however, were varied, and their desire to control the art and the artists was extremely heavy-handed. They wanted to make sure that they "got what they paid for." As Hughes' biographer, Faith Berry, makes clear, Charlotte Osgood Mason had specific ideas about black folk and black art: ". . . she subscribed to his [her deceased husband, Dr. Rufus Osgood Mason's] beliefs that the most magnificent manifestations of the spiritual were found in "primitive" "child races."[3]

Mason, starting in the summer of 1927, would eventually subsidize Langston Hughes for three years. She felt that of all the HR writers, Hughes possessed the most natural gift and could delineate her wishes about primitivism through his art. But their relationship proved to be extremely constraining for Hughes; Mason required strict obedience. She requested, for instance, that Hughes write her almost daily. She also "chose the books he read, the music he listened to, and the plays he saw."[4] In fact, Mason would soon ask Hughes to answer only *her* letters, pressure him to change the title of his novel, try to select a composer for one of his earliest plays, and take Zora Neale Hurston's side against him in their infamous dispute over their collaborative theatrical work, *Mule Bone.*[5] When Hughes finally realized the price he was paying for Mason's financial and maternalistic support and ended their relationship in 1930, Mason predicted his downfall:

> She lectured him on the limitations of his talent, reminded him of all the things she had done for him. But for her he would never have written his novel. But for her his foster brother would not have had the privilege of attending a New England school. She predicted that, lacking her support, Hughes would fall. . . . The unpleasant goodbye was traumatic for Hughes and irrevocable for both concerned.[6]

The Hughes-Mason relationship was merely one of many similar artist-patron associations that marked the second phase of the HR: a phase during which Harlem was "in" and rich whites, for a variety of not too altruistic reasons, flocked to Harlem to participate in the Harlem nightlife. The underwriting of black art, however, was just as much a matter of Lost Generation sentiment for things primitive and "natural" (which was fading from American life as a result of industrialization) as it was an open acknowledgement of black creativity. As David Levering Lewis contends in his informative and entertaining *When Harlem Was in Vogue* (1981), patronage was widespread but rarely if ever admitted:

White capital and influence were crucial, and the white presence, at least in the early years, hovered over the New Negro world of art and literature like a benevolent censor, politely but pervasively setting the outer limits of its creative boundaries.[7]

Another HR writer who had patrons, but of a different sort, was the Jamaican-born Claude McKay (1889-1947).

Unlike Hughes, McKay's linkages and associations to and with whites were with those of "the left," principally Max Eastman, then editor of the radical periodical *The Liberator.* McKay made his way to New York after his "vagabond" days in other parts of the United States. He had an affection for his leftist colleagues and friends while simultaneously he was alienated from the New Negro group just as much for his age as his Jamaican and radical roots:

I was an older man and not regarded as a member of the renaissance, but more as a forerunner. Indeed, some of them [those abroad in Paris during McKay's sojourn there] had aired their resentment of my intrusion from abroad into the renaissance set-up.[8]

In his autobiography, *A Long Way from Home* (1937), McKay did not really describe or allude to patronage as a separate issue or critique those most responsible for giving him the opportunities to display his work. He generally had very warm words for most of his associates during the era; he characterized whatever rifts he had with those at *The Liberator* as artistic differences or a clash of personalities, e.g., his disagreements with Michael Gold over which pieces should go into the magazine.[9] Instead, he leveled his sharpest criticism at the HR writers for what he considered their mistaken ideas about the New Negro renaissance:

The Negroes were under the delusion that when a lady from Park Avenue [Mason lived on Park Ave.] or from Fifth Avenue, or a titled European, became interested in Negro art and invited Negro artists to her home, that was a token of Negroes breaking into upper-class white society. I don't think that it ever occurred to them that perhaps such white individuals were searching for a social and artistic significance in Negro art which they could not find in their own society.[10]

McKay's assertion is obviously a reference to Mason and Hughes; yet it also underscores his accurate and less sentimental understanding of what patrons wanted from black art and artists. But McKay also had an association, despite his failure to mention it, with the patron Mason:

McKay, another "precious child," was one of Locke's . . . stiffest challenges. . . . But after a few months of righteous silence, he and Locke were corresponding again, for McKay was always care-

ful not to break irrevocably with people who could help him. As for Godmother, the poet accepted her checks gratefully and wrote adoringly, thanking her for news clippings and renewed magazine subscriptions, and in return penning vivid descriptions of "primitive" life in North Africa.[11]

One of the most interesting comments McKay makes on the Harlem artists is his revelation of intense competition between HR writers for the leading role in the New Negro play. In essence, the Awakening writers were engaged in a battle for ascendancy to a separate and elevated status as *the* black writer most respected by white patrons, critics, editors and publishers; they sought the designation of "best" of the brightest:

Also, among the Negro artists there was much of that Uncle Tom attitude which works like Satan against the idea of a coherent and purposeful Negro group. Each one wanted to be the first Negro, the one Negro, and the only Negro *for the whites* instead of for their group. Because an unusual number of them were receiving grants to do creative work, they actually and naively believed that Negro artists as a group would always be treated differently from white artists and be protected by powerful white patrons.[12]

McKay's last point about "protection" seems just as much a political critique as an aesthetic one. For early in McKay's career, as a result of his most famous poem, "If We Must Die," as well as his associations with Communists, Marxists and black nationalists (he wrote articles for Marcus Garvey's *Negro World*), he was branded "bitter" and a black radical.[13] Consequently, his relations with whites were more politically dangerous and radical than those of his pro-integrationist HR counterparts. But McKay would discover, as did Richard Wright some twenty years later, that the American Communist Party was supportive of black artists only if those artists parroted the party line in their public speeches and their work:

He returned to Paris ill and with the American Communists hostile toward him for refusing to join their ranks and submit to party discipline.[14]

A larger issue, however, as it pertains to white patronage—and I am saying that radical whites and the Communist Party in the U.S. constituted a support group, a patron group, and publication outlets for black writers—is that neither shared ideological beliefs nor aesthetic sensibilities would alter the patron(s)' desire to have the artist recreate what they viewed as important about the black experience. For the HR writers and painters, once they agreed to a patron-artist relationship—especially a financial one—it seemed to obligate them to produce a certain kind of product that would meet the patron(s)' approval. Hence, it is difficult to imagine just what kind of art might have been produced had not the artists been under such covert pressure to please their supporters. The best example of this transactional arrangement was the contract which Charlotte Osgood Mason had her lawyer create for Zora Neale Hurston, whom she subsidized for five years. Only a portion of it is provided below:

> This agreement made and entered into this 1st day of December, 1927, by and between Charlotte L. Mason, of New York City, first party, and Zora Hurston, of the same place, second party:
>
> *WITNESSETH:*
>
> Whereas said first party, Charlotte L. Mason is desirous of obtaining and compiling certain data relating to the music, folklore, poetry, voodoo, conjure, manifestations of art, and kindred matters existing among American Negroes but is unable because of the pressure of other matters to undertake the collection of this information in person. . . .[15]

Although Zora Neale Hurston would be able to create without worrying about finances, the actual Afro-American artifacts which could have been used to produce her art would, ultimately, belong to Mason. Such artifacts could have ended up in a proposed museum for Afro-American art that Mason's procurer for the arts, Alain Locke, worked on creating during the latter years of the HR.

In his role as Mason's procurer of black art no HR figure is more representative of patron-middleman-artist relations than the ubiquitous Locke. He had the dubious role of carrying out Mason's wishes regarding the most well-known writers and artists of the era: Langston Hughes, Zora Neale Hurston, Claude McKay, and the painter/illustrator Aaron Douglas. Operating in the shadows of Du Bois and Charles S. Johnson (who was singularly responsible for bringing together quite a few artists and publishers via his *Opportunity* magazine awards banquets),[16] Locke was able to carry out his personal vision of *The New Negro* (1925) with financial support that, at least for a time, seemed unlimited. As Mason's steerer he was responsible for direct communications to the artists which not only fulfilled Mason's wishes but his own aesthetic ideas as well:

> Locke's bondage to Charlotte Mason, despite patronizing lectures and occasional acts of rank tyranny, was more apparent than real. He walked a tightrope between obsequious accomodation to the old lady and nervous fidelity to his own beliefs, dissembling masterfully and taking the cash. His strategem was to use Mason's money to prove how like well-bred, intelligent whites, well-bred, intelligent Afro-Americans were.[17]

In fact, more than occasionally, Locke functioned as a kind of "spy" for Mason on those artists who had defected from the Mason camp, such as Langston Hughes. Years after Hughes severed his ties with Mason, Locke was still reporting regularly to his Godmother on Hughes' work and activities with some of his correspondence personally vindictive and cruel:

> Locke, still harboring deep resentment for Hughes and perenially expressing it in letters to Godmother, had even harsher words for *The Ways of White Folks* (1934) in his correspondence to her. . . . Forever eager to turn up anything he could to give Langston a verbal flogging, that March (1934) he had sent Godmother a clipping of Hughes's caustic essay "Would You Fight for the U.S. in the Next War?"—with a note attached: "The latest blast from Langston—in which his megolamania grows to ridiculous proportions—Aesop's Frog."[18]

Fortunately for Zora Neale Hurston, Locke's support was, typically, unwavering; quite possibly though, he supported Hurston because her loyalty to their mutual benefactor was unquestionable. Note Locke's support of Hurston in the *Mule Bone* incident as well as his disparagement of Arthur Spingarn (of the NAACP and Hughes' lawyer in the case):

> I don't think I should write the Cleveland people [the Jelliffes, founders of Karamu House]—but just send Z[ora]'s introduction, showing absolute confidence in her. . . . Moreover, Locke's willingness to embrace the doctrinaire anti-Semitism of Mrs. Mason would have added to the poet's disillusionment and disappointment with the critic-professor (and Rhodes Scholar) he had once trusted as a friend. Locke's remark to her—"it shows what you say about jews"—was meant to cast an aspersion on Arthur Spingarn, whom the professor resented for wiring him that Langston had justifiable rights to *Mule Bone*.[19]

Although Locke and McKay interacted with one another cordially in public, they engaged in a rather protracted disagreement over Locke's alteration of McKay's poem "White House." Locke made it plural, changing it to "White Houses," and in the process this enraged McKay:

> I wrote him saying that the idea that my poem had reference to the official residence of the President of the United States was ridiculous. . . . It changed the whole symbolic intent and meaning of the poem. . . . But Dr. Locke high-handedly used his substitute title of "White Houses" in all the editions of his anthology.[20]

Just as Locke had secured the services of Hughes, Hurston, and McKay for Mason, he would also get the painter Aaron Douglas on Mason's payroll:

> Painting murals at a Harlem club, Aaron Douglas remembered being ordered down from his scaf-

folding after his repeated refusals to appear at 399 Park Avenue compelled Godmother to motor to Harlem. To his later regret, Douglas became a retainer in Mason's court, frequently compelled to delay and even withdraw from major commissions offending his patron's sense of what was "proper Negro art"—until, at last, Douglas fled to Merion, Pennsylvania, on a fellowship at the New Barnes Foundation.[21]

Locke's manner and extremely refined and sophisticated appearance, as well as his impeccable academic credentials, clearly overshadowed his behind-the-scenes role as a middleman between black artists and his patron/Godmother. In retrospect, Locke's roving ambassadorship of the HR obscured the most obvious, yet far-reaching, historical precedent for his true role—procurer of the black arts. For Locke's relationship to Mason is clearly similar to those "anonymous *sensali*" who worked on behalf of the Medici family in fifteenth- and sixteenth-century Florence, Italy. Indeed, if Mason perceived herself as a twentieth-century financial and spiritual Medici for obscure yet soon-to-be-famous black essayists, poets, novelists, folklorists, and painters, then certainly Locke, who is sometimes credited with coining the term "Renaissance," saw himself as a twentieth-century Paolo del Sera. Locke, like del Sera, was both *dilettante* and *professori* and acquired numerous works of art on behalf of Mason as did del Sera for Leopoldo de Medici.[22] Locke was also noted for his "good taste and incisive understanding of the local art market," a characterization identical to del Sera's.[23] If there was to be a Renaissance, Locke probably reasoned that someone would have to be the courtier and courier to secure its financial and aesthetic underpinnings. He seemed, for reasons of upbringing, personality, and his simultaneous beliefs in racial integration and the significance of folk art, to be ideally suited for the job. Nonetheless, just as the Medicis have come to be known as rather infamous owners of art and artists, so too would figures like Mason. In typical *quid pro quo* fashion she wanted to play, like other white patrons of black arts and artists, a major role in the creation of black art and not just be a monetary nursemaid for its growth:

> Nor was the Negro artist assumed to be the final judge of truth and relevant statement. The patron—as best illustrated by Van Vechten—was a teacher, guide and judge; his search for authentic Negro voices was dictated by his own needs. . . . But white guidance and encouragement probably prevented those few men and women of real talent from wrestling with their senses and plodding through to those statements which the thrust of their lives and experience would force them to make. Whatever other burdens Negro artists carried, this arrangement stigmatized Negro poetry and prose of the 1920s as being an artistic effort that was trying to be like something other than itself.[24]

One of the more significant means, beyond the Locke-Mason connection, for artists and patrons to come together for mutual benefit during the HR were the *Opportunity* awards banquets. Ironically though, many of those who did in fact win awards but who did not have the financial ties to white patrons beyond the banquets achieved their place in the limelight only during the HR and plunged—literally like shooting stars—into obscurity when the Great Depression had a firm grip on the country. Writers like Joseph Cotter, Jr., Warren MacDonald, John Matheus and Frank Horne, all *Opportunity* awards winners, for instance, are rarely even mentioned in the chronicles of the HR or its lists of literary figures. Eventually, after 1933, the "Urban League would mount one more annual literary gala before concluding that the money and interest to sustain the tradition were lacking."[25]

To be sure, those artists who were able to cultivate separate ties to individual white patrons were obviously better off when the interest of large numbers of whites in black art faded after the stock market crash of 1929. It could also be said, however, that any folk art which is not sustained and/or supported by the folk it purportedly represents and is instead bought and paid for by significant others is inevitably and inherently doomed to failure. It is not surprising that we know so much about Hughes, McKay, and Hurston and so little about Horne and Matheus. At any rate there are clearly some lessons which can be learned from the failure of the Harlem Renaissance to sustain itself.

A primary point would obviously be the need for art and artists to be independent and autonomous if their work is to be inspirational and truly representative. Moreover, as this pertains to black people, if they want believable imagery of themselves and consider those images to be important, and if they desire art about themselves that is uplifting and seeks to deliver the "truth," then they have to be willing to pay for it, institutionalize it, and support its creators. Yet, some of the tensions between black creative artists and their older black intellectual peers were sparked by the issue of artistic freedom and whether the black art they created did more harm than good for the black masses. Ironically, however, the black middle class, the group most desirous of black artists creating "uplift" fiction depicting refined and "successful" blacks in the HR, was too small in number and lacked the financial clout to support the black artists and art produced in the 1920s. Then, as now, without this group's support—the group most able to create, financially sustain, and promote black publishing institutions and creative outlets—the black artist is forced to go to the dominant culture for the publication of her/his work and the recognition and visibility that accrues from such critically recognized endeavors. Thus, white patronage of black art during the Harlem Renaissance was crucial if the art were to ever be exposed. Nonetheless, such aesthetic and commercial support from either left or right political circles and/or individuals inherently makes it difficult for artists to be truly free to create. It is clear today, as it has been throughout the twentieth century, that black writers need black publishers of books and periodicals if their art is to be honest and uplifting for their people.

### Notes

1. Sterling Brown, *Southern Road* (Boston: Beacon, 1974), p. xxxiv.

2. W. E. B. Du Bois, "The Negro College," in *A Reader,* ed. Meyer Weinberg (New York: Harper, 1970), p. 181.

3. Faith Berry, *Langston Hughes: Before and Beyond Harlem* (Westport, Conn.: Lawrence Hill, 1983), p. 87.

4. Ibid., p. 92.

5. Ibid., p. 102.

6. Ibid., p. 107.

7. David Levering Lewis, *When Harlem Was in Vogue* (New York: Knopf, 1981), p. 98.

8. Claude McKay, *A Long Way from Home* (New York: Harcourt, 1970), p. 321.

9. Ibid., pp. 50-56.

10. Ibid., p. 321.

11. Lewis, pp. 153-54.

12. McKay, p. 322.

13. See U. S. Congress, Senate, 66th Congress, 1st Session, Senate Document No. 153 (Washington, D.C.: U.S. Government Printing Office, 1919) for a discussion of the work of McKay and other HR writers the Congress classified as "Radical" and "Seditious."

14. McKay, p. xiv.

15. Berry, p. 90.

16. Lewis, p. 95.

17. Ibid., p. 154.

18. Berry, p. 205.

19. Ibid., p. 116.

20. McKay, p. 314.

21. Lewis, p. 152.

22. See Edward L. Goldberg, *Patterns in Late Medici Art Patronage* (Princeton, N.J.: Princeton Univ. Press, 1983).

23. Ibid., p. 57.

24. Nathan Huggins, *Harlem Renaissance* (New York: Oxford Univ. Press, 1971), pp. 128-29.

25. Lewis, p. 294.

## ELINOR DES VERNEY SINNETTE (ESSAY DATE 1989)

**SOURCE:** Sinnette, Elinor Des Verney. "Arthur Schomburg and the Harlem Renaissance." In *Arthur Alfonso Schomburg: Black Bibliophile & Collector,"* pp. 103-30. Detroit: The New York Public Library & Wayne State University Press, 1989.

*In the following excerpt, Sinnette details Schomburg's role as documentor of the Harlem Renaissance and as promoter of some of its greatest authors.*

\* \* \*

*To skeptic and believer alike, to scholar and school child, to proud black and astonished white, "Here is the evidence."*[1]

An early arrival to Harlem, Arthur Schomburg lived for many years on West 140th Street, where he maintained both his private collection and that of the Negro Society for Historical Research. In 1918 the Schomburg family moved from Harlem to Brooklyn. Their final residence was on Kosciusko Street in a house that eventually proved inadequate to the needs of the family and the size of the collection. Although he lived in Brooklyn for twenty years, Schomburg's ties to the Harlem community continued. He was especially involved in the budding literary and social movement that started in Harlem and spread through black communities across the country—the Negro or Harlem Renaissance.[2]

The roots of the new movement can be traced to the reactions of the black population to events of the "Great War." Black American troops had fought and died on the battlefields of France, and the hopes and aspirations of those who returned might be summarized in a 1918 letter Schomburg wrote to the New York *Sun.* He called attention to the blacks who had sacrificed their lives on American battlefields half a century earlier "to secure the integrity and preservation of the Union" and singled out the battle-proven troops of the Fifty-fourth Massachusetts Regiment for their heroic role in that conflict. Noting that members of the all-black 369th Regiment had marched proudly up New York City's Fifth Avenue in the victory parade at the end of World War I, Schomburg called upon President Woodrow Wilson to guarantee to these men, and others like them, the opportunity to live and work anywhere without let or hindrance.[3] It soon became apparent that such pleas fell on deaf ears and that once again blacks would be denied full citizenship.

The influx of immigrant labor to the United States from Europe decreased markedly during World War I, and from 1917 on, blacks from the rural South flocked to northern cities seeking employment in wartime industry. They adjusted to city life, and an active black press encouraged other blacks to follow. On a 1923 trip to Chicago, Schomburg was so impressed by the large number of recently transplanted blacks who were employed in that city that he wrote, "[the] Ku Klux Klan might have been a blessing in disguise" since it helped to force rural blacks to migrate north where opportunities were greater.[4] During this period Schomburg had great faith in the North, but his hopes were soon dashed when the white population of the northern cities reacted with hostility to what they considered a black invasion of their neighborhoods. They rampaged through city streets attacking blacks indiscriminately and engaged in other acts of destruction. In the summer of 1919 alone, there were some twenty-six race riots throughout the country. In the nation's capital, bands of white servicemen went on a three-day spree of killing and maiming blacks. Fully aware of the irony and hypocrisy of the term "the American way of life," Schomburg wrote that he was "glad [that the] riot had occurred when the President [Woodrow Wilson] had just come back from Europe [where he had told] Europeans how to conclude a lasting peace."[5] Schomburg was particularly incensed with the double standards of white American officials. In 1920, as Grand Secretary of the Prince Hall Masons of New York State, he petitioned the U. S. Department of Justice for the enactment of federal antilynching legislation. The Masons were deeply concerned about the lawlessness and mob violence in the southern states, and he informed the Justice Department that these acts "picture to the other nations the low estimate which Americans have for the majesty of the law." To this, the government agency callously replied that lynching was a local matter.[6]

The race riots and lynchings were a prime concern of the major black leadership organizations such as the National Association for the Advancement of Colored People (NAACP) and the National Urban League. They were at the forefront in promoting legislation and developing programs to improve conditions for blacks and to lessen racial strife. Through their respective journals, the *Crisis: A Record of the Darker Races* and *Opportunity: A Journal of Negro Life,* blacks across the nation were informed of personalities, events, and issues affecting them and their communities. In addition to providing political and social commentary, these publications soon became vehicles for creative expression. The latter came at a time when a black cultural awakening was being encouraged with financial support from white intellectuals who themselves were seeking new experiences to enliven the Roaring Twenties. Although the new wave of cultural consciousness spread quickly to other "black enclaves throughout the country," it was Harlem that became a mecca, attracting black writers and artists from many corners of the world. Poet Langston Hughes described this remarkable comingling of black life and culture:

> Harlem—Southern Harlem—the Carolinas, Georgia, Florida—looking for the Promised Land. . . . West Indian Harlem—warm, rambunctious, sassy. . . . Haitian Harlem, Cuban Harlem, little pockets of tropical dreams in alien tongues. Magnet Harlem, pulling an Arthur Schomburg from Puerto Rico. . . . Melting pot Harlem. . . .[7]

Commenting on the friction between American-born blacks and those from the Caribbean (particularly the English-speaking West Indies), historian Gilbert Osofsky described Harlem as a "battleground of intraracial antagonisms."[8] There were indeed tensions among the various black ethnic groups, but not of the magnitude that Osofsky suggests. Schomburg was aware of these tensions and knew from previous experience how destructive these divisions could be. He worked actively to bridge the differences, with the result that under his guidance and leadership one of the more active organizations of an earlier period, the "Negro Society for Historical Research had brought together for the first time . . . African, West Indian and Afro-American scholars."[9]

The confluence of culturally diverse populations unleashed new and powerful black voices of creative expression. Harlem became known for its talented artists and writers who were determined to explore their historical past and who were equally determined to use the black experience as a legitimate instrument of artistic expression. This era of the "New Negro" lasted approximately from 1918 to 1930, with the period from 1920 to 1928 being most productive. In recent years the Harlem Renaissance has been a subject of considerable discussion and debate. During the period itself, Langston Hughes, then a young poet and one of the era's better-known participants, summed up the spirit and intent of his fellow artists when he wrote in the *Nation:*

The younger Negro artists who create now intend to express our individual dark-skinned selves without fear or shame. If white people are pleased, we are glad. If they are not, it doesn't matter. We know we are beautiful. And ugly too. . . . If colored people are pleased we are glad. If they are not, their displeasure doesn't matter either. We build our temples for tomorrow, strong as we know how and stand on the top of the mountain free from within ourselves.[10]

One of the most significant publications of the Renaissance was Alain Locke's anthology *The New Negro,* published in 1925, a banner year for the movement. Paul Kellogg, editor of *Survey Graphic,* a bi-monthly magazine with a primarily white, professional audience interested in social conditions, asked Locke to edit a special issue on "Harlem, Mecca of the New Negro." Locke gathered stories, essays, poems, and art work by and about blacks for the issue, which appeared on the newsstands and in bookshops in March. It sold forty thousand copies and went into ten printings, the most popular issue in the magazine's history. Locke, one of the movement's leading sponsors and advocates, outlined its goals in his introductory essay. Whereas Hughes's statement was the personal credo of individual black artists, Locke's exposition could be regarded as the manifesto of the Harlem Renaissance:

The intelligent Negro of today is resolved not to make [racial] discrimination an extenuation of his shortcomings in performance, individual or collective; he is trying to hold himself at par, neither inflated by sentimental allowances nor depreciated by current social discounts. For this he must know himself and be known for precisely what he is, and for that reason he welcomes the new scientific rather than the old sentimental interest in [him].

Recognizing that race was the issue that constituted the core of black life in America, Locke believed that black Americans were developing "the consciousness of acting as the advance guard of the African peoples in their contact with twentieth-century civilization . . . rehabilitating the race in world esteem from that loss of prestige for which the fate and conditions of slavery have so largely been responsible." Although he taught at Howard University in Washington, D.C., Locke maintained a second residence in New York City, and he commuted between the two locations almost weekly. His numerous activities in New York and his extensive contacts with many of the city's leading black figures convinced him that "the pulse of the Negro world has begun to beat in Harlem," which he saw as the logical place for the emergence of "a spiritual coming of age."[11]

With considerable justification, Alain LeRoy Locke might be described as the doyen of the Harlem Renaissance. Similarly, Arthur Alfonso Schomburg deserves to be considered as the documentor of the movement. By 1925 the friendship between the two men had flowered. They belonged to many of the same organizations and on more than one occasion shared the same platform. On January 21 1926, Wendell P. Dabney's Cincinnati newspaper, the *Union,* carried a banner headline declaring the evening of February 9 1926, as a "Red Letter Night" because Locke and Schomburg were to speak. "In deference to many requests," the article stated, "the joint meeting for Dr Alain LeRoy Locke and Arthur Schomburg has been changed from a subscription to a public affair, so that all may have an opportunity to hear these distinguished gentlemen." Under a handsome photograph, Schomburg was described as a "famous . . . bibliophile and collector of Negro art and literature [and] an authority on Masonry." With an element of hyperbole Schomburg was also described as "the executive head of the foreign correspondence department of one of the biggest banking institutions in this country." Schomburg's presentation was to be the "History of Negro Masonry." On the right side of the newspaper's front page, the photograph of a dreamy-eyed Locke appeared over a brief biographical sketch of his life and accomplishments. Locke was scheduled to discuss his recently published anthology, *The New Negro.*

While Schomburg had a high regard for Locke's erudition, he often resented Locke's frosty manner. Steeped in the formal intellectual tradition and coming from a cultivated, middle-class background, Locke, like Du Bois, could not relate easily to the black masses. Locke's pedantic mannerisms and the scholarliness of his subject matter prompted Dabney to refer to his presentations as "philosophical disquisitions."[12] Schomburg also found Locke at times to be a gossip, an opinion he voiced only to close friends, in contrast to his open criticism of Du Bois, James Weldon Johnson, and Carter Woodson. Throughout their lives, Schomburg and Locke remained "bosom friends." Locke appreciated Schomburg's "Latin ideas of scholarship, [his] voracious reading, accurate memorization, phenomenally detailed memory and his tireless patience."[13]

For Arthur Schomburg, the Harlem Renaissance proved to be an excellent environment for conducting his bibliophilic research and an ideal opportunity to promote interest in black history and culture. Responding to the urgent desire of black writers and artists to use "black themes," Schomburg supplied information both from his encyclopedic knowledge and from his private collection. He was much sought after, and his home on Kosciusko Street became a popular gathering place.

The Harlem Renaissance also stimulated Schomburg himself to write more for publication, and this proved to be his most prolific period. His earlier written efforts, apart from the tract in 1910 about the Cuban poet Plácido and two notices in José Marti's newspaper, *Patria,* in 1892 and 1895, were confined to a dozen or so letters published in various newspapers. He readily admitted that the brief bibliography of Afro-American poetry he had prepared for Mississippi bookdealer Charles Heartman in 1916 fell far short of what was needed. In fact, in his discussions with young black writers, Schomburg used the bibliography as an example of shoddy work. Schomburg never wrote a lengthy work although many times he seemed on the verge of attempting such an effort. He dreamed of acquiring the five editions of Benjamin Banneker's almanacs and writing a book about them. He longed to compile a complete set of Ira Aldridge's playbills and theater notices, to be introduced by a review of the black actor's life and work. After his trip to Europe, Schomburg wanted to complete a thorough study of references and other documentary evidence confirming the contributions of blacks to sixteenth- and seventeenth-century Spanish history and culture.

Despite his scholarly limitations and numerous other commitments, Schomburg managed to prepare a number of articles for submission to the two leading black journals of the period. The *Crisis,* founded in 1910 by the NAACP, was published under the visionary editorship of W. E. B. Du Bois. Schomburg had greatly admired Du Bois' scholarship since their first meeting in 1904, and in the following years Du Bois regularly called on Schomburg for specific documentation. Schomburg's May 1911 article about the Caribbean island of St Lucia appeared in the seventh issue of the *Crisis.* The black poets William Stanley Braithwaite and Leslie Pinkney Hill had been published in earlier issues, but Schomburg's article and another by Mrs A. W. Hunton, organizer of the National Association of Colored Women's Clubs, were the first essays by blacks to be accepted by Du Bois. Entitled "The Fight for Liberty in St. Lucia," the brief treatise described an unsuccessful slave revolt on the island, with Schomburg pointing out that "much has been told of Haiti's fight

## ON THE SUBJECT OF...

### ARTHUR SCHOMBURG

Arthur Alfonso Schomburg (January 24, 1874-June 10, 1938) was born in San Juan, Puerto Rico, to a German merchant and an unmarried Black laundress who was a native of St. Thomas, Virgin Islands. He emigrated to the United States in 1891, moving to New York City. Schomburg worked in a law office and began his lifelong quest to amass a collection of African American books and other materials in order to demonstrate the existence and significance of Black history. With his broad knowledge and passion for African American history, Schomburg became a leading spirit in the Harlem Renaissance and an inspiration to a generation of historians. In 1925 the New York Public Library established a special Negro Division at the 135th Street Branch, and the next year the Carnegie Corporation purchased for $10,000 Schomburg's vast and unequalled collection of books, manuscripts, and art works, and donated it to the library. Schomburg, who was a librarian at Fisk University from 1930 to 1932, became curator of his own collection with another Carnegie grant, which he received in 1932. His collection forms the core of the present Schomburg Center for Research in Black Culture, the largest collection of materials by and about people of African descent.

for liberty under the inspiration of the French Revolution, but little is known of the desperate struggle that took place about the same time on the island of St. Lucia."[14]

A year later another article by Schomburg appeared in the *Crisis.* It dealt with the life of Evaristo Estenoz, a black Cuban general who had "taken up the gage of battle for the rights of his dark fellowmen," thereby precipitating a political and military crisis in Cuba. "Estenoz was born," Schomburg wrote, "in the birthplace of revolutionary conspiracies, Santiago de Cuba" (destined later to be the cradle of Fidel Castro's revolution). At first, Cubans of all colors had fought together to establish the republic so that "they should enjoy in common the burdens and the benefits of the country." For reasons never explained, Estenoz later abandoned the pluralistic philosophy and adopted a black nationalist stance. In 1905 Estenoz visited New York City, where he met with former members of the Cuban and Puerto Rican revolutionary groups. Upon his return to Cuba he formed the Independent Colored Party to "promote the interests of the colored race, to urge the government to recognize their rights as citizens and taxpayers and to accord them a fair proportion of the elective and appointive offices." Estenoz also edited a weekly party newspaper. His movement became so successful that the government took measures to destroy it. Using a black senator as its spokesman, the government introduced a "notorious amendment" that forbade the formation of any political party along racial lines. Black leaders were thrown into prison as the predominantly white Cuban leadership became "determined that [blacks] should not have any representation save that which was bestowed on them as a charity." In Schomburg's opinion the "infamous and despicable" amendment could be compared only to the odious Dred Scott decision in the United States.[15]

In a third article for the *Crisis,* in 1916, Schomburg discussed the Spanish mulatto artist Sebastian Gomez, observing that "among the great painters who have achieved honor and recognition by their talents, the least has been said of Sebastian Gomez of the city of Sevilla in Spain." Gomez' slavemaster, the artist Bartolomeo Esteban Murillo, recognized the latent talent of his enthralled servant and gave him instruction and encouragement. Under Murillo's tutelage, Gomez produced works of "good taste, a heavy brush on his canvases and an exactness in his drawing." Schomburg noted that some of Gomez' works could be found in churches and convents in Seville, the city in which he died and was buried in 1680.[16]

In 1922 the *Crisis* published a portrait of Schomburg with a biographical sketch that included a description of his private collection. It was not until 1927, however, that a fourth Schomburg contribution appeared in that journal. Entitled "In Quest of Juan de Pareja," the article was accompanied by a portrait of the black Spanish artist and a copy of one of his paintings. Schomburg wrote of his own visits a year earlier to Cordoba and Granada in Spain where, in addition to uncovering the works of Gomez, he also encountered those of Juan de Pareja. Like Gomez, Pareja was a slave. His master was the renowned Spanish artist Diego Velázquez. In his description of

Granada, Schomburg vividly captured his walk through the "cloisters of the University where one may still see the minutes attesting the fact that a black man, Juan Latino, received here on May 4, 1546 his B.A. degree before the Archbishop of Granada, the learned men of Spain and the elite of the city." Schomburg saw the home of Leo Africanus, "a Moor born in Granada," and wrote how he thoroughly enjoyed walking through the Alhambra. During his stay in Granada he hoped to find pictures of Latino and Africanus but was unsuccessful. Schomburg went on to describe his visit to the Prado in Madrid, where he became friendly with the museum's director. Portrayed by Schomburg as "a suave Castillian," the director allowed him to view exhibits in sections of the museum that were closed to the general public. Schomburg marveled at the splendid collection, especially the works of Pareja, declaring, "what a treasure house is this great museum!" He viewed Pareja's large painting "The Calling of Matthew" and stated that he had "journeyed thousands of miles to look upon the work of this colored slave who had succeeded in the face of every discouragement." Obviously moved by the experience, Schomburg "sat in reverent silence before this large canvas . . . glad of the opportunity thus given [him] to see this work and to tell people in America [of its existence]."[17] It must have been greatly satisfying for Schomburg to see a broad selection of the artist's work, for earlier he had found one of Pareja's religious paintings in a New York City furniture-storage warehouse. The present whereabouts of that painting is not known, but Schomburg had planned to offer it to one of the Harlem churches before "its value became too greatly stressed."[18]

Schomburg's final *Crisis* articles—a series of biographical sketches of General Antonio Maceo, an Afro-Cuban military figure, and Alessandro, a Florentine Duke sometimes referred to as the "Negro Medici," appeared in the May and December 1931 issues. The article on Maceo was prompted by a photograph in an American publication showing Secretary of State Charles Evans Hughes posing in Cuba at the base of a statue of General Maceo. Since the face of the Cuban hero did not appear in the photograph, Schomburg used the pages of the *Crisis* not only to inform readers of the general's African lineage but also to describe his great deeds. The article about Alessandro de Medici was carefully edited by Du Bois, who indicated that he had added "dates and historical connections." Alessandro, the first hereditary Duke of Florence, whose "woolly hair and Negro-like

The Abyssinian Baptist Church.

appearance had already caused him to be called the Moor," was described by Schomburg as the son of Pope Clement VII and an "African Venus, whom some claimed was a slave, others a trusted servant in the ducal household."[19]

The other major black periodical, *Opportunity*, first appeared January 19, 1923. Published by the National Urban League, it had as editor the black sociologist Charles Spurgeon Johnson, who later, at Fisk University, conducted important research on black life and culture. The journal's initial objective was "to present . . . facts of Negro life," and it soon became one of the chief outlets for the works of Harlem Renaissance figures. Johnson was impressed by Schomburg's knowledge and his perspective on world history and soon began to rely on the bibliophile's ability to recall the minutiae that so often provide vital clues in the interpretation of historical data. In an early *Opportunity* article Schomburg took serious issue with the notion that Africans generally were savages until rescued by Christianity, and he declared that slavery was a blot on the "banner of religion." He believed the Islamic religion to be "more akin to

the nature of the African," and seemed unwilling to mention the lucrative slave trade carried on by many followers of Islam over the course of centuries.[20]

The developing tensions between black Americans and West Indian blacks led Johnson to devote the entire issue of November 1926 to the peoples of the Caribbean. A lengthy editorial about the approximately eighty-five thousand "foreign born Negroes," nearly half of whom lived in New York City, decried "the American Negro who dislikes West Indians and applies to them offensive names [matched] by the West Indian who can outlaw a fellow countryman for associating too much with American Negroes." The special issue carried biographies of prominent West Indians and the proceedings of a symposium that discussed West Indian-black American relations. Schomburg contributed a brief study, "West Indian Composers and Musicians," in which he traced to Africa the roots of black American and West Indian song and dance and discussed the subsequent transfer of these art forms to the Americas and the Carribean by way of the transatlantic slave traffic. He named Claudio de Salas Brindis, born in Havana in 1800, as "the earliest Negro violin player," and noted that another black Cuban, José Silvestro Lafitte White, had at the age of fifteen composed a "mass for the orchestra of the Catholic Church at Matanzas his home town." Chevalier de Saint Georges, another West Indian, was born on the island of Guadeloupe during the eighteenth century and was said to have composed a number of pieces that became popular in European music halls.[21] After his return from Europe in September 1926, Schomburg's contributions to *Opportunity* dealt solely with information he had uncovered during his visit to the city of Seville. In both his 1927 and 1928 articles he focused on the colony of blacks he had found in that city.[22]

In 1928 *Opportunity* published Schomburg's lengthy "Notes on Panama and the Negro: Luna y Victoria, First Native Born Bishop of the Catholic Church of America." Schomburg described the eighteenth-century Bishop Francisco Xavier Luna y Victoria as "the obedient son of a poor black woman" and told how he rose to become head of the Catholic Church in Panama. He also described his research in Seville, where he unearthed documents "dealing with the ecclesiastical regime of Panama" and "actually held in my hands" papers and documents belonging to Luna y Victoria. The article was accompanied by a fine etching of the Catedral de Panama by artist Albert Smith.[23] Schomburg's final article in *Opportunity* appeared in 1933 and described his visit to Cuba three years earlier "in quest of Negro books."[24]

Two years after publication of *The New Negro,* Charles S. Johnson, whom some called the "entrepreneur" of the Harlem Renaissance, produced for *Opportunity* a special issue entitled *Ebony and Topaz: A Collectanea.* This compilation of stories, articles, and illustrations by Renaissance figures provided an additional forum for expressing the philosophy of the era. Johnson labeled the issue as "a venture in expression," and in his introduction he echoed Langston Hughes's earlier manifesto statement.

> It is not improbable that some of our white readers will arch their brows. . . . Some of our Negro readers will doubtless quarrel with certain of the Negro characters who move in these pages . . . [but] the most that will be claimed for this collection is that it is a fairly faithful reflection of current interests and observations in Negro life. . . .[25]

Schomburg, described in the issue as "perhaps the greatest of Negro bibliophiles," permitted Johnson to reproduce several items from his pri-

vate collection: two mezzotints, one of Jacobus Eliza Capitein and another of Ignatius Sancho; photographs of four paintings by Sebastian Gomez; facsimiles from Juan Latino's first book of poetry; and a Phillis Wheatley poem. In addition, Schomburg contributed an article, "Juan Latino, Magister Matinus." Schomburg described his pleasure in finding "a copy of Juan Latino's own book on the library shelf of [Latino's] alma mater." He also mentioned his discussions with Professor Marin Ocete, whose doctoral dissertation, a critical biographical essay on Latino (*El Negro Juan Latino*) was published in Granada in 1925. Describing Latino's rise from slavery to a position of power and influence at the university, Schomburg pointed out that Latino's verse was engraved on the "arches erected to commemorate the defeat of the Turks at the battle of Lepanto." Schomburg also told of examining other books of verse by Latino that he found in the National Library in Madrid. He summed up Latino's writing style as "exact and precise, like fine steel with all the strength yet with all ductibility [sic] . . . with inspiration without artifices to give exact tone, measure and softness. . . . The whole book can be summed up as a work of a historian who was also a poet."[26]

Schomburg's articles also appeared in other publications, including the *A.M.E. Review,* the organ of the African Methodist Episcopal Church; *Light,* a weekly newspaper out of Chicago; and the *Messenger,* the socialist journal of Chandler Owen and A. Philip Randolph. In the *Messenger,* in a review of a book about Russia, Schomburg pointed out that many white New York City reviewers (whom he labeled "metropolitan quill pushers") failed to mention that the mother of Russia's celebrated author Alexander Pushkin was a mulatto, and he added that "American book reviewers get nervous when dark faces appear."[27]

Schomburg's major literary contribution, "The Negro Digs Up His Past," appeared in Locke's special Harlem edition of the *Survey Graphic* in March 1925. Reprinted in *The New Negro,* Schomburg's fourteen-page essay represents a distillation of his major themes, including his oft-quoted admonition that "the American Negro must remake his past in order to make his future." It was a prophetic article for it foretold the rise of Marcus Garvey's "back to Africa" movement as well as the "black is beautiful" and "roots" phenomena of the 1960s and 1970s respectively. In the article, Schomburg expressed his belief that blacks were "thinking more collectively, more retrospectively" and that in the process of exploring their historical past they might become "enthusiastic antiquarian[s]." Schomburg recognized the urgency many blacks attached to establishing their racial identity. Nonetheless, he urged that their research should be "well documented . . . and administered as a stimulating and inspiring tradition for the coming generation." In particular, he deplored those "less discriminating compendiums [about] exceptional men and women of African stock [that were] pathetically overcorrective, ridiculously overlaudatory . . . apologies turned into biography." Schomburg also referred to items in his private collection and in the collections of other black bibliophiles as illustrations of the materials scholars might use to document their research. These resources, he asserted, could serve not only as a basis for the "first true writing of Negro history but [also] for the re-writing of many important paragraphs of the common American history." In calling for an objective, scientific approach to the study of black history, Schomburg repudiated "the blatant Caucasian racialist with his theories and assumptions of race superiority and dominance." At the same time he cautioned against the rise of "an Ethiopian counterpart—the rash and rabid amateur who glibly tries to prove half of the world's geniuses to have been Negroes and to trace the pedigree of nineteenth-century Americans to the Queen of Sheba."[28]

Although he never completed a major, full-length work himself, Schomburg and his collection played a highly significant role in the Harlem Renaissance. Through him the black writers and artists of the period were inspired to see themselves "against a reclaimed background, in a perspective that [gave them] pride and self-respect."[29] Among the many writers who consulted Schomburg were Gwendolyn Bennett, Georgia Douglas Johnson, Arna Bontemps, Langston Hughes, and Jessie Redmon Fauset. Hughes would become a celebrated figure of the Renaissance, but it was not until the mid-1930s, when Hughes traveled to Russia and later to Mexico, that he and Schomburg solidified their friendship and exchanged correspondence. In addition to providing information, advice, and encouragement, Schomburg gave financial assistance to young black writers and artists. On one occasion he even gave one of his overcoats to a struggling painter.[30]

In 1924 an informal guild was formed by a group of "younger Negro litterateurs" who described themselves as "the most dynamic of the present generation of Negro creative writers." Schomburg was invited by writer Eric Walrond to attend their first meeting. "We're all expecting you, so please come and be prepared to enrich us with a mite of your immense knowledge of our subject."[31] Countee Cullen, Jessie Fauset, Langston Hughes, and Gwendolyn Bennett were among the guild members, and Schomburg repeatedly urged them to join the American Society of Composers, Authors and Publishers (ASCAP) in order to protect their royalties. Artist Aaron Douglas, who came to New York in 1925 and whose home became a gathering place for the spirited young creative artists, commented: "We younger people knew Schomburg was there, we knew what he was doing . . . about his books and all . . . but much of [the Renaissance] was fun and parties. Perhaps we were not ready for what he had to offer."[32]

Douglas recalled that Schomburg rarely participated in the "Bohemian" social life of the Renaissance. But although he did not appear at the "hell raisers and noisy celebrations of the times," Schomburg did attend many of the cultural events. At the awards dinner sponsored by *Opportunity* on May 1 1925 to honor "Negro writers now dealing with the sparkling materials of their own group life," Schomburg was one of the guests on the dais.[33] When Claude McKay left the United States for Russia in 1922, his farewell party at the home of James Weldon Johnson was a major social event. Recalling the event, Johnson wrote, "you know that was the first getting together of the black and white literati on a purely social plane. . . . There were present Heywood Broun [and] Carl Van Doren . . . on our side, Du Bois, Walter White, Jessie Fauset, Schomburg. . . . I think that party started something. . . ."[34] It is not surprising that of all the Renaissance figures Schomburg befriended, and there were many, he was closest to and extremely supportive of McKay, appropriately described by critic Robert Bone as "l'enfant terrible" of the Negro Renaissance. Their close friendship may be partially explained by a common Caribbean background and their similar reactions to the blatant racism they encountered in the United States. They also shared a particular vision of the black man's future. Black historian George Kent's statement about McKay could apply equally to Schomburg since they both "anticipated all the stands taken today by those who think of themselves as conscious black men, and [they] understood more deeply than most . . . that the blacks' salvation must come from within."[35]

Claude McKay, considered a seminal writer of the Harlem Renaissance, was born on September 15 1889 in Jamaica, British West Indies, and came to the United States in 1912. Deeply resenting American racism, he was attracted to the philosophy of Booker T. Washington and enrolled at Tuskegee Institute. Disillusioned with life at the Institute, he left to complete his education at an agricultural school in Kansas. After two years he abandoned thoughts of a career in agriculture and decided to become a writer. In 1919 he went to England, but after a short period there he returned to the United States. A collection of poems, *Harlem Shadows,* published in 1921, was received favorably. He soon became restless again, and in 1922 he began a twelve-year exile, during which he spent time in Russia, Spain, Morocco, and France. During McKay's years abroad Schomburg served as his main link to the United States. He sought out publishers for McKay's work, sent McKay money and materials, and patiently answered McKay's numerous queries, which were often difficult and time-consuming. Complaining about the brevity and relative infrequency of some of Schomburg's letters, McKay wrote: "Even if you won't write you are doing the next best thing by [supplying] practical help so I won't quarrel with you."[36]

As often occurs with exiled writers, the themes and settings of the works McKay produced while abroad were those of the land he had fled. As time passed, his memory of the physical characteristics and customs of the United States grew less reliable. Without ready access to reference sources, McKay bombarded Schomburg with requests and questions. "I warned you that I shall make many demands on you to finish my book and do it well. I want a little map of the United States with the boundary of each state clearly marked. Then I want the fauna and flora of Alabama, Texas and Florida—especially the chief garden flowers. . . ." In his typical brazen manner, McKay continued: "What is the salary of the Governor of New York? . . . Can you tell me if Smith, Vassar and Wellesley take colored girls and the exact location of each college and . . . I should like to have a copy of that novel called *White and Black*." McKay concluded: "And now Schomburg please do not fail me. It is absolutely necessary for me to have the map. . . . I have finished the first half of my book and want to revise it. But I cannot do it without the map and some clearer knowledge of the flora and fauna of the South. I have forgotten so much."[37]

Schomburg did not fail him, but after three years McKay, now penurious, began to complain about other friends in the United States who did not reply to his letters. Increasingly he depended on Schomburg to help him keep in touch with publishers and to send him the money that had accrued from the publication of his books. Schomburg was solely responsible for submitting McKay's articles to various publications and for redirecting to other publications those that were rejected. McKay steadfastly refused to return to the United States: "I haven't the money, besides I don't want to. I want to stay abroad and write more things." Gradually McKay became more embittered with many of his black friends and associates in the United States. With the exception of Arthur Schomburg they "had stopped writing . . . when a word of encouragement from a member of my own [race] would have meant so much to me. . . . The white friends in America whom I thunder against send me all their interesting literature."[38] McKay's letters to Schomburg continued to include a long series of questions and requests for reference sources. Although Schomburg's meager income did not always permit him to send the books that McKay requested, he seemed usually to answer McKay's questions.

In August 1924, McKay sent Schomburg a collection of poems that he wanted published. Schomburg repeatedly but unsuccessfully submitted the work to publishers. In desperation Schomburg finally offered to publish the poems privately. In a sudden turnabout, McKay objected, stating: "I do not want the poems published now in any form." He added testily: "I thought I told you that . . . in a letter sometime back . . . I am acting on good 'white American' advice and it is a matter of material urgency to me that those poems should not be published. . . . Nor do I want [them] shown around to anybody." Schomburg, angered by the tone of the letter, apparently sent McKay a sharply worded reply, for on April 8 1925 McKay apologized for the overbearing tone of his previous letter.[39]

Shortly thereafter, McKay reported exuberantly that at last he had finished another book and called upon Schomburg to negotiate for him with several well-known publishing houses, especially Alfred A. Knopf, Harcourt, Brace, and Boni-Liveright. He instructed Schomburg that the manuscript, entitled "Color Scheme," was to be kept secret and that he should go immediately to a publisher to make the best possible financial arrangements. McKay added: "Schomburg, I think you will like my novel. It is a comedy, a satire on white and black and I don't make virgins of my colored girls. No sir! It will shock some of our ultra respectable, hypocritical Negroes but I think I'm nearer the truth and tragedy and gaiety of Negro life than Miss Jessie Fauset."[40] Schomburg scanned the manuscript, and despite having found "some erotica," he declared that it was "some book!!!"[41]

Promising not to reveal its existence to any of McKay's Renaissance confreres, Schomburg took the manuscript to Alfred A. Knopf, the first publisher on McKay's list. It was rejected. For the next several months Schomburg tried diligently to find a publisher willing to accept the manuscript. After exhausting McKay's list without success, Schomburg suggested Viking, a new and lesser-known press, to McKay, who, however, would not consider it. Not only would he settle for nothing less than one of the leading publishing houses, McKay was particularly insistent that Schomburg not permit "the NAACP crowd" to find out about the manuscript. He considered them all to be hypocrites who would regard his book as immoral; the leading critic, he alleged, would be Du Bois. Claiming to be financially destitute, yet unable to seek work because of his anxiety over the manuscript, he wrote: "Schomburg, my whole life is in your hands."[42]

By late autumn 1925, McKay was resigned to having his manuscript returned. In the meantime, despite McKay's instructions about secrecy, Schomburg had decided that the situation of his exiled writer friend was such that the help of others would be necessary. More than likely Schomburg did not obtain McKay's approval before he consulted a few of the black writers. When it was apparent that they would not be of much assistance, Schomburg approached Walter White, then Executive Secretary of the NAACP. He also wrote on McKay's behalf to the "Sage of Baltimore," H. L. Mencken, who replied that the work fell outside the field of *American Mercury,* the journal he edited. Finally, and this time with McKay's approval, Schomburg took the manuscript to Eric Walrond, editor of the *Negro World,* the newspaper of Marcus Garvey's Universal Negro Improvement Association. Walrond found the novel "static," and he sent Schomburg a lengthy criticism. "Reading a novel, I unconsciously put myself in the position of one on a journey. Am I going anywhere? That's the thing—I don't care a whit where I am going but by God I must be going somewhere."[43] Neither Schomburg nor Walrond wanted to break the bad news to McKay. Finally, Walrond persuaded a white literary couple to return the manuscript to its owner. On his trip to Europe, Schomburg, still troubled by McKay's financial predicament, sent his friend one hundred francs and asked McKay to join him in Paris.

McKay replied that he wanted to see Schomburg but did not have suitable clothes to wear. Schomburg even offered to buy either the "Color Scheme" manuscript or a handwritten copy of a poem, "Spring in New Hampshire," which McKay had written in 1921. McKay, however, did not accept Schomburg's offer.

Perhaps McKay's lack of interest had to do with his preoccupation with another novel, *Home to Harlem,* published in 1928, which received immense praise from some, including James Weldon Johnson, but drew scathing criticism from others, notably Locke and Du Bois. Schomburg took an intermediate position in his review in the Philadelphia *Tribune.* He recognized the novel's wholesome attributes, but expressed a preference for less sex and promiscuity. Schomburg noted that "with [Carl] Van Vechten's 'Nigger Heaven,' the colored people got a shock—with Claude McKay we have received a full charge of currents of electricity. . . ." Schomburg believed that McKay's was "a very creditable work," but as there was a positive side to Harlem life, "could [the book] not have been written on the promising side of life rather than on the saturnalia, the rotten, and corrupted? . . . Harlem is not as McKay painted it." Schomburg, not surprisingly, accused McKay of writing the book for financial gain—"the artist is solely after shekels, shekels and still more shekels"—and although he was reasonably pleased with its message, he concluded that, "the book is out in substantial garment too clean for the subject within its covers."[44] Much later Schomburg apologized for criticizing what McKay maintained to be "my best prose work to date." Although McKay lashed out viciously at other critics, he graciously accepted Schomburg's retraction.[45]

In 1934 the virtually penniless McKay returned to a poverty-stricken Harlem and almost immediately recruited Schomburg to help him plan a new black literary journal. Throughout their relationship, despite the writer's erratic behavior and unreasonable demands, Schomburg remained loyal to McKay, and it was only to Locke that Schomburg revealed his annoyance. It is Claude McKay who provided a vivid and revealing description of his friend Schomburg:

> his private taste in books was inclined to be esoterically erotic. . . . [Schomburg] was not typically literary [but] possessed a bloodhound's nose in tracing any literary item about Negroes. He could not discourse like a scholar, but he could delve deep and bring up nuggets for a scholar which had baffled discovery.

More than any other Renaissance figure, McKay could attest to Arthur Schomburg's being "full of wonderful love and admiration and hate—positively liking his friends and positively disliking his foes."[46]

Deeply involved in the cultural and intellectual life of the Harlem Renaissance, Schomburg also played a significant role in the nationalist movement that came to the fore during this period. Indeed, he helped to create it. The philosophy of race-consciousness and "black is beautiful" formed an ideal setting for the emergence of a leader who would advocate race pride, self-help, and a back-to-Africa scheme. Marcus Mosiah Garvey strode across the stage of world history, and the impact of his presence and message reached blacks in almost every corner of the world, including Arthur Schomburg.

Garvey, like McKay, was born in Jamaica, British West Indies, but two years earlier, in 1887. Also like McKay, Garvey was inspired by the self-help doctrine of Booker T. Washington, and he immigrated to the United States in 1916, four years after McKay. Garvey made one of his first public speeches on June 12 1917 at a meeting in Harlem. Called upon unexpectedly and said to have been totally unprepared, Garvey captivated the audience with his magnetism, forceful delivery, and persuasive message. Soon his mass movement became a dominant feature of the Harlem Renaissance.[47]

Schomburg became a staunch supporter of many of Garvey's programs, although later he would express reservations about the back-to-Africa plan. Garvey impressed Schomburg as "a man of principles . . . [whose] name will go down in history . . . for integrity in the Negroes [sic] cause. . . ."[48] By 1921, by which time his mentor John Edward Bruce, after initial antagonism, had become Garvey's secretary and trusted confidant, Schomburg too had become a Garvey disciple. He was enthusiastic about Garvey's plans for black development and impressed by Garvey's financial acumen in arranging for the acquisition of the Black Star Line of steamships. "The Black Star Line is going to increase its capital from $500 to $10,000!!! then there will be an unusual howl from the doubters . . . Garvey is the man!" Although he wrote, "Garvey, veni, vidi, vici,"[49] Schomburg chose not to risk criticism from his colleagues in the American Negro Academy and turned down Bruce's request to have Garvey address the body. In a letter to John Wesley Cromwell, Schomburg wrote, "I have just returned from 'all over' the state to find Bruce's letter pleading

for the opportunity to hear Garvey express his ideas. I think he put the matter before A[lain] L[eroy] L[ocke]—I have no objection whatever to hearing Garvey but I am reluctant to bring the matter before the Executive Committee and be turned down. If you think I will receive a favorable reception good and well, drop me a line."[50] Many members of the Negro Society for Historical Research, on the other hand, were either members of Garvey's Universal Negro Improvement Association (U.N.I.A.) or, like Schomburg, were advocates of the organization's plans and goals. Schomburg did not join the U.N.I.A., but he did entertain Garvey in his home, lend him items from his collection, translate letters and documents for him, and contribute articles to Garvey's newspaper, the *Negro World*.[51]

There was considerable rivalry and antagonism between the black nationalist members of Schomburg's Negro Society for Historical Research and those of Carter Woodson's Association for the Study of Negro Life and History. Members of the latter considered Schomburg's group too strident in their pro-black attitude and too subjective and unscholarly in their approach to black history and culture. When Woodson's *The Negro in Our History* was published in 1922, several black intellectuals reviewed it for newspapers and journals. Referring to the study as "a compendium of facts with little interpretation," Alain Locke nonetheless found its fourth edition to be "temperate and objective."[52] Eugene Kinckle Jones, the executive secretary of the National Urban League, while questioning whether miscegenation and fornication were suitable topics, noted that the book contained many handsome photographs and old prints.[53] Over a period of years Schomburg had given Woodson generous access to his collection to select prints and photographs for the book. Often Woodson would leave Schomburg's home with batches of material, and more than once Schomburg had to remind him to return the borrowed items. Nevertheless, Woodson's brief preface made no acknowledgment of Schomburg's assistance and generosity.

Schomburg felt this was a deliberate slight and not simply an oversight. He vented his anger on Woodson, perhaps intending also to excoriate the entire group of credentialed black scholars who he believed did not appreciate his efforts on their behalf. In a lengthy review in Garvey's newspaper, under the headline "Schomburg Tears Woodson to Pieces for Historical Narrowness," Schomburg accused Woodson of not understanding the nature of slavery in the West Indies. He chided

Woodson for referring to Esteban, the alleged discoverer of the city of Cibola in Central America, by the diminutive form of his name, Estevanico, adding that "even George Parker Winship in his work on the Coronado Expedition (1540-1542) . . . holds to the dignity of the proper name of Esteban." Schomburg took both Woodson and Du Bois to task for certain assumptions he claimed they had made about the black population of fifteenth-century Seville. Finally, like Kinckle Jones, Schomburg questioned "the propriety of the extensive treatment of miscegenation . . . for school children" and added, "we need not parade before their eyes the palpable sins of omission and commission for which they are as a race [not responsible]." Although Schomburg acknowledge that the book was profusely and splendidly illustrated, he stated that it was "out of tune with the rules of chronology." Leaving no doubt in the reader's mind that the omission of an acknowledgment played a prominent role in his negative comments, Schomburg concluded, "a charitable appreciation for those who helped Dr. Woodson with rare prints, engravings, etc., would not in anyway [have] harmed . . . the preface."[54] Schomburg's visceral comments were not in keeping with his usual generous spirit and gentlemanly behavior. In fact, historian Lawrence Reddick, who would work with Schomburg at Fisk University some nine years later, found it difficult to believe that his avuncular colleague had written such blunt criticism.[55] This episode, however, did not prevent Schomburg from participating in activities for Negro History Week that were sponsored by Carter Woodson's association. Later, Woodson acknowledged the importance of Schomburg's contribution to the study of black history, declaring the sale of the Schomburg collection to The New York Public Library to be "the outstanding event of the year."[56]

Shortly after Schomburg turned over his collection to The New York Public Library, Locke wrote to him with words of praise: "Splendid!, that's a Spingarn achievement you should and shall be nominated."[57] There is little doubt that Schomburg would have been extremely pleased to receive the coveted Spingarn medal awarded by the NAACP each year since 1915 to the individual who had attained "the highest and noblest achievement of an American Negro."[58] He even mentioned the possibility of being the Spingarn recipient in a letter to McKay in Europe.

McKay wrote that "the very thought of a Spingarn medal to reward the intelligence of American Negroes" annoyed him, adding that Schom-burg could quote him to whomever and whenever he pleased. McKay regarded the Spingarn medal as "the cheapest of decorations . . . an insult to the intelligence of the American Negro."[59] It must have been a blow to Schomburg when Woodson was designated the Spingarn medalist for 1925. *Opportunity* announced Woodson's selection in its July 1926 issue; the unkindest cut of all for Schomburg must have been the editorial praising Woodson's "difficult task of rescuing from a threatened oblivion, records largely ephemeral and carelessly preserved, on a most important period of American history and on one of the most significant experiences of this nation—its dealings with its Negro population." The editorial praised *The Negro in Our History,* calling it a significant contribution as a text for students of black history.[60]

Marcus Garvey's trial for misuse of the U.S. Postal Service and his subsequent deportation led to the gradual decline of the U.N.I.A. Schomburg never denounced Garvey, as did so many others; rather he continued to support the ideals of Garvey and to assist those who were in the forefront of the movement. "We cannot forget Marcus Garvey who for several years gave us much inspiration in trying to awaken the dormant mind of our people and in so doing arouse the ire of his enemies. . . . We must admire his indomitable courage."[61]

The author and librarian Arna Bontemps, commenting on the Harlem Renaissance, pointed out that it was supported by "elder statesmen like W. E. B. Du Bois and James Weldon Johnson, scholars and bibliophiles like Alain Locke and Arthur Schomburg [who] gave it their blessing and helped to point directions." He emphasized the importance of the Garvey movement, which, despite its rejection by many black intellectuals, was, Bontemps felt, an important element underlying much of the Renaissance writing. Bontemps cited Schomburg's "The Negro Digs Up His Past" as a seminal statement of the period.[62]

In a letter to Claude McKay, Walter White of the NAACP described the climate of the times. "The Negro artist is really in the ascendancy just now. There is unlimited opportunity and I think you would be amazed at the eagerness of magazine editors and book publishers to get hold of promising writers."[63] Carl Van Doren and Martha Gruening, white intellectuals who were keenly interested in the period, observed that the Renaissance was an important literary phenomenon. Both noted the patronizing attitude of some whites toward black artists. Van Doren even went so far as to brand the sudden upsurge of apparent white interest in things black as merely "a fad."[64] Schomburg, perhaps for different reasons, continued to distrust many of the whites who during the Renaissance seemed so eager to support black talent. In 1916 he had told John Bruce that "white people call our efforts clever too readily," adding, "beware of those whites who lavish our every effort with praise. I think we should be careful and realize that in the long run they will give us nothing. We must work hard and earn each token."[65]

The poet Sterling A. Brown was one of the young writers of the Harlem Renaissance. Although he later renounced its premise and refused to acknowledge its importance, Brown provided a cogent summary of what occurred during that time. He wrote that the Harlem Renaissance was concerned with "a discovery of Africa as a source of race pride . . . a use of Negro heroes and heroic episodes from American history . . . [the] propaganda of protest . . . a treatment of the Negro masses . . . with more understanding . . . [and a] franker and deeper self-revelation [by black artists]."[66] Schomburg contributed to each of these aspects and left one of the period's most tangible legacies. If, indeed, "today's young writers, while conceding that the Renaissance left them a foundation, look askance at its failure to build lasting institutions,"[67] it will be because they, as well as others who arrive at the same conclusion, have overlooked Arthur Alfonso Schomburg's bibliophilic and bibliographic efforts during the period.

## Notes

1. Schomburg "The Negro Digs Up His Past" *The New Negro* ed Locke 232.

2. Several important studies deal with different aspects of the Harlem Renaissance, among them: Nathan Irvin Huggins *Harlem Renaissance* (NY: Oxford Univ Press 1971); and *Voices of a Black Nation: Political Journalism in the Harlem Renaissance* ed Theodore G. Vincent (San Francisco: Ramparts Press 1973). A readable volume edited by a participant in the events in *Harlem Renaissance Remembered, Essays Edited with a Memoir by Arna Bontemps* (NY: Dodd, Mead 1972); see also Anderson *This Was Harlem*; David Levering Lewis *When Harlem Was in Vogue* (NY: Alfred A. Knopf 1981); and *The Harlem Renaissance: An Historical Directory for the Era* comp Bruce Kellner (Westport, Conn.: Greenwood Press 1984).

3. Schomburg to City Editor, NY *Sun,* Mar 1918, in box 123, folder 5, Schomburg Papers, SCRBC.

4. Schomburg to Cromwell, Sept 1 1923, box 24-2, folder 28, Cromwell Family Papers, MSRC. A leader in this campaign was Robert Abbott's newspaper, the Chicago *Defender,* in which articles and editorials held forth glowing promises of jobs and prosperity awaiting blacks who moved north.

5. Schomburg to Cromwell, July 28 1919, box 24-1, folder 23, Cromwell Family Papers, MSRC.

6. Muraskin *Middle-class Blacks in a White Society* 221-22.

7. James Weldon Johnson "Harlem: The Culture Capital" *The New Negro* 301-11 and Langston Hughes "My Early Days in Harlem" *Harlem, a Community in Transition* ed John Henrik Clarke (NY: Citadel Press 1964) 64. Former curator Jean Blackwell Hutson's article about the history of The New York Public Library's Schomburg Collection is also in this volume.

8. Osofsky *Harlem: The Making of a Ghetto* 135. Osofsky's study is an historical account of the birth of black Harlem and presents a picture of the community during the Renaissance period; for contrast, see James Weldon Johnson *Black Manhattan* (NY: Atheneum 1969) 145-59. *Opportunity* devoted its entire Nov 1926 issue to Harlem's West Indian population.

9. Schomburg "The Negro Digs Up His Past" *The New Negro* ed Locke 236. Schomburg's bibliography of "Notable Early Books by Negroes" is included in this volume. "The Negro Digs Up His Past" was reprinted in other Renaissance publications; see *Anthology of American Negro Literature* ed V. F. Calverton (NY: Modern Library 1929) and *Negro* ed Cunard. It is also included in Huggins *Harlem Renaissance.*

10. Langston Hughes "The Negro Artist and the Racial Mountain" *Nation* 122 (June 23 1926) 692-94.

11. Locke *The New Negro* 8, 14, 16.

12. Dabney to Schomburg, Nov 23 1927, Schomburg Papers, SCRBC.

13. Locke "In memoriam: Arthur Alfonso Schomburg 1874-1938."

14. A. A. Schomburg "The Fight for Liberty in St. Lucia" *Crisis* 2 (May 1911) 33-34. See also Charles Johnson "Rise of the Negro Magazine" *Journal of Negro History* 13 (Jan 1928) 7-21 and Du Bois to Schomburg, Oct 21 1912, Aug 13 1915, Nov 16 1916, and Oct 13 1917, Schomburg Papers, SCRBC.

15. Arthur A. Schomburg "General Evaristo Estenoz" *Crisis* 4 (July 1912) 143-44.

16. Arthur A. Schomburg "Sebastian Gomez" *Crisis* 11 (Jan 1916) 136-37.

17. Madeline G. Allison "The Horizon" *Crisis* 23 (Mar 1922) 220 and Arthur A. Schomburg "In Quest of Juan de Pareja" *Crisis* 34 (July 1927) 153-54, 174.

18. "Arthur Schomburg" *Opportunity* 4 (June 1926) 175.

19. Arthur A. Schomburg "General Antonio Maceo" *Crisis* 38 (May 1931) 155-56, 174 and "Alessandro, First Duke of Florence, the Negro Medici" *Crisis* 38 (Dec 1931) 421-22.

20. Arthur Schomburg "The Negro and Christianity" *Opportunity* 2 (Sept 1924) 362-64. A study of the Urban League and its role during the Harlem Renaissance is Guichard Parris and Lester Brooks *Blacks in the City: A History of the Urban League* (Boston: Little, Brown 1971).

21. *Opportunity* 4 (Nov 1926) 334; 355-56; 353-55, 363.

22. Arthur A. Schomburg "The Negro Brotherhood of Sevilla" *Opportunity* 5 (June 1927) 162-64 and "Negroes in Sevilla" *Opportunity* 6 (Mar 1928) 70-71, 93.

23. Arthur A. Schomburg "Notes on Panama and the Negro" *Opportunity* 6 (July 1928) 207-09.

24. Arthur A. Schomburg "My Trip to Cuba in Quest of Negro Books" *Opportunity* 11 (Feb 1933) 48-50.

25. Charles S. Johnson, ed *Ebony and Topaz: A Collectanea* (NY: National Urban League 1927) ii. See also Patrick J. Gilpin "Charles S. Johnson, Entrepreneur of the Harlem Renaissance" *Harlem Renaissance Remembered* 215-24.

26. Arthur A. Schomburg "Juan Latino, Magister Latinus" *Ebony and Topaz* ed Charles S. Johnson 69, 72.

27. Arthur A. Schomburg, review of *The Penitent* by Edna Worthley, *Messenger* 2 (May 1923) 712. Schomburg made exceptional efforts to gather material about Pushkin.

28. Arthur A. Schomburg "The Negro Digs Up His Past" *The New Negro* ed Locke 231, 236.

29. *The New Negro* 237.

30. Interview with Regina Anderson Andrews, July 18 1973. Both Nathaniel and Fernando Schomburg mentioned the overcoat story in their interviews.

31. Eric D. Walrond to Schomburg, Nov 3 1924, Schomburg Papers, SCRBC.

32. Interview with Aaron Douglas [now deceased], Nov 13 1973, Fisk University, Nashville, Tenn.

33. Douglas interview and James Weldon Johnson to Schomburg, Apr 20 1925, Schomburg Papers, SCRBC.

34. James Weldon Johnson to Claude McKay, Aug 21 1930, Claude McKay Papers, James Weldon Johnson Memorial Collection, Yale University. Langston Hughes further described these parties—formal and informal—in his autobiography *The Big Sea* (NY: Hill and Wang 1940) 243-49.

35. Robert A. Bone *The Negro Novel in America* rev ed (NY: Yale Univ Press 1965) 67 and George E. Kent "The Soulful Way of Claude McKay" *Black World* 20 (Nov 1970) 37-51. *The Passion of Claude McKay: Selected Poetry and Prose, 1912-1948* ed Wayne F. Cooper (NY: Schocken Books 1973) 139-43 contains three letters from McKay to Arthur Schomburg.

36. McKay to Schomburg, Mar 1 1920, Schomburg Papers, SCRBC.

37. McKay to Schomburg, Mar 1 1920, Schomburg Papers, SCRBC.

38. McKay to Schomburg, Sept 25 1923 and Feb 4 1924, Schomburg Papers, SCRBC.

39. McKay to Schomburg, Jan (?) 1926 and Apr 8 1925, Schomburg Papers, SCRBC.

40. McKay to Schomburg, Apr 28 1925, Schomburg Papers, SCRBC.

41. Schomburg to McKay, June 22 1925, Claude McKay Papers, James Weldon Johnson Memorial Collection, Yale University.

42. McKay to Schomburg, see June 3 1925; also July 17, July 22, and Aug 3 1925, Schomburg Papers, SCRBC.

43. Waldron to Schomburg, Dec 24 1925, Schomburg Papers, SCRBC.

44. "Home to Harlem" rev by A. A. Schomburg, typescript, box 13, folder 10, Schomburg Papers, SCRBC; also clipping, Philadelphia *Tribune* Mar 15 1928, box 12, folder 5, Schomburg Papers, SCRBC.

45. McKay to Schomburg, May 7 1933, Schomburg Papers, SCRBC.

46. McKay *Harlem: Negro Metropolis* 141, 142.

47. James Weldon Johnson *Black Manhattan* 253. More about Garvey's influence during this time is found in John Henrik Clarke "The Impact of Marcus Garvey on the Harlem Renaissance" *Marcus Garvey and the Vision of Africa* ed John Henrik Clarke (NY: Vintage Books 1974) 180-88. See also Martin *Race First.*

48. Schomburg to Cromwell, July 28 1919, box 24-1, folder 23, Cromwell Family Papers, MSRC.

49. Schomburg to Cromwell, undated, box 24-2, folder 32, Cromwell Family Papers, MSRC.

50. Schomburg to Cromwell, Oct 27 1921 and Nov 12 1921, and see also Aug 4 1921, box 24-2, folder 24, Cromwell Family Papers, MSRC.

51. Fernando Schomburg's interview with Ruth Ann Stewart and author's interview with James E. Allen [now deceased], Jan 22 1972. See also Martin *Race First* 86, 288; Du Bois to Schomburg, Nov 9 1920, and Du Bois to W. A. Domingo, Nov 9 1920, Schomburg Papers, SCRBC.

52. Alain Locke, review of *The Negro in Our History* by Carter G. Woodson, *Journal of Negro History* 12 (Jan 1927) 99.

53. Eugene Kinckle Jones, review of *The Negro in Our History—Messenger* 5 (May 1923) 704-22.

54. Arthur A. Schomburg, review of *The Negro in Our History—Negro World* (Nov 4 1922) 3; rpt in *Voices of a Black Nation* 340-42.

55. Telephone conversation with Lawrence Reddick, Feb 5 1974.

56. Carter Woodson "The Celebration of Negro History Week 1927" *Journal of Negro History* 12 (Apr 1927) 108. See also *Crisis* 33 (Mar 1922) 200, *Opportunity* 6 (Aug 1928) 249 and 7 (July 1938) 197.

57. Locke to Schomburg, n.d., Schomburg Papers, SCRBC.

58. Langston Hughes *Fight for Freedom: The Story of the N.A.A.C.P.* (NY: W. W. Norton 1962) 192. See also "Spingarn Medal" *Crisis* 8 (May 1914) 88 and "Survey of the Month" *Opportunity* 4 (July 1926) 230.

59. McKay to Schomburg, July 17 1925, Schomburg Papers, SCRBC.

60. "The Spingarn Medalist" *Opportunity* 4 (July 1926) 207.

61. Arturo A. Schomburg "Negroes in the League of Nations" NY *Age* (Sept 4 1935).

62. Arna Bontemps, Oral History interview, pt I, Oral History Project, Fisk University Library, Nashville, Tenn.

63. Walter White to Claude McKay, May 20 1925, Claude McKay Papers, James Weldon Johnson Collection, Yale University.

64. Carl Van Doren "The Negro Renaissance" *Century Magazine* 3 (Mar 1926) 635; Martha Gruening "The Negro Renaissance" *Hound and Horn* 5 (Apr-June 1932) 504.

65. Schomburg to Bruce, July 14 1916, Bruce Papers, SCRBC. See also Schomburg to Cromwell, Mar 5 1924, box 24-2, folder 29, Cromwell Family Papers, MSRC.

Both Regina Anderson Andrews and Ethel Ray Nance, Charles S. Johnson's former secretary, mentioned that during the period some blacks displayed a cynical distrust of the "supportive whites."

66. Sterling Brown *Negro Poetry and Drama* (Washington, D.C.: Associates in Negro Folk Education 1937) 61.

67. George Kent "Patterns of the Harlem Renaissance" *Harlem Renaissance Remembered* ed Bontemps 49.

# ELINOR DES VERNEY SINNETTE (ESSAY DATE 1989)

**SOURCE:** Sinnette, Elinor Des Verney. "The Library, Harlem's Cultural Center." In *Arthur Alfonso Schomburg: Black Bibliophile and Collector*, pp. 131-48. Detroit: The New York Public Library & Wayne State University Press, 1989.

*In the following essay, Sinnette discusses the development of the Harlem branch of the New York Public Library, focusing on Authur Schomburg and on the librarians and civic leaders who helped organize the Schomburg exhibit and the famous Arthur A. Schomburg Collection of Negro Literature and Art.*

\* \* \*

*Effective branch librarians tried to make the library an active part of the community, to participate in neighborhood life by going beyond the mere provision of books and information in an attractive setting.*[1]

The influx of immigrants into certain areas of New York City during the 1890s and the decade preceding World War I compelled librarians in neighborhood branch libraries to find ways to attract these newcomers to use the services of the library, including special programs for the foreign born. Phyllis Dain's history of The New York Public Library indicates that the "librarians viewed themselves as active agents in the acculturation of these immigrants," and the new services they provided turned many of the branch libraries into educational centers.[2]

Dain's observation is an accurate description of the New York Public Library's 135th Street Branch in Harlem in 1925. The branch was officially opened on January 14 1905. Harlem at this time was rapidly becoming a Jewish community, and the Hebrew Orphan Asylum Band entertained an enthusiastic white middle-class audience at the library's opening ceremony. By September 1919 a new migration had occurred, and the Harlem community presented a decidedly different picture. Ernestine Rose, who was appointed librarian of the 135th Street Branch in 1920, reported that the elementary school opposite the library had an enrollment of "over 2000 children . . . [and] over 90% . . . are colored. There are 8 colored teachers. . . ." The school's principal had suggested to her that "colored help would be [an] advantage to the work of the branch library across the street,"[3] so she encouraged the hiring of black librarians

and cooperated with them in establishing many innovative programs. Before coming to Harlem, Rose had worked in lower Manhattan with the foreign born at both the Chatham Square and Seward Park branches of The New York Public Library.[4] Although Harlem was not an immigrant community in the traditional sense, it displayed many of the characteristics and problems of the city's foreign enclaves and could benefit from library services similar to those provided to the typical immigrant communities. Concerned about the need to provide these services to America's black citizens, Rose participated actively in the American Library Association's special programs devoted to this issue.[5]

Richard B. Moore, a longtime Harlem resident, friend of Arthur Schomburg, and a fellow collector, described Rose as "an exceptional person, seeking to maintain a relationship with the community in which she worked and in that relationship aiding the community's cultural development and self-expression. . . ."[6] Rose had a long, distinguished career in librarianship, which, unfortunately, has received little public recognition and whose contributions to the profession have gone largely unheralded.[7]

The 135th Street Branch served a twenty-block area in central Harlem with a population of approximately 125,000 when poet Langston Hughes arrived in September 1921.[8] Within hours of checking into the YMCA, Hughes walked to the library just down the street. He later remarked: "There a warm and wonderful librarian, Miss Ernestine Rose, white, made newcomers feel welcome, as did her assistant . . . Catherine Latimer, a luscious café au lait."[9]

Catherine Allen Latimer was the first black librarian hired by The New York Public Library and was assigned to the 135th Street Branch. Proudly acknowledging that she had "African blood in her veins," Latimer conscientiously kept a file of clippings on black history and set up a small separate collection of books dealing with the subject.[10] Soon other black librarians were assigned to the branch, among them poet Countee Cullen's cousin, Roberta Bosely, who was in charge of children's services,[11] and Regina Anderson, whose apartment was a frequent meeting place for Harlem Renaissance writers and artists. Anderson set aside a small work area for them in the library, and Langston Hughes, Eric Walrond, and Claude McKay were among its users.[12] In 1922, when Ernestine Rose discovered, on one of her neighborhood walking tours, that a Spanish-speaking community was forming in close proximity to the library, she recruited Pura Belpré, the

Lenox Avenue in Harlem.

branch's first Puerto Rican-born librarian, to help the Hispanic newcomers.[13]

During the Harlem Renaissance years, heavy use by readers of books and journals about black history and culture resulted in rapid deterioration of the branch's material, much of which was irreplaceable. Latimer and Rose decided to place all of this valuable material in a reference collection on the library's third floor. They then asked a few community leaders to assist in formulating a plan for the collection.

On Tuesday, December 16 1924, with Arthur Schomburg as chairman, a group met in the library to begin work on the plan. Besides Schomburg, the group included James Weldon Johnson; the latter's brother-in-law, John A. Nail, a prominent black real estate and business entrepreneur; and Hubert Harrison, "intellectual giant and freelance educator."[14] Schomburg had already loaned a large portion of his private library to the branch,[15] and the group decided to continue "to build up a collection which would give the Harlem community a sense of background [with an] accent on achievement."[16] In May 1925, the Division of Negro History, Literature and Prints was inaugurated at the 135th Street Branch "to preserve the historical records of the race; to arouse the race consciousness and race pride; to inspire art students [and] to give information to everyone about the Negro. . . ."[17] The original planning committee remained intact, with Schomburg now serving as president, Johnson as vice-president, Harrison as secretary, and Nail as treasurer. Gilbert Osofsky's study of the Harlem community described the 135th Street Branch as "Harlem's cultural center," and, indeed, the library played a key role in the black Renaissance.[18] Centrally located between Lenox and Seventh Avenues near one of Harlem's main thoroughfares, the branch not only provided reading material for the community, it also established a busy schedule of cultural and educational programs. With a large elementary school across the street, the YMCA up the block, Harlem Hospital one block away, the YWCA two blocks away, and two of Harlem's largest churches within easy walking distance, the library and its meeting facilities were ideally situated at the hub of community activities.

Hubert Harrison, well-known sidewalk speaker in the Wall Street area as well as in Harlem, conducted weekly lectures on black history in the library, and listeners were encouraged to borrow books. There was a dramatic rise in circulation of books in 1925, and the 135th Street Branch led all other branches of the New York Public Library system in the number of community meetings and cultural events sponsored. The library's annual exhibition of black artists was an eagerly awaited event. In an article, "Art and the Public Library," Rose wrote, "the function of a library in any community is to act as a natural center for the development of the community's intellectual life; it will be the library's duty and privilege to search out and encourage any activity which quickens . . . aesthetic interest."[19] Over 100 paintings were exhibited annually, which included over the years the works of Laura Wheeler Waring, Louise Latimer, William Ernest Braxton, and Albert Smith, while both Hale Woodruff and Aaron Douglas were given one-man shows in the library. Schomburg served energetically on the exhibition planning committee, believing that the annual displays provided "evidence of the technical capacity and competence of the Negro artist."[20]

A small display of materials illustrating the "historical and geographical sources which feed the racial life of Harlem [and highlight] the library's place in Harlem life," organized in 1925 at The New York Public Library's Fifth Avenue building by members of the staff of the 135th Street Branch, noted that "much of the source material in this field was lent by Mr. Arthur A. Schomberg [sic], a collector of long standing, as were also all the manuscripts, letters and books dealing with the Negro in old New York."[21] Of the white press, the *Christian Science Monitor* gave the event the fullest coverage, under the headline, "New York Public Library Shows Exhibit of New Achievements." The *Monitor*'s article observed:

> There is a Negro exhibit at the New York Public Library. Within a dozen cases there lies the story of a race. A dozen cases, narrow, shallow, compressed and yet through their clear glass tops there shines that which arrests, challenges, commands attention. . . ."[22]

The exhibition, the first of its kind in the history of The New York Public Library, remained open for four months and was a great success. Although disappointed that more Harlemites had not traveled downtown to see it, Schomburg was pleased, nevertheless, by the numbers of whites who came. The organizers considered the exhibition a landmark event, and Charles S. Johnson wrote to Schomburg, "you have marvelled the town."[23]

Schomburg's collection was, by this time, widely recognized for its great value and inestimable importance to black studies. Schomburg, of course, shared this opinion, and early in December 1925 he confided to John Wesley Cromwell that "overtures for the purchase of my library [are] now on the way. [J. E. Kwegyir] Aggrey wanted it for [Achimota] University in West Africa and since then the offer has been intercepted by more friendly spirits [advising me] against such a course. In the meantime it is preferable that such a collection remain at home."[24]

It is said that on several occasions Schomburg remarked jokingly that his wife had given him an ultimatum regarding the books that were crowding their home—either they or she and the children would have to leave![25] During this period Schomburg received other offers from persons interested in buying the collection; one prospective purchaser allegedly offered him several times the amount for which it was eventually sold. Reportedly Schomburg angrily rejected the offer when the buyer made clear his position that the amount he was prepared to pay gave him the prerogative to do whatever he saw fit with the collection.[26] Whether or not this actually happened is incidental. The undeniable fact is that there is ample evidence that Schomburg had long harbored feelings that he wanted his collection to remain in the Harlem community where it could be accessible to scholars and, more important, to Harlem youth.

In February 1926 Schomburg offered his collection to the New York City office of the National Urban League. It is not known if he asked a specific price, but it appears that Schomburg's primary interest was in finding a proper home for the collection. The league was unable to accept the offer because it had neither the staff nor the facilities to accommodate the collection.[27] Schomburg then met with the National Urban League president, L. Hollingsworth Wood, and staff members Charles S. Johnson and Eugene Kinckle Jones, and they unanimously agreed that the collection should be placed in the 135th Street Branch of The New York Public Library. Since the Library chose not to purchase the collection outright, it was further recommended that the Library apply for a grant from the Carnegie Corporation to make the purchase possible.

The positive response and efficient arrangements for purchase and transfer of the collection were due in large measure to the efforts of three men: Frederick P. Keppel, president of the Carnegie Corporation, L. Hollingsworth Wood, and Franklin Hopper, chief of the Circulation Department for The New York Public Library (responsible for managing the branch library system). In March 1926 the Carnegie Corporation appropriated the sum of $10,000 to The New York Public Library for the purchase of Schomburg's collection. Shortly thereafter Wood suggested to Edwin H. Anderson, director of The New York Public Library, that the collection be named for Schomburg and recommended the formation of an advisory committee to expand and further promote the collection.

Between May 1926 and January 1927 the Board of Trustees of The New York Public Library adopted certain resolutions concerning the collection. One authorized The New York Public Library to accept the sum of $10,000 from the Carnegie Corporation and to use these funds to purchase Schomburg's collection. Another contained a number of important provisions. The collection was to be known as "The Arthur A. Schomburg Collection of Negro Literature and Art" to be kept as a separate reference collection to which additions would be made periodically (however, it continued to be part of the Division of Negro History, Literature and Prints until the entire unit was officially renamed in Schomburg's honor after his death). A key clause stipulated that the Schomburg Collection would be deposited in "such library of the New York Public Library system as shall seem advisable for the purpose of making [it] of the greatest use to the interested public." A final clause in the second resolution stated that although the collection would remain at the 135th Street Branch "for the time being," it was a part of the entire Reference Collection of The New York Public Library. This clause would prove a source of friction with the Harlem community when, on several occasions, The New York Public Library was suspected of wanting to transfer the collection from the 135th Street Branch to what is now called the Central Research Library at Fifth Avenue and 42nd Street. The final resolution wisely accepted Wood's suggestion and authorized the establishment of an Advisory Committee to oversee the administration of the collection. The trustees asked Arthur Schomburg to serve as one of the five founding members of the committee.[28]

The day following the authorization meeting, Anderson sent a copy of the resolution to Keppel at the Carnegie Corporation, stating in a cover letter that "as soon as the collection is catalogued we shall place it on the third floor of our 135th Street branch, which is in the midst of the colored district . . . but . . . if the cultural center of the colored population should change, we can move the collection to another branch." He added, "Mr. Wood and Mr. Schomburg seem to be anxious to put this deal through as soon as possible. I think Mr. Schomburg is intending to go to Europe soon to buy more books for the collection at his own expense."[29] The collection was delivered to the central building of The New York Public Library in more than one hundred packing cases on May 19 1926. It was the library's plan to prepare the books and materials at the central building during the summer of 1926 and then transfer them to the 135th Street Branch ready to be made available to the public by January of 1927.[30] In early June, Schomburg received a check from the Library for ten thousand dollars.

There is still widespread feeling among blacks that Schomburg did not receive a fair price for his collection. It is not known whether the collection was appraised before the sale, but even had it been, given the low regard for black literature at the time it is doubtful that it would have been valued at as much as $10,000. In his later years at Fisk Schomburg himself would be negotiating with owners of similar collections on relatively comparable terms. Recently, black books and documents have begun to appreciate in value, but it is still unusual to find a single item appraised at more than $500. Shortly after the collection was sold, Arthur Spingarn wrote to Schomburg, "I realize your feeling about parting with what has almost become a part of you, and as a collector I know the financial sacrifice you made in letting the collection go at such a figure. You have done a fine thing which should inure to your happiness and the welfare of your race."[31]

Years later, in an interview with Gustavo Urrutia, editor of the Cuban newspaper *Diario de la marina,* Schomburg himself remarked that the sum he received for the sale of his collection did not reflect its true value—although there is every indication that he readily accepted the payment, not a small one for the time. "[$10,000] is hardly what the books cost me. Some of [them] are actually priceless and cost a great deal of money . . . the amount hardly gives me back the money I spent to get [the books]. My time, labor and effort

[were] not considered." Schomburg's primary concern, however, was to make his collection available to a wide reading public, and the amount of money he realized from the sale was only a secondary consideration. "Of the books I would have said 'go free, I give them gladly.' I am proud to be able to do something that may mean inspiration for the youth of my race. I would have gladly given the books outright had I not felt [that] in a way it would have been unfair to the public . . . as a gift they might not have been deeply appreciated as they are by having cost something. Those who know what they cost naturally feel there must be some real value attached to them."[32]

Neither Schomburg nor his colleagues had the financial resources to provide an endowment for the collection's upkeep, but the resolutions adopted by the Library's Board of Trustees gave reasons for confidence that the collection would be well housed at the 135th Street Branch. Besides, Schomburg had fulfilled a long-cherished "desire to have [his] collection available in a strategic center for students of Negro life and . . . to stimulate the aspirations of young Negro literary talent."[33] In recognition of his outstanding efforts, on January 1 1927, Arthur Schomburg received one of the first awards made by the Harmon Foundation for nationally significant contributions in the fields of literature, art, music, science, education, and race relations. For his achievement in the area of education Schomburg was awarded a bronze medal and one hundred dollars. Among other recipients that first year were Countee Cullen, James Weldon Johnson, and the artist Hale Woodruff.[34]

The New York Public Library reported that the collection consisted of "2,932 volumes, 1,124 pamphlets and many valuable prints and manuscripts."[35] Part of the Schomburg Collection was catalogued and classified by the staff of the Library's central building, while the remainder was transferred to the 135th Street Branch to be handled there. Edward Christopher Williams, a scholar and librarian at Howard University, "a handsome, charming man from Washington [went] twice a month" to the 135th Street Branch to assist the staff in the classification and cataloging efforts.[36]

With the sale of the collection safely behind him, Schomburg was now ready to embark on the trip about which he had so long dreamed. As a self-taught historian who realized that black history was but a part of world history, Schomburg

felt a need to uncover some of the important missing links—the black history links—that lay buried among the documents of Europe, particularly Spain. Schomburg knew that to vindicate and reinforce his historical viewpoint he would have to search through European archives, museums, and catalogues. Before sailing from New York on June 25 1926 aboard the Spanish steamer *Manuel Arnus,* Schomburg wrote to his friend John Wesley Cromwell:

> On the eve of my departure for Seville, Spain, I wish to express my sincere regards for the many years we have labored in the vineyards of usefulness to the race. I depart now on a mission of love to recapture my lost heritage.[37]

As noted earlier, most of Schomburg's two-month stay in Europe was spent searching for black historical material and was described in some detail in Schomburg's articles for the *Crisis* and *Opportunity.* The search for a lost black Hispanic heritage had another, more personal dimension. During his stopover in Seville, Schomburg came across a small section of the city inhabited by descendants of the African slaves brought to Spain as early as the sixteenth century who had gradually coalesced into an informal group known as the Negro Brotherhood of Seville. Schomburg took photographs of the "streets where yesteryear's Negroes lived near their chapel." On one street, which he referred to as "Calle del Conde Negro" (street of the black chief), Schomburg had a glimpse of a time long gone when the black population was larger and there were black children "playing in the streets." So moved was he by the experience that he took special pains to obtain a photograph of a man alleged to be "the last direct descendant of a member of the Negro Brotherhood of Seville."[38]

Virtually all of Schomburg's time in Europe was occupied in one way or another with his self-appointed mission. He did attend some concerts and take an occasional short sightseeing trip while in Spain, but it was only in Paris, near the end of his stay, that he enjoyed a bit of relaxation. There he met Alain Locke, and on several occasions they joined a few friends at a favorite bistro, "Le Rat Qui N'est Pas Mort," for an evening of dining and sparkling conversation. Although he would have liked a few more weeks to continue his mission, when Schomburg left Paris to return home, he felt that the trip had been a success.

Schomburg returned to New York in late August or early September 1926 on the *Paris.* Among his shipboard companions were Alain Locke, the Rev Frederick Asbury Cullen, and the latter's adopted son, Countee. Schomburg counselled the Reverend Cullen to encourage Countee to enter the teaching profession rather than devote his time to journalism. Countee did become a teacher eventually, but only after he explored a career in the Fourth Estate including a stint with *Opportunity*.[39]

From acquisitions made during his trip, Schomburg presented a case of 185 books and other materials to the Division of Negro History, Literature and Prints at the 135th Street Branch Library, for which Franklin Hopper expressed appreciation. "It is a mighty nice lot of material and the Library and the Schomburg Collection are everlastingly indebted to your great generosity. Please don't ever expect us to make adequate thanks because I know full well that is impossible. You are doing so much for us."[40]

The Arthur A. Schomburg Collection was formally opened on January 20 1927 at a ceremony before a large gathering in the auditorium of the 135th Street Branch Library. Among the speakers that evening were Dr Henry Goddard Leach, editor of *Forum Magazine* and president of the collection's advisory committee, Ernestine Rose and Franklin Hopper, representing The New York Public Library, and Elise Johnson McDougald, black assistant principal of the neighborhood elementary school. Leach remarked that the collection was "the largest of its kind in the world" and predicted that it would assume nationwide importance to both blacks and whites. Hopper, in turn, viewed the Library's acquisition of the collection as a positive step toward the resolution of the nation's racial problems. He also stated that the public library should be at the forefront in promoting cultural understanding among peoples. McDougald stressed the educational and motivational value of the collection, declaring: "Colored people . . . lack inspiration because they don't know what their historical background has been and here [in the Schomburg Collection] they will find evidence to prove that it has been as great as any other race." She predicted that the collection would be helpful to New York City's white teachers as well as to the "five hundred colored teachers in the city." Schomburg, the evening's principal speaker, discussed some of his early book-collecting experiences and reported several highlights of his recent European tour.[41]

A familiar figure in the library, Arthur Schomburg was generally referred to as "Doctor" Schomburg, a title the library staff and the Harlem community conferred upon him out of genuine respect. He was at the library at least three or four days each week to carry on his own work as well as to participate in the library's civic and cultural activities. He served as an advisor to the Krigwa Players and the Negro Little Theater, two dramatic groups that met regularly at the library. He contributed a paper on Alexander Crummell to the "Famous Negro Men and Women" lecture series and was a member of the Library Forum, a discussion group. At one forum meeting Schomburg took Eric Walrond to task for what he considered a risqué theme in a short story Walrond had read to the group.[42] Naturally, he spent a great deal of time with his collection in the Division of Negro History, Literature and Prints, where his presence was felt by many members of the library staff. Pura Belpré commented that "he used to come in the evening . . . to me, up there was a Sanctum Sanctorum . . . I loved to be assigned there while he was working." She added, however, that Schomburg neither spoke to her in Spanish nor discussed their mutual Puerto Rican backgrounds.[43] Some staff members recall that Schomburg was not reluctant to corner them while on duty for an impromptu lecture on some aspect of black history—usually telling them more than they cared to know. Ernestine Rose frequently called upon him to address monthly library staff meetings that were conducted like formal tea parties, with prominent persons as invited guests.

During the 1920s Rose and her staff transformed the 135th Street Branch Library into a black cultural center, and it became a focal point of the black Renaissance. The Division of Negro History, Literature and Prints, especially with the acquisition of Schomburg's collection, became the intellectual showpiece and over the years rendered increasingly important research services.

### Notes

1. Phyllis Dain *The New York Public Library: A History of Its Founding and Early Years* (NY: The New York Public Library 1972) 294.

2. Dain 288-95.

3. This information was found in a coverless photograph album/scrapbook compiled by branch librarian Ernestine Rose. I found the scrapbook in a basement workroom of the Countee Cullen Regional Branch Library, successor to the former 135th Street Branch and built adjoining it.

4. See Ernestine Rose *Bridging the Gulf: Work with the Russian Jews and Other Newcomers* (NY: Immigrant Publication Society 1917). See also her "Serving New York's Black City" *Library Journal* 46 (Mar 15 1921) 255-58; "A Librarian in Harlem" *Opportunity* 1 (July 1923) 206-07, 220; "Books and the Negro" *Library Journal* 52 (Nov 1 1927) 1012-14.

5. See Ernestine Rose "Work with Negroes Round Table" *A.L.A. Bulletin* 15 (July 1921) 200-01; George G. Settle "Work with Negroes Round Table" *A.L.A. Bulletin* 17 (Jan 1923) 45. One solution to the "vexing" problem of serving black patrons was the establishment of separate facilities for them, staffed by black librarians. A "colored" branch library, opened in Roanoke, Va. in 1921, soon became a popular community social center. The "Colored Department" of the Louisville Free Public Library in Kentucky opened two branches in 1905. See Thomas F. Blue "A Successful Library Experiment" *Opportunity* 2 (Aug 1924) 244-46. A school to train black librarians was established at Hampton Institute in Virginia in 1925.

6. Moore interview.

7. *Who's Who in Library Service* (NY: H. W. Wilson Co 1933) 49, provides a brief biographical sketch. Rose was the author of *The Public Library in American Life* (NY: Columbia Univ Press 1954), a work emphasizing the leadership and educational roles of the librarian.

8. "Report of the Director" *Bulletin of The New York Public Library* 25 (Apr 1921) 240.

9. Langston Hughes "My Early Days in Harlem" *Freedomways* 3 (Summer 1963) 312.

10. Elise Johnson McDougald "The Task of Negro Womanhood" *The New Negro* 376. McDougald wrote about Catherine Latimer's career, pointing out the "opportunities in the field of trained library work for Negro women."

11. As a youth, artist Jacob Lawrence participated in an art workshop at the library, where librarian Roberta Bosely Hubert hung one of his early drawings in an exhibition. On viewing it, Carter Woodson predicted that Lawrence did not have sufficient talent to be successful in the art world. Interview with Roberta Bosely Hubert, Oct 15 1973.

12. Andrews interview.

13. Belpré interview.

14. See "Hubert Henry Harrison, Intellectual Giant and Free-Lance Educator" *World's Great Men of Color* ed John Henrik Clarke (NY: Macmillan Co 1972) II and Richard B. Moore "Harrison, Hubert Henry" *DANB*.

15. Mollie E. Dunlap "Special Collections of Negro Literature in the United States" *Journal of Negro Education* 4 (Oct 1935) 486.

16. Rose "Books and the Negro" and Pittsburgh *Courier* (Sat, Dec 27 1924).

17. "Opening of Negro Department at One Hundred and Thirty Fifth Street Branch" *Opportunity* 3 (May 1925) 159.

18. Osofsky *Harlem: The Making of a Ghetto* 181.

19. Ernestine Rose "Art and the Public Library" *The Harmon Foundation Presents an Exhibition of the Works of Negro Artists* (NY: Harmon Foundation 1931).

20. Arthur Schomburg "Some Historical Reflections" *The Harmon Foundation Presents an Exhibition* 9.

21. "The Negro Harlem Exhibition" *Bulletin of The New York Public Library* 30 (Mar 1926) 157.

22. Marjorie Shuler "New York Public Library Shows Exhibit of Negro Achievements" *Christian Science Monitor* (Wed, Aug 30 1925).

23. Charles S. Johnson to Schomburg, Jan 8 1926, Schomburg Papers, SCRBC.

24. Schomburg to Cromwell, Dec 1 1925, box 24-2, folder 30, Cromwell Family Papers, MSRC.

25. Richard B. Moore, Dorothy Homer, and Augusta Baker mentioned this during their interviews. During his interview with Ruth Ann Stewart, Fernando Schomburg said there were, in the house on Kosciusko Street, "books from the cellar to the top floor, in every room including the bathroom."

26. Reginald Schomburg and Nathaniel Schomburg interviews. It has been suggested that the man who wanted to purchase the collection and place some of Schomburg's material in a time capsule on his Dearborn, Mich. estate was Henry Ford.

27. Parris and Brooks *Blacks in the City* 186 and Parris interview.

28. Board of Trustees, The New York Public Library (hereafter, Bd of Trustees and NYPL): Minutes 1920-27, May 12 1926 and Bd of Trustees: Executive Committee Minutes 1912-28, June 4 1926, NYPL Archives.

29. Anderson to Keppel, May 13 1926, Carnegie Corporation Archives, New York.

30. Bd of Trustees: Executive Committee Minutes 1912-28, Jan 7 1927, NYPL Archives.

31. Spingarn to Schomburg, June 8 1926, Schomburg Papers, SCRBC.

32. Gustavo E. Urrutia "Schomburg" typescript, box 16, folder 60, Schomburg Papers, SCRBC.

33. "The Schomburg Library Opened to Students" *Opportunity* 4 (June 1926) 187.

34. *Opportunity* 5 (Jan 1927) 20-22.

35. *Bulletin of The New York Public Library* 31 (Apr 1927) 295.

36. Belpré interview.

37. Schomburg to Cromwell, June 1 1926, box 24-2, folder 31, Cromwell Family Papers, MSRC.

38. This photograph is contained in an album with captions in Arthur Schomburg's handwriting deposited by Doris Chambers Thompson, Aug 1975, at SCRBC . . .. See also Arthur A. Schomburg "The Negro Brotherhood of Sevilla" *Opportunity* 5 (June 1927) 162 and "Negroes in Sevilla" *Opportunity* 6 (Mar 1928) 70.

39. Schomburg to W. W. Alexander, Nov 28 1934, Schomburg Papers, SCRBC.

40. Hopper to Schomburg, Mar 10 1927, Schomburg Papers, SCRBC.

41. "Schomburg's Rare Negro Library Now at 135th Street Branch" NY *Amsterdam News* (Jan 25 1927). The article quoted Hopper as saying that the collection would serve to redress "the bareness of American life [due to] the cramming of Anglo-Saxonism indiscriminately down the throats of the people."

42. "Library Notes" *Negro World* (Jan 22 1927) 5.

43. Belpré interview.

# JEAN BLACKWELL HUTSON (ESSAY DATE 1990)

**SOURCE:** Hutson, Jean Blackwell. "The Schomburg Center for Research in Black Culture." In *Black Bibliophiles and Collectors: Preservers of Black History,* edited by Elinor Des Verney Sinnette W. Paul Coates, and Thomas C. Battle, pp. 69-80. Washington, D.C.: Howard University Press, 1990.

*In the following essay, Hutson writes of her three decades of work on the Schomburg Collection at the New York Public Library*

## Background

In 1925, through the efforts of the branch librarians and a number of concerned black citizens, the Division of Negro Literature, History and Prints was established at the 135th Street Branch of the New York Public Library in Harlem. Bibliophiles John E. Bruce, George Young, Reverend Charles D. Martin, and Arthur Schomburg were joined by artist Louise Latimer and teacher/orator Hubert Harrison to form an advisory committee to librarian Ernestine Rose and her able staff. Together a collection of books and other resources dealing with the history and culture of black people was placed in a separate area of the building and designated as a reference collection.

At this period of history, Negroes (as we were then called) were moving into Harlem from lower Manhattan, the deep South, and the Caribbean and a new, predominately black community was established. The 135th Street Branch Library, situated close to the corner of Lenox Avenue, became a cultural center, as literary, dramatic, and artistic programs were sponsored by community groups and held in the library. *The New Negro,* an anthology of black writing edited by Alain Locke in 1925, and the special issue of *Survey Graphic* entitled "Harlem, Mecca of the New Negro" epitomized the Harlem Renaissance, a period of black expression that reverberated within the library as well as within Madame C. J. Walker's famous salon, "The Dark Tower." The Division of Negro Literature, History and Prints sponsored an extensive exhibition of books, manuscripts, and art work highlighting achievements by blacks in these areas. During the opening ceremony, Miss Rose stressed the importance of housing such a collection in a public library, "available equally to scholars, to the man in the street and to school children of all races."

The following year, 1926, the private library of Arthur Alfonso Schomburg was purchased by the New York Public Library with funds obtained from the Carnegie Corporation with the assistance of the Urban League. Mrs. Catherine Latimer, who may have been the first black professional librarian in the New York Public Library System, was the main force in the integration of this valuable collection into the assemblage of black books already housed in the 135th Street library. She was an energetic and talented cataloger who also delighted in receiving and instructing young visitors. In 1932 Arthur Schomburg came to the library as curator of the collection.

Arthur Schomburg, Alain Locke, and the librarian Miss Rose played a dynamic role in Works Project Administration (WPA) sponsored adult education and cultural and artistic programs that took place in the 135th Street library. When I was first employed by the New York Public Library in 1936, a part of the general staff was funded by the WPA and Catherine Latimer supervised them in researching and calendaring manuscripts. From 1932 to 1938, Arthur Schomburg lectured and encouraged a wide range of cultural activities in the community. Following his death in 1938, the Negro Division, renamed in his honor, became the Schomburg Collection.

Dr. Lawrence D. Reddick succeeded Mr. Schomburg as curator and placed an even greater emphasis on the library's participation in community events than his predecessor. Reddick launched a lecture series, set up topical exhibits, and took an interest in the observance of special occasions and the commemoration of significant events in African and African American history. Probably his most successful project was the Schomburg Collection's "Honor Roll in Race Relations," which issued annual awards. During the 1940s, persons named to the Honor Roll considered this one of their greatest achievements. The collection won wide recognition and the enduring friendship of its awardees.

Under Dr. Reddick's leadership, the Schomburg Collection became involved with the activities of the NAACP and the National Urban League. The lecture series it sponsored often featured outstanding black scholars discussing and debating the issues of the day. The theatrical productions staged in the library's auditorium under the aegis of the American Negro Theatre proved to be a training ground for such well-known performers as Frederick O'Neal, Sidney Poitier, and Harry Belafonte. Thus in the 1940s the Schomburg Collection became far more than a reference collection. It was a civic and cultural agency or institution playing an activist role in a community that by that time had become national in scope and varied in interest.

# ON THE SUBJECT OF...

## ERNESTINE ROSE AND HARLEM'S NEGRO REFERENCE LIBRARY

As Harlem became the focal point for Black artistic and intellectual activities, the 135th Street branch of the New York Public Library took on a new dimension. The library had opened the branch in 1905 in a neighborhood that was predominantly Jewish; within fifteen years it was half Black. Ernestine Rose, who had developed services in other ethnic neighborhoods, was assigned to adapt the library's resources to meet the needs of the changing community. In 1921 the branch began to sponsor annual art exhibitions, which were planned by committees including cultural leaders such as W. E. B. Du Bois, James Weldon Johnson, and Arthur Schomburg. It also sponsored lectures and book discussions. By 1924, however, the library was facing a serious dilemma. The community's heightened interest in materials by and about Black people had begun to strain its limited resources. To meet this challenge Rose called a community meeting in December 1924, during which a citizen's committee elected Schomburg, Johnson, Hubert H. Harrison, and John Nail as officers. The group recommended that the rarest books be set aside as a Negro reference library. Gifts and loans for the special collection came from the private libraries of noted Black collectors, including John Bruce, Louise Latimer, Harrison, George Young, Charles D. Martin, and Schomburg.

When Dr. Reddick resigned in 1948, the library administration appointed Dr. Dorothy Williams to succeed him. Although Dr. Williams remained only a few months as curator of the Schomburg Collection, she conducted a survey and reevaluation of the facility's role during that time that resulted in a set of recommendations that ultimately served as guidelines for the collection's growth and development during the following two decades. Dr. Williams suggested that the "activist" stance the facility had assumed under Dr. Reddick be "abandoned" for a more reference and research-oriented posture.

## Growth and Development

I came to the Schomburg to substitute for Dr. Williams when she was granted a six-month leave of absence. I stayed for thirty-two years, leaving only one year to serve as assistant librarian at the University of Ghana, where I developed the Africana library. My first decade at the Schomburg was comparatively peaceful because I concentrated my efforts in processing the four storerooms of acquisitions that had accumulated since the retirement of Catherine Latimer. I was the first one responsible for such matters following the termination of the WPA Project in 1940. In addition, I publicized the contents and activities of the collection to local groups, many of whom were unaware of its rich resources.

The circumstances of Dr. Reddick's resignation alienated some members of the community who had worked closely with him, and I set out to win other users. Fortunately, I had the support of the National Urban League as well as the New York chapter of that organization. Two friends who were most helpful were Dr. Marguerite Cartwright, a teacher at Adelphi and Hunter colleges, and the author Langston Hughes. Hughes began by urging me to sponsor an evening program based on the works of Nicolás Guillén, Cuba's national poet, and Eusebia Cosme, an Afro-Cuban singing and dramatic artist. Translations of Guillén's poetry by Langston Hughes were read. Another outstanding program was based on the book *Selected Poems of Claude McKay* and another on Langston Hughes and Arna Bontemps's *Poetry of the Negro*.

I continually stubbed my toe on the budget problem, which was one of the reasons for Reddick's departure. He had had connections with the General Education Fund, whose grant to the collection had expired, and I tried to obtain another grant from Dr. Channing Tobias, then educational director of the Phelps Stokes Fund. I was greatly chagrined by the manner in which he turned down my request. However, as the result of Dr. Tobias's strongly worded letter to the New York Public Library, I was given an increased budget for the Schomburg. Up until then the growth of the collection was largely due to gifts, but Dr. Tobias's letter forcefully made the point that it was about time the library purchased the books needed for the Schomburg Collection. Among the important acquisitions that were processed in this period were the papers of the Negro Writers Project, *The Negro in New York,* and the papers of the National Negro Congress.

I recall the turmoil I caused among the staff for having the collection inventoried; such mundane duties had not been performed in twenty years. When the inventory was complete, I had the satisfaction of getting all the holdings in sequential order. At this time the collection was housed on the top floor of the new library building on 136th Street named for poet Countee Cullen in 1950. To enter the Schomburg, one had to climb four steep flights of stairs, a fact that barred Dr. Alain Locke from completing his last work and caused asthmatic attacks in others. Then in 1954 the collection was given quarters in the old 135th Street building, usurping space formerly allotted to the children's collection; the children did the climbing to the second floor of the Countee Cullen building.

Also in 1954 came the historic Supreme Court decision on school desegregation. Much of the research for the legal brief preceding that decision had been prepared in the Schomburg. The small staff had a real sense of participating in that event. But then came the scary suggestion within the New York Public Library Administration that the Schomburg Collection would not be needed any longer because Negro history would be integrated into the general collections!

One friend of the Schomburg, Robert Kingery, who was then chief of the Preparation Division of the New York Public Library, arranged for the G. K. Hall Company to film the catalog of the Schomburg Collection. This was done in spite of the misgivings of the perfectionist cataloger who dreaded having any mistakes so preserved. To the surprise of all concerned, this publication, *The Dictionary Catalog of the Schomburg Collection of Negro Literature and History* (1962), sold to libraries throughout the United States, Europe, and Africa. Mr. Hall had undertaken this publication as a somewhat philanthropic gesture, but was pleased and surprised that it sold.

It didn't do the Schomburg any harm to have the *Dictionary Catalog* available when black studies emerged in the 1960s as a result of the so-called black revolution. Libraries that had seemed unable to afford books purchased the catalog and before long G. K. Hall issued a supplement in 1967 and in 1972.

A dramatic event that I now recognize as typical of my story was the joyful way I entered into the plan to observe the ninetieth birthday of Dr. W. E. B. Du Bois in 1958. At this period, Du Bois had been indicted by the federal government for failing to register as a Communist under the Alien Registration Act. A bust of Du Bois sculpted by William Zorach was placed in the Schomburg Collection and historian Van Wyck Brooks delivered an appreciative lecture for the celebration. The reading room was jammed with FBI agents watching the Communists, and the Communists watching anti-Communists to such an extent that most of the readers who usually attended such programs were left on the sidewalk. The event was climaxed by a coalition of anti-Communist forces writing threats to cut off contributions to the New York Public Library.

### Funding Concerns

Meanwhile, in March 1971, a corporation was formed by individuals and organizations concerned with the Schomburg Collection's needs and future. Some personal history forms a background for this corporation. The seed for its development was planted in my mind by Dr. Carleton Sprague Smith, who had known Arthur Schomburg and witnessed the collection's early development. He had also participated in fund raising for the Library for the Performing Arts as it developed as a part of Lincoln Center. Dr. Smith visited my flat in Ghana while I was working at the university there in the academic year of 1964-65, and said: "When you come home we'll have to do something about the Schomburg." Sure enough, he did meet with me when I came home in 1965. Then with the help of Whitney Young of the National Urban League (through his friendship with the Rockefeller brothers), I attended the First World Festival of Negro Arts in Dakar, Senegal, in April 1966. My chief intent was to acquire, for the Schomburg, publications I had spied in Dakar when I was on my way down the coast of West Africa going to Ghana in 1964.

Through my friendship with Langston Hughes, who was the center of much admiration in Dakar, along with Leopold Senghor and Amie Cesaire as the historical and literary trio responsible for the festival, I came to the attention of *Ebony* magazine. An *Ebony* staff writer who relied upon the Schomburg Collection for his research was Allen Morrison, who had tried without success to convince *Ebony* editors to run a story on the Schomburg Collection. Not until I was noticed by the *Ebony* representatives at the festival was the Schomburg considered newsworthy. Thus, Ponchita Pierce, with whom I shared the plane traveling overnight to Dakar, wrote the influential story titled "Schomburg's Ailing Collection" in the October 1967 edition of *Ebony*.

Of course, this was also the period in which the concern about black history was stirring college students. During the students' strike at Columbia University, the Harlem community threatened to take over the Schomburg and to make it independent of the New York Public Library: that demand was taken seriously by the library administration.

I may have played a part in arousing concern about the future welfare of the Schomburg because I spoke of the need for an endowment when I was given an award by the Association for the Study of Negro Life and History in February 1966. Dr. Kenneth B. Clark received an award on that same occasion and said, I recall, that "accepting an award for past behavior is making a commitment for the future," and he pledged himself to work to ensure the future of the Schomburg. Earlier, Clark had written in the *Wilson Library Bulletin,* September 1965, an essay on what an inspiration Arthur Schomburg had been to him when as a small immigrant boy he was not permitted to play in the streets of Harlem. He met Schomburg when he ventured upstairs to the third floor of the library, where Schomburg explained to him the significance of the heroes whose pictures adorned the walls and emphasized the fact that one need not be physically tall and large to be heroic.

After this award ceremony, the Schomburg Endowment Fund was established under Dr. Clark's leadership. Members met and raised funds and became involved with yet other groups that met at the Harlem YMCA, discussing what to do about the Schomburg Collection. Out of such discussions there emerged another organization, the Schomburg Corporation, incorporated in March 1971, and concerned about the condition, needs, and future of the Schomburg Collection.[1] The purposes of the Schomburg Corporation were to raise funds for the conservation and preservation of material in the collection, to work toward the construction of a new building that would adequately house the collection, and to solicit new material for the collection.

The Schomburg Corporation helped to obtain a grant from the National Endowment for the Humanities in 1972, and it raised funds to meet the requirements of that grant. The grant continued through June 30, 1974, and was followed by a second and third grant from the NEH for 1974-76 and 1976-78. The corporation, with cooperation from the New York Public Library and interested political figures, secured an award under the Federal Public Works Employment Act of 1976 to give the Schomburg Collection its vitally needed new home.

One little-known aspect of the recent history of the Schomburg is the vital support of the New York State Legislature, which has enabled the Schomburg to maintain longer hours of opening than many other units of the New York Public Library and has substantially augmented funds for staff, acquisitions, and preservation. The first grants in 1973 were largely spearheaded by State Senator Sidney von Luther, but his effectiveness has been continued and even extended by Senator Carl McCall and Assemblyman George Miller, with the support of the Black and Puerto Rican Legislative Caucus.

A national fund-raising campaign by mail, under the leadership of Mrs. Ralph Bunche and Drs. John Hope Franklin and Robert Weaver, raised matching funds for two grants from the National Endowment for the Arts. It initiated an annual fund-raising dinner and produced a quarterly journal mailed to donors and national educational institutions. Today the Schomburg is a living monument to the efforts and concerns of those who helped transfer the private library of Arthur Schomburg to a public center for research in black culture.[2] In addition, 1972 was the year in which the administration of the Schomburg Collection was transferred to the Research Libraries (formerly the Reference Department) of the New York Public Library. The collection was renamed the Schomburg Center for Research in Black Culture and I, the former curator, became the chief. As Stanton Biddle, the center's archivist has said quite aptly, "We gained something and we lost something" by that change.[3] The Schomburg gained professional recognition as a national resource with the January 1972 grant from the National Endowment for the Humanities, which literally gave a new lease on life to much of the Schomburg's holdings by enabling the staff to clear up a cataloging backlog of nonbook materials and a wide range of 89 monographs, 29 archival record groups and 340 titles on microfilm.

In its 1973-74 legislative session, the State of New York provided $250,000 in state aid to the Schomburg Center as a result of legislation introduced by then State Senator Sidney von Luther. Another grant was received for 1974-75. Included in the 1974-75 appropriation were funds for the maintenance and expansion of services and the acquisition, preservation, and restoration of materials and collections, which enabled the center to employ more professional staff.

Late in 1973, the National Cash Register Corporation developed a proposal to convert the extensive vertical file maintained under some 10,000 subject headings to microfiche. The vertical file consisted of clippings from nonblack periodicals, newspaper clippings, broadsides, programs, playbills, leaflets, pamphlets, newsletters, book reviews, typescripts, post cards, menus, and other types of ephemera. This file has been maintained from the beginning of the collection in 1925 up to the present.

The Schomburg Center was designated as one of the Research Libraries of the New York Public Library system. This administrative change provided conservation consultants to the center through the staff of the Conservation Division, and the grant from the National Endowment provided funding for a technical staff that could be trained in the preparation of materials for filming. Meantime, the National Endowment for the Humanities awarded a new two-year matching grant (July 1974-June 30, 1976) to the Schomburg Center, which ensured continued funding for the technical staff. A proposal was drafted, forwarded, and funded by the Ford Foundation for filming the vertical file.

### The New Building

The new building, as described by its architect J. Max Bond, Jr., of Bond Ryder Associates,

> was designed to retain the existing Schomburg building, enhance the Lenox Avenue frontage with an art gallery and street trees, provide a sense of the library's purpose by opening the reading rooms, garden and amphitheatre to public view and provide pleasant workable spaces for those who use the Center.
>
> Three reading areas . . . are housed one above the other in an octagonal drum. . . . This was our way of expressing African tradition in the design element. As an additional reflection of the cultural and also economic links between Africans and African American and because of its beauty, sapele wood imported from West Africa was the material chosen for the shelves and wall paneling of the two major reading rooms. Brick was used for the exterior of the building not only to reflect the materials of most of the nearby buildings but also because the largest proportion of minority workers in the construction trades are masons. And we wanted to ensure their participation in the building's construction.
>
> Simply put, the design and materials are intended to support the purposes of the Schomburg Center itself, which are, as we understand them, to reflect and reinforce the culture and work of African people throughout the world.[4]

This lovely new building provides only for rehousing the archival and library collections. "New Technology for Old Treasures," by James Briggs Murray, in *The Schomburg Center Journal* for Winter 1983, describes the audiovisual documentation that has grown remarkably in its new home. However, the new building was planned to supplement the old 135th Street structure, and that structure remains a challenge to the community and the library to be renovated for proper preservation and display of the art collection and also to provide ample space for lectures and other types of meetings. The basement of that old building was the home of the American Negro Theatre, from which many of our most successful actors graduated. At present, the new building is overused by community activities it was not prepared to house. Book parties and exhibitions are crowded into the archival "search" room, the reference room, the tiny gallery, and the lobby on off-hours. Thus the tradition of serving the community is continued and the need for renewed support is still very great.

### Notes

1. "The Schomburg Corporation," *The Schomburg Center for Research in Black Culture Journal,* 1, no. 2 (Spring 1977), 3. Reprinted by permission of *The Schomburg Journal.*

2. Jean Blackwell Hutson, "The Schomburg Center for Research in Black Culture," *Encyclopedia of Library and Information Science,* 26 (New York: Marcel Dekker, Inc., 1972). Reprinted by permission of Marcel Dekker, Inc.

3. Stanton F. Biddle, "A Partnership in Progress," *The Schomburg Center for Research in Black Culture Journal,* 1, no. 4 (Spring 1978), 2. Reprinted by permission of *The Schomburg Journal.*

4. J. Max Bond, Jr., "Schomburg's New Home," *The Schomburg Center Journal,* 2, no. 1 (Winter 1983), 1. Reprinted by permission of *The Schomburg Journal.*

# WOMEN OF THE HARLEM RENAISSANCE

## CHERYL A. WALL (ESSAY DATE 1995)

**SOURCE:** Wall, Cheryl A. "On Being Young—A Woman—and Colored: When Harlem Was in Vogue." In *Women of the Harlem Renaissance,* pp. 1-32. Bloomington, Ind.: Indiana University Press, 1995.

*In the following excerpt, Wall contrasts the "New Negro" sensibility defined by Alain Locke—and associated primarily with male writers—with the racial and gendered identity articulated by Marita Bonner.*

Harlem, the fabled cultural capital of the black world, gave its name to the awakening among African-American artists during the 1920s and

1930s. The Harlem Renaissance with its outpouring of literature, art, and music defined a new age in African-American cultural history. To a degree, the difference was formal; artists' explorations of vernacular culture yielded new genres of poetry and music. The transformation was, however, larger than that. Proclaiming the advent of the "New Negro" in 1925, Alain Locke argued for a revised racial identity. The migration of thousands of blacks from the rural South to northern cities reflected and produced a renewed race consciousness and pride. As his lead essay in the landmark anthology *The New Negro* announced, African-Americans had achieved at long last a spiritual emancipation, "shaking off the psychology of imitation and implied inferiority" that were slavery's legacy. Locke's essay, also titled "The New Negro," defined the terms in which the Harlem Renaissance has been discussed ever since.[1]

Writing that "the day of 'aunties,' 'uncles' and 'mammies' is equally gone" (5), Locke argued that the imposed and anonymous identities these appellations denoted belonged to the "Old Negro," a term that had always signified more myth than man, more formula than human being. As such, the Old Negro was properly the concern of the sociologist, the philanthropist, and the race leader. To see beyond the formula and to grasp the transformations that were occurring within the race required the insights of psychology. Locke's analysis shifted uneasily between individual and group characteristics.[2]

The New Negro was self-defined; indeed, "self" appears as a hyphenated prefix in the essay eleven times in thirteen pages. Self-understanding, self-direction, self-respect, self-dependence, and self-expression supplanted the self-pity that is the sole emotion to which the Old Negro seems to have been entitled. Ironically, the new positive sense of self was motivated by a "deep feeling of race," not altogether unlike the one that had inspired the self-hatred it replaced. But heretofore only a common condition and the fears and shame it produced had bound blacks to each other; now a common consciousness became "the mainspring of Negro life." To a degree only tacitly acknowledged in reality and in Locke's analysis, New Negro consciousness resulted from "an attempt, fairly successful on the whole, to convert a defensive into an offensive position, a handicap into an incentive" (11).

Perhaps more paradoxically, only by reclaiming a positive racial identity would the New Negro be empowered to struggle for his rights as an American. In this revision of Du Bois's famous formulation of African-American identity ("one ever feels his twoness,—an American, a Negro . . ."), Locke looks forward first to a suspension, then to a release, of the tension in which the terms of racial identity and deferred citizenship are held. The "forced attempt to build his Americanism on race values is a unique social experiment," Locke conceded, and "its ultimate success is impossible except through the fullest sharing of American culture and institutions" (12). Having raised the question, Locke broached no answer regarding the dominant society's willingness to permit such participation.

To have done so would have undercut the optimism that defines Locke's tone in "The New Negro." However qualified his assertions and cautious his predictions for success, Locke was persuaded that the "New Negro" was indisputably a sign of progress. Evidence of progress was everywhere. The Great Migration was itself "a deliberate flight not only from countryside to city, but from medieval America to modern" (6). This interpretation was echoed elsewhere in Locke's volume in essays by Charles S. Johnson and James Weldon Johnson, although the former emphasized the economic motive rather than the "new vision" that Locke avers inspired black people's flight. Having escaped southern feudalism, blacks needed no longer to be preoccupied with racial problems; rather, in the process of their acculturation to urban life, they would wrestle with "the large industrial and social problems of our present-day democracy" (5).[3]

A symbol of their fitness for the task was Harlem, the physical embodiment of New Negro consciousness. Nothing symbolized better the black's entrance into the modern age.[4] Harlem was, or would be, the race capital, drawing blacks from throughout the African diaspora: from the American North and South, the West Indies, and even Africa itself. Not yet typical, Harlem was the augury of the future. It was the home alike of the cosmopolite and the peasant, the worker and the professional, the artisan and the artist, the preacher and the criminal. For the first time since the advent of slavery had ruptured the ancestral community, people of African descent could through their group expression—and the art it generated—forge a new unity.

Art inscribes the transformation from the Old Negro to the New. Like the migrant masses, "shifting from countryside to city," the young black artists "hurdle several generations of experience at a leap." The result was the "Negro Renaissance" that the volume named and proclaimed. Thinking perhaps of Countee Cullen's poem "Heritage," or Aaron Douglas's drawings and decorative designs, among other contributions to the volume, Locke considered New Negro art reflective of the New Negro's "consciousness of acting as the advance-guard of the African peoples in their contact with Twentieth Century civilization" (14). But as important as the African reconnection was, and as necessary in Locke's view for the eventual rehabilitation of the image of the race, the immediate benefit of New Negro art did not depend on its content, but derived simply from the fact that it existed. The new generation of artists would be seen and cause the race to be seen not as society's wards, but as "collaborator[s]" and "participant[s]" in American civilization. With far more optimism than prescience, Locke concluded that "the especially cultural recognition [artists] win should in turn prove the key to that revaluation of the Negro which must precede or accompany any considerable further betterment of race relationships" (15).

Locke does not directly contemplate issues of gender in his essay, but with its imagery drawn from industry, technology, and war, and the extended citations of poems by Langston Hughes, Claude McKay, and James Weldon Johnson, the essay takes on a masculinist cast. Consider, for example, the terms in which Locke couches his analysis of the Negro's "racialism": "it is only a constructive effort to build the obstructions in the steam of his progress into an efficient dam of social energy and power" (12). Whatever had become of the "aunties" and "mammies," the New Negro seemed to be gendered male.[5]

In 1925, the same year that Locke published *The New Negro,* Marita Bonner published the essay "On Being Young—A Woman—and Colored"; her perspective was far less sanguine. Preponderant images in Bonner's essay evoke stasis and claustrophobia, not change and movement. Bonner addresses a female reader, presumably as well educated and refined as she, who cannot plan even an excursion from Washington to New York. To travel alone would offend propriety. "You decide that something is wrong with a world that stifles and chokes; that cuts off and stunts; hedging in, pressing down on eyes, ears and throat." This pressure is applied by blacks. Its intensity is explained by their sensitivity to whites' perception of black women as "only a gross collection of desires, all uncontrolled." The essay concludes with the speaker's comparing herself to a Buddha, "motionless on the outside. But on the inside?"[6]

Alain Locke, Harvard, Ph.D., Rhodes Scholar, and professor of philosophy at Howard University was a major figure in the Harlem Renaissance and beyond. He edited a special issue of *Survey Graphic* magazine, which in expanded form became the anthology *The New Negro,* widely accepted as the manifesto of the period. Shuttling regularly between Washington and New York, he was both a cultural critic and an intermediary between the community of black artists and the white patrons on whom several were dependent for financial support.

Marita Bonner, Radcliffe, B.A., short story writer and playwright, published her work regularly in black journals during the 1920s and 1930s. Her early stories were about "passing," but her more memorable pieces, written after she moved to Chicago in 1930, explored the dislocation southern blacks experienced in northern cities and the consequent disruption in family life, as well as the concomitant social, economic, and cultural conflicts between black migrants and European immigrants. Despite publishing more than a score of stories and several plays, Marita Bonner remained almost unknown until 1987, when her writing, including several never-before-published pieces, was first collected in book form under the title *Frye Street & Environs.* The publication was posthumous. Marita Bonner died in 1971. Bonner's notebooks had been kept by her daughter, who wrote the introduction to the volume.[7]

The contrast I want to develop is not between the careers of Alain Locke and Marita Bonner, two gifted individuals, but rather between the sense of the Renaissance that their two essays convey. The paradigm set forth in "The New Negro" overstates the case for male writers, but it contradicts the experience of many women. Although Harlem was "a magnet" for Negro intellectuals, as Langston Hughes put it, few of them were migrants from the rural South. Zora Neale Hurston is the outstanding exception. Unlike Hurston, the literary women were mostly northern born and bred; they knew little of rural southern black culture, and what they did know they had been trained to deny. Despite being born in Atlanta and rural Virginia respectively, Georgia Douglas Johnson and Anne Spencer wrote poetry that neither spoke in the accents of the region nor represented its social reality. Less innovative in form and less race conscious in theme, black women's writing generally does not seem to "hurdle several generations of experience in a leap."

Moreover, much of it, like Bonner's essay, reflects a strong sense that the stereotypes Locke dismissed continued to haunt. Many of these stereotypes, of course, were sexist as well as racist. But the heightened race consciousness of the period made issues of sexism more difficult to raise. Paula Giddings points to "the rise and subsequent decline of Black militancy, and the decline of feminist consciousness after passage of the Nineteenth Amendment" as factors that made black women in the twenties subordinate their concerns about sexism.[8] Amid the effort to forge a revised racial identity, a woman who persisted in raising such concerns might see them dismissed as irrelevant or trivial; she might herself be perceived as disloyal to the race.

In her title, Bonner makes it plain, nevertheless, that she wants to claim a racial *and* a gendered identity. Writing from a position of privilege—the opening line of the essay reads "You start out after you have gone from kindergarten to sheepskin covered with sundry Latin phrases"—Bonner leaves no doubt that she knows exactly what she desires. First is a career, then time, (in her phrase the one real thing that money buys) and of course "a husband you can look up to without looking down on yourself." But only youth, Bonner quickly adds, makes things appear so simple. Race is the first problematic. Gender is the second. "All your life you have heard of the debt you owe 'Your People' because you have managed to have the things they have not largely had." The effort to discharge that debt entraps her in a doubled ghetto—the ghetto of race and the ghetto within the ghetto that is the gilded cage of the middle class. Bonner writes acidly of the endless rounds of parties and cards and poignantly of the metaphorical bars that prevent escape. The price of escape is the loss of respectability, which for the black woman Bonner apostrophizes carries a racial as well as an individual cost.

Bonner's attack on bourgeois vacuity might be considered in the context of another well-known essay of the Harlem Renaissance: Langston Hughes's often reprinted "The Negro Artist and the Racial Mountain." Published in 1926, just four months after his first volume, *The Weary Blues* appeared to mainly admiring reviews, Hughes's essay brims with the brio of youth and the authority of authorship. He chides his fellow poets and African-Americans in general for "their desire to pour racial individuality into the mold of American standardization." If, for Hughes, the empty and imitative culture of the black middle class represented "a very high mountain indeed for the would-be racial artist to climb in order to discover himself and his people," there was a definite alternative.

> But then there are the low-down folks, the so-called common element, and they are the majority—may the Lord be praised! The people who have their hip of gin on Saturday nights and are not too important to themselves or the community, or too well wed, or too learned to watch the lazy world go round. They live on Seventh Street in Washington or State Street in Chicago and they do not particularly care whether they are like white folks or anybody else. Their joy runs, bang! into ecstasy. Their religion soars to a shout. Work maybe a little today, rest a little tomorrow. Play awhile. Sing awhile. O, let's dance![9]

Hughes leaves a term as problematic as "racial individuality" undefined. And, his representation of the poor veers close to familiar stereotypes. But however much he romanticizes the lives of the urban masses, Hughes as an artist is clearly revitalized by their example. Not only is he inspired by the specific vernacular forms—spirituals, blues, and jazz, which he goes on to cite and which become essential elements in his poetry—but by the broader example of an autonomous self-concept. He ends his essay with one of the most stirring declarations of artistic autonomy in African-American letters:

> We younger Negro artists who create now intend to express our individual dark-skinned selves without fear or shame. If white people are pleased we are glad. If they are not, it doesn't matter. We know we are beautiful. And ugly too. The tom-tom cries and the tom-tom laughs. If colored people are pleased we are glad. If they are not, their displeasure doesn't matter either. We build our temples for tomorrow, strong as we know how, and we stand on top of the mountain, free within ourselves.

(309)

What a sharp contrast Bonner presents. Never referring to herself as an artist, but more and more often toward the end of her essay referring to women, Bonner concludes with a cluster of images of silence, entrapment, and paralysis. Rather than building a temple, she images herself a god, a Buddha, who, in an aside, she thinks perhaps is a woman. Like Buddha, she sits "still; quiet; with a smile, ever so slight, at the eyes so that Life will flow into and not by you. And you can gather as it passes, the essences, the overtones, the tints, the shadows; draw understanding to yourself" (7).

To a notable degree, Bonner's essay anticipates themes and metaphors that inform much of the fiction written by women during the Renaissance. Like several of the texts discussed in this study, particularly the novels of Jessie Fauset and Nella Larsen, Bonner's essay images the consequences of racial prejudice, gender bias, and class stratification in metaphors of confinement and self-division. It provides therefore a useful context in which to read black women's fiction. Moreover, "On Being Young—A Woman—and Colored" defines as well major contrasts between the Harlem Renaissance memorialized by male writers and that remembered by women.

The Harlem Renaissance was not a male phenomenon. A substantial number of literary women played significant roles: Jessie Fauset and Zora Neale Hurston were among the most prolific writers of the era; Nella Larsen's two novels, published in successive years, were widely read and reviewed; and a host of lesser-known poets published regularly in journals and magazines. Long ignored, their work is now being rescued from obscurity. Alongside such men as Langston Hughes, Sterling Brown, Countee Cullen, and Jean Toomer, black women writers struggled to claim their own voices. The voice of novelist and folklorist Zora Neale Hurston is by far the most distinctive; belatedly, she has become the first woman to be added to the list of "major" writers of the period.[10]

Hurston's recuperation intensifies the need to examine the lives and works of her female contemporaries: to identify common themes and metaphors in their writings, to determine who they were and where and how they lived, and to study the level of interaction among them. Hurston's achievement in *Their Eyes Were Watching God* and other books was the end result of a struggle enjoined by a generation of literary women to depict the lives of black people generally and of black women in particular, honestly and artfully.

As these facts are filled in, new questions are raised about the history of the Harlem Renaissance we have at hand. "Harlem Renaissance" is, of course, a contested term, with some scholars arguing that no renaissance occurred and others asserting that one did, but Harlem was not its principal setting.[11] Although some have sought to substitute labels such as "New Negro Renaissance" or "New Negro Movement," which are in fact more accurate historically, no term has come close to displacing "Harlem Renaissance." When one focuses on the participation of women writers, the limitations of the term are clear. Few of the women lived in Harlem for any length of time. Jessie Fauset and Nella Larsen did. But Anne Spencer lived in Lynchburg, Virginia; for much of her

life, Alice Dunbar-Nelson called Wilmington, Delaware, home. Indeed, Washington, D.C., where Georgia Douglas Johnson hosted her Saturday Nighters in her S Street home, rivals Harlem as a center for the female literary community. Marita Bonner, Alice Dunbar-Nelson, Jessie Fauset, Angelina Grimké, and Zora Neale Hurston (who spent much of the Renaissance on the road) all frequented Johnson's salon at one time or another.

Literary and cultural historians have debated the dates of the Harlem Renaissance as vigorously as its name. As Huggins observes, periodization is always a fiction of sorts; the moment a movement begins or ends can never be absolutely identified. So while some scholars apply the term strictly to the decade of the twenties, Huggins's dates are somewhat elastic: he refers to a "decade of change—roughly between World War I and the Great Depression." Rejecting the Harlem label, Arthur P. Davis and Michael Peplow date the New Negro Renaissance from 1910, the year in which the National Association for the Advancement of Colored People and its journal *The Crisis* were founded, to 1940, the year that saw the publication of Richard Wright's *Native Son* and preparation for World War II. Following David Lewis, Bruce Kellner marks the rise and fall of the Renaissance in terms of political events: the silent protest march through Harlem in 1917 and the Harlem riot of 1935.[12]

When one considers women central to the movement, a more expansive definition is clearly preferable. Jessie Fauset and several other female poets wrote and published well before World War I. All of Hurston's novels and one of Fauset's were published after the start of the Great Depression. As a consequence, neither Huggins nor Lewis in their studies of the Harlem Renaissance considers Hurston's major fiction. With good reason, Gloria Hull has written that "women writers are tyrannized by periodization."[13] In an effort to undo that tyranny, this study will draw flexible perimeters.

Convenient, if arbitrary, literary markers of the Harlem Renaissance are the publication of two significant anthologies: James Weldon Johnson's pioneering *The Book of American Negro Poetry,* first published in 1922, and the massive anthology *The Negro Caravan,* edited by Sterling Brown, Arthur P. Davis, and Ulysses Lee, issued in 1941. They are also useful measurements of the shifts in the critical status of women writers. Johnson presented the work of Jessie Fauset, Anne Spencer, and Georgia Douglas Johnson alongside that of their male peers, including Claude McKay, the poet whose lyrics seemed to the editor to break most dramatically with the past. Johnson's assessments of the women's poetry were measured but laudatory. Two decades later, *The Negro Caravan* included most of the women writers of the Harlem Renaissance, but the editors' introductory essays and headnotes often devalued their work. For example, after asserting that during and after World War I, "poetry by Negroes was a fairly sensitive barometer of [social] changes," the editors declare that "delicate lyricism was still present in the works of such poets as Georgia Douglass [*sic*] Johnson and Angelina Grimké, but in general a more vigorous, socially aware poetry was produced." Similarly, the paragraph that follows the description of Fauset's and Larsen's novels begins: "During the New Negro movement, many young artists stepped free from the 'problem,' or rendered it implicitly rather than explicitly. That is, they tried to be novelists rather than lecturers."[14] More comprehensive than any anthology of African-American literature before or since, *The Negro Caravan* not only offered an influential version of the canon of African-American literature, it set the tone for much of its criticism.

Despite the emphasis on novelty, the art of the Harlem Renaissance was not as new as its press agents claimed. Necessarily, much of the writing echoed precursor texts in both the African-American and Anglo-American traditions. What those echoes register is open to debate. Too often critics, like the editors of *The Negro Caravan,* have used them to relegate women writers to the "Rear Guard" of the movement, or to the so-called "Best Foot Forward" or "genteel" schools. I would suggest instead that black women's writing, like African-American writing generally, exists on a continuum.

Albeit in more subdued tones than their turn-of-the-century fore-mothers, the women of the Harlem Renaissance continued to explore creatively the implications of what Anna Julia Cooper called the "colored woman's" unique position. "She is confronted by both a woman question and a race problem," Cooper wrote in 1904, "and is as yet an unknown or an unacknowledged factor in both."[15] The same situation obtained two decades later, although the social climate was less congenial to feminism and more preoccupied with racial politics. As the vogue for Harlem subsided, black women writers probed the

social and psychological meanings of their positionality in ever increasing depth. In so doing, they reappropriated "old" definitions of the race, "colored" for example, and figured new definitions of a racial "home."

Understandably, as the most visible promoter of the New Negro Renaissance, Alain Locke stressed the discontinuities between the race's past and present cultural contributions. Although the value of African-American folk art had too long been unacknowledged, Locke argued, it was important in ways that would be recognized eventually. More vital, however, was "a second crop of the Negro's gifts" (15). These gifts were the harvest of the younger generation. For Locke, the "New Negro" was synonymous with youth. He dedicated the volume to the "younger generation" and chose as its epigraph several bars of a spiritual: "O, rise, shine for Thy Light is a'coming." "Youth speaks," he wrote in another essay in the volume, "and the voice of the New Negro is heard" (47). Despite the emphasis on youth, however, many of the New Negroes were not young. Yet no man felt compelled to take years off his age. Several of the women did. Fauset, Georgia Johnson, and Larsen all invented later birth dates. Hurston, as usual, was the most dramatic; she was a full decade older than her contemporaries believed her to be.

Even those general conclusions that remain persuasive are complicated when the experience of women writers is added to the evidence. For example, the exploration of the vernacular—the incorporation of folk speech and folk forms such as spirituals, gospel, and blues—is a hallmark of the Harlem Renaissance. These forms are indeed the building blocks of African-American modernism. The hesitation of women to experiment with these forms is certainly a major reason so many women have been consigned to the "Rear Guard" of the period. But, significantly, even when women writers like Hurston embrace these forms, they modify and extend them in what I consider to be gender-inflected ways.

Strikingly, even in *The New Negro* anthology, Elise Johnson McDougald offers a perspective not wholly congruent with editor Locke's. A social worker and educator, McDougald was one of eight female contributors and the only one to address gender issues.[16] Her essay, entitled "The Task of Negro Womanhood," is both a survey of black women's employment in the New York City labor force and a charge to successful black women to take up the cause of racial uplift. In both these aspects, the essay requires the reader to differentiate among black women, to see them and their problems individually, rather than en masse. McDougald delineated four groups of black women: a leisure group made up of the wives and daughters of successful men, the women in business and professions, the women in trades and industry, and the preponderance of black women "struggling on in domestic service"; the second, "a most active and progressive group," garnered most of her attention. To some degree, this emphasis mirrored McDougald's own class identity, but in keeping with the volume's theme, she used it to mark racial advancement as well.

Whatever progress life in New York afforded blacks, however, McDougald concluded that the race was free "neither economically, socially, or spiritually." One passage responds tellingly to Locke's declaration that two generations after slavery the New Negro could finally proclaim his spiritual emancipation. Demurely, McDougald recounts what she felt the African-American woman had to be emancipated from:

> She is conscious that what is left of chivalry is not directed toward her. She realizes that the ideals of beauty, built up in the fine arts, have excluded her almost entirely. Instead the grotesque Aunt Jemimas of the street-car advertisements proclaim only an ability to serve without grace or loveliness. Nor does the drama catch her finest spirit. She is most often used to provoke the mirthless laugh of ridicule; or to portray feminine viciousness or vulgarity not peculiar to Negroes. This is the shadow over her.
>
> (369-70)

Although McDougald was not a writer, her concerns were shared by some black women who were. As a group, the female poets bore the burdens of the past most visibly. Not only does their work project a version of the feminine ideal glorified in the dominant society's literature and culture, it reveals more than a little of the defensiveness that underlay the words of race women like Elise Johnson McDougald. What strikes many as their conservatism reflects in part a determination not to conform in even the slightest manner to hateful stereotypes. In a society reluctant to recognize sexuality in most women, black women were burdened with an almost exclusively sexual identity. Not surprisingly, then, in their poetry certain subjects, particularly sex, were taboo, and the language was mostly genteel.[17] Perhaps reflecting the restrictions on their mobility in life, these women took imaginative journeys in their verse.

Consider, for example, the poem "Wishes," first published in *The Crisis* in April 1927, by Georgia Douglas Johnson (1880-1966):

> I'm tired of pacing the petty round of the ring of the thing I know—
> I want to stand on the daylight's edge and see where the sunsets go.
>
> I want to sail on a swallow's tail and peep through the sky's blue glass.
> I want to see if the dreams in me shall perish or come to pass.
>
> I want to look through the moon's pale crook and gaze on the moon-man's face.
> I want to keep all the tears I weep and sail to some unknown place.[18]

After its brief opening reference to the world of social reality, "Wishes" transports the reader on a journey through a dreamscape. In contrast to the constraint and tedium of a life represented by "the petty round of the ring," the poem introduces images of physical and psychological freedom. Sailing through the limitless expanse of the sky, in flight as graceful as a bird, the speaker transcends time as well as space. From the point at which she stands "on the daylight's edge," she visualizes the night sky and her future. The desire simply to look seems as strong as the yearning to sail; it seems to underscore the extent of the speaker's current confinement. The nature of that confinement is left undefined of course, as is the cause of her tears. Defined or not, the forces that confine her will keep the speaker earthbound. Her wishes will remain dreams deferred.

Like most of Johnson's poems, "Wishes" is written in a pattern of meter and rhyme that aspires to be as regular as the swallow's flight. Typical too are the use of the first person pronoun and the absence of racial references. The images please; they do not startle. "Wishes" might be read as a pretty lyric expressing a speaker's longing to escape from some personal anguish. In the 1920s, Johnson's admirers eagerly compared her poems to those of Sara Teasdale, a then fashionable poet. That comparison is significant, if only to show how completely Johnson relied on the safest, least controversial models.

Yet the knowledge that Johnson is an African-American woman writing in 1927 invites alternative interpretations of "Wishes." For example, "the thing I know" and "all the tears I weep" might allude to the burdens of racism that are unceasing and inescapable except through flights of the imagination and the spirit. Johnson's journeys of the imagination, like the images of stasis and deferral in poems by Alice Dunbar-Nelson and Angelina Grimké might be read as statements of protest.[19]

The desire to invent another world in poetry is the topic of the aptly titled sonnet "Substitution," by Anne Spencer (1882-1975). In the sestet of the poem, as the speaker and auditor wrestle with philosophical imponderables, the addressee is lifted clear "Of brick and frame to moonlit garden bloom,—/ Absurdly easy now our walking, dear, / Talking, my leaning close to touch your face. / His All-Mind bids us keep this sacred place."[20] Neither racism nor any other problem will invade this idealized world where beauty and love flourish. The principle of substitution is central to Spencer's aesthetic.

In most of her poems, her speakers and subjects find at least momentary release from the real world of ugliness, impurity, and hate. For example, one of her freshest and most striking poems, "At the Carnival," offers a finely hued, evocative description of a tawdry street fair. Onlookers like "the limousine lady" and the "bull-necked man," "the unholy incense" of the sausage and garlic booth, the dancing tent where the "quivering female-thing gestured assignations," and the crooked games of chance combine to produce an atmosphere of unrelieved ugliness and depravity. Yet the possibility of beauty exists even here, in the person of a young, female diver, the "Naiad of the Carnival tank." Her presence transforms the scene.

Despite her work as a civil rights activist in Lynchburg, Virginia, Anne Spencer makes few references to race or racism in her poetry.[21] Gardens, by comparison, are a frequent setting and metaphor. (Along with her civil rights activism, the garden she cultivated was the chief source of her local fame.) In an autobiographical statement composed for Cullen's anthology, *Caroling Dusk*, Spencer proposes this artistic credo: "I write about the things I love. But have not civilized articulation for the things I hate. I proudly love being a Negro woman—it's so involved and interesting. *We* are the problem—the great national game of TABOO."[22] In fact, however, very few of Spencer's poems present black women as speakers or subjects. The juxtaposition of "Negro woman" and "TABOO" in her statement suggests a tension that Spencer never reconciles in her art.

An important exception is "Lady, Lady." Here Spencer subverts the class connotations of the title by applying it to a washerwoman. Investing her subject with a dignity the world denies, Spencer addresses the poem to her. The poem protests the exploitation of black women's labor, but in the final quatrain it does more: "Lady, Lady, I saw your heart, / And altared there in its darksome

place / Were the tongues of flames the ancients knew, / Where the good God sits to spangle through."[23] Anticipating the impulse of present-day black women writers, Spencer not only claims nobility for her subject, she attributes the gift of poetry to her as well. That gift is stated; however, it is not represented in the poem. The subject, unlike Paule Marshall's "poets in the kitchen," does not speak. Indeed, Spencer's language and her allusions serve to hold both the subject's condition and her voice at a distance.

When one thinks of the women of the Harlem Renaissance, one does not think of Bessie Smith, Alberta Hunter, Ida Cox, or Ma Rainey. Yet these women achieved artistic maturity and enjoyed tremendous popular success during the same years that their literary sisters published their books, short stories, and poems. They too grappled with issues of identity, sought forms that could encompass the reality of their experience as black women, and struggled to control their own voices. Unlike the literary women, however, the blueswomen worked within an aesthetic tradition that recognized their right to speak. Free of the burdens of an alien tradition, a Bessie Smith could establish the standard of her art; in the process she would compose a more honest poetry than any of her literary sisters. Consider, for example:

"YOUNG WOMAN'S BLUES"
Woke up this mornin' when chickens was
    crowin' for days
And on the right side of my pilla my man had
    gone away
By the pilla he left a note reading I'm sorry Jane
    you got my goat
No time to marry, no time to settle down
I'm a young woman and ain't done runnin'
    round
I'm a young woman and ain't done runnin'
    round.

Some people call me a hobo, some call me a bum
Nobody knows my name, nobody knows what
    I've done
I'm as good as any woman in your town
I ain't high yeller, I'm a deep killa brown
I ain't gonna marry, ain't gonna settle down
I'm gonna drink good moonshine and run these
    browns down.

See that long lonesome road
Lord, you know it's gotta end
I'm a good woman and I can get plenty men.[24]

The poem's language and references immediately define the speaker and her setting as black and southern. Her tone expresses a complex mixture of bravado and vulnerability. She is a woman who, though resigned to life's broken promises and disappointments, refuses to let them defeat her ("I'm a young woman and ain't done runnin' round"). Still, she is painfully aware of the judgement the world assigns: "hobo" is most assuredly a euphemism. In the end, she draws strength only from an implicit faith that the future is not as bleak as it appears—the "long lonesome road" must only *seem* endless. In the meantime, she boasts of her ability to attract new lovers; it is the only boast she has to make. She pledges to take joy where she can find it, and her words condemn a world that offers so little.

Musicologist Ortiz Walton has written that "the blues as lyric/sung poetry is a medium through which passes the essence of the life experience, both its travails and its ecstasies."[25] The truth of this statement is verified when one listens to Bessie Smith's recording of "Young Woman's Blues," which despite its lyric is anything but despairing. When she sings, "I'm gonna drink good moonshine and run these browns down," the listener recognizes that life's pleasures, though transitory, are nonetheless real.

According to one historian of the Great Migration, "migrants, though harsh in their criticism of the South and its peculiar form of 'justice,' nonetheless retained an attachment to and a longing for the region."[26] To Alain Locke, Charles Johnson, and James Weldon Johnson, the South represented political oppression, economic exploitation, and social degradation; to the blues singers and to the masses of black people who heard in their songs a reflection of their lives, the South was also home.[27]

In the year of the New Negro, Bessie Smith wrote and recorded a blues that registered the disillusionment with Harlem and other northern cities that many migrants had already begun to feel. "Dixie Flyer Blues" began in the imperative mood. In a spoken introduction, Smith commands the conductor to "hold that train." Then she sings:

Hold that engine, let sweet mama get on board,
Hold that engine, let sweet mama get on board,
Cause my home ain't here, it's a long ways down
   the road.

On that choo choo, mama's gonna find a berth,
On that choo choo, mama's gonna find a berth,
Goin' to Dixie land, it's the greatest place on
   earth.

Dixie Flyer, come on and let your drivers roll
Dixie Flyer, come on and let your drivers roll
Wouldn't stay up North to save nobody's dog-
   gone soul.

Blow your whistle, tell 'em Mama's coming too,
Blow your whistle, tell 'em Mama's coming too,
Take it up a little bit, cause I'm feelin' mighty
   blue.

Here's my ticket, take it please conductor man,
Here's my ticket, take it please conductor man,
Goin' to my mammy, way down in Dixie land.[28]

Smith allows her listeners to fill in their own reasons for wanting to leave: low wages, poor working conditions, lack of opportunity, higher cost of living, or family problems.[29] But, whatever the specific complaint, the disenchantment with northern urban life was sufficiently widespread that Smith counted on an audience who would empathize with her lyrics. To be sure, the event the song depicted, the actual return to the South, was at best a fantasy for most of her northern listeners; at worst, it was a nightmare. But many of them, like the singer's persona, were linked to the South by family and communal ties. Claude McKay's title *Home to Harlem* notwithstanding, when asked where "home" was, black New Yorkers were more likely to name a southern town than give a street address in Harlem.

In "Sonnet to a Negro in Harlem," Helene Johnson (1907-) expresses this sense of emotional displacement. She writes in the octave:

You are disdainful and magnificent—
Your perfect body and your pompous gait,
Your dark eyes flashing solemnly with hate;
Small wonder that you are incompetent
To imitate those whom you so despise—
Your shoulders towering high above the throng,
Your head thrown back in rich, barbaric song,
Palm trees and mangoes stretched before your
   eyes.[30]

Rather than blaming the migrant for his failure to adapt to the requirements of urban life and granting him the right to his anger as well as his pride, the speaker concludes exultantly, "You are too splendid for this city street!" The home the Boston-born poet evokes through her references to palm trees and mangoes is more likely Africa than the American South, however. In this respect, the sonnet belongs to a cluster of poems including Cullen's "Heritage," Waring Cuney's "No Images," Claude McKay's "Africa," and Gwendolyn Bennett's "To a Dark Girl." Yet in other poems, Helene Johnson is more likely than any of these poets to treat the African reconnection with an irony that problematizes, even as it affirms, it.

Born in Harlem to southern migrants in 1924, James Baldwin once told an interviewer, "I am, in all but in technical fact, a Southerner. My father was born in the South—my mother was born in the South, and if they had waited two more seconds I might have been born in the South. But that means I was raised by families whose roots were essentially southern rural. . . ."[31] Members of Baldwin's parents' generation established social organizations in the North that maintained relationships among migrants premised on links to communities in the South. They founded new chapters of the lodges, fraternal and sororal organizations that had flourished "down home." In their churches, they preserved the ceremonies and rituals, the ideals, and the vision that had sustained them in the past. On a more practical note, they exploited their nostalgia to raise funds for building churches; one common gambit was a rally of the states in which, for example, the Virginia club and the Georgia club might vie for first place. Entrepreneurs—from chefs to morticians—attempted to capitalize on the migrants' nostalgia for their southern homes. Not only did cafes specialize in southern "barbeque," one Harlem undertaker advertised his establishment as "the Carolina Chapel."

To claim a southern home without enumerating the factors that mitigated against the claim could be problematic, however, even in a three-minute blues record. Not even Bessie Smith can quite pull off the line about Dixie land being "the greatest place on earth." Yet, despite the strong overlay of commercialism in the spoken introduction, the trite sound effects imitating the train whistle and roar, and the untroubled references to the stereotypes of "Mammy" and "Dixie" within a single line, "Dixie Flyer Blues" might have connected with its audience on a more profound level.[32] Its most resonant line—"Cause my home ain't here, it's a long ways down the road"—comes directly from the storehouse of blues and spiritual lyrics. Its theme, that in leaving the South blacks might have left the closest thing to a home they would know in the United States, looks forward to the writing of Zora Neale Hurston.

The raw material from which Bessie Smith refined her art was alien to most of the women of the Harlem Renaissance. Almost to a woman, they abhorred the raunchiness so much a part of Bessie's public persona and, unlike her audiences, could hear nothing of the spirituality or the art in her work. Hurston was the one literary woman who was free to embrace Bessie's art and who was also heir to the legacy she evoked.

Hurston's meditation on racial identity, "How It Feels to Be Colored Me," was published in May 1928. The title, with its colloquial tone and emphasis on the personal, differentiates it from the

formal essays Locke anthologized in *The New Negro*. The contrast is reinforced when Hurston opens her essay with a joke: "I am colored but I offer nothing in the way of extenuating circumstances except the fact that I am the only Negro in the United States whose grandfather on the mother's side was *not* an Indian Chief."[33] The joke is aimed both at those whites who would assume that blackness is a condition requiring some apology or explanation and at those blacks, almost certainly including race-conscious New Negroes, who want it understood that they are not *merely* black. Hurston claims her color gladly.

The essay's next paragraph, with its striking assertion—"I remember the very day that I became colored"—reveals Hurston's understanding that racial identity is not grounded in biology; it is socially constructed. Racial identity for African-Americans might be constructed in response to the harsh racism of the deep South, manifested in the system of legal segregation, or it might be shaped by the more benign racism expressed through and stimulated by the vogue for the Negro, a climate that was both supportive of and crippling to artistic expression by blacks. "How It Feels to Be Colored Me" explores a third possibility.

Hurston's often-cited declaration not to be embittered by either form of racism—her refusal to be "tragically colored"—is premised on her assertion of a prior identity that was constituted before she encountered racism, an identity she achieved at "home." Out of this prior identity, Hurston drew the strength to acknowledge, even to celebrate, racial and cultural differences, while affirming the commonalities that underlay them.

Home for Hurston was Eatonville, Florida, the all-black town that became the privileged site of her fiction. According to the essay, the only white people in Eatonville were those passing through, and of these only the Northerners were worth watching. The townspeople, Hurston asserts, "got just as much pleasure out of the tourists as the tourists got out of the village." The townspeople and their chronicler, Hurston, derive the confidence that makes this reciprocity possible from their sense of being "at home."

For herself, Hurston affirms the identity of "Everybody's Zora"—an identity that makes her one with the community. Yet she asserts some distance from it as well. For example, she acknowledges a certain uneasiness with the community's values—the townspeople, she charges, "deplored any joyful tendencies in me"—but she was "their

Zora nevertheless" (153). In her adult recollection, the "everybody" who claimed her extends to include white tourists motoring through, guests in the nearby hotels, and "the county." While the blacks listened for free, she recalls whites giving her "small silver" for "speaking pieces," singing, and dancing. The offer of money is a gesture that strikes the child Zora as strange as well as generous, because performing made her so happy that she needed "bribing to stop." Retrospectively, her uneasiness with her black neighbors stemmed perhaps in part from their failure to share her joy in performances that partook of a communal cultural heritage—the heritage to which Hurston was to devote her subsequent career to reclaiming.[34] Almost certainly, the joy she remembers here is an impetus to that reclamation.

Describing as a "sea change" her relocation from Eatonville to Jacksonville, Florida, Hurston defines its most traumatic aspect: "I was not Zora of Orange County any more, I was now a little colored girl. I found it out in certain ways. In my heart as well as in the mirror, I became a fast brown—warranted not to rub nor run" (153). A fixed racial identity imposed from outside becomes stigmatized inwardly as well. The persona who reveled in the possibility inscribed by the adjective "colored" becomes vulnerable to the kind of negative self-definition that the New Negro movement was striving to displace.

Tellingly, this recognition of a diminished sense of self in racial terms also occasions the first explicitly gendered reference in the essay. "Zora of Orange County" becomes a "little colored girl" after changes occurred in her family when she was thirteen. In her autobiography, *Dust Tracks on a Road,* Hurston identifies those changes, unspecified here, as the death of her mother and the dissolution of her family home. Although the essay emphasizes the impact of her delayed racial awareness, Hurston's sense of constricted possibilities may have derived as well from the experience of puberty and the recognition of the limitations and dangers to which her emergent womanhood made her vulnerable. Indeed, especially given the unmentionability of "the certain ways" through which she became aware of her gender identity, the reference to "fast brown" might be heard as a muted echo of Bessie Smith's phrase in "Young Woman's Blues."

What makes the tone and texture of Hurston's meditation on identity so different from the others considered here is the sense of home that gives rise to an identity that is not constructed in re-

sponse to racism and sexism. Her term for it is the "unconscious Zora of Eatonville before the Hegira." In his article "The Trope of a New Negro and the Reconstruction of the Image of the Black," Henry Louis Gates argues that "the register of a New Negro was an irresistible, spontaneously generated black and sufficient self. A rhetorical figure and a utopian construct, the term New Negro signified 'a black person who lives at no place and at no time.'"[35] I would argue that partly in response to this term, Hurston invents a mythic autobiographical self that she derives from her ability to claim a very specific place, her "home," Eatonville.[36] Moreover, unlike even those unreconstructed black people who claimed their homes in the South with a deep-rooted ambivalence, Hurston seemed to claim hers with an uncomplicated pride. Eatonville was, as she never tired of pointing out, the first all-black town incorporated in the United States, "the first attempt at organized self-government on the part of Negroes in America" (*Dust Tracks,* 3). Hurston roots her literary persona in this historical anomaly.

Wherever she journeyed, the essay implies, Hurston was able to draw on this heritage and find the strength to remain herself. At least on occasion, she could reclaim or, as she prefers, "*achieve* the unconscious Zora of Eatonville before the Hegira*" (my emphasis). Her flight takes her eventually to New York—to Barnard, to "Harlem City," and to the site that becomes the essay's symbolic antithesis of home, the New World Cabaret. The cabaret is a basement speakeasy, complete with a jazz orchestra and jazz waiters, perhaps like those who made Smalls' Paradise a favorite twenties haunt. There, sitting with a white companion and listening to the music's "narcotic harmonies," Hurston's "color comes."

This passage depicts a second moment of cultural performance and cultural exchange in the essay. This time Hurston is spectator, rather than performer, and African-American music and dance have become commodities in the cultural marketplace of New York. The description of the jazz performance relies on jungle metaphors, as does the description of the writer's response: "I dance wildly inside myself; I yell within, I whoop; I shake my assegai above my head, I hurl it true to the mark *yeeeeooww!*" (154). When the song ends, she "creeps back slowly to the veneer we call civilization," and her white friend, whose race has made her sharply aware of her own, sits "motionless in his seat, smoking calmly" (154).[37]

The scene Hurston draws is a staple in the literature of the Harlem Renaissance and in the popular mythology of the 1920s, the Jazz Age. For those white Americans with the time, money, and sophistication to make the trip, Harlem at night seemed a world apart. In contrast to their own world, discipline, hard work, and frugality were counterfeit coin in the realm of imaginary Harlem. Nothing symbolized its otherness more than the cabaret.

Fiction writer and physician Rudolph Fisher satirized the vogue for Harlem night life in a 1927 essay, "The Caucasian Storms Harlem." Tongue in cheek, he describes his return to his old stomping ground after a five-year absence, and finding no familiar faces, he concludes: "The best of Harlem's black cabarets have changed their names and turned white." He notes the popularity of black art on Broadway, on the concert stage, and even in the galleries of the Metropolitan Museum: "Negro stock is going up, and everybody's buying." The fad for the cabaret remains peculiar. Reflecting on the spectacle of whites doing black dances in Harlem nightclubs while blacks watch, he concludes: "This interest in the Negro is an active and participating interest. It is almost as if a traveler from the North stood watching an African tribe-dance, then suddenly found himself swept wildly into it, caught in its tidal rhythm."[38]

Metaphors of travel and exploration, primitivism and civilization were intrinsic to the mythology. Commenting sardonically on its convenience, Nathan Huggins describes Harlem night life as "merely a taxi trip to the exotic for most white New Yorkers." Once there they listened to "jazz, that almost forbidden music," in cabarets decorated in tropical and jungle motifs or in establishments, like the Cotton Club, that evoked the old plantation. For these Harlem night visitors, "it was a cheap trip. No safari! Daylight and a taxi ride rediscovered New York City, no tropic jungle. There had been thrill without danger. . . ."[39]

As Hurston's description makes clear, blacks could take the same trip, although the price of the ticket was higher. The psychic journey required a denial of the reality they could not escape when the music ended. Familiar as they were with actual Harlem, they recognized that survival there depended on work and sacrifice. Indeed, according to inveterate Harlem booster James Weldon Johnson, "of a necessity the vast majority of [Harlemites] are ordinary, hard-working people. . . . Most of them have never seen the inside of a nightclub."[40] Whether they had or had not, most knew that the poshest cabarets earned big money for gangsters, who lived far from Harlem. They

knew no tourist would trade his position of privilege for the supposed license of the Harlem dandy. They knew as well that black women on or off the chorus line might become objects of exchange between the tourist and the dandy. Most important, they knew that New York was no more exotic or primitive uptown than it was down.[41]

On one level, Hurston seems, through her exaggerated metaphors, to parody the myth of exotic primitivism. On another, she insists that the power of the music, so often expropriated to propel the myth, is genuine. But its power is undefinable and unspeakable—at least in the context in which it is heard. Extravagant as her response to the music is, it is wholly internalized. In fact, the key to survival in the mecca of the New Negro seemed to be to play the part the cultural script assigned and keep one's feelings safely hidden.

But, in contrast to Marita Bonner's persona, Hurston's does not lose access to the feelings she suppresses. Instead of imaging herself a Buddha, she can "set [her] hat at a certain angle and saunter down Seventh Avenue, Harlem City. . . . The cosmic Zora emerges" (154-55). At these moments, she contends, she has no race. Rather than the Du Boisian conflict between one's identity as an American and a Negro, she draws the distinction between a racial or "colored" identity and "me." "Me" is at one point associated with the "eternal feminine," but its definition is never fixed.

Racial identity, expressed through the metaphor of a brown bag, becomes merely the container that holds a multiplicity of elements out of which an individual identity is constituted. Instead of a divided self, Hurston images an inner space filled with such disparate pieces as "a first-water diamond, an empty spool, bits of broken string, a key to a door long since crumbled away . . ." (155). This jumble of elements, "both priceless and worthless," both unique and interchangeable, constitutes a self that is at once individual and transcendent. Thus, "cosmic Zora" shares a bond with humanity ("other bags, white, red and yellow"), yet remains unmistakably herself.

In "How It Feels to Be Colored Me," Hurston demonstrates the utility of the biomythography she continued to elaborate throughout her life. What Claudine Raynaud writes of Audre Lorde's "biomythography," *Zami: A New Spelling of My Name*—"the reflexiveness and the individualism of the autobiographical gesture give way to the construction of a mythic self"—is also true of several of Hurston's texts, including the volume of folklore, *Mules and Men,* and *Dust Tracks on a Road.*[42] Like Lorde, Hurston fuses the three modes of consciousness that critic Chinosole discerns in *Zami:* collective memory rendered through myth and legend (for Hurston, read "folklore"), the memory of personal experience, and the memory accessible through dream (for Hurston, read "spiritual experience").[43] Unlike Lorde, Hurston does not develop her biomythography in a single text, but produces it in fragments throughout her oeuvre; it informs her fiction as well.

Its earliest expression was "How It Feels to Be Colored Me." Even as Hurston wrote the essay for a white periodical in 1928—recreating the situation that obtained in her girlhood—being paid by whites for her words, her sense of her mythic self, the "cosmic Zora," was strong enough that she believed she could dictate the terms of exchange. It was out of this self-authorizing posture that she could proclaim:

> BUT I AM NOT tragically colored. There is no great sorrow dammed up in my soul, nor lurking behind my eyes. I do not mind at all. I do not belong to the sobbing school of Negrohood who hold that nature somehow gave them a lowdown dirty deal and whose feelings are all hurt about it. . . . No, I do not weep at the world—I am too busy sharpening my oyster knife."[44]

Despite the earlier references to sauntering down Seventh Avenue, by the time this essay was published, Hurston was shucking oysters in rural Florida, where she had begun to collect the folk tales, songs, and sermons that would eventually constitute the volume *Mules and Men.* It was as if she heeded the lyrics of "Florida Bound Blues," a song recorded by Bessie Smith that began, "Goodbye North, Hello South, / Goodbye North, Hello South, / It's so cold up here that the words freeze in your mouth."[45] Although she would return to New York intermittently over the next two decades, she wrote and lived most of her life in her native state. There she was, figuratively and literally, at home.

The idea of "home" has a particular resonance in African-American expressive tradition, a resonance that reflects the experience of dispossession that initiates it.[46] In the spirituals, blacks had sung of themselves as motherless children "a long way from home." Images of homelessness—souls lost in the storm or the wilderness—abound. In the absence of an earthly home, the slaves envisioned a spiritual one, a home over Jordan, for example; or they laid claim defiantly to "a home in dat

rock." As Melvin Dixon observes, the images of home, self, and freedom in the spirituals reflect a manipulation of language that "thwarts the dehumanizing effects of slavery by depicting alternative spaces and personae slaves could assume" (14). "This reconstruction of self and space" through language is a hallmark of twentieth-century secular traditions as well. Hurston's contemporary, Jamaican expatriate Claude McKay entitled his memoir *A Long Way from Home.* The efforts to claim Harlem as home found voice in texts such as James Weldon Johnson's *Black Manhattan* and McKay's *Harlem: Negro Metropolis.* In the political realm, Marcus Garvey sought through his visionary rhetoric to inspire a New Negro who would fight to redeem Africa, the ancestral home.

Hurston was well aware of this legacy, as her manipulations of the Eatonville setting in her nonfiction and novels make clear.[47] But her relationship to "home" is problematic. Whether in the process of documenting the expressive traditions of her people or considering the usefulness and implications of those traditions for her own writing, or in the physical reencounter with the landscape of her childhood, Zora Neale Hurston confronted anew the ways in which women were silenced in the performances she recorded, the ways in which sexism in the African-American community stunted female (and male) potential, and perhaps the ways in which she had herself first become aware she was a little colored girl. She did not deny the impact of racism on the community, but she was iconoclast enough to find it most cruelly manifested in African-Americans' adoption of the inferior values of the dominant culture.

For women, feminist theorists Biddy Martin and Chandra Mohanty argue, home often offers only "an illusion of coherence and safety, based on the exclusion of specific histories of oppression and resistance, the repression of differences even within oneself."[48] But for cultural and personal reasons, home was too valuable an illusion for Hurston to relinquish. What she attempted to do instead was to reconstruct a home in language that acknowledged but did not dwell on the history of racial oppression, counted African-American creative expression as a powerful mode of resistance, and fostered the recognition of differences without and within oneself. Hers was an effective solution to the literary dilemma posed by being young, a woman, and colored when Harlem was in vogue.

## Notes

My title alludes to the essay by Marita Bonner discussed below and to the title of David Lewis's history of the Harlem Renaissance, *When Harlem Was in Vogue* (New York: Knopf, 1981); Lewis's title was itself an allusion to Langston Hughes's designation for the 1920s as the time "When the Negro Was in Vogue" in *The Big Sea* (New York: Knopf, 1940).

1. *The New Negro* (1925; rpt. New York: Atheneum, 1992), 4. The standard intellectual history of the period is Nathan Huggins, *Harlem Renaissance* (New York: Oxford University Press, 1971). Lewis's volume is unparalleled in its delineation of the period's social, political, and cultural life. Other general studies and anthologies include Arna Bontemps, ed., *The Harlem Renaissance Remembered* (New York: Dodd, Mead, 1971); Nathan Huggins, ed., *Voices from the Harlem Renaissance* (New York: Oxford University Press, 1976); Arthur P. Davis and Michael Peplow, eds., *The New Negro Renaissance* (New York: Holt, Rinehart & Winston, 1975); Victor Kramer, ed., *The Harlem Renaissance Re-examined* (New York: AMS Press, 1987); Amritjit Singh, William Shiver, and S. Brodwin, eds., *The Harlem Renaissance: Revaluations* (New York: Garland, 1989); and Cary D. Wintz, *Black Culture and the Harlem Renaissance* (Houston: Rice University Press, 1988). For revisionist analyses, see Houston Baker, *Modernism and the Harlem Renaissance* (Chicago: University of Chicago Press, 1987) and Hazel Carby, *Reconstructing Womanhood: The Emergence of the Afro-American Woman Novelist* (New York: Oxford University Press, 1987).

2. Locke's analysis follows the model of Sigmund Freud, *Group Psychology and the Analysis of the Ego,* published in 1921. For discussions of earlier interpretations of "the New Negro," see Huggins, 52-72; Henry Louis Gates, "The Trope of the New Negro and the Reconstruction of the Image of the Black," *Representations* 24 (Fall 1988): 129-55, and Hazel Carby, 165.

3. These interpretations were somewhat at odds with the facts. To be sure, the numbers were dramatic. Over 400,000 blacks left the South between 1916 and 1918. Between 1915 and 1930, New York's black population grew over 250 percent, from 91,709 in 1910 to 327,706 in 1930. Although New York's black population was largest in absolute numbers, rate of growth in midwestern cities including Chicago, Detroit, and Cleveland was even higher (Wintz, 14). But many of the migrants did not come directly from rural areas; they had previously migrated to southern cities. A substantial number of the men were skilled laborers; they found jobs in the North not unlike those they held previously. Especially after the war, during which some women were able to obtain factory jobs, the majority of black women were domestic workers; although certain conditions of employment were different in the North—e.g., they were more likely to be "day workers" than live-in workers as they had been in the South—the character of the work was not dissimilar. For further analysis of this point, see Carole Marks, *Farewell—We're Good and Gone* (Bloomington: Indiana University Press, 1989), chap. 2. Despite the distinctive regional differences then, the journey from the South to the North was not quite analogous

to a flight from "medieval America to modern." And, of course, although there was less racist terrorism in the North, blacks were hardly free of "racial problems."

4. Scholars have written extensively on Harlem's historic and symbolic significance. See, for example, Jervis Anderson, *This Was Harlem: A Cultural Portrait, 1900-1950* (New York: Farrar Straus Giroux, 1982); John Henrik Clarke, ed., *Harlem: A Community in Transition* (New York: Citadel Press, 1969); Harold Cruse, *The Crisis of the Negro Intellectual* (New York: Morrow, 1967); James de Jongh, *Vicious Modernism: Black Harlem and the Literary Imagination* (New York: Cambridge University Press, 1990); and Gilbert Osofsky, *Harlem: The Making of a Ghetto* (New York: Harper, 1971). Two pioneering studies of the community are James Weldon Johnson, *Black Manhattan* (New York: Knopf, 1930); Claude McKay, *Harlem: Negro Metropolis* (New York: Dutton, 1940).

5. The iconography of the first edition of *The New Negro* includes more representations of women than does the text, but it depicts them mainly in traditional roles. The most extreme example is the volume's frontispiece, "The Brown Madonna," by the German painter Winold Reiss. It depicts a youthful brown-skinned woman, hair curled into a pageboy, eyes looking downward, holding a plump curly-haired infant of indeterminate gender; the child's eyes, not the mother's, confront the viewer. Reiss also produced a series of portraits of Harlem Renaissance notables, including Locke, Jean Toomer, Cullen, Paul Robeson (as "Emperor Jones"), Roland Hayes, Charles S. Johnson, James Weldon Johnson, Robert Russa Moton, and Du Bois. The women in the series were the educators Elise Johnson McDougald and Mary McLeod Bethune. Female figures were the focus of other sketches entitled "African Phantasie: Awakening," "Type Sketch: 'Ancestral,'" "From the Tropic Isles," "The Librarian," and "The School Teachers." The last three are notable for their depiction of dark-skinned women with distinctively Negroid features. Reiss's student Aaron Douglas drew abstract female figures in African-inspired motifs. Miguel Covarrubias drew the figure of a blues singer to illustrate poems by Langston Hughes.

6. "On Being Young—A Woman—and Colored," in *Frye Street & Environs: The Collected Works of Marita Bonner* (Boston: Beacon Press, 1987), 5. Subsequent references to this edition will be cited in the text.

7. The story of Bonner's notebooks is reminiscent of the publishing history of Alice Dunbar-Nelson's diary edited by Gloria Hull, *Give Us Each Day: The Diary of Alice Dunbar-Nelson* (New York: Norton, 1984). Hull recounts her discovery of the manuscript and her relationship with the diarist's niece who preserved it in "Researching Alice Dunbar-Nelson: A Personal and Literary Perspective," in *All the Women Are White, All the Blacks Are Men, But Some of Us Are Brave: Black Women's Studies,* ed. Gloria Hull, Patricia Scott, and Barbara Smith (Old Westbury: Feminist Press, 1982).

8. *When and Where I Enter: The Impact of Black Women on Race and Sex in America* (New York: Morrow, 1984), 183. Giddings asserts that "femininity, not feminism

was the talk of the twenties." The idea that black women could be beautiful fit both the call to race pride and the dominant culture's emphasis on glamour.

9. 1926; rpt. in Nathan Huggins, ed., *Voices from the Harlem Renaissance* (New York: Oxford University Press, 1976), 306. Subsequent references to this edition will be cited in the text.

10. In addition to biographical and critical works on individual authors, feminist revisions of Harlem Renaissance studies include Maureen Honey, ed., *Shadowed Dreams: Women's Poetry of the Harlem Renaissance* (New Brunswick, NJ: Rutgers University Press, 1989); Gloria Hull, *Color, Sex, and Poetry: Three Women Writers of the Harlem Renaissance* (Bloomington: Indiana University Press, 1987); Lorraine Roses and Ruth Elizabeth Randolph, *Harlem Renaissance and Beyond: Literary Biographies of 100 Black Women Writers, 1900-1945* (Boston: G. K. Hall, 1990); Ann Allen Shockley, *Afro-American Women Writers, 1746-1933* (New York: New American Library, 1989); Cheryl A. Wall, "Poets and Versifiers, Singers and Signifiers: the Women of the Harlem Renaissance," in Kenneth Wheeler and Virginia Lussier, eds., *Women, the Arts, and the 1920s in Paris and New York* (New Brunswick: Transaction Press, 1982), 74-98; Mary Helen Washington, *Invented Lives: Narratives of Black Women 1860-1960* (New York: Anchor Books, 1987).

11. For a cogent summary of these debates, see Robert Stepto, "Sterling A. Brown: Outsider in the Harlem Renaissance?" in *The Harlem Renaissance: Revaluations,* ed. Amritjit Singh et al.

12. Nathan Huggins, *Voices from the Harlem Renaissance,* 3; Davis and Peplow, xxi; Kellner, *The Harlem Renaissance: A Historical Dictionary for the Era* (New York: Methuen, 1984), xxiv. Perhaps the most open-ended dates come from Houston Baker. In *Modernism and the Harlem Renaissance,* he perceives the awakening as a moment on a continuum that embraces Booker T. Washington and Charles Chesnutt on one end, and Richard Wright on the other. To my mind, Washington is at most a precursor of the Renaissance and one against which a number of authors write, while Wright represents a sharp break with the movement's prevailing trends. I find the notion of continuum very useful nonetheless.

13. Hull, *Color, Sex, and Poetry,* 30.

14. Sterling Brown, Arthur P. Davis, and Ulysses Lee, eds., *The Negro Caravan.* (1941; rpt. New York: Arno Press, 1969), 279; 142. The comments on Hurston's fiction are most positive. One notes that she "has written more fully than any other Negro of Southern rural life." Another judges that "sympathy and authenticity mark her work" (143). Significantly, all of the folktales in the anthology are taken from *Mules and Men*; a folk sermon from Hurston's novel *Jonah's Gourd Vine* is also reprinted in the "Folk Literature" section. The introductions do not draw attention to the fact that Hurston is among the best-represented authors in the volume.

15. *A Voice from the South* (1892; rpt. New York: Oxford University Press, 1988), 134. Cooper anticipated many of the themes Locke would use to promote the New Negro. For example: "Everything to this race is new and strange and inspiring. There is a quickening of its pulses and a glowing of its self-consciousness. Aha, I can rival that! I can aspire to that! I can honor my name and vindicate my race! Something like this, it strikes me, is the enthusiasm which stirs the genius of young Africa in America. . . ." (144-45). But she insisted that the regeneration of the race must begin with the black woman (28).

16. Gwendolyn Bennett, Jessie Fauset, Angelina Grimké, Zora Neale Hurston, Georgia Douglas Johnson, Helene Johnson, and Anne Spencer were the other female contributors. Fauset was the only other essayist. Hurston was represented by a short story, "Spunk," while the other women contributed poems. Total contributors to *The New Negro* numbered thirty-six, including Locke.

17. An important exception to this rule was the lesbian poet Mae Cowdery, whose work is notable for its exploration of erotic themes. For examples of these, see Honey, *Shadowed Dreams,* 129-39; Cowdery published a volume of poems, *We Lift Our Voices* (Philadelphia: Alpress Publishers, 1936).

18. *The Crisis* (April 1927): 49. The poem is reprinted in Maureen Honey, *Shadowed Dreams,* 60.

19. I think, for example, of Dunbar-Nelson's "I Sit and Sew" and Grimké's "Little Grey Dreams" and "Under the Days." For a detailed study of the lives and work of Johnson, Dunbar-Nelson, and Grimké, see Gloria Hull, *Color, Sex, and Poetry.*

20. J. Lee Greene, *Time's Unfading Garden: Anne Spencer's Life and Poetry* (Baton Rouge: Louisiana State University Press, 1977), 176.

21. In his biography . . ., J. Lee Greene details Spencer's successful efforts to organize a Lynchburg affiliate of the NAACP, to hire black teachers for the high school, and to organize the first public library to serve Lynchburg's black community.

22. Cullen, *Caroling Dusk: An Anthology of Verse by Negro Poets* (New York: Harper, 1967), 47.

23. Greene, 179.

24. Written by Bessie Smith. Recorded October 26, 1926, with Joe Smith, cornet; Buster Bailey, clarinet; Fletcher Henderson, piano; and Bessie Smith, vocals. Columbia 14179-D.

25. Ortiz Walton, *Music: Black, White & Blue* (New York: William Morrow, 1972), 28.

26. Carole Marks, 159.

27. Remarks by northern-born artist/intellectual Paul Robeson may illustrate the point. Speaking to an integrated audience in New Orleans in 1942, Robeson acknowledged that he "had never put a correct evaluation on the dignity and courage of my people of the deep South until I began to come south myself. . . . Deep down, I think, I had imagined Negroes of the South beaten, subservient, cowed." But his visits changed the view of the prominent actor, concert singer, and activist. He concluded, "I find that I must come south again and again, again and yet again. It is only here that I achieve absolute and utter identity with my people." "We Must Come South," in Robert Yancy Dent, ed., *Paul Robeson: Tributes and Selected Writings* (New York: Paul Robeson Archives, 1976), 64.

28. Written by Bessie Smith. Recorded on May 15, 1925, with Charlie Green, trombone; Buster Bailey, trumpet; Fred Longshaw, piano; James T. Wilson, miscellaneous sound effects; and Bessie Smith, vocals. Columbia 14079-D.

29. Marks cites all but the last of these in *Farewell—We're Good and Gone,* 123. One depiction of the negative impact of the migration on family life in *The New Negro* is "Vestiges," a series of sketches by Rudolph Fisher.

30. *The Book of American Negro Poetry,* 281.

31. Kenneth Clark, "A Conversation with James Baldwin," in Clark, ed., *Harlem: A Community in Transition,* 124.

32. In her entry for "mammy" in "Glossary of Harlem Slang," Zora Neale Hurston wrote "a term of insult. Never used in any other way by Negroes." Reprinted in *Spunk: The Selected Short Stories of Zora Neale Hurston* (Berkeley: Turtle Island Foundation, 1985), 94.

33. "How It Feels," in Alice Walker, ed., *I Love Myself When I Am Laughing . . . And Then Again When I Am Looking Mean and Impressive: A Zora Neale Hurston Reader* (New York: Feminist Press, 1979), 152. Subsequent references to this edition will be cited in the text.

34. In *Dust Tracks on a Road,* Hurston elaborates on the tensions operative in her relationships with her Eatonville neighbors. She considered herself too curious, too imaginative, too unladylike, and too bold a child to be at ease with the dull, hardworking townspeople, who enforced their discipline with a palmetto switch. She escaped through books: "My soul was with the gods and my body in the village. People just would not act like gods. Stew beef, fried fat-back and morning grits were no ambrosia from Valhalla" (1942; Second Edition. Urbana: University of Illinois Press, 1984), 56. Hurston's views seem based in equal measure on her egotism, the town's provincialism, and her distaste for her family and neighbors' acceptance of racial and gender restrictions.

35. Gates, "Trope of a New Negro," 132.

36. Although I know of no specific reference to the term "New Negro," Hurston's impatience with the rhetoric of racial advancement is well documented. She enjoyed referring satirically to race leaders as "Negrotarians." In his description of her relationship to her colleagues on the journal *Fire!!,* Robert Hemenway notes that Hurston, "probably the quickest wit in a very witty lot . . . proclaimed herself 'Queen of the Niggerati'" (22-23, 44).

37. In a fascinating reading of Hurston's essay, Barbara Johnson glosses this passage thus: "The move into the jungle is a move into mask; the return to civilization is a return to veneer. Either way, what is at stake is an artificial, ornamental surface." Moreover, Johnson views Hurston's manipulation of color in this scene as a subversion of the binary oppositions (black/white, jungle/civilization) it addresses. See "Thresholds of Difference," 177.

38. Fisher, "The Caucasian Storms Harlem," in *Voices from the Harlem Renaissance,* 75, 80, 81.

39. *Harlem Renaissance,* 89-90.

40. James Weldon Johnson, *Black Manhattan* (New York: Knopf, 1930), 161.

41. In his critique of Harlem fiction, Sterling Brown described as "exotic primitives" those characters "whose dances—the Charleston, the 'black bottom,' the 'snake hips,' the 'walking the dog'—were tribal rituals; whose music with wa-wa trumpets and trombones and drum batteries doubled for tom-toms; whose chorus girls with bunches of bananas girding their shapely middles nurtured tourists' delusions of the 'Congo creeping through the black.'" He castigated as opportunists those black writers who, cashing in on the Negro vogue, treated "*joie de vivre* as a racial monopoly." See Brown, "A Century of Negro Portraiture in American Literature," 1966. Rpt. Abraham Chapman, ed., *Black Voices* (New York: New American Library, 1968) 564-89. No literary text offers a more scathing indictment of this cultural exploitation than Brown's own poem "Cabaret."

42. "'A Nutmeg Nestled Inside Its Covering of Mace': Audre Lorde's *Zami,*" in Bella Brodzki and Celeste Schenck, eds., *Life/Lines: Theorizing Women's Autobiography* (Ithaca: Cornell University Press, 1988), 221. Another similarity worth considering is the way in which Hurston and Lorde image "home." Note for example Lorde's representation of Carriacou, the birthplace of her mother: "But underneath it all as I was growing up, *home* was still a sweet place somewhere else which they had not managed to capture yet on paper, nor to throttle and bind up between the pages of a schoolbook. It was our own, my truly private paradise of blugoe and breadfruit hanging from the trees, of nutmeg and lime and sapadilla, of tonka beans and red and yellow Paradise Plums." See *Zami: A New Spelling of My Name* (Freedom, CA: Crossing Press, 1982), 14.

43. Chinosole, "Audre Lorde and Matrilineal Diaspora," in Joanne Braxton and Andree McLaughlin, eds., *Wild Women in the Whirlwind: Afra-American Culture and the Contemporary Literary Renaissance* (New Brunswick, NJ: Rutgers University Press, 1990), 379-94.

44. *I Love Myself,* 153. Not only was Hurston being paid for her own words; she was writing to pay for the words of a group of fellow artists. She wrote the article for *World Tomorrow,* a "progressive" white journal, to earn money to pay the bills still outstanding for *Fire!!,* the avant-garde black journal edited by Wallace Thurman, et al., in 1926.

See Priscilla Wald, "Becoming 'Colored': The Self-Authorized Language of Difference in Zora Neale Hurston," for a discussion of Hurston's rhetoric on race. *American Literary History* 2, 1 (1990): 79-100.

45. Written by Clarence Williams. Recorded on November 17, 1925, with Clarence Williams, piano, and Bessie Smith, vocals. Columbia 14109-D.

46. This notion of "home" is ancestral or spiritual; it does not denote the domestic sphere. For some of Hurston's contemporaries, notably Jessie Fauset, the ancestral home and the domestic hearth are one.

47. Analyzing the importance of Eatonville in what she terms "Hurston's mythology," Nellie McKay asserts: "In respect to race, the community Hurston claims might strike us as romantically idealized, but the specialness of its history is in the depriveleging of and liberation from the supremacy of American slave his-

tory over other aspects of the black American experience." ("Race, Gender, and Cultural Context," in Brodzki and Schenck, *Life/Lines: Theorizing Women's Autobiography,* 183).

48. In "Feminist Politics: What's Home Got to Do with It?" Martin and Mohanty analyze the autobiography of Minnie Bruce Pratt, a white, upper-class southerner, whose feminist politics and lesbianism force her to deconstruct the illusion that is her southern home. A signal difference between Hurston and Pratt is that Hurston, even in the awareness of its sexism and the destructive impact of the dominant society's racism, never rejects her Eatonville home. "Feminist Politics," in Teresa de Lauretis, ed., *Feminist Studies, Critical Studies* (Bloomington: Indiana University Press, 1986), 191-212.

# FURTHER READING

## Criticism

Bamikunle, Aderemi. "The Harlem Renaissance and White Critical Tradition." *College Language Association Journal* 29, no. 1 (Sept. 1985): 33-51.

*Studies the artistic compromises made by Black writers of the Harlem Renaissance in response to constraints imposed by white critical standards, particularly involving the use of the Black vernacular.*

Coles, Robert A. and Diane Isaacs. "Primitivism as a Therapeutic Pursuit: Notes toward a Reassessment of Harlem Renaissance Literature." In *The Harlem Renaissance: Revaluations,* edited by Amritjit Singh, William S. Shiver, and Stanley Brodwin, pp. 3-12. New York: Garland, 1989.

*Discusses primitivism as a set of cultural values set in opposition to those of Western civilization which after World War I were perceived as spiritually bankrupt and self-destructive.*

De Souza, Pauline. "Black Awakening: Gender and Representation in the Harlem Renaissance." In *Women Artists and Modernism,* edited by Katy Deepwell, pp. 55-69. Manchester: Manchester University Press, 1998.

*Examines the formulation of a new Black identity during the Harlem Renaissance through visual images and the philosophical writings of Du Bois, Locke, Garvey, and Thurman.*

Fabre, Michel. *From Harlem to Paris: Black American Writers in France, 1840-1980.* Urbana: University of Illinois Press, 1991, 358 p.

*Examines the Paris years of many important figures of the Harlem Renaissance, including Langston Hughes, Alain Locke, Countee Cullen, Claude McKay, Jessie Fauset, and Gwendolyn Bennett, as well as a number of minor writers.*

Feuser, Willfried F. "Black Reflections in a White Mirror. Literature and Culture in the Twenties." *Neohelicon* 20, no. 1 (1993): 289-306.

*Suggests that the Harlem Renaissance was part of a larger literary and cultural movement that included white writers in America and other parts of the world, particularly France and Germany.*

Franklin, John Hope and Alfred A. Moss, Jr. "The Harlem Renaissance." In *From Slavery to Freedom: A History of African Americans,* pp. 401-17. New York: Alfred A. Knopf, 2000.

*Offers a survey of key Harlem Renaissance writers, playwrights, musicians, painters, and filmmakers.*

Hart, Robert C. "Black-White Literary Relations in the Harlem Renaissance." *American Literature* 44, no. 4 (Jan. 1973): 612-28.

*Explores the literary and social relationships between the major figures of the Harlem Renaissance and a number of white writers of the era.*

Honey, Maureen, ed. Introduction to *Shadowed Dreams: Women's Poetry of the Harlem Renaissance.* New Brunswick, N.J.: Rutgers University Press, 1989, 238 p.

*Introduction to a poetry anthology that includes many of the lesser-known female poets associated with the Harlem Renaissance.*

Johnson, Eloise E. "What Are the Reasons for Exclusion of Harlem Artists from Major Art Texts?" In *Rediscovering the Harlem Renaissance: The Politics of Exclusion,* pp. 23-35. New York: Garland, 1997.

*Examines the role of art historians and scholars, of museums and universities, in excluding Black artists from the American and modern artistic canons.*

Kent, George E. "Patterns of the Harlem Renaissance." In *The Harlem Renaissance Remembered,* edited by Arna Bontemps, pp. 27-50. New York: Dodd, Mead & Company, 1972.

*Discusses the attempt by Black writers of the Harlem Renaissance to establish a cultural sensibility separate and distinct from the intellectual and artistic conventions of America.*

Knopf, Marcy. Introduction to *The Sleeper Wakes: Harlem Renaissance Stories by Women,* pp. xix-xxxix. New Brunswick, N.J.: Rutgers University Press, 1993.

*An overview of the Harlem Renaissance and a discussion of the female artists and writers associated with the movement.*

Kramer, Victor A., ed. *The Harlem Renaissance Re-Examined.* New York: AMS Press, 1987, 362 p.

*A collection of essays on various aspects of the Harlem Renaissance, from aesthetic theories to analyses of specific writers and their texts.*

Lewis, David Levering, editor. *The Portable Harlem Renaissance Reader.* New York: Viking, 1994, 766 p.

*Collection of significant writings from the Harlem Renaissance, including drama, fiction, essays, and poetry.*

Marks, Carole and Diana Edkins. *The Power of Pride: Stylemakers and Rulebreakers of the Harlem Renaissance.* New York: Crown Publishers, 1999, 272 p.

*Individual studies of the important artists, writers, and performers of the Harlem Renaissance period, including those in Chicago, Washington, D.C., and Paris.*

Martin, Tony. *Literary Garveyism: Garvey, Black Arts and the Harlem Renaissance.* Dover, Mass.: The Majority Press, 1983, 204 p.

*Traces the literary and artistic influence of Marcus Garvey during the Harlem Renaissance, suggesting that the Black aesthetic advocated by Garvey had much in common with the Black Arts movement of the 1960s.*

Stephens, Judith L. "The Harlem Renaissance and the New Negro Movement." *The Cambridge Companion to American Women Playwrights*, edited by Brenda Murphy, pp. 98-117. Cambridge: Cambridge University Press, 1999.

*Explores the work of four Black women playwrights of the Harlem Renaissance: Georgia Douglas Johnson, May Miller, Eulalie Spence, and Zora Neale Hurston.*

Tyler, Bruce M. "The Art Ideology of the Harlem Renaissance." In *From Harlem to Hollywood: The Struggle for Racial and Cultural Democracy 1920-1943*, pp. 3-33. New York: Garland, 1992.

*Discusses the role of writers of the Harlem Renaissance in breaking down racial stereotypes and presenting positive images of African Americans in literature and art.*

Wintz, Cary D. "Black Writers and White Promoters." In *Black Culture and the Harlem Renaissance*, pp. 154-89. Houston: Rice University Press, 1988.

*Explores the sometimes strained relationships between Black writers of the Harlem Renaissance and members of the white literary community who served as their publishers, patrons, and friends.*

Wintz, Cary D., editor. *Black Writers Interpret the Harlem Renaissance*. New York: Garland Publishing, 1996, 471 p.

*Reprints essays from the Harlem Renaissance, including works by Countee Cullen and Sterling A. Brown.*

# SOCIAL, ECONOMIC, AND POLITICAL FACTORS THAT INFLUENCED THE HARLEM RENAISSANCE

The events leading up to the Harlem Renaissance formed the consciousness of a new generation of Blacks. This generation, raised during the decades of reconstruction following the Civil War, was the first not to have experienced slavery directly. Among these first free Blacks from the United States and the Caribbean emerged cultural, literary, and political leaders who would define the Harlem Renaissance and the New Negro.

Black migration from the South was a key factor in the development of the Renaissance. The years 1890 to 1914 saw huge numbers of Blacks migrating from the Jim Crow South to northern and western cities. These Blacks migrated to escape segregation and lynchings, which were then occurring in greater numbers than at any other time in the nation's history, and to seek better employment opportunities that the increasingly industrialized urban areas provided. These urban areas offered something else that was equally important: an outlet for Black political organization. Harlem soon hosted the development of several key political groups. In 1910 W. E. B. Du Bois, a rising Renaissance leader from Atlanta, Georgia, formed the NAACP (National Association for the Advancement of Colored People). Marcus Garvey, from Jamaica, formed the UNIA (Universal Negro Improvement Association) and moved it to Harlem in 1916. Publications like *The Crisis*, the monthly magazine for the NAACP, and

*Opportunity*, the publication for the National Urban League, along with others like *The Messenger, Challenge, The Voice, The Crusader*, and *The Negro World* provided Blacks with a written forum and a way to distribute their ideas and messages to the community. The 135th branch of the New York Public Library, which opened in 1905, was in Harlem. By 1920, when librarian Ernestine Rose was appointed, the branch had become an indispensable educational and cultural center, and played an unparalleled role in the preservation of Black history.

Scholars write that a Negro settlement in New York City was inevitable, but that certain conditions in and around the city and the country aided in the creation of Harlem, a city within a city, the "Black capital of the world." The Dutch first settled the area; by the 1890s it consisted primarily of wealthy white residents. But new subway routes connecting the area to the lower part of Manhattan, along with land speculation and subsequent overconstruction of apartment buildings, deflated property values. Phillip A. Payton's Afro-American Realty Company gained control of 134th and 135th streets. After initial settlement, Black businesses took hold—a few of them very profitable. Lillian Harris Dean ("Pig Foot Mary") sold pigs' feet before becoming a real estate tycoon. "Madam" C. J. Walker, a poor washerwoman, became a millionaire by inventing a hair-straightening process. Salons opened. The music and cultural venues of the Tenderloin area, sensing greener pastures, moved a hundred blocks north to Harlem. So did churches, newspapers, and clubs.

The Great Migration (1916 to 1919) further increased the Black population in Harlem. During the World War I years, Blacks took jobs in new areas that had previously included the comparatively privileged European immigrants. Blacks (notably the Harlem Hell Fighters) fought heroically in Europe for a democracy they didn't experience. When the Harlem Hell Fighters returned from war, they were perturbed to learn that their efforts were not acknowledged or appreciated. Many Blacks who were being exposed to new economic opportunities were, like women after World War II, expected to resume the status quo. But they wouldn't. The "red summer" of 1919 was filled with major riots in New York City and in twenty-five cities throughout the country. Booker T. Washington's strategy in the early part of the century had urged Blacks to live "respectable lives," but now Du Bois and Garvey dominated Black political and philosophical thought, and they advocated militancy. Blacks, let down again by their own country, were ready to rise up. They did so on the streets, but also in a way that college-educated Blacks were now prepared to do: with their pens.

Alain Locke, mentor for the Harlem Renaissance, wrote that Blacks had "common problems without a common consciousness." The rising writers, artists, and intellectuals of the postwar years quickly and effectively ushered in the Harlem Renaissance, now a developed, self-conscious movement. Though the term "New Negro" had been used as early as the late 1800s, it was now a mainstream concept that was more defined, understood, and embraced. The Harlem Renaissance of the 1920s is considered to be the time when many already existing opinions and tensions about the Black situation were given literary expression. Social trends helped this expression find a ready audience. It was the great Jazz Age, a time when whites were embracing life and living it up, and Harlem provided a fashionable realm in which to indulge their free-flowing idealism and exuberant postwar celebrations. Moneyed whites flocked to Prohibition-era cabarets, like the Cotton Club, to view a world considered "exotic" and to witness for themselves what they believed was the Blacks' inherent "joy of living." They poured money into Black culture and into publishing houses, which promptly fed their bottom line by sponsoring a steady stream of Black novels, nonfiction, and poetry. Harlem was in vogue.

With these conditions, creativity flourished and couldn't be stemmed. Claude McKay published militant poetry. Alain Locke compiled the *New Negro* anthology, which was published in 1925. Other writers like Zora Neale Hurston, Langston Hughes, Countee Cullen, Jessie Redmon Fauset, Charles S. Johnson, James Weldon Johnson, and Nella Larson were providing their own interpretations of the Black situation. The charismatic Marcus Garvey, the Pan-Africanist visionary who shook the Black nation with his back-to-Africa movement, gained a huge following. Garvey embraced all the poor, Black or white. He spoke out against capitalism and colonialism, giving his outlook a distinct Marxist flavor. His views differed in some areas from those of Du Bois, who focused on protest, civil and political rights, and the "talented tenth," a group of college-educated intellectual elites who would bring new culture to the Black race.

But not all was well. Widespread support of Black creativity was fraught with misunderstandings. The people of Harlem were mythologized as the ideal outcasts. As author Jessie Redmon Fauset commented, "the fascination of whites with Harlem was a revisionist rendering of the traditional romantic conception of blacks as cultural primitives and exotics." Whites seemed to embrace only the Black art that didn't challenge them too much. And the white patrons who embraced Black creativity nevertheless maintained the fundamental Euro-American criteria and standards for judging it. Zora Neale Hurston dubbed these whites and others who too-readily accepted Black art the "Niggerati." And even though Harlem possessed Black business owners, Black property owners, and even Black policemen, segregation still dominated. White-owned clubs and restaurants did not allow Blacks to enter. The Cotton Club, a popular Lenox Avenue hot spot, did not allow Black patrons inside. Blacks struggled mightily with being Jim Crowed in their own "capital." It seemed that even Harlem existed primarily for whites and for white entertainment.

What further complicated life for Black writers and artists was the problem of artistic identity. They debated about the reliance on whites—the very people they were struggling to free themselves from—for their art, about whether to embrace or deny their Black heritage and traditions, and about whether to fight to prove themselves and their talents to the white world or to demand to be accepted as themselves. The immediate popularity that Blacks found by writing "acceptable" books and producing "acceptable" art was criticized by some as a dangerous catering to the white world, at the expense of truth. In addition, some Blacks, particularly Garvey, accused Du Bois's "talented tenth" of neglecting the common person and of ignoring the poverty and struggles that plagued Blacks living in Harlem. Harlem in the 1920s, as one expert points out, was rapidly becoming a slum. Rents were high, overcrowding was prevalent, infant mortality was high, and because there were relatively few Black-owned enterprises, a stable middle class never took hold.

The not-so-glamorous side of Harlem was not readily acknowledged, but a few writers addressed it. The famous short story "The City of Refuge," by Rudolph Fisher, explicitly revealed the dishonesty and contradictions of Harlem. It is difficult to blame these writers and artists, however, for taking advantage of a socio-political climate that allowed them, for once, to speak out and be heard, even if their products were somewhat tame.

The stock market crash of 1929 brought the economy and thus the Harlem Renaissance to a halt. The Great Depression of the 1930s further eroded the great strides made during the 1920s. Some of the writers and artists who flourished during the 1920s fell into obscurity, but many continued with their successful careers. The Harlem Renaissance, though short-lived, was the result of a fortuitous blend of talent and socio-political events, and produced some of the best literature and art America has known.

## REPRESENTATIVE WORKS

**Edmund David Cronon**
*Black Moses: The Story of Marcus Garvey and the Universal Negro Improvement Association* (nonfiction) 1955

**W. E. B. Du Bois**
*The Souls of Black Folk* (fiction, nonfiction, and folklore) 1903

*The Gift of Black Folk* (nonfiction) 1924

*Black Reconstruction: An Essay Toward a History of the Part Which Black Folk Played in the Attempt to Reconstruct Democracy in America, 1860-1880* (nonfiction) 1935

*Black Folk, Then and Now: An Essay in the History and Sociology of the Negro Race* (nonfiction) 1939

**Marcus Garvey**
*The Philosophy and Opinions of Marcus Garvey; or, Africa for the Africans.* 2 vols. (political philosophy) 1923-25
*The Tragedy of White Injustice* (poetry, political philosophy) 1927

**Langston Hughes**
*The Big Sea* (autobiography) 1940

**Charles S. Johnson**
*The Negro in Chicago: A Study of Race Relations and a Race Riot* (nonfiction) 1922

*The Negro in American Civilization* (nonfiction) 1930

*The Economic Status of Negroes* (nonfiction) 1933

*Race Relations: Adjustment of Whites and Negroes in the United States* [with Willis D. Weatherford] (nonfiction) 1934

**James Weldon Johnson**
*Black Manhattan* (nonfiction) 1930

*Along This Way* (autobiography) 1933

**Robert Thomas Kerlin**
*Voice of the Negro* (nonfiction) 1920

**Nella Larsen**
*Quicksand* (novel) 1928

*Passing* (novel) 1929

**Alain Locke**
*The New Negro* [editor] (poetry and essays) 1925

**Claude McKay**
*Negry v Amerike* [*The Negroes in America*] (essays) 1923

*Sudom lincha* [*Trial by Lynching: Stories about Negro Life in North America*] (short stories) 1925

*Home to Harlem* (novel) 1928

*A Long Way from Home* (autobiography) 1937

*Harlem: Negro Metropolis* (nonfiction) 1940

**Carl Van Vechten**
*Nigger Heaven* (novel) 1926

**Walter White**
*The American Negro and His Problems* (nonfiction) 1927

*The Negro's Contribution to American Culture* (nonfiction) 1927

## PRIMARY SOURCES

### NEW YORK TIMES (ESSAY DATE 1925)

**SOURCE:** "Charleston a Hit in Home, Dance Hall, and Ballroom." *New York Times* (24 May 1925).

*In the following essay, the popularity of the Charleston—a dance step that originated in African American dance halls—is examined.*

"Can you Charleston" is the question, but with unconcealed anxiety these days, by women-folk seeking a cook or wielder of mop and duster from the ranks of Negro household workers. For the Charleston, as the latest dance innovation is called, is all the rage both for ballroom and exhibition, and being of African origin, is naturally best known by darkies.

Proprietors of employment agencies are being importuned to supply cooks, waitresses, laundresses and maids "who can Charleston." Women who employ Negro servants adept in the combination wing and step are implored by friends to obtain for them servants similarly skilled. The domestic helper who works by one day and "sleeps out" and she who is always at hand and "sleeps in" need offer no excuses for tasks uncompleted if they can show their employers how to do a passable Charleston. The visiting laundress will hear no complaint about her slowness if she can "shake a leg." Burned food, late luncheon or dinner, dust in the corners and even forays on the icebox and the disappearance of the remains of Sunday's ham intended for Monday consumption are forgiven if the offender can only impart to her mistress that elusive winging movement of the legs without which there is no authentic Charleston.

The mistress humbles herself in her own domain and seeks with eagerness as a pupil the approval of her social inferior. Broom and vacuum cleaner gather dust instead of routing it while the rug is turned back, the music machine is started and maid and matron, holding their skirts above their knees, go through the evolutions of a modern version of a form of primeval jungle ritual.

The new excuse which greets the husband inquiring why dinner is not on the table is, "Sally has been showing me how to do the Charleston."

Debutantes are practicing it at the Colony Club; society matrons are panting over it in Park Avenue boudoirs; department store clerks are trying to master it in the restrooms at the lunch hour; the models of the garment industry dance it together in the chop suey palaces at noontime; the flats of the West Side and the tenements of the East Side are not immune to the contagion. Wherever there's a pier glass, in front of it is a feminine or masculine form striving with the utmost earnestness to make both legs simultaneously and at the same time step forward, back or to the side. Many a man has forsaken his daily dozen for the Charleston. Darky youth and pickaninnies dance

it on the street corners for both profit and pleasure. Even sharks of the bridge table trump each other's tricks while listening to an exposition of the fad of the hour. "My maid is teaching me the Charleston," is a cry of triumph sure to rouse heartburnings of envy.

What is this dance in which amateurs and professionals are competing for ballroom and stage I prizes, which just now is danced almost to the exclusion of all others with varying degrees of proficiency in public dance hall, cabaret, night club and private as0semblies, and is sending a new crop of pupils to the studios of instructors? It is kin of buck and wing, of turkey trot and fox trot, a relative of all the dances of peculiarly Negro origin which have from time to time been modified and adapted to ballroom and stage. It may be danced as a solo by indvidual or couple in either exhibition or social dancing. It is danced to jazz music played either in 2-4 time and one-step rhythm or in the 4-4 tempo of the slow fox trot, as a part of which it is often introduced. In many of the smart dance clubs frequented by professional dancers, according to a committee designated to report on dance tendencies by the New York Society of Teachers of Dancing, a modified Charleston combined with the plain walking step of the one-step is the dance of the hour, while in the Broadway cabarets the straight Charleston is the ruling favorite, danced to the 4-4 time of a "blues."

As in all dances of this type where there are fundamental positions and movements, there is ample scope for individual invention and embroidery with the result that especially among exhibition dancers, there are many combinations of steps unrelated to the genuine Charleston. Nevertheless the opportunity for originating novel evolutions, which has made the fox trot of the present so different from the type which first bore that name, is one of the most alluring features of the Charleston, and already the college and high school youths who devise the predominating movements of social dancing have put their wits and legs together in embellishing the figures of the dance which, as its name implies, first attracted attention and became labeled through its popularity at the social assemblies of Charleston's dusky society several years ago. In fact, the sudden fascination which the Charleston has exercised on white folks has surprised the colored population of Harlem, who gave it up for the fox trot but are now reviving their childhood lore and finding it a valuable asset.

# FRED DE ARMOND (ESSAY DATE 1925)

**SOURCE:** De Armond, Fred. "A Note on the Sociology of Negro Literature." In *The Politics and Aesthetics of "New Negro" Literature,* edited by Cary D. Wintz, pp. 265-67. New York: Garland Publishing, 1996.

*In the following essay, originally published in 1925, De Armond suggests that "race literature" can only be understood in the context of its creators' background and social history.*

No people can be understood without some study of their literature and other artistic expression. And the literature of a race, group or nationality, to be rightly appraised and interpreted must be considered with reference to the facts of that people's history, religion and sociology. A failure to appreciate these basic truths is, I believe, a strong contributing cause for the complete ignorance of the Negro on the part of white America, as well as the Negro's lack of conception as to his own powers.

The average Nordic, particularly in the South, has become so accustomed to wearing that attitude of lofty superiority and amused tolerance toward blacks that he knows no more about their mental processes than he does about Chinese ideals or Brahman theology. To the rude mind, Negro poetry, art and religion are no more serious than the diverting antics of a favorite pet animal. A great fiction has thus grown up around the Negro character and the Negro himself, with his unusual histrionic ability, has accepted the false conception and fostered it with his feigned burlesque and mimicry. There are few even of our college professors, congressmen and D. D.'s discerning enough to perceive that the "good nigger" is merely a good actor, that all this extravagant deference, feudal manners and Ham Bone humor is merely a form of guile and subtle flattery by which Negroes secure those privileges which other men are expected to stand up and demand as their rights.

To attain the understanding that will straighten all such distorted views, race literature must be studied not by direct comparison, but in the light of the influences that have affected it. American literature proper, not only has a brilliant provincial history of over two hundred years, but it is a direct branch both in blood and tradition, of that stalwart oak, the roots of which go back to the England of Chaucer's day. If I may be excused for using the metaphor still further, I would say that the writing of the American Negro is a healthy sprout that has sprung up within the shade of its mighty progenitor. Sixty-five years ago the race languished in a bondage so hopeless that only by the slyest stealth could any person of color learn to read and write. "Negroes by law are prohibited from learning to read and write," wrote Rev. John Aughey, a Northern clergyman sojourning in Mississippi in 1861. "I had charge of a Sabbath school for the instruction of blacks in Memphis, Tennessee, in 1853. The school was put down by the strong arm of the law, shortly after my connection with it ceased. In Mississippi a man who taught slaves to read or write would be sent to the penitentiary instanter." Frederick Douglass relates in his autobiography how he was deprived of the only real pleasure he ever remembers during his slave days in Maryland, when the school that he was teaching on Sundays was broken up and suppressed by his master. He had previously, by many subterfuges and by the assistance of a kind mistress, succeeded in getting for himself a smattering of the rudiments. At one time he had over forty pupils meeting with the greatest secrecy in a barn, in order that they might taste the delights of knowledge. One of the men who helped to suppress the school by force was a very religious character who had taught the neighboring slaves about the Bible, professing much interest in saving their souls.

But it is not so much the educational development of the Negro under enormous difficulties that constitutes the outstanding feature of his artistic accomplishment, as it is his marvelous adaptability to Caucasian civilizaton. In reading one of Claude McKay's poems, or listening to Roland Hayes singing, or admiring the pictures of Tanner, one should remind oneself of the vast gulf that the artist has bridged between his art and his savage African ancestry—at most only a few generations away. Wherever the Ethiopian has been transplanted to other parts of the world, he has shown himself remarkably adaptable to foreign civilization.

The record of "America's subject race" has given a flavor of the exotic to our history, an element of color that creates a most enchanting background for literature. Drama and romance are conjured in the imaginative mind by such events as the slave trade, the underground railroad, the gallant dash of colored troops in the war of the rebellion, emancipation and the aftermath of reconstruction with all those bizarre incidents of poetic justice to the former masters. All epochs in the struggle for human liberty have had their interpreters; the Negro people believing as they do that they are still in process of emancipation from the disabilities imposed by race prejudice, have never had such able, eloquent and sincere spokesmen as at this time.

The blighting effect of slavery can hardly be appreciated in its full influence on artistic expression as well as social life. Consciously or unconsciously it imposed on the race a servile feeling of inferiority that centuries will not wipe out. Thus it is only from a feeling of great power that a Negro writer can assert himself with any of that confident ego that we have been wont to expect from genius. There is discernible in Dunbar's poetry a sort of hesitating modesty that causes the reader to feel that some hereditary race consciousness was restraining the highest flights of his genius. It is something of the same inferiority complex that prompted a Negro teacher of an industrial school appearing before a committee of the legislature in a Southern state to apologize for wearing such a good suit. Socially the taint of bondage has exerted a tremendous influence. It should not be forgotten that the institution of marriage properly dates only from Reconstruction. Booker Washington, sitting down to write his autobiography did not even know his father's name. Frederick Douglass could not remember having seen his mother but a few times in his life and then only when she had stolen away at night and walked many miles that she might snatch a few hours with her child. The word "father" was not in the slave child's vocabulary. Many of the first families of Virginia maintained their aristocratic station by the refined and lucrative business of breeding slaves for the southern markets.

White observers have made much of the Negro moral code but said little about these causes that account for a distinction in that respect. In T. S. Stribling's "Birthright." Peter Siner, an educated and refined Negro laments the low standards and the atavism of his race. No such pessimism is justified. It is rather with satisfaction and pride that Negroes should contemplate the progress of sixty years. Most characterizations by white observers are gross exaggerations and caricatures and will be recognized as such by those who see and think for themselves. The lascivious stories set to the familiar Rastus-Liza cast are an example. As they are related with loud guffaws to groups of male hearers by those verbose gentlemen who know "the niggers" so thoroughly, these anecdotes have about as much realism as the raptures of a California realtor.

James Weldon Johnson, the distinguished colored poet, has called attention to what he considers the greatest obstacle in the way of artistic expression by his race. This is, in the South at least, the all-consuming tensity of the race struggle. Not only does this problem dissipate the intellectual energy of the Negroes, he says, but also in almost equal degree of the Southern whites, accounting for H. L. Mencken's somewhat exaggerated statement: "In all this vast region . . . there is not a single poet, not a serious historian, not a creditable composer, not a critic good or bad, not a dramatist dead or alive." Heywood Broun called the Southern fear of the Negro "an intensified specialization that atrophies the mind of the South."

There has been an absence of objective thought on this subject, either written or spoken, throughout the South; a dogmatism built on such stale repetitions as "The Southern white man is the only person that understands the Negro", "We need no meddling interference from the North", "The Negro is an irresponsible child", etc. The Southern Negroes on their part, while making great strides industrially, have left the intellectual leadership to the North, where the dominant race, instead of hostility, has shown only indifference.

The great migration to the North seems to be one of the practical economic forces working toward a solution of the race problem. This movement, by better distributing the Negro population, is certain to make the question more nearly what it should always have been—national and not sectional in scope and interest. The changing order is already finding expression in the race literature. Bards are singing more of Harlem dance halls and less of Mississippi plantations. The new setting is the big industrial centers of the North which are soon to vie with the cotton belt as the black center of population. Jean Toomer, the new star on the firmament of Negro prose fiction, picks many of his characters from the flotsam of the big city. Miss Fauset scorns precedent by writing a novel of polite Negro society, minus dialect and other thought-to-be indispensable ear-marks of race literature. Poets like Countee Cullen bare their souls and display secret emotions long repressed. A freedom from the inhibitions of the Southland is shown by the Negro press, the pulpit and by publicists, black and white.

Most Southern white men have professed to see in the exodus from the late Confederacy only rainbow-chasing, bound to end in disillusionment for the emigrants. But this opinion is not concurred in by the Negro observers nor by such white writers as Rollin Lynde Hartt and Frank Tannenbaum. Hartt's conclusion is that the principal incentive is the hope of increased security and equal protection of the law. In his new home we see the Negro's facility for adapting himself to changed environment. Every year this quality is enabling thousands to surmount vocational barriers, as it will eventually be the means of overcoming discrimination.

The continuing improvement in inter-racial relations will have the effect of turning Negro thought away from channels of controversy and propaganda. It will release the writers of philippics for more creative work, just as the final abolition of slavery turned Whittier and Lowell from fiery abolition poems to the greater and broader classics on which their fame chiefly rests in our day.

A study of the colored press such as Robert T. Kerlin has made in *The Voice of the Negro,* reveals an undeniably aggressive and bitter feeling against mob-law, disfranchisement, peonage and "Jim-Crowism." Most of the periodicals are strongly pessimistic and cynical. L. M. Hussey writes in *The American Mercury:* "This cynicism distinguishes all his current utterances. It informs and enlivens the propaganda that he prints in his periodicals. These periodicals are seldom naive. They make use of the weapon of irony. To the white brethren seeking civilized amusement, to the Nordic overman a bit soured by the pallid timidities of his accustomed journals, I recommend a trial glance at such Negro papers as *The Crisis, The Messenger* and *Opportunity.* Taken after a dose of the usual savorless blather of white journalism, their effect is akin to that of four ounces of ethyl hydroxide."

The bellicosity of those journals like *The Chicago Defender, The Black Dispatch* of Oklahoma City and *The Houston Informer* will surprise all those who have been deceived by the stage deference of the blacks into thinking that the race as a whole is quiescent and contented. According to a writer in *World's Work,* in some parts of the black belt of the South the radical Chicago papers are considered as vicious contraband by the authorities, which necessitates their being smuggled in surreptitiously and sold among the Negroes much in the same manner that Garrison's *Liberator* was circulated during slavery. But even in the South there are few of the colored organs that follow the idea of non-resistance. In expressing opinions that are anathema to the orthodox Southerner they seem to encounter less intolerance than would be vented on the white man who gave voice to the same heresies. While we are a long way from having a free press in these United States, it is at least gratifying to reflect on our improvement since the time of Elijah Lovejoy.

Religious fervor is strongly reflected in the literature of the Negro. There is a faith deeply emotional and strictly fundamentalist, imbued with the imagery of a personal Savior, a very real Satan and Hell and a literal construction of the Scriptures. Booker Washington related that he found a pathetic aspiration to learn reading and writing among the older men and women who had spent their youth in slavery. They attended his night schools faithfully and repeatedly told him that they did so solely with the ambition of reading The Bible for themselves before they died.

This strong spiritual craving is traceable to slavery. It was very deliberately cultivated by the masters with the object of providing an emotional outlet that would keep them quiescent. According to Frederick Douglass, drunkenness was encouraged for the same reason. On the Maryland plantations it was customary to give all the field hands a week or two of holiday during the Christmas season, when it was expected that the slaves would waste their time and their money if they happened to have any, in riotous carousing. Then it was certain that no dangerous ideas would occupy their minds and turn their thoughts to freedom.

There is also a close connection between this fervid Christianity inherited by the freedman from the slace, and the Negro spirituals, the most distinctive artistic contribution of the race to our American civilization. Mr. Kerlin in his essay on *Contemporary Negro Poetry* has shown the undoubted kinship between the new Negro poetry and the old spirituals. Both, he says, "bear the stamp of African genius." In the course of evolution we may well expect that the musical theme of the spirituals will be further interpreted in our generation.

In those feeling old hymns, legacy from "Black and Unknown Bards of Long Ago," there is much to provoke the interest of all students of original sources in American life and history. Whether considered as poetry, music or religion, the force and originality of the spirituals are striking. As poetry they symbolized the intense yearning of a people for freedom; as music they were the flight of troubled spirits in spontaneous, melancholy song; as religion they were the primitive appeal of tortured slave souls to a higher power.

Various Negro leaders have charged their people with being too self-conscious and urged them not to exhibit diffidence in displaying their own distinctive qualities, to cease aping white customs and develop themselves in their own way; in short to take a pride in their race and in preserving its entity. They insist that the black race has a very distinct place in the future of America, and in the fullest realization of that future there should be no real clash of interests.

## AMY JACQUES GARVEY (ESSAY DATE 1926)

**SOURCE:** Garvey, Amy Jacques. "Black Is Beautiful." In *Voices of a Black Nation: Political Journalism in the Harlem Renaissance,* edited by Theodore G. Vincent, pp. 373-75. Trenton: Africa World Press, 1990.

*In the following essay, originally published in 1926, Garvey condemns Blacks who try to be white.*

Too much cannot be said in denouncing the class of "want-to-be-white" Negroes one finds everywhere. This race-destroying group are dissatisfied with their mothers and with their Creator. Mother is too dark "to pass" and God made a mistake when he made black people. With this fallacy uppermost in their minds, they bleach their skins and straighten their hair in mad efforts to look like their ideal type. To what end, one asks? To the end that they may be admitted to better jobs, moneyed circles, and, in short, share the blessings of the prosperous white race. They are too lazy to help build a prosperous Negro race, but choose the easier route—crossing the racial border. It is the way of the weakling, and in their ignorance and stupidity they advise others to do like-wise. As if 400,000,000 Negroes could change their skins overnight. And if they could, would they? Seeing that the bulk of Negroes are to be found on the great continent of Africa, and they, thank Heaven, are proud of their black skins and curly hair. The would-be-white few are fast disappearing in the Western World, as the entire race, through the preachments of Marcus Garvey, has found its soul, and is out to acquire for itself and its posterity all that makes other races honored and respected.

This urge for whiteness is not just a mental gesture, it is a slavish complex, the remnant of slavery, to look like "Massa," to speak like him, even to cuss and drink like him. In last week's issue of the Nation Magazine, Langston Hughes, a poet, wrote a splendid article on the difficulties facing the Negro artist, in which he described the racial state of mind of a Philadelphia club woman, which is typical of the group under discussion. He states:

"The old subconscious 'white is best' runs through her mind. Years of study under white teachers, a lifetime of white books, pictures and papers, and white manners, morals and Puritan standards made her dislike the spirituals. And now she turns up her nose at jazz and all its manifestations—likewise almost everything else distinctly racial. She does not care for the Weinold Reiss portraits of Negroes, because they are 'too Negro.' She does not want a true picture of herself from anybody. She wants the artist to flatter her, to make the white world believe that all Negroes are as smug and as near white in soul as [she] wants to be."

We are delighted with the frank statement of Mr. Hughes in a white magazine; we do not know if he is a registered member of the Universal Negro Improvement Association; in any event his closing paragraph marks him as a keen student of Garveyism, and with stamina enough to express its ideals:

"To my mind, it is the duty of the younger Negro artist, if he accepts any duties at all from the outsiders, to change through the force of his art that old whispering, 'I want to be white,' hidden in the aspirations of his people, to 'Why should I want to be white? I am a Negro—and beautiful!' . . . We younger artists who create now intend to express our individual dark-skinned selves without fear or shame. If white people are pleased we are glad. If they are not, it doesn't matter."

Bravo, Mr. Hughes! From now on under your leadership we expect our artists to express their real souls, and give us art that is colorful, full of ecstasy, dulcent and even tragic; for has it not been admitted by those who would undervalue us that the Negro is a born artist. Then, let the canvas come to life with dark faces; let poetry charm the muses with the hopes and aspirations of our race; let the musicians drown our sorrows with the merry jazz; while a race is in the making, and steadily moving on to nationhood and to power.

Play up, boys, and let the world know "We are Negroes—and beautiful."

## FRANK BYRD (DOCUMENT DATE 1938)

**SOURCE:** "Harlem Rent Parties." Federal Writers' Project (23 August 1938).

*The following document examines the cultural phenomenon of the rent party, a social gathering that gained prominence in Harlem culture for the musical forum it created; many famous musicians came to prominence through their rent party appearances.*

The history of the Harlem house-rent party dates back as far as the World War. To understand what gave such an impetus and community wide significance to this institution, it is necessary to get a picture of living conditions as they were in Harlem at that time.

During the early nineteen twenties it is estimated that more than 200,000 Negroes migrated to Harlem: West Indians, Africans and American Negroes from the cotton fields and cane brakes of

Black Cross nurses parade through Harlem, opening the Universal Negro Movement Association convention, supporting the Back-to-Africa movement.

the Deep South. They were all segregated in a small section of Manhattan about fifty blocks long and seven or eight blocks wide; an area teeming with life and activity. Housing experts have estimated that, sometimes, as many as five to seven thousand people have been known to live in a single block.

Needless to say, living conditions under such circumstances were anything but wholesome and pleasant. It was a typical slum and tenement area little different from many others in New York except for the fact that in Harlem rents were higher; always have been, in fact, since the great war-time migratory influx of colored labor. Despite these exhorbitant rents, apartments and furnished rooms, however dingy; were in great demand. Harlem property owners, for the most part Jews, began to live in comparative ease on the fantastic profits yielded by their antiquated dwellings. Before Negroes inhabited them, they could be let for virtually a song. Afterwards, however, they brought handsome incomes. The tenants, by hook or crook, managed to barely scrape together the rents. In turn they stuck their roomers for enough profit to yield themselves a meagre living.

A four or five room apartment was (and still is) often crowded to capacity with roomers. In many instances, two entire families occupy space intended for only one. When bedtime comes, there is the feverish activity of moving furniture about, making down cots or preparing floor-space as sleeping quarters. The same practice of overcrowding is followed by owners or lesees of private houses. Large rooms are converted into two or three small ones by the simple process of stragetically placing beaverboard partitions. These same cubby holes are rented at the price of full sized rooms. In many houses, dining and living rooms are transformed into bed rooms soon after, if not before, midnight. Even "shift-sleeping" is not unknown in many places. During the night, a day-worker uses the room and soon after dawn a nightworker moves in. Seldom does the bed have an opportunity to get cold.

In lower Harlem, sometimes referred to as the Latin Quarter and populated mostly by Cubans, Puerto Ricans and West Indians, accommodations are worse. The Spanish seem to require even less privacy than their American cousins. A three or four room apartment often houses ten or twelve people. Parents invariably have the two or three youngest children bedded down in the same room with themselves. The dining room, kitchen and hallway are utilized as sleeping quarters by relatives or friends.

Negroes constitute the bulk of the Harlem population, however, and have (as was aforementioned) since the War. At that time, there was a great demand for cheap industrial labor. Strongbacked, physically capable Negroes from the South were the answer to this demand. They came North in droves, beginning what turned out to be the greatest migration of Negroes in the history of the United States. The good news about jobs spread like wildfire throughout the Southlands. There was money, good money, to be made in the North, especially New York. New York; the wonder, the magic city. The name alone implied glamour and adventure. It was a picture to definitely catch the fancy of restless, over-worked sharecroppers and farmhands. And so, it was on to New York, the mecca of the New Negro, the modern Promised Land.

Not only Southern, but thousands of West Indian Negroes heeded the call. That was the beginning of housing conditions that have been a headache to a succession of political administrations and a thorn in the side of community and civic organizations that have struggled valiantly, but vainly, to improve them.

With the sudden influx of so many Negroes, who apparently instinctively headed for Harlem, property that had been a white elephant on the hands of many landlords immediately took an upward swing. The majority of landlords were delighted but those white property owners who made their homes in Harlem were panic-stricken. At first, there were only rumblings of protest against this unwanted dark invasion but as the tide of color continued to rise, threatening to completely envelop the caucasion brethen, they quickly abandoned their fight and fled to more remote parts; Brooklyn, Bronx, Queens and Westchester. As soon as one or two Negro families moved into a block, the whites began moving out. Then the rents were raised. In spite of this, Negroes continued to pour in until there was a solid mass of color in every direction.

Harlemites soon discovered that meeting these doubled, and sometimes tripled, rents was not so easy. They began to think of someway to meet their ever increasing deficits. Someone evidently got the idea of having a few friends in as paying party guests a few days before the landlord's scheduled monthly visit. It was a happy; timely thought. The guests had a good time and entered wholeheartedly into the spirit of the party. Besides, it cost each individual very little, probably much less than he would have spent in some public amusement place. Besides, it was a cheap way to help a friend in need. It was such a good, easy way out of one's difficulties that others decided to make use of it. Thus was the Harlem rent-party born.

Like the Charleston and Black Botton, it became an overnight rage. Here at last, was a partial solution to the problem of excessive rents and dreadfully subnormal incomes. Family after family and hundreds of apartment tenants opened wide their doors, went the originators of the idea one better, in fact, by having a party every Saturday night instead of once a month prior to the landlord's call. The accepted admission price became twenty five cents. It was also expected that the guests would partake freely of the fried chicken, pork chops, pigs feet and potato salad (not to mention homemade "cawn") that was for sale in the kitchen or at a makeshift bar in the hallway.

Saturday night became the gala night in Harlem. Some parties even ran well into Sunday morning, calling a halt only after seven or eight o'clock. Parties were eventually held on other nights also. Thursday particularly became a favorite in view of the fact that "sleep in" domestic workers had a day off and were free to kick up their heels without restraint. Not that any other weekday offered Saturday any serious competition. It always retained its popularity because of its all round convenience as a party day. To begin with, the majority of working class Negroes, maids, porters, elevator operators and the like, were paid on Saturday and, more important than that, were not required to report to work on Sunday. Saturday, therefore, became the logical night to "pitch" and "carry on", which these pleasure-hungry children did with abandon.

The Saturday night party, like any other universally popular diversion, soon fell into the hands of the racketeers. Many small-time pimps and madames who, up to that time, had operated under-cover buffet flats, came out into the open and staged nightly so-called Rent Parties. This, of course, was merely a "blind" for more illegitimate activities that catered primarily to the desire of travelling salesmen, pullman porters, inter-state truck drivers, other transients, for some place to stop and amuse themselves. Additional business could always be promoted from that large army of single or unattached males and females who prowled the streets at night in search of adventure in preference to remaining in their small, dingy rooms in some ill-ventilated flat. There were hundreds of young men and women, fresh from the hinterlands, unknown in New York and eager for the opportunity of meeting people. And so, they would stroll the Avenue until they saw some flat with a red, pink or blue light in the window, the plunk of a tin-panny piano and sounds of half-tipsy merry making fleeting out into the night air; then they would venture in, be greeted volubly by the hostess, introduced around and eventually steered to the kitchen where refreshments were for sale. Afterwards, there was probably a night full with continuous drinking, wild, grotesque dancing and crude lovemaking. But it was, at least, a temporary escape from humdrum loneliness and boredom.

The party givers were fully aware of the conditions under which the majority of these boys and girls lived and decided to commercialize on it as much as possible. They began advertising their get-togethers on little business cards that were naive attempts at poetic jingles. The following is a typical sample:

There'll be brown skin mammas
High yallers too
And if you ain't got nothin to do
Come on up to
ROY and SADIE'S
228 West 126 St. Sat. Night, May 12th.
There'll be plenty of pig feet
An lots of gin
Jus ring the bell
An come on in.

They were careful, however, to give these cards to only the "right" people. Prohibition was still in effect and the police were more diligent about raiding questionable apartments than they were about known "gin mills" that flourished on almost every corner.

Despite this fact, the number of personal Saturday night responses, in answer to the under-cover advertising, was amazing. The party hostess, eager and glowing with freshly straightened hair, would roll back the living room carpets, dim the lights, seat the musicians, (usually drummer, piano and saxophone player) and, with the appearance of the first cash customer, give the signal that would officially get the "rug-cutting" under way. Soon afterwards she would disappear into the kitchen in order to give a final, last minute inspection to the refreshment counter: a table piled high with pig-feet, fried chicken, fish and potato salad.

The musicians, fortified with a drink or two of King Kong (home made corn whiskey) begin "beating out the rhythm" on their battered instruments while the dancers keep time with gleeful whoops, fantastic body-gyrations and convulsions that appear to be a cross between the itch and a primitive mating-dance.

After some John buys a couple of rounds of drinks, things begin to hum in earnest. The musicians instinctively improvise as they go along, finding it difficult, perhaps, to express the full intensity of their emotions through a mere arrangement, no matter how well written.

But the thing that makes the house-rent party (even now) so colorful and fascinating is the un-equalled picture created by the dancers themselves. When the band gets hot, the dancers get hotter. They stir, throw or bounce themselves about with complete abandon; their wild, grotesque movements silhouetted in the semi-darkness like flashes from some ancient tribal ceremony. They apparently work themselves up into a frenzy but never lose time with the music despite their frantic acrobatics. Theirs' is a coordination absolutely unexcelled. It is simple, primitive, inspired. As far as dancing is concerned, there are no conventions. You do what you like, express what you feel, take the lid off if you happen to be in the mood. In short, anything goes.

About one o'clock in the morning; hilarity reaches its peak. "The Boys", most of whom are hard-working, hard-drinking truck drivers, longshoremen, moving men, porters or laborers, settle down to the serious business of enjoying themselves. They spin, tug, and fling their buxom, amiable partners in all directions. When the music finally stops, they are soaked and steaming with perspiration. "The Girls", the majority of whom are cooks, laundresses, maids or hair-dressers, set their hats at a jaunty angle and kick up their heels with glee. Their tantalizing grins and the uniformly wicked gleam in their eyes dare the full blooded young bucks to do their darndest. They may have been utter strangers during the early part of the evening but before the night is over, they are all happily sweating and laughing together in the beat of spirits.

Everything they do is free and easy; typical of that group of hard-working Negroes who have little or no inhibitions and the fertility of imagination so necessary to the invention and unrestrained expression of new dance-steps and rhythms.

The dancers organize little impromptu contests among themselves and this competition is often responsible for the birth of many new and original dance-steps. The house-rent party takes credit for the innovation of the Lindy-Hop that was subsequently improved upon at the Savoy Ballroom. For years, it has been a great favorite with the regular rug-cutting crowd. Nothing has been able to supplant it, not even the Boogie-Woogie that has recently enjoyed a great wave of popularity in Uptown New York.

Such unexpected delights as these made the house-rent party, during its infancy, a success with more than one social set. Once in awhile a stray ofay or a small party of pseudo-artistic young Negroes, the upper-crust, the creme-de-la-creme of Black Manhattan society, would wander into one of these parties and gasp or titter (with cultured restraint, of course) at the primitive, untutored Negroes who apparently had so much fun wriggling their bodies about to the accompaniment of such mad, riotously abandoned music. Seldom, however, did these outsiders seem to catch the real spirit of the party, and as far as the rug-cutters were concerned, they simply did not belong.

With the advent of Repeal, the rent-party went out, became definitely a thing of the past. It was too dangerous to try to sell whiskey after it became legal. With its passing went one of the most colorful eras that Harlem has ever known.

## VIVIAN MORRIS (DOCUMENT DATE 1939)

SOURCE: "The Harlem Swing Club." Federal Writers' Project (17 January 1939).

*The Harlem Swing Club was typical of many dance halls and clubs in Harlem that became noteworthy for their contributions to music and dance innovations.*

The Harlem Swing Club is located in a stately white building at 41 West 124th Street, Mount Morris Park North. It is a place where Negro and white workers congregate and have a bit of Sunday night pleasure by resorting to the terpsichorean art or relaxing in the chairs lining the walls and delving deeply into these serious economic and political crises that are staring us in the face today. Because tomorrow, those who are fortunate begin paying their pound of flesh, for which they will at the end-of the week receive a pittance that will keep the dispossess away for a few days longer. They realize that it's dog eat dog and notwithstanding the seemingly carefree air of the people who make up the Swing Club, one feels that the smiles are artificial; the brains behind them are restless, seeking solution to the unfair tangled state of things.

The dancers glide over the cozy hall with an agile tread and seem to feel the spine-tingling music which the Swing Club orchestra sends forth. One notices the ease with which the individuals in the orchestra handle their instruments, the finesse with which the piano player coaxes the tones from his piano. Some of the greatest musicians of our day are before you—the personnel of the "Harlem Swing Club Band" are men from the great name bands of national and international fame. The men drop in and play a while and if

they have other engagements they leave and join their band; but if they have the night off they usually spend the evening at the Swing Club where there is such a friendly tone in the surroundings that anyone feels at ease.

The band plays some torrid swing music and a little brown man, a scant four feet tall, proves to be the most phenomenal untiring dancer on the floor. His partner is a young lady, with an engaging personality, who tops him in height about four inches. The little man dances with abandon. He runs the gamut of the latest swing crazes; the perspiration sticks to his back but he doesn't let up.

A pretty girl, with an aquiline nose, joins hands with her tall, loose-jointed partner and they give a dance exhibition with such scintillating ease that it gives the impression that anyone could emulate them.

The room becomes warm and smoke congested as the music ceases and the dancers find seats or drift toward the walls and stand earnestly talking in little groups.

A brawny man, with a booming voice, walks to the center of the floor and asks for silence. With flowing adjectives and tremor in his voice he introduces a speaker whose greatness and worth to the working class could not be bared with all of the superlatives in the English language. He is a living martyr. Who? Angelo Herndon.

There is ear-splitting applause! Herndon is an idol of the working man. He's the fearless Negro youth who was remanded to the Atlanta Georgia chain gang, for life; he dared to interfere with the shameless infringements by southern law enforcers, on the Constitutional rights of Negro and white workers.

Herndon appealed to the Georgia Supreme Court, but it broadly winked at justice and upheld the Atlanta court's decision. But Herndon was not to be so easily daunted—he appealed to the Supreme Law of the land. The Supreme Court saw the joker in the case and said, "Free Herndon."

Herndon is a clean-cut, soft spoken Negro, who incessantly puffs on a cigarette. His physique doesn't lead one to believe that he could stand the physical and mental brutalities which were heaped upon him. A man's heart must be elephantine in proportion for him to calmly state, in the face of almost certain death, as Herndon did while in that filth-ridden prison in Georgia, "I am not one, I am millions; if they kill me, a million more will rise in my place." He's a man.

Herndon's speech is about another martyr—Tom Mooney. Mooney was released from a California prison yesterday, after serving over twenty-two years on a trumped up charge. Those two men have something in common—Angelo and Tom. Herndon modestly spent his speech extolling the amount of courage and spirit it took Tom Mooney to come through his experiences so physically sound and mentally alert and abreast of the political and economic trend of the outside world. Herndon's speech was short but packed with dynamite. He was cheered to the echo.

Wait! Wait! The powerful voice introduces some other heroes. Some of the American lads who served in the Loyalist lines in Spain are in our midst. Let's give them a hand. They are men, every one of them.

Give a moment's silence for the boys who did not return from Spain. Silence.

The music began and the dancers resumed dancing; I slipped out of the Harlem Swing Club feeling pleasantly surprised. I did not see the usual collection of light-brained, swing-crazed American youth. Meeting such a serious-minded group caused the cockles of my heart to throb in ecstasy.

## VIVIAN MORRIS (DOCUMENT DATE 1939)

**SOURCE:** "Harlem Beauty Shops." Federal Writers' Project (19 April 1939).

*In the following document, Morris describes how beauty parlors provided not only a means of subsistence for African American women but also provided a gathering place for exchanging stories and ideas.*

The largest and most profitable profession indulged in by the Negro women in Harlem is the beauty shops. Beauty Culture takes care of over fifty percent of the Negro professional women as well as supplying jobs for a goodly portion of the male populace in the role of salesman, advertisers and in the actual field of male beauticians.

The most widely known of the persons who took advantage of the knowledge that Negro women desire beautiful hair and soft attractive skin was Mme. C.J . . . Walker who cleared over a million dollars, through the sale of her skin bleaches, hair pomades, etc. The better known systems that are used by the several hundred beauty shops that are sprinkled through Harlem are The Apex, Poro, Nu Life, and Hawaiian Systems and the money made by the owners of the schools conducted by these systems contributes greatly toward the economic life of Harlem, and were they stopped it would leave a big vacuum in the community's budget.

There are four general headings under which the shops of Harlem may be listed according to clientele. From 135 Street down to 110 Street known as lower Harlem on Eighth, Seventh, and Lenox Avenues, may be listed as the shops where the "average Harlemite" gets her work . . . done . . . , from 135-138 Streets on Seventh Avenue may be cataloged as the section where the theatrical group gets its hair "done", from 138 Street North on Seventh and Lenox Avenues to "Sugar Hill" which is above 145 Street is the location of the shops that cater to the Negro elites who dwell in fashionable "Sugar Hill" section, the numbered streets contain beauty shops which draw the bulk of their patrons from the particular locality from which the operators come; if the operator is from Columbia, South Carolina then the persons who are the clients in that particular shop are from that section or as close as possible. Hence there are four Classifications of shops, "Average Harlemite", "Theatrical", "Elite", and "Hometown."

I happen to be in a shop in the "Average Harlemite" areas on a Thursday just before the afternoon rush of the women who do domestic work and stay on the premises where they work and get a half Thursday off. I heard a grumbling conservation going on between two apprehensive operators. "Well it's Thursday again," says the tall one. Soon the place will be so crowded with "kitchen mechanics" you can't move.

"Yeh, . . . it wouldn't be so bad, . . ." sighs the stocky one looking at her feet reflectively "if you didn't have to work so long. We won't be able to leave this shop until two o'clock tomorrow morning."

"The Union did do a little bit of good by saying that we had to close the doors at 10 pm because we used to get out at five and six in the morning before," said the first speaker.

"One of these days," said the stocky speaker, "when this place is full of people who come in just before closing time, without an appointment, I'm gonna "jump salty" (fly off the handle) and "Throw up both hands and holler."

"It's sure no bed of roses," agreed the tall operator. "We learned beauty culture to get away from sweating and scrubbing other peoples floors and ran into something just as bad—scrubbing peoples scalps, straightening, and curling their hair with a hot iron all day and smelling frying hair."

"Yeh," answers the short woman, "and you sweat just as much or a damn sight more and most of 'em are in a hurry—but I think it's a little better than housework—it's cleaner and you don't have no white folks goin' around behind you trying to find a spec of dirt."

"Oh—here comes one of my calkeener broads" (a woman who cooks in a private family).

If she mentions her madam I'll choke her. You'd think on their day off they'd forget their madams. "Hello Miss Adams. Your on time," said the tall operator.

"Yeh," says Miss Adams popping chewing gum and all in a dither. "Got to make time. Me and my boyfriend got a little matter to straighten out this afternoon. He's got to tell me one thing or another. Then, we're gonna "dig that new jive" (see the new show) down the Apollo; then we'll "cut out" (go) to the Savoy and "beat out a few hoof rifts" (dance) till the wee hours then I'll fall on back to the "righteous mansion" (job) "dead beat for shut eye" (sleepy) but willing to "carry on" (work).

"You sure are making the most of your day off," avers the operator, covering the woman's head with a bubbling shampoo and dousing her head in the sink scrubbing vigourously with a stiff brush.

"I didn't tell you what my madam said—hey take it easy on the "top piece" (head), yells Miss Adams as the operator scrubs vigorously and looks at the other operator meaningly as Miss Adams mentions her madam.

"My, madam" resumes Miss Adams, "asked me what I had done to my hair last Friday when she saw it all curly and pretty. I told her I'd been to the hair dresser. She asked me how much it cost and when I told her she just looked funny and started to ask me how I could afford it. She needn't worry 'cause I'm dead sure I'm gonna ask her for a raise 'cause this little money she pays me ain't a "drop in the bucket." (not much).

I dropped in one of the "hometown" shops and saw a breezy well groomed man enter and make his way to the back of the shop saying "They're at the post. Don't get left."

The operators excused themselves handed the man a piece of paper which he copies. "Hey Ann", he asks "Is this 517 or 511? Your figures are so hard to figure out."

"517" retorts Ann, "You can't read. Better get them numbers right, "cause they're hot."

"Is that the number man?" asks a customer, "Give me 370 for a dime. I dreamed about my dead uncle and everytime I dream about him 370 comes out."

The mentioning of the "number" as a dream "number" causes most of the customers and the operators to play it because they all believe in dreams. When the "writer" leaves his book is "loaded" with the 370 which thereby becomes a "hot number" (a number favored to come out which seldom does).

In another "Hometown" shop I found operators selling tickets to a Beauticians Ball, while the customers sell them tickets to a supper for the church or their own house rent parties.

When I entered a shop in the "Theatrical" area a male operator washing a person's hair whom you assume to be a woman in slacks. When the person turned around it was a man. Yes, the theatrical men and a few non-theatrical men get their hair straightened and waved.

The conversation was about a currently popular star. The fellow who is getting his hair washed says, "Chick Webb sure pulled some "hep jive" when he signed Ella Fitzgerald up. I hear from good source that Benny Goodman offered gangs of money for her contract. Chick said "no can do." (no).

"Yeh," answers a dreamy eyed girl getting wavy ringlets pressed over her entire head. "I remember Ella when—ain't changed a bit towards little Fifi."

"The Swing Mikado's been sold I hear", says one girl as a hot comb is pulled through her hair.

"The actors think that's "weird jive" (bad) says another, "They ain't commin' up to that tab." (Don't want to work for a private owner.)

I know what the jive is. W. P. A. says the sale is left up to the cast. They want to put us back on relief. Too many of us on Broadway at the same time. 110 of us in "Hot Mikado" and 75 of us in "Swing Mikado." They'll either take us out on the road or fire us here. If Equity takes us in then we have some protection, but they'll ditch us before Equity gets around to us. What the hell is the difference anyway? They got the money and they'll keep you right where they want to, unless we have a God damn riot, and how much good would that do? A hell of a lot don't fool yourself. Didn't we get jobs on 125 Street after the March 19th riot?

In the "Sugar Hill' area I found well dressed women pulling up in big cars. Their topics are the grave international situation, the latest plays, the teachers discuss schools. I see where "Address Unknown" was a best seller for last month. The copies were sold almost as soon as they reached the book stores," says one.

"Oh yes," remarked another woman (wearing two diamonds and an imported wrist watch), from under her application of bleach cream. "The author was very fortunate. At another time it would just have been another book—interesting reading of course but the story—then the book was published at the precise, psychological time when the "Madman of Europe" was shedding blood all over Germany. Result? A best seller."

Suddenly a man darted in the swanky shop with a bag and made his way to the rear, with significant nods to each other. The operators went to the rear singly. He was peddling "hot stuff" (stolen goods). The operator's make their purchase and hurried back to their customers. A nosey customer asks "What is he selling? Last time I was here I got some lovely perfume very cheap."

"Lingerie" says the operator.

"Reasonable?" asks the inquisitive one. "They have ten dollar . . . tags . . . He sells them for three," answers the operator.

"Please tell him I want to see them," says the customer jumping out of the chair, with her beauty treatment half finished. With the apron around her neck she goes to the rear of the shop followed by more interested customers.

INTERESTING PLACES—THESE BEAUTY SHOPS.

# OVERVIEWS

## C. C. BARFOOT, HANS BERTENS, THEO D'HAEN, AND ERIC KOOPER (ESSAY DATE 1994)

**SOURCE:** Barfoot, C. C., et al. "The New Negro in Context." In *Wallace Thurman's Harlem Renaissance*, pp. 17-54. Amsterdam: Editions Rodopi B. V., 1994.

*The following essay relates five central forces that defined the New Negro Movement and the Harlem Renaissance: the Great Migration, Marcus Garvey, Black magazines and literary outlets, Alain Locke's groundbreaking anthology* The New Negro, *and Carl Van Vechten's support of the Black race.*

No single event, historical, political, or cultural, can by itself mark the onset of the "New Negro Movement."[1] The movement evolved over a long period of time and was stimulated by a variety of loosely related and parallel developments, both in and outside the United States. It took the First World War to generate a particular configuration and environment out of which the New Negro Movement and its artistic dimension, the Harlem Renaissance, could emerge.

Over the years the New Negro Movement has come to be known under a variety of names, including the New Negro Renaissance, the Black Renaissance, and even the "Cullud Renaissance" as Langston Hughes would call it.[2] What all of these have in common is a new emphasis on race as a source for identity and pride and the importance of Harlem as the black capital of the world.

For the purpose of this study the term "New Negro Movement" will be used to indicate the development of a temper of racial pride and defiance which manifested itself collectively and openly among African-Americans following the end of the Great War. The term "Harlem Renaissance" will be reserved to indicate an outburst of creative activity which marked the intellectual and artistic expression of this new temper during the 1920s. The main centre of black artistic activity was concentrated in Harlem, New York. The traditional perception of the Harlem Renaissance as primarily a literary movement will be retained.

Just as scholars cannot agree upon a single name for the renaissance, they cannot agree upon its dates. Attempts to place the movement in a historical time frame mark its beginning as early as 1903 and its end as late as 1940. As a starting point for both the New Negro Movement and the Harlem Renaissance, I suggest 1919. This was the year in which early manifestations of a new postwar temper became apparent. Notable indicators with regards to the emergence of the New Negro Movement and the Harlem Renaissance include the return of the Harlem Hell Fighters from the war in Europe, the rise of Marcus Garvey's Back-to-Africa Movement, the publication of Claude McKay's militant poetry, and the appointment of Jessie Redmon Fauset as literary editor of *Crisis* magazine.[3]

The end of the Harlem Renaissance as essentially a group phenomenon was the result of the dissolution of the very group which had encouraged its birth and early development. Again, no one event marks the onset of this process. Yet, just as the first world war had played a critical role in the movement's inception, the economic depression of the 1930s precipitated its demise. The spirit of the New Negro Movement, however, prevails to this day.

Like the New Negro Movement, African-Americans associated with the Harlem Renaissance were not unified in their efforts and goals. Both movements included a number of strong-minded intellectuals, writers and artists with radically different ideas about how their race should be represented and how racial parity could be achieved in a white supremacist society. The older generation traditionally believed that their goals were best pursued by exhortation and propaganda emphasizing the uniqueness of the African-American experience and the solidarity of the race. The younger generation was more inclined

African American soldiers of the 368th Infantry.

to believe that the cumulative effect of individual intellectual and artistic achievement would ultimately dispel racism.

Wallace Thurman, the typical Jazz-Age figure of cosmopolitan, hedonistic "flaming youth,"[4] was a strong voice for the power of the individual. His rejection of the genteel tradition of Victorian bourgeois attitudes connected him to the new temper of scepticism which scorned middle-class values and advocated intellectual, artistic, and sexual freedom. These sympathies also linked him, at least in spirit, with the Greenwich Village avant-garde. But unlike his white peers from the Village, or indeed his light-skinned bohemian friends in Harlem, Thurman's affinity with the spirit of the avant-garde, as we shall see, was part of his life-long struggle to free himself from a debilitating preoccupation with colour.

* * *

The first and introductory Chapter of this study examines some of the defining forces which informed the New Negro Movement and the Harlem Renaissance:

1. The Great Migration and the development of black Harlem.[5]

2. Black leadership and the Great War.

3. Marcus Garvey and black nationalism.

4. Black magazines and the advancement of the arts.

5. Alain Locke and *The New Negro* Anthology.

6. Carl Van Vechten and interracial cultural elitism.

The first three sections provide a political and socio-economic context for the New Negro Movement. The final three sections reconstruct and assess the cultural climate in which the Harlem Renaissance could develop.

* * *

### 1. The Great Migration and the Development of Black Harlem

At the end of the American Civil War (1861-1865), blacks slowly began to move out of the Deep South. Between 1870 and 1890 some 40,000 persons per decade left the region. This figure almost doubled during the last ten years of the nineteenth century.[6] Behind this migration lay a complex of motives. With the failure of Reconstruction (1865-1877), race relations in the South deteriorated rapidly. Despite the ambitious educational ideals of a small core of mostly northern liberals and progressive southern blacks the majority of former slaves remained poorly educated or wholly illiterate. By the end of the century the newly emancipated black population was still for the most part excluded from higher education, business, government, and other means of personal, social, economic, and political development. Southern politicians such as governor James Vardaman of Mississippi, who in 1906 urged the legislature to stop wasting half a million dollars per year on "the vain purpose of trying to make something of the negro which the Great Architect . . . failed to provide for in the original plan of creation," were no exception.[7] Not surprisingly, the black press pointed at the worsening racial conditions as the major cause of the growing exodus of blacks after 1870.[8] A later sociological study by Charles S. Johnson, however, suggested that the main impetus for this collective migration was, in the best American tradition, economic.[9]

When towards the end of the nineteenth century the predominantly agricultural southern States could no longer produce crops without the aid of expensive machinery and fertilizers, people began to move to industrial centres within the South, or they went to potentially more productive land outside the region. Some left for the North. Of the 60,534 blacks living in Manhattan in 1910, for example, only 14,309 were born in New York State. The majority had migrated from Virginia, the Carolinas, Georgia, and Florida.[10] During the 1910s, black emigration from the South was precipitated by a series of natural disasters. Between 1914 and 1916 long periods of drought were followed by seasonal flooding which in turn provoked plagues of insects thriving in wet conditions and feeding on cotton crops. The bleak economic situation in the South coincided with increasing labour shortages in the North. Immigration from Europe had come to a virtual standstill following the outbreak of the Great War. With the traditional source for industrial labour all but cut off, northern manufacturers turned to America's southern States to find a new work force for their rapidly expanding war industry. The massive response to their advertising campaigns set into motion a pattern which

would continue until the onset of the Great Depression in 1929. In *The New York World* of 5 November 1917 the six main reasons which motivated black migration to the North are listed as follows:

1. The natural desire to get a promised increase of wages, accompanied by a free ride to the new field of labor.

2. To gratify a natural impulse to travel, and see the country.

3. To better the condition of the Negro by a freer use of schools and other advantages offered in the North, East and West. The desire of some Negroes to escape the persecution of thoughtless and irresponsible white people who mistreat them.

4. To see the fulfilment of a dream to be on a social equality with white people.

5. The Negro who is educated wants to go where he can vote and take part in running the Government.[11]

In Chicago, Detroit, Cleveland, Philadelphia, Pittsburgh, and New York, major black concentrations began to develop. Between 1910 and 1920 the black population of New York City, for example, grew from 91,709 to 152,467. Of these, some 73,000 were living in Harlem at the beginning of the 1920s.[12]

The development and growth of Harlem, which had begun as early as the 1870s, was a by-product of the expansion of commercial and industrial activity of New York City as a whole. In 1880 the population of Manhattan had passed the one million mark, and Harlem, then a predominantly white rural suburb, had become, as some of the locals would have it, "the choicest residential section of the city."[13] At the turn of the century, the construction of new underground lines connecting Harlem with the downtown business centres was announced. The prospect of improved public transport turned the neighbourhood into a target for real estate speculation. Between 1898 and 1904, when the so-called Lenox Avenue line finally opened, Harlem was overbuilt and housing prices had soared to unrealistic heights. The inevitable collapse of the real estate market came in 1904. In an effort to avoid bankruptcy, real estate agents turned to New York's black population then concentrated in the overcrowded and crime infested Tenderloin and San Juan Hill neighbourhoods on Manhattan's West Side.[14] Here, regardless of social or economic distinctions, blacks were packed together in small ghettos and forced to pay higher rents than other ethnic minorities.[15] The exodus from these parts of the city, which began as early as 1905, was initiated by organizations such as the Afro-American Realty Company which secured the acquisition of entire apartment blocks in Harlem for occupation by blacks.[16] The following advertisement, for example, appeared in Newark and Baltimore newspapers:

> Colored people: Chance of a life-time to acquire elegant, newly furnished rooms, single or en suite, in the beautiful Garden Courts, occupying nearly one whole square block on St. Nicholas Avenue, 118th Street and 119th Street; over 650 rooms to be turned over to the use of colored people; electric light, steam heat, hot and cold water; handsomely decorated, marble stairs, tiled bathrooms, etc.; near subway and Eight Avenue elevated station. Call at once in office of Charles Klein, 164 St. Nicholas Avenue, corner 118th Street.[17]

Apart from new and better housing, Harlem also offered the prospect of greater distance between the various social layers without the black community itself. Indeed, the newly created distance in terms of the variety in living quarters functioned as an illustration of intraracial social stratifications. Some streets became decidedly more upper class than others. In a section of 139th Street called "Strivers Row," houses originally designed by Stanford White for a well-to-do white clientele now came to be inhabited almost exclusively by upper-middle-class blacks. This mainly light-skinned so-called Talented Tenth[18] lived on Harlem's higher grounds in well-appointed apartment buildings while the average black family lived in cramped quarters "down in Harlem."

To Harlem's new residents, sophisticated living was important. It symbolized, at least on the surface, the race's potential for upward mobility, both economically and socially. Yet in socioeconomic terms it was the concentration of predominantly lower-class blacks which provided a base for a black middle class, including business and professional men and a black intelligentsia.[19] African-American businessmen began to enter occupations from which they had previously been barred. West Indians in particular became prominent in this respect. Their business acumen earned them the label of "Jews of the race."[20] Despite a relatively large number of West Indians engaged in business, only 2% of the entire black professional class were categorized as businessmen in 1925.[21] Harlem's nightclubs and theatres, a major source of revenue throughout the 1920s, were largely owned and run by whites. Indeed, one of Harlem's major problems appears to have been its inability to generate an effective black business community.[22] In February 1930, some time before the effects of the stock market crash began to affect Harlem, Beverly Smith in *The New York Herald Tribune* offered the following numbers:

> 90 per cent of the night clubs in Harlem are owned by white people. Nearly 92 per cent of the speakeasies are operated by white racketeers downtown. . . . nine-tenths of the work that white folks do is closed to Negroes. If the chief trades open they are taken on only after the supply of white labour is exhausted. . . . Men who employed both races tended to fire the Negro worker first.[23]

The accuracy of Smith's data is difficult to establish, yet there can be no doubt that racial discrimination played a significant role in the allocation of jobs in New York City. The average black worker was unlikely to ever rise above a marginal economic status.

Others, like Wallace Thurman, who lived in Harlem more or less permanently from September 1925 until his death in December 1934, painted a more favourable picture of the district. Although Thurman acknowledged that black Harlemites did not own banks, theatres, dance halls, or saloons, he stressed their achievements as real estate operators.[24] In Thurman's estimation, blacks owned over $60,000,000 in property, including houses, restaurants, and shops.[25] Thurman also maintained that a prosperous and socially prominent black middle class flourished in Harlem, occupying expensive houses and apartment buildings, employing maids and butlers, and sending their children to select academic institutions such as Harvard, Yale, Columbia, Barnard, Vassar, and Wellesley.[26]

Thurman's account of the economic strength and social standing of Harlem's middle class was optimistic. Even in the early days of the Harlem Renaissance the district bore all the marks of an expanding urban slum. Many of the immigrants, which included African-Americans, Africans, blacks from British, Spanish, Portugese, and Dutch colonies, Cubans, Puerto Ricans, and East Indians, whom Thurman also lists,[27] found no further use for their skills and joined the ranks of the unemployed. The rising unemployment rate brought not only poverty but also juvenile delinquency, drugs, and disease.

With the beginning of the 1920s many of Harlem's white inhabitants, unable to halt the tidal wave of blacks, had decided to move elsewhere.[28] Over the next decade Harlem's African-American population grew to 164,566 in 1930 and became what Osofsky described as the world's largest black melting pot.[29] Despite the precarious economic position of a large percentage of Harlem's population, their concentration within a small urban setting produced, among other things, a new political awareness particularly among those who had been virtually disenfranchised in the South. This awareness was reflected in the growing influence of racial uplift organizations such as the National Association for the Advancement of Colored People (N.A.A.C.P.), the National Urban League (N.U.L.), and their respective magazines.[30]

Both organizations were staffed and supported by white as well as black Americans. The N.A.A.C.P., founded in 1909, fought racial injustice primarily through the courts, opposing, defending, and sponsoring legislation in the best interests of the race as a whole. The N.A.A.C.P. also offered legal help to individual blacks. The Urban League, established in 1911, focused primarily on social welfare among African-Americans, including housing, education, and employment. Both the N.A.A.C.P. and the Urban League employed a small but effective group of intellectuals and journalists to bring out their respective monthly magazines, *The Crisis: A Record of the Darker Races,* (1910-) and *Opportunity: A Journal of Negro Life,* (1923-49). A third journal of note was *The Messenger: The World's Greatest Negro Monthly,* (1917-28). Initially *The Hotel Messenger,* this black socialist monthly magazine became the official journal of The Brotherhood of Sleeping Car Porters in 1925.[31] All three magazines had a national readership, yet by conducting their activities from Harlem they brought attention to this city within a city and made it the focal point of black America. Of particular importance in this respect was *The Crisis.* The oldest and largest of the black periodicals (with a circulation of over 100,000 by 1919), was headed by W. E. B. Du Bois (1868-1963), one of America's most influential civil rights leaders of the day.

## 2. Black Leadership and the Great War

Du Bois' prominence relatively early in life was directly related to his reputation as an intellectual and a political activist, and his opposition to Booker T. Washington (1856-1915).[32] Born in Great Barrington, Massachusetts, of mixed French Huguenot and Haitian descent, Du Bois received a B.A. degree from Fisk University and an M.A. degree from Harvard. Later, in 1892, Du Bois travelled to Europe to read history and economics at the University of Berlin. Back at Harvard two years later, he published his Ph.D. dissertation, *The Suppression of the African Slave Trade to the United States of America, 1638-1870.* Various teaching positions followed: Professor of Greek and Latin at Wilberforce University, Ohio; Assistant Instructor in Sociology at the University of Pennsylvania; and Professor of Economics and History at Atlanta University in Georgia. In 1910, as one of the founding members of the N.A.A.C.P., Du Bois became Director of Publications and Research and editor of the organization's magazine *The Crisis.*

The interracial N.A.A.C.P. (1910) and its precursor the Niagara Movement (1905) were established as a reaction to what some considered the domineering and at times manipulative racial politics of Du Bois' rival Booker T. Washington. Although both Washington and Du Bois devoted their lives to the advancement of the black race, they approached their objectives from what they perceived as irreconcilable positions. The dissimilarity in their views and methods can to some extent be explained in the context of their respective social and intellectual backgrounds. Unlike Du Bois, who had been educated in the New England tradition, Washington was educated in the South at the Hampton Normal and Agricultural Institute in Virginia. Born a slave on a small farm in Franklin County, Virginia, in 1856, Washington would focus on rudimentary racial advancement policies best suited to the needs of the recently freed southern black population. The educational methods of the Tuskegee Institute in Alabama, established by Washington in 1881 and modelled on his alma mater in Hampton, Virginia, were motivated by a pragmatic approach to learning. Stressing the importance of economic self-reliance and self-sufficiency, Tuskegee emphasized industrial and agricultural training over the liberal arts and sciences, much to the satisfaction and possibly the relief of the white philanthropic institutions which funded the school.[33] The Tuskegee Institute, it was felt by Du Bois' and his supporters, had become the facade behind which Washington maintained and extended his influence with powerful white philanthropists and through which he controlled, at least in part, the policies of black businesses and newspapers.[34]

By 1903, Du Bois disagreed openly with what he considered Washington's shortsighted and self-limiting advocacy of economic advancement at the expense of civil rights. He articulated both his criticism of Washington as well as the tenets of his own position on racial uplift and black leadership in *The Souls of Black Folk* (1903).[35] Washington's accommodationist strategy, in Du Bois' estimation, not only further disenfranchised African-Americans but also perpetuated their status as second-class citizens and a servile caste.[36]

Du Bois' own approach to America's race problem, not surprisingly, was equally a reflection of his own background. As a well-educated, sophisticated northern black, born a free man, Du Bois conceived of black leadership in terms of a Talented Tenth. The black race, like all races, Du Bois contended, "was going to be saved by its exceptional men."[37] Through his criticism of Washington, Du Bois, after Washington's death in 1915, became a prominent driving force in black America's transition from an attitude of submission and accommodation traditionally associated with the mentality of the "old negro" to the more defiant and proud temper of the "new negro."

Of critical significance in this respect was Du Bois' appeal to African-Americans to join the war effort in Europe. When in April 1917 the United States declared war on Germany, some 20,000 black soldiers were available for active duty.[38] About 50% of these troops were part of the army. The other half were members of black regiments in the National Guard. One of these, the 15th New York, was nicknamed the Harlem Hell Fighters.[39] Officially the United States 369th Infantry Regiment, the Harlem Hell Fighters engaged in active duty for ten months as part of the 16th and 161st divisions of the French Army. The Hell Fighters' record in the Battle of Meuse-Argonne earned them the Croix de Guerre not only for their regimental colours but also for one hundred and fifty of their men.[40] Upon their return on 17 February 1919, the thirteen hundred black soldiers and their eighteen white officers were greeted by an enthusiastic crowd of New Yorkers, black and white alike. As feelings of solidarity, pride, and hope swept through Harlem, one of the bystanders, Dan Block recorded his impressions of the event in a poem which appeared in *The Messenger* under the title "When the Colored Troops Got Back":

> When the colored troops got
> back,
> And the whites "joined in" with
> them
> In the hurricane of laughter,
> Which stirred the city to its depths
> And thrilled all hearts with pater-
> nalness,

> I felt—if only for a moment—
> "The Great International Spirit of Brothers."[41]

In addition to the feeling of brotherhood which informed Block's poem, it was felt that the patriotism and striking war record of these black soldiers would also generate respect for America's black population as a whole.

This was also the view of Du Bois at *The Crisis*. In his role as the N.A.A.C.P.'s most public and most vocal spokesman, Du Bois' response to President Woodrow Wilson's battle cry to "make the world free for democracy" had greatly influenced public opinion on black participation in the war in Europe.[42] Du Bois believed that through the black war effort America might at last live up to its own alleged democratic ideals. In 1918, in one of his *Crisis* editorials, he argued:

> We of the colored race have no ordinary interest in the outcome [of the war]. That which the German power represents today spells death to the aspirations of Negroes and all darker races for equality, freedom and democracy. Let us, while this war lasts, forget our special grievances and close our ranks shoulder to shoulder with our own white fellow-citizens.[43]

Clearly Du Bois had a vital interest in the reverberations of the returning Hell Fighters. Determined to profit from the unprecedented political momentum he now urged black Americans to fight for democracy at home. In another of his fiery editorials for *The Crisis,* by now selling over one hundred thousand copies per month,[44] Du Bois characterized The United States as a country where black citizens were insulted, degraded, and lynched. Aiming specifically at African-Americans themselves, Du Bois declared: "We are cowards and jackasses if now that the war is over, we do not marshal every ounce of our brain and brawn to fight a sterner, longer, more unbending battle against the forces of hell in our own land."[45]

But "the forces of hell," in the most literal sense, were to prevail throughout the so-called Red Summer of 1919. Violent race riots erupted in more than twenty-five cities all across the United States. In Chicago, for example, the rioting lasted for five days. When hostilities ended, fifteen whites and twenty-three blacks were dead, five hundred and thirty-seven people were wounded, and about one thousand families were left homeless.[46] The causes of this uncontrollable fury were both economic and racial. During the final years of World War I, conditions on the labour market had deteriorated steadily. In the absence of new war contracts, manufacturers had begun to lay off part of their mainly black workforce. The ranks of the unemployed were swelled by the still uninterrupted flow of migration from the agricultural South. After the war, the demobilization of thousands of soldiers, both black and white, further glutted the labour pool. The subsequent massive unemployment directly affected living conditions in the black belts of major industrial centres.

Before long, the optimism surrounding the homecoming of the Harlem Hell Fighters turned into disillusion and despair. Once back in the United States, many black war veterans found themselves without a job and with little evidence of progress in the struggle for racial equality. Indeed, the sight of blacks in uniform often provoked an angry response from those whites who considered the status of soldier incompatible with what they perceived as the black man's proper station in life.

Riots and lynchings continued all through the summer. They were widely reported in the black press and aroused collective indignation and public censure from African-Americans on a national scale. One of the first outspoken interpretations of this new temper of anger and defiance, in a purely literary voice, was Claude McKay's sonnet "If We Must Die," published, ironically, in Max Eastman's white, liberal magazine *The Liberator*.

> If we must die, let it not be like hogs
> Hunted and penned in an inglorious spot,
> While round us bark the mad and hungry dogs,
> Making their mock at our accursed lot.
> If we must die, O let us nobly die,
> So that our precious blood may not be shed
> In vain; then even the monsters we defy
> Shall be constrained to honor us though dead!
> O kinsmen! we must meet the common foe!
> Though far outnumbered let us show us brave,
> And for their thousand blows deal one
>     deathblow!
> What though before us lies the open grave?
> Like men we'll face the murderous, cowardly
>     pack,
> Pressed to the wall, dying, but fighting back![47]

In a critical assessment of McKay's poem, Wallace Thurman identified the sonnet as an accurate expression of the essence of the New Negro temper. "There is no impotent whining here," he declared, "no mercy-seeking prayer to the white man's God, no mournful jeremiad, no 'ain't it hard to be a nigger,' no lamenting of or apologizing for the fact that he is a member of a dark-skinned minority group."[48]

McKay's assurance that blacks could win the respect of their white countrymen by first of all showing respect for themselves was not shared by all. Some were convinced that black participation in the American Dream was highly unlikely. One

of the more uncompromising manifestations of this position was Marcus Garvey's crusade for an all-black African homeland.[49]

## 3. Marcus Garvey and Black Nationalism

In 1914, the then twenty-seven year old, largely self-taught, Marcus Garvey established the first branch of the Universal Negro Improvement Association (U.N.I.A) in his native Jamaica. Two years later, Garvey moved his racial uplift organization to the United States. Garvey's message, based on Booker T. Washington's ideology of self-help and economic independence, was directed primarily at the black lower class. Capitalizing on the deteriorating economic and racial climate, Garvey began to stir the imagination of his audience with a utopian vision of motherland Africa where all "exiled" blacks, as he put it, would ultimately return.[50] A failed attempt on Garvey's life in 1919 further added to his charisma. By the end of the decade, Garvey was perceived by many as the black Moses of the race.[51]

African-Americans joined the U.N.I.A. by the thousands, participating in a wide variety of all-black enterprises and institutions such as the Black Eagle Flying Corps and the Universal Black Cross Nurses. The most remarkable of U.N.I.A. commercial establishments was the Black Star Line through which black repatriation to the motherland was to be achieved. The Black Star Line's first ship, the *Yarmouth*, attracted thousands of sightseers (at one dollar per ticket). The ships clearly functioned as visible symbols of African-Americans' imminent return to their African homeland. Through various advertising campaigns African-Americans were further encouraged to support the shipping line by buying stocks at five dollars each. In the end almost $800,000 was spent on the acquisition of substandard ships which never came in sight of the African coast.

For the national and international dissemination of his ideas, Garvey established the weekly magazine *Negro World* (1918-1933). The success of the magazine was overwhelming. Through the offices of a highly qualified editorial staff which at one time included the historian and literary critic Professor William H. Ferris and one of Harlem's oldest and most respected radical intellectuals Hubert Harrison, Garvey, who refused to bow in any way to the requirements of a non-black readership, insisted on the portrayal of black life in wholly positive terms.[52] Unlike the other racial uplift organizations of the day, Garvey's was opposed to the assimilation of the black and the white races. His enmity towards whites was only surpassed by his loathing for African-Americans with a light complexion. Adam Clayton Powell, Sr., then the pastor of Harlem's Abyssinian Baptist Church, observed how Garvey succeeded in making those with lighter skin-tones ashamed of their colour.[53] This emphasis on racial purity, however, eventually led Garvey to agree publicly with the Ku Klux Klan in its advocacy of an all white Anglo-Saxon Protestant United States.

After 1922, Garvey's mass-movement began to decline. In January 1922 Garvey was charged with income tax evasion and mail fraud. Garvey, who dismissed his lawyer and argued his own case, was sentenced to five years in prison and a $1,000 fine in 1923.[54] After an unsuccessful appeal, he entered Atlanta Penitentiary in February 1925. Two years later, in November 1927, he was pardoned by President Coolidge, anxious to gain the black vote, on condition that Garvey leave the country. Garvey was released from Atlanta prison in December 1927 and returned to Jamaica where he died in 1940.

Although Marcus Garvey never gave up his efforts to return "Africa to the Africans," it was only during the spectacular years in Harlem, roughly from 1919 to 1925, that his activities played a role as part of the New Negro Movement. According to Wallace Thurman, Garvey's forthright advocacy of black pride and self-reliance generated an affirmative race-consciousness among the black masses. Thurman also suggested that Garvey's insistence on the cultivation of the black population's natural and racially distinctive endowment made him a significant contributor to the inception of the Harlem Renaissance.[55]

Despite Garvey's impressive support, his ideology of emancipation through separatism was not without opposition. The N.A.A.C.P. (damned by Garvey as the National Association for the Advancement of *Certain* People) as well as the National Urban League were relieved to see him go.[56] They resented what they considered his manipulation of mass emotion. More importantly, however, Garvey's ideology and methods, like Booker T. Washington's before him, were incompatible with the image of the New Negro they themselves were trying to project to the outside world.[57]

During the Harlem Renaissance period the integrationist approach of the Talented Tenth was built, at least in part, on black intellectual and artistic achievement. The promotion of African-American art was contained in their struggle for civil rights and racial equality.[58] This perception

explains the old guard's determination to oversee and regulate the Harlem Renaissance' artistic product. After 1926, the idealism of the old guard[59] and their efforts to control the artistic representation of black life would provoke a powerful opposition from members of Harlem's younger generation of artists and writers. This rebellion against a propagandist motivation in the arts was led by Wallace Thurman. As was to be expected black magazines functioned as the prime medium for the expression of the differences between the two competing factions.

## 4. Black Magazines and the Advancement of the Arts

Black leaders used the magazines of their respective organizations as a means to generate and influence a new racial disposition among the rapidly growing black urban population. Similarly, the artistic expression of the New Negro Movement also developed under the auspices of black periodicals. The three most prominent New York-based journals in this respect were *The Crisis, Opportunity,* and *The Messenger.* Carefully orchestrated and highly self-conscious, these periodicals helped to create a movement in the arts which came to be known as The Harlem Renaissance. In 1919, the first significant step in the advancement of the black race through sponsorship of the arts was initiated by W. E. B. Du Bois with the appointment of Jessie Redmon Fauset as literary editor of *Crisis* magazine.[60] Fauset, of solid Talented Tenth extraction, was educated at Cornell (Phi Beta Kappa) and at the University of Pennsylvania. From 1912 onwards, she had contributed reviews, essays, short stories, and poems to *The Crisis* on a regular basis. Convinced that the artistic interpretation of black life could best be done by blacks themselves, she now, in her capacity as literary editor, began to encourage young writers to submit their materials for publication.[61]

Like other black intellectuals of the day, Fauset and Du Bois advocated what came to be known as cultural elitism, the social intermingling of blacks and whites of compatible educational background and cultural taste. They held the view that social and intellectual interaction between the races would ultimately help to bring about the breakdown of racism in the United States. Interracial integration could be further stimulated, it was felt, if blacks were to show themselves worthy equals of their white counterparts through intellectual and artistic parity.

Although *The Crisis* had published black literature almost from its inception in 1910, it was only with Fauset's appointment to the staff that the advancement of the arts became one of the magazine's serious objectives. Between Fauset's arrival at *The Crisis* in 1919 and her departure from the magazine in 1926, *The Crisis* published one hundred and twenty-six poems, twenty pieces of fiction, and two plays.[62] The magazine also began to organize literary contests. In December 1922, *The Crisis* announced a fifty-dollar prize for the best short story on black life written by a student. The first full-scale competition, which included such categories as poetry, the graphic arts, drama, short stories, and essays, was announced in November 1924, only two months after a similar contest had been called by *Opportunity* magazine. Before long a spirit of competition developed between *The Crisis* and *Opportunity* magazine. Prize money was frequently increased to attract submissions and the magazines vied with each other to find distinguished personalities for their respective panels of judges. The splendour of the award dinners and dances to which New York's intellectual elite, both black and white, were invited, was also a conscious effort to entice participation.[63]

Despite *The Crisis'* lead in soliciting and publishing artistic work by blacks, the magazine encountered considerable rivalry from *Opportunity* magazine. The first of the three major *Opportunity* contests was announced in September 1924 and included such categories as short stories, essays, poetry, plays, and personal experience sketches.[64] The rules of the contest restricted participation to African-Americans only. In addition, all entries with the exception of the poetry category had to deal with aspects of black life.[65] In a response to the debate provoked by these restrictions, the magazine pointed out that a keen interest in black life had occurred among white readers and that white authors were eager to capitalize on this latest fad.[66] The treatment of black life by black artists had become a matter of some urgency.

The third prominent black periodical of the day, *The Messenger,* never explicitly functioned as a forum for the arts. Yet the magazine reserved space for literary publications and employed influential Harlem Renaissance figures such as George Schuyler, Theophilus Lewis, and Wallace Thurman on its editorial staff. *The Messenger,* however, did not engage in literary contests, nor in any of the interracial social functions promoted by *Crisis* and *Opportunity.*

One of the earliest and most notable of these social gatherings by New York City's interracial cultural elite was organized by Charles S. Johnson,

# ON THE SUBJECT OF...

### THE CIVIC CLUB DINNER

On March 21, 1924, *Opportunity* editor Charles S. Johnson organized a gathering with the hope that African Americans could eventually gain equality through artistic achievement. With that goal in mind, he sought to gain the influence of the white literary establishment. He chose the Civic Club (a venue notable for allowing white and black patrons to intermingle) as the location and invited 110 guests, including such Harlem luminaries as Walter White, Du Bois, and Countee Cullen, as well as white literary figures like Frederick Lewis Allen, Carl Van Doren, and Paul Kellogg.

Director of the Department of Research and Investigations for the National Urban League and editor of *Opportunity*. It was held on 21 March 1924 at Manhattan's Civic Club. The Club, established by some of the founding members of the N.A.A.C.P., among others, was one of the few public places which admitted both black and white membership.[67] Ostensibly to celebrate the publication of Jessie Fauset's first novel *There Is Confusion,*[68] Johnson brought promising black writers into contact with the established white publishing world, represented by, among others, *Scribner's, Harper's, World Tomorrow,*[69] and *Survey Graphic.*[70]

At the Civic Club gathering, black writers were encouraged to capitalize on the post-war Jazz-Age spirit, with its revolt against idealism and puritanism and its call for liberation and change. Carl van Doren, the white editor of the *Century Magazine* and one of the speakers at the event, declared: "What American literature decidedly needs at the moment, is color, music, gusto, the free expression of gay or desperate moods. If the Negroes are not in a position to contribute these items, I do not know what Americans are."[71]

The most important publication to come out of the Civic Club dinner was proposed by Paul Kellog, editor of the white journal *Survey Graphic.* Kellog's advice to publish the evening's papers and speeches in a special Harlem issue reflected an editorial policy change at *Survey Graphic*. The magazine's traditional reluctance to discuss African-Americans had been overcome by its white readership's growing interest in the supposedly primitive and exotic lives of Harlem's black population.[72] To edit the proposed issue, Charles Johnson enlisted the help of Alain Locke, professor of philosophy at Howard University and master of ceremonies at the dinner.

In March 1925, the birth of the New Negro was formally announced by *Survey Graphic*'s special issue entitled "Harlem Mecca of the New Negro." The Harlem number sold 40,000 copies within two weeks, a record unmatched until the 1940s.[73] The publication, furthermore, established Alain Locke as one of the leading figures of the Harlem Renaissance.

### 5. Alain Locke and the New Negro Anthology

Despite Locke's intention to focus on the work of the younger generation of black artists[74], many of the articles in the special issue of *Survey Graphic* were written by established academics. Moreover, the illustrations of "Harlem Types" were the creation of the white Bavarian artist Winold Reiss. In November 1925, expanding on the core of writings in *Survey*'s Harlem issue, Locke published his anthology *The New Negro*.[75] The aim of the anthology, as Locke stated in his foreword, was "to document the New Negro culturally and socially, to register the transformations of the inner and outer life of the Negro in America that have so significantly taken place in the last few years."[76] This time, Locke's intention was clear. By dedicating his anthology to "the Younger Generation," Locke stressed the responsibility of young black writers to interpret what he called the truly racial elements in the lives of the as yet inarticulate masses. Locke further advised aspiring writers to ignore all politically motivated social and propagandistic pressures and to turn to Harlem's proletariat for inspiration.[77] It was in the milieu of the recently arrived migrant population, Locke maintained, that black life must be explored. Contact with and interpretation of the folk culture of southern blacks brought to Harlem by the Great Migration, Locke believed, would yield the distinctive character and soul of the African-American.[78]

Locke's appreciation of folk culture was at odds with the traditional understanding of black folk art. As Robert Hemenway notes in his biography of Zora Neale Hurston, folk art as perceived by the majority of blacks was a shameful relic from their former condition in slavery and better forgotten.[79] Others suggested that folk art merely commercialized African-American "backwardness."[80] The initial rejection and later acceptance of negro spirituals by members of the all-black Howard University student choir may serve as an illustration of this anxiety. Perceiving themselves as Americans rather than African-Americans, the students initially refused to perform black songs, generally regarded as degrading and primitive. Their objection was based not only on the spirituals' roots in slavery, non-standard grammar, and dialect lyrics, but also on the fact that they were never performed at white universities.[81] These students, not surprisingly, had accepted white American cultural tastes and criteria for the assessment and appreciation of art.

There were, however, some exceptions. The white writer and critic Carl Van Vechten pointed out that some black colleges were unique in their relatively early public appreciation of the artistic value of black folk art, including music.[82] As an example, Van Vechten recalled the highly acclaimed European tour of the Fisk Jubilee Singers who in 1871 gave performances of spirituals before Queen Victoria, among others. Van Vechten acknowledged, however, that it had taken blacks half a century to overcome their aversion to their own musical heritage.[83]

According to the black writer and anthropologist Zora Neale Hurston, even Locke himself had to be convinced of the spirituals' artistic value. Hurston, in one of her unpublished articles, remembers how Locke at first had been "one of the leaders in a hullabaloo against the singing of Negro spirituals. That was before so many people in high places had praised them."[84] Hurston's evaluation parallels Wallace Thurman's contention that only after white music critics began to recognize and discuss the beauty and power of the spirituals did the black cultural elite "join in the hallelujah chorus," as he put it.[85] Thurman further points out that blacks were no different in this respect from those American whites who would only appreciate authors such as Edgar Allan Poe and Walt Whitman after they had been endorsed and sanctioned by literary critics in Europe.[86]

Whatever Locke's initial reservations may have been, in his own contributions to his anthology *The New Negro* he clearly set out to instruct the uninitiated. In his essay "The Negro Spiritual," for example, he attempted to circumvent black sensibilities by incorporating the spirituals into a European cultural tradition. The negro spiritual, he argued, must be praised as "a classic expression of the religious emotion also found in Gregorian and German chorals," and as such part of the American conception of High Art.[87] Locke believed that a new respect for the spiritual was long overdue; he also implied that the appreciation of this indigenous art form demonstrated the discriminating taste of an expert: "Thematically rich, in idiom of rhythm and harmony richer still, in potentialities of new musical forms and new technical traditions so deep as to be accessible only to genius, they have the respect of the connoisseur even while still under the sentimental and condescending patronage of the amateur."[88]

Locke's strategy to endow the spirituals with prestige was intended to reduce the existing aversion among blacks to their own cultural heritage. Hemenway points out that black interpreters of the spirituals began to perform them in formal dress, including black tie and tails, with only a piano for accompaniment, and without stage settings. Such a setting which removed the musical form from its true context in the black church helped to "elevate" the spirituals up to the concert stage and into the Anglo-American cultural tradition.[89]

Locke's artistic tastes, illustrated by his selections for his *New Negro* anthology, provoked critical reactions particularly from the side of the prime representative of the old guard, W. E. B. Du Bois. Du Bois' comments reveal some of the differences between factions within the Talented Tenth. For example, Du Bois disagreed with Locke's perception of black literature as first and foremost an aesthetic expression of the black experience. Instead, Du Bois believed that the arts must function as a means to influence public opinion in the interest of the black race.[90] In his review of *The New Negro*, Du Bois was quick to point out what he called the falseness of the idea that "Beauty rather than Propaganda should be the object of Negro literature."[91] Although relieved to find Locke's anthology "bursting with propaganda," Du Bois also sounded a warning note.[92] Re-emphasizing his own conviction that black art must at all times be politically relevant, he argued that Locke's exclusively aesthetic evaluation of art would turn the Renaissance into decadence.[93] "It is the fight for Life and Liberty," Du Bois declared, "that is giving birth to Negro literature and art today."[94] Other noteworthy comments from outside the old guard, both favourable and unfavourable, came from H. L. Mencken, Wallace Thurman and Leon Whipple. H. L. Mencken welcomed the book as "the American Negro's final emancipa-

tion from his inferiority complex."[95] Thurman, with characteristic scepticism, looked upon the publication of *The New Negro* as the beginning of a new fad for white intellectuals which would provide the white publishing world with a new source of income.[96] Leon Whipple of *Survey Graphic*, like Thurman, sensed the potential for exploitation by what he termed the seekers after commercial, social, or literary aggrandizement. It would be the ultimate tragedy, Whipple declared, "if after exploiting the Negro's body for two centuries we ended by exploiting his art and soul."[97] Most of the critical attention devoted to *The New Negro*, however, was favourable, and despite its relatively high price of five dollars, the anthology sold well and rapidly became the standard book for the decade. Or as Arnold Rampersad puts it: "*The New Negro* seemed not only to certify the existence of a great awakening in black America but also to endow it with a Bible."[98]

Locke's *Survey* issue and the subsequent publication of *The New Negro* anthology expedited the onset of the second stage of the Harlem Renaissance. This stage, ironically, was characterized by a declining interest of the three leading black magazines in their support of the arts and by a growing white interest and influence in the Harlem Renaissance movement. Although the literary component of Locke's anthology brought together many of the winning entries of the literary contests organized by these very periodicals, young black authors now began to move on to more prestigious white magazines and publishing houses. In addition, conflicting ideas over the role of the black artist in the portrayal of black life which had divided the Talented Tenth along generational lines intensified during the second half of the decade. *The Crisis* and *Opportunity*, as the official magazines of racial uplift organizations, were anxious to show the black race as compatible with the rest of America. By 1926, however, the avant-garde of young Renaissance writers and artists had begun to focus on Harlem's urban underclass. Their subsequent interpretation of black life projected images which were clearly incompatible with the ideals advanced by the leading civil rights organizations and their respective magazines. The traditional old guard black leadership now began to look upon their young charges as a potential hindrance to their idea of racial advancement.

In February 1926, the controversy concerning the portrayal of black life in the arts developed into a public debate. A questionnaire was sent out to a wide range of prominent Americans, both black and white, and was published simultaneously in *The Crisis*.[99] Some of the questions were indicative of the growing frustration of the old guard:

1. When the artist, black or white, portrays Negro character is he under any obligations or limitations as to the sort of character he will portray?

2. Can any author be criticized for painting the worst or the best characters of a group?

3. Can publishers be criticized for refusing to handle novels on the ground that these characters are no different from white folk and therefore not interesting?

4. What are Negroes to do when they are continually painted at their worst and judged by the public as they are painted?

5. Does the situation of the educated Negro in America with its pathos, humiliation and tragedy call for artistic treatment at least as sincere and sympathetic as "Porgy" received?

6. Is not the continual portrayal of the sordid, foolish and criminal among Negroes convincing the world that this and this alone is really and essentially Negroid, and preventing white artists from knowing any other types and preventing black artists from daring to paint them?

7. Is there not a real danger that young colored writers will be tempted to follow the popular trend in portraying Negro character in the underworld rather than seeking to paint the truth about themselves and their own social class?[100]

In the course of the following nine months, *Crisis* magazine printed a selection of reactions under the title: "The Negro in Art: How Shall He Be Portrayed; a Symposium." Most of the contributors to the debate offered viewpoints which went beyond the limitations of the questions. H. L. Mencken, a great favourite with the younger Harlem Renaissance writers, reacted with characteristic directness. In response to *The Crisis'* introductory suggestion that only the black writer is in a position to portray the black man without caricature, Mencken declared that it was nonsense to argue that whites must always see blacks as blacks see themselves.[101] Another respondent, Langston Hughes, dismissed the entire discussion as irrelevant. In his answer to Fauset he wrote:

the true literary artist is going to write about what he chooses anyway regardless of outside opinions. You write about the intelligent Negroes; Fisher about the unintelligent. Both of you are right. Walpole pictures the better class Englishman; Thomas Burke the sailors in limehouse. And both

are worth reading. It's the way people look at things, not what they look at that needs to be changed.[102]

The *Crisis* debate further alienated the old guard and their racial uplift institutions from the younger generation who resented *The Crisis'* efforts to define what was proper and suitable material for artistic treatment. In November 1926, in a spirited defence of artistic freedom, Harlem's Young Wits, as they were called, launched their own little magazine *Fire!!: A Quarterly Devoted to the Younger Generation of Negro Artists*.[103] Of the magazine's seven editors, which included Langston Hughes, Wallace Thurman, Zora Neale Hurston, Richard Bruce Nugent, Gwendolyn Bennett, John Davis, and Aaron Douglas, Thurman was the driving force.

## 6. Carl Van Vechten and Interracial Cultural Elitism

The rebellion which arose from the side of Harlem's younger generation during the second half of the 1920s was not an isolated development. It can be viewed as one of the manifestations of the spirit of the era, the origins of which are perhaps best described by the philosopher George Santayana. Santayana, in his influential public address at the University of California at Berkeley in October 1911 entitled "The Genteel Tradition in American Philosophy," argued that young America was rejecting the so-called genteel tradition in American culture.[104] America, he explained, was not simply, "a young country with an old mentality," but rather "a country with two mentalities, one a survival of the beliefs and standards of the fathers, the other an expression of the instincts, practice, and discoveries of the younger generations."[105]

During the 1910s and 1920s, the concept of "the younger generation" came to indicate a temper of intellectual and artistic rebellion which was centred in Manhattan's Greenwich Village. As one of the villagers, Ralph Oppenheim, explained, the new and distinguishing elements in the disposition of the younger generation were a lack of respect for their elders, the effects of the triumph of materialism and realism over Victorian idealism, the impact of the theory of evolution, and the influence of Nietzsche and his pronouncements on the death of Christianity and its specific moral dictates.[106]

Optimism and idealism, the two defining characteristics of the genteel tradition, as Malcolm Cowley has pointed out, were countered by a non-idealistic generation determined to narrow the gap between the reality of their lives as they knew it and the artistic interpretation of it. Marx, Freud, and Darwin together had helped to generate a new *Zeitgeist,* the essence of which was decidedly post-Victorian and anti-middle class. Its proponents advocated a sceptical approach towards so-called traditional values. This new disposition would only be further intensified by the impact of the First World War.[107]

One of the defining events used to mark the onset of the temper of modernity associated with the younger generation was the establishment of a social, intellectual and artistic centre at the house of the "creator of creators," Mabel Dodge Luhan, at 23 Fifth Avenue, New York.[108] The establishment of Dodge's salon followed her first meeting and subsequent friendship with Carl Van Vechten. Van Vechten first called on Dodge early in 1923 to interview her about Gertrude Stein's "Portrait of Mabel Dodge at the Villa Curonia."[109] Over the next few months, the two would meet almost daily, and although the intensity of their friendship fluctuated over the years they always remained friends. It was Van Vechten who introduced two black performers to Dodge's first "Evening" where guests, regardless of social class, political persuasion, or economic status freely mingled.[110]

The establishment of Greenwich Village as America's avant-garde cultural centre had a direct bearing on the development of the Harlem Renaissance after 1926. Almost simultaneously with Charles S. Johnson's interracial dinner party at the Civic Club in March 1924, Van Vechten began inviting black guests to his own social functions, first at West 55th Street and later at Central Park West. Van Vechten, who, as James Mellow points out, "had a penchant for championing whatever was new and shocking," was not specifically interested in the advancement of the black race.[111] Yet he was fully aware of the potential of his gatherings to promote the assimilation of the black and white cultural elite.[112]

Van Vechten's interest in African-Americans was not new. By the time he left home to go to college, Kellner explains, he had been "inoculated against racial prejudice to whatever extent was possible in turn-of-the-century America."[113] His family's connection with blacks dated back to 1638 when an ancestor emigrated from The Netherlands in the company of two black servants. Two and a half centuries later the two black servants in the Van Vechten household in Cedar Rapids, Iowa, were treated with uncommon deference and respect.

During his years at the University of Chicago, Van Vechten continued to socialize with blacks, a practice which occasionally resulted in the assumption that he must be one of the many light-skinned blacks who lived in Chicago at the time. Van Vechten reported how in black circles he was "invariably taken for a coon."[114] In 1904, Carl Van Vechten's first publications on black entertainers appeared in *The Chicago American.* In the spring of 1906, he arrived in New York City where, in November of the same year, he was appointed assistant music critic for *The New York Times.* In 1912, Van Vechten left the *Times* and for one year became the drama critic for *The New York Press,* reviewing over one hundred dramatic performances.[115]

In 1922, Van Vechten embarked on his new career as a novelist with the publication of *Peter Whiffle* which brought him instant recognition. Four years later, his fifth novel entitled *Nigger Heaven* would become one of the most controversial novels of the decade.[116] From 1924 until his death in 1964, Van Vechten, a firm believer in Du Bois' concept of the Talented Tenth, "popularized" the black American by creating an atmosphere of acceptance. Following his example, it became *bon ton* for sophisticated white New Yorkers to include prominent blacks in their social affairs. Indeed, Van Vechten became Harlem's chief public relations man. According to the black journalist and writer George Schuyler, Van Vechten and his actress wife Fania Marinoff,

> devoted themselves as assiduously as any sincere revolutionist could. With Machiavellian design the doyen of the dilettanti made it smart to be interracial. Once the idea took hold it spread in geometrical progression. Racial snobbery was eliminated on the higher levels and the Van Vechten philosophy spread like a forest fire, consuming great stands of racial bias along the way. Where there had been doubt and scepticism, there grew tolerance, curiosity, understanding and appreciation on both sides. Those who came as mere faddists left as fellow travellers of interracialism.[117]

Van Vechten's first contact with a member of the black cultural elite was established through his friend and publisher Alfred Knopf. After Knopf's publication of Walter White's novel *Fire in the Flint* (1924), Van Vechten requested an introduction to the author. Shortly after their first meeting, he made the following observations in a letter to the writer Edna Kenton: "Walter White . . . spent two hours with me the other day. He speaks French and talks about Debussy and Marcel Proust in an offhand way. An entirely new kind of Negro to me. I shall, I hope, see something of these cultured circles."[118]

SOCIAL, POLITICAL, AND ECONOMIC TRENDS

It did not take Van Vechten long to become an honorary member of Harlem's Talented Tenth.[119] In 1925, Alain Locke invited him to write the introduction to his magnum opus *The New Negro*. Although Van Vechten declined Locke's request he later would publish several introductory articles to promote the work of black writers, especially the younger generation. This avant-garde of the Harlem Renaissance included Zora Neale Hurston, Aaron Douglas, Richard Bruce Nugent, Langston Hughes, and Wallace Thurman.

## Notes

1. The expression New Negro dates back to the end of the 19th century. In an editorial in the Cleveland *Gazette* 28 June 1895, for example, the term was used to identify a new class of educated blacks which began to emerge after the end of the Civil War. In 1900, N. B. Wood, F. Barrier Williams, and Booker T. Washington published a collection of essays entitled *A New Negro for a New Century: His Political, Civil and Mental Status, and Related Essays;* and in 1916, William Pickens published a study entitled *The New Negro*. Rayford W. Logan, Eugene C. Holmes, and G. Franklin Edwards, eds., *The New Negro Thirty Years Afterward* (Washington: Howard UP, 1955) 18.

2. Langston Hughes, letter to Wallace Thurman, n.d.; internal evidence suggests Aug. 1929. Langston Hughes Papers, James Weldon Johnson Memorial Collection, Beinecke Rare Book and Manuscript Library Collection, Yale University. Hereafter JWJ. The Langston Hughes Papers from this collection will be referred to hereafter as JWJ/LHP.

3. *The Crisis* (1910-), monthly magazine of the interracial National Association for the Advancement of Colored People. In one of its advertisements, the magazine identified itself as "the most hated, most popular and most widely discussed magazine dealing with questions of race prejudice." *Survey Graphic* March 1925: 624.

4. Samuel Hopkins Adams' novel *Flaming Youth* (New York: Boni and Liveright, 1923) went through twelve printings between Jan. and Aug. 1923. The novel portrays the early 1920s as a cynical, reckless, hurried, hedonistic, egoistic and neurotic time.

5. The Great Migration was a massive migratory movement of African-Americans from the agricultural South to industrial centres in the North and West of the United States between 1916-1919. Estimated numbers of migrants from the various demographic sources used for this section range from approximately 500,000 to almost 1,500,000.

6. Gilbert Osofsky, *Harlem: The Making of a Ghetto. Negro New York, 1890-1930* (New York: Harper, 1971) 18.

7. Florette Henri, *Black Migration: Movement North 1900-1920* (New York: Doubleday, 1975) 55.

8. The first so-called Jim Crow laws were passed in the South in the beginning of the 1880s. The term *Jim Crow* appears to have become a popular household word after a song (and dance) by a crippled black farm worker was adapted for the stage by the American entertainer Thomas Dartmouth Rice (1808-60). Chris-

tine Ammer, *It's Raining Cats and Dogs and other Beastly Expressions* (New York: Dell, 1989) 178-79.

9. Charles S. Johnson, "How Much Is the Migration a Flight from Persecution?" *Opportunity* Sept. 1927: 272-73.

10. Osofsky 18.

11. Quoted in: A. Schoener, ed., *Harlem on My Mind* (New York: Random, 1968) 29.

12. Osofsky 123.

13. Osofsky 75.

14. Manhattan's Tenderloin and San Juan Hill districts stretched from around 21 St. to 64 St. west of Broadway. Jervis Anderson, *This Was Harlem: A Cultural Portrait, 1900-1950* (New York: Farrar, 1987) 8.

15. Anderson 8.

16. Harold Cruse points out that virtually all of the prominent businessmen and politicians associated with the Afro-American Realty Company were protegees of Booker T. Washington and as such part of Washington's so-called Tuskegee Machine. Harold Cruse, *The Crisis of the Negro Intellectual: A Historical Analysis of the Failure of Black Leadership* (New York: Quill, 1984) 19.

17. Quoted in: Schoener 51.

18. Term used by Du Bois to indicate a leadership class of educated African-Americans devoted to the advancement of the race through legal action, protest, and propaganda, who could guide, as Du Bois put it, "the American Negro into a higher civilization." W. E. B. Du Bois, *The Autobiography of W. E. B. Du Bois* (1968; New York: International Publishers Co., Inc., 1986) 236.

19. Gorham Munson, in his memoir-history of the 1920s, points out that in The United States the term *intelligentsia* came into use only towards the end of the First World War. The term *Intellectuals* (with a capital I), Munson writes, "had entered journalistic writing about 1914 when *The New Republic* was founded and obtained a vogue for a while when used in an elite sense. . . . The Intellectuals did much to foster the literary revival" of the 1920s. Gorham Munson, *The Awakening Twenties* (Baton Rouge: Louisiana State UP, 1985) 22.

20. Osofsky 133. Wallace Thurman suggests in one of his articles on Harlem that West Indians, the second largest group of blacks living in Harlem, were also resented by their fellow Harlemites because of their reluctance to conform to the American way of life. *Negro Life in New York's Harlem: A Lively Picture of a Popular and Interesting Section* (Girard: Haldeman-Julius, Little Blue Book 494, 1928) 35. This article was previously published in *The Haldeman-Julius Quarterly* Oct., Nov., Dec., 1927.

21. Cary Wintz, *Black Culture and the Harlem Renaissance* (Houston: Rice UP, 1988) 25, 26. Osofsky points out that the population flow from the West Indies was not affected by the tightening of immigration laws in the early 1920s which significantly decreased European immigrants and almost banned the immigration of Asians into the United States. After 1924, when restrictions came into effect for the immigration of West Indians, the quotas were never filled. Osofsky 131.

22. Osofsky 131.

23. Quoted in: Schoener 126.

24. Wallace Thurman, "Harlem Facets," *The World Tomorrow* Nov. 1927: 466-67.

25. Thurman, "Harlem Facets" 466.

26. Thurman, "Harlem Facets" 466.

27. Thurman, *Negro Life* 5.

28. In 1920, African-Americans occupied about two square miles in Harlem, between 130th and 145th St. and Fifth and Eighth Avenue. Osofsky 128.

29. Osofsky 131.

30. For a discussion of the foundation of the N.A.A.C.P., see August Meier and Elliott Rudwick, *From Plantation to Ghetto* (New York: Hill, 1976). The interracial National Urban League advertised its objectives as follows: The League seeks to improve "the relations between the races in America. It strives to improve the living and working conditions of the Negro. Its special field of operation embraces cities where Negroes reside in large numbers." *Survey Graphic* March 1925: 623.

31. For a further discussion of the role of African-American magazines in the twentieth century, see Abby Arthur Johnson and Ronald Maberry Johnson, *Propaganda and Aesthetics: The Literary Politics of Afro-American Magazines in the Twentieth Century* (Amherst: U of Massachusetts P, 1979).

32. For my discussion of W. E. B. Du Bois I have made extensive use of Arnold Rampersad, *The Art and Imagination of W. E. B. Du Bois* (New York: Schocken Books, 1990). John White, *Black Leadership in America 1895-1968* (New York: Longman, 1985) and David Lewering Lewis, *W. E. B. Du Bois: Biography of a Race 1868-1919* (New York: Holt, 1993).

33. In Apr. 1940, Booker T. Washington became the first African-American to have his portrait on a United States stamp (10 cents), U.S. Post Office, Williamsburg, Va.

34. Rampersad, *Du Bois* 82-87.

35. W. E. B. Du Bois, *The Souls of Black Folk* (1903), Rpt in *Three Negro Classics* (N.Y.: Avon, 1965) 240-47. Du Bois' essay "Of Mr. Booker T. Washington and Others" is his most succinct discussion of Washington's leadership and politics.

36. Du Bois, *Souls* 246.

37. Quoted in: E. Franklin Frazier, *Black Bourgeoisie: The Rise of the Middle Class in the United States* (New York: Collier, 1957) 62.

38. Benjamin Quarles, *The Negro in the Making of America* (New York: Macmillan, 1987) 180.

39. Quarles 180.

40. Anderson 108.

41. Dan Block, "When the Colored Troops Got Back," *The Messenger* May/June 1919: 25.

42. Ironically, Woodrow Wilson would be one of the more racist Presidents of the United States. He sanctioned segregation in Washington and removed blacks from important federal positions. Wilson, furthermore, refused to speak out in public against lynching. Efforts to appoint black officials in the South he described as "a social blunder of the worst kind." In 1921, Wilson's successor Warren C. Harding promoted civil rights for African-Americans but by no means social equality. Martin Bauml Duberman, *Paul Robeson* (New York: Knopf, 1988) 31.

43. W. E. B. Du Bois, Editorial, *The Crisis* July 1918. *The Messenger* with its radical anti-war stance was critical of Du Bois. The magazine's editors A. Philip Randolph and Chandler Owen described Du Bois as "reactionary on economic and political questions, and compromising in the face of cheap honors and extended epaulets." Quoted in: Manning Marable, *W. E. B. Du Bois: Black Radical Democrat* (Boston: Twayne, 1986) 109.

44. By 1919 *The Crisis* had reached a circulation of 104,000. *Opportunity*'s peak circulation of 11,000 was reached in 1927 and 1928. Until 1928, *Opportunity* was supported by a grant from the Carnegie Foundation. *The Crisis* was always self-supporting. Jabulani Kamau Makalani, "Why Harlem?" *Black World* Feb. 1976: 12.

45. W. E. B. Du Bois, Editorial, *The Crisis* May 1919: 14.

46. John Hope Franklin and Alfred A. Moss, Jr., *From Slavery to Freedom: A History of Negro Americans* (1947; New York: McGraw, 1988) 315. No race riots occurred in New York City in 1919.

47. Claude McKay, "If We Must Die," *The Liberator* July 1919. In Sept. 1919, the poem appeared in *The Messenger,* and in 1922 it was included in a collection of McKay's poetry entitled *Harlem Shadows*. Shortly after its first publication in 1919, the Republican Senator of Massachusetts Henry Cabot Lodge read the poem in Congress as an illustration of so-called black radicalism. George Kent, "The Soulful Way of Claude McKay," *Black World* Nov. 1970: 38. See also Wayne F. Cooper, *Claude McKay: Rebel Sojourner in the Harlem Renaissance* (Baton Rouge: Louisiana State UP, 1987) 101.

48. Wallace Thurman, "Negro Poets and their Poetry," *The Bookman* July 1928: 560.

49. Charles S. Johnson, "After Garvey-What?" *Opportunity* May 1924: 6.

50. The idea of a return to Africa was not new. Martin R. Delany, a physician educated at Harvard, visited Liberia in 1859 to investigate the remigration of African-Americans. Cruse 5.

51. Bruce Kellner, ed., *The Harlem Renaissance: A Historical Dictionary for the Era* (New York: Methuen, 1987) 133-34.

52. For further information on both Ferris and Harrison see Kellner, *Dictionary* 121, 158.

53. John Henrik Clarke, "The Neglected Dimensions of the Harlem Renaissance," *Black World* Nov. 1970: 123.

54. Anderson 189.

55. Wallace Thurman, "Marcus Garvey," ts. 13 pp., n.d.; internal evidence suggests 1929. Thurman included his biographical portrait of Garvey in his collection of essays entitled "Aunt Hagar's Children" (1929), JWJ. The essays were never published. The Wallace Thurman Papers from the JWJ collection will be referred to hereafter as JWJ/WTP.

56. Cooper 145.

57. June Sochen, *The Unbridgeable Gap: Blacks and their Quest for the American Dream, 1900-1930* (Chicago: Rand McNally, 1972) 88.

58. During the first decades of the twentieth century the perception of the black race as sub-human and inferior was still widespread. John W. Burgess, founder of what later would become the School of Social Science at Columbia University refers to black suffrage as "monstrous." Burgess further asserts that "a black skin means membership of a race of men which has never of itself succeeded to reason, has never, therefore, created any civilization of any kind." Quoted in: Stanley Coben, *Rebellion Against Victorianism: The Impetus for Cultural Change in 1920s America* (New York: Oxford UP, 1991) 39.

59. Despite the distinguished roles of prominent members of the Talented Tenth old guard such as James Weldon Johnson, Charles S. Johnson, William Stanley Braithwaite and Benjamin Brawley and others, a lengthy discussion of their respective contributions to the Harlem Renaissance is outside the scope of this study.

60. Jessie Fauset worked for *The Crisis* in this capacity from Nov. 1919 to May 1926. Johnson and Johnson 42.

61. Abby Arthur Johnson, "Literary Midwife: Jessie Redmon Fauset and the Harlem Renaissance," *Phylon* 39 (1978): 143-53.

62. Jean Fagan Yellin, "An Index of Literary Materials in *The Crisis*, 1910-1934; Articles, Belles Lettres, and Book Reviews," *CLA Journal* June, Dec. 1971: 452-65, 197-233.

63. From 1924 to 1926, annual competitions were organized by both *The Crisis* and *Opportunity* magazine. Mrs. Amy Spingarn, active member in the N.A.A.C.P., donated significant financial awards for all three *Crisis* competitions. For *Opportunity* most of the prize money came from Mrs. Henry Goddard Leach, member of the board of the N.U.L., and the black businessman Casper Holstein. Judges for *The Crisis* competitions included Sinclair Lewis, H. G. Wells, and Eugene O'Neill. The *Opportunity* contests were judged by, among others, Theodore Dreiser, Robert Frost, Van Wyck Brooks, and Vachel Lindsay. Johnson and Johnson 44, 54.

64. The first contest opened 1 Sept. 1924 and closed four months later on 31 Dec. *Opportunity* Oct. 1924: 291.

65. *Opportunity* Aug. 1924: 253.

66. *Opportunity* Aug. 1925: 227-28.

67. The Civic Club was located at 14 West 12th St.

68. Between 1924 and 1933, Jessie Fauset published four novels. This accomplishment makes her one of the more prolific Harlem Renaissance writers. According to Fauset, the idea to celebrate the publication of her first novel had originated with Charles S. Johnson's secretary Regina Anderson and the writer Gwendolyn Bennett. Jessie Fauset, letter to Alain Locke, 9 Jan. 1933, Alain Locke Papers, Moorland Spingarn Research Center, Howard U, Washington. Hereafter Howard/ALP. Although Fauset's novel was applauded by the old guard, Wallace Thurman identified it as "an ill-starred attempt to popularize the pleasing

news that there were cultured Negroes deserving of attention from artists, and of whose existence white folk should be appraised." Wallace Thurman, "Negro Artists and the Negro," *The New Republic* 31 Aug. 1927: 39.

69. *The World Tomorrow*, a Christian, socialist, and pacifist magazine of the Fellowship of Reconciliation, came out with a special black issue as early as 1923. This well-respected journal published early materials by black writers. In Oct. 1926, the magazine hired Wallace Thurman as its publication manager. *The World Tomorrow* was combined with *The Christian Century*, an ecumenical weekly, in 1934.

70. Editorial, *Opportunity* Sept. 1924. *Opportunity* magazine described the Civic Club dinner as a coming out party for the Writers' Guild. The Guild was defined as a group of writers which included Countee Cullen, Eric Walrond, Langston Hughes, Jessie Fauset, Harold Jackman, Regina Anderson, and Gwendolyn Bennett.

71. The occasion initiated, as Johnson put it, "the first significant transformation of vague hopes for the future into a material means for making that future possible." Editorial, "The Younger Generation of Negro Writers," *Opportunity* May 1924: 144-45.

72. Editorial, *The Crisis* Jan. 1926: 141.

73. Johnson and Johnson 72.

74. Alain Locke, letter to Langston Hughes, 22 May 1924, JWJ/LHP.

75. Alain Locke, ed., *The New Negro* (1925; New York: Atheneum 1968) xv.

76. Locke, *New Negro* xv.

77. Locke, *New Negro* xv.

78. Locke, *New Negro* xv.

79. Robert E. Hemenway, *Zora Neale Hurston: A Literary Biography* (London: Camden, 1986) 52-54.

80. Duberman 106.

81. Hemenway 52-54.

82. Bruce Kellner, ed., *"Keep A-Inchin' Along" Selected Writings of Carl Van Vechten about Black Art and Letters* (Westport: Greenwood, 1979) 35, 43.

83. Kellner, *Selected Writings* 35.

84. Zora Neale Hurston, "The Chick with One Hen," ts., 2 pp., n.d.; external evidence suggests 1937, JWJ.

85. Wallace Thurman, "This Negro Literary Renaissance." ts., 18 pp., n.d.; external evidence suggests 1929, JWJ/WTP. This article, included in "Aunt Hagar's Children," combines, with some changes, two previously published articles by Thurman: "Negro artists and the Negro," *The New Republic* 31 Aug. 1927: 37-39 and "Nephews of Uncle Remus," *The Independent* 24 Sept. 1927: 296-298. In his comment, Thurman does not mention African-Americans such as Hall Johnson and James Weldon Johnson (no relation) who had promoted the spirituals long before they were "discovered."

86. Thurman, "This Negro Literary Renaissance."

87. Locke, *New Negro* 201. A similar idea had been expressed some 10 years earlier by James Weldon Johnson. In his anonymously published novel *The*

*Autobiography of an Ex-coloured Man* (1912), Johnson's protagonist suggests the transformation of black folk music "into classical masterpieces somewhat in the vein of what Dvorak did with the spirituals in his 'New World Symphony.'" S. P. Fullinwider, *The Mind and Mood of Black America: 20th Century Thought* (Dorsey P, 1969) 87.

88. Locke, *New Negro* 200.

89. Hemenway 52-54.

90. Du Bois' expertise as a literary critic was called into question by Claude McKay. In a reaction to Du Bois' review of *Home to Harlem* (1928), McKay accused him of incompetence in matters concerning the arts: "Nowhere in your writings," McKay alleged, "do you reveal any comprehension of aesthetics, and therefore you are not competent nor qualified to pass judgment upon any work of art." Quoted in: Johnson and Johnson 47.

91. W. E. B. Du Bois, Editorial, *The Crisis,* Jan. 1926: 141.

92. Du Bois, Editorial, Jan. 1926.

93. Du Bois, Editorial, Jan. 1926.

94. Du Bois, Editorial, Jan. 1926.

95. Charles Scruggs, *The Sage in Harlem: H. L. Mencken and the Black Writers of the 1920s* (Baltimore: Johns Hopkins UP, 1984) 156.

96. Dorothy West, "Elephant's Dance: A Memoir of Wallace Thurman," *Black World* Nov. 1970: 78.

97. Leon Whipple, "Letters and Life," *The Survey* Aug. 1926: 517.

98. Arnold Rampersad, *The Life of Langston Hughes: Volume 1: 1902-1941; I, Too, Sing America* (New York: Oxford UP, 1986) 105.

99. Kellner indicates that the idea of a public debate was initiated by Van Vechten in an attempt to prepare the reading public for his novel *Nigger Heaven,* scheduled for publication in the summer of 1926. It was Van Vechten, according to Kellner, who formulated the questionnaire. Kellner, *Selected Writings* 53. Bruce M. Tyler also attributes the *Crisis* questionnaire to Van Vechten in his study *From Harlem to Hollywood: The Struggle for Racial and Cultural Democracy, 1920-1943* (N.Y.: Garland Publishing, Inc., 1992) 13. Another source for an insight into Van Vechten's role in the debate on the responsibilities of the black artist is Leon D. Coleman, "The Contribution of Carl Van Vechten to The Negro Renaissance: 1920-1930," diss., U of Minnesota, 1969.

100. Editorial, "The Negro in Art: How Shall He Be Portrayed," *The Crisis* Feb. 1926: 113.

101. Editorial, "The Negro in Art: How Shall He Be Portrayed," *The Crisis* March 1926: 219.

102. Editorial, "The Negro in Art: How Shall He Be Portrayed," *The Crisis* Apr. 1926: 278. Other authors who responded included Mary White Ovington, Sinclair Lewis, Georgia Douglas Johnson, Sherwood Anderson, Charles Chesnutt, and Vachel Lindsay.

103. A discussion of *Fire!!* (1926) and some of Thurman's other magazine publications will follow in Chapter 4 [in Barfoot, C. C., et al. *Wallace Thurman's Harlem Renaissance.* Amsterdam: Editions Rodopi B. V., 1994].

104. Douglas L. Wilson ed., "The Genteel Tradition in American Philosophy," *Nine Essays by George Santayana* (London: Oxford UP, 1967) 39.

105. Wilson 39.

106. Ralph Oppenheim, "The Younger Generation Speaks: An American Youth Tells about its Attitude to Life," *Haldeman Julius Quarterly* Apr. 1927: 63-80.

107. Malcolm Cowley, "The Revolt Against Gentility," *After the Genteel Tradition; American Writers 1910-1930,* ed. Malcolm Cowley (1936; Carbondale: Southern Illinois UP, 1964) 10.

108. Steven Watson, *Strange Bedfellows: The First American Avant-Garde* (New York: Abbeville P, 1991) 131.

109. Watson 131.

110. Watson 136-37.

111. James R. Mellow, *Charmed Circle: Gertrude Stein and Company* (Boston: Houghton, 1974) 195.

112. Carl Van Vechten, interview trans., Columbia U, Oral History Collection, New York, 1960. Hereafter CU/ Oral/CVV.

113. Kellner, *Selected Writings* 1-16.

114. Kellner, *Selected Writings* 1-16.

115. Kellner, *Selected Writings* 1-16. Over the following years, Van Vechten published several collections of critical essays on music and drama under the titles *Music after the Great War* (1915), *Music and Bad Manners* (1916), *Interpreters and Interpretations* (1917), *The Merry-Go-Round* (1918), *The Music of Spain* (1919), *In the Garret* (1919), and two collections of cat tales entitled *A Tiger in the House* (1920) and *Lord of the Housetops* (1921).

116. In 1930, Van Vechten's seventh and final novel *Parties* was published. From the early 1930s until his death in 1964, Van Vechten worked as a photographer establishing, among other things, one of the most extensive photographic collections of prominent African-Americans. In 1941, Van Vachten established the James Weldon Johnson Memorial Collection of Negro Arts and Letters at Yale University. Other Library Collections established by Van Vechten are: the George Gershwin Memorial Collection of Music and Musical Literature at Fisk University (1944), the Rose McClendon Memorial Collection of Photographs of Celebrated Negroes at Howard University (1946), and the Jerome Bowers Peterson Collection of Photographs by Carl Van Vechten of Celebrated Negroes at the University of New Mexico (1954). Kellner, *Dictionary* 367-68.

117. George Schuyler, interview trans., Columbia U, Oral History Collection, New York, 1960. Hereafter CU/ Oral/Schuyler.

118. Carl Van Vechten, letter to Edna Kenton, postmarked 28 Aug. 1924, JWJ. The Carl Van Vechten Papers from this collection will be referred to hereafter as JWJ/ CVVP.

119. As Harold Jackman wrote in a letter to Carl Van Vechten shortly after their first meeting: "You are the first white man with whom I have felt perfectly at ease. You are just like a colored man! I don't know if you will consider this a compliment or not, but that's the only way I can put it." Harold Jackman, letter to Carl Van Vechten, 14 Feb. 1925, JWJ.

# CARY D. WINTZ (ESSAY DATE 1996)

**SOURCE:** Wintz, Cary D. "The Social and Political Background." In *Black Culture and the Harlem Renaissance*, pp. 6-29. College Station: Texas A & M University Press, 1996.

*In the following essay, Wintz discusses racial violence, migration patterns, and settlement in Harlem.*

Two of the most significant elements in the black experience around the turn of the century were the steady deterioration of the race's social and political position in America, and especially in the South, and the steadily growing exodus of blacks from their homes in the rural South to the industrial cities of the South and North. The effect of these developments on black history must not be underestimated. Besides the obvious changes evidenced by the growth of black ghettos in northern cities and the resurgence of black militancy in the face of an apparently unremitting chain of racism, violence, and injustice, there was also a more subtle shift of attitude among blacks. By the 1920s few black intellectuals still believed that the future of their race lay in the South. As they turned their attention northward and focused their hope on the emerging black communities in northern cities, however, they also were turning their backs on their southern heritage.

The basic political experience of blacks at the turn of the century was that during the two decades following the end of Reconstruction they had witnessed the systematic erosion of the rights they had achieved under the Fourteenth and Fifteenth Amendments and through the various acts of Congress and the Reconstruction governments in the South. Although in the half century following emancipation a number of blacks successfully accumulated property and acquired an education, most remained poorly educated and mired in rural poverty. Even those who had achieved some material success saw these accomplishments threatened by the growth of segregation and racial violence. Supreme Court reinterpretations of the Fourteenth and Fifteenth Amendments left blacks defenseless against the segregationist enactments of southern legislatures. In *Williams* v. *Mississippi* (1898), *Giles* v. *Harris* (1903), and *Giles* v. *Teasley* (1904) the Court endorsed various strategies that southern states devised to disenfranchise blacks, while *Plessy* v. *Ferguson* (1896) was the most dramatic of a series of decisions that legitimized laws segregating public facilities—from schools, railroad cars, and restrooms to public parks and residential neighborhoods.[1]

Northern blacks fared hardly better than their southern counterparts. Throughout the North, theaters, restaurants, and hotels discriminated against blacks, often in violation of northern civil rights laws. Many communities also established segregated school systems in spite of state law. Blacks who attempted to challenge this growing segregation were so often unsuccessful that most chose simply to try to live with the situation. Even more serious was the discrimination blacks faced in the workplace. For example, in Philadelphia in the late nineteenth century employers were reluctant to hire blacks for any but the worst jobs because to do so would precipitate trouble with white workers and their unions. As a result of the refusal of most unions to admit blacks to membership, blacks were excluded from entire industries and generally found employment in "the two worst categories in the occupational lexicon: 'domestic and personal service' and 'unskilled labor.'"[2]

Black participation in northern politics also declined in the early twentieth century. Although blacks never constituted a powerful force in local or state politics, they were a visibly present minority in public office throughout the North as late as the early 1890s. By the turn of the century blacks in elected office had become quite rare. Nowhere was the declining political status of blacks more apparent than in Washington during Theodore Roosevelt's administration. During his first term Roosevelt won black approval by praising the valor of black troops during the Battle of San Juan Hill, by dining with Booker T. Washington at the White House, and by standing by his controversial black political appointments in the South. Before the end of his second term, however, Roosevelt had done a complete about-face. The troops he had earlier praised he now branded as cowards, and more and more he linked his political machine to the conservative, lily-white faction in the southern Republican party. In 1905 he toured the South and publicly praised former Confederate leaders and the Confederacy; in 1906 he infuriated blacks with his harsh treatment of the black troops who were involved in the Brownsville riots and by his statements to Congress falsely asserting that lynchings were caused by black sexual assaults on white women. Conditions deteriorated further under Roosevelt's successors. William Howard Taft publicly endorsed restrictions on black suffrage and refused to appoint blacks to office when whites objected. Taft also began the practice of segregating federal offices in Washington, a policy that was expanded under President Wilson. By the time that World War I began, blacks had seen their political rights and political influence almost totally evaporate in the North as well as in the South. Conditions did not improve in the early 1920s. President Harding, while promising to enforce civil rights, denounced racial amalgamation and social equality.[3]

More alarming even than this decline in political and civil rights was the upsurge in racial violence and terrorism. Lynchings, while declining in number from approximately 150 per year in the early 1890s to about half that number after 1905, continued to outrage as well as terrorize the black community. Far more ominous was the marked increase in the number of race riots around the turn of the century. In 1898, for example, a highly emotional campaign to eliminate black suffrage triggered a riot in Wilmington, North Carolina, which resulted in thirty-six black casualties. In 1904 racial violence swept through the small town of Statesboro, Georgia. Following the conviction of two blacks for the murder of a white family, a white mob took action against the growing "insolence" of local blacks. After capturing and burning the two murderers, the mob turned its wrath on the entire black community. They attacked blacks indiscriminately, burned their houses, and drove a number from the town. Two years later an even more serious riot erupted in Atlanta. Like the Wilmington riot, trouble began in Atlanta during a campaign to disenfranchise blacks. For several months before the election on the suffrage provision, local newspapers inflamed the public with racial hatred. Finally, on September 22, 1906, a white mob gathered and began attacking every black in sight. In the four days of violence that followed four blacks died, many others were injured, and there was wholesale destruction of black property.[4]

The racial violence of this period was not confined to the South. There were large-scale race riots in New York (1900), Springfield, Illinois (1904), and Greensburg, Indiana (1906). In addition, white gangs frequently assaulted blacks in large northern cities, while several small towns in Ohio and Indiana sought to avoid racial disorder by simply preventing blacks from settling there.[5]

The most serious northern riot before World War I took place in Springfield, Illinois, in 1908. Trouble began when a black man, George Richardson, was accused of raping a white woman. By the time that a grand jury cleared Richardson of the charges, whites in Springfield were determined to seek vengeance on their own. Unable to get their hands on Richardson, they vented their anger on the entire black community. It took 5,000 state militia to restore order, but not before two blacks were lynched, four whites were dead, and more than seventy persons were injured. As usual, there was widespread destruction of black property. The Springfield riot also struck a symbolic blow to the hopes of black Americans, coming so close to the centennial of Lincoln's birth and occurring just two miles from the great emancipator's burial place.[6]

In many ways these riots sounded an ominous warning about the state of race relations in the country. Even more than lynchings, they expressed an intense and highly advanced form of racial prejudice. Lynching, as barbaric as it was, constituted violence committed against an individual in response to a specific transgression, real or imagined. Lynching targeted "bad" blacks to serve as an example for all blacks. On the other hand, the race riots that occurred at the turn of the century were characterized by indiscriminate, wholesale violence directed against all blacks regardless of their actions. A law-abiding, accommodating black could reasonably expect to be safe from lynching, but there was no protection from the random violence unleashed by these riots.

More depressing, and ultimately more threatening to blacks, was the almost complete acceptance of scientific and pseudo-scientific theories of racism in America at the turn of the century. Racist ideology, in fact, was a dominant theme in both America and Europe at this time. The anti-Negro literature of the period was only one aspect of a generally racist outlook in western thought in the late nineteenth century. Other examples included concepts such as the "white man's burden" and the poetry of Rudyard Kipling, both of which were used to justify a racially based imperialism, and the emergence of a racially based anti-semitism that was fueled by monographs such as Houston Stewart Chamberlain's *Foundations of the Nineteenth Century* (1900), and that was reflected in outbursts of anti-semitic prejudice such as that which surfaced dramatically in France during the Dreyfus affair. In the United States men like Josiah Strong and Henry Cabot Lodge used theories of Anglo-Saxon racial superiority to justify acquisition of the Philippines; these same theories were manifested in the Chinese Exclusion Act of 1882, the anti-Japanese hysteria that swept California in 1905, and the growing demand for immigration restriction voiced by nativists.

Anti-black propagandists at the turn of the century often took extreme positions. Thomas

Dixon popularized concepts of black inferiority in his widely read novels, *The Leopard's Spots* (1902) and *The Clansman* (1905). Dixon's open racism, however, was surpassed by the fanatical and often fantastic arguments advanced in pseudo-scientific studies such as Charles Carroll's *The Negro, Beast or in the Image of God* (1900), which was one of three books that Carroll wrote that combined scientific and biblical evidence to argue that blacks (indeed all nonwhite races) were subhuman hybrid species that lacked souls but had been granted the power of speech so that they might better serve (white) mankind; or in the work of Frederick L. Hoffman, whose *Race Traits and Tendencies of the American Negro* (1896) used demographic data to postulate that the high death rate among blacks, caused primarily by their innately inferior physical structure, their moral decline, and their high rate of illegitimacy, ultimately would lead the race to extinction.[7]

The predominant racial theory in the South at the turn of the century depicted blacks as an inferior and immoral race that would never achieve parity with whites. Slavery, it was argued, had Christianized blacks and restrained their baser tendencies, but freedom had resulted in a rapid reversion toward barbarism. Some southern writers even justified lynching as the only effective check against the black man's increasing tendency to rape, and argued that the only solution to the race problem was either colonization or extermination. Even the most tolerant southerners generally accepted the basic superiority of the white race, and dreamed of the old South—magnolia trees and contented slaves serenading "ole Marsa" and his family in the warm southern sunset—a South kept alive in the romantic novels of writers such as Thomas Nelson Page.[8]

Northern social scientists were hardly more tolerant than their southern counterparts. Armed with theories of eugenics and with IQ data gathered from recruits during World War I, they expressed concern about the intellectual and physical inferiority of blacks and alarm over miscegenation and a mongrelized America. They supported racist doctrines and interpreted history in a manner that justified white supremacy and the disenfranchisement of blacks. Even anthropologist Franz Boas, who generally advocated a cultural relativism which rejected the view of Western or European cultural superiority and who reacted against claims that the black race as a whole was anatomically or psychologically inferior to whites, believed that black Americans were genetically inferior to whites and that only

through intermarriage and the subsequent modification of the black genetic inheritance would America solve its racial problems.[9]

The outbreak of World War I only intensified racial conflict in America. Traditionally blacks have supported America's war efforts in hopes that a display of loyalty and battlefield gallantry would win them popular support in their quest for equality. And, in their efforts to participate fully in their country's battles, blacks have traditionally confronted a government reluctant to accept their services. During World War I the already existing racial strife intensified these problems.

Most black leaders responded to the onset of the war by urging blacks to support their country wholeheartedly. Even W. E. B. Du Bois set aside his struggle for integration and asked his people to "close ranks" with white America and to "forget our present grievances" for the duration of the war, even though this meant accommodation with the segregationist policies of America's military forces. For some blacks, though, this was asking too much. Socialist and labor leader A. Philip Randolph was sentenced to thirty months in prison for publishing antiwar articles, while Francis Grimké argued bitterly that the atrocities which allied propagandists attributed to German troops could not equal the very real atrocities committed by white Americans against their black neighbors. Most blacks, however, made every effort to comply with Du Bois's request in spite of the openly discriminatory policies of their government. At the outset of the war, for example, Colonel Charles Young, the ranking black regular Army officer, was forced to resign. The Navy allowed blacks to serve only as mess boys, while the Marines would not accept blacks in any capacity. The Army eventually accepted blacks in all branches except for the pilot section of the Air Corps, and, after considerable agitation by the NAACP, established a segregated officer training camp for blacks. Of course the entire military was segregated.[10]

As serious as segregation was, the majority of wartime racial problems did not result so much from the problems of the military as from the unrealized expectations and frustrations of black soldiers. Blacks hoped that the uniform they wore and the sacrifices they were willing to make for their country would win them some measure of respect and equal treatment. They were proud of their military accomplishments and more reluctant than ever to accept a second-class position in society. From the beginning of the war, however, whites responded to black soldiers with hostility and fear. They did not view the black soldier as a friendly ally; instead, they saw him as a potentially dangerous element which in the future would have to be even more carefully kept under control. These worries seemed quite realistic when racial strife erupted in towns surrounding several training bases before the first black troops even left for Europe. These base towns, especially those in the South, strongly resented the presence of black troops, usually refused to admit them to restaurants and theaters, and provided few, if any, recreational facilities for them. In addition the YMCA recreational units attached to Army camps restricted their services to whites and made no provisions for black soldiers.[11]

The most serious incident during the war occurred in 1917 in Houston. Trouble began when northern black soldiers stationed in the city confronted the overt segregation of the South. The riot began when rumors circulated that a popular black soldier had been arrested or killed by Houston police. Although the rumor was false, previous confrontations with the city's police made it believable. That night approximately a hundred black soldiers, with rifles and fixed bayonets, marched into the city seeking vengeance against the police and whites in general. Before the Army restored order, sixteen whites and four blacks were dead; eleven more whites were seriously wounded. In the series of court martials that followed, nineteen black soldiers were executed, sixty-three received life sentences, twenty-eight received lesser prison terms, and seven were acquitted. At Spartanburg, South Carolina, Fort Riley, Kansas, and other bases around the country similar incidents were narrowly averted. The Army did nothing to improve facilities or protect black troops from discrimination; instead, whenever trouble threatened they either disarmed the soldiers or quickly dispatched them to Europe.[12]

The Atlantic Ocean did not dilute the Army's discriminatory policies. In Europe black troops experienced the same sort of inequity and prejudice at the hands of the military that they had encountered in the United States. White entertainment groups almost always bypassed their units, and they did not receive the same benefits from service organizations like the YMCA and the Federal Council of Churches. But what really underscored this discrimination was the contrast between the way black troops were treated by their own countrymen and by the French. With few exceptions the French received American blacks warmly and with no visible prejudice. In fact French women associated so freely with blacks that white officers attempted to intervene. The most extreme examples of this were an order issued by General James Erwin forbidding blacks to associate with French women and a document, *Secret Information Concerning Black Troops,* which was circulated among the French in 1918 warning that racial separation was necessary to prevent blacks from assaulting and raping white women.[13]

The equality black soldiers enjoyed in their association with the French contrasted sharply with developments on the home front. During the war lynchings rose from thirty-eight in 1917 to fifty-eight in 1918. In Tennessee three thousand spectators responded to the invitation of a local newspaper to come out and watch a "live Negro" being burned, while in East St. Louis the employment of blacks in a factory holding government contracts sparked a race riot that left at least forty blacks dead, including a two-year-old who was shot and thrown into a burning building.[14]

These incidents were only a prelude to the racial violence that greeted the troops on their return from war. During the long hot summer of 1919 race riots erupted in more than twenty cities, in both the North and the South. In most cases these riots, like the earlier ones at the turn of the century, were characterized by white mobs indiscriminately attacking blacks with little or no interference from local police. However, there was a new element in the 1919 riots, as blacks, no longer willing to rely on ineffective police protection and no longer believing that the government would provide justice for them, armed themselves and fought back against white mobs. In Washington, Chicago, and even in southern towns like Elaine, Arkansas and Longview, Texas, blacks shot back when fired upon or even shot first to protect themselves and their property. The pride engendered by their wartime service and the self-confidence resulting from their military training combined with frustration over apparently unending racial injustice to give birth to a new militancy among American blacks.[15]

The second major social development that dominated the black experience during the first quarter of the twentieth century was the vast migration which brought tens of thousands of blacks from the rural South into northern industrial cities. Although the early signs of this population shift can be detected in the 1890s, as late as 1910 census figures show that 75 percent of American blacks lived in rural areas and that 90 percent lived in the South. Before 1910 most of the black migration was within the South, and generally in a westward direction from one agricultural region to another more prosperous one, or from a rural area to a small town or city. Although several northern cities did substantially increase their black population before 1910, with New York growing from 60,666 in 1900 to 91,709 in 1910, most of this new black population came from the border states. The real mass migration of blacks northward began about 1915 and continued through the 1920s. During this period New York's black population grew over 250 percent, from 91,709 in 1910 to 327,706 in 1930. Although New York would attract more blacks than any other city, other industrial centers such as Chicago, Detroit, and Cleveland saw their black population grow at an even faster rate.[16]

Like most major population relocations in American history, the black migration was influenced by both "push" and "pull" factors and affected most by economic developments. The push factors included an economic depression which spread across the South in 1914 and 1915 and which undermined the economic position of black farmers and farm workers; the ravages of the cotton boll weevil in the summers of 1915 and 1916 and the devastating flooding of the lower South during the summer of 1915 added to the misery and aggravated the economic problems of rural blacks. Finally, the outbreak of the war caused food prices in the South to increase more rapidly than farm wages. These developments intensified the general dissatisfaction of blacks with their economic status in the rural South and provided the major motivation for the exodus. When these economic factors are combined with the deteriorating racial situation, it is no surprise that thousands of blacks chose to seek a better life elsewhere. It is important to note, however, that economic factors dominated the decision to migrate. Also, 1930 census figures indicate that three border states of the upper South—Virginia, Kentucky, and Tennessee—continued to lose the largest percentage of their black population, suggesting that proximity to northern employment centers was the major factor influencing migration patterns.[17]

From the days of slavery the North had held a special position in the mythology of southern blacks as a place of refuge where equality and racial justice abounded. However, the pull factors for the upsurge in black migration in 1915, like the push factors, were primarily economic. W. E. B. Du Bois and the Chicago *Defender* might urge blacks to come north to escape the oppression of the South, but the voice that called the loudest and attracted the attention of most southern blacks was the voice of the advertising pages of newspapers like the *Defender* which promised better jobs at higher pay. The *Defender* and other black newspapers that circulated widely in the South were filled with ads offering jobs at wages that were two or three times those paid in the South. Women domestics, for example, who received $2.50 per week in the South, could earn from $2.10 to $2.50 per day in the North, while their husbands could increase their earnings from $1.10 per day to $3.75 per day by taking a job in a northern factory. The reason for this sudden increase in the demand for labor was that northern industry, stimulated by war contracts, found that the war also cut off its traditional source of industrial labor, the European immigrant. Many companies responded to this labor shortage by actively recruiting southern blacks for the low-paying, unskilled jobs that newly arrived immigrants had previously filled.[18]

It is important to remember that as significant as the black migration was, its major impact, particularly in terms of how it affected the racial or ethnic mix of a community, was on northern cities and not on the South. Even after 1910 most of the movement of blacks was within the South, to southern cities or to other southern or southwestern states that were experiencing economic growth. For example, the 1930 census figures indicate that more blacks had moved into Florida and Arkansas than had moved out of those states, and Texas had gained almost as many as it had lost. . . . The overall pattern is that blacks who did leave their home state, especially in the deep South or Southwest, tended to migrate to another southern state rather than to a northern one. For example, 6.6 percent of the blacks born in Louisiana were living in Texas in 1930 and 3.3 percent of them were living in Arkansas, while a greater percentage of blacks from Mississippi moved to Arkansas than to Ohio. In addition, more than 50 percent of the blacks who migrated to New York before 1930 came from the six states of the South Atlantic region—Virginia, Maryland, North Carolina, South Carolina, Georgia, and Florida.[19]

One effect of the black migration was the emergence of Harlem as the black metropolis and the social and cultural center of black America. Before 1900 Harlem had been an extremely desirable upper-middle-class neighborhood of fine homes and apartment houses. It also housed a significant number of the city's more prosperous Jewish residents. Confidence in the future of this area of the city led to extensive development and speculation there in the 1890s. When the speculative building boom collapsed in the early twentieth century, a number of investors discovered that many of the homes and apartments they had constructed were standing empty. The depressed housing market and the initiative of a number of black realtors brought a steadily increasing flow of black residents into West Harlem, beginning in 1903.[20]

In the late nineteenth century New York's sixty thousand blacks were scattered through the five boroughs, with the largest concentration living in the Tenderloin and San Juan Hill sections of the west side of Manhattan. While some romanticized the west side area between Twenty-seventh and Fifty-third streets as "black bohemia," there was nothing glamorous about life in these segregated slums. Most inhabitants paid exorbitant rent for the privilege of space in one of the tiny apartments, rooming houses, and boarding houses that lined narrow, congested streets. In the Tenderloin district they had to contend with the fact that their neighborhood was the center of prostitution and gambling in the city, as well as home to most of its underworld elements. San Juan Hill was as bad or worse. It enjoyed the distinction of being perhaps the most densely populated area in the city, with 3,580 people living on just one of its streets.[21]

As newcomers from the South swelled the city's black population, pressure for additional and hopefully better housing pushed blacks northward up the west side toward Harlem. Ambitious blacks, who had achieved some economic success, were eager to move their families out of the congested, vice-ridden slums. The racial violence that swept through the Tenderloin during the 1900 riots intensified their determination to escape, while Harlem, with its abundance of good housing, seemed to be the logical place to move.

Harlem's transition, once it began, followed fairly traditional patterns. As soon as blacks started moving onto a block, it became more and more difficult to maintain property values, and whites began to move out. Both black and white realtors took advantage of declining property values in Harlem, the panic selling that resulted when blacks moved in, and the pressure to provide housing for the city's rapidly growing black population, to acquire, subdivide, and lease Harlem property to black tenants. Some white residents of Harlem attempted to block the black invasion. They established organizations like the Harlem Property Owners' Improvement Association and the West Side Improvement Association

to protect their neighborhood. The latter organization tried to evict blacks from the area between West 90th and 110th Streets, claiming that they were not racially prejudiced but worried about the declining value of their property. In spite of these efforts, year by year the line between white and black Harlem moved steadily north, as blacks, desperate for decent housing, streamed into Harlem as quickly as housing was made available to them. By 1910 they had established themselves as the majority group on the west side of Harlem north of 130th Street.[22]

During the next two decades black Harlem continued to grow as tens of thousands of migrants from the South were joined by thousands of black immigrants from the West Indies. All seemed to find their way to Harlem's streets and tenements. In 1920 black Harlem extended from 130th Street to 145th Street and from Fifth to Eighth Avenue, and it contained approximately 73,000 blacks (66.9 percent of the total number of blacks in the borough of Manhattan); by 1930 black Harlem had expanded north ten blocks to 155th, spread from the Harlem River to Amsterdam Avenue, and housed approximately 164,000 blacks (73.0 percent of Manhattan's blacks). In 1930 the heart of black Harlem, bounded roughly by 126th Street on the south, 159th Street on the north, the Harlem River and Park Avenue on the east, and Eighth Avenue on the west, had a population of more than 106,000 that was 95.1 percent black. By 1920 Harlem, by virtue of the sheer size of its black population, had emerged as the capital of black America; its name evoked a magic that lured all classes of blacks from all sections of the country to its streets. Impoverished southern farmers and sharecroppers poured northward, where they were joined in Harlem by black intellectuals such as W. E. B. Du Bois and James Weldon Johnson. Although the old black social elites of Washington, D.C., were disdainful of Harlem's vulgar splendor, and while it housed no great black university as did Washington, Atlanta, and Nashville, Harlem still became the race's cultural center and a Mecca for its aspiring young. It was the headquarters for the NAACP and the Urban League, Marcus Garvey launched his ill-fated brand of black nationalism among its masses, and it became the geographical focal point of the black literary movement of the 1920s. Harlem, in short, was where the action was in black America during the decade following World War I.[23]

More important, perhaps, than the reality of Harlem as a city within a city—as an emerging ghetto in the nation's greatest city—were the various images associated with this community of more than 100,000 blacks. Rudolph Fisher, for example, captured one aspect of Harlem when he described it as seen through the eyes of a recently arrived southern black in his short story "City of Refuge":

> Gillis set down his tan-cardboard extension case and wiped his black, shining brow. Then slowly, spreadingly, he grinned at what he saw: Negroes at every turn; up and down Lenox Avenue, up and down One Hundred and Thirty-fifth Street; big, lanky ones; men standing idle on the curb, women, bundle-laden, trudging reluctantly homeward, children rattle-trapping about the sidewalks; here and there a white face drifting along, but Negroes predominately, overwhelmingly everywhere. There was assuredly no doubt of his where-abouts. This was Negro Harlem.[24]

This passage illustrates the awe and excitement that Harlem's sheer magnitude generated in most newcomers. "Harlem must be a better world," reasoned most blacks. The reason was clearly visible as Fisher's Gillis turned and noticed to his astonishment that a *black* policeman was directing traffic, and white drivers obediently followed his commands:

> Yet most of the vehicles that leaped or crouched at his bidding carried white passengers. One of these overdrove bounds a few feet and Gillis heard the officer's shrill whistle and gruff reproof, and saw the driver's face turn red and his car draw back like a threatened pup. It was beyond belief—impossible. Black might be white, but it couldn't be that white![25]

For thousands of blacks Harlem was just that—a city of refuge where, at least it was thought, one could escape from the white control that was omnipresent in the South.

Another young poet saw Harlem only slightly differently. Like many would-be black writers, Langston Hughes was strongly drawn to the black metropolis. When his father offered to send him to college in Europe, Hughes balked and then suggested Columbia University as a compromise "mainly because I wanted to see Harlem. . . . More than Paris, or the Shakespeare country, or Berlin, or the Alps, I wanted to see Harlem, the greatest Negro city in the world."[26] Like Fisher's Gillis, Langston Hughes was transfixed as he ascended from the subway into the heart of Harlem:

> I went up the steps and out into the bright September sunlight. Harlem! I stood there, dropped my bags, took a deep breath and felt happy again. I registered at the Y.
>
> When college opened, I did not want to move into the dormitory at Columbia. I really did not want

to go the college at all. I didn't want to do anything but live in Harlem, get a job and work there.[27]

After his first year at college Hughes did exactly that. He dropped out of school and moved into Harlem. Hughes was enraptured of the place because of the masses who lived, toiled, and played there. Many of his early poems captured the life of the ghetto's streets and cabarets. Hughes always recognized that Harlem was a slum where one did not really escape racial oppression, but he nevertheless loved the vitality and life of the blacks who resided there.

James Weldon Johnson saw a still different Harlem. In 1930 he published *Black Manhattan,* in which he described the black metropolis as the race's great hope and its grand social experiment: "So here we have Harlem—not merely a colony or a community or a settlement—not at all a 'quarter' or a slum or a fringe—but a black city located in the heart of white Manhattan, and containing more Negroes to the square mile than any other spot on earth. It strikes the uninformed observer as a phenomenon, a miracle straight out of the skies." Johnson was so blinded by the image he held of the Harlem that could be that he saw the ghetto in only the most glowing terms, and described that area of Manhattan as "one of the most beautiful and healthful in the whole city. It is not a fringe, it is not a slum, nor is it a 'quarter' consisting of dilapidated tenements. It is a section of new-law apartment houses and handsome dwellings, with streets as well paved, as well lighted, and as well kept as in any other part of the city."[28]

Johnson concluded his study with the claim that Harlem would prove to be the great laboratory in which all of the racial misconceptions of white America would be laid to rest. He argued that Harlem proved that large numbers of blacks could live together in the North without creating racial disorder, and that it demonstrated the ability of blacks to create a viable community which offered its inhabitants opportunity and decent living conditions. He further maintained that Harlem and the literary movement associated with it would obliterate the stereotype that the Negro was a "beggar at the gates of the nation waiting to be thrown the crumbs of civilization," and would instead place blacks in an entirely new light that would ultimately eliminate the discrimination and disadvantages which had oppressed the race for centuries.[29]

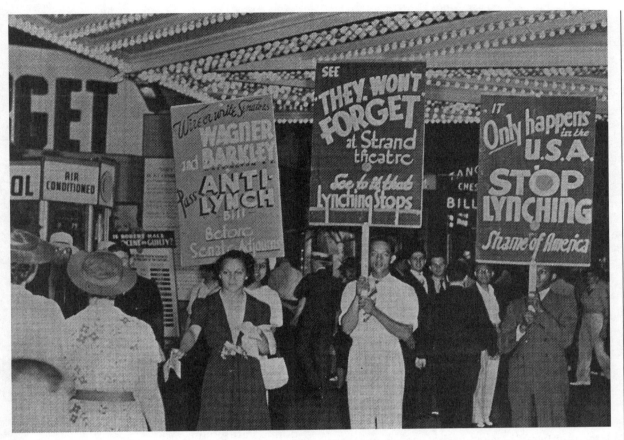

Members of the NAACP New York City Youth Council picket for anti-lynching legislation in front of the Strand Theatre in Times Square.

Unfortunately, Johnson's idealism and optimism masked reality and prevented him from recognizing that in the 1920s Harlem was rapidly deteriorating. Granted, Harlem was a rapidly growing black metropolis, but, as Gilbert Osofsky documented, "the most profound change that Harlem experienced in the 1920s was its emergence as a slum. Largely within the space of a single decade Harlem was transformed from a potentially ideal community to a neighborhood with manifold social and economic problems called 'deplorable, unspeakable, incredible.'" Exorbitant rents in Harlem led to subdividing apartments and extreme overcrowding, making it the most congested area in the nation. This, in turn, resulted in serious health problems, which gave Harlem the highest infant mortality and general mortality rates in New York City. In addition the rapid influx of blacks made it difficult for many Harlem residents to find decent jobs. Job discrimination, which ironically was practiced in the heart of the black ghetto, exacerbated these employment problems. During the 1920s the vast majority of Harlem's retail establishments would only

hire blacks for menial jobs such as porter, maid, or elevator operator. As a result of this and similar job discrimination most of Harlem's residents lived, at best, on the verge of poverty, a situation which contributed to the emergence of this area as the city's leader in vice, crime, juvenile delinquency, and drug addiction.[30]

Many of the pathologies of ghetto life are those linked to the breakup of the black family in American slums. While Herbert Gutman's study of the black family effectively refutes Osofsky's claim that slavery had undermined the black family prior to the great migration, the vitality of the black family in Harlem in the 1920s is not so clear. Gutman's argument that large numbers of lower-class southern blacks had effectively adapted familial and kinship ties to life in the ghetto may be accurate, but there is still evidence that indicates that the black family was a victim of ghetto life and that the ghetto, in turn, was adversely affected by the weakening of family ties. One problem confronting the black family in Harlem in the 1920s was the growing number of families or subfamilies that were headed by a female. While the percentage of female-headed households and subfamilies among blacks in New York City declined slightly from 17 percent in 1905 to 15 percent in 1925, it may be more significant that in the samples studied by Gutman the total number of male-absent families and subfamiles had grown from 587 in 1905 to 2,089 in 1925. In a congested urban area the absolute number of male-absent families (and the number of children raised in families where the father is absent) can have as great an impact on the community as the percentage of male-absent families does. The growing congestion of Harlem also impacted on family structure. Between 1905 and 1925 nuclear families became less prevalent, declining from 49 percent to 39 percent, while the number of households containing subfamilies increased from 12.7 percent to slightly over 30 percent; in addition, by 1925 nearly half of the black households contained a boarder or lodger.[31]

The most significant problem that confronted Harlem was the failure to establish a viable black middle class there. While Harlem attracted a substantial number of black intellectuals, writers, and poets in the 1920s, and it became the home of a large number of black churches, newspapers, and civil rights organizations, it housed relatively few black businesses. In 1930, for example, Manhattan, with a population of 224,670 blacks, contained only 258 black-owned retail stores, one fewer than Houston, with only 63,337 blacks, and significantly fewer than existed in either Atlanta, New Orleans, or even Detroit. Black-owned retail stores in Manhattan also had significantly lower sales per capita (of the black population) than did those in the other cities surveyed. . . . Black-owned retail businesses were involved primarily in food-related activities (groceries, restaurants, lunch counters), although these businesses were somewhat more diversified in Manhattan than in other cities. A survey of economic activity in Harlem in the mid-1930s found that blacks owned less than 19 percent of the 10,300 enterprises operating in Harlem, and the ones that blacks did operate were usually personal service businesses or businesses in fields that required little capital and little labor; in 1930 the average black-owned retail store in Manhattan employed only 1.49 full-time workers, including the proprietor. In 1925 less than 2 percent of Manhattan blacks were classified entrepreneurial, while 89 percent were employed as skilled, unskilled, or service workers.[32]

Undermining the emergence of a black middle class in Harlem was widespread discrimination in employment and education. Even corporations that made their money from black patronage often refused to hire blacks. For example, in 1935 the Metropolitan Life Insurance Company, which insured more than 100,000 blacks in Harlem alone, did not employ a single black. Utility companies in the New York City area employed almost 135,000 persons, but only 1 percent were black (and most of these held janitorial positions), while discrimination was perpetuated even by the New York State Employment Service, which required racial identification on all applications and listed only menial jobs at its Harlem office, and both the city and state civil service systems. The New York educational system completed the pattern of discrimination that held blacks out of the middle class. Vocational schools in the city consistently refused to offer training to blacks in fields that were reserved for whites, while the practice of zoning school districts was manipulated effectively to segregate the public schools. As a result, most Harlem blacks attended high schools where the curriculum assumed (and assured) that they would occupy a marginal economic status in life.[33]

The available housing in Harlem, which had initially seemed so attractive, soon deteriorated. Existing brownstones and roomy apartments were quickly subdivided, and then developers threw up cheap tenements to cash in on the area's burgeoning growth. Rents and demand for housing remained so high that many black families were forced to take in boarders or hold rent parties in order to afford even low-quality housing. Over-crowding and segregation combined to undermine the neighborhood. Faulty maintenance, violation of municipal codes, and outright vandalism accelerated the process. By the late 1930s, 30 percent of the area's dwellings lacked bathing facilities. The inevitable consequence of overcrowding and inadequate sanitation was the deterioration of public health. For example, in 1930 the death rate of blacks from tuberculosis in New York City was almost five times greater than it was for whites, and substantially higher than it was for blacks in large southern cities like Atlanta, Houston, and New Orleans; the average infant mortality rate for blacks in New York City between 1926 and 1931 was more than twice as high as it was for whites, and substantially higher than it was for blacks in other large northern industrial cities, while the gap between white and black rates for infant mortality was greater in New York than in other major cities in the North or the South. In short, the day-to-day realities that most Harlemites faced differed dramatically from the image of Harlem life presented by James Weldon Johnson. Perhaps Johnson finally became aware of how far reality had diverged from his dream, or perhaps he did not, but in 1931 Harlem's greatest booster abandoned black Manhattan for a position in Nashville at Fisk University.[34]

Harlem, then, was not so much a black metropolis as a black ghetto. If, as Johnson observed, racial tension had declined in New York during the twenties, it was because whites had succeeded in confining most blacks to a separate, self-contained section of New York with institutions and services inferior to those in other parts of the city, had limited them to the more menial jobs, and had isolated them from the mainstream of the city's social and political life. As one character in Carl Van Vechten's novel *Nigger Heaven* bitterly remarked:

> Nigger Heaven! Byron moaned. Nigger Heaven! That's what Harlem is. We sit in our places in the gallery in this New York theater and watch the white world sitting down below in the good seats in the orchestra. Occasionally they turn their faces up towards us, their hard, cruel faces, to laugh or sneer, but they never beckon. It never seems to occur to them that Nigger Heaven is crowded, that there isn't another seat, that something has to be done. It doesn't seem to occur to them either, he went on fiercely, that we sit above them, that we can drop things on them and crush them, that we can swoop down from Nigger Heaven and take their seats. No, they have no fear of that! Harlem! The Mecca of the New Negro! My God![35]

Harlem, then, symbolized different things to different blacks. It was both their hope and their despair. More important, Harlem reflected the confusing and contradictory position of blacks in the early twentieth century. It was a symbol of the black migrant who left the South and went north with dreams of freedom and opportunity. It also symbolized the shattered pieces of those dreams which lay half-buried beneath the filth and garbage of the city slum. Harlem reflected the self-confidence, militancy, and pride of the New Negro in his or her demand for equality; it reflected the aspirations and genius of the writers and poets of the Harlem Renaissance; but Harlem, like the black migrant, like the New Negro, and like the Renaissance writers, did not resolve its problems or fulfill its dreams. Everything, it seemed, fell short of its goal.

## Notes

1. For a discussion of the deterioration of the racial situation following reconstruction see August Meier, *Negro Thought in America, 1880-1915: Racial Ideologies in the Age of Booker T. Washington* (Ann Arbor: University of Michigan Press, 1968), 69-82, 161-63; see also Leon F. Litwack, *Been in the Storm So Long: The Aftermath of Slavery* (New York: Vintage Books, 1979) for a discussion of the often troubled efforts of blacks and whites to adjust to the end of slavery.

2. Roger Lane, *Roots of Violence in Black Philadelphia, 1868-1900* (Cambridge, Mass.: Harvard University Press, 1986), 40-41. Lane documents the exclusion of blacks from labor unions, and hence from the better industrial jobs, in late nineteenth-century Philadelphia. Ibid., 35-41.

3. Lane, 35-41; Meier, 164-65; Henry Pringle, *Theodore Roosevelt: A Biography* (New York: Harcourt, Brace & World, Inc., 1956), 261, 322-27; Dwight W. Hoover, *The Red and the Black* (Chicago: Rand McNally College Publishing, 1976), 221.

4. It is very difficult to pinpoint accurately the number of lynchings in any given year. The figures cited here are those used by John Hope Franklin, *From Slavery to Freedom: A History of Negro Americans,* 5th ed. (New York: Knopf, 1980), 313-14, which were based on studies done between 1913 to 1933. More recent work by George C. Wright on racial violence in Kentucky suggests that these figures are very conservative. See George C. Wright *Life Behind a Veil: Blacks in Louisville, Kentucky, 1865-1930* (Baton Rouge, Louisiana State University Press, 1985), 71-76, 254-57. Wright developed his theories of lynching, including "legal lynching," even further in a paper, "Racial Violence in Kentucky: Lynching, Legal Lynching, and Mob Rule," that he delivered at Rice University, February 5, 1987.

5. Franklin, 316.

6. Ibid., 317.

7. Thomas Dixon, Jr., *The Leopard's Spots* (New York: Doubleday, Page, 1902); Thomas Dixon, Jr., *The Clansman* (New York: Doubleday, Page, 1905); Charles Carroll, *The Negro Not the Son of Ham; or Man Not a Species Divisible* (Chattanooga, TN, 1898); Charles Carroll, *The Negro, Beast or in the Image of God* (St. Louis: American Book and Bible House, 1900); Charles Carroll, *The Tempter of Eve or the Criminality of Man's Social, Political, and Religious Equality, with the Negro, and the Amalgamation to Which These Crimes Inevitably Lead* (St. Louis: Adamic Publishing, 1902); Frederick L. Hoffman, *Race Traits and Tendencies of the American Negro* (New York: Published for the American Economic Association by Macmillan, 1896). For a survey of racial thought in the United States in the late nineteenth and early twentieth centuries see Hoover, 164-90, 218-52.

8. S. P. Fullinwider, *The Mind and Mood of Black America: 20th Century Thought* (Homewood, IL: Dorsey Press, 1969), 4.

9. Hoover, 241-53; the most notable historians who argued this position were James Ford Rhodes, John W. Burgess, and especially William A. Dunning in *Reconstruction* (New York: Harper & Brothers, 1907); see also Hoover, 211-17, 233-34; Franz Boas, "Industries of the African Negroes," *The Southern Workman,* April 1909, 217-19; and Franz Boas *The Mind of Primitive Man* (New York: Macmillan, 1911).

10. [W. E. B. Du Bois], "Close Ranks," *Crisis*, July 1918, 111; Franklin, 342; *The Works of Francis J. Grimké*, ed. Carter G. Woodson, vol. 3 (Washington, D.C.: Associated Publishers, 1942), 44, 67.

11. Franklin, 325-31; for a thorough discussion of the problems faced by black troops during World War I see Stetson Conn, ed., *The United States in World War II*, vol. 8, part 8, *The Employment of Negro Troops*, by Ulysses S. Lee (Washington, D.C.: Government Printing Office, 1966), 8-14; and Stephen E. Ambrose, "Blacks in the Army in Two World Wars," in *The Military in American Society: Essays and Readings*, ed. Stephen E. Ambrose and James A. Barber, Jr. (New York: Free Press, 1972).

12. See Robert V. Haynes, *A Night of Violence: The Houston Riot of 1917* (Baton Rouge: Louisiana State University Press, 1976) for a detailed account of the Houston riot. August Meier and Elliot M. Rudwick, *From Plantation to Ghetto* (New York: Hill and Wang, 1970), 219.

13. Franklin, 336; see also Lee, 10-11, and Ambrose, 183.

14. Franklin, 341.

15. Meier and Rudwick, 220-21.

16. Thomas J. Woofter, *Negro Migration: Changes in Rural Organization and Population of the Cotton Belt* (New York: Negro Universities Press, 1920), 170; Gilbert Osofsky, *Harlem: The Making of a Ghetto: Negro New York, 1890-1930* (New York: Harper & Row, 1966), 18. From 1870 to 1890 there was a small but steady movement of blacks northward, averaging approximately 41,000 per decade. From 1890 to 1910 this number increased to more than 100,000 per decade.

17. Emmett Scott, *Negro Migration During the War* (New York: Oxford University Press, 1920), 14; U.S. Department of Commerce, Bureau of the Census, *Negroes in the United States, 1920-1932* (Washington, D.C.: Government Printing Office, 1935), 40-43.

18. Scott, 17; Osofsky, 29; Arna Bontemps and Jack Conroy, *Anyplace but Here* (New York: Hill and Wang, 1969), 160.

19. *Negroes in the U.S., 1920-1932*, 34-36, 40-43.

20. Osofsky, 81-104; Roi Ottley and William J. Weatherby, eds., *The Negro in New York: An Informal Social History* (Dobbs Ferry, NY: Oceana Publications, 1967), 179-83.

21. The "Tenderloin" district was an ill-defined area that included scattered pockets of black settlement stretching from Twentieth Street to Fifty-third Street on the west side of Manhattan; San Juan Hill had more precise boundaries, along Tenth and Eleventh avenues from Sixtieth to Sixty-fourth streets. See Osofsky, 12-13; *The Negro in New York*, 182-83.

22. Jeffrey S. Gurock, *When Harlem Was Jewish, 1870-1930* (New York: Columbia University Press, 1979), 146-47;

23. *Negroes in the U.S., 1920-1932*, 68; Osofsky, 123, 130.

24. Rudolph Fisher, "The City of Refuge," in *The New Negro*, ed. Alain Locke (New York: Atheneum, 1969), 57-58.

25. Ibid., 59.

26. Langston Hughes, *The Big Sea: An Autobiography* (New York: Hill and Wang, 1963), 62-64.

27. Ibid., 81-82.

28. James Weldon Johnson, *Black Manhattan* (New York: Atheneum, 1968), 3-4, 146.

29. Ibid., 284-85.

30. Osofsky, 127-49; Herman D. Bloch, "The Employment Status of the New York Negro in Retrospect," *Phylon* 20, December 1959, 327; and Thomas J. Woofter, *Races and Ethnic Groups in American Life* (New York: McGraw-Hill, 1937), 133.

31. Herbert G. Gutman, *The Black Family in Slavery and Freedom, 1750-1925* (New York: Vintage Books, 1977), 443-44, 450-55, 509-515, 643n; Osofsky, 134. Gutman defined a subfamily as either a husband and wife, two parents and their children, or a single parent and children living in the same household with another nuclear family.

32. *Negroes in the U.S., 1920-1932*, 520-26, 578; Dominic J. Capeci, Jr., *The Harlem Riot of 1943* (Philadelphia: Temple University Press, 1977), 37; Gutman, 512.

33. Capeci, 35-36, 40.

34. Ibid., 48; *Negroes in the U.S., 1920-1932*, 374-75, 452-57.

35. Carl Van Vechten, *Nigger Heaven* (New York: Harper & Row, 1971), 149.

# ELOISE E. JOHNSON (ESSAY DATE 1997)

**SOURCE:** Johnson, Eloise E. "When Harlem Was in Vogue: History of the Harlem Renaissance." In *Rediscovering the Harlem Renaissance: The Politics of Exclusion*, pp. 9-21. New York: Garland Publishing, 1997.

*In the following essay, Johnson provides a brief survey of early Harlem and its role in the Harlem Renaissance. She writes of how Harlem was created, of the intellectual differences between Booker T. Washington and W. E. B. Du Bois, and of important Renaissance figures.*

The 1920's were the years of Manhattan's black Renaissance. It began with *Shuffle Along, Running Wild,* and the Charleston. Perhaps some people would say even with The Emperor Jones, Charles Gilpin, and the tom-toms at the Provincetown. But certainly it was the musical revue, *Shuffle Along,* that gave a scintillating send-off to that Negro vogue in Manhattan, which reached its peak just before the crash of 1929, the crash that sent Negroes, white folks, and all rolling down the hill toward the Works Progress Administration.

Langston Hughes, *The Big Sea*

This [essay] will trace the historical circumstances that led to the phenomenon called the Harlem Renaissance. This is not an attempt to give a total historical review of the period, but the material will inform the reader of the many historical details that shaped the era. Unfortunately, many events and characters who played a part in the making of Harlem will have to be omitted. A number of factors contributed to Harlem's becoming the "Negro metropolis" of the world. By the mid 1920s, with the Jazz Age in full swing, Harlem was, according to James Weldon Johnson, "the great Mecca for the sight-seer, the pleasure-seeker, the curious, the adventurous, the enterprising, the ambitious and the talented of the whole Negro world . . ."[1] This change in Harlem was due to the influx of artists, writers, philosophers, educators, actors, immigrants from the south, and voyeurs. But how did a small genteel community inhabited by Dutch immigrants at the turn of the century become a "black phenomenon"? The beginning of this [essay] will look at the history of African Americans in New York, the black immigrants from the south and their subsequent movement to Harlem, and the artists, writers and philosophers who contributed to the Harlem Renaissance.

## Harlem

According to Gilbert Osofsky, at the turn of the century there were 60,666 blacks living in New York City with the highest concentration living in Manhattan.[2] African Americans had migrated to New York from the six states of the South Atlantic region—Virginia, Maryland, North Carolina, South Carolina, Georgia and Florida.[3] But according to Osofsky, there were more foreign-born blacks in New York City than in any other city in America.[4] In the early nineteenth century, New York blacks lived in the Five Points district. The Sixth Ward, located in the Five Points district, consisted of working class blacks. The black section within it was popularly called "Stagg Town" or "Negro Plantations." This was the first place in which freed slaves settled. By the 1830s the population of Five Points began to decline. Gradually the majority of the people moved north and west into Greenwich Village.[5]

Like that of Five Points the black community in Greenwich had a bad reputation. Greenwich was an area known for its alleged vices. This stereotype continued to exist although there were hundreds of menial workers who built churches in the community. In 1920, the few hundred Blacks living in Greenwich Village were janitors living in basements of tenement buildings housing whites.[6]

The black population was concentrated in the Tenderloin and San Juan Hill areas in the 1890s. The Tenderloin was a vague area. Therefore, its boundaries were not clearly defined. The black sections scattered within this general area began at approximately Twentieth Street and ended at Fifty-third. It was given the romantic name of "black bohemia." The boundaries of San Juan Hill were easily delineated. They stretched from Sixtieth to Sixty-fourth Streets, between Tenth and Eleventh Avenues. San Juan Hill gained notoriety as being one of the most congested areas in America's most populated city: 3,580 people lived on just one street. Its nomenclature came from the Spanish-American War, and it was often the site of interracial skirmishes. These took place in the neighborhood on the steep slope leading to Sixtieth Street. Meanwhile, the construction of Pennsylvania Station further reduced residential land space for blacks citizens living there.[7]

During the last three decades of the nineteenth century, Harlem was populated by Dutch, French, and English descendants. Harlem expanded gradually and was annexed to New York City in 1873, becoming a community of upper- and upper-middle-class people. Luxurious houses and apartments with elevators created a "genteel" community. The inevitable bust came in 1904-1905. Harlem was inundated with too many houses and commercial buildings. By 1905 financial institutions stopped making loans to Harlem speculators and building loan companies.[8]

## The Afro-American Realty Company

Rather than face financial ruin, landlords and corporations in Harlem began renting to blacks, charging the usual high rent. Others used the threat of renting their property to black tenants to frighten their neighbors into buying property at a higher than market price.[9]

Black newcomers from the South created a demand for housing in Harlem. Also, blacks who had achieved economic success were eager to move to a better neighboorhood. Furthermore, the destruction of many all-black neighborhoods in the Tenderloin when Pennsylvania Station was built dislocated the black inhabitants. Black tenants, offered decent housing for the first time in the city's history, flocked to Harlem in droves.[10]

This unique situation provided a profitable opportunity for a black realtor, Phillip A. Payton, Jr. His plan was to lease Harlem apartment houses from white owners and assure them a regular income. In turn, he would rent these homes to blacks and make a profit by charging rents ten percent above the then deflated market.[11]

Payton's activities in Harlem real estate reached a peak in 1904 with his founding of the Afro-American Realty Company. The company had a partnership that consisted of ten blacks organized by Payton. This partnership specialized in acquiring five-year leases on Harlem property owned by whites and subsequently renting them to blacks.[12] The Afro-American Realty Company was founded with the promise of success, but after four years it failed due to Payton's speculations. Nevertheless, this company helped to lay the foundations for the largest "Negro ghetto in the world".[13]

## The Great Migration

Another reason for Harlem's becoming one of the most important cities in the 1920s was the arrival of newcomers. The Great Migration of rural blacks from the south owed its beginning to economic crisis and a quest for social equality. The impetus to migrate was brought on by racism, lynchings, race riots, low wages, agricultural mechanization, and a demand for laborers in the north. Blacks began migrating north in 1915 and 1916, searching for jobs due to a decrease in European immigration during World War I.[14] The war brought a decrease in foreign immigration due to a diminished pool of unskilled laborers and domestic servants. Also, desperately needing laborers because of the induction of skilled and unskilled men into the armed forces, manufacturers began hiring black men and women.[15] By 1920 thousands had arrived in New York, Chicago, Indianapolis, Detroit, Philadelphia, Cleveland, and other urban areas. The flow continued throughout the 1920s and began to taper off during the Depression. The move to the north could often be a traumatic experience for the rural black American. Often seeking social equality, the migrants found out that the north was not the "promised land" they envisioned. Nevertheless, the Harlem Renaissance would not have been possible if not for this influx of migrants flowing into the city from the south.

## Philosophers and Educators

Two important leaders who emerged from the twenties had a great impact on the Harlem Renaissance, though they were in opposing camps in terms of political and social ideology. They were Booker T. Washington and W. E. B. DuBois.

Washington, who came from humble origins, attended Hampton Institute in Virginia. He became the founder of Tuskegee Institute in Alabama, where he established a vocational educational plan which was antithetical to the liberal arts education proposed by W. E. B. DuBois. Washington believed that blacks could only achieve a sort of racial equality by becoming skilled wage-earners in society; not by political means. Tuskegee's mission was to turn black students into

manual laborers, no matter what their real propensity might be. Washington believed that this type of industrial education would transform the American black into an economic force whose base would be self-sufficiency. He was also a "separatist." In his famous speech delivered in Atlanta in September 1895, he stated, "In all things that are purely social we can be as separate as the fingers, yet one as the hand in all things essential to mutual progress." He urged blacks to become self-sufficient in his "Cast down your bucket where you are" speech and urged whites to assist them in their endeavors. Under Washington's leadership, Tuskegee was able to gain more philanthropic support from white patrons than any other black school. But Washington's economic program was limited. His outdated formula for an economically independent artisan did not prepare blacks for the industrialization that was taking place in America. His conciliatory policy had failed to achieve any sort of economic and political goals. Clearly, a new ideology had to be initiated to obtain some type of progress for blacks.[16]

William Edward Burghardt DuBois was not interested in conciliation, but the full integration of blacks into American society. He "would stress the beauty of the folk, the necessity of liberal learning, the value of culture, the importance of a leading class, the spirituality of life, and . . . the perfectibility of man."[17] He studied at Fisk University and the University of Berlin, and received three degrees from Harvard, becoming in 1895 the first black ever to receive a Ph.D. His doctoral dissertation, "The Suppression of the African Slave Trade," became the first published work in the Harvard Historical Studies series. Possessed of an intellectual approach different from Washington's, DuBois was a pioneer in the sociological study of the African American. His book entitled: *The Soul of Black Folks* deals with a sociological investigation of blacks living in this country. Here he identified the underlying problem of blacks living in the twentieth century as "the problem of the color line." In an essay in his book entitled "Of Mr. Booker T. Washington and Others," DuBois accused Washington's program of accepting black inferiority. DuBois also charged Washington with being hostile to Negro liberal arts colleges and their graduates. He believed that a "Talented Tenth" would rise from the ranks of the black community and would become part of the black intelligentsia. Washington's program of industrial education would deny the existence of this group.[18]

## The Talented Tenth

The pre-World War I migration has sometimes been called the "Migration of the Talented Tenth."[19] According to DuBois, "The Negro race, like all races, is going to be saved by its exceptional men. The problem of education, then among Negroes must first of all deal with the Talented Tenth . . . ."[20] This ten per cent of college-educated students would contribute intellectually to the Harlem Renaissance. Black schools were established after slavery by white missionaries following the Union army. They taught the ideals of industry, thrift, and morality. After Reconstruction the Freedmen Bureau was concerned with the education of blacks. Because of the need for black teachers, the Bureau established schools of higher education. Among the institutions established were Atlanta University, Fisk University, and Howard University which are some of the oldest institutions dedicated to the education of African Americans. Various religious organizations also established institutions for the education of African Americans.[21] There were 2,132 African Americans in college in 1917. Ten years later, there were 13,580. Only 200 or 300 of these were in white schools. By 1927, 39 had won doctorates. There were few professional African Americans in the fields of dentistry, medicine, law, college teaching and administration and banking. And the fields of architecture, engineering, art, and science were practically non-existent in the black community. Meanwhile, black colleges were becoming oppressed by the vocational education program of Booker T. Washington which taught students outmoded trades.[22]

The General Education Board presided over black education backed by Rockefeller and other philanthropic money. The board's first chairman argued that higher education would not be useful to blacks. Booker T. Washington agreed with this sentiment. Thus, while the endowment of vocational Hampton and Tuskegee institutes grew until they were among the richest schools in America, the three outstanding African American liberal arts colleges—Atlanta, Fisk, and Lincoln funds were depleted by the Carnegie, Jeanes, Phelps-Stokes, and Slater foundations, and by the General Education Board. Fisk and Atlanta barely survived. When in 1916 the United States Bureau of Education and the Phelps-Stokes Fund issued a joint 724-page definitive report on African American higher education proclaiming vocational education as paramount, things seemed quite bleak. The African American seemed doomed to a life of stagnation and drudgery. Nevertheless, Booker T. Washington's death and the War slowed the implementation of the anti-liberal arts policy. Fate had intervened.[23]

When the war was over, the Talented Tenth began to gather its defenses for a counterattack, headed by DuBois, the two Grimke brothers, Archibald and Frances, Alain Locke, Kelly Miller, and a few others. DuBois complained that academies like Hampton and Tuskegee were designed by "rich and intelligent people, and particularly . . . those who masquerade as the Negroes' friend . . . to educate a race of scullions and then complain of their lack of ability."[24]

If not for the protestation of the "Talented Tenth" on college campuses, the Harlem Renaissance would not have been the arts and letters phenomenon it was. Some of the students who later became a part of academia in the 1920s, and who went on to fame and fortune, were E. Franklin Frazier, Rudolph Fisher, Ruth Anne Fisher, Arthur H. Fauset, Sterling A. Brown, Aaron Douglas, Hubert T. Delaney, Roy Wilkins, Benjamin Quarles, Charles Drew, Ralph Bunche, Gwendolyn Bennett, Jessie Fauset, Arna Bontemps, Langston Hughes, and Countee Cullen. This was not a silent generation.[25]

## The New Negro

Alain Locke was temporarily fired in 1925 for his courage in representing the grievances of the faculty salary committee at Howard University. Locke, a Rhodes scholar and professor of philosophy, was a champion of the younger generation. In 1925 he published a book entitled *The New Negro* which contained poems, essays, and pictures representing the new outlook of the African American. Locke encouraged writers and artists alike to live up to their intellectual potential. He became the father of the New Negro movement in America. Writers such as Langston Hughes and Countee Cullen became his proteges. Locke acknowledged that a change had occurred in black America and that these young writers would reflect that change. The New Negro was often militant in outlook and filled with a sense of racial pride. According to Locke, the Negro would no longer be a "foundling" in this country but a participant and contributor. Locke believed that by looking to the past—that is, an African past—the Negro could reclaim his heritage and free himself from the stigma of slavery. It was an age of rediscovery led by Locke and his contemporaries. The influx of college-educated students added to the militancy and self-assertiveness of the New Negro.

Marcus Garvey, another contributor to the black movement in the 1920s, also added to the militancy of the New Negro. Born in Jamaica, Garvey came to New York in 1916. He dreamed of re-establishing the African American within his African homeland. Garvey's message appealed to the masses. He founded the Universal Improvement Association in 1917 which immediately attracted a following. With a grandiose sense of theatricality, Garvey utilized plumed hats and cockades, street parades, and the conferring of titles such as "knight" and "duke" on his followers. But pageantry and theatricality were not Garvey's ultimate goals. He appealed to his followers' sense of racial pride and gave meaning to their lives, which were often shaped by hopelessness. His message to the black masses was that they should be proud of their African heritage; it was a glorious page in the history of the world. He made the common black man feel like somebody. Garvey sought to eliminate self-hatred from the African American's consciousness and to establish a sense of self-worth. His ultimate goal was to return with his followers to Africa.[26]

Another contributing factor to the New Negro movement was World War I. Black troops returning from the war and bringing with them a new sense of pride agitated for change. Woodrow Wilson's claim of global democracy did not ring true for African Americans. After a less-than-glorious start, 200,000 black soldiers were shipped to France. Black soldiers could not be trained with white troops, and most worked as menials within the armed services. But finally, in a training camp in Des Moines, Iowa, black troops were trained for battle and eventually shipped out to Europe. The 369th Regiment, which had been instructed in Des Moines, achieved an outstanding record for valor in combat. It was the first Allied unit to reach the Rhine and having fought in the trenches for 191 days, it was awarded the Croix de Guerre for exceptional bravery in action. Even though the American army had warned the French in a secret document not to fraternize with black troops, the French citizens treated the black soldiers as "full Americans." Returning in 1919 in a parade in New York City, the 369th, with Lt. James Europe's band, stepped proudly to a ticker-tape parade in their honor. This new sense of pride and militancy from the war-weary soldiers contributed to the mood of the New Negro. They had seen what it was like to be men; now this new sense of manhood would not be easily taken away.[27]

## The Writers

The four major Renaissance writers who achieved their first major recognition in the 1920s—Claude McKay, Jean Toomer, Countee Cullen and Langston Hughes—were diverse in background, personality, and style though there were certain common themes that brought them together as members of the Harlem literary movement. McKay and Toomer were a decade older than Cullen and Hughes, but all four wrote much of their best work before the age of thirty.[28]

In addition to McKay, Toomer, Cullen, and Hughes, other writers contributed to the quest for the New Negro in the 1920s. Jessie Fauset, Walter White, and Nella Larsen wrote novels concerned with the problems of the black middle class, especially the concept of "passing". Others by George Schuyler and Wallace Thurman took a satirical look at the paradox of color consciousness. Two short story writers, Eric Walrond, whose *Tropic Death* reveals a gloomy view of black life in the Caribbean, and Rudolph Fisher, who dealt with vignettes of Harlem, made literary contributions to this renaissance. In poetry Arna Bontemps, Waring Cuney, Sterling Brown, Frank Horne, Gwendolyn Bennett, Helene Johnson, and others contributed to the youthful idealism of the era.[29]

## The Artists

The Harlem visual artists did not constitute a "school" in which a distinct style can be seen. Indeed, in his book *Negro Art,* James Porter criticizes these artists for being too "individualistic." Among the artists who participated in this renaissance were Lois Mailou Jones, Aaron Douglas, Hale Woodruff, Palmer Hayden, Archibald Motley, William H. Johnson, Richmond Barthe, and Elizabeth Prophet. These artists did not coalesce into a distinct group until the formation of the Harmon Foundations.

## Early Exhibitions

Black artists at the beginning of this period found it difficult to find space for exhibitions. Often white-owned galleries were segregated, a practice observed throughout the social structure of this country in the beginning of this century. Therefore, space had to be found to display the work of these fledgling artists. The problem was solved by the erection or expansion of public libraries in black communities around the country. These buildings provided the necessary space, due to the generosity of Andrew Carnegie, who maintained a special program for building libraries in black communities as part of his general library building program. These libraries, as well as a network of Y.M.C.A. buildings, provided the opportunity for the exposure of black artists.[30]

The Colored Branches of the International Committee of Young Men's Christian Associations was first organized in 1853. It occupied a prominent position in the cultural life of black communities and colleges during the 1920s. This organization often provided the space for lectures, concerts, exhibitions, and educational programs.[31]

Arthur Schomburg, historian and bibliophile, was the force behind the Carleton Avenue Y.M.C.A. exhibitions. Schomburg was perhaps the greatest collector of books on the history of blacks in the United States, Spain, and Latin America. Born in 1874 in San Juan, Puerto Rico, he journeyed to America in 1891. He worked as a law clerk and researcher for five years and later worked for the Bankers Trust Company of Wall Street as head of the mailing department. But most of his time was spent collecting books, pamphlets, manuscripts, and other items related to the history of black people throughout the world. He traveled to Europe in 1924 to do research and to collect more material. While in Spain he established that two famous Spanish painters, Juan Pareja and Sebastian Gomez, were black.[32] In 1926, with a grant from the Carnegie Foundation, The New York Public Library purchased his collection of books, manuscripts, and artwork for $10,000. These works were placed in the 135th Street Branch that now bears his name.[33]

In 1911, Schomburg founded the Negro Society for Historic Research and appointed William E. Braxton as art director. Later in 1914, Schomburg and John E. Bruce began the Negro Library Association, which cooperated with the Carleton Y.M.C.A. in organizing exhibitions of African and African American art. Exhibitions were also held in 1918, and in 1921 exhibitions that had been held in Brooklyn were now housed in the 135th Street Branch of the New York Public Library. In Harlem the library and the branch of the Y.M.C.A. that was located across the street from it provided facilities for a variety of social, cultural, and political activities. It also held an extensive collection of African and African American materials. Exhibitions held in 1921, 1922, and 1923 had a showing of sixty-five artists with 261 paintings, sculptures and work on paper. While museums and galleries were rejecting these artists on the basis of race, artists' societies and exhibitions whose primary objective was to show the work of black artists were usually supported by institutions whose purposes bridged social and artistic interests.[34]

The black artist also participated in individual exhibitions in the early part of the twentieth century. For example, in 1903 Samuel O. Collins, a landscape painter, organized with Eliza Hawkins a two-person exhibition at his home at 11 Gay Street in Greenwich Village. The sculptor Meta Warrick Fuller was invited to exhibit in group shows at the Pennsylvania Academy of Fine Arts in 1906, 1908, 1920, and 1928. May Howard Jackson also exhibited at the Emancipation Exposition as well as at the Corcoran Gallery in 1915, Veerhoff's Galleries in Washington D.C., in 1919, and at the National Academy of Design in 1916 and 1928.[35]

### The Harmon Foundation

The Harmon Foundation was created in 1922 by William E. Harmon, philanthropist and real estate magnate. The purpose of the award was to stimulate interest in self-improvement and character development. By late 1925, he and his foundation had been convinced by Alain Locke and George Edmund Haynes to give a considerable sum to endow the William E. Harmon awards for black achievement. In December 1925 the foundation announced that it would award annually to blacks two prizes—a gold medal and $400 to the winners and a bronze medal and $100 to the runner-up. The categories included literature, fine arts, science, education, industry, religion, and music. In January 1928 the foundation sponsored its first all-black exhibition at the International House in New York City. The gold award winner was Archibald Motley.[36]

Each year the jury consisted of five experts, including one black juror. Artists were required to present examples of work executed within the last year and also provide letters of recommendation, biographical information, and a recent photograph. Applications could be obtained at Dr. Haynes' office at the Council of Churches. The jurors were unpaid but were reimbursed for travel expenses. The outcome of this condition resulted in a selection of judges who lived either in New York City or within easy commuting distance. Over the years the group came to include a number of well-known American painters and sculptors: Francis C. Jones, Laura Wheeling Waring, Charles Dana Gibson, May Howard Jackson, F. Ballard Blashfield, Charles C. Curran, Arthur Lee, Meta Warrick Fuller, George Luks, and Winold Reiss. Especially during its early years, the Foundation chose well-known artists with strong ties to established institutions such as the National Academy of Design. Francis C. Jones, F. Ballard Williams, Charles C. Curran, and Edwain H. Blashfield were essentially academic figure painters whose aesthetic sensibilities had been formed at the end of the nineteenth century. There was no need to look for innovation or for avant gardism to be praised by these jurors. The portraitist Wayman Adams was a popular choice for conservative businessmen and politicians at the time. As a group, these artists wielded considerable power in the New York art world and often served on juries and advisory committees. Their work and taste emphasized traditional values, which led them into conflict with the early modernists.[37]

The foundation sponsored numerous exhibitions including traveling ones. By 1933 five such exhibitions had been held, and traveling exhibitions of the work of nearly 150 artists had been sent to fifty cities and an audience of more than 150,000 viewers.[38]

The Harmon awards later were criticized for their failure to achieve the goal of helping black artists ease into the mainstream. By the early 1930s, criticism of the annual exhibition focused on the quality of the art and artists. Sometimes professional artists' work was exhibited along with that of amateurs and dilettantes. Aaron Douglas accused the foundation of literally "dragging" people off the streets. While this notion might be far-fetched, there were some legitimate grievances with the foundation. Another argument centered on the exhibition being segregated from mainstream art by holding separate exhibitions, although the reason for this practice was apparent. Romare Bearden criticized the Harmon Foundation for its paternalistic handling of black artists. Nevertheless, the Harmon Foundation was considered one of the most influential organizations contributing financial support to blacks in America.

I have tried in this [essay] to capture some of the moments that eventually became great events in this historical period. Harlem's becoming a "black metropolis," the influx of black immigrants from the south, the influence of DuBois and Washington, the rebellion of the college students, and the imminent impact of World War I, these events, although small in the total picture of American history, become exquisite gems in the setting of the Harlem Renaissance. The visual artists, despite the many barriers they had to face in studying, exhibiting, and selling their work, survived and their work survived. This survival,

above anything else, is reason enough to study and consider their efforts. Adversity is a well-known ailment in the black community, but it is not a fatal condition.

## Notes

1. Henry Drewry and Cecelia H. Drewry, *Afro-American History: Past to Present* (New York: Charles Scribner's Sons, 1971), 358.

2. Gilbert Osofsky, *Harlem: The Making of a Ghetto* (New York: Harper and Row Publishers, 1963), 3.

3. Cary D. Wintz, *Black Culture and the Harlem Renaissance* (Houston: Rice University Press, 1988), 17.

4. Osofsky, 3.

5. *Ibid,* 9.

6. *Ibid,* 11-12.

7. *Ibid,* 13

8. *Ibid,* 87-91.

9. *Ibid,* 92.

10. *Ibid,* 93.

11. *Ibid.*

12. *Ibid,* 96.

13. *Ibid,* 98-104.

14. Richard Barksdale and Keneth Kinnamon, *Black Writers of America: A Comprehensive Anthology* (New York: The MacMillan Company, 1972), 468.

15. Benjamin Quarles, *The Negro in the Making of America* (London: Collier MacMillan Publishers, 1964), 193-4.

16. *Ibid,* 170-1.

17. Arnold Rampersad, *The Art and Imagination of W.E.B. DuBois* (New York: Schoeken books, 1990), 1.

18. Quarles, 172-73.

19. Osofsky, 20.

20. E. Franklin Frazier, *Black Bourgeoisie* (New York: MacMillan Publishing Company, 1962), 62.

21. *Ibid.,* 56-58.

22. David Levering Lewis, *When Harlem Was In Vogue* (New York: Oxford University Press, 1979), 158.

23. *Ibid,* 158.

24. *Ibid,* 159

25. Herbert, Aptheker, *Afro-American History: The Modern Era* (New Jersey, The Citadel Press, 1971), 184.

26. Quarles, 195-96.

27. Nathan Huggins, *Harlem Renaissance* (London: Oxford University Press, 1971), 54-55.

28. Barksdale and Kinnamon, 472.

29. *Ibid,* 474.

30. Gary Reynolds and Beryl J. Wright, *Against the Odds: African American Artists and the Harmon Foundation* (New Jersey: The Newark Museum, 1989), 15.

31. *Ibid.*

32. Bruce Kellner, *The Harlem Renaissance: A Historical Dictionary For the Era* (New York: Methuen, 1987), 317-18.

33. *Ibid,* 16.

34. *Ibid,* 16-17.

35. *Ibid,* 18.

36. Kellner, 156-57.

37. Reynolds and Wright, 30.

38. Kellner, 157.

# SOCIAL AND ECONOMIC FACTORS

## JABULANI KAMAU MAKALANI (ESSAY DATE 1976)

SOURCE: Makalani, Jabulani Kamau. "Toward a Sociological Analysis of the Renaissance: Why Harlem?" *Black World* 25, no. 4 (February 1976): 4-13, 93-97.

*In the following essay, Makalani examines the economic events that allowed Blacks to prosper in Harlem.*

During the decade of the 1920's, a flowering of artistic activity centered in the Black community of Harlem. Such creative spirit had earlier antecedents, but did not become a recognized self-conscious movement until this decade, and while earlier important advances had been made in all Black creative forms (dance, theater, the visual arts, *etc.*), the Harlem Renaissance was primarily a literary movement.[1]

Over time, certain complex socio-historical events combined to create the conditions for a concentration of artists and writers in one location. Linkages (face-to-face communications among artists and the creation of outlets for artistic creativity) developed among them which fostered a group consciousness supported by the consciousness, ethos, and economic prosperity of the Harlem community. Similarly, other factors contributed to the decline of these linkages so that the Harlem Renaissance took on a less self-conscious and locally defined character. Cultural activity among Blacks did not cease, but became more geographically and ideologically dispersed and less symbolic of a singular community (Harlem) ethos.

Certain important questions raised by this artistic movement are:

1. Why should a cultural and artistic flowering be important for Black people at that particular point in history?

2. Who were the primary participants of the Renaissance; where did they come from; why did they come; and what was their involvement, contribution, or impact on Black artistic creativity?

3. Why did this event occur in the northern city of New York, within the community of Harlem?

4. What factors facilitated a communications network among artists and the development of a self-conscious artistic movement? How was this network altered over time and what effects did it have on the character of the movement?

5. How has the Renaissance been characterized in terms of its successes, failures, goals, *etc.*? Have these characterizations been correct? These questions are not exhaustive, but represent some major concerns if one is to understand the sociological significance of the Harlem Renaissance.

The importance to Black people of a cultural and artistic flowering in the decade of the Twenties is based upon the serious disruption and/or destruction of African cultural traditions and institutions, resulting from the historical experiences of colonialism, the Middle Passage and chattel slavery.[2] The Renaissance symbolized the fact that Black people in America, freed from the constraints of chattel slavery, were now able to seriously grapple with the question of culture (a way of life) and a collective direction for themselves. Blacks now had the opportunity to move into colleges and universities and for the first time to create a substantial intellectual class.[3]

Charles S. Johnson, in his extensive study of Black college graduates first published in 1938, provides some valuable information with respect to the rapid growth of the Black intelligentsia. He notes[4] that from all available records from 1826 to 1936, there were 43,821 Black graduates of colleges and professional schools in America. The increase in the number of Black graduates did not really begin until about 1885 (following Reconstruction) and accelerated considerably after 1920. These graduates were distributed between northern colleges and Black colleges in the South. Of the total number of Black graduates (43,821), 14.7 percent (6,424) graduated from northern colleges and 85.3 percent (37,397) graduated from Black colleges in the South.

The largest increase in the number of Blacks graduated from northern and Black colleges occurred from 1920 onward.[5] This increase was without doubt a reflection of Black migration, urbanization, and industrialization. For example, there were more graduaates during the 11 years from 1926 through 1936 than there were during the 100-year period from 1826 to 1925. Between 1920 and 1933, the annual number of Black graduates from northern colleges increased from 156 to 439, an increase of 181 percent. For the same period, the annual number of graduates from Black colleges increased from 497 to 2,486 or 400 percent. There was a decline in the number of graduates listed for the years 1934, 1935 and 1936, partly because of the Depression and partly because of the difficulty in getting complete reports on graduates for this period.

Besides the accelerated growth of college graduates in the 1920's[6] there was a much higher rate of growth among the number of Black graduates when compared to the rate of growth of all college graduates. In 1920, for example, there were 38,552 bachelors degrees granted by all colleges and 381 degrees granted to Blacks. In 1928, there were 83,065 bachelors degrees granted to all colleges and 1,152 granted to Blacks. Thus, there was a 115.5 percent total increase compared to a 296.9 percent increase for Blacks.

The development of a Black intelligentsia was a significant requisite to the cultural and artistic flowering which took place in Harlem. Much of the biographical material on major writers of this period[7] shows that college training was a primary characteristic. In addition, New York, Illinois, Ohio, and Pennsylvania, respectively, ranked highest in the number of southern-born graduates who went north to live.[8] Thus, we begin to see migratory trends which placed Black intellectuals in the North. In addition, colleges and universities, both Black and white, gained ascendancy as important socializing forces upon Black artists.

Degreed Blacks were undoubtedly more acceptable (legitimate) to white entrepreneurs who controlled artistic markets. The socializing impact of colleges and universities and the demands of European and Euro-American artistic standards required to make one's art acceptable to whites contributed to much of the ambivalence of Black artists concerning their own identities and the direction and character of their art.

Although a definitive statement on this question cannot and will not be attempted here, I contend that at the very least the increase in college-trained Blacks reflected a concomittant increase in Black creative intellectuals (artists) and

symbolized sociological conditions which freed the creative potential of Black people on a larger scale—a creative potential previously stifled by chattel slavery.

* * *

The Harlem Renaissance, a northern and urban phenomenon, could not have taken place without the rapid northern and urban migration of Blacks from the rural South. This migration was the result of certain push-and-pull factors, *i.e.*, the boll-weevil infestation which sharply reduced cotton production, segregation policies, lynchings and other violence perpetrated against Blacks, and increasing job opportunities in the North brought about by wartime requirements for increased industrialization and urbanization.[9] In all likelihood, a decreasing job market in the South (Blacks were tied primarily to the cotton industry) and an expanding job market in the North provided the greatest impetus for Black migration, since few Blacks left the South immediately following the Civil War.[10]

During World War I, the gross national product and manufacturing employment increased by about one-quarter. From 1910 to 1914, European immigration to the United States had averaged over one-million persons per year. This ended in 1916 (a combination of the war and changing immigration laws in the 1920's). When this occurred, labor recruiters were sent into the South to secure Blacks to fill the subsequent shortage of labor.[11] For example, the Pennsylvania Railroad alone brought 12,000 Black men North to maintain tracks and equipment, and 50,000 were counted in Chicago, arriving from the South in an 18-month period from 1917 to 1918. This emigration of Blacks from the South continued after World War I, primarily because of continuing prosperity in the North and economic depression in the South. In fact, during the 1920's, the number of Blacks who left was greater than during the previous decade.[12] Within the northern and western states, the Black population grew more rapidly than in the southern states and there was also a movement to the cities. By 1940, the greatest concentration of Blacks was in the North, in New York and in Chicago.[13]

The experiences of the war, urbanization and northern migration were important factors shaping the lives of Blacks during this period. Those experiences included: 1. rejection by unions, 2. extreme violence from whites as evidenced by the so-called "red summer" of 1919 when race riots occurred in 25 cities,[14] and 3. the war provided a large number of Blacks with the experience of being abroad, where they appeared, for once, to be respected as men.[15]

Employment was a dominant factor in bringing all classes of Blacks North. The writer and artist were attracted to New York because it offered the best publishing opportunities. Downtown major houses such as Alfred A. Knopf, Boni and Liveright, Harper, Viking Press, and Harcourt, Brace were opening up to Black writers.[16] Other attractions were the theaters on Broadway and in Greenwich village and the charisma of Harlem itself.[17]

Once the Black writer/artist reached New York, the only place to live was Harlem. The creation of Black Harlem was only one example of the general development of large, segregated Black communities in many American cities.[18] The creation of a Black community in New York based upon the thousands of Black people streaming into the city during World War I was inevitable. The economic prosperity which followed the war, plus the specific conditions internal to New York and to the Harlem community, resulted in the development of Harlem not only as the largest Black community in America, but also as a uniquely diverse and cosmopolitan community with a developing lifestyle and ethos.[19]

Gilbert Osofsky points out that in the late 19th century (1890's) Harlem was a prosperous white community of luxury and wealth.[20] Three decades prior to this, it had been an isolated and poor community. Paralleling the general development and prosperity of New York, Harlem was transformed into New York's first suburb. This prosperity was the result of an urban revolution characterized by improvements in the methods of transportation, sanitation, water supply, communication lighting and building. The expansion of New York's population (in 1880 the population of Manhattan alone passed the one million mark—1,164,673) coincided with an expansion of business and industrial activity. This expansion created the need for people to move beyond New York's bustling inner core, and Harlem was to become a choice residential section.

One obstacle to Harlem's development in the early nineteenth century had been its distance from lower Manhattan. However, the expansion of subway routes into Harlem between 1879 and 1881 solved much of this problem. The character of Harlem began to change when a rash of land speculation and over-construction of apartment

buildings was brought on by an anticipation of new subway routes in the 1890's. Not enough people were attracted to the area, and landlords began to compete for tenants, cutting rents.

It was this period that created the conditions for Blacks to gain a foothold in Harlem.

> The individuals and companies that were caught in Harlem's rapidly deflated real estate market were threatened with financial ruin. Rather than face destruction, some landlords and corporations were willing to rent their houses to Negroes and collect the traditionally high rents that colored people paid. Others, instead of accepting their losses, used the threat of bringing in Negro

tenants to frighten their neighbors into buying them out at a higher than market price . . . Negroes offered decent living accommodations for the first time in the city's history, "flocked" to Harlem and filled houses as fast as they were open to them.[21]

Johnson[22] points out that the move to Harlem by Blacks was largely engineered by Philip A. Payton, a Black real-estate man. Payton was determined to obtain better housing for Black people in New York. This "became the dominating idea of his life, and he worked on it as long as he lived." Payton approached landlords and presented them with the proposal to fill their empty houses. Thousands of Blacks poured into Harlem each month, creating a physical pressure for room. New York was riding on a wave of prosperity. Newcomers found work as fast as they arrived at wages they had never dreamed of before. There was plenty of money for renting and for buying property, which Blacks did with rampant contagion.[23]

> In 1914 Negroes lived in at least 1,100 different houses within a twenty-three block area of Harlem. The Negro population of Harlem was then conservatively estimated at just under 50,000—the entire Negro population of Manhattan in 1910 had been 60,534. By 1920 the section of Harlem bordered by 130th Street on the south, 145th Street on the north, and west of Madison and Fifth Avenue to Eighth Avenue was predominantly Negro—and inhabited by some 80,000 people. . . . By 1930 Negro Harlem had reached its southern limit, 110th Street—the northern boundary of Central Park. Its population was then approximately 200,000.[24]

The white residents of Harlem showed little concern about the expansion of Blacks into their community until they began to spread west and across Lenox Avenue.[25] Whites took steps to block this expansion by formulating a financial concern with the expressed purpose of purchasing from the Hudson Realty Company all property occupied by Blacks and then evicting them. Payton responded by organizing the Afro-American Realty Company, which would buy and lease houses to be let to Black tenants. This held whites in check for several years. However, the Afro-American Realty Company lacked large amounts of capital and became defunct. Nevertheless, several Black individuals carried on.

> Philip A. Payton and J. C. Thomas bought two five-story apartments, dispossessed the white tenants, and put in coloured ones. John B. Nail bought a row of five apartments and did the same. St. Philips Episcopal Church, one of the oldest and richest coloured congregations in New York, bought a row of thirteen apartments on One Hundred and Thirty-Fifth Street between Lenox and Seventh Avenues and rented them to coloured

> tenants. . . . They [whites] felt that Negroes as neighbors not only lowered the values of their property, but also lowered their social status. Seeing that they could not stop the movement, they began to flee. . . . The presence of a single coloured family in a block, regardless of the fact that they might be well bred people, with sufficient means to buy their new home, was a signal for precipitate flight.[26]

Harlem's white residents[27] organized formal opposition to Black settlement through a number of local associations of landlords. Some were committees representing individual blocks and others were community-wide in structure. Between 1907 and 1915, the last years in which there was significant organized opposition to Black settlement, a number of protective associations were founded. Property owners on West 140th, 137th, 136th, 131st, 130th, 129th (in descending order as the Black community spread southward, and along the avenues), signed agreements not to rent to Blacks for 10 or 15 years. All of these efforts eventually failed because no single organization was able to gain total support of all white property owners in the neighborhood.

Once the takeover of Harlem was complete, it exhibited a uniqueness absent from other Black ghettos. Harlem was not a slum, but a symbol of prosperity and elegance. For the first time, Black people in New York were able to live in decent housing in a respected neighborhood. As a result, Harlem became a magnet attracting all types of Black-owned and Black-oriented economic, social and political organizations within its boundaries.

> Practically every major Negro institution moved out of its downtown quarters and came to Harlem by 1920: churches, insurance companies, small businesses, real estate firms, fraternal orders, settlement houses, social service agencies, the Y.M.C.A. and Y.W.C.A., branches of the Urban League and N.A.A.C.P. The "Fighting Fifteenth," Harlem's Negro National Guard unit, was outfitted in 1916. Harlem's first Negro assemblyman was elected in 1917. Harlem hospital hired its first Negro nurse and a Negro doctor in 1919.[28]

Harlem remained prosperous, and a multiplicity of institutional structures came to exist within its geographic boundaries. Harlem attracted the African, the West Indian, the southerner, the northerner, the man from the city, the man from the town, the student, the businessman, the artist, the writer, *etc*. Foreign-born Blacks (West Indians and Africans) formed a little less than 20 percent of the total Black population of New York, of which 28,184 lived in the Borough of Manhattan.[29]

Harlem was developing a distinctive way of life which reflected a growing radicalism, a consciousness of Africa and developing cultural styles. For example, the Marshal hotel (reflective of fashionable life on West 53rd Street) became famous as a headquarters for Black talent. The first modern jazz band ever heard in New York was organized there.[30] This band, called the Memphis Students, was a playing, singing, and dancing orchestra which made the first combined major use of banjos, saxophones, clarinets and trap drums. These and other musical innovations made their way to Harlem as New York's Black population shifted to the Harlem community.

Research conducted by Ira De A. Reid (an important Renaissance figure) for the National Urban League showed that there was a rapid growth in the number of religious sects that "studied and practiced esoteric mysteries."[31] The multitude of churches in Harlem was reflective of that institution's role in Black life. Beyond its spiritual and religious function, the church was a social center and a place where Blacks could construct their own reality, exercise power and find self-realization. Churches grew and prospered with the prosperity of Harlem itself and were important contributors to the character of Harlem life.

Harlem had developed a substantial *bourgeois* class, a Black proletariat, an underworld and an intellectual class all within its geographic boundaries. Its spirit was reflected in its street life and developing cultural forms (*e.g.,* jazz, ballroom dancing, *etc.*). During the first two decades of the twentieth century, Harlem had developed an African consciousness,[32] as evidenced by the literature sold on the streets of Harlem and the character of its religious, political, economic and social organizations. Harlem was also a parade ground during the warmer months of the year. No Sunday (parades were not just limited to Sundays) passed without a parade, and almost any excuse was sufficient—"the funeral of a member of the lodge, the laying of a corner-stone, the annual sermon to the order, or just a desire to 'turn out!'"[33]

In the next few years following the war, radicalism flourished in Harlem.[34] Indicative of the spirit of the times, Harlem's famed regiment, the Fifteenth, was shipped out of town when they became enraged over the treatment of one of their men by a white hotel owner (November 12th, 1917). On July 28th, 1917, ten thousand Blacks (men, women and children) silently marched down the streets of New York. This was the famous "Silent Parade," a courageous act, given the violence being perpetrated against Black people dur-

ing this period in history. Radical newspapers such as The Messenger, Challenge, The Voice, The Crusader, The Emancipator and The Negro World either came into existence during this period or took on a new character. The span of time following the war and extending a few years into the Twenties saw the growth of the Garvey movement, the largest modern mass movement to occur among Blacks in America. Conservative estimates of membership in his Harlem-based organization (The Universal Negro Improvement Association) placed the number at three million, and Garvey himself claimed six million.[35]

\* \* \*

By the time whites re-discovered Harlem in the 1920's, it had developed an ethos and an identity created by a history of struggle, radicalism and cultural diversity. It was this historical movement and diversity which created the conditions for the Harlem Renaissance. Whites became fascinated with Harlem's exotic character, and Black creativity became in demand. This concern for Black creativity paralleled a period of questioning by white writers and artists of their own cultural reality, who thus took a closer look at Black life. White interest helped to unlock doors to prestigious publishing houses, since Black creativity now had a market and audience among whites.[36]

Langston Hughes, an important Renaissance writer, relates in his autobiography the changes made in the life of the Harlem community in order to adjust to a newly developed market among whites:

> White people began to come to Harlem in droves. For several years they packed the expensive Cotton Club on Lenox Avenue. But I was never there, because the Cotton Club was a Jim Crow club for gangsters and monied whites. They were not cordial to Negro patronage, unless you were a celebrity like Bojangles. So Harlem Negroes did not like the Cotton Club and never appreciated its Jim Crow policy in the very heart of their dark community. Nor did ordinary Negroes like the growing influx of whites toward Harlem after sundown, flooding the little cabarets and bars where formerly only colored people laughed and sang, and where now the strangers were given the best ringside tables to sit and stare at the Negro customers—like amusing animals in a zoo.[37]

Harlem and its exciting night-life became an important tourist attraction:

> The lindy-hoppers at the Savoy even began to practice acrobatic routines, and to do absurd things for the entertainment of the whites, that probably never would have entered their heads to attempt merely for their own effortless amusement. Some of the lindy-hoppers had cards

printed with their names on them and became dance professors teaching the tourists. The Harlem nights became show nights for the Nordics.[38]

Harlem was in vogue by the 1920's. This fact, combined with developing entrepreneurial support for Black artists and writers, the formal and informal mechanisms for bringing the Harlem writers into face-to-face contact with one another, and the previously mentioned ethos, cultural diversity and segregated geography of Harlem, produced a self-conscious movement called the Harlem Renaissance. The earliest acknowledgement of this movement appears to have been 1924[39]; by 1925 Alain Locke had compiled an edited volume (*The New Negro*) which contained a representative number of Renaissance writers and statements on the philosophy of this movement; and by 1926 one could go to the Renaissance Casino (indicative of the spirit of the times),[40] a favorite spot for practitioners of the Charleston and the Big Apple.

In the days of the 1920's, there were a great many parties given in and out of Harlem which brought Black writers and artists together. In addition, these parties included white writers, artists, celebrities and potential patrons of Black art. The most important party-giver outside of Harlem was Carl Van Vechten, a white writer who had devoted his life to promoting Black writers.[41] James Weldon Johnson, another important Renaissance writer, states, "Carl Van Vechten had a warm interest in colored people before he even saw Harlem. In the early days of the Negro literary and artistic movement, no one in the country did more to forward it than he accomplished in frequent magazine articles and by his many personal efforts in behalf of individual Negro writers and artists."[42] Van Vechten was symbolic of white patronage without which there probably would have been little production of commercial Black art.[43]

In Harlem the most important Black party-giver and promoter of the arts was A'Leilia Walker, heiress to millionaire Madame C. J. Walker (famous for her method of hair care). A'Leilia Walker gave lavish parties which were usually crowded because she wanted to give artists a chance to meet people who could help them. She sought out wealthy men and women who would become patrons and invited agents, producers and publishers to promote their interests in Black artists and writers. Among her other properties she owned a house on 136th Street where she welcomed writers, sculptors, musicians, *etc.* There

were other lesser parties given in and out of Harlem, but Van Vechten and Walker were the most well known and were symbolic of the spirit of the times.

The Crisis and Opportunity magazines, official publications of the National Association for the Advancement of Colored People and the National Urban League, respectively, were important supporters of the Renaissance. During its early stages, these publications provided the greatest exposure for young Black writers. W. E. B. Du Bois (a Harvard-trained sociologist) became editor of The Crisis at its inception in 1910. In an autobiographical sketch, he tells of his desire to promote young Black writers through the pages of Crisis:

> More especially I tried to encourage other Negro writers through the columns of *The Crisis*. In the next few years we published work from Claude McKay, Langston Hughes, Jean Toomer, Countee Cullen, Anne Spencer, Abram Harris, and Jessie Fauset. In 1924, through the generosity of Amy Spingarn, wife of Joel, we were enabled to offer a series of prizes for young Negro writers, and our contemporary, *Opportunity*, organ of the Urban League, offered similar prizes. For several years this competition went until it grew into what has been called the renaissance of Negro literature, late in the twenties.[44]

Similarly, Charles S. Johnson (a University of Chicago-trained sociologist) became editor of Opportunity at its inception in 1923. Johnson immediately moved to promote Black writers and artists through the pages of Opportunity and moved deliberately to bring white publishers and Black writers together.[45] However, Johnson was most successful as an entrepreneur through the literary contests and dinners sponsored by his magazine. The first of the dinners was in 1924. Quoting from the May 1924 issue of Opportunity,

> Interest among the literati in the emerging group of younger Negro writers found an expression in a recent meeting of the Writer's Guild, an informal group whose membership includes Countee Cullen, Eric Walrond, Langston Hughes, Jessie Fauset, Gwendolyn Bennett, Harold Jackman, Regina Anderson, and a few others. The occasion was a "coming out party" at the Civic Club, on March 21 . . . (p. 143).

The entire May 1924 issue of Opportunity was devoted to African Art with special emphasis on the debut of Harlem's young Black writers. At least one scholar of this period[46] has noted that Opportunity captured more of the spirit of the Renaissance than Crisis. The former's pages, from 1924 to the early Thirties, contained many literary and artistic articles. However, Opportunity had a much smaller circulation than The Crisis (*e.g.*, by 1919, Crisis had reached a circulation of 104,000, while Opportunity's peak circulation in 1927 and 1928 was only 11,000).[47]

Following the initial support by these publications, wealthy philanthropist William C. Harmon became one of the first benefactors to recognize this group of young Black writers and in December of 1926, the first Harmon Foundation awards were announced. Thus, by the second decade of the twentieth century, the Harlem writers had acquired entrepreneurial support, a market largely among whites,[48] and a collective self-consciousness.

\* \* \*

The decline of the Harlem Renaissance is usually associated with the Depression of the Thirties. A depressed economy quickly discouraged whites from spending money on the night life of Harlem and from buying the creations of Black writers and artists. Nevertheless, more study is needed on this part of the Renaissance in order to make even preliminary statements on variables specific to Harlem and New York which brought the Renaissance to an end. In all likelihood there was a gradual erosion of the sources of support for Black writers, including their outlets for publication.

In 1928, Charles S. Johnson left as editor of Opportunity to take a position at Fisk university. In addition, Opportunity lost its funding from the Carnegie Foundation and was in financial difficulty. A'Leilia Walker died in 1931; the end of prohibition deprived Harlem of much of its exclusive appeal; and there is some indication that Harlem's writers began to spread out over the country and abroad in pursuit of employment and additional educational opportunities. Finally, some Black artists and writers continued under different sponsorship and promotion, *e.g.*, the W.P.A. and the Communist Party.

In summary, the rise and decline of the Harlem Renaissance were in many ways linked to broader socio-historical events (*e.g.*, World War I, the Depression). However, there were specific and unique determinants to the movement (*e.g.*, the circumstantial development of Harlem as a prosperous community). This study has touched only lightly upon the complexity of events which led to the Harlem Renaissance and makes even more explicit the need for further research. For example, further analysis is needed to assess the relationship between entrepreneurial support and ideological orientations. Also, more data is needed to determine the specific factors which led to the decline of the Renaissance, as well as analyses of the ideologies and the goals of the movement.

## Notes

1. See, for example, *The New Negro,* edited by Alain Locke (New York: Atheneum, 1969), and *Ebony and Topaz* (1927), edited by Charles S. Johnson, for a representative sample of the major writers of this period.

2. See E. Franklin Frazier, *The Negro Family in the United States* (Chicago: University of Chicago Press, 1939).

3. The first Black graduate in America was John Russwurm, who founded the first Black newspaper (*Freedom's Journal*). He graduated from Bowdoin in Maine, in 1826. For 20 years after this, there were only seven more graduates of recognized colleges. In 1860, at the outbreak of the Civil War, there had been only 28.

4. Charles S. Johnson, *The Negro College Graduate* (New York: Negro Universities Press, 1969), pp. 7-21.

5. *Ibid.*, pp. 9-10, 20.

6. *Ibid.*, pp. 10, 20.

7. See Nathan Irvin Huggins, *Harlem Renaissance* (New York: Hill and Wang, 1940).

8. Johnson, *op. cit.*, pp. 54-55.

9. Reynolds Farley, *Growth of the Black Population: A Study of Demographic Trends* (Chicago: Markham Publishing Co., 1970), p. 46.

10. *Ibid.*, p. 44.

11. *Ibid.*, p. 47.

12. *Ibid.*, pp. 47-48. Farley notes (p. 47) that it is difficult to determine the number of Blacks migrating north during the war, but that it was probably much less than the number of immigrants entering the country each year prior to the war. The 1920 census only showed a net emigration from the South of one-half million.

13. *Ibid.*, p. 75.

14. During the first year following World War I, whites lynched 70 Blacks (10 were soldiers still in uniform). Fourteen Blacks were publicly burned—11 while still alive.

15. George E. Kent, "Patterns of the Harlem Renaissance, in *The Harlem Renaissance Remembered,* Arna Bontemps ed. (New York: Dodd, Mead & Co., 1972), p. 31.

16. Richard Barksdale and Kenneth Kinnamon eds., *Black Writers of America: A Comprehensive Anthology* (New York: Macmillan, 1972), p. 471.

17. See Bontemps, *op. cit.*, pp. 1-26, and Warrington Hudlin, "The Renaissance Re-examined," in Bontemps, pp. 268-277.

18. See Gilbert Osofsky, "Harlem: The Making of A Ghetto," in *Harlem, U.S.A.*, John Henrik Clarke ed. (New York: Collier Books, 1946), pp. 7-19.

19. See Locke, *op. cit.*; Osofsky, *op. cit.*; and James Weldon Johnson, *Black Manhattan* (New York: Alfred R. Knopf, 1930).

20. Osofsky, *op. cit.*

21. *Ibid.,* p. 12.

22. James Weldon Johnson, *op. cit.,* pp. 147-148.

23. *Ibid.,* p. 153.

24. Osofsky, *op. cit.,* p. 19.

25. James Weldon Johnson, *op. cit.,* p. 148.

26. *Ibid.,* pp. 149-150.

27. Osofsky, *op. cit.,* pp. 13-16.

28. *Ibid.,* p. 18.

29. W. A. Domingo, "Gift of the Black Tropics," in Locke, *op. cit.,* p. 341.

30. James Weldon Johnson, "Harlem: The Culture Capital," in Locke, *op. cit.,* pp. 302-303.

31. James Weldon Johnson, *Black Manhattan, op. cit.,* p. 165.

32. Richard B. Moore, "Africa-Conscious Harlem," in Clarke, *op. cit.,* pp. 37-56.

33. James Weldon Johnson, *Black Manhattan, op. cit.,* p. 168.

34. *Ibid.,* pp. 233-51.

35. C. L. R. James, *A History of Pan African Revolt* (Washington, D. C.: Drum and Spear Press, 1969), pp. 78-79.

36. See Huggins, *op. cit.;* Kent, *op. cit.;* and Harold Cruse, *The Crisis of the Negro Intellectual* (New York: William Morrow & Co., 1967).

37. Langston Hughes, *The Big Sea: An Autobiography* (New York: Hill and Wang, 1940), p. 225.

38. *Ibid.,* p. 226.

39. Bontemps, *op. cit.,* pp. 1-11.

40. Blanche E. Ferguson, *Countee Cullen and the Negro Renaissance* (New York: Dodd, Mead & Co., 1966), p. 83.

41. Hughes, *op. cit.,* p. 243.

42. James Weldon Johnson, *Along This Way: The Autobiography of James Weldon Johnson* (New York: The Viking Press, 1933), p. 382.

43. Huggins, *op. cit.,* p. 129.

44. W. E. B. Du Bois, *Dusk of Dawn: An Essay Toward an Autobiography of A Race Concept* (New York: Schocken Books, 1968), p. 271.

45. Patrick J. Gilpin, "Charles S. Johnson: Entrepreneur of the Harlem Renaissance," in Bontemps, *op. cit.,* p. 224.

46. *Ibid.,* p. 223.

47. Opportunity was supported by a grant from the Carnegie Foundation, while The Crisis was self-supported.

48. Fire, a shortlived literary magazine, was the only independent Black publication, but folded because of a lack of money (see Hughes, *op. cit.,* p. 235).

## SIDNEY H. BREMER (ESSAY DATE 1996)

**SOURCE:** Bremer, Sidney H. "Home in Harlem, New York: Lessons from the Harlem Renaissance Writers." In *The Harlem Renaissance, 1920-1940: Analysis and Assessment, 1980-1994,* edited by Cary D. Wintz, pp. 1-10. New York: Garland Publishing, 1996.

*In the following essay, Bremer explores Harlem Renaissance writers' relationship with the urban space of Harlem.*

America's mainstream culture has long lodged "home" in the mythic permanency of a rural cottage. There the kinship circle, sense of belonging, and implicit responsibilities that define "home" are tended by a purely white, motherly wife. As an imaginary bulwark against industrial urbanization, this mythic image of home took shape in the nineteenth century's mass periodicals. It later expanded into the small-town Main Streets of Hollywood movies and the privatized suburban fantasies of television. It is an unrealistic, even dangerously deceptive image, as many American authors—from Mark Twain and Charles Chesnutt to Sinclair Lewis to Joyce Carol Oates—have shown. Few of us are wived and familied white men commuting to some privileged space apart. Even for those few, the cottage front hides the complexities of familial and social relations. The rural rootedness of our mythic home ignores, moreover, the predominantly mobile, urban realities of modern American life. Indeed, "movement over a variety of county" may well be Americans' "largest common background," as a wise though little remembered Chicago novelist named Edith Wyatt affirmed as early as 1914; and most of us have been doing our moving and working and living in cities since the 1930 census.

If we are to feel at home in our changing urban world, we need images of home that are more fitting to our experience—not for reasons of sentiment but in order to feel realistically grounded, belonging, and responsible there. We need specifically urban images of home to be able to see ourselves at home with—even when at odds with—our own experience, with others, and with our dreams in cities. First, we need to know the city as a physical home place, with the power to evoke sensory memory, what William Faulkner calls the "memory [that] knows before knowing remembers" (111). Second, we need to recognize that, like it or not, we belong to urban home communities—those families and neighborhoods and birthright groups with which we share our history, images, social circumstances, and physical experience. Third, we need to be able to find a symbolic home for our aspirations in the city, as F. Scott Fitzgerald once could in Edmund Wilson's book-lined New York apartment.

But that homelike "apartment [where] life was mellow and safe" was a city whose *loss* Fitzgerald lamented in his 1932 essay "My Lost City" (25).

Just when cities were becoming de facto home for most Americans, much American literature despaired of an urban "home." It conceded to ethnic minority writers the imaginative home that Walt Whitman had offered for mobile urban Americans when he "loved well those cities" of Manhattan and Brooklyn, with their sensory vitality, embracing crowds, and visionary unities, in "Crossing Brooklyn Ferry" (160-62). The wake of World War I swamped the Progressive dream of a "civic family" that turn-of-the-century Chicago's residential writers like Henry Blake Fuller, Edith Wyatt, and Elia Peattie had shared with Jane Addams (Bremer 39). It also upset the thrust toward realistic comprehension and technological progress that had mitigated the newcomer's reaction to the city's strangeness in turn-of-the-century works by William Dean Howells, Theodore Dreiser, Upton Sinclair, Henry James, and others. Only the latter group's alienating images survived in the Euro-American vision of the living-dead megalopolis—its physical landscape reduced to a "valley of ashes," its society and psyches to grotesque "fragmentation," and its dreams to "gruesomely preserved" artifacts and mass-produced clichés (Fitzgerald, *Great Gatsby* 23; Dos Passos, qtd. in Wagner 63; Wharton 50; West). The megalopolitan world epitomized by these images of Greater New York offers no home to the human body, social spirit, or soul.

But our literature does include an alternative stream of urban imagery. During those same megalopolitan 1920s, some of New York's most powerful ethnic minority writers bravely claimed the city—at least, their neighborhood microcosm of the city—as a home for the transient outcasts of American society. Like the Jewish immigrants crowded into the Lower East Side before them, Harlem's African American newcomers constituted a critical mass large enough to sustain a subculture and to achieve high visibility. Harlem, too, had its own cultural resources of language, folkways, and ritual aesthetic forms. Although seriously compromised by poverty, undependable white patronage, and a colonized color consciousness, Harlem also had its own cultural institutions—political organizations, clubs and cafés and theaters, newspapers, and places of worship. Like the Lower East Side, it was touted as a "city within a city" (Cahan 51; White 187; see also Ellison 122). Like Jewish immigrants from the pogroms of Eastern Europe, too, Harlem's migrants from the Jim Crow South viewed the city as a "promised land"—as Jewish American Mary Antin also proclaimed Boston in the title of her 1912

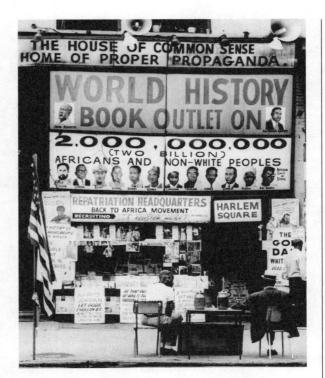

Harlem bookstore, known as the "House of Common Sense and the Home of Proper Propaganda," hosting the registration for the Back-to-Africa movement.

autobiography and as Claude Brown, a second-generation Harlem autobiographer, confirmed even in 1965 in *Manchild in the Promised Land*. Brown referred to that vision with some conscious irony, however. For Harlem's African Americans, like the Jews before them, were also subject to continuing minority exclusions—not only from American society's daily goods and powers but also from such common dreams as the sentimental, rural-cottage image of home. So they were predisposed to a critical perspective on the dominant cultural values that World War I had bankrupted. Indeed, as in Jewish American literature, a strong tension between hope and oppression grounds the Harlem Renaissance vision of urban neighborhood-ghetto as a home away from home.

The writers of the Harlem Renaissance were an extremely mobile crew, who felt joined, not estranged, by their wanderings, because they were part of the great migration of black people to the urban Northeast around World War I. Collectively they developed a vision of an urban home that was at once an organic place, a birthright community, and a cultural aspiration. In all three of these dimensions, the vitality of their home reached out even across continents joined in oppression. And Harlem, New York, their capital city within a city, was the center. Whether or not they happened to be living there at any particular time, the Harlem Renaissance writers regarded Harlem as their primary, symbolic home. Thus their Harlem focused an exemplary attempt to make a home for modern urban transients.[1] Their lives and works tried Harlem's strengths as well as its limitations as home place, community, and aspiration. Their Harlem Renaissance was a civic, as well as an aesthetic, enterprise.

Nearly all the Harlem Renaissance writers were urban wanderers. Even those who were raised in small towns came to Harlem via other cities—Northerner W. E. B. Du Bois from the faculty of Atlanta University, Southerner Zora Neale Hurston from service as a manicurist in Washington, DC, Westerner Wallace Thurman from the post office in Los Angeles. Young Langston Hughes arrived from Cleveland, Nella Larsen from Chicago, Rudolph Fisher from Washington, DC, Dorothy West from Boston; and before them, James Weldon Johnson came from Jacksonville, Walter White from Atlanta, Jessie Fauset from Philadelphia, and Claude McKay from Kingston, Jamaica. They were from cities and on the move.

In fact, the best publicized "New Negro" leaders of the Harlem Renaissance were more often away than in residence during the 1920s: Claude McKay took off in 1922 for a twelve-year vagabondage through major cities of Europe and Africa; loyal Langston Hughes just kept coming back from sea or college for Harlem weekends, vacations, and special occasions; and Countee Cullen, the only leader of the Harlem Renaissance raised in New York City, was away over half the time at Harvard, then in Paris. So many Renaissance Harlemites flocked to Paris that Alain Locke once called it a "transplanted Harlem."[2] Even for the senior writers who were also political organizers, editors, and its most stable residents, Harlem was a rather brief hegira. Nearly all, young and old alike, had moved on by 1932, as the Depression stripped away the Jazz Age excess to expose Harlem's underlying poverty.

The writers' urban wanderlust, however, only increased their identification with Harlem as the hub of a dynamic world. Harlem was the goal of many African American migrants in the 1910s and 1920s, collecting over 200,000 black residents by 1930. Because the city's economy was service-oriented rather than industrial, Manhattan did not draw the predominantly rural, unskilled blacks who migrated to other Northern cities. The new Harlemites, like their writers, came mostly from other cities—one-fourth from the West Indies, like McKay and Arthur Schomburg (J. W. Johnson, *Black Manhattan* 14-53; C. S. Johnson 279). And they came because Harlem was the symbolic center of African America generally—the "Negro Capital" or "Mecca" or "Promised Land," as it was variously dubbed.

Indeed, Harlem's symbolic status knew few circumstantial limits. Wherever they might be, the wandering citizens of Harlem felt its presence whenever they came into contact with its characteristic textures, persons, or arts. Distance could even increase African Americans' sense of identification with Harlem, as a place to go to or aspire to or think toward. McKay published his superb 1928 novel, *Home to Harlem,* from abroad, then wrote Hughes in 1930, "I am thinking of coming home next fall or winter. I write of America as home [although] I am really a poet without a country."[3] Longing from abroad for the "refuge" of an American city's Black Belt (*Long Way* 304), McKay could see a home in America where he had previously seen only imperial oppression. And he identified America-as-home specifically with Harlem, whereas he had previously associated America-as-oppressor with the surrounding city of New York—for instance, in his 1922 poem "The White City" (*Harlem Shadows* 23). Thus in tension with the oceanic reach of Harlem's symbolic home, New York implicitly defined Harlem's limits for McKay. In this imagistic distinction between Harlem and New York, he was profoundly visionary, as we shall see.

McKay was typical in his use of sensory images to present Harlem as home place. In Harlem Renaissance literature, African America's capital city is organic, not mechanical. It is fleshy—and embodied in lively colors, tastes, and sounds. This basic organicism is the first noteworthy strength of Harlem as home. Its sensory elements are basic enough to be found anywhere and portable enough to go anywhere, although they concentrate most vividly in Harlem's streets. The organicism of Harlem's street life is life-giving, too. More earthy than its perversions in Anglo-American exotica, this Harlem is nurturing as well as sexually exciting. When McKay's fictional double in *Home to Harlem,* Jake Brown, longs back to Harlem from abroad, he longs for the sexual edibles that its streets offer: "Fifth Avenue, Lenox Avenue, and One Hundred and Thirty-fifth Street, with their chocolate-brown and walnut-brown girls, were calling him" (5). While McKay's masculinist fantasy of women as food offers a troubling glimpse into the sexual politics of the Harlem Renaissance, its sensory intensity was embraced by his female compatriots, too. Another major work also published in 1928, Nella Larsen's novel *Quicksand*, similarly describes its heroine's "magic sense of having come home" in Harlem "as if she were tasting some agreeable, exotic food . . ." (65). So Harlem's street life excites and feeds its homecoming participants—as it also gave life's breath to Langston Hughes on his arrival there in 1921: "At every subway station I kept watching for the sign: 135TH STREET. When I saw it, I held my breath. . . . I went up the steps and into the bright September sunlight. Harlem! I looked around. Negroes everywhere! . . . I took a deep breath and felt happy again" (*Big Sea* 81). A rather basic equation: Harlem's streets = sex + food + breath = life-giving home.

In its organic embodiedness, Harlem as home denies the mainstream American image of the city as a machine boxed off from nature. Its urban streets are continuous with Walt Whitman's "Song of the Open Road" (1855)—just as sensory and dynamic, connecting rural with urban folk life and generating new life in the city. The Harlem Renaissance writers simply did not share in America's standard idealization of the countryside—as a rural home to be held especially dear and apart from the alien city. Few of the Harlem Renaissance writers had had childhood homes in any rural places or small towns, nostalgic memories of which they might find hard to shake. Conversely and collectively, the historical memory of slavery had soured all of them on America's rural past. It is perhaps not surprising, then, that they challenged America's cultural habit of rural nostalgia.

But it is surprising that they affirmed the pastoral values of organic energy and Edenic belonging that the pastoral tradition associated with rural settings, that they brought those values into the urban setting of Harlem, and that, in the process, they undercut assumptions about urban artificiality and alienation. Those assumptions were undoubtedly reinforced by the personal and historical experience of many African Americans under the domination of whites in urban as well as rural America. Nonetheless the countercultural experience of organic vitality in Harlem was powerful—and reinforced by two academic movements, which Du Bois and Alain Locke led and younger renaissance writers like Hurston, Hughes, and Cullen followed: the aesthetic cult of African primitivism and the anthropological exploration of African American folklore. Each of these schools of thought located organic vitality not in a particular setting but in the people themselves, in a racial heredity of primitivism or in an ethnic heritage of song and story. Together with the Harlem Renaissance writers, they simultaneously extended and challenged the pastoral tradition by suggesting that its values of organic energy and belonging are more a matter of inner human development than of external environments. Thus the vision of Harlem as home brings the transcendent power of the pastoral to bear on city life.

The very streets of Harlem come to life with human personalities in the third great Harlem Renaissance novel of 1928, *The Walls of Jericho,* by Rudolph Fisher. Fifth Avenue is a "fallen" aristocrat above 125th Street; Seventh Avenue is a "promenade" of "triumphant" Sunday churchgoers in all their "self-righteousness"; and fictitious Court Avenue, where "dicty" middle-class Harlemites live, is "a straight, thin spinster" (3-4, 44-45, 188-89). In all their variety, these streets are both home to Harlem residents and Harlem residents themselves, at home there. "Such skillful humanization of inanimate objects" (Singh 86) breaks down the distinction between human beings and their urban environment. It envelops people in an organic vitality that is compatible, even coterminous with their physical and emotional life.

The streets of the Harlem Renaissance are indeed magical in their sensory life-force. Like totems, they are repeatedly invoked by name and imbued with transcendent power in Harlem Renaissance literature. Gathering together the life of the folk, parading it, and publicizing it abroad, they transcend limits of place—making Harlem an "[i]sland within an island, but not alone," as Hughes later wrote in a poem he sent to McKay in 1943 ("Broadcast to the West Indies"). Harlem's streets transcend time and weather, too. Seventh Avenue especially accomplishes this feat. The parade of dark skins on Seventh Avenue makes "the frigid midwinter night . . . warmer," while the "rainbow" hues of its costumes make the noontime "sun grin . . . more brightly" at two important points in the first black mystery novel, *The Conjure-Man Dies,* written by Rudolph Fisher and published in 1932 (3, 86-87). A Seventh Avenue parade of organic, colorful vitality appears in almost every Harlem Renaissance novel. In other Harlem streets, too, children's dances promise future life and inspire art, as Jessie Fauset's novel *There Is Confusion* (1924) and Wallace Thurman's short story "Terpsichore in Harlem" (1930?) both insist.

Filled with children as well as adults, women as well as men, Harlem's streets are a neighborhood extension of family life and generation. That does not mean that the Harlem streets are happy—any more than families are always happy. But they are alive, generative. In explicit, repeated contrast to the deadening subway machines and dwarfing skyscraper streets of Anglo New York, Harlem's streets are defined by people walking. They are a "stream of life" in Fauset's 1929 novel, *Plum Bun* (97; cf. 87), "rivers" in Larsen's *Quicksand* (253). Even death confirms the generativity of life, as blues spawn the laughter of jazz and street life spills into the cabarets in Langston Hughes's first book of poems, *The Weary Blues* (1925).

Beyond Hughes's lyrics, however, the open-ended vitality of the streets rarely breaks into Harlem's interior spaces, those overcrowded containers where sensory richness becomes sensory overload. In the cabaret and rent-party scenes that are as standard as street parades in Harlem Renaissance literature, the many colors and edibles and sounds become kaleidoscopic, dizzying, explosive. Harlem's churches, too, can get caught up in this confusion. They regularly mix spiritual with sensory vitality—dangerously so in Nella Larsen's deep *Quicksand*. There the heroine is self-divided—both Danish American and African American—and unable to express her full life in the race pride that Harlem's streets celebrate. Accelerating into a "torrent" of passion, the streets' "rivers" of organic life sweep her into a storefront church, where she is welcomed as a "scarlet 'oman" and lured into wild "rites" that drain her spiritual resources for merely physical ends (253-63).

Perhaps the Harlem Renaissance women saw most clearly the power of Harlem's organic vitality of place to enslave people in merely sensory existence (see Carby 170-75). But the men reluctantly recognized, too, that Harlem was finally not open-ended but materially bound—a promised land in a ghetto. As their white fellow traveler Carl Van Vechten spelled it out in the title of his 1926 novel, Harlem's sensory surfaces might seem like "nigger heaven," but "nigger heaven" was slang for the segregated back balconies that African Americans had to occupy in theaters. So Van Vechten's hero protests:

> Nigger Heaven! That's what Harlem is. We sit in our places in the gallery of this New York theatre and watch the white world sitting down below in the good seats in the orchestra. Occasionally they turn their faces up towards us, their hard, cruel faces, to laugh or sneer, but they never beckon. It never seems to occur to them that Nigger Heaven is crowded, that there isn't another seat, that something has to be done.
>
> (149)

Enforced crowding: that was the prison in which the Harlem Renaissance paraded its colors and music, the ghetto that was the "Negro Capital" of America, the source of the tears in Harlemites' laughter.

Van Vechten's black friends objected that he was giving away "family secrets."[4] And so he was. The Harlem Renaissance writers walked a delicate line. While emphasizing the fertile dirt in which their dreams grew, they resisted recognizing the extent to which white ghettoization limited the spread of Harlem's sensory vitality, even turned it back on itself. Instead they asserted the magic of that vitality and its sole dependence on their own community.

For that sensory power could be carried wherever—albeit only where—black people could congregate. It was part and parcel of their birthright community. And Harlem as home was as much a locus of communal association—its second noteworthy strength—as a place of residence for them. As a community to which they belonged by right of birth, Harlem anchored the personal contacts and the institutions that linked its artists to its political activists, librarians, partygoers, even gangsters, and just plain folks. Those communal associations were what kept them coming back to be grounded in its sensory life. Human community was the germ of that life. So the Southern-born author of its first generation, James Weldon Johnson, implied in 1931 when he proclaimed himself "a New Yorker" by a kind of "blood tie," because his "father and mother met in this city" (Speech 2).

Especially did street blues and jive and jazz and sermons express that community. Johnson, Hughes, and Fisher made these rhythms into the central stuff of their literary art. Many Harlem Renaissance writers appended glossaries of "Harlemese" to their novels as regularly as they included Seventh Avenue parades and cabarets and rent parties. But *The Walls of Jericho* showed that the lively idiom of Harlem's community also hid Harlem's full humanity. As Fisher's text explained, "[b]eneath the jests, the avowed fear, the merriment, was a characteristic irony, a markedly racial tendency to make light of what actually was grave" (29)—namely, the social separation of blacks from whites, of Harlem from the rest of New York City, of a part of humanity from the whole. This separation was the most serious limitation on Harlem as home.

The walled city is Fisher's synthesizing metaphor for these communal limits. It stands for both the divided city of Harlem, New York, and for the divided self. Fisher's streetwise hero, Joshua Jones, brashly yet stereotypically nicknamed Shine, describes the biblical outlines of the story:

> Well, this Joshua thought he was the owl's bowels, till one day he run up against a town named Jericho. Town—This place was a flock o' towns. It was the same thing to that part o' the country that New York is to this. . . . But try and get in. This burg has walls around it so thick that the gals could have their jazz-houses on top. . . . And here this red hot papa, Joshua, who's never had his damper turned down yet—here he is up against that much wall—and the damn thing don't budge.
>
> (181-82)

He continues his namesake's story until the walls come tumbling down, but he doesn't report to his street buddies the still deeper lesson drawn from it in the church service he attended with his fiancée. There the minister explained:

> You, my friend, are Joshua. You have advanced through a life of battle. . . . And then you find yourself face to face with a solid blank wall—a wall beyond which lies the only goal that matters—the land of promise.
>
> Do you know what that goal is? It is the knowledge of man's own self.
>
> (186-87)

Wrapped up in Harlem's jive, Joshua had been walled off from himself. The segregation of one part of humanity from another is not just an external division, then; it divides each part internally too. Not only is Harlem divided from Greater New York, Fisher reveals; Harlem is self-divided as well. And so, by implication, is the rest of New York.

That canker at the root of this home community also limits Harlem's effectiveness as a home of dreams. Zora Neale Hurston explained the aspirations of the Harlem Renaissance in specifically urban terms in 1934: it sought to find the "fabulous cities of artistic concepts . . . within the mind and language of some humble Negro." As itself a "fabulous city of artistic concepts," Harlem was also home to its writers in this sense: it expressed African America's cultural aspirations in public voice. As a literary center, the wellspring of a creative movement its writers proclaimed a renaissance, and as a recurring, central subject in their art, Harlem offered them this third, spiritual home strength. In celebrating the organic place and community of Harlem in fiction, poetry, plays, autobiographies, and histories, they were simultaneously realizing, and reflecting on, Harlem as an expression of their creative spirit.

As Harlem's sensory life and communal rituals were both expressive and ghettoized, however, so its dreams were both profound and deceptive. For the most part, Harlem Renaissance writers accepted the ambiguities of make-believe. Rather than aspire to some unvarnished truth, the renaissance writers offered Harlem's own self-dramatization in place of racist stereotypes imposed from without. They considered the make-believe of the "signifying monkey" (Gates 286-88) part of Harlem's home power to generate art and symbolize aspiration. *Quicksand, The Walls of Jericho,* and most other Harlem Renaissance novels explicitly embrace the fusions of truth and pretense—even of paradise and damnation—in the rites of storefront churches and the rhythms of cabarets. It seems as wonderful as it is awful that Wallace Thurman's heroine in *The Blacker the Berry* (1929) could not "tell whether the cast was before or behind the proscenium arch" in the Lafayette Theater, what with all "the spontaneous monkey shines" of the audience and "stereotyped antics of the hired performers" (202-03). Such Harlem Renaissance literature presents Harlem as a masquerade.

In some sense, any art is a masquerade—the more deceptive the more profound, as Vladimir Nabokov argues over and over in his expatriate novels. Insofar as Harlem Renaissance literature recognizes and even celebrates the mix of sex and soul, of jazz and blues, of promise and limitation, of truth and deception in the heart of Harlem, it offers an image of home wondrously adequate to the ambiguities of human life. Insofar as the Harlem Renaissance writers recognize that they are both a divided and a connected people—and ritualize that tragicomedy in their art—they are closer to the home truth of modern life than are other Americans who think that home is undivided, simple, and pure.

But that home truth needs its special place in the human community. As aspiration gave boundary-breaking meaning to Harlem as sensory place and birthright community, so the place and community legitimized Harlem as home vision in Harlem Renaissance art. Not to be rescued *from* poverty or the people, Harlem's aspirations were viewed as living *in* its poverty and people. Indeed, painter Aaron Douglass proclaimed the primary goal of the Harlem Renaissance to achieve the "spiritually earthy" quality of "mediating between dung and God."[5] In their Harlem home, dreams were rooted in the dirt and grit of physical and communal life—and could be ruined there, too, as Douglass's close friend Langston Hughes would dramatize forty years later, in his most famous poem, by figuring forth "a dream deferred" as spoiled food and broken skin.

The three dimensions of Harlem as home—place, community, aspiration—needed one another. And unfortunately, Harlem as place, community, and aspiration was finally limited by Greater New York. A civic as well as an aesthetic moment, the Harlem Renaissance realized both the strengths and the limitations of home in Harlem, New York. But its Anglo-American compatriots did not. And that Anglo-American failure was both civic and aesthetic, too. In particular, the artistic aspirations of the Harlem Renaissance were often denied place and citizenship in Greater New York—even by friends, and even in the name of art itself. Such civic denial was the outcome when Carl Van Vechten had his way with money raised to memorialize James Weldon Johnson.

James Weldon Johnson had already written the first black New York novel, *The Autobiography of an Ex-Coloured Man* (1912), coauthored African America's "national anthem," "Lift Every Voice," and served as United States consul to Venezuela and Nicaragua, when he moved north from Jacksonville, Florida, in 1914 to "become a citizen of New York." He came to regard the city as "home," and he continued to do so even after he moved on to Nashville in 1931. He felt related to the city as a godson might or as if the bond were even "closer to a blood tie" (J. W. Johnson, Speech 2). In New York he assumed leadership of the NAACP—as its first black executive secretary—in time to help act out the "cherished belief" he shared with so many others of the renaissance, that African American art could "destroy race prejudice" by presenting "the Negro as a creator and a contributor to American civilization."[6] As he had written Walter White a few years earlier, art "is the approach that offers the least friction" (qtd. in Waldron 116). But Harlem Renaissance art may have gone so far so smoothly only because, in the last analysis, as Angela Davis has also recently argued (21), Anglo-Americans continue to separate art from civics—and in the process, continue to deny art's full power.

When Johnson died in 1938, Van Vechten, his literary executor, formed the James Weldon Johnson Memorial Committee, including Johnson's honorary pallbearers and other luminaries like Mayor La Guardia, W. E. B. Du Bois, Eleanor Roosevelt, Langston Hughes, Duke Ellington, and Marian Anderson. They adopted an idea proposed by Harlem sculptor Augusta Savage, that a statue be erected at Seventh Avenue and 110th

Street—at the corner of Central Park "where Harlem meets the rest of Manhattan," Hughes later explained in a 1941 fund-raising appeal.[7]

Johnson's widow, Grace Nail Johnson, was particularly emphatic about this "large N. Y. idea," "this civic expression," and she proposed that the monument be inscribed with a poem that Johnson had sent his dear friend Van Vechten back in 1925, "wonder[ing]," as he put it then, "if we love the city in about the same way." "My City," his widow now wrote, was the poem in which he had "declared" New York his "home."[8] "My City" is typical of the Harlem Renaissance in locating the organic energy and belonging associated with "home" in an urban, as contrasted with a rural, setting. It is unusual in extending that imagery beyond the city's black neighborhoods to embrace all Manhattan:

> "MY CITY"
> When I come down to sleep death's endless
>     night,
> The threshold of the unknown dark to cross,
> What to me then will be the keenest loss,
> When this bright world blurs on my fading
>     sight?
> Will it be that no more I shall see the trees
> Or smell the flowers or hear the singing birds
> Or watch the flashing streams or patient herds?
> No. I am sure it will be none of these.
>
> But, ah! Manhattan's sights and sounds, her
>     smells,
> Her crowds, her throbbing force, the thrill that
>     comes
> From being of her a part, her subtle spells,
> Her shining towers, her avenues, her slums—
> O God! the stark, unutterable pity,
> To be dead, and never again behold my city!
>                                 (*Saint Peter* 37)

But Van Vechten proposed instead that the monument be inscribed with Johnson's sonnet to African American artists, "O Black and Unknown Bards"; and the Committee for a James Weldon Johnson Memorial adopted that idea at a meeting attended by only six committee members, all men.[9] The same meeting endorsed the Harlem-Manhattan location proposed by Augusta Savage but chose African American Richmond Barthé to sculpt an allegorical statue quite different from the representational death mask of Johnson that Savage had already completed. These decisions limited the civic dimensions of the project and turned it toward more abstract aesthetic ends. And it is quite possible that the men who made the decisions lacked some more profound respect for embodiment—in place and in human form—that Grace Johnson and Augusta Savage shared as women. Toni Morrison has recently suggested such a gendered sensitivity by describing her own "strong sense of place . . . [of] the mood of the community":

> I think some of it is just a woman's strong sense of being in a room, a place, or a house. Sometimes my relationship to things in a house would be a little different from, say, my brother's or my father's or my sons'. I clean them and I move them and I do very intimate things "in place": I am sort of rooted in it. . . .
>
> (167-68)

In any case, New York City's powerful park commissioner, Robert Moses, jammed the whole works. In 1941 he rejected the proposal to site Barthé's allegorical nude at Seventh Avenue and 110th Street—because, he proclaimed, the statue would be a bad influence on the children of Harlem. In 1942 Moses suggested placing the statue inside Central Park—near a Puerto Rican and black area where "no white man or dicty Negro has ever set foot," Van Vechten objected. Then Moses suggested saving the statue for a proposed postwar housing project deep inside Harlem, since World War II had made it impossible to divert metal from guns to statues anyhow. When Moses finally did agree to the original proposal in late 1945, the costs of casting had increased far beyond the funds that had been raised before the war.[10] That blow sounded the death knell for the statue. It would have been the first public monument to a black person in the city of New York.

But that is not the end of the story. In 1941, just before the committee approached Moses, Van Vechten took up another, related cause. He discovered that Yale University did not have "any Negro books at all"; and Yale, he wrote the memorial committee's secretary, Walter White, was "in the thickest part of the collegiate world." When Van Vechten later concurred with Moses that a statue was "rather a waste of time" and finally "decided to do something else" himself—as he recalled in a 1960 Columbia oral-history interview ("Reminiscences" 344-45)—he chose not only to endow a literary archive rather than a public statue but also to separate what became the James Weldon Johnson Memorial Collection from the thickest part of the African American world, a Harlem home. Van Vechten determined that Harlem's Schomburg Collection, purchased by the New York Public Library in 1926, was "already . . . outstanding" and not in need of help (unlike poor Yale?). He also opted for Yale's commitment to archival preservation to perpetuate "the fame of the Negro" and against the Schomburg Center's commitment to "dissemination and widespread use" of black literature (Hutson 17) in "the largest Negro city in the world"—where "the black masses can read and follow in [their forebears'] footsteps," as Arthur Schomburg put the case for the New York Public Library's Harlem branch.[11]

The decisions of Anglo-Americans Robert Moses and Carl Van Vechten, then, finally denied Johnson's public citizenship—his home—in greater New York. So his statue was not built, and he was memorialized in an academic library away from the city he claimed as home. Similarly, the Harlem Renaissance itself has been treated more often as a merely aesthetic moment rather than as a civic enterprise, too—and its image of home has consequently been ignored. Cut off from the surrounding island of New York, Harlem could only be an imperfect home to African Americans—and no home at all to other mobile, urban Americans. Segregated from and subordinated to Greater New York, the sensory place, the birthright community, and the cultural aspirations that Harlem expressed as home could not be fully joined. When New York lost the 110th Street statue of James Weldon Johnson, it lost a complex symbol for celebrating Harlem's uniqueness and Harlem's connection to Greater New York. Today, too, when we treat Harlem's art apart from that art's place and community, we obscure the power and poignancy of its vision of Harlem as home.

The Harlem of renaissance literature and life nonetheless offers us important suggestions for making our cities home for mobile Americans. Its street forms dramatize the power of crowded open-ended spaces—of continuities and possibilities, rather than of separations and end points. Filled with the generative energy of people of both sexes and all ages, its central streets overflow with sensory accents too—vivid colors, tastes, and sounds that celebrate pedestrian interaction. That sensory base helps to enhance and celebrate group identities—in ways that are transferable to other places. The community includes artists as self-dramatizing, masquerading participants in all this—and encourages them to reflect on its meaning. Harlem's opening and enriched place, its celebrant community groups, and its arts all interconnect, moreover. For the Harlem Renaissance writers essayed to make Harlem their home in all these ways at once. If not in their own segregated lives, then at least within the works of their civic art, Harlem did give its people "that magic sense of having come home."

## Notes

1. See Houston Baker's admiring description of *The New Negro* as an "inscription of Afro-American modernity in mass, urban, national, and international terms" (83).

2. Alain Locke, letter to Langston Hughes, 2 Sept. 1926, Hughes Papers, James Weldon Johnson Memorial Collection, Beinecke Library, Yale U.

3. Claude McKay, letter to Langston Hughes, 30 Aug. 1930, Hughes Papers, Johnson Memorial Collection.

4. Charles S. Johnson, letter to Carl Van Vechten, 10 Aug. 1926, Van Vechten Correspondence—*Opportunity,* Johnson Memorial Collection.

5. Aaron Douglass, letter to Langston Hughes, [21 Dec. 1925], Hughes Papers, Johnson Memorial Collection.

6. J. W. Johnson, letter to Carl Van Vechten, 6 Mar. 1927, Van Vechten Correspondence, Johnson Memorial Collection.

7. List, 15 Dec. 1938; Augusta Savage, letter to Walter White, 14 Apr. 1940, Van Vechten Correspondence—Johnson Memorial, Johnson Memorial Collection. Langston Hughes, "In Memory of a Man," ms., 4 Apr. 1941, Hughes Mss. Collection 529, Johnson Memorial Collection.

8. Grace Nail Johnson, letters to Carl Van Vechten, 19 Dec. 1938 and 4 Jan. 1939; James Weldon Johnson, letter to Van Vechten, 28 Feb. 1925, Van Vechten Correspondence—Johnson Memorial, Johnson Memorial Collection.

9. Minutes, 12 Dec. 1939, Van Vechten Correspondence—Johnson Memorial Collection.

10. Robert Moses, letter to Walter White, n.d., enclosed in White, letter to Carl Van Vechten, 2 Apr. 1942; Van Vechten, letter to White, 9 May 1942; minutes, 4 Dec. 1942; White, letters to Johnson Memorial Committee, 25 Oct. 1945 and 5 Feb. 1947, Van Vechten Correspondence—Johnson Memorial Collection.

11. Carl Van Vechten, letter to Walter White, 14 Aug. 1941, Van Vechten Correspondence, Johnson Memorial Collection; Arthur Schomburg, letter to Langston Hughes, 16 Feb. 1933, and letter to Nancy Cunnard, 23 Oct. 1935, Schomburg Papers 7: 3, 8, Schomburg Center for Research in Black Culture, New York Public Library.

## Works Cited

Antin, Mary. *The Promised Land.* Boston: Houghton, 1912.

Baker, Houston A., Jr. *Modernism and the Harlem Renaissance.* Chicago: U of Chicago P, 1987.

Bremer, Sidney H. "Lost Continuities: Alternative Urban Visions in Chicago Novels, 1890-1915." *Soundings* 64 (1981): 29-51.

Brown, Claude. *Manchild in the Promised Land.* New York: Macmillan, 1965.

Cahan, Abraham. *Yekl.* New York: Appleton, 1896.

Carby, Hazel V. *Reconstructing Womanhood.* New York: Oxford UP, 1987.

Davis, Angela. "'Strong beyond all definitions. . . .'" *Women's Review of Books* 4 (July-Aug. 1987): 1, 21.

Ellison, Ralph. *Invisible Man.* New York: Random, 1952.

Faulkner, William. *Light in August.* New York: Random, 1932.

Fauset, Jessie Redmon. *Plum Bun.* New York: Stokes, 1929.

———. *There Is Confusion.* New York: Boni, 1924.

Fisher, Rudolph. *The Conjure-Man Dies: A Mystery Tale of Dark Harlem.* 1932. Facsim. ed. New York: Arno and New York Times, 1971.

———. *The Walls of Jericho.* New York: Knopf, 1928.

Fitzgerald, F. Scott. *The Great Gatsby.* New York: Scribner's, 1925.

———. "My Lost City." *The Crack-Up.* Ed. Edmund Wilson. 1934. New York: New Directions, 1945. 23-33.

Gates, Henry Louis, Jr. "The Blackness of Blackness: A Critique of the Sign and the Signifying Monkey." *Black Literature and Literary Theory.* New York: Methuen, 1984. 285-321.

Hughes, Langston. *The Big Sea: An Autobiography.* New York: Knopf, 1940.

———. "Broadcast to the West Indies." Letter to Claude McKay. 23 July 1943. McKay Papers. James Weldon Johnson Memorial Collection. Beinecke Library, Yale Univ.

———. *The Weary Blues.* New York: Knopf, 1925.

Hurston, Zora Neale. "Race Cannot Become Great until It Recognizes Its Talent." Clipping from *Washington Tribune.* 29 Dec. 1934. Julius Rosenwald Fund Archives 423: 9. Fisk Univ.

Hutson, Jean. Interview. With Barbara Kline. 16 Mar. and 5 May 1978. Oral History Collection. Butler Library, Columbia Univ.

Johnson, Charles S. "The New Frontage on American Life." *The New Negro: An Interpretation.* Ed. Alain Locke. New York: Boni, 1925. 278-98.

Johnson, James Weldon. *The Autobiography of an Ex-Coloured Man.* Blue Jade Ed. New York: Knopf, 1927.

———. *Black Manhattan.* 1930. Facsim. ed. New York: Atheneum, 1958.

———. *Saint Peter Relates an Incident.* New York: Viking, 1935.

———. Speech of Resignation, NAACP. 1931. Johnson Papers 103. James Weldon Johnson Memorial Collection. Beinecke Library, Yale Univ.

Larsen, Nella. *Quicksand.* New York: Knopf, 1928.

McKay, Claude. *Harlem Shadows: The Poems of Claude McKay.* New York: Harcourt, 1922.

———. *Home to Harlem.* New York: Harper, 1928.

———. *A Long Way from Home.* New York: Furman, 1937.

Morrison, Toni. "'Intimate Things in Place': A Conversation with Toni Morrison." With Robert Stepto. 19 May 1976. *The Third Woman.* Ed. Dexter Fisher. Boston: Houghton. 167-82.

Singh, Amritjit. *The Novels of the Harlem Renaissance.* University Park: Pennsylvania State UP, 1976.

Thurman, Wallace. *The Blacker the Berry.* 1929. Facsim. ed. New York: Arno and New York Times, 1969.

———. "Terpsichore in Harlem." *Aunt Hagar's Children*. Ms. N.d. Thurman Collection 1-16. James Weldon Johnson Memorial Collection. Beinecke Library, Yale Univ.

Van Vechten, Carl. *Nigger Heaven*. New York: Knopf, 1926.

———. "The Reminiscences of Carl Van Vechten." Interviews. With William T. Ingersoll. Mar.-May 1960. Oral History Collection. Butler Library, Columbia Univ.

Wagner, Linda W. *Dos Passos: Artist as American*. Austin: U of Texas P, 1979.

Waldron, Edward W. *Walter White and the Harlem Renaissance*. Port Washington: Kennikat, 1978.

West, Nathanael. *Miss Lonelyhearts*. New York: New Directions, 1933.

Wharton, Edith. *The Age of Innocence*. 1920. New York: Modern Library-Random, 1943.

White, Walter. *Flight*. New York: Knopf, 1926.

Whitman, Walt. *Leaves of Grass*. Comprehensive Reader's Ed. Ed. Harold W. Blodgett and Sculley Bradley. New York: New York UP, 1965.

Wyatt, Edith Franklin. "Overland." Newspaper clipping. 27 June [1914]. Scrapbook 1914-16. Wyatt Mss. (1873-1958). Newberry Library, Chicago.

# MARIA BALSHAW (ESSAY DATE 2000)

**SOURCE:** Balshaw, Maria. "New Negroes, New Spaces." In *Looking for Harlem: Urban Aesthetics in African American Literature*, pp. 14-29. London: Pluto Press, 2000.

*In the following essay, Balshaw examines what a heavily Black Harlem space meant to its residents. She argues that this "racial urbanity" was brought about in part by key Renaissance literary works, such as* The New Negro *and* Fire!! *magazine.*

Huh! de wurl' ain't flat,
An' de wurl' ain't roun',
Jes' one long strip
Hangin' up an' down—
Since Norf is up,
An' Souf is down,
An Hebben is up,
I'm upward boun'.

> Lucy Ariel Williams, 'Northboun', *Opportunity* (June 1926).

Lucy Williams's celebration of the heaven that is the North echoes a utopian strain to be found in much African American writing of the 1920s, particularly in the sense that the reputation of Harlem draws writers to this famed 'city within a city'.[1] This sense of excitement can be found in a wide variety of Harlem Renaissance writers and cultural commentators, from Alain Locke's celebration of the new spirit in Negro life in *The New Negro* (1925) to James Weldon Johnson's *Black Manhattan* (1930), the controversial avant-gardism of *Fire!!* magazine and the sophisticated wit of Rudolph Fisher's urban tales. For these and many other Harlem writers the definitive changes brought about by large-scale migration to the Northern urban centres by African Americans after the First World War, and the subsequent expansion of Harlem, are registered as a barely contained excitement with the city these writers situate themselves in.[2]

We see a very good example of this thrill of the urban in a story by Rudolph Fisher called 'City of Refuge', published in 1925 in *Atlantic Monthly*.[3] This shows us the shocking newness of Harlem through the eyes of a typical urban ingenue, a migrant from rural Georgia, King Solomon Gillis. 'City of Refuge' demonstrates that despite the economic hardships, racism and exploitation which existed at the time, Harlem does act at this point as a fantasy space of freedom, pleasures and opportunities for African American citizens (as well as acting as the legendary space of exoticism and license for the white imagination). Gillis, the putative hero of Fisher's story, is on the run from the South after killing a white man and comes to Harlem 'with the aid of a prayer and an automobile' (p. 3) to escape being lynched. His arrival sees him propelled into a carnivorous city of disorienting sounds, speed and subways until, like Jonah out of the whale, he is burped up into a sunny, calm and all-black Harlem:

> Then slowly, spreadingly, he grinned at what he saw: Negroes at every turn; up and down Lenox Avenue, up and down 135th Street; big, lanky Negroes, short, squat Negroes; black ones, brown ones, yellow ones; men standing idle on the curb, women, bundle-laden, trudging reluctantly homeward, children rattle-tapping about the sidewalks; here and there a white face drifting along, but Negroes predominantly, overwhelmingly everywhere. There was assuredly no doubt of his whereabouts. This was Negro Harlem.
>
> (p. 3)

As the quotation aptly demonstrates Gillis is dumbfounded at the sight of so many African Americans gathered together and it catches very well the Harlem street scene; a feature of many of Fisher's short stories. Part of the newness of Harlem for Gillis is the comfortable occupation of public space by African Americans and the experience of Harlem as mass phenomenon. The sense of shock at the all-black space Gillis experiences is perhaps a little deceptive, since his Southern home will have assuredly been a segregated community. What is remarkable to him about Harlem is the occupancy of *urban* space as racial space. The story conveys his shock that the social organisation of the space, from shops to landlords to traffic cops, is in the hands of African Americans and he cannot get over the sight of a thoroughly developed, socially progressive urban race capital. In terms that will be developed through this [essay], Gillis is profoundly disturbed and deeply delighted at African Americans pursuing the practice of urbanity.

For Gillis, Harlem offers all the opportunities conventionally associated with the modern city: anonymity, entertainment, work, pleasure and mobility. It is, furthermore, a place of safety, because the modernity of Harlem offers the possibility that Gillis will be able to disappear into the mêlée:

> In Harlem, black was white. You had rights that could not be denied you; you had privileges, protected by law. And you had money. Everybody had money. It was a land of plenty . . . The land of plenty was more than that now; it was also the city of refuge.

> (p. 4)

The city eventually consumes the naive Southerner, but not before the story catches the elation of arrival to this turned around, 'black is white' world of Harlem, registered in Gillis's amazed exclamation: 'Even got cullud policemen' (p. 5). This elation underlines the extent to which Harlem is not simply Gillis's port of refuge but is a projection of a state of mind about urban aspirations for African Americans. Fisher uses indirect discourse to allow Gillis's amazed perceptions to in part take over the narrative voice of the story to convey a larger-than-life perception of Harlem. We see, for example, the policeman directing traffic as 'a handsome brass-buttoned giant' (p. 4). The story ends with Gillis being duped by a rather more street-wise Harlemite into trafficking drugs, but the apparent failure of the 'city of refuge' to save Solomon Gillis is presented by Fisher in complex terms. As he is seized by policemen in a night-club Gillis finds himself face-to-face with the gigantic apotheosis of his Harlem aspirations, an African American policeman. Instead of continuing to fight: 'Very slowly King Solomon's arm's relaxed; very slowly he stood erect; and the grin that came over his features had something exultant about it' (p. 16).

This strange ending underlines the most notable feature of the story, that the urban space in which Gillis finds himself is a utopian projection of his own psyche, at least as much as it is a reflection of the conditions of Harlem life at the time. In this sense the ending represents not the failure of urban promise but the limits of powerful psychic and social realities for African Americans in this period when Harlem comes to be claimed as a 'race capital'.[4] The attitude to the city in Fisher's story sees African Americans as part of a narrative of modernity associated with movement away from the perceived backwardness of the South and the (premodern) history of slavery and Southern racism; a narrative which sees the South as an anachronism which will be replaced by a new age, represented particularly by Harlem. To echo Paul Gilroy's suggestions in *The Black Atlantic,* this clearly places African Americans as insiders to an essentially Enlightenment narrative of modernisation and progress.[5] It critiques the myths of modernity not through asserting that African Americans are outside or exiled by these myths, but by pointing out how the experience of migration to the North, and the subsequent narratives of urban life generated by these migrants, place African Americans as players in the story of the making of America and the American city despite the material and racial prohibitions encountered in the urban environment.[6]

The Harlem presented in the texts that form the basis of this [essay] is a city of urbanity and urban sophistication, particularly as this defines a race capital in Harlem in opposition to the rural or Southern history of African Americans. This raises important questions about the centrality of urban experience in understanding the meanings of race in the writing of this period. It also implicitly raises questions about the relationship between African American writing and critical conceptions of modernity and of that problematically related term, modernism.[7] While the 'discovery' of African American modernism in the writers and writing I examine functions as little more than academic name calling, I do want to suggest that the Harlem writing privileged in this [essay] . . . demands consideration in terms which we might *loosely* categorise as modernist: that is, defined through its fascination with urbanity as a key shaping element in the development of a racialised aesthetic commensurate to the experience of African American life in Harlem.[8]

This race aesthetic presents African American subjectivity as mediated by the impact of new forms of urban organisation that develop in the Northern urban centres and most typically and substantially in Harlem. Representations of Harlem typically articulate the dislocated and unsettling aspects of urban life as a characteristically modern fragmented subjectivity. There is a fascination with the visual impact of Harlem and with the imbrication of race and sexuality in the formation of subjectivity. This writing often features the spectacular experience of Harlem night-life, a primitivist celebration of racial and sexual exoticism, or Africanist otherness, but I do not want to move too quickly to dismiss these representations of Harlem's legendary exotic spaces. To condemn them as irretrievably compromised by the taint of white influence is to impose an after-the-fact self-consciousness about the politics of the black liberation struggle.[9] This does a disservice in both cultural and literary terms to the aims and agendas of the New Negro movement . . .. It is also very important to weigh things carefully when one considers the kinds of sexual freedoms offered in Harlem's largely unlicensed and unregulated entertainment economy. The work of Lillian Faderman and Eric Garber points out the importance of Harlem as a gay scene at this time and the position of women within the burgeoning race capital is as interesting as it is problematic.[10] It would be a mistake to underestimate the significance of the exploration of sexual identity in the shaping of African American urban identity merely because the writing often does not conform to conventional ideas of authentic black expression.[11] These issues will be explored as the study unfolds, for now we must simply note that while Harlem was not by any means a free expressive space, interesting configurations do emerge out of the conscious understanding in the period of its status as an urbane and cosmopolitan race capital.

### Racialised Urbanity

The notion of urbanity as the expression of a peculiarly modern form of urban consciousness—the projection of an urban mode of being and self-awareness of what it means to be a citizen in a rapidly changing urban polis—has been the subject of much critical analysis.[12] The modern origins of this concept can be traced back to the writings of Robert E. Park and his contemporaries (particularly Louis Wirth) and the foundations of the Chicago School of sociology.[13] The meanings of urbanity are manifold, but what emerges most clearly from the writings of Park and his contemporaries is that it refers to the evolution of civic consciousness and responsibility and stresses the importance of the life of the mind, in terms of everyday customs, artistic endeavour, human communication and philosophy, in the construction of what it means to live in the city. It is also crucially dependent on the idea of the coming together of strangers who construct the city through social interaction that is not based on kinship or group membership.[14] In Park's most famous formulation the city is,

a state of mind, a body of customs and traditions, and of the organised attitudes and sentiments that inhere in these customs and are transmitted with this tradition. The city is not, in other words, merely a physical mechanism and an artificial construction. It is involved in the vital processes of the people who compose it; it is a product of nature, and particularly of human nature.[15]

This notion of the civilised and civilising human organisation of the city is one which has been questioned profoundly in the years since Park wrote, both in terms of the subsequent development of the cities he wrote about and his theoretical conception of it. The concept of urbanity has also accrued rather different meanings as the twentieth century has progressed, coming to stand less for the active striving toward civic responsibility and more for a social and cultural sophistication, a self-consciousness about how to project the manners and mores of urban living: being urbane rather than practising urbanity.[16] It is useful though, at least for this study, to remember the connections between urbanity and civic consciousness, and being urbane as self-consciousness, because the Parkian stress on the importance of communication and social interaction, with the arts as an integral part of this urban social interchange, does connect importantly to the other sense of urbanity as proficiency in negotiating cultural capital. These connections can provide us with one way of understanding the motivations and aspirations of at least one strain of New Negro writing.

Tracing the importance of urbanity to New Negro writing might at first seem a rather odd task given that it is not a concept held to have much relevance to African American urban experience. This is understandable given that the subsequent history of African American life in the northern urban centres such as New York or Chicago might be cited as the antithesis of the experience of urbanity. The optimism of Park's understanding of urban space is most easily undermined if one considers the lack of progress in cultural, economic or political terms that has characterised black urban experience in the decades since the 1920s. This is borne out if one looks at the 1922 Report of the Chicago Commission on Race Relations, *The Negro in Chicago,* which featured a Parkian stress on the eventual resolution of urban strife through social cooperation and the civic-minded behaviour of Chicago's different communities.[17] The Report, steered by the dynamic Charles S. Johnson, a student of Park and one of the foremost African American sociologists of his age as well as the editor of *Opportunity* magazine in the New Negro years, makes depressing retrospective reading, especially if one considers that more than half of its recommendations refer directly to the responsibility on the part of Chicago citizenry to cultivate a fair-minded tolerance between racial groups.[18] That these hopeful admonitions toward a racially tolerant urbanity do not materialise in Chicago or anywhere else is the subject of any number of historical and sociological analyses; for the purposes of this text we shall see the unfulfilled promise of urbanity marked clearly enough in the texts of Marita Bonner, Ann Petry and Richard Wright . . ..

Yet, urbanity does have key significance to African American writing, particularly during the 1920s. The influence of Parkian thinking on the key players in the Harlem Renaissance can be traced in direct terms through figures like Charles S. Johnson, as George Hutchinson and others have shown.[19] It has a broader influence, however, if one sees that the particular mode of 'uplift' or racial improvement that leaders of the New Negro movement like Alain Locke advocated was one which was plainly concerned with the cultivation of urbanity as both civic responsibility and as an artistic attitude of mind. In this sense the race aesthetic advocated by New Negro philosophers could be termed racialised urbanity. Furthermore, the stress in Chicago School work on the significance of the coming together of strangers in the public spaces of the modern metropolis gives us a useful context for understanding the fascination with racial spectacle, in the form of cabarets, balls, dances and bars, in the work of many Harlem Renaissance writers. While one must allow that this in part reflects awareness of what white (and black) readers expected of Negro Harlem and its writers, one should also see these representations as part of an urge toward urbanity which is an important element of African American thinking about the city.

### From the Harlem Special Issue to The New Negro

I want to trace the construction of this racial urbanity by looking first at the most famous of all Harlem Renaissance texts, Alain Locke's collection The New Negro.[20] This text developed from the Survey Graphic Special Issue on Harlem which Locke had edited and it has come to stand as the apotheosis of the New Negro Renaissance (indeed to a large degree it was regarded as such at the time).[21] It included stories, poetry, essays and polemic and featured virtually every black writer of note in the period. For commentators of all

theoretical and political persuasions Locke's collection stands as the New Negro document, representing (variously) the most definitive statement of black modernism, a trickster mastery of form, the highpoint of the Negro vogue, a pragmatist expression of desires for social change through artistic excellence, as well as the first seeds of the eventual compromise of New Negro hopes.[22] To paraphrase George Hutchinson, it is likely that all these views are mostly right but partly wrong.[23] While I do not want to knock The New Negro from pride of place in the pantheon of Harlem Renaissance texts, I want to draw attention to elements of the collection that reveal an abiding concern with the construction of urbanity as a racial attitude and as an artistic impetus.[24]

The genesis for the Survey Graphic Special Issue came from the famous Civic Club dinner in March 1924 organised by Charles S. Johnson and hosted by Alain Locke. This event, which has been as much studied as the collections which grew out of the meeting, gathered together most of the younger African American writers and artists of note for a kind of launch party for the New Negro, ostensibly in celebration of the publication of Jessie Fauset's novel There Is Confusion.[25] The speeches at this gathering, the essay which Locke himself wrote as introduction to the Survey collection, and the more numerous essays which punctuate The New Negro, make it clear that the cultural awakening that these collections herald is one which breaks with the tradition of genteel fiction that was associated with Fauset's work. Indeed, as George Hutchinson points out, Fauset was explicitly sidelined by Locke because he saw her conservatism as being at odds with the new spirit that he wished to capture in his anthologies.[26] In Hutchinson's view this new spirit, or cultural racialism, was part of more general cultural tendencies that saw New Negro writing as part of a resurgent cultural nationalism, which drew out racial and ethnic distinctiveness at the same time as articulating American values as they were being shaped in the work of philosophers like William James and ethnographers like Franz Boas, developing what Hutchinson calls a 'rhetoric of Americanism'.[27] The idea of a race spirit, and the racial aesthetic which forms the basis of Locke's New Negro essays and gives critical shape to this incredibly diverse (some would say antagonistic) collection, should undoubtedly be viewed in this light and Locke makes explicit claims about the New Negro's American credentials. He argues, 'the choice is not between one way for the Negro and another way for the rest, but between American institutions frustrated on the one hand and American ideals progressively fulfilled and realized on the other' (p. 12).

The modernist aspirations of the collection are also clearly evident in Locke's essays. In a preface to the fiction in the collection he says: 'It has been their achievement also to bring the artistic advance of the Negro sharply into stepping alignment with contemporary artistic throught, mood and style. They are thoroughly modern, some of them ultra-modern, and Negro thoughts now wear the uniform of the age' (p. 50). Whether one chooses to go along with Locke's assessment of the fiction (and not all of it fits this 'ultra-modern' description), or for that matter whether one sees Locke's integrationist modernism as a useful strategy for African American artists in this period, was the subject of at least as much comment in Locke's time as it has been in the decades since the collection was published. Documenting the intensity of contemporary or subsequent spats over Locke's rather programmatic shaping of the collection goes beyond the remit of this study, even if this had not already been the subject of excellent and extensive scholarly debate.[28] What I want to draw out is the extent to which Locke draws on a notion of urban civic culture as a means to articulate a national and racial identity and literature.

Locke undertook substantial revisions between the *Survey Graphic* issue and the expanded collection. While the first collection bears Locke's imprint in terms of the fiction and poetry he solicited as well as in his own keynote essays, it is also shaped by the social work agenda of the *Survey*. So, a number of the pieces have a sharp sociological edge rather at odds with the broader artistic and cultural optimism that underpins Locke's framing pieces. He subsequently found himself subject to a number of critiques about the negativity of some of the essays in the *Survey* issue as well as to lobbying from powerful middle-class interest groups (who wished to see the race represented by institutions such as Howard University rather than through the bars and tenements of working-class Harlem). Locke also harboured his own agenda about what should be projected as a representative image of the race and his response was to remove many of the pieces which reflected the mass urban phenomenon of Harlem when he expanded the edition on the grounds that they might confirm the worst (white) preconceptions about Harlem and its citizenry. So Winthrop

Lane's article 'Ambushed in the City: The Grim Side of Harlem', as well as Kelly Miller's 'The Harvest of Race Prejudice' and Eunice Roberta Hunton's 'Breaking Through' (which drew out an interpretation of Harlem as a modern ghetto very close to the picture we will see later of Chicago in Marita Bonner's work) were all excluded from the later collection.[29] However, contrary to criticisms of Locke's collection offered by scholars such as Charles Scruggs, I suggest that while pieces which foreground African American social problems in the race capital are excised, the collection retains a focus on the social organisation of African American urban life. This is reflected in the fiction and the poetry but also, at a deeper rhetorical level, in essays by Locke, James Weldon Johnson, J. A. Rogers, Melville Herskovits and Elise Johnson McDougald, which draw on urban experiences as the foundation for a new race aesthetic and for renewed race pride.[30]

In a passage which survives the transition from *Survey* to book edition Locke lays claim to a series of international precedents which allow him to formulate the spirit of the New Negro as well as to place African American artistic renaissance in line with other national cultures the *Survey* had taken as subjects in the preceding years.[31] Following his claim that Harlem is a race capital he goes on to say: 'Harlem has the same role to play for the New Negro as Dublin has had for the New Ireland or Prague for the New Czechoslovakia' (p. 7). What is interesting in terms of this study is the way in which Locke sees cultural renaissancism, or the building of a race spirit, as part of the development of urbanity as a key marker of progressive national identity. Caught up with this is his understanding of African American modernism as a projection of New Negro aspirations toward cultural renewal as well as a reflection of the changing conditions of black urban life. This places the Negro as the most forward looking of American citizens at the same time as claiming a kinship with artistic and cultural innovations in an international frame.

This can be seen if one looks again at Fisher's 'City of Refuge'. Locke supplemented 'The South Lingers On', Fisher's original submission to the *Survey* issue, with 'City of Refuge', previously published in *Atlantic Monthly*. As the first piece in Locke's fiction section it sets a dynamic urban tone for the rest of the collection, as well as most adequately fulfilling Locke's grand statements about the ultra-modern tendencies of the writing.[32] This urban tone is continued in the second

Fisher piece 'Vestiges' (a revised version of 'The South Lingers On'), which presents a number of short snapshots of African American urbanism, highlighting episodes that were to become key issues in Fisher's writing: night-life, sexual relationships, the significance of the church to African American urban life and the peculiar persistence of superstition within city culture. These are in many ways precisely those issues that disappear in sociological form between the *Survey* issue and *The New Negro,* but are maintained in a more attenuated yet still powerful way in the fiction, poetry and drama. While one might note that the majority of the pieces which make up the official poetry section is of the Countee Cullen mode of traditional lyric expression of African American spiritualism, one can see a more populist and urban driven poetry interspersed through other sections of the collection, for example in Langston Hughes's 'Jazzonia' and 'Nude Young Dancer', in Gwendolyn Bennett's 'Song', or Claude McKay's 'Negro Dancers', which precedes an essay by J. A. Rogers on jazz and its urban locale.[33] This attention to the material urban scene surfaces only intermittently through the entire document but it powerfully connects to the ideas of urbanity and racial progress which Locke seeks to foreground as the primary mode for New Negro literature and culture.

In revising the collection Locke works hard to foster a self-conscious urbanity as the characteristic tone of the pieces. He, in essence, presents a collection fit for Harlem as the 'race capital' he wants to claim. The essays and stories in the collection have always offered ammunition to those who wish to damn the Harlem Renaissance for its capitulation to white dictated norms and values (particularly in terms of the largely middle-class orientation of the pieces).[34] These charges are true in part but also substantially misleading. In the changes Locke made between the two collections one can see a striving after an urban self-consciousness. If one holds this in mind and entertains the idea that urbanity is the central note that runs through the collection then the manifold and diverse opinions contained within it seem to make more sense. This would also make explicit the influence of progressive sociological narratives of urban space, drawn from the work of Robert E. Park and filtered through Charles S. Johnson, as an important background to Harlem Renaissance urban optimism.

## Fire!! *Magazine*

Viewing *The New Negro* in this light places it in line with another 1926 text, *Fire!!* magazine—a text it is usually held to be in direct opposition to.[35] *Fire!!* was edited by one of Harlem's more controversial figures, Wallace Thurman, whose disparagement of Harlem's intelligentsia almost certainly led to his not being asked to contribute to *The New Negro.*[36] This magazine represents the most deliberate attempt during the Harlem Renaissance to foster an African American modernism. It attempted to emulate the style of modernist little magazines like the Greenwich Village-based *Quill,* and was a self-conscious attempt to break with the orthodoxy of race writing in the period in thematic and stylistic terms. Thurman clearly believed that the magazine should be a statement of aesthetic position taking, commenting: '*Fire!!* would burn up a whole lot of old, dead, conventional Negro-white ideas of the past, *épater le bourgeoisie* into a realisation of younger Negro writers and artists.'[37] This idea of a flaming intervention became a rather lamentable reality for the magazine. The financing of the venture was always insecure and Thurman was forced to leave the majority of the issue with the printer until he could raise the required funds. This didn't happen quickly enough unfortunately, as before he could get the copies released the printer's store went up in flames.

The contributors to the magazine included most of the notable younger Negro writers: Thurman, Fisher, Zora Neale Hurston, Countee Cullen, Arna Bontemps, Gwendolyn Bennett, Langston Hughes, Aaron Douglas and Bruce Nugent amongst others, but excluded many of those older, more established (and more conservative in Thurman's opinion) writers who featured in *The New Negro.* The subject matter was resolutely and rigorously urban in focus, and dealt with elements of working-class life that are largely absent from *The New Negro,* particularly in Wallace Thurman's short story of the encounter between a naive New Negro and a young potential prostitute; Langston Hughes's poems, including his wonderful but much reviled 'Elevator Boy'; and Gwendolyn Bennett's 'Wedding Day', which dealt with a relationship between a black boxer and a white prostitute.[38] The front page of the magazine designed by Aaron Douglas featured a stark geometric representation of a Sphinx in blocks of red and black. Viewed across its vertical axis the design revealed a stylised man's face adorned with an Africanist earpiece. The design is a more clearly abstract version of the African-inspired artwork Douglas produced for *The New Negro* and shows a style he was to develop more fully for covers for *Opportunity* magazine during 1926 and 1927.[39]

The Sphinx-face of Douglas's design underlines the magazine's central premise, that this challenge by 'Younger Negro Artists' to accepted models of African American writing was conceived as a stylistic break as much as a change in subject matter. Douglas's motifs ran throughout the magazine, a technique that was adopted intermittently by *The Crisis* and *Opportunity* in the later 1920s as well as being a feature of Locke's collection. In the case of *Fire!!*, the integration of typeface, story and poetry layouts, page headers and portrait pieces is a much more thoroughgoing design principle and one which deliberately fosters the integration of avant-garde form and content and works away at the distinction between the two. The foreword which takes up the first page proper continues this stress on aesthetic innovation adorned as it was with a credo which began: 'FIRE . . . flaming, burning, searing, and penetrating far beneath the superficial items of the flesh to boil the sluggish blood.' It also echoes key modernist motifs of primitivism and exoticism, reconceptualised from an African American perspective, as the polemic goes on to dissolve boundaries between material, flesh and action in crusading modernist abandon as well as taking up a distinctly pagan African style and an African American blues-inflected spiritualism. As the last passage of the foreword proclaimed:

> FIRE . . . weaving vivid, hot designs upon an ebon bordered loom and satisfying pagan thirst for beauty unadorned . . . the flesh is sweet and real . . . the soul an inward flush of fire . . . Beauty? . . . flesh on fire—on fire in the furnace of life blazing . . .
>
> Fy-ah
>
> Fy-ah, Lawd,
>
> Fy-ah gonna burn ma soul!
>
> (p. 1)

A good example of how *Fire!!* stands in relation to the aesthetic strategies of Locke's *Survey* issue and *The New Negro* can be seen in the drawings that feature in each of them. The *Survey* issue included a number of portraits by the German artist Winold Reiss which made up a kind of roster of African American urban types, including a picture of a mother and child and of two African American school teachers. These pictures of Negro women caused something of a furore, with many of the middle-class black readers of the issue objecting that the naturalistic style adopted by Reiss was not representative of Negro womanhood as they saw it.[40] The dark skin and natural hair depicted were rather far from beauty ideals of the period however beautiful they may appear to us now. It is perhaps not the images themselves that caused offence so much as the suggestion that they should be considered representative of Harlem's model citizens—the new urban African American. This drive toward urban typing through the artwork is something picked up directly in *Fire!!* as we shall see in a moment, and both magazines stand as useful examples of the racial urbanity I am tracing.

In *The New Negro* the issue of representativeness is taken up in a slightly different fashion. Reiss's artwork is replaced by that of Aaron Douglas, who had studied under him for some time.[41] He moves the idea of urban typing in a different direction, drawing on African motifs and designs to thematise the collection as an Africanist urban celebration. This is entirely in line with Locke's internationalist framing of the collection, as well as providing a working example of the relationships between the ancestral arts of Africa and African American culture, which are the subject of a number of the essays in the collection.[42] Douglas's striking illustrations provide the most concentrated example of the aesthetic tendencies I have been highlighting in that they present an urban scene mediated through an international context of black history and culture *and* modernist interest in primitivism. Douglas was to go on to paint large-scale murals for the walls of the 135th Street library (now the Schomburg Library) which utilised the technique he initiates in these drawings to portray the journey of Africans to the New World and into modernity. His work provides one of the best examples of a simultaneous dialogue with African traditions and white modernism, which produces a unique and dynamic representation of African American culture.[43] His figuration of the black body in these pictures is very far from the naturalism of Reiss's portraits, utilising a semi-abstract style of symmetrically organised extended limbs, angular head and torso shape and blocks of colour, notably black against white or cream. Presumably, the Africanism of the art didn't offend in the same way as Reiss's portraits since it was not assumed to represent anyone actually residing in Harlem. What is interesting is that Douglas's style, which captures movement and energy very well, especially in the 'Emperor

Jones' and 'Music' drawings, clearly goes on to influence the ways in which Harlem's cabarets and street life become codified in painting by subsequent white and African American artists, forms of representation to which the better class of New Negro would surely have objected.[44]

In *Fire!!* Douglas provides another set of urban figures, rather different from those already examined. Douglas's caricatures of urban figures in the magazine extend the principle of urban typing—his pictures are of the race leader, the artist and the barmaid—but they break with the representational mode, this time drawing aesthetic inspiration from popular urban experience to construct a line-drawn jazz style.[45] The drawings also break with the noble tradition of representative portraits of these New Negroes as Douglas develops black-qua-black stereotyping, emphasising big lips, long limbs and styled-out posing in an attempt to catch the mood of the high and low cultural elements of Harlem life. The other drawings in the magazine, by Bruce Nugent, were still more provocative as they featured nude black women with the lithe bodies of dancers and kinky hair in a stylised African setting of palm trees and abstract patterned black and white surrounds.[46] While this is in line with Douglas's drawings in *The New Negro* they go considerably further than he does toward a celebration both of African primitivism and exotic sexuality. Although it is almost too easy to seize on those recorded comments by rather conservative African American critics like Benjamin Brawley and Rean Graves, we should note that neither Douglas's nor Nugent's pictures pleased them at all—both felt that the drawings were not worth the paper they were printed on.[47] Moreover, the difficulty around the question of representation is precisely that which Thurman would take up in his bitingly satirical editorial commentary, which closes the magazine.[48] Taking issue with the responses by black intellectuals to Van Vechten's *Nigger Heaven*, which Thurman believed showed the fundamental hypocrisy of those figures who promoted the uplift message, he argues that to claim that a jazzer or con-man misrepresents the New Negro is as fatuous as claiming that all African American women resemble the heroines of Jessie Fauset's novels. Of course, he intends to provoke by defending the most vilified of white-authored Harlem novels, but at the same time the editorial is a defence of the content and formal aesthetic of the magazine which it concludes.

The magazine's combination of art, poetry, polemic and distinctly salacious fiction certainly provoked reaction from the African American intelligentsia, though not generally a favourable one, and this extended beyond a few reactionary complainants.[49] The *Fire!!* philosophy was one that presented itself as avant-garde radicalism, even if it now seems rather overblown and pretentious (particularly since the magazine only survived one issue). The controversy generated by the magazine seems to justify Thurman's feeling that things needed radically shaking up. What is interesting in terms of the writing examined in this book is the stories which caused most offence among the African American establishment and media were those which were concerned with urban sexuality, particularly Thurman's 'Cordelia the Crude', the story of a young prostitute, and Bruce Nugent's 'Smoke, Lilies and Jade'. Nugent's piece caused the greatest fuss when *Fire!!* was published and was hailed by some as the most signal evidence of the magazine's degenerate tendencies.[50] The delight the text exhibits in Alex's idleness and the frank celebration of inter-racial homo- and bisexuality was a step too far for many contemporary commentators. Rean Graves, of the *Baltimore Afro-American,* in an article headlined 'Writer Brands *Fire!!* As Effeminate Tommyrot', documents his pleasure at tossing the first edition of the magazine into the fire.[51] Complaints about the piece, and about *Fire!!,* were however rarely kept to moral objections at the level of content. The pursuit of what we might recognise as modernist experimentation with literary form also seemed to cause offence. The following comment by Benjamin Brawley in *Opportunity* magazine makes it clear that stylistic transgression ranks high on the taboo list for the responsible African American artist:

> Another matter is that of the jerky, hectic, incoherent composition that some people are cultivating today, but that is nothing more than the workings of the Bolshevistic spirit in literature. With some people the sentence has lost its integrity altogether, and writing is nothing more than a succession of coarse suggestive phrases.[52]

We can only speculate on who these 'people' were, but evidence such as 'Smoke' would give one a pretty good idea.

'Smoke' concerns the story of the hero Alex's affair with a white man, referred to as Beauty, and a black woman called Melva. It is written in free indirect discourse and eschews conventional punctuation, joining fragmented observations through sets of ellipses. There is little narrative progression, the text working instead through the repetition of key phrases, colours, and feeling, forcing a synathesic attention to the words as they construct a kind of empty artificiality conveying a decadent and delirious city scene. The story's fragmented meanderings are, it becomes clear, the disconnected musings of the superbly camp Alex, as he pursues a night-time existence and sexual relationships with Beauty and Melva. Alex's bisexual and inter-racial relationships are made possible by an attitude to the city that insists on the pleasures of this urban environment. Awareness and indeed exploitation of the spectacle of Harlem finds its most outrageous expression in the story as it cultivates an obsessive fascination with looking relations, decadence and the city scene.

Alex rarely gets off his couch, where he puffs contentedly on a cigarette held in a red and green jade inlaid cigarette holder; when he does it is to move through the anonymous modernist city space of the flaneur. Moving from one briefly articulated bohemian scene to another, he encounters various members of Harlem's literati, all presented as endlessly substitutable names which flicker across Alex's consciousness; an errant progress which leads him to a chance street encounter with a stranger, whom he christens Beauty,

> . . . the echo of their steps mingled . . . they walked in silence . . . the castanets of their heels clicking accompaniment . . . the stranger inhaled deeply and with a nod of content and a smile . . . blew a cloud of smoke . . . Alex felt like singing . . . the stranger knew the magic of blue smoke also . . . they continued in silence . . . the castanets of their heels clicking rhythmically . . . Alex turned in his doorway . . . up the stairs and the stranger waited for him to light the room . . . no need for words . . . they had always known each other . . . [sic] as they undressed by the blue dawn . . . Alex knew he had never seen a more perfect being . . . his body all symmetry and music . . . and Alex called him Beauty . . .
>
> (p. 35)

Nugent's piece depends most crucially on the elaboration of desire as the exchange of looks between characters in a city space that is both commodified and aestheticised; being and looking urbane is Alex's primary goal. In its obsessive cultivation of the rare, the beautiful and the artificial, and its understanding of identity as nothing more than the chance encounter or the surface apprehension of difference, Nugent's story is exceptional within Harlem Renaissance writing. Indeed, we might say thankfully so, in that Alex's

exceptionalism seems to offer little except a rampant snobbery and intellectual one-upmanship. However, I am unwilling to let the story go that easily. Perhaps the fact it was so vilified at the time (and since) is what appeals to me, and perhaps also I'm unwilling to dismiss one of the only explicit representations of homosexuality generated within Harlem Renaissance culture (despite the number of central figures who were gay).[53] We see attention to a cultivated scene of urbanity, and the cultivation of a decidedly rarefied form of urbane behaviour, in the development of a race literature worthy of a rapidly expanding race capital. But more than this, the spectacular urban playground so fundamental to Nugent's story is refracted through a range of writings and writers in variously provocative ways.

## Notes

1. See James Weldon Johnson, 'Harlem: The Culture Capital' in Alain Locke, *The New Negro* (1925; rpt, New York: Atheneum, 1968), p. 301.

2. Arna Bontemps, one of the foremost chroniclers of Harlem literary life, recorded his sense of the dynamism of Harlem in the 1920s, which had drawn him all the way from California: 'In some places, the autumn of 1924 may have been an unremarkable season. In Harlem it was like a foretaste of paradise. A blue haze descended at night and with it strings of fairy lights on the broad avenues. From the window of a small room in an apartment on Fifth and 129th Street I looked over the rooftops of Negrodom and tried to believe my eyes. What [a] city! What a world! . . . full of golden hopes and romantic dreams.' Preface to *Personals* (London: Paul Bremen, 1963), p. 4.

3. Rudolph Fisher, 'City of Refuge', *Atlantic Monthly*, Vol. 135 (1925), pp. 178-87. Rpt in *City of Refuge: The Collected Stories of Rudolph Fisher*, ed. McCluskey, pp. 3-16. All further page references to Fisher's work will be to this edition and incorporated in the text.

4. See Locke, *The New Negro*, p. 6: 'In Harlem, Negro life is seizing upon its first chances for group expression and self-determination. It is—or promises to be—a race capital.' The term race capital becomes a widely used one in writings on Harlem from the mid-1920s. On the concept of a race capital and its links to ideas of urban civility see Scruggs, 'City Cultures' in his *Sweet Home*, pp. 38-67.

5. Gilroy, *The Black Atlantic*. See in particular pp. 41-71, pp. 187-223.

6. For analyses of the role of race in the construction of 'America' and concomitant debates over citizenship and national identity, see Walter Benn Michaels, *Our America: Nativism, Modernism, and Pluralism* (Durham: Duke University Press, 1995); Lauren Berlant, 'National Brands/ National Body: *Imitation of Life*' in Hortense J. Spillers (ed.), *Comparative American Identities: Race, Sex and Nationality in the Modern Text* (New York, London: Routledge, 1991), pp. 110-40; Hortense J. Spillers, 'Introduction: Who Cuts the Border? Some

Readings on "America"' in *Comparative American Identities*, pp. 1-25; Robyn Wiegman, *American Anatomies: Theorizing Race and Gender* (Durham, London: Duke University Press, 1995).

7. For contemporary critical accounts which address the cultural significance of the Harlem Renaissance phenomenon and its relationship to debates about modernity and modernism in the US context see Houston A. Baker, *Modernism and the Harlem Renaissance* (Chicago: University of Chicago Press, 1987); Benn Michaels, *Our America*, pp. 85-94; Ann Douglas, *Terrible Honesty: Mongrel Modernism in the 1920s* (London: Picador, 1996), pp. 73-107; pp. 303-45; Hutchinson, *The Harlem Renaissance in Black and White*.

8. The 1997 *Rhapsodies in Black* exhibition at the Hayward Gallery, London, clearly revealed the extent to which Harlem artists both drew on modernist motifs and critically reformulated them to suit the new urban context of Harlem. See David A. Bailey's introduction to the exhibition book and essays by Richard J. Powell, 'Re/Birth of a Nation' and Henry Louis Gates Jr, 'Harlem on our Minds' in David A. Bailey (ed.), *Rhapsodies in Black: Art of the Harlem Renaissance* (London: Hayward Gallery, 1997), pp. 10-13; pp. 14-33; pp. 160-7.

9. See Huggins, *Harlem Renaissance*, pp. 84-136; Bruce Kellner, '"Refined Racism": White Patronage in the Harlem Renaissance" in Victor A. Kramer (ed.), *The Harlem Renaissance Re-Examined* (New York: AMS Press, 1987), pp. 93-106; Levering Lewis, *When Harlem Was In Vogue*, pp. 240-81.

10. See Lillian Faderman, *Odd Girls and Twilight Lovers* (Harmondsworth: Penguin, 1992), pp. 66-8; Eric Garber, '"A Spectacle in Color": The Lesbian and Gay Subculture of Jazz Age Harlem' in Martha Baum Duberman, Martha Vicinus and George Chauncey Jr (eds), *Hidden From History* (New York: New American Library, 1989), pp. 318-31; Gregory Woods, 'Gay Rereadings of the Harlem Renaissance Poets' in Emmanuel Nelson (ed.), *Critical Essays: Gay and Lesbian Writers of Color* (New York: Haworth, 1993), pp. 25-41.

11. The literature on black authenticity and the black vernacular is extensive. For key interventions see Houston A. Baker Jr, *Blues, Ideology and Afro-American Culture* (Chicago, London: University of Chicago Press, 1984); Henry Louis Gates Jr, *The Signifying Monkey* (New York, Oxford: Oxford University Press, 1980); Paul Gilroy, *Small Acts* (London: Serpent's Tail, 1993); bell hooks, *Yearning: Gender and Cultural Politics* (London: Turnaround Press, 1991); Isaac Julien, '"Black Is, Black Ain't": Notes on De-Essentializing Black Identities' in Dent (ed.), *Black Popular Culture*, pp. 255-63; Kobena Mercer, *Welcome to the Jungle* (New York, London: Routledge, 1994), pp. 233-58.

12. See Kevin Robins, 'Prisoners of the City: Whatever Could a Postmodern City Be?' in Erica Carter (ed.), *Space and Place: Theories of Identity and Location* (London: Lawrence and Wishart, 1993), pp. 303-30; Michael Walzer, 'The Pleasures and Costs of Urbanity' in Phillip Kasinitz (ed.), *Metropolis: Centre and Symbol of Our Times* (London: Macmillan, 1995), pp. 320-30; Iris Marion Young, 'City Life and Difference' in Kasinitz (ed.), *Metropolis*, pp. 250-70.

13. See Robert E. Park, Ernest W. Burgess, Roderick D. McKenzie, *The City* (1925; rpt Chicago, London: University of Chicago Press, 1967); Louis Wirth, 'Urban-

ism as a Way of Life' (1938) in *On Cities and Social Life: Selected Papers* (Chicago, London: University of Chicago Press, 1964), pp. 60-83.

14. See Louis Wirth, 'Urbanism as a Way of Life', pp. 71-7. See also Iris Marion Young: 'By "city life" I mean a form of social relations which I define as the being together of strangers.' 'City Life and Difference', p. 264.

15. Park, 'The City: Suggestions For The Investigation of Human Behaviour In The Urban Environment' in Park, Burgess and McKenzie, *The City*, p. 1.

16. For an analysis of the changing meanings attached to the term urbanity and the sense of a contemporary crisis of urbanity, see Robins, 'Prisoners of the City', pp. 314-15.

17. Chicago Commission on Race Relations, *The Negro in Chicago: A Study of Race Relations and a Race Riot* (1922; rpt New York: Arno Press, 1968). See in particular the summary report, pp. 595-651.

18. See *The Negro In Chicago*, pp. 640-51.

19. On Park see Hutchinson, *The Harlem Renaissance in Black and White*, pp. 50-60; Scruggs, *Sweet Home*, pp. 50-4. For discussion of Charles S. Johnson's influence on the New Negro movement see Hutchinson, pp. 173-80; Levering Lewis, *When Harlem Was In Vogue*, pp. 88-9; pp. 125-9.

20. Locke, *The New Negro*. All further references will be incorporated in the text.

21. *Survey Graphic*, Vol. VI, No. 6 (March 1925), Harlem Number.

22. These positions belong to Henry Louis Gates Jr, 'The Trope of the New Negro and the Reconstruction of the Image of the Black' in Philip Fisher (ed.), *The New American Studies: Essays From Representations* (Berkeley, Los Angeles, Oxford: University of California Press, 1991), pp. 319-45; Baker, *Modernism and the Harlem Renaissance*; Levering Lewis, *When Harlem Was In Vogue*; Hutchinson, *The Harlem Renaissance In Black and White*; Huggins, *Harlem Renaissance*.

23. Hutchinson, *The Harlem Renaissance in Black and White*, p. 16.

24. Recent provocative reassessments of *The New Negro* which have been important to this study include Hutchinson, *The Harlem Renaissance in Black and White*, pp. 387-433; Benn Michaels, *Our America*, pp. 85-94; Scruggs, *Sweet Home*, pp. 38-67.

25. See Hutchinson, *The Harlem Renaissance in Black and White*, pp. 389-95 on the development of *The New Negro* from the Civic Club dinner. For an account of the dinner see 'The Debut of the Younger School of Negro Writers', *Opportunity*, Vol. 2, No. 5 (May 1924), pp. 143-4. See also Patrick J. Gilpin, 'Charles S. Johnson: Entrepreneur of the Harlem Renaissance' in Arna Bontemps (ed.), *The Harlem Renaissance Remembered* (New York: Dodd, Mead, 1972), pp. 224-50; Levering Lewis, *When Harlem Was In Vogue*, p. 93.

26. Hutchinson, *The Harlem Renaissance in Black and White*, p. 390; pp. 394-5, n. 523.

27. Ibid. p. 400.

28. See Hutchinson for an excellent summary of scholarly work on *The New Negro*, particularly 'Introduction' and 'Producing *The New Negro*', pp. 1-28; pp. 387-434;

see also Scruggs, *Sweet Home*, pp. 56-7. For responses contemporary to *The New Negro* see John E. Bassett, *Harlem In Review: Critical Reactions to Black American Writers, 1917-1939* (London, Toronto: Associated University Presses, 1992), pp. 60-1.

29. See *Survey Graphic* Vol. IV, pp. 692-4; pp. 713-15; pp. 682-3; pp. 711-12; p. 684.

30. See Locke, 'The New Negro' and 'Negro Youth Speaks', pp. 3-16, pp. 47-53; J. A. Rogers, 'Jazz At Home', pp. 216-24; James Weldon Johnson, 'Harlem: The Culture Capital', pp. 301-11; Melville J. Herskovits, 'The Negro's Americanism', pp. 353-60; Elise Johnson McDougald, 'The Task of Negro Womanhood', pp. 369-82. All page references refer to *The New Negro*.

31. As a magazine of social work, *Survey Graphic* had run special issues on cultural movements in a number of different countries including Ireland, Russia and Mexico as well devoting issues to ethnic and racial groups within the US.

32. Hutchinson's analysis of 'City of Refuge' is one of the few which notes the innovativeness of the story. See *The Harlem Renaissance in Black and White*, pp. 403-4.

33. *The New Negro*, p. 226; p. 227; p. 225; pp. 214-15; pp. 216-24.

34. This attack starts with Langston Hughes, *The Big Sea: An Autobiography* (New York, London: Alfred A. Knopf, 1940) and has come to be a largely uninvestigated truism of Harlem Renaissance study. Hutchinson's *The Harlem Renaissance in Black and White* dislodges some of the more persistent myths about white influence on the Harlem phenomenon, but he does not explore the importance of ideas of urbanity which are the basis of my analysis here.

35. *Fire!! A Quarterly Devoted To the Younger Negro Artist*, Vol. 1, No. 1 (November 1926).

36. For a detailed study of Wallace Thurman's life and writing see Eleonore Van Notten, *Wallace Thurman's Harlem Renaissance* (Amsterdam: Rodopi, 1994); see also David Wadden, '"The Canker Galls . . ." or the Short Promising Life of Wallace Thurman' in Kramer (ed.), *The Harlem Renaissance Re-Examined*, pp. 201-21.

37. Quoted in Hughes, *The Big Sea*, pp. 235-6.

38. *Fire!!*, p. 20; pp. 25-8. 'Elevator Boy' upset many since it appeared to lack any sense of a respectable American work ethic. Benjamin Brawley, the embodiment of conservative middle-class African America, thundered, 'the running of an elevator is perfectly honorable employment and no one with such a job should leave it until he is reasonably sure of getting something better.' 'The Negro Literary Renaissance', *Southern Workman*, Vol. 56 (April 1927), p. 183.

39. Aaron Douglas designed a number of modernist-Africanist covers for *Opportunity* starting in December 1925 (Vol. 3, No. 12) and running through 1926 to July 1927 (Vol. 5, No. 7).

40. See Hutchinson, *The Harlem Renaissance in Black and White*, pp. 394-5 for details of this controversy. See also Jeffrey C. Stewart, *To Color America: Portraits by Winold Reiss* (Washington, DC: Smithsonian Institute Press, 1989) pp. 50-4.

41. For Douglas's drawings see *The New Negro*, p. 54; p. 56; p. 112; p. 128; p. 138; p. 152; p. 196; p. 198; p. 216; p. 228; p. 270.

42. See Albert C. Barnes, 'Negro Art and America', pp. 19-28; Locke, 'The Legacy of the Ancestral Arts', pp. 254-70; Arthur Schomburg, 'The Negro Digs Up His Past', pp. 231-7.

43. See Hutchinson, *The Harlem Renaissance in Black and White*, pp. 398-9 for more on Douglas's embrace of white modernist ideas and African traditions.

44. See for example the work of William H. Johnson, Archibald J. Motley or Edward Burra. Their work is reproduced and discussed in Mary Schmidt Campbell (ed.), *Harlem Renaissance: Art of Black America* (New York: Studio Museum in Harlem and Abradale Press, Harry N. Abrams, Inc., 1987), pp. 105-54. See also Bailey (ed.), *Rhapsodies in Black*, pp. 111-17.

45. Aaron Douglas, 'Three Drawings', *Fire!!*, pp. 29-32.

46. Bruce Nugent, 'Drawings', *Fire!!*, p. 4; p. 24.

47. See Abby Arthur Johnson and Ronald Maberry Johnson, *Propaganda and Aesthetics: The Literary Politics of Afro-American Magazines in the Twentieth Century* (Amherst: University of Massachusetts Press, 1979), pp. 82-4 for details of the responses by Graves and Brawley.

48. *Fire!!*, p. 47.

49. In general the younger reviewers and writers liked the magazine but Du Bois, though gracious about its publication, let it be known that he was upset by its tone, and Alain Locke disapproved of its deliberate decadence. See Johnson and Johnson, *Propaganda and Aesthetics*, pp. 77-84 for full details of African American critical response to *Fire!!*

50. 'Smoke, Lilies and Jade', *Fire!!;* rpt in Nathan Huggins (ed.), *Voices From the Harlem Renaissance* (New York: Oxford University Press, 1976) pp. 99-110. All further references will be to this edition and incorporated in the text.

51. Quoted in Johnson and Johnson, *Propaganda and Aesthetics*, p. 83.

52. Benjamin Brawley, 'The Writing of Essays', *Opportunity*, Vol. 4, No. 9 (September 1926), p. 284.

53. Isaac Julien's 1989 film *Looking For Langston*, . . . still remains the most comprehensive, if elliptical, examination of the sexuality of major Harlem Renaissance figures. It is fitting that Nugent's text is taken as inspiration for a sexual fantasy within the film.

# BLACK INTELLECTUAL AND POLITICAL THOUGHT

## FAITH BERRY (ESSAY DATE 1970)

**SOURCE:** Berry, Faith. "Voice for the Jazz Age, Great Migration, or Black Bourgeoisie." *Black World* 20, no. 1 (November 1970): 10-16.

*In the following essay, Berry writes of how the "Black literati" of the Harlem Renaissance tended to portray life in Harlem as idealistic, ignoring the real-life situations of most Blacks in the area at the time.*

Some still like to believe that the period referred to as the Harlem Renaissance was indeed a spiritual and intellectual awakening when Harlem became a kind of cultural Timbuktu of the 1920's. Both history and Renaissance literature would indicate that was not entirely so. Although it was a time of inspiration and recognition for many Black artists and scholars, it also turned Harlem into a setting most Harlemites never knew existed. As the late Langston Hughes once remarked about the epoch in *The Big Sea:* "ordinary Negroes hadn't heard of the Negro Renaissance." Unlike most of the artists and writers who had come to Harlem from as far away as California, much of the newly-settled Black population had been attracted not by the Renaissance but had arrived on the wave of the Great Migration. Evidence that the Renaissance years and the Great Migration nearly coincided is not often reflected in the great bulk of Renaissance expression. If "ordinary Negroes hadn't heard of the Negro Renaissance," knowledge of their existence doesn't show up much in Renaissance literature either.

Black scholar Alain Locke, in a long piece in 1926, "The New Negro, An Interpretation," tried to make readers aware of the importance of the increasing numbers of black Americans moving from rural to city areas—especially to Harlem. But very little from the era's poetry and prose appears about Harlem's Black masses—let alone the increasing segment straight from the South to the New York metropolis—except that almost everybody seemed to have a great lust for life in dancehalls and cabarets. Although no Black American poet so loved the Harlem black community as Langston Hughes, only in a few of the many poems written during the Twenties, such as "South," "Bound No'th Blues," or "Po' Boy Blues," is the attempt made to express the feeling of Blacks leaving the South or arriving North. Most of his poems of this *genre* were later. Wallace Thurman, in a play called *Harlem* (coauthored with William Jordan Rapp), made an effort to show the impact of Harlem life on a family from the South, but the script was so altered for box office purposes that the outcome was not Thurman's original intention. Rudolph Fisher, in a short story, "The City of Refuge"—which first appeared in The Atlantic Monthly and later in *The Best Short Stories of 1925*—revealed a Southern character who arrives in Harlem discovering that instead of a city of refuge it is one where greed and dishonesty overcome and change the lives of many Black people. Only a few such glimpses of the period exist.

In assessing the writing and intentions of Renaissance authors who, instead, preferred to emphasize the gay side of Harlem, poet-critic Sterling Brown comments in *The Negro In American Fiction:*

What resulted was a search for the exotic and an insistence that Negroes were peculiarly marked by a "joy of living." Dancehalls, rent-parties, gambling, sprees, casual love-affairs crowded out more serious realism. The cabin was exchanged for the cabaret, but Negroes were still described as "creatures of joy." Even Negro propagandists urged this, seeking to find some superior "racial gift." To look for the true life of a Negro community in cabarets, most often run by white managers for white thrill seekers, is like looking for the truth about slavery in the off-time banjo-plunking and capers before the big house. Focusing upon carefree abandon, the Harlem school, like the plantation tradition, neglected the servitude. Except for brief glimpses, the drama of the workaday life, the struggles, the conflicts, are missing. And such definite features of Harlem as the lines of the unemployed, the overcrowded schools, the delinquent children headed straight to petty crime, the surly resentment—all of these seeds that bore such bitter fruit in the Harlem riot are conspicuously absent.

Because the economic and social condition of most blacks during the 1920's made the great majority unaware that any such event as a "Renaissance" was occurring in Harlem, the existence of such a cultural movement was dependent upon white recognition and approbation. It also required a black readership and, as it happened, this came largely from what then existed of a Black middle class. The latter, however, more often than not striving toward respectability, was not in search of the same elements in Negro fiction most often sought after by its white counterpart. The concept of the "New Negro" to most middle class Black readers meant an increased articulateness and an end to old stereotypes. To the young Black writers of the Harlem School, most of whom had broken from their more traditional backgrounds, the concept meant freedom from racial stereotypes, but also a return to cultural roots. Some of the cultural roots were soon depicted, as Sterling Brown wrote, in "an insistence that Negroes were peculiarly marked by a 'joy of living.'" Such a depiction was the one many white readers sought. Especially was this so during the Jazz Age of the Roaring Twenties. Thus, it was no paradox that the flowering of the Renaissance paralleled such a decade. During an age of Charleston-flapperism, when much of what white America had previously swept under the rug suddenly became vogue, an overwhelming interest by many whites in jazz and Harlem seemed to go right along with the times. The sprouting interest had no minor effect on certain members of the Harlem *literati* whose work was just what the Jazz Age ordered. The era was one in which pleasureseeking white people enjoyed as much living-it-up in Harlem cabarets as reading about them in fiction. Talented Black authors, therefore, describing the exotic primitive and the picturesque, had no trouble finding sponsors, publishers and immediate popularity.

In 1925, one year before publication of his *Nigger Heaven,* Carl Van Vechten, white critic and patron of Afro-American arts, requested permission of Langston Hughes, then 23, to submit some of Hughes' poems to Alfred A. Knopf for publication. The submission resulted soon after in Hughes' first book of poetry, *The Weary Blues*—accompanied by a long introduction of praise from Van Vechten. A second volume of poetry, *Fine Clothes To The Jew,* one year later, was dedicated to Van Vechten. Other Hughes works in succeeding years were likewise published by Knopf. Although his poems of the 1930's changed distinctly from exotic primitivism to social protest, the fascination for Van Vechten of the earlier Hughes poems—in addition to talent—was the likeness some of them bore to the exotic images portrayed in *Nigger Heaven.* A few descriptive lines of cabaret scenes in *Nigger Heaven* as compared to Hughes' poems, "Harlem Nightclub," "To Midnight Nan at Leroy's," or "Nude Young Dancer," leave little doubt about Van Vechten's acceptance—despite the latter's interest in seeking to have Alfred A. Knopf publish other black authors whose work differed greatly from that of the early Hughes. In 1927, Van Vechten wrote an introduction to a reissued edition of James Weldon Johnson's *Autobiography of An Ex-Coloured Man,* originally published in 1912. The Van Vechten-Johnson admiration appeared mutual. One year earlier, in an October 1926 issue of Opportunity magazine, Johnson had described Van Vechten's *Nigger Heaven* as "the most revealing, significant and powerful novel based exclusively on Negro life yet written."

Unlike some other black critics, Wallace Thurman in 1926 in The Messenger—of which he was then managing editor—also had great praise for Van Vechten's novel. But he likewise did not go without imitating some of its sexual exploitation in his own novel, *The Blacker the Berry,* published several years later. A brooding but multi-talented writer, he believed it was necessary to use the current Harlem fad to his advantage—even if against his own will. In his second novel, *Infants of the Spring,* a character expresses thoughts which were Thurman's own about the period:

> Being a Negro writer these days is a racket and I'm going to make the most of it while it lasts, I find queer places for whites to go in Harlem . . . and they fall for it.

If he knew the Harlem vogue was a fad, he also realized it was ephemeral, with little being accomplished to establish lasting standards in art. Two years after publication of *Infants of the Spring,* he was dead of tuberculosis at age 32, having contributed to his own end by a steady consumption of gin.

Claude McKay, another lion of the Renaissance, indicated in his autobiography, *A Long Way From Home,* that his 1928 novel, *Home To Harlem* (written in France), was in no way influenced by Van Vechten. It was not Van Vechten but white critic-writers Frank Harris and Max Eastman who helped and encouraged him in his career—though the two novels bear great resemblance. McKay's main character, Jake Brown, a war veteran, is involved in many Harlem night spots and sexual escapades not unlike those in *Nigger Heaven.* But because on occasion it tended toward even greater sensationalism and often presented more insight, *Home to Harlem* became the most popular novel of the Harlem Renaissance, selling more than 50,000 copies. Although his 1922 volume of poems, *Harlem Shadows*—inclusive of the militant "If We Must Die," inspired by the Harlem riots of 1919—might be termed a forerunner to the Renaissance, McKay chose to live abroad from 1922-1934, in Russia, France, Spain and Morocco. Referred to as a writer of the Renaissance, but one who was absent from it—and often castigated by some members for *Home To Harlem*—McKay, a native of Jamaica, in later years described his ambivalence toward the Harlem *literati:*

> They were nearly all Harlem conscious, in a curious synthetic way, it seemed to me—not because they were aware of Harlem's intrinsic values as a unique and popular Negro quarter, but apparently because white folks had discovered black magic there . . . I thought it might be better to leave Harlem to the artists who were on the spot; to give them their chance to produce something better than *Home To Harlem.* I thought I may as well go back to Africa.

If his desire was to leave to other Harlem Renaissance writers a chance—as his autobiography also indicated—not only to produce something better than *Home To Harlem* but to arrive at a creative consensus as a homogeneous group, that was not the final result. Though variety was necessary for such a literary movement, one has only to discover from the literature of the period what dissimilarities existed: how the poetry and prose of Countee Cullen contrasted with that of Hughes or McKay; or the novels of Rudolph Fisher contrasted with those of Wallace Thurman or George

Schuyler; or the features which distinguished the fiction of Arna Bontemps from that of Jean Toomer; or the ways in which all of these differed from the novels of Jessie Fauset, Nella Larsen, Walter White or W. E. B. Du Bois. Black writers for the first time disassociated themselves from old stereotypes apparent in earlier fiction, but no new ultimate overall aim was displayed for a literary focus which could be called typical of the group. But among the critics, Benjamin Brawley argued in 1927 that the Harlem School advocates presented "new stereotypes hardly better than the old."

If there was one distinguishing feature, it was that almost all wrote as individualists without any collective literary credo—even though some would have preferred there be one. Throughout the decade, opposing views were exchanged between writers and critics as to what the best image of the Negro should be—genteel, folk, or exotic-primitive. Statements and disagreements became a matter of public debate: Langston Hughes made known the direction he preferred in a now-famous piece in the Nation: "The Negro Artist and the Racial Mountain"; others did so in issues of the Crisis, which in 1926 published opinions on "The Negro in Art: How Shall He Be Portrayed?"; and still others appeared from time to time in The Messenger and Opportunity, in addition to the nation's leading newspapers and magazines. None of these, however, introduced the issue of how the life of the new urban black masses might most truthfully be portrayed. As it happened, the first Black writer to do it appeared not during the Harlem Renaissance, but during the Depression days of the South Chicago slums: Richard Wright. Otherwise white essayist-novelist Maxwell Bodenheim with his *Naked On Roller-Skates* in 1934 was one of the few novelists of the time, Black or white, who attempted to show Harlem not as joy-filled but as just the opposite.

Although various autobiographies and articles of the period suggest open camaraderie, if not lasting friendship among most of the Renaissance generation, it is doubtful if the literary disputes didn't also affect some of their social relationships. It is difficult to imagine all members of this overwhelmingly independent literary coterie getting along together all the time while disagreeing most of the time. While Jessie Fauset (whom much of the Harlem School often admired in her positions taken in the Crisis), Nella Larsen, Walter White and Du Bois, amongst others, were trying to portray respectable, well-educated, aspiring members of society (which the authors them-

selves were), Langston Hughes was stating in his 1926 Nation piece that, "We younger Negro artists who create now intend to express our individual dark-skinned selves without fear or shame. If the white people are pleased we are glad. If they are not, their displeasure doesn't matter . . . If colored people are pleased, we are glad. If they are not, their displeasure doesn't matter either." Simultaneously, Countee Cullen was deploring the exotic primitive and demanding "types that are truly representative of us as a people." Not far behind, Wallace Thurman was satirizing and indicting the entire Renaissance generation with his characters of Nigeratti Manor. Speaking through his character Taylor in *Infants of the Spring,* he says of the generation: "We all get side-tracked sooner or later. The older ones become warped by propaganda. We younger ones are mired in decadence. None of us seems able to rise above our environment."

The Renaissance stressed pride in Blackness (except in novels about "passing") and a definite search for cultural heritage was a pronounced feature. Yet the Garvey Movement of the 1920's can be said to have had no great effect on the cohorts of the Harlem School. Nowhere did the Back-To-Africa movement take hold in their arguments on the search for roots. Satirist George Schuyler in his novel, *Black No More,* blatantly spurned black nationalism.

Almost all the figures prominent during the Harlem Renaissance were of modest-income families and had a college education. Some had more than one university degree. Critic and educator Alain Locke, who studied at Harvard, Oxford and the University of Berlin, was the first Black Rhodes scholar. Du Bois—much of whose literary activity preceded the Renaissance—received a B. A. from Fisk, another B. A. and an M. A. from Harvard, then later studied two years at the University of Berlin before returning to Harvard for a Ph.D. Rudolph Fisher earned two degrees from Brown before finishing Howard Medical School to practice medicine. Countee Cullen graduated from N.Y.U. and took a master's degree at Harvard before later studying in France on a Guggenheim Fellowship.

Several others also studied or spent time abroad. Nella Larsen, born in the Virgin Islands of a Danish mother and West Indian father, also lived for a time in Scandinavia; Jessie Fauset lived three years in France and studied at the Sorbonne; Jean Toomer spent a summer at Fontainebleau studying under the Russian mystic Gurdjieff; Claude McKay first made his way to London in 1919 before later becoming an expatriate for 12 years; and by the time his first book was published Langston Hughes had lived in Mexico and worked his way to Europe and Africa on a steamer.

Whether internationalist, bohemian, satirist, folksy, or politely respectable, the Renaissance as a whole had a middle-class orientation. The period rushed in when *Shuffle Along* was on Broadway and crashed with the stock market going out as quickly as the Depression came in. It began with a day when many of its artists could associate as freely with most socially influential downtown New Yorkers as with uptown Harlemites. But the Harlem of the 1930's was no longer a place for a middle-class literary movement, nor could downtown white New Yorkers any longer afford to support it. A movement which mirrored an age, but could not always see its own reflection ended. With it came many personal literary successes, some distinct contributions, and a long overdue notice for Black artists. The Black masses, however, from which it was removed, have since displayed that the Renaissance image of Harlem existed in fiction more than life—and that even such an image in fiction could not endure forever.

## JOHN RUNCIE (ESSAY DATE 1986)

SOURCE: Runcie, John. "Marcus Garvey and the Harlem Renaissance." In *The Harlem Renaissance, 1920-1940: Analysis and Assessment, 1980-1994*, edited by Cary D. Wintz, pp. 321-42. New York: Garland Publishing, 1996.

*In the following essay, originally published in 1986, Runcie writes about the many differences between Garveyism and the beliefs of the Harlem Renaissance elite.*

During the 1920s Afro-American history was dominated by two developments. Black intellectuals, who believed that a display of cultural achievements by black writers and artists would foster pride within the black community and win respect and other more tangible benefits from white America, launched the Harlem Renaissance. Meanwhile, Marcus Garvey organized and led a very different type of movement. His Universal Negro Improvement Association attracted a large following, especially among the black masses of the urban north. Both these movements contributed to the idea of the "New Negro" which flourished during the 1920s. They seemed to have much in common in their attitudes to race pride and the African past and yet the relationship between them was frequently characterized by mutual hostility or indifference.

Antagonism towards black intellectuals was certainly a recurring theme in Garvey's speeches and writings during the 1920s. In the early years

of the decade his attacks were not directed at the Harlem Renaissance as such but at intellectuals in general and at such individuals as W. E. B. DuBois and James Weldon Johnson in particular. DuBois and Johnson incurred Garvey's enmity because they were among his principal rivals for leadership within the black community; their status as important figures in the Renaissance movement was largely coincidental. However, though it may not have been deliberate, Garvey's criticism of these "rogues and vagabonds" effectively contradicted one of the central tenets of the Renaissance—that cultural achievement would pave the way for black social and political equality.[1] In a speech delivered during July 1924 at Liberty Hall in New York, Garvey scorned the idea that "the solution of the race problem depends upon our development in music, in art, in literature . . . and in poetry."[2] Over a year earlier in the course of a U.N.I.A. meeting in Carnegie Hall, Garvey had identified himself with a quite different set of priorities. "You talk about music and art and literature, as such men like DuBois and Weldon Johnson take pride in doing. A nation was not founded first of all on literature or on writing books, it is first founded upon the effort of real workers."[3] Clearly sensitive to the charge that his followers were "rude, ignorant and illiterate",[4] Garvey argued that "Philosophy and the ability to write books were not going to bring to the Negro the recognition for which he was looking."[5] Instead he emphasized the value of the practical knowledge and skills of the ordinary worker which could be translated into industrial and commercial progress for the black race. "They call us the common people," Garvey sneered, "They say we are illiterate. Let us see if they can live without the so-called illiterates."[6] On another occasion he stressed that "when we can provide employment for ourselves, when we can feed ourselves, then we can . . . find time to indulge in the fine arts."[7]

By the late 1920s Garvey's criticisms of the Harlem Renaissance had changed direction and become more specific. His skeptical dismissal of intellectuals in general and his particular dislike of the older upper-middle class elitist wing of the Renaissance gave way to a virulent attack on the movement's younger, more radical writers, who sought to exploit the folk culture of the black lower class and the primitive exotica of the black experience.

The publication in 1928 of Claude McKay's controversial novel *Home to Harlem* furnished Garvey with the occasion for an attack on this

A follower of Marcus Garvey stands ouside the UNIA club in New York.

trend, but his bitter comments were clearly directed at the Harlem Renaissance movement and not just at McKay. In a front page *Negro World* editorial Garvey contended that "It is my duty to bring to your attention this week a grave evil that afflicts us as a people at this time. Our race, within recent years, has developed a new group of writers who have been prostituting their intelligence, under the direction of the white man, to bring out and show up the worse (sic) traits of our people. . . . They have been writing books, novels and poems under the advice of white publishers, to portray to the world the looseness, laxity and immorality that are peculiar to our group. . . ."[8]

There was nothing particularly original in Garvey's remarks. Many other blacks had attacked this trend in the race's literature from a variety of political and cultural perspectives. Writers like Claude McKay and Langston Hughes had been widely criticized for pandering to depraved white tastes, succumbing to the demands of white publishers, and publicizing everything that was coarse, brutal and grotesque in the lives of the superstitious, illiterate dregs of black society.[9] Garvey's criticisms were inaccurate and uninformed as well as unoriginal. To link the short story writer Eric Walrond with Claude McKay was perhaps not inappropriate, but to include DuBois,

Johnson and Walter White in the same group of writers suggests that Garvey had personal rivalries and political propaganda in mind, as much as objective literary criticism. The work of writers like Hughes and McKay did not always conform to the "high art" expectations of this older generation and indeed DuBois had been just as critical of the direction of the Harlem Renaissance as Garvey. However, none of this detracts from the significance of Garvey's position. In the space of four years he had progressed from an unfocused tirade against all black intellectuals to a much more specific attack on some of the principal luminaries of the Harlem Renaissance in which he denounced them as "literary prostitutes" and demanded a boycott of their works.[10]

Garvey's hostility to the intellectuals of the Harlem Renaissance is more easily described than explained. It was the product of a complex combination of circumstances and influences. One would, for example, hardly have expected Garvey to endorse a movement whose very existence was so dependent on the approval and support of white patrons, publishers, critics and readers.

White involvement in the Harlem Renaissance was complemented by the support, encouragement and publicity given to the movement by such black magazines as the *Crisis, Opportunity,* and the *Messenger.* These were the mouthpieces of organizations and individuals who were vying with Garvey for influence in the black community and who were critical of his policies and his personality. Support for the Renaissance by magazines whose editors dismissed Garvey as a "monumental monkey," an "unquestioned fool and ignoramus," "the most dangerous enemy of the Negro race in America and in the world," was unlikely to dispose Garvey favorably towards it.[11] It was also partly as a result of their connection with these magazines and the organizations they represented that some of the Renaissance intellectuals identified the movement with the kind of integrationist interracial philosophy which was incompatible with Garvey's separatist black nationalism. This in turn helps to explain why the writers of the Renaissance, whose work appeared so frequently in other black publications, rarely submitted any material to the *Negro World.*

Another vital clue to Garvey's apparent anti-intellectualism lies in the dramatic contrast between his comparatively deprived educational background and the high level of formal education enjoyed by virtually all the participants in the Harlem Renaissance. The educational attainments of the Renaissance artists were remarkable by any standards. By those applicable to the black community in the 1920s their record was positively astonishing. DuBois and Alain Locke both held Ph.D.s from Harvard University. Countee Cullen and Sterling Brown had earned their Master's degree from the same university. James Weldon Johnson, John Matheus, Zora Neal Hurston and Jessie Fauset had also completed their M.A.; while Rudolph Fisher held both an M.A. from Brown University and an M.D. from Howard. Most of the others had completed their first degree and many of them had spent some time as graduate students. Someone like George Schuyler who never attended any university or college was a rare exception to this characteristic pattern.

Garvey enjoyed none of these advantages. Most of his formal education was acquired at an elementary school in Jamaica which he was forced to leave at the age of fourteen as a result of his father's financial difficulties. Garvey's enemies frequently contended that the U.N.I.A. attracted only ignorant and illiterate blacks and they did not allow Garvey to forget his own educational deficiencies. DuBois, in particular, placed considerable emphasis on this fact. Garvey, he contended, was ". . . a poor black boy . . . He received little training in the Church of England grammar school . . . he had no chance for a university education. . . . Garvey had no grasp of high education and a very hazy idea of the technic of civilization."[12]

Garvey reacted to this situation in a number of fairly predictable ways. He claimed to be better educated than he was;[13] he evolved a pretentious pseudo-intellectual style of speaking and writing; he frequently addressed his audiences wearing the cap and gown of the academic, and he invented degrees as well as impressive-sounding titles for himself. Garvey's attempts to compensate for the inadequacies of his formal education also led him to question the value of this kind of training. In his *Philosophy and Opinions* he wrote, "Many a man was educated outside the school room." "Develop your mind," he argued, "and you become as great and full of knowledge as the other fellow without even entering the class room."[14] Education according to Garvey was "not so much the school that one has passed through, but the use one makes of that which he has learned."[15] Garvey did not approve of the use which many of the Harlem Renaissance intellectuals were making of their many formal qualifications. His attack on them was another form of compensation for his own shortcomings and those of his followers.

Color prejudice further widened the gulf between Garvey and the Negro intellectuals. Garvey viewed the American racial situation from a West Indian perspective and insisted on dismissing light-skinned mulattoes as a separate and hostile caste. He repeatedly denounced racial amalgamation and called for "pride and purity of race."[16] Hitherto, light-skinned Negroes had enjoyed certain advantages in America and there was a disproportionate number of them in the better educated upper strata of Afro-American society. This fact is at least partially reflected in the membership of the Harlem Renaissance. The point should not be exaggerated. The physical appearance of Claude McKay, Wallace Thurman, and Countee Cullen could hardly have offended Garvey's inverted racial prejudices. However, the fact remains that the movement did attract a significant percentage of light-skinned Negroes. Langston Hughes had so much white blood in him that native Africans did not even recognize him as a negro.[17] Nella Larsen had a Danish mother. The appropriately named Walter White was blond-haired, blue-eyed and could very easily have passed for white. Jean Toomer was a very pale-skinned mulatto who twice married white women, and for whom color was so unimportant that he once declared, "I am of no particular race. I am of the human race."[18] Finally, two of the leading figures in the Renaissance, DuBois and Weldon Johnson clearly belonged to the mulatto group.

Garvey exploited the possibilities of this situation. He dismissed Walter White as someone "whom we can hardly tell from a Southern gentleman . . . ,"[19] and referred scathingly to DuBois as "This unfortunate mulatto," "this near white or colored man."[20]. According to Garvey, DuBois represented a group that "hates the Negro blood in its veins . . ."[21] This was a charge which was clearly inapplicable to many of the extremely race-conscious Renaissance artists, but for reasons of ignorance or expediency Garvey showed no understanding of the complexities of this movement. Without any attempt to distinguish between one artist and another he accused all the authors and poets of the Renaissance of being unworthy of their race and of feeling no pride in their color. Instead, said Garvey, "they are prostituting their intelligence and ability as authors and writers against their race for the satisfaction of white people."[22]

Garvey's hostility towards the Harlem Renaissance was reciprocated in full. To the more politically involved members of the movement Garvey represented a threat to their leadership which had to be met, and they responded with a stream of critical essays, articles and editorials. Many of the important figures in the Renaissance were not politically active. Their lives and their correspondence were often dominated by literary and cultural concerns and reveal little interest in Garvey or his Universal Negro Improvement Association. However, Garvey was too important a figure to be ignored even by the most a-political of writers. He provided a rich source of subject matter for light-hearted satire as well as for serious analysis. The Renaissance reaction to Garvey was expressed in novels by Countee Cullen, Claude McKay and George Schuyler, in essay and short story form by Zora Neal Hurston, Rudolph Fisher and Eric Walrond, and in Wallace Thurman's unpublished play "Jeremiah the Magnificent," just as effectively as in the critical analyses of W. E. B. DuBois and James Weldon Johnson.

The intellectuals of the Harlem Renaissance attacked Garvey in many different ways and on many different levels. His aims and objectives, his policies and programmes were all subjected to critical scrutiny. Assessments of Garvey's character and personality and references to his physical appearance were particularly abusive. In his satirical novel *Black No More,* George Schuyler depicts Santop Licorice, head of the Back to Africa Society, and clearly a fictional version of Garvey, as "250 pounds, five-feet-six inches of black blubber."[23] Schuyler's description of the real-life Garvey in his autobiography as "a short, smooth, black, pig-eyed, corpulent West Indian," was scarcely less offensive.[24] Garvey, according to Schuyler, was an "ignorant mountebank," a rabble rouser and a megalomaniac who in many respects "anticipated Hitler."[25] These views were shared to a greater or lesser degree by many other members of the Renaissance. DuBois, himself the subject of so much of Garvey's contempt, retaliated by describing his tormentor as "A little, fat black man, ugly, but with intelligent eyes and big head."[26] In DuBois' eyes Garvey was a dangerous demagogue, "dictatorial, domineering, inordinately vain and very suspicious." DuBois also referred to Garvey's penchant for "bombast and exaggeration," identified an element of paranoia in his behavior and dismissed him as "either a lunatic or a traitor."[27] To Wallace Thurman, Garvey was in certain respects like "a primitive child, arrogant, egotistical and lacking any real mental depth."[28] Claude McKay was less restrained. He described Garvey as a "West Indian charlatan" who cowed his audiences with "his huge ugly bulk," and who "wasn't worth no more than the good boot in his bahind that he don got."[29]

Garvey's success in the early 1920s owed much to his realization that policies had to be supplemented by the colorful pageantry of massive parades, gaudy uniforms, marching bands, banners, ostentatious titles and "court receptions." This dimension of Garveyism attracted mass support to the U.N.I.A. It also attraced the attention of several members of the Harlem Renaissance. Claude McKay referred to Garvey's activities as a form of "stupendous vaudeville",[30] while James Weldon Johnson saw them as "the apotheosis of the ridiculous."[31] Even the normally sober DuBois saw the humor in the knighting of U.N.I.A. members at a specially organized reception. "A casual observer," he said of the ceremony, "might have mistaken it for the . . . rehearsal of a new comic opera . . ."[32] Characteristically, George Schuyler went further. His satirical "Shafts and Darts" column in the *Messenger* frequently poked fun at Garvey. To Schuyler, Garvey was a suitable candidate for the "Nobel Mirth Prize. Certainly no man or woman living today has contributed more to the mirth of the world than the little octoroon admiral. He has outdistanced Falstaff, Don Quixote and Bert Williams in the production of guffaws."[33]

This resort to humor in dealing with everything that was most ostentatious and pretentious in Garvey's behavior is also apparent in some of the literature of the Renaissance. In his only novel, *One Way to Heaven,* Countee Cullen gently mocks the elevation of an undistinguished elocution teacher to the rank of Duchess of Uganda in Garvey's self-created nobility.[34] The much more abrasive Zora Neal Hurston dealt less gently with Garvey's conceited arrogance in an unpublished essay titled appropriately, "The Emperor Effaces Himself." Using the language of exaggerated irony, Hurston argued that "Self-effacement was typical of Mr. Garvey and his organization. He would have no fuss nor bluster—a few thousand pennants strung across the street overhead, eight or nine bands, a regiment or two, a few floats, a dozen or so titled officials and he was ready for his annual parade."[35] Hurston also directed her irony at Garvey's weakness for bestowing the most grandiloquent-sounding titles on himself. Garvey, she suggested, granted titles to others "till it hurt them to carry all that he gave them. . . . For himself he kept almost nothing. He was merely Managing Editor of the Negro World, President of the Black Star Steamship and Navigation Line, President-General of the Universal Negro Improvement Association, Supreme Ruler of the Sublime Order of the Nile, Provisional President of Africa and Commander in Chief of the African Legions."[36]

Garvey was attacked in a similar vein in the unpublished satirical play "Jeremiah the Magnificent, co-authored by the white writer William Jourdan Rapp and the important Harlem Renaissance figure, Wallace Thurman." The central character in the play, Jeremiah Saunders, is very obviously based on Garvey and nowhere is this more apparent than when the authors describe their hero's exaggerated sense of his own importance. Jeremiah strikes poses before a mirror and practices his oratory with such modest statements as "The Jews had their Moses, the Italians their Caesar, the French their Joan of Arc, the Americans their George Washington . . . the Russians their Lenin, and now the black man has Jeremiah."[37] Jeremiah also shared with Garvey a weakness for ostentatious and colorful costumes. He addresses his followers wearing "a purple robe lined with red and trimmed with imitation ermine."[38] In his lavishly furnished private office the walls "are literally covered with flag draped full length pictures of Jeremiah in his various costumes of state; one in an emperor's robes, another in an admiral's regalia, another in a general's outfit, and another in a religious habiliment worthy of a high priest."[39] It was left to Claude McKay to deflate Garvey's pretentions completely and to see the man from an altogether different perspective. The hero of McKay's novel, *Banjo,* says of Garvey, "I guess he thought . . . that he was Moses or Napoleon or Frederick Douglass, but he was nothing but a fool, big-mouf nigger."[40]

Treating Garvey as a buffoon, as someone to be mocked and ridiculed, was one way of reacting to the excesses of the man and his organization, but Garvey was a source of concern and embarassment as well as of amusement to the Renaissance intellectuals. Eric Walrond grasped the fact that Garvey's use of pageantry, of colorful parades, and impressive-sounding titles was enabling him to manipulate increasing numbers of the repressed black proletariat, by bringing an element of excitement into their otherwise drab lives.[41] Both Cullen and Johnson saw sinister implications behind the creation of Garvey's nobility. If he ever fulfilled his African ambitions, the government he would establish there would be based upon the hereditary class distinctions which he had experienced as a colonial in the British West Indies and far removed from the democratic republican system favored in America.[42] Finally, to the more conservative wing of the Renaissance in particular, Garvey's antics were intolerable. He threatened their power and status in the black community, and at a time when they were seeking to prove something to white society through their artistic achievements, Garvey's excesses seemed likely to confirm many of the contemptuous white prejudices and stereotypes about blacks. At one point in Thurman and Rapp's play, Jeremiah is visited by a group of leaders of other black organizations. One of the characters, clearly based on DuBois, expressed precisely these anxieties when he complained that "We feel that your organization is a detriment to the whole race. It holds the Negro up to ridicule. Because of you, the world is laughing at us."[43]

Many people were also laughing at Garvey's numerous ambitious business ventures. The idea of promoting economic self-sufficiency among. Afro-Americans was an important part of the U.N.I.A. programme. Garvey contended that businesses owned and operated by the black community would create more employment for blacks and free them from white domination and exploitation. With these aims in mind he established U.N.I.A. factories, stores, laundries and restaurants. The organization also operated its own hotel, newspaper and university. The piece de resistance in Garvey's programme of economic nationalism was his steamship company, the Black Star Line, which it was envisaged would promote trade between the colored people of the world and carry U.N.I.A members back to Africa. Garvey's failures were as spectacular as his ambitions and attracted the attention of the Renaissance satirists. Wallace Thurman was of the opinion that the history of the S.S. Yarmouth, Garvey's first purchase, had "a Gilbertian flavor which makes it one of the major maritime comedies."[44] George Schuyler lamented the fact that Gilbert and Sullivan were no longer alive "to do justice to the U.N.I.A. fleet."[45] In 1924, when Garvey revived his commercial ambitions in the form of the Black Cross Line, Schuyler noted the fact in the *Messenger.* "Marcus Garvey is again entering the scrap iron business. The Black Cross Line is to succeed the wharf-hugging Black Star Line of joke book fame. Merely for the sake of accuracy, we suggest that the adjective 'Double' be used in the new name instead of 'Black'."[46] Several years later

Schuyler reviewed Garvey's various business ventures and concluded that "The result was and is a tragic farce highly amusing to the gods."[47]

Schuyler was not alone in his perception that there was tragedy as well as farce inherent in the failure of Garvey's business and commercial enterprises. Other members of the Harlem Renaissance condemned Garvey for his complete lack of business sense, for failing to keep proper accounts, for paying exorbitant salaries and expense accounts and for indulging in impractical and wild schemes. Eric Walrond accused Garvey of being incompetent and dishonest, and contended that in business affairs he was no more than "a hopeless nincompoop."[48] Garvey's inexperience was also evident in his unfortunate choice of assistants. He alienated many able blacks and in Thurman's opinion, "perversely placed himself in the hands of a few sycophants, who eventually played Judas to his Messiah."[49] Garvey had squandered money as well as opportunities. He was guilty, according to Claude McKay, of "wasting the wealth of the Negro masses."[50] This wastefulness was especially galling to someone like DuBois, who was interested in leadership as well as art and whose efforts failed to attract the same kind of support as Garvey's, and were dependent on white philanthropy. DuBois was astute enough to recognize the feasibility of some of Garvey's schemes but this simply made their failure even more intolerable. To someone as image-conscious as DuBois, Garvey's business failures seemed as damaging to black prospects as his other extravagent indulgences.[51]

Africa was another bone of contention between Garvey and the intellectuals of the Harlem Renaissance. Garvey argued that America was a white man's country and that Afro-Americans should seek to establish an independent nation in Africa, their ancestral homeland. To many of the period's black intellectuals Garvey's ideas on African redemption, his creation of the U.N.I.A.'s African Legion, and his pretentious styling of himself as "Provisional President of Africa," constituted another of his wild fantasies. During the 1920s many black creative artists were interested in and influenced by their African heritage. They extolled Africa's culture and its contribution to civilization and this sensitivity to their racial past was reflected in their poetry, novels, essays and graphic art. Africa was important in more immediate ways. Unlike Garvey, George Schuyler, W. E. B. DuBois and Langston Hughes all visited Africa and were much moved by the experience. However, the intellectuals of the Renaissance were primarily interested in the aesthetic meaning of Africa and in the idea of Africa as a symbol of primitivism, and this kind of interest, which was in any case not shared by all the Renaissance writers, was far removed from the back-to-Africa activities of Marcus Garvey. This central part of the U.N.I.A. program was criticized by many different members of the Renaissance for a wide variety of reasons.

Claude McKay, for example, emphasized just how naive and ill-informed Garvey's understanding of the African situation really was. "He talks of Africa as if it were a little island in the Caribbean Sea. Ignoring all geographical and political divisions, he gives his followers the idea that that vast continent of diverse tribes consists of a large homogenous nation of natives struggling for freedom and waiting for the Western Negroes to come and help them drive out the European exploiters."[52] Some of McKay's points were taken up by George Schuyler and Wallace Thurman. Schuyler pointed out that the whites who controlled most of Africa would prevent any large scale immigration of American or West Indian Negroes, and that there was no reason to anticipate that native Africans would be any more enthusiastic about it. According to Schuyler, "The experience of the American Negro colonists in Liberia who have had to fight off the natives for almost a century proves that."[53] Thurman also had something to say about the Liberian situation. He made the point that Abyssinia and Liberia were the only independent states in Africa. The former excluded foreign blacks and the latter "was too much in debt to America and American financiers to risk incurring their displeasure by becoming a colonization center for empire building Garveyites."[54] The failure of Garvey's negotiations with the Liberian government partly affirmed the accuracy of Thurman's analysis.

Events also confirmed that Afro-Americans were no more interested in emigrating to Africa than the native Africans were in having them there. Garvey's African vision received as little popular support as its various nineteenth century incarnations. Rudolph Fisher got to the root of this problem in his short story, "Ringtail," in which a group of West Indians living in Harlem discuss the merits of African emigration. One of them argues the U.N.I.A. line of America as a white man's country and Garvey as the "Moses of his people," but the response of one of the others, a naturalized American, is more convincing. "'Back to Africa!' snorted Payner. . . . I stay right here! . . . How de hell I'm goin' back where I never been?"[55] This same point runs through much of the literature of the Renaissance. James Weldon Johnson emphasized that despite their African origins black Americans "were as much American as anyone in the nation."[56] Langston Hughes shared this sense of an American identity. Despite the African activism which runs through much of Hughes' early poetry, despite his image of himself as "Black like the depths of my Africa,"[57] and despite his long-standing interest in Africa, he recognized that he was fundamentally American. The tom-toms of the jungle might beat in Hughes' blood but as he conceded in his autobiography, "I was only an American Negro—who loved the surface of Africa and the rhythms of Africa—but I was not Africa. I was Chicago and Kansas City and Broadway and Harlem."[58] This kind of self-knowledge was hardly likely to breed enthusiasm for Garvey's programme of repatriation to the African motherland. Instead it led more typically to the attitude assumed by one of the characters in Nella Larson's novel, *Passing,* who rejected the idea of emigration on the grounds that "She was an American. She grew from this soil, and she would not be uprooted."[59] In typically pungent fashion George Schuyler underlined this fundamental weakness in the Garveyite program, "Africa for the Africans is all right, but we are not, and have not been for 300 years Africans."[60]

With the exception of West Indians like Claude McKay and Eric Walrond the Renaissance writers all shared a sense of their identity as Americans and from this stemmed a commitment to priorities quite different from Garvey's. DuBois spoke even for the politically inarticulate members of the renaissance when he emphasized that "the battle of Negro rights is to be fought right here in America . . . we must unite to fight lynching and 'Jim Crow' cars, to settle our status in the courts, to put our children in school and maintain our free ballot. . . . Africa needs her children, but she needs them triumphant, victorious, and not as poverty-stricken and cowering refugees."[61]

W. E. B. DuBois had his own particular reasons for opposing Garvey's African policies. Of all the intellectuals identified with the Harlem Renaissance he was the one most interested in Africa. DuBois' interest was not confined to the complex history and sophisticated cultures of Africa. He was also a leading figure in the Pan-African movement during the 1920s. Pan-Africanism shared with Garveyism an interest in the idea of redeeming Africa for the African people but it hoped to accomplish this through the efforts of black leaders on an international basis. The idea of international cooperation working for gradual reforms which would lead to independence and self-determination for the countries of Africa was incompatible with the separatist fantasies of the Provisional President of Africa. It annoyed DuBois that the U.N.I.A. attracted much more support than the Pan-African movement, and that foreigners sometimes confused the two. He felt that Pan-Africanism had been "seriously harmed by the tragedy and comedy of Marcus Garvey."[62] In this area as in others, DuBois was clearly embarrassed by Garvey's behaviour and by the impracticability of his schemes.

Garvey's African policies have to be seen in the context of his belief in the importance of racial solidarity and his exaltation of everything black. This emphasis on race and color, and Garvey's West Indian way of viewing these matters were further sources of annoyance to some of the Renaissance intellectuals. For someone with socialist sympathies, like Claude McKay in the early 1920s, Garvey's emphasis on race rather than class stood in the way of cooperation between black and white workers in their struggle against the capitalist system. McKay complained that Garvey had "never urged Negroes to organize in industrial unions."[63] From a totally different conservative, middle-class, perspective George Schuyler made a similar point when he argued that racial differences between blacks and whites were less important than cultural and class differences which cut across racial boundaries. According to Schuyler, blacks and whites in America shared a common culture and a common language and consequently "the Aframerican is just a lamp-blacked Anglo-Saxon."[64] When Garvey's preoccupations with racial purity and black separatism led him into dealings with the Ku Klux Klan, Schuyler used similar terminology to express a distaste which was shared by other black intellectuals. He dismissed the Garveyites as "nothing more than lamp-blacked Ku Klux Klansmen, leading their followers astray with absurd doctrines of fanatical racialism. . . ."[65]

The fact that Garvey and many of his supporters in America were West Indian was a further source of annoyance. The level of black West Indian migration to America was high in the early 1920s and this generated various nativist prejudices and resentments among the Afro-American group. Without in any way identifying himself with these feelings, Rudolph Fisher described them in one of his short stories. Having expressed the hope that Garvey would take all the West

Indian "monkey-chasers" back to Africa with him, one of Fisher's characters justifies this hope on the grounds that the foreigners are "too damn conceited. They're too agressive. They talk funny. They look funny. . . . An' there's too many of 'em here."[66] There is no evidence that the intellectuals of the Harlem Renaissance ever held prejudices quite as blatant as this, but many of them valued their American identity, and their descriptions of Garvey as a "West Indian Charlatan," a "black, pig-eyed, corpulent West Indian from Jamaica," and a "West Indian agitator," suggest that his foreign birth contributed to their hostility towards him.[67] This was certainly true in the case of Johnson and DuBois both of whom resented Garvey's influence and dwelt on the fact that he was not an American citizen, and that his followers, in DuBois' words were "the lowest type of Negroes, mostly from the Indies."[68]

The enmity between Marcus Garvey and the intellectuals of the Harlem Renaissance was deep rooted and mutual, but it was far from absolute. To interpret the relationship between the two purely in terms of their hostility and indifference towards each other fails to recognize the complexity and subtlety of the situation. To some members of the Renaissance, Garvey was more than simply a figure of fun, a source of embarrassment or a target for criticism. Garvey was equally ambivalent in his attitudes to culture and his opinions of intellectuals.

Garvey's scathing comments on black intellectuals must be off-set by the clear understanding of the potential importance of this group to the success of the U.N.I.A., which he and other members of his organization occasionally displayed. In October 1924, for example, the *Negro World* carried "An appeal to the Intelligentsia" on its front page. "I appeal," wrote Garvey, "to the higher intelligence as well as to the illiterate groups of our race. We must work together . . . for the higher development of the entire race."[69] The reasoning behind this appeal is clear enough. When it suited him to do so Garvey sang the praises of the illiterate common people and the ordinary workers but he understood with T. Thomas Fortune, the editor of the *Negro World* from 1923 until 1928, that "No movement that amounts to anything can get anywhere without intelligent leadership."[70]

In the light of these opinions it is not surprising to find that in its heyday the U.N.I.A. attracted a diverse group of individuals who clearly qualify as members of the black intelligentsia, and who in some instances had important connections with the Harlem Renaissance.

This group included such people as William Ferris who held Masters degrees from both Yale and Harvard, who served for a year as Assistant President General of the U.N.I.A. and who was literary editor of the *Negro World* from 1919 to 1923. During this same period the paper was edited by the orator and lecturer, Hubert Harrison, described by one of his contemporaries as "perhaps the foremost Afro-American intellect of his time."[71] Also identified with the *Negro World* and hence with Garvey were T. Thomas Fortune who edited the paper from 1923-1928, and the essayist, short story writer and important Harlem Renaissance figure, Eric Walrond, who was one of the paper's associate editors from 1921-1923. The most committed of Garvey's supporters among the black intellectuals was the journalist, historian and co-founder of the Negro Society for Historical Research, John E. Bruce. Other black intellectuals of the period enjoyed a much looser relationship with the Garvey movement. Without actually joining the U.N.I.A. respected figures like Carter G. Woodson, Joel Rogers, and Arthur Schomburg contributed to the *Negro World* and lectured to meetings of Garvey followers.

The implications of this situation should not be exaggerated. For all their qualities people like Bruce and Harrison had enjoyed little formal education. They and the mildly eccentric Ferris were not part of the intellectual mainstream represented by the Harlem Renaissance. Renaissance writers who did have something to do with Garvey, like Eric Walrond, who wrote short stories and book reviews as well as editorials for the *Negro World,* Claude McKay who contributed a series of articles to the *Negro World* in 1919, and Zora Neal Hurston, three of whose earliest peoms were published in successive April 1922 editions of the paper, were motivated by considerations other than a belief in Garveyism. McKay admitted this when he noted that by 1920 "I had stopped writing for the *Negro World* because it had not paid for contributions."[72] For Hurston the *Negro World* offered an opportunity to have some of her poems published. There is no evidence that she was interested in or influenced by Garvey's ideas and in different circumstances she was perfectly willing to ridicule the man and his movement. Walrond's involvement with Garveyism went deeper and lasted longer but in the end he too displayed a similar lack of commitment and consistency. He joined the ranks of Garvey's critics and within a year of leaving the *Negro World* had become business manager of *Opportunity,* the magazine issued by the Urban League, which was a rival organization to the U.N.I.A.

However, the fact remains that men of intelligence did participate in Garvey's movement in a variety of different ways, and this in turn meant that Garvey and the Harlem Renaissance were not two totally unrelated phenomena. Someone like Eric Walrond provided an obvious link between the two movements, but the roles of John Bruce and Arthur Schomburg were more durable and more important. The papers of these two men reveal the extent of their involvement with the activities and personalities of the Renaissance.

The example of John Bruce is particularly interesting. This important figure in the U.N.I.A. was a member of the prestigious American Negro Academy which included such prominent Renaissance intellectuals as DuBois and James Weldon Johnson and was presided over by the pro-Garvey Arthur Schomburg. He was also on friendly terms with Alain Locke, the patron-saint of the Renaissance.[73] In addition, although Bruce was not a profound thinker or a highly educated man, this one-time slave and self-taught journalist was a person of sufficient intelligence and culture to collect African art objects and to turn his hand to the writing of essays, pamphlets, plays, short-stories, poetry, song lyrics and even music. Activities of this kind by the most pro-Garvey of black intellectuals indicate that the movement's attitude to black culture was as ambivalent as its attitude to black intellectuals.

This ambivalence is certainly reflected in Garvey's own writings. When it suited him to do so Garvey attacked intellectuals and dismissed the idea that art, literature and music could be as important in the solving of black problems as industrial and commercial strength. On other occasions, however, his priorities were rather different. In a speech delivered in Washington in 1923, Garvey emphasized that unless Negroes evolved their own education system, philosophy, civilization and culture they would remain "mental slaves." "You must first emancipate your mind," he contended, "and then only can you emancipate your bodies."[74] Garvey developed this theme in other speeches and in his articles and editorials. He argued that all the world's ethnic groups had developed their own cultures and that the Negro should do likewise,[75] and he resorted to ideas reminiscent of those used by the theorists of the Harlem Renaissance when he expressed the belief that cultural achievement would encourage respect for the black man. According to Garvey, "The Negro will have to build his own government, industry, art, science, literature and culture, before the world will stop to consider him."[76]

Garvey's nationalism embraced economics and politics as well as culture and as such it went far beyond anything contemplated by even the more radical members of the Renaissance. But whatever his social, political and economic objectives, Garvey shared with the Renaissance intellectuals some understanding of the importance of creating a rich black culture. This concern was apparent, for example, in the program of Garvey's 4th International Convention, held in the summer of 1924, which included discussion of "The promotion of an independent Negro literature and culture."[77] Some of the means used to promote culture by the U.N.I.A. during this period cast further light on the interrelationship between Garvey and the Harlem Renaissance. The *Negro World* had pioneered the idea of encouraging black writers by inviting them to participate in a literary competition which it sponsored in December, 1921. This idea had subsequently been developed with such success by magazines like *Opportunity* and *Crisis* that The *Negro World* revived the practice and sponsored its own "Great Literary Contests" in 1926 and 1927.[78]

The outcome of these various attitudes, objectives and incentives was predictable enough. There was a significant cultural dimension to the activities of the Garvey movement. The U.N.I.A. contained its own artists, essayists, dramatists and poets, just as it evolved its own musicians, choirs, bands and orchestras. U.N.I.A. meetings in Liberty Hall and in all the local divisions were invariably preceded by a musical program. Theatrical evenings and poetry readings were fairly common. Garvey himself emulated John Bruce and wrote plays, song lyrics and poetry. Much of Garvey's literary output was published in the *Negro World,* which frequently offered its readers a remarkable selection of book reviews, short stories and poems alongside accounts of U.N.I.A. activities and reproductions of Garvey's speeches.

These cultural activities helped to reduce the distance between Garvey and the Harlem Renaissance, but they also reveal how different the two movements really were. Culture in the context of the U.N.I.A. was frequently quite different in content, quality and motivation from the efforts of the Renaissance. Artists like Professor Packer Ramsey, "the celebrated Basso-profunda," and Miss Carolina Reed, the "song bird of the East," could captivate audiences in New York's Liberty

Hall,[79] but it is unlikely that they would have been as well received by more discerning audiences as were Roland Hayes or Marian Anderson. Similarly, although the Renaissance produced more than its share of inferior, derivative literature, its artists rarely sank to the depths of cultural ineptitude regularly reached by contributors to the *Negro World.* It is hardly surprising that Ethel Trew Dunlap, "the poetess-laurente" of African redemption, appears in no anthologies of Afro-American poetry from this period, though her efforts were superior to those of many others including Garvey himself. Garvey in his *Poetic Meditations* and in lengthy works like *The Tragedy of White Injustice* vacillated between the bombastic pretention which characterized so many of his speeches and a kind of banal saccharine naivete. Thomas Fortune could claim that Garvey was "a poet of high order,"[80] but his wife showed more insight when she conceded that "he never learned versification."[81] This fact was everywhere apparent in Garvey's poetry, for example in a poem like "Loves Morning Star," which contained the immortal lines

> I've waited patiently for you,
> And now you come to make me glad
> I shall be ever good and true
> And be the dearest sweetest dad.[82]

The motives underlying Garvey's encouragement of cultural activities were fairly complex. They were both similar to and quite different from the purposes of the Harlem Renaissance. Both groups shared a common interest in fostering race pride among blacks through artistic achievement and by glorifying African history and culture. Garvey's motives also coincided with those of at least a faction of the Renaissance in one other respect. Although their objectives were totally different, Garvey shared with the elitist conservatives of the Renaissance the belief that art could prove the black man's worth and further his cause. As he put it on one occasion, "let us build up a culture of our own, and then the whole world will fall down in appreciation and respect before the black man."[83] This objective required a certain kind of art, and the Renaissance conservatives would certainly have endorsed the suggestion that the best way to educate white public opinion was by promoting "such songs, plays, paintings, motion pictures and literature as will fully interpret the true ideals and aspirations of the Negro."[84] Garvey had similar considerations in mind in 1928 when he attacked Claude McKay's *Home to Harlem* for its misrepresentation of black life, and insisted that "We must encourage our own black

authors . . . who are loyal to their race, who feel proud to be black. . . ." These were the people who would "advance our race through healthy and decent literature."[85] There was more than a little irony in the fact that Garvey's position on these matters should have aligned him with his arch-enemy DuBois in opposition to those Renaissance writers who were seeking to explore the culture and life-style of the black proletariat, so well represented in Garvey's own movement.

The element of irony and confusion in the relationship between Garvey and the Harlem Renaissance was reinforced by another part of Garvey's cultural philosophy—his belief that culture should reach and influence a mass audience. This belief differentiated Garvey from the bourgeois elitists of the Renaissance who were committed to the concept of "high" culture, and took him closer to artists like Claude McKay and especially Langston Hughes. Hughes was certainly active in trying to take his poetry to a larger black audience by means of poetry readings and by making available special cheap editions of his poems, which he claimed on one occasion "sold like reefers on 131st Street."[86] However, on the subject of culture and the black masses the priorities of Garvey and Hughes were quite different. Hughes was primarily interested in utilizing and legitimizing in his poetry the language and folk culture of the black ghetto, and in providing blacks with an alternative to the middle-class consciousness which permeated so much of the Renaissance. Garvey was primarily interested in capturing and manipulating a mass audience in the interests of the U.N.I.A. This objective was not immediately reconcilable with Garvey's hopes of advancing the race by artistic achievement, but he overcame this problem skillfully. Garvey's bid for respect combined with his British West Indian background to encourage the kind of art which strove to be impeccably "decent," Europeanized and middle-class. This is reflected, for example, in Garvey's own poetry, and in the kind of music invariably performed at U.N.I.A. functions. There was little trace of the colloquial speech, or of the jazz and blues, so dear to Langston Hughes. At the same time, however, Garvey catered to the masses by exploiting a different more popular kind of culture, in the form of mass meetings, political rhetoric, colorful parades, marching bands, banners, uniforms and impressive-sounding titles.

One final motive remains to be considered. It can be discerned in much of the cultural activity of the U.N.I.A. and it is totally absent in the work of the Harlem Renaissance. It was the degree to which art was deliberately used as propaganda on behalf of Marcus Garvey and his organization. The propaganda value of U.N.I.A. pageantry is obvious enough, but the manipulation of culture went much further than this. When the *Negro World* urged its readers to "Read Good Books During the Vacation," it was Garvey's *Philosophy and Opinions* which was recommended.[87] When the *Negro World* sponsored its "Great Literary Contest" in 1926 it stipulated that all entries were to be essays on the subject of "Why I Am A Garveyite," and when the winning entries were subsequently published in the paper they all emphasized Garvey's important role in arousing race pride and race consciousness.[88] The 1927 contest offered more choice. Entrants were to select what they felt to be the most forceful passage from Garvey's *Philosophy and Opinions,* and to explain their choice.[89] In similar vein, songs were sung in praise of Garvey at U.N.I.A. meetings and he was defended and applauded in poems and plays written by U.N.I.A. members. John Bruce's work was typical in this respect. In his short play *Soundings,* one of the characters describes Garvey as "one of the common people. . . . He is honest, brave hearted and true blue to his race. . . ."[90]

No member of the Harlem Renaissance ever expressed sentiments of this kind. Neither the ambivalence of Garvey's attitudes towards intellectuals and black culture, nor the cultural activities of the U.N.I.A.'s own intellectuals and artists were enough to resolve the considerable differences and mutual hostility between the two movements. However, the cultural dimension of Garveyism, plus the limited interests and objectives which it shared with the Renaissance, did have some influence on the relationship between the two. Occasionally the abuse which they hurled at each other was qualified by an element of mutual recognition and respect.

Though he modified his views on the role of intellectuals in the struggle for black liberation Garvey himself never retracted his criticisms of the Renaissance writers. However, the *Negro World,* his mouthpiece, publicized poetry readings, lectures and other events involving Renaissance artists, and it recorded the triumphs of people like Roland Hayes and Countee Cullen.[91] The paper's editor, T. Thomas Fortune, praised the Renaissance in general terms and singled out Walter White's novel *The Fire in the Flint* for special mention as "a masterpiece . . . an epoch-making novel."[92] Garvey's friend John Bruce found occasion to commend the work of Claude McKay, James Weldon Johnson and in particular of W. E. B. DuBois, whom he described in 1921 as "unquestionably the greatest living Negro scholar today in America."[93] Even Garvey's wife joined in with an enthusiastic description of Langston Hughes as "a keen student of Garveyism"[94] following the publication of his 1926 article, "The Negro Artist and the Racial Mountain," which insisted that Negroes should produce an identifiably black art. The following week Mrs. Garvey's women's page in the *Negro World* included one of Hughes' poems.

No journal associated with the Harlem Renaissance ever published any of Garvey's poems. But if the people involved in the Renaissance were not prepared to recognize Garvey as a fellow artist and intellectual, some of them were at least able to identify his strengths as well as his weaknesses and one or two of the most discerning realized how important he was for the Renaissance itself.

Even Garvey's most bitter critics occasionally paid him compliments. George Schuyler described him as a "charismatic character," and Claude McKay conceded that he possessed "a very energetic and quick-witted mind."[95] Both of them recognized Garvey's abilities as propagandist, orator and organizer, and so too did men like James Weldon Johnson and W. E. B. DuBois who admired and envied the great influence which Garvey enjoyed among the black masses. In 1920 DuBois referred to Garvey's "tremendous vision" and "great dynamic force," and even some years later when the relationship between the two men was one of almost unrelieved hostility he conceded that his enemy's "plan to unite Negrodom by a line of steamships was a brilliant suggestion and Garvey's only original contribution to the race problem."[96] Alain Locke also recognized the significant implications of Garvey's African policy. He emphasized how important and potentially constructive it was that Garvey had "stirred the race mind to the depths with the idea of large-scale cooperation between the variously separated branches of the Negro peoples." The Garvey movement in Locke's view had served to arouse a serious interest in Africa among American and West Indian Negroes and had effectively "built bridges of communication for the future."[97]

Alain Locke was also a perceptive enough observer of the Afro-American scene during the 1920s to grasp the fact that for some of the period's artists these "bridges of communication" were related parts of the phenomenon which he identified as the "New Negro." Although he never mentioned Garvey by name, Locke clearly had him in mind when in his analysis of the background to the Renaissance he emphasized the importance of the current upsurge of race-pride, race-consciousness and race-solidarity in the black community. "The younger generation," Locke wrote, "is vibrant with a new psychology; the new spirit is awake in the masses."[98]

What Locke had implied about the relationship between Garvey and the Harlem Renaissance was much more forcefully stated by Wallace Thurman. Thurman had been among the most articulate of Garvey's Renaissance critics and had condemned most aspects of the U.N.I.A. leader's personality and policies. One of the characters in Thurman's novel *Infants of the Spring* describes Garvey as "a great man with obvious limitations,"[99] and although Thurman himself found the limitations much more obvious than the greatness he was objective enough to recognize the importance of Garvey's role. For Thurman, Garvey's "one great contribution to the American Negro" was his insistence that Negroes should reject white standards and be "proud of their black skins, thick features, and kinky hair."[100] It was precisely this issue which formed the core of Thurman's novel *The Blacker the Berry* in which the central character Emma Lou Brown suffers much pain and humiliation until she comes to terms with her color. Thus Thurman drew on his own experience as an artist as well as on his familiarity with the work of his contemporaries when he summed up the relationship between Garvey and the Harlem Renaissance in this way: "Garvey did much to awaken 'race consciousness' among Negroes . . . The alleged Negro renaissance which has been responsible for the great number of suddenly articulate Negro poets, novelists, etc. (sic), owes much to Garvey and to his movement. He laid its foundation and aroused the need for its inception."[101]

## Notes

1. Amy Jacques Garvey, ed., *The Philosophy and Opinions of Marcus Garvey* (London, 1967), II, p. 123.

2. *Negro World,* July 12, 1924, p. 3.

3. Ibid., March 3, 1923 p. 7.

4. Ibid.

5. Ibid., March 17, 1923, p. 3.

6. Ibid., August 23, 1924, p. 1.

7. Ibid., September 27, 1924, p. 1.

8. Ibid., September 29, 1928, p. 1.

9. For the views of Arthur Schomburg see the *Philadelphia Tribune,* March 15, 1928. William Ferris attacked McKay and Hughes in the *Pittsburgh Courier,* March 31, 1928. DuBois criticized McKay in language similar to Garvey's in *Crisis,* 35 (June 1928), 202.

10. *Negro World,* September 29, 1928, p. 1.

11. These quotations are from A. Philip Randolph, *Messenger,* V (January 1923), 561; W. E. B. DuBois, *Crisis,* 28 (May 1924), 8; and Charles S. Johnson, *Opportunity,* 1 (August 1923), 232.

12. W. E. B. DuBois, "Back to Africa," *Century Magazine,* 105 (February 1923), 540-41.

13. This issue is discussed in Edmund David Cronon, *Black Moses: The Story of Marcus Garvey and the Universal Negro Improvement Association* (Madison, Wisc., 1955), pp. 7-8.

14. Amy Jacques Garvey, *Philosophy and Opinions,* I, pp. 15-16.

15. Ibid., II, p. 318.

16. Ibid., I, p. 17.

17. Langston Hughes, *The Big Sea* (New York, 1963), p. 11.

18. Cited in Margaret Perry, *Silence to the Drums. A Survey of the Literature of the Harlem Renaissance* (Westport, Conn., and London, 1976), p. 32.

19. Amy Jacques Garvey, *Philosophy and Opinions,* II, p. 59.

20. Ibid., II, pp. 310, 84.

21. Ibid., II, p. 57.

22. *Negro World,* 29 September 1928, p. 1.

23. George S. Schuyler, *Black No More* (New York and London, 1971), p. 103.

24. George S. Schuyler, *Black and Conservative: The Autobiography of George S. Schuyler* (New Rochelle, N.Y., 1966), p. 120.

25. Information from Schuyler's "Views and Reviews" column in the *Pittsburgh Courier* contained in the George Schuyler section of the Schomburg Collection Clipping File, New York Public Library. Schuyler, *Black and Conservative,* p. 120. The term megalomaniac was also applied to Garvey by Eric Walrond. See Walrond, "The New Negro Faces America," *Current History,* XVII (February 1923), 787.

26. Cited in Tony Martin, *Race First: The Ideological and Organizational Struggles of Marcus Garvey and the Universal Negro Improvement Association* (Westport, Conn., and London, 1976), p. 297.

27. *Crisis,* 21 (December 1920), 58, 60; 24 (September 1922), 214; 28 (May 1924), 8.

28. Wallace Thurman, "Marcus Garvey," pp. 11-12. This undated and presumably unpublished article is in the Thurman Collection, Box I, Folder 15, The Beinecke Rare Book and Manuscript Library, Yale University.

29. Claude McKay, *A Long Way From Home* (New York, 1969), p. 354. See also McKay, *Banjo* (New York, 1957), p. 76.

30. Claude McKay in *The Liberator,* 5 (April 1922), 9.

31. James Weldon Johnson in his "Views and Reviews" column in the *New York Age,* August 19, 1922.

32. W. E. B. DuBois, "Back to Africa," *Century Magazine,* 105 (February, 1923), 539.

33. George S. Schuyler in *Messenger* VI, (July 1924), 213.

34. Countee Cullen, *One Way to Heaven* (New York and London, 1932), p. 190.

35. Zora Neale Hurston, "The Emperor Effaces Himself," p. 1. A typed carbon of this incomplete and presumably unpublished essay is in the Hurston Collection, Box I, Folder 16, The Beinecke Rare Book and Manuscript Library, Yale University.

36. Ibid., p. 3.

37. Wallace Thurman and William Jordan Rapp, *Jeremiah the Magnificent*, Act I, p. 36. A Microfilm of the typescript of this unpublished play is in the Schomburg Collection, New York Public Library.

38. Ibid., Act I, p. 10.

39. Ibid., Act II, p. 1.

40. McKay, *Banjo*, p. 77.

41. Eric Walrond, "Imperator Africanus. Marcus Garvey: Menace or Promise," *The Independent*, 114 (January 1925), 9.

42. Cullen, *One Way to Heaven*, p. 191. James Weldon Johnson, *New York Age*, August 19, 1922.

43. Thurman and Rapp, *Jeremiah*, Act II, p. 30.

44. Thurman, "Marcus Garvey," p. 6.

45. *Messenger*, VI (February 1924), 41.

46. *Messenger*, VI (May 1924), 138.

47. *Pittsburgh Courier*, August 10, 1929.

48. Walrond, "Imperator Africanus," 10.

49. Thurman, "Marcus Garvey," p. 11.

50. McKay to James Weldon Johnson, Marseille, April 30, 1928, James Weldon Johnson Correspondence, Series I, Folder 308, The Beinecke Rare Book and Manuscript Library, Yale University.

51. W. E. B. DuBois, "Marcus Garvey and the NAACP," *Crisis*, 35 (February 1928), 51. See also *Crisis*, 22 (May 1921), 8.

52. Claude McKay in *The Liberator*, 5 (April 1922), 9.

53. George S. Schuyler, "A Negro Looks Ahead," *American Mercury* (February 1930), 214.

54. Wallace Thurman, "Marcus Garvey," p. 1.

55. Rudolph Fisher, "Ringtail," *Atlantic Monthly*, 135 (May 1925), 657.

56. Cited in Eugene Levy, *James Weldon Johnson. Black Leader, Black Voice* (Chicago and London, 1973), p. 231.

57. From Hughes' poem "Negro," *Crisis*, 23 (January 1922), 113.

58. Hughes, *The Big Sea*, p. 325.

59. Nella Larsen, *Passing* (New York and London, 1971), p. 178.

60. *Pittsburgh Courier*, January 7, 1928. Essentially the same point was made by Wallace Thurman in his article, "Nephews of Uncle Remus," *The Independent*, 119 (September 1927), 297. See also his novel, *Infants of the Spring* (Freeport, N.Y., 1972), pp. 234-241.

61. *Crisis*, 22 (May 1921), 8. In fairness to Garvey, it should be mentioned that he proposed to be selective in his choice of those members of his organization who were to go back to Africa. He emphasized that his program was one of African redemption rather than "Back to Africa" and argued that "we do not want all the Negroes in Africa. Some are no good here and naturally will be no good there." Garvey clearly saw the need in Africa for scientists, engineers, doctors, teachers and businessmen, but he also talked, less selectively, of repatriating "hundreds of thousands" of men and women. See Amy Jacques Garvey *Philosophy and Opinions*, II, p. 122, *Negro World*, January 12, 1924, p. 1, and January 19, 1924, p. 1.

62. *Crisis*, 27 (November 1923), 9.

63. *The Liberator*, 5 (April 1922), 9. See also Wayne F. Cooper, ed., *The Passion of Claude McKay. Selected Poetry and Prose, 1912-1948* (New York, 1973), pp. 15, 53.

64. George S. Schuyler, "A Negro Looks Ahead," *American Mercury* (February, 1930), 217.

65. *Pittsburgh Courier*, July 23, 1927.

66. Fisher, "Ringtail," 656-57.

67. . . . Also, DuBois, cited in Tony Martin, *Race First*, 295.

68. Cited in Ibid., p. 287. See also pp. 276, 299.

69. *Negro World*, October 25, 1924, p. 1.

70. Ibid., April 27, 1928, p. 4.

71. Joel Rogers, *World's Great Men of Color* (New York, 1972), II, p. 432.

72. McKay, *A Long Way From Home*, p. 87.

73. John E. Bruce Papers, Bruce 430, Schomburg Collection, New York Public Library.

74. *Negro World*, April 28, 1923, p. 10.

75. Ibid., July 17, 1926, p. 1.

76. Amy Jacques Garvey, *Philosophy and Opinions*, II, p. 24. See also *Negro World*, January 26, 1924, p. 3.

77. *Negro World*, June 7, 1924, p. 1.

78. Ibid., December 17, 1921, August 28, 1926, February 5, 1927.

79. Ibid., March 3, 1923, p. 3; March 7, 1925, p. 5.

80. Ibid., October 22, 1927, p. 4.

81. Amy Jacques Garvey, *Garvey and Garveyism* (London, 1970), p. 168.

82. Marcus Garvey, *Selections from the Poetic Meditations of Marcus Garvey* (New York, 1927), p. 20.

83. *Negro World*, April 28, 1923, p. 1.

84. Ibid., August 23, 1924, p. 20.

85. Ibid., September 29, 1928, p. 1.

86. Hughes to Carl Van Vechten, February 17, 1932, Carl Van Vechten Correspondence, Beinecke Rare Book and Manuscript Library, Yale University.

87. *Negro World*, September 4, 1926, p. 9.

88. Ibid., August 28, 1926, p. 5, January 8, 1927, p. 3.

89. Ibid., February 5, 1927, p. 5.

90. Bruce Papers, B 9-87.

91. See, for example, *Negro World,* March 31, 1923; April 7, 1923; October 6, 1923; December 1, 1923; December 15, 1923, p. 6; November 22, 1924, p. 4; December 13, 1924, p. 4.

92. Ibid., October 4, 1924, p. 4; November 22, 1924, p. 4.

93. Bruce Papers, B5 3-5.

94. *Negro World,* July 10, 1926, p. 5.

95. Schuyler, *Black Conservative,* p. 120. McKay in *The Liberator,* 5 (April 1922), 8.

96. *Crisis,* 21 (December, 1920) 58, Ibid., 24 (September, 1922), 210.

97. Alain Locke, "Apropos of Africa," *Opportunity,* 2 (February 1924), 37-38.

98. Alain Locke, *The New Negro. An Interpretation* (New York and London, 1968), pp. 3, 7, 8.

99. Thurman, *Infants of the Spring,* p. 219.

100. Thurman, "Marcus Garvey," p. 2.

101. Ibid., pp. 11-12.

## CARY D. WINTZ (ESSAY DATE 1988)

**SOURCE:** Wintz, Cary D. "Booker T. Washington, W. E. B. Du Bois, and the 'New Negro' in Black America." In *Black Culture and the Harlem Renaissance,* pp. 30-47. Houston: Rice University Press, 1988.

*In the following essay, Wintz examines the many strains of intellectual thought that developed among Black leaders during the years before World War I.*

During the period that Harlem was emerging as a black ghetto, a transformation was also underway in black social and political thought. It was the consensus of most black intellectuals that a "New Negro" emerged among black youth in the years immediately following World War I. As Alain Locke observed in 1926, "the younger generation is vibrant with a new psychology" which was manifested in a shift from "social disillusionment to race pride." Locke went on to note that this new psychology rejected the old stereotypes of black "aunties, uncles, and mammies" and substituted instead self-respect, self-dependence, and racial unity. Locke's New Negroes centered their hopes on a new vision of opportunity, social and economic freedom, and a chance to organize and fight for improved racial conditions. The New Negroes were unwilling to place their future in the hands of white America; they were no longer content to turn the other cheek when confronted with discrimination and prejudice. They were not really radical—in fact, their values and objectives were basically middle class; all they demanded

was an end to American racial prejudice and the institution of equal opportunity and social justice. However, they often assumed a posture of militancy when they voiced these demands, such as when one cried, "the next time white folks pick on black folks, something's going to drop—dead white folks."[1]

Actually the term "New Negro" and the ideas associated with it did not originate in the 1920s. The first use of the term seems to have been on June 28, 1895, when the Cleveland *Gazette* editorialized about a new class of blacks with education, class, and money that had arisen since the Civil War. From the moment that this concept originated around the turn of the century there were conflicting interpretations about precisely what the term meant. Some maintained that the essence of the New Negro was his commitment to the idea of self-help, while others argued that the New Negro was ready to protest against discrimination or any abridgment of his civil rights. Still others insisted that the New Negro was Pan-African in outlook and determined to link the future of black Americans with the other colored peoples of the world. What all agreed on was the belief that large numbers of black Americans had become proud of their race, self-reliant, and assimilated to American middle-class values, and that they were demanding their rights as American citizens. The term can be understood best as the culmination of extensive social and intellectual developments within the black community in the years following Reconstruction, and as the synthesis of a number of divergent strains that had dominated black thought prior to the First World War. This synthesis would then find literary expression in the Harlem Renaissance.[2]

The fundamental political reality that influenced the development of black thought during the last quarter of the nineteenth century was the steady deterioration of the position of blacks in American society. The black community responded to the increased racial tension in part by turning inward and developing attitudes of self-help and racial pride. Blacks reacted in a quite reasonable fashion to the political and social realities as white society defined them. Faced with growing hostility, characterized by the emergence of segregation and an increase in racial violence, blacks focused their energies on developing their own community and their own institutions. Faced with declining support from even liberal whites, blacks banded together in separate organizations to advance their cause. As political avenues of advancement were eliminated by disenfranchisement, blacks sought equality through economic and moral growth; when whites argued black inferiority, blacks attempted to demonstrate their equality by publicizing their past achievements, by cultivating racial pride and a sense of their own worth, and by competing successfully with whites in the economic arena. Most of all, in times of white hostility, blacks had to turn to each other and rely on themselves.

The most prominent early advocate of black self-help was Alexander Crumwell, the rector of St. Luke's Episcopal Church in Washington, D.C. For twenty years, beginning in 1853, Crumwell lived in Liberia, where he was a militant advocate of black nationalism and a back-to-Africa movement. Following his return to America, Crumwell turned his attention to black social and economic development within the United States. He retained his militant black nationalism, but his goal of colonizing blacks in Africa gave way to a philosophy of racial pride, solidarity, and self-help within America. What Crumwell stressed was that blacks must recognize that until prejudice disappeared they constituted a distinct nation within the country. Therefore, rather than seeking a common heritage or destiny with white America, blacks must strive for advancement along racial lines. Crumwell hoped that this strategy would be a temporary one, lasting only until racial justice prevailed, but until that day arrived blacks must help themselves, not by political agitation, but through carefully coordinated economic effort aimed at establishing a strong black economic force in America. A corollary to black economic development was mental and moral improvement; taken together, accomplishments in these areas ultimately would bring power and social justice for blacks in America.[3]

Crumwell's self-help ideology reverberated through the black community in the 1870s and 1880s. Conventions of black business and fraternal groups as well as most black newspapers endorsed self-help as the only realistic strategy for blacks to improve their status in America. The National Conference of Colored Men that met in Nashville in 1879, while concerned about the erosion of civil rights, focused most of its attention on self-help and argued:

> We are to a great extent the architects of our own fortune, and must rely mainly on our own exertions for success. We, therefore, recommended to the youth of our race the observation of strict morality, temperate habits, and the practice of the acquisition of land, the acquiring of agriculture,

of advancing to mercantile positions, and forcing their way into the various productive channels of literature, art, science and mechanics.[4]

The black press echoed this theme. Leading magazines such as the African Methodist Episcopal (A.M.E.) Church *Review* and the A.M.E. *Christian Recorder* printed numerous articles stressing economic development, self-help, and racial solidarity. Among black newspapers, the Washington *Bee* took the lead in developing this argument. Although blacks did not unanimously endorse this point of view, generally Crumwell's ideas dominated black thought during the last two decades of the nineteenth century.[5]

It is essential to remember that during the last quarter of the nineteenth century blacks were on the defensive in America, and their ideologies reflected this defensiveness. While arguments for self-help and racial pride are not inherently defensive in nature, they took this form in the two decades following Reconstruction. The tone of black speeches and pronouncements and of black editorials and articles reflected this. So did the black history that was written at the turn of the century.

Black history emerged concurrently with the self-help movement, and, like the latter, was part of the expression of racial pride. Early black historians used historical evidence to counter the racial stereotypes that characterized mainstream history and provided a basis for discrimination, and they presented historical arguments to support their claims of racial equality. These efforts took two forms: some attempted to establish a basis for racial equality through scriptural interpretation (and by refuting through logical argument scripturally based justifications for black inferiority) or by depicting the past greatness of black civilizations; others apologized for the backwardness of black culture by linking culture with environment.[6]

The first targets for black historians were the theological arguments that many whites used to justify discrimination. Edward A. Johnson developed the standard counter-argument in *A Short History of the Negro Race in America* (1890). Johnson refuted the interpretation that Ham, afflicted with Noah's curse, ceased to be the brother of Shem and Japeth, thus separating the races and providing a justification for prejudice. Johnson reasoned that since Noah was drunk when he cursed Ham, the curse could not have been an expression of God's will. Furthermore, since the Bible later identified the Babylonians and Canaanites as descendants of Ham, the curse was

Parade of Black men at the opening of the annual convention of the Provisional Republic of Africa in Harlem.

obviously invalid. Like most other black historians of the late nineteenth century, Johnson used his scriptural analysis as merely a prelude to his work and gave added emphasis to more scientific historical arguments. The most noted black historian of the period, George Washington Williams, in his *History of the Negro Race in America, from 1619 to 1880* (1883), sought to establish a basis for Negro greatness by demonstrating how the civilizations of Egypt, Greece, and Rome borrowed their culture from ancient black civilizations; the tragedy of Africa and the black race was that following their early greatness they had turned their backs on God, experienced moral decline, and lost their civilization. Perhaps the most interesting (and bizarre) claim of black greatness came from William T. Alexander, who advanced the theory that mythical Atlantis, the home of an advanced civilization which at one time had controlled the world, was inhabited and controlled by blacks.[7]

After establishing the past greatness of their race, black historians attempted to account for the racial disparity that characterized the world in the late nineteenth century. Most maintained, first, that in America, despite the handicap of slavery,

blacks had made tremendous advancements, and, second, that Africa had declined from greatness into savagery because of environment or because they had incurred the wrath of God. Implicit in these arguments was the assumption that Africa had fallen far behind Western civilization in morality and social organization as well as in technology; that, in short, African history was a story of degeneration and devolution that ran counter to the Western story of evolution and progress. For Africa and the black race to rise again, they must re-acquire civilization from white society. This diagnosis fit well into the philosophy of self-help and economic advancement outlined by Crumwell.[8]

Similar attitudes were emerging in the field of black education. By the early 1890s Crumwell's self-help ideology, embodied in the concept of industrial education, had largely supplanted classical or liberal arts education as the principal focus of America's black colleges. The American Missionary Association and most other religious and secular bodies that supported black education in the post-Reconstruction South committed themselves to industrial education in the early 1880s.

Their arguments for doing so were: first, industrial education more effectively addressed the needs of a majority of the students, who came to colleges from underdeveloped agricultural or industrial backgrounds; second, since few students arrived with adequate academic preparation, there was little demand for liberal arts courses; and, third, industrial and vocational classes provided immediate economic return to financially strapped institutions by raising crops and livestock, constructing buildings and furniture, and in other ways contributing directly to the survival of the institution. By the early 1890s the trend toward industrial education had become so pervasive that even prominent liberal arts colleges such as Fisk and Atlanta felt compelled to add courses in agriculture and the industrial arts.[9]

Industrial education enjoyed widespread popularity not only because it addressed the real needs of many black colleges and their students, but also because it met the needs of dominant elements in both the black and the white communities. Among blacks it was compatible with the concepts of self-help and racial solidarity. Industrial education had as its goal the creation of a race of thrifty, hard-working, industrious men and women focusing their energies on economic advancement rather than on political equality. In addition industrial education appeased whites who had criticized classical or liberal arts curricula at black colleges as either not addressing the educational needs of blacks or, even worse, creating black college graduates who refused to work as manual laborers.[10]

Conservative black clergymen also contributed to the development of the self-help ideology in the late nineteenth century. They developed an image of blacks which incorporated the patience, humility, and easygoing nature that had been one of the survival strategies during slavery and that was a defense mechanism against the racial hostility that was so widespread at the turn of the century. As S. P. Fullinwider explained:

> The "Christ-like" image (stereotype) of the Negro was born out of the formation of ego-defense mechanisms contrived in the slave's unconscious to maintain self-respect during a time when the choice in handling aggression was either to repress it or be destroyed. The slave's patience, humility, and good nature were necessary for his survival. Now, these were the very traits that the Christian religion set before the slave and the post-Emancipation generation as the ideal for which all men should strive—they were the traits of Christ, himself. It was not difficult, therefore, for the oppressed Negro to interpret his subservient behavior as being Christ-like. In fact it was necessary for his self-esteem (ego-defenses) that he see himself as not servile; that he see himself, rather, as the realization of the Christian ideal.[11]

With this image blacks could maintain their self-respect while avoiding a direct confrontation with racism. They could glorify their meekness, patience, and humility, while still condemning the inhumanity of white racism. Furthermore this image gave blacks a special mission—to carry the values of Christianity to a hostile and unChristian world, to save Africa, America, or both.[12]

Although these arguments for self-help and racial pride were rapidly becoming dominant in black thought in the 1880s, as long as Frederick Douglass lived, he served as a strong counterbalance to these views. In the three decades that followed the Civil War Douglass stood at the very apex of black leadership in America. His credentials were impeccable; he was the undisputed leader of his race from the time of his emergence during the abolitionist movement until his death in 1895. Throughout his career Douglass symbolized protest and political agitation, although until the early 1880s he had combined protest for political rights with a call for racial pride, economic independence, and self-help. But, as most of the black community responded to the deteriorating racial situation by moving away from protest and toward self-help, Douglass moved in the opposite direction. During the last years of his life he increasingly expressed doubts about the effectiveness of self-help and concentrated instead on the struggle against segregation and disenfranchisement. For Douglass the racial problem was not merely a black problem but an American one; the fundamental issue was whether American justice applied equally to all citizens or only to some. In addition Douglass pointed out that black racial pride differed little from the arguments of white racists; instead of racial solidarity he stressed assimilation.[13]

When Douglass' dominating presence was removed by his death, his ideas quickly faded into the background, and the self-help ideology of men like Crumwell became dominant. This process was accelerated by the emergence of a successor to Douglass who embraced this ideology. By the mid-1890s Booker T. Washington had taken over the position recently vacated by Douglass as the most powerful man in black America.

Booker T. Washington had been born in slavery in 1856. Following emancipation he received an education at Hampton Institute in Virginia, where he became a disciple of Samuel Chapman Armstrong's brand of industrial education. In 1881 he established Tuskegee Institute and made it his power base as well as a major center of agricultural and industrial education. Washington was an educator, a spokesman, and an organizer, but not an originator of ideas. His biographer, Louis R. Harlan, saw him as "not an intellectual, but a man of action. Ideas he cared little for. Power was his game."[14] The concepts usually associated with his name, self-help and industrial education, had become dominant ideologies in the black community some time before he rose to prominence. Washington himself had been thoroughly indoctrinated in those views while a student at Hampton Institute, which had pioneered the program of industrial education for blacks in the late 1860s under the leadership of Samuel Chapman Armstrong.

Booker T. Washington's philosophy, as it was publicly expressed, was fairly simple and remarkably consistent over the course of his career. Essentially he argued that thrift, industry, and Christian morality would eventually earn blacks their Constitutional rights. The first essential step toward equality must be for blacks to learn trades so that they might compete effectively with whites in the economic arena. Therefore, blacks must make, as their educational objectives, the acquisition of those practical skills that would promote their economic development. Thus far Washington merely echoed the call for industrial education that was already widely accepted in the black community. Far more controversial was the corollary to his thesis for racial advancement that urged accommodation with segregation. The best-known public expression of this was his 1895 Atlanta speech in which he followed his call for economic self-help with the proclamation: "In all things that are purely social we can be as separate as the five fingers, yet one as the hand in all things essential to mutual progress. . . . The wisest among my race understand that the agitation of questions of social equality is the extremist folly."[15] Washington in Atlanta proposed that blacks put aside, for the time being, their quest for desegregation and the vote; in return they would be permitted to develop their own separate but equal economic, social, and educational institutions within the framework of the expanding southern economy. Although a few blacks criticized this approach as accommodationist, it was embraced by most of the black intellectual elite at the turn of the century and almost universally praised by white Americans.[16]

Washington would continue to stress the principles he outlined in his Atlanta speech. He consistently counseled patience in matters of racial injustice; he pronounced protest and racial agitation ineffective tactics and advised instead that living respectable lives and acquiring wealth was a much surer route to equality. In addition, in spite of the steadily deteriorating racial situation and the upsurge in racial violence, he continually expressed faith in the good will of southern whites. Late in his career Washington went so far as to argue that, notwithstanding the obvious racial problems, southern blacks enjoyed greater opportunity than blacks anywhere else and that American blacks were better off than the European poor.[17] Throughout his life Washington gave little public attention to racial injustice. Instead he directed his energies toward winning the good will of southern whites, whose support he believed was vital for racial advancement.

Although on the basis of most of his public statements and activities Washington earned the reputation of an extreme accommodationist, there was another, less public side to the man. While he was sincere in his commitment to self-help and industrial education and while he truly believed that racial progress depended on the support of southern whites, he often involved himself clandestinely in behind-the-scenes activities to combat racial injustice. While publicly denouncing protest and preaching patience, Washington secretly diverted funds to help finance court battles against segregation. In 1895, for example, he lobbied against black disenfranchisement in Georgia, and in the years that followed he supported the legal fight against discriminatory laws in several southern states, by both soliciting funds and contributing from his own pocket. Before the Atlanta speech he had been even more outspoken, condemning racial segregation of public transportation and as late as 1894 urging blacks to boycott segregated streetcars. Even after he donned his accommodationist cloak, his public statements, if examined very carefully, reveal a subtle protest against racial inequality. In the Atlanta speech itself, beneath the call for patience and ambiguous references to justice, progress, and uplift, Washington indicated that ultimately he expected blacks, through moderate means, to gain their full and unrestricted political and social rights. This theme was never dominant in Washington's rhetoric; most whites, distracted and seduced by his moderate tone and conciliatory phrases, remained blind to it, but the Tuskegeean's supporters stressed this side of his philosophy.[18]

Within a few months of his Atlanta speech Washington had become politically the most powerful black in America. There were several reasons for his rapid accumulation of power. First,

Washington emerged as nationally prominent before anyone else had moved to fill the power vacuum left by the death of Frederick Douglass. Even more important, Washington's philosophy, and especially his association with industrial education, fitted well with the prevailing attitudes of both whites and blacks. The Tuskegeean reflected Crumwell's self-help ideology and the educational policies of his mentor at Hampton, Samuel Chapman Armstrong. His conciliatory tone and stress on an economic approach to racial problems placated whites and gained their enthusiastic support. President Grover Cleveland saw in the Atlanta speech a "new hope" for black Americans, while the Atlanta *Constitution* called Washington a "wise counselor and a safe leader."[19] Finally, Washington's position of leadership among blacks was secured by the fact that whites, in both the North and the South, elevated him to the position of spokesman for his race. Washington discovered soon after the Atlanta speech that politicians consulted him before they dispensed patronage to blacks, and more importantly, philanthropists sought his advice before they funded black institutions.

Washington's power increased rapidly after the turn of the century. During Theodore Roosevelt's administration few blacks received political appointments without clearance from Tuskegee; black colleges, churches, and other institutions found it almost impossible to obtain contributions without his endorsement. Washington's power was also manifested in the control that he exerted over the editorial policy of the black press, especially the influential New York *Age,* and his influence over appointments in the black church and in black colleges. By 1905 Washington had become the virtual dictator of black America.

To complicate matters, as he grew in eminence, Washington became increasingly sensitive to criticism, especially by blacks, and used his influence to suppress those who opposed his policies or who threatened his personal position or prestige. He employed every means at his disposal against his critics. He placed spies in their organizations, used his influence with the press to discredit them and their policies, deprived them of their political, church, or college positions, and made it difficult for them to obtain financial support for their programs. If it had been within his power, Washington undoubtedly would have excommunicated his antagonists from the black race.

Initially Washington's tactics for dealing with his critics were relatively mild. In the late 1890s he used his control over patronage to lure more radical blacks into his camp. For example, in 1901 in an effort to muzzle one of his more outspoken critics, civil rights activist Mary Church Terrell, he arranged for her husband to become the first black federal judge in Washington, D.C.; he also headed off a move by James Weldon Johnson in late 1905 to affiliate a group of black writers and poets with the Niagara Movement, and in the process bought Johnson's loyalty by arranging for him to be appointed United States Consul to Venezuela and Nicaragua. As opposition coalesced against the "Tuskegee Machine," Washington's tactics became more aggressive. He used Melvin Chisum to spy on William Monroe Trotter and on the Niagara Movement in 1905-1906; he used his influence in the White House to block the appointment of W. E. B. Du Bois as assistant superintendent of Washington, D.C., schools in 1906, and to arrange the removal of Judson W. Lyons from his position as register of the U.S. Treasury. Lyons had made the mistake of voicing moderate support for Trotter.[20]

As Washington became more and more dictatorial, opposition to both his policies and his style of leadership grew within the black community. It is essential to remember that the ideas that Washington championed in the years following his Atlanta speech, although accepted by a majority of blacks, never enjoyed unanimous support. There were always those who remained within the more militant tradition of Frederick Douglass and who were unwilling to accept the accommodation that the Tuskegeean preached. Although as late as 1900 Washington was almost free of criticism, within three years opposition surfaced which ultimately split the black intellectual community into warring factions of Bookerites and anti-Bookerites. Men like Francis J. Grimké, while embracing many of the tenets of self-help and racial pride, carried these principles to militant rather than accommodationist conclusions. Grimké, for example, accepted self-help largely because he distrusted whites, whom he characterized as savage barbarians dedicated to re-enslaving blacks.[21] Thus, he could not accept Booker T. Washington's confidence that through self-help and industry blacks could win the admiration of whites. Grimké and other critics of Washington had only to point to the fact that during the Tuskegeean's ascendancy, while he preached moderation and patience, blacks were being disenfranchised and lynched without letup.

Francis Grimké and his brother Archibold formed the nucleus of a growing circle of black intellectuals who were dissatisfied with Washington. The split first surfaced because of the continuing question of whether black political strategy should be based on accommodation or agitation, but it soon spread to encompass a criticism of Washington's educational philosophy and his style of leadership—especially the heavyhanded tactics which he used to silence his opponents within the black community. In many respects Washington's critics returned to Douglass' emphasis on political action rather than on economic or moral improvement as the most effective way to achieve racial justice in America; in some ways, however, they accepted the Tuskegeean's emphasis on economic improvement, but combined self-help with a call for political action. Actually, it is difficult to define precisely the political and social ideology of Washington's opponents (whom some labeled the anti-Bookerites), because the group consisted of numerous elements with divergent views who often were united only in their antagonism toward Washington and his dominance of black America. August Meier presented the best description of these divisions in the black community when he characterized the Bookerite versus anti-Bookerite conflict as resulting in numerous groups "roughly correlated with each other, so that gradualism, conciliation, the middle-class virtues, racial solidarity, self-help, and sympathy for Washington tended to cluster together to form a 'conservative' outlook, while agitation for civil and political rights, advocacy of immediate and complete integration, interest in the labor movement, and opposition to the Tuskegeean also tended to cluster together to form a 'radical' outlook."[22] It is important to add that the conservative faction did not have a monopoly on racial pride and self-help; both factions endorsed those values.

Organized opposition to Washington first became significant during 1903. Several events that year underscored that deep divisions had developed in the black community. The first occurred during the annual meeting of the Afro-American Council. The Afro-American Council, which had originally been founded as the Afro-American League by T. Thomas Fortune in 1890 as a militant organization committed both to racial solidarity and agitation for equal rights, had, by the turn of the century, fallen under the control of the Tuskegeean. At the 1903 meeting militants attempted, unsuccessfully, to regain control of the organization. The blatant manner in which Washington retaliated to suppress his critics (who were not really all that militant) alienated a number of blacks.

This opposition strengthened in the aftermath of the so-called Boston riot. On July 30, 1903, as Washington addressed two thousand listeners in Boston, a small group of dissidents led by William Monroe Trotter disrupted the speech, and police were called in to restore order. Several of the anti-Washington hecklers were arrested, including Trotter, who spent a month in jail. This incident had a major impact on the politics of black America by driving a wedge between Booker T. Washington and W. E. B. Du Bois. Although Du Bois had no involvement in the disturbance, he spent time as a guest in the Trotter home later that summer, and he criticized his host's jail term; this convinced Washington that the young Atlanta professor was behind the riot and prompted the Tuskegeean to launch a campaign to discredit his opponent and punish him by denying him access to funding and by threatening his employer with a loss of funds.[23] This, plus the publication earlier in the year of *The Souls of Black Folk* with its chapter "Of Mr. Booker T. Washington and Others," intensified the philosophical differences between Washington and Du Bois, crystallized the growing split in the black intellectual community, and propelled Du Bois to the forefront of the anti-Bookerite faction.

Washington's opponents coalesced, first in the Niagara movement and then in the National Association for the Advancement of Colored People. In July 1905 Du Bois and twenty-eight other black leaders, impatient with accommodation, met in Fort Erie, Ontario, to organize a more militant civil rights organization. The resulting Niagara movement selected Du Bois as its general secretary and dedicated itself to universal manhood suffrage and the elimination of "all caste distinctions based simply on race or color."[24] The major target of the movement was Booker T. Washington's domination of black America; in turn the Tuskegeean used his control of the black press to discredit the organization and his political influence and prestige to sabotage the careers of the Niagaraites. Faced with Washington's relentless opposition, the Niagara movement never gained sufficient funds or enough influence to achieve much success, and it disbanded in 1909.[25] Most of the blacks associated with it shifted their affiliation to the NAACP following its establishment in 1910 under the leadership of Du Bois and a number of white progressives. This bi-racial group was strong enough and well enough funded to withstand Washington's attacks and, after the Tuskegeean's death in 1915, succeeded in reconciling and uniting most of the factions in the black community.

During the first two decades of the twentieth century W. E. B. Du Bois was the man who symbolized an alternative to the philosophy and leadership of Booker T. Washington. The contrasting educational backgrounds of these two men reflect clearly their ideological differences. While Washington was immersed in industrial education at Hampton and Tuskegee, Du Bois graduated from Fisk and then pursued graduate study in history, philosophy, and psychology at Harvard and the University of Berlin. At Harvard, Du Bois studied with the best minds of late nineteenth-century America—William James, Josiah Royce, George Santayana, and Albert Bushnell Hart—and emerged with a deep commitment to scholarship and convinced that intellectual and scientific study were essential in countering racial prejudice and dispelling racial myths. After completing his Ph.D. he published his dissertation, *The Suppression of the African Slave Trade* (1896), and *The Philadelphia Negro: A Social Study* (1899), works which established his reputation as both a historian and a sociologist. He also became a professor of sociology at Atlanta University, where he attempted to instill a scientific approach to the study of black America.

In spite of their very different backgrounds, Du Bois initially supported Washington and his positions. He congratulated the Tuskegeean for the 1895 Atlanta speech, and he defended the Atlanta Compromise as offering the basis for a real settlement between whites and blacks in the South. As late as 1903 the Bookerites still hoped to recruit Du Bois for the faculty at Tuskegee and wed him to their faction. By that time, however, Du Bois had begun to express reservations about Washington's educational and political philosophies. In his assessment of Washington in *The Souls of Black Folk* he acknowledged that the Tuskegeean was the "most distinguished Southerner since Jefferson Davis, and the one with the largest personal following"; furthermore, Du Bois insisted that he sincerely valued his achievements and recognized the political realities in the South that forced moderation. However, he sharply criticized Washington for actually perpetuating the alleged inferiority of blacks through his educational system and for counseling blacks to give up temporarily their claims for political power, civil rights, and higher education for their youth. The most damning indictment of the Washington program, Du Bois maintained, was that during the ten years that it had dominated black thought, blacks indeed had been disenfranchised, had been legally segregated in a distinct and inferior civil status, and had witnessed the steady withdrawal of funds from liberal arts programs at black colleges.[26]

Du Bois responded to the shortcomings in Washington's program with his own agenda for American blacks. He based his approach on the conviction that blacks needed well-educated leadership to direct the uplifting of the race. To accomplish this, black colleges and universities should not focus their efforts exclusively on industrial education but should continue to offer a strong liberal arts program to produce the class of teachers and professionals necessary to carry out this task. Du Bois had no objections to practical education in the industrial arts (so long as it did not perpetuate skills that were becoming obsolete in industrial America), but he warned that it would be dangerous to ignore classical education because ultimately it would be the educated elite, the "talented tenth," that would bring culture and progress to the race. As Du Bois put it, "if we make money the object of man-training, we shall develop moneymakers but not necessarily men; if we make technical skill the object of education, we may possess artisans but not, in nature, men. Men we shall have only as we make manhood the object of the work of the schools—intelligence, broad sympathy, knowledge of the world that was and is, and of the relation of men to it—this is the curriculum of that Higher Education which must underlie true life."[27]

In addition to challenging Washington's ideas about education, Du Bois also rejected the Tuskegeean's political tactics. Du Bois insisted that protest, not accommodation, was the only viable way for blacks to secure their civil and political rights. He argued that blacks could never gain self-respect until they fought for their rights; they could never secure and defend their position as property owners until they achieved and exercised the right to vote. Du Bois never accepted segregation on even a temporary basis during this period of his life. Instead, he argued that "separate but equal" was never equal, but a system designed to foster inequality and perpetuate the subordination of blacks. Although he urged blacks to develop their own businesses and to patronize the businesses of other blacks, and while he recognized that integration might undermine the economic development of the black community, he insisted that the evils of segregation more than offset its short-term economic advantages.[28] Du Bois believed in racial solidarity, but not as an end in itself; rather, racial solidarity should be used as a weapon to protest disenfranchisement and segregation and to win the struggle for civil rights.

Thus far the differences between Du Bois and Washington, though substantial, were differences in degree rather than substance, differences in means rather than ends. Both men were committed to uplifting their race, instilling racial pride, and securing political and civil rights. However, Du Bois, the greatest black intellect of the prewar period, constantly explored concepts that were alien to the more conservative Washington. In 1910, for example, Du Bois shocked many moderates of both races when he condemned the prohibition of interracial marriage (although he qualified his stand with the observation that current conditions did not encourage widespread marriage between the races). He also flirted with the belief that there were inherent differences between the races and that strong ties existed between American blacks and other colored peoples.[29] Du Bois also examined socialism and attempted to explain racial discrimination in terms of class conflict. In 1911 he joined the Socialist party, and by the end of the decade he had become convinced that the ultimate solution of racial problems would be found through the elimination of class antagonisms and a union of black and white workers.

While Du Bois was challenging Washington's leadership, black historians also distanced themselves from the Tuskeegean, related to the more militant stance of black intellectuals in the early twentieth century, and helped popularize another concept that would characterize the New Negro. Whereas their colleagues in the late nineteenth century had been preoccupied with defending blacks against the attack of racially biased historians and anthropologists and had generally accepted the interpretation that their race lagged behind the West in terms of culture, after 1910 black historians became more aggressive and chauvinistic. They remained committed to the concepts of self-help and racial pride, but they were far less defensive in their interpretation of black history than their predecessors had been. One of their principal concerns was making sure that black history was included in the curricula of black schools. Organizations such as the Negro Society for Historical Research, founded in 1912, reflected this growing interest in black history. In addition to their interest in the history of black Americans, members of this organization also reinterpreted African history and placed new emphasis on the African roots of black culture. For example, A. A. Schomburg, the West Indian book collector and librarian at the Harlem branch of the New York Public Library, stressed the ties between American blacks and African and Arabic cultures and suggested that black history should be used to stimulate black patriotism; another member, John Edward Bruce, argued that whites feared black history because they knew that it would prove that African civilization predated European civilization and that the white man stole his alphabet and other tools of culture from blacks.[30]

This belief that their African heritage should be a source of pride and the basis of a racial solidarity that linked all colored people was another ingredient in the emerging black consciousness that would be known as the New Negro. Unlike an earlier generation that had addressed the decline and corruption of African culture, and in doing so apologized for their African roots, the New Negro embraced Africanism.

We can see elements of pan-Africanism as early as the 1890s in the thought of several prominent blacks, including both Du Bois and Washington. Alexander Crumwell, along with several other black leaders, participated in the Chicago Congress on Africa in 1893, where the idea of black emigration to Africa was a major topic of discussion, and four years later he promoted efforts of a group of African and Caribbean students to establish an African Association in London. Even Booker T. Washington endorsed pan-Africanism. Like a number of his contemporaries, he supported the idea of a pan-African conference during his 1899 visit to London. On a more concrete level Washington established an agricultural project in Togo, invited African dignitaries to speak at Tuskegee, and sent a number of graduates to jobs in several African countries. Ironically, W. E. B. Du Bois, who would become a major advocate of pan-Africanism, initially was suspicious of the idea. In 1897 he rejected as premature a plan calling for the migration of American blacks to the Congo Free State and proposed instead a more conservative effort to establish contacts between black Americans and Africa. Within a few years, however, he had embraced pan-Africanism. He served as a delegate to an international pan-African conference in London in 1900 and was selected to direct the American branch of the Pan-African Association. Du Bois's other obli-

SOCIAL, POLITICAL, AND ECONOMIC TRENDS

gations and interests would keep his commitment to pan-Africanism in the background until after the First World War. Nevertheless, the relationship between black Americans and the colonial peoples of Africa and the Caribbean would become an increasingly important concern during the first quarter of the twentieth century, especially following the war, when Marcus Garvey would base a mass movement on this issue.[31]

Marcus Garvey was born in a small town on the northern coast of Jamaica in 1887. As a young man, he worked as a printer and briefly operated a newspaper, *Garvey's Watchman,* in 1909. In 1910 he left Jamaica, traveling first to Central America and then to England, where he took courses at a college for working-class youth and observed British politics, from the debates in Parliament to the speeches in Hyde Park, while he lived among the small but diverse groups that made up London's ethnic community in the early twentieth century. In these surroundings Garvey first encountered pan-Africanism.[32]

When Garvey returned to Jamaica in 1914, he founded his Universal Negro Improvement Association (UNIA), which in its early years combined the ideas of pan-Africanism with the self-help and industrial education program of Booker T. Washington. Garvey did not enjoy much success as an organizer in Jamaica. After two years the UNIA had only about a hundred members, while his efforts to establish an institution modeled after Tuskegee did not get off the ground. In 1916 he left for the United States, primarily in an effort to raise funds for his school.

By 1917 Garvey had settled in Harlem, where he reestablished his UNIA and made contacts among other black political leaders, especially those who shared his commitment to pan-Africanism, but also black socialists and labor leaders like A. Philip Randolph. Garvey's goal was to unite (under his leadership) the four hundred million black people of the world; he preached a message that drew on the self-help doctrines of Washington and called for the creation of a black economy within the white capitalist world, that would both liberate the blacks of America from the oppression of discrimination and redeem the peoples of Africa from the oppression of colonialism. Garvey's genius was his ability to capture the loyalty of the black masses in America. By August 1921 he reported a membership of over four million; even if these claims were inflated, before his organization began unraveling in 1923 Garvey had created and controlled the only large-scale organization among the black urban masses in America.

As the 1920s began, the various strains of prewar black thought each contributed to the new black consciousness that would be labeled the New Negro. The militancy symbolized by Du Bois become an integral part of this concept. While the accommodationist approach to racial problems associated with Washington was scorned by the new generation of black intellectuals, the New Negro accepted his doctrines of self-help and racial pride. Likewise, while most black intellectuals rejected the flamboyant and vulgar style of Garvey and his movement, they were attracted by the ideology of pan-Africanism. The New Negro was never a simple or comfortable blend of these ideologies; it was rather a dynamic ideology filled with internal conflicts and even contradictions whose fundamental questions remained unresolved. What was the true identity and nature of black Americans? Were they black, American, or African? Could they best achieve their destiny through integration and assimilation into American culture, or should they attempt to identify and preserve their own special traits—even through segregation? The New Negro emerged from the war years determined to be assertive and to stand up for his or her rights, but the New Negro also struggled with the diverse alternatives that blacks faced. These conflicts fueled black intellectual debates during the 1920s, and they fueled the artistic endeavors of black writers and poets. These conflicts, and the quest for their resolution, are the underlying themes of the Harlem Renaissance.

## Notes

1. James Weldon Johnson, *Along This Way* (New York: Viking, 1961), 158-59.

2. For the most complete information about Johnson's early life see Eugene Levy, *James Weldon Johnson: Black Leader, Black Voice* (Chicago: University of Chicago Press, 1973), 3-73; see also Johnson, *Along This Way,* 3-156.

3. Johnson, *Along This Way,* 188-89. Eugene Levy contends that the deteriorating racial situation in Jacksonville and the declining support for black education were major factors in Johnson's decision. See Levy, 68-79.

4. Johnson, *Along This Way,* 177, 221.

5. Placing blacks in consular posts was a major problem for Anderson and Washington. President Roosevelt had difficulty identifying locations where the appointment of a black would not cause undue friction;

blacks, in turn, often were reluctant to accept low-paying positions in out-of-the-way places. Given this situation Johnson became a major figure in Anderson's and Washington's efforts to keep blacks in the foreign service. See Levy, 105-108.

6. Johnson, *Along This Way*, 193, 237.

7. James Weldon Johnson to Brander Mathews, [November] 1908, JWJ; James Weldon Johnson to Carl Van Doren, December 28, 1922, JWJ.

8. For the best account of McKay's life see Wayne F. Cooper, *Claude McKay: Rebel Sojourner in the Harlem Renaissance, A Biography* (Baton Rouge: Louisiana State University Press, 1987), 1-62.

9. James Weldon Johnson, ed., *The Book of American Negro Poetry* (New York: Harcourt, Brace & World, 1959), 165-66.

10. Cooper, 64-73.

11. Ibid., 78-81, 93-95.

12. Claude McKay, "The Harlem Dancer," in *Selected Poems of Claude McKay* (New York: Bookman Associated, 1953), 61.

13. Claude McKay, *A Long Way from Home* (New York: Harcourt, Brace & World, 1970), 26.

14. Ibid., 99, 110-12, 114.

15. James Weldon Johnson, "American Negro Poets and Their Poetry," unpublished manuscript of a speech given at Howard University, April 10, 1924, JWJ.

16. For an account of Hughes's childhood see James A. Emanuel, *Langston Hughes* (New Haven: College & University Press, 1967), 18-19.

17. Langston Hughes, *The Big Sea* (New York: Hill and Wang, 1963), 16, 26.

18. Ibid., 40.

19. Ibid., 61-66.

20. Ibid., 92-94.

21. Ibid.; Johnson, "American Negro Poets."

22. Langston Hughes, "The Weary Blues," in *The Weary Blues* (New York: Knopf, 1926), 23-24.

23. Arna Bontemps, "The Negro Renaissance: Jean Toomer and the Harlem Writers of the 1920s," in *Anger and Beyond: The Negro Writer in the United States*, ed. Herbert Hill (New York: Harper & Row, 1968), 24; Countee Cullen to Jean Toomer, September 29, 1923, JTP.

24. Quoted in Arna Bontemps, "Introduction" in Jean Toomer, *Cane* (New York: Harper & Row, 1969), viii. The best biographical information on Toomer is found in Cynthia Earl Kerman and Richard Eldridge, *The Lives of Jean Toomer: A Hunger for Wholeness* (Baton Rouge: Louisiana State University Press, 1987), and in Toomer's various unpublished autobiographies, especially "Book of Parents," JTP.

25. Kerman and Eldridge, 65-75.

26. Jean Toomer, "From Exile into Being," unpublished manuscript of the second volume of Toomer's autobiography, JTP, 97-98.

27. Kerman and Eldridge, 80-81.

28. Ibid., 91-92.

29. Jean Toomer, "Exile into Being," 98-99.

30. Kerman and Eldridge, 102-103.

31. Ibid., 99-100, 108; Allen Tate to Jean Toomer, November 7, 1923, JTP.

32. Alain Locke to Jean Toomer, n.d., JTP; Alain Locke to Jean Toomer, January 4, 1923, JTP; William Stanley Braithwaite, "The Negro in American Literature," in *The New Negro*, ed. Alain Locke (New York: Atheneum, 1969), 44.

# FURTHER READING

## *Criticism*

Balshaw, Maria. Introduction to *Looking for Harlem: Urban Aesthetics in African American Literature*, pp. 1-13. London: Pluto Press, 2000.

*Discusses how novels written by Blacks during the 1920s, 1930s, and 1940s treat urbanism. Also provides an introduction to the criticism and reevaluation of Black literary history that can be found in writings of recent decades.*

Cunard, Nancy. "Harlem Reviewed." In *The Politics and Aesthetics of 'New Negro' Literature*, pp. 183-91. New York: Garland Publishing, 1996.

*Portrays the Harlem of the 1930s.*

De Jongh, James. "The Legendary Capital" and "City of Refuge." In *Vicious Modernism: Black Harlem and the Literary Imagination*, pp. 5-32. Cambridge: Cambridge University Press, 1990.

*Characterizes the Harlem of the 1920s. Studies several key literary works and analyzes how New Negro poets and writers of the first decades of the twentieth century evoked and interpreted Harlem.*

Elmes, A. F. "Garvey and Garveyism: An Estimate." *Opportunity* 3, no. 29 (May 1925): 139-41.

*Discusses the successes and failures of Marcus Garvey and of Garveyism.*

Huggins, Nathan Irvin. "Harlem: Capital of the Black World." In *Harlem Renaissance*, pp. 13-51. London: Oxford University Press, 1971.

*Explores why Harlem drew major Black thinkers like James Weldon Johnson, W. E. B. Du Bois, and Marcus Garvey and how these figures, especially Du Bois and Garvey, interpreted the events and politics of World War I as well as the internal struggles and antagonisms that existed among the Black intellectual progressives.*

Hughes, Langston. "My Adventures as a Social Poet." *The Politics and Aesthetics of "New Negro" Literature*, edited by Cary D. Wintz, pp. 325-32. New York: Garland Publishing, 1996.

*Hughes relates how his poems have bred hostility. Originally published in 1947.*

Johnson, Charles S. "After Garvey—What?" *Opportunity* 1, no. 8 (August 1923): 231-33.

*Comments on Marcus Garvey's thought and leadership.*

Jones, Eugene Kinckle. "The Negro's Opportunity Today." *Opportunity* 6, no. 1 (January 1928): 10-12.

*Summarizes the inroads African Americans have made in all areas of life.*

Matthews, Mark D. "Perspective on Marcus Garvey." *Black World* 25, no. 4 (February 1976): 36-48.

*Outlines Garvey's political thought, especially his interpretation of communism, and points out common misconceptions about it.*

Maxwell, William J. "Kitchen Mechanics and Parlor Nationalists: Andy Razaf, Black Bolshevism, and Harlem's Renaissance." In *New Negro, Old Left: African-American Writing and Communism between the Wars,* pp. 13-61. New York: Columbia University Press, 1999.

*Examines Andy Razaf and the first Black bolsheviks in the Harlem Renaissance, arguing that bolshevism was an "invited guest," rather than an imposition, in Harlem. Studies how Black art of the time expressed bolshevism and refutes the assertation that communism killed the New Negro Movement.*

Osofsky, Gilbert. "'Come Out from Among Them': Negro Migration and Settlement, 1890-1914." In *Harlem: The Making of a Ghetto,* pp. 17-34. New York: Harper and Row, 1971.

*Discusses the reasons behind Black migration and traces the migration patterns of Southern Blacks moving west and north, particularly to New York City, over a period of three decades.*

Taylor, Clyde. "Garvey's Ghost: Revamping the Twenties." *Black World* 25, no. 4 (February 1976): 54-67.

*Discusses the portrayal of Garvey and Garveyism in the following books:* The Harlem Renaissance Remembered, *by Arna Bontemps,* Marcus Garvey and the Vision of Africa, *by John Henrik Clarke,* Voices of a Black Nation: Political Journalism in the Harlem Renaissance, *by Theodore G. Vincent,* Mumbo Jumbo, *by Ishmael Reed, and* Good Morning Revolution: Uncollected Writings of Social Protest, *by Faith Berry.*

Wagner, Jean. "The Negro Renaissance." In *Black Poets of the United States: From Paul Laurence Dunbar to Langston Hughes,* pp. 149-93. Urbana: University of Illinois Press, 1973.

*Addresses the forces that aided in the creation of the Negro Renaissance, what the Negro Renaissance was, and the role Black poets played in that movement.*

# PUBLISHING AND PERIODICALS DURING THE HARLEM RENAISSANCE

As a cultural and intellectual movement among African Americans in the 1920s, the Harlem Renaissance offered a growing number of men and women of color the opportunity to write, publish, and express their ideas as never before. Still, the movement came about not only in response to new concepts promoted by African American writers, artists, and intellectuals, but also due to a generally heightened mainstream awareness of Black contributions to American literature and culture. These realizations led to the establishment and growth of a variety of Black cultural institutions, many of which still function today. As African American organizations in the United States gained recognition and influence, they launched new periodicals, including *Opportunity*, the journal of the National Urban League, and *The Crisis*, published by the National Association for the Advancement of Colored People (NAACP). Through such publications African American writers found an audience and a cultural forum for their works. Meanwhile, major publishing firms began to take notice, reversing a trend toward the exclusion of Black authors and capitalizing on a new vogue for the increasingly popular literary expressions emanating from the vibrant center of Harlem. The publication of Jean Toomer's novel *Cane* by the well-known publisher J. B. Lippincott in 1923 attested to the viability of fiction written by Black authors and dealing with African American life. Two years later, with the appearance of Alain Locke's groundbreaking anthology *The New Negro,* a collection that included representative poetry, fiction, and prose from a range of outstanding African American authors of the period, the Harlem Renaissance movement reached what many critics view as its literary highpoint.

The history of publication by Blacks during the Harlem Renaissance period is one of a relatively slow recognition, followed by a broad expansion during the mid-1920s, and an eventual decline by the early 1930s. Critics have identified several writers as the most significant literary precursors to the movement, including Claude McKay, William S. Braithwaite, and James Weldon Johnson. These three men, whose works began to appear in established literary periodicals prior to the 1920s, are generally viewed as transitional figures in the African American poetic tradition. During this period, Black writers were largely unable to publish in any but the most liberal magazines. Securing book publication with major publishing houses, likewise, was extremely difficult for African Americans before the early 1920s. However, the rise of the African American press, led by such magazines as *Opportunity* and *The Crisis,* helped elicit interest in the works of such writing talents as Langston Hughes, Countee Cullen, Sterling A. Brown, and Zora Neale Hurston, and drew the attention of editors at prominent publishing companies and mainstream periodicals. Yet, the process of discovery was measured. Joining Jean Toomer's *Cane* of the previous year, Jessie Fauset's novel *There Is Confusion* was printed by Boni and Liveright in 1924. That same year, Alfred Knopf published Walter White's novel *The Fire in the Flint* and later works by Langston Hughes and James Weldon Johnson. Meanwhile, a new form of literary patronage began to develop in New York City during the 1920s, as a few wealthy whites, newly aware of African American authors, sponsored several young Black writers. Zora Neale Hurston, who had arrived in Harlem in 1925 with little money, was discovered by the affluent Fannie Hurst, who offered Hurston a job as her personal secretary and helped finance the struggling young writer's education. The poet Langston Hughes, similarly, enjoyed the patronage of Charlotte Osgood Mason, but commentators note that the cases of Hurston and Hughes were exceptional. With the close of the 1920s and the deepening of economic depression in the ensuing years, such support began to vanish. Hurston's major works, including her skillfully narrated collection of African American folktales *Mules and Men* (1935), did not appear until the following decade, when the pace of Black publishing had slackened. Soon, after the Renaissance excitement had abated and Black authors struggled to find work, Hurston was to mourn what she called "the Anglo-Saxon's lack of curiosity about the internal lives of Negroes," and described the accumulated burden of racial stereotypes in the United States as "The American Museum of Unnatural History."

Among the principal intellectual proponents of the Harlem Renaissance, author and editor Alain Locke stands out as a seminal figure. Locke's 1925 anthology of African American literature entitled *The New Negro: An Interpretation* collected the works of all the major Black authors of the period, from more established writers like Claude McKay to newer figures such as Langston Hughes and Zora Neale Hurston. The collection also popularized the so-called "New Negro Movement," as the Renaissance was designated at the time. Featuring fiction by Jean Toomer, Hurston, and Jessie Fauset; the poetry of Hughes, McKay, and Countee Cullen; essays by James Weldon Johnson, W. E. B. Du Bois, and Charles S. Johnson; along with works by numerous other contributors, *The New Negro* became the standard by which the literary contributions of Blacks in America would be judged. With it, Locke had articulated a fresh vision of African American art and creativity. The collection arose from the publication of a special issue of the journal *Survey Graphic* that appeared in March of 1925 with the subtitle *Harlem; The Mecca of the New Negro*. This unique edition, which included literary works by whites and Blacks, as well as drawings by the noted Austrian anthropological artist Winold Reiss, proved to be one of the most successful ever for *Survey Graphic*. Locke expanded the material he had accumulated for the periodical to produce his anthology, which he suggested would chronicle the cultural development of the African American in the early twentieth century. Reviews of *The New Negro* were generally approving, with none more so than that of Carl Van Vechten, an enthusiastic white supporter of the Negro Renaissance and author of the 1926 novel *Nigger Heaven*—which, despite alienating some with its controversial title, helped popularize Harlem and African American literature in the 1920s. Van Vechten's review in the *New York Herald Tribune* celebrated Locke's "remarkable" collection as it surveyed the anthology's wide-ranging contents. Subsequent assessments of *The New Negro* emphasized the anthology's central importance to the Harlem Renaissance and studied the new attitudes and creative spirit celebrated in it. In his 1928 essay on the New Negro movement entitled "Beauty instead of Ashes," Locke declared, "Like a fresh boring through the rock and sand of racial misunderstanding and controversy, modern American art has tapped a living well-spring of beauty." In addition to Locke's influential volume, two outstanding poets of the era edited noteworthy collections of African American verse in the 1920s. James Weldon Johnson produced *The Book of American Negro Poetry* in 1922 and Countee Cullen edited *Caroling Dusk: An Anthology of Verse by Negro Poets* in 1927. Together, these works trace the growing contribution of Black writers to the American poetic tradition.

Commentators on the Harlem Renaissance almost invariably acknowledge the role of several African American periodicals in stimulating the development of literature by Blacks in the 1920s. Chief among these publications, *Opportunity: Journal of Negro Life* was founded in 1923 by the National Urban League. Its first editor, Charles S. Johnson, encouraged young Black writers such as Zora Neale Hurston to publish their works by offering them both a literary medium and a reading public. While not devoted solely to literature, the periodical became one of the two most significant outlets for new works of poetry and fiction by "undiscovered" African American writers. In the mid-1920s, its editors conducted a series of highly successful literary contests that served to popularize new authors and draw the attention of non-Black audiences. The poetry prize for *Opportunity*'s first contest in 1924 was awarded to Langston Hughes for his "The Weary Blues," a poem that gave its name to Hughes's 1926 verse collection. Later winners included Countee Cullen and the then relatively unknown poet and novelist Arna Bontemps. The success of these contests transformed *Opportunity* from a predominantly sociological journal into the leading African American literary periodical of the day. It shared this designation to a degree with its chief competitor, *The Crisis: A Journal of the Darker Races.* Established by sociologist and Black leader W. E. B. Du Bois in 1910, *The Crisis* was the journalistic organ of the newly created NAACP, an organization cofounded by Du Bois, who was also its director of publications. Not principally a literary magazine, *The Crisis* nevertheless regularly featured works by a number of Black poets and novelists throughout the 1920s, including the fiction of Jessie Fauset, who would later become the magazine's literary editor. Together with *Opportunity,* Du Bois's *Crisis* encouraged Black writers to focus on African American subjects and to eschew the condescending or sentimentalizing attitude that mainstream works generally demonstrated toward Blacks. *The Crisis* also held literary contests, including a series that ran concurrently with those of *Opportunity* between 1924 and 1927.

A third journal that ranks among the most influential of the period, *The Messenger* began publication in Harlem in 1917. Its editorial focus was even more broadly social than that of either *Opportunity* or *The Crisis*: it tended to focus on art and music, especially promoting jazz and blues, which steadily grew in popularity during the period. While the content of *The Messenger* was mostly economic and political, it did publish short stories as well as verse, including poetry by Claude McKay. Interestingly, its editorial page also featured broadsides that mocked the nascent New Negro literary movement in the early 1920s, although such attacks were rare by mid-decade. The first issue of the journal *Fire!!* was published with the subtitle *A Quarterly Devoted to the Younger Negro Artists* in November of 1926, but a second issue never appeared. A collaborative effort between Langston Hughes, Zora Neale Hurston, Wallace Thurman, and several others, *Fire!!* sought to create a medium for a more radical and individualistic artistic ethos, but it elicited only negative criticism from conventional Black periodicals, and was almost completely ignored by the white press. Nevertheless, scholars have since recognized that this ephemeral publication was a significant manifestation of artistic experimentalism during the Harlem Renaissance. Other African American periodicals of note from the period include two small-scale magazines—*The Stylus,* published in Washington, D.C., and the Boston-based *New Era.* Both publications were established in 1916, and served to promote Black literature and art outside of the acknowledged center of the movement in Harlem. Another periodical, *The Crusader,* which ran from 1918 to 1922, is an early representative of more culturally oriented magazines like *The Messenger* that supported African American music, heralding innovations in jazz, blues, and Black theater in the early Renaissance period. Also prominent among Black publications of the era focused exclusively on cultural development, W. E. B. Du Bois's short-lived *Brownie's Book* was designed to encourage self-respect among juvenile readers.

# REPRESENTATIVE WORKS

*\*The Crisis: A Journal of the Darker Races* (periodical) 1910-

*\*\*Opportunity: Journal of Negro Life* (periodical) 1923-1949

## Sterling Allen Brown
*The Negro Caravan* [editor with Arthur P. Davis and Ulysses Lee] (poetry) 1941

## V. F. Calverton
*The Modern Quarterly* (periodical) 1923-1940

*An Anthology of American Negro Literature* [editor] (anthology) 1929

## Countee Cullen
*Caroling Dusk: An Anthology of Verse by Negro Poets* [editor] (anthology) 1927

## W. E. B. Du Bois
*Brownie's Book* (periodical) 1920-1922

## Marcus Garvey
*Negro World* (newspaper) 1918-1933

## Charles S. Johnson
*Ebony and Topaz: A Collectanea* [editor] (anthology) 1927

## James Weldon Johnson
*The Book of American Negro Poetry* [editor] (anthology) 1922; revised 1931

## Robert T. Kerlin
*Negro Poets and Their Poems* [editor] (anthology) 1923

## Alain Locke
*The New Negro: An Interpretation* [editor] (anthology) 1925

*Four Negro Poets* [editor] (poetry) 1927

*Plays of Negro Life: A Source-Book of Native American Drama* [with Montgomery Gregory: editor] (dramas and essays) 1927

### A. Phillip Randolph and Chandler Owen
*The Messenger* (periodical) 1917-1928

### Wallace Thurman
*Fire!! A Quarterly Devoted to the Younger Negro Artists* (periodical) 1926

### Dorothy West
*Challenge* (periodical) 1934-1937

### Newman Ivey White and Walter Clinton Jackson
*An Anthology of Verse by American Negroes* [editors] (anthology) 1924

\*     This periodical was published by the National Association for the Advancement of Colored People (NAACP).

\*\*    This periodical was published by the National Urban League.

## PRIMARY SOURCES

### ALAIN LOCKE (ESSAY DATE 1928)

**SOURCE:** Locke, Alain. "Beauty Instead of Ashes." *The Nation* 126, no. 3276 (18 April 1928): 432-34.

*In the following essay, Locke stresses the promise of African American artistic and literary development in the 1920s, commenting on the contemporary trend toward the writing and publication of fiction and poetry that portrays a broader range of Black life and culture in the United States.*

Like a fresh boring through the rock and sand of racial misunderstanding and controversy, modern American art has tapped a living wellspring of beauty, and the gush of it opens up an immediate question as to the possible contribution of the soil and substance of Negro life and experience to American culture and the native materials of art. Are we ever to have more than the simple first products and ground flow of this wellspring, and the fitful spurt of its released natural energies, or is the wellhead to be drummed over and its resources conserved and refined to give us a sustained output of more mature products and by-products?

To produce these second-process products is the particular *raison d'être* of a school of Negro poets and artists, and what most of our younger school really mean by an "acceptance of race in art" is the consciousness of this as an artistic task and program. Its group momentum behind the individual talent is largely responsible, I think, for the sudden and brilliant results of our contemporary artistic revival. The art movement in this case happens to coincide with a social one—a period of new stirrings in the Negro mind and the dawning of new social objectives. Yet most Negro art-

ists would repudiate their own art program if it were presented as a reformer's duty or a prophet's mission, and to the extent that they were true artists be quite justified. But there is an ethics of beauty itself; an urgency of the right creative moment. Race materials come to the Negro artist today as much through his being the child of his age as through his being the child of his race; it is primarily because Negro life is creatively flowing in American art at present that it is the business of the Negro artist to capitalize it in his work. The proof of this is the marked and unusually successful interest of the white writer and artist in Negro themes and materials, not to mention the vogue of Negro music and the conquest of the popular mind through the dance and the vaudeville stage. Indeed in work like that of Eugene O'Neill, Ridgely Torrence, and Paul Green in drama, that of Vachel Lindsay and a whole school of "jazz poets," and that of Du Bose Heyward, Julia Peterkin, Carl Van Vechten, and others in fiction, the turbulent warm substance of Negro life seems to be broadening out in the main course of American literature like some distinctive literary Gulf Stream. From the Negro himself naturally we expect, however, the most complete and sustained effort and activity. But just as we are not to restrict the Negro artist to Negro themes except by his own artistic choice and preference, so we are glad that Negro life is an artistic province free to everyone.

The opening up and artistic development of Negro life has come about not only through collaboration but through a noteworthy, though unconscious, division of labor. White artists have taken, as might be expected, the descriptive approach and have opened up first the channels of drama and fiction. Negro artists, not merely because of their more intimate emotional touch but also because of temporary incapacity for the objective approach so requisite for successful drama and fiction, have been more effective in expressing Negro life in the more subjective terms of poetry and music. In both cases it has been the distinctive and novel appeal of the folk life and folk temperament that has first gained general acceptance and attention; so that we may warrantably say that there was a third factor in the equation most important of all—this folk tradition and temperament. Wherever Negro life colors art distinctively with its folk values we ought, I think, to credit it as a cultural influence, and as in the case of Uncle Remus, without discrediting the interpreter, emphasize nevertheless the racial contribution. Only as we do this can we see how constant and important a literary and artistic influence Negro life has exerted, and see that the recent developments are only the sudden deepening of an interest which has long been superficial. After generations of comic, sentimental, and *genre* interest in Negro life, American letters have at last dug down to richer treasure in social-document studies like *Birthright* and *Nigger,* to problem analysis like *All God's Chillun Got Wings,* to a studied but brilliant novel of manners like *Nigger Heaven,* and finally to pure tragedy like *Porgy* and *Abraham's Bosom.* Negro intellectuals and reformers generally have complained of this artistically important development—some on the score of the defeatist trend of most of the themes, others because of a "peasant, low-life portrayal that misrepresents by omission the better elements of Negro life." They mistake for color prejudice the contemporary love for strong local color, and for condescension the current interest in folk life. The younger Negro artists as modernists have the same slant and interest, as is unmistakably shown by Jean Toomer's *Cane,* Eric Walrond's *Tropic Death,* Rudolph Fisher's and Claude McKay's pungent stories of Harlem, and the group trend of *Fire,* a quarterly recently brought out to be "devoted to younger Negro artists."

These critics further forget how protectively closed the upper levels of Negro society have been, and how stiffly posed they still are before the sociologist's camera. Any artist would turn his back. But in the present fiction of the easily accessible life of the many, the few will eventually find that power of objective approach and self-criticism without which a future school of urbane fiction of Negro life cannot arise. Under these circumstances the life of our middle and upper classes is reserved for later self-expression, toward which Jessie Fauset's *There Is Confusion,* Walter White's *Flight,* and James Weldon Johnson's *Autobiography of an Ex-Colored Man* are tentative thrusts. Meantime, to develop the technique of objective control, the younger Negro school has almost consciously emphasized three things: realistic fiction, the folk play, and type analysis, and their maturing power in the folk play, the short story, and the *genre* novel promises much for the future.

Though Negro genius does not yet move with full power and freedom in the domain of the novel and the drama, in the emotional mediums of poetry and music it has already attained self-mastery and distinguished expression. It is the popular opinion that Negro expression has always flowed freely in these channels. On the contrary, only recently have our serious artists accepted the folk music and poetry as an artistic heritage to be used for further development, and it is not quite a

decade since James Weldon Johnson's "Creation" closed the feud between the "dialect" and the "academic" poets with the brilliant formula of emancipation from dialect plus the cultivation of racial idiom in imagery and symbolism. Since then a marvelous succession of poets, in a poetry of ever deepening lyric swing and power, have carried our expression in this form far beyond the mid ranks of minor poetry. In less than half a generation we have passed from poetized propaganda and didactic sentiment to truly spontaneous and relaxed lyricism. Fifteen years ago a Negro poet wrote:

> The golden lyre's delights bring little grace,
> To bless the singer of a lowly race,
> But I shall dig me deeper to the gold—
> So men shall know me, and remember long
> Nor my dark face dishonor any song.

It was a day of apostrophes and rhetorical assertions; Africa and the race were lauded in collective singulars of "thee's" and "thou's." Contrast the emotional self-assurance of contemporary Negro moods in Cullen's

> Her walk is like the replica
> Of some barbaric dance,
> Wherewith the soul of Africa
> Is winged with arrogance

and the quiet espousal of race in these lines of Hughes

> Dream singers,
> Story tellers,
> Dancers,
> Loud laughers in the hands of Fate,
> My people.

It is a curious thing—it is also a fortunate thing—that the movement of Negro art toward racialism has been so similar to that of American art at large in search of its national soul. Padraic Colum's brilliant description of the national situation runs thus: "Her nationality has been a political one, it is now becoming an intellectual one." We might paraphrase this for the Negro and say: His racialism used to be rhetorical, now it is emotional; formerly he sang about his race, now we hear race in his singing.

Happily out of this parallelism much intuitive understanding has come, for the cultural rapprochement of the races in and through art has not been founded on sentiment but upon common interests. The modern recoil from the machine has deepened the appreciation of hitherto despised qualities in the Negro temperament, its hedonism, its nonchalance, its spontaneity; the reaction against oversophistication has opened our eyes to the values of the primitive and the importance of the man of emotions and untarnished instincts; and finally the revolt against conventionality, against Puritanism, has fought a strong ally in the half-submerged paganism of the Negro. With this established reciprocity, there is every reason for the Negro artist to be more of a modernist than, on the average, he yet is, but with each younger artistic generation the alignment with modernism becomes closer. The Negro schools have as yet no formulated aesthetic, but they will more and more profess the new realism, the new paganism, and the new vitalism of contemporary art. Especially in the rediscovery of the senses and the instincts, and in the equally important movement for re-rooting art in the soil of everyday life and emotion, Negro elements, culturally transplanted, have, I think, an important contribution to make to the working out of our national culture.

For the present, Negro art advance has one foot on its own original soil and one foot on borrowed ground. If it is allowed to make its national contribution, as it should, there is no anomaly in the situation but instead an advantage. It holds for the moment its racialism in solution, ready to pour it into the mainstream if the cultural forces gravitate that way. Eventually, either as a stream or as a separate body, it must find free outlet for its increasing creative energy. By virtue of the concentration of its elements, it seems to me to have greater potentialities than almost any other single contemporary group expression. Negro artists have made a creditable showing, but after all it is the artistic resources of Negro life and experience that give this statement force.

It was once thought that the Negro was a fine minstrel and could be a fair troubadour, but certainly no poet or finished artist. Now that he is, another reservation is supposed to be made. Can he be the commentator, the analyst, the critic? The answer is in process, as we may have shown. The younger Negro expects to attain that mastery of all the estates of art, especially the provinces of social description and criticism, that admittedly mark seasoned cultural maturity rather than flashy adolescence. Self-criticism will put the Negro artist in a position to make a unique contribution in the portrayal of American life, for his own life situations penetrate to the deepest complications possible in our society. Comedy, tragedy, satire of the first order are wrapped up in the race problem, if we can only untie the psychological knot and take off the somber sociological wrappings.

Always I think, or rather hope, the later art of the Negro will be true to original qualities of the folk temperament, though it may not perpetuate them in readily recognizable form. For the folk temperament raised to the levels of conscious art promises more originality and beauty than any assumed or imitated class or national or clique psychology available. Already our writers have renewed the race temperament (to the extent there is such a thing) by finding a new pride in it, by stripping it of caricaturish stereotypes, and by partially compensating its acquired inferiority complexes. It stands today, one would say, in the position of the German temperament in Herder's day. There is only one way for it to get any further—to find genius of the first order to give it final definiteness of outline and animate it with creative universality. A few very precious spiritual gifts await this releasing touch, gifts of which we are barely aware—a technique of mass emotion in the arts, a mysticism that is not ascetic and of the cloister, a realism that is not sordid but shot through with homely, appropriate poetry. One wonders if in these sublimated and precious things anyone but the critic with a half-century's focus will recognize the folk temperament that is familiar today for its irresistibly sensuous, spontaneously emotional, affably democratic and naive spirit. Scarcely. But that is the full promise of Negro art as inner vision sees it. That inner vision cannot be doubted or denied for a group temperament that, instead of souring under oppression and becoming materialistic and sordid under poverty, has almost invariably been able to give America honey for gall and create beauty out of the ashes.

## CRISIS (ESSAY DATE 1928)

SOURCE: "Communists." *Crisis* (September 1928): 320-21.

*In the following essay, an anonymous author explains the position of the American Communist Party, reprinting the party's manifesto and offering some explanation as to why the organization attracted so many African Americans in the 1920s and 1930s.*

### Communists

The Workers' (Communist) Party of America, through its executive committee in New York, has issued the following manifesto in the Negro problem.

The manifesto is the election campaign pronouncement of the Workers (Communist) Party on this important question. It contains the following demands, which are taken from the platform of the Workers (Communist) Party and which demands clearly indicate the position of the Party on the lynchings and on the Negro question:

1. A Federal law against lynching and the protection of the Negro masses in their right of self-defense.

2. Abolition of the whole system of race discrimination. Full racial, political and social equality for the Negro race.

3. Abolition of all laws which result in segregation of Negroes. Abolition of all Jim-Crow laws. The law shall forbid all discrimination against Negroes in selling or renting houses.

4. Abolition of all laws which disfranchise the Negroes.

5. Abolition of laws forbidding intermarriage of persons of different races.

6. Abolition of all laws and public administration measures which prohibit or in practice prevent, Negro children or youth from attending general public schools or universities.

7. Full and equal admittance of Negroes to all railway station waiting rooms, restaurants, hotels, and theaters.

8. Abolition of discriminatory practices in courts against Negroes. No discrimination in jury service.

9. Abolition of the convict lease system of the chain gang.

10. Abolition of all Jim-Crow distinctions in the army, navy and civil service.

11. Immediate removal of all restrictions in all trade unions against the membership of the Negro workers.

12. Equal opportunity for employment, wages, hours and working conditions for Negro workers and white workers. Equal pay for equal work for Negro and white workers.

The manifesto clearly states the position of the Democratic and Republican Parties in their attitude towards lynching and comes to the conclusion that these two parties are not opposed to the lynching system but instead support it. It also points out that the candidates of the Republican and Democratic Parties, Hoover and Smith, are both more interested in maintaining the lynching system than in fighting it. In addition, it exposes the role of the Socialist Party on the Negro question, particularly its support of the segregation process as far as the Party itself is concerned, its support of the opposition to the organization of Negro workers by Mr. Green and other officials of the American Federation of Labor, and the fact that the Socialist Party does not oppose the role of Randolph, the leader of the Negro porters, in coming out for the support of Governor Smith, who is the candidate of the Party of the Southern lynchocrats.

# W. E. B. DU BOIS (ESSAY DATE 1951)

SOURCE: Du Bois, W. E. B. "Editing *The Crisis.*" In *Black Titan: W. E. B. Du Bois: An Anthology by the Editors of "Freedomways,"* edited by John Henrik Clarke, *et al.*, pp. 268-73. Boston: Beacon Press, 1970.

*In the following essay, originally published in 1951, Du Bois recounts his formation and editorship of* The Crisis.

From the time I entered High School at Great Barrington, Massachusetts, in 1880, I have had the itch to edit something. The first fruition was a school paper, in manuscript, called the *High School Howler,* edited by me and illustrated by Art Benham, who could draw caricatures. It had as I remember but one issue.

My next effort was while I was a student at Fisk University and I became, first, exchange editor and then editor of the *Fisk Herald,* during my junior and senior years, 1887-1888.

The next adventure was the monthly called *The Moon,* which was published by Harry Pace and Edward Simon in Memphis and edited by me in Atlanta in 1906. From 1907 to 1910, I was joint editor of a miniature magazine, published monthly in Washington, D.C. My co-laborers were H. M. Hershaw and F. H. M. Murray.

In 1910, I came to New York as Director of Publications and Research in the NAACP. The idea was that I should continue the kind of research into the Negro problem that I had been carrying on in Atlanta and that eventually I should become Secretary of the NAACP. But I did not want to raise money, and there were no funds for research; so that from the first, I urged that we have a monthly organ.

This seemed necessary because the chief Negro weekly *The New York Age* was then owned by friends of Mr. Washington, and the Tuskegee organization had tight hold of most of the rest of the Negro press. The result was that the NAACP got a pretty raw deal from the colored press and none at all from the white papers.

In addition to that the Negro press was at the time mainly organs of opinion and not gatherers of news.

I had the idea that a small publication would be read which stressed the facts and minimized editorial opinion, but made it clear and strong; and also published the opinion of others.

There were many on the board of directors who did not agree with me. I remember Albert Pilsbury, former Attorney General of Massachusetts, wrote to me and said: If you have not already determined to publish a magazine, for heaven's sake drop the idea. The number of publications now is as many as the "plagues of Egypt!" But I was firm, and back of me stood William English Walling, Paul Kennedy, Charles Edward Russell, and John E. Mulholland and other members of the board.

But there again the matter of money was difficult. It was hard enough to raise the salaries of our two executive officers, and certainly we had no capital for investment in a periodical. I was persistent and two persons helped me: Mary Maclean, an English woman who was a writer on the *New York Times* and a loyal and efficient friend; and Robert N. Wood, a printer who was head of the Negro Tammany organization at that time.

Wood knew about printing and I knew nothing. He advised me, helped me to plan the magazine, and took the risk of getting me credit for paper and printing. The Board agreed that it would be responsible for debts up to but not exceeding $50.00 a month. It has always been a matter of pride to me that I never asked for that $50.00.

Finally after what seemed to me interminable delays on various accounts, the first number of *The Crisis* appeared in November 1910. It had sixteen 5 x 8 pages, with a cover which carried one little woodcut of a Negro child; as one of my critics facetiously said: "It is a shame to take the ten cents which this issue costs."

First because of the news which it contained, in four pages of "Along the Color Line;" then because of some blazing editorials which continually got us into hot water with friends and foes; and because of the pictures of Negroes which we carried in increasing number and often in color, *The Crisis* succeeded.

We condensed more news about Negroes and their problems in a month than most colored papers before this had published in a year. Then we had four pages of editorials, which talked turkey. The articles were at first short and negligible but gradually increased in number, length, and importance; but we were never able to pay contributors. Pictures of colored people were an innovation; and at that time it was the rule of most white papers never to publish a picture of a colored person except as a criminal and the colored papers published mostly pictures of celebrities who sometimes paid for the honor. In general the Negro race was just a little afraid to see itself in plain ink.

The circulation growth of *The Crisis* was extraordinary, even to us who believed in it. From a monthly net paid circulation of 9,000 copies in 1911, it jumped to 75,000 copies in 1918, and from an income of $6,500 to an income of $57,000. In January 1916, *The Crisis* became entirely self-supporting, paying all items of its cost including publicity, light, heat, rent, etc., and the salaries of an editor and business manager and nine clerks. It circulated in every state in the union, in all the insular possessions, and in most foreign countries including Africa.

We doubled the size of the tiny first issue in December 1910. We increased the number of pictures, trying two-color jobs on the cover in 1911 and three colors in 1912, 1917-1918. Our special education and children's numbers began in 1914. From time to time we issued special numbers on localities like Chicago and New Orleans; on "Votes for Women" and the pageant "Star of Ethiopia."

During this period two persons were indispensable in the conduct of *The Crisis*: Mary Maclean, editorial assistant, who died in harness and worked without pay; and Augustus Dill, business manager, who organized a model office. In November 1919, Jessie Fauset became literary editor and gave us inestimable help for seven years. Mattie Allison and Lottie Jarvis as secretaries, and Hazel Branch as head of the clerical staff, helped make an ideal family. Frank Turner was our bookkeeper from 1910 until the NAACP took him over in 1922.

We reached a circulation of 100,000 in 1919, following my revelation of the attitude of American army officers toward the Negroes in France. I shall never forget the circumstances of that scoop. I was in the office of Blaise Diagne in the spring of 1919. Diagne was a tall, thin, black Senegalese, French Under-Secretary of State for Colonies, and during the war, French Commissioner in West Africa, outranking the Colonial Governor. Diagne saved France by the black shock troops which he brought from Africa and threw against German artillery. They held the Germans until the Allies could get ready for them.

Diagne was consequently a great man and it was his word which induced Prime Minister Clemenceau to let the First Pan-African Congress meet in Paris against the advice of the Americans. Diagne did not like white Americans.

"Did you see," he stormed, "what the American Mission told the French about the way Negroes should be treated?" Then he showed me the official document. I read it and sat very still. Then I said, as carelessly as possible, "Would it be possible to obtain a copy of this?" "Take that," said Diagne.

Having the precious document, the problem was what to do with it. I dare not carry it nor trust it to the mails. But a white friend who was sailing home offered to take anything I wished to send. I handed him the document sealed, neglecting to say what dynamite was in it. *The Crisis* office and NAACP officials read it and dropped it until I returned. I published it in May 1919. The Post Office promptly held *The Crisis* up in the mails. But it proved too hot for them; if the Government held it that would be acknowledging its authorship. They let it go. We sold 100,000 copies!

Our income in 1920 was $77,000; that was our high-water mark. Then began a slump which brought the circulation down to 35,000 copies in 1924 and a cash income of $46,000.

The causes of this were clear and strike every modern periodical: the reading public is not used to paying for the cost of the periodicals which they read; often they do not pay even for the cost of the paper used in the edition. Advertisers pay for most of the costs and advertisers buy space in periodicals which circulate widely among well-to-do persons able to buy the wares offered. *The Crisis* was known to circulate among Negro workers of low income. Moreover it antagonized many white powerful interests; it had been denounced in Congress and many respectable Negroes were afraid to be seen reading it. Mississippi passed laws against it and some of our agents were driven from home.

We got some advertising, especially from Negro businesses; some advertisers we refused because we did not like the wares they offered or suspected fraud. The "Big" advertisers remained aloof; some looked us over, but nearly all fell back on the rule not to patronize "propaganda" periodicals. Besides they did not believe the Negro market worth entering.

Our only recourse was to raise our price of subscription. In December 1919 we raised our price to a dollar and a half for a year and fifteen cents a copy; also we increased our size to sixty-four pages and cover. This might have extricated us if the prices of everything else had not gone up, while wages went down. The depression which burst on the nation in 1929, started among Negro workers as early as 1926. It struck the workers of the Negro race long before the country in general dreamed of it. I remember bringing the matter to the attention of the president of the board of directors, but he said "the country is unusually prosperous!" Nevertheless, I retorted, the Negro worker is losing old jobs and not getting new ones.

There was a wider underlying cause: How far was *The Crisis* an organ of opinion and propaganda; and of whose opinion and just what propaganda? Or how far was it an organ of an association catering to its immediate plans and needs? The two objects and methods were not incompatible with each other in the earlier days of beginnings. Indeed from 1910 to 1925 or later *The Crisis* was the predominant partner, with income and circulation larger than the income and membership of the NAACP. For just this reason the NAACP became known outside its membership, and with the energetic work of Shillady, Johnson, and White, the membership and income increased and the question of the future relation of *The Crisis* and the NAACP had to be settled. Their complete separation was proposed; or if the income of *The Crisis* continued to fall, the subsidy of *The Crisis* by the NAACP; or further attempts to prolong the present relations and increase *The Crisis* income and circulation.

From 1925 to 1934, the latter method was tried. Various efforts were made to increase *The Crisis* circulation, by change of form and content. Considerable success ensued, but the depression which now fell heavier on the nation, convinced me that *The Crisis* could not be made to pay again for a long period and that meantime the only way to keep it alive was by subsidy from the NAACP. For this reason in 1934, I gave up my position as editor and publisher of *The Crisis* and went back to teaching and writing at Atlanta University.

In the nature of the case, there is a clear distinction between an organ of an organization and a literary magazine. They have different objects and functions. The one is mainly a series of reports and records of organizational technicalities and news notes of methods and routine notices. All large organizations need such a publication. But it is never self-supporting nor widely read. So far as it tries to be literary and artistic, it misses its main function and is too narrow to achieve any other.

On the other hand, a literary and news journal must be free and uncontrolled; in no other way can it be virile, creative, and individual. While it must follow an ideal, and one of which one or more organizations approve, yet its right to deviate in particulars must be granted, else it misses its function of provoking thought, stimulating argument, and attracting readers. For many years the NAACP gave me such freedom and the public repaid them and me by wide support. But when public support lagged and the NAACP must furnish a large part of the supporting funds, it would have called for more faith than any organization was likely to have in one man, to leave me still in untrammeled control. And as for me, I had no interest in a conventional organ; I must be free lance or nothing.

Against, therefore, the strong pleas of close friends like Joel Spingarn; and against the openly expressed wish of the whole board, which did not wholly agree with me, but were willing to yield much to retain me, I resigned. And I resigned completely and not in part. I was not only editor and head of a department which was separate from that of the Executive Secretary, with my own office and staff and separate bank account; I was also one of the incorporators of the NAACP and member of the board of directors since its beginning. Its officials from the first had come to consideration and election on my recommendation. I was a member of the Spingarn Medal Committee, and chief speaker at every annual conference. It was fair to say that the policy of the NAACP from 1910 to 1934 was largely of my making.

I would not have been honest therefore with my successors to have resigned in part and hung on to remnants of my former power. I went out completely. I think some sighed in relief. But many were genuinely sorry. Among the latter was myself. For I was leaving my dream and brainchild; my garden of hope and highway to high emprise. But I was sixty-five; my life work was practically done. I looked forward to a few final years of thought, advice, and remembrance, beneath the trees and on the hills beside the graves and with the friends where first my real life work had begun in 1897.

# OVERVIEWS

## CHIDI IKONNÉ (ESSAY DATE 1981)

**SOURCE:** Ikonné, Chidi. "Black Journals and the Promotion of the New Negro Literature." In *From Du Bois to Van Vechten: The Early New Negro Literature, 1903-1926*, pp. 91-123. Westport, Conn.: Greenwood Press, 1981.

*In the following essay, Ikonné surveys the principal journals associated with the Harlem Renaissance—including* The Crisis, Opportunity, Fire!!, *and* The Messenger—*considering their combined contribution to the New Negro Movement of the 1920s.*

### Opportunity

The first black magazine that comes to mind when one thinks of the promotion of the New Negro movement of the 1920s is *Opportunity: Journal of Negro Life.* Founded in January 1923 by the National Urban League, it came into being at a time when there were, as Dr. Charles S. Johnson puts it, many "young Negro writers and scholars whose work was not acceptable to other established media because it could not be believed to be of standard quality despite the superior quality of much of it."[1] Thus, although the magazine was not established specifically for the propagation of black literature, it soon felt the necessity for "a revolution and a revelation sufficient in intensity to disturb the age-old customary cynicisms."[2] It intensified the campaign for the development of black literature and culture by arousing the spirit of competition in other black magazines interested in the promotion. Recognizing "a most amazing change in the public mind on the question of the Negro . . . a healthy hunger for more information—a demand for a new interpretation of characters long and admittedly misunderstood,"[3] it went beyond the "revelation" of other Negro "uplift" magazines and newspapers to aid young black writers who, according to it, "had dragged themselves out of the deadening slough of the race's historical inferiority complex, and . . . are leaving to the old school its labored lamentations and protests, read only by those who agree with them, and are writing about life."[4] For instance, its editor, Charles S. Johnson, addressed letters of encouragement to young promising writers like Zora Neale Hurston who, in her own words, "came to New York through *Opportunity,* and through *Opportunity* to Barnard."[5] On 21 March 1924 Johnson arranged a "coming-out party" for the new group of writers.[6]

The list of guests present at the party reads like a miniature *Literary Market Place*: Horace Liveright, publisher; Carl Van Doren, editor of the *Century*; Paul Kellogg, editor of the *Survey*; Devere Allen, editor of *The World Tomorrow*; Freda Kirchwey and Evans Clark of the *Nation*; Mr. and Mrs. Frederick L. Allen of Harper Brothers; Louis Weitzenkorn of the *New York World.* There were messages of goodwill from Oswald Garrison Villard, editor of the *Nation*; Herbert Bayard Swope, editor of the *New York World*; George W. Ochs Oakes, editor of *Current History.* Also represented were established writers (both white and black) including Alain Locke who had demonstrated his interest in the new writers when he looked for Langston Hughes in New York and France after reading the young author's poems in *The Crisis.*[7] He was rightly "selected to act as Master of Ceremonies and to interpret the new currents manifest in the literature of this younger school."[8]

The results of the party and the publicity given to it were immediate. The Writers' Guild was established—at least in name. Its membership included Countée Cullen, Eric Walrond, Langston Hughes, Jessie Fauset, Gwendolyn Bennett, Harold Jackman, Regina Anderson, and a few others. Frederick Allen of *Harper's* offered to publish Countée Cullen's poems. The *Survey Graphic* which, in the words of W. E. B. Du Bois, "has always been traditionally afraid of the Negro problem and has usually touched it either not at all or gingerly,"[9] volunteered to bring out a special Harlem number "which will express the progressive spirit of contemporary Negro life in its new aspects and settings, using Harlem as a stage."[10] To illustrate the issue, it announced "a Prize of *Fifty Dollars* for the best original interpretation in painting, sculpture, etching, or black and white drawings."[11] According to Charles S. Johnson, "this fumbling idea lead [sic] to the standard volume of the period, the *New Negro.*"[12] In November 1924 Countée Cullen saw four of his poems published simultaneously in four leading magazines: "*Youth Sings a Song of Rosebuds*" in *Bookman*; "*Fruit of the Flower*" in *Harper's* ("a magazine," in the words of *The Crisis,* "whose relation to black folks resembles that of the Devil to Holy Water"[13]); "*Yet Do I Marvel*" in *Century Magazine* and "*The Shroud of Color*" in *American Mercury.* Mrs. Henry G.

Leach's "conviction of the capacity" of the Negro was heightened. She gave *Opportunity* five hundred dollars for a literary contest.[14]

This last result enabled the magazine to sustain the flame of "revolution" which it had kindled. To judge the entries, which were to deal mainly with various aspects of the Negro life, it invited such important men and women of letters as John Farrar, editor of the *Bookman*; Carl Van Doren, editor of *Century Magazine*; Clement Wood, author; John Macy, author and editor; Montgomery Gregory, scholar; Robert Hobart Davis, dramatist and editor of *Munsey's*; Dorothy Scarborough, author, book reviewer and critic; Zona Gale, author; Edna Worthley Underwood, author and linguist; Blanche Colton Williams, author and editor.[15] For the awards it gave a dinner, the importance of which is best felt in the *New York Herald-Tribune's* characterization of it: A novel sight, that dinner—white critics, whom "everybody" knows, "Negro writers, whom "nobody" knew—meeting on common ground."[16]

The results, therefore, were as impressive as those of the "coming-out party." John Matheus's "Fog" (which won the first prize in the short story division) was recommended to the O. Henry Memorial Prize committee by Dr. Blanche Colton Williams.[17] Langston Hughes's poem, "*The Weary Blues,*" which had won the first prize in the poetry section of the contest, appeared in the August number of *Forum,*[18] accompanied by an illustration by Winold Reiss, the famous Bavarian artist. Such major journals as the *Nation* and *Vanity Fair* solicited more poems from him than Hughes could write.[19] His first book of poems came out a few months later, and he was invited from various parts of the country, by both black and white groups, to read his poetry.[20] Jazz poems poured in from all parts of the country for his comments; he could not help wondering whether he had "started a new school [of writing] or something."[21] Above all, Casper Holstein, a New York Negro merchant, "bursting with joy and appreciation for what [the editor of *Opportunity* had] so nobly and unselfishly undertaken," gave Charles S. Johnson a check for five hundred dollars to enable him to conduct another literary prize contest which he was sure would "prove just as productive of desirous results as this one has undoubtedly proven to be."[22] He later doubled his original gift, while the Federation of Colored Women's Clubs offered prizes for constructive journalism.[23] Thus, the revolutionary promotion continued. The awards were increased, and the departments extended to include musical composition, constructive journalism, and the Alexander Pushkin Poetry Prize. After the contest, Edward J. O'Brien chose Eugene Gordon's "Rootbound" (which had won a prize of fifteen dollars in the contest) for his *Best Short Stories of 1927*. "This means," as Gwendolyn Bennett quickly and proudly pointed out, "that 'Rootbound,' winner of the fourth prize in the short story division . . . has been designated . . . as one of the stories printed in 1926 which . . . may fairly claim a position in American literature." Blanche Colton Williams also picked "Rootbound," along with Zora Neale Hurston's "Muttsy" and Dorothy West's "Typewriter" (two stories which had won the second prize in the contest) in her *O. Henry Memorial Award Volume of Short Stories for 1926*.[24] Casper Holstein once again volunteered to sponsor the 1927 competition which, incidentally, was to be the last of the first series of *Opportunity*'s literary contests.

Perhaps the greatest achievement of the last two contests (those of 1926 and 1927) was the launching of Arna Bontemps, poet, novelist, scholar, and one of the most authoritative chroniclers of the Harlem Renaissance. Bontemps had already been published by *The Crisis* before his association with *Opportunity*,[25] but it was his winning of the Alexander Pushkin Prize in 1926 and 1927 that rolled his popularity beyond the Negro world and its immediate white friends. His life, he acknowledged shortly before his death in 1973, "has never been the same since."[26] There are many other young black writers who could say the same thing about their association with *Opportunity*. *Opportunity* itself achieved its aim to some extent. It went in for "a revolution and a revelation sufficient in intensity to disturb the age-old customary cynicisms," and succeeded in making the work of many black writers "acceptable to other established media."[27]

Whether the tone of this achievement was worth the energy expended is still an open question. Its answer depends on one's attitude towards the whole phenomenon: Harlem Renaissance. One thing, however, is certain: it was not immune from the period's patterns of attitudes towards the black man as an artist and as a subject matter. While many white men and women of letters were loud in their praise of the work *Opportunity* was doing, Benjamin Brawley and several other articulate blacks were dissatisfied with the literature it sponsored. For instance, while Howard W. Odum found, in the literary trend, a commendable "new self-discovery on the part of the Negro,"[28] Wallace Thurman, who was in fact one of the key figures of the New Negro movement, maintained that "the results of the renaissance have been sad rather than satisfactory, in that critical standards have been ignored, and the measure of achievement has been racial rather than literary."[29] While Carl Van Vechten, in order to show his appreciation of its "editorship and at the same time . . . encourage young writers to continue to give their best to *Opportunity*,"[30] offered a prize of two hundred dollars for the best signed contribution published in the magazine, critics like Thomas Millard Henry challenged the award of the first prize for poetry to Langston Hughes in the 1925 contest: "The *story* called "The Weary Blues" is *not* poetry; it is a *little story* of action and life . . . the kind of stuff that Alexander Pope called *prose* run mad. . . . Perhaps it is not bad to call such stuff doggerel. It is a product of the inferiority complex."[31] Eugene F. Gordon saw the award as a "Nordic" conspiracy "which required Negroid poetry from Negroes,"[32] thus driving *Opportunity* to a desperate explanation of how "The Weary Blues" had earned the prize:

> The contest placed no restriction as to theme on poetry. The poems were rated by the most accurate method known, the votes of the judges being arranged by a mathematical formula. It so happened that the judge giving "The Weary Blues" the highest rating was a Negro, whose record as a poet, as well as a calm student of social affairs, and leader in a quite positive movement of race improvement is wholly beyond question.[33]

Countée Cullen, in his column "The Dark Tower," almost suggested that Arna Bontemps's poem, "The Return," did not merit the Alexander Pushkin Poetry Prize which it had received[34]— possibly because of its amateurishness as revealed in its faulty rhymes and clumsy syntax. Witness the first stanza where almost all the clauses dangle; and it is not clear what the word "leaves" is supposed to rhyme with:

> Once more, listening to the wind and rain,
> Once more, you and I, and above the hurting
>     sound
> Of these comes back the throbbing of
>     remembered rain,
> Treasured rain falling on dark ground.
> Once more, huddling birds upon the leaves
> And summer trembling on a withered vine.
> And once more, returning out of pain,
> The friendly ghost that was your love and
>     mine.[35]

In any case, Cullen was at this time the assistant editor of *Opportunity*, and his apparent dissatisfaction with the success of the magazine seems to reflect that of the magazine itself. It had repeatedly affirmed its belief in the Negro creative genius. Many a person who could read and wield the pen had interpreted this belief as an invitation to submit anything in words and on paper. Consequently, *Opportunity*'s offices were flooded with what it described as "grotesqueries." It progressively lost its temper. It warned: "The encouragement that they [the new writers] are receiving from established writers is a gracious and valuable aid . . . but this does not mean that simply because they are Negroes they can sing spirituals or write stories and verse or even dance *instinctively*."[36]

Its courage failed it; it suspended the literary contests to "allow for our aspiring writers a margin for experimentation with more than one manuscript, in the search for the most effective channels of expression."[37] The contests were not revived until 1931 and then *Opportunity* was alarmed. The manuscripts it received, in its own words, "show a marked inclination to follow the formalism of the English essayists of the eighteenth century or to slavishly follow the style of the literary elect of the nineteenth century. As a result the writing lacks spontaneity and vigor or what is popularly called 'punch.'"[38]

The young writers had moved from writing "instinctively" to turning out things that lacked "spontaneity." *Opportunity* had lost its hold on them; and as if that was not bad enough for the black literature which it was trying to revolutionize, it seemed to have lost its own sense of direction. In one breath it condemned the apparent triumph of the Brawley school, and in the same breath it discussed the new writing as a Benjamin Brawley would:

> We do not mean that *Opportunity* merely wishes to stimulate the adoption of those cheap devices of the new realism which currently pass for literature, nor the bizarre technique of some of the so-called modernists.[39]

> Another matter is that of the jerky, hectic, incoherent composition that some people are cultivating today, but that is nothing more than the working of the bolshevistic spirit in literature. With some people the sentence has lost its integrity altogether, and writing is nothing more than a succession of coarse suggestive phrases.[40]

Yet, on the whole, the achievement of *Opportunity* was intact. The vacillation and the apparent indecision of the journal as to what it really wanted notwithstanding, it compelled some other black publications, through its successes, to adopt its revolutionary stance.

## The Crisis

Founded in November 1910 as an organ of the NAACP, *The Crisis: a Record of the Darker Races* was already in existence, before the establishment of *Opportunity,* as a step forward in "the weary struggle of the Negro population for status through self-improvement and recognition, aided by their friends."[41] Although its main function was not publication of creative writing, it provided an outlet for young black writers, like Langston Hughes,[42] who for one reason or another had not been published by "other established media." Thus by April 1920 it could boast that "it [had] helped to discover the poetry of Roscoe Jamison, Georgia Johnson, Fenton Johnson, Lucian Watkins, and Otto Bohanan; and the prose of Jessie Fauset and Mary Effie Lee."[43]

Although not all these readily come to mind when one thinks of the New Negro writers, each of them made valuable contributions to the literary awakening and some of them, in a way, belonged to the movement. Fenton Johnson, for instance, anticipated not only the attempt to convert the demeaning traits attributed to the Negro into positive values but also the adoption, by some New Negro writers, of the whitmanesque departure from the conventional forms of poetry. Even in tone some of his poems, like "Tired" and "The Scarlet Woman,"[44] can bear comparison with some of the representative poems of the renaissance. Although Lucian Watkins died in 1921—before the formal launching of the New Negro—at least one of his poems, "Star of Ethiopia," belongs with the New Negro writings.[45] While her novels, poems, and short stories belong to the old school, Jessie Fauset, as literary editor of *The Crisis,* was a source of inspiration and encouragement to the budding writers.[46] Langston Hughes describes her, Charles S. Johnson, and Alain Locke as "the three people who midwifed the so-called New Negro literature into being."[47]

In any event, *The Crisis* was a major force in the black literary awakening. It endorsed its parent organization, the NAACP's, encouragement of Afro-Americans in all fields of activity (including literature) by its annual award of the Spingarn medal, as well as its occasional parties and conferences at which black writers and important white artists and publishers often met. Countée Cullen and Langston Hughes, for instance, were introduced to Carl Van Vechten by Walter White at one of these parties.[48] In a 1920 editorial *The Crisis* called to the attention of its black readers the existence of enough material for

# ON THE SUBJECT OF...

**BLACK SOLDIERS WHO SERVED IN WORLD WAR I**

Make way for Democracy! We saved it in France, and by the Great Jehovah, we will save it in the United States of America, or know the reason why.

**SOURCE:** W. E. B. Du Bois, writing on the return of Black soldiers who served in World War I, in *Crisis,* May, 1919, p. 14.

"a renaissance of American Negro literature."[49] In December 1922 it organized a short story competition on behalf of the Delta Omega Chapter of Alpha Kappa Alpha Sorority at Virginia Union University.[50] Above all, after the establishment of *Opportunity* in 1923, it refused, so to speak, to yield to that organ of the National Urban League in the promotion of the renaissance.

Thus, in May 1924, *Opportunity* devoted an entire issue to one aspect of the New Negro movement: African art. In June of that same year, *The Crisis* called for manuscripts for its August issue which, according to the magazine, "will be . . . devoted this year exclusively to the products and achievements of the younger group of Negro writers."[51] In August 1924 *Opportunity* announced its first literary contest. In September *The Crisis* hinted at its own contest and formally announced it in October.[52] *Opportunity* announced its winning contestants at a special meeting in New York on the evening of 1 May 1925.[53] *The Crisis* contest did not coincide with *Opportunity*'s only because W. E. B. Du Bois wanted, as he put it, "to give young authors every chance . . . so that there will be no unnecessary rivalry and all can have full benefit of this great generosity and foresight on the part of friends."[54] At any rate, it extended its own field of contest to include illustration and song.[55] It invited such an international figure as René Maran, the winner of the 1921 Prix Goncourt (whom its literary editor, Jessie Fauset, must have met personally in Paris in October 1924[56]), to be one of its judges. Among other judges were H. G. Wells, Sinclair Lewis, Charles Waddell Chesnutt, Mary White Ovington, J. E. Spingarn, Benjamin Brawley, William Stanley Braithwaite, and Winold Reiss.[57]

*The Crisis* increased its awards from $600 in 1925 to $2,035 in 1927.[58] In 1928 it expanded the Charles Waddell Chesnutt honoraria which it had established the year before, making them monthly awards: "prizes of $50 each month, $600 for a year."[59] In the same year, and thanks to eight colored banks and five colored insurance societies, it introduced "economic prizes" for "short stories, essays or cartoons, which will illustrate or study or tell the story of the economic development of the Negro: of Negroes as laborers, as farmers, as skilled workers, as business men, in all the different lines of business."[60] As if its supporters, too, were determined to see that it was not beaten by *Opportunity* in their common struggle to promote the literary movement, one of them, Mrs. E. R. Matthews, established a yearly award of $1,000 to be known as the Du Bois Literary Prize in honor of its famous editor.[61] It was in the same spirit that Amy E. Spingarn had started the current round of literary awards when she donated $300 "with the hope of assisting *The Crisis*" to promote "the contribution of the American Negro to American art and literature."[62]

It launched the *Krigwa,*[63] a workshop by which the magazine tried its best to help and guide young writers and artists. For instance, after the 1925 contest, the guild undertook to assist those "who did not win prizes this time but who may later; and also those who may never win but who will also wish to study and help the development of beauty in the souls of black folk."[64] It addressed letters to "the five hundred and ninety-nine [persons] who tried and received neither word nor prize" telling them what it thought of their "effort and what Krigwa advises and how the advice may best be followed."[65] By June 1926 the guild had established about six branches in different parts of the country. Some of these offered plays, especially the Krigwa Players of New York who, establishing a Little Negro Theatre at the 135th branch of the New York Public Library, gave three plays in three performances in May 1926.[66] Its "four fundamental principles" further demonstrate the effort of *The Crisis* to fix the tone of the New Negro production, and strengthen the self-possessedness and self-expressiveness of the movement as a whole:

> The plays of a real Negro theatre must be: 1. *About us.* That is, they must have plots which reveal Negro life as it is. 2. *By us.* That is, they must be written by Negro authors who understand from birth and continual association just what it means to be a Negro today. 3. *For us.* That is, the theatre must be supported and sustained by their enter-

tainment and approval. 4. *Near us.* The theatre must be in a Negro neighborhood near the mass of ordinary Negro people.[67]

In 1927 it formed the Krigwa Academy made up of "all persons who have received two prizes, first and second, in any one class of entries in *Crisis* contests." Members of the academy were apparently going to serve as judges in future *Crisis* contests.[68]

Still acting in its own name, *The Crisis* instituted a symposium "The Negro in Art: How Shall He Be Portrayed (?)" to make sure the renaissance was not "entirely off on the wrong foot."[69] Participants included important publishers and writers. Their responses reflect their sociopolitical attitudes and justify their individual literary practices. The following summaries and excerpts constitute an index of the bases of the patterns of reaction to the New Negro literature.[70]

*Carl Van Vechten*: To capture what is genuinely negroid in the Afro-American, the artist should focus on the unpolished black American.

*H. L. Mencken*: "The artist . . . should be free to depict things exactly as he sees them." Even exaggerations like those in Cohen's stories "always keep some sort of contact with the truth." Scientific criteria should not be applied to works of art.

*DuBose Heyward*: The portrayal of the Negro in art should not have propaganda as its main aim. If a moral or a lesson should be present in any work of art it should be subordinated to the artistic aim.

*Mary W. Ovington*: Stereotypes and propaganda in art should be condemned. "What publishers, at least the best, want today is art, not propaganda. They don't want to know what the writer thinks on the Negro question, they want to know about Negroes." Happily "white artists are beginning to see the true Negro and colored writers are beginning to drop their propaganda and are painting reality."

*Langston Hughes*: "You [Du Bois] write about the intelligent Negroes; Fisher about the unintelligent. Both of you are right."

*J. E. Spingarn*: Presently many works by Afro-Americans are published because of their indigenous cultural values as distinct from "contribution to the literature of the world." Nevertheless, "the Negro race should not sniff at the *Uncle Tom's Cabins* and the *Jungles* of its own writers, which are instruments of progress as real as the ballot-box, the school-house or a stick of dynamite."

*Walter White*: The idea that "the only interesting material in Negro lives is in the lives of the lower or lowest classes—that upper-class Negro life is in no wise different from white life and is therefore uninteresting" in literary creation is questionable. The truth is that "it makes no difference . . . what field a writer chooses if he has the gift of perception, of dramatic and human material and the ability to write about it."

*Alfred A. Knopf*: No artist, black or white, should be limited in his or her choice of subject.

*John Farrar*: "The Negro should be treated by himself and others who write about him with just as little self-consciousness as possible." Stories like those of Octavius Roy Cohen can be "untrue" and amusing without constituting "any very great libel on the Negro."

*William Lyon Phelps*: "The only obligation or limitation that an artist should recognize is the truth. He cannot be criticized unless he takes the worst [Negro characters] as typical."

*Vachel Lindsay*: With "truth and beauty" as guiding principles, an author "should be free to choose his characters according to his desire and purpose."

*Sinclair Lewis*: "There is the greatest danger" that the obsession with "economic and social problems of the colored race" will lead black authors to the writing of novels that are "fundamentally alike." A good example of this is the appeal of the subject "passing" to them. But all of them must not "go on repeating the same novel (however important, however poignant, however magnificently dramatic) about the well-bred, literate and delightful Negro intellectual finding himself or herself blocked by the groundless and infuriating manner of superiority assumed by white men frequently less white than people technically known as Negroes."

*Sherwood Anderson*: It is "a great mistake for Negroes to become too sensitive." They should "quit thinking of Negro art [.] If the individual creating the art happens to be a Negro and some one wants to call it Negro Art let them. . . . I have lived a good deal in my youth among common Negro laborers. I have found them about the sweetest people I know."

*Jessie Fauset*: While any writer should be free to choose his or her characters and situations, the development of a large black reading audience will compel publishers to "produce books, even those that depict the Negro as an angel on earth." Experience has shown that white "people are keenly interested in learning about the better class of colored people. They are quite willing to be shown." The obstacle is the publisher who in many cases has "an idée fixe" as to what is good for the public.

*Benjamin Brawley*: While the freedom of the artist to choose his subject must be acknowledged, it is regrettable that "many artists . . . prefer today to portray only what is vulgar. There is beauty in the world as well as ugliness, idealism as well as realism."

*Robert T. Kerlin*: "The duty of the black artist is to be a true artist and if he is such he will show the 'sordid,' the 'foolish,' and the 'criminal' Negro in the environment and the conditions—of white creation, of course—which have made him what he is. Let the black artist not hesitate to show what 'civilization' is doing to both races."

*Haldane MacFall*: (No direct answer to the questions. Only tries to prove that his portrayal of the Negro in his novel did not stem from contempt or hatred.)

*Georgia Douglas Johnson*: All Afro-Americans cannot "reach the high levels *en masse*." Therefore "the work of the artist" is to portray "the few who do break thru the hell-crust of prevalent conditions to high ground." He should stop capitalizing "the frailties of the struggling or apathetic mass—and portray the best that offers."

*Countée Cullen*: The Negro writer should be allowed "the one inalienable right" enjoyed by "all other authors": freedom to choose his subject and treat it as he wishes. Nevertheless, unlike "all other authors" whose races have "a large enough body of sound, healthy race literature" behind them, he should not "speculate in abortions and aberrations." If, in any case, he wants to write about the unpolished Negroes let him go ahead "only let him not pander to the popular trend of seeing no cleanliness in their squalor, no nobleness in their meanness and no common sense in their ignorance."

*J. Herbert Engbeck*: "The obligation of the artist is not to his race but to his talent." Certainly "there is a false notion among a great number of peoples that the sordid-foolish-criminal side is all there is in the Negro. The Negro will have to fight that down as the Jew has had to fight down the same impression by proving the contrary."

*Julia Peterkin*: "The minute any one becomes an advocate he ceases to be an artist." The Negro should be proud of himself and of his heritage, for example, the "Black Negro Mammy." "I write about Negroes because they represent human nature obscured by so little veneer; human nature groping among its instinctive impulses and in any environment which is tragically primitive and often unutterably pathetic. But I am no propagandist for or against any race."

*Otto F. Mack*: (From Stuttgart, Germany) Although many thinking people no longer take the uncomplimentary image of the Negro in American literature seriously, the Negro writer should fight to correct it.

*Charles W. Chesnutt*: The artist should be free to choose his subject. But "a true picture of life would include the good, the bad and the indifferent." The weakness of Negro writings is that they tend to be "too subjective. The colored writer, generally speaking, has not yet passed the point of thinking of himself first as a Negro, burdened with the responsibility of defending and uplifting his race." There is no reason why "a Negro oil millionaire" should be preferred by a black writer to an ordinary Negro. "A Pullman porter who performs wonderful feats in the detection of crime has great possibilities."

Unfortunately, the symposium was overtaken by a bitter quarrel engendered by the appearance of Carl Van Vechten's *Nigger Heaven* in August of that year (1926) and so was unable to settle the question as to how the black man should be portrayed in art. Nevertheless, it achieved two main things. Firstly, it brought into sharp focus the attitudes underneath the writings and criticisms of the Harlem Renaissance—attitudes which ranged from Jessie Fauset's call for a literary exhibition of "the better class of colored people" to Carl Van Vechten's recommendation of the use of the most unpolished Negroes as subject matters; from Countée Cullen's advice that a black writer should not "speculate in abortions and aberrations" to H. L. Mencken's plea that an artist should be allowed to depend completely on his or her own perception of reality. Secondly, the fact that it was instituted, along with *Opportunity*'s suspension of its literary prizes, demonstrates the effort of black journals themselves to control the direction of the literary movement.

In this connection *The Crisis* perhaps went too far. Although the magazine was a major force in the initiation of the all-out promotion of black literature by black journals, its sensitiveness and skepticism regarding the trend of the movement often dampened the enthusiasm of the young writers to express themselves as they saw fit. Beginning with little or no control over the participants in its literary contests, it progressively held them so tightly that their desire to compete was apparently stifled.

The rules of the first contest in 1924 were few and flexible. In addition to those dealing with mechanics and the submission of the entries, the main ones were: (1) The competition was open only to "persons of Negro descent in order to encourage their aptitude for art expression." (2) "Plays must deal with some phase of Negro history or experience." (3) "Essays . . . may deal with personal experience, biography, history, scientific research, art, criticism or any subject." (4) Poetry "may be on any subject." (5) "Illustrations may be for covers of *The Crisis* or for decorations of *The Crisis* page, cartoons or general illustrations."[71]

The rules for the 1926 contest were less flexible. The announcement of the contest itself was accompanied by a restrictive statement of policy:

> We want especially to stress the fact that while we believe in Negro art we do not believe in any art simply for art's sake. We want the earth beautiful but we are primarily interested in the earth. We want Negro writers to produce beautiful things but we stress the things rather than the beauty. It is Life and Truth that are important and Beauty comes to make their importance visible and tolerable.[72]

The rules for the 1927 competition were still more restrictive: (1) All entrants who "must be of Negro descent" were "urged to become subscribers to *The Crisis Magazine*" so that they might know what was happening to the entries. (2) Persons who had "received two prizes, first and second, in any class of entries in *Crisis* contests" should not compete.

The prizes themselves were divided into carefully regulated categories: Negro Business Prizes, Prizes in Literary Art and Expression, Prizes for Poetry, Prizes for Songs, Covers for *The Crisis,* and the Charles Waddell Chesnutt Honorarium. More than ever the emphasis was on utility, for the journal wanted to make sure that the youths were not engaging in "any art simply for art's sake." The declaration of the aim of the "Business Prizes" almost said as much: "The object of these prizes is to stimulate general knowledge of banking and insurance in modern life and specific knowledge of what American Negroes are doing in these fields; and to collect facts and impressions concerning Negro workers and their relation to Negro business."[73]

As if all these were too weak to let *The Crisis* influence the subjects and forms of the entries, the journal assumed what amounted to an absolute control of the competition. No judges were announced. The November issue of the magazine carried a cover drawing which had been entered by one Vivian Schuyler, even though the final selection of prize winners had not been made. An announcement within the number itself revealed that the editor—at least at that stage—was the sole judge of the entries. It said among other things:

> The entries are of a higher order of merit than in any previous contest. The editor has undertaken to read every single manuscript personally and instead of the drudgery he anticipated, the work has been a joy and inspiration. He has marked all the manuscripts on a scale as follows:
>
> A - Excellent. Only these are considered for prizes.
>
> B+ - Good and worth publication.
>
> B - Good.
>
> C - Fair.
>
> D - Poor, but with some points to commend.
>
> E - Impossible.
>
> *After the editor has personally chosen the A manuscripts* (and he has already chosen most of them), he will call in expert outside aid to confirm or criticize his decisions.[74]

The customary award dinner was suspended; checks were mailed to prize winners[75] who, obviously by accident, happened to be almost all women. The December issue carried their names, and also confirmed the determination of *The Crisis* to have full control over the award of its prizes. No judges were mentioned. Instead the introductory paragraph attached to the list of winners only said that "the Editors of *The Crisis,* with aid and suggestion of various authors, artists and experts with whom they consulted, have decided to distribute *The Crisis* prizes. . . ."[76] Not all the awards, however, were made. The "Business Prizes" were postponed because, according to the announcement, "to our great surprise only 13 of the 375 entries were made for this competition. This, we think, is much too small a number and with the consent of the donors, therefore, we are extending the time of entry for these prizes until July 1st, 1928."[77]

The 1928 contest narrowed the field of competition to "The Charles Waddell Chesnutt Honoraria," and "the Economic Prizes"—a division which the young contestants apparently found unappealing. General rules included the use of real names instead of pen names, and the fact that "the Editors of *The Crisis* in consultation with the donors (as distinct from "authors, artists and experts" of the previous year) will decide upon the prize winners."[78]

Entries closed on 31 December 1928. When prize winners were announced in June 1929 contestants learned that the award of some of the "Economic Prizes" had once again been postponed—this time indefinitely, for the "balance" was "to be distributed from time to time as we receive such contributions on the economic development of the American Negro as seem to merit recognition."[79] Nothing much was heard about *The Crisis*'s prizes thereafter, until the institution of "The Du Bois Literary Prize" in 1931 and the attempt in August 1932 to revive the "Literary Dinners."[80] The attempt, however, did not bear much fruit in spite of *The Crisis*'s optimistic remark, "Despite depression, the Kingdom of the Spirit still lives."[81]

Depression, certainly, contributed to the death of *The Crisis*'s contests. The principal cause, nevertheless, was the excessive control assumed by the journal over its contestants. All in all, what its editor said about himself personally while accepting "The Du Bois Literary Prize" could be applied to *The Crisis*. W. E. B. Du Bois declared:

> I have been striving in recent years to induce the stream of Negro-American literature, especially of our younger writers, to return to a normal, human and truthful channel, rather than to be led astray by considerations of income and sensationalism.[82]

Having said all this, it must be affirmed that the control was well-meant and, given the innocence of Black art and literature in the Roaring Twenties, justifiable. The temptation to misplace emphasis was real. *The Crisis* wanted to make sure that the Negro self-expressiveness of the renaissance was not sacrificed to its glamour.

## The Messenger

*The Messenger,* founded in November 1917 by A. Philip Randolph and Chandler Owen, never pretended to be an enthusiastic promoter of the Harlem Renaissance writing. It was too preoccupied with socioeconomic issues to concern itself with a race-conscious literary movement per se. Indeed, its column "Shafts and Darts" ridiculed the New Negro literature as it did Marcus Garvey and W. E. B. Du Bois whenever the initiator of the Niagara Movement appeared soft, too conciliatory, or unassimilationist. Witness George S.

Schuyler's "Ballad of Negro Artists" where Negro artists are portrayed as getting rich and fat at the expense of the American Negro's right to full American citizenship:

I

Now old Merlin the wizard had nothing on us,
Though he conjured a castle up out of the dust;
For with nothing but gall and a stoutness of
    heart,
On the public we've foisted this New Negro Art.

CHORUS:

Oh! this New Negro Art;
This "peculiar" art;
On the gullible public
We've foisted our "Art."

II

If old Kinkle and "Rusty" of mendicant fame,
Grabbed off wads of cash in the panhandle
    game;
Cannot we alleged writers and singers and such,
Playing on "racial differences," cash in as much?

CHORUS:

We *can* cash in as much—
Very *nearly* as much;
Though we know we're all hams,
We can cash in as much.

III

By stupendous logrolling and licking of boots,
And fawning around influential galoots;
We have gotten a place 'neath the calcium flare.
And paying our room rent and eating good fare.

CHORUS:

Oh, we're eating good fare;
Eating mighty good fare;
Though once we went hungry,
We now eat good fare.

IV

Our pet "racial differences" theory can
Be indorsed, it is true, by the Knights of the Klan;
But we care not for trifling matters like that,
When as "racial interpreters" we can grow fat.

CHORUS:

Yes, we can grow fat;
Get flabby and fat;
Eating three squares a day—
And all paid for at that![83]

The *Messenger* had no more encouraging words for the development of jazz and the blues—two of the features of the New Negro mood—which it believed was detrimental to the status of the black man in the United States. "A race that hums opera will stay ahead of a race that hums the 'blues,'" it contended editorially in March 1924.[84] It had in July 1918 ridiculed Du Bois's interest in literature and vaunted its own preference for "Economics and Politics". Its leading critic, Theophilus Lewis, dissociating himself later from what he called "the current jubilee in celebration of the 'Renaissance' of Negro culture," emphatically denied "that the spirituals are triumphs of art."[85] For the journal, the New Negro "spirit" which was artistically à la mode was an inaccurate reflection of the New Negro "spirit" as it saw and felt it. U. S. Poston, its reviewer of Alain Locke's volume, *The New Negro,* almost spoke for it:

> Is not the spirit of Garveyism, the N.A.A.C.P. and the Labor Movement agitations by A. Phillip Randolph, Frank Crosswaith, and Chandler Owen, Hubert Harrison and other radicals more expressive of the spirit of the new Negro than the Sorrow Song and the spirit of Hampton and Tuskegee? . . . as a volume designed to express the spirit of the new Negro, this *New Negro* [Alain Locke's] is wanting in many respects. That virile, insurgent, revolutionary spirit peculiar to the Negro is missing. The recent gesture on the part of Roland Hayes to not sing whenever his group is segregated, is far more expressive of the spirit of the new Negro.[86]

Yet the *Messenger* did not stand on the sidewalk and watch the bandwagon of the literary promotion roll by. It had, before the literary awakening took any recognizable form, published short stories and poems by black writers, including Claude McKay. These, however, seem to have been printed because of their sociopolitical stance. But with the formal launching of the New Negro by *Opportunity* in March 1924 it started to print pieces that were more interested in art than in sociopolitical issues. It offered Langston Hughes a platform to experiment in a new genre when it bought and published his first short stories, although its managing editor, Wallace Thurman called them "very bad stories."[87] Through Theophilus Lewis's theatre column, which was inaugurated in September 1923, it provided the New Negro drama with the most searching and the most disinterested, if unscholarly, monthly commentary on plays and their production. Despite its belief in the universal and international brotherhood of man, despite its contention that "humanity is one," and that "the Negro in France, is a Frenchman, in England, an Englishmen [sic], and so on,"[88] it persistently called for "stories of Negro life."[89] It even submitted, at least for some time, to the editorship of Wallace Thurman, the editor of *Fire,* a magazine which looked for its material and characters among those whom Wallace Thurman himself described as "people who still retained some individual race qualities and who were not totally white American in every respect save color of skin."[90]

The *Messenger* had no literary contests and award dinners. It was not a happy rider on the race-conscious literary bandwagon. Nonetheless, it did its best to assist the young writers, before its demise in June 1928.

### Fire

The young authors were not idle as the competition to promote them went on. Although they were grateful to the three major black journals for publishing their works, they were not, as Wallace Thurman puts it, "satisfied to be squeezed between jeremiads or have [their] works thrown haphazardly upon a page where there was no effort to make it look beautiful as well as sound beautiful."[91] They were also unhappy with what they regarded as their elders' "shoddy and sloppy publication methods . . . patronizing attitudes . . . editorial astigmatism and . . . intolerance of new points of view."[92] Thus, beginning with *Fire,*[93] various groups of them founded little magazines such as *Black Opals* (published in Philadelphia[94]) and the *Quill* (published in Boston) which unfortunately could not in several cases go beyond the first issue.

The story of *Fire* illustrates this attempt on the part of the young writers to help promote their own works. Early in the summer of 1926 seven of them—Langston Hughes, Zora Neale Hurston, Wallace Thurman, Aaron Douglas, John P. Davis, Bruce Nugent, and Gwendolyn Bennett—got together and decided to found their own journal "to be called *Fire*—the idea being," as Langston Hughes points out, "that it would burn up a lot of old, dead conventional Negro-white ideas of the past, *épater le bourgeois* into a realization of the existence of the younger Negro writers and artists, and provide us with an outlet for publication not available in the limited pages of . . . the *Crisis, Opportunity,* and the *Messenger.*"[95] They taxed themselves fifty dollars each and elected Wallace Thurman, John P. Davis, and Bruce Nugent as editor, business manager, and director of distribution respectively.[96]

The magazine came out in November. Its unconventional foreword defined its radical aims. It ended as follows:

> FIRE . . . weaving vivid, hot designs upon an ebon bordered loom and satisfying pagan thirst for beauty unadorned . . . the flesh is

sweet and real . . . the soul an inward flush
of fire. . . . Beauty? . . . flesh on fire—on
fire in the furnace of life blazing. . . .
      "Fy-ah,
      Fy-ah, Lawd,
      Fy-ah gonna burn ma soul!"[97]

Unfortunately for the youths, however, because of difficulties in distribution the existence of the journal was hardly noticed by white critics. Black critics who noticed it threw, to use Hughes's phrase again, "plenty of cold water . . . on it.[98] For instance, under the heading "Writer Brands Fire as Effeminate Tommyrot," Rean Graves in the *Baltimore Afro-American* informed his readers that he had "just tossed the first issue of *Fire*—into the fire, and watched the crackling flames leap and snarl as though they were trying to swallow some repulsive dose," and went on to comment on the contributors in terms hardly complimentary:

> Aaron Douglas who, in spite of himself and the meaningless grotesqueness of his creation, has gained a reputation as an artist, is permitted to spoil three perfectly good pages and a cover with his pen and ink hudge pudge. Countee Cullen has written a beautiful poem in his "From a Dark Tower," but tries his best to obscure the thought in superfluous sentences. Langston Hughes displays his usual ability to say nothing in many words.[99]

The result of the black critics' hostility to, and the white critics' unawareness of, *Fire* was the failure of the first and only issue of the magazine which was eventually consumed by real fire in a basement apartment where several hundred copies of it had been stored.[100]

Yet, in spite of flaws and weaknesses of individual contributions, *Fire* achieved its artistic aim: expression of the young writers' "individual dark-skinned selves without fear or shame."[101]

Richard Bruce's two nudes with well-defined contours, Aaron Douglas's pen-and-ink sketches of a Negro preacher, a Negro painter, and a highly sensuous "serving" lady, as well as his "Incidental Art Decorations" obviously inspired by African masks and statues, underscore the young artists' intention to use any available Negro material even if it meant gratifying or hurting the feelings of parts of their audience.

This is also true of the written contributions which fall under four headings—fiction, drama, poetry, and essay—even though, with the exception of the poems which are grouped under "Flame from the Dark Tower," they are not categorized.

The first piece is Wallace Thurman's story which seems to have been chosen leader to em-phasize the fact that *Fire* did not care which foot Afro-Americans, for "diplomatic" reasons, wanted to put forward. Entitled "Cordelia the Crude," it describes the life of a sixteen-year-old black prostitute. In addition to giving details as to how and where Cordelia operates, the story teems with whore houses in Harlem, and with Negroes who are only superficially clean, Negroes with "well-modeled heads, stickily plastered hair, flaming cravats, silken or broadcloth shirts, dirty underwear. . . ."[102] The tone is candid; but the story is bad stylistically. Besides other flaws, the point of view is wobbly; the first-person narrator speaks as if he lived with Cordelia and her parents and were omniscient.

Zora Neale Hurston's play *Color Struck* and story "Sweat" . . . capitalized on the Negro folk culture, and are, in a way, forerunners of the folklorist's later novels.

The ten-piece "Section of Poetry" is a potpourri of poems which range from Countée Cullen's sonnet "From the Dark Tower" (with the author's usual muted "protest") to Langston Hughes's experiment with jazz rhythm in "Elevator Boy," and "Railroad Avenue." Other contributors in this section are Helene Johnson ("A Southern Road"), Edward Silvera ("Jungle Taste" and "Finality"), Waring Cuney ("The Death Bed"), Arna Bontemps ("Length of Moon"), and Lewis Alexander ("Little Cinderella" and "Streets").

Gwendolyn Bennett, a talented young woman who, in addition to being in charge of *Opportunity*'s literary gossip column, "The Ebony Flute," had published poems and drawings in *The Crisis, Opportunity* and the *Messenger,* contributed a story, "Wedding Day," in which she focuses on what she calls "the Harlem of Paris" and, in a considerably detached manner, lets her black Americans react to life in a non-American environment, thereby expressing some hidden parts of their selves.

The most experimental story, as far as form is concerned, comes from Richard Bruce. Written without any paragraph indentation and punctuation marks save the many ellipses, "Smoke, Lilies and Jade"[103] operates within that basic vehicle of black cultural heritage: the oral tradition.

Arthur Huff Fauset's *Intelligentsia,* which is alone in the class of "essay," is a frontal attack on the intelligentsia as distinct from what the author calls "the true intellectuals who are accomplishing things."[104] The attack, however, is not directed against any group of persons of any particular race. While it mentions Sinclair Lewis, Theodore Dreiser, H. L. Mencken, and G. B. Shaw as examples of true intellectuals, it contents itself with delineating the characteristics of the intelligentsia. The following is only one of the many traits:

> They simply give art and artists a black eye with their snobbery and stupidity; and their false interpretations and hypocritical evaluations do more to heighten suspicion against the real artist on the part of the ordinary citizen than perhaps any other single factor in the clash of art and provincialism.[105]

The magazine ends as boisterously as it started with Wallace Thurman's "Fire Burns," an "editorial comment" on the reaction of blacks to Carl Van Vechten's *Nigger Heaven*—a novel for which, Wallace Thurman contends, Afro-Americans should be grateful:

> Some time ago, while reviewing Carl Van Vechten's lava-laned Nigger Heaven I made the prophecy that Harlem Negroes, once their aversion to the "nigger" in the title was forgotten, would erect a statue on the corner of 135th Street and Seventh Avenue, and dedicate it to this ultrasophisticated Iowa New Yorker.

> So far my prophecy has failed to pan out, and superficially it seems as if it never will. . . .

> Yet I am loathe to retract or to temper my first prophecy. . . . I defiantly reiterate that a few years hence Mr. Van Vechten will be spoken of as a kindly gent rather than as a moral leper exploiting people who had believed him to be a sincere friend.[106]

Thus *Fire* does exactly what its foreword claims for it. It flames, burns, sears, and penetrates "far beneath the superficial items of the flesh to boil the sluggish blood." The standard of the contributions is uneven; their collective tone is discordant. But this is to be expected of a journal interested in unregulated "individual" artistic expression. *Fire* is an adequate manifestation of the daredevil attitude of some of its founders towards Art.

## Conclusion

The role of black journals in the birth and growth of the New Negro cannot be overemphasized. Some of them (including *The Crisis* and *Opportunity*) were, however, Negro "uplift" magazines,[107] and so could not completely avoid the current Negro "uplift" literary concept: the Negro must be portrayed as *un homme pareil aux autres*[108] and at his best; or, as Countée Cullen, the assistant editor of *Opportunity,* put it:

> Whether they relish the situation or not, Negroes should be concerned with making good impressions. They cannot do this by throwing wide every

---

# ON THE SUBJECT OF...

**WILLIAM WARING CUNEY**

Born in Washington, D.C., on May 6, 1906, William Waring Cuney was one of the "second echelon" transitional poets of the Harlem Renaissance, along with writers Frank S. Horne, Georgia Douglas Johnson, Donald Jeffrey Hayes, Helene Johnson, Gwendolyn Bennett, Arna Bontemps, and Anne Spencer. He is often critically overlooked, although he made substantial contributions to the New Negro movement. Best known for his minor masterpiece "No Images," which won first prize out of 1,276 entries in the *Opportunity* poetry contest in 1926, Cuney used his musical and literary talents to depict the Black experience in a career that spanned half a century. Many of Cuney's poems are simple vignettes, sketches, or opinions written in a straightforward language that makes them seem like artifacts of folk life in urban Black America. These more prosaic pieces in his canon are, in their way, as representative of the modern movement in Black literature as "No Images" is representative of the Harlem Renaissance, since they open to scrutiny a unique perspective of Afro-American life.

---

door of the racial entourage, to the wholesale gaze of the world at large. Decency demands that some things be kept secret; diplomacy demands it; the world loses its respect for violators of this code. . . . Let art portray things as they are, no matter who is hurt, is a blind bit of philosophy.[109]

The works of Benjamin Brawley and William Stanley Braithwaite, the main leaders of opposition to the New Negro literature, are the best examples of the adherence to this "code" in poetry. Brawley's best known poems are on Chaucer and Robert Gould Shaw.[110] Braithwaite wrote about leaves, flowers, and concepts. He advised Claude McKay "to write and send to the magazines only such poems as did not betray [his] racial identity"[111]—a piece of advice which points to another aspect of the "code" style.

In addition to regulating the choice of subject, it also determined the treatment of the subject chosen. The writer should sound as learned as possible. Beautiful, if abstract, expressions should be preferred to folksily down-to-earth, but concrete, language. Thus we have the following lines from William Stanley Braithwaite's *Exit*:

> No, his exit by the gate
>     Will not leave the wind ajar;[112]

and the following with its archaism "trow" from the second stanza of Brawley's *My Hero*:

> This was the gallant faith, I trow,[113]

and the beautiful sound of the second stanza of Jessie Fauset's *Dead Fires,* that does not say much:

> Is this pain's surcease? Better far the ache,
>     The long-drawn dreary day, the night's
>     white wake,
> Better the choking sigh, the sobbing breath
>     Than passion's death![114]

The position of the black man in America, and not an awareness of the inauthenticity of what was being produced, was mainly at the root of the "code" and its opposition to the new trend of Negro literature. Because of the peculiarity of that position the black man, it was argued, must try to make "good impressions."

Yet through their awareness of the beauty of the black self, and their strong belief that that self had an important role to play in the general American culture, the black journals succeeded, to some extent, in bringing "new Negro voices into tune with the larger world of letters—to help them discover themselves."[115]

It is true that they were not completely responsible for their success since they and their prizes could hardly have thrived without a white audience and white financial support. Up to 1927 *Opportunity,* for instance, depended almost completely on a yearly grant of eight thousand dollars from the Carnegie Foundation to the Department of Research and Investigation of the National Urban League. The list of "Persons Who Acted as Patrons for the First Issue" of *Fire* contains at least one white man.[116] The *Stylus* was supported by Howard University. The Spingarn Medal, the Amy Spingarn Awards, the Harmon Award, the Van Vechten Award for published contributions, the Albert and Charles Boni Prize for Negro Novel, the Du Bois Literary Prize, all had white men and women behind them.

However, a careful study reveals that the most effective among the contests and prizes existed more because of black men and women's support than that of white men and women. Albert and Charles Boni's prize of one thousand dollars "for the best novel of Negro life written by a man or woman of Negro descent"[117] was never awarded because, according to Gwendolyn Bennett in her column "The Ebony Flute," there was without doubt no one worthy of the prize."[118] Its greatest achievement was that it nearly brought René Maran into more direct participation in the Harlem Renaissance when Alain Locke and Charles S. Johnson, encouraged by the Bonis themselves, submitted for the competition his novel, *Roman d'un Nègre,* which had been translated for the purpose by Mrs. Underwood.[119] René Maran, however, saw the movement as too race-conscious and race-motivated. He was too French to accept such a "racial" honor; he politely declined:

> Quelle que soit la valeur du prix en question,—prix Albert and Charles Boni, —il m'est très difficile d'y prendre part. Elle amoindrirait en France ma situation littéraire, qui est très forte, malgré et en raison même des oppositions qu'on ne cesse de dresser contre moi, mais aussi ma situation morale, qui jusqu'ici est irréprochable. On me reprocherait d'être racial. Et je n'aurai plus qu'à disparaître.[120]

*Fire* cost about one thousand dollars to produce. If the "patrons" offered it any financial assistance, that assistance does not seem to have been adequate. In any case, Langston Hughes describes how the cost was defrayed:

> I think Alain Locke, among others, signed notes guaranteeing payments. But since Thurman was the only one of the seven of us with a regular job, for the next three or four years his checks were constantly being attached and his income seized to pay for *Fire.* And whenever I sold a poem, mine went there, too—to *Fire.*[121]

Wallace Thurman's later attempt to resuscitate and expand the creative stance of *Fire* started and ended with the one-issue *Harlem: A Forum of Negro Life* in November 1928—ended because of lack of money.[122] After being supported by its publishers in 1928 and 1929, *The Quill* in 1930 offered itself for sale. It never reappeared. The *Poet's Journal,* a magazine which Helene Johnson and her club, The Colored Poetic League of the World, planned to launch did not see the light of day, perhaps because of lack of money.[123] Mrs. E. R. Matthews's "Du Bois Literary Prize" announced for the fall of 1932 never got off the ground because the nominating committee could not find any "work of first-rate importance"—work worthy of "this important prize."[124]

The Harmon Award, the Spingarn Medal, and the Carl Van Vechten Award were actually given out; but they were not, as instruments of literary promotion among the young black writers, as effective as the *Opportunity* and *The Crisis* prizes which, as demonstrated above, were almost completely taken over, and sponsored by Negro businessmen and businesswomen after they had been initiated by white well-wishers.

In conclusion, therefore, one can safely say that while the taste of a white audience helped to fix the color of the products of the literary campaign by the black journals, the choice of the basic material used in the products was controlled by the journals and the young writers. As for the young authors' wish to produce in the first place (if it owed anything to prizes), it depended more on black businessmen and businesswomen than on white philanthropists. Thus, contrary to the impression often created by some critics, the involvement of whites in the literary contests and award dinners did not detract much from the self-motivation and self-expressiveness of a literary movement which developed essentially from within.

## Notes

1. Patrick J. Gilpin, "Charles S. Johnson: Entrepreneur of the Harlem Renaissance" in Arna Bontemps, ed., *The Harlem Renaissance Remembered* (New York: Dodd, Mead & Co., 1972), p. 222.

2. Ibid.

3. *Opportunity* 2, no. 15 (March 1924): 68.

4. Ibid.

5. Zora Neale Hurston, *Dusk Tracks on a Road: An Autobiography* (1942; reprint ed., Philadelphia: J. B. Lippincott, 1971), p. 168. *See also* Langston Hughes, *The Big Sea: An Autobiography* (New York: Hill and Wang, 1940), p. 218.

6. *Opportunity* 2, no. 17 (May 1924): 143.

7. Hughes, *Big Sea*, pp. 92-94; 184-86.

8. *Opportunity* 2, no. 17 (May 1924): 143.

9. *The Crisis* 31, no. 3 (January 1926): 141.

10. *Opportunity* 2, no. 20 (August 1924): 253. For the controversy on who actually suggested the publication of the issue to Paul Kellogg, *see* Abby Arthur Johnson and Ronald Maberry Johnson, *Propaganda and Aesthetics; The Literary Politics of Afro-American Magazines in the Twentieth Century* (Amherst: University of Massachusetts Press, 1979), pp. 69-70.

11. *Opportunity* 2, no. 20 (August 1924): 253. Emphasis in the original.

12. Bontemps, *Harlem Renaissance*, p. 228.

13. *The Crisis* 29, no. 2 (December 1924): 81.

14. *Opportunity* 3, no. 25 (January 1925): 3.

15. Ibid., 2, no. 21 (September 1924): 277, 279.

16. Ibid., 3, no. 30 (June 1925): 176.

17. Ibid., 3, no. 34 (October 1925): 291.

18. Ibid., pp. 238-39.

19. *See* Hughes to Van Vechten, Monday, 18 May 1925, and Thursday, 4 June 1925, Yale University.

20. *See,* for example, Hughes to Van Vechten, 23 August 1925, and 20 January 1926, Yale University.

21. Ibid.

22. *Opportunity* 3, no. 30 (June 1925): 177.

23. Ibid., 3, no. 34 (October 1925): 292.

24. Ibid., 5, no. 7 (July 1927): 212. The growing interest in black literature is further evidenced by the fact that in October 1926 Countée Cullen was invited by Idella Purnell and Witter Bynner to edit a special issue of their magazine *Palms* which was devoted to black poets. *Carolina Magazine* (published at the University of North Carolina) also brought out Negro numbers in May 1927, May 1928, and April 1929. For a discussion of these issues and the influence of *Opportunity* literary contests on their contents, *see* Johnson and Johnson, *Propaganda and Aesthetics,* pp. 74-77.

25. Bontemps, *Harlem Renaissance,* pp. 14-15.

26. Ibid., p. 20.

27. Patrick J. Gilpin, "Charles S. Johnson: Entrepreneur of the Harlem Renaissance," in Arna Bontemps, ed. *The Harlem Renaissance Remembered,* p. 222.

28. "Welcoming the New Negro," *Opportunity* 4, no. 40 (April 1926): 113.

29. Wallace Thurman, "Nephews of Uncle Remus," *Independent* 119, no. 4034 (24 September 1927): 296.

30. *Opportunity* 5, no. 1 (January 1927): 6.

31. Thomas Millard Henry, Letter to the Editor, *Messenger* 7, no. 6 (June 1925): 239. Emphasis added. Hughes's poem, *The Weary Blues,* is discussed in chapter 5.

32. *Opportunity* 3, no. 31 (July 1925): 219.

33. Ibid.

34. Ibid., 5, no. 7 (July 1927): 210.

35. Ibid., p. 194.

36. Ibid., 4, no. 39 (March 1926): 80. *Opportunities'* italics.

37. Ibid., 5, no. 9 (September 1927): 254.

38. Ibid., 9, no. 11 (November 1931): 331.

39. Ibid.

40. Benjamin Brawley, "The Writing of Essays," *Opportunity* 4, no. 45 (September 1926): 284. He had earlier discussed some other weaknesses of the new writers.

41. Ibid., 1, no. 1 (January 1923): 3.

42. Langston Hughes's first (published) poem, *The Negro Speaks of Rivers,* appeared in *The Crisis* 22, no. 2 (June 1921): 71.

43. *The Crisis* 19, no. 6 (April 1920): 298-99. Apart from the works of the writers mentioned in this passage, *The Crisis* published several stories and poems which definitely anticipated the writing of the Harlem Renaissance. *See,* for instance, Virginia P. Jackson's poem *Africa* where the speaker hears the "voice" of Africa asking her to return home. Ibid., 17, no. 4 (February 1919): 166.

44. James Weldon Johnson, ed., *The Book of American Negro Poetry* (1922, 1931; reprint ed., New York: Harcourt, Brace & World, 1959), pp. 144, 145.

45. Ibid., p. 211. *See The Crisis* 13, no. 3 (January 1917): 118.

46. *See also* chapter 2. Jessie Fauset was literary editor of *The Crisis* from November 1919 to May 1926.

47. Hughes, *Big Sea,* p. 218.

48. Ibid., p. 202; *see also* Carl Van Vechten's "Introducing Langston Hughes to the Reader," in Langston Hughes, *The Weary Blues* (New York: Alfred A. Knopf, 1926), p. 11.

49. *The Crisis* 19, no. 6 (April 1920): 299. The interest of *The Crisis* in the development of black literature, long before the 1920s, is also evident in its editor's comments in the issues of April 1911 (p. 21), November 1915 (p. 28), and November 1918 (p. 22).

50. Ibid., 25, no. 2 (December 1922): 56.

51. Ibid., 28, no. 2 (June 1924): 82.

52. Ibid., 28, no. 5 (September 1924): 199; ibid., 28, no. 6 (October 1924): 247.

53. "Contest Awards," *Opportunity* 3, no. 29 (May 1925): 142.

54. "To Encourage Negro Art," *The Crisis* 29, no. 1 (November 1924): 11.

55. Ibid., 33, no. 4 (February 1927): 192.

56. Maran to Locke, 18 October 1924, Alain Locke Papers, Moorland-Spingarn Research Center, Howard University, Washington, D.C.

57. *The Crisis* 29, no. 2 (December 1924): 74.

58. Ibid., 33, no. 4 (February 1927): 191.

59. *The Crisis* 35, no. 3 (March 1928): 76.

60. Ibid. *The Crisis*'s precise definition of the types of material that should be submitted reflects Du Bois's attempt to control the direction of the movement.

61. Ibid., 34, no. 4 (April 1931): 117. *See also* "The Donor of the Du Bois Literary Prize: An Autobiography," *The Crisis* 40, no. 5 (May 1931): 157.

62. Ibid., 28, no. 5 (September 1924): 199.

63. This organization was originally called CRIGWA (Crisis Guild of Writers and Artists). Ibid., 28, no. 6 (October 1924): 247.

64. Ibid., 30, no. 5 (September 1925): 215.

65. Ibid., 30, no. 6 (October 1925): 278.

66. Two plays by Willis Richardson: "Compromise" (published in the *New Negro*); "The Broken Banjo" (first-prize winner in *The Crisis* contest of 1925); and Mrs. R. A. Gaines-Shelton's "The Church Fight" (second-prize winner, *The Crisis* contest of 1925), performed on 3, 10, and 17 May.

67. "Krigwa Players Little Negro Theatre: The Story of a Little Theatre Movement," *The Crisis* 32, no. 3 (July 1926): 134. *The Crisis*'s italics.

68. Ibid., 33, no. 4 (February 1927): 191.

69. This phrase is from Sinclair Lewis's contribution, ibid., 32, no. 1 (May 1926): 36.

70. The responses appeared in *The Crisis* between March and November 1926. In March Van Vechten, Mencken, Heyward (pp. 219-20); in April Hughes, Spingarn, White, Knopf, Farrar, and Phelps (pp. 278-80), in May Lindsay, Lewis, Anderson (pp. 35-36); in June Fauset, Brawley, Kerlin, and MacFall (pp. 71-73); in August Johnson, Cullen, and Engbeck (pp. 193-94); in September Peterkin, Mack (pp. 238-39), and Chesnutt (pp. 28-29).

71. "The Amy Spingarn Prizes in Literature and Art," *The Crisis* 29, no. 1 (November 1924): 24.

72. Ibid., 31, no. 3 (January 1926): 115.

73. Ibid., 33, no. 4 (February 1927): 191-93.

74. Ibid., 34, no. 9 (November 1927): 312. Emphasis added.

75. Ibid.

76. Ibid., 34, no. 10 (December 1927): 347.

77. Ibid.

78. Ibid., 35, no. 3 (March 1928): 76.

79. Ibid., 36, no. 6 (June 1929): 214.

80. Ibid., 39, no. 10 (October 1932): 331.

81. Ibid.

82. "The Donor of the Du Bois Literary Prize: An Autobiography," *The Crisis* 38, no. 5 (May 1931): 157.

83. George S. Schuyler, *Shafts & Darts: A Page of Calumny and Satire, Messenger* 8, no. 8 (August 1926): 239. Schuyler's italics.

84. Ibid., 6, no. 3 (March 1924): 71.

85. Ibid., (July 1918): 27: ibid., 8, no. 10 (October 1926): 312.

86. U. S. Poston, "Review of The New Negro," ibid., VIII, (April 1926), 118.

87. Hughes, *Big Sea,* p. 234.

88. J. A. Rogers, "The Critics: Do They Tell the Truth," *Messenger* 8, no. 2 (February 1926): 44.

89. *Messenger,* 8, no. 5 (May 1926): 131, 157.

90. Wallace Thurman, "Negro Artists and the Negro," *New Republic* 52, no. 665 (31 August 1927): 37.

91. Editorial, *Harlem: A Forum of Negro Life* 1, no. 1 (November 1928): 21.

92. Ibid.

93. Strictly speaking, *Fire* was not the first Afro-American little magazine during the period under review. *Stylus* (Washington, D.C.) and *New Era* (Boston) were founded in 1916. But while *New Era* disappeared after two issues in February and March 1916, *Stylus* was as good as dead until June 1929 when its third issue appeared. The first and second numbers had been published in June 1916 and May 1921.

94. In its first issue, *Black Opals* 1, no. 1 (Spring 1927) described itself as "the expression of an idea . . . the result of the desire of the older New Negroes to encourage younger members of the group who demonstrate talent and ambition." Contributors to the

maiden issue included such well-known New Negro writers as Langston Hughes, Arthur Huff Fauset, Lewis Alexander, and Alain Locke whom it called "the father of the New Negro Movement." Gwendolyn Bennett of *Opportunity* was guest editor of the second number (Christmas 1927) in which Jessie Fauset's "Nostalgia" appeared.

Although *Black Opals* was established to serve young residents of Philadelphia, by Christmas of 1928 it had started publishing material from all parts of the country. All in all, its literary stance was conservative. Subject matters were most of the time nonracial. When they were distinctively Negro, they often dripped with tears or tumbled from pulpits. Nonetheless, some of its contributors achieved some recognition as evidenced by the prizes they received in 1927:

> *Opportunity* contest—Idabelle Yeiser (First Prize for Personal Experience Sketch); James H. Young (Second Prize for Essay); Allan Randall Freelon (Second Prize in Art as well as two honorable mentions); Nellie R. Bright (Third Prize for Personal Experience Sketch as well as an honorable mention).

> *The Crisis* contest—Mae V. Cowdery (First Prize for Poetry), Allan Randall Freelon (Fourth Prize in Art).

*Goal,* a poem by Mae V. Cowdery, which appeared in the Spring 1927 number of the magazine was selected by William S. Braithwaite for his 1928 anthology. *See Black Opals* 1, no. 2 (Christmas 1927): 16.

95. Hughes, *Big Sea*, pp. 235-36.

96. Ibid., p. 236.

97. *Fire!! A Quarterly Devoted to the Younger Negro Artists* 1, no. 1 (November 1926).

98. Hughes, *Big Sea*, p. 237.

99. Thurman, "Negro Artists and the Negro," p. 37; Hughes, *Big Sea*, 237.

100. Hughes, *Big Sea*, p. 237.

101. Langston Hughes's phrase: "The Negro Artist and the Racial Mountain," *Nation* 122, no. 3181 (23 June 1926): 694.

102. *Fire*, p. 5.

103. For an account of how Richard Bruce wrote his story, *see* Robert E. Hemenway, *Zora Neale Hurston: A Literary Biography* (Urbana: University of Illinois Press, 1977), p. 46. Langston Hughes met (Richard) Bruce (Nugent) for the first time in the summer of 1925 in Washington, D.C. He relates how he amused himself with him and one other young man, "going downtown to white theatres 'passing' for South Americans, and walking up Fourteenth Street barefooted on warm evenings for the express purpose of shocking the natives." Hughes to Van Vechten, 24 June 1925, Yale University, New Haven, Conn.

104. *Fire*, p. 46.

105. Ibid.

106. Ibid., p. 47.

107. Wallace Thurman describes them as "pulpits for alarmed and angry Jeremiahs spouting fire and venom or else weeping and moaning as if they were either predestined or else unable to do anything else." In the editorial, *Harlem*, p. 21.

108. The title of an autobiographical novel by René Maran, in which the black writer tries to show that the black man is like everyone else.

109. *Opportunity* 6, no. 3 (March 1928): 90.

110. Benjamin Brawley, *Chaucer, My Hero,* in Johnson, *The Book of American Negro Poetry*, pp. 150-51.

111. Claude McKay, *A Long Way from Home* (1937; reprint ed., New York: Harcourt, Brace & World, 1970), p. 27.

112. Johnson, *The Book of American Negro Poetry,* p. 101.

113. Brawley, p. 150.

114. Ibid., p. 207.

115. *Opportunity* 2, no. 24 (December 1924): 355.

116. *Fire,* n.p.

117. "A Prize for Negro Novel," *Opportunity* 4, no. 39 (March 1926): 105. *See also* ibid., 4, no. 40 (April 1926): 113; "For A Prize Novel, $1000," *The Crisis* 31, no. 5 (March 1926): 217-18.

118. *Opportunity* 5, no. 4 (April 1927): 123.

119. Locke to Maran, 23 December 1926, Alain Locke Papers, Moorland-Spingarn Research Center, Howard University, Washington, D.C.

120. Translation: Whatever is the value of the prize in question,—Albert and Charles Boni Prize,—it will be very difficult for me to take part in it. It will weaken, in France, not only my literary situation, which is very strong, in spite and even because of the continual opposition against me, but also my moral position which until now has been irreproachable. I will be accused of being racial. And I will only have to disappear. Maran to Locke, 25 July 1926, Alain Locke Papers, Moorland-Spingarn Research Center, Howard University, Washington, D.C.

121. Hughes, *Big Sea*, pp. 236-37.

122. Although *Harlem* retained *Fire*'s interest in unregulated individual artistic expression, it solicited material from both black and white writers and went beyond purely literary matters to deal with political and economic questions. Thus while its essays ranged from Walter White's political statement in "For Whom Shall the Negro Vote" (pp. 5-6) to Richard Bruce's critique of black middle-class attitudes towards the portrayal of the Negro in art, the list of its future contributors, whose contributions unfortunately were never published, included blacks and whites from all fields of activity: Claude McKay, Countée Cullen, Rudolph Fisher, Eva Jessaye (author of *My Spirituals*), Eugene Gordon, Heywood Broun, Clarence Darrow, William Stanley Braithwaite, Charles S. Johnson, Frank Alvah Parsons (president, New York Schools of Fine and Applied Arts), Arthur Fauset, A. Philip Randolph, James Weldon Johnson, Jean Toomer, Jessie Fauset, Nella Larsen, H. L. Mencken, Dorothy Peterson, and Dr. R. Nathaniel Dett (a composer).

123. Johnson & Johnson, *Propaganda and Aesthetics,* p. 219, footnote 71.

124. Oliver LaFarge, trustee, "The Du Bois Literary Prize", *The Crisis* 40, no. 2 (February 1933): 45.

# AFRICAN AMERICAN WRITERS AND MAINSTREAM PUBLISHERS

## ERA BELL THOMPSON (ESSAY DATE 1950)

**SOURCE:** Thompson, Era Bell. "Negro Publications and the Writer." *Phylon* 11, no. 4 (1950): 304-06.

*In the following essay, Thompson emphasizes the increased opportunities available to Black journalists and writers in the post-Harlem Renaissance era.*

As soon as my berth was made up, I asked the porter for a table. The look of surprise turned into a big proud grin as I opened my typewriter case and went to work. I had noticed how carefully he had handled the machine the night before, how he had said a little louder than necessary, "Do you want your typewriter with you, Miss?"

Busy as I was with my notes, I could not help noticing the interest I was attracting. Hardly a passenger or trainman passed who did not stare at the spectacle of a Negro girl who could not only read reading, but type writing. One or two stopped to satisfy their curiosity, others sent the porter, a more than willing emissary.

"Got everything you need?" he began, solicitously. I had. "Got a lot of work there," he ventured, coming closer. Then, "What kind of work do you do, if I may be so bold?"

"I write for a magazine," I told him.

"Oh! You are that lady who writes! I've heard about you." He reared back, his eyes twinkling. He raised his voice so that the white passengers could hear. "Well, well! What do you know about that! I've already had on my train the beautiful movie star, Lena Horne, the great Negro educator, Mrs. Bethune, the come-upper Mae West, and now I've got you. Yes, sir, I've done carried all the notorious women!"

That was a great day for the Negro in journalism, the day he reached professional status among his own people—with or without notoriety (and I do not know how Mae West got into the act), for on that day a porter gave notice to the world that we, too, have correspondents hopping trains and pounding typewriters; that our magazines and newspapers are now to be reckoned with, no longer ridiculed.

Merchandisers, already vying for the newly discovered Negro buying market, were made even more aware of black dollar potentialities when the colored Associated Publishers, Inc., (seventeen of their twenty-four papers are members of the Audit Bureau of Circulations) acquainted them with the power of the Negro press during last year's American Manufacturer's Association meeting at the Waldorf Astoria. A tape recording told the story of fourteen million Americans with an eleven billion dollar annual income—an untapped market right at their own doorstep which requires no foreign language, no special package labeling, and which annually buys more than the total value of United States domestic exports below the Rio Grande.

Such demonstrations plus intensive campaigns by individual publishers have resulted in increased national advertising which, in turn, has raised our periodicals out of mediocrity and given them a scope and status never before attained. No longer dependent solely upon subscriptions, political handouts and the meager income derived from advertising cheap and questionable products, the Negro press for the first time has the wherewithal to improve itself. National advertising enables it to compete with established newspapers and magazines which have heretofore included Negro readership in with their total circulation count, but made no effort to recognize its vast buying importance.

By the same token the Negro press is also competing with the white press for Negro stories. Seldom does a month go by that some white publication does not carry an article or picture spread extolling the achievements of a darker brother. On the other hand, stories (especially technical and scientific) that appear in Negro publications require the same painstaking preparations given to stories for white publications. So when a white organization, institution or agency tells a Negro editor that his coverage of its activity was better than that of any other publication, that editor knows that although his is a specialized press, aimed at the Negro millions, the quality of his work is no longer measured by a separate rule.

This has resulted in better layout, better printing and greatly improved pictures as well as larger staffs. It spells less sensationalism and race-baiting, more features and fiction. Even humor is finding its rightful place in the pages of the Negro press.

What does all this mean to the Negro writer? It means more markets and also greater competition. It means better training and consequently higher salary. Within the Negro field alone, there are some two hundred weeklies, a daily, several scholarly and specialized periodicals, three major picture magazines, one digest, a comic, and now a slick confession magazine—all kinds of markets for all kinds of writing.

Both the *Afro-American* and the *Courier* have large magazine sections, and a few of the other weeklies use short stories. The Negro angle is desirable, say most editors of the emancipated Negro press, but they warn against belaboring the subject. Pay among the best of these markets compares favorably with that of white publications. Journalism classes and writers' magazines regularly canvass the Negro field for their literary needs. The Negro press today represents a four million dollar investment, boasts of a two million circulation. But the Negro writer need not stop there.

White journalism has always been open to the Negro, but never to the extent that it is today. Negro and white Abolitionists worked side by side on propaganda journals before the Civil War, and as early as the 1880's Thomas Fortune, founder of the New York *Age,* became assistant editor of the New York *Evening Sun.* During the same period, John S. Durham was a member of the staff of the Philadelphia *Evening Bulletin.* Both Lester A. Walton and Eugene Gordon worked on large Eastern dailies. Charles W. Chesnutt's short stories began to appear in the *Atlantic Monthly* in 1887, but it was a decade and a half later before readers discovered his racial identity. For many years the renowned poet and anthologist William Stanley Braithwaite was a critic for the Boston *Evening Transcript,* interviewing every foremost contemporary British poet who visited America and every foremost American poet.

Today it is quite common in the North for the larger white dailies to employ a Negro reporter and even some of the more liberal Southern papers are following suit. Top white magazines have been more reluctant to accept Negroes on their staffs—or perhaps qualified Negroes have not applied. As far as we know, Earl Brown of *Life* is the only Negro writer on the staff of a leading white magazine. E. Simms Campbell has been one of *Esquire's* most celebrated cartoonists for a good many years, and photographer Gordon Parks is a regular member of the lens crew at *Life.* Walter White broke ground for syndicated columns.

How many other Negroes are similarly employed, or that make their cake and Cadillac money free lancing for the p  )s, we do not know.

White editors are not as interested, it would seem, in the color of the author as they are in the quality of his work. It is no longer unusual to see the byline of a Negro on a story or article in a white magazine.

Opportunity for Negro writers is here, but far too few are ready. Too few have bothered to prepare themselves for such openings when they do occur. Like the ministry, which is finding less room for the untutored Man of God whose only qualification is his "call" to preach, journalism is also no place for those with only the "urge" to write.

Judging from the unsolicited manuscripts that pass over the desk of the Negro editor, the rate of illiteracy is nearly as high as the number of would-be lions of literature. Second to inability to write correct and effective English is an unwillingness to think in terms other than The Problem. And high on the list are a lack of literary imagination and a sense of humor.

Schools of journalism and special courses in writing are accessible to most potential writers. Certain fellowships and grants are available to those with talent.

Negro journalism has at last come of age. Current opportunities for the Negro writer are more than good and the future holds for those who qualify even greater success—if not downright notoriety.

## ZORA NEALE HURSTON (ESSAY DATE 1979)

**SOURCE:** Hurston, Zora Neale. "What White Publishers Won't Print." In *I Love Myself When I Am Laughing . . . And Then Again When I Am Looking Mean and Impressive: A Zora Neale Hurston Reader,* edited by Alice Walker, pp. 169-73. Old Westbury, N.Y.: The Feminist Press, 1979.

*In the following essay, Hurston laments the fact that perceptions of African Americans and other minorities in the United States continue to be based upon stereotypes, to the detriment of Black publishing and American society in general.*

I have been amazed by the Anglo-Saxon's lack of curiosity about the internal lives and emotions of the Negroes, and for that matter, any non-Anglo-Saxon peoples within our borders, above the class of unskilled labor.

This lack of interest is much more important than it seems at first glance. It is even more important at this time than it was in the past. The internal affairs of the nation have bearings on the international stress and strain, and this gap in the national literature now has tremendous weight in world affairs. National coherence and solidarity is implicit in a thorough understanding of the various groups within a nation, and this lack of knowledge about the internal emotions and behavior of the minorities cannot fail to bar out understanding. Man, like all the other animals fears and is repelled by that which he does not understand, and mere difference is apt to connote something malign.

The fact that there is no demand for incisive and full-dress stories around Negroes above the servant class is indicative of something of vast importance to this nation. This blank is NOT filled by the fiction built around upper-class Negroes exploiting the race problem. Rather, it tends to point it up. A college-bred Negro still is not a person like other folks, but an interesting problem, more or less. It calls to mind a story of slavery time. In this story, a master with more intellectual curiosity than usual, set out to see how much he could teach a particularly bright slave of his. When he had gotten him up to higher mathematics and to be a fluent reader of Latin, he called in a neighbor to show off his brilliant slave, and to argue that Negroes had brains just like the slaveowners had, and given the same opportunities, would turn out the same.

The visiting master of slaves looked and listened, tried to trap the literate slave in Algebra and Latin, and failing to do so in both, turned to his neighbor and said:

"Yes, he certainly knows his higher mathematics, and he can read Latin better than many white men I know, but I cannot bring myself to believe that he understands a thing that he is doing. It is all an aping of our culture. All on the outside. You are crazy if you think that it has changed him inside in the least. Turn him loose, and he will revert at once to the jungle. He is still a savage, and no amount of translating Virgil and Ovid is going to change him. In fact, all you have done is to turn a useful savage into a dangerous beast."

That was in slavery time, yes, and we have come a long, long way since then, but the troubling thing is that there are still too many who refuse to believe in the ingestion and digestion of western culture as yet. Hence the lack of literature about the higher emotions and love life of upper-class Negroes and the minorities in general.

Publishers and producers are cool to the idea. Now, do not leap to the conclusion that editors and producers constitute a special class of unbelievers. That is far from true. Publishing houses and theatrical promoters are in business to make money. They will sponsor anything that they believe will sell. They shy away from romantic stories about Negroes and Jews because they feel that they know the public indifference to such works, unless the story or play involves racial tension. It can then be offered as a study in Sociology, with the romantic side subdued. They know the scepticism in general about the complicated emotions in the minorities. The average American just cannot conceive of it, and would be apt to reject the notion, and publishers and producers take the stand that they are not in business to educate, but to make money. Sympathetic as they might be, they cannot afford to be crusaders.

In proof of this, you can note various publishers and producers edging forward a little, and ready to go even further when the trial balloons show that the public is ready for it. This public lack of interest is the nut of the matter.

The question naturally arises as to the why of this indifference, not to say scepticism, to the internal life of educated minorities.

The answer lies in what we may call THE AMERICAN MUSEUM OF UNNATURAL HISTORY. This is an intangible built on folk belief. It is assumed that all non-Anglo-Saxons are uncomplicated stereotypes. Everybody knows all about them. They are lay figures mounted in the museum where all may take them in at a glance. They are made of bent wires without insides at all. So how could anybody write a book about the non-existent?

The American Indian is a contraption of copper wires in an eternal war-bonnet, with no equipment for laughter, expressionless face and that says "How" when spoken to. His only activity is treachery leading us to massacres. Who is so dumb as not to know all about Indians, even if they have never seen one, nor talked with anyone who ever knew one?

The American Negro exhibit is a group of two. Both of these mechanical toys are built so that their feet eternally shuffle, and their eyes pop and roll. Shuffling feet and those popping, rolling eyes denote the Negro and no characterization is genuine without this monotony. One is seated on a stump picking away on his banjo and singing and laughing. The other is a most amoral character before a share-cropper's shack mumbling about injustice. Doing this makes him out to be a Negro "intellectual." It is as simple as all that.

The whole museum is dedicated to the convenient "typical." In there is the "typical" Oriental, Jew, Yankee, Westerner, Southerner, Latin, and even out-of-favor Nordics like the German. The Englishman "I say old chappie," and the gesticulating Frenchman. The least observant American can know all at a glance. However, the public willingly accepts the untypical in Nordics, but feels cheated if the untypical is portrayed in others. The author of *Scarlet Sister Mary* complained to me that her neighbors objected to her book on the grounds that she had the characters thinking, "and everybody know that Nigras don't think."

But for the national welfare, it is urgent to realize that the minorities do think, and think about something other than the race problem. That they are very human and internally, according to natural endowment, are just like everybody else. So long as this is not conceived, there must remain that feeling of unsurmountable difference, and difference to the average man means something bad. If people were made right, they would be just like him.

The trouble with the purely problem arguments is that they leave too much unknown. Argue all you will or may about injustice, but as long as the majority cannot conceive of a Negro or a Jew feeling and reacting inside just as they do, the majority will keep right on believing that people who do not feel like them cannot possibly feel as they do, and conform to the established pattern. It is well known that there must be a body of waived matter, let us say, things accepted and taken for granted by all in a community before there can be that commonality of feeling. The usual phrase is having things in common. Until this is thoroughly established in respect to Negroes in America, as well as of other minorities, it will remain impossible for the majority to conceive of a Negro experiencing a deep and abiding love and not just the passion of sex. That a great mass of Negroes can be stirred by the pageants of Spring and Fall; the extravaganza of summer, and the majesty of winter. That they can and do experience discovery of the numerous subtle faces as a foundation for a great and selfless love, and the diverse nuances that go to destroy that love as with others. As it is now, this capacity, this evidence of high and complicated emotions, is ruled out. Hence the lack of interest in a romance uncomplicated by the race struggle has so little appeal.

This insistence on defeat in a story where upperclass Negroes are portrayed, perhaps says something from the subconscious of the majority. Involved in western culture, the hero or the heroine, or both, must appear frustrated and go down to defeat, somehow. Our literature reeks

with it. Is it the same as saying, "You can translate Virgil, and fumble with the differential calculus, but can you really comprehend it? Can you cope with our subtleties?"

That brings us to the folklore of "reversion to type." This curious doctrine has such wide acceptance that it is tragic. One has only to examine the huge literature on it to be convinced. No matter how high we may *seem* to climb, put us under strain and we revert to type, that is, to the bush. Under a superficial layer of western culture, the jungle drums throb in our veins.

This ridiculous notion makes it possible for that majority who accept it to conceive of even a man like the suave and scholarly Dr. Charles S. Johnson to hide a black cat's bone on his person, and indulge in a midnight voodoo ceremony, complete with leopard skin and drums if threatened with the loss of the presidency of Fisk University, or the love of his wife. "Under the skin . . . better to deal with them in business, etc., but otherwise keep them at a safe distance and under control. I tell you, Carl Van Vechten, think as you like, but they are just not like us."

The extent and extravagance of this notion reaches the ultimate in nonsense in the widespread belief that the Chinese have bizarre genitals, because of that eye-fold that makes their eyes seem to slant. In spite of the fact that no biology has ever mentioned any such difference in reproductive organs makes no matter. Millions of people believe it. "Did you know that a Chinese has . . ." Consequently, their quiet contemplative manner is interpreted as a sign of slyness and a treacherous inclination.

But the opening wedge for better understanding has been thrust into the crack. Though many Negroes denounced Carl Van Vechten's *Nigger Heaven* because of the title, and without ever reading it, the book, written in the deepest sincerity, revealed Negroes of wealth and culture to the white public. It created curiosity even when it aroused scepticism. It made folks want to know. Worth Tuttle Hedden's *The Other Room* has definitely widened the opening. Neither of these well-written works take a romance of upper-class Negro life as the central theme, but the atmosphere and the background is there. These works should be followed up by some incisive and intimate stories from the inside.

The realistic story around a Negro insurance official, dentist, general practitioner, undertaker and the like would be most revealing. Thinly disguised fiction around the well known Negro names is not the answer, either. The "exceptional" as well as the Ol' Man Rivers has been exploited all out of context already. Everybody is already resigned to the "exceptional" Negro, and willing to be entertained by the "quaint." To grasp the penetration of western civilization in a minority, it is necessary to know how the average behaves and lives. Books that deal with people like in Sinclair Lewis' *Main Street* is the necessary metier. For various reasons, the average, struggling, non-morbid Negro is the best-kept secret in America. His revelation to the public is the thing needed to do away with that feeling of difference which inspires fear and which ever expresses itself in dislike.

It is inevitable that this knowledge will destroy many illusions and romantic traditions which America probably likes to have around. But then, we have no record of anybody sinking into a lingering death on finding out that there was no Santa Claus. The old world will take it in its stride. The realization that Negroes are no better nor no worse, and at times just as boring as everybody else, will hardly kill off the population of the nation.

Outside of racial attitudes, there is still another reason why this literature should exist. Literature and other arts are supposed to hold up the mirror to nature. With only the fractional "exceptional" and the "quaint" portrayed, a true picture of Negro life in America cannot be. A great principle of national art has been violated.

These are the things that publishers and producers, as the accredited representatives of the American people, have not as yet taken into consideration sufficiently. Let there be light!

## CARY D. WINTZ (ESSAY DATE 1996)

**SOURCE:** Wintz, Cary D. "Black Writers and White Promoters." In *Black Culture and the Harlem Renaissance*, pp. 154-89. College Station: Texas A & M University Press, 1996.

*In the following essay, Wintz documents relationships between many of the outstanding writers of the Harlem Renaissance and their white publishers, patrons, and supporters.*

While the black intelligentsia played a major role in the Harlem Renaissance, their efforts alone were not enough to create a major literary movement. Black America in the 1920s did not possess the resources to develop a full-fledged literary movement. Blacks did not control the publishing houses, they could not mobilize a large enough body of book buyers, and they lacked the capital and contacts in their own community to sustain a major literary movement. Consequently, while the Harlem Renaissance was a black literary movement, it had significant and indispensable links to the white literary community.

White involvement in the Renaissance took several forms. First, a number of white publishers centered in New York and led by firms like Alfred Knopf played a major role in identifying and promoting black literary talent. White publishers worked through their contacts with black writers and the black intelligentsia, or through white writers and literary promoters who had such contacts. The link between black writers and white publishers is itself an interesting aspect of the black literary movement. A second group of whites involved in the movement were those who provided financial support to black writers and black literary activity. They included patrons who established individual associations with specific black writers as well as those whose funding activities affected larger numbers of Renaissance participants. The relationship between white patrons and their black protégés, while often cordial, sometimes resulted in misunderstandings and problems. The third category of whites involved in the movement was the handful who found that the Renaissance overlapped their own literary or political activities. Theirs was generally a brief but occasionally intense involvement. Obviously these categories are not mutually exclusive. Some white supporters of the Renaissance could be placed in two categories; Carl Van Vechten fell into all three. Whatever its nature and however well intentioned, white involvement in the Renaissance always generated a certain amount of suspicion and resentment, some of which was warranted, some of which was not.

Of all the whites involved in the Renaissance the most necessary were the publishers. In the early twentieth century blacks were almost totally dependent on white-owned publishing houses for the publication and distribution of their literature. Except for black-owned newspapers and periodicals and a few small publishing ventures usually affiliated with black newspapers or churches, this industry was exclusively white. While black poets could see their verses in black newspapers and magazines and while black short story writers could occasionally place a piece with *Opportunity* or *Crisis,* true literary success, measured by the production of a book, required working with white publishers.

The dependence of black literature on white publishers is easily documented by examining the experiences of pre-Renaissance black writers. Relatively successful writers like Chesnutt and Dunbar established close contacts with white publishers, while those who were less successful, like James Edwin Campbell and Raymond Dandridge, failed to convince the major white publishing houses of the quality of their work. Throughout the period preceding the Renaissance, black writers struggled to get their work published. Chesnutt, for example, negotiated with Houghton Mifflin for five years before it agreed to publish his first book of poetry. Then, after the commercial failure of his first two novels, he shifted to Doubleday for his last novel. Dunbar, on the other hand, privately printed his first two volumes of poetry and attracted the attention of a major commercial publisher, Dodd, Mead, only after William Dean Howells had identified him as a major poetic talent.

James Weldon Johnson had a similar experience. Even though he had enjoyed some success as a songwriter, he had great difficulty placing and marketing his first literary works. *The Autobiography of An Ex-Colored Man* was issued by a small, virtually unknown Boston publishing house, Sherman, French, but received no real promotion and consequently did not sell well until it was reissued by Knopf during the Renaissance. Johnson had even more trouble with his first book of poetry, *Fifty Years and Other Poems*. His mentor, William Stanley Braithwaite, finally arranged for the volume to be published by Cornhill Publishers, a Boston firm of which he was part owner. Again, the marginal resources of the publishing house prevented the book from being adequately promoted and achieving any popular success. In both instances Johnson had to become financially involved in the publication process. He helped pay promotional costs for his novel, and he had to subsidize the cost of printing his first book of poetry.[1]

The growing public fascination with blackness that was reflected in the Harlem vogue and the higher quality of literature produced by young black writers in the mid-1920s helped open the doors of the major publishing houses to black literature. No longer were black writers forced to raise money to publish their material; no longer did they have to rely on the disorganized and inadequate resources of the black community to promote and market their work.

The degree to which white publishers opened their doors to black writers before and during the Renaissance is clear from the publishing experiences of individual black writers. Except for Dunbar and Chesnutt, before 1920 black writers had

to rely on small, unknown, local presses or else publish their own works. If there was a center for the publication of black literature, it was Boston, where Braithwaite's Cornhill Company and several other small presses published the work of four of the nine black writers who were unable to attract the attention of the major companies. Marketed primarily by the authors themselves, these books suffered from poor distribution and consequently had no real impact on black literature. After 1920, however, major publishing houses, most of which were located in New York, were much more accessible to black writers. Each of the Renaissance writers listed after 1920 published with a major press; all but Zora Neale Hurston published with a New York City publishing house. Of the seven publishers involved in the movement, two (Alfred A. Knopf, which published six Renaissance authors, and Harcourt Brace, which published five) dominated but did not monopolize the publication of black literature.

Although the door to the major white publishing houses was open to black writers during the Harlem Renaissance, they rarely gained entrance on their own. As in the case of Chesnutt and Dunbar, the dynamics of the process through which a black author obtained a contract with a major publishing house still required someone to run interference—to introduce the unknown black writer to the white publisher, vouch for the literary merit of his or her work, and generally serve as liaison between writer and publisher. During the Renaissance this position was almost always filled by a white.

Examples of this process abound. Although Alain Locke arranged for the publication of two of Jean Toomer's poems in *Crisis* in the Spring of 1922, and Claude McKay accepted three of his pieces for *Liberator* late that summer, it was Waldo Frank who wrote the foreword for *Cane*, took the manuscript to Horace Liveright in December of 1922, and then telegraphed Toomer on January 2, 1923, with the information that Boni & Liveright had agreed to publish the book. A year earlier, in the fall of 1921, Joel Spingarn, chairman of the board of the NAACP and associated with the new publishing firm of Harcourt, Brace, arranged for that company to publish *Harlem Shadows*, Claude McKay's first American book of poetry. This was not the first time that Spingarn had promoted McKay's career. Five years earlier he had introduced him to Waldo Frank, who eventually accepted several of his poems for *The Seven Arts*. Max Eastman wrote the introduction for *Harlem Shadows*.[2]

# The Book of American Negro Poetry

CHOSEN AND EDITED
WITH AN ESSAY ON THE
NEGRO'S CREATIVE GENIUS

BY

JAMES WELDON JOHNSON
Author of "Fifty Years and Other Poems"

NEW YORK
HARCOURT, BRACE AND COMPANY

Title page from *The Book of American Negro Poetry,*
edited by James Weldon Johnson.

Alfred and Blanche Knopf would be the most active publishers of the works of the Harlem Renaissance. They not only published more of the writers associated with the movement than did any other publisher, but also, more than the others, they were active promoters of the Renaissance. The Knopfs were close friends with the Van Vechtens and with the James Weldon Johnsons. Indeed, the friendship of the multiethnic threesome—Carl Van Vechten (the WASP), Alfred Knopf (the Jew), and James Weldon Johnson (the black)—reached an intimacy of great depth that encompassed far more than their common literary interests and endured far longer than the Harlem Renaissance. This friendship and the professional association that went with it placed the Knopfs and their firm in a position from which they could greatly influence the development of black literature. Not only did Van Vechten publish his novels with Knopf (including the blockbuster *Nigger Heaven*), but he served as talent scout, critic, photographer, and at times almost a

partner for the firm, especially in developing black literature. James Weldon Johnson provided the link between Knopf and the black intellectual establishment.

Harcourt, Brace also had close ties with the black community. Joel E. Spingarn, one of the founders of that publishing company, provided a strong link between the white publishing world and Harlem. The descendant of a wealthy German Jewish family and a former professor of literature at Columbia University, Spingarn was best known as a civil rights activist. He was a founding member of the NAACP, and he served that organization through the 1920s alternately as treasurer, president, and board chairman. He had also headed a drive at the outset of World War I to recruit black officers for the army. He provided the funding for the initial *Crisis* literary prize in 1925 and, along with Alfred Knopf, published and promoted the work of talented black writers. Together, the two firms published the majority of Renaissance writers.[3]

Despite the new opportunity that firms like Knopf and Harcourt, Brace offered it was still not always easy for black writers to get their work published, especially in the early and mid-1920s, before the Renaissance had established the popularity and marketability of black books, and especially during this early period if the subject matter was controversial. Walter White's early efforts to get his work published clearly illustrates this situation.

By the early 1920s Walter White had achieved a degree of prominence as an officer of the NAACP, and he would be remembered by Langston Hughes for his fine apartment overlooking the Hudson and for the hospitality he showed to the "hungry literati." In 1922, largely at the urging of H. L. Mencken, White began writing a novel that chronicled the experiences of a college-educated black in the South and concluded with an exposé of the brutality of southern prejudice. Initially things went well for White—he wrote the book in one marathon twelve-day stint and, with the assistance of John Farrar, editor of *The Bookman,* he received the promise of a publishing contract from Doran. For a time it looked as if White would publish the second book of the emerging Renaissance.[4]

Unfortunately, Doran began having second thoughts about the book. Although associate editor Eugene Saxton liked it, as did John Farrar, George Doran worried about the impact the book might have on the South and, more importantly, on the business his company did there. In a meeting that included Saxton and Farrar, Doran asked White to make revisions, because the "Negro characters . . . are not what the readers expect." White did make a few revisions and even moderated the racist views of one of the southern characters, but this was not enough. Doran sought the opinion of Kentucky humorist Irvin S. Cobb, who warned that the publication of such an outspoken novel would trigger race riots in the South and make it impossible for Doran to sell any more books there. Saxton, who still liked the book and acknowledged the accuracy of its description of the racial situation in the South, wrote White in August 1923 that Doran was withdrawing from the project. Although "disheartened and disillusioned," White tried to change Doran's mind. At Saxton's suggestion he collected affidavits from prominent civil rights leaders attesting to the validity of *The Fire in the Flint*'s descriptions of racial violence and assuring the publishing house that there was no basis for libel or court action against the novel. These efforts fell flat. In October Saxton passed on the news that George Doran still refused to publish the novel.[5]

White's experiences indicate that as late as mid-1923 at least some major publishing houses still were reluctant to print a book by a black author that they considered racially inflammatory, even though it had the support of industry figures like John Farrar and Eugene Saxton. Southern criticism, whether real or imagined, intimidated Doran—the warnings of a Kentucky humorist carried more weight than the recommendations of one of his senior editors or the publisher of a prominent literary magazine. The publication of Jean Toomer's *Cane* a few months earlier had not yet broken the ice. Despite the fact that it was clearly a book which addressed the realities confronting black Americans, *Cane* still veiled much of its social criticism with extensive and occasionally obscure symbolism; it was more avant-garde than incendiary. White, always more of a reporter than an artist, openly confronted southern racism with realism rather than symbolism, to a degree that no one had since Chesnutt. Doran lacked the will or the courage to pioneer with such a book.[6]

After the rejection from Doran, White sent his manuscript to H. L. Mencken, who urged him to send it to his own publisher, Alfred Knopf. Mencken advised White that "I have already told Knopf that I think it would be good business to publish the novel." Knopf issued White a contract in December 1923, and *The Fire in the Flint* appeared in September 1924. While the book created something of a stir, it was generally well received. White and Knopf were able to mobilize considerable support in their efforts to promote the book. Lawrence Stallings, critic for the *New York World* and a native of Georgia, praised the book, affirming the accuracy of its setting, characters, and plot; Sinclair Lewis, Carl Van Vechten, and Carl Van Doren joined Mencken in acclaiming the book in reviews and publicity statements prepared for Knopf. The ever irascible Mencken devised the strategy of sending review copies to the most "Negrophobe" southern newspapers; the ensuing controversy boosted sales in the South, while the strong endorsements by northern writers and critics generated curiosity and sales in that region of the country. The result, as White noted, was that the book became "a modest best seller far beyond its literary merits," and, consequently, "Knopf and I will be able to pay our bills for some time." The novel and the surrounding publicity also made White something of a minor celebrity in both Harlem and Manhattan and enabled him to establish contacts with men like Alfred Knopf and Carl Van Vechten that would later blossom into valuable and useful friendships.[7]

*The Fire in the Flint* appeared about six months after Boni & Liveright brought out Jessie Fauset's *There Is Confusion* along with Claude McKay's *Harlem Shadows* (Harcourt, Brace, 1922) and Toomer's *Cane* (Lippincott, 1923). These books opened the doors to the white publishing houses. While none became best sellers, their sales were respectable, as were the reviews. Similar success greeted Countee Cullen's first volume of poetry, which Harper brought out in 1925. However, the real flood of black books followed the appearance of Carl Van Vechten's *Nigger Heaven* in 1926. That novel and the rancor that surrounded its publication opened the gates. *Nigger Heaven* launched the "Negro vogue" and established the popularity of books about Harlem. It also suggested that no theme or subject matter was too controversial to be included in black literature—indeed many concluded that controversy and exposé were necessary ingredients for popular success. In the six years that followed . . . thirty-one books, representing the major works of the Harlem Renaissance, appeared.

Publishing houses like Knopf, Harper, and Harcourt Brace not only provided a new level of opportunity for black writers to publish their work but also promoted black literature, and in some cases actually attempted to influence the output of their writers. For this the publishers relied on their contacts with interested white literary figures like Carl Van Vechten and with black writers and intellectuals like James Weldon Johnson and Walter White. To say that white publishers controlled the literary output of the Harlem Renaissance is not accurate; black writers were dependent on white publishers, but white publishers like Knopf were sincerely interested in black literature, and they worked closely with black writers and intellectuals to achieve a viable literary movement. Of course, they were also interested in making money.

Examples of the efforts of publishers to promote black literature are numerous. Alfred Knopf was particularly sensitive to the need to promote black literature. His organization worked closely with its authors to place review copies of their books in appropriate hands and to solicit promotional endorsements and friendly reviews from other writers and well-known critics. For example, when Knopf reissued James Weldon Johnson's *The Autobiography of an Ex-Colored Man* in 1927 the company closely coordinated promotional efforts with the author; Knopf agents set up appearances for Johnson to read selections from his novel on three New York radio stations, arranged for an autograph session at Gimbels department store, synchronized publicity and appearances in Chicago bookstores to take advantage of a Johnson lecture tour there, and solicited from Johnson a portrait photograph by Carl Van Vechten and a quote from a congratulatory note from Clarence Darrow to use in their promotion. Johnson was an active participant in these efforts. He suggested linking his speaking tour with a promotional campaign in Chicago, urged Knopf to send publicity material to bookstores in towns where newspapers had featured reviews or articles about the book (and to Great Barrington, Massachusetts, where he was well known and had a part-time residence), and supplied Knopf with the names of appropriate reviewers for his books.[8]

Alfred Knopf was not the only publishing firm to promote its black writers energetically. Countee Cullen, who was much younger and less sophisticated about the business of marketing books when he published his first collection of poems with Harper in 1925, also benefited from the strong promotional support provided by his publisher. In the fall of 1925, when the Jordan Marsh department store in Boston asked Harper to provide one or two writers for their book week celebration, Frederick Lewis Allen, chief editor at Harper, asked Cullen, who had just published

*Color* and was attending classes at Harvard, to represent the publishing company. Harper also promoted Cullen's first collection of poetry by arranging for Walter White to review the book in *Saturday Review* and Mark Van Doren to review it in the New York *Herald Tribune.* In addition the firm's publicity department worked closely with Walter White in "the exploitation" of the book. In December 1925, obviously pleased with both the early sales and the critical response to *Color,* Allen informed Cullen that Harper was entering his book in the Pulitzer Prize competition. Alluding to Cullen's recent receipt of the Witter Bynner undergraduate poetry prize, Allen quipped that the Pulitzer "would be the next logical step in your prize-winning career."[9]

Harper paid close attention to the interests of their young poet. During 1925 and 1926 they supplied him with regular and encouraging reports of the book's sales. When they decided to print a second edition in late 1925, Allen pointed out to Cullen that his was the only second edition for a volume of poetry in recent years, except for "Miss Millay's." Such praise certainly must have been pleasing to the young writer. Harper also assisted Cullen in other ways. When Cullen was having difficulty getting into Professor Copeland's popular course at Harvard, Allen intervened on his young client's behalf. In early 1926, when Cullen was approached by a musician who wanted to obtain exclusive rights to set several of the poems from *Color* to music, Harper's editorial staff, while willing to accede to any arrangements that Cullen might want to make, cautioned him that by granting exclusive rights he might be giving away too much, and eventually they entered directly into the negotiations (which dragged out for almost a year) in an effort to guarantee that the poet shared in any profits that might be made from his creations. Harper also helped promote Cullen's financial well-being by helping arrange a lecture tour, under the management of Lee Keedrick, which the publishers felt "should bring in a substantial income."[10]

Meanwhile, Harper continued to encourage Cullen's writing efforts. A few months after it published *Color,* Allen began soliciting poems for *Harper's* magazine. In 1927 Allen wrote to Cullen that the magazine staff had "broken a record" accepting one of his poems after only ten minutes of deliberation. Indeed, the success of his first book relieved Cullen of most of the difficulties that previous black writers experienced with their publishers. In 1926, for example, when Cullen proposed editing an anthology of black poetry,

Harper responded promptly, "we are all enthusiastic about your suggestion for the Anthology. . . . Let me thank you for thinking first of Harper's." The anthology, *Caroling Dusk,* appeared in 1927, as did Cullens's second and third volumes of poetry, *Copper Sun* and *The Ballad of the Brown Girl,* making that year a banner one for the young poet and illustrating Harper's commitment both to Cullen and to black poetry.[11]

Success also brought queries from other publishers. Back in 1925 when the popularity of *Color* was at its peak, Carl Van Vechten wrote Cullen congratulating him and soliciting future work for Knopf: "I shall never cease to regret that we [Knopf] did not publish *Color,* but that was not my fault, if you recall. However, if you would send your next book to Knopf, I think they will only be too delighted to welcome it." Such a solicitation undoubtedly flattered the young poet. The experience of having rival publishers compete for yet unwritten manuscripts was at this time unique among black writers, and it was not common for poets of any hue. While Cullen did not switch publishers, he did maintain cordial relations with Van Vechten, even though he disapproved of *Nigger Heaven,* and with the Knopfs, and he helped that firm promote Langston Hughes's first book of poetry by preparing a prepublication review for *Opportunity.* Van Vechten, in turn, also helped Cullen find a management firm that could arrange lecture tours for him.[12]

While there was nothing unusual or extraordinary in these promotional efforts, they do contrast greatly with the experiences of black writers a decade or two earlier. These differences are perhaps most vividly evident in the problems that James Weldon Johnson had faced with his novel *The Autobiography of an Ex-Colored Man* in 1912. The original publisher, Sherman, French of Boston, lacked either the resources, the skill, or the will to promote the book effectively. Johnson blamed the sluggish sales on the failure of what he termed an "ultra-conservative publishing house" to market the book effectively. Arna Bontemps caught the essence of the situation when he observed that "one could almost say it was published in secret." When he returned to New York in 1914, Johnson took on the promotional duties himself. In late 1914 he openly acknowledged his authorship of the novel and suggested strategies to his publisher for selling the remaining copies of the book; in 1915 he personally paid for the printing and distribution of Brander Matthews's favorable review of the book. Through these efforts Johnson did sell off the remaining

stock of the novel, but the *Autobiography* was hardly a success until it was revived in 1927 by Knopf. This time, effectively marketed by a major publishing house and enjoying the popularity of black literature generated by the Renaissance, it sold respectably, and it has remained in print for more than fifty years. Johnson seemed almost relieved that his only novel was finally in the hands of a publisher that appreciated it.[13]

In addition to the major publishing houses, a number of relatively small literary magazines joined in the campaign to promote black literature during the 1920s. Generally this took the form of actively soliciting materials from black writers. For example, Ralph Cheney, editor of *Contemporary Verse,* asked Countee Cullen to submit any poems that he might have—and apologized in advance for being unable to pay anything. Harriet Monroe, on the other hand, not only sought material from Cullen—"your work interests us," she wrote—but also awarded him the John Reed Memorial Prize of $100 for the "general promise and quality of your work" that had been published in her magazine, *Poetry: A Magazine of Verse,* in May 1925.[14]

The little magazine that had the greatest impact on the Harlem Renaissance was Idella Purnell's *Palms: A Magazine of Poetry.* Purnell was born in Guadalajara but educated in Baltimore and Los Angeles. After she graduated from the University of California at Berkeley, where she studied under poet and critic Witter Bynner, she returned to Mexico and began publishing her magazine. With some support from her mentor at Berkeley, who became associate editor and undoubtedly contributed the resource of his extensive literary contacts, Purnell made *Palms* a rather influential magazine in the field of avant-garde American poetry.[15]

Countee Cullen was the first Renaissance poet to appear in *Palms.* Cullen, who had placed second in the Witter Bynner undergraduate poetry contests in both 1923 and 1924, was directed to *Palms* by the Berkeley critic. In its early summer issue of 1924 *Palms* published Cullen's "Ballad of the Brown Girl," a seven-page poem—the longest in the magazine. Cullen placed three more poems in the magazine that fall, and several more the following year. Furthermore, Cullen received twenty dollars from the magazine when his contributions were selected as the second most popular poems by a poll of *Palms* readers in both 1924 and 1925, and another $150 as winner of the Witter Bynner

Undergraduate Poetry Prize which, beginning in 1925, was administered jointly by the Poetry Society of America and *Palms*.[16]

In its January 1926 issue *Palms* made a major commitment to the Harlem Renaissance. First, it published two poems by Langston Hughes, who now joined Cullen as one of the magazine's up-and-coming young black poets. Second, *Palms,* which rarely reviewed books of poetry, published a lengthy and very favorable review of Countee Cullen's *Color*. The reviewer, John M. Weatherwax, celebrated Cullen as "one of the greatest of the younger American poets," noted that "there are enough *good* poems in this 'little collection' for five ordinary books of verse," and concluded with the terse proclamation, "Countee Cullen. Twenty-two. Watch him." Finally, the magazine announced that it intended to devote an entire issue to black poetry. The review of *Color* was followed by the notice: "PALMS takes great pleasure in announcing that Countee Cullen has consented to act as Editor for a Negro Poets' Number of the magazine."[17]

Idella Purnell's announcement in January 1926 of her plan to publish a black poetry issue of *Palms* was well timed to relate to the Harlem Renaissance at a critical time when the black literary movement was just gathering momentum. During the preceding eighteen months Cullen had published his first volume of poetry and Fauset and White had published their first novels; Langston Hughes's first book of poetry would appear early in 1926. The *Opportunity* literary contests were under way, and Locke had edited the "Harlem: Mecca of the New Negro" issue of *The Survey Graphic* and his own anthology, *The New Negro*. In the fall of 1926, while Du Bois was wrapping up his *Crisis* symposium on the role of blacks in art and literature, and only a few weeks after the publication of Van Vechten's *Nigger Heaven,* which did so much to launch the "Negro Vogue" and popularize black literature, Purnell and Cullen released their "Negro Poets" issue.

The black poetry issue of *Palms* appeared in October 1926. Purnell described it as containing work by "every negro [sic] poet of note in the U.S." and observed that it "came like a dark constellation, shining in the American world of letters with a new light." While much of this "new light" had been preempted by *The Survey Graphic,* Cullen did take special care to include work from a broad spectrum of black poets, ranging from the most conservative "old school" poets like Braithwaite and Du Bois, to newcomers like Arna Bontemps and Helene Johnson. As an introduction, Cullen

arranged for Walter White to write an essay on the Negro Renaissance, and the issue contained Carl Van Vechten's review of *The Weary Blues*. It also announced that Langston Hughes had won $150 for first place in the Witter Bynner American Undergraduate Poetry Prize, making this the second consecutive year that a black poet had won this prestigious award.[18]

The black poetry issue of *Palms* was well received in almost all quarters. Cullen reported from New York that the issue was the talk of all Harlem, and he sent Purnell a list of black and white periodicals that should receive review copies. The best indication of success, though, was the fact that the issue entirely sold out in only a month and that over a hundred requests for copies could not be met. Purnell admitted that it had never occurred to her that the issue could be so extraordinary, but "it seems that most people find the idea breathtaking—and when they recover from their surprise, like it." In November 1926 Cullen wrote Purnell that popularity of the project had convinced him to prepare an anthology of black poetry based largely on the *Palms* issue, and he announced that Harper had already agreed to publish it.[19]

As soon as the success of the Negro Poets' issue of *Palms* became apparent, both Purnell and Cullen indicated their interest in repeating the project. They continued to discuss this for more than two years and even began making concrete plans in 1928, but the issue never appeared. Purnell continued to publish black poetry and even began listing Cullen as an assistant editor of the magazine in 1927, but following her marriage in August 1927, the magazine seemed to lose its focus. *Palms* went though several changes in its editorial direction as it moved from Guadalajara to Washington state, to New York, and then back to Mexico, and as her husband, John M. Weatherwax, assumed a more active role as the magazine's publisher. Purnell continued her interest in black poets, and especially helped Sterling Brown by publishing some of his first verses in 1930, but by that time, neither Idella Purnell nor her magazine wielded the influence that they once had in the literary world. *Palms* ceased publication in 1930.

In the early 1930s, as the Harlem Renaissance was beginning to decline, another literary magazine, *Contempo,* attempted to attract black writers from the Harlem Renaissance to its pages and to develop a relationship with Harlem writers similar to that of *Palms*. *Contempo* was a somewhat daring southern literary magazine published in Chapel Hill, North Carolina, initially under the leadership of Anthony J. Buttitta. Buttitta and his staff were determined to involve black writers in his magazine in order to make the publication "more representative." They implored black writers to submit poems, essays, and short stories to them, and they reviewed most books written by blacks. Countee Cullen, Langston Hughes, James Weldon Johnson, Walter White, and Wallace Thurman were among the Renaissance writers who either submitted material to *Contempo* or were requested to. Langston Hughes visited the *Contempo* offices on his tour through the South in November 1931, and he stayed with Buttitta during his three days in Chapel Hill. That trip cemented a relationship between the two that would soon be reflected in the magazine. The December issue of *Contempo* listed Hughes as one of its six contributing editors, and the April 1932 issue announced that Hughes would edit a special forthcoming "Negro Arts Edition" of the magazine. Throughout the summer of 1932 *Contempo* carried an advertisement for *Scottsboro Limited,* which it described as "4 poems and a play in verse by Langston Hughes . . . for the benefit of the Scottsboro Boys."[20]

Unfortunately *Contempo*'s efforts to become a southern outlet for the literature of the Harlem Renaissance did not succeed. Symbolic of its failure was the fact that its "Negro Arts Edition," conceived as the major expression of its commitment to black literature, never materialized. A variety of circumstances combined to prevent this and to weaken the relationship of the magazine with the Harlem Renaissance and, indeed, to undermine the magazine itself. First, the editors of *Contempo* simply did not possess the gift of timing that Idella Purnell and *Palms* did. By 1932 the appearance of another anthology of black literature in a regional literary magazine (even a southern one) would do little to help the Renaissance. A decade earlier such an event would have been significant, but the "Negro Arts" issue of *Vanity Fair,* the Negro issue of *Palms,* Alain Locke's *New Negro,* Charles S. Johnson's *Ebony and Topaz,* and anthologies by Countee Cullen and James Weldon Johnson had effectively saturated the market as well as filled the need for such an edition. The announcement of the *Contempo* number was met, therefore, with a real lack of enthusiasm. Walter White, for example, credited *Contempo* for bringing a "new note into the South which is sorely needed," but then said that he had no material ready to contribute and that, because of his demanding work schedule, "I have had to abandon all thought of writing for the present." Countee

Cullen echoed these sentiments almost verbatim: "I am glad that you are going to do a Negro number of *Contempo.* . . . Unfortunately, I have not been writing lately, and have nothing at the moment which I can send you." If this lack of excitement among black writers undermined the project, internal dissension at *Contempo* finished it off. By mid-October Buttitta was no longer associated with the magazine. Three months later the new editors warned their readers that any paper that Buttitta might publish, whether called *Contempo* or not, would not be the "original and authentic" *Contempo.* The magazine did not survive this schism. In early 1934 it ceased publication.[21]

In addition to publishing and marketing black literature during the Renaissance, white publishing houses and the editors of literary magazines also served as literary advisers and critics for black writers. Ideally this relationship was one between equals or colleagues in the literary world, and neither race nor the distinction between writer and editor and publisher intruded; occasionally the positions in the relationship were reversed, and the black writers assisted their white colleagues. Sometimes, however, the relationship was strained or even shattered by economic or racial differences.

Usually the literary advice that white editors offered black writers focused on details related to the style or content of their work. For example, when Cullen submitted the poem "Spirit Birth" to the *American Mercury,* H. L. Mencken accepted it but suggested that the title be changed to "Shroud of Color" or "The Black Man Speaks"; similarly, John Farrar accepted one of the young poet's pieces on the condition that he improve the rhyme in one of its lines. Idella Purnell urged Sterling Brown to send examples of his work to Witter Bynner for assessment, and she suggested that he work on the "diffuseness" which marred much of his poetry. This kind of criticism was widespread and a common aspect of the editor-writer relationship.[22]

On several occasions, however, editors attempted to become much more involved in the literature of their writers. In the fall of 1927, shortly after Knopf reissued *The Autobiography of an Ex-Colored Man,* Blanche Knopf suggested that James Weldon Johnson write a new novel for the firm. Flattered by the suggestion, Johnson agreed to meet with Mrs. Knopf to talk about the idea. However, Johnson was preoccupied, first with speaking engagements, and then with his study of blacks in New York, and on several occasions postponed the meeting to discuss the novel. Blanche Knopf remained persistent. In December 1927 she suggested a topic—a fictionalized account of the life of boxer Jack Johnson. Although James Weldon Johnson seemed interested in the idea, he remained engrossed in his own projects. Eventually, in 1928 Blanche Knopf got Walter White to go to work on the "prize-fighter novel," but she still attempted to convince Johnson to do a novel for Knopf. In August 1930, after Johnson had finished *Black Manhattan,* his study of New York, she even sent him a contract for the still undefined novel. In spite of these efforts, Johnson did not write the novel. Johnson politely declined the contract and concentrated his literary energies on a revision of his earlier anthology of black poetry and on his autobiography.[23]

In January 1930 Eugene F. Saxton, now editor for Harper, made an even more detailed proposal for a book to Countee Cullen. Saxton wanted Cullen to write a long, book-length poem which would chronicle the history of blacks in America, beginning with "the pageant of the Negro's arrival from Africa, his period of slavery, and his eventual emergence into the highways of the New World." The project was to be elaborate—Harper would commission original wood blocks to illustrate the poem; Saxton envisioned a book similar to "Steve Benet's 'John Brown's Body.'" Cullen indicated his interest in the project but never really began work on it. Instead, like Johnson, he became sidetracked by a project of his own, his novel *One Way to Heaven.*[24]

The determination of black writers to pick their own subject matter (a right they also demanded from their black critics) was a sign of the growing maturity of black literature. It certainly contrasted with Dunbar's need to continually produce the dialect poetry demanded by his editors. It also indicated that at least in some ways black writers achieved a parity with their editors and with the white literary world in the late 1920s. While it is important not to read too much into this, the popularity of black writers during the hey-day of the Renaissance gave them a freedom and, at least in literary areas, an equality which has rarely been seen in any area of American life.

One sign of this equality was an interesting parity in the relationship of many black writers with their editors, especially those connected with the small literary magazines. While blacks certainly depended on these magazines to publish their work, the magazines and their editors also needed the black writers, and often solicited their services. Idella Purnell, for example, not only

utilized Countee Cullen's talents and his contacts in the black literary community to create the most popular issue in *Palms* history, but she also asked for his help in raising money, selling subscriptions, and finding patrons for *Palms* in the black community. Anthony J. Buttitta not only published black writers in an effort to broaden the appeal of *Contempo* (and establish its credentials as an avantgarde literary magazine in the South), but he also asked both James Weldon Johnson and Langston Hughes to help promote *his* literary career by critically evaluating the manuscript of his novel. And, Norman W. Macleod, the editor of *Palo Verde Southwestern Poetry Magazine,* asked Countee Cullen to serve as the sole judge for selecting the best poem in their magazine.[25]

There were of course limits to this equality. The relationship between writer and publisher is not always a relationship of equals; likewise, racial prejudice did not vanish in the twenties. Indeed, to one degree or another it colored all relationships. Sometimes racial considerations, real or imagined, created a rift between black writers and their publishers. The conflict between Walter White and George Doran over the publication of *The Fire in the Flint* was only one example of this friction. Ironically Alfred Knopf, who ultimately came to White's rescue and published his controversial novel, did not always get along with his black writers. Claude McKay, in particular, was extremely bitter about what he viewed as Knopf's biased handling of the manuscript of "Color Scheme," which he sent to Knopf in 1925. "Color Scheme" was McKay's first attempt to write a novel. He wrote the manuscript in 1924 and 1925 while in France, drawing largely on his experiences in Harlem. Walter White and Louise Bryant, McKay's most reliable patron during the mid-1920s, contributed to the Jamaican's support while he was writing, while White and James Weldon Johnson convinced the Garland Fund to provide him with a monthly stipend during 1924. White also arranged for Sinclair Lewis to provide critical advice, and Lewis persuaded the Garland Fund to extend McKay's grant through the summer of 1925. When McKay finished the manuscript, he sent it to Arthur Schomburg and instructed him to send it on to Alfred Knopf. In August Knopf rejected the manuscript because its literary quality was "uneven" and because the firm was concerned that its explicit sexual references would be found obscene by the courts.[26]

McKay did not accept the stated reasons for the rejection. McKay wrote to H. L. Mencken for assistance in getting the manuscript published.

McKay admitted that the novel was flawed but felt that its realistic portrayal of Harlem life and the fact that it was a first novel compensated for its unevenness. Mencken provided no help. In his frustration McKay saw himself the victim of a conspiracy. Knopf, he believed, had held his novel for six months to guarantee that Van Vechten's novel of Harlem life was published first; Walter White, "an unreliable mulatto," was loyal to Van Vechten, and consequently McKay had been deprived of the fame and wealth that he should have received as the author of the first novel of Harlem local color.[27]

This was not McKay's first or last encounter with Knopf, nor was it the only time that he felt betrayed by the firm. In 1919 he thought that Knopf had agreed to publish his first American volume of poetry. A year later he wrote Braithwaite that Knopf had "failed me at the last moment." Knopf failed him again in 1933 when McKay was down on his luck in Tangier and trying without any success to find a publisher for his new novel, "Savage Love." Few liked the novel. Even his friend and benefactor Max Eastman was critical, as was Eugene Saxton of Harper, who had published McKay's first four novels but now advised the Jamaican that he was an "expired fad." Knopf for a time considered publishing the manuscript, but finally rejected it because it was poorly constructed, dated, and likely to "lose a good deal of money."[28]

Claude McKay, who was frequently penniless, often in ill health, and almost always in the midst of some sort of life crisis over his work, his philosophy, or his friends, often saw a conspiracy behind his misfortune, and consequently he could be a very difficult person to work with. A more accurate picture of the difficulties that sometimes arose between black writers and their publishers, and how these difficulties affected the writer-publisher relationship, can be seen in the conflict that developed between Langston Hughes and Alfred Knopf over a collection of poems that Hughes wrote in the early 1930s.

Between 1931 and 1933 Hughes was out of the country on an around-the-world jaunt that began when he accepted an invitation to join a film company attempting to make a movie in the Soviet Union. While he was abroad, Hughes was especially dependent on his publisher, Alfred Knopf, to handle his business affairs. For two years the Knopfs served as Hughes's primary link with the Renaissance. They received and forwarded mail, received and stored the manuscripts that he sent back to the United States, served temporarily

as his literary agent, placed one of his short stories with H. L. Mencken and the *Mercury,* and finally found him a full-time literary agent.[29]

Hughes, of course, was grateful for this assistance. However, his experiences abroad, especially in the Soviet Union, strengthened Hughes's leftist tendencies and his perception of himself as a "proletariat" or "social poet." For example, while he expressly deferred to Blanche Knopf's judgment in the selection of a literary agent, he wrote that a friend in Moscow suggested that he attach himself to Liberman, a New York agent who was in touch with "the liberal and left-wing publications who are most likely to print my stuff," and observed that *Scribners* had recently rejected one of his stories because "it would shock our good middle class audience to death." Wisely, Blanche Knopf ignored the advice that Hughes received in Moscow and placed him with a mainstream New York literary agent. However, Hughes's leftward shift would create a more difficult problem for his publishers.[30]

Among the material that Langston Hughes sent the Knopfs from Moscow was the manuscript for a book of political poems. Blanche Knopf immediately sent the book to Carl Van Vechten for his opinion. Van Vechten, who was not at all pleased with Hughes's flirtation with communism, described the manuscript as a very weak collection of poems whose revolutionary pieces were "more hysterical than lyrical" and predicted that if this were published, it would hurt Hughes's reputation. When Blanche Knopf forwarded Van Vechten's evaluation to Hughes, along with her suggestion that he try to revise the manuscript, the poet was not pleased. He responded that he would be happy to undertake revisions if Knopf was really interested in eventually publishing the collection, but he could not base his revisions on Van Vechten's critique: "Carlo, as you know, did not like the book at all except for a few lyrics, so I could hardly revise it on the basis of his letter. There wouldn't be anything left in it afterwards." Hughes sent the Knopfs "two Moscow opinions on the book," and, implying that most of Van Vechten's comments were politically biased, he added, "I trust you have given it to some left-wing critics for a reading."[31]

Both the Knopfs and Van Vechten were very concerned about the reaction and the feelings of their young poet. Alfred Knopf suggested that they send the manuscript to another reader, and even expressed regret for having sent it to Van Vechten in the first place. Blanche attempted to distract Hughes away from the poetry book with another project. She suggested that he continue working on his "black and white" series of short stories but provide them with enough continuity so that they could easily be combined into a book; she even proposed a title for the collection, *The Ways of White Folks*. Hughes agreed to the plan and sent in fifteen stories, "most written from the Negro point of view concerning situations derived from conditions of inter-racial contact." Van Vechten, who also reviewed this manuscript for the Knopfs, seemed almost relieved when he read it: "I am delighted to be able to report at once that I find myself tremendously enthusiastic about Langston's book. . . . I am glad to feel that way after my reaction to that communist poetry book." Van Vechten went on to call the book Hughes's "best work to date," and concluded his report with the observation that "I have long believed that Ethel Waters and Langston Hughes had more genius than any others of their race in this country. . . . This boy grows under your eye." When *The Ways of White Folks* neared publication, Blanche Knopf worked closely with Hughes to guarantee that the book did not interfere with the sale of several of the stories to magazines—she even delayed the publication date several months so that he could sell stories to *Esquire* and *Scribners*.[32]

The publication of Hughes's collection of short stories did not resolve the issue of his poetry collection. In February 1934 he sent a revised manuscript to Knopf with a note stating he had received favorable comments on the poems from Lincoln Steffens and several other leftist literary figures in California and that he believed there was a market for the book. Van Vechten still disagreed. He argued that the book was not nearly so good as Hughes's other volumes of poetry, and he asserted that in his opinion Hughes had gone as far as he could go as a poet—that he should be advised "to leave the Muse alone henceforth." Van Vechten urged Knopf to reason with Hughes, to point out that it would be difficult to sell a book of these poems because "communists do not buy books and few others will want to hang a book in which the communist sentiment is stronger than the art." However, Van Vechten advised that if Hughes still wanted the book published, Knopf should publish it.[33]

The same day that she received Van Vechten's recommendation, Blanche Knopf communicated her decision to Hughes. Knopf would publish the collection of poetry if Hughes insisted, but she strongly and frankly advised against it:

I have given the question of your book of poetry a good deal of thought and have come to the following conclusion, which I write you because I think we know each other well enough to be completely frank and have no pretense as a barrier.

I don't think that this is the moment for you to publish a book of poems—I think that you have become much more important than this poetry is and that the publication of such a book now would tend to hurt your name rather than help it. This in my very humble opinion, is not as good a book of poetry as your earlier ones. Definitely I think the place for these poems is between magazines and not book covers, now. By this I don't mean that ultimately at some future time the poetry should not or cannot be published; but I don't believe that a propaganda book in verse is wise for you nor do I think that the communists would back you up and buy it. From a publishing point of view I would much rather not do your poems now and do your next prose book when it comes along if we both agree on that.

Now that I have written my worst I want to add that if you still feel definitely that you want us to publish the book of poetry, we are your publishers and I would not want to let you go elsewhere, so if you insist on the publication, of course we will do it. I am merely giving my best advice and my opinion and I hope you will take it in the way that I mean, which is in deepest friendship.

Hughes did not insist that Knopf publish the poems. Instead he decided to arrange for a radical press to bring out an inexpensive edition and distribute it through workers' book shops and union halls. Van Vechten concurred with this decision.[34]

Significantly, the dispute over Hughes's radical poetry did not affect his relationship with either the Knopfs or Van Vechten. The Knopfs remained Hughes's primary publisher, and Hughes, Van Vechten, and the Knopfs continued to work closely together throughout the 1930s and the 1940s. Van Vechten provided the promotional material for *The Ways of White Folks,* and Hughes suggested the use of Van Vechten's photographs to publicize his autobiography which Knopf published at the end of the decade.[35]

While white editors and publishers played an obvious and visible role in the Harlem Renaissance, they were not the only whites involved in the movement and not the only ones to have a significant impact on it. Nor were they the only whites to assist and befriend black writers or to endure a sometimes stormy relationship with them. White patrons of black literature, both individuals and institutions, also were involved in the Renaissance and with individual black writers.

White patronage of the black arts took several forms, but generally it consisted of providing money for prizes, grants, scholarships, and the support of individual writers. Occasionally this could take the form of an anonymous contribution to a young artist. In December 1923, for example, Countee Cullen was surprised to receive a five-dollar check from an unknown benefactor who identified himself as Jedediah Tingle. Tingle, the pseudonym for an unidentified person who sent contributions to individuals for something they said, did, or wrote, mailed Cullen the check because he was impressed with a poem and story about the young poet he had read in the *New York Times.* Most patrons of the Harlem Renaissance were more organized or more specifically involved in the promotion of black literature than was the mysterious Mr. Tingle.[36]

Many of the awards and contests that helped launch the Harlem Renaissance were funded by white contributors. White liberals associated with the Urban League, for example, were largely responsible for convincing *The Survey Graphic* to let Alain Locke produce the Harlem issue in 1925. Joel Spingarn funded the Spingarn medal, which was awarded annually to the black who had done the most to promote the cause of his or her race, and he funded the initial *Crisis* literary competition. Other literary prizes funded by white patrons included the Van Vechten award of $200 for the best poem, short story, or essay appearing each year in *Opportunity,* and the $1000 W.E.B. Du Bois literary prize. The most prestigious awards presented to black writers during this period were the prizes bestowed annually for five years beginning in 1926 by the William E. Harmon Foundation for "distinguished achievement among Negroes in creative endeavors." Each year the foundation offered a $400 gold prize and a $100 bronze prize in each of eight fields, including the fine arts and literature. Countee Cullen, Claude McKay, James Weldon Johnson, and Nella Larsen were among the black writers who received Harmon prizes during the Renaissance. In 1926 the publishing house of Boni & Liveright announced a $1000 prize for the best novel on "Negro life" written by a black author.[37]

The various literary contests and prizes were designed to stimulate the development of black literature by holding out the promise of public recognition and financial windfall. In addition, philanthropic agencies like the Guggenheim Foundation, the Julius Rosenwald Fund, and the Garland Fund provided fellowships that several black writers used either to finance their education or to support themselves while writing. Virtually every writer associated with the Harlem Renaissance benefited in some way from these contests, prizes, grants, and fellowships. Langston Hughes, for example, received the following awards during his long career:

> First *Opportunity* poetry prize
> Witter Bynner undergraduate poetry award
> Harmon Gold Medal for literature
> Guggenheim fellowship
> Rosenwald Fund fellowship
> American Academy of Arts and Letters grant

This institutional patronage provided Renaissance writers with a source of economic support that pre-Renaissance blacks never saw. Furthermore, except for the unsuccessful efforts of Du Bois and Braithwaite to manipulate the prizes in their efforts to divert black literature away from ghetto realism, black writers received these benefits while surrendering little of their artistic freedom.[38]

This was not always the case, however, with the more direct and personal patronage that was also widespread during the Harlem Renaissance. In some instances the gifts or support that patrons provided had few strings attached. Claude McKay, for example, received financial assistance from Louise Bryant off and on from 1924 to 1928. Bryant, the widow of revolutionary John Reed and later the wife of a wealthy Philadelphian, not only assisted McKay financially, but also helped market the essays and short stories he wrote during his years in France, and provided him with emotional support and guidance during a difficult and frustrating time in the Jamaican writer's life. Despite his tendency to quarrel with his friends and benefactors, McKay and Bryant remained friends throughout this period.[39]

Zora Neale Hurston also benefited from the support of several benefactors, especially that of her patron and friend Fannie Hurst, who maintained contact with her long after the Renaissance ended. Hurston arrived in New York from Howard University in January 1925 with only $1.50 in her pocket. She headed straight for the offices of *Opportunity,* which had already published two of her short stories. Charles S. Johnson took her under his wing, and Hurston achieved rapid success, largely because of the intervention of two white patrons. Annie Nathan Meyers arranged for her to attend Barnard College and funded her education; Fannie Hurst hired her to be her live-in secretary, driver, and traveling companion. The arrangement between Hurston and Hurst was mutually advantageous. Hurston received room and board and a place to live and write while acquiring a first-rate education as an anthropologist and folklorist; Hurst, on the other hand, gained a crash course in black life and culture from the mercurial Hurston, who became the inspiration for and the model for her later best-selling novel of black life, *Imitation of Life.* Both Meyer and Hurst maintained interest in and involvement in Hurston's career long after she left Barnard, and the relationship between Hurst and Hurston evolved into a deep friendship. In addition to providing references for Hurston when she applied for Guggenheim fellowships in 1934 and 1935 and in other ways promoting her career, Hurst exchanged frequent chatty letters with Hurston throughout the 1930s and early 1940s, and in the summer of 1940 Hurston offered to come to New York to take care of Hurst during an illness.[40]

Hurston also benefited from the patronage of Charlotte Osgood Mason, an aged, very wealthy, somewhat mysterious white woman, who held court in her Park Avenue apartment as the self-styled "godmother" of the Renaissance and provided generous support for her favorites. Mason's fascination with the "primitive" nature of blacks attracted her to Hurston, who by virtue of her studies with Franz Boas had become an accomplished folklorist. Hurston delighted Mason with her animated stories of rural black folk; Mason responded by providing her with a grant of $200 per month for two years to collect black folk material. Hurston's relationship with Mason was very close. In her autobiography Hurston wrote that "there was and is a psychic bond between us." Hurston credited her with forcing her to be intellectually honest—to Mason the most serious crime was insincerity, no matter how cleverly it might be disguised—and impressing her with the significance and beauty of primitive cultures.[41]

The relationship between black writer and white patron was not always so idyllic. While black writers undoubtedly reaped considerable financial and professional benefit from the attention that whites showered on them during the Renaissance, they also occasionally faced the risk of becoming snared by their benefactors. Although a patron might provide a writer with the economic freedom to pursue his or her profession, this same patron might, at the same time, either consciously or unconsciously, limit the artistic freedom that his or her protégé required to produce really first-rate work.

The most widely publicized conflict between patron and writer over these issues occurred between Langston Hughes and his patron, the same Charlotte Osgood Mason, whom Zora Neale Hurston praised so unequivocally. Hughes met Mason through Alain Locke during one of his trips to New York City while he was in his third year at Lincoln University. When Mason learned that Hughes was working on a novel, she offered to support him during the summer so that he could focus entirely on his writing. After he graduated from Lincoln, she provided him with a monthly allowance sufficient to allow him to spend a year free from economic worry. Like most other writers who knew her, Hughes was quite taken with this woman. Years after he had broken with her he still remembered her with a mixture of awe and affection:

> My patron (a word neither of us liked) was a beautiful woman, with snow-white hair and a face that was wise and very kind. She had been a power in her day in many of the movements adding freedom and splendor to life in America. She had great sums of money, and had used much of it in great and generous ways. She had been a friend of presidents and bankers, distinguished scientists, famous singers, and writers of world renown. Imposing institutions and important new trends in thought and in art had been created and supported by her money and her genius at helping others. Now she was very old and not well and able to do little outside her own home. But there she was like a queen. Her power filled the rooms. Famous people came to see her and letters poured in from all over the world. . . .
>
> She was an amazing, brilliant, and powerful personality. I was fascinated by her, and I loved her. No one else had ever been so thoughtful of me, or so interested in the things I wanted to do, or so kind and generous toward me.

Although she was quite elderly, Mason remained up-to-date in her ideas and outlook. In the twenties she added an interest in the New Negro to her long-standing commitment to racial justice. Like many other patrons of the Renaissance, she was not only concerned about the well-being of blacks in America, but she possessed certain well-defined attitudes concerning the nature of blacks and their potential contribution to American civilization. Like Zora Neale Hurston, Hughes discovered Mason's fascination with the primitive:

> Concerning Negroes, she felt that they were America's greatest link with the primitive, and that they had something very precious to give to the Western World. She felt that there was mystery and mysticism and spontaneous harmony in their souls, but many of them had let the white world pollute and contaminate that mystery and harmony, and make something of it cheap and

ugly, commercial and, as she said, "white." She felt that we had a deep well of the spirit within us and that we should keep it pure and deep.[42]

The characteristics that Hughes so admired in his patron—wealth, a strong will, and a belief in the primitive nature of black Americans—were also the source of their estrangement. Unlike Zora Neale Hurston, Hughes became uncomfortable with the economic gulf that separated him (and the blacks among whom he lived) from Mason, and he became increasingly troubled by her focus on the primitive. The differences between the two intensified as Hughes became more and more political in the late 1920s and early 1930s. Although he appreciated the economic freedom that Mason's generosity provided him, he grew increasingly uncomfortable with the disparity between the poverty of Harlem and the luxury of Park Avenue, especially in the months following the stock market crash, and he became frustrated with his patron's insistence that he focus his art on the primitive element in black life. As the economic situation worsened, Hughes became particularly sensitive to the plight of the unemployed. As he recalled, "it was impossible for me to travel from hungry Harlem to the lovely homes on Park Avenue without feeling in my soul the great gulf between the very poor and the very rich in our society."[43]

Hughes expressed his growing alienation indirectly, through two political poems. The first, "Advertisement for the Waldorf-Astoria," was a fairly long poem satirizing an advertisement announcing the opening of New York's finest and most luxurious hotel. Hughes considered the Waldorf an obscene flaunting of wealth at a time when thousands of homeless slept in doorways and had little to eat, and he was further incensed by the fact that the hotel neither employed blacks nor admitted them as guests. The second poem, "Park Bench," was a short, incisive indictment of Park Avenue wealth with clear revolutionary implications, and a thinly veiled attack on Mason herself:

> I live on a park bench.
> You, Park Avenue.
> Hell of a distance
> Between us two.
>
> I beg a dime for dinner—
> You got a butler and a maid.
> But I'm wakin' up!
> Say, ain't you afraid.
>
> That I might just maybe,
> In a year or two,

> Move on over
> To Park Avenue?

Years later Hughes recalled clearly that Mason was not pleased by "Advertisement for the Waldorf-Astoria." "It's not you," she complained, "It's a powerful poem! But it's not you." However, it was Hughes, at least at this stage in his career. Poet and patron never reconciled their differences, and in December 1930 they severed their relationship. As Hughes simply stated, "in a little while I did not have a patron anymore."[44]

Hughes felt that Mason objected to his political poems, not merely because of their political content, but because they focused on politics instead of the primitive nature of black life. Nowhere did these verses express the soul of Africa or the jungle rhythms that she looked for in black poetry; nor did they give voice to the "mystery and mysticism and spontaneous harmony" that she had come to expect. The problem was that Mason was looking for something in Hughes that did not really exist:

> She wanted me to be primitive and know and feel the intuitions of the primitive. But, unfortunately, I did not feel the rhythms of the primitive surging through me, and so I could not live and write as though I did. I was only an American Negro—who had loved the surface of Africa and the rhythms of Africa—but I was not Africa. I was Chicago and Kansas City and Broadway and Harlem. And I was not what she wanted me to be.[45]

Primitivism was a complex issue for participants in the Renaissance. Many whites expected to find it in black writing. Zora Neale Hurston felt very comfortable dealing with it, and some of her peers did develop primitive African themes in their literature (including Langston Hughes in "A Negro Speaks of Rivers"). Others were simply amused or shared Hughes's discomfort or were even hostile to those who seemed to be confining blacks to a stereotype of primitiveness and sensuality. Mary Love expressed these feelings in Carl Van Vechten's *Nigger Heaven*; so did Harold Jackman, who admitted, half seriously and half in jest, that he did not get the same thrill from jazz that blacks were reputed to experience, and he questioned the validity of the new racial stereotypes that many whites had imposed on blacks during the Renaissance. Writing to Claude McKay, he asked:

> Tell me, frankly, do you think colored people feel as primitive as many writers describe them as feeling when they hear jazz? So many writers, Negro and white, assert this. I know that we are a rhythmic people. It doesn't take much observation to see that, but this business of feeling the music so deeply that we almost become intoxicated is be-

yond me. . . . I always wish I could enjoy such an experience. There is so much hokum and myth about the Negro these days (since the Negro Renaissance, as it is called) that if a thinking person doesn't watch himself, he is liable to believe it.[46]

When the relationship between black writers and white patrons (or editors and publishers) was based on such stereotypes, there was always the danger that black writers would pay too high a price for the financial support that they received, and consequently that the quality of black literature would suffer.

Another potential source of conflict between black writers and their white patrons, publishers, and supporters was the question of money. The major publishing houses had few problems in this area because their financial relationship with the black writers was handled on a purely contractual basis, and most publishers were careful to protect the economic interests of all of their authors. But for the editors of small literary magazines and anthologies, who generally had limited economic resources, and for some patrons economic questions and misunderstandings about economic arrangements were a source of potential conflict with black writers.

Usually misunderstandings were avoided. Most literary magazines announced up front that they could not afford to pay for the poetry they published, and few black writers seemed surprised by this information. Early in his career Cullen expressed his understanding of the situation philosophically when he wrote Idella Purnell at *Palms,* "Mr. Bynner explained to me that *Palms* does not pay for contributors, but what poet is ever concerned about money?" Several free copies of the magazine containing one's poems was the usual payment that novice poets received from small magazines. However, despite Cullen's comments to Purnell, no Renaissance writer was uninterested in money; indeed, all of them hoped to make a living from their craft. Several years later Cullen demonstrated more concern about the earning potential of his writing when he instructed his publishers not to allow any of his poems to be reprinted in anthologies without remuneration, noting that this was the situation he faced when he collected material for *Caroling Dusk.* In the mid-1930s he again demonstrated his sophistication about the publishing business when he negotiated with Harper to reprint *Copper Sun* by agreeing to reduce his royalty to make the project economically feasible.[47]

The best-documented misunderstanding over money occurred between heiress Nancy Cunard and Claude McKay in the early 1930s. Cunard, whose interest in the Renaissance grew out of both her personal life (her well-publicized love affair with a black American musician) and her revolutionary politics (which involved her in the crusade to liberate the nonwhite peoples from European imperialism), devoted considerable energy in the early 1930s to the collection of material for a new anthology of black art and literature. In pursuing this goal, Cunard came in contact with a number of black writers. Sterling Brown, who was just beginning his writing career, was particularly infatuated by her, while Langston Hughes, who initially agreed to send her a couple of his poems and help her identify other potential contributors to the anthology, especially among lesser-known black writers, discovered that she was a kindred soul, at least in terms of her revolutionary politics, and the relationship between the two blossomed into a friendship that lasted into the 1960s.[48]

Initially the relationship between Cunard and McKay was equally close. The two began corresponding in 1931 while Cunard was soliciting contributions for her anthology and McKay was living in North Africa. They exchanged a rather extensive correspondence of lengthy letters in which McKay discussed in detail his political views and his frustrations over the criticism of his work and his politics in Harlem, the commercial failure of most of his books, and his failing health. Cunard, in turn, recounted the unpleasant reception that she and her lover received in Harlem. The two also assisted each other. McKay arranged for his brother U'Theo to be her host when she visited Jamaica, and Cunard helped McKay cash checks and get funds transferred to Tangier; she also tried to arrange for the publication of *Banana Bottom* in London.[49]

This increasingly intimate relationship was shattered when McKay finally sent his manuscript to Cunard and asked when he might anticipate payment. Cunard responded that she had expected the contributors to write without compensation, out of a shared commitment to the project's goal, "to throw light on the appalling way the entire color question is handled." McKay, who had written Cunard only two months earlier of his poor health and poverty, was taken aback. As he explained, "I told you once in a letter that I was 'romantic' about artists and creative work, but my romanticism is different from those nice people who ask and expect artists to write, sing, act, and perform in other ways freely and charitably for a cause while they would not dream of asking the carpenter and caterer, others who do the manual tasks, to work for nothing." When Cunard reiterated that she was unable to pay contributors, McKay angrily demanded the return of his manuscript:

> Writing is my means of livelihood. I wrote the article "Up To Date" for payment. You are not paying for articles, you say. Well, the very obvious way out is to *leave my article altogether out of your Anthology.* . . . I have not the slightest wish now to appear in your anthology, and I hope you will respect that wish.

That was the end of the friendship. McKay's article did not appear in Cunard's anthology, *Negro*.[50]

McKay was not the only Renaissance writer who refused to contribute to *Negro* without payment. Eric Walrond also boycotted the project, while Cunard pressured Cullen to release the poems without his customary charge, with the threat that otherwise she would be forced to leave him out of the book. Jean Toomer refused to contribute anything on the grounds, "I am not a Negro." On the whole, however, Cunard's project was supported by most black writers and poets, and the volume was very favorably received when it appeared in 1934, despite the fact that it contained Cunard's rather critical article on Du Bois and the NAACP, "A Reactionary Negro Organization." Alain Locke sent his congratulations and promised to promote the book among his acquaintances, while Arthur Schomburg promised that his review of the book would appear in three hundred black newspapers and offered his services as an agent for the book among black Americans. He also castigated Walrond, and especially McKay, for refusing to participate in the project without pay.[51]

Misunderstandings like that between McKay and Cunard had the potential of sowing discord between black writers and their white supporters, especially in the early 1930s as the Harlem vogue began to dissipate and the onset of the Great Depression intensified the economic pressures that black writers faced. Sometimes blacks could joke about their dependence on white capital, but these jokes were often bittersweet. For example, the black journal, *The Messenger,* which relied heavily on white funds, had earned the dubious reputation among blacks of vacillating between a radical or socialist paper and a black society sheet, depending on who was paying the bills at the moment. While black writers could laugh about *The Messenger,* they lost their sense of humor when they faced the loss of their own patronage. As the Renaissance began to lose its popularity in the mid-1930s and white interest and white funds began to dry up, several black writers became bitter about the turn of events. To many it seemed that they had only been a fad, and now that the moment had passed, no one had much interest in their writing or their careers.[52]

In spite of the occasional problems associated with it, patronage was a vital and necessary element in the development of the Harlem Renaissance. While some patrons inhibited the freedom of their protégés, most placed few strings on their financial support. Amy and Joel Spingarn, for example, generously supported black art and literature without restricting the creativity of the artists and writers. Almost every participant in the Renaissance acknowledged that not only was Carl Van Vechten the most important white contributor to the movement, but that his association was more that of a friend and colleague than a patronizing banker. The sincerity of Van Vechten's support can easily be demonstrated by the fact that his interest in black literature transcended the Renaissance. He first became involved with black writers in the early 1920s before there was a literary movement, he was one of the handful of whites who deserve credit for helping to establish the movement, and he continued his interest and his help long after the "fad" had run its course.[53]

Van Vechten's contributions to the movement took several forms. The public side of his involvement was well known. It ranged from providing financial support to one of the *Opportunity* literary prizes and serving as one of the patrons of *Fire!!,* to almost singlehandedly generating the Negro vogue with *Nigger Heaven* and then perpetuating it with the infamous "tours" of Harlem night spots that he conducted, always with a crowd of white celebrities in tow. He was equally famous for the parties that became so important to the Harlem literary scene and "so Negro" that they were reported "as a matter of course in the colored society columns, just as though they occurred in Harlem" instead of at the West 55th Street apartment that he shared with his wife, actress Fania Marinoff. In addition Van Vechten was always ready to assist black writers in any way he could. In 1925, for example, he helped Langston Hughes publish his first book of poetry and quickly gained the reputation among black writers as a friend they could turn to if they had difficulty finding a publisher for their work. When Zora Neale Hurston had her first novel accepted in 1933, she asked him to write an advance review and help promote the book. Van Vechten also worked behind the scenes with Blanche Knopf as an unofficial but de facto editor at Knopf for black literature. The Knopfs regularly sent manuscripts from known and unknown black writers to him for his critical evaluation, and they almost always followed his recommendations.[54]

What truly distinguished Van Vechten's involvement in the Harlem Renaissance and set him apart from other white editors and patrons was the fact that, more than any other white man, he developed close, personal friendships with a number of Renaissance figures. His correspondence with black writers and intellectuals reflected not only a concern for their professional careers but also a genuine interest in their personal lives and personal problems. Novelist Nella Larsen and her husband felt close enough to confide in Van Vechten when they were having marital problems. Zora Neale Hurston valued Van Vechten's friendship more than his patronage and even expressed concern that he might mistake her friendship for favor-seeking. Van Vechten's personal relationships with blacks were so close and so well known that a number of his friends joked that he was more black than white. In Van Vechten's favorite caricature of himself, artist Covarrubias gave substance to the jest by portraying him with distinctly Negroid features.[55]

Van Vechten was especially close to James Weldon Johnson, Walter White, and Langston Hughes. Historian David Lewis graphically described these friendships: "James Weldon Johnson, as dear to him as his own father and possessing greater 'tact and discretion'; Walter White, with whom he got on like 'a house afire' and who was soon to bestow Van Vechten's name on his son; and Langston Hughes, who was like a son and a colleague." James Weldon Johnson and Van Vechten formed a personal understanding that whoever lived longer would assume control over the papers and literary material of the other. When Johnson died in 1938, Van Vechten honored the arrangement by establishing the James Weldon Johnson Collection of Negro Arts and Letters at Yale University. Despite their political differences, Hughes and Van Vechten remained close long after the end of the Renaissance. Hughes, perhaps, best captured the depth and simplicity of Van Vechten's racial views and his relationship with his black friends in his description of a birthday celebration:

> For several pleasant years, he [Van Vechten] gave an annual birthday party for James Weldon Johnson, Young Alfred A. Knopf, Jr., and himself, for their birthdays fall on the same day. At the last of these parties, the year before Mr. Johnson died, on the Van Vechten table were three cakes, one red, one white, and one blue—the colors of our flag. They honored a Gentile, a Negro, and a Jew—friends and fellow Americans. But the differences of race did not occur to me until days later, when I thought back about the three colors and the three men.
>
> Carl Van Vechten is like that party. He never talks grandiloquently about democracy or Americanism. Nor makes a fetish of those qualities. But he lives them with sincerity—and humor.[56]

Carl Van Vechten represented white support of black literature at its best—sincere and with unselfish intentions. However, even unselfishness and sincerity could not always prevent misunderstandings between black writers and white patrons, nor could it prevent white support from imposing restrictions, as unintentional as they might be, on black literature. There were always elements that strained the relationship between blacks and whites—political disagreements, disparate views about the purpose and appropriate nature of black literature, economic misunderstandings, and ultimately the racial differences that underlie almost every aspect of American life. Even a person as totally dedicated to helping the development of black literature as Van Vechten, and one who did as much as anyone to popularize and aid the Renaissance, did conflict with Hughes over politics and also unwittingly helped establish the stereotypes about ghetto life and the primitive nature of blacks which ensnared some black writers. Indeed, Van Vechten, *Nigger Heaven,* and the whole Negro vogue reflected the major dilemma of the Harlem Renaissance: no matter how committed to giving expression to the black experience, the Renaissance was, in the final analysis, dependent on white audiences, white magazines, white publishers, and white money. What is amazing is that on the whole the black-white literary partnership worked fairly well and fairly equitably.

### Notes

1. Eugene Levy, *James Weldon Johnson: Black Leader, Black Voice* (Chicago: University of Chicago Press, 1973), 126-28, 161-63.

2. Cynthia Earl Kerman and Richard Eldridge, *The Lives of Jean Toomer: A Hunger for Wholeness* (Baton Rouge: Louisiana State University Press, 1987), 91-92, 99-100; Claude McKay, *A Long Way from Home* (New York: Harcourt Brace & World, 1970), 147-48.

3. David Levering Lewis, *When Harlem Was in Vogue* (New York: Vintage Books, 1982), 10, 97.

4. Langston Hughes, *The Big Sea* (New York: Hill and Wang, 1963), 247-48; Walter White, *A Man Called White: The Autobiography of Walter White* (Bloomington, IN: Indiana University Press, 1970), 65-66; Lewis, 133.

5. White, 66-67; Lewis, 133-35.

6. There is another interpretation of this episode. Charles Scruggs suggests that Doran rejected the manuscript for aesthetic reasons and that White, from the moment he met Mencken in the spring of 1922 (a year before he wrote *The Fire in the Flint*), shrewdly manipulated him, first by planting the seed that prompted Mencken to suggest that White write a novel of southern life, and then deluding him about the reason Doran rejected the manuscript. In the process White triggered Mencken's antipathy toward the South by suggesting that a southern conspiracy was at work attempting to suppress the novel and recruited him as an ally in getting the manuscript published. See Charles Scruggs, *The Sage in Harlem: H. L. Mencken and the Black Writers of the 1920s* (Baltimore: Johns Hopkins University Press, 1984), 117-20. While White's recollection of the situation in his autobiography is not very detailed and undoubtedly a bit biased, it is also far-fetched to assume that a young man recently arrived from Georgia could completely bamboozle Mencken, as well as Saxton, Farrar, Knopf, and practically the entire literary establishment. Doran may have been concerned about the literary quality of White's book (White himself had been reluctant to send his unrevised twelve-day-wonder to Farrar), but he did consult with Cobb and was concerned about southern reaction to the manuscript. See White, 66; and Lewis, 133.

7. White, 68; Scruggs, 117-20; Lewis, 135-36.

8. See James Weldon Johnson to Myriam Sieve, September 8, 1927, September 11, 1927, and September 27, 1927; Myriam Sieve to James Weldon Johnson, September 21, 1927, October 1, 1927, and October 21, 1927; Myriam Sieve to Mr. Smith, October 10, 1927; Blanche Knopf to James Weldon Johnson, July 6, 1927, and December 30, 1927, Alfred Knopf, Inc. Collection, HRHRC; see also a draft of a letter from Myriam Sieve to twenty-two Chicago bookstores informing them of Johnson's itinerary in their city and offering publicity materials for the *Autobiography of an Ex-Coloured Man,* October 28, 1927, Alfred Knopf, Inc. Collection, HRHRC.

9. Frederick Lewis Allen to Countee Cullen, October 19, 1925, December 16, 1925, and Ruth Raphael to Countee Cullen, January 26, 1926, Countee Cullen Papers, ARC-TU. Unfortunately, the event at Jordan Marsh was canceled by the department store. See Frederick Lewis Allen to Countee Cullen, October 27, 1925, ARC-TU.

10. See Frederick Lewis Allen to Countee Cullen, December 9, 1925, September 30, 1925, February 11, 1926, Countee Cullen Papers, ARC-TU; Eugene F. Saxton to Countee Cullen, March 9, 1926, May 21, 1926, June 1, 1926, November 16, 1926, and May 26, 1927, Countee Cullen Papers, ARC-TU.

11. Frederick Lewis Allen to Countee Cullen, October 27, 1925, and January 11, 1927; William H. Briggs to Countee Cullen, October 27, 1926, Countee Cullen Papers, ARC-TU.

12. Carl Van Vechten to Countee Cullen, December 11, 1925, and October 13, 1925, Countee Cullen Papers, ARC-TU. For years Cullen received a substantial income presenting lectures under the management of W. Colston Leigh, the firm that Van Vechten recommended.

13. Levy, 127-28, 305; Arna Bontemps, "Introduction" in James Weldon Johnson, *Autobiography of an Ex-Coloured Man* (New York: Hill and Wang, 1960), v; James Weldon Johnson to Blanche Knopf, April 23, 1926, Alfred Knopf, Inc. Collection, HRHRC. The Knopf edition made a few minor changes in the novel—the most visible was changing the spelling of "Colored" to "Coloured" in the title. See Levy, 305n.

14. Ralph Cheney to Countee Cullen, December 17, 1926, and Harriet Monroe to Countee Cullen, October 16, 1925, Countee Cullen Papers, ARC-TU.

15. Idella Purnell Stone, "Autobiographical Sketch," handwritten manuscript, Idella Purnell Stone Papers, HRHRC.

16. See *Palms* 2, Early Summer 1924; *Palms* 2, Early Fall 1924; *Palms* 3, Summer 1925; *Palms* 3, November 1925; *Palms* 3, December 1925, 93.

17. *Palms* 3, January 1926. John W. Weatherwax, who was a principal financial supporter of *Palms* and who would later marry Idella Purnell, reviewed Cullen's book.

18. Stone, "Sketch," *Palms* 4, October 1926.

19. Countee Cullen to Idella Purnell, October 5, 1926, and November 4, 1926, Idella Purnell Stone Papers, HRHRC; Idella Purnell to Countee Cullen, November 24, 1926, Countee Cullen Papers, ARC-TU.

20. See Clifton Cuthbert to Countee Cullen, August 6, 1931, and Milton Abernathy to Countee Cullen, September 21, 1931, Countee Cullen Papers, ARC-TU; Langston Hughes to Anthony J. Buttitta, November 11, 1931, and Langston Hughes to *Contempo*, April 21, 1932, *Contempo* Collection, HRHRC; Walter White to Anthony J. Buttitta, February 9, 1932, *Contempo* Collection, HRHRC; George S. Schuyler to Milton Abernathy, October 25, 1931, *Contempo* Collection, HRHRC; Countee Cullen to Anthony J. Buttitta, February 4, 1932, *Contempo* Collection, HRHRC, James Weldon Johnson to Anthony J. Buttitta, October 4 [1931], *Contempo* Collection, HRHRC. *Contempo* began listing Langston Hughes as a contributor beginning with the September 15, 1931, issue of the magazine and as one of six contributing editors beginning with the December 15, 1931, issue; they also began listing Countee Cullen as a contributor beginning with the November 1, 1931, issue. See *Contempo*, between September 15, 1931, and December 15, 1932, for an indication of its commitment to black literature.

21. White to Buttitta, February 9, 1932; Cullen to Buttitta, February 4, 1932; *Contempo* 3 (25 October 1932) and (10 January 1933). *Contempo* undoubtedly was hurt by the economic crisis of the early 1930s. In addition to the Depression's most obvious effects, it made it difficult for small magazines like *Contempo* to get review copies of books from publishers. See Blanche Knopf to Anthony J. Buttitta, March 31, 1932, *Contempo* Collection, HRHRC.

22. H. L. Mencken to Countee Cullen, August 13, [1924], and John Farrar to Countee Cullen [1923], Countee

Cullen Papers, ARC-TU; Sterling Brown to Idella Purnell, March 9, 1930, Idella Purnell Stone Collection, HRHRC.

23. See Blanche Knopf to James Weldon Johnson, October 12, 1927, November 14, 1927, December 14, 1927, December 29, 1927, Alfred Knopf, Inc. Collection, HRHRC; James Weldon Johnson to Blanche Knopf, October [25], 1927, November 20, 1927, and August 24, 1930, Alfred Knopf, Inc. Collection, HRHRC; Blanche Knopf to Walter White, March 12, 1928, Alfred Knopf, Inc. Collection, HRHRC; Walter White to Blanche Knopf, March 18, 1927, Alfred Knopf, Inc. Collection, HRHRC.

24. Eugene F. Saxton to Countee Cullen, January 31, 1930, and February 27, 1930, Countee Cullen Papers, ARC-TU.

25. Idella Purnell to Countee Cullen, November 24, 1926, Countee Cullen Papers, ARC-TU; Countee Cullen to Idella Purnell, December 4, 1926, Idella Purnell Stone Papers, HRHRC; Langston Hughes to Anthony J. Buttitta, December 7, 1933, and James Weldon Johnson to Anthony J. Buttitta, October 26, 1933, and May 30, 1934, *Contempo* Collection, HRHRC; Norman W. Mcleod to Countee Cullen, June 1928, Countee Cullen Papers, ARC-TU.

26. Lewis, 140-41; Wayne F. Cooper, *Claude McKay: Rebel Sojourner in the Harlem Renaissance* (Baton Rouge: Louisiana State University Press, 1987), 216-17.

27. Cooper, 221-22; Lewis, 141-42. After Mencken failed to offer assistance, McKay burned the manuscript. However, with some financial assistance from Max and Crystal Eastman, whom he ran into in France, he began work on *Home to Harlem.*

28. Cooper, 288-89; Lewis, 296; Alfred Knopf to Carl Van Vechten, July 9, 1934, quoted in Lewis, 296; see also Claude McKay to Max Eastman, November 10, 1934, in *The Passion of Claude McKay: Selected Prose and Poetry, 1912-1948*, ed. Wayne Cooper (New York: Schocken Books, 1973), 206-208 for an example of McKay's continuing frustration with his publisher. McKay also had problems with black editors. When Alain Locke was assembling material for the Harlem issue of *Survey Graphic* in 1924, McKay submitted several short stories along with his poems. When Locke rejected one, "Mulatto," because of its extreme radical tone, McKay warned him not to publish his poems without his short stories or "you may count upon me as an intellectual enemy for life." Locke ignored the warning and published the poems anyway. McKay, of course, would become one of Locke's most outspoken critics. See Cooper, *McKay: Rebel,* 225.

29. Langston Hughes to Blanche Knopf, March 6, 1933, and April 20, 1933; Blanche Knopf to Langston Hughes, March 23, 1933, and May 2, 1933; Memo, Blanche Knopf to Alfred Knopf, May 2, 1933, Alfred Knopf, Inc. Collection, HRHRC.

30. Langston Hughes to Blanche Knopf, April 20, 1933, and June 11, 1933, Alfred Knopf, Inc. Collection, HRHRC; Blanche Knopf to Langston Hughes, May 2, 1933.

31. Blanche Knopf to Carl Van Vechten, March 24, 1933; Carl Van Vechten to Blanche Knopf, April 3, 1933; Blanche Knopf to Langston Hughes, April 6, 1933; Langston Hughes to Blanche Knopf, June 11, 1933, Alfred Knopf, Inc. Collection, HRHRC.

32. Memo, Blanche Knopf to Alfred Knopf and handwritten reply from Alfred Knopf, July 14, 1933, Alfred Knopf, Inc. Collection, HRHRC. Alfred Knopf was concerned that the political gulf was so wide between Hughes and Van Vechten that Van Vechten was biased against Hughes's political pieces, and Hughes, therefore, would pay no attention to his critical comments. Blanche Knopf to Langston Hughes, August 21, 1933, October 3, 1933, January 10, 1934, January 26, 1934, February 2, 1934; Carl Van Vechten to Blanche Knopf, December 15, 1933; Langston Hughes to Blanche Knopf, November 6, 1933, January 22, 1934, January 30, 1934, and February 21, 1934, Alfred Knopf, Inc. Collection, HRHRC.

33. Langston Hughes to Blanche Knopf, February 27, 1934, and Carl Van Vechten to Blanche Knopf, March 12, 1934, Alfred Knopf, Inc. Collection, HRHRC.

34. Blanche Knopf to Langston Hughes, March 12, 1934; Langston Hughes to Blanche Knopf [1934], Alfred Knopf, Inc. Collection, HRHRC. *New Song* was published in New York by the International Workers Order in 1938.

35. Langston Hughes to Blanche Knopf, January 30, 1934, and Memo, March 17, 1941, Alfred Knopf, Inc. Collection, HRHRC.

36. Jedediah Tingle to Countee Cullen, December 3, 1923, Countee Cullen Papers, ARC-TU. Cullen had clipped to the letter an undated item from the *New York Times* which described Tingle's exploits.

37. August Meier and Elliott M. Rudwick, *From Plantation to Ghetto: An Interpretative History of American Negroes* (New York: Hill and Wang, 1965), 207; Evelyn S. Brown, "The Harmon Awards," *Opportunity,* March 1933, 78; Lewis, 179.

38. Lewis, 100-103, 179; See the list of Langston Hughes's awards, Uncataloged Permanent Title Folders, Langston Hughes, Alfred Knopf, Inc. Collection, HRHRC.

39. Cooper, *McKay: Rebel,* 209-211, 228-29, 231, 236, 265.

40. Zora Neale Hurston, *Dust Tracks on a Road* (New York: Arno Press and the New York Times, 1969), 175-77; Lewis, 129; Annie Nathan Meyer to Zora Neale Hurston, January 13, 1935; Fannie Hurst to Henry Allen Moe, December 1, 1933, and [December 1935]; Zora Neale Hurston to Fannie Hurst, August 4, 1940, Fannie Hurst Collection, HRHRC; see other correspondence between Fannie Hurst and Annie Nathan Meyer, Zora Neale Hurston, and Carl Van Vechten in Fannie Hurst Collection, HRHRC.

41. Lewis, 151-53, Hurston, 183-85. The material Hurston collected resulted in her first two books, a collection of folk stories, *Mules and Men* (Philadelphia: Lippincott, 1935), and a novel, *Jonah's Gourd Vine* (Philadelphia: Lippincott, 1934).

42. Langston Hughes published several accounts of this relationship. The most complete were in Hughes, *Big Sea,* 312-26; and Hughes, "My Career as a Social Poet," *Phylon* 8, September 1947, 206-207. See also Nathan Irvin Huggins, *Harlem Renaissance* (New York: Oxford University Press, 1971), 315-16; and Clare Bloomgood Crane, "Alain Locke and the Negro Renaissance" (Ph.D. diss., University of California, San Diego, 1971), 174. Hughes, *Big Sea,* 314-15, 316.

43. Hughes, "Adventures as a Social Poet," 206.

44. Hughes, *Big Sea*, 320-21, 323; Hughes, "Adventures as a Social Poet," 206-207. Hughes's political poetry was also the source of his difficulties with Knopf and Van Vechten a few months later. Indeed, "Advertisement for the Waldorf-Astoria" and "Park Bench" were two of the poems in the "revolutionary" collection that so disturbed Van Vechten and created such problems for Blanche Knopf. See Carl Van Vechten to Blanche Knopf, April 3, 1933, Alfred Knopf, Inc. Collection, HRHRC.

45. Hughes, *Big Sea*, 325.

46. Harold Jackman to Claude McKay, April 22, 1928, JWJ.

47. Clifton Cuthbert to Countee Cullen, August 6, 1931; Ralph Cheney to Countee Cullen, December 17, 1926, Countee Cullen Papers, ARC-TU; Countee Cullen to Idella Purnell, May 6, 1924, Idella Purnell Stone Collection, HRHRC; Countee Cullen to Eugene F. Saxton, August 9, 1927, Countee Cullen Papers, ARC-TU; Amy Flashner to Countee Cullen, June 6, 1935, and June 10, 1935, Countee Cullen Papers, ARC-TU.

48. Cooper, 283; Lewis, 302-303; Sterling Brown to Nancy Cunard, February 7, 1932, [May 10, 1932]; Langston Hughes to Nancy Cunard, September 30, 1931, December 27, 1931, Nancy Cunard Collection, HRHRC. Hughes also sent several of his political speeches to Cunard in the late 1930s and maintained a steady correspondence with her into the 1960s.

49. Cooper, 283; McKay to Nancy Cunard, February 26, 1932, March 29, 1932, April 30, 1932, August 30, 1932, September 18, 1932, September 29, 1932, October 15, 1932, and November 28, 1932, Nancy Cunard Collection, HRHRC; Nancy Cunard to Claude McKay, September 20, 1932, JWJ.

50. Nancy Cunard to Claude McKay, January 28, [1933]; Claude McKay to Nancy Cunard, January 12, 1933, January 25, 1933, and n.d. [February 1933], Nancy Cunard Collection, HRHRC. McKay would later accuse Cunard of using her association with blacks as a club with which to beat her mother. See McKay, *Long Way from Home*, 343-45.

51. Lewis, 303; Jean Toomer to Nancy Cunard, February 8, 1932, JTP; Alain Locke to Nancy Cunard, April 14, 1934; Arthur Schomburg to Nancy Cunard, March 21, 1934, and May 8, 1934, Nancy Cunard Collection, HRHRC; Nancy Cunard to Countee Cullen, February 7, 1932, Countee Cullen Papers, ARC-TU. Ironically, although both McKay and Walrond boycotted Cunard's anthology, the two West Indian writers had long ceased to be friends. Indeed, McKay had discussed his estrangement from Walrond at length with Cunard. See Claude McKay to Nancy Cunard, September 18, 1932.

52. Hughes, *Big Sea*, 233-34; Claude McKay to James Weldon Johnson, August 8, 1935, JWJ.

53. Meier and Rudwick, 207. Of all the Renaissance writers, only Claude McKay failed to acknowledge the contribution of Van Vechten to the movement and to his own career. McKay, who was absent from Harlem during most of the Renaissance, encountered Van Vechten only once, in Paris. McKay recalled that he had expected to find Van Vechten patronizing, and instead found him friendly, but boring. McKay, *Long Way from Home*, 302. Of course, McKay might still

have been bitter that *Nigger Heaven* reaped the popular and financial rewards as the first novel of Harlem life, instead of one of his pieces.

54. Lewis, 182-83; Hughes, *Big Sea*, 216, 251; Alain Locke to Carl Van Vechten, May 24, 1925; Jessie Fauset to Carl Van Vechten, October 21, 1925; and Zora Neale Hurston to Carl Van Vechten, December 4, 1933, JWJ. See Blanche Knopf to Carl Van Vechten, March 16, 1931, June 26, 1931, September 25, 1931, and November 19, 1931, Alfred Knopf, Inc. Collection, HRHRC, for examples of the relationship between Van Vechten and Knopf.

55. Elmer Imes to Carl Van Vechten, September 12, 1930; Nella Larsen Imes to Carl Van Vechten, May 22, 1930; and Zora Neale Hurston to Carl Van Vechten, October 23, 1937, and July 24, 1945, JWJ; James Weldon Johnson, *Along This Way* (New York: Viking, 1961), 382. Van Vechten included this sketch in his papers in the James Weldon Johnson Collection, JWJ.

56. Lewis, 188; Edward Leuders, *Carl Van Vechten* (New Haven: College & University Press, 1965); Johnson, *Along This Way*, 382; Hughes, *Big Sea*, 254-55.

## *Abbreviations Used*

ARC-TU: The Amistad Research Center, Tulane University

HRHRC: The Harry Ransom Humanities Research Center, The University of Texas at Austin

JTP: The Jean Toomer Papers, Fisk University Library

JWJ: James Weldon Johnson Memorial Collection of Negro Literature and Art, Beinecke Rare Book and Manuscript Library, Yale University

# ANTHOLOGIES: *THE NEW NEGRO* AND OTHERS

## CARL VAN VECHTEN (REVIEW DATE 1925)

**SOURCE:** Van Vechten, Carl. Review of *The New Negro*, edited by Alain Locke, and *Mellows, Negro Work Songs, Street Cries and Spirituals*, edited by R. Emmet Kennedy. *New York Herald Tribune Books* (20 December 1925): 5-7.

*In the following review of Alain Locke's 1925 anthology* The New Negro *and R. Emmet Kennedy's* Mellows, Negro Work Songs, Street Cries and Spirituals, *Van Vechten evaluates the range of African American literary art reprinted in these volumes, with particular emphasis on Locke's influential collection.*

New York is celebrated for its transitory crazes. For whole seasons its mood is dominated by one popular figure or another, or by a racial influence. We have had Jeritza winters, Chaliapin winters, jazz winters, Russian winters, Spanish winters. During the current season, indubitably, the Negro is in the ascendency. Harlem cabarets are more popular than ever. Everybody is trying to dance the Charleston or to sing spirituals, and volumes of arrangements of these folksongs drop from the press faster than one can keep count of them. At least four important white fiction writers have published novels dealing with the Negro this fall, while several novels and books of poems by colored writers are announced. Florence Mills, Bill Robinson, Taylor Gordon, Paul Robeson, Roland Hayes and Ethel Waters are all successful on the stage or concert platform. *The New Negro* should serve as the most practical guidebook to those who are interested in this popular movement.

This is, indeed, a remarkable book. I am not certain but, so far as its effect on the general reader is concerned, it will prove to be the most remarkable book that has yet appeared on the Negro. Alain Locke, the editor, has done a superb job. Basing his material on the Negro number of the *Survey Graphic,* he has expanded here, cut down there, substituted in the third instance. He has put not merely the best foot of the new Negro forward; he has put *all* his feet forward. Herein is included, in fact, work by every young American Negro who has achieved distinction or fame in the literary world—Rudolph Fisher, Walter White, Jessie Fauset, Eric Walrond, Claude McKay, Countée Cullen, Langston Hughes, Jean Toomer and many others are represented. There are also contributions from the pens of a few of the older men, James Weldon Johnson, W. E. B. Du Bois and William Stanley Braithwaite. Several excellent reasons might be adduced to justify the inclusion of James Weldon Johnson's poem, "The Creation." Not only is it a fine poem, but also it was the poem that broke the chains of dialect which bound Paul Lawrence Dunbar and freed the younger generation from this dangerous restraint.

I think the fiction and poetry in this volume will amaze those who are cognizant only in a vague sort of way of what Negro youth is doing. Rudolph Fisher's "The City of Refuge," which appeared in the *Atlantic Monthly* for February, 1925, is, I am convinced, the finest short story yet written by a man of Negro blood, except Pushkin, and Pushkin, save in one instance, did not write stories dealing with Negroes. It is, moreover, an ironical story a fact perhaps worthy of note, considering that Dr. Fisher is the only American Negro story teller I know who has employed this device save Charles W. Chesnutt, a writer only too little known, especially among Negroes, who has not published a book for twenty years. *The Wife of His Youth* is an extraordinary collection of short stories. I gape with astonishment when I recall that it was published in 1899. It is no wonder that it fell flat, especially among Negroes, for Negroes are no

lovers of irony. They do not, for the most part, even comprehend it and are likely to read literalness where it is not intended.

Negro sensitiveness and fear of ridicule, justifiable enough, God knows, in the circumstances, have driven many a Negro writer into literary subterfuge. Mr. Locke's reference in his preface to "the gradual recovery from hypersensitiveness and 'touchy' nerves" is both a little optimistic and a little premature. Dr. Fisher, however, has had the courage to treat his subject with the same objectivity that he might if he were dealing with Australians or Hindus. It is not likely that his work, for some time to come, at least, will be widely popular among members of his own race. I hope that any internal pressure brought to bear upon him will not cause him to deviate from his present splendid artistic purpose. It is a pity that Mr. Locke saw fit to include Dr. Fisher's "Vestiges." Inferior work, this, and an anticlimax after "The City of Refuge."

Eric Walrond is an uneven writer. A good deal of his work is actually bad; some of it is passable and a little of it brilliant. "The Palm Porch," in this collection, is by far the best story of his that I have read. It appeared originally in the *New Age* and it is worthy of appearance anywhere. It is perhaps more of a picture than a short story, but it is a picture vividly observed and set down in a coruscant and exotic style. I do not think it will be readily forgotten by any one who reads it.

Of Jean Toomer's work it is unnecessary to speak at length. The character studies included in this anthology were selected from *Cane,* and they are well chosen. Mr. Braithwaite, justifiably, describes *Cane* as "a book of gold and bronze, of dusk and flame, of ecstasy and pain." Zora Neale Hurston is more or less of a newcomer. She has published comparatively little. The story in the volume, "Spunk," won the second prize in the 1925 short story contest instituted by *Opportunity Magazine.* Miss Hurston may be highly commended for her intimate knowledge of dialect and for her expert use of free and natural dialogue, but her work is still somewhat diffuse in form. I think however, that "Spunk" is far superior to Mr. Matheus's "The Fog," which won the first prize in the same contest.

Countee Cullen and Langston Hughes are the youngest and the best of the contemporary Negro poets. Both have sprung into prominence within the last year. Both are already famous. Harper's recently issued Mr. Cullen's book, *Color,* and Alfred A. Knopf will presently publish Mr. Hughes's

*The Weary Blues.* I do not think either of these young poets is here represented by his best work, but the level is sufficiently high, in both instances, to offer a taste of their fine talents.

If I were to attempt to discuss adequately the points raised in the various articles in *The New Negro* I could fill an entire number of "Books." The opportunities for controversy are endless. I must perforce content myself with reference to a few of the more prominent papers. "The Negro in American Literature," by William Stanley Braithwaite, presents in a few pages an able survey of the range of American Negro literature from the time of Phillis Wheatley to the contemporary hour. I agree with Mr. Braithwaite's judgments in almost every respect; I would say that he lays exactly the proper emphasis where it belongs. I am especially pleased that he deals so justly with the work of Charles W. Chesnutt, a writer, I repeat, who, in spite of his faults, cannot much longer be neglected, especially by those Negroes who pretend to an interest in the striking literary figures of the race. He came, as Mr. Braithwaite explains, at the wrong time, when the world, white or black, was quite unwilling to accept a "realistic representation of the Negro, more especially an ironic realism. There was a demand for the conventional comic or sentimental darkey. It was the day of Paul Lawrence Dunbar.

On one point, however, I would take decided issue with Mr. Braithwaite. He repeats the old cliché that Negro novels must be written by Negroes. Now I have said repeatedly that the Negro writer should deal with Negro subjects. In the first place, generally speaking, he knows more about them. In the second place, the Negro world, in spite of a popular misconception to the contrary, is largely unexplored, and if the Negro writers don't utilize the wealth of material at their finger tips, white writers, naturally, will be only too eager to exploit it.

And there is no reason why the white writer should not be successful in this experiment. The difference between the races, as a matter of fact, is largely a matter of an emotional psychology, created on either side by the social barrier. Nearly all the idiosyncratic reactions of the Negro are caused by an extreme sensitiveness, nearly all the reactions of the white man by an excessive self-consciousness, an almost pathetic attempt to do what is decent, so often construed by the alien race as condescension or patronage. Negroes among themselves, I am inclined to believe, behave and react very much as white people, *of the same class,* behave and react among themselves.

In this connection it is well to remember that colored owners of human property in slavery days were among the most cruel masters.

If a white writer is cognizant of these facts I see no reason why he should not undertake to write a Negro novel. Charles W. Chesnutt wrote his novels from the white point of view, and if they are not wholly successful that is not the reason. He understood the point of view well enough. No one has informed the world that Lafcadio Hearn was impertinent when he wrote about the Japanese or Marmaduke Pickthall when he wrote about the Arabs.

I confess I was somewhat startled to discover that Mr. Locke had chosen Miss Jessie Fauset to write an article about the Negro theater. If I had been the editor of *The New Negro* I am certain that she would have been about the last person I should have considered for the job. Not that Miss Fauset is lacking in literary talent; rather because I have never thought of her in connection with the theater. My pleasure, perhaps, was doubled in reading her article by the realization that Mr. Locke had been wise in selecting her to write it. It is an extremely stimulating article; ideas spring out of every line. What she has to say is originally expressed and delightfully phrased. On the whole, I think it is the best discussion of the Negro in the theater with which I am familiar.

With Miss Fauset, too, however, I must interpose a couple of objections. She states that Bert Williams became melancholy because he was constrained by the nature of his race to remain a clown. Here she overlooks a very general condition. All comedians are sad in private life. Is Miss Fauset familiar, I wonder, with the well-known anecdote concerning Grimaldi? Does she know anything about the personality of Charles Spencer Chaplin? It was not because of his color that Bert Williams was constrained to be funny; no such obstacle has beset the way of that fine actor Paul Robeson. The fact is that so few authentic clowns are born into the world that when one comes along no manager will consent to his appearance in other than farcical situations.

Miss Fauset states truly "There is an unwritten law in America that though white may imitate black, black, even when superlatively capable, must never imitate white," and suggestively, referring to the wide range of colors among Negroes, she pleads for a brown Othello, a yellow Butterfly, a near white Hamlet. There is certainly no cogent excuse to offer for the state of a theater which makes this sort of thing difficult of accomplishment. On one or two occasions it has actually happened I remember Evelyn Preer's Salome very vividly to this day. The Negro writer, however, has as yet been very feebly represented in the drama; most of the successful colored plays have been written by white men. I should hate to see Negro acting talent turned in this conventional direction therefore, until the play-writing and histrionic talents of the race have been more fully exploited in actual racial fields. There will never be a true Negro theater until it is founded on racial heritage. When we have that, by all means let Negroes play anything they please; before we have that I regard it as a mistaken aim to experiment with *The School for Scandal.*

Mr. Locke's paper on the Spirituals is rhapsodic and critical rather than historical. I think he is a little too condescending in his attitude toward the folk-poetry of these songs. In this respect, indubitably, they are not on an equal plane with the Blues, themselves far inferior as music. Nevertheless, it would be hard to find folk-poetry with deeper feeling or more imaginative imagery than that which exists in some of the Spirituals. He pleads for choral arrangements of the Spirituals after the manner of the arrangements Russian musicians have made of the Russian folksongs, forgetting that the Russian folksong is sung as melody, while the Spirituals, although probably created as melody, so soon fell into harmonic form that they are scarcely ever sung in any other fashion in that quarter of the country where they were born. I applaud his desire to hear these elaborate choral arrangements, but there will be time enough for that after a few of them are taken down in the authentic manner in which they are at present performed in the South. So far as I know, only quartet versions—and those usually after the singing of college men—have been set down. It is well to remember that a large Negro chorus sings in many more than four parts.

There is an unaccountable omission of the name of J. Rosamond Johnson. I suppose that *The Book of American Negro Spirituals* was not yet off the press when Mr. Locke wrote this article (it is listed in the bibliography), but this is not the first work that Mr. Johnson had accomplished in connection with the Spirituals. As for *The Book of American Negro Spirituals,* I should say that it has already done more to popularize these songs, not only with the great public, but also with musicians and critics, than the work of any other ten men. It is not technical books like H. E. Krehbiel's *Afro-American Folksongs* (a very faulty work, more-

over, hastily thrown together from casual newspaper articles) or Ballanta-Taylor's pedantic *Saint Helena Island Spirituals* that interest the musician—unless he be actively engaged in arranging versions of the Spirituals—it is the real thing in practical form, just as the true musician is much more interested in the scores of Mozart's operas than he is in thematic guides to them. I have seen more copies of Mr. Johnson's book on the piano racks of my musical friends during the last two weeks than I have seen of Mr. Krehbiel's book in libraries since the day in 1914 when it first appeared.

Mr. Locke supplies three other interesting and provocative contributions. In his preface he paints a brilliant picture of the general intellectual attitude of the new literary figures, contradictory at that, for the New Negro does very little group thinking. "If it ever was warrantable," Mr. Locke very sensibly says, "to regard and treat the Negro *en masse,* it is becoming with every day less possible, more unjust and more ridiculous". In another paper Mr. Locke discusses at length the subject of African primitive sculpture.

But little space remains to devote to the many other excellent papers in this volume. I should like, however, to touch on a few. James Weldon Johnson offers a picture of the growth of the new Harlem, with its economic and cultural achievements and possibilities. Dr. Du Bois is represented by a scholarly account of the American Negro's point of view in regard to the French, German, Belgian and English colonies in Africa. He points out bitterly that, while the slave trade has ended, these governments find it equally advantageous to exploit their natives in their own land. The condition remains. Elsie Johnson McDougald tells what it means to be a colored woman in the modern business and professional worlds. Walter White describes the psychology arising from race prejudice. He also goes beneath the surface and drags out the fact that this prejudice creates certain internal disagreements among the Negroes themselves. Charles S. Johnson explains why Negroes leave the South. "Enoch Scott was living in Hollywood, Miss., when the white physician and one of the Negro leaders disputed a small account. The Negro was shot three times in the back and his head battered—all this in front of the high sheriff's office. Enoch says he left because the doctor might some time take a dislike to him." He fills several pages with such incidents.

J. A. Rogers's article about jazz is disappointing and occasionally inaccurate. He has comparatively little to say about the Harlem cabarets—surely among the most interesting features of the Negro's new Mecca—and there should be a great deal more to write about W. C. Handy, the "father of the Blues," Clarence Williams and other popular composers, but I don't suppose it would be possible to do Justice to all sides of the new Negro in one volume.

The bibliography, by no means complete, but certainly the most complete bibliography of the subject available, was compiled by Arthur B. Schomburg, Arthur H. Fauset and Alain Locke. The volume is bountifully illustrated with reproductions of paintings, many in color, by Winold Reiss, Miguel Covarrubias and Aaron Douglas, the last a Negro.

The latest addition to the rapidly growing literature dealing with spirituals is *Mellows,* a large, handsome volume, bound in bandanas and embellished with numerous drawings in black and white by Simmons Persons. The book is the work of R. Emmet Kennedy, a white man from Louisiana. Many songs are given with piano arrangements. Most of these will be found to be perversions—nearly all of the spirituals are sung differently in different localities—of melodies familiar in other forms. A few of them—I especially recommend "If you can't come, send one angel down"—are new and deserving of more familiarity. The novel interest in the book consists in the ingenious forewords Mr. Kennedy has supplied to each song, telling where and when and how and from whom it was recorded. This is not one of the more important books about the spirituals, but it is one of the most pleasant.

## COUNTEE CULLEN (ESSAY DATE 1927)

**SOURCE:** Cullen, Countee. Foreword to *Caroling Dusk: An Anthology of Verse by Negro Poets,* edited by Countee Cullen, pp. vii-xii. New York: Harper & Row, 1974.

*In the following foreword to the first edition of* Caroling Dusk: An Anthology of Verse by Negro Poets, *originally published in 1927, Cullen considers the significance of poetry to African American cultural development and comments on the qualities of the works contained in his collection.*

It is now five years since James Weldon Johnson edited with a brilliant essay on "The Negro's Creative Genius" *The Book of American Negro Poetry,* four years since the publication of Robert T. Kerlin's *Negro Poets and Their Poems,* and three years since from the Trinity College Press in Durham, North Carolina, came *An Anthology of Verse by American Negroes,* edited by Newman Ivey White and Walter Clinton Jackson. The student of verse by American Negro poets will find in these three anthologies comprehensive treatment of the work of Negro poets from Phyllis Wheatley, the first American Negro known to have composed verses, to writers of the present day. With Mr. Johnson's scholarly and painstaking survey, from both a historical and a critical standpoint, of the entire range of verse by American Negroes, and with Professor Kerlin's inclusions of excerpts from the work of most of those Negro poets whose poems were extant at the time of his compilation, there would be scant reason for the assembling and publication of another such collection were it not for the new voices that within the past three to five years have sung so significantly as to make imperative an anthology recording some snatches of their songs. To those intelligently familiar with what is popularly termed the renaissance in art and literature by Negroes, it will not be taken as a sentimentally risky observation to contend that the recent yearly contests conducted by Negro magazines, such as *Opportunity* and *The Crisis,* as well as a growing tendency on the part of white editors to give impartial consideration to the work of Negro writers, have awakened to a happy articulation many young Negro poets who had thitherto lisped only in isolated places in solitary numbers. It is primarily to give them a concerted hearing that this collection has been published. For most of these poets the publication of individual volumes of their poems is not an immediate issue. However, many of their poems during these four or five years of accentuated interest in the artistic development of the race have become familiar to a large and ever-widening circle of readers who, we feel, will welcome a volume marshaling what would otherwise remain for some time a miscellany of deeply appreciated but scattered verse.

The place of poetry in the cultural development of a race or people has always been one of importance; indeed, poets are prone, with many good reasons for their conceit, to hold their art the most important. Thus while essentially wishing to draw the public ear to the work of the younger Negro poets, there have been included with their poems those of modern Negro poets already established and acknowledged, by virtue of their seniority and published books, as worthy practitioners of their art. There were Negro poets before Paul Laurence Dunbar, but his uniquity as the first

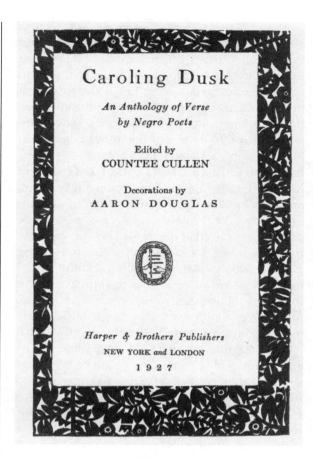

Title page from *Caroling Dusk,* edited by Countee Cullen.

such a fever, or the symptoms of such an ague, will prove on closer examination merely the moment's exaggeration of a physician anxious to establish a new literary ailment. As heretical as it may sound, there is the probability that Negro poets, dependent as they are on the English language, may have more to gain from the rich background of English and American poetry than from any nebulous atavistic yearnings toward an African inheritance. Some of the poets herein represented will eventually find inclusion in any discriminatingly ordered anthology of American verse, and there will be no reason for giving such selections the needless distinction of a separate section marked Negro verse.

While I do not feel that the work of these writers conforms to anything that can be called the Negro school of poetry, neither do I feel that their work is varied to the point of being sensational; rather is theirs a variety within a uniformity that is trying to maintain the higher traditions of English verse. I trust the selections here presented bear out this contention. The poet writes out of his experience, whether it be personal or vicarious, and as these experiences differ among other poets, so do they differ among Negro poets; for the double obligation of being both Negro and American is not so unified as we are often led to believe. A survey of the work of Negro poets will show that the individual diversifying ego transcends the synthesizing hue. From the roots of varied experiences have flowered the dialect of Dunbar, the recent sermon poems of James Weldon Johnson, and some of Helene Johnson's more colloquial verses, which, differing essentially only in a few expressions peculiar to Negro slang, are worthy counterparts of verses done by John V. A. Weaver "in American." Attempt to hedge all these in with a name, and your imagination must deny the facts. Langston Hughes, poetizing the blues in his zeal to represent the Negro masses, and Sterling Brown, combining a similar interest in such poems as "Long Gone" and "The Odyssey of Big Boy" with a capacity for turning a neat sonnet according to the rules, represent differences as unique as those between Burns and Whitman. Jessie Fauset with Cornell University and training at the Sorbonne as her intellectual equipment surely justifies the very subjects and forms of her poems: "Touché," "La Vie C'est la Vie," "Noblesse Oblige," etc.; while Lewis Alexander, with no known degree from the University of Tokyo, is equally within the province of his creative prerogatives in composing Japanese *hokkus* and *tan-*

Negro to attain to and maintain a distinguished place among American poets, a place fairly merited by the most acceptable standards of criticism, makes him the pivotal poet of this volume.

I have called this collection an anthology of verse by Negro poets rather than an anthology of Negro verse, since this latter designation would be more confusing than accurate. Negro poetry, it seems to me, in the sense that we speak of Russian, French, or Chinese poetry, must emanate from some country other than this in some language other than our own. Moreover, the attempt to corral the outbursts of the ebony muse into some definite mold to which all poetry by Negroes will conform seems altogether futile and aside from the facts. This country's Negro writers may here and there turn some singular facet toward the literary sun, but in the main, since their is also the heritage of the English language, their work will not present any serious aberration from the poetic tendencies of their times. The conservatives, the middlers, and the arch heretics will be found among them as among the white poets; and to say that the pulse beat of their verse shows generally *kas.* Although Anne Spencer lives in Lynchburg, Virginia, and in her biographical note recognizes the Negro as the great American taboo, I have seen but two poems by her which are even remotely concerned with this subject; rather does she write with a cool precision that calls forth comparison with Amy Lowell and the influence of a rock-bound seacoast. And Lula Lowe Weeden, the youngest poet in the volume, living in the same Southern city, is too young to realize that she is colored in an environment calculated to impress her daily with the knowledge of this pigmentary anomaly.

There are lights and shades of difference even in their methods of decrying race injustices, where these peculiar experiences of Negro life cannot be overlooked. Claude McKay is most exercised, rebellious, and vituperative to a degree that clouds his lyricism in many instances, but silhouettes most forcibly his high dudgeon; while neither Arna Bontemps, at all times cool, calm, and intensely religious, nor Georgia Douglas Johnson, in many instances bearing up bravely under comparison with Sara Teasdale, takes advantage of the numerous opportunities offered them for rhymed polemics.

If dialect is missed in this collection, it is enough to state that the day of dialect as far as Negro poets are concerned is in the decline. Added to the fact that these poets are out of contact with this fast-dying medium, certain sociological considerations and the natural limitations of dialect for poetic expression militate against its use even as a *tour de force*. In a day when artificiality is so vigorously condemned, the Negro poet would be foolish indeed to turn to dialect. The majority of present-day poems in dialect are the efforts of white poets.

This anthology, by no means offered as *the* anthology of verse by Negro poets, is but a prelude, we hope, to that fuller symphony which Negro poets will in time contribute to the national literature, and we shall be sadly disappointed if the next few years do not find this collection entirely outmoded.

. . . . .

The biographical notices carried with these poems have been written by the poets themselves save in three cases (Dunbar's having been written by his wife, the younger Cotter's by his father, and Lula Weeden's by her mother), and if they do not reveal to a curious public all it might wish to know about the poets, they at least reveal all that the poets deem necessary and discreet for the public to know.

## ROBERT HAYDEN (ESSAY DATE 1968)

**SOURCE:** Hayden, Robert. Preface to *The New Negro*, edited by Alain Locke. 1968. Reprint, pp. ix-xiv. New York: Atheneum, 1975.

*In the following preface to the first Atheneum Edition of Alain Locke's* The New Negro, *Hayden explains the integral importance of this literary anthology to the Harlem Renaissance movement and enumerates some of its principal themes.*

Dr. Alain Locke's interpretive anthology, *The New Negro,* first published in 1925, was the definitive presentation of the artistic and social goals of the New Negro movement. Perhaps it is no exaggeration to say that this book helped to create the movement. Certainly it had the effect of a manifesto when it appeared, and it remains an invaluable document of the cultural aspects of the Negro struggle as they were revealed by the work of artists and writers in Harlem during the 1920s.

The New Negro movement, known also as the Harlem Renaissance and the Negro Renaissance, was less a movement, as we generally use the term, than a configuration of "new" racial attitudes and ideals and the upsurge of creativity inspired by them and by the iconoclastic spirit of the times. In his introductory essay to *The New Negro* Dr. Locke described the movement as representing a new spiritual outlook, as having "inner objectives." And he saw the Negro's "newness" as the product of psychic and social forces that had been gathering strength since the nineteenth century.

The New Negro movement had no formal organization, and it was more aesthetic and philosophical—more metaphysical, let us say—than political. Such political implications as it now may be seen to have had arose from the fervid Negro nationalism which was its background and which became significant after the First World War. One of the most zealous voices of black nationalism was Marcus Garvey, West Indian leader of The [Universal] Negro Improvement Association. He is mentioned only briefly, and somewhat disparagingly, in the pages of *The New Negro*. Yet Garveyism had tremendous appeal for American Negroes, winning thousands of ardent followers who saw in its program of separatism and its vision of a mass "return" to Africa their best hope for liberation and autonomy.

Africa was a recurrent theme of the Harlem writers, whose atavistic poems and stories later came to be classified, more or less humorously, as "literary Garveyism." African art as a vital source of inspiration for the Negro artist was discussed by Dr. Locke in "The Legacy of the Ancestral Arts." And although he considered Garveyism a "transient, if spectacular phenomenon," he believed nonetheless that "the possible role of the American Negro in the future development of Africa is one of the most constructive and universally helpful missions that any modern people can lay claim to."

The Negro Renaissance was of short duration, beginning in the mid-twenties and ending with the decade. Harlem was its acknowledged center. A Negro city within a city, bohemian, cosmopolitan, "fast"; vibrant locus of a variety of racial strains, nationalities, languages, dialects, folkways; a "city of refuge" where "group expression and self-determination" would be possible, Harlem attracted young Negro artists and intellectuals from all over the United States and from foreign countries as well. They came, together with hosts of less articulate migrants fleeing southern oppression, to seek fulfillment in the Negro "Culture Capital," as Harlem was designated by the Renaissance group.

Too often the Harlem Renaissance, when given any attention at all in the textbooks, is approached as though it had no organic relationship to the developments taking place in American culture generally during the twenties. That the converse was true is amply illustrated by this anthology.

"The Jazz Age" was a period of disillusionment and revolt, of experimentation in life styles and in the various forms of imaginative expression. The accent was on the "new" and untried. Old modes were either rejected or were revaluated and adapted to the uses of an often self-conscious modernism. Americans, black and white, sought to discover or to reclaim their native spiritual resources. Mary Austin looked for the authentic "American rhythm" in Indian poetry and song. The Negro became a "vogue," partly as the result of a growing interest in his jazz, spirituals, and folklore, partly as the result of the glamour and notoriety brought to the Harlem Renaissance by wealthy dilettantes who "took it up" as a sort of amusing hobby.

The Negro Renaissance was clearly an expression of the *Zeitgeist,* and its writers and artists were open to the same influences that their white counterparts were. What differentiated the New Negroes from other American intellectuals was their race consciousness, their group awareness, their sense of sharing a common purpose. Arna Bontemps, poet and novelist, has said in the foreword to his book of poems, *Personals* (London, 1963):

> It did not take long to discover that I was just one of many young Negroes arriving in Harlem for the first time and with many of the same thoughts and intentions. Within a year or two we began to recognize ourselves as a "group" and to become a little self-conscious about our "significance." When we were not too busy having fun, we were shown off and exhibited and presented in scores of places to all kinds of people. And we heard the sighs of wonder, amazement and sometimes admiration when it was whispered or announced that here was one of the "New Negroes."

But if it arouses nostalgia in those who once shared in its novelty and excitement, the movement also elicits the animadversions of a later generation that feels it was essentially bourgeois, genteel, and lacking in political dynamism. Some critics have charged that the New Negroes "went in" for a fashionable exoticism, cultivating a species of primitivism in the arts which was calculated to appeal to a jaded white audience. The Harlem writers, it is often said, simply exchanged one set of racial clichés for another. And, further, their identification with Africa was a mere pose, a literary convention.

In March, 1925, Dr. Alain Locke, then Professor of Philosophy at Howard University and one of the chief mentors of the Renaissance, edited the Harlem number of the *Survey Graphic.* The materials originally gathered for the magazine became the nucleus for *The New Negro.* Dr. Lock's stated purpose was to "register the transformations of the inner and outer life of the Negro in America that [had] so significantly taken place in the last few years."

Including sociological and historical essays, poetry, fiction, drama, and criticism, this handsomely designed book covered every phase of recent Negro cultural achievement. There had been nothing like it before. Sophisticated and urbane, race conscious without being chauvinistic—there were several white contributors, for instance—it presented facets of Negro life and thought which stimulated the imagination and challenged traditional prejudices. One of its most exciting and unusual features was the work of the Austrian artist Winold Reiss and the rising young

Negro artist Aaron Douglas. Their illustrations, portraits of racial types, and African-inspired decorative motifs constituted a fresh and original approach to materials hitherto little explored. Together with the photographs of African sculpture also included, the work of these artists added considerably to the total effect of the volume as a testimonial to Negro beauty, dignity, and creativity. Stressing the role of the Negro writer as the interpreter of his people, Dr. Locke drew upon the work of Countée Cullen, Jean Toomer, Langston Hughes, and Claude McKay, all of whom had won recognition. Older writers whose work was considered to have prepared the way for the Harlem *avant-garde* were represented by James Weldon Johnson and W. E. B. DuBois, among others.

The cachet of the modern mode, still in process of becoming during this period, reveals itself in *The New Negro* with varying degrees of luster. Realism and satire are characteristic styles, as are also symbolism and impressionism. Disenchantment and skepticism are present too. An interest in the experimental and a concern with new forms and techniques are much in evidence. Certain poems and stories, notably those of Jean Toomer and Eric Walrond, have an exotic flavor, a tropical lushness. Others achieve distinctive rhythms and individuality of tone and idiom through the use of Negro folk motifs.

The New Negro writers rejected the "minstrel tradition" in American literature, with its caricatures and southern dialect, and they likewise rejected overt propaganda and "racial rhetoric" for the most part as obstacles to literary excellence and universal acceptance. They eschewed the stereotypes and easy moral solutions of the past. Hence, the personae of the stories by Rudolph Fisher, Zora Neale Hurston, Toomer, and Walrond are neither virtuous "stuffed shirts" created to win the approval of white readers nor stock-in-trade embodiments of racial woes and aspirations. They have human strengths and frailties, are villains as well as heroes. Protest, explicit or implicit, is to be found of course in a number of the poems included here, but there are also many poems in which it either does not appear or has been made subordinate.

Not all the imaginative writing in *The New Negro* is of uniformly high quality. Some of it is flawed by a lingering Victorianism, some of it "arty" or technically gauche. Many of the critical essays, particularly those by Dr. Locke himself, are

still required reading and contain valuable insights, although recent events have in some cases given a wry twist to the hopes expressed.

*The New Negro* articulates the crucial ideas of a generation in rebellion against accepted beliefs and engaged in racial self-discovery and cultural re-assessment. It affirms the values of the Negro heritage and expresses hope for the future of the race in this country, stressing the black man's "Americanism." This hope was not shared by Garvey and other nationalists, as we know, and today's black revolutionists repudiate Negro "Americanism" in favor of separatism.

The main thrust of *The New Negro* is clearly integrationist, not separatist. Dr. Locke and most of his collaborators thought of race consciousness and race pride as positive forces making the Negro aware of the true worth of his contributions to American society and helping him to achieve his rightful place in it. His task was interpreted as being twofold. He must be, in Dr. Locke's words, "a collaborator and participant in American civilization," and he must at the same time preserve and implement his own racial traditions.

One is impressed by the optimism which is the prevailing mood of this anthology. That a new day for the Negro has arrived; that he is experiencing a spiritual Coming of Age; that, as Langston Hughes wrote, "we have tomorrow bright before us like a flame"—these are dominant themes. But there are counterthemes as well. We hear them in the protest poems of Claude McKay, for example, and in "The Negro Mind Reaches Out," the essay by W. E. B. DuBois which ends the volume: "And thus again in 1924 as in 1899 I seem to see the problem of the 20th century as the Problem of the Color Line."

## RICHARD A. LONG (ESSAY DATE 1976)

**SOURCE:** Long, Richard A. "The Genesis of Locke's *The New Negro.*" *Black World* 25, no. 4 (February 1976): 14-20.

*In the following essay, Long examines the publication history of Alain Locke's anthology* The New Negro—*a work he calls "the keystone of the Harlem Renaissance"—and surveys its contents.*

I think there is no doubt that the anthology *The New Negro*, edited by Alain Locke, is the keystone of the Harlem Renaissance. This towering work of over 450 pages had a momentous and seminal effect. Its appearance at the end of 1925 was the imprimature of a movement and sensibil-

W. E. B. Du Bois (top right) and others working in the offices of the NAACP's *Crisis* magazine.

ity that had been "in the air." The anthology made concrete what had seemed evanescent and fugitive to many. It is important, then, for the sake of cultural history, to document as carefully as possible the circumstances and personalities which led to the appearance of the anthology.

Several works, events, phrases, should be regarded as preliminary. In 1922, James Weldon Johnson had edited *The Book of American Negro Poetry,* known today in its 1931 revision. In 1923, the Urban League had begun the publication of *Opportunity* under the editorship of Charles S. Johnson. *The Crisis,* under the editorship of W. E. B. Du Bois, and with the aid of Jessie Fauset, had taken on an increasingly cosmopolitan and artistic turn after the First Pan African Congress of 1919 and was a part of the reading of virtually every articulate Afro-American.

Already in 1916, William Pickens had used *The New Negro* as the title of a book. The phrase, perhaps initiated by the title, was current coin in the speeches of Garvey and in his articles in The Negro World.

At some point in late 1923, the year in which he had published the article "Apropos of Africa"

in *Opportunity,* Dr. Locke had a conversation with Paul Underwood Kellogg, the editor of *Survey Graphic,* in which the current cultural ferment in the Harlem community was a topic. Kellogg, a journalist who had studied at Columbia University and the New York School of Social Work, had founded around 1912 a journal, *The Survey,* which would treat in succeeding issues topics of intellectual and humanitarian concern which did not receive treatment elsewhere. It was to be a thoroughly serious organ of social enlightenment. In 1921, the title of the journal was changed to *Survey Graphic* and, in 1923, an additional publication, *Survey Mid-Monthly,* issued from the same organization, known as Survey Associates. Kellogg was later a founder of the still-existing quarterly, *Foreign Affairs.* He was active in League of Nations and International Social Work activities. It was perfectly natural, then, that he should be in touch with Alain Locke, who shared many of the same concerns, tinctured of course by Locke's deep interest in the race question at home and abroad.

In January 1924, there was a letter from Kellogg to Locke asking for a list of topics for a special issue of *Survey Graphic* based upon their earlier conversation. In the next few months such a list was discussed and consideration of persons who might be helpful was made. By May 1924, the collection of articles was in process, some had already been read by Locke and Kellogg, and the decision was made to have illustrations done by Winold Reiss, a German artist living in New York. Of Reiss Locke says, in a note in the *New Negro*:

> With ever-ripening skill he has studied and drawn folk types of Sweden, Holland, of the Black Forest, and his own native Tyrol, and in America, the Black Foot Indians, the Pueblo people, the Mexicans, and now, the American Negro.
>
> (p. 419)

(After doing the illustrations for the *New Negro,* Reiss continued his graphic study of Negro types by working in St. Helena Island in the Sea Islands area.)

By December 17, 1924, the Harlem issue of *Survey Graphic* had been substantially gathered. On that date, Kellogg wrote to Locke that the business office of the magazine had decided that, in view of the special promotion activities to be undertaken, the issue would have to come out in March 1925 instead of February as originally hoped.

On December 23, Kellogg wrote to Locke that Countee Cullen had called and expressed dismay over the proposed payment of $40.00 for the poems which he had agreed to let be published. This matter was eventually regulated to everyone's satisfaction.

On January 15, 1925, Kellogg wrote to Locke: "Albert Boni of Boni Brothers (called) asking if it would be possible to arrange for the republication of the materials in our Harlem number in book form, perhaps next fall."

At this point correspondence from *Survey Graphic* to Alain Locke becomes quite heavy. During late 1924 and early 1925, there is also extensive correspondence from the *Survey* editor most directly concerned with the details of the issue, Geddes Smith. For example, on January 26, Smith reports difficulties with Melville Herskovits over revisions proposed by the editors and on January 28 announces that Herskovits had rejected the revisions.

On February 5, Kellogg wired Locke to state that it was the opinion of "Sales and advertising Experts" that sales of the Harlem issue would be doubled if the Reiss head of Roland Hayes could be used on the cover. Locke wired Hayes immediately for permission, which was granted.

On the editorial side, prose sketches expected from Eric Walrond had still not arrived. In the meantime Robert Russa Moten had agreed to do an article for the April issue of *Survey Graphic.* This was to compensate for the absence of a representative of the Tuskegee tradition in the Harlem issue. Moten also agreed to sit for a sketch by Winold Reiss. On February 12, it was announced that Dr. Du Bois had also agreed to sit (or perhaps just pause) for a similar sketch. Eugene Kincle Jones of the Urban League also consented to be sketched.

Kellogg announced on February 20 that an exhibition of the Reiss sketches had been arranged for the Public Library in Harlem to begin on March 1.

The March issue was published in a run of 30,000 copies and was an immediate sensation. On March 20, it was decided to print a second edition of 12,000 copies. Of these, 1000 were paid for by Albert C. Barnes, 1000 by George Foster Peabody, 1000 by Professor and Mrs. Spingarn. These copies were to be distributed free to a wide sector of Black students and organizations.

The March 1925 issue of *Survey Graphic* (Volume VI, No. 6), entitled, "Harlem—Mecca of the New Negro," was approximately 66 pages of text and illustration in large format, numbered consecutively from page 629. It was divided into three sections: I. The Greatest Negro Community in the World; II. The Negro Expresses Himself; III. Black and White—Studies in Race Contacts.

In Part I there is an unsigned statement on Harlem by Locke, articles by Locke ("Enter the New Negro"), James Weldon Johnson ("The Making of Harlem"), and W. A. Domingo ("The Tropics in New York"); there are also sketches by Rudolph Fisher ("The South Lingers On"). These pieces, except for the unsigned statement, were republished in the anthology under the following titles: Locke, "The New Negro"; Johnson, "Harlem—The Culture Capital"; Domingo, "Gift of the Black Tropics"; Fisher, "Vestiges."

In addition to illustrations and poems, Part II offered the following articles: W. E. B. Du Bois, "The Black Man Brings his Gifts"; J. A. Rogers, "Jazz at Home"; A. C. Barnes, "Negro Art and America"; Dr. Schomburg, "The Negro Digs up his Past"; A. L. Locke, "The Art of the Ancestors" (unsigned). The article by Du Bois, obviously a section from an historical work, does not appear in the anthology, but is replaced by his long essay "The Negro Mind Reaches Out," revised from an article in *Foreign Affairs.* The other articles appeared under the title given above, except that Locke's article, now signed, is retitled, "The Legacy of the Ancestral Arts."

Part III includes the following articles: Herskovits, "The Dilemma of Social Pattern"; Bercovici, "The Rhythm of Harlem"; Walter White, "Color Lines"; Kelly Miller, "Harvest of Race Prejudice"; Eunice Roberta Hunton, "Breaking Through"; Elise Johnson McDougald, "The Double Task"; Winthrop Lane, "Ambushed in the City"; George E. Haynes, "The Church and the Negro Spirit." Both the articles by Herskovits and Konrad Bercovici had given trouble or disappointment to the editors. Herskovits' article is used, however, under the title "The Negro's Americanism" in the *New Negro,* as was Walter White's. Kelly Miller substituted another article for the anthology, "Howard: The National Negro University," obviously done to balance Moton's "Hampton-Tuskegee: Missioners of the Masses" which had appeared in the April *Survey Graphic* under the title "Hampton, Tuskegee and Points North." None of the other articles from this section reappears in the anthology except Elise McDougald's, retitled, "The Task of Negro Womanhood."

There can be no doubt that the spectacular impact of the Harlem issue was due in large measure to the poetry and to the illustrations. Apart from the sketches by Rudolph Fisher, there was no fiction, Walrond's pieces not having arrived in time. In Part II there was a section, "Youth Speaks," which offered poems by Cullen, Anne Spencer, A. Grimké, McKay, Toomer, and Hughes. In addition, there were poems elsewhere in the special issue by McKay and Hughes, who with Cullen dominated the poetry section. There were in all nine poems by Cullen, including "Heritage"; six by McKay; and 10 by Hughes.

Apart from an illustration by Mahonri Young which does not reappear in the *New Negro* and by Walter von Ruckteschell ("Young Africa") which does, the other illustrations are by Winold Reiss and include cubistic designs as well as portrait drawings and drawings of Negro types (*e.g.,* "The School Teachers," the "Librarian"). The cover drawing of Roland Hayes has already been referred to. One illustration which invited much favorable comment was "A College Lad," which is a portrait of the young Harold Jackman. Eight photographs of African sculpture in the Barnes Foundation Collection were used to illustrate Locke's piece on the Ancestral Arts.

The success of the Harlem issue confirmed the Boni Brothers in their resolution to have Locke make a book of it. Further conversations took place on the subject in March 1925. In April, Kellogg notes in a letter to Locke that Winold Reiss was having some difficulties with the publishers and he cautions: ". . . you better have everything copper riveted before going ahead." Kellogg was still ecstatic over the success of the issue, though he had to defend himself and Locke at a forum in Harlem where "a speaker challenged our having an outsider like yourself edit the number."

On May 8, Kellogg reports the happiness with which the *Survey* staff received a commemorative cup presented to the magazine by contributors to the Harlem number. On May 21, he wrote to Locke:

> Mrs. McDougald has written me of her suggestion to you that you include if possible work by Negro artists in the new book, and I most warmly second her motion.

This pointed up an anomaly which was not resolved by the publication of the *New Negro* itself. For there, too, the chief illustrator was Reiss. However, the *New Negro* does include six sketches by Aaron Douglas, which show a considerable influence of Reiss' cubistic manner. The *New Negro* also includes three illustrations by the Mexican artist Miguel Covarrubias. Reiss is conspicuously represented by his portrait sketches of the following people: Alain Locke, Jean Toomer, Countee Cullen, Paul Robeson, Roland Hayes, Charles S. Johnson, James Weldon Johnson, Robert Russa Moten, Elise J. McDougald, Mary McCleod Bethune, and W. E. B. Du Bois.

The *New Negro* appeared at the very end of 1925, in December. It was a modified and greatly expanded version of the March *Survey Graphic.* Some of the changes and carry-overs have already been noted. Following are the new features of the anthology. It was divided into two basic sections: Part I. The Negro Renaissance, and Part II. The New Negro in a New World.

Part I included "The New Negro" by Locke and the article by Barnes: in addition, there was William Stanley Braithwaite's "The Negro in American Literature," which had appeared in the *Crisis* in 1924. Then follows sections devoted to fiction and poetry, drama and music. The fiction section presents Rudolph Fisher, adding his story, "The City of Refuge," to his earlier sketches. There are two stories by Jean Toomer from *Cane*; John F.

Matheus' 1925 *Opportunity* Prize Story, "Fog"; as well as stories by Zora Neale Hurston, Bruce Nugent, and Eric Walrond.

The poetry section offers poems mainly from the Harlem issue. The drama section has two essays, one by Montgomery Gregory and the other by Jessie Fauset, as well as a play by Willis Richardson, *Compromise*.

The music section consists of an essay by Locke on the Spirituals, the essay on Jazz by J. A. Rogers and poems inspired by Negro Music and dance.

The last section of Part I is headed by Schomburg's essay, followed by Arthur Huff Fauset's folklore essay, and two stories collected from Cugo Lewis. Cullen's poem "Heritage" is published here and Alain Locke's essay on the ancestral arts.

Part II is not nearly so innovative. From *Survey Graphic* come James Weldon Johnson's essay on Harlem, Moton's on Hampton and Tuskegee (from the April issue), Domingo's essay on West Indian immigrants, as well as the articles by Herskovits, Walter White, and Elise McDougald. As already mentioned, Kellogg, Miller and W. E. B. Du Bois are represented by substituted essays.

Completely new are three essays: "The Negro Pioneer," by Paul U. Kellogg, editor of *Survey Graphic*; "The New Frontage on American Life," by Charles S. Johnson, editor of *Opportunity*; and "Durham: Capital of the Black Middle Class," by E. Franklin Frazier, then Director of the Atlanta School of Social Work.

Of enormous importance to the success of the *New Negro* was the comprehensive bibliography attached to it, 31 pages in small type. It was entitled, "A Select List of Negro-Americana and Africana." Arthur A. Schomburg contributed "Notable Early Books by Negroes." "Negro Folklore" was compiled by Arthur Huff Fauset. All other sections were Alain Locke's: "The Negro in Literature," "Negro Drama," "Negro Music," "A Selected List of Modern Music, Influenced by American Negro Themes or Idioms," "The Negro Race Problem." This bibliography was the most comprehensive to appear since Du Bois', published by Atlanta University early in the century. It was to remain the best available until Alain Locke's subsequent updating of it in the early Thirties in an American Library Association publication.

This account, which has been largely textual, has had as its object the revelation of the steps by which a monumental survey and testament to Afro-American life was compiled. It does not have to be reiterated that the energies expended by Alain Locke, as well as the creativity and erudition he demonstrated, were the essential ingredients in the production of this most impressive and influential landmark.

# GEORGE HUTCHINSON (ESSAY DATE 1995)

**SOURCE:** Hutchinson, George. "V. F. Calverton, *The Modern Quarterly*, and an Anthology." In *The Harlem Renaissance in Black and White*, pp. 278-88. Cambridge, Mass.: The Belknap Press of Harvard University Press, 1995.

*In the following essay, Hutchinson surveys V. F. Calverton's support for African American writers during the 1920s as editor of the journal* The Modern Quarterly— *which published works by such authors as W. E. B. Du Bois and Alain Locke—and as the compiler of* An Anthology of American Negro Literature *(1929).*

Closely related to *The Masses* and *The Liberator,* and perhaps initiated because the demise of *The Liberator* in 1922 left room in the market, V. F. Calverton's magazine, *The Modern Quarterly* (1923-40), . . . showed significant interest in the "Negro renaissance." According to Sidney Hook, *The Modern Quarterly* was one of the major expressions of "an independent American revolutionary Marxism," thus provoking virulent attacks in the 1930s from the Communist Party and its front organizations, when it was also one of the few journals in which Max Eastman could get published.[1] Until 1930 Calverton (born George Goetz in 1900) contributed regularly to *The New Masses,* and he also wrote for *The Nation.* In his own magazine, as a matter of policy, Calverton featured at least one piece by a black author in each issue, in a journal that usually included only eight or nine articles.

An admirer of people like Max Eastman, Floyd Dell, Van Wyck Brooks, Waldo Frank, Langston Hughes, and Claude McKay, Calverton ran the magazine roughly along the lines of Eastman's magazines; it took a more insistently ideological line in its literary criticism but was undoctrinaire enough to call down the wrath of the same people (Joseph Freeman and Michael Gold, for example) who began attacking Eastman in the late twenties and the thirties. Buckling under to pressure from the hard-line International Union of Revolutionary Writers, *The New Masses* went to the trouble of devoting almost an entire issue to attacking Calverton and his magazine.[2] Because of his focus on American conditions, Calverton was attuned to the relevance of Marxism to African Americans and vice versa; but, as Harold Cruse argues, Communist Party attacks on him prevented black

Marxists from giving him the attention he deserved. Black writers, however, found a welcoming atmosphere in his pages; he allowed "more uncensored comment" than communist publications and a greater range of topics.[3]

In the opening number *The Modern Quarterly* set itself off against *The Nation* and *The New Republic,* calling those "liberal" rather than "radical" magazines; but *The Modern Quarterly* adhered to the same cultural nationalist and anti-"high" modernist line that characterized them.[4] The white contributors also are often familiar: Eastman, Dell, Dewey, and Herskovits, for example. Among black writers, between 1925 and 1929 the magazine published Abram L. Harris, Jr., Charles S. Johnson ("The Negro Migration" and "The New Negro"), W. E. B. Du Bois ("The Social Origins of American Negro Art"), Langston Hughes ("Listen Here Blues"), Alain Locke ("American Literary Tradition and the Negro"), Hubert Harrison, Clarence Cameron White ("Labor Motif in Negro Music"), Thomas Dabney, E. Franklin Frazier ("La Bourgeoisie Noire"), and George Schuyler. Nothing in any of these pieces exploited the white fixation on traditional black stereotypes, as the list of contributors alone would suggest—which is not to say that the editor himself was immune to unrecognized stereotypes in his own mind, as we will see.

Calverton placed advertisements in *The Messenger, Opportunity,* and *The Crisis,* in hopes of attracting a black readership; and both *Opportunity* and *The Crisis* advertised in *The Modern Quarterly* under the impression that its readership would be interested in the magazines that were promoting, as one *Opportunity* advertisement put it, "A New Negro Aesthetic." Using a practice typical of the period, the editors of *Opportunity, The Crisis,* and *The Modern Quarterly* also offered combined subscriptions at a reduced price, hoping to attract one another's audiences.

Calverton's interest in black writing (like the interest of Carl and Irita Van Doren, Ridgely Torrence, Robert Morss Lovett, Max Eastman, and so on) predated the Civic Club dinner of 1924 that is often credited with introducing white editors to black arts. In January 1924—almost immediately after the founding of his magazine—he contacted Charles S. Johnson, and solicited articles on Negro subjects for *The Modern Quarterly.* What he was looking for was a "frank and unapologetic discussion of subjects long tabooed."[5] While getting his own magazine off the ground Calverton also tried to strengthen his ties to black publications. At the

end of September 1925 he asked to review *The New Negro* for *Opportunity,* and Johnson wrote to Locke for advice: "I had thought to ask some person like Zona Gale or Carl Van Doren [to review the book] or—someone who had already had a hand in the fostering of this school represented in the book, and at the same time commands attention."[6] Locke suggested letting Calverton do the review, and Johnson decided to get Van Doren to do one for a different publication.

As it turned out, Calverton also published his review of *The New Negro* in *The Nation,* where he stated: "This book marks an epoch in the hectic career of the Negro. . . . In undermining and annihilating the Negro myth it functions as a clarifying and signal contribution to contemporary thought."[7] He worked hard to draw attention to the book, inviting Locke to give a lecture entitled "The New Negro" at his home in Baltimore, which would be attended by twenty to thirty selected people.[8] Five days earlier Calverton had solicited an article from Locke on "the new literature growing up about and by the Negro," treating both white- and black-authored works.[9] Ultimately Locke contributed "American Literary Tradition and the Negro," a "survey" of American attitudes to the Negro as expressed in works of literature.[10] Meanwhile, Calverton kept stumping for *The New Negro*: "You see I am doing everything I can to boost this book of yours, and I do hope it will sell in no mean way."[11] He had both Charles S. Johnson and Howard Odum do reviews of the book for *The Modern Quarterly* (knowing pretty well what they would have to say about it) and suggested that Locke send a review copy to Odum for the *Journal of Social Forces.* He even told Locke to send copies to Havelock Ellis and Bertrand Russell—two of the intellectual celebrities of the age—"and write to me immediately, special delivery, so that I can know they have been dispatched. I shall take care of the rest" (Ellis was a friend of Calverton's, as well as an author whose work Locke had followed for some years).[12] Still Calverton was not done pushing the book; he wrote yet another article on it for *Current History.*[13] Locke liked the article but suspected it would get Calverton in trouble with the *Crisis* crowd. Calverton planned to "wear extra armour" for a lecture he was to give at the Sun Rise Club in Harlem on April 19, 1926.[14] Having made the "New Negro" cause his own, Calverton went on to lecture on the subject at Syracuse University in February 1926 and to spark the organization of a "racial cooperative group" there. He even asked Locke about the advisability and possibility of his getting a job teaching sociology or literature at Howard University.[15]

It is clear from his solicitations to Locke and Charles S. Johnson, as well as from the nature of the work carried in the magazine generally, that Calverton asked his contributors for "social" approaches to literature. *Modern Quarterly* essays by W. E. B. Du Bois and Alain Locke are worth a close look for the ways they fit Calverton's critical approach and his interests in black American literary tradition.

Du Bois's contribution, "The Social Origins of American Negro Art," explains the "social compulsion" behind the development of a distinct African American tradition in literature, which he predictably locates not in *formal* characteristics but rather in content. To Du Bois, a new American Negro "school" of art is inevitable, as he explains with a thoroughly pragmatistic rationale: "They may not bring anything particularly new in method, but the content of such an art contribution must always be new because as every individual differs from another so every group and set of group experiences differs, and the truth about them has something fundamentally new and different from anything else in the world."[16] Just as the social oppression of the Negro has to a large extent determined the nature of Negro arts to the present, concludes Du Bois, social conditions "are going to determine its future very largely." Either social oppression will continue, shutting out the light from the black writer-prophets, or the wall of oppression may be broken, "so that the very blaze of coming light may illuminate the former darkness and make the intricate path over which this group has come all the more thrilling for its shadows, turns and twists. The American who wants to serve the world has unusual opportunity here."[17] Du Bois's aesthetics do not match Calverton's, insofar as Du Bois does not recognize a transformation in aesthetic form as a necessary aspect of the development of a new literary tradition. Neither does Du Bois come anywhere near suggesting the development of a proletarian art; on the contrary, he thinks of artists as Old Testament or Romantic prophets. On the other hand, his emphasis on the close link between social conditions and the production of art, along with the corollary of the "Americanness" of black American art, fall very easily into the general critical orientation of *The Modern Quarterly*.

Alain Locke's "American Literary Tradition and the Negro" examines "the literary treatment of Negro life and character" as a record of the social history of the Negro in America.[18] Such an investigation, Locke believes, reveals "fundamental attitudes of the American mind," changing in seven major phases determined by social history: "a Colonial period attitude (1760-1820), a pre-Abolition period (1820-45), the Abolitionist period (1845-65), the Early Reconstruction period (1870-85), the Late Reconstruction Period (1885-95), the Industrial period (1895-1920), and the Contemporary period since 1920."[19] In each period, the figure of the Negro in American literature has dramatized two aspects of white psychology: "first, the white man's wish for self-justification, whether he be at any given time anti-Negro or pro-Negro, and, second, more subtly registered, an avoidance of the particular type that would raise an embarrassing question for the social conscience of the period."[20] Locke finds the image of the Negro in literature all the more revealing insofar as it is not deliberately propagandistic but is actually considered "accurate" by the white authors and audiences of any given period; it thus expresses an "unconscious social wish" responding to socioeconomic conditions.

Locke's explanation for the sudden "liberation" of Negro literary portraiture in the twenties must have pleased Calverton. The growth of literary realism played its role, as did the interest in "local color" and the "exotic tendencies of conscious aestheticism."[21] However, "the really basic factor in the sharp and astonishing break in the literary tradition and attitude toward the Negro came in the revolt against Puritanism. . . . The release which almost everyone had thought must come about through a change in moral evaluation, a reform of opinion, has actually and suddenly come about merely as a shift of interest, a revolution of taste. From it there looms the imminent possibility not only of a true literature of the Negro but of a Negro Literature as such."[22]

The contrasts between Locke's thinking and Du Bois's are revealing. Whereas Du Bois, the prophet-propagandist and moralist, looks for a moral conversion that will liberate black literature from its hidden and oppressed circumstances, Locke (also an ethicist as well as aesthetician and, not coincidentally, a homosexual) finds such liberation resulting instead from a revolution in aesthetic taste—that is, a transformation in structures of "feeling" encouraged by the revolt against "Puritan" repression of the sensual body. While recognizing that this development has led to a fascination for "the primitive and pagan and emotional aspects of Negro life and character," Locke remains hopeful that an independent literature of greater authenticity will emerge; for, in contrast to the sensationalistic fictions of paganism, "the work of Waldo Frank, Jean Toomer, Walter White, Rudolph Fisher, and DuBose Heyward promises greatly."[23]

Locke's list of authors is interesting today in that he differentiates between the white exploiters of exotic primitivism and such white authors as Frank and Heyward, whom more recent critics usually lump in with the white fans of the primitive Negro. Locke was not merely making concessions to his white audience; in black periodicals and letters to black friends, he regularly mentioned selected white novelists as important pioneers of and participants in the black literary movement. What differentiates Frank from other white novelists, presumably, is the greater social consciousness that informs his novel—it is, if nothing else, a direct attack upon the contradictions of Southern white racial mythology, which the novel links to economic oppression, the sexual unconscious, and white evangelical Christianity. Heyward, on the other hand, was an important precursor of the "folk school" of black fiction. Overall, Locke's critical methodology—though less hospitable to economic determinism—fits more closely with Calverton's critical and ideological orientation than does Du Bois's, as Locke's review in *Opportunity* of Calverton's book, *Sex Expression in Literature* (1927), would later show.[24]

Calverton's support of the "Negro renaissance" did not stop with his editorial decisions at *The Modern Quarterly* and his lecturing. He helped found the short-lived American Inter-Racial Association, intending to launch a more radical economic attack on American racial oppression than the NAACP or the Urban League.[25] Perhaps even more important, he compiled and edited one of the most significant anthologies of black literature ever published, in Henry Louis Gates's estimation: "Calverton's was the first attempt at black canon-formation to provide for the influence and presence of black vernacular literature in a major way."[26]

In compiling *An Anthology of American Negro Literature* (1929), Calverton expressed his own vision of the history and possibilities of African American literature, but he also solicited the advice and criticism of black authors such as Alain Locke and Walter White.[27] Calverton based his selections on his sense of the history of black literary forms, believing that this history constituted a distinctive African American expressive tradi-

tion.[28] At the same time, he thought this tradition constituted the most original contribution to a truly "American" literature:

> The white man in America has continued, and in an inferior manner, a culture of European origin. He has not developed a culture that is definitely and unequivocally American. In respect of originality, then, the Negro is more important in the growth of American culture than the white man. . . . While the white man has gone to Europe for his models, and is seeking still a European approval of his artistic endeavors, the Negro in his art forms has never gone beyond America for his background and has never sought the acclaim of any culture other than his own. This is particularly true of those forms of Negro art that come directly from the people.[29]

Gates notes that "Calverton couched his argument in just that rhetoric of nationalism, of American exceptionalism, that had long been used to exclude, or anyway occlude, the contribution of the Negro. In an audacious reversal, it turns out that *only* the Negro is really American, the white man being a pale imitation of his European forebears."[30] By 1929, however, as we have seen, this reversal was no longer "audacious"; it informed much of the criticism of the American cultural nationalists when they concerned themselves with black arts.

Calverton did not regard what he called the "primitivism" of black folk forms as expressive of a racial essence or even an African cultural background. Rather, the folk forms were "a singular evolution of our American environment. In describing them as primitive, we do not mean that they are savage in origin, or that the instincts of savagery linger in them, but that they are untutored in form and unsophisticated in content."[31] Calverton was hardly a perceptive student of black folk arts, but neither can his views on black art be slotted neatly into the usual categories of white racism. In fact, he was quick to point out the long history of black culture and literature, noting the extensive if neglected history of African civilizations such as Songhay and Mali and great universities such as that in Timbuktu. African art is "rigid," less "exuberant," and more classically disciplined than American Negro art—in short, more the product of a traditional culture than of a modernist "New World."[32] On the other hand, free of age-old traditions and conventions, the American Negro created art without thought of what was "Art" and what was not; "he" was thus able to create art from his "soul," art springing from the life of "the people," "an artless art," "the most genuine art of the world." This art stands in stark contrast to white American art as well as to

African art. "The exuberance of sentiment, the spirited denial of discipline, and the contempt for the conventional, that are so conspicuous in the art of the American Negro, are direct outgrowths of the nature of his life in this country."[33] A variety of romantic primitivism invests Calverton's comments, combined with his cultural nationalism; but the terms of his praise are virtually identical in these particular respects to the terms he used in characterizing the work of his great poetic hero, Walt Whitman—another New World artist, in the fullest sense, according to Calverton. Whitman, however, was a lonely voice, hardly a true proletarian or folk poet; in vain had he longed to be the voice of "the people." The Negro folk poets enjoyed advantages he never had. By extension, African American poets to come, building on the work of their precursors rather than upon feeble "white" models (as Calverton felt most poets in the literary tradition had so far done), would be the harbingers of a real American literature.

In developing his anthology, Calverton stayed in close touch with Locke, who encouraged the project and agreed to contribute, if Calverton would in turn contribute to a volume Locke was thinking of publishing in Europe about "the movement."[34] It was a suggestion from Locke that led Calverton to include a section in his anthology on "artificial blues" by Langston Hughes and other young poets, in addition to the blues and labor songs he had already planned to include. Calverton also asked for Locke's advice on which plays to use in the volume.[35] Calverton had been a fan of Hughes's blues since early 1926, when he had invited the poet to his home for a reading before the *Modern Quarterly* group; and he published "Listen Here Blues" in the magazine. Hughes was, of course, just the sort of poet Calverton would have been looking for—writing alternately in a Midwestern free-verse style and in folk forms, often advancing a political message (implicit when not explicit), and flouting "bourgeois" and "Puritan" attitudes to sex and social convention. Calverton stayed in touch with Hughes for years, continuing to review his work, soliciting reviews from him, and inviting him to visit. In 1929, newly an editor for the Macauley Company, Calverton even tried to lure Hughes away from Knopf, perhaps suspecting that the Knopfs' distaste for proletarian writing was making Hughes restless.[36]

Representative of the breadth of Calverton's interest in black writing is his relationship with Hughes's chief antagonist, George Schuyler.[37]

After soliciting work from the then-socialist satirist, who particularly enjoyed ridiculing notions of radical "racial" or cultural differences between black and white Americans, he published Schuyler's "Emancipated Woman and the Negro" in the fall 1929 *Modern Quarterly*. Schuyler also published a review of the book *Black Genesis* and, in 1934, the article "When Black Weds White."[38] Calverton encouraged Schuyler to write his first book, *Black No More* (1931)—surely the most iconoclastic (not to mention hilarious) product of the Harlem Renaissance—and was instrumental in getting the book published by the Macauley Company.[39] The important point to notice here is that Calverton was actively promoting an author, and a novel, that attacked with devastating satire the stereotypes of African Americans as primitives or as exotic "pagans" in the urban jungles of America, fundamentally different in nature or nurture from white Americans. The revolt against "Puritanism," insofar as the latter is perceived as one aspect of the "colonial complex" (to borrow Calverton's term) that also fosters racism, does not shade seamlessly or inevitably into a racialist vision of Negroes as exotic primitives; and even when it does, it does not necessarily entail a strong resistance to other types of black fiction. No doubt Calverton was largely responsible for Macauley's hiring of Wallace Thurman for an editorial position at the firm.

Calverton's role in Melvin Tolson's career was also noteworthy, and reveals the continuities between Harlem Renaissance networks and the next generation. (The strongest influences on Tolson's early poetry were Hughes and Schuyler, and his M. A. thesis, written in the 1930s, was entitled "The Harlem Group of Negro Writers.") In the 1930s Tolson came across a copy of *The Modern Quarterly* that impressed him and informed him that the editor had published a book of Negro poetry. Tolson sent Calverton some poems, and they soon became friends. In fact, "throughout his life, Tolson referred to Calverton as 'the best friend I ever had.'"[40] When visiting New York, Tolson even had a key to Calverton's home. Calverton published several of Tolson's poems in *Modern Monthly* in 1937, his first appearance except for one poem published in a Dillard University arts magazine.[41] Subsequently, in a column for *Current History* Calverton introduced him to a wider audience as a poet "who in his *Harlem Gallery* is trying to do for the Negro what Edgar Lee Masters did for the middlewest white folk over two decades ago."[42] Indeed, Tolson himself said Masters, Sandburg, Frost, and Robinson had been the inspirations that turned him, in 1932, away from writing Anglo-Saxon sonnets in the form of a "dead classicism."[43]

Calverton's treatment of black literature in his most significant book of criticism, *The Liberation of American Literature,* reveals even more persuasively than his anthology his view of the importance of African American culture to the national identity as a whole. The most important development in modern American literature, for Calverton, was the long-needed liberation from a "colonial" mentality; the next needed development, in his view, was a break from "petty bourgeois individualism" into a revolutionary "proletarian ideology."[44] This final liberation had been approached by *The Masses,* but Eastman, Dell, and company had not matched their revolutionary ideology with a suitable validation of proletarian *art*; moreover, they had failed to reach beyond a bourgeois audience of intellectuals. Calverton's culture-heroes from what we now call the American canon were Whitman, Mark Twain, and Theodore Dreiser. He applauded the "rediscovery of America" in the first two decades of the twentieth century, pioneered by writers from outside the orbit of New England—particularly Midwestern muckrakers, critical realists, and free-versifiers. By the mid-teens, the nation finally had a poetry in the language of the American people, "rooted in the American soil,"[45] and this "native" thrust of the literature survived into the twenties undiminished.

Along with the literary movement, Calverton emphasizes, came a serious study of American folklore; John A. Lomax first hunted up cowboy songs and ballads (which "belong as definitely and natively to American literature" as the old English ballads belong to English literature) before turning to other folk traditions, and these works became the basis for more "self-consciously" artistic treatment. Similarly, interest in Native American songs and tales grew. "But more important than either the Indian or the cowboy literature which has been recovered, and added to the native stock of our tradition, is the growth of Negro literature which has made a far greater contribution to American culture. The contributions of the Negro to American culture are as indigenous to our soil as the legendary cowboy or gold-seeking frontiersman. In fact, I think it can be said without exaggeration, that they constitute a large part of whatever claim America can make to originality in its cultural history."[46] Black folklore presents a rich resource for the development of an authentic as well as revolutionary American cultural tradition.

Calverton tended toward an emerging political view of black intellectuals as the vanguard of proletarian revolution—even when he viewed black people as more spontaneous, joyous, and rhythmic, than the repressed "Nordics." For Calverton, capitalism and the repression of sexuality were intimately intertwined, and black folk culture had particular significance because of its inherent subversion of these deep structural afflictions of the bourgeois psyche and society. Predictably, however, Calverton found that, like white American cultural nationalists, the "New Negro" writers failed to be sufficiently suffused with class consciousness; their work, with a few exceptions like works of the thirties by Langston Hughes and Eugene Gordon, did not go "beyond" a bourgeois "racial" emphasis. For black as for white writers, then, cultural nationalism—crucial as it was to the "liberation of American literature"—had so far failed to develop into the needed ideology of scientific socialism. Calverton could be crude in his sweeping applications of "vulgar Marxism" to literary history, but his brand of Marxism always served a cultural nationalist vision. That vision informed his promotion of a distinctive African American literary tradition, socialism, and racial equality.

## Notes

1. Sidney Hook, "Preface" to reprint of *Modern Quarterly.* Eric Homberger, *American Writers and Radical Politics, 1900-1939: Equivocal Commitments* (London: Macmillan, 1986), 125. For a brief sketch of Calverton's relationship to Eastman, see Daniel Aaron, *Writers on the Left: Episodes in American Literary Communism* (New York: Avon, 1965), 335. Aaron (335-346) also gives a very informative general treatment of Calverton's position on the cultural left in the 1920s and 1930s. For a useful overview of V. F. Calverton's relationships with African American intellectuals, see Haim Genizi's "V. F. Calverton: A Radical Magazinist for Black Intellectuals, 1920-1940," *Journal of Negro History* 57 (1972): 241-253; Harold Cruse discusses Calverton's unappreciated grasp of the black situation in *The Crisis of the Negro Intellectual* (New York: William Morrow, 1967), 152-158. Leonard Wilcox discusses Calverton's distinctively "American" synthesis of political and sexual radicalism, Marxism and Freudianism, in "Sex Boys in a Balloon: V. F. Calverton and the Abortive Sexual Revolution," *Journal of American Studies* 23 (1989): 7-26; and in his *V. F. Calverton: Radical in the American Grain* (Philadelphia: Temple University Press, 1992), with brief remarks on Calverton's relationship to the Harlem Renaissance, 89-91.

2. David Ramsey and Alan Calmer, "The Marxism of V. F. Calverton," *New Masses* 8 (1933): 9-27. For the story of how this came about, on orders from Moscow, see Aaron, *Writers on the Left,* 340.

3. Cruse, *Crisis,* 152-158.

4. Richel North, "The Limitations of American Magazines," *Modern Quarterly* 1 (1923): 2-12.

5. Charles S. Johnson to Alain Locke, 10 January 1924, correspondence files, Alain Locke Papers, Moorland-Spingarn Research Center, Howard University.

6. Charles S. Johnson to Alain Locke, 1 October 1925, Alain Locke Papers.

7. V. F. Calverton, review of *The New Negro, Nation* 121 (1925): 761.

8. V. F. Calverton to Alain Locke, 25 October 1925, Alain Locke Papers. Locke did in fact give the lecture; see Calverton to Locke, 5 November 1925, Alain Locke Papers.

9. V. F. Calverton to Alain Locke, 20 October 1925, Alain Locke Papers.

10. Alain Locke, "American Literary Tradition and the Negro," *Modern Quarterly* 3 (1926): 215-222.

11. V. F. Calverton to Alain Locke, 30 November 1925, Alain Locke Papers.

12. V. F. Calverton to Alain Locke, 5 December 1925, Alain Locke Papers.

13. V. F. Calverton to Alain Locke, 30 December 1925, Alain Locke Papers.

14. V. F. Calverton to Alain Locke, 1 February 1926, Alain Locke Papers.

15. V. F. Calverton to Alain Locke, 31 March 1926, Alain Locke Papers.

16. W. E. B. Du Bois, "The Social Origins of American Negro Art," *Modern Quarterly* 3 (1925-26): 54.

17. Ibid., 56.

18. Locke, "American Literary Tradition," 215.

19. Ibid., 216.

20. Ibid.

21. Ibid., 221.

22. Ibid.

23. Ibid., 222.

24. Alain Locke, review of *Sex Expression in Literature, Opportunity* 5 (1927): 57-58. The review is detailed and enthusiastic, though objecting to Calverton's overemphasis upon economic determinism.

25. See V. F. Calverton, "The American Inter-racial Association," *Opportunity* 5 (1927): 23.

26. Henry Louis Gates, Jr., "The Master's Pieces: On Canon Formation and the African-American Tradition," *South Atlantic Quarterly* 89 (1990): 97.

27. On Calverton's relationship with Walter White, see Waldron, *Walter White and the Harlem Renaissance* (Port Washington, N.Y.: Kennikat Press, 1978), 164-165; White read the first few chapters of the anthology at an early stage. Calverton also sent the book to Elmer Carter of *Opportunity,* who enthusiastically praised it.

28. Gates, "Master's Pieces," 35.

29. V. F. Calverton, "Introduction," *An Anthology of American Negro Literature* (New York: Modern Library, 1929), 4-5.

30. Gates, "Master's Pieces," 98.

31. Calverton, "Introduction," 8.

32. Ibid., 8.

33. Ibid., 4, 8-9.

34. Alain Locke to V. F. Calverton, 19 October 1928, Alain Locke Papers.

35. V. F. Calverton to Alain Locke, 24 November 1928 and 20 November 1928, Alain Locke Papers.

36. V. F. Calverton to Langston Hughes, 19 July 1930, 21 January 1929, 16 April 1929, Langston Hughes Papers, James Weldon Johnson Collection, Beinecke Rare Book and Manuscript Library, Yale University.

37. Aaron, *Writers on the Left,* 335-338, emphasizes how Calverton wanted *The Modern Quarterly* to be a forum for diverse views of the radical left, to help unite warring factions. Thus Calverton's embrace of opposite poles of the Harlem Renaissance (Hughes and Schuyler, Locke and Du Bois) fits the general aim of the magazine.

38. George S. Schuyler, *Black and Conservative: The Autobiography of George S. Schuyler* (New Rochelle, N.Y.: Arlington House, 1966), 170.

39. Ibid., 170. See also Schuyler's "Preface" to *Black No More* (1931; Boston: Northeastern University Press, 1989), 14, which thanks Josephine Schuyler and V. F. Calverton for their help and encouragement.

40. Joy Flasch, *Melvin B. Tolson* (Boston: Twayne, 1972), 29.

41. Robert M. Farnsworth, *Melvin B. Tolson, 1898-1966: Plain Talk and Poetic Prophecy* (Columbia: University of Missouri Press, 1984), 57.

42. Quoted in ibid., 58.

43. Ibid., 42.

44. V. F. Calverton, *The Liberation of American Literature* (New York: Scribner's, 1932), 406-450, 479.

45. Ibid., 417.

46. Ibid., 438.

# AFRICAN AMERICAN PERIODICALS AND THE HARLEM RENAISSANCE

## GEORGE S. SCHUYLER (ESSAY DATE 1951)

**SOURCE:** Schuyler, George S. "Forty Years of *The Crisis.*" *The Crisis* 58, no. 3 (March 1951): 163-64.

*In the following essay, Schuyler encapsulates the publishing history of the NAACP's journal* The Crisis.

The Crisis was born near the end of the most parlous period in post-Civil War history. The bright promise of Reconstruction which for ten

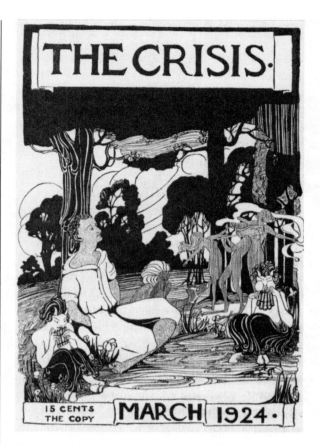

Cover of the March 1924 issue of *Crisis,* illustrated by Gwendolyn Bennett.

years had inspired high hopes in the hearts of millions, began to tarnish after the Hayes-Tilden compromise of 1876, when the freedmen were returned to the tender mercies of the unreconstructed South. By 1890 the Ku Klux elements were firmly in the saddle almost everywhere below the Smith and Wesson Line, and the ensuing succession of anti-Negro legislation indicated the political decline of *Homo Africanus.* Jim Crowism, lynching, disfranchisement, peonage and mobbism became epidemic in Dixie, and in the remainder of the Republic the Negro was only half a man. Colored Americans were losing hope, depressed by increasingly fell circumstances and the campaign of ridicule and calumny which presented them as having no past, a degrading present, and an ominous future.

Then came *The Crisis,* like a clear, strong breeze cutting through the miasma of Negrophobism. Here for the first time with brilliance, militancy, facts, photographs and persuasiveness, a well-edited magazine challenged the whole concept of white supremacy then nationally ac-

cepted. There had been and were Negro newspapers but nothing on so high a journalistic level had so far appeared. It was a revelation to America and particularly colored America. It is no exaggeration to say that the early *Crisis* created an intellectual revolution in the most out-of-the-way places. Its impact was similar to that created fifteen years later by *The American Mercury.* It became the bible of the militant Negro of the day and "must" reading for the growing number of his white champions. What it lacked in typography it made up in content. It was the rallying point for the new interracial deal.

In its pages was the first encouragement of Negro writers and artists. Here were the first literary contests, the first section devoted to Negro children, the first presentation of Negro art work, the first feature stories about successful Negroes, the first full-fledged drive for Pan-Africanism, the first special numbers devoted to Negro educational advancement, the first articles on consumers' cooperation. Here were scathing denunciations and flaming defense. It was a magazine that passed through ten times more hands than bought it, and it is not surprising that after World War I it boasted a circulation of over 100,000 copies, one of the largest in the land.

Through the years it has hewed to the line with commendable consistency. More sophisticated but no less militant than when it was launched in 1910, it continues to the present to attack the same dragons it ventured forth to destroy. They are weaker dragons and not so numerous because the work started by *The Crisis* has borne fruit, and where forty years ago it fought alone, it now shares the vanguard with many. Indeed, there are thousands of newspapers and periodicals now fighting for the goals *The Crisis* announced in 1910.

It has been an inspiration of Negro rights, and perusal of its files is like marching back through the battlefields of yesteryear. Too often we forget that what is now taken for granted was burning issue not so long ago. Its pages are peopled with men and women now gone and generally forgotten who were devoted workers, flaming fighters, dedicated champions of a new interracial order. Today as in the past it welds together the same kind of people for the same cause with the same singleness of purpose. Rich in years but young in spirit, it stands as a unique example of what a militant magazine should be.

# WALTER C. DANIEL (ESSAY DATE 1976)

**SOURCE:** Daniel, Walter C. *"Challenge Magazine*: An Experiment That Failed." *CLA Journal* 19 (1976): 494-503.

*In the following essay, Walter discusses Dorothy West's short-lived literary journal* Challenge, *highlighting the difficulties faced by African American publications in the mid-1930s.*

Dorothy West intended her new magazine, *Challenge,* to recapture, in the mid-thirties, the literary vitality of the Harlem Renaissance which had not survived the Depression. It appeared irregularly from its first number in March, 1934, to its final issue in the Fall of 1937. The ambitious editor hoped to establish a "new movement" in Afro-American writing. Established writers responded admirably to her call and some significant post-Renaissance literary works appeared in *Challenge.* The editor had expected a higher quality of writing from Black college students than she found to exist. The old names could hardly mount a new Renaissance; and, significantly, the race, the nation, and large parts of the world were leaning toward a proletarian artistic vision which Miss West never fully understood. She believed the Chicago School of writers very well might set the tone and purpose of a great deal of American writing for the future; so she cheerfully—even if naively—changed her "pale pink" *Challenge,* which survived totally on subscriptions and which did not pay its contributors, into *New Challenge* which ceased publication after one issue, although its roster of contributing editors listed Sterling Brown, Robert Hayden, Langston Hughes, Margaret Walker and others. Its new associate editor was Richard Wright, whose literary success seemed assured at the time.

This paper does not intend to provide reasons for the demise of a magazine whose editors had reason to believe that, at long last, the proper combination of influences and talents and interests had been forged for a successful publication. But a fairly detailed study of the several issues of *Challenge,* with particular emphasis on contributors and on editorial comment in most numbers, can focus upon some of the tensions which were created as a small magazine—seldom mentioned and little remembered—sought to reflect the Black experience in the United States during that somewhat uncertain literary climate of the mid-thirties. And it can provide in capsule form what Keneth Kinnamon considers "An obstructive example of the general change in Afro-American

# ON THE SUBJECT OF...

## JAMES WELDON JOHNSON'S ADVICE TO YOUNG WRITERS

It is one thing just to dabble in writing and another thing to be a writer. To those who really desire to become writers let me say: Writing is not only an art, it is also a trade, a trade that demands long, arduous and dogged effort for mastery.

**SOURCE:** James Weldon Johnson, in the foreword to the first issue of the *Challenge,* March 1934, p. 1.

writing from the exotic bohemianism of the Harlem Renaissance to the social consciousness of Wright and other WPA writers."[1]

James Weldon Johnson, then professor of creative writing at Fisk University, provided the "Foreword" for the first issue of *Challenge* with commendation for its editor and for the promise he felt the new magazine offered, as he wrote:

It is a good thing that Dorothy West is doing in instituting a magazine through which the voices of younger Negro writers may be heard. The term "younger Negro writers" connotes a degree of disillusionment and disappointment for those who a decade ago hailed with loud huzzas the dawn of the Negro literary millennium. We expected much; perhaps too much. I now judge that we ought to be thankful for the half-dozen younger writers who did emerge and make a place for themselves. But we ought not to be satisfied; many newer voices should be constantly striving to make themselves heard. But these younger writers must not be mere dilettantes; they have serious work to do. They can bring to bear a tremendous force for breaking down and wearing away the stereotyped ideas about the Negro, and for creating a higher and more enlightened opinion about the race. To do this, they need not be propagandists; they need only be sincere artists, disdaining all cheap applause and remaining always true to themselves. . . . It seems to me that the greatest lack of our younger writers is not talent or ability, but persistent and intelligent industry. That, I think, explains why the work of so many of them was but a flash in the pan. It is one thing just to dabble in writing and another thing to be a writer. To those who really desire to become writers let me say: Writing is not only an art, it is also a trade, a trade that demands long, arduous and dogged effort for mastery.

Miss West considered the magazine "primarily an organ of the new voice," and announced a plan to "bring out the prose and poetry of the newer Negroes," claiming that "we who *were* the New Negroes challenge them to better our achievement . . . for we did not altogether live up to our fine promise." Clearly, both Dorothy West and James Weldon Johnson believed at the time that the passing of the Harlem Renaissance did not signal the decline of talent among Negro writers, but that a new magazine would provide a renewal for their talent and would encourage their output. For several issues of the publication, their faith seemed justified. Hughes' short story "Little Dog" was the lead item and Arna Bontemps' "Barrel Staves" appeared in the March, 1934, issue. Harry T. Burleigh wrote a special article on the "serious menace to the artistic standing of the race" which he saw in the growing tendency of some musicians to utilize the melodies of spirituals for fox trots, dance numbers and sentimental songs. Pauli Murray, then a student at Hunter College and considered by Miss West "a writer of much promise," sent an eight line poem, "Song." Helene Johnson, called in the issue "the most highly rated of the women poets," published her rather lengthy "Widow with a Moral Obligation." Two of Countee Cullen's sonnets—"In Absence" and "Sonnet"—occupied a special place in the magazine. Cullen, who never conducted the book review column for *Challenge* which was promised, advised the editor to get in touch with Langston Hughes because he had been doing some good prose recently. "I wish I had his objectivity," he wrote. "Lord knows, I wish we could recapture the spirit of '25; I hope the bird hasn't flown forever," he continued. And he wrote that there must be ever so many new recruits who would flock to the banner *Challenge.*

Arna Bontemps wrote:

. . . with the chickens to be fed and the fall garden to be tended I'm a busy man. Then there is the Scottsboro thing at our door, and the production of 'St. Louis Woman' in Cleveland (for my fancy), and the new book (only begun) which, of course, is my daily meat and drink, and withal I am a busy man and a lazy one. . . . I have just one poem of recent date that has not been published. I am holding it as one sometimes holds a good-luck penny, lest he should go completely broke. But I had a short story that might do, and if you will give me time to find it and make a copy, I'll gladly send it along for your brave new project.

The second issue of *Challenge* did not appear until September, 1934. Miss West explained that the magazine had become a quarterly, rather than a monthly, as she had originally planned, largely because she was disappointed in the contributions that came in from the new voices, which provided little that she wanted to print, because some of the bad writing was unbelievably bad. "We felt somewhat crazily that the authors must be spoofing and that they didn't really mean us to take their stuff for prose and poetry," she wrote. So, admitting embarrassment, she had to fall back on the "tried and true voices." Arna Bontemps, though, was not surprised that the outpouring from the "younger writers" was not coming forth. "We're not washed up by a jugful," he boasted, and continued:

It is a pretty pose, this attitude about 'old before our time'. I will not have it. We left Egypt in the late twenties and presently cross the Red Sea. Naturally the wandering in the wilderness followed. The promised land is ahead. Why Langston (Hughes) had just recently been spying it out for us, and the grapes are promising. Furthermore we are well able to go over and possess it. Now if the "Younger writers" can take our crowns, here is a chance and here is our challenge. But they will have to take them. We have just achieved our growth. Nobody knows our strength.

In the same vein, Carl Van Vechten criticized the claim that the great Negro Renaissance that was launched so bravely in 1926-27 had not continued its voyage on the seas of art as triumphantly as might have been wished. To him, the Negro of 1934 was "on a much more solid base as an artist as a social individual" than he was in the mid-twenties. James Weldon Johnson's newly published *Along This Way,* Langston Hughes' *The Ways of White Folks,* and Zora Neale Hurston's *Jonah's Gourd Vine* proved his conclusion. The Spring number (May, 1935) pleased the editor; for most of the authors were new and not all of them were Negroes; most were young, but few of the new names became well known writers. Arna Bontemps' short story, "Dang Little Squirt"; Frank Yerby's two poems, "To a Seagull" and "Drought"; Pauli Murray's poem, "Inquietude"; and Helen Johnson's poem, "Let Me Sing My Song," provided the best works in the issue. Apparently the paucity of satisfactory material did not disappear, though, but a different kind of problem arose— one which surfaced in the editorial comments for the January, 1936 issue in which Miss West wrote:

Somebody asked us why *Challenge* was for the most part so pale pink. We said because the few red articles we did receive were not literature. We care a lot about style. And we think a message is doubly effective when effectively written without bombast or bad spelling . . . We would like to print more articles and stories of protest. We have daily contact with the underprivileged. We know their suffering and soul weariness. They have only the meager bread and meat of the dole, and that will not fail their failing spirits. Yet the bourgeois youth on the southern campus, who should be conscious of these things, is joining a fraternity instead of the brotherhood of serious minds. Leadership of the literate is infinitely preferable to the blind leadership of the blind.

Two issues later (April, 1937), Miss West explained that *Challenge* had not appeared for nearly a year because of financial reasons. But to her, those delays should not become months rather than weeks. This time the delay was almost entirely due to the lack of "even fair material," she explained. This was a circumstance she could not understand, and she hoped it was only because "*Challenge* may not be known to the young writing people we want to reach," for, "it would cause us no little despair to believe there was a dearth in good writing, and that even if *Challenge* were on every newsstand and was in a position to pay its contributors, there would be no inflow of readable stuff." Her editorial policies had not changed since the first issue, she explained, and she wrote that her own personal preferences and political opinions in no way influenced her judgment of material. Although she wanted to publish a "progressive magazine," she had no intention of dictating style, choice of subject, or content. At the same time, she wrote, "we would defeat the purpose of the magazine, mainly to foster developing talents, if we rejected these early gropings toward style, social consciousness and adulthood.' She repeated rather forcefully her special hope for the young Negro to grow to complete awareness of his heritage, his position as a member of a minority group, and his duty to take some active part in social reform; "he must not escape, through his university training, to himself as an entity apart"; and he must "know the South whose centre is not the campus," and the North "whose main stem is not Sugar Hill."

The poor examples of writing she received from the Negro colleges disappointed her, but she believed her explanatory letters and complimentary copies of *Challenge* which she sent to English department heads often never reached their students. She preferred to believe the younger generation would have responded to her requests for stories and poems if they had known she had requested them. She was not discouraged, however, for she had become greatly interested in a young Chicago group, which held regular meetings where their works were read in open discussion. She wrote that *Challenge,* she understood, had "come in for considerable dispraise" by the Chicago writers, and that, although she never

resented honest opinion, she had retaliated by offering them a special section in a forthcoming issue that may "show us what we have not done by showing us what they can do."

The special edition to which Miss West referred appeared as the Fall issue in 1937 under the title, *New Challenge,* with Marian Minus as one of its editors and Richard Wright as associate editor. The editorial explained that the organ was designed to "meet the needs of writers and people interested in literature which cannot be met by those Negro magazines which are sponsored by organizations and which, therefore, cannot be purely literary;" and it would "break down much of the isolation which exists between Negro writer and the rest of the writing world." She also hoped the magazine could point social directives and provide a basis for the clear recognition of and solution to problems which face the contemporary writer. Clearly, these editorial purposes transcended the "pale pink" hue of the magazines which has been referred to earlier. At the same time, she stated that she was not attempting to "restage the 'revolt' and 'renaissance' which grew unsteadily and upon false foundations ten years ago"; for, a literary movement among Negroes . . . should, first of all, be built upon the writer's placing his material in the proper perspective with regard to the life of the Negro masses." For that reason, she wrote, "we want to indicate, through examples in our pages, the great fertility of folk material as a source of creative material." She wanted *New Challenge* to provide a medium of literary expression for all writers who realize the present need for the realistic depiction of life through the sharp focus of social consciousness. She went so far as to write that Negro writers themselves and the audience which they reach must be reminded, and in many instances taught, that writing should not be *in vacuo* but placed within a definite social context. In order to carry out these new editorial policies, the reorganization of the magazine had been carried through in terms of the "best way to fulfill our plans for relating it to communities beyond New York City"; for she wanted *New Challenge* to become the organ of regional groups composed of writers opposed to fascism, war, and general reactionary policies. She thought that other groups of writers, similar to those working at the time in Chicago, should be fostered by the magazine in order that regional contributing editors may make available to *New Challenge* young writers who were seriously concerned with the problems facing them "in their defense of existing culture and in their sincere creation of higher cultural values." Yet, the magazine would not adhere to the prescriptions of any one dogma, and it would ask "that the bigot and potential fascist keep away from our door." Its new directions were clearly set, but it would be "non-political"; it would not be subsidized by any political party nor receive huge contributions from individuals.

The special issue which was fashioned to represent these new editorial directions contained short stories written by Norman MacLeod, Benjamin Appel, Valdemar Hill, George B. Linn, and Clarence Hill. Poetry was contributed by Frank Marshall Davis, Sterling A. Brown, Owen Dodson, Charles Henri Ford, Robert Davis, and Margaret Walker.

Allyn Keith's article, "A Note on Negro Nationalism," and Eugene Holmes' essay, "Problems Facing the Negro Writer Today," implemented parts of the new editorial purposes. But Richard Wright's "Blueprint for Negro Writing" represents perhaps the most significant article which appeared during three years of the magazine's publication.

By the time the special issue of *New Challenge* appeared, most of Wright's revolutionary poetry had already been published in *Left Front, The Anvil, New Masses, Midland Left,* and *International Literature.* In an article in *The Daily Worker* (June 8, 1937) Wright elaborated upon the purposes of *New Challenge.* It would become a new audience of thousands of Negro workers and students and intellectuals who had been touched by recent social and economic changes. Most importantly, this new direction in writing would "contradict the Harlem School of expression which was complemented by the World War and post-war conditions" which he believed had been exploited in "publishing for the jaded appetites of New York Bohemians." The new movement among Negro writers "is receiving its stimulus from below rather than above," he wrote. For the first time in Negro history, he believed, such problems as nationalism in literature and the relation of Negro writer to politics and social movements which were formulated and discussed at the National Negro Congress in Chicago a year earlier would become the focus of a magazine.

In Washington, Memphis, and Detroit, Wright wrote, similar organizations were emerging to organize young writers on a plan similar to the purpose and structure of the John Reed Clubs which, he thought, "influenced so many young white writers during the previous seven years."

And although, the contributors would in the main be Negroes, white readers "dealing definitively with minority themes and depicting conditions of life common to the Negro people will be welcomed." That one of the most hopeful and profound symptoms of the new movement is the deep desire on the part of the Negro writers for unity and at the same time the alliance with all that is progressive in American life seemed to motivate Wright to associate himself actively with the new quarterly. Wright's article in *The Daily Worker* further amplified his proposal that *New Challenge* should become a significant organ for proletarian literature. Thus, his own "Blueprint for Negro Writing" becomes an important document in the development of an ethnic center for Black writers. Understandably, then, he dismissed previous Negro literature as "humble novels, poems, plays, prim and decorous ambassadors who went a-begging to white America"; which "entered the Court of American Public Opinion dressed in the knee-pants of servility, curtsying to show that the Negro was not inferior, that he was human, and that he had a life comparable to that of other people." Accordingly, white America never offered these Negro writers any serious criticism, and even the majority of literate Negroes looked upon this writing with pride when, in fact, the best of it was "something external to the lives of educated Negroes themselves." No Negro writers had taken advantage, in their literature, of the uniquely hard conditions of the life of the Negro worker, and in doing so they had actually lagged behind their own people's struggles for one another. A view of society as "something becoming rather than as something fixed and admiring" is the one which points the way for Negro writers to stand shoulder to shoulder with Negro workers in mood and outlook became an integral part of Wright's "blueprint." The inner resources for such writing lay mainly in the Negro church, and in the folklore of the people, he wrote.

Aspects of Negro life were to Wright, as sharply manifest in the social institutions of Negro people as in folklore—the Negro church, the Negro press, the Negro social world, the Negro sporting world, the Negro school system, the Negro professions—all of which make up a Negro world which, they did not ask for, but which provided a way for them to express themselves and adhere to this special way of life. Negro writers must accept the nationalist implications of their lives, not in order to encourage them, but in order to change and transcend them, he wrote.

Appearing, as it does, previous to his major successes as a writer, this essay becomes an important touchstone to the student of Richard Wright, but its analysis is not actually the purpose of this paper. Instead, the problem of giving the reasons for the sudden death of *New Challenge* becomes all the more interesting when one believes that Miss West willingly modified rather radically the purposes of her magazine in order to gain added stature for it by fashioning it into an organ of proletarian literature with Richard Wright, a high name on the horizon of developing Black writers, as her associate editor. Yet, the ambitious venture failed, and even the precarious publication of the magazine ceased altogether with this issue. Most of the Black writers whose works survived into the next generation were conspicuously absent from the list of contributors to the new quarterly, with the notable exception of the poems of Sterling Brown and Margaret Walker.

Most importantly, though, the history of the editorial policies of *Challenge* and the types of literary works it published gives rise to some interesting questions about the problems involved in prescribing trends for people's literature. For, quite possibly, the decision to enter into the John Reed Club pattern of conscious literature did not work out well with an editor who wanted to be able to continue a non-political magazine while, at the same time, it sought to implement Richard Wright's theory of racial literature. As a result of this experiment which failed, *Challenge* could no longer provide a publishing source for young Negro writers whose works the editor wanted to choose solely on the basis of their literary qualities and place them before a reading public.

## Note

1. *The Emergence of Richard Wright,* (University of Illinois Press, Urbana, 1973), p. 69.

## ABBY ARTHUR JOHNSON AND RONALD MABERRY JOHNSON (ESSAY DATE 1979)

**SOURCE:** Johnson, Abby Arthur and Ronald Maberry Johnson. "Black Renaissance: Little Magazines and Special Issues, 1916-1930." In *Propaganda and Aesthetics: The Literary Politics of Afro-American Magazines in the Twentieth Century,* pp. 65-96. Amherst: University of Massachusetts Press, 1979.

*In the following excerpt, Johnson and Johnson survey the small-scale African American periodicals and special issues that appeared after* The Crisis *had made its mark in 1916, addressing the ways in which these publications contributed to the Black cultural revolution in 1920s America.*

The first black little magazines of the twentieth century came immediately after *Crisis* had achieved financial independence from the NAACP. In November 1915, Du Bois announced that *Crisis* was solvent. In January 1916, the journal paid his entire salary, and all other operational expenses, for the first time. Two small black journals appeared shortly thereafter, as if the success of Du Bois had bolstered the confidence of others who wanted to start periodicals. *New Era* of Boston emerged in February and *Stylus* of Washington, D.C., in June of that year. Other black little magazines followed, as did Afro-American issues of essentially white periodicals, but they arrived after the war had ended and the postwar depression had eased. *Survey Graphic,* a journal published in New York and concerned broadly with social questions, featured in 1925 a special number on Harlem, its literature and its people. Established in Guadalajara, Mexico, a little poetry magazine called *Palms* published an issue devoted to Afro-American literature in 1926. The next year saw the first Afro-American number of the *Carolina Magazine,* a student publication at the University of North Carolina. Inspired by the quality and influence of that number, the students followed with a special issue of black literature in 1928 and also in 1929. The black little magazines began in Harlem with two radical and short-lived publications, *Fire* in 1926 and *Harlem* in 1928. More conservative Afro-American journals appeared elsewhere on the East Coast, as did *Black Opals* in Philadelphia during 1927 and 1928, and the *Saturday Evening Quill* in Boston during 1928 to 1930.

Pauline Hopkins came to the fore again with *New Era.* She established the journal because she sensed the beginning of "a really new era in America," and wanted to be part of that beginning. She did not succeed in addressing the contemporary scene, however, and the magazine collapsed after its first two issues of February and March. In the opening number, she introduced her compeers, saying "the roll of the staff presents a few familiar names, but for the most part we are as young in public life as is the new year."[1] The controlling voices came out of the past, though, for Hopkins was listed as editor and Walter Wallace, her colleague on the staff at *Colored American Magazine,* as managing editor. The contributors even included Sarah Allen, or Hopkins writing under the maiden name of her mother, her previous practice when she lowered her profile.

In both issues Hopkins elaborated on the functions of *New Era.* Her commentary indicates that she envisioned the journal in three roles: as an agitator for race rights, as an historian of race progress, and as a promoter of black literature and arts. Her accents rang as of old when she placed the journal firmly within the protest tradition: "We know that there are able publications already in the field, but the pang that has set our active world a-borning is the knowledge that the colored man has lost the rights already won because he was persuaded and then bullied into lying down and ceasing his fight for civil liberty."[2] Hopkins understood the importance of journals as preservers of tradition. As editor of *New Era* she voiced sentiments reminiscent of those expressed much earlier by Max Barber. "We are," she claimed, "sparing neither time nor money to make this Magazine the most authentic historian of the race's progress." She recognized the importance of black journals in providing an outlet for Afro-American writers. She promised, then, that *New Era* would "do its utmost to assist in developing the literature, science, music, art, religion, facts, fiction and tradition of the race throughout the world." In this connection, she hoped to establish a "Race Publishing House" in Boston which would "stand as a permanent and lasting monument of race progress."[3] Undoubtedly she envisioned the publishing house along the lines of the Colored Co-operative Publishing Company which had issued the *Colored American Magazine,* as well as books by and about blacks.

In many respects, the contents of *New Era* paralleled the contents of the *Colored American Magazine* when edited by Hopkins. *New Era* emphasized biography, with each issue featuring several sketches of prominent persons. Hopkins probably wrote all the sketches, those left unsigned as well as those carrying her name, because the pieces bore her stylistic idiosyncrasies, with didactic introductions and conclusions stressing the value of individual effort. She envisioned the biographical essays as a continuation of her earlier effort, as indicated in the February issue: "The series of sketches prepared by Miss Hopkins some years since on 'Famous Men of the Negro Race,' will have a worthy sequel in this series entitled 'Men of Vision.'"[4] She likewise planned a series on "sacrificing women" of the race, including Frances Harper, Sojourner Truth, and Harriet Tubman. As in the past, her favorite subjects were New Englanders, men like John Trowbridge whom she identified as the "Last of the Famous Group of New England Authors."[5]

She continued to feature fiction and verse. The table of contents for each issue noted two short stories and one poem, and then Hopkins went ahead and included several other creative pieces which were not announced. Foremost among the poets was William Stanley Braithwaite, whose "picture adorn[ed] our cover" for the February issue, and whose lyrics appeared in prominent positions in the March issue.[6] The most significant fiction came from Pauline Hopkins, who was engaged once again with a serialized novel, this time called "Topsy Templeton." She planned her effort to "run through several issues," and consequently readers never did learn what finally happened to Topsy. The first two installments were sufficient, however, to show that Hopkins had not changed as a creative writer. Once again she concentrated on interracial relations, in this story between the white Newbury sisters and Topsy, the little black girl they adopted. She ended the first episode with much suspense and an apparently dead Topsy. In the second issue, she revived a scene which had figured significantly in *Of One Blood,* serialized in *Colored American Magazine.* A physician having psychic powers recognizes Topsy's condition as "suspended animation" and "reanimates" her before some wondering colleagues and two very grateful Newbury sisters.[7]

Not all of the journal was a look backward. Hopkins had the foresight to include a regular column, headed "Helps for Young Artists," by the sculptor, Meta Warrick-Fuller, who was art editor for the journal. In her column, Fuller urged black artists to form groups in order to experiment with suggestions advanced in the column. By so doing, she became one of the first writers in a black journal to stress the need for such organization. Only Du Bois had preceded her, with his call one year earlier for Horizon clubs dedicated to Afro-American pageantry. Hopkins recognized the merit in Fuller's comments and encouraged involvement by announcing a prize to be awarded "to the individual or group of persons . . . who will have tried out any one or more of the instructions offered in this series."[8] The journal collapsed before the plans matured, but Hopkins nevertheless anticipated Du Bois and Charles S. Johnson who later realized the value of artistic competitions and prizes.

*New Era* went quietly. Du Bois never alluded to its demise in *Crisis,* but then he had never announced its initial appearance. He kept a fine eye on the press, so he probably knew about *New Era.* Most likely he did not welcome the magazine because he saw it as a potential rival to *Crisis.* He would not have criticized Hopkins because she had battled long and hard in the past for a free black press and for other concerns he himself endorsed. It would have been ungracious to express satisfaction over the failure of her later attempt with a magazine rivalling his own. And so Du Bois said nothing. No one else said much about the magazine either. As a result, it slipped out of memory, forgotten by editors and literary historians.[9]

Whereas much of *New Era* echoed the past, *Stylus* looked to the future. The support for the journal came in the winter of 1915-16, when Professors Alain Locke and Montgomery Gregory organized a literary society at Howard University. Called Stylus, the group included students, to be selected from biannual competitions, and several faculty and honorary members. From the beginning, members wanted to stimulate writing based on Afro-American culture and to encourage artistic expression in the black community, especially among youth. Gregory remembered that the society had "a vision, a vision which embodied in the not too distant future a Negro literature that should secure recognition along with that of other peoples."[10] The *Howard University Record* recalled in later years that the efforts of Stylus were not limited to Howard University, but that they extended "to the Negro race and to civilization." Benjamin Brawley noted that the organization "hoped to make a genuine contribution to racial advance."[11] To further their ends, Locke and associates issued a journal which bore the same name as the organization and which was the first purely literary magazine published at any black college. Appearing in June 1916, *Stylus* featured student efforts and special contributions by honorary members, such as Braithwaite, Brawley, and James Weldon Johnson.

World War I interrupted the work, sending Stylus members and supporters to distant parts. Efforts did not resume until peace returned and a handful of the former participants came back to campus. With that nucleus Professors Locke and Gregory attracted new student members, including Zora Neale Hurston, and additional honorary members, notably Charles W. Chesnutt, W. E. B. Du Bois, Alice Moore Dunbar, and Arthur A. Schomburg. The second number of *Stylus* appeared in May 1921.

In his "Foreword" to that issue, Montgomery Gregory voiced sentiments which would be echoed by New Negroes emerging in the latter half of the decade. "It becomes clearer daily," he stated, "that it must be through the things of the Spirit that we shall ultimately restore Ethiopia to her seat of honor among the races of the world. The Germans have amply demonstrated the futility of force to secure a place in the sun. Any individual or people must depend upon the universal appeal of art, literature, painting, and music—to secure the real respect and recognition of mankind." Gregory urged his colleagues onward with promise of better days ahead: "*The Stylus* is on the right track although like all bearers of Truth they are in a minority for a day. Theirs are the future years, rich with the promise of a fulfilment of the visions of those whose love for their race embraces humanity."[12] *Stylus* reserved further statements for future years. The third number, to be discussed later, did not appear until 1929.

Du Bois lent his name to *Stylus,* but he was not much impressed with the journal. He mentioned it only once in *Crisis,* and then with faint praise. "The poems of Otto Bohanan seem to be the only notable contributions," he asserted about the publication in 1916. Du Bois did not say so, but *Stylus* launched the careers of writers much more influential than Bohanan. Probably the most outstanding student published in the journal during its early years was Zora Hurston. In her autobiography, *Dust Tracks on a Road,* she traced her literary career from her involvement in the Howard group. She explained how Charles Johnson, who was then planning the first issue of *Opportunity,* read a short story of hers included in *Stylus* and asked her to contribute to his magazine. Hurston sent him "Drenched in Light," which he published. Later he published a second story, "Spunk," and counselled her to move to Harlem, which he considered the hub of literary activity. Hurston responded enthusiastically to his promptings: "So, beginning to feel the urge to write, I wanted to be in New York."[13] *Stylus* also served as the testing ground for Locke. From his editorial experience at Howard, he went on to involve himself in the more significant black journals of the 1920s. He related well to numerous, often conflicting groups and became the most ubiquitous Afro-American literary presence in that period.

The Harlem number of *Survey Graphic* appeared in March 1925, edited by Locke. Contemporaries applauded Locke for his role but then dickered over who gave Paul Kellogg, editor of the magazine, the idea for the issue. Du Bois claimed the credit for his own staff. At the Civic Club Dinner of March 21, 1924, he explained, Kellogg had sat next to Augustus Dill, business manager of *Crisis,* who acquainted him with those in attendance.

Then "it occurred to the editor of *The Survey*," wrote Du Bois, "that here was material for a *Survey Graphic*." Despite his own cautions, "still he hesitated and feared the 'social uplifters' of the United States with a mighty fear," he acted on the inspiration encouraged by Dill and went ahead with plans for the special issue.[14]

Charles S. Johnson saw it differently, as indicated in a speech made in 1955 at Howard University. He explained that Locke had written a series of important essays for *Opportunity,* variously entitled "The Black Watch on the Rhine" (1921), "Apropos of Africa" (1924), and "Back Stage on European Imperialism" (1925). Johnson found the essays so insightful that he offered to share publication with *Survey Graphic* in order to find them a larger audience. Kellogg gladly published the articles at hand and requested further essays from Locke. "Thus began," declared Johnson, "an important relationship with the editor of the *Survey* and *Survey Graphic*." At the Civic Club affair, which Johnson carefully distinguished as an *Opportunity* dinner, Kellogg asked Locke to edit an issue of *Graphic* which would "carry the entire evening's readings."[15] Johnson does deserve a large share of the credit, since ideas for the number originated during the occasion he had staged, and since the editor was the essayist he had introduced to Kellogg.

The catchword in the issue became "Harlem," with essays, stories, poems, and drawings considering life in that urban center. The cover of the number bore the designation, "Harlem: Mecca of the New Negro." In the lead editorial, entitled "Harlem," and in another article, Locke ascended the scale to near religious ecstasy, labeling the area "a race capital," "the sign and center of the renaissance of a people," and finally, "the home of the Negro's 'Zionism.'" In Harlem, he believed, "the masses" would lead black writers toward the making of a vital folk literature. "In a real sense," he noted, "it is the rank and file who are leading, and the leaders who are following. A transformed and transforming psychology permeates the masses."[16] With such an emphasis, Locke enunciated ideas which would become increasingly prevalent throughout the decade and which would emerge, recast, as dominant in the 1930s with the pronouncements of Richard Wright and others.

Locke reinforced his ideas with an essay by James Weldon Johnson, "The Making of Harlem"; an essay by Konrad Bercovici, "The Rhythm of Harlem"; with portraits by the German artist, Wi-nold Reiss, on "Harlem Types"; with seven well-wrought poems by Countee Cullen on "Harlem Life"; and with "The South Lingers On," sketches of life in Harlem by Rudolph Fisher. The south lingered in the new migrants, in Jake Crinshaw who came from "Jennin's Landin'," Virginia, in unsuccessful pursuit of work in Harlem, in Reverend Ezekiel Taylor who followed his congregation north—"But where were they?"—in a grandmother who thinks her Jutie has lost her soul in Harlem, "this city of Satan."[17]

Another slogan in the issue was "the New Negro." After "Harlem," the Table of Contents listed Locke's essay, "Enter the New Negro." Revised, the piece became the lead article in Locke's edition of *The New Negro*. "Enter the New Negro" illustrates the balanced prose and memorable phrases Locke used to capture the attention of his contemporaries. Gone, he declared, is the "Old Negro," who was more fiction than actuality: "The day of 'aunties,' 'uncles' and 'mammies' is equally gone. Uncle Tom and Sambo have passed on, and even the 'Colonel' and 'George' play barnstorm roles from which they escape with relief when the public spotlight is off. The popular melodrama has about played itself out, and it is time to scrap the fictions, garret the bogeys and settle down to a realistic facing of facts." The facts included a "younger generation . . . vibrant with a new psychology," a black population "awake" in a "new spirit." The awakened generation was conscious, he explained, of being "the advance-guard of the African peoples in their contact with Twentieth Century civilization."[18]

He wrote again about the New Negro in "Youth Speaks," an essay printed midway in the issue. In expanding upon his ideas, he entered headlong into the controversy over art and propaganda. He talked about literary pioneers—Du Bois, along with Chesnutt, Dunbar, James Weldon Johnson, Lucian Watkins, and others—and said they had spoken "for the Negro," meaning they had tried to interpret the race to others. The new generation wrote instead "as Negroes" and attempted to express the quality of Afro-American life to Afro-Americans. Thus had come "the happy release from self-consciousness, rhetoric, bombast, and the hampering habit of setting artistic values with primary regard for moral effect." Among the New Negroes were Rudolph Fisher, Willis Richardson, Eric Walrond, and the young poets published on the very next pages, including Countee Cullen, Langston Hughes, Claude McKay, and Jean Toomer.[19]

The issue featured a heady sampling of those influential in interracial circles. There were essays from Melville Herskovitz, the cultural anthropologist; Arthur Schomburg, who was establishing his collection of books on black history and culture; Walter White, who was assistant secretary of the NAACP. The number also included an essay by Charles S. Johnson, on "Black Workers and the City," and a piece by Du Bois, called "The Black Man Brings His Gifts." Du Bois used an ironic style, by then familiar to *Crisis* readers. He developed a story to illustrate the pretensions of some white midwesterners who believe they have the best of everything. "We've got a pretty fine town out here in middle Indiana," the white persona declares at the beginning of the story. When told of the contributions blacks had made to American life, she and her friends become huffy and shun the speakers, who include a white professor and an educated black woman. The persona confides to the reader that the ideas of the black speaker especially "made me sick and I turned and glared right at her."[20]

The Harlem number of *Survey Graphic* was important for several reasons. The issue sold over 40,000 copies, thereby establishing a circulation record which the magazine did not match until the 1940s. The number led immediately to Locke's *The New Negro*, which was published by Boni in the fall of 1925 as an expanded form of the issue. The book was also significant, considered by Charles S. Johnson to be the "standard volume of the period," "the portal to a new world of adventure."[21] The editors of *Messenger* praised the Harlem number of the magazine for something far less tangible, for "the spirit which gave it birth." They saw in it the sign of a new day, as expressed in an editorial for April 1925: "It marks an interesting turn in the attitude of intellectual white America toward the Negroes. It was planned by black and white intellectuals. This is as it should be." Writing much later, in his study of Paul Kellogg, Clarke Chambers emphasized the uniqueness of the magazine: "In focusing on the contributions rather than the problems of the American Negro, in stressing the constructive cultural advances emerging in Harlem, in using Negro authors and critics to set forth the truths of the Negro renaissance, the *Survey Graphic* was far ahead of its time. Other journals might publish sympathetic articles now and again, but the *Graphic*'s adventure stands alone as a classic account."[22]

The Harlem number was unique, but it did not stand alone in the 1920s. By its example, it encouraged other magazines to feature issues on black literature and life. In October 1926, Idella Purnell and her associate editor, Witter Bynner, published a special number of *Palms,* a poetry journal issued six times a year from Guadalajara.[23] The October table of contents carried this statement: "Countee Cullen is the editor of this issue of *Palms* which is entirely the work of Negro poets." The comment was apt in that the emphasis was on black poets rather than on black poetry. The writers included the best of the day: Lewis Alexander, Gwendolyn Bennett, Arna Bontemps, William Braithwaite, Countee Cullen, W. E. B. Du Bois, Jessie Fauset, Langston Hughes, Helene Johnson, and Bruce Nugent. Most of them wrote about love and nature, not about topics specifically pertinent to Afro-American readers. The first stanza of Du Bois's "Poem" did not, for example, run true to his customary ejaculations:

> O Star-kissed drifting from above,
> On misty moonbeams, sunshine shod,
> Dim daughter of the lips of God,
> To me and angels—Thou art Love!

Two other verses followed, one addressed to Life and the other to Truth.

There were exceptions in the issue, such as the other poem by Du Bois. In "The Song of America," Du Bois sounded a familiar theme, as a few lines from the persona, the U.S.A., indicate: "I writhe, I rave, / To chain the slave / I do the deed, I kill!" The most notable exception was "Black Madonna," by Albert Rice. The particular emphasis emerged clearly in the first two stanzas:

> Not as the white nations
>   know thee
>     O Mother!
>
> But swarthy of cheek
>   and full-lipped as the
>     child races are.[24]

Du Bois liked the composition so much that he published it, along with an announcement of the *Palms* issue, in the November 1926 *Crisis*. In the next number, he reprinted Braithwaite's "Age and Autumn," one of the best-crafted poems in the October *Palms*.

The special issue of *Palms* figures in the cultural renaissance of the 1920s. It publicized contemporary work with two timely essays: a discussion of "The Negro Renaissance" by Walter White, and a favorable review of Hughes's *The Weary*

*Blues,* by Alain Locke.[25] It encouraged the best from young writers with two poetry contests open to anyone who cared to apply. As announced in *Palms,* Langston Hughes won the Witter Bynner Undergraduate Poetry Prize Award for 1926, as well as the John Keats Prize one year later. In her *Opportunity* column, "Ebony Flute," Gwendolyn Bennett acknowledged Hughes's award and reminded readers that they could still enter the Witter Bynner competition for 1927. In retrospect she declared that "of no small importance was the Negro issue of *Palms.*"[26] The number not only provided further support for black writers, but it also indicated the widespread interest in Afro-American literature.

With their literary journal, *Carolina Magazine,* the students at the University of North Carolina gave further testimony to that interest. They published a "Negro Number" in May 1927, a "Negro Poetry Number" in May 1928, and a "Negro Play Number" in April 1929. The editors, who changed with each new year, received materials for each special issue from Lewis Alexander, a poet, an actor, and a member of both the Washington Saturday Nighters and the Quill Club of Boston. Alexander managed to include most writers who had been published in other black magazines and issues, save for Du Bois, who did not appear in any of the numbers. He clearly favored the efforts of Charles S. Johnson, whom he identified as the founder of *Opportunity,* "the ablest Negro journal in America." Johnson wrote the lead article, "The Negro Enters Literature," for the 1927 issue and one of the featured essays, "Jazz Poetry and Blues," for the 1928 number.[27] The lead article for the "Negro Poetry Number" of May 1928 was Alain Locke's "The Message of the Negro Poets."

The underlying theme in the essays of both Johnson and Locke was that New Negro poets had gained immeasurably by leaving the old propaganda emphases behind. Both men echoed statements they had made elsewhere. Locke's commentary, for example, recalled opinions he had asserted in *Survey Graphic* and made basic to *The New Negro*: "Yesterday it was the rhetorical flush of partisanship, challenged and on the defensive. This was the patriotic stage through which we had to pass. Nothing is more of a spiritual gain in the life of the Negro than the quieter assumption of his group identity and heritage; and contemporary Negro poetry registers this incalculable artistic and social gain."[28]

Some of the plays, stories, and poems included characters and situations which would not have been acceptable to Du Bois or others concerned with respectability. "The Hunch," a play by Eulalie Spence, gave a lesson in the numbers game:

MRS. REED. Ah dream Ed an' me—Ed's mah fus husband—Ah dream Ed an' me was lyin' in bed—

MITCHELL. Is he dead?

MRS. REED. Bin dead five years.

MITCHELL. That's 9.

MRS. REED. The door opened an' in walks Joe, mah secon' husban'—Lookin' mad tuh kill.

MITCHELL. Is he dead, too?

MRS. REED. Yeah. Died las' year.

MITCHELL. That's 2. Your number's 295. Play the combination an' yuh can't lose.[29]

Hughes, represented by several poems, wrote about a "Boy" who preferred to be "a sinner . . . and go to hell," about a "Boy on Beale Street" who lost his dream in "dice and women / And jazz and booze," and about an "African Dancer in Paris" who traded her native lover "for coins of gold." Waring Cuney sang the blues about "Once Bad Gal":

Ah'd go straight if
Ah thought Ah could,
Say Ah'd go straight
If Ah thought Ah could,
But a once bad gal
Can't never be good.[30]

Alexander put together the special issues by relying extensively on prizewinning literature from the *Crisis* and especially the *Opportunity* literary contests. The May 1927 number carried such pieces from *Opportunity* in each of the major genres: Arthur Huff Fauset's "Symphonesque" had placed first in the short story section for 1926; Helene Johnson's "Fulfillment" was first honorable mention in the poetry division for the same year; and Spence's "The Hunch" took second place in the 1927 drama competition. The editorial for the April 1929 issue identified the playwrights—Eulalie Spence, Willis Richardson, John F. Matheus, and May Miller—by their previous success: "All won prizes in *The Crisis* and *Opportunity* contests." In the same number, Alexander reflected on the meaning of those competitions, since they had by then ceased. "The contests and prizes offered reassured the race writers that it was worth while," he explained; "for some of them . . . had been writing a decade or more with little or no attention at all. The new spirit of the contests reincarnated the old writers and moved aspiring young dreamers to take up their pens and write."[31]

*Crisis* never acknowledged the compliment. In the November 1929 issue, Du Bois simply mentioned the drama number and then added that it included a drawing by Aaron Douglas "done for *The Crisis* and reprinted without credit." *Opportunity* responded graciously, with several laudatory reviews of the special issues. In June and July of 1927, Countee Cullen and Gwendolyn Bennett wrote in a similar vein about North Carolina University and the black number for that year. Cullen, in June, called the school and its journal "oases in that barren land," while Bennett praised the institution for its "fine liberality of thought." By July, both had recognized the number as a pioneering effort. Cullen spoke at greater length than Bennett, saying the May *Carolina Magazine* was "a number of historical importance in race relations in this country. For the first time, as it were, in the time of man, a Southern university magazine has given over one of its numbers to the work of Negro writers."[32]

Cullen was particularly impressed because he recalled an ugly episode he had written about in the December 1926 installment of "Dark Tower." He had noted that Julian Starr and R. K. Fowler, "erstwhile" editors of *Carolina Magazine,* had been "deposed" in 1926 for publishing a story having a white girl and a mulatto as principal characters. The incident had seemed, to Cullen, an immense step backward: "And this just after we had been turning double somersaults and triple handsprings because that same issue carried a sketch by Eric Walrond, along with a pronunciamento asking for contributions from people of all races, colors, creeds, and political leanings!"[33]

For some time, there had been students and teachers at North Carolina University interested in black literature and folklore. The special numbers of *Carolina Magazine* stressed this interest, describing it as part of a rich cultural legacy. The dedication to the May 1928 number called it "fitting" that the journal should feature black poetry. One of the earliest Afro-American poets, George Horton, had been a familiar figure on campus, and one of the New Negroes represented in the issue, Donald Hayes, was a native of Raleigh, North Carolina. In the April 1929 number, Lewis Alexander stated that "it is quite fitting" for the magazine to emphasize black drama, "for the University of North Carolina, thru [sic] its organization The Carolina Playmakers has done more for the development of the folk play in America than any other University." He urged students at North Carolina to remain true to the example set by Paul Green, a native North Carolinian who wrote *In Abraham's Bosom*; Professor Howard Odum, who edited the *Journal of Social Forces,* which was published at the University and which included several timely articles on black culture; and, among others, Newman I. White and Walter C. Jackson, editors of the *Anthology of Verse by American Negroes* published by Trinity College Press of Durham, North Carolina.[34]

Much of the excitement of the period appears in the black little magazines, which came in the second half of the 1920s, as did the special issues from journals with white management. The little magazines represented a new stage in the evolution of Afro-American culture. In the past, political and organizational concerns had dominated purely literary interests. After World War I the emerging generation sensed opportunities never seriously considered by earlier generations, partly because of the groundwork done by the NAACP and the NUL. To many New Negroes it seemed no very difficult matter to launch an entirely new type of black periodical, one concerned primarily with the arts. In November 1926, Wallace Thurman broke with tradition and issued *Fire.* As the first black magazine that was both independent and essentially literary, *Fire* deserves a place in surveys of American cultural history. It has been excluded from most studies of the 1920s, however, and mentioned only briefly in the others. Nathan Huggins, for example, took just two paragraphs to label *Fire* as a "short-lived" journal, one of "Harlem's attempts" at a little magazine.[35] One of the few to comment at length and with insight about the journal is Langston Hughes, who discussed it in *Big Sea* and in an article published later.

In his recollections he paused fondly over memories of Sugar Hill, in Harlem. At 409 Edgecombe, the address of the "tallest apartment house" on the hill, lived Walter and Gladys White, who gave frequent parties for their friends; Aaron and Alta Douglas, who "always had a bottle of ginger ale in the ice box for those who brought along refreshments"; Elmer Anderson Carter, who succeeded Charles S. Johnson as editor of *Opportunity*; and actor Ivan Sharpe and his wife Evie. Just below the hill, in the Dunbar Apartments, lived W. E. B. Du Bois as well as E. Simms Campbell, the cartoonist. Nearby was Dan Burley, a black journalist and a boogie-woogie piano player. Hughes recalled the excitement of those days: "Artists and writers were always running into each other on Sugar Hill and talking over their problems" and the ways to fellowships and grants from benevolent organizations. One evening, Hughes and six friends gathered in the Aaron Douglas apartment and made plans for a literary magazine. Hughes remembered their motives, saying generally that they wanted "to express" themselves "freely and independently—without interference from old heads, white or Negro," and specifically that they hoped "to provide . . . an outlet for publishing not existing in the hospitable but limited pages of *The Crisis* or *Opportunity*." They readily divided responsibilities for the new magazine, establishing Wallace Thurman as editor, Aaron Douglas as artist and designer, John P. Davis as business manager, and Gwendolyn Bennett, Zora Hurston, Bruce Nugent, and Hughes as the other board members.

They selected *Fire* as a title because, in Hughes's words, they desired to "*épater le bourgeois,* to burn up a lot of the old stereotyped Uncle Tom ideas of the past. . . ."[36] Hughes did not expand further on the meaning of the name, which merits brief examination. It represented a significant contrast with the quieter labels, such as "Colored American Magazine" and "Voice of the Negro," appearing in earlier generations. It broke as well with the import of "Crisis," which suggested that a crucial moment must be met, and "Opportunity," which implied that possibilities were at hand for the observant black. *Fire!!* with two exclamation marks in the full title, sounded an alarm that the old way would be destroyed in preparation for a new world.

The group was confident, even though members had little money of their own and no benefactors in sight. They planned to share expenses, with each of the seven contributing an initial fifty dollars. The bills mounted quickly as the board selected an expensive format. Hughes noted that "only the best cream-white paper would do on which to print our poems and stories. And only a rich crimson jacket on de luxe stock would show off well the Aaron Douglas cover design." As it turned out, Thurman became responsible for the expenses since he, with a job at *World Tomorrow*, was the only one who had steady although hardly profitable employment. Thurman wrote to Hughes that "*Fire* is certainly burning me,"[37] and Hughes wondered how the number ever left the printer's office, "how Thurman was able to persuade the printer to release the entire issue to us

on so small an advance payment." The available funds went to the printer, thereby leaving no money for advertising or distributing the journal. The board hoped that the magazine would quickly attract a loyal constituency who would assure solvency and a second number. They quietly asked for help on the first page of the issue: "Being a non-commercial product interested only in the arts, it is necessary that we make some appeal for aid from interested friends. For the second issue of FIRE we would appreciate having fifty people subscribe ten dollars each, and fifty more to subscribe five dollars each. We make no eloquent or rhetorical plea. FIRE speaks for itself."[38]

After November 1926, *Fire* never reappeared. "When the editorial board of *Fire* met again, we did not plan a new issue," Hughes narrated, "but emptied our pockets to help poor Thurman whose wages were being garnished weekly because he had signed for the printer's bills." Thurman's wages continued to be "garnished" for three or four more years, even after "the bulk of the whole issue" burned to ashes in the basement of the apartment in which it was stored.[39]

The end was ironic, particularly because fire had been the unifying metaphor in the periodical. Thurman autographed special copies with "Flamingly, Wallace Thurman." The "Foreword," with its provocative challenge, established the dominant motif:

> FIRE . . . flaming, burning, searing, and penetrating far beneath the superficial items of the flesh to boil the sluggish blood.
>
> FIRE . . . a cry of conquest in the night, warning those who sleep and revitalizing those who linger in the quiet places dozing.
>
> FIRE . . . melting steel and iron bars, poking livid tongues between stone apertures and burning wooden opposition with a cackling chuckle of contempt.
>
> FIRE . . . weaving vivid, hot designs upon an ebon bordered loom and satisfying pagan thirst for beauty unadorned . . . the flesh is sweet and real . . . the soul an inward flush of fire. . . . Beauty? . . . flesh on fire—on fire in the furnace of life blazing. . . .
>
> Fy-ah,
> Fy-ah, Lawd,
> Fy-ah gonna burn ma soul![40]

The poetry section announced itself with the title from Countee Cullen's poem and appeared as "Flame From the Dark Tower." The issue concluded with "A Department of Comment" by Thurman, called "Fire Burns."

Thurman indicated the literary aesthetic behind the magazine in his comments. He began by recalling his controversial review of *Nigger Heaven,* published two months earlier in *Messenger.* Instead of being honored with a statue on 135th Street and Seventh Avenue, he explained, Van Vechten had become a likely candidate for a lynching. The wheel would revolve in a few years and Van Vechten, he predicted, would then be "spoken of as a kindly gent rather than as a moral leper." For the time being, Thurman ridiculed the detractors of *Nigger Heaven* and cried freedom for black writers: "Any author preparing to write about Negroes in Harlem or anywhere else . . . should take whatever phases of their life that seem the most interesting to him, and develop them as he please."[41]

As author and editor, Thurman was primarily interested in aspects of black life generally considered disreputable by the more proper Afro-Americans, as his inclusions in *Fire* indicate. The three short stories featured characters falling far short of standards dear to the bourgeoisie, both black and white. "Cordelia the Crude: A Harlem Sketch," by Thurman, followed directly after the table of contents and Bruce Nugent's drawing of a naked African woman. The story traces the development of "a fus' class chippie," from the italicized first word of the opening sentence: "*Physically,* if not mentally, Cordelia was a potential prostitute, meaning that although she had not yet realized the moral import of her wanton promiscuity nor become mercenary, she had, nevertheless, become quite blasé and bountiful in the matter of bestowing sexual favors upon persuasive and likely young men." Later in the issue came Gwendolyn Bennett's "Wedding Day," which portrays the unsuccessful relationship between a black boxer and a white prostitute; and Zora Hurston's "Sweat," which tells the tragic end of Sykes, a loafer who loses everything, including his life, because of an obsession with fat black women: "Gawd! how Ah hates skinny wimmen!"[42]

The number also included the first part of a novel, "Smoke, Lilies and Jade," by Bruce Nugent writing under the pseudonym of Richard Bruce. In his narration, Nugent detailed the amours of bisexual black artist Alex, known to his male lover Adrian (alias Beauty) as Duce. One scene, involving an interracial relationship, particularly violated the sensibilities of the middle class on both sides of the color line: "Alex ran his hand through Beauty's hair . . . Beauty's lips pressed hard against his teeth . . . Alex trembled . . . could feel Beauty's body . . . close against his . . . hot . . . tense . . . white . . . and soft . . . soft . . . soft. . . ."[43] No other black literary magazine had previously included an explicit portrayal of a homosexual affair.

The poetry section, headed by Cullen's "From the Dark Tower," included "Elevator Boy," a controversial poem by Langston Hughes. The selection bothered many, because the protagonist showed no evidence of the American work ethic: "I been runnin' this / Elevator too long. / Guess I'll quit now." "Flame From the Dark Tower" featured other poets worthy of comment, such as Lewis Alexander, Arna Bontemps, Waring Cuney, Helene Johnson, and Edward Silvera. Alexander contributed two poems, one of them about a prostitute ironically called "Little Cinderella," a girl who did not wait for her prince:

> Look me over, kid!
> I knows I'm neat,—
> Little Cinderella from head to feet.
> Drinks all night at Club Alabam,—
> What comes next I don't give a damn! . . .[44]

Reaction to *Fire* was mixed. As Hughes noted, the white-owned press largely ignored the journal. An exception was *Bookman,* which reviewed the periodical in November 1926. In *Big Sea,* Hughes called that appraisal "excellent," an adjective he wisely removed from his subsequent discussion of the same material. The *Bookman* review shifted in tone, telling blacks first to lift themselves into the middle class by their own bootstraps and then suggesting that Afro-American writing should be separate and distinct from "American literature." The anonymous author, perhaps editor John Farrar, initially commended *Fire* for appearing "at a time when the Negro shows ominous signs of settling down to become a good American." He continued: "As the Negro begins more and more to measure up to the white yardstick of achievement, he will gain a merited position in American society." By his conclusion, the reviewer was complimenting *Fire* for encouraging "separate but equal" in the arts: "It is to be hoped that he [the black writer] will find in this new Negro quarterly the thing he needs to keep his artistic individuality."[45]

*Fire* brought a greater response from black magazines and reviewers. *Opportunity* endorsed the journal enthusiastically, as it did the other black little magazines of the period. Cullen, in the January 1927 issue of "Dark Tower," suggested that the journal would offend only the unsophisticated: "There seems to have been a wish to shock

PUBLISHING AND PERIODICALS

in this first issue, and, though shock-proof our-selves, we imagine that the wish will be well real-ized among the readers of *Fire.*" He called the journal "the outstanding birth of the month" and looked to the future with anticipation: "This sort of success," particularly the contributions of Hur-ston and Aaron Douglas, "augurs good for the development of Negro artists." Gwendolyn Ben-nett wrote in the same month, with the same opinion as Cullen's, but with more temperate phrasing. She undoubtedly felt constrained in us-ing her position at *Opportunity* to trumpet her concerns elsewhere. Thus, she simply defined *Fire* as "the new literary venture of the newer Ne-groes," and as a quarterly which had been "hailed with enthusiasm." She kept silent about her own involvement in the journal. "To Wallace Thur-man goes the praise for the editorship of this first number," she declared.[46]

*Crisis* did not have so much to say about *Fire.* Hughes claimed that "Dr. Du Bois in the *Crisis* roasted it," although he provided no supporting quotation. Hughes remembered inexactly, prob-ably because he and others had wanted and ex-pected Du Bois to respond with indignation. "As we had hoped—even though it contained no four-letter words as do today's little magazines—the Negro bourgeoisie were shocked by *Fire,*" Hughes recalled. In his January 1927 review of the maga-zine, Du Bois showed that he was still capable of surprising contemporaries who tried to push him to the periphery of artistic circles. He graciously accepted the magazine: "We acknowledge the receipt of the first number of *Fire* 'devoted to Younger Negro Artists.'" He praised the format and the contributions by Douglas: "It is strikingly illustrated by Aaron Douglas and is a beautiful piece of printing." And he even endorsed the publication: "We bespeak for it wide support."[47]

Some unexpected criticism came later in the year from Alain Locke, who reviewed the maga-zine in *Survey,* August 15-September 15, 1927. Ever the diplomat, Locke commended before he corrected. He began with a statement which would please Thurman and the others, saying that with *Fire,* "the youth section of the New Negro movement has marched off in a gay and self-confident manoeuver of artistic secession." "Ob-vious artistic cousins" of the journal were, he observed, the *Little Review,* edited by Margaret Anderson, and the *Quill,* a magazine of Greenwich Village. Then he came to the sore point. True, *Fire* was "a charging brigade of literary revolt, espe-cially against the bulwarks of Puritanism," but it raised the wrong standard. Simply put, *Fire* ex-ceeded Locke's limits: "If Negro life is to provide a healthy antidote to Puritanism, and to become one of the effective instruments of sound artistic progress, its flesh values must more and more be expressed in the clean, original, primitive but fundamental terms of the senses and not, as too often in this particular issue of *Fire,* in hectic imitation of the 'naughty nineties' and effete echoes of contemporary decadence."[48]

The commentary appeared eight months after Hughes had sent his own bemused reactions to bourgeois readers in a note to Locke, dated De-cember 28, 1926. He chortled over the review in the *Afro-American,* especially the part saying that at least Locke had been left out of the magazine. Under the heading, "Writer Brands *Fire* as Ef-feminate Tommyrot," Rean Graves of the Balti-more *Afro-American* had declared: "I have just tossed the first issue of *Fire*—into the fire, and watched the cackling flames leap and snarl as though they were trying to swallow some repul-sive dose."[49]

Benjamin Brawley provided the most hostile review in "The Negro Literary Renaissance," pub-lished in the April 1927 issue of the *Southern Work-man.* He did not believe black writers and artists were undergoing any especial awakening, even though promise was shown in the efforts of Claude McKay, Jean Toomer, Eric Walrond, and Walter White. The sign of the times appeared in jazz, "a perverted form of music," and in *Fire,* a magazine he considered the work of decadent loafers, not artists at all. By way of example, he quoted a passage from "Smoke, Lilies and Jade." "I certainly hope the compositor will set it up exactly as we give it to him," he added:

> he wondered why he couldn't find work . . . a job . . . when he had first come to New York he had . . . and he had only been fourteen then was it because he was nineteen now that he felt so idle . . . and contented . . . or because he was an art-ist . . . but was he an artist . . . was one an artist until one became known . . . of course he was an artist . . . and strangely enough so were all his friends . . . he should be ashamed that he didn't work . . . but . . . was it five years in New York . . . or the fact that he was an artist . . .

About "Cordelia the Crude," he claimed it "ought not to have been written, to say nothing of being published"; about Hughes's "Elevator Boy," he "submit[ted] simply that the running of an elevator is perfectly honorable employment and that no one with such a job should leave it until he is reasonably sure of getting something better." The last paragraph expended on *Fire* gave

324

HARLEM RENAISSANCE: A GALE CRITICAL COMPANION, VOL. 1

his summary comment: "About this unique periodical the only thing to say is that if Uncle Sam ever finds out about it, it will be debarred from the mails."[50]

Thurman commented on the outrage over *Fire* in "Negro Artists and the Negro," an essay published in the August 1927 number of *New Republic*. He explained, essentially, that the more conservative readers had been shocked once too often, first by *Nigger Heaven* and then by *Fine Clothes to the Jew*, "a hard, realistic" volume of poems by Hughes. The latter book appeared when "Negroes were still rankling" from *Nigger Heaven* and thereby uncovered "a store of suppressed invective that not only lashed Mr. Van Vechten and Mr. Hughes, but also the editors and contributors to *Fire*." The magazine was "experimental," noted Thurman, who went on to define the term for those confused about the magazine: "It was not interested in sociological problems or propaganda. It was purely artistic in intent and conception. Its contributors went to the proletariat rather than to the bourgeoisie for characters and material." Unlike Jessie Fauset and Walter White, those contributors were interested in black Americans, not Negroes who were "totally white American in every respect save color of skin."[51]

As the ashes settled, some of the younger writers began to think of a new journal. And thus Zora Hurston turned to Alain Locke, whose reputation survived intact from the *Fire* controversy. In a letter to him, dated October 11, 1927, she touched on the past lightly, saying *Fire* had been a good idea which failed for lack of "better management." In surveying the present, she reiterated complaints heard previously about *Crisis* and *Opportunity*, that they were "house organ[s]" of political groups and were consequently "in literature" only "on the side." Before soliciting his aid, she asked him a rhetorical question: "Dont you think . . . that it is not good that there should be only two outlets for Negro fire?" She followed with another question, posing an intriguing triumvirate: "Why cant our triangle—Locke—Hughes—Hurston do something with you at the apex?" She concluded with a statement which flattered but which also gave testimony to Locke's influence among diverse literary circles: "I am certain that you can bind groups with more ease than any other man in America." "Will you think it over?" she added.[52]

The "triangle" never did get together. Locke had too many responsibilities with his writing and his work at Howard, which included sponsorship of *Stylus*, a magazine needing some atten-

tion. Hughes was no longer interested, for the demise of *Fire* had educated him in the ways of literary periodicals: "That taught me a lesson about little magazines. But since white folks had them, we Negroes thought we could have one, too. But we didn't have the money." And then a member outside the threesome was already setting the basis for another journal.

After the collapse of *Fire*, Thurman "laughed a long bitter laugh," Hughes remembered, and set to work again.[53] Determined to avoid problems that had ended *Fire*, he planned for a journal that both looked professional and lasted. He secured an office on Seventh Avenue and peopled it with young writers who wanted to handle the business affairs of the journal. He kept the managing board small, with himself as editor of the magazine, Aaron Douglas as art editor, and S. Pace Alexander as managing editor. He tried to repair communication with influential persons disturbed by *Fire*. In a letter of October 3, 1928, sent on *Harlem* letterhead stationery, he asked Locke to support the venture with a short article "of some kind" for the first number. He assured Locke that *Harlem* would be no *Fire*. He described the effort as a "general magazine," with all types of literature, creative and critical, and for all kinds of people: "We are not confining ourselves to any group either of age or race." The journal would, though, fill a gap left by the larger race journals: "*The Crisis* and *The Messenger* are dead. *Opportunity* is dying. Voila here comes *Harlem*, independent, fearless and general, trying to appeal to all." Thurman had not fully considered his plans, as his unlikely conjunction of "fearless" with "general" indicated. Of one matter, however, he was sure: "I am mighty glad of the chance to be able to edit a magazine and let someone else worry about the financial end, in fact, after *Fire*, that is the only way I would ever venture forth again."

Locke responded with a letter dated October 8. He was "committed" to the new magazine, he said, because "dear friends," whom he did not specify, were promoting it. Then, too, he agreed with Thurman over the need for an "independent journal—especially a journal that will recognize that there is more than one side to most issues." He would contribute to the first issue with an article called "Art or Propaganda,—Which?"[54]

Thurman carefully organized the one and only issue of *Harlem*, published in November 1928. He alternated the essays, which explicitly indicated the focus of the magazine, with poems, stories, and illustrations. As if to emphasize the contrast between *Harlem* and his previous little magazine, he started the issue with a political discussion he had solicited from Walter White. At the onset of his essay, "For Whom Shall the Negro Vote?" White quoted from Thurman's letter to him, which had asked for an examination of "the dilemma of Negro voters today—surveying the attitude of the old guard toward loyalty to the Republican party and the attitude of another group which is openly advocating a bolt from the traditional party of our fathers." In his analysis, White adopted a moderate, well-balanced tone, seemingly in keeping with Thurman's approach to his new journal. He acknowledged great inadequacies in Al Smith and Herbert Hoover, candidates for the United States presidency, but he did not call for new political parties. Seeing that black voters held a balance of power in about ten states, he urged them to "trade ballots for justice," to make white candidates listen to the needs of black people.[55]

After the political discussion came artistic considerations, including a story by Hughes, a poem by Helene Johnson, and the essay from Locke. With diplomacy, Locke considered the most debatable aesthetic matter of the times, and from the opening sentence: "Artistically it is the one fundamental question for us today,—Art or Propaganda. Which?" The query was rhetorical to anyone who had read Locke's earlier pronouncements. He asserted that "After Beauty, let Truth come into the Renaissance picture,—a later cue, but a welcome one." He distinguished between truth and propaganda, saying that the latter is monotonous and that it encourages feelings of "group inferiority even in crying out against it." Metaphors followed theory, with Locke comparing Afro-American propagandists with "too many Jeremiahs" occupying too much "drab wilderness." He likened the larger black journals to Jeremiahs and the black little magazines to David, confronting the Philistines with confidence and with "five smooth pebbles." He thought *Harlem* could be a most valuable magazine if it developed as "a sustained vehicle of free and purely artistic expression."[56]

The editorial came midway in the issue, after Locke had calmly discussed the matter of art and propaganda. Thurman considered the same issue in a basically similar way, echoing some of Locke's imagery and much of his approach. He sketched the history of black magazines, beginning with "the old propagandistic journals," such as *Crisis, Opportunity,* and *Messenger,* which had served their day but were "emotionally unprepared to serve a new day and a new generation." They had

been "Jeremiahs," either "alarmed and angry," or "weeping and moaning." All they could offer the aspiring young writer was an occasional page, "but the artist was not satisfied to be squeezed between jeremiads or have his work thrown haphazardly upon a page where there was no effort to make it look beautiful as well as sound beautiful." The only recourse, until the latter 1920s, was the white press. Few blacks, though, would continually buy "white magazines" in order to read an occasional poem or story by an Afro-American writer.[57]

In 1926, *Fire* seemed to herald a new era. As Thurman remembered, it "was the pioneer of the movement. It flamed for one issue and caused a sensation the like of which had never been known in Negro journalism before." Wisely, he did not elaborate on the "sensation" but went on to credit more moderate magazines which had since developed—*Black Opals* in Philadelphia, "a more conservative yet extremely worthwhile venture," and the *Saturday Evening Quill* in Boston, published by and for members of a literary group. These little magazines had problems, however, as Thurman so well recalled: "The art magazines, unsoundly financed as they were, could not last."

With *Harlem,* Thurman thought he had the formula for success. He would lower his own profile, become relaxed, genial, tolerant. The magazine "enters the field without any preconceived editorial prejudices, without intolerance, without a reformer's cudgel," he told readers. He stated his goal with modesty, saying the journal "wants merely to be a forum in which all people's opinions may be presented intelligently and from which the Negro can gain some universal idea of what is going on in the world of thought and art."[58] He subtitled the magazine, "A Forum of Negro Life."

Thurman was not so balanced in his other contributions which appeared later in the number, after poems by Georgia Douglas Johnson, Alice Dunbar Nelson, and Effie Lee Newsome, a story by George Little, and essays by Theophilus Lewis and Bruce Nugent. When tucked into the back of the issue, Thurman felt free to be outspoken and controversial. He attacked the aesthetics of Du Bois in a review ostensibly directed towards *The Walls of Jericho,* by Rudolph Fisher, and *Quicksand,* by Nella Larsen. In the opening paragraph, he recalled that Du Bois had criticized Fisher in *Crisis* for not portraying the people he knew best, the "better class Negroes." Thurman had "chanced" upon the review, which "set my teeth on edge and sent me back to my typewriter hopping mad." He thought Du Bois ought to have known better, to have realized that "the entire universe is the writer's province." Du Bois had served his race "so well," asserted Thurman, "that the artist in him has been stifled in order that the propagandist may thrive." Thurman also came to the next novelist through a consideration first of Du Bois: "The author of *Quicksand* no doubt pleases Dr. Du Bois for she stays in her own sphere and writes about the sort of people one can invite to one's home without losing one's social prestige."[59]

Thurman was unrestrained in the "Harlem Directory: Where To Go And What To Do When in Harlem," included among the advertisements in the last pages. The initial line, with its neat parallelism, surely offended the same persons shocked by *Fire.* "There are four main attractions in Harlem," he announced with some glee: "the churches, the gin mills, the restaurants, and the night clubs," which he considered in order. He went for the exotic in churches, listing first the "largest congregations" and mentioning then "a great number of Holy Roller refuges, the most interesting of which is at 1 West 137th Street." Prohibition had made the "gin mills" more appealing, if anything: "As a clue to those of our readers who might be interested we will tell them to notice what stands on every corner on 7th, Lenox, and 8th Avenues. There are also many such comfort stations in the middle of the blocks." The most attractive night clubs, he said, were best seen in company "with some member on the staff of *Harlem.*" "Only the elect and the pure in heart are admitted to these places," he explained.[60]

Perceptive readers would have detected the old Thurman not only in the last part of *Harlem* but also in the stories and poems included throughout the issue. Hughes contributed three poems dealing with drunkenness, boredom, and jazz, and a short story called "Luani of the Jungles," which portrays the fatal attraction between a white European man and a black African woman. The other short stories offered pictures no more appealing to the black bourgeoisie. Roy de Coverly's "Holes" and George W. Little's "Two Dollars" both consider prostitution and murder. Only George Schuyler offered a respectable character in "Woof," a story about the courageous and commanding First Sergeant William Glass of Company H, Twenty-fifth U.S. Infantry.

Thurman had planned succeeding issues of *Harlem.* With this in mind, he challenged readers to support his effort. In the last page of his editorial he wrote: "It now remains to be seen whether the Negro public is as ready for such a publication as the editors and publishers of *Harlem* believe it to be."[61] He gave further evidence of his plans at the end of the journal, when he listed prominent writers who had been asked to contribute to future issues, such as Heywood Broun, a columnist for the New York *Telegram* and the *Nation*; Clarence Darrow, "noted liberal and attorney"; Eugene Gordon, editor of the *Saturday Evening Quill*; Charles Johnson, former editor of *Opportunity*; Claude McKay, author of *Home to Harlem*; H. L. Mencken, editor of the *American Mercury*; and Frank Alvah Parsons, President of the New York Schools of Fine and Applied Arts.

As a literary editor, Thurman failed once again. In part he himself was responsible, since he had not been able to develop a magazine sufficiently different from *Fire.* Thurman had a bad name with many readers, who merely shook their heads knowingly when they saw his book review, his tips on the town, and his friends sandwiched in among more respectable contributors. It was not in Thurman to edit a truly "general magazine." He had an uncontrollable urge toward controversy, of a type which readers were not buying, especially in the face of the Great Depression. In 1932, upon the appearance of Thurman's *Infants of the Spring,* Theophilus Lewis wrote that *Fire* and *Harlem* came to their end for financial reasons. "It was a lack of money," he explained, "not a dearth of merit which caused the . . . magazines to disappear."[62] Lewis did not elaborate. Thurman lacked funds because times were hard, especially for Afro-Americans, but also because he was too outspoken to attract the type of support he needed.

Lewis was one of the few to note the demise of *Harlem.* Contemporary responses were negligible, with neither *Crisis* nor *Opportunity* venturing a comment. So many enterprises were collapsing in those days that another unsuccessful attempt by Thurman raised few eyebrows. Lewis covered essentially new ground in 1932, when he reviewed Thurman's editorial career for the New York *Journal and Guide.* The title of the piece reflects the reputation Thurman had acquired: "Wallace Thurman Adores Brown Women Who Have Beauty Mark On Shoulder; Prefers Sherry To Gin." As an editor, Thurman went from the *Outlet* in Los Angeles, to five periodicals in New York—*Looking Glass, Messenger, World Tomorrow, Fire,* and *Harlem.* The first magazine had been his most successful, wrote Lewis, because it lasted for six months. Editorial longevity remained his dream, as Lewis added: "His ambition, he says, is to be the editor of a financially secure magazine."[63]

The ambition went unmet. Disillusioned by the loss of *Harlem,* Thurman never again attempted a literary journal, and he became more and more convinced that the black renaissance had failed. In *Infants of the Spring,* he compared the 1920s to a scene at a drunken party. Raymond, who represents Thurman in this novel, describes the situation: "Whites and blacks clung passionately together as if trying to effect a permanent merger. Liquor, jazz music, and close physical contact had achieved what decades of propaganda had advocated with little success." Raymond concludes that "this . . . is the Negro renaissance, and this is about all the whole damn thing is going to amount to." Through his protagonist, Thurman also reevaluated some of the main figures of the period. He reserved gentle satire for Alain Locke, who "played mother hen to a brood of chicks, he having appointed himself guardian angel to the current set of younger Negro artists."[64]

## Notes

1. "Announcement and Prospectus of the *New Era Magazine,*" and "Editorial and Publisher's Announcements," *New Era Magazine* 1 (February 1916): 3, 60.

2. "Editorial and Publisher's Announcements," Ibid., p. 60.

3. "Editorial and Publisher's Announcements," *New Era Magazine* 1 (March 1916): 124; "Announcement and Prospectus of the *New Era Magazine,*" p. 1.

4. "Announcement and Prospectus of the *New Era Magazine,*" p. 4.

5. "Editorial and Publisher's Announcements," and "John Trowbridge," *New Era Magazine* 1 (March 1916): 124, 112.

6. "William Stanley Braithwaite," *New Era Magazine* 1 (February 1916): 61.

7. "Announcement and Prospectus of the *New Era Magazine,*" p. 2; "Topsy Templeton," *New Era Magazine* 1 (March 1916): 77.

8. "Prize Contest," *New Era Magazine* 1 (March 1916): 111.

9. *Crisis* acknowledged the death of Hopkins on August 23, 1930, at Cambridge, Massachusetts. The brief obituary noted only that Hopkins had been an "authoress and poetess" and that she had worked as a stenographer at the Massachusetts Institute of Technology. "Along the Color Line," *Crisis* 37 (October 1930): 344.

Ann Allen Shockley says nothing of *New Era* in her brief article on Hopkins. "Pauline Elizabeth Hopkins: A Biographical Excursion into Obscurity," *Phylon* 33 (Spring 1972): 22-26.

If included anywhere, the magazine should have been mentioned in the dictionary of *Black American Writers,* compiled by Theressa Gunnels Rush, Carol Fairbanks Myers, and Esther Spring Arata. The editors did note Hopkins's association with the *Colored American*

*Magazine,* but they made no reference to *New Era* (Metuchen, New Jersey: Scarecrow Press, 1975), vol. 1, pp. 389-90.

10. "Foreword," *Stylus* 1 (May 1921): 6.

11. "The Stylus," *Howard University Record* 19 (May 1925): 372; "Visions of the Dawn," *Stylus* (June 1934): 1. The issues of *Stylus* following May 1921 were assigned neither a volume nor a number.

12. Gregory, "Foreword," p. 6.

13. "The Looking Glass," *Crisis* 12 (August 1916): 182; *Dust Tracks on a Road* (1942: rpt. Philadelphia: Arno Press, 1969), pp. 175-76; Robert E. Hemenway, *Zora Neale Hurston* (Urbana: University of Illinois Press, 1977), pp. 18-20.

14. "Our Book Shelf," *Crisis* 31 (January 1926): 141.

Within the discussion, Du Bois essentially cast Kellogg and associates as inconsistent liberals who advocated social reform for all groups save for the black. He recalled that the editors had wanted, for a 1914 issue of *Survey,* a statement concerning the aims of the NAACP. Du Bois sent back a militant, but routine comment, as his conclusion indicates: "Finally, in 1914, the Negro must demand his social rights. His right to be treated as a gentleman when he acts like one, to marry any sane, grown person who wants to marry him, and to meet and eat with his friends without being accused of undue assumption or unworthy ambition." He never expected the subsequent uproar, the calls from *Survey* editors to the NAACP office, the demand that the offending passage be excised, if the piece was to appear in the magazine. Among the NAACP leadership, Du Bois remembered, "they found easily several who did not agree with this statement and one indeed who threatened to resign if it were published." The unnamed objectors must have included those trying to intimidate Du Bois into subservience to the organization. Du Bois, stubborn from the beginning of his editorship, would not comply and thus *Survey* rejected his entire statement.

In 1923, Kellogg divided the *Survey* into two magazines: the *Survey Graphic,* which appeared on the first of each month and reached a popular audience with general information and analysis of social problems, and *Survey,* which served as a professional bulletin for the field of social work.

15. "The Negro Renaissance and its Significance," in *The New Negro Thirty Years Afterward: Papers Contributed to the Sixteenth Annual Spring Conference of the Division of the Social Sciences,* ed. Rayford W. Logan, Eugene C. Holmes, and G. Franklin Edwards (Washington, D.C.: Howard University Press, 1955), pp. 85-86. Clarke Chambers said nothing about the Civic Club Dinner but stressed Kellogg's own motivation for the Harlem number. He noted that Kellogg had always liked "folk," that he had previously published special issues on the Gypsies, the Irish, and the Mexican peasants, and that his "favorite artists were always those who worked with folk themes, especially when their styles reflected the primitive strength of the common folk." *Paul U. Kellogg and the Survey* (Minneapolis: University of Minnesota Press, 1971), pp. 112-13.

16. "Harlem," and "Enter the New Negro," *Survey Graphic* 6 (March 1925): 629-30, 633.

17. "The South Lingers On," Ibid., 645, 644, 646.

18. "Enter the New Negro," Ibid., 631, 633.

19. "Youth Speaks," Ibid., 659.

20. "The Black Man Brings His Gifts," Ibid., 655, 710.

21. "The Negro Renaissance and its Significance," in *The New Negro Thirty Years Afterward,* p. 86; "The Negro Enters Literature," *Carolina Magazine* 57 (May 1927): 48.

22. "Editorials," *Messenger* 7 (April 1925): 156; Chambers, *Kellogg and the Survey,* p. 115.

23. The first issue of *Palms* appeared in October 1923 and the last in April 1927. Idella Purnell commented, in the last number, that *Palms* would emerge again in the fall: "The editors feel it necessary to bring forcibly to the attention of *Palms'* readers that the magazine has continued and will continue." Despite such protestations, *Palms* never again reappeared. See "Notice," *Palms* 4 (April 1927): 190.

24. "Poem," "The Song of America," and "Black Madonna," *Palms* 4 (October 1926): 19, 18, 8.

25. In a letter dated September 27, 1925, Countee Cullen asked James Weldon Johnson if he would contribute a short article on black poets to the issue. Committed elsewhere, Johnson could not supply the essay; hence, the discussion by White. Cullen to Johnson, James Weldon Johnson Papers, James Weldon Johnson Collection, Yale University.

26. "Ebony Flute," *Opportunity* 5 (April 1927): 123; "Ebony Flute," *Opportunity* 5 (January 1927): 28.

27. "Contributors," *Carolina Magazine* 58 (May 1928): 48. Virginia Lay, acting editor of *Carolina Magazine* and also sister of Paul Green, had originally asked James Weldon Johnson either to write a survey of Afro-American literature for the May 1927 issue or to suggest someone else who could contribute the essay. Apparently, Johnson did not have time to author the piece and thus recommended Charles S. Johnson for the lead article. Lay to James Weldon Johnson, April 18, 1927, Series C, Container 83, NAACP Papers, Manuscripts Division, Library of Congress (hereafter cited as NAACP Papers).

28. "The Message of the Negro Poets," *Carolina Magazine* 58 (May 1928): 11.

29. "The Hunch," *Carolina Magazine* 57 (May 1927): 24.

30. "Boy," "Boy on Beale Street," "African Dancer in Paris," and "Once Bad Gal," *Carolina Magazine* 58 (May 1928): 38, 36, 22.

31. "Comment," and "Plays of Negro Life," *Carolina Magazine* 59 (April 1929): 4, 46.

32. "The Negro in Literature," *Crisis* 36 (November 1929): 377; "Dark Tower," and "Ebony Flute," *Opportunity* 5 (June 1927): 181, 183; "Dark Tower," *Opportunity* 5 (July 1927): 211.

33. "Dark Tower," *Opportunity* 4 (December 1926): 388. Starr and Fowler were still listed in their official capacities in the May 1927 issue of *Carolina Magazine,* even though Virginia Lay was serving as editor. In her letter to James Weldon Johnson, she indicated that Starr had to attend to business in New York for an indeterminate period. She also indicated that Starr had made plans and Lewis Alexander had gathered materials for the first special issue of black literature. Lay to Johnson, April 18, 1927, Series C, Container 83, NAACP Papers.

34. "Dedication," *Carolina Magazine* 58 (May 1928): 4; Alexander, "Plays of Negro Life," p. 47.

35. *Harlem Renaissance* (New York: Oxford University Press, 1971), p. 29. John W. Blassingame called the Huggins's study "hardly definitive," saying that *Harlem Renaissance* "ignores the internal dynamics of the black community which fostered and nurtured the movement." Blassingame concluded that there still exists undiscovered "a different kind of renaissance than that which Huggins found. "The Afro-Americans: Mythology to Reality," in *The Reinterpretation of American History and Culture,* ed. William H. Cartwright and Richard L. Watson, Jr. (Washington, D.C.: National Council for the Social Studies, 1973), p. 69.

36. "The Twenties: Harlem and its Negritude," *African Forum* 1 (Spring 1966): 18-19; also see Hemenway, *Hurston,* pp. 43-50.

37. Hughes, "The Twenties," 19; Thurman to Hughes, December 8, 1927, Wallace Thurman Folder, James Weldon Johnson Collection, Yale University.

38. Hughes, "The Twenties," p. 19; *Fire* 1 (November 1926); introductory page.

39. Hughes, "The Twenties," p. 20; *Big Sea* (1940; rpt. New York: Hill and Wang, 1963), p. 237.

40. Thurman so autographed the copy of *Fire* in the Moorland-Spingarn Research Center of Howard University; "Foreword," *Fire,* p. 1.

41. "Fire Burns," Ibid., pp. 47-48.

42. "Cordelia the Crude," "Wedding Day," and "Sweat," Ibid., pp. 5, 25-28, 41.

43. "Smoke, Lilies and Jade," Ibid., p. 38.

44. "Elevator Boy" and "Little Cinderella," Ibid., pp. 20, 23.

45. Hughes, *Big Sea,* p. 237; "A Challenge to the Negro," *Bookman* 64 (November 1926): 258-59.

46. "Dark Tower," and "Ebony Flute," *Opportunity* 5 (January 1927): 25, 28.

47. Hughes, *Big Sea,* p. 237; Hughes, "The Twenties," pp. 19-20; "Looking Glass," *Crisis* 33 (January 1927): 158.

48. "Fire: A Negro Magazine," *Survey* 58 (Aug. 15-Sept. 15, 1927): 563.

49. Hughes to Locke, December 28, 1926, Literary Series, Alain Locke Collection, Howard University (hereafter cited as Locke Collection); Hughes, *Big Sea,* p. 237.

50. "The Negro Literary Renaissance," *Southern Workman* 56 (April 1927): 177-79, 183.

51. "Negro Artists and the Negro," *New Republic* 52 (August 31, 1927): 37.

52. Hurston to Locke, October 11, 1927, Locke Collection.

53. Hughes, *Big Sea,* p. 238.

54. Thurman to Locke, October 3, 1928, Locke Collection; Locke to Thurman, October 8, 1928, Locke Collection.

55. "For Whom Shall the Negro Vote?" *Harlem* 1 (November 1928): 5, 45.

56. "Art or Propaganda?" Ibid., p. 12.

57. "Editorial," Ibid., p. 21.

58. Ibid., pp. 21-22.

59. "High, Low, Past and Present," Ibid., pp. 31-32.

60. "Harlem Directory: Where To Go And What To Do When In Harlem," Ibid., p. 43.

61. "Editorial," Ibid., p. 22.

62. "Wallace Thurman Adores Brown Women Who Have Beauty Mark On Shoulder; Prefers Sherry to Gin," New York *Journal and Guide,* March 5, 1932. The article is included in the Wallace Thurman Folder, Vertical File, Schomburg Collection of Black History, Literature and Art, New York Public Library.

63. Ibid.

64. *Infants of the Spring* (New York: Macaulay Company, 1932), pp. 186-87, 180.

# ADDELL P. AUSTIN (ESSAY DATE 1988)

**SOURCE:** Austin, Addell P. "The *Opportunity* and *Crisis* Literary Contests, 1924-27." *CLA Journal* 32, no. 2 (December 1988): 235-46.

*In the following essay, Austin assesses the differing approaches taken by Charles S. Johnson of* Opportunity *and W. E. B. Du Bois, editor of* The Crisis, *in encouraging African American writers during the mid 1920s.*

In the early 1920s, stories on Negro life written primarily by whites had become quite popular; however, blacks failed to appreciate them. William Stanley Braithwaite commented:

> [A]lmost every one of these stories is written in a tone of condescension. . . . Many of these writers live in the South or are from the South. Presumably they are well acquainted with the Negro, but it is a remarkable fact that they almost never tell us anything vital about him, about the real human being in the black man's skin. . . . Always the Negro is interpreted in the terms of the white man. White man psychology is applied and it is no wonder that the result often shows the Negro in a ludicrous light.[1]

Blacks believed that their own writers could portray themselves more realistically. What was needed were vehicles to promote these writers and their works. *Opportunity* and *Crisis* magazines and their respective editors, Charles S. Johnson and W. E. B. Du Bois, were to play significant roles in the development and promotion of black artists.[2] Years after Johnson resigned as *Opportunity* editor, he stated:

> [T]he importance of the *Crisis Magazine* and *Opportunity Magazine* was that of providing an outlet for young Negro writers and scholars whose work was not acceptable to other established media because it could not be believed to be of standard quality despite the superior quality of much of it.[3]

Furthermore, Du Bois believed that the magazines' literary contests "grew into" the Harlem Renaissance.[4] While both Johnson and Du Bois wanted to encourage black writers, other objectives for the literary contests were incompatible. The *Opportunity* editor wanted to use black literature to affect white attitudes toward Afro-Americans. In contrast, the *Crisis* editor seemed less concerned about influencing whites and instead directed black literary efforts to an Afro-American readership. Throughout the history of the literary competitions, antagonisms between Johnson and Du Bois were reflected in the design and execution of their respective contests.

Arna Bontemps recalled that Johnson "spoke of his aim to conduct a literary contest through *Opportunity*" at a party during the summer of 1924.[5] In the August issue of *Opportunity,* news of the contest was made public with the following announcement:

> To stimulate creative expression among Negroes and to direct attention to the rich and unexploited sources of materials for literature in Negro life, *Opportunity* will offer prizes for short stories, poetry, plays, essays, and personal experience in the amount of FIVE HUNDRED DOLLARS.[6]

The cash prizes were donated by Mrs. Henry Leach, an Urban League board member and, according to Johnson, a "long, thorough sympathizer with the struggles of Negroes for social as well as artistic status."[7] Her husband was the editor of the influential *Forum* magazine.

Accompanying the contest announcement was an editorial by Johnson, "On Writing About Negroes." Here, the editor provided his views on black literature and its writers and affirmed the role of literature as the "liason between races." He also stated that blacks were dissatisfied with literature on black life "written by persons other than Negroes, who have never yet been wholly admitted to the privacy of Negro thoughts." While he did not contend that blacks should be restricted to writing about their own race, Johnson believed that in order to treat black themes "competently," black writers, "knowing them best, should be the ones to do it."[8]

At *Crisis,* Du Bois was surprised by *Opportunity*'s contest announcement. According to David Lewis, although a *Crisis* literary competition "had been widely discussed in Harlem circles," Du Bois had no forewarning of *Opportunity*'s contest. Lewis further contended that this "was an early example of Charles S. Johnson's gloved ruthlessness. For the pragmatic sociologist . . . the appropriation of a rival's idea was hardly a misdemeanor if it promoted racial progress through the arts."[9]

*Crisis* announced its contest in its October 1924 issue. Referred to as "The Amy Spingarn Prizes in Literature and Art," it offered $100 more in prizes than *Opportunity*'s competition. Still upset over its rival's contest, Du Bois reprinted a 1920 editorial in *Crisis*' November 1924 issue. The editorial boasted of how the magazine had sought to promote black literature "since its founding," thirteen years before the first issue of *Opportunity*. Du Bois then provided an impressive list of writers published by *Crisis* since 1920. The list included such authors as Jean Toomer, Countee Cullen, Claude McKay, and Walter White. He concluded with the following paragraph, which must have been read with an underlying sense of bitterness to those who knew of Du Bois's true feelings about the *Opportunity* contest:

> Today and suddenly $1,000 are offered in prizes to Negro writers and artists. Without either knowing the other's plans or intentions, both *The Crisis* and the magazine published by the Urban League, *Opportunity,* have offered a series of prizes. Mrs. Spingarn's offer was made to us in July, but *Opportunity* first gave publicity to its prize offer. In order, therefore, to give young authors every chance we have put the date of our competition well on in the spring so that there will be no unnecessary rivalry and all can have the full benefit of this great generosity and foresight on the part of friends.[10]

According to the Du Bois editorial, it appeared as if the total cash prizes and deadline dates were the only differences between the competitions. Of course, there were similarities between the contests. The competitions had four common categories: short story, poetry, playwriting, and essay.[11] The contests were restricted to black writers. Contestants were to use pseudonymns, allowed to compete in more than one division, and could submit more than one entry per category. The contests allotted the greatest cash awards to the short story category.[12] Both journals stated that they would publish the prize-winning entries.[13] Length or text limitations were given for most categories. Both contests utilized distinguished black and white judges, such as Alain Locke, James Weldon Johnson, William Stanley Braithwaite, Zona Gale, John Macy, Alexander Woollcott, and Eugene O'Neill.

Nevertheless, the contest differed in several important ways. Unlike *Opportunity*, *Crisis* ran articles on the writing of short stories and plays before its contest deadline. *Opportunity* stated that

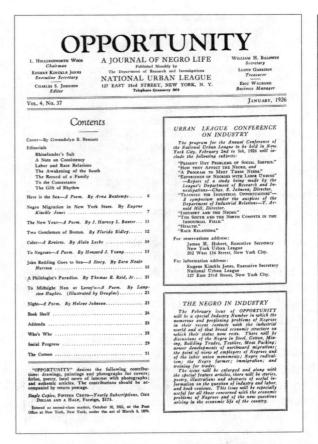

Title page of the January 1926 edition of *Opportunity*.

the short stories, plays, and essays "must deal with some phase of Negro life." The personal experience sketch must also be related to black life since the work had to a be based on a true experience of the writer who by contest rule must be black. *Crisis* only restricted the subject of the plays to "deal with some phase of Negro history or experience." Eighteen of the twenty-four judges used by *Opportunity* were white, as compared to the nine white and seven black judges employed by *Crisis*.

Why would there be such a difference between the contests in subject restrictions and racial composition of the panel of judges? By looking at the stated purposes of the competitions, it can be seen that Johnson had grander objectives in mind than Du Bois. The purpose of the *Crisis* contest was simply to "encourage their [black writers'] aptitude for art expression."[14] However, Johnson provided the following statement of purpose for the *Opportunity* competition:

> It hopes to stimulate and encourage creative literary effort among Negroes; to locate and orient Negro writers of ability; to stimulate and encourage interest in the serious development of a body of literature about Negro life, drawing deeply

upon these tremendously rich sources; to encourage the reading of literature by Negro authors and about Negro life, not merely because they are Negro authors but because what they write is literature and because the literature is interesting; to foster a market for Negro writers and for literature by and about Negroes; to bring these writers into contact with the general world of letters to which they have been for the most part timid and inarticulate strangers; to stimulate and foster a type of writing by Negroes which shakes itself free of deliberate propaganda and protest.[15]

The *Opportunity* editor wanted to take advantage of the current vogue for works on black life. Therefore, Johnson structured the contest to generate these writings. To ensure that these works received the attention of influential whites, he loaded the jury with many more prominent whites than blacks. Johnson may have believed that the competition would appear to be more legitimate with such a ratio of whites to blacks on the panel of judges.

*Opportunity* announced the winners of its contest in the May 1925 issue. Johnson stated that "the average quality of the manuscripts was high in all divisions of the contest."[16] Fifteen of the seven hundred and forty-seven entries were awarded cash prizes. The winning authors included some names—such as Langston Hughes, Zora Neale Hurston, and Countee Cullen—already known in New York and Washington, D.C., literary circles. However, the contest did elicit award-winning works from previously unknown writers, such as George Dewey Lipscomb, G. A. Stewart, and Fidelia Ripley.

*Opportunity* held a dinner for the contestants at the Fifth Avenue Restaurant in New York. Besides the contestants, the three hundred and sixteen attendants included Johnson, the judges, and other distinguished guests. Impressed by the dinner, the *New York Herald-Tribune* included an editorial on the event in its May 7, 1925, edition. Entitled, "A Negro Renaissance," the editorial provided the following comments:

> [The *Opportunity* dinner] was only a somewhat more conclusive indication of a phenomenon of which there have been many symptoms—of the fact that the American Negro is finding his artistic voice and that we are on the edge, if not already in the midst, of what might not improperly be called a Negro renaissance. . . . These young people—and youth was another striking thing about this gathering—were not trying to imitate the white man nor repeating the professional white story-teller's dreary stencils of the "darkey."[17]

Regardless of the editorial's few patronizing remarks, Johnson must have been elated by this publicity because the editorial also included a statement appearing to affirm that others had recognized the potential for racial understanding through the arts:

> A novel sight, that dinner—white critics, whom "everybody" knows, Negro writers, whom "nobody" knew—meeting on common ground. The movement behind it doubtless means something to the race problem in general; certainly it means something to American literature.[18]

Johnson reprinted the *Herald-Tribune* editorial in *Opportunity*'s June 1925 issue.

*Crisis* held a similar dinner for its contestants at the Renaissance Casino in New York on August 14, 1925. Besides the announcement of award winners, the program also featured a presentation of the first-place winning play, *The Broken Banjo,* by Willis Richardson. Strangely, in its September issue, *Opportunity* listed its rival's contest winners one month before *Crisis.*[19] *Crisis* provided a list of the award winners and selected comments from its judges in its October 1925 issue. Winners were to receive free membership in the Crisis Guild of Writers and Artists (KRIGWA) and Du Bois claimed that each contestant would receive a letter from KRIGWA to provide advice on his or her work.[20] As in the *Opportunity* contest, Langston Hughes, Countee Cullen, and G. A. Stewart also won awards in the *Crisis* competition. However, the *Crisis* contest seemed to award more prizes than *Opportunity* to previously unknown writers, such as Marie French, Anita Scott, and Ruth Gaines Shelton.

For the 1926 *Opportunity* contest, the cash awards were donated by Casper Holstein. The donor was a Harlem numbers banker who shared Johnson's beliefs on the potential role of black arts in American society. According to Langston Hughes:

> [The West Indian native] did good things with his money, such as educating boys and girls at colleges in the South, building decent apartment houses in Harlem, and backing literary contests to encourage colored writers. Mr. Holstein, no doubt, would have been snubbed in impolite Washington society, Negro or white, but there he was doing decent and helpful things that it hadn't occurred to lots of others to do.[21]

Due to Holstein's generosity, the prizes now totaled $1,000. A musical composition category was added to the competition. Furthermore, the white-to-black ratio of judges was lower than it had been in the previous year, 1.5:1 (sixteen whites/ten blacks). The 1926 *Opportunity* contest received one thousand two hundred and seventy-six entries as compared to seven hundred and thirty-two works submitted to the 1925 competition.

Again, *Opportunity* announced the awards at a dinner with an impressive guest list. One of the guests—Leon Whipple, a Columbia University professor and journalist for *The Survey*—called the event "a glory for the thousand or more Negroes there, the prize winners and their loving admirers. It was warm with good hope for the serious friends of Negro art."[22] However, Whipple expressed concern at the "profiteers and parasites" who were also present at the dinner:

> This sorry crew are not important in themselves. Next year they will be flittering round the candle of some new fad. But they may misguide the Negro for a time unless he can steel himself in anger or wrap himself in his own guffaws against their flattery, false witness, and bribes. It would be the final tragedy if after exploiting the Negro's body for two centuries we ended by exploiting his heart and soul.[23]

At *Crisis,* Amy Spingarn again donated money for the awards, still totaling $600. This year, cash prizes were only awarded for first and second places to allow larger cash awards for these winners. Nine blacks and six whites served as judges. In a January 1926 editorial, Du Bois provided advice for the contestants. He stated, "We want especially to stress the fact that while we believe in Negro art we do not believe in any art simply for art's sake."[24] Clearly, the contestant who read this statement would believe that his or her entry would have a better chance of winning if it had propagandistic leanings.

The dinner for the contestants included presentations of the awards and plays—*Foreign Mail* and *Mandy,* poetry and short story readings, a performance by the Negro String Quartet, and dancing. It was announced that the awards would be increased to $1,000 for the 1927 competition (matching the awards offered by *Opportunity*). Also, since there were several repeat winners, it was ruled that those who had won two first- or second-place prizes would be ineligible for next year's contest.[25]

In 1927, Casper Holstein again donated $1,000 for the *Opportunity* literary contest. The ratio of white to black judges was about the same as the 1926 competition (sixteen whites/nine blacks). The January 1927 issue of *Opportunity* included an editorial by Johnson citing some of the recent achievements of short story and poetry contest winners. Their works were now being published in magazines and anthologies.[26] How-

ever, the playwriting division disappointed the *Opportunity* editor. Johnson stated that the play section "seems yet farthest behind the possibilities of its field of all the literary divisions."[27] The awards were announced at a dinner described in an article by short story award winner Eugene Gordon in *Opportunity*'s July 1927 issue.[28]

Four months after the magazine announced its 1927 award winners, Johnson suspended the contest. He wrote:

> Examination of the mass of manuscripts shows that there has been improvement over the mass of other years, and that in general they are not very much worse than those of other general contests. We have concluded, however, that with the point of the contests known, more time for the deliberate working of manuscripts will yield vastly more valuable results. Most important, this extension of time should allow for our aspiring writers a margin for experimentation with more than one manuscript, in the search for the most effective channels of expression.[29]

As he had written in the January 1927 issue, he commended the poetry and short story sections, since some of these works were being published in "standard" literary journals (magazines with a predominately white readership). Also, he stated that he was displeased with the results of the drama and essay divisions.

While *Opportunity* eventually sponsored other literary contests, none matched the scale of prestige of the ones conducted from 1924 to 1927. Johnson left *Opportunity* in 1928 to become the Chairman of the Department of Social Sciences at Fisk University.[30]

At *Crisis,* Du Bois changed the format of the literary contest without notifying the contestants. The editor personally read all of the three hundred and seventy-five entries. Clearly, this year's number of entries represented a significant drop from the six hundred and twenty-seven entries of 1925.

For the 1927 contest, divisions were eliminated as writers competed against each other regardless of the form used. Du Bois graded each entry using the following scale:

A—Excellent
B +—Good and worth publication
B—Good
C—Fair
D—Poor, but with some points to commend
E—Impossible[31]

Only those manuscripts with the grade of "A" would be considered for prizes.

There was no formal dinner to announce the award winners. Instead, contest results were cited in the editorial section of *Crisis*. Du Bois selected the winners in consultation with (unnamed) "experts." There were only three cash award winners: First place ($200) went to Marita Bonner for her collection of two plays, short story, and essay; Brenda Ray Moryck received the second place award of $100 for three short stories; and Eulalie Spence won the third place award of $50 for two plays.

Without warning, the literary contests were eliminated. In their place, monthly honoraria of fifty dollars were awarded to the best literary works published in *Crisis*. According to David Lewis, Amy Spingarn (the donor of the cash awards) "must have been surprised to see white writers Zona Gale and Clement Wood among the first recipient of prizes intended for ambitious Afro-American writers."[32]

Nevertheless, despite the brief history of the *Opportunity* and *Crisis* literary contests from 1924 to 1927, it can be said that the competitions were a major factor in the development of black literature of the period. Many of the major writers of the Harlem Renaissance were introduced to the general public through these contests. Furthermore, the publishing contacts made via the competitions greatly enhanced their fledgling careers.

Charles S. Johnson took advantage of the current vogue for black literature. The *Opportunity* editor promoted black writers and made sure that influential whites became acquainted with their writings via the contest juries and awards dinner. W. E. B. Du Bois appeared less concerned about pleasing white audiences. Unlike *Opportunity*'s contests, *Crisis*'s 1925 and 1926 literary competitions used nearly an equal number of black and white judges. For the 1927 competition, Du Bois acted as the primary judge. He also eliminated the awards dinner, which was an important way for black writers to make contacts with established writers, editors, and publishers. Thus, although both Johnson and Du Bois sought to encourage black writers, they used different strategies to achieve this goal.

## Notes

1. William Stanley Braithwaite, "The Negro in Literature," *Crisis*, 29 (November 1924), 24.

2. *Opportunity* and *Crisis* were house organs of the National Urban League and National Association for the Advancement of Colored People, respectively.

3. Patrick J. Gilpin, "Charles S. Johnson: Entrepreneur of the Harlem Renaissance," in *The Harlem Renaissance Remembered*, ed. Arna Bontemps (New York: Dodd, 1972), p. 22.

4. W. E. B. Du Bois, *Dusk of Dawn* (New York: Schocken, 1968), p. 270.

5. Arna Bontemps, "The Awakening: A Memoir," in *The Harlem Renaissance Remembered*, ed. Arna Bontemps (New York: Dodd, 1972), p. 20.

6. Charles S. Johnson, "*Opportunity* Literary Contest," *Opportunity*, 2 (August 1924), 228.

7. Charles S. Johnson, "The Donor of the Contest Prizes," *Opportunity*, 3 (January 1925), 3.

8. Charles S. Johnson, "On Writing About Negroes," *Opportunity*, 3 (August 1925), 227-28.

9. David Lewis, *When Harlem Was in Vogue* (New York: Knopf, 1981), pp. 97-98.

10. W. E. B. Du Bois, "To Encourage Negro Art," *Crisis*, 29 (November 1924), 11.

11. The *Opportunity* contest also featured a personal experience sketch category. The *Crisis* competition also offered prizes for illustrations.

12. Total cash awards for short story category—$150 (*Opportunity*) and $170 (*Crisis*). In the *Opportunity* contest, playwriting was allotted the second highest cash awards ($110). The playwriting and illustration categories offered the second highest cash awards ($125 each) in the *Crisis* competition.

13. Actually, the magazines published many but not all of the winning entries.

14. "The Amy Spingarn Prizes in Literature and Art," *Crisis*, 29 (November 1924), 24.

15. Charles S. Johnson, "An Opportunity for Negro Writers," *Opportunity*, 2 (September 1924), 258.

16. Charles S. Johnson, "The Contest," *Opportunity*, 3 (October 1925), 291-92.

17. "A Negro Renaissance," *New York Herald-Tribune*, 7 May 1925, p. 16.

18. Ibid.

19. "The Amy Spingarn Prizes," *Opportunity*, 3 (September 1925), 287.

20. W. E. B. Du Bois, "Krigwa," *Crisis*, 30 (October 1925), 278.

21. Langston Hughes, *The Big Sea* (New York: Hill and Wang, 1940), p. 214.

22. Leon Whipple, "Letters and Life," *The Survey*, 56 (1 August 1926), 517.

23. Ibid.

24. W. E. B. Du Bois, "Krigwa, 1926," *Crisis*, 31 (January 1926), 115.

25. Because of this rule, poet Countee Cullen and dramatist Willis Richardson could not enter the 1927 *Crisis* competition.

26. Charles S. Johnson, "Stories and Poetry," *Opportunity*, 5 (January 1927), 5.

27. Charles S. Johnson, "On the Need of Better Plays," *Opportunity*, 5 (January 1927), 5-6.

28. Eugene Gordon, "The *Opportunity* Dinner: An Impression," *Opportunity*, 5 (July 1927), 208-09.

29. Charles S. Johnson, "The *Opportunity* Contest," *Opportunity*, 5 (September 1927), 254.

30. Johnson became Fisk's first black president in 1947.

31. W. E. B. Du Bois, "Krigwa," *Crisis*, 34 (November 1927), 312.

32. Lewis, p. 200.

# ROLAND E. WOLSELEY, ALICE A. TAIT, AND TODD STEVEN BURROUGHS (ESSAY DATE 2002)

**SOURCE:** Wolseley, Roland E., Alice A. Tait, and Todd Steven Burroughs. "Black Journalism Enters the Twentieth Century." From a revised and corrected version of the chapter in *The Black Press, U.S.A.*, pp. 43-78. Ames: Iowa State University Press, 1990.

*In the following excerpt from their study of African American journalism, Wolseley, Tait, and Burroughs concentrate on the roles of W. E. B. Du Bois and Marcus Garvey as influential editors of the 1920s.*

## The Crisis *and W. E. B. Du Bois*

So controversial was William Edward Burghardt Du Bois's life—he was the center of disagreements as a teacher, as an NAACP executive, and as a political partisan—that his close association with Afro-American journalism is submerged. He founded five magazines, two of which still are published; he was a correspondent for four newspapers, columnist for numerous both Black and white papers, and contributor of articles to many general as well as scholarly periodicals, Black and white.

Journalism to Du Bois, it is true, was only a tool to advance his sociological studies of the Black race or to aid him in his plans to help the race. But he used it effectively and far more than some others who considered themselves journalists but engaged in that profession as entrée to another: politics.

A New Englander, he was born in . . . 1868. Du Bois's first journalism was the editorship, with a white classmate, of a short-lived hand-produced high school paper called *Howler*. A local bookshop operator got him his first professional news job—as correspondent for *The Springfield Republican*, a famous white daily. He also wrote for the notable Black weeklies, *The New York Age, The Freeman*, and *The New York Globe*. When he went to Fisk University in 1886, his first venture into the South, he edited *The Fisk Herald*. Many years later, in 1924, he helped bring out what might be called an off-campus version of it in New York in support of a student rebellion at his alma mater.

From Fisk he went to Harvard, but did no journalistic work there, nor again until his return late in the century from graduate study in Germany.

He began contributing sociological articles to *The Atlantic Monthly* and *World's Work,* two of the most important white periodicals then being published. A clue to his developing concept of journalistic responsibility appeared when a committee made up of several dignitaries, including Walter Hines Page, editor of *The Atlantic,* approached him about editing a magazine to be published at Hampton Institute. When he said, in submitting his plans, that he would expect all editorial decisions to be his own only, the project was dropped. This position was to disturb his journalistic life ever after but also may account for the effectiveness of several of the publications he edited.

By 1905 Du Bois had become fully aware of the power of the press. He wrote to a wealthy man he had met two years before, he relates in an autobiography, about the need for "a high class journal to circulate among the Intelligent Negroes. . . ." In his letter he characterized the African-American press of the time thus: "Now we have many small weekly papers and one or two monthlies, and none of them fill the great need I have outlined." He thus described that need: "The Negro race in America today is in a critical condition. Only united, concentrated effort will keep us from being crushed. This union must come as a matter of education and long continued effort."

The publication he had in mind would tell Black readers of their own and their neighbors' needs, "interpret the news of the world to them, and inspire them toward definite ideas." And it would be a monthly. But the wealthy men he approached expressed sympathy and nothing more. There it ended until a few years later.

Du Bois's proposal of a magazine reflected his social views. They put him into conflict with Booker T. Washington, the most powerful Black leader of the day. Du Bois himself "believed in the higher education of a talented tenth who through their knowledge of modern culture could guide the American Negro into a higher civilization." Washington believed that Blacks would gain their best place by being skilled workers and businesspeople and finally capitalists.

Du Bois saw his plans for a publication born at last in 1906. With the help of two Atlanta University graduates, he had started in Memphis a small printing establishment. It now produced *The Moon Illustrated Weekly,* and may have given the editor the formula for the magazine he edited later, *The Crisis. The Moon* soon ranged itself against Washington. It contained miscellany, much of it reprinted from other Black publications but also original editorials and biographical articles. After a year it was discontinued and in 1907 replaced by *Horizon*, which its founder dismissed by merely calling it "a miniature monthly." Rudwick (1968), one of Du Bois's biographers, reported that *Horizon* was begun as a voice for the Niagara Movement. It failed, he believed, because the Black people of the period were not ready for the Niagara philosophy. But producing this periodical laid more of the foundation for Du Bois's later editorial work. *Horizon,* in turn, gave way in his affections to *The Crisis.*

That magazine came from Du Bois's decision to resign his faculty post at Atlanta University and become director of publications and research for the NAACP, of which he had been an incorporator. His work brought him into association with Oswald Garrison Villard, publisher of *The Nation* and editor of *The New York Evening Post* as well as a grandson of William Lloyd Garrison. He began *The Crisis* on his own and despite, as he put it, "the protests of many of my associates." He saw in the magazine a chance to interpret to the world "the hindrances and aspirations of American Negroes." His work with it was a deep interest for nearly a quarter of a century: 1910 to 1934. During those years he made the magazine a vigorous critic of any national policy or event which resulted in harm to African-Americans—whether it was discrimination in the military services or the wartime lynchings of the 1914-19 conflict.

"As *Crisis* editor," Bennett has written. "Du Bois set the tone for the organization and educated a whole generation of Black people in the art of protest" (Bennett, 1969). But he was so possessive of the magazine and so prone to use it to comment on the NAACP itself (of which, it should be remembered, it was the official organ) that there was dissension within the organization. Through the magazine he advocated a program of economic self-help, which he called "economic segregation." The NAACP balked, and after a turbulent war of words between Du Bois and the NAACP in the pages of *The Crisis,* Du Bois resigned in 1934, returning to Atlanta University as head of its sociology department. At Atlanta, one of his purposes, he said, was "to establish . . . a scholarly journal of comment and research on world race problems." It took six years for this goal to be reached. The result was *Phylon,* being published until recently at the university as a scholarly and literary quarterly. He was editor for four years. It was to be his last major journalistic editorial work. Thereafter he wrote articles for Black as well as

white publications: *New York Times Magazine, New Masses, The Nation, Journal of Negro Education, Negro Digest, Freedomways, Masses,* and *Mainstream,* among others. He was the author, from 1896 to 1963, of a score of books, editor of a dozen more, author of countless articles, and regularly contributed newspaper columns.

Because he placed his confidence in college-educated Blacks to "save the race," as Rudwick puts it, Du Bois naturally believed in the use of books, magazines, and newspapers as vehicles of communication.

Toward the end of his life, Du Bois joined the Communist party, moved to Ghana, and became a citizen of that African nation. He died there in 1963, aged ninety-five. He was not to live to finish his newest publishing project—"The Encyclopaedia Africana"—which he had been commissioned to direct. In 1999, Harvard professors Henry Louis Gates and Kwame Anthony Appiah dedicated their "Africana" encyclopedia to Du Bois.

### Other Magazines of the Period

Du Bois's magazines were not the only important ones of the first few decades of the century. One group now remembered because of the social climate then and today was what might be called mildly leftist in sympathies. These included *Opportunity, Crusader, Promoter, Triangle, Messenger, Black Man,* and *Negro World,* most issued from New York City. Like so much of the Black press, several of these were organs of protest. Some were asking for a Black state. Others espoused a vague radicalism that avoided both socialism and communism of the brands then current, a radicalism centered on battling for the rights of Blacks or for Blacks to be in all government departments. But others supported some brand of socialism as a social order, with stronger labor and farmers' unions and cooperatively owned businesses (Detweiler, 1969).

One of the most feared publications of its day was *The Messenger.* At first it was edited jointly by Chandler Owen and A. Philip Randolph, the latter a revered Black leader long identified with the labor movement. Openly Marxist, a dangerous position for those days of government interference with the press, it opposed Du Bois as much as Washington, although they were in sharp disagreement. Representative James Byrnes, of South Carolina, attacked *The Messenger* (as well as *The Crisis*) in the House and blamed Black journalists for the postwar race riots. Consequently it was investigated by the Department of Justice. Its report named *The Messenger* as "the most dangerous" (Detweiler, 1969).

An important magazine of the era of the 1920s was *Opportunity*, from 1923 until 1949 of the National Urban League. Black scholar Charles S. Johnson began and edited *Opportunity*, making it one of the best in its day. He saw the need to give the magazine an auxiliary activity by sponsoring the Harlem Writers' Guild and set up literary competitions. As Frank W. Miles, a writer on Black periodical journalism, noted of it, "thus living up to the Urban League's motto—not alms but Opportunity" (Miles, 1946). Bearing the subtitle *Journal of Negro Life*, it was a quarterly of about fifty pages an issue, carried serious articles on Black problems, reviewed books, and reported on business and professional opportunities. Personality sketches and literary work were staples, as was League news. When it ceased publication in 1949, it had a circulation of 10,000. The Urban League would re-establish *Opportunity* in the 1990s, and it would continue in 2002.

During the 1920s new magazines of a more specialized type than *Opportunity* appeared quickly: *American Musician, Master Musician, Music and Poetry,* and *Negro Musician* were those particularly devoted to music. In another decade, a dozen and a half more were begun, including *Brown American* and *Challenge,* but did not live to see the last of the 1930s. But in the 1940s, as to be seen later, came the surge that produced several highly successful consumer magazines and the rise of various more specialized periodicals, these dealing with the trades, education, travel, and other topics. *Pulse, Negro, Spotlighter,* and *Headlines,* among the general ones, did not survive; *Negro Digest* did, although it was buried for a decade and in 1970 became *Black World*. The magazine, which strove to reflect the Black Power era of the early 1970s, ceased publication in 1976.

## Booker T. Washington and Marcus Garvey

The newspapers during this period had just as unsteady a history. Prominent in the first quarter of the century were two figures, one an educator, the other a politician-editor-churchman, both interested in newspapers rather than periodicals as tools for their purposes. These men were Booker T. Washington and Marcus Garvey.

Washington's vague connections with Black newspapers already have been noted. He was thought, according to Rudwick, to have provided some with financial assistance; it may or may not be significant that his articles appeared in those particular papers. Du Bois accused him, as early as 1905, of having provided several with three thousand dollars in hush money the year before. In time Du Bois even named them: *The New York Age, Chicago Conservator, Boston Citizen, Washington Colored American, Indianapolis Freeman,* and *Colored American* magazine, all now defunct. Rudwick asserts that Washington secretly invested that sum in the magazine and assumed its operations.

Rudwick writes that advertisements were bought in papers which supported him, such support including publication of editorials sent to the editors. Among the papers so favored, he declares, were *The Charleston Advocate* and *The Atlanta Independent*. These editorials appeared in several papers simultaneously, a situation to be expected in chain or group papers but not in those independently owned and separate. To these assertions Ottley adds the view that Washington gained press support by persuading supporters to buy financially weak papers; at one time as many as thirty-five were available to publicize his work or that of supporters. Among them were the Chicago *Broad Ax* and *Chicago Conservator* (Ottley, 1955).

Washington did more than operate behind the scenes, however. After publication of his classic of Black literature, "Up From Slavery," which was inspired by magazine articles he had written, he was asked to write more articles. Ever his opponent, Du Bois declared in one of his autobiographies that these were prepared by Black and white ghost writers, with their headquarters at Tuskegee, of which Washington was president (Du Bois, 1968). Perhaps, like many a presidential and gubernatorial speech and article, his were composed with the help of others. Nevertheless, they were important in advancing Washington's views, especially that the Black man was best able to improve his lot by using the worlds of labor and business as the paths to power.

If Washington was largely on the fringe of Black journalism, Marcus Garvey, at least in the early part of his life, was steeped in it. One of his first jobs was as a printer, at which he worked from his fourteenth to his twentieth year in Kingston. In 1907 he became a master printer and a foreman. When he took part in a printers' strike that year he lost his job, an experience that led him to begin what was to be a lifelong career as an organizer for members of his race to improve their social, political, and economic condition. Black journalism played an important part in Garvey's life. His first venture into publishing began while he was on a government printing office job in 1910 in Jamaica. He started a magazine, *Garvey's Watchman*, the first of a series of short-lived publications he was to sponsor. Next came a fortnightly, *Our Own*, a political organ.

By now he had concluded that organization was needed if he was to help improve the conditions of his people. He quit his job, went to Costa Rica and while there started *Nacionale*, but it too failed through lack of response. Then came another Spanish-language paper, *La Prensa*, likewise short of life. He traveled through South America, where he saw more exploitation of Black workers. Eventually he reached England, where he spotted Washington's classic autobiography, called "Up From Slavery." It inspired him to more efforts to lead his race; it was then that he returned to Jamaica to form the Improvement Association. In two years he went to the United States, and in another two he started the New York paper which was his most important journalistic contribution: *The Negro World*, the Association organ.

A weekly, *The World* rapidly became popular and went to a circulation of about 200,000 at its best, perhaps 50,000 in an average week, with a wide distribution. Garvey was responsible for the paper, writing editorials and at times longer articles, but the bulk of the writing was done by others (Cronon, 1955). It was more an opinion organ than a newspaper, hitting hard for the nationalistic aims of Garvey's group, harking frequently back to Africa. Among the several capable journalists who wrote for it were T. Thomas Fortune and John E. Bruce. *The Negro World*, in fact, for a time was a rival for the *Chicago Defender* as a leading Black paper. Garvey's strong personality and the actions of some followers put *The Defender* in the opposite camp. *The Negro World* naturally espoused Garvey's major campaigns for his shipping company, a Black House to match the White House, Black generals, Black congressmen, and even a Black God.

Garvey wrote forcefully and convincingly. An example of his writing is this portion of an article in *The Negro World* in 1921:

> Some people ask, "Why hasn't the Universal Negro Improvement Association protested against so-and-so, and why hasn't it sent a telegram to the President denouncing lynching? Why hasn't it asked for interviews from Congressmen and Senators over the question of injustice to the Negro?" Why should you want to do this when other organizations have been doing this for the last twenty years without any result (Schoner, 1968)?

*The Negro World* was suspended in 1933, a depression year, outliving several other short-lived Garvey ventures, such as *Negro Times*, a daily; *Black Man*, a monthly magazine; *African World*, a paper distributed in South Africa; the monthly *Negro Churchman*; and the *Negro Peace Echo*. When Garvey died in 1940 a follower revived *The World* in Cleveland as *The New Negro World*, in magazine form, but it soon ceased.

Garvey's plans were to unite all African people everywhere. The organization for which he is most remembered, the Universal Negro Improvement Association, he formed and headed in 1914. It was his platform. Garvey had a sense of the dramatic that made his own and his followers' activities newsworthy. In appearance they were attention-getting. The men were part of what he called the African legion; they wore blue and red uniforms. The women belonged to a Black Cross Nurse Society (Bennett, 1969).

Garvey's following was large among working class Blacks but not among middle class or its leaders, many of whom were disaffected by such bombast as calling himself the Provisional Ruler of Africa in Exile. His plans were very ambitious, involving establishment of a Black Star Line, a steamship company with small vessels in poor condition. African-Americans invested $750,000 in the firm, which could not carry out his glowing plans. Garvey, indicted on fraud charges, was accused of making rosy promises that were not kept. He received a five-year sentence and later was deported to Jamaica. (Decades later, Dr. Robert A. Hill, editor of the Marcus Garvey Papers project at the University of California, found new papers in the National Archives that show Garvey was the victim of Hoover's practice of seeing both Blacks and communists as conspirators against the United States.) The account in his paper, *The Negro World*, on August 11, 1926, carried the headline: "150,000 Honor Garvey" and the story began: "Harlem, the largest Negro community in the world, paid a tribute today to the greatest Negro in the world." He died in London in 1940.

Garvey's political and journalistic contributions are fondly remembered and studied by those who believe that nationalism will save and build a Black movement against white supremacy. Garvey is regarded as a great ancestor in Harlem and other cities.

### Works Cited

Bennett Jr., L., (1969). *Pioneers In Protest*. Baltimore: Penguin Books, 221.

Cronon, E. D. (1955). *Black Moses: The Story of Marcus Garvey And The Universal Negro Improvement Association*. Madison: University of Wisconsin Press, 1955, 46.

Detweiler, F. G. (1922/1968). *The Negro Press In The United States.* Chicago: University of Chicago Press, 1922; College Park, MD: McGrath, 1968, 55–56.

Du Bois, W. E. B. (1968). *The Autobiography of W. E. B. Du Bois.* New York: International Publishers, 238. Material for this chapter was drawn not only from this autobiography but also from Francis L. Broderick, *W. E. B. Du Bois: Negro Leader in Time of Crisis,* Elliot M. Rudwick's *W. E. B. Du Bois: Propagandist of the Negro Protest,* and the chapter on Du Bois in Bennett, *Pioneers in Protest.*

Miles, F. W. (1946). "Negro Magazines Come of Age," *Magazine World* 2, no. 8 (1 June 1946); 12–13.

Rudwick, Elliott M. (1968). *W. E. B. Du Bois, Propagandist of the Negro Protest.* New York: Athenaeum, 1968, 390 pp.

Schoner, Allon, ed., (1968). *Harlem On My Mind: Cultural Capital Black America, 1900–1968.* New York: Random House, 54.

# FURTHER READING

## Bibliography

Daniel, Walter C. *Black Journals of the United States.* Westport, CT: Greenwood Press, 1982, 432 p.

*Provides an alphabetical listing of periodicals from Abbott's Monthly to The Western Journal of Black Studies, including relevant statistical information and a short descriptive sketch.*

## Criticism

Broderick, Francis L. *W. E. B. Du Bois: Negro Leader in a Time of Crisis.* Stanford, CA: Stanford University Press, 1959, 259 p.

*Recounts Du Bois's political agenda in the second decade of the twentieth century, including his use of the editorial page of The Crisis to promote social advancement for African Americans.*

Brown, Sterling A. "The Negro Author and His Publisher." *Quarterly Review of Higher Education Among Negroes* 9, no. 3 (July 1941): 140-46.

*Enumerates the considerable barriers to publication faced by Black writers in the United States.*

Burks, Mary Fair. "The First Black Literary Magazine in American Letters." *CLA Journal* 19, no. 3 (March 1976): 318-21.

*Briefly relates the publication history of the first known Black literary journal, The Anglo-African Magazine, established in 1859 and discontinued six years later.*

Cooper, Wayne F. "With the *Liberator,* 1921-1922." In *Claude McKay: Rebel Sojourner in the Harlem Renaissance,* pp. 134-70. Baton Rouge: Louisiana State University Press, 1987.

*Examines poet Claude McKay's editorial relationship with the New York-based, left-wing journal The Liberator in the early 1920s.*

Fishbein, Leslie. "The Exotic Other." In *Rebels in Bohemia: The Radicals of 'The Masses,' 1911-1917,* pp. 160-81. Chapel Hill: University of North Carolina Press, 1982.

*Views the anti-racist program of the NAACP in the context of U. S. socialist journalism of the early twentieth century.*

Fultz, Michael. "'The Morning Cometh': African-American Periodicals, Education, and the Black Middle Class, 1900-1930." In *Print Culture in a Diverse America,* edited by James P. Danky and Wayne A. Weigand, pp. 129-48. Urbana: University of Illinois Press, 1998.

*Surveys educational themes in nine Black monthly journals published between 1900 and 1930.*

Johnson, Charles S. "The Rise of the Negro Magazine." *Journal of Negro History* 13, no. 1 (January 1928): 7-21.

*Brief history of the African American periodical from its 1827 origins with the appearance of* Freedom's Journal *to the era of* Opportunity *in the 1920s.*

Kornweibel, Theodore, Jr. "The *Messenger* and the Harlem Renaissance." In *No Crystal Stair: Black Life and the "Messenger," 1917-1928,* pp. 105-31. Westport, CT: Greenwood Press, 1975.

*Discusses the Harlem Messenger as an organ of Black literary and cultural development in the 1920s.*

Lash, John S. "The Anthologist and the Negro Author." *Phylon* 8, no. 1 (1947): 68-76.

*Observes the frequent omission of black authors from literary anthologies and remarks on important collections of works by African American writers from James Weldon Johnson's* The Book of American Negro Poetry *(1922) to anthologies of the 1940s.*

Martin, Tony. "Book Reviews." In *Literary Garveyism: Garvey, Black Arts and the Harlem Renaissance,* pp. 91-105. Dover, MA: The Majority Press, 1983.

*Affirms the quality of literary reviews that appeared in the Negro World between 1920 and 1923.*

Meier, August. "Booker T. Washington and the Negro Press: With Special Reference to the *Colored American Magazine.*" *Journal of Negro History* 38, no. 1 (January 1953): 67-90.

*Chronicles Washington's unprecedented control over the Black press in the United States during the first decade of the twentieth century.*

Miles, Frank W. "Negro Magazines Come of Age." *Magazine World* (1 June 1946): 12-14, 21.

*Offers short profiles of such publications as The Crisis, Opportunity, The Journal of Negro Education, Negro Digest, and Ebony.*

Muraskin, William. "An Alienated Elite: Short Stories in *The Crisis,* 1910-1950." *Journal of Black Studies* 1, no. 3 (March 1971): 282-305.

*Describes several works of short fiction that depict the educated, middle-class African American as estranged from both the Black community and mainstream, white culture.*

"Twenty-Six Years of Opportunity." *Opportunity* 27, no. 1 (winter 1949): 4-7.

*Presents an overview of the publication history of Opportunity, noting its rapid growth during the Harlem Renaissance of the 1920s.*

Partington, Paul G. "The *Moon Illustrated Weekly*—The Precursor of *The Crisis.*" *Journal of Negro History* 48 (1963): 206-16.

*Observes the significance of W. E. B. Du Bois's first national magazine, the Moon Illustrated Weekly (1905-1907).*

Redding, J. Saunders. "The Negro Author: His Publisher, His Public and His Purse." *Publishers Weekly* 24 (March 1945): 1284-88.

*Focuses on barriers to Black literary publication in the United States, identifying problems first apparent in the post-Civil War era that extended into the twentieth century.*

Streator, George. "Working on *The Crisis.*" *The Crisis* 58, no. 3 (March 1951): 159-61.

*Remembrance of W. E. B. Du Bois and of a low point in public support for the African American civil rights movement in the mid 1930s by a former editor of* The Crisis.

Vincent, Ted. "The *Crusader Monthly*'s Black Nationalist Support for the Jazz Age." In *The Harlem Renaissance 1920-1940,* edited by Cary D. Wintz, pp. 251-64. New York: Garland Publishing, 1996.

*Chronicles the promotion of jazz, blues, and Black theater in the pages of the* Crusader, *a Harlem-based periodical published between 1918 and 1922.*

Young, P. Bernard, Jr. "News Content of Negro Newspapers." *Opportunity* 7, no. 12 (December 1929): 370-72, 387.

*Endeavors to categorize and assess the journalistic content of African American newspapers in the late 1920s, concluding that representative dailies printed less than ten percent "sensational" news and approximately forty percent news of socializing or cultural value, with the remainder of the publications given to opinion, human interest, sports, and miscellaneous material.*

# PERFORMING ARTS DURING THE HARLEM RENAISSANCE

The Harlem Renaissance is widely considered one of the most significant events in the development of African American literature and culture in the twentieth century. Although the movement manifested itself most clearly in the writings of Black authors of the time, it is especially significant because it touched almost all aspects of African American life, redefining Black music, theater, and the arts in the process. Partially rooted in a growing awareness among Black Americans regarding racial consciousness and pride, the movement is generally dated as an event that occurred during the 1920s, sandwiched between World War I and the Great Depression. However, many critics consider the Harlem Renaissance a fluid and developing artistic and cultural consciousness that blossomed in the 1920s and evolved into a more defined and established Black aesthetic over the course of the next several decades. Regardless of critical disagreement surrounding the dating of the Harlem Renaissance, there is consensus among scholars that the movement was self-conscious, with participants acutely aware that they were in the process of defining parameters and aesthetics of an entirely new era in African American arts, culture, and literature.

In addition to its artistic, literary, and political implications, the Harlem Renaissance exemplified the struggle amongst artists and authors to establish an appropriate aesthetic for African American writing and art. This was characterized most often by an exploration of southern and African roots of Black culture, as well as in the focus on the impact of race and urbanization on the African American experience. Writings of the time drew strongly on the cultural and historic roots of Black Americans, as evidenced in the influence of music on contemporary writing. The early 1920s also saw the burgeoning popularity of Black music, especially jazz, which had hitherto been considered an underground musical movement that only appealed to a narrow section of society. With the advent of such musicians as Duke Ellington, who performed at the Hollywood Club in 1923, jazz now began to emerge as a significant part of the mainstream musical scene in America. The landmark stages for this type of music and the epicenter of the development of Black entertainment, however, was Harlem itself; it flourished in such places as the Cotton Club, the Apollo Theatre, the Savoy Ballroom, Smalls, and the Kentucky Club. Devotees of jazz included both Black and white patrons, and although many Harlem nightclubs admitted Black patrons, it is significant and characteristic of the culture of the time that many places, especially the Cotton Club, a key venue for Black performers, did not. Joseph M. McLaren notes that critics of the arts during the Harlem Renaissance, including W.E.B. Du Bois, W.S. Braithwaite, and others, did not consider the development of jazz representative of "high" African American art. Of the many Black writers active during that time, Langston Hughes was one of a very small number of authors who did laud jazz, using both jazz and the blues in his writing and poetry. Eventually, jazz and other African American music forms were incorporated into the movies as well, indicating the acceptance of this type of music in popular culture.

While many Black intellectuals of the time did not perceive jazz and other Black musical forms as significant contributors to the development of a new Black aesthetic, they felt strongly about encouraging the development of Black theater. However, because of financial constraints as well as the massive collaboration required for successful productions, their vision of a vibrant Black theater did not materialize. Regardless, there were several authors who wrote groundbreaking scripts that both featured Black characters and focused on Black experiences in their writing. One of the leading proponents of the development of Black theater was W.E.B. Du Bois, who argued for a theater "about blacks, by blacks, for blacks, and near blacks." In order to sponsor this development, Du Bois formed the Krigwa Players Little Negro Theater in Harlem, with the group performing several plays during the early twentieth century. Other significant sponsors of African American theater included Alain Locke, who advocated a new Black drama of discussion and social analysis, arguing for a theater that provided a depth and authenticity of experience that he considered missing on the white American stage. Although the two men differed in their opinions regarding the purpose and source of art, they both achieved significant success at the time in encouraging dramatic activity in Harlem and elsewhere. In addition to Du Bois and Locke, Theophilus Lewis, a critic for the *Messenger,* also encouraged the development of African American theater, basing his philosophy for the creation of a national Black theater not only on philosophical concepts but also on his own observation of what was happening with popular Harlem theater at the time. Interestingly, Black theater did flourish somewhat away from New York, in small university theaters in Chicago and Cleveland, among other places.

Although the dream of a vibrant Black theater did not evolve as leaders of the Harlem Renaissance envisioned it, there was enough activity in the arena that by the late 1920s, there was no doubting the increasing popularity of Black themes in the performing arts. This trend was picked up by the movies as well, and in 1928, studios began launching films that were clearly influenced by both Black music and writing. One

of the more significant films of the period was *The Green Pastures.* Based on a play written by Marc Connelly, the work featured Blacks in significant and dignified roles and, as Thomas Cripps notes in his introduction to the play, it "became a powerful document in the history of popular art." Despite wide acceptance of both the film and play by Black and white critics, many of whom jumped at the chance to offer praise for a work by a white person that offered a sympathetic view of Blacks, there were several among the community who saw the film as patronizing, a work that "corrupted more than it cultivated art." Another landmark film made during the Harlem Renaissance was D. W. Griffith's on-screen adaptation of *The Clansman* by Thomas Dixon. Set in the American Civil War, *Birth of a Nation* presented Griffith's vision of the war and its aftermath, focusing on interracial issues. Widely acknowledged as a significant event in the history of Hollywood cinema for its technical innovations, the movie caused great furor among Black intellectuals for its racist portrayal of African Americans, resulting in riots across major cities in the U.S. Today, the film continues to inspire heated debate over its message, the intention of its director, and the effect it had on race relations in the United States. In addition to movies that featured Black themes and characters, albeit in ways unacceptable to modern society, Hollywood also incorporated Black music, notably jazz, widely in productions, beginning with *The Jazz Singer* in 1927. According to Bruce M. Tyler, despite the controversy surrounding such films as *Birth of a Nation* and the continued inequality between Black and white actors, Hollywood and the Harlem Renaissance boomed at the same time during these years, with the film industry providing a means for the greatest and most lucrative exposure for Black artists at that time.

## REPRESENTATIVE WORKS

### Marita Bonner
"One Boy's Story" [as Joseph Maree Andrew] (essay) 1927

*The Purple Flower* (play) 1928

*Exit: An Illusion* (play) 1929

### Marc Connolly
*The Green Pastures: A Fable* (play) 1930; adapted to film in 1936

**W. E. B. Du Bois**
*The Star of Ethiopia* (play) 1911

*The Gift of Black Folk: The Negroes in the Making of America* (essays) 1924

**Edward Kennedy ("Duke") Ellington**
"East St. Louis Toddle-O" (song) 1924

"Mood Indigo" [with Barney Bigard] (song) 1930

**Paul Green**
*White Dresses* (play) 1923

*In Abraham's Bosom* (play) 1927

*The House of Connelly* (play) 1931

**D. W. Griffith**
*The Birth of a Nation* [adapted from *The Clansman*, by Thomas Dixon] (screenplay) 1929

**DuBose Heyward**
*The Emperor Jones* [adapted from Eugene O'Neill's play] (screenplay) 1933

**Langston Hughes**
*The Weary Blues* (poetry) 1926

*Little Ham* (play) 1936

*Don't You Want to Be Free?* (play) 1938

*Mulatto* (play) 1939

**Claude McKay**
*Negroes in America* (play) 1923

*Home to Harlem* (play) 1928

*Banjo: A Story without a Plot* (play) 1929

**Oscar Micheaux**
*Body and Soul* (film) 1924

**Aubry Lyles and Flournoy Miller**
*Shuffle Along* (musical) 1921

**Willis Richardson**
*The Chip Woman's Fortune* (play) 1923

*Negro History in Thirteen Plays* (plays) 1935

**Bessie Smith**
"Reckless Blues" (song) 1925

**Jean Toomer**
*Natalie Mann* (play) 1922

*Song of the Sun* (poetry) 1923

**Ridgely Torrence**
"Granny Maumee," "The Rider of Dreams," "Simon the Cyrenian": Plays for a Negro Theater (plays) 1917

*Hesperides* (play) 1925

*The Story of Gio from the Heike Monogatari, Retold by Ridgely Torrence* (play) 1935

# PRIMARY SOURCES

## PAUL ROBESON (ESSAY DATE 1924)

**SOURCE:** "Reflections on Eugene O'Neill's Plays." *Opportunity* (December 1924): 368–70.

*In the following excerpt, Paul Robeson, one of the most respected actors of the early-twentieth century, offers his recollections of working as a Black actor on the plays of Eugene O'Neill.*

All this seems so very strange to me—writing about the theatre. If, three years ago, someone had told me that I would be telling of my reactions as an actor I would have laughed indulgently. Even now the whole chain of events has a distinct dreamlike quality. To have had the opportunity to appear in two of the finest plays of America's most distinguished playwright is a good fortune that to me seems hardly credible. Of course I am very, very happy. And with these things there has come a great love of the theatre, which I am sure will always hold me fast.

In retrospect all the excitement about *All God's Chillun* seems rather amusing, but at the time of the play's production, it caused many an anxious moment. All concerned were absolutely amazed at the ridiculous critical reaction. The play meant anything and everything from segregated schools to various phases of intermarriage.

To me the most important pre-production development, was an opportunity to play the *Emperor Jones*, due to an enforced postponement. This is undoubtedly one of *"the great plays"*—a true classic of the drama, American or otherwise. I recall how marvelously it was played by Mr. Gilpin some years back. And the greatest praise I could have received was the expression of some that my performance was in some wise comparable to Mr. Gilpin's.

And what a great part is "Brutus Jones." His is the exultant tragedy of the disintegration of a human soul. How we suffer as we see him in the depths of the forest re-living all the sins of his past-experiencing all the woes and wrongs of his people-throwing off one by one the layers of civilization until he returns to the primitive soil from which he (racially) came. And yet we exult when we realize that here was a man who in the midst of all his trouble fought to the end and finally died in the "'eighth of style anyway."

In *All God's Chillun* we have the struggle of a man and woman, both fine struggling human beings, against forces they could not control,—indeed, scarcely comprehend—accentuated by the almost Christ-like spiritual force of the Negro husband,—a play of great strength and beautiful spirit, mocking all petty prejudice, emphasizing the humanness, and in Mr. O'Neill's words, "the oneness" of mankind.

I now come to perhaps the main point of my discussion. Any number of people have said to me: "I trust that now you will get a truly heroic and noble role, one portraying the finest type of Negro." I honestly believe that perhaps never will I portray a nobler type than "Jim Harris" or a more heroically tragic figure than "Brutus Jones, Emperor," not excepting "Othello."

The Negro is only a medium in the creation of a work of the greatest artistic merit. The fact that he is a Negro Pullman Porter is of little moment. How else account for the success of the play in Paris, Berlin, Copenhagen, Moscow and other places on the Continent.

Those people never heard of a Negro porter. Jones's emotions are not primarily Negro, but human.

Objections to *All God's Chillun* are rather well known. Most of them have been so foolish that to attempt to answer them is to waste time. The best answer is that audiences that came to scoff went away in tears, moved by a sincere and terrifically tragic drama.

The reactions to these two plays among Negroes but point out one of the most serious drawbacks to the development of a true Negro dramatic literature. We are too self-conscious, too afraid of showing all phases of our life-especially those phases which are of greatest dramatic value. The great mass of our group discourage any member who has the courage to fight these petty prejudices.

I am still being damned all over the place for playing in *All God's Chillun*. It annoys me very little when I realize that those who object most strenuously know mostly nothing of the play and who in any event know little of the theatre and have no right to judge a playwright of O'Neill's talents.

I have met and talked with Mr. O'Neill. If ever there was a broad, liberal-minded man, he is one. He has had Negro friends and appreciated them for their true worth. He would be the last to cast any slur on the colored people. . . .

## DOROTHY WEST (DOCUMENT DATE 1938)

**SOURCE:** "Amateur Night in Harlem." Federal Writers' Project (December 1, 1938).

*As part of the Federal Writers' Project, writers such as West were charged with chronicling the folk history of specific regions of the U.S. In this piece, West describes the scene during an amateur night performance at Harlem's Apollo Theater. Such events became a hallmark of Harlem culture and continue to the present.*

The second balcony is packed. The friendly, familiar usher who scowls all the time without meaning it, flatfoots up and down the stairs trying to find seats for the sweethearts. Through his tireless manipulation, separated couples are reunited, and his pride is pardonable.

The crowd has come early, for it is amateur night. The Apollo Theater is full to overflowing. Amateur night is an institution. Every Wednesday, from eleven until midnight, the hopeful aspirants come to the mike, lift up their voices and sing, and retire to the wings for the roll call, when a fluttering piece of paper dangled above their heads comes to rest—. . . determined by the volume of applause—. . . to indicate to whom the prizes shall go.

The boxes are filled with sightseeing whites led in tow by swaggering blacks. The floor is chocolate liberally sprinkled with white sauce. But the balconies belong to the hardworking, holidaying Negroes, and the jitterbug whites are intruders, and their surface excitement is silly compared to the earthy enjoyment of the Negroes.

The moving picture ends. The screen shoots out of sight. The orchestra blares out the soulticking tune, "I think you're wonderful, I think you're grand."

Spontaneously, feet and hands beat out the rhythm, and the show is on.

The regular stage show preceds Amateur Hour. Tonight an all-girls orchestra dominates the stage. A long black girl in flowing pink blows blue notes out of a . . . clarinet. It is hot song, and the audience stomps its approval. A little yellow trumpeter swings out. She holds a high note, and it soars up solid. The fourteen pieces are in the groove.

The comedians are old-timers. Their comedy is pure Harlemese, and their prototypes are scattered throughout the audience. There is a burst of appreciative laughter and a round of applause when the redoubtable Jackie Mabley states that she is doing general housework in the Bronx and adds, with telling emphasis, "When you do housework up there, you really *do* housework." It is real Negro idiom when one comedian observes to another who is carrying a fine fur coat for his girl, "Anytime I see you with something on your arm, somebody is without something."

The show moves on. The . . . Sixteen . . . girls of sixteen varying shades dance without precision but with effortless . . . joy. . . . The best of their spontaneous steps will find their way downtown. A long brown boy who looks like Cab Calloway sings, "Papa Tree-Top Tall." The regular stage show comes to an end. The act file on stage. The chorus girls swing in the background. It is a free-for-all, and to the familiar "I think you're wonderful, I think you're grand", the black-face comic grabs the prettiest chorine and they truck on down. When the curtain descends, both sides of the house are having fun.

A Negro show would rather have the plaudits of an Apollo audience than any other applause. For the Apollo is the hard, testing ground of Negro show business, and approval there can make or break an act.

It is eleven now. The house lights go up. The audience is restless and expectant. Somebody has brought a whistle that sounds like a wailing baby. The cry fills the theater and everybody laughs. The orchestra breaks into the theater's theme song again. The curtain goes up. A [WMCA?] announcer talks into a mike, explaining to his listeners that the three hundred and first broadcast of Amateur Hour at the Apollo is on the air. He signals to the audience and they obligingly applaud.

The emcee comes out of the wings. The audience knows him. He is Negro to his toes, but even Hitler would classify him as Aryan at first glance. He begins a steady patter of jive. When the audience is ready and mellow, he calls the first amateur out of the wings.

Willie comes out and, on his way to the mike, touches the Tree of Hope. For several years the original Tree of Hope stood in front of the Lafayette Theater on Seventh Avenue until the Commissioner of Parks tore it down. It was . . . believed . . . to bring good fortune to whatever actor touched it, and some say it was not Mr. Moses who had it cut down, but the steady stream of down-and-out actors since the depression who wore it out.

Willie sings "I surrender Dear" in a pure Georgia accent. "I can' mak' mah way," he moans. The audience hears him out and claps kindly. He bows and starts for the wings. The emcee admonishes, "You got to boogie-woogie off the stage, Willie." He boogie-woogies off, which is as much a part of established ritual as touching the Tree of Hope.

Vanessa appears. She is black and the powder makes her look purple. She is dressed [in black?], and is altogether unprepossessing. She is the kind of singer who makes faces and regards a mike as an enemy to be wrestled with. The orchestra sobs

out her song. "I cried for you, now it's your turn to cry over me." Vanessa is an old-time "coon-shouter." She wails and moans deep blue notes. The audience give her their highest form of approval. They clap their hands in time with the music. She finishes to tumultous applause, and accepts their approval with proud self-confidence. To their wild delight, she flings her arms around the emcee, and boogie woogies off with him.

Ida comes out in a summer print to sing that beautiful lyric, "I Let a Song Go Out of My Heart," in a nasal, off-key whine. Samuel follows her. He is big and awkward, and his voice is very earnest as he promises, "I Won't Tell A Soul I love you." They are both so inoffensive and sincere that the audience lets them off with light applause.

Coretta steps to the mike. Her first note is so awful that the emcee goes to the Tree of Hope and touches it for her. The audience lets her sing the first bar, then bursts into cat-calls and derisive whistling. In a moment the familiar police siren is heard off-stage, and big, dark brown Porto Rico, who is part and parcel of amateur night, comes on stage with nothing covering his nakedness but a brassiere and panties and shoots twice at Coretta's feet. She hurriedly retires to the wings with Porto Rico switching after her, brandishing his gun.

A clarinetist, a lean dark boy, pours out such sweetness in "Body and Soul" that somebody rises and shouts, "Peace, brother!" in heartfelt approval. Margaret follows with a sour note. She has chosen to sing "Old Folks", and her voice quavers so from stage . . . fright . . . that her song becomes an unfortunate choice, and the audience stomps for Porto Rico who appears in a pink and blue ballet costume to run her off the stage.

David is next on the program. With mounting frenzy he sings the intensely pleading blues song, "Rock it for Me." He clutches his knees, rolls his eyes, sings away from the mike, and works himself up to a pitch of excitement that is only cooled by the appearance of Porto Rico in a red brassiere, an ankle-length red skirt, and an exaggerated picture hat. The audience goes wild.

Ida comes out. She is a lumpy girl in a salmon pink blouse. The good-looking emcee leads her to the mike and pats her shoulder encouragingly. She snuggles up to him, and a female onlooker audibly snorts, "She sure wants to be hugged." A male spectator shouts, gleefully, "Give her something!"

Ida sings the plaintive, "My Reverie". Her accent is late West Indian and her voice is so bad that for a minute you wonder if it's an act. Instantly here are whistles, boos, and handclapping. The siren sounds off stage and Porto Rico rushed on in an old fashioned corset and a marabou-trimmed bed jacket. His shots leave her undisturbed. The audience tries to drown her out with louder applause and whistling. She holds to the mike and sings to the bitter end. It is Porto Rico who trots sheepishly after her when she walks unabashed from the stage.

James come to the mike and is reminded by the audience to touch the Tree of Hope. He hasn't forgotten. He tries to start his song, but the audience will not let him. The emcee explains to him that the Tree of Hope is a sacred emblem. The boy doesn't care, and begins his song again. He has been in New York two days, and the emcee cracks that he's been in New York two days too long. The audience refuses to let the lad sing, and the emcee banishes him to the wings to think it over.

A slight, young girl in a crisp white blouse and neat black skirt comes to the mike to sing "A Tisket". She has lost her yellow-basket, and her listeners spontaneously inquire of her, "Was it red?" She shouts back dolefully, "No, no, no, no!" "Was it blue?" No, it wasn't blue, either. They go on searching together.

A chastened James reappears and touches the Tree of Hope. A woman states with grim satisfaction, "He teched de tree dat time." He has tried to upset a precedent, and the audience is against him from the start. They boo and whistle immediately. Porto Rico in red flannels and a floppy red hat happily shoots him off the stage.

A high school girl in middy blouse, jumper and socks rocks "Froggy Bottom." She is the youngest thing yet, and it doesn't matter how she sings. The house rocks with her. She winds up triumphantly with a tap dance, and boogie woogies confidently off the stage.

A frightened lad falls upon the mike. It is the only barrier between him and the murderous multitude. The emcee's encouragement falls on frozen ears. His voice starts down in his chest and stays here. The house roars for the kill, Porto Rico, in a baby's bonnet and a little girl's party frock, finishes him off with dispatch.

A white man comes out of the wings, but nobody minds. They have got accustomed to occasional white performers at the Apollo. There was a dancing act in the regular stage show which received deserved applause. The emcee announces the song, "That's Why—" he omits the next word "Were Born." He is a Negro emcee. He will not use the word "darky" in announcing a song a white man is to sing.

The white man begins to sing, "Someone had to plough the cotton, Someone had to plant the corn, Someone had to work while the white folks played, That's why darkies were born." The Negroes hiss and boo. Instantly the audience is partisan. The whites applaud vigorously. But the greater volume of hisses and boos drown out the applause. The singer halts. The emcee steps to the house mike and raises his hand for quiet. He does not know what to say, and says ineffectually that the song was written to be sung and urges that the singer be allowed to continue. The man begins again, and on the instant is booed down. The emcee does not know what to do. They are on a sectional hook-up-the announcer have welcomed Boston and Philadelphia to the program during the station break. The studio officials, the listening audience, largely white, has heard a Negro audience booing a white man. It is obvious that in his confusion the emcee has forgotten what the song connotes. The Negroes are not booing the white man as such. They are booing him for his categorization of them. The song is not new. A few seasons ago they listened to it in silent resentment. Now they have learned to vocalize their bitterness. They cannot bear that a white man, as poor as themselves, should so separate himself from their common fate and sing paternally for a price of their predestined lot to serve.

For the third time the man begins, and now all the fun that has gone before is forgotten. There is resentment in every heart. The white man will not save the situation by leaving the stage, and the emcee steps again to the house mike with an impassioned plea. The Negroes know this emcee. He is as white as any white man. Now it is ironic that he should be so fair, for the difference between him and the amateur is too undefined. The emcee spreads out his arms and begins, "My people—."

He says without explanation that "his people" should be proud of the song. He begs "his people" to let the song be sung to show that they are ladies and gentlemen. He winds up with a last appeal to "his people" for fair-play. He looks for all the world like the plantation owner's yellow boy acting as buffer between the black and the big house.

The whole house breaks into applause, and this time the scattered hisses are drowned out. The amateur begins and ends in triumph. He is the last contestant, and in the line-up immediately following, he is overwhelmingly voted first prize. More of the black man's blood money goes out of Harlem.

The show is over. The orchestra strikes up, "I think you're wonderful, I think you're grand." The audience files out. They are quiet and confused and sad. It is twelve on the dot. Six hours of sleep and then back to the Bronx or up and down an elevator shaft. Yessir, Mr. White Man, I work all day while you-all play. It's only fair. That's why darkies were born.

# FRANK BYRD (DOCUMENT DATE 1939)

**SOURCE:** "Harlem Personalities: Cliff Webb and Billie Day." Federal Writers' Project (January 19, 1939).

*Working for the Works Progress Administration's Federal Writers' Project, Byrd was one of many writers chronicling the social and cultural life of Harlem. Here he describes an after-hours cabaret performance by two musicians specializing in ethnic folk songs.*

In the Charles Dillingham production of "New Faces" last season, that played to admiring, capacity audiences for many months, were two faces that were once well known in the vicinity of the Park Avenue Market in Harlem. They were the faces of Cliff Webb and Billie Day who at one time provided almost all the after-dark entertainment for the peddlers in the Latin Quarter.

In a little basement cabaret in East 111th Street, they gathered nightly to hear these two croon their plaintive Negro, West Indian and Spanish songs to the accompaniment of an out-of-tune piano and a battered but tuneful guitar. Cliff played the piano and Billie accompanied her own singing with the guitar obligatos. Occasionally there was dancing. Then these two vivacious kids acted as chorus and orchestra for the pleasure-seeking peddlers. The fact that they were able to earn a living solely on the tips they received was a tribute to their popularity. They never received a definite salary. In fact, it was very peculiar how they even happened to get the job.

The two kids had a habit of wandering from one little restaurant or cabaret to another, singing their songs, dancing (if asked) and passing the hat (if the proprietor had no objections) and filing out as quietly as they had appeared. One night they went to the Casa Diablo, the small basement place in 111th Street, and were such a huge success with the peddlers and other transient guests that the owner of the place, a Puerto Rican whom everyone called El Gato, asked them to come in every night and sing for tips. The only incentive offered them was all they wanted to eat and drink. They stayed.

Not long afterwards, the place became quite popular and one night some friends of Leonard Stillman, the director, stumbled accidentally into the place. They listened to the two rollicking youngsters and tipped Stillman off to their whereabouts. He engaged them for his show and they were an immediate success. The very first night they "stopped" the show; were forced to take curtain after curtain call. The blase first nighters were simply mad about them. They were so new, so fresh and unspoiled.

El Gato's place remained the favorite retreat for the market peddlers but the atmosphere was never the same after Cliff and Billie left. Night after night, the peddlers used to sit around talking about the good times they had when these two kids were about and how different it was without them.

# EDWARD KENNEDY ELLINGTON (ESSAY DATE 1973)

**SOURCE:** Ellington, Edward Kennedy. "The Big Apple." In *Music Is My Mistress*, pp. 69–89. New York: Doubleday & Company, Inc., 1973.

*In the following excerpt from his autobiography, Duke Ellington recalls the Cotton Club during its heyday, offering a brief history of the fabled Harlem nightclub.*

The Cotton Club was a classy spot. Impeccable behavior was demanded in the room while the show was on. If someone was talking loud while Leitha Hill, for example, was singing, the waiter would come and touch him on the shoulder. If that didn't do it, the captain would come over and admonish him politely. Then the headwaiter would remind him that he had been cautioned. After that, if the loud talker still continued, somebody would come and throw him out.

The club was upstairs on the second floor of the northeast corner of 142nd Street and Lenox Avenue. Underneath it was what was originally the Douglas Theatre, which later became the Golden Gate Ballroom. The upstairs room had been planned as a dance hall, but for a time the former heavyweight champion, Jack Johnson, had run it as the Club De Luxe. It was a big cabaret in those days, and it would seat four to five hundred people. When a new corporation took it over in the '20s, Lew Leslie was put in charge of producing the shows, and the house band was led by Andy Preer, who died in 1927.

Sunday night in the Cotton Club was *the night.* All the big New York stars in town, no matter where they were playing, showed up at the Cotton Club to take bows. Dan Healy was the man who staged the shows in our time, and on Sunday night he was the m.c. who introduced the stars. Somebody like Sophie Tucker would stand up, and we'd play her song, "Some of These Days" as she made her way up the floor for a bow. It was all done in pretty grand style.

Harlem had a tremendous reputation in those days, and it was a very colorful place. It was an attraction like Chinatown was in San Francisco.

"When you go to New York," people said, "you mustn't miss going to Harlem!" The Cotton Club became famous nationally because of our transcontinental broadcast almost every night. A little later, something similar happened with Fatha Hines at the Grand Terrace in Chicago. But in Harlem, the Cotton Club was the top place to go.

The performers were paid high salaries, and the prices for the customers were high too. They had about twelve dancing girls and eight show girls, and they were all beautiful chicks. They used to dress so well! On Sunday nights, when celebrities filled the joint, they would rush out of the dressing room after the show in all their finery. Every time they went by, the stars and the rich people would be saying, "My, who is that?" They were tremendous representatives, and I'm darned if I know what happened to them, because you don't see anybody around like that nowadays. They were absolutely beautiful chicks, but the whole scene seems to have disappeared. . . .

During the prohibition period, you could always buy good whiskey from somebody in the Cotton Club. They used to have what they called Chicken Cock. It was in a bottle in a can, and the can was sealed. It cost something like ten to fourteen dollars a pint. That was when I used to drink whiskey as though it were water. It seemed so weak to me after the twenty-one-year-old corn we had been accustomed to drinking down in Virginia. That was strong enough to move a train, but I paid no attention to this New York liquor. I just drank it, never got drunk, and nothing ever happened.

The episodes of the gangster era were never a healthy subject for discussion. People would ask me if I knew so-and-so. "Hell, no," I'd answer. "I don't know him." The homicide squad would send for me every few weeks to go down. "Hey, Duke, you didn't know so-and-so, did you?" they would ask. "No," I'd say. But I knew all of them, because a lot of them used to hang out in the Kentucky Club, and by the time I got to the Cotton Club things were really happening!

# OVERVIEWS

## JOSEPH M. MCLAREN (ESSAY DATE 1989)

**SOURCE:** McLaren, Joseph M. "Early Recognitions: Duke Ellington and Langston Hughes in New York, 1920-1930." In *The Harlem Renaissance: Revaluations,* edited by Amritjit Singh, William S. Shiver, and Stanley Brodwin, pp. 195-208. New York: Garland Publishing, 1989.

*In the following essay, McLaren analyses the emerging acceptance of African American music and drama during the early 1920s in the context of Langston Hughes's and Duke Ellington's success.*

In the 1920s, when Edward Kennedy (Duke) Ellington and Langston Hughes launched their careers in New York City, American artistic and popular culture had begun to accept and promote Afro-American literature and music in some measure. In assessing the contributions of Ellington and Hughes, it is essential to consider the outlines of American literary and musical culture in the post-World War I era. American writers such as Hemingway and Fitzgerald, as well as musicians such as Gershwin and Whiteman, had established, or were beginning to establish, reputations by the late 1920s that were international in scope and that assured for them economic and artistic success. However, when one takes a broad view of the American artistic scene, one becomes aware of certain levels of taste characteristically divided into the categories of "serious" and "popular." Literature and music can of course be divided into these categories, and it is sometimes fruitful to do so because the definitions of "serious" and "popular" (or "highbrow" and "lowbrow") can often reveal the aesthetic preferences of certain critics who are considered spokesmen for their particular constituencies of American artistic culture.

Ellington and Hughes certainly fall into both these realms of taste, the "serious" and the "popular," and in the burgeoning years of their careers, their acceptance was heralded by critics to varying degrees. For example, Duke Ellington's engagement at the Hollywood Club in 1923 with his first group of sidemen, then called the Washingtonians, was not mentioned in the American journals of "serious" orchestral music because this band was part of an underground musical cult growing out of and representing the post-World War I era of the "roaring twenties" when jazz came of age and donned the cloak of respectability for many white Americans—especially after Paul Whiteman's introduction of symphonic jazz to New York in 1924.[1]

During the early 1920s, Ellington had not yet made a significant impact on popular musical culture, although he appeared to be destined to help maintain a style of raw jazz-playing that had its source in New Orleans ragtime and the blues. As a relatively unknown group, the Washingtonians were mentioned in local newspapers that announced upcoming engagements. Ellington's reputation as a New York bandleader was especially solidified by his long engagement at the Cotton Club (1927-1933), the underworld-owned showplace of Afro-American entertainment in Harlem. Duke Ellington's name then became firmly associated with American popular musical entertainment, just as jazz itself began to be accepted. Although the Harlem Renaissance, the era during which both Hughes and Ellington began their careers, received a serious setback from the depression of the 1930s commencing with the stock market crash of 1929, jazz continued to flourish with commercialization and symphonic elaboration.

One significant cultural reality in a comparative study of the acceptance of Hughes and Ellington is that Hughes, as a representative and practitioner of Afro-American literary expression, was reviewed by white critics of the "serious" literary world during his early career and especially with the publication of his first volume of poetry, *The Weary Blues* (1926). Reviews of Hughes's *Weary Blues* and his next volume of published poetry, *Fine Clothes to the Jew* (1927), appeared in the *New York Times Book Review* and the *New York Herald Tribune* as well as in Afro-American journals such as *Opportunity* and *The Crisis*.[2]

Criticism of the arts during the Harlem Renaissance, by such figures as W.E.B. DuBois, W.S. Braithwaite, Benjamin Brawley, and Alain Locke, did not discuss the development of jazz as an expression of "high" Afro-American art, and it is significant that Langston Hughes was one of the few Afro-American writers who lauded jazz and in fact structured much of his poetry on the blues form, a musical style that permeated the development of jazz during the 1920s and afterward.

As for Duke Ellington, the 1920s witnessed his rapid growth as one of the leading jazz bandleaders in America, a bandleader who in many ways

## ON THE SUBJECT OF...

**ELLINGTON'S UNQUENCHABLE THIRST**
Roaming through the jungle of "oohs" and "ahs," searching for a more agreeable noise, I live a life of primitivity with the mind of a child and an unquenchable thirst for sharps and flats.

**SOURCE:** Duke Ellington, excerpt from his autobiography, *Music Is My Mistress*, Doubleday, 1973.

surpassed such contemporaries as Don Redman, Fletcher Henderson, Jimmie Lunceford, and Chick Webb. It is significant that Ellington's growth can be measured in terms of his recorded works, his radio broadcasts from the Cotton Club, his night club performances and stage shows, and his popularity abroad, which proved especially consequential as the Ellington band made its first European tour in 1933.

If the success of Hughes and Ellington is any indication of the increasing acceptance of Afro-American literature and music, we must ask to what extent this acceptance contributed to the American artistic scene and American art forms. The Afro-American writer, from Wheatley to Dunbar, had been read and appreciated as an Afro-American. The nineteenth-century black American writer had been, for the most part, an imitator of European-American forms, a spokesman of protest as in Horton and Douglass, or a practitioner of plantation themes as in Dunbar and Chesnutt. Hughes's early work was published and promoted mainly because the American reading public, primarily whites, wanted to hear about the Afro-American experience, and publishers saw this experience as commercially profitable. Hughes is part of an Afro-American literary tradition of imitative art, of protest writing and of folk orientation. The Harlem Renaissance, however, brought to the fore a number of Afro-American writers whose race-consciousness found expression in works of radical artistic form. Originality in music at this time was exemplified by Duke Ellington.

Ellington's contribution to Afro-American music in the 1920s was in many ways a modification of essential elements of New Orleans jazz—

African rhythmic and tonal qualities, blues structures, antiphony and polyphony—and a transference of these modified elements to a new mode of Northern jazz as played in New York. As a form of Afro-American music, jazz dates from Reconstruction and the post-Civil War period. Many jazz critics, such as Hobsen, Blesh, Jones, and Stearns, have demonstrated that blues, worksongs, and spirituals contributed to the development of jazz. Ellington's improvisational music, however, had its early and direct inspiration in the types of ensemble-playing that developed in New Orleans in the 1880s and afterward. It must be said that improvisation, altered tones, and blues elements had not been a primary concern of Afro-American musicians who, particularly in the North, had formed bands in the nineteenth century and were competent practitioners of traditional set-form band presentations. Departing from this, Ellington, it is clear, was working with the same kind of instrumentation as was found in the early jazz groups of New Orleans.[3]

As a product of American culture, jazz prospered through and along with many new mediums of entertainment—radio, motion pictures, and, especially for Ellington, recorded performances. That Ellington led one of the first bands to take part in a Hollywood film, *Check and Double Check,* in 1930, is significant, for it indicates that jazz was becoming part of cinematic popular culture.

Regarding Afro-American literature, the spirit of the 1920s favored artistic expression by Afro-Americans; the Harlem Renaissance was proof of the craving for such expression. A number of scholars have attributed this growing interest in Afro-American literature to the hedonistic spirit of the 1920s and a resurgence of "primitivistic" ideas.[4] Although these conditions were certainly present—with the speakeasy, bootleg gin, and organized crime as a backdrop—the growth of urbanization and the fact that many Afro-Americans had access to higher education allowed room for artistic talent and the creation of forums for its expression. In short, Harlem was the mecca of black entertainment in the 1920s and there is a connection between its cultural milieu and the emergence of literary artists such as Langston Hughes.

If the 1920s can be viewed in American culture as an era of immigration and recession, of "do-nothing" presidents such as Harding, it can also be viewed as a period that marks the artistic and political reawakening of Afro-Americans. The relationship of American culture as a whole to the Afro-American literary renaissance is that its audience—the buyers of books and patrons of black writing—was formed mostly of white American intellectuals. In search of sensation and novelty, this literary elite found enjoyment in Afro-American literature that limned, for the most part, the conditions and cultural make-up of Afro-Americans. It is true, nonetheless, that many writers of the Harlem Renaissance were supported by Afro-American journals.

The acceptance and recognition of Afro-American literature and jazz in the 1920s and the elements that link these two manifestations of artistic expression raise important questions. Indeed, it appears that the poetry of Langston Hughes and the music of Duke Ellington satisfied a certain need: the need to experience the Afro-American reality that seemed grounded in an African "reality" or "primitive" folk qualities of expression. So the increasing taste for Afro-American literature and music showed a connection not only with the new political and social awareness gained by Afro-Americans but also with the realities of destruction brought on by World War I and its aftermath of widespread financial speculation. That taste appeared integral in the 1920s to this era of re-adjustment and rebellion. The white intellectuals who read Langston Hughes's poetry and listened to Duke Ellington's musical entertainment were moved to do so by dominant cultural forces of the times. Langston Hughes especially, among the Afro-American writers, wrote a kind of urban blues that had particular appeal for this urban audience concerned with the conditions of social change. It was an audience that supported Hughes's work because in this era when "the Negro was in vogue," it was "the thing to do." The taste of these patrons was anticipated by publishers who found new themes and new subjects of literary exploration in Afro-American life.

The Harlem Renaissance writers, including Hughes, were also encouraged by black periodicals such as *The Crisis* and *Opportunity*. The rising socialist press of the 1920s, notably *The Messenger* and *The Liberator,* could also be counted on to support the burgeoning efforts of Afro-American authors. It is clear, then, that Afro-American literature of the 1920s, with its themes of race pride, prejudice, folk ancestry, the African past, and the urban predicament, as well as traditional poetic lyricism, was supported by whites, encouraged by intellectual blacks, and published for the most part by the established publishing houses of the dominant literary culture.

The devotees of jazz, or Afro-American music, were also both black and white. Many of the Harlem nightclubs such as Smalls and the Kentucky Club, which could be called platforms for the presentation of "raw" types of ensemble playing that characterized Ellington's organization, allowed black patrons, but the Cotton Club, which was certainly the key booking in the development of Ellington's reputation, did not admit blacks; it was an entertainment arena for wealthy whites and gangland leaders. The Cotton Club is, thus, appropriately symbolic of the entertainment culture of Harlem in the 1920s that catered primarily to white audiences.

One other aspect of American popular culture in the late 1920s helped contribute to the growth of jazz and to the development of Duke Ellington and his orchestra. This phenomenon was the rise of the recording industry and the mass production of phonograph records. During the late 1920s, Ellington and various sidemen recorded widely for many labels such as Okeh under the management of Irving Mills, the promotional agent and businessman who was responsible for securing the Cotton Club engagements and who rapidly accelerated the popularity of Ellington and provided key contacts for the band in the recording industry.[5] The first years of Ellington recordings were on various labels, some of them the so-called "race records" that had a specific audience and a particular method of release and sales. And yet the Duke's connection with a popular form of disseminating musical entertainment can be viewed as a major breakthrough in the history of jazz. It provided for him an audience that could share in and begin to be influenced by the kinds of musical expression that he and others were creating in the late 1920s.

The cultural importance of recordings that, unlike published sheet music, required no particular expertise in order to hear the reproduction, was similar to the aesthetic impact of the motion picture industry, for in both cases the audience needed only to let the product provide the entertainment. It was not essential to participate in the experience, although in the case of recorded music, the participation of the audience often took the form of dance. Recordings were also a way of bringing jazz to areas of the country that might not have been exposed to live performances of jazz, for many of the emerging black bands of the 1920s could not be booked in some areas of the country, especially the South, because of the then prevalent racial practices.

Afro-American literature as represented by Hughes and jazz as represented by Ellington wore different cloaks of respectability and acceptance among most white American patrons of popular culture—in literature and in music—during the 1920s. Like black intellectuals, socially conscious white intellectuals enjoyed *The Weary Blues* and *Fine Clothes to the Jew*. In certain respects, however, Ellington's music and Langston Hughes's poetry corresponded to a rebellious spirit on the part of certain segments of white America and on the part of Afro-American artists. The rebellious college-aged youth and upper-class whites listened to "The Mooch" and "Black and Tan Fantasy" and "East St. Louis Toodle-O."

A consideration of the level of the American population that appreciated the creations of Hughes and Ellington leads to a recognition of the cultural level exemplified by Hughes's poetry and Ellington's music. As mentioned earlier, the writers of the Harlem Renaissance were, for the most part, non-supportive of jazz and considered it "low art." Writers such as Countee Cullen and W.E.B. DuBois saw themselves as promoters of a "higher culture" of the Afro-American experience, and the development of big band jazz was often viewed as an attempt to use coarser elements of Afro-American culture for the purpose of art. Clearly, there had been an ideological split in the attitudes of Afro-American intellectuals toward jazz and its use of loud, so-called raucous effects, especially in its development during the 1920s. In fact, Hughes was perhaps the only writer of the Harlem Renaissance who integrated an essential musical component of jazz into his early poetry and into much of his later work; this essential element is, of course, the blues.

If Ellington's brand of jazz in the 1920s was viewed by some as a frivolous sort of background entertainment, as an outgrowth of vaudeville entertainment, and as a purely popular music designed to produce sensations of pleasure, Hughes's work was regarded in some circles as a serious attempt to promote the Afro-American contribution to American literature. Hughes and Ellington were at different stages of their artistic development in the 1920s, which is evidenced by the types of critical responses their works evoked. Again, jazz and Afro-American literature were not exactly at the same point in their impact on various levels of the culture. (Certainly, symphonic jazz had become by the late 1920s a kind of general popular music of America, but it must be remembered that it was Paul Whiteman who had been a major proponent of this adaptation of jazz

Duke Ellington and Louis Armstrong.

characteristics to the symphonic form. At the same time, white American literary figures such as Eugene O'Neill, Sherwood Anderson, and Paul Green were exploring Afro-American themes and characters in their works of fiction and drama.)[6] It appears, however, that the dissemination of Afro-American cultural ideas that related to literature and music were unequally accepted and reproduced in the 1920s, so that by the time the stock market crashed in 1929, the American reading public had begun to move away from the creations of the Harlem Renaissance writers but had not, and would not, in fact, equally reject and move away from those elements of Afro-American musical expression that were popularly known as jazz.

Since the 1920s represent the development of Hughes and Ellington in their primary stages of artistic recognition, it is significant to examine some of the critical responses and references to their output in this period. For Duke Ellington, the 1920s (especially the first half of the decade) showed that the American musical world was not yet aware of or responsive to the talents and the innovative material presented by the Washingtonians (later known as "Duke Ellington and His Famous Orchestra"). In fact, if we survey two important American periodicals of the time, *Metronome* and *Etude,* we find hardly any mention of

Duke Ellington in the beginning years of his career in New York City and the East. It is revealing to begin looking at these music periodicals from the year 1924, and, although it is practically impossible to find any mention of Ellington or other Afro-American jazz masters such as Louis Armstrong, one does become aware of the aesthetic issues of the times and the relevance of Afro-American music and jazz to American musical consciousness.[7] *Etude* and *Metronome* can serve as clear barometers of the opinions of the established voices of the American musical world of the time, of both the so-called "highbrow" and "lowbrow" levels.[8] Significantly, there appears to be only one mention of Ellington in the late 1920s and this is a reference to his name in the newly added section of *Metronome* called "Where They Are," a listing of club dates for bands and orchestras of the day: "Ellington, Duke—Cotton Club, N.Y." (October 1928). However, with the decline in the debate over jazz and an increased interest in Hollywood motion pictures, one begins to see the incorporation of musical advertisements in *Metronome* that used jazz personalities as "bait."

Certain *Metronome* issues of the 1920s had used important white dance bands and orchestral musicians as spokesmen for musical instruments and accessories—Whiteman and Wiedoeft, for example—but the "night club" hot musician had not yet been "taken up" as a popular selling, promotional and testimonial device. In addition to a general interest in the future of "bands," mostly high school and popular groups, by the close of the decade came the commercial advertising of "hot bands" and musicians. Bix Beiderbecke was part of a Holton trumpet advertisement and by April 1930, a number of Ellington tunes—"The Mooch" and "Birmingham Breakdown," "East St. Louis Toddle-O," and "Black Beauty"—appeared in an Irving Mills music advertisement.[9]

Unlike the development of Ellington's early career, Langston Hughes's recognition in the 1920s was both boldly apparent and significant. The differences in recognition are linked to previously discussed reasons, which suggest that Afro-American literature had progressed at a faster rate than Afro-American music, and that Langston Hughes first began to be published in periodicals that were controlled and edited by Afro-Americans, mainly W.E.B. DuBois's *The Crisis,* admittedly an organ of the "talented tenth" thinkers of the postwar generation. In comparing the development of Ellington and Hughes, it is critical to recognize that Hughes formed part of a tradition of Afro-American authors, beginning with Phillis Wheatley, who had been supported by certain "establishment" publishing houses and who were often considered spokesmen of the Afro-American experience.

Generally speaking, Hughes was lauded by both white and black literary critics. Because Hughes employed blues forms and themes in his first published work of poetry, *The Weary Blues* (1926), he was considered both innovative and radical, a poet of the people, a rhythmic syncopator. As early as 1924, DuBois had recognized the "exquisite abandon of a new day," and Alain Locke's landmark work, *The New Negro* (1925), had praised Hughes's "fervency of color and rhythm; and biblical simplicity of speech."[10]

In short, Hughes was a new poetic voice to be reckoned with by the critics, both black and white. The criticism of Hughes in the 1920s represents a dilemma expressed by both black and white critics over the value and importance of urban folk themes and "lowdown blues" elements in his work. This is particularly apparent in the responses to Hughes's second volume of poetry, *Fine Clothes to the Jew* (1927). Richard Barksdale has described the way in which *The Crisis* set out to defame and rebuke Hughes and other writers of the Harlem Renaissance who employed the facts of urban folk life as themes and structures of their works. Regarding an essay by Allison Davis in a 1928 *Crisis* issue, Barksdale comments:

> The objective of the essay was not only to censure with "learned rebuke" young writers like Hughes and Fisher and McKay but to end forthwith the diabolical influence of Carl Van Vechten on these writers.[11]

Clearly, both black and white critics were split over the significance of blues themes and style in Hughes's works that drew on the "real situation" of urban blacks in an undisguised form. The mention of Van Vechten reminds one that a cult of primitivism, although seemingly Afro-American, was in fact promoted by certain whites who saw the urban blues life as significant and exotic.

Like the issues surrounding the acceptance of jazz in the 1920s, the issues regarding the aesthetic correctness of Hughes's approach to verse point to the development of a black aesthetic as defined by Afro-American artists and critics. Ellington's brand of hot jazz was maligned by certain music critics because of its so-called "unrefined elements," just as Hughes's jazz and blues poetry was disliked because of its "raw folk" elements. Clearly, those Afro-American critics who deplored these elements in Hughes saw the development of unrefined jazz as equally denigrating

to the image of the Afro-American in relation to white American society. And yet, as some others saw it, jazz represented a new form and a new approach to rhythm and tone, and Hughes's urban blues represented an emphasis on folk culture as the basis for poetry. And thus, despite lack of recognition by some contemporaries, both Hughes and Ellington were part of a whole wave of "newness" that influenced American cultural standards in the 1920s.

By examining the underpinnings of the critical approaches to Ellington's type of jazz and Hughes's type of poetry in this period, one is forced to return to what has now become a standard dualistic approach to judging the merits and cultural relevance of American art forms. The dualistic approach is based on a recognition of "high art" and "low art," of "serious" and "popular" culture. If "high art" became associated with the best artistic expression, the definition of "high" was closely linked to the class level of the audience that supported a particular form of "high art." If "low art" was associated with "popular" artistic expression, then "low" was closely connected with distinctly folk-oriented American models, which were offshoots of or improvisations on African and European designs and models. The poetry of Hughes and the music of Ellington were evidence of a re-emergence of contemporary folk expression that used rhythms and themes derived from the life of the folk as the basis of artistic material.

Although Ellington and Hughes developed their early careers in Harlem during the 1920s, they were not necessarily part of the same coterie of creative artists. However, as Faith Berry has pointed out, the two artists did collaborate during the 1930s in the writing of the musical play *Cock o' the World*.[12] Despite differences in critical recognition and reception, both Ellington and Hughes developed their individual artistic visions along similar aesthetic and cultural paths. This is demonstrated not only in their later collaborative efforts but also in the sources and designs of their early creative achievements.

### Notes

1. Much of the factual information on Ellington and the orchestra has been collected from Barry Ulanov, *Duke Ellington* (London: Musicians Press Ltd., 1946), and from the chronology of events in Derek Jewell, *A Portrait of Duke Ellington* (New York: Norton, 1977).

2. Hughes's two volumes of poetry published in the 1920s are *The Weary Blues* (New York: Knopf, 1926); and *Fine Clothes to the Jew* (New York: Knopf, 1927).

3. Four works on the development of jazz have been used for general factual information: Wilder Hobsen, *American Jazz Music* (New York: Norton, 1939); Rudi Blesh, *Shining Trumpets* (New York: Knopf, 1946); Marshall Stearns, *The Story of Jazz* (New York: Oxford University Press, 1956); LeRoi Jones, *Blues People* (New York: Morrow, 1963).

4. See Nathan Huggins, *Harlem Renaissance* (New York: Oxford University Press, 1971), ch. 3, for a discussion of primitivism. See also Amritjit Singh, *The Novels of the Harlem Renaissance* (University Park: Pennsylvania State University Press, 1976), pp. 21-25, 55-57.

5. Ulanov, pp. 73-74.

6. See Doris E. Abramson, *Negro Playwrights in the American Theatre, 1925-1959* (New York: Columbia University Press, 1967), ch. 2.

7. Editions of *Metronome, Etude,* and other jazz periodicals were found in the Library of Performing Arts at Lincoln Center, New York Public Library.

8. See Neil Leonard, *Jazz and the White Americans* (Chicago: University of Chicago Press, 1962), ch. 2. Leonard's is a cogent treatment of the controversy regarding the acceptance of jazz.

9. *Metronome*, 46 (April 1930), 10.

10. W.E.B. DuBois, "Younger Literary Movement," *Crisis*, 27 (February), 161-163; partially reprinted in R. Baxter Miller, *Langston Hughes and Gwendolyn Brooks: A Reference Guide* (Boston: G.K. Hall, 1978), p. 7; Alain Locke, *The New Negro* (New York: Charles Boni, 1925), pp. 4-5.

11. Richard K. Barksdale, *Langston Hughes: The Poet and His Critics* (Chicago: American Library Association, 1977), p. 26.

12. Faith Berry, *Langston Hughes: Before and Beyond Harlem* (Westport: Lawrence Hill, 1983), pp. 263, 285, 313. Although this collaborative effort is mentioned a number of times, it is not clear how this effort was accomplished or exactly when it was initiated and completed. Evidently, Hughes had arranged for Ellington to write the musical score, and the project underwent revision during the latter half of the 1930s while Hughes attempted to find a producer. A later collaborative project, the writing of *Heart of Harlem* in 1945, also shows the compatibility of their artistic visions and styles.

## PETER BROOKER (ESSAY DATE 2000)

**SOURCE:** Brooker, Peter. "Modernism Deferred: Langston Hughes, Harlem, and Jazz Montage." In *Locations of Literary Modernism: Region and Nation in British and American Modernist Poetry,* edited by Alex Davis and Lee M. Jenkins, pp. 231-47. Cambrdige, England: Cambridge University Press, 2000.

*In the following essay, Brooker discusses the juxtaposition of interracial conflicts and undercurrents and the excitement of a newly-emerging cultural identity for African Americans during the Harlem Renaissance. This essay also appears in Brooker's* Modernity, Writing, Film, and Urban Formations *(Palgrave, 2000, pp. 55–74).*

On 15 January 1926, Langston Hughes read first at the Washington Playhouse, then in Baltimore, and at the end of the month at a venue in Claremont Avenue near Columbia University in New York from his newly published first volume of poetry, *The Weary Blues.*[1] The volume was published by Alfred A. Knopf in a striking red, black and yellow wrapper. It carried a drawing of an angular blues pianist on its front by the Mexican caricaturist Miguel Covarrubias and an introduction by the white author, Harlem impresario, friend to Hughes and others of the 'Negro Renaissance', Carl Van Vechten. Vechten had been instrumental in securing the publication of Hughes' book with Knopf and had hosted a party in Hughes' honour in November 1925. His own controversial novel *Nigger Heaven* was also to appear later in 1926.

The reading in Washington was presided over by Alain Locke, Professor of Philosophy at Howard University in Washington and editor the previous year of the special issue of the *Survey Graphic* on black arts and culture and of the celebrated collection *The New Negro: An Interpretation* based upon it.[2] This had announced the arrival of a 'new group psychology' and 'collective effort, in race co-operation' and a social project led by 'the more advanced and representative classes' to reclaim the inspiration and advantages of American democracy.[3] 'The Negro mind', wrote Locke, 'reaches out as yet to nothing but American wants, American ideals.'[4] Locke's emphasis upon the signs of cultural renewal, the evidence of this in the pages of the collection in work by poets, fiction writers, illustrators and essayists on the spirituals, jazz, Africanism and the uniqueness of Harlem made *The New Negro* the symbolic representative text of what came to be called the Harlem Renaissance.

Some of the excitement of this new cultural identity for American blacks must have been in the air at the time of Hughes' reading, but so too undoubtedly were some of the tensions and friction comprising this formation. Many of the familiar positions and cross-currents of the Renaissance move across the face of this moment and it is this dynamic, conflictual, intra- and interracial composition of the Renaissance as a whole that I mean to draw attention to. In itself, this evening in January 1926 stretched back, in a still modestly defined period, to the composition of the title poem 'The Weary Blues' in 1920 and pulled a crowded set of events and experiences forward into itself: amongst them the experience of Hughes' first published poems, notably 'The Negro Speaks of Rivers'; his final break with his father in Mexico; his travels to Africa and Europe; his first meetings with Locke and Countee Cullen, with W. E. B. Du Bois, Jessie Fauset, Blanche Knopf and others, at Harlem parties and literary events; his 'discovery' as a new young Negro poet by Vachel Lindsay at the Wardman Park Hotel in November 1925; and his recent decision to attend Lincoln, a black university, when his contemporaries pressured him to return to Columbia or apply to Harvard.

In one emerging antagonism, Van Vechten had suggested the title of Hughes' volume but this had disappointed Hughes' fellow poet Countee Cullen as catering to whites 'who want us to do only Negro things'[5] and who wondered in reviewing the volume whether blues made for poetry at all.[6] Cullen who was 'in certain ways Hughes' exact opposite'[7] preferred traditional European stanzaic forms and diction to folk forms and idioms. Like Du Bois, eminent editor of *Crisis* magazine and leader of the NAACP (National Association for the Advancement of Colored People), Cullen felt the new Negro must show the race's best artistic and intellectual side. Du Bois' opinion appeared in his offended reviews of Van Vechten's *Nigger Heaven* and of *Home to Harlem,* the uninhibited novel of the lives, loves and music of Harlem blacks by the Jamaican-born Claude McKay, whose example and contribution as associate editor of the socialist journal the *Liberator* had much impressed Hughes.[8]

There were, that is to say, profoundly conflicting views on the proper sources and definition of 'art' circulating at the very outset of the movement. These differences were compounded by the relation of black intellectuals and writers to white friends, supporters and patrons, of whom Van Vechten was one. Patronage was common but, not surprisingly, often thought to risk personal and artistic integrity and a loss of 'race pride'. Much of this thinking was targeted at Van Vechten who it was later felt had distorted Hughes' work; a charge refuted by Hughes who had, for his part, spoken out in defence of *Nigger Heaven.* They remained lifelong friends, whereas Van Vechten's friendships with Cullen and with Locke evidently cooled. One factor was that all three men were homosexual, though Van Vechten and Cullen both married. Hughes' sexuality remains mysterious, but it is clear he was propositioned by both Cullen and Locke. Locke had met him in Paris to ask for a contribution to the *Survey Graphic* and both men had travelled to Italy before separating there. On his return Hughes was affronted by Cullen's advances. This personal history of affection, ardour, misunder-

standing also preceded the publication of Hughes' volume and was no doubt a further undertow on 1814 North St as Hughes read his verse.

The moment of Hughes' arrival as a poet of the Negro Renaissance with his first published volume was a moment therefore of genuine common purpose but also of less evident internal differences, upon key matters of race, art and sexuality. As such, I suggest, it provides a picture of the complex configurations of this cultural formation as a whole. There are three factors, either immediately or more distantly active in these months in 1925 and 1926, which filtered out into Hughes' work and the identity of the 'Renaissance' which I want to expand upon. The first is the major site of this formation in Harlem; the second, the role of the blues and jazz in developing a racialised black aesthetic and identity; and the third the meanings given (and which we might give) in this specifically located context and history to modernism.

One of the most striking facts about the young Hughes is the extent of his travels—in one way anticipating his prolific output across genres as one of the first self-declared professional black writers. Before *The Weary Blues* in 1926 when he was twenty-four, he had lived in Cleveland, Mexico and Washington, sailed as cabin boy on a six-month trip to West Africa, sailed twice to Holland, lived, worked and hustled in Paris and Italy.[9] Harlem was hailed in *The New Negro* as the 'race capital', 'a city within a city' and Hughes had felt its affirmative impact on first arriving for his abortive period of study at Columbia in 1921. In *The Big Sea* he writes in what was a common trope in writings of the period, of arriving at the subway of 135th Street in 1921: 'Hundreds of coloured people! . . . I went up the steps and out into the bright September sunlight. Harlem! I stood there, dropped my bags, took a deep breath and felt happy again.'[10] However, Hughes did not reside for any length of time in Harlem until later years. After reading in New York in January 1926, for example, he returned immediately on the night train to Washington where his mother was living. Either side of this date in the twenties, when he was not travelling outside the United States, he lived as a student at Lincoln University in Philadelphia and later in New Jersey, coming into Harlem for the weekends. Here—judging from the accounts in *The Big Sea*—he joined a round of literary and social gatherings, readings, shows, 'parties and parties'[11] in which he sometimes felt out of place and disenchanted by the bourgeois airs of the proceedings.

For Hughes, therefore, Harlem was a vibrant centre, 'a radiant node or cluster' in the language of European Imagism; a vortex, even, 'through which ideas were constantly rushing', and through which he himself moved, in an irregular pattern of departure and return. Just as James Weldon Johnson wished to define the area as neither colony nor ghetto but 'a city within a city',[12] so too for Hughes, as for a figure like McKay who opted for self-exile in Paris, it was a centre within a broader geo-social and artistic network, whose energies travelled back and forth along the lines of force of their lives and work. Hughes' connections with other places and peoples, including artists and writers, consorts with the view of the diasporic nature of the Renaissance, elaborated especially by James de Jongh in his *Vicious Modernism*. This was clear from the outset, however, in the recognition in *The New Negro* of the mixed West-Indian and Afro-American identities of Harlem blacks; in the connection with Europe, and especially Paris, of intellectuals like Du Bois and Locke and of jazz entertainers and celebrities like Paul Robeson and Josephine Baker.

Harlem was therefore the dynamic hub in a dispersed 'travelling' culture: at once a definite place on the map, where artists and residents discovered an enriching cultural community, 'a paradise of my own people' as Claude McKay had put it on his arrival in 1914,[13] but whose symbolic value was felt beyond itself and beyond this immediate sense of a utopian belongingness. We need to recall too how these meanings and connections radiated outwards from an evolving rather than fixed physical locale, how the place on the grid map of Manhattan dramatically changed its literal shape as well as its economic and cultural identity over these two or more decades. In the 1900s blacks lived in the Tenderloin district of lower Manhattan. By 1910, with the migration to the North from the rural South, New York's black population had increased from a few hundred to 5,000. It was at this point that blacks began to move North within the city into Harlem, first into rented accommodation, then as a house-owning bourgeoisie into what Kellner calls the 'beige colony' of the first block West of Fifth Avenue.[14] Whites resisted and then deserted the neighbourhood and house prices dropped. In the early 1920s black Harlem comprised six blocks between 125th and 131st Sts, bounded by the overcrowded crime- and poverty-stricken tenements of Fifth Avenue to the East and the luxury middle-class apartments of Eighth Avenue and Sugar Hill to the West. To the North, from 145th St, the less than two square miles of 'Coogans Bluff' was also black and contained some 200,000 residents. Lenox Avenue was a line of pool halls, cabarets and dives with some restaurants and theatres. The show piece, however, was 'Black Broadway' on Seventh Avenue from 127th to 134th Sts: a fanfare of churches, theatres, businesses, restaurants, speakeasies. Seventh Avenue, writes Kellner, 'was thriving and well groomed and active all day, and from five in the afternoon until after midnight it was brilliant and glamorous and exciting'.[15]

This is the Harlem James Weldon Johnson described in *The New Negro*, expanded now to 'twenty five solid blocks' North of 125th St;[16] an 'inner city' of fine, well-priced housing and economic independence, booming entertainment and active artistic cultural life. Even so, *The New Negro* omitted to describe the poverty and discrimination originally reported in the *Survey Graphic*, and other writers—Wallace Thurman, Hughes and McKay, for example—were in their turn to represent even the Harlem of the heyday of the Renaissance differently. By the end of the decade Harlem was sliding into the recession and the further dramatic decline into the ghetto of the 1930s described by Gilbert Osofsky.

In the twenties, Harlem, we might say, 'jes grew', but, as above, this dynamism brought with it both an intensely felt collective unity and a complex pattern of social and racial differentiation. By the mid-twenties Harlem was unquestionably black. Its population numbered 175,000 black residents and in the most densely populated areas around Lenox and Fifth Avenue it supported 233 residents per acre, compared with 133 per acre in Manhattan. Most were employed as manual labourers or in menial, servicing or domestic work. Many were destitute and trapped in crowded, crime- and vice-ridden tenements without the mobility of the elite blacks of the literary and artistic intelligentsia.[17] Like whites the latter came and went; though, once again, on different terms and even at different times of day. There were 120 entertainment spots in the ten-block area off Lenox Avenue, 25 or so along 'Jungle Alley' along 133rd St,[18] but, as is well known, some were for mixed audiences and some, notably the Cotton Club, were for whites only. Rent parties for blacks took place in Harlem, other kinds of parties downtown.

A revealing illustration of these kinds of differences, involving Hughes, occurred, casually enough so it would seem, on an occasion in May 1925. Charles S. Johnson hosted an impressive banquet to announce the winners of a poetry competition run by *Opportunity* magazine in a Fifth Avenue restaurant near 24th St in downtown Manhattan. Here, writes Rampersad, was 'the greatest gathering of black and white literati ever assembled in one room'.[19] Hughes won first prize for the poem 'The Weary Blues' and after the banquet accepted Van Vechten's invitation to meet him and some others 'for a night on the town' in Harlem at the Manhattan Casino and then the Bamville Club. Musicians from the Cotton Club were going on to the more egalitarian Bamville where blacks and whites danced in mixed couples.

Evidently, Harlem—in its internally differently coded sites and protocols—was for whites a place of spectacle: an exotic 'marginal zone'[20] or 'erotic utopia'[21] where whites could explore their late-night darker selves. Van Vechten, whom Hughes visited the next day with his manuscript of poems, lived downtown on West 55th St. Here Hughes often stayed or attended Van Vechten's celebrated parties. Another guest and herself a party-giver *extraordinaire* was the black heiress A'Leila Walker. She had asked Wallace Thurman to secure her an autographed copy of Hughes' *Weary Blues* in January 1926 and decorated a wall of the elaborate 'Dark Tower' tea room at her mansion on 126th St with a section of the title poem. Harlem too had its wealthy black middle class.

The 'city within a city' was itself internally coded, therefore, as a residential area (for poor, working-class blacks) and entertainment centre (for middle-class blacks and whites): intimately connected to the white and black world of Manhattan and beyond. Emerging technologies and modes of production reinforced this social and spatial hybridity. The offices of the important journals and white-owned publishing industries, for example, were in Manhattan and the NAACP and National Urban League had been established there since the 1910s. It was this materially based cultural apparatus of (in Harlem) theatres, clubs, fugitive magazines, the important meeting place of the 135th St branch of the New York Public Library, and (in Manhattan) of patrons, publishers and related organisations which supported the Renaissance writers and brought them to public attention. And it was this development which at the same time distinguished Harlem from Washington where Hughes first read *The Weary Blues*. Harlem was more 'modern' than Washington because New York was more modern, in its technologies, communications and more egalitarian culture: a locus for the publication of ideas of the modern 'New Negro' and in the NAACP and National Urban League a centre for reform and organised resistance to racial injustice.

Within the larger modernising metropolis Harlem was more of a magnet, a 'Mecca' in the sub-title of the special number of the *Survey Graphic,* than an enclave. It drew peoples and ideas toward it but also expanded and exhaled in ways that re-shaped and patterned the developing city in a series of indentations and cross-hatched lines of communication. The picture emerges of a stratified and permeable heteropolis, experienced simultaneously as an autonomous but dependent, and in significant ways subordinate community within the metropolis. As such, the dynamic physical site of Harlem itself expressed the very 'twoness' of the American Negro as famously described by W. E. B. Du Bois; embodying in its spatial relations the paradox and hope of being at once black and American. In James Weldon Johnson's description, in what turns out to be an unintended but telling echo of aesthetic modernism, Harlem was 'a large scale laboratory experiment in the race problem'.[22]

In January 1926 at the Washington reading, once more, Hughes had planned a jazz performance for the interval. His chosen musician was from the slum area of Seventh Avenue. Alain Locke had however stepped in and hired a performer who could provide more polite jazz.[23] The incident clearly reveals how differences of class and artistic sensibility helped determine the public image and consumption of the new Negro art. That this should be expressed through music is especially significant. Hughes had already decided on an aesthetic which drew upon African American and 'folk' sources, but folk art and music, most conspicuously, had an ambiguous status for Renaissance intellectuals and supporters. Locke, like Du Bois, looked more to the spirituals for this folk source, the 'kernel' indeed for Locke of black folk song, praised for its 'universality', intricacy and 'tragic profundity'.[24] As such, spirituals promised to stand not only as the 'classic folk expression' of the Negro but as 'America's folk song'.[25] His thoughts were accompanied in *The New Negro* by an essay on jazz by J. A. Rogers. Hutchinson and Gilroy have stressed Rogers' case for the democratising influence of jazz but this view in his essay is combined with much else which echoes contradictorily through his own and others' arguments.[26]

This tension surfaces especially in Rogers' view of 'the jazz spirit' as 'being primitive'.[27] In one set of associations where 'being primitive' is

# ON THE SUBJECT OF...

## W. C. HANDY

William Christopher "W. C." Handy (November 16, 1873-March 28, 1958) co-founded a music-publishing company with Harry Pace in Memphis in 1908. After moving to New York in 1918, the Pace and Handy Music Company became the leading publisher of music by African Americans. Handy served variously as a musical consultant, concert program producer, and booking agent. He also continued playing trumpet, composing, arranging, touring, and recording. During his life as a performer, Handy played with such popular groups as W. A. Mahara's minstrels, with Jelly Roll Morton, and with other jazz and popular-music luminaries. He appeared at theaters, dance halls, and concert venues as an instrumentalist and as a bandleader.

Handy's first published blues, "Memphis Blues," in 1912, started a fad; by 1914 he had published the song for which he is best known, "St. Louis Blues." Later he published "Beale Street Blues," making a third Handy "standard" in America's published blues canon. A consensus among jazz historians is that some compositions popularly attributed to Handy are derivative. Some esteem him more highly as a collector, publisher, and popularizer than as a creator of blues. Handy was a pioneer in bringing folk blues to the public. This led to his being called "the Father of the Blues," which was later used as the title of his autobiography.

equated with 'frankness and sincerity' and 'naturalness', it can be extrapolated as 'a leveller [which] makes for democracy'. On the other hand, where the spontaneity and 'physical basis' of jazz's primitivism is responsible for 'its present vices and vulgarizations, its sex informalities, its morally anarchic spirit', it stands in need of musical refinement and cultivation. This is provided, says Rogers, by 'white orchestras of the type of the Paul Whiteman and Vincent Lopez organizations that are now demonstrating the finer possibilities

of jazz music' and in the flattering adoption of American Negro jazz in 'serious modernistic music' notably by French composers. What in one sentence is 'vulgarization' becomes 'primitive new vigor' in another. Rogers ends with a call 'to lift and divert it into nobler channels'[28]—a sentiment and mission echoed, without the tensions of his essay, in the evolutionary schema proposed later by Locke, by which the crudities of Chicago's 'hot jazz' are put through the sieve of the more melodic 'sweet jazz' of New York to produce the third, elevated category of the 'jazz classics' of the big orchestras and the 'symphonic' or 'classical jazz' of Paris. Though Negro, Locke comments, jazz is 'fortunately . . . human enough to be universal in appeal and expressiveness'.[29]

Locke was wary of commercialisation and, for all his evident cultural elitism, positively acknowledged the technical expertise of jazz performers. Others like Countee Cullen would ignore the folk source altogether. Reviewing *The Weary Blues*, Cullen questioned whether blues or jazz poetry should be admitted to 'that select and austere circle of high literary expression which we call poetry'.[30] He wished, he said, repeatedly, to be 'a poet, not a Negro poet'.[31] His theme was taken up by George Schuyler and Hughes replied to both positions in his famous essay 'The Negro Artist and the Racial Mountain' in June 1926. Here he hit out at 'the smug Negro middle class' dogged by the subconscious whisper that 'white is best'.[32] Instead he turns to the 'common people' and to jazz, 'their child', an 'inherent expression of Negro life in America' and 'the tom-tom of revolt against weariness in a white world'.[33]

Hughes' riposte to Cullen and Schuyler served as a manifesto of 'American Negro' poetry; a call to re-articulate blackness in a white America—at the risk of offending either (or both) whites or blacks. Two contemporary incidents suggested how fraught this enterprise was, however. Van Vechten had hailed jazz as 'the only indigenous American music of true distinction',[34] and as part of his researches into its black roots had consulted Hughes on the blues for an article in *Vanity Fair*. After reading in Washington, Hughes met Bessie Smith at Baltimore and asked her opinion of Van Vechten's essay. She was dismissive and saw the blues as a means to making money, not art. If Hughes meant to be in touch with this black blues sensibility he was not, any more than he shared Van Vechten's innocent new enthusiasm and taste for light jazz. As an 'American Negro' poet he was positioned somewhere between and to the side of both raw blues singer and white essayist, while in quite another world from most American Negro leaders.

At the heart of differences on the new Negro, therefore, there were problematic constructions of folk art, the blues and jazz: the culture of 'the black folk' or 'masses' who artists and intellectuals sought to represent and direct. The ambiguities were such that spirituals or blues or jazz could be either esteemed as a positive and authentic cultural expression or rejected as a demeaning presentation of racial identity. The uncomprehending 'coloured near-intellectuals' of Hughes' essay tended to view spirituals, pre-eminently, and the blues, less comfortably, in primitivist or essentialist terms as expressions of an Africanist or Southern rural folk culture, and to see jazz as the degraded culture of modern urban blacks. For those seeking uplift, jazz was too evidently tainted with inartistic and untutored performance, with an unabashed display of sexuality and with juke joints, drink and prostitution: in short with 'low' parts of the city, mind and body. But jazz too was constructed in divergent ways. The dives and cabarets arguably comprised the core of Harlem's symbolism, the compound 'chronotope' of its identity in space and time, and the jazz performed there echoed Harlem's ambiguities: at once in Rogers' terms 'a joyous revolt', the 'release of all the suppressed emotions'[35] and the scene of vice, vulgarity and anarchy.

What Renaissance leaders feared was that 'jazz abandon', in Rogers' coinage,[36] confirmed the worst stereotypes of the Negro to white voyeurs and cultural arbitrators, and thus to themselves; hence the arguments for its necessary refinement and the defence of its diluted and European 'classical' forms. On the other hand, 'the primitive' was esteemed for being precisely this. Both Hughes and Zora Neale Hurston were on this count recruited by the immensely rich white patron Mrs Charlotte (Rufus Osgood) Mason to recover the lost African essence of the American Negro. From 1928 she financed Hughes at college, on his travels and in his New Jersey lodgings. The experience was to prove traumatic and the relationship broke down (with some conniving by both Hurston and Locke) over the issue precisely of 'being primitive'. In Hughes' own, evidently selective and compressed account in *The Big Sea*,[37] Mrs Mason had objected to the poem 'Advertisement for the Waldorf Astoria' which exposed how the new hotel exacerbated discrepancies between the poor blacks of Harlem and the vast wealth of whites on Park Avenue. He sat silently while she told him how he had failed himself and her. It came down, he reflected later, 'to the old impasse between white and Negro'.[38] But if this was the governing division, it carried with it manifest differences of social class, competing notions of the primitive black and artistic creativity, and the personal psychological needs on both sides: of the young brown man, estranged from his family, and the dowager patron who insisted on being called 'godmother'. The involvement of Hurston and Locke, throughout, and more distantly of Van Vechten in the final squabbles and separation in this episode, confirm how these general issues were woven once more into the fabric of gendered, sexual and professional relationships between friends and collaborators. The cultural and artistic movement we unify under the name of the 'Harlem Renaissance' proved once more to be a mutable formation showing all the marks, on these different levels of personality and idea, of divergent and common endeavour, of support and rivalry, and of unequal power.

The traumatic break with Mrs Mason in 1930 was a break with a sentimentalised version of Hughes' own project and the accompanying appeal to an essentialised blackness. 'I did not feel the rhythms of the primitive surging through me', he wrote, 'I was only an American Negro—who had loved the surface of Africa and the rhythms of Africa—but I was not Africa. I was Chicago and Kansas City and Broadway and Harlem.'[39] He emerged with the socially grounded sense of black cultural identity of the 'Negro Mountain' essay and his own class-based allegiance confirmed. It was out of this, I believe, paradoxically as the Renaissance neared its end, that Hughes came to produce an urban-based populist modernism.

The thirties underlined Hughes' allegiance to black proletarian experience and cultural forms, now more emphatically expressed in favour of jazz rather than blues. J. A. Rogers had equated jazz with Americanism: it 'ranks with the movie and the dollar as a foremost exponent of modern Americanism', it had absorbed 'that tremendous spirit of go, the nervousness, lack of conventionality . . . of the American, white or black, as compared with the more rigid formal nature of the Englishman or German'.[40] For their part Europeans, and the German avant-garde, in particular, welcomed jazz and America as joint symbols of the machine age.[41] The black jazz entertainer and America were admired as discordant emblems of an exotic otherness and frenetic modernity combined: a fevered collision of the primitive and the new world. Meanwhile, the vocabulary of 'newness' and 'renaissance' which percolated through the decade, the association of jazz particularly with urban life and with the developing technologies of transport (conveying musicians on an emerging 'circuit' from city to city and continent to continent), of radio, recording and promotion, only confirmed this metaphorical association with progress and social modernity.[42]

But if Harlem and the new Negro and jazz were 'modern' was the latter also 'modernist'? The answer I think is that the jazz of the 1920s was new but evolutionary rather than revolutionary, that its sexual aura was an affront to middle-class respectability in the way that some European modernisms were, but that for all the differences of colour and commercialism between, say, the Fletcher Henderson and Paul Whiteman bands, it was primarily a dance music and, unlike those modernisms, a broadly social, popular art. A 'modernist' jazz appeared, I believe, in the 1940s and 1950s, well after the generally recognised period of the Renaissance, and along with it the most conspicuous and sustained examples of modernist 'jazz poetry' by Hughes, in the sequences *Montage of a Dream Deferred* (1951) and *Ask your Mama* (1961). I want to discuss the first poem in these terms below. Much depends in this, of course, on how we conceive of modernism. At its least controversial this implies a marked degree of formal experimentation within the terms of a given medium. Modernist art comes therefore to claim a self-regarding autonomy—in a way that jazz and swing bands did not. More depends, however, on how this internal innovation addresses the newness of social modernity, on how it is received in this society, on its ideological inflection by class, gender and ethnicity and on its relation to popular culture. The terms of debate in the present instance on the construction of modernism in relation to black writing and culture are most usefully mapped in the positions taken by Houston Baker and George Hutchinson, both of which bear interestingly on Hughes' poem. I want to consider these first.

In *Modernism and the Harlem Renaissance,* Baker directly challenges the hegemony of the Anglo-American-Irish canon of literary modernism. In place of its limited ideas of 'civilisation' and supporting critical categories, he proposes a '"renaissancism" in Afro-American expressive culture as a whole'[43] stretching across the longer modern period of the 1880s to the 1930s. He views this black tradition as exercising either a 'mastery of form' or 'deformation of mastery': discursive strategies by which African-American culture has assimilated and remobilised dominant white dis-

course in the interests of a 'quintessential' Afro-American spirit or racial 'genius'.[44] Hutchinson, rightly, critiques the binarism of Baker's model and the essentialist notion of black identity it invites. He stresses instead the 'diverse interracial and interethnic cultural resources' impinging upon and in tension with a conviction of the 'cultural wealth of black America'.[45] However, this is in the end itself unpersuasive. Firstly, because the description of an 'intercultural matrix' and of *'kinship'* across 'ostensibly opposite racial traditions'[46] risks flattening out what are artistic, social and racialised inequalities, and, secondly, because while he speaks of 'American modernism' and of 'African American modernism', Hutchinson does not define these sufficiently in aesthetic or formal terms.[47] Modernism abuts in his study upon the leading 'problematic of cultural nationality' and is composed of tendencies in pragmatist philosophy, anthropology and democratic theory which he tends to assume were an active part of the thinking of the participants.[48] No doubt he avoids a definition of aesthetic modernism because this has been corralled by advocates of European high modernism. The result, however, is that this domain of artistic activity is surrendered rather than reoccupied.

In fact, the kind of description one wants throughout is less a formalist definition than an account of the terms and criteria by which and when 'high modernism' was established as a settled orthodoxy. What this would make clear is that, excepting Graves and Riding's *Survey of Modernist Poetry* in 1927, definitions of modernism, as such, did not appear until American critics of the 1950s began to ruminate on the *passing* of this paradigm.[49] 'Modernism' was therefore a retrospective construction which did not exist in the mind of its participants in the same terms as it did for its conservers. It was only at this later point also that alternative modernisms and 'post modernism' began to come into view. Baker's 'renaissancism' of 1987 refutes this already waning model and the limitations of its historical as much as racialised perspective. In reconfiguring black writing and arts of the earlier twentieth century (and thus beyond this era) he is in effect refuting the criticism of the midcentury. Though this critical orthodoxy is his opponent, he tends, like Hutchinson, to ignore it; and by the same token to ignore the literature it construed this way.

If we have this historicised cultural construction of modernisms in mind, the idea of 'renaissancism' and an emphasis upon an interethnic intertextuality both become appropriate to Hughes. Hughes had modelled his verse upon American, populist or democratic examples, both black and white: namely, Walt Whitman, Carl Sandburg and Claude McKay. In *Montage of a Dream Deferred* the resources of this tradition were joined with jazz idioms and structure under the organising concept of 'montage' drawn from the vocabulary of European film and painting. Hughes had entitled a poem 'Montage' in *One-Way Ticket* (1948) and might have been influenced by the explicitly montaged composition of John Dos Passos' *USA* (1938). Rampersad reports anyway that Hughes felt that montage was 'the crucial medium of the twentieth century' and that this coincided with his awareness of the transformation in jazz by Dizzy Gillespie, Thelonius Monk and other musicians producing bop and be-bop.[50] This was the modernist moment of jazz composition, when New York became known as 'the jazz capital' rather than 'race capital' of the world and a moment too when leading black musicians, notably Miles Davis at the end of the forties, began to play with white musicians such as Gerry Mulligan, Gil Evans and Kenny Baker.

Hughes' intentions are clear in the original prefatory note to the sequence of poems:

> In terms of current Afro-American popular music and the sources from which it has progressed—jazz, ragtime, swing, blues, boogie-woogie, and be-bop—this poem on contemporary Harlem, like be-bop is marked by conflicting changes, sudden nuances, sharp and impudent interjections, broken rhythms, and passages sometimes in the manner of the jam session, sometimes the popular song, punctuated by riffs, runs, breaks, and disc-tortions of the music of a community in transition.[51]

*Montage* consequently tracks this community through the psychogeography of Harlem locales (Lenox, Minton's, Small's, The Harlem Branch Y), following life on the street and in time through the passage from morning to night in an echo of the twilight areas and stark contrasts between black and white. The poem's social content, vernacular idiom and jazz form are unmistakable. As a poem of sound and speech, its jazz riffs, trills, neologisms ('combinate', 'trickeration') and the occasional blues refrain punctuate a sequence of often juxtaposed 'conversationing' voices—of children, women and men expressing resignation, defiant self-affirmation, cynicism, and the humour of laughing back 'in all the wrong places'.[52]

These voices speak of the embedded inequalities of this world ('I know I can't be president'), of its racism and discrimination and the relative safety of Harlem ('Not a Movie'); the passing equivalence of white and black (at 'Subway Rush Hour', 'mingled so close . . . so near no room for fear') and most profoundly of their persistent, complex, reluctant interdependence ('a part of you, instructor. / You are white—/ Yet a part of me, as I am part of you / That's American'; 'Theme for English B'). So the poem moves in a zig-zag of single notes, asides and solos against the emotional drumbeat ('Harlem's Heartbeat')[53] of the dream and the dream deferred which rumbles underneath, breaks the surface, and runs the poem to its cumulative end in a jam session of its structuring motifs, themes and phrasing.

We can think with some justice of the poem as being at once 'dialogic', in the full sense of combining consensual and dissident voices in Bakhtin's use of this term, and as a 'jazz poem' which matches the rhythms, harmonies and dissonance of jazz performance.[54] One of the best descriptions of jazz so conceived remains Ralph Ellison's—who felt he had played a role in introducing Hughes to bop and to whom, with Fanny Ellison, 'Montage' was dedicated. Ellison wrote of jazz, with bebop and Charlie Parker in mind, as a dialogic and combative art in which each improvised solo flight springs from a challenge with other musicians; 'each true jazz moment' he saw as 'a definition of identity: as individual, as member of a collectivity and as a link in the chain of tradition'.[55]

Ellison's account closely echoes the general description of modernism offered above and by Harvey.[56] Jazz is 'modernist' by virtue of its internal formal experiment and bebop answers especially to this definition. We can go beyond this, however, if we read into relations between the innovative solo, group dynamics and tradition of jazz, the tensions between the individual and the social mass marking social modernity. Indeed, Nanry's account of jazz and modernity suggests just such a homology between jazz composition and the relation of the individual to the social collective in the new modern city. Jazz, and bebop in particular, comes to model the 'disjunction and uprootedness' experienced by city dwellers and their enforced, 'often painful' search for 'commonality'.[57]

We might want to distinguish between the weaker or stronger, more exploratory and questioning forms that either jazz or jazz poetry can take along these lines. In which case we would need to think in terms of a critical transformation rather than a reflexive homology between artistic and social forms. Any judgment of Hughes' *Montage* in these terms must take account of its internal form, as above, and social content, but also of its critical purpose and the relation between this 'modernist' jazz poem by a black poet and the prevailing modernist orthodoxy.

The 'boogie-woogie rumble' of the dream runs underneath, is passed on to become common knowledge ('ain't you heard?'); an acquired rhythm shaping a shared consciousness that recognises this deferral as its own experience. The poem's vignettes present strategies for survival and sociality (to 'Dig and Be Dug / In Return');[58] seizing the times which interrupt this rhythm and bring a sunny Sunday (when 'Harlem has its / washed-and-ironed-and-cleaned-best out') or money or love: the lucky break in lives ruled by chance. Sometimes these are stories of individuals, often of couples or of the community who realise a moment of joy and oneness in song or dance or in a street parade. Toward its close, the poem extends its sympathies toward other ethnicities, to Jews and Hispanics in Harlem and (though barely) to whites downtown ('Likewise', 'Good Morning', 'Comment on Curb').

The sense of community here is splintered and unequal but these groups are felt, if fleetingly, to experience a common frustration of their desires. The poem asks 'What happens to a dream deferred? Does it dry up, fester, sag, *Or does it explode*?'[59] The poem warns, therefore, of unrest and riot, such as had occurred in Harlem in the 1930s, but there is no sense that this would be mobilised through any organised social agency. Here, evidently, the poem stumbles. As an expression of collective frustration it seeks a collective solution. This was provided in the poem's first appearance in the credo of America's political character and destiny embodied in the poem 'Freedom Train'. However, this was removed from the sequence by Hughes for the *Selected Poems* of 1959. What remains of the *'Dream within a dream'* of American democracy is a fantasy of jitterbugging, singing unity in Harlem ('Projection') and of its two-tone 'gold and brown' wrapped in 'dancing sound' ('College Formal', 'Renaissance Casino', 'Island'). The change withdraws the earlier belief in the inevitability of the American way but does not abandon the ideal of democracy. The resulting tension, we might say, embodies its eventual structure of feeling, an unresolved duet of black in white, white in black ('a part of me, as I am a part of you').

We might argue too that this tension—felt in the registration of a fragmented, expectant consciousness and an uneasy, because willed and rhetorical, conviction in a renewed cultural and ideological unity—is characteristic of many 'classic' modernist poems. I do not want to suggest that Hughes' *Montage* is finally or fundamentally like *The Waste Land* or the *Cantos*. It shares a topology or problematic with these and other modernist texts, a structure of aspiration and failure to achieve coherence, but there is much too that it does not share; in its sources, its social complaint and democratic sympathies. It is odd perhaps too to think of a modernist poem being produced in 1951. If it is this, it would seem to confirm Baker's argument that black writing renews itself outside the confines of the orthodox Anglo-Irish/American paradigm. The point, however, once more, is that 'canonic' modernism was constructed after the event and that white culture is also (of course) engaged in a process of renewal and consolidation; indeed, that both cultures were involved at this moment, as earlier, in the process of cultural re-definition.

What makes this clear is the appearance in the early 1950s of Ellison's 'modernist' *Invisible Man* and Melvin B. Tolson's 'high modernist' 'E & O.E' and *Libretto for the Republic of Liberia,* a work Rampersad describes as 'the most hyper-European, unpopulist poem ever penned by a black writer'.[60] Both writers offer versions of 'black modernism' which contrast significantly with Hughes' work, as was clear at the time. I want to comment briefly on the example of Tolson. His highly allusive fifteen-page 'E & O.E' appeared with footnotes in *Poetry* magazine (which had had a long association with literary modernism). It was championed there by Karl Shapiro who had earlier rejected poems by Hughes. The same number also ran an essay by William Carlos Williams damning Carl Sandburg, one of Hughes' major inspirations. Tolson's *Libretto* was hailed by the *New York Times* as the equal of Eliot's *Waste Land,* Crane's *The Bridge* and Williams' *Paterson.* Allen Tate praised Tolson as the first Negro poet to have 'assimilated completely the full poetic language of his time and by implication the language of the Anglo-American poetic tradition'.[61] Tolson had succeeded in producing an erudite and inaccessible modernism for a minority and in producing himself as a latter day version of Countee Cullen who wanted to be 'a poet, not a Negro poet'. The assumption in such an aim is that poetry is above race and ethnicity; that it is 'colourless'. But this apparent invisibility is the very power which whiteness as a received and unseen norm possesses.[62] Had Tolson, though a black poet, produced a 'white modernism' for the admirers of T. S. Eliot, or in Baker's terms performed a 'deformation of mastery', re-appropriating hegemonic modernism for the purposes of black culture? The reception of the poem would suggest the first.

What, to put this matter in other terms, seemed to be at issue at this moment was a prevailing cultural 'taste': a compound of the power of the critic, a now 'modernist' tradition, and an aesthetic which esteemed complexity, seriousness and artistic dedication and dismissed simplicity, commercialism and the use of 'folk' idioms. Hughes was accused of all of the latter, but this 'taste' will not break into white versus black. If Tolson succumbed to the example of Eliot, Ellison committed himself to a serious dedication to art and distanced himself from Hughes on that count. Likewise, the jazz of the 1940s and 1950s sought to create a taste for complexity so as to outrun the white business industry and the standardised black and white jazz of the previous era and so establish itself as a black avant-garde art form. Hughes aimed in *Montage* to negotiate between this experimentalism and a common black experience in the name of a future for the American Negro. Such were the terms of his 'populist modernism'.

We may be abe to recognise finally, however, that in the 1990s these quarrels over definition are behind us. Raymond Williams suggests that we can make the necessary move beyond the fixities of modernism (and postmodernism) by thinking of how we make 'a modern *future* in which community may be imagined again'.[63] Hughes' 'populist modernism' was generally, and in the terms of one of the poems of *Montage*, a 'Projection', oriented, in its directness, whimsy and unresolved complexities, toward the future—as Williams' remarks are and as the work of Walt Whitman, Hughes' consistent inspiration, also was. To be modern, black and American—this in the end was the deferred common dream of a future democracy upon which Hughes improvised.

## Notes

1. See Arnold Rampersad, *The Life of Langston Hughes*, vol. 1: *1902-1941. I, Too, Sing America*, 2 vols. (New York and Oxford: Oxford University Press, 1986), vol. 1, pp. 123-4. I draw on this and the subsequent volume for much of the biographical information which appears in this chapter.

2. See George Hutchinson, *The Harlem Renaissance in Black and White* (Cambridge, Mass.: The Belknap Press of Harvard University Press, 1995), for an extensive discussion of *The New Negro* and a consideration of the differences between this volume and the special issue of the *Survey Graphic*.

3. Alain Locke (ed.), *The New Negro: An Interpretation* (1925) (New York: Johnson Reprint Corporation, 1968), pp. 10, 11.

4. Ibid., pp. 11-12.

5. Rampersad, *The Life of Langston Hughes*, vol. 1, p. 113.

6. Edward J. Mullen (ed.), *Critical Essays on Langston Hughes* (Boston: G. K. Hall, 1986), pp. 37-9.

7. Rampersad, *The Life of Langston Hughes*, vol. 1, p. 63.

8. Du Bois viewed *Nigger Heaven* as 'a caricature . . . a mass of half truths . . . a blow in the face' and complained that *Home to Harlem* 'nauseates me'. See Amrijit Singh, *The Novels of the Harlem Renaissance* (Pennsylvania State University Press, 1976), pp. 30, 44-5, and Kathy J. Ogren, *The Jazz Revolution: Twenties America and the Meaning of Jazz* (Oxford University Press, 1989), pp. 126-9.

9. Gilroy cites Hughes on these grounds as a symptomatic figure in the 'Black Atlantic'. Paul Gilroy, *The Black Atlantic* (London: Verso, 1994), p. 13.

10. Langston Hughes, *The Big Sea: An Autobiography* (1940) (London: Pluto, 1986), p. 81; and see Christopher Mulvey, 'The Black Capital of the World', in Christopher Mulvey and John Simons (eds.), *New York: City as Text* (London: Macmillan, 1990).

11. Hughes, *The Big Sea*, p. 247.

12. James Weldon Johnson, 'Harlem: The Culture Capital', in Locke, *The New Negro*, p. 301.

13. Wayne F. Cooper, *Claude McKay: Rebel Sojourner in the Harlem Renaissance. A Biography* (Baton Rouge: Louisiana State University Press, 1987), pp. 70-1.

14. Bruce Kellner (ed.), *The Harlem Renaissance: A Historical Dictionary for the Era* (London: Routledge, 1987), p. xv.

15. Ibid., p. xviii.

16. Johnson, in Locke, *The New Negro*, p. 301.

17. Gilbert Osofsky, *Harlem: The Making of a Ghetto, Negro New York, 1890-1930* (New York and Evanston: Harper Torchbooks, 1963), pp. 137-8.

18. Ogren, *The Jazz Revolution*, p. 62; Arnold Shaw, *The Jazz Age: Popular Music in the 1920s* (New York: Oxford University Press, 1987), pp. 59-60.

19. Rampersad, *The Life of Langston Hughes*, vol. 1, p. 107.

20. Ogren, *The Jazz Revolution*, p. 57.

21. Osofsky, *Harlem*, p. 186.

22. Johnson, in Locke, *The New Negro*, p. 310.

23. Rampersad, *The Life of Langston Hughes*, vol. 1, p. 123.

24. Locke, *The New Negro*, pp. 210, 199-200.

25. Ibid., p. 199.

26. Hutchinson, *The Harlem Renaissance in Black and White*, p. 423; Gilroy, 'Modern Tones', in *Rhapsodies in Black: Art of the Harlem Renaissance* (London: Hayward Gallery; and University of California Press, 1997), p. 108.

27. J. A. Rogers, 'Jazz at Home', in Locke, *The New Negro*, p. 223.

28. Ibid., pp. 223, 223, 221, 222, 224.

29. Alain Locke, *The Negro and His Music* (1936) (New York: Arno Press, 1969), p.72. See Paul Burgett, 'Vindication as a Thematic Principle in the Writings of Alain Locke on the Music of Black Americans', in Samuel A. Floyd, Jr (ed.), *Black Music in the Harlem Renaissance: A Collection of Essays* (Knoxville: University of Tennessee Press, 1993).

30. Countee Cullen, review of *The Weary Blues,* rpt in Mullen, *Critical Essays on Langston Hughes,* p. 38.

31. Onwuchekwa Jemie, *Langston Hughes: An Introduction to the Poetry* (New York: Columbia University Press, 1973), p. 7.

32. Langston Hughes, 'The Negro Artist and the Racial Mountain' (1926), rpt in August Meier *et al.* (eds.), *Black Protest Thought in the Twentieth Century* (Indianapolis: Bobbs Merrill, 1965), p. 115.

33. Ibid., p. 112, p. 114; and see Peter Brooker, *New York Fictions: Modernity, Postmodernism, The New Modern* (London: Longman, 1996), pp. 181-2, p. 187.

34. Rampersad, *The Life of Langston Hughes,* vol. 1, p. 109.

35. Rogers, in Locke, *The New Negro,* p.217.

36. Ibid., p. 220.

37. See Rampersad, *The Life of Langston Hughes,* vol. 1, pp. 185-94.

38. Hughes, *The Big Sea,* p. 325.

39. Ibid, p. 325.

40. Rogers, in Locke, *The New Negro,* p. 216, p. 220.

41. See Beeke Sell (ed.), *Envisioning America* (Cambridge, Mass.: Busch-Reisinger Museum, Harvard University, 1990).

42. Nanry confirms the association of jazz, capitalist expansion, the technologies of mass production and the modern city. The 'modernism' of his title, however, refers to these processes of modernity and 'modernization' rather than to aesthetic modernism: Charles Nanry, 'Jazz and Modernism; Twin-Born Children of the Age of Invention', *American Review of Jazz Studies* 1 (1982), 146-54. Rogers' view is echoed also in Harvey, who identifies the 'modernism' of 1920s jazz with its revolt against tradition: Mark S. Harvey, 'Jazz and Modernism: Changing Conceptions of Innovation and Tradition', in Reginald T. Buckner and Steven Weiland (eds.), *Jazz in Mind* (Detroit: Wayne State University Press, 1991), pp. 128-47.

43. Houston A. Baker, Jr, *Modernism and the Harlem Renaissance* (Chicago University Press, 1987), p.8.

44. Houston A. Baker, Jr, *Afro-American Poetics: Revisions of Harlem and the Black Aesthetic* (Madison: University of Wisconsin Press, 1988), p. 5.

45. Hutchinson, *The Harlem Renaissance in Black and White,* p. 25.

46. Ibid., p. 31.

47. Hutchinson later cites Hughes' poem 'I, Too', included in *The New Negro* as an example of this 'kinship'. This misses the position of disadvantage from which this claim is made in the poem. Where he approaches the question of definition, Hutchinson speaks of Harlem Renaissance modernism as drawing upon traditions of realist and naturalist discourse. This is interesting and relevant to Hughes. But why we should call this or the intellectual traditions he discusses 'modernist' rather than 'modern' is unclear: Hutchinson, *The Harlem Renaissance in Black and White,* pp. 414, 117-20.

48. Hutchinson, *The Harlem Renaissance in Black and White,* pp. 7, 30.

49. Peter Brooker (ed.), *Modernism/Postmodernism* (London: Longman, 1992), pp. 5-13.

50. Arnold Rampersad, *The Life of Langston Hughes.* Vol. 11: *1941-1967. I Dream a World,* 2 vols. (New York and Oxford: Oxford University Press, 1988), vol. 11, p.151.

51. Quoted in Jemie, *Langston Hughes,* p. 63.

52. Langston Hughes, *Selected Poems* (1959) (London: Pluto, 1986), p. 230.

53. Ibid., pp. 223, 265, 248, 227.

54. See Brooker, *New York Fictions,* pp. 182-7.

55. Ralph Ellison, *Shadow and Act* (London: Secker and Warburg, 1967), p. 234.

56. Harvey, in Buckner and Weiland, *Jazz in Mind,* p. 149.

57. Nanry, 'Jazz and Modernism', p. 149.

58. Hughes, *Selected Poems,* p. 234.

59. Ibid., p. 268.

60. Rampersad, *The Life of Langston Hughes,* vol. 11, p. 235, and see 193 and 201.

61. Ibid., p. 235.

62. See Richard Dyer, *White* (London: Routledge, 1997), pp. 2-3.

63. Raymond Williams, 'When Was Modernism?' in his *The Politics of Modernism: Against the New Conformists,* ed. Tony Pinkey (London: Verso, 1989), p. 35.

# DRAMA OF THE HARLEM RENAISSANCE

## JOHN M. CLUM (ESSAY DATE 1972)

**SOURCE:** Clum, John M. "The Negro Plays." In *Ridgely Torrence,* pp. 100-17. New York: Twayne Publishers, 1972.

*In the following essay, Clum notes that although Torrence's plays are virtually unknown today, they were a landmark achievement in the early twentieth century because they provided, for the first time in history, an opportunity for Blacks to play a significant part in the American dramatic scene.*

I have sometimes imagined that the Negro, other things being equal, might produce the greatest, the most direct, the most powerful drama in the world.[1]

The five-year span preceding the premiere of Torrence's play *Granny Maumee* in 1914 was a time of inactivity for Torrence, and there are a number of possible explanations for his creative doldrums. Moody's death was undoubtedly one of the reasons for the silence, but it can hardly be considered the primary one. A more likely factor would be the disillusionment Torrence felt over his lack of success with his dramatic writing, for none of his prose plays had been produced or published.

He was out of work and dependent financially upon the generosity of his family and friends. Any of these factors could have led to this period of disillusionment or depression which hampered his creativity.

Torrence still considered New York his home during these years, but he was forced to spend a good deal of time in Xenia where he was supported by his family. He also spent some time at a roominghouse in Cos Cob, Connecticut, where living was less costly than in the city. Records and correspondence from the years 1909-14 are scarce, and what does exist is of little importance to a study of Torrence's literary career.

## I. Marriage

The years from 1914 to 1917, however, were also crucial years for Torrence personally; moreover, they did more than any other period to establish his place in the inner circle of American literary figures. On the evening of February 3, 1914, Torrence's parents were awakened by the following telegram: "Was married this evening to Olivia Dunbar and stole march on Findley."[2] Torrence and Miss Dunbar had been friends since the young poet had moved into the Judson in 1906. In fact, he was infatuated with the young, attractive writer of short stories during the first months of their acquaintance, but their correspondence shows little mention of marriage. It seems possible that their decision to get married at this time was linked to Torrence's hopes for his new Negro plays. Jobless as he had been for so many years, he saw the plays as the new hope for a financial return from his work. Whatever their reasons for marriage after such a delay, time proved it to be a happy one. Of course, one of their well-wishers was their old friend from the Judson days, Edwin Arlington Robinson. Robinson's note seems strangely reserved, but it is not atypical of the poet:

> I have no means of knowing how much or how little my best wishes are worth to either of you, but you may be sure that you have them, and that they are entirely genuine. I was not very much surprised by the news, for the occurrence seemed in the order of things likely to happen.
>
> I hope most sincerely that all will go well with you, and that you will forgive me for not saying so in more brilliant language.[3]

Chard Powers Smith, in his recent biography of Robinson, reports that Torrence, not long before his death, had admitted that Robinson was in love with Olivia and was upset on returning from Peterborough, New Hampshire, in the fall of 1912 to find Olivia engaged to Torrence. Smith cites this incident as the cause for the "lapse in their (R.T. and E.A.R.) former intimacy" that followed.[4] This statement might be convincing were it not for Torrence's report next year (1915) that he and Olivia had been seeing "a good deal" of Robinson.[5]

## II. The Significance of the Negro Plays

Although Torrence's plays about Negroes did have great success at the box office, their place in the memory of this generation of theatergoers is virtually nonexistent. However, his three *Plays for a Negro Theatre* made a place for the Negro in serious American dramatic literature. As Edith J. R. Isaacs notes in her study, *The Negro in the American Theatre,* "They marked . . . a turning point in Negro theatre history. They broke completely with all theatre stereotypes of Negro character. They gave Negro actors a first fine opportunity. They made Negroes welcome in the audience. They showed that Negroes could appreciate a white man's contribution to the literature of their life, if it were written in truth and beauty."[6] These plays, then, opened the door for the Negro in our theater.

Soon other serious playwrights, both white and Negro, turned to the Negro as a rich source of dramatic material. In the 1920's, Eugene O'Neill wrote *The Emperor Jones,* that brilliant study of man's descent from king to savage through fear and superstition. The 1930's brought Marc Connelly's delightful folk play, *Green Pastures;* DuBose Heyward's picture of life in Charleston's Catfish Row, *Porgy,* later to become Gershwin's great folk opera; and the federal theater's brilliant all-Negro *Macbeth.* More recently we have seen Langston Hughes, Lorraine Hansberry, Ossie Davis, and LeRoi Jones depict the Negro with an honesty that is at times delightful but often unsettling.

We have come to take the Negro's place on the American stage for granted; but, before Torrence's plays, the Negro and his problems were rarely presented on the legitimate stage in any form. Of course, *Uncle Tom's Cabin* had been a standby during the previous century, but it was popular when its antislavery theme was safely out of date. The only previous twentieth-century play to consider the Negro was Edward Sheldon's *The Nigger,* which had enjoyed a fair amount of success in the 1909-10 season. The play was not really about Negroes but about the crisis that occurs when the governor of a southern state is discovered to have some Negro blood. The problem is treated in a tabloid fashion that makes good theater, but it has little relation to real social concerns. The only

Negro who appears is an old mammy, the sister of our hero's quadroon grandmother, and she emerges as nothing more than a stereotype of the faithful Negro servant. The play does not suggest that the hero should be accepted as he was before the discovery of his origins, despite his Negro blood. As a matter of fact, the hero himself rejects this idea: "Black's black, an' white's white. If yo' not one, yo' the othah, Geo'gie. I've always said that, an' I reckon I'll have to stick to't now!"[7]

If Torrence's plays did not explore the social problems of the Negro in America, such as poverty and inequality, in a way that would satisfy the Negro in our era of civil rights protests, they did for the first time present the Negroes as human beings with all the dignity and potential for both comedy and tragedy that they deserve. Moreover, their production was the first all-Negro performance of a serious play in the legitimate theater.

There seem to be two reasons for Torrence's new interest in Negro drama, both of which are presented in a statement he made in *Crisis* in 1917:

> I have sometimes imagined that the Negro, all other things being equal, might produce the greatest, the most direct, the most powerful drama in the world.
>
> And then, of course, it was not only the capacities of the Negro as actor that I wished to exploit in my plays. It was also the extraordinary dramatic richness of his daily life. . . . In modern life, the Negro comes face to face with many tragedies unknown to the Anglo-Saxon. And then, of course, his natural buoyancy of disposition produces a wealth of comedy which all the world has now learned to love. The parallel of all this with the Irish race and its national drama made a deep impression on me. I wanted to make the experiment, and try to contribute something, if I could, to a possible Negro drama, as vital and charming as the Irish.[8]

The first reason, then, is Torrence's enthusiasm for Irish folk drama, caused by the American visits of the Abbey Theatre. The Irish Players from the Abbey had made their first appearance in New York at the Maxine Elliott Theatre on Thirty-ninth Street on November 20, 1911. The repertoire included the greatest products of the Irish renaissance: Synge's *Riders to the Sea* and *The Playboy of the Western World*, Lady Gregory's *The Workhouse Ward*, Yeats's *Kathleen na Houlihan*, and Shaw's *The Shewing-Up of Blanco Posnet*. Because of the success of their engagement, the company returned the next season to present a repertory, beginning on February 4, 1913, at Wallack's Theatre. Torrence was strongly impressed by the folk drama the Irish had developed and saw great possibilities for such a form on the American stage.

We must remember, however, that the Irish players merely strengthened an interest in folk material that was already evident in Torrence's earlier plays, *The Madstone* and *The Thunder Pool*. In both those plays folk legends provided the central symbol. Yet it had been six years since these plays were completed. In all probability the impact of the Irish players was enough to counteract Torrence's disillusionment with the failure of his two prose plays and to kindle his desires to create an American folk drama.

His new interest in the Negro as the source for his plays is not difficult to explain. Before the Civil War, Torrence's home town of Xenia, Ohio, was an important stop on the underground railroad, the route by which runaway slaves escaped to Canada with the aid of Northern Abolitionists. Because of this, and because of its southwestern position in the state, not far from the Kentucky border, many Negroes also came to Xenia to settle after the Civil War. Near it, one of the country's major Negro colleges, Wilberforce University, developed. Thus Negroes played an important part in the life of Xenia, and in Torrence's childhood:

> When I was a boy, I saw a great deal of my colored townsmen who occupied Xenia's "East End." Xenia, by the way, is a concentrated patch of Southern flavor and tradition, having been the focal point of immigration from all the Southern states for sixty years before the Civil War.
>
> I didn't deliberately seek the Negroes out. They were there and they were entertaining playmates. Their ways became as familiar to me as the ways of my own relatives. Their speech, their voices, their laughter, evoked an unconscious but perfectly sympathetic mimicry; so that Negro dialect became the only language not my own that I have ever learned to speak with facility and I believe with pretty complete accuracy.[9]

In his unpublished autobiography, Torrence tells of his later contact with the Negroes of Xenia while working on his father's farm during his periodic visits home during the early years of this century:

> In October, as soon as the black frost came, it was time to have the pigs to market. This was always a little earlier by day and in the slow horse drawn trucks under the early afternoon sun, the pigs would "drift" and reduce their poundage by many degrees. But by night, usually under the moon, these treks were not only the wisest but also filled with romance. Usually the drivers consisted of my brother, four Negroes—Zachariah Letts, the tenant on our farm, a tall gaunt brown man unquestionably of Arab descent; Milo Alexander, also an evident Arab or Moor, with a hawk nose and majestic curly beard; Cal Hatcher, foreman in our lumber yard, a mulatto; Alec Morgan, a powerful

full blooded black elder—and myself. Behind us all, in the low phaeton, sat my father, driving our wise old mare, Gipsy, a household deity, proceeding at a snail's pace, always adapting her sensitive discernment to the situation. As we passed the various sleeping homesteads, the Negroes would converse with each other regarding their owners past and present.

"Das de old Conklin place. Man, many's de time I wuk in dem fields for ole man Conklin. Well, man, you never hear word from him no more."

"Well, you ain' goin' to wuk fer him no more."

"How come?"

"He done fell asleep in Jesus."

"Man, you're telling me somethin'. I ain' never hear dat. When was dis?"

"Way back yondah."

"Now look at his here place, beyont. Who live here now?"

"Man, dat's de sheepinest-raisin' man dat we ever had. But I thought dat was de ole Galloway place?"

"It uster be but Sheep Macmillan took it from de court."

"How come dat?"

"De farm finally come down to Bill Galloway an' you know about him?"

"Dat drinkin' man?"

"Drinkinest man I ever knew. Drink it all up."[10]

As with most of Torrence's experiences in his native region, it was quite a while before he decided to use his knowledge and memories of the Negroes of Xenia as the basis of a literary creation. Just as his poetry showed a greater freedom and mastery of his medium when he used familiar, regional material, his Negro plays, stemming as they did from his own experiences, displayed an economy and mastery of dramaturgy absent from his earlier poetic dramas. Moreover, just as his shorter lyric poems showed a decided improvement over his more ambitious pieces, the one-act Negro plays are much more successful than the early attempts at full-length dramas. Torrence had obviously discovered for himself that he was a miniaturist as well as a regionalist. Most important, however, was the fulfillment of the attempts made in the earlier prose plays to achieve poetic drama in prose as Moody had in *The Great Divide.*

## III. The Production of the Negro Plays

The late winter of 1914 brought with it the first stage presentation of one of Torrence's Negro plays, *Granny Maumee,* the first of his plays to be produced. In February, Torrence wrote Harriet Moody of the proposed production: "The pieces are both Negro plays. One I have now written

PERFORMING ARTS

## ON THE SUBJECT OF...

**RIDGELY TORRENCE**

Frederick Ridgely Torrence was born 27 November 1874 in Xenia, Ohio. Although he is little studied today and is perhaps best remembered as a poet, Torrence was among the first white American dramatists to write serious roles for Black actors. As an admirer of the Irish Abbey Theatre, which helped revitalize the Irish dramatic tradition, Torrence hoped that his *Granny Maumee, The Rider of Dreams, Simon the Cyrenian: Plays for a Negro Theater* (1917) would be similarly successful in establishing an African American theater. The playwright's home town of Xenia was a great influence on his work. Having been an Underground Railroad stop during the Civil War, Xenia became home to many former slaves and their descendants. Torrence knew his Black neighbors, and his unfinished memoir *Reminiscences,* quoted in John M. Clum's 1972 monograph, reflects his appreciation for their culture: "Their ways became as familiar to me as the ways of my own relatives. Their speech, their voices, their laughter, evoked an unconscious but perfectly sympathetic mimicry; so that Negro dialect became the only language not my own that I have ever learned to speak with facility and I believe with pretty complete accuracy." Torrence later drew upon his knowledge of African American speech and folklore in writing his *Plays for a Negro Theater.*

within the past ten days and handed in yesterday. The other is already on the way. The producer is an organization called the Play Society. It pays no money and gives but two performances of each play but the productions are made to give plays a start and try to create a popular demand for popular performances. The Society is composed of practical professional people and the Frohmans furnish the Lyceum Theatre."[11]

The play was presented during the last week in March; and, in accordance with the policy of the Play Society, it was given a public matinee on Monday preceded by an invitational dress rehearsal the night before. As is usually the case with special Sunday performances, the audience for the unveiling of *Granny Maumee* was composed largely of theater people on a busman's holiday. *Granny Maumee* was preceded on the bill by a heavily cut revival of *A Woman Killed with Kindness,* Heywood's Jacobean potboiler, which was probably intended to be the chef d'œuvre. Typical of the enthusiastic critical reception of *Granny Maumee* was the review by Carl Van Vechten in the New York *Press:*

> There has been no more important contribution made to American dramatic literature than Ridgeley [*sic*] Torrence's "Granny Maumee." It opened up entirely new fields.
>
> The audience at the Sunday night rehearsal, which was made up entirely of well known people, made the theatre resound with bravos after the curtain had fallen on the piece, and Dorothy Donnely, the principal interpreter (a white actress) was called before the footlights again and again.
>
> Mr. Torrence in "Granny Maumee" has written a serious play entirely about the negroes from the negro point of view. The whole thing is as real, as fresh, as the beginning of the Irish theatre movement must have been in Dublin.[12]

Of course, the critical acclaim must have been most gratifying for the poet, but the excitement of the marriage and the production of *Granny Maumee* proved to be too large a strain on his weak constitution. In May, Torrence was hospitalized for nervous exhaustion. He and Olivia went to Xenia in late June, where they stayed through the end of the year while he recuperated. During this convalescence, Torrence continued to write poetry and to gather material for his Negro plays. The poems were short lyrics with settings inspired by his native Greene County. Like "Evensong" and "Three O'Clock," they show a mastery of technique that is seldom felt in his verse plays. These and other poems of the period are discussed, however, in the next chapter.

Despite the impressive poetic output at this time, Torrence's main goal was a professional production of *Granny Maumee* before it was forgotten. Harrison Grey Fiske, husband of the famous actress, planned a production for April 19, 1915. The leading lady was to be the French actress Mme Jolivet. Unfortunately, the production never materialized, but there was still hope. An audition performance of the play was arranged for vaudeville bookers, with the idea that the play would be booked as an attraction on the major vaudeville circuits. Such a "road" production had a precedent, as The Manhattan Players had presented *Granny Maumee* at the Lyceum Theatre in Rochester, New York, in May, 1914, on a double bill with Frank Mandel and Helen Kraft's contemporary comedy, *Our Wives.* Once again, *Granny Maumee* received appreciative responses from the critics. The reviewer for the Rochester *Evening Times* had this to say: "There is genuine inspiration in Mr. Torrence's drama, its strength, its sense of mystery, its tragic intensity and its novelty making it one of the very few real sensations of the year in the theatre."[13] The producers, too, were happy with the results, but neither this success nor the audition performance on the afternoon of April 22, 1915, seemed to impress the two vaudeville bookers:

> There were just two men who were to see it and judge and they both came. They control the bookings. Well the fact is that the blazing asses were too stupid to see the merit of the play and consequently wouldn't offer Mr. Fiske enough per week to have it in their theatres. They looked like a couple of gunmen and of course that was their calibre. They were only used to judging the usual vaudeville act consisting of slapstick men or trapeze performers or trained animals and they frankly said that it was "beyond them." . . . And this play has been delayed entirely through the stupidity of those two vaudeville asses.[14]

So, despite the new recognition of Torrence the poet, the dramatist had to wait for his moment in the sun. Torrence and Olivia were living at this time in an apartment at 107 Waverly Place, the building owned by Harriet Moody. Mrs. Moody had given them the apartment and financial aid, as she had done for many of her struggling friends. A new opportunity came to them in the spring of 1915, probably through the good offices of Robinson, when Mrs. Edward MacDowell invited them to spend the summer at the MacDowell Colony in Peterborough, New Hampshire. The colony at Peterborough had already become the favorite summer home of Robinson, who first visited there in 1911; by 1915, it was the place where most of his creative work was accomplished.[15]

Torrence's visit to the artist's colony at Peterborough was cut short by bad news from Xenia about the health of his father. Torrence returned home to be with his father during his last days (he died on June 24) and to assist with the family business which was eventually taken over by Ridgely's younger brother, Findley, who also had held hopes of becoming a writer and who had to his credit a large number of feature articles in one of the Dayton papers.

The winter found Torrence back on Waverly Place working on some new lyrics and making plans for the presentation of his Negro plays. In

February, 1917, he wrote his mother of a possible production: "This afternoon I am expecting to go out to Groton to talk over darky plays with Bobby Jones (Robert Edmond Jones) who wants to put on the stage and costuming [sic] of some pieces of mine."[16] It was not long before the plans made at that discussion began to materialize. Torrence had four plays completed, but the actual production was not going to be easy. The first problem was the assembling of a Negro acting company—a difficult task, because few Negroes had entered the legitimate theater as anything but musical performers, comedians, or stage domestics. Harlem was obviously the first place to look for Negro performers: "I and my scenic man Robert Edmond Jones are going up to Harlem to attend a performance of colored people so that we may look over the ground."[17]

Despite the seemingly fertile ground of Harlem for casting a Negro play, Torrence and Jones found the task difficult. On March 2, Torrence wrote his family: "We have lots of discouragement in trying to assemble a company of colored people. We have the plays and Mrs. Hapgood [Emilie Hapgood, former wife of journalist Norman Hapgood, who invested in serious modern drama] has the money and readiness to hire a theatre and pay all expenses and Jones has his costumes and scenery designed but we are blocked so far by not being able to find the proper people available for casts."[18]

By March 12 things were looking up, but Torrence was still skeptical, as he wrote to Harriet Moody:

I am still whittling at that proposed production of Negro plays but it is a long task and I don't know when the presentation will be made. At present we are still without a cast, two of the leading characters in one of the pieces are without actors to suggest them and we try out numbers of candidates every day. Meanwhile, two other plays are being rehearsed with fairly competent casts. But we are so far left in the dark as to whether we can make the production at all that we haven't had the scenery or costumes made yet.[19]

Still, the plays were ready to open at the old Garden Theatre on Thursday night, April 5, 1917. The preceding Sunday they had received an important advance notice from Robert Benchley in the New York *Tribune* in his article "Can this be the Native American Drama?":

It may be that Thursday night will see the beginnings of a new movement on the American stage. Potentially, it is as rich in possibilities as any that have preceded it. It all depends on the spirit in which the public receive it. If they go expecting to see burlesque they will not only be disappointed;

they will be ashamed. If they go with a sympathy for the attempt and an appreciation of its difficulties and aspirations, they may be witnessing the first stirrings of a really distinctive American drama.[20]

The three plays presented on that night were *Granny Maumee*, a folk tragedy obviously influenced by Synge's *Riders to the Sea;* a comedy, *The Rider of Dreams,* whose dreamer hero reminds one of Synge's Christy Mahon; and a historical pageant, *Simon the Cyrenian.* The performers came from just about every area except the Broadway "legitimate" theater. Some came from Negro companies such as the Lafayette in Harlem which played light drama, comedy, and musicals with Negro casts; others, from vaudeville and night clubs; and many had no acting experience at all. But under the painstaking direction of Robert Edmond Jones, the assembled cast appeared to be quite professional. Between the plays, a singing orchestra sang and played folk music and spirituals in such a compelling way that few people took advantage of the intermission.

There was unanimous enthusiasm for the plays, especially for *The Rider of Dreams*. The comments of Francis Hackett in *The New Republic* are typical of the enthusiastic reception afforded this lyrical little comedy:

The way Mr. Torrence has caught the poet in his Rider of Dreams, has kept the rollick and lilt of Madison Sparrow without disturbing his innocence, is proof that with delicate art any kind of personality may be established on the stage. But in the intoxicated romance of Madison Sparrow, in the gallop of his imagination, there is no dependence on the popular idea of the Negro. . . . No one reared on the fodder of newspapers is prepared for such a burst of poetry, but the domestication of it by Mr. Torrence is as completely convincing as it is enchanting.[21]

Enthusiasm for the performers was more tempered. Hackett wrote that "Besides their gracious speech there is, despite much amateurishness, a real capacity for creating illusion." Alexander Woolcott was complimentary about the plays but less so about the players:

Two of them [the plays] developed, from rich and almost entirely neglected material, such fine poetic and dramatic values that they fairly cried aloud for expression on the stage. One of them had been played here before, an unforgettable experience for the few who saw it. But when the hour came the plays were offered to the public with a company of players who naturally looked the important roles to perfection, who made possible a most successful visual appeal, who were all you could ask in the matter of externals, but who, as it happened, had neither the endowment nor the training to express adequately the really big dramatic moments of the evening. These were blandly, almost complacently, forfeited.

It must be quite clear that the complaint here made against the decision of the producers was not that they decided to employ Negro actors, but that they decided to employ Negroes, whether they were actors or not.[22]

The plays moved uptown from the Garden Theatre to the Garrick on April 16 but survived there for only a week. An important factor in the failure of the plays at the box office may well have been the United States' declaration of war on the day after the plays' opening. With such momentous front-page news, few people probably bothered to read the reviews. Despite the lack of success, Torrence still had faith in the production: "It hasn't made a cent so far although it has been a great artistic success, that is, the papers have been unanimous in their approval and praise and all who have seen them have been enthusiastic but the audiences are slim. The thing is sure to go sooner or later but the time may not be ripe for it just now while the war is at this stage."[23]

For one critic, however, the declaration of war enhanced the power of one of the plays. Randolph Bourne wrote of seeing the plays on that eventful Friday:

It was Good Friday. And it was the day of the proclamation of war. As the solemn tones pealed out in the last play *Simon, the Cyrenian,* with its setting for the Crucifixion—"They that take the sword shall perish by the sword"—you could hear the audience catch its breath as it realized the piercing meaning of this heroic little drama of non-resistance played before a Christian nation that was going into a world war on the very day that its churches celebrated devoutly the anniversary of this very warning. . . . It seems imperative that no person with imagination miss this genuine dramatic experience.[24]

## IV. The Plays

Each of the three plays was unique not only in its treatment of the life and attitudes of the Negro, but also in the form in which Torrence chose to present his characters and themes.[25] The first play, *Granny Maumee,* is a domestic tragedy; the setting is the living room of an old Negro cabin that is dominated by a large fireplace. Contrasted with the dinginess of the walls of the old cabin are many touches of bright red: curtains, tablecloth, chairs, geraniums. Here Torrence's predilection for color imagery has been translated into effective visual terms.

Granny Maumee, who lives with her granddaughter Pearl, has been blinded while trying to save her son Sam from being burned alive by a white lynch mob. Since that time, a generation before, she had been consumed by two passions:

hatred for the white man, and the desire for a male in the family to replace her lost son. As the play begins, Granny is eagerly awaiting the homecoming of her granddaughter Sapphire and the fulfillment of all Granny's hopes, Sapphire's son. Sapphire arrives with her new child, but the child is half white—the offspring of an illicit union with the grandson of the murderer of Granny's son. For an instant Granny's sight is restored, and she discovers the awful truth that not only has the family's pure black blood been tainted but that it has been mixed with the blood of murderers. Distraught, the old woman loses her veneer of white man's Christianity and begins a voodoo rite that culminates in the death of the white man who tainted the blood of her family. During the rite, however, a vision of Sam, Granny's son, appears to her and begs her to be merciful. When Sapphire and Pearl awake from the stupor induced by the old woman's potion, they find Granny dead.

We may readily see that there is too much dependence upon coincidence for *Granny Maumee* to be a great play, but Torrence presented his highly emotional plot with such skill that each moment is fully exploited. The setting, with its splotches of red, symbolizing passion, blood, and fire, mirrors the highly passionate nature of the superstitious old woman. Moreover, the entire action of the play can be seen as a series of rituals. It opens with an almost ritualistic presentation. The finest sheets are being placed on the bed. Granny dresses herself in a red gown. Then comes the recognition scene in which Granny's sight is momentarily restored, and she sees the child's light skin. Finally, there is the highly dramatic voodoo rite with the two dazed granddaughters drumming in the background as Granny Maumee stabs the wax effigy of the white father of her great-grandchild. The scene builds to a fever pitch as the young women echo Granny's chants:

By de w'ip an' de rope an' de chain dat swung,
By de bloody mouf an' de bit off tongue,
By de eat-up heaht an' de spit out gall,
We scream, we beg, we whoop, we squall
Tuh git poweh, tuh git stren'th tuh put de trick
     on um all.

(27)

When the child's father arrives at the cabin door—the man Granny wanted to burn as his grandfather had burnt her son—Granny cries from within: "Go back w'ite man. Roll back w'ite wave er de fiery lek. Once you lit de fieh an' bu'n me. Once you po' de blood an' pizen me, but dis time Sam an' me we's de stronges' an' we leaves you go, we leaves you live tuh mek yore peace wif Gawd. We're poure bloods heah, royal black—all but one an' we'll do de bes' we kin erbout him. He shill be name Sam. Go back w'ite man, an' sin no mo'" (30).

If the action proceeds in a ritualistic fashion, the language, too, is highly formalized. Torrence has attempted to use not only the Negro dialect, but also the simple colorful language and highly emotional nature of these people who were only one generation removed from the slaves when Torrence grew up. The language of the play is a result of Torrence's fine ear for the cadences of Negro speech as he heard it in and around Xenia.

We do not wonder at the enthusiasm *Granny Maumee* engendered at its first performance in 1914 and again in 1917, for this was the first time that a New York audience was presented with a picture of a Negro's bitterness toward the white man, much less a depiction as powerful as *Granny Maumee*. Granny's horror that the blood of her race would be tainted with white blood must have had a great deal of dramatic impact in 1917.

Just as *Granny Maumee* presents an embittered old woman at odds with the white world because of her desire for vengeance and her pride in her race, *The Rider of Dreams* presents a man whose conflict stems from his own irresponsibility. Madison Sparrow dreams of the wealth of the white man, but he does not have the energy to earn a decent living or the responsibility to hold on to the money his wife has saved to buy their house. His goal is that of the dreamer: "I goin' to lan' us all in a sof' place on dat Easy Street I heah' 'em singin' 'bout so long wifout seein'" (48). Madison, with the help of a white ne'er-do-well, has taken his wife's savings to buy a stolen guitar. Fortunately, their landlord, who resolves the problem as if he were a deus ex machina, has recovered the money and accepts it as full payment for the house. His only stipulation is that Madison use the guitar to his advantage: "I'm goin' to give you dat guitar—but—dere's suhtinly goin' to be a string tied to it. You kin take dat guitar but you got to make somethin' outer yourself wif her or back she'll come to me. You kin give lessons an' learn folks music or you kin write down de music you make, but you got to do somethin' wif it fer Lucy. You got to wake up or I'll take de guitar" (72).

We expect the play to end here, with everyone happy and all problems solved, but it does not. Madison Sparrow, the dreamer, is not that quick to accept the stringent requirements the world imposes upon him:

I don' undehstan' dis worl'. If I wants to make music why can't folks lemme alone to make music? If I dream a fine dream why is it I always wake up? Looks to me like somebody's always tryin' to crown me out an' git me in a tight place.

*Lucy* (his wife): . . . De trouble wuz dat dis dream of youahs wasn't a good dream.

*Madison:* Yes, but not all of my dreams is bad ones. All I wants is room to dream my dreams an' make my own music.

(75-76)

The critics liked *The Rider of Dreams* best, and it is not hard to understand why. Madison Sparrow's lyrical telling of his dreams makes it impossible for the audience to judge him harshly for his irresponsibility. He is a universal character, as old as comedy itself: he lies, he travels with the wrong people, he is constantly being duped, but he remains likable. A half-century before, he was a favorite character in the folk tales of the American Frontier, and, transferred again to the Negro world twenty years later, he became the irrepressible George "Kingfish" Stevens of "Amos and Andy." Unfortunately, the developing popularity of this type of character is partially a result of the white man's image of the Negro. Madison Sparrow, then, seems to us to be a stereotype; but his effectiveness is enhanced by the Negro setting of *The Rider of Dreams*. In it, we find a man who dreams of things he, as as Negro, cannot have; but the social implications of this problem are not explored in the play. It does not question the justice of Madison Sparrow's static position in society; rather, it operates within the existent framework of values. We cannot censure Torrence for this fact, for his interest in the Negro was more esthetic than social; moreover, his attitude was that of his time. In this context, the play remains a winning one.

*Simon the Cyrenian* provides a strong contrast with the other plays. A religious drama, it is set in the garden of Pontius Pilate on the day of Christ's crucifixion. The play is based on the verse from Saint Luke: "And as they led him away, they laid hold upon one Simon, a Cyrenian, coming out of the country, and on him they laid the cross, that he might bear it after Jesus" (Luke 23:26). Although we do not usually think of the characters involved in this incident as Negroes, Torrence's intention was that they should be depicted as such. His directions were explicit:

Although Cyrene was in Northern Africa, the wall-paintings in the vast Cyrenian tombs depict black people instead of brown.

That Jesus' cross bearer was a black man, as the early painters represented him, is a fact that holds a certain suggestion bearing upon a phase of modern society.

It has been the author's design that all the characters in this play should be represented by persons entirely or partly of Negro blood; and this intention has been carried out in the original stage production. Simon is a full-blooded Negro, Battus is a little less dark, Acte is a mulatto as were most Egyptians of the latter dynasties. Her attendants comprise both mulattos and Negroes. The Roman characters are played by persons of a slighter Negroid strain.

(78)

When the play begins, Procula, Pilate's wife, is disturbed because of the ominous dreams she has had regarding the consequences of Christ's crucifixion, and she has sent Simon, the leader of the recent slave uprisings in Rome, to rescue Christ if he is condemned. When Simon arrives, he discloses the fact that he is already a believer in Christ:

> . . . I had summoned to a garden
> The bravest of the slaves to help them plan
> A new sedition that would free Barabbas.
> There as I roused the jungles against Rome
> I saw lights in another part of the garden,
> I saw men come with torches and seize a man.
> I hurried near and through the olive leaves
> His eyes looked into mine,
> His eyes burned into mine. I have seen them
>     since,
> Waking or sleeping.

(93)

When Christ is sentenced to death, Simon rushes to save him, but he is transfixed when he sees Christ and hears Him speak: "Put up the sword. For they that take the sword shall perish by the sword" (108). Centurions take Simon and order him to carry Christ's cross up the hill for him, and the play ends with Simon's being taunted by the three mockers: The Mocker with the Scourge, The Mocker with the Robe, and The Mocker with the Crown of Thorns. As the crown of thorns is placed on Simon's head, Christ's voice is heard once more: "If any man will come after me let him take up the cross and follow me," to which Simon answers as he takes up the cross: "I will wear this, I will bear this till he comes into his own" (111).

Although it is difficult to know just exactly how much Torrence intended to say in this short work, it certainly showed his belief in the strength of human love and in pacifism; but it is difficult not to see Simon as the oppressed Negro, just freed from slavery, accepting Christian love and pacifism as the only solutions to his problems. It may be, however, that Torrence only intended to say that Christ spoke to Negroes as well as to whites—and that his message was, therefore, for both races.

Unlike the other two plays, much of *Simon the Cyrenian* is in verse; but, unlike his earlier verse dramas, the meter is free; and there is no attempt at rhyme. The result is a much more natural flow of language. Like many religious plays, *Simon the Cyrenian* shows a greater concern for the communication of an idea than with logical motivation of character, and we feel that the mockers contribute little to the effectiveness of the drama. The play's power, then, resides in its message—a message that was of particular import in April, 1917.

Torrence's *Plays for a Negro Theatre* were not great successes at the box office, nor was their subsequent publication by Macmillan profitable. Moreover, their lack of concern for the social, economic, and political position of the Negro in American society, and their acceptance of the Negro race as one apart from the mainstream of American life make them seem quite irrelevant to a reader of half a century later. Still, if the plays did not sound a battle cry, they did show an acceptance and a respect that the Negro had not yet been afforded in American society or on the American stage. They were a beginning for the Negro in our theater. For Torrence, they marked the culmination of all his dramatic hopes and efforts—a promise fulfilled.

## Notes

1. Letter from R. T. to W. O. Walker, editor of Cleveland *Call Post,* January, 1939.

2. Telegram from R. T. to his parents, February 3, 1914.

3. Letter from Edwin Arlington Robinson to R. T., February 9, 1914.

4. Chard Powers Smith, *Where the Light Falls; A Portrait of Edwin Arlington Robinson* (New York, 1965), p. 239. Smith seems to find the idea of an affair between E. A. R. and Olivia Dunbar doubtful (see note, p. 404).

5. Letter from R. T. to Harriet Moody, May 5, 1915.

6. Edith J. R. Isaacs, *The Negro in the American Theatre* (New York, 1947), p. 60.

7. Edward Sheldon, *The Nigger* (New York, 1910), p. 245. The play was first performed December 4, 1909.

8. "The New Negro Theater," *The Crisis: A Record of the Darker Races,* XIV (June, 1917), 80.

9. From typescript of unpublished memoir, Ridgely Torrence Papers, Princeton University Library.

10. *Ibid.*

11. Letter from R. T. to Harriet Moody, February, 1914.

12. Carl Van Vechten, review *Granny Maumee,* New York *Press,* March 31, 1914.

13. Anon. review *Granny Maumee,* Rochester *Evening Times,* May 19, 1914.

14. Letter from R. T. to his parents, May 1, 1915.

15. Hermann Hagedorn, *Edwin Arlington Robinson: A Biography* (New York, 1938), p. 295.

16. Letter from R. T. to his family, February 2, 1917.

17. Letter from R. T. to his family, February 23, 1917.

18. Letter from R. T. to his family, March 2, 1917.

19. Letter from R. T. to Harriet Moody, March 12, 1917.

20. Robert C. Benchley, "Can This Be the Native American Drama?," New York *Tribune,* April 1, 1917, pt. 5, p. 6.

21. Francis Hackett, "After the Play" (review Negro Plays), *The New Republic,* XI (April 14, 1917), 325.

22. Alexander Woolcott, "The Colored Players," *The New York Times,* April 29, 1917, sec. 8, p. 7.

23. Letter from R. T. to his family, April 20, 1917.

24. Randolph Bourne, Letter to the Editor of *New York Tribune,* April 10, 1917, p. 10.

25. Ridgely Torrence, *Granny Maumee, The Rider of Dreams, Simon the Cyrenian: Plays for a Negro Theatre* (New York, 1917). All citations will be from this text.

## Works Cited

*Granny Maumee, The Rider of Dreams, Simon the Cyrenian: Plays for a Negro Theatre.* New York: The Macmillan Company, 1917.

*Poems, by Ridgely Torrence.* New York: The Macmillan Company, 1952.

Isaacs, Edith J. R. *The Negro in the American Theatre.* New York: Theatre Arts Books, 1947. Devotes much attention to Torrence's plays.

Moody, William Vaughn. *Letters to Harriet.* Ed. Percy MacKaye. Boston: Houghton Mifflin and Company, 1935. Contains many references to Torrence.

[Gale, Zona] "Mr. Torrence's Metrical Art," *The Atlantic,* XCVIII (September, 1906), 325-35.

Sinclair, May. "Three American Poets of Today," *Fortnightly Review,* LXXXVI (September, 1906), 421-37, reprinted in *The Atlantic,* XCVIII (September, 1906), 325-35. Discusses Moody, Robinson, and Torrence.

## THOMAS CRIPPS (ESSAY DATE 1979)

**SOURCE:** Cripps, Thomas. "Introduction: A Monument to Lost Innocence." In *The Green Pastures,* by Marc Connelly, edited by Thomas Cripps, pp. 11-39. Madison: University of Wisconsin Press, 1979.

*In the following essay, Cripps presents a detailed overview of both the film and stage versions of Marc Connelly's* The Green Pastures, *characterizing the work as an important social document.*

In order to appreciate the achievement of Marc Connelly's *The Green Pastures,* the play and the motion picture must be seen as two points along the continuum of American social and political life. The film is important to us not only as a monument to a lost past and as a prophecy but also as a cinematic accomplishment; similarly, the play is important as both a social document and a theatrical moment.

Like many other Pulitzer Prize winners, the play carried a message that spoke more to its own times than to the ages. By 1930, the year Connellys "fable" began its long run, urban Afro-America had begun to achieve a self-conscious social identity that had often been denied in the rural South, and with this newly citified black life had come a certain fame for "the new Negro." For white Americans, the increasingly visible evidence of the breadth and variety of black culture began to give the lie to generations of invidious stereotypes that had caricatured Negroes in advertising, performing arts, popular fiction, doggerel, and jokes. Coincident with the migration of southern blacks to northern cities, Hollywood movies began to redirect their depictions of blacks on the screen away from abject slaveys and toadies toward sentimental tributes to such presumed "good Negro" virtues as loyalty and fortitude in the face of hard times. Six months before *The Green Pastures* appeared on Broadway, two black Hollywood films reflected the new sensibility: MGM's *Hallelujah!* and Fox's *Hearts in Dixie.* These interacting forces of black urbanization and white attention to it together provided an intellectual and social environment in which Connelly wrote *The Green Pastures* and directed the movie five years later.

In times of social upheaval, romance has often been the vehicle for conveying a sense of lost innocence. Wordsworth's pastoral lyrics, Scott's Gothic novels, and Constable's great green landscapes spoke to the sense of loss and provided respite from the wrenching forces of the British industrial revolution. So too, Connelly's fable of black folk religion appeared at the end of the first decade in which blacks and whites self-consciously confronted each other across the boundaries of their urban neighborhoods. The sense of lost innocence and of disappearing rural, primitive folklore that would soon be no more informed and colored Connelly's scenes.

*The Green Pastures* came to Broadway just as economic depression began to dampen optimism, impoverish the cities blacks had begun to fill, and dry up the sources of wealth that had fueled the "Harlem Renaissance." Connelly's fable romanticized and memorialized the history of the rural black South that had been decimated by the

A scene from the film version of Marc Connelly's Pulitzer-Prize-winning play, *The Green Pastures.*

northern black diaspora and, in disarming style, brought it to a broad national white audience for whom black life had been exotic.

Connelly's dramatic strategy was a simple one. Taking as his source Roark Bradford's local-color genre stories of black southern life, *Ol' Man Adam an' His Chillun,* he created a company of black characters who wrestled with the universal problem of man's nature and his place in the cosmos. Gone were the black brutes, mindless Topsies, and blindly loyal uncles of southern legend. Taking a critical moment in Old Testament theology, the metamorphosis of Jehovah from a wrathful tribal God into the merciful God promised by the prophet Hosea, Connelly recast the myth into terms that a southern black preacher might have used to explain Genesis to his Sunday school pupils. From Connelly's pristine heaven, God descends to earth in four crucial episodes of Judeo-Christian legend: the creation and fall from grace, the deluge, the Hebrew exodus from Egypt and captivity in Babylon, and an apocryphal tale that foreshadows the crucifixion. The resulting structure allowed audiences to see man's growth toward a modern spirit as part of a black myth that

conveniently held white America blameless for the plight of blacks, because as surrogates for all of mankind the black characters struggled, not against external enemies, but against their own nature expressed as inner weakness to be overcome through prayer and faith. Thus the black company of more than one hundred characters became a collective symbol of man's hope and spirit. Connelly's movie, then, is to be studied not only as cinema but as a document of American social history and as a well-meaning attempt to present the best of the black soul in a pleasing way to an urbane white audience.

The drama from which the film emerged arrived at the end of an era during which white New Yorkers, long before the rest of their countrymen, had seen urban, prepossessing black Americans who were far removed from the southern rural blacks of American legend. In the 1920s, major white publishers had brought black novelists and poets to the attention of a white readership, preparing the way for a modification of American race relations. The trend took two forms, one intellectual, the other popular. The former used the art of Countee Cullen, Claude McKay, Rudolph Fisher, and Jean Toomer to bring home the social reality of black life; the latter won the affection of a broad popular white audience through the vaudeville and film work of Bert Williams and later Stepin Fetchit and Bill Robinson.

This is not to say that America's racial attitudes and customs were transformed by a few black poets sipping tea in bohemian salons or by a couple of hoofers clicking their ways across vaudeville stages. Nevertheless, independently of each other, and often burdened with mutual cross-purposes and antipathies, through their arts and through intellectual inquiry or the mere winning of affection across racial lines, black writers and performers contributed to the withering away of outmoded nineteenth-century racial behaviors. To expect more is to ignore the stamina of segregation customs.

## Negro Theater in the Twenties

Connelly's play provided a neat punctuation to the end of the era of the Harlem Renaissance by paying homage to black folk religion while taming white anxieties aroused by the northward migration of southern Negroes. The 1920s had begun with a blossoming of Negro theater and ended with a romantic white version of it for a large and appreciative white audience. By speaking to this mood, Connelly clearly earned his Pulitzer.

James Weldon Johnson, the executive secretary of the National Association for the Advancement of Colored People and a shrewd observer of black theater, reckoned the beginning of the era at the appearance of Ridgely Torrence's *Three Plays for a Negro Theatre* on April 5, 1917, one day before America entered World War I. For Johnson it was the Negro's "first opportunity in serious legitimate drama." He wrote in the *New York Age:* "We do not know how many colored people of greater New York realize that April, 1917, marks an epoch for the Negro on stage."[1] Torrence, a white man, was soon joined in the trend by other whites: Eugene O'Neill with *The Emperor Jones* (with Charles Gilpin in the title role) and *All God's Chillun Got Wings* at the Provincetown Playhouse; Paul Green with his Pulitzer-winning play, *In Abraham's Bosom;* and young Charles MacArthur and Edward Sheldon (author of the notorious *The Nigger*) with the flashy Harlem melodrama *Lulu Belle.*[2]

Away from white Broadway, black theater also bloomed. University theaters, such as Howard's Ira Aldridge Players, were joined by the Pekin stock company in Chicago, Karamu House in Cleveland, and the Lafayette Players in Harlem. They intruded into white circles in two ways: white visitors came to black preserves, especially Harlem, and black productions, such as *Shuffle Along,* played Broadway during the off months. Negro revues that lent themselves to formulaic repetition perpetuated the trend. Two performers in the cast of *Shuffle Along,* for example, soon wrote their own *Chocolate Dandies,* which was in turn followed by annual productions of Lew Leslie's *Blackbirds* and lesser known musical rambles.[3]

The rage for black performing arts coincided with the maturing of American theater from its nineteenth-century days of melodrama and flamboyant actor-managers. After World War I, the Playwrights' Company, the American National Theatre, the Theatre Guild, and the Group Theatre helped bring substantive social themes to the boards. Thus Connelly's *The Green Pastures* arrived on Broadway after audiences had received ten years of tutelage in social drama. Indeed, Connelly may have been inspired as much by DuBose and Dorothy Heyward's *Porgy,* a 1926 Theatre Guild production directed by Rouben Mamoulian that owed its own inspiration to the black folk life of the Sea Islands of South Carolina, as by Roark Bradford's book.[4] Eight years later, *Porgy* may have attracted Warner Brothers to Connelly's script when the Heywards' play reappeared as an opera, possibly assuring the studio of the continuing popularity of Negro themes.

Movies followed the trend. In 1928, King Vidor, after months of pleading, persuaded MGM to produce *Hallelujah!,* fulfilling his longtime urge to film rural Negro life. At Fox, Paul J. Sloane expanded a short subject into still another fragile rendering of Negro folk life, the studio's "prestige" film of the year, *Hearts in Dixie.* While the other studios avoided such risky themes, they made a long cycle of two-reelers featuring black music if not black life.[5]

## Connelly and the Play

Like many middle-class Americans, Connelly maintained an affectionate neutrality toward Afro-Americans, sympathizing with their plight, enjoying the company of the few blacks who served them, and condemning the worst of "southern outrages." Like another Pittsburgher, Stephen Foster, he perceived Negro life as a romance for which his own life had done little to prepare him. Of his only early contact with a black he recalled: "We had a Negro porter called Jim with whom I had the intimacy of a nine-year-old boy. He had an almost slavelike care and concern for me. . . . That's my only experience with Negroes."[6]

His childhood in McKeesport and Pittsburgh, in comfortable circumstances, was filled with gentle good times leavened by talks with actors, like Richard Mansfield, who stayed at his father's hotel. Until the "rich man's panic" of 1907, nothing, not even the death of his father in 1902, disturbed the tranquility. Then in 1908, his mother lost the hotel and opened a small shop in Pittsburgh, and Connelly, instead of going to Harvard, joined in turn the *Pittsburgh Press* as a collector of advertising fees, the Associated Press as a rewrite man, and the *Pittsburgh Gazette-Times* as a humor columnist in the style of Franklin P. Adams. Along the way he tinkered with skits, plays, songs, and stories that led him to Broadway where, as World War I ended, he began a collaboration with another Pittsburgher, George S. Kaufman, the *Times* drama critic. *Dulcy,* their first script (a light comedy intended as a vehicle for young Lynn Fontanne), began Connelly's celebrated career, which was punctuated by evenings at the opera, drinks at W. C. Fields's private bar, and long lunches with a circle of young writers at the Algonquin Hotel and the studio of the magazine illustrator Neysa McMein.[7]

A life so successful as to resemble a bad play seemed to leave no room for attention to black life, at least until a warm day, probably in 1928, when his friend Rollin Kirby, the Pulitzer-winning cartoonist, pressed upon him a copy of *Ol' Man Adam an' His Chillun,* which he read in a single night's sitting.[8] Late in the year, Connelly signed a contract with Harper and Brothers publishers assigning him the right to make a play from Bradford's book, in return for which Bradford was to receive a generous thirty percent of the royalties and a quarter of the sale of motion picture rights.[9]

Bradford's book accelerated the calm rhythm of Connelly's stroll toward success. Trained by a decade of theatrical collaboration that coincided with a pervasive boom in racial productions on Broadway, Connelly took up the challenge of bringing *Ol' Man Adam an' His Chillun* to the stage as *The Green Pastures.* Unschooled in black lore, he set sail on the steamer *Dixie* to see Louisiana, hear the local dialect, and learn the lore at the feet of Bradford.

Like other southern white writers of his day, Bradford viewed black life from the verandah of the big house, a fact reflected in the illustrations of the first edition, which depicted God not as black but "as a stereotype southern planter with black fedora hat, goatee, and cane." Yet, if Connelly cleaved to Bradford's conception of pious, long-suffering Negro folk, he also wisely saw that God must emerge as a strong black figure. In addition, he provided his own apocrypha in which he sketched an archetype of the new Negro who spoke to the question of a militant black future in urban America: his Hezdrel defends Jerusalem against a nameless enemy.

It is Hezdrel who marks the thematic difference between *Ol' Man Adam an' His Chillun* and *The Green Pastures,* as shown most vividly in the denouement of the two pieces. Through Hezdrel, Connelly was able to close on a note of affirmation that, while it lacked specific political conviction or affiliation, clearly promised, to black audiences at least, a future in which they could become activists in their own cause. In this sense, any reasonably "good race man" could view *The Green Pastures* as an allegory in which his own activism was in a great tradition of fighters for Hebrew and Negro freedom from bondage. Connelly brought this special relationship between the Jewish and Negro heritages into the present by ending with the fulfillment of the biblical prophecy of a messiah. This beginning of the salvationist ethic of the New Testament and its merciful God to whom blacks may pray for redemption occurs in the last moment off stage in the drama and out of frame in the film. Thus the great history of Jews is inherited by modern blacks.

Bradford's book of stories, on the other hand, promises only business as usual as far as blacks are concerned. Joshua's assault on Jericho is merely one of a series of God's stunts rather than an embryonic political expression, as in the film. Bradford's younger generation is represented not by militant Hezdrel but by Ehud, whose courage is displayed not in combat but in a street-style stabbing. And his promise of the future is that nothing will change. His Nigger Deemus, for example, knows God represents the status quo. "Lawd, you knows and I knows I ain't got no business goin' round de wilderness wid you and all dem white folks," he says. "I knows my place in dis man's town." Only in heaven does he expect a reward that includes the knowledge that "won't nobody know is I white or black." In fact, God is as devious as other white men in racial matters. While pleading that "I ain't got no Jim Crow law 'mongst my disciples," he treats Nigger Deemus to a display of racial discrimination that reminds the

Negro of the white-primary election laws and "grandfather clauses" used to deny blacks the franchise in the South. Miraculously, God transforms rocks into food for his disciples, while denying food to Nigger Deemus on various disingenuous pretexts. At last, after each disciple has received his fried chicken, ham, cake, and beans, old Nigger Deemus is left with "a little bitty hard lump er cold cawn bread."

It may be seen from Bradford's reportage of southern life as it was that Connelly performed a considerable feat of creative imagination by taking his inspiration from a work in which whites had their accustomed place at the top and reworking it into a fable possessed of a warm black soul. Perhaps Hezdrel was Connelly's northern sensibility grafted onto Bradford's deep South.

He finished the first act on board the *Dixie* and, after a day's warm acquaintance with Bradford, began to select the music, with the help of Negro musicians near Bradford's home in the Vieux Carré. A few visits to black churches and the Mississippi Valley to the north, and Connelly began to shape the stylized dramaturgy of *The Green Pastures*.[10]

Connelly's Yankee sensibility, somewhat like the intense but surface view of the tourist, both helped and hindered his work. His sympathetic liberalism brought dignity to his black characters. But he missed much. Myriad historical, social, and doctrinal reasons for the splintering of Negro churches were reduced to petty quarrels over social dancing. He met not a spectrum of preachers but "a dozen Mr. Deshees" on his rural jaunts. For his notion of sin he turned to a few "'barrelhouse' dives" in New Orleans and, "in a way, possibly," his recollections of Harlem hustlers and criminals. Out in the countryside, he read dialogue to the field hands for their approval, much as he imagined "Robert Burns's habit of reading his poems in dialect to the peasants for criticisms of their authenticity." After a year that included tinkering with the script on a cruise through the Greek islands, he completed an acceptable draft and began making the rounds of producers.[11]

Not only had the Great Crash decimated the ranks of prospective producers, but veterans of "the street" greeted *The Green Pastures* with skepticism because of the "bad business" promised by its black and possibly sacrilegious theme. Successful black shows had always laid claim to jazzy music and scandalous characters, or, like *Shuffle Along*, they had survived a tryout in some disused theater. Besides, there was no hope for an eventual sale to Hollywood; *Hearts in Dixie* and *Hallelujah!* had not stimulated a trend.[12]

Nevertheless, Rowland Stebbins, a retired stockbroker with an itch for show business, became an "angel." His bridge partner, George S. Kaufman, had touted the script and caught Stebbins's interest, and by December 29 rehearsals began for an opening on February 26, 1930.

Of all the problems, including working in the shabby halls available to Negro companies, casting was the most difficult. They were agreed that native dignity should matter as much as acting experience and therefore searched outside the thin ranks of Negro thespians. Connelly reached into the South, inquiring after the availability of Robert Russa Moton, the principal of world-famous Tuskegee Institute, to play God. Failing that, and with only four days left before the opening of rehearsals, they just missed signing Adam Clayton Powell, Sr., of Harlem's Abyssinian Baptist Church, for the role of God. At the last moment, they auditioned Richard B. Harrison, a touring platform speaker and dramatic reader and a perfect typecast as a patriarchal God, who agreed to play the role only after assurances that the play would in no way slander the race.[13]

*The Green Pastures* immediately began its career as an American classic, an event that memorialized, celebrated, romanticized, and embalmed lost values while offering them as the foundation of the present. It presented Afro-Americans as interracial ambassadors of goodwill whose charming flaws of dialect and naiveté allowed white audiences to admire their unthreatening dignity under duress. For blacks, at least those who praised it, the play fulfilled an ambition that most black leaders, even the most nationalistic, had come to embrace—the eventual carving of a black place in American society based upon individual dignity and merit. It was as though Marc Connelly spoke for the achievement-oriented black middle class.

*The Green Pastures,* like Stepin Fetchit's movie roles, became a tactic in a kind of advertising campaign designed to evoke inter-racial affection. As Fetchit often described his act as a device for relieving white unease in dealing with racial matters, so Connelly felt that his play and Harrison's performance stimulated "the audience's affectionate responses."[14] A typical friendly reviewer accounted for the success of the play with reference to its ambassadorial intent: "All the way through it is permeated by affection for and understanding of the half-developed negro yearning" for biblical truth.[15] James Weldon Johnson agreed that affection was at the center of both Fetchit and *The Green Pastures*—with a caveat that neither should be taken as the reality of Negro life.

Generally, white critics praised Connelly's attempt at affectionate universality, his sincerity, and his lack of patronizing—sometimes by patronizing *him*. As Richard Watts wrote in the *New York Post* (March 22, 1930): "Perhaps the most amazing thing about the play is that its author should be a white man, a sophisticated New Yorker, hitherto distinguished chiefly as a wit and a satirist."

Watts was also the only urban critic who demurred from the praise of *The Green Pastures,* having been discomfited by his misunderstanding of Connelly's apocryphal Hezdrel who symbolized a modern teleology in which the new Negro took up arms against his oppressors. He found Hezdrel's scene the "one place in the narrative where the author appears to lose, for a moment, his objective view-point; where you begin to suspect that he is stepping out of character and showing you something, not as it appears to an old Negro preacher, but as the more sophisticated playwright has fabricated it." For him Hezdrel conveyed the message of the play "that is not quite in the mood of strict simplicity that the rest of the play maintains." In other words, where an aggressive Negro appears, Watts blamed Connelly's loss of balance, perhaps because Hezdrel's assault on a nameless enemy broke the spell of the audience's warm feelings toward Negroes.

The black press leapt at the opportunity to praise a white liberal theatrical production that accomplished the black goal of dampening white antipathy. Few of them ventured to attack that which whites had praised; they too romanticized slavery into an epoch that tempered the survival powers of the race. Others routinely praised any black achievement, whatever its merits, especially if white intellectuals had put their imprimatur upon it or white entrepreneurs had bought advertising lineage for it.

Through the medium of show business, the black press also discovered a way of mythologizing black performers into icons that symbolized the two goals of individual success and racial integration, without sacrificing claims to Negro cultural nationalism. The *Pittsburgh Courier*

(February 22, 1930), a pioneer in its coverage of theater, for example, praised Jules Bledsoe's work in *Show Boat* as "ample proof that real ability knows no color barrier" while admiring the chorus line for its "haunting rhythm and melody which is a heritage of the Negro." Expressed as formula, blacks were entitled to the same opportunities accorded other Americans while retaining preternatural traits to which whites were not privy.

Turning to *The Green Pastures,* the *Courier*'s Chappie Gardner paid tribute to both elements of the myth, white homage and black attainment. He gave credit to Connelly for rendering black religion "in a lovable and simple way" unspoiled by "irreverence" while accurately recreating "a fishfry in heaven much the same as we [blacks] give picnics today. . . . Everyone," he reckoned, "should see this play."[16]

With variations, other black papers agreed. New York's *Amsterdam News* headlined its story: "Green Pastures Takes Broadway by Storm." Claude A. Barnett's Associated Negro Press, which reached a nationwide sample of black papers, celebrated the event as the occasion on which black and white liberals could agree. One such story that appeared in the *Norfolk Journal and Guide* (March 8, 1930) quoted a platoon of white New York critics whose praise was ratified by Walter White of the NAACP, who pointed out that Connelly's "moving pageant" illustrated the affinity between the plight of ancient Jews and modern Negroes.

Even if black critics demurred from the praise of *The Green Pastures,* they agreed that the race benefited from the employment it brought black actors. Bennie Butler in the gossipy *Inter-State Tatler* (March 14, 1930), for example, predicted that "this triumph will eventually mean to the colored entertainers . . . [a] harvest" of jobs derived from road companies and imitators. "While things look bad for the rest of the country," he wrote, "the sepia theatre entertainers can look forward to an era of prosperity."

As the bearers of the theatrical fable, the actors became a focal point of discussion that threatened to spoil the journalistic unanimity. When Connelly, intending a bit of well-meaning praise, claimed that "almost every Negro is a good actor," the *Journal and Guide* (March 15, 1930) challenged the "press agents and white producers . . . pernicious habit of depriving Negro talent of any recognition of its past achievements" by asserting that blacks were no more than "uncultivated talent found in kitchens and divers other menial jobs." The *Courier* (May 24, 1930) carried the argument to the actors themselves, asking them, in view of their public roles, to abstain from the gambling, tardiness, and scandals that always threatened the survival of plays like *The Green Pastures*. "It is always the same with colored casts," said the *Courier*'s critic. "They cry for opportunities, but when they are fortunate enough to get hold of one, they deliberately throw it away."

As the most influential black voices of organized, affiliated, middle-class Negroes, the house organs of the NAACP and the Urban League reached the broadest audience of black intellectuals and spoke with the clearest authority. The Urban League not only used the drama as the occasion for a benefit performance, but its magazine, *Opportunity,* praised it as an uplifting experience that "transcends the color line."[17] *Crisis,* the NAACP organ, hedged because of "the embargo which white wealth lays on full Negro expression," but concluded that *The Green Pastures* was "beautiful and beautifully done, . . . the beginning of a new era, not simply in Negro art but in the art of America."[18]

Even after a half year's reflection, few black intellectuals damned the play. The *Chicago Defender,* Theophilus Lewis, and George S. Schuyler took sharpest issue with the majority. Lewis found it a merely "fair to middling play" saved by "astute direction," while Schuyler refused to see it at all because of the old-fashioned stereo-typing that had been reported to him. One of the actors, Salem Tutt Whitney, reminded black critics of the old Negro custom of refraining from intraracial criticism within earshot of whites. "There are some things that a critic should not write even if he thinks them," wrote Whitney, but Schuyler waived the rejoinder aside as a self-serving defense of his "meal ticket."[19]

Connelly himself had taken pains to avoid such division even before the play opened. Against the advice of his producer, he cut the parable of David and Goliath during rehearsals. If the Egyptian captivity of the Hebrews symbolized slavery in Negro minds, then David's clash with the champion of the Philistines could only stand for oppressive whites bent on reenslaving blacks. On the eve of the fight, Samuel wails, "An' now de Chosen People is abandoned." Can he mean, unconsciously, that Republicans had abandoned the Negro during Reconstruction at the end of their American captivity? God answers by help-ing David. Are we to believe that God helps blacks make war on whites? If so, then the principle of universality is an empty one.[20]

*The Green Pastures* embarked upon a five-year career on Broadway and the road, with the blessing of black and white critics. As a fable that symbolized the American accommodation to a racial history that granted black suffering without requiring whites to feel guilt, the drama became a powerful document in the history of popular art. Unfortunately for its prospects as a movie, by the time it lumbered into production in 1935, American racial sensibility had begun to change under the liberal, if inconsistent, prodding of New Deal rhetoric. The movie could make only a fraction of the monumental impact of the Broadway production; it neither celebrated nor memorialized racial history; it merely repeated itself.

### Production of the Film

By 1935, the year Connelly signed his contract with Warner Brothers for a $100,000 advance against the profits, too much had changed. Only two months before the pact, Rose McClendon, the doyenne of Negro theater, had written an angry letter not to the black *Amsterdam News* but to the white *New York Times* (June 6, 1935), announcing that the day was past when blacks contented themselves with a mere presence on the stage. Instead, they demanded that theater "deal with Negroes, with Negro problems, with phases of Negro life, faithfully presented and accurately delineated." As evidence she contrasted a "doomed" black version of *The Front Page* at Harlem's Lafayette with Clifford Odets's agitprop *Waiting for Lefty,* which attracted four thousand to the Negro People's Theatre.

American films had also slipped to the left between 1930 and 1935. At first, blacks appeared in largely ceremonial roles depicting their fortitude in the face of southern racism or as natural men prossessed of wisdom inaccessible to effete white men. *Hearts in Dixie, Hallelujah!,* Universal's *Uncle Tom's Cabin* (1927), a revival of *The Birth of a Nation* with a sound track, and even films inspired by blackface minstrelsy spoke for the era. But after 1935, black roles broadened to include the outraged black family of Odets's *Golden Boy,* the smooth gunman of *The Petrified Forest,* and musical numbers inspired by Etta Moten's singing of "Remember My Forgotten Man" in *Gold Diggers of 1933.* Some of them conveyed mild propaganda messages such as the antilynching tracts, Mervyn LeRoy's *They Won't Forget,* and Fritz Lang's *Fury.* Others, like *Show Boat,* were merely strengthened by fresh performers, like Paul Robeson, who offered alternatives to the work of such Hollywood regulars as Bill Robinson, who supported Shirley Temple in *The Little Colonel* and *The Littlest Rebel.*[21] In *Slave Ship, So Red the Rose,* and *The Prisoner of Shark Island,* slavery received less than its often rose-tinted treatment. Moreover, Negroes often took note of the events. As the white literateur Carl Van Vechten wrote to his black friend James Weldon Johnson: "Have you seen 'Slave Ship'? This goes a little further in the direction of realism than most movies on this subject and you get a glimpse of how the Africans were packed into the holds of ships and treated."[22]

Sometimes the pace of change seemed too rapid. The usually liberal *Variety* complaied of an interracial routine played by Martha Raye and Louis Armstrong in *Artists and Models:* "This intermingling of the races isn't wise, especially as she lets herself go into the extremist manifestations of Harlemania torso-twisting and gyrations. It may hurt her personally."[23]

Stepin Fetchit's sad career may be taken as a barometric index of the period. In 1930 he was a hero to many blacks, as a result of appearing in a handful of stylized burlesques of southern Negroes and their responses to racial etiquette. But by 1936 his career at Fox came to an end after a flurry of roles in Will Rogers's rural local colorist films, *Judge Priest, The County Chairman, David Harum,* and *Steamboat Round the Bend.* Thenceforward, he slumped into B pictures, short films, and eventually "race movies," having fallen victim to increasingly urbane tastes that did not include the excessive sycophancy that had marked older Negro roles.

This mid-decade burst of Negro activity must not be taken as a revolution in racial attitudes. A glance at the script of Paramount's *So Red the Rose* (1935) is instructive. A high moment comes when Cato, a rebellious slave modeled, it was said, on Nat Turner, harangues the slaves. But the script merely instructs the extras to "laugh like school children released from school" and set upon Cato "laughing like imbecilic animals." When a house servant helps put down the insurrection, he is seen as "loyal and righteous" and "wearing the pride of his race upon his features." Cato can only whine abjectly: "I just a slave nigger that don't know nuthin'."[24]

If the racial temper of the times had changed in ways that would make *The Green Pastures* seem slightly antique, Connelly too had matured and grown settled. In the years since the opening of the play, he had become a resident wit, an elder statesman of the theater, and even a professor in the Yale drama school, all of which helped mold Connelly into an established and lionized figure with a diminished concern for innovation.

Warner Brothers shared the mood as though seeking to produce a "prestige" film that would neither disappoint nor challenge its audience, who would see the movie as a replica of the play they had seen six years earlier. "It was a disappointment to me; I wanted to make it down south; I wanted to do it out of doors," Connelly recalled. "I had an idea of making it into a picture, not to transcribe the play onto film, which was what the Warner Brothers wanted."[25]

Despite Connelly's wishes, his own training and experience in the theater prevailed and the film retained a striking theatrical quality. Most changes from script to screenplay, even those that heightened its visual quality, were strategic decisions in favor of theatrical, as opposed to cinematic, effects. God's entrances, for example, are always appropriately quiet and simple rather than accompanied by peals of special effects thunder-and-lightning. Even the central episode of Genesis is conveyed by acting rather than special effects, except for a simple camera-stop insertion of Eve into the scene. Those sequences in which secular sin is depicted are carried almost entirely by the actors' flair and personae, assisted by effective costumes rather than self-conscious cinematic devices. Visual rhetoric and embellishment were restricted to the main titles, various special effects that enhanced the biblical deluge, and other "exteriors." The price of such visual augmentation included minor matters, such as the loss of a certain amount of local color, picturesque debates over the merits of minnows and worms as fish bait, a ceremonial awarding of Sunday school diplomas, as well as major losses in theological foundations that had given political meaning and thrust to the stage play.

Unintentionally, Warner Brothers and Connelly reinforced each other in making *The Green Pastures* into a well-made photographed play. No matter how much he wished to make a movie from his script, Connelly's psyche was rooted in theater from earliest childhood. For the Warner brothers' part, the production of a "prestige" classic imported from Broadway dictated that the play come to the screen with few changes. In a candid moment, Connelly remembered the Warners, Harry and Jack, as "terrified people [who] were afraid of originality," and "money men" interested mainly in Connelly's ability to bring in the negative under its $800,000 budget and return an estimated three or four million dollars.[26]

At every turn, the studio appeared to allow Connelly his head while denying him such wishes as the location shooting that might have opened up the action. In the end, he felt the studio regarded the project as a routine film beset by the "cheap" decision of the Warners to lease studio space from themselves. The arrangement so "handicapped the production" that Connelly "hated it" because it grew into a mere "stencil" of his stage play. Warners capped its parsimony by releasing the film in the dog days of summer, earning the polite praise reserved for "classics." *Variety*'s review, written by editor Abel Green himself, found the movie "a credit to Warner Bros., and the entire motion picture industry,"[27] a tribute as hollow as finding Joe Louis a credit to his race. Connelly muted his disappointment behind press releases praising the studio for its "cooperation."[28]

The press books also played up *The Green Pastures* for its prestige as a long-running American classic in the tradition of *Uncle Tom's Cabin, Abie's Irish Rose,* and *Rip Van Winkle.* As though its audience was a respectable, informed, white middle class capable of perceiving black folk-religion with a cultural relativity that might have been acquired through reading the then popular anthropology of Ruth Benedict's *Patterns of Culture,* the ad copy stressed the rich simplicity of "primitive" religion.

Along with the usual tie-ins with department stores and radio programs, Warners' press books encouraged testimony from "lecturing friends," society-page writers, a local "big shot" who had seen the play, and clergymen, providing they were handled "with kid gloves." In the schools, pupils were the targets of a campaign complete with a sixteen-page study guide that tied the movie to the studio's own classics—*A Midsummer Night's Dream* and *Anthony Adverse.*

No "race angle" intruded. In Harold Cox III's illustrations, the actors can barely be taken for Negroes and are never identified as to race. Not until page nineteen did press releases take up the superstitions and dialect of "dusky angels." Even then racial references were disguised by such euphemisms as "the aborigines of Louisiana's bayou." Only as the plot is told at the end, does the exhibitor see clearly the racial identity of the motion picture he is about to put on the market. The capsule narrative opens: "A dozen pickaninnies . . ."

To the dismay of black professionals, the press releases characterized several of the actors as fey, winsome amateurs. Ida Forsyne is "discovered" dusting and running an elevator in a New York store; Abraham Gleaves is Connelly's porter on the Santa Fe *Chief* on a journey to the West Coast; and so on. In Rex Ingram's case, the copywriters used a reverse strategy that eventually embarrassed the actor by presenting him as an urban version of the self-sacrificing agronomist George Washington Carver. Ingram, according to the story, was born on the Mississippi steamer *Robert E. Lee,* earned a Phi Beta Kappa key at Northwestern, took a medical doctorate, and turned away from a career as a surgeon only after his hands were crushed by a trunk lid. Such paragons of accuracy as the *New York Times* were taken in by many of the stories, and only *Time* magazine exposed Ingram's overblown autobiography. Most newspapers ran the stories as uncritical reinforcement of the popular acceptance of the Negro as a natural actor whom Connelly had merely provided opportunity.

### Reaction to the Film

As though taking their cue from the press books, the nation's white magazines lavished praise on the movie. *Time* led off with a spread of ten stills and a recounting of *The Green Pastures*'s phenomenal success on the road, predicting with faint praise that it should do well in the same medium-sized cities that had enjoyed the road show. *Literary Digest* and *Canadian Magazine* lifted from the whole cloth of the press book such tales as the casting from the ranks of Pullman porters and a synopsis of "the modern Southern Negro conception of heaven" complete with "pickaninnies." Most of them, like *Commonweal*'s James P. Cunningham, praised its broad range from tragedy to "honest negro humor." Those magazines that were unenthusiastic, like the educational trade paper *Scholastic* and the leftist *Nation,* remained neutral or carped at its constricted mise-en-scène caused by translating a play from stage to screen. The daily press, typified by the *New York Times,* praised the film makers for embalming an American classic on film, holding each detail up to the light and comparing it with its dramatic source or assaying each cinematic device according to its faithfulness to the original conception. If the reviewer had cause for regret it was only that Rex Ingram's roles as God, Adam, and Hezdrel were made possible by the death of Richard B. Harrison.[29]

*The Green Pastures* elicited an even more deeply felt approbrium from the Afro-American press, including the many regional papers whose readers had never seen the play but who read criticism of the arts in the form of "boiler plate" sent out to provincial papers by the Associated Negro Press. Its often effusive praise and its transparent efforts to spur racial pride maximized the impact of *The Green Pastures* and minimized its flaws.

The black press was a longtime voice of the literate, churched, socially and politically affiliated black middle class. As such, it enthusiastically retailed to blacks the myths of American aspiration, personal worth, and success. Such stories included J. A. Rogers's chauvinistic columns on the successful figures from history whom he considered "black": Cleopatra, Hannibal, Abraham Lincoln, and Warren Harding; America's largest black bank or first black millionaire; and the frequent obituaries that began with slavery and ended with prosperity, all of which taught readers a bedrock faith in the American sense of fair play that promised soon to extend to Afro-Americans. In the 1930s, success in Hollywood became a variant on the legend in the form of well-photographed parties, friendships with white stars, long-nosed automobiles, and escapades in usually all-white preserves such as Los Angeles hotels. At first, the reportage merely acknowledged jobs won by armies of black bitplayers and extras or, in fan magazines, the careers of Stepin Fetchit or Hattie McDaniel, but after 1930 the stories took up instances of black penetration into the ranks of assistant directors, script doctors, and confidants of the Hollywood elite.

As *The Green Pastures* went into production, it provided the black press with supplemental nutrients that fed the legend. The *Pittsburgh Courier*'s theater pages, with a readership that extended through the Ohio and Mississippi valleys, ran many such stories. Early preproduction stories played up veteran actor George Randol's duties as assistant director and Hall Johnson as musical director. As casting got under way, black reporter Bernice Patton plugged each lucky actor who won a role. Rex Ingram served both sides of the legend: admired as a medical scholar, yet chided as a rake caught in the snares of paternity suits, bigamy, sexual escapades, and bankruptcy.[30]

Each new film release promised a cycle of imitators. *The Green Pastures* was no exception: Patton predicted that "with the screening of 'Green Pastures' a cycle of Biblical folklore with a Negro cast is on." Already, she reported, Randol and Johnson had been signed by RKO; Billy Rowe, a *Courier* writer, heard that Warners planned a musical set in the Cotton Club; and another report touted Connelly as a likely maker of a movie on the Haitian revolution.[31]

At least one black group, Claude Barnett's Associated Negro Press, tried to use the production as a means of advancing the cause of the blacks in Hollywood. The ANP's movie correspondent, Fay M. Jackson, was among the first black reporters to notice the difference between accommodating Hollywood Negroes and more socially conscious New York black actors. When the major roles went to the politically conscious Rex Ingram, she described him to Barnett as an interloper "to whom all the smokes [in Hollywood] object." One of the stories she filed charged the studio with not only stinting on black salaries but employing Connelly as a kind of white straw boss who succeeded because he knew "how to handle Negroes," an account that brought forth an outraged denial from the studio.[32]

Thus the success myth was applied to the Hollywood experience in a way that promised a glowing future—both professionally and politically—to black performers. In reporting on preproduction activities, most of the black press played yet another angle that flattered the urban black bourgeoisie and affirmed their social values by contrasting them with the lowly state of the Negroes depicted in *The Green Pastures*. They described the film as a reverent work that "symbolizes the simple and childlike beliefs of many untutored Negroes," thereby paying tribute to their own rise from slavery and poverty.[33]

Only one preproduction story spoiled the ritual: Fay Jackson's report of discriminatory pay scales that threatened to grow into a scandal. But most of the black press headed off the story by accepting the studio's defense, either by quoting unrefuted statements by executives or by reporting from the point of view of Oscar Polk, who played Gabriel in the movie. Polk, a trained and accomplished professional, pointed to his own good pay as a sign of the blacks' well-being. Fortunately for the production, if not the black actors, the newspapers gave the studio the benefit of the doubt.[34]

When the movie appeared, the black press urged it upon its readers as an important cultural event and a monument to black fortitude. Earl J. Morris, who covered Detroit for the *Courier*, exemplified the enthusiasm. "See Warner Brothers' screen classic, 'The Green Pastures,'" he wrote. "It is highly entertaining. . . . The divine comedy will live for years. Marc Connelly did a good job. . . . Rex Ingram stands out in his role of De Lawd . . . but you will love his fighting characterization of Heddrel [sic]" (August 8, 1936). Of all the critics, Morris understood Hezdrel and saw him as a symbol of the new Negro temper. Throughout the land, the regional black press echoed his encomiums, filled columns with press book copy, and wrote headlines like that in the *Norfolk Journal and Guide:* "'The Green Pastures' Achieves Immortality and Fulfillment in Its Depiction on the Screen."

Two urban newspapers took sharp issue with the black fans of *The Green Pastures:* the Baltimore *Afro-American,* which reached black communities from South Carolina through New Jersey, and the *Amsterdam News,* which spoke to blacks in Greater New York. Although both papers found much to be desired, the *Afro*'s review caused more dismay among distributors because the show business trade paper *Variety* ran a summary of it along with an assertion that *The Green Pastures* had received the worst review in the *Afro*'s history. Ralph Matthews, the *Afro*'s man, caught the film in Radio City Music Hall remote from Baltimore's segregated houses, and pronounced it a disgrace to Hollywood and to Negroes and a shoestring production little different from those of the "race movie" maker Oscar Micheaux. The blow was only slightly softened when *Variety* checked the story and found that in northern cities blacks had given the film a friendly reception. A week later the *Afro* ran a story from Chicago that minimized the worst and judged the film as merely "an interesting and entertaining spectacle with a cast of underpaid colored actors portraying Marc Connelly's conception of Roark Bradford's impression of unlearned earlier-day beliefs."[35]

Roi Ottley in the *Amsterdam* took up deeper issues, perhaps in keeping with the interests of his urbane audience. Under a characteristically flippant bannerline—"'Green Pastures' Is Punk"—Ottley not only sneered at the acting, pacing, direction, haste, studio parsimony, muddy make-up, and "amateurish" photography, but also blasted the friendliness with which Negro critics customarily regarded white attempts to render black life on stage and screen. Although the *Amsterdam,* perhaps to mollify advertisers, also ran an ANP piece headlined "Praise Certain for Pastures," Ottley came back with a second attack on Negro critics of the film who, in his view, were corrupted by their urge to praise any well-meaning white treatment of black life, no matter how shabbily done. "*The Green Pastures* will no doubt, receive magnificent and glowing accounts in the Negro press . . . and unhappily so for the Negro public," he wrote. "Negro newspapers on the whole have a false sense of values. . . . They seem to work from the premise that any time a Negro appears in a play or picture which the whites have produced it should be applauded regardless of its merits."[36] Such patronizing praise, he claimed, corrupted more than it cultivated art.

The box-office success of *The Green Pastures* is more difficult to assess than its critical reception. Connelly recalled that he had brought in the film under the $800,000 that had been budgeted as a negative cost. If he is correct in remembering that it grossed "three or four million dollars," then the movie version of his play earned a profit of perhaps two million. Yet *The Green Pastures* started no trend. Despite the outward signs of success, Hollywood executives were chary of controversial films, especially those with racial themes. They believed that no matter what the merits of the film, it stood to lose the box-office grosses of the South and the small towns that often carried films into the profit column, thus placing the burden of money making on a handful of large urban markets. Thus even fairly successful all-black films such as *Hallelujah!* and *Hearts in Dixie* rarely inspired cycles or sequels. Indeed, one year after the release of *The Green Pastures, Variety* reported that Lew Leslie had almost sold Hollywood on making a movie based on his annual *Blackbirds* revues, "but sales departments of the film companies have stymied at least two deals that were all set to go through . . . because of merchandising qualms."[37]

Despite the black critics and the unclear box-office returns, Connelly had, nonetheless, succeeded in capturing a moment in American racial history and casting it in bronze. Indeed, he and the black critics may have reached a common ground if he had only been more successful in presenting his apocryphal and militant Hezdrel as a metaphor for increasingly self-conscious and aggressive urban Negroes. Without a clearly defined Hezdrel, Connelly had achieved only the limited goal of building a monument to past black dignities that spoke little to the modern black temper. His hope for the play—"I feel that it is offered as an honest inquiry into man's attempt to find dignity and virtue within himself"—simply offered less to blacks than did the potentially powerful allegorical figure of Hezdrel.[38]

As it was, with God presiding over the heavenly fish fry—the master-scene of the film—Hezdrel's place was correspondingly reduced in scale. Yet, as testimony to his potential social meaning, at least one black critic saw and admired Connelly's half-formed intention. And at least one white critic who saw the same thing needled him for his lapsed "objectivity." Without a powerful Hezdrel, *The Green Pastures* led nowhere, either politically or artistically, inspired no trend, and helped label Connelly a one-play author. Later on, like most monuments to the past, *The Green Pastures* was further distorted by time and spoke little to succeeding generations.

Nevertheless, Connelly had taken an element of Negro religion and reshaped it into a sympathetic portrayal through which whites glimpsed the darker side of their arrogant history, and blacks derived race pride from his sentimental treatment of their culture. If later social changes rendered his achievement old-fashioned, *The Green Pastures* should be judged no more harshly than Daniel Chester French's monumental *Lincoln*, Augustus St. Gaudens's allegorical *Grief*, or Horatio Greenough's toga-clad *Washington*. Monuments are monuments.

It should be said in fairness to *The Green Pastures* that at least some of its latter-day reputation as an icon of the old order may be traced to its use as a shorthand expression used by popular critics when speaking against some other bête noir. In its way it suffered the fate of Harriet Beecher Stowe's Uncle Tom. Created as a well-meaning indictment of slavery, Tom came to represent not fortitude in the face of misfortune but blind loyalty in the face of oppression. As early as 1930, when Bishop W. J. Walls attacked popular depictions of Afro-American life as "the jazzy, staccato, expression [and] commercialization of primitive weakness," he included Wallace Thurman's drama *Harlem*, the radio show *Amos 'n' Andy*, the Heywards' *Porgy*, and *The Green Pastures* all in the same broad swath.[39] And when Langston Hughes searched for a metaphor that characterized the end of the Harlem Renaissance, he chose Connelly's play: "The cycle that had charlestoned into being on the dancing heels of *Shuffle Along* now ended in *Green Pastures* with *De Lawd*."[40] Over the years, the reputation of the play took on a life of its own, gradually changing its meaning in the minds of later generations. Through Hezdrel it had promised a militant, hopeful black future; by reputation it seemed an apologist for changelessness.

In later years, Connelly and his advisers did not always understand this changing meaning of *The Green Pastures*. By 1951 a revival on Broadway for an audience made sensitive to the budding civil rights movement closed within a month, an anachronism in the age of social "message movies" and assertive Negroes. In 1957, George Schaefer's television version produced for *Hallmark Hall of Fame*—a series that embalmed "classics" into a bland format suitable for framing the commercials of a manufacturer of sentimental greeting cards—received poor ratings despite Connelly's efforts to "clean up" the writing for the occasion.[41]

## Notes

1. Edith J. R. Isaacs, *The Negro in the American Theatre* (New York: McGrath, 1947), p. 59.

2. Isaacs, *Negro in American Theatre*, p. 82. *Lulu Belle* was an ambiguity. On the one hand, Isaacs claimed that it "hastened the presentation of other plays of Negro life especially those with Harlem as a background," but on the other, the producer, David Belasco, hedged by casting it with the white actors Lenore Ulric and Henry Hull.

3. Isaacs, *Negro in American Theatre*, pp. 61, 63, 66. At least one black historian looked with indifference upon the opening of Broadway to black talent. In the view of Loften Mitchell, the trend was merely a restoration of the Negro to the stage from which he had been segregated as a consequence of the 1896 monopoly of Broadway by the Theatrical Trust Syndicate. Blacks were driven to indigenous theater such as the Krigwa Players and the Negro Art Theatre. See Loften Mitchell, *Black Drama: The Story of the American Negro in the Theatre* (New York: Hawthorn, 1967), chapter 7, and John Selby, *Beyond Civil Rights* (Cleveland: World, 1966).

4. Mitchell, *Black Drama*, pp. 83-86. It must be remembered that romance has its uses. Seen through the mists of time and place, *The Green Pastures*, in the words of the critic, Kenneth Burke, carried audiences "into a region of gentleness, this in contrast with the harsh demand of our day." Quoted in Doris E. Abramson, *Negro Playwrights in the American Theatre*, 1925-1959 (New York: Columbia University Press, 1969), p. 53.

5. Thomas Cripps, *Slow Fade to Black: The Negro in American Film, 1900-1942* (New York: Oxford University Press, 1977), chapter 10.

6. Interview with Marc Connelly, New York, April 15, 1978. Like many northern liberals of his day, Connelly associated racism with southern provincialism, which he held in obvious contempt.

7. Marc Connelly, *Voices Offstage: A Book of Memoirs* (New York: Holt, Rinehart & Winston, 1968), chapter 4.

8. Connelly's recollection of this incident varies. See Connelly, *Voices Offstage*, p. 144; Oral History Collection, Columbia University, Popular Arts Series II, p. 527; Connelly interview; Paul T. Nolan, *Marc Connelly* (New York: Twayne Publishers, 1969), pp. 79-80. See Roark Bradford, *Ol' Man Adam an' His Chillun: Being the Tales They Tell About the Time When the Lord Walked the Earth Like a Natural Man*, with drawings by A. B. Walker (New York: Harper, 1928).

9. Letter from Eugene F. Saxton to Connelly, September 28, 1928.

10. Connelly, *Voices Offstage*, p. 148; Connelly interview. Connelly chose the steamer rather than the train in order to allow him time to concentrate on writing.

11. Connelly, *Voices Offstage*, pp. 150, 153, 164. In interview, Connelly provided an addendum to his recollection of "sin" in New Orleans. He cited his visits to Harlem "when there was something to see" as at least a possible additional source for his depiction of evil.

12. Columbia Oral History Collection, p. 527; Connelly, *Voices Offstage*, p. 165.

13. Columbia Oral History Collection, pp. 527-28; Connelly, *Voices Offstage*, pp. 167-79, 171-72, 175, 190.

14. Connelly, *Voices Offstage*, p. 187.

15. *Tatler* (London), June 25, 1930, Carl Van Vechten Collection, Yale University.

16. That Connelly's play inadvertently gave him a reputation as a racial ambassador may be seen in later events. During World War II, when the Army was beset by racial violence surrounding and even on its reservations, the Pentagon asked Connelly to study the problem and to submit suggestions that eventually grew into the training film *The Negro Soldier*. And when Walter White of the NAACP opened a wartime campaign to compel Hollywood to broaden the range of black roles, MGM hired Connelly to do a draft of *Cabin in the Sky*. White also proposed that Connelly write a film biography of black agronomist George Washington Carver (Correspondence in NAACP Records, Library of Congress).

17. Howard Bradstreet, "A Negro Miracle Play," *Opportunity*, May 1930, pp. 150-51.

18. *Crisis*, May 1930, pp. 162, 177.

19. *Amsterdam News* (New York), March 5 and October 8, 1930.

20. In an interview, Connelly found the scene merely "gratuitous." It may be found in Connelly, *Voices Offstage*, pp. 178-83.

21. The films are in 16-mm release. For journalistic reviews and comment, see *Variety*: May 16, 1929, p. 4; October 9, 1929, pp. 31, 34; April 16, 1930, p. 23; August 27, 1930, pp. 4, 14-15; September 10, 1930, p. 17; July 16, 1930, p. 15; *New York Times*: March 10, 1929; September 5, 1930. See also Cripps, *Slow Fade to Black*, chapter 11.

22. Van Vechten to Johnson, June 26, 1927, James Weldon Johnson Collection, Yale University.

23. August 4, 1937, p. 18. The scene was directed by Vincente Minnelli, without credit. In 1943 he directed MGM's *Cabin in the Sky*.

24. Script in Doheny Library, University of Southern California. Interview with King Vidor, by telephone, spring 1970.

25. Connelly interview.

26. Connelly interview.

27. July 22, 1936, p. 17.

28. Connelly's recollections vary, perhaps depending on his mood, from resigned patience with the Hollywood system to snappish remembrances of its eternal attention to money, its "banker's eye for percentages." See note 8 for various sources.

29. *Time*, June 29, 1936, pp. 38-40; *Literary Digest*, July 18, 1936, pp. 18-19; *Canadian Magazine*, August 1936, pp. 34-36; James P. Cunningham, "Green Pastures," *Commonweal*, June 5, 1936, p. 160; *Scholastic*, September 19, 1936, p. 17; "Marc Connelly—Moving Man," *Nation*, July 25, 1936, p. 110; *New York Times*, March 8 and July 17, 1936. Also *Variety*, October 23, 1935, p. 8.

30. *Pittsburgh Courier*, January 18, January 25, February 8, March 7, and March 14, 1936; *Afro-American* (Baltimore), August 22, 1936.

31. *Pittsburgh Courier*, June 20 and August 29, 1936. Even those older regional papers reduced by poverty to four-page formats, such as the *Cleveland Gazette*, ran occasional photographs as "teasers," although they had no space for lengthy press book copy. See also *Norfolk Journal and Guide*, February 15, 1936, for pre-release copy.

32. "Fear 'Green Pastures' New Yorkers May Spoil Hollywood," mimeographed press release; Edward Selzer, Warner Brothers, to Jackson, copy, February 3, 1936; Jackson to Barnett, January 15, 1936, Barnett Papers, Chicago Historical Society.

33. In still other stories, black newspapers such as the *Gary American* (November 1, 1935) linked achieving blacks with white symbols of success. One story reported that the blackface singer Al Jolson had been put forth as a candidate for the role of God, while another rumor held that *The Green Pastures* would be shot in Technicolor as a hedge against the box-office failure that was "the curse which has befallen all pictures with exclusive Negro casts" (*Norfolk Journal and Guide*, February 15, 1936).

34. *Norfolk Journal and Guide*, February 15, 1936. Earl J. Morris reported from another angle that Ingram's pay for his three key roles came to a mere eight thousand dollars. See *Pittsburgh Courier*, August 8, 1937.

35. *Variety*, July 29, 1936, p. 12; *Afro-American*, August 8, 1936; *Amsterdam News*, May 30 and June 6, 1936, A. A. Schomburg Collection, New York Public Library.

36. *Amsterdam News*, May 30, June 6, and June 20, 1936.

37. August 18, 1937, p. 1. Whatever the success of *The Green Pastures*, at least a few black critics predicted that its impact would eventually throttle the threadbare little industry known as "race movies" that manufactured films for exclusively black ghetto audiences. So that even to those blacks who regarded the film as an affirmative accomplishment, it was at the expense of the unstable, shabby, often mediocre, but all-black movie industry. See Cripps, *Slow Fade to Black*, chapters 7 and 12.

38. Connelly's estimate, made late in his career, is quoted in Nolan, *Marc Connelly*, p. 84.

39. Bishop W. J. Walls, "What About Amos 'n' Andy?" *Abbott's Monthly*, December 1930.

40. Langston Hughes, *The Big Sea: An Autobiography* (New York: Knopf, 1945), p. 334.

41. The best that could be said of it appeared in the trade paper *Scholastic Teacher*: "The Hallmark Hall of Fame further endears itself to the nation's English teachers" (October 11, 1957). For commentary on subsequent productions of the play in other media or in revivals, see Connelly to Barrett H. Clark, Dramatists' Play

Service, July 6, 1938; November 12, 1938, in Barrett H. Clark Papers, Yale University; Nolan, *Marc Connelly,* p. 84; Columbia Oral History Project, p. 526; *Scholastic Teacher,* October 11, 1957; *New York Times,* July 31, 1957; Morning Telegraph, March 25, 1959, all clippings in Schomburg Collection.

## Selected Bibliography

Sources for the study of *The Green Pastures* are widely, almost elusively, scattered, perhaps because its author's reputation as a "one-shot" playwright has discouraged study. Of the materials that have been collected, most are ephemera that shed more light on its reception than its production. Marc Connelly's own papers remain in his possession. The most useful bibliography, now ten years old, is found in Paul T. Nolan, *Marc Connelly,* Twayne's United States Authors Series, no. 149 (New York, 1969). Although Nolan takes up *The Green Pastures,* he devotes his attention to its production on the stage rather than the screen, so we lack a thorough study of the play-as-film.

Nolan's bibliography also neglects the film in favor of a literary and theatrical angle. The most primary of the works is Connelly's own essay, "This Play's the Thing: Green Pastures," *Theatre Magazine* (May 1930), pp. 32-35, 66-70. A treatment of the 1951 revival of the play may be found in Marion Kelley, "Backstage: Marc Connelly Back with Prize Play," *Philadelphia Inquirer,* March 24, 1951, pp. 21, 24, and Ward Morehouse, "Broadway After Dark: Prof Connelly (Yale) Talks of 'Pastures'," *New York Sun,* February 1, 1951, p. 20.

Criticism from a black perspective ranges from the near sycophancy of the weekly press to the biting commentary of recent times. A sensitive contemporary appreciation appears in James Weldon Johnson, *Black Manhattan* (New York: Knopf, 1930), pp. 218-24. Another friendly treatment is in Edith J. R. Isaacs, *The Negro in the American Theatre* (New York: McGrath, 1947), pp. 86-88. More acidly etched judgments appear in Loften Mitchell, *Black Drama: The Story of the American Negro in the Theatre* (New York: Hawthorn, 1967), pp. 95-96; and in Nick Aaron Ford's more scholarly essay, "How Genuine Is *The Green Pastures,*" *Phylon* (Spring 1960), 67-70. In Doris E. Abramson, *Negro Playwrights in the American Theatre, 1925-1959* (New York: Columbia University Press, 1969), *The Green Pastures* receives scattered attention as a kind of antithesis of genuine black drama. More general comment may be found in Brooks Atkinson, *Broadway* (New York: Macmillan, 1970), pp. 238 ff., and in Nolan's bibliography, along with a selection of uniformly favorable reviews and two of Nolan's own essays on the play.

By way of contrast, the journalistic sources are seemingly infinite. In addition to the accounts, reviews, appreciations, biographical sketches, and gossip that may be found in the *New York Times Index* and the *Readers' Guide to Periodical Literature* volumes for the 1930s, several collections of clippings and other ephemera are available. *The Green Pastures* is disappointingly represented in the James Weldon Johnson Collection in the Beineke Library at Yale, although there are a few reviews and some fugitive letters in the manuscripts of William Lyon Phelps, Frederick B. Millett, and Barrett H. Clark. A small cache of clippings is in the George P. Johnson Collection at the Research Library of the University of California at Los Angeles; a microfilm copy of the collection is on deposit in, among other libraries, the Soper Library of Morgan State University.

Volume 33 of the L. S. Alexander Gumby Collection in the Butler Library of Columbia University is devoted to *The Green Pastures,* as is a folder in the vertical file of the A. A. Schomburg Collection in the New York Public Library. The New York Public Library Performing Arts Collection has *The Green Pastures* ephemera in individual collections, all of which are accessible through cross-indexing under the title of the play. Among them are the Laurence Rivers scrapbooks and the Vandamm Collection. Included among the items are clippings, photographs, posters, souvenir programs, scrapbooks, press books, television studio floor plans, and copies of much of the more ambitious journalistic coverage such as that in *London Mercury, Theatre Magazine,* the French language *Correspondant, Vanity Fair, Theatre Arts, Creative Reading,* and many regional and racial serials.

Connelly's own testimony appears in fragmentary form in several places. Nolan quotes from apparently lengthy interviews between Connelly and himself. In the Oral History Collection of Columbia University there is an interview between Connelly and Robert C. Franklin recorded in March 1959. My interview with Connelly on April 15, 1978, is recorded on tape. Connelly has never taken seriously the writing of a thoroughgoing autobiography, but he has turned out *Voices Offstage: A Book of Memoirs* (New York: Holt, Rinehart, and Winston, 1968), which is far more informative about his years among the Algonquin wits than it is on his Hollywood tenure.

# NELLIE MCKAY (ESSAY DATE 1996)

**SOURCE:** McKay, Nellie. "Black Theater and Drama in the 1920s: Years of Growing Pains." In *The Harlem Renaissance, 1920-1940: Analysis and Assessment, 1980-1994,* edited by Cary D. Wintz, pp. 75-86. New York: Garland Publishing, 1996.

*In the following essay, McKay describes the reasons behind the slow development of African American theater and drama during the Harlem Renaissance.*

Drama more than any other art form except the novel embodies the whole spiritual life of a people; their aspirations and manners, their ideas and ideals, their fantasies and philosophies, the music and dignity of their speech—in a word, their essential character, and it carries this likeness of a people down the centuries for the enlightenment of remote times and races.[1]

Our ideal is a national Negro Theater where the Negro playwright, musician, actor, dancer, and artist in concert shall fashion a drama that will merit the respect and admiration of America. Such an institution must come from the Negro himself, as he alone can truly express the soul of his people . . . in . . . the rich veins of folk-tradition of the past and the portrayal of the authentic life of the Negro masses of today.[2]

These statements, the first by Theophilus Lewis, and the, second by Montgomery Gregory, both made in 1926, underline the importance that Afro-Americans place on the role of drama in the development of culture, and the predominant attitudes of black critics of the form in the 1920s. In a heritage that spans centuries, from Africa through the Middle Passage, and permeating the diaspora—from the slave community to the rituals of contemporary religious ceremonies—drama has been at the center of day-to-day black activities, meeting the demands of black spiritual life in the face of multiple oppressions.

Little wonder, then, that literary and cultural historians, as well as critics of black theater and drama unanimously bemoan the poverty of Afro-American formal theater and drama in the first two decades of the twentieth century. Black intellectuals, conscious of the need to strengthen all areas of cultural influences, tried hard but failed to bring a vibrant black theater to birth, and to make that theater a significant part of the history of the Harlem Renaissance. Serious, authentic black theater that attracted public attention did not emerge from the Afro-American community until the 1930s and 1940s with such playwrights as Owen Dodson and Langston Hughes. With the benefit of hindsight, we can point to some of the reasons for the slow progress of black dramaturgical/theatrical development in comparison to other branches of the arts. One was the fact that theater and drama required the collaboration of many people; another, the persistence of negative racial stereotypes of black people; and a third, the economics of theater production. At the same time, concerned critics did their bit to overcome these obstacles by vigorously proposing active directions in which black theater and drama could develop. This essay examines ideas that three such critics expressed between 1926 and 1927: W. E. B. DuBois, editor of the *Crisis;* Alain Locke, another central figure of the Harlem Renaissance; and Theophilus Lewis, drama critic of *The Messenger.* It concludes with a brief look at some achievements of the period. In the case of DuBois, in particular, his views on all areas of Afro-American art evolved through earlier uncertainties to a fixed and stable position by 1925.

Among others, historian/critic Nathan Huggins has noted that while there was no black tradition of theater in America at the turn of the century, for almost a hundred years prior, Afro-Americans "had a very substantial [if distorted and grotesque] place in the American theatrical tradition."[3] Put another way, Clinton Oliver wrote that the black American "was in American theater long before he was a genuine part of it."[4] "Black" characters—as stereotypes that were the butt of white ridicule—appeared on the American stage as early as 1769, while, for more than half a century, white-originated black minstrelsy was the most popular form of mass entertainment in the country. The black character (on and off stage), defined in the white American mind by minstrelsy—lazy, comic, pathetic, childlike, idiotic, etc.—embodied an image that was disastrous to the advancement of serious black theater, and one not easily reversed. For openers, although there were nineteenth century Afro-American entertainers who repudiated it, many blacks, at all levels in turn-of-the-century theater, continued to accommodate themselves to minstrelsy because it was lucrative. Those like Bob Cole tried to alter that form through various creative innovations, including shows that were organized, written, produced and managed by blacks. By adding African themes to the form in 1902, the Williams and Walker show, *Dahomey,* achieved another step away from the stock qualities of minstrelsy. The black musical comedy reached its highest watermark in 1921 with *Shuffle Along,* also written, produced, and performed by blacks, and initially opening to black audiences in Washington, D.C. and Philadelphia before its smashing success on Broadway. One of the great ironies of the minstrel tradition is the manner in which contemporary black playwrights have transformed the "old form into a vehicle for anger and satire" in such plays as Douglas Turner Ward's *Day of Absence* and Ed Bullins' *Gentleman Caller.*[5]

A large part of the controversy that black intellectuals, dramatists and actors argued in the years leading up to and through the 1920s was connected to disagreements surrounding a definition of black theater, its cultural role and function, and the relationship between black playwrights, producers, actors, and black audiences. Loften Mitchell illustrated the dimensions of the first question in his essay, "Harlem Has Broadway on Its Mind," in which he indicated that more than a dozen major theater groups were formed there between 1910 and 1930. Some groups, like the Lafayette and Lincoln Players, wanted the freedom to perform plays unrelated to the black experience. Others, like DuBois' Krigwa Players and the Negro People's Theater, championed "dignified" plays of Negro life; and a number, like the Rose McClendon Players and the Pioneer Drama Group, wanted to illustrate that, given similar circumstances, blacks and whites reacted alike.[6] Such fundamental differences of opinion do not blur the evidence of ferment, and clearly indicate the interest that many Afro-Americans had in the establishment of "black" theater—however they perceived the nature of the productions they offered their audiences.

From its beginning in 1910, the *Crisis,* under DuBois's editorship, although deeply involved in the politics of race, made clear its support of the arts, including theater and drama. Its influence was large, appealing to a wide black readership with information not otherwise readily available to them. Beginning in 1910 with a circulation of 1,000 copies, by 1919 it reached a peak of 95,000. DuBois set the literary tone in his editorials and essays, blending stories, travel accounts, and character portraits into these different forms, and often using sarcasm, satire, and irony to make his point. In addition, he made the journal easily accessible by publishing works by new as well as already known writers. From 1925 through 1927 the *Crisis* ran annual literary and artistic competitions for first, second, and third place winners in five categories: stories, plays, poetry, essays and illustrations. In 1928, when the readership of the *Crisis* had declined substantially, the contests were discontinued, and instead small prizes were given for the best contributions of each month.

There is little question that the bias of the *Crisis* was toward race pride, and DuBois' attitudes were toward the primacy of the role and function of black art within the Afro-American community. In 1926 he made his now-famous declaration that "all Art is propaganda, and ever must be . . . for gaining the right of black folk to love and enjoy."[7] Not everyone agreed with DuBois, and the differences of opinions on art and propaganda became the legacy for intellectuals of every succeeding generation to debate. The issue for us may be a reconciliation with DuBois's definition of propaganda, and its relationship to Beauty, Truth, and Justice.

Not the least of DuBois' artistic concerns was the representation of Afro-Americans in drama. "As the renaissance of art comes among American Negroes" he wrote, "the theater calls for new birth."[8] He felt that, as minstrels, comedians, singers, etc., Afro-American performers had been trained to entertain white audiences, and black audiences had not demanded authentic black drama of them. Black actors would only do their "best" he noted, when that best was "evoked" by black people who wanted to see their own lives accurately depicted by their own writers and performers.

To this end, in 1926 he organized the first of the Krigwa Players Little Negro Theater groups, one-act black play groups that performed plays of black life in black schools and churches across the country. In the philosophy behind these groups we have his definition of black theater and drama:

> The plays of a real Negro theater must be: 1. *About us.* That is, they must have plots which reveal Negro life as it is. 2. *By us.* That is, they must be written by Negro authors who understand from birth and continual association just what it means to be a Negro today. 3. *For us.* That is, the theater must cater primarily to Negro audiences and be supported and sustained by their entertainment and approval. 4. *Near us.* The theater must be in a neighborhood near the mass of ordinary Negro people.[9]

DuBois saw the Krigwa groups as building blocks in the foundation of a folk-play movement in America. He pointed to the appropriateness for the Krigwa movement of many of the plays that surfaced in the literary contests sponsored by the *Crisis* and other agencies (underlining the cultural contribution that the *Crisis* made by initiating these competitions); and to the need for interested persons to identify dramatic talent. In New York, the Harlem branch of the New York Public Library offered one of its basement lecture rooms to the Krigwa Players, built a stage and dressing rooms for the actors, and supplied them with lighting equipment. The players furnished the props and secured their own audiences. Krigwa premiered with two tragedies (one a first prize winner in a *Crisis* competition) and a comedy (also a *Crisis* prize-winner). The players gave three performances, each to a full house of approximately 200 people, and they cleared "something over $240." DuBois concluded that the venture met with undisputed success, and proved the rightness of his program for an authentic Afro-American theater. A central issue here was a theater sufficiently inexpensive to permit its support by black audiences. He plunged ahead to encourage the organization of the second group in Washington, D.C.

The 1920s controversy among intellectuals and writers over the merits of propaganda as a function of art is clear in the separate position that DuBois and Alain Locke took on this issue. Still, both men were partly responsible for nurturing the flowering of Afro-American arts in that period. DuBois followed up his strong 1926 statement on black theater by implementing his theories with the Krigwa Players Little Negro Theater. Locke helped to establish a dramatic laboratory at Howard University in Washington, D.C. His position on black theater and drama is clear in his

1927 essay, "The Negro and the American Theater," originally published in *Theater: Essays on the Arts of the Theater,* edited by Edith J. R. Isaacs.[10]

Like DuBois, Locke called for new directions in the development of an Afro-American tradition in drama, but where the first gave scant information on the steps of the process, Locke unveiled a detailed agenda. Like DuBois, he felt that the "likeliest soil" for an American "dramatic renascence" as in the folk art of Afro-America, but he went farther to suggest the path "should lead back over the trail of the group tradition to an interest in things African. . . . [For] African life and themes," he said, "apart from any sentimental attachment, offer a wonderful field and province for dramatic treatment." In general, he thought, the white American stage was bereft of action, instinct and emotion, qualities that black performers would bring to black drama if it existed as "expression and artistic interpretation," outside of "propaganda," which he called the "drama of discussion and social analysis."

Like DuBois, Locke's blueprint for a new black drama wedded playwrights and actors to the roots of black culture and the black idiom. He challenged both groups to break with already established dramatic conventions, and to strike out on new experimental ground. Black drama had to "grow in its own soil and cultivate its own intrinsic elements; . . . [in order to] become truly organic, and cease being a rootless derivative." He identified the "art of the Negro actor" as "the free use of body and voice as instruments of feeling," and urged its liberation from old ways (e.g., minstrelsy and buffoonery) in the interests of vibrant artistic revelations. He envisioned the evolution of a truly "great" black drama in two stages. The first, he thought, should look to the folk play, which, realistically and imaginatively, was "drama of free expression and imaginative release . . . with no objective but to express beautifully and colorfully race folk life. . . ." He suggested that "more . . . poetic strain . . . more of the joy of life even when life flows tragically, . . . more of the emotional depth of pity and terror" would give it the vitality it needed. The technical model of this drama would become the foundations for serious black theater.

Locke's second stage in the development of a dramatic tradition was the point at which he broke with DuBois. While both men dismissed the musical comedies as buffoonery and pathos, Locke's disenchantment with Afro-American playwriting revolved around the social problem

PERFORMING ARTS

## ON THE SUBJECT OF...

### ANITA BUSH AND HER THEATRICAL COMPANIES

Anita Bush (c. 1883-February 16, 1974) was an actress who organized the Colored Dramatic Stock Company in 1914; the company was later renamed the Anita Bush Stock Company. Bush's mission for her company was to introduce serious drama to African American audiences. Originating at Harlem's Lincoln Theatre, the company moved in 1915 to the Lafayette Theatre, where, as the Lafayette Players, they performed for seventeen years. With a repertory of 250 plays, some 300 actors and actresses worked with Bush over the years. Among the dramatic works staged by company were *The Girl at the Fort, Over the Footlights,* and *About 2 O'Clock.* Members of the company included Dooley Wilson, Charles S. Gilpin, Carlotta Freeman, Lawrence E. Chenault, and Ida Anderson. Bush herself continued to act when the company failed to survive the depression. She appeared in several pioneering Black films, including *The Crimson Skull* (1921), one of the first all-Black westerns, and *The Bull Dogger,* based on the career of Black cowboy Bill Pickett. In 1937 Bush was in *Swing It,* sponsored by the government's Works Progress Administration.

plays—with what he called their tendency toward "moralistic allegories or melodramatic protests as dramatic correctives and antidotes for race prejudice." Admitting that black dramatists had the advantage of "psychological intimacy" with their subject, he denied them the objectivity that "great art" requires in dealing with these issues, and decried their counter partisanship and propagandistic attitudes. The black playwright, he said, needed to "achieve mastery of a detached, artistic point of view, and reveal the inner stresses and dilemmas of these situations." In time, he hoped for a "race" drama that served as an imaginative channel of escape and spiritual release, and by some process of emotional re-enforcement to cover life with the illusion of happiness and spiritual freedom."

DuBois, who, as noted above, championed the folk-play as the starting point for authentic black drama, and who was also deeply concerned with the refinements of art, was not in accord with Locke's views on objectivity and emotional detachment in art. Among other things, his *Crisis* writings were, on one hand, propagandistic; on the other, often intimate and self-revelatory. In 1926 he wrote that Locke's new book, *The New Negro,*[11] articulated

> better than any book that has been published in the last ten years the present state of thought and culture among American Negroes and it expresses it so well and so adequately, with such ramification into all phases of thought and attitude, that it is a singularly satisfying and inspiring thing.[12]

But he criticized Locke's position on art and propaganda, pointing out that the book, "filled and bursting with propaganda," proved Locke's thesis wrong. He noted that its propaganda was "for the most part beautifully and painstakingly done," and he (DuBois) doubted if "in any renaissance there can be a search for disembodied beauty which is not really a passionate effort to do something tangible, accompanied and illumed and made holy by the vision of eternal beauty." DuBois's now famous survey on the role and function of black art, "The Negro in Art, How Shall He Be Portrayed," which took place in the *Crisis* between February and October 1926, brought many reactions from white and black writers and critics, but did little to resolve a dilemma in which opinions were so firmly fixed.

Theophilus Lewis had an entirely different background from Harvard-educated DuBois and Locke, recognized men of great refinement, erudition and letters. In contrast to them, Lewis had little formal education, no claims to fame, and worked in the Post Office. However, even as a child he loved theater, and when he arrived in New York after the war he patronized the Harlem houses. His career as drama critic for *The Messenger* began unexpectedly when he submitted an essay on the subject to that journal and it was accepted (without remuneration). But A. Phillip Randolph, the editor, invited him to join the company of *The Messenger's* regular contributors, and he agreed.[13]

Unlike the *Crisis* and *Opportunity,* with which Locke was closely associated, in its early years (1917-23) the general editors of *The Messenger* had somewhat of a bias against "art." They published verse, but only if it served the social and economic ends of the journal.[14] However, between 1923 and 1928, when Lewis and George Schuyler took over many of the editorial prerogatives of the publica-tion, socialist verse disappeared from its pages in favor of more artistic works by well-known litterateurs like Countee Cullen, Langston Hughes, and Georgia Johnson. From July 1923 to July 1927 Lewis contributed a regular monthly column under the title, "The Theater, The Souls of Black Folks" (echoing DuBois's famous work although never showing any reverence for the older man). In so doing he was not only the first but the only regular black drama critic of that era. As others have noted, he did not simply review plays; like DuBois and Locke he also attempted to evolve an ideology for a national black theater.[15] Unlike them, he based his theories not only on philosophical concepts of a tradition in black drama, but also on analyses of close observations of what was occurring at the grassroots level of popular Harlem theater of the day.

In the 1926 July, September, and October issues of *The Messenger,* Lewis' columns analyzed current conditions of black theater and drama. His most precise definition of black theater did not come until his final "Theater" column in July 1927 in "Main Problems of the Negro Theater." His prescription for black theater and drama was less rigid than DuBois', but somewhat less flexible than Locke's:

> Negro drama, reduced to a simple statement, is . . . the body of plays written by Negro authors. The kind of life represented in the play is immaterial. The scene may be in Norway or Spain, and the characters presumably natives of one or the other country. Nevertheless it will be a Negro play if it is the product of a Negro mind. Hamlet is not a Danish play. . . . The Phaedra of Euripides is Greek, while the Phaedra of Racine is French. . . . A play is a work of art and . . . to maintain that Negro drama consists merely of plays about Negro life, regardless of who writes them, is to alter the accepted meaning of terms.[16]

DuBois, Locke and Lewis agreed that the responsibility for vital authentic black theater rested with dramatists, players and audiences, perhaps in different proportions, but with each group assuming weighty responsibilities. The stage, said Lewis, was the "vehicle for two important arts—drama and acting," and the black stage "should be a vital force in the spiritual life of the race," delighting and exalting the audience at the same time.[17] But while DuBois and Locke essentially attacked past traditions in which they saw contemporary Afro-American drama mired, and promoted visionary theories for change, Lewis first looked more closely at the reasons behind the failures of each element of the theater of his day. He examined the roles of dramatists, actors, and audience in the light of the economics of black theater in a way that neither Locke nor DuBois came close to doing. He realized that while the audience, through its financial support, influenced the type of theater that existed, that the dramatist gave it enduring features and actors made it what it was, there was an economic structure that pre-determined the outcome of the whole.

Lewis blamed the black middle class for three areas of negligence toward promoting authentic Afro-American theater. The first was for its nonsupport of existing black dramatic activities. While the group freely criticized black theater, it did not support possibilities for change through its presence or financial resources. As a result, the lesser educated audience kept black theater alive. Equally irresponsible was the middle-class lack of critical insight into the economic politics of theater. Theater took on the character of those who supported it, and in this case, since most black theater was economically controlled by whites interested only in profits, promoters catered to those who supported their ends by their presence, applause, and money. In addition, Lewis accused the middle class of ambivalence toward authentic black theater. Instead of promoting serious black drama, the educated classes often demanded a theater that imitated the white American stage. Such a demand, Lewis said, fostered artificiality and did nothing to create a tradition in Afro-American theater. At the same time, black actors and dramatists, anxious for work, often accommodated themselves to the travesty of the economic exploitation of their talents and were also responsible for contributing to the abysmal state of black theater. In the final analysis, it was the lower classes who kept black theater alive, assuring, on some level, an evolution of a tradition. Lewis warned that without economic autonomy the black theater would never become the "medium for the expression of the spirit of Negro people" that everyone wanted it to be.[18] In its failure to develop indigenous drama, said Lewis, black theater contributed nothing to the culture of the race, nor gave it anything to pass on as a gift to the general culture of humanity.[19]

His solution to the problems echoed DuBois and Locke. He called for a national theater and a repertory system that, isolated from the white stage, addressed its appeal to colored audiences. In this theater dramatists would be at home creating race character, which he said was "the real meaning of Negro drama"; and actors would lift their audiences to a "beauty they were not previously conscious of . . . gradually creat[ing even

in the lower classes] a demand for a higher standard of entertainment."[20] It is interesting to note that all three critics found most to be optimistic about in the craft of the performers, especially in the energy of their dancing and the rich ribaldry of their comedy.

Yet, in spite of the bleak picture of the state of the art that emerges from these reports, the situation was not as barren as they suggest. The promotion of all branches of literary endeavor by the *Crisis* and *Opportunity* yielded a number of one-act dramas, including many folk plays. Before the end of the decade, anthologies of drama on black life also appeared, including *Plays of Negro Life* (works not exclusively by black playwrights) edited by Alain Locke and Montgomery Gregory (1923), and *Plays and Pageants from the Life of the Negro*, edited by Willis Richardson (1930). At the University of North Carolina, the *Carolina Magazine* did a "Negro Play Number" with plays of black life in 1929. Notably too, several black women were prominent among the new dramatists of the time. Between 1918 and 1930 eleven black women published twenty-one plays between them, in comparison to no more than half-a-dozen men who saw their works in print during these years. However, this count does not include plays that were performed although never published. Most of those that ended up in print were one-act in length and suitable to the Little Theater Movement. Themes varied from conflicts of race, class, and gender (the latter in women's plays), to struggles for self within the black community, and comedy on black folk life.

Among the most interesting playwrights of this period of experimentation were Marita Bonner, Jean Toomer, and Willis Richardson. Richardson, who wrote more than twenty one-act dramas and several longer ones, mostly folk-plays, won first prizes in the Krigwa Players and the Amy Spingarn *Crisis* magazine contests, and was the first black dramatist whose work appeared on Broadway, with *The Chip Woman's Fortune* (1923). His 1935 anthology, *Negro History in Thirteen Plays* is the first such collection devoted exclusively to black playwrights. Richardson's plays were performed in New York, in Washington, D.C., and in St. Paul as well.

Both Marita Bonner and Jean Toomer also wrote folk-plays, but are most interesting to contemporary scholars because of their experimentations with expressionist drama. Bonner's *The Purple Flower* used symbol, dance, and rhythm, with characters who are representations of qualities of human nature—good and bad—that depict various people of color joining efforts to over-throw white supremacy. The drama is impressive both for its technical apparatus, which was then known only to a small number of American play-wrights, as well as for its ideas. The play concludes with the characters of color resigned to the inevi-tability of a race war, ready to shed their blood for freedom and human dignity. Toomer wrote three expressionist plays, *Natalie Mann, The Sacred Fac-tory,* and *The Gallonwerps. Natalie Mann* concen-trates on the loss of black identity that occurs among middle-class Afro-Americans who imitate white European cultural habits. The other two plays, written after Toomer became involved with the mystic George Gurdjieff, address the sterility of the world at large from the perspective of the philosophy that informed the teachings of that man.

The 1920s were years of growing pains in the development of a tradition in Afro-American the-ater and drama. As it is often the case, the intel-lectuals and others who determine trends are often much more advanced in their vision than those who make them come true. By the 1920s there was a solid, urban, educated, sophisticated black middle class, and men like DuBois and Locke felt the responsibility to help to direct the group away from narrow self-interests and into directions that would raise the cultural aspira-tions of the black masses. Fiction, poetry, paint-ing, music, and sculpture flourished as drama seemed not to, largely because, unlike other areas of the arts, it was not an individualistic venture, but one that required the involvement of many people for its success. The goals of the critics were ambitious: to overturn the almost century-old black public performance tradition as the major-ity of white and some black people had conceived it. This was the task that they set about to ac-complish. If their successes were slow in coming, they were no less significant. It is heartening to know that first they turned to the black experi-ence—to the folk-play, the spirit life of black people—for the model on which to lay the foun-dations of authentic Afro-American drama. This is a heritage of which we can well be proud.

### Notes

1. Theophilus Lewis, "Survey of the Negro Theater—III," *The Messenger,* Vol. VIII, no. 10 (October 1926), p. 302.

2. Montgomery Gregory, "The Drama of Negro Life," *The New Negro, An Interpretation,* ed. Alain Locke (New York: Albert and Charles Boni, 1925), p. 159.

3. Nathan Huggins, *Harlem Renaissance* (New York: Ox-ford University Press, 1971), p. 286.

4. Clinton Oliver and Stephanie Sills, eds. *Contemporary Black Drama from* A Raisin in the Sun *to* No Place to Be Somebody (New York: Scribner's Sons, 1971), p. 4.

5. Oliver and Sills, p. 8.

6. Loften Mitchell, "Harlem Has Broadway On Its Mind," *Theater Arts,* Vol. XXXVII (June 1953), pp. 68-69.

7. W. E. B. DuBois, "Criteria of Negro Art," *Crisis,* Vol. 32, no. 6 (October 1926), p. 296.

8. DuBois, "Krigwa Players Little Negro Theater," *Crisis,* Vol. 32, no. 3 (July 1926), p. 134.

9. DuBois, "Krigwa Players Little Negro Theater," p. 134.

10. Alain Locke, "The Negro in the American Theater," *The Black Aesthetic* (New York: Doubleday, 1971), pp. 263-71. The quotations from Locke that follow are from this essay.

11. Locke, *The New Negro, An Interpretation* (New York: Al-bert and Charles Boni, 1925).

12. DuBois, Review of Locke, *The New Negro, Crisis,* Vol. 31, no. 3 (January 1926), p. 140.

13. Theodore Kornweibel, Jr., "Theophilus Lewis and the Theater of the Harlem Renaissance," *The Harlem Re-naissance Remembered,* ed. Arna Bontemps (New York: Dodd, Mead and Company, 1972), p. 171.

14. Abby Arthur Johnson and Ronald Mayberry Johnson, *Propaganda and Aesthetics, The Literary Politics of Afro-American Magazines in the Twentieth Century* (Amherst: University of Massachusetts Press, 1979), p. 58.

15. Johnson and Johnson, p. 60; Kornweibel, Jr., p. 171.

16. Lewis, "Main Problems of the Negro Theater," *The Messenger,* Vol. IX, no. 7 (July 1927), p. 229.

17. Lewis, "Bird's Eye View of the Negro Theater," *The Messenger,* Vol. VIII, no. 7 (July 1926), p. 214.

18. Lewis, "Survey of the Negro," *The Messenger,* Vol. VIII, no. 9 (September 1926), p. 279.

19. Lewis, "Survey of the Negro Theater—III," p. 302.

20. Lewis, "Survey of the Negro Theater—III," p. 301.

# FILM AND THE HARLEM RENAISSANCE

## BRUCE M. TYLER (ESSAY DATE 1992)

**SOURCE:** Tyler, Bruce M. "Harlem Meets Hollywood." In *From Harlem to Hollywood: The Struggle for Racial and Cultural Democracy, 1920-1943,* pp. 87-136. New York: Garland Publishing, 1992.

*In the following essay, Taylor provides an overview of Hol-lywood's relationship to Blacks, particularly in Harlem and New York City, during the early twentieth century.*

Starting in the 1920s and reaching a water-shed during World War II, black New York artists and entertainers made a steady trek to Hollywood.

Fame and fortune could be won in Hollywood, and one stood a better chance in Hollywood if he or she had won a reputation elsewhere, especially in New York. Blacks who had already gained fame, if not fortune, in New York, Harlem, and the Cotton Club increasingly looked to the new entertainment capital. In 1925 George S. Schuyler said that "today I believe it fair to say Negro America looks to New York for advanced leadership and opinion."[1] Harlem was the home of the Harlem Renaissance, W.E.B. Du Bois, and Walter White, and the NAACP's national headquarters was located in New York. From Harlem to Hollywood became the road to success.

Black and white critics continued to debate the images and performances of blacks who themselves were divided over what constituted antiblack stereotypes in films. The struggle for cultural democracy and racial pluralism in the film industry still remains a central issue for blacks and some whites. During the Great Depression, blacks in Los Angeles looked especially to Hollywood for employment. Black leaders demanded more jobs in the film industry, especially in non-stereotype roles. They argued that stereotype roles limited employment opportunities for blacks. Increasingly, blacks looked to Harlem's renowned entertainers to come to Hollywood to challenge and alter black caricature images.

James Reese Europe had built a fine jazz tradition in New York that continued to blossom under Duke Ellington, Fletcher Henderson, Cab Calloway, and many others. The Cotton Club, the Savoy Ballroom, Smalls' Paradise, and the Apollo Theatre were located in Harlem, and all shared an international reputation for high-quality entertainment and lavish floor shows with beautiful chorus line girls, dancers, and exotically dressed performers and patrons.

Walter White and Mayor Fiorello La Guardia worked together to promote civil rights and cultural pluralism in New York, which became a model for the whole nation. As a result, New York's Harlem emerged as the political, social, fashion, literary, and cultural capital of black America in the 1920s and remained so until the end of the 1940s.

Harlem's pervasive influence during that time had a dramatic impact on blacks in Los Angeles who looked to Harlem for political and cultural leadership. The proximity of black Los Angeles to Hollywood led to a keen desire among many blacks to imitate the already established and highly acclaimed social and cultural achievements of Harlem, with its proximity to Broadway, in order to break into Hollywood films. In fact, blacks in Los Angeles and around the country, especially New York, went to Hollywood seeking fame and fortune. Reputations earned in New York on Broadway or in the exclusive night clubs in Harlem carried more weight in Hollywood because of the high state of the performing arts and traditions there. Hollywood also maintained its connections with New York's entertainment world. The emergence of Hollywood as an entertainment center opened the door to blacks who had gained international recognition in the performing arts or those just entering the field.

Hollywood and theaters around the country employed musicians for movie scores. Motion picture musical scores exploded from 1928 onward after the success of the talking film *The Jazz Singer* (1927) starring Al Jolson. His singing of one song in blackface indicated Hollywood's interest in jazz. Jazz music had a different style than music associated with films. Joseph Carl Breil, a white man, had scored the music for *Queen Elizabeth* (Sarah Bernhardt) in 1912, *The Birth of a Nation* (1915), and *Intolerance* (1916). His attitude embodied a style of music opposite to that of the jazz style. He said, "Motion picture music is essentially program music, for it is a commentary and illustration of the play, entirely subservient to the action presented. It should be subtle, suggestive, and seductive.[2] Jazz as played by most blacks was just the opposite. It was often described as hot, frantic, and with a biting attack.

Hollywood producers hired musicians who played at such local Los Angeles theaters as Grauman's, Clune's Auditorium, the Orpheum, Kinema, and Miller's California. They played the type of music described by Breil. In 1918 Hollywood employed 100 musicians.[3] German music tended to dominate the classical music field and theaters, but World War I led to a powerful backlash. Los Angeles staged a downtown parade to celebrate the ending of the war. Bands and paraders sang. Some displayed signs with inscriptions as: "To Hell with the Kaiser" and "Goodbye France, Hello Broadway" as a signal to reject foreign influences and praise everything American. American music and black spirituals experienced a dramatic revival.[4] The rise of a formal musical community in Los Angeles and the rise of Hollywood as a movie and radio empire made the city a mecca for entertainers of every race, creed, color, sex, and national origin.

Los Angeles's musical community matured rapidly and developed the Los Angeles Philhar-

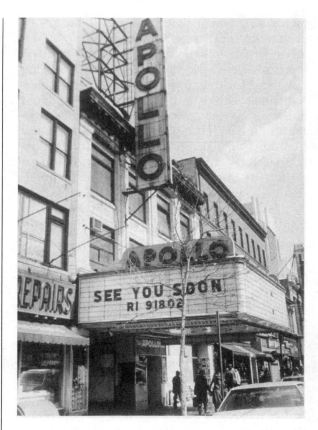

The Apollo Theater, Harlem.

monic Orchestra and the Hollywood Bowl. Len E. Behymer conducted the Philharmonic between the two world wars. He supplied artists from his orchestra to the Southwestern states. The Shrine Auditorium was built in 1927 and offered another outlet for musicians and concerts. Behymer supplied the major motion picture studios with musicians from 1928 onward after Hollywood shifted to sound following the success of *The Jazz Singer* (1927) with Al Jolson. Behymer signed with Fox Film Corporation to provide its film musical scores. He served as a "master press agent" for Hollywood studios, and his work and musicians (for whom he served as a hiring agent) were in high demand. He performed for the Los Angeles Olympic Games in 1932.[5] Black musicians were not included in Behymer's group because of the prevalent racism.

The advent of the sound picture also led Hollywood's Sunset Boulevard and Vine Street to become an industry center for radio broadcasting. Earle C. Anthony, owner of the first big radio station in Los Angeles, announced a broad musical policy on January 15, 1923: "In the musical end we want to be able to broadcast from opera to jazz. . . ."[6] Musicians often played live on radio,

which also used recorded music. This shift in musical policy proved hospitable for black jazz artists who made records or played live on the radio.

In 1927 and 1928 the advent of the sound picture led many theater operators to fire their bands and organists. About 5,000 musicians across the nation lost their jobs as a result. Joseph N. Weber, president of the American Federation of Musicians, was alarmed. He went to Los Angeles to organize and supervise the deluge of unemployed musicians converging on Hollywood studios for work. He established minimum wages and maximum hours as work standards. He told musicians to share the work. He said in June 1929 that a musician "should willingly lend his aid that more musicians be employed instead of a mere handful earning huge wages."[7]

Behymer and his well-trained classical orchestra musicians early monopolized Hollywood studio film work because of their superior training and organization. Hollywood grew rapidly and so did jobs for studio musicians. The competition was fierce. Racism limited blacks in the competition and blacks had a small number of formally trained musicians compared to whites.

The Harlem Renaissance and Hollywood boomed at the same time in the 1920s. Hollywood for blacks became one of the few outlets—and the most lucrative—and offered the greatest exposure for artists. Harlem artists started going to Hollywood in the 1920s just as New York Broadway stars did in search of fame and fortune. These black and white New Yorkers set the standards which many others imitated in their attempts to break into show business. Competition grew fierce among blacks as opportunities exploded in Hollywood, Harlem, and on Broadway. The entertainment industry expanded to accommodate escapism, and jobs became lucrative and plentiful in the black entertainment market. Many blacks in Los Angeles caught the Harlem and Hollywood fever for the performing arts in quest of fame and fortune.

Central Avenue was the main street and residential area where blacks clustered. It became an important cultural and entertainment center, and its connection with Hollywood films resulted in its most spectacular growth and recognition. It looked to Harlem and its Renaissance as a model to imitate. Hollywood provided a crucial outlet for black entertainers in need of employment.

In the 1920s, Charles Butler became one of "the original talent agent[s] and scout[s] for Hollywood" to recruit blacks primarily for "G-string and African" native roles, "cottonfield" workers, and menial labor roles. Butler had an office at 1315 E. 12th Street, a few steps off Central Avenue, the heart of the black residential and entertainment community. He and his wife Sarah dominated the "cattle calls" (calls for work as "extras" who usually played background scenes or "bit" talking roles) for large numbers of blacks to play bit parts in Hollywood films. Butler positioned himself to take advantage of managing. He later moved his business to his residence in the 1100 block of East 52nd Street. Butler's wife was a pioneer as a minister of a church in the middle 1930s. Undoubtedly, because she and her husband recruited black choirs to sing spirituals and songs in films, it was an advantage to maintain a church and choir for film roles. Since most blacks lived and socialized in the Central Avenue district, it was convenient and easy to spot blacks who might fit a casting-type for certain film roles. For example, Darby Jones, a tall black native of Los Angeles, got frequent calls to play African warrior and buck roles because of his appearance. "Mammy types," "African bucks," and blacks with "a certain look" often received "cattle calls." Maids and butlers were considered prestigious roles by blacks in the 1920s because they were casting-types in regular demand and, therefore, provided the most days of employment. Earl Dancer became an agent and worked as a master of ceremony in the Central Avenue night spots. He moved in with his aunt, Bertha Dunigan, a native of Columbia, Texas, who had lived in Los Angeles since 1918. Since she lived at 840 Birch Street, just two blocks east of Central Avenue, Dancer wanted to take advantage of the talent and blacks who frequented the area as potential recruits for Hollywood "cattle calls." Besides, his aunt was well known in social circles. Earl Broady, who delivered mail to the Butler and Dancer residences, remembered Dancer as "an impresario for plays and actors."[8] Dancer used his family connections and his own experience in New York to promote his career in the entertainment world of Central Avenue and Hollywood.

It was a distinct advantage to live near Central Avenue, the black social and entertainment section of the black community. Promoters and entertainers worked the clubs and talent scouts looked to Central Avenue to hire blacks for Hollywood films. Hollywood periodically hired large numbers of blacks from Los Angeles's "Black Broadway," Central Avenue, as film extras. "Hollywood Movie Colony Studios Resembles League of Nations: Cosmopolitan Air Vogue at Smart Film Colony; Race Actors Are Plentiful," a black newspaper reported in 1929. It noted that Hollywood and Los Angeles had settlements of almost every race, ethnic group, and talent from around the world. Hollywood's Central Casting Bureau recruited Orientals for the film *Dr. Fu Manchu* from Chinatown in Los Angeles. Also, "Seventy-five Negroes appear in a Harlem Cabaret scene of George Bancroft's new starring picture, *Thunderbolt,* as well as varied types of Americans. The Negroes were recruited from Central Avenue, Los Angeles," reported the *Pittsburgh Courier.*[9]

Harlem's racial, economic, and political trends developed early among blacks in Los Angeles and affected the way blacks perceived Hollywood. In 1921 in Los Angeles Noah Thompson led a majority splinter group out of the Universal Negro Improvement Association of Marcus Garvey, a Pan-Africanist, whose headquarters was located in Harlem. Garvey and Booker T. Washington developed plans to develop the economy of the black community. Thompson organized his group into the Pacific Coast Negro Improvement Association in November 1921. He and anti-Garvey crusader Chandler Owen in 1924 organized The California Development Company as a cooperative economic venture. They bought an apartment building in the black community which they called "the Harlem of Los Angeles." Other blacks started businesses that resulted in the emergence of a number of substantial black business institutions modeled on Garvey's plans and Booker T. Washington's National Negro Business League, which also was located in New York City.[10] Blacks in Los Angeles continued to imitate Harlem trends, especially in entertainment. During the Great Depression, Los Angeles blacks copied Harlem and Chicago demands for employment by verbal protests, threat, and boycotts first initiated by black militants.

Curtis Mosby, a Los Angeles musician, made the sound track for an obscure movie called *Thunderbolt* (1919) by George Bancroft. He played sound tracks for other film shorts in this period as well. His band played and appeared in the first all-black film musical, *Hallelujah* (1929), which starred Daniel Haynes and Nina Mae McKinney. Mosby's band played "Introduction," "Swanee Shuffle," and "Blue Blowers Blues" on the sound track. His regular band was called "Curtis Mosby and His Dixieland Blue-Blowers." Black Hollywood actress Nina Mae McKinney also sang with his regular band. Benjamin "Reb" (for rebel) Spikes, another black Los Angeles musician and businessman, had a group called Spikes' Seven

Josephine Baker in a scene from the 1934 film *Zou Zou*.

Pods of Pepper Orchestra. They recorded in 1922 and the late 1920s. Les Hite played with this group, then formed the house band for Frank Sebastian's prestigious Cotton Club (named after the famed Harlem club) on Washington Boulevard in Culver City, a suburb of Los Angeles and a center of Hollywood film studios.[11] Black musicians performed at Sebastian's club but could not enter as patrons because it practiced racial discrimination and segregation. Black musicians and a few select notables, however, were allowed to sit on the bandstand as observers as a courtesy of the management.[12]

Nina Mae McKinney's life epitomized the from-country-to-urban trek, the from-Harlem-to-Hollywood phenomenon, and the eventual rise to stardom when she made her first film, *Hallelujah,* in 1929. "I was born in South Carolina on the estate where our family had lived several generations. My grandmother was an old and trusted servant of this household." She "reared me until I was about 12 years old. Then my father, who was in New York, sent for me." She recalled, "Imagine my delight at this big metropolitan city. I was constantly thrilled by the wonder unfolded to me. Its skyscrapers, its parks, the theatres, anything, everything was a veritable fairyland, and I beheld its glories in wide-eyed amazement."[13] She dreamed, danced, and play-acted before her mir-

ror. Three years later, "I joined the chorus of 'Lew Leslie's Blackbirds of 1928.'" She had taught herself to dance. "The phenomenal success of Florence Mills and Josephine Baker stimulated me. I longed to hold a place in the hearts of the world as they did."[14]

King Vidor, a Hollywood director, saw McKinney in the Broadway musical hit *Blackbirds* and called her to Memphis, Tennessee, where he was shooting *Hallelujah.* He had studied Louisiana's black countryside and religion in order to make his film. McKinney said, "I was thrilled. There I began the fascinating work of acting for the movies." She played the role of cabaret dancer "Chick," who seduced "Zeke" (Daniel Haynes), an evangelical minister. The film became a hit. McKinney praised Vidor and Hollywood for the 2,000 black extras who were hired for the film from the Memphis area plantations. One scene used the whole black population of a town of 500. Vidor said, "I am trying to do for Negro talent what we did for the doughboys in the *Big Parade*": Make them respected heroes. And he added, "Much depends upon the Negro pioneers in this field of art." McKinney was impressed. "He is very sympathetic to us."[15] Thus some blacks felt they had a future in films.

The *Chicago Defender* reported that the success of *Hallelujah* led to talk of another producer making another "race epic," boasting that "many of our group are finding steady employment in the pictures, not only in character, but as members of mob scenes in which their racial characteristics may not be seen."[16] Thus very early blacks appreciated employment in films and recognition.

*Hallelujah*'s plot starkly revealed that the black, rural folk culture, including its ministry, quickly collapsed when confronted with the urban culture symbolized by the cabaret. King Vidor discovered that cabaret culture was so pervasive in black society that its exact counterpart existed in the most rural and backward regions of the South. Urbane hustlers preyed on the rural blacks by using exotic women, gambling, liquor, and jazz music to cheat them out of their wages. Country girls used hustling to escape a life of poverty and drudgery in the countryside. One reviewer noted that "the fate of Zeke (played by Daniel Haynes), a contented cotton picker and eldest son of a large family, is analogous to that of any country boy who enters the city 'green' as far as experience is concerned [and] whose pockets were lined with 'greenbacks,' representing his year's labor." He was cheated out of his money by the urbane McKinney and her pimp.[17]

The cabaret symbolized urban life and the Harlem which Carl Van Vechten in his novel, *Nigger Heaven* (1926), and Claude McKay in *Home to Harlem* (1928), had made famous, leading many whites to trek to Harlem to enjoy its entertainment. Vidor made the rural cabaret famous with *Hallelujah.* Cabaret and entertainment culture emerged early in Los Angeles, too. Hollywood's proximity to Central Avenue encouraged blacks to seek fame and fortune in entertainment and cabaret culture. McKinney and many other blacks went to Los Angeles to pursue acting and entertainment careers.

In the 1920s Mosby and Spikes both had music stores on Central Avenue, at 2315 and 1203 South Central respectively. The Spikes brothers, Benjamin and Johnny, sold their records but concentrated on selling music publications from their record-store firm called Sunshine Record Company. Their biggest hit was "Someday Sweetheart" (1919), which they sold to the Melrose brothers (Melrose Avenue was named after them) in 1924. The Spikes brothers wrote the lyrics and music for the musical comedy *Steppin' High* (1924), which went on the road and disbanded in Amarillo, Texas, in December of 1924. Benjamin Spikes also used his record store as a referral service for musicians, placing them in night clubs around the city and elsewhere. In November 1924 Reb's Legion Club Forty-Fives recorded a tune, "Sheffield Blues," in tribute to Maceo Sheffield, a feared Los Angeles black police officer who became an actor, "supervisor," and management agent for actors. Mosby and various local musicians were among the first blacks to record sound tracks for Hollywood films. William Rogers Campbell "Sonny" Clay was born in Phoenix, Arizona, on May 15, 1899, but moved to Los Angeles around 1915. He organized Sonny Clay's Plantation Orchestra, a popular Los Angeles band. He was the most recorded black in Los Angeles in the middle and late 1920s. Clay claimed his band appeared in sixty-five films in his heyday.[18]

Lawrence "Speed" Webb and his Hollywood Blue Devils started out in Toledo, Ohio, in 1926 as a jazz band. They played in three films, *Riley the Cop, Sables and Furs,* and *On with the Show,* from 1927 to 1929 while in Los Angeles for ballroom engagements. Webb made a record with a flashy front cover that played up his Hollywood film connections: "Speed Webb and His Nationally Famous Hollywood Blue Devils"; "America's Smartest Colored Band"; "Direct from Warner Bros., M-G-M and Fox Studios"; "14 Radio and Screen Artists."[19]

Lionel Hampton, a drummer then, went to Los Angeles in 1927 and built his reputation at Frank Sebastian's Cotton Club in Culver City. Paul Howard's Quality Serenaders was regarded as the "most musical band" in Los Angeles in the 1920s. Howard came from Steubenville, Ohio, and formed his quartet at the Quality Cafe on 12th Street and Central Avenue, in the heart of black Los Angeles. In 1927 his band played at the Cotton Club in Culver City. They recorded for the Victor label such tunes as "The Ramble," "Stuff," "Quality Shout," and "Moonlight Blues" with Lionel Hampton on drums. The band played regularly at the Kentucky Club on Central Avenue but got a date and played at "Eddie Brandstatter's swank Montmartre on Hollywood Boulevard." The band recorded the tunes "California Swing," "Cuttin' Up," and "Harlem" before it broke up in the summer of 1930.[20] The Harlem and Hollywood connections meant the big time in entertainment, and individuals and groups more and more paid homage to them in name and song.

Louis Armstrong came to the Culver City Cotton Club to perform in July 1930. While there he made his first film, *Ex-Flame,* which starred Neal Hamilton, for the Liberty Film Company. He recorded with Les Hite, the Cotton Club house band, such songs as "Ding Dong Daddy," "I'm in the Market for You," "I'm Confessin'," and "Just a Gigolo," all of which were popular songs or were featured in current movies. Armstrong stayed in Los Angeles nine months because the Cotton Club was broadcast by radio from coast to coast, and Hollywood movie stars filled the club nightly. He and Vic Berton were arrested and jailed ten days for possession of marijuana. Earl Broady, a pianist and mailman who saw Armstrong during this period, recalled that Armstrong made marijuana popular among some musicians in Los Angeles. Armstrong returned in 1932 and remained for a three-month engagement at the Cotton Club because he was so impressed with Los Angeles and its emergence as a cultural capital.[21] Recording for Hollywood films and even playing "bit" parts became a regular feature of big name entertainers and their bands while traveling to Los Angeles.

Liquor and marijuana increasingly became part of the jazz and entertainment world, and for some blacks, it was a response to the Jim Crow system. In 1933, while on a ship to England, Louis Armstrong's white manager, Johnny Collins, called him a "nigger." John Hammond, the great jazz impresario, who was present, defended Armstrong's honor and, to Armstrong's dismay, knocked Collins down. Armstrong remained with his manager for another year. Armstrong had a reputation of smoking marijuana daily. He said, "It makes you feel good, man. It relaxes you. Makes you forget all the bad things that happen to a Negro. It makes you feel wanted, and when you're with another tea smoker it makes you feel a special kinship."[22] Many racists and critics used drug and alcohol abuse by musicians and cabaret culture to denounce jazz and its cultural recognition, cultural pluralism, and democracy.

Les Hite played with all the regular and big name Los Angeles musicians such as Curtis Mosby and Paul Howard. He played at Los Angeles City Hall in 1933. He played for Fats Waller in 1935 when Waller went to the Cotton Club in Culver City. One newspaper reported: "Les Hite and his famous Hollywood Orchestra is probably the most famous Negro band on the Pacific Coast!" Moreover, "Millions of movie fans have heard their music and seen the shadowy outline of their faces in cinema productions." Hite played on the air coast to coast from the Culver City Cotton Club on Sundays. He played the big Los Angeles theaters. "Now Playing at the Orpheum downtown is Les Hite and his orchestra in the Black and Tan Revue of 1938 starring Peg Leg Bates, Hattie Noel, Chocolate Brown Sisters and 16 Sweethearts. Two first run pictures are also on the bill." Hite disbanded his group in 1943 and died in 1962.[23] Among blacks, Hite and "Reb" Spikes made the most Hollywood films, at least sixty-five each, because they were first-rate band leaders, were organized, controlled large numbers of musicians through employment, and were based in the Los Angeles area. They were the mainstays and conduits for employment of black musicians in early Hollywood films.

Floyd Ray's Harlem Dictators went to Los Angeles in 1936 with a Miller and Slayter show that was organized in Scranton, Pennsylvania, in 1934. They became very popular at the Warner Brothers studio lot, where blacks often gave weekend dances. In 1936 Cab Calloway and his band went to Los Angeles. Eddie Barefield left that band to remain in Los Angeles because, in his view, there were so few first-rate bands in the city.[24] The opportunities were improving for work, especially in Hollywood, because it increasingly employed local talent as well as performers visiting the city.

Charlie Christian, the great black jazz guitar player, in August of 1939 left Oklahoma City for Los Angeles to play for Benny Goodman. Christian arrived wearing a "purple shirt and yellow shoes" and Goodman was dismayed. His apprehension was allayed after he told the band to play "Rose Room," a tune he thought Christian did not know. To his surprise Christian played so well that he not only inspired Goodman and the band, but the audience gave them the loudest applause ever for their performance at the Victor Hugo Restaurant in Beverly Hills.[25] Thus blacks participated very early and at every level in the Hollywood and Los Angeles area entertainment culture. Moreover, they promoted cultural pluralism and integration of the races.

Increasingly, Los Angeles attracted blacks, especially those traveling to the city for work or pleasure. Many returned to stay. Black railroad workers often boasted across the country about the city and spread its reputation. Some brought family and girlfriends to the city to live. In 1933 about 100,000 blacks lived in Southern California, and 50,000 of these clustered around Central Avenue. Few black Pullman porters lived in Los Angeles, but many other transportation workers, like "red caps" and cooks, did. The Southern Pacific dining car employees had an "elaborate headquarters at Twelfth and Central" that was presided over by its president, Clarence Johnson. They were second in number in the work force to domestic workers. Many black domestics worked for whites in Hollywood's film industry, especially for the stars and moguls. Blacks working for the city and county of Los Angeles ranked third, "although the motion-picture industry sometimes leads" because of the large numbers of extras employed periodically in films. In 1932 blacks in films earned $35,000. The black community had "six motion picture theaters all conducted by its own people."[26] Thus Hollywood played a significant role in the social life and economy of black Los Angeles.

Local blacks in Los Angeles first got jobs in Hollywood. Hazel Augustine Washington, the wife of Roscoe Washington, a Los Angeles Police Department officer who was highly respected in the department and the black community, was one of the first black hairdressers and personal maids to white female Hollywood stars. She was a "licensed operator" (hairdresser) and a union member, and worked out of the union hall at a time when most unions excluded blacks. She first was an "aide" for Greta Garbo "when they had no Negroes around." "In the 1920s," Washington said, "Hollywood started hiring a lot of blacks." She later worked for years as a personal aide to actress Rosalind Russell. (As a pioneer "black Angeleno" and as the wife of a black policeman, which was high status in black Los Angeles, she never called herself a "servant" or allowed herself to be treated like one because she was a "licensed" and unionized "operator," unlike most other blacks in her field, who were at the mercy of the personal whims of their employers.) Russell helped her open a customized leather-goods store and even became a partner. In 1943 Hazel Washington was the hairdresser for the actors in *Stormy Weather* and *Cabin in the Sky,* and she became a close friend of Lena Horne.[27]

Hazel Washington's position was exceptional. Most blacks were traditional domestic servants and chauffeurs. For many blacks then it was a status symbol to work for prominent employers or Hollywood's film industry moguls or professionals.

Los Angeles had a small number of black males regularly employed (under contract) as actors and showmen in 1930. Out of a total of 4,451 actors, only 128 were black. Three blacks were among the 1,106 "directors, managers, and officials, motion picture production" in the 1930 census. Of 2,909 actresses and showwomen, only 85 were black. The census did not even list a category for female directors, managers, officials, and motion picture production workers.[28] In 1940 the United States Census listed the total number of actors in Los Angeles as 2,426, of whom 51 were black. Male dancers, showmen, and athletes were classed together for a total of 910, with 33 blacks. The total number of males seeking work as experienced actors in Los Angeles amounted to 1,271, with 42 blacks in this number. Similarly, male dancers, showmen, and athletes seeking work amounted to a total of 226, with 21 blacks. The total number of females employed in 1940 as actresses amounted to 743, with 15 blacks. No second category was listed.[29]

Clearly, only a small number of blacks were regularly employed in these fields at any given time. It is not clear if they were largely the same persons employed or different ones. A larger pool of blacks was employed from time to time as extras in Hollywood. Black workers in Los Angeles were largely unskilled and suffered frequent unemployment in the depression years. Hollywood often became a periodic employer for blacks unemployed and underemployed.

"When *King Kong* was filming at RKO in 1933, every out-of-work black musician, singer, actor, and dancer rushed to that lot for work on 'Skull Island'" as natives in the traditional stereotype "G-string" or "loin cloth" roles reserved for blacks from the Central Avenue community. Light-skinned blacks were not hired for these roles. Jazz trumpeter Buck Clayton was turned away from the *Kong* film for this reason. The best white musicians could get work in Hollywood studios, which paid good wages and where work was steady. Black musicians, however, had a rough time because of discrimination and because some lacked the musical literacy the studios demanded.[30]

In February of 1937, 1,500 blacks were hired in Hollywood as extras in *A Day at the Races* filmed by Metro-Goldwyn-Mayer and featuring the Marx Brothers. The song "All God's Chillun Got Rhythm" was to be used in the film. Harpo Marx insisted that black entertainers be used in the scene in which the song was used. Freita Shaw worked on the casting of blacks with the help of Ben Carter. Hundreds of juvenile dancers and bit players were signed as well. However, the weekly payroll amounted to only $800 since only a small percentage of the blacks were used at any one time. Duke Ellington and his band with Ivy Anderson, a singer and native Californian, were featured in the film. Other black acts were headlined, too.[31]

In the film *Slave Ship* 750 blacks were hired by 20th Century-Fox. This broke the record for the number of blacks ever hired by the studio. Blacks were jammed into a slave ship. "There were 400 men and 350 women, a larger number of colored players than has ever worked at one time in any picture in the history of Hollywood." The 350 women were cast in "bit" parts that paid them "$15 per day." Charles Butler played a key role in recruiting these blacks as the Central Casting Office's director for blacks. As usual, he recruited them from his Central Avenue office.[32] Many blacks looked more and more to employment and recognition from Hollywood.

The black press took a closer look at Hollywood's projection of the black image and sought more employment for black entertainers because of the possibility of earning fabulous fortunes. Also, recognition of the race could be won in this medium, and there were reasonable wages and work for blacks recruited for bit roles. Then, too, black pride had to be defended publicly, and Hollywood's projection of blacks in a favorable light was crucial. Also, substantial incomes often came with stardom. The Great Depression made employment a central concern of blacks. The economic crisis also made blacks more politically conscious as left-wing politics spread within the black urban communities.

The film *Green Pastures* (1936) resulted in the more socially and politically conscious New York blacks going to Hollywood to play lead roles. Among these were some old veteran Hollywood film actors such as Rex Ingram, who played the "De Lawd," George Randol as the "High Priest," and assistant director Hall Johnson and his Hall Johnson Choir, who provided the choral music arrangement. Johnson was also the conductor for the film. Ernest Whitman played "Pharaoh."

Los Angeles-based black actors resented the hegemony of New York blacks. When the Associated Negro Press theatrical correspondent, Fay M. Jackson, revealed that Rex Ingram was chosen to play the key role, her opinion was that Ingram was "to whom all the smokes [blacks] [in Hollywood] object." Moreover, she and Claude Barnett, president of the Associated Negro Press, attempted to use the film to advance the cause of black Hollywood actors by protesting the low pay scales and some scenes considered objectionable. Warner Brothers responded with a press release, "Fear 'Green Pastures' New Yorkers May Spoil Hollywood," which impressed some black critics, who felt Jackson's criticisms had been answered. The play and film of *Green Pastures* in Los Angeles resulted in some actors returning to stay in the city. It was such migrants who formed the nucleus of "Hollywood's Harlem" film colony that began "reproducing it [Harlem nightlife] in Hollywood and on Central Avenue," reported the *Chicago Defender*.[33] This influx of actors from New York overshadowed and threatened the black Los Angeles actors and promoters as second-rate imitators.

Blacks tended to resent plantation epics because of the negative connection of rural life with slavery, and especially the slander associated with *The Birth of a Nation* (1915). *Green Pastures* (1936) was generally well received because it had won fame as a play first. Broadway plays and Harlem cabaret shows of distinction would often later be reproduced as films in Hollywood. Marc Connelly's play, *Green Pastures* (1930), was well received by many blacks. It became a "sensational hit" on Broadway and dealt with black religious practices with respect. One critic, Sharon Kane, thought Connelly's play of black rural religious life and culture reflected "absolute originality." Moreover, "this extraordinary play" was a new "dimension" because Connelly had "produced a magnificently imaginative and absolutely new type of Race drama." Black actors were "coming into their own in the world of theater."[34] Another critic was impressed with *Green Pastures* because "the Negro is being taken seriously in drama in this epoch of ours—as a person, not as a caricature." Blacks and their religion were portrayed sympathetically. Nevertheless, Salem Tutt Whitney, presumably a black critic writing for the *Chicago Defender,* "the Harlem complex" (critical of and defensive toward racial slights and caricatures that offended Harlem blacks) "must be allowed to stalk a while" because *Green Pastures* had not completed "the work of exorcism" of prejudice and stereotyping of blacks.[35]

The ministry praised *Green Pastures* lavishly. Bishop Shipman, Bishop Wallace, Dr. W.A. Nichols, religious editor of the *New York Telegram,* and the Rev. Russell J. Clinchy of the Broadway Tabernacle Church attended the play at the Mansfield Theater and wrote raving reviews. Ministers attended every showing and were impressed. Bishops Shipman and Wallace came backstage to congratulate the performers. Dr. Nichols wrote in his column, "Instead of being shocked I was thrilled throughout." He confided, "I went there prepared to be shocked, I came away with the determination to be a better priest. And let it be added, no conscience need be violated by anyone seeing it during Lent, for it is a devotion in itself."[36] Rev. Clinchy said in the press, "May I commend to your readers the play which is now running at the Mansfield theater, entitled 'The Green Pastures,' because my interest in this is simply to aid in spreading news concerning one of the most significant dramas of modern times. . . ."[37] These ministers' approval was important in the reception of the play.

The National Association for the Advancement of Colored People (NAACP) honored Marc Connelly, the play's writer and director, as the guest of honor of the New York Men's Committee of the NAACP at a "smoker" in April 1930. Connelly was introduced by Heywood Broun, a columnist of the *New York Telegram* and Scripps-Howard newspapers. Connelly said he had used Roark Bradford's "Ol' Man Adam and His Chillun" to write his play and he had traveled to Louisiana to study black country life and religion, which were reflected in his play.[38] In 1931 Richard (Rex) Harrison won the NAACP's highest award, the Spingarn Medal, for his acting. Lieutenant Governor Herbert H. Lehman of New York presented Harrison with the medal on March 22, 1931, at the Mansfield Theater, where the play had been presented.[39] The play in 1930 and the film version in 1936 of *Green Pastures* were a relief and well received by most blacks and many whites. It became a standard by which they would judge other plantation epics.

Washington, D.C.'s black population was a proud and dignified group with many educated at Howard University as doctors, lawyers, teachers, dentists, and other professionals. Howard was the leading black college in the country. On February 26, 1933, the *Green Pastures* play was scheduled at the National Theatre for a two-week run. The National did not allow black patrons. Tickets had to be purchased in person to prevent blacks from buying by telephone or mail. Blacks mobilized rapidly to deal with their exclusion. The NAACP and a delegation of black ministers went to Baltimore, where the cast was then playing, to petition the cast not to play at the National Theatre unless blacks were allowed to freely buy tickets and attend the performance. Marc Connelly wrote a letter of protest against the Jim Crow policy, but only the Washington, D.C., *Daily News* published it. Others refused to do so, and the National stopped advertising in the *Daily News* as a protest against its liberalism. Black and white protesters were refused permits by the police to picket the play. A Jim Crow performance was arranged by the Black Elks who quickly had to renounce their role in the matter after an angry protest by key sectors of black leaders. A plot was hatched to kidnap Harrison in order to sabotage the play. Four or five hundred blacks, nevertheless, showed up for the performance and outraged those who had advocated a boycott.[40] Blacks demonstrated again that no broad consensus had been achieved within black society over protest and racial accommodations or how blacks should be portrayed and under what conditions they should perform.

The cast and Richard B. Harrison were under contract, wanted to work, received an income, and dared not refuse to play because their careers might be ruined. Many black and white civil rights activists were severely divided over the incident.[41] No consensus was ever reached among blacks and whites on this issue. Militant blacks, and some white allies, were sorely disappointed. They thought that many blacks by their passive accommodation to Jim Crow were, in effect, co-conspirators in their own oppression and degradation. W.E.B. Du Bois of New York and Loren Miller of Los Angeles held this view.

Many blacks felt embarrassed by their rural past, which was often associated with slavery and passive accommodation to oppression. Migration to cities, especially in the North, brought greater freedom and job opportunities. Racial pride often increased along with a willingness to insist on public and media respect for the race. Harlem became the black urban capital because of its large black population and its racial militancy. As a result, the "Harlem complex" became well known throughout the country. Harlem as a black social and cultural capital was reflected in its pervasive influence and attempts at creating "little Harlems" across the country, and even back into history, which was evident with the film *Harlem on the Prairie* (1937) by prominent blacks of Los Angeles under the leadership of Maceo Sheffield.

A white film company under Jed Buell made *Harlem on the Prairie,* billed as "The first all-Negro musical Western." A reviewer noted, "The cast is an interesting cross-section of the upper crust of Los Angeles' South Central Avenue [Negro district]." Flournoy E. Miller, who played a key role in *Shuffle Along,* which ran on Broadway successfully for two years and opened up new artistic and cultural opportunities for blacks for generations, appeared in the film. *Harlem on the Prairie* merged a cowboy yarn with flashy Western dress outfits to reflect the Harlemites who adored fine dress along with dramatic acting and first-rate songs.[42] It was a radical departure from the highly resented plantation epics. Black Western films provided an alternative to Southern slavery epics that often portrayed negative "Uncle Tom" stereotypes with "dog-like devotion" to their slavemasters.

A reviewer of *Harlem on the Prairie* wrote, "It brings to life a cow-country as fabulous as the version of some Holy Roller prophet. In this apocalyptic land everybody—the prospectors and stage-coach drivers, the medicine men, outlaws, sheriff, the hero with the silver-plated stock saddle—is a gentlemen of color." Moreover, "it is in no sense a burlesque." It had a real plot that unfolded with dramatic acting. Its first-rate songs were written by a white man, Lew Porter. "Romance in the Rain," the Four Tones harmonizing "Albuquerque," and Herb Jeffries, who sang "The Old Folks at Home," were outstanding.[43]

*Harlem on the Prairie* was a jazzed-up black dude cowboy film with an urbane flavor designed to appeal to urbane blacks who resented Southern plantation films and caricatures. It romanticized the rural past that many black Harlemites felt ashamed of and were disturbed over—its poverty and peonage, which severely hampered blacks' social and economic mobility. Many blacks, as a result, eagerly sought to adopt a sophisticated urban culture as a means of seeking status and acceptance. Harlem had inaugurated the Harlem Renaissance to combat negative black stereotypes and usher in a "New Negro," an urban and sophisticated black, educated, talented, worldly, and able to secure his own status and social mobility by acquiring and skillfully applying sophisticated urban skills—often in the art and entertainment worlds.

The Club Alabam, run by Ralph Roberts, and later by Curtis Mosby, and the Dunbar Hotel located at 42nd Street and Central Avenue were the two main anchors of the nightlife on Central Avenue. Bill Robinson did a guest show in August of 1938 and the press noted, "Maxine Wows 'Em on L.A.'s Central Avenue: Bojangles Puts on One of His Famous Shows at Club Alabam—Sends Police Escort for Jeni LeGon's Shoes" so she could dance, too. Robinson was made an honorary "lieutenant of police" in Los Angeles (just as New York's Mayor La Guardia had honored him as "the Mayor of Harlem") which gave him petty special privileges. Earl Dancer served as master of ceremonies. Jeni LeGon came from Chicago but now, it was noted, "Jeni LeGon, the dancing darling of the films, carved her way into the hearts of Hollywood's Harlem" that centered on Central Avenue and served as a staging ground for blacks aspiring to get into Hollywood films as well as a showcase for those who had made it.[44]

Entertainers such as "Luther Thompson and Director Tom Jacobson, along with three pretties from his studio doing Hollywood's Harlem" were popular on Central Avenue.[45] Earl Dancer and Flournoy E. Miller had made it big, even if only briefly, in New York on Broadway and at the Apollo Theatre. They took Harlem entertainment culture to Los Angeles and became the founders and pacesetters of "Hollywood's Harlem" social and cultural movements. It represented class, style, and professional accomplishment. It became one of the elite black status groups in Los Angeles and on Central Avenue.

One contemporary observer noted in Los Angeles that Earl Dancer "tried to impress people. He was a promoter, manager and director." He was a master of ceremonies at nightclubs and acted as an agent for entertainers, movie actors, and singers. He spent money lavishly. He talked confidently about breaking into the "big time" by getting into "the white time" entertainment world and money—that meant Hollywood films.[46] Dancer's big city talk, style, and goals impressed the local blacks who lacked the background, Broadway, and magical Harlem connections that he and Miller could boast about.

The *California Eagle* newspaper advertised in August 1938, "South East Harlem Aristocrat of Night Spots, Featuring T-Bone Walker, 11812 Par-

malee Avenue, 2 blocks East of Central off Imperial Highway, JE-7434." Another read, "Dunbar Cocktail Lounge, Host Harry Spates, 4227 So. Central, Adams 4201." And visitors were solicited with "Summer Visitors! Los Angeles' 'Night Life' Is Found at the Club Alabam, Gala Opening July 9th, Fun-Freedom-Hilarity—Lavish Floor Show Produced by Mantan Moreland, For Reservations call Je-4569." In 1940 T-Bone Walker played at the popular Little Harlem nightclub located at 114th Street and Central Avenue. Also, a club named the Plantation was patronized and Harlem itself had a club called the Plantation.[47] The *California Eagle* ran a huge advertisement, saying "Hollywood Meets Harlem": "Grand Studio Ball & Movie Classics. Sponsored by Golden West Lodge No. 86, I.B.P.O.E.W. Championship Big-Apple-Contest. The Pick of Harlem-Harlem's Elect. Sepia Bathing Beauty Parade. California's Most Charming and Graceful Maidens. Directed by Clarence Muse. Warner Bros. Studio. Sunset Blvd. and Van Ness Ave., Hollywood. Thurs. Nite, July 21st, 1938, 9 P.M. Movie Stars, Radio Favorites, Famous Directors and Camera-men, the Baker, Butcher and Even the Ice Man will join hands when Hollywood Meets Harlem. Gen. Adm. $.75, Reserve Section $1.00, Boxes Seating six $7.00. For Reservations Call Room 200 Elks Bldg. Phone Adams 7578."[48] This ad was one of the most dramatic and lavish presentations of the social and cultural movement of "Hollywood Meets Harlem."

Other ads noted that Clarence Muse was the only male who met with the black women's Social Committee for the "Hollywood Meets Harlem" celebration at the Elks' Hall on Central Avenue. Still another ad noted: "Hollywood to Meet Harlem" on Stage Six "in a gigantic movie ball." Muse said the winner among sixty black bathing beauty contestants would receive a movie contract. The "Hollywood Meets Harlem" celebration included a "Big Apple Swing Session" at this "movie jamboree." The *California Eagle* society editor, Helen F. Chappell, wrote a column called "Chatter and . . . Some News" in which she called Central Avenue "the Angel City Harlem."[49]

Los Angeles in Spanish means "the angels" and many commentators called it "The City of the Angels." The Angel City Harlem was the Central Avenue black entertainment colony. Blacks found many ways to express the Hollywood/Harlem connection, and Hollywood proper was often used very loosely to mean Central Avenue or just blacks in Hollywood films. In short, black Hollywood or "Harlem in Hollywood" most often meant blacks with the Harlem entertainment style working in Hollywood films or on Central Avenue.

Clarence Muse had good reason to promote dances at Hollywood movie lots. A reporter noted, "Mr. Muse says the only hope for young Negro actors is the loyal support of colored audiences. If they fail to come to the theatre the young Negro artist is doomed." He won success in New York at the Lafayette Theatre because blacks heavily patronized the shows. He believed that Earl Dancer "is one of America's best Negro theatre thinkers" in the country.[50] Such "Harlem in Hollywood" leaders as Dancer and Muse were cultivating their own black Los Angeles audiences to ensure their success in Hollywood films. Central Avenue played a key role in their efforts to cultivate a sophisticated black entertainment culture and they attempted to duplicate the black cabaret culture of Harlem there and in Hollywood.

The Elks Golden West Lodge No. 86, which sponsored the "Hollywood Meets Harlem" celebration, was a black fraternal organization that engaged in social and political activity. It was a significant institution in the emergence of the Harlem in Hollywood movement. Many of the black Los Angeles elite were members of the Elks or the Masons. The Elks had a huge hall at 40th Place and Central Avenue which was used for meetings, community affairs, ballroom dances, and jazz concerts. Many of the nightlifers and party-goers associated with the Elks because of the fun and social status at their huge and successful dances at the Elks' Auditorium, which often featured nationally renowned black entertainers and hosted black Hollywood stars.[51] The Elks promoted the glamour of urban life and cabaret culture. Its social and cultural activities helped rural blacks make the transition to urbane culture and sophistication.

Despite many blacks' misgivings about their rural past, they still reveled in the rural cabaret tradition, which they transferred to cities, where it reached new levels of cultivation. This was reflected in stage shows and parades. *Dixie Goes Hi-Hat* was an "all-colored musical comedy" produced by Charles K. Gordon. He and Flournoy E. Miller wrote the book, and the music and lyrics were by Otis and Leon Rene. Miller and black actor Mantan Moreland sponsored the show at the Wilshire Ebell Theatre—a prestigious white theater in Los Angeles off Wilshire Boulevard. Admission cost 50 cents, 75 cents, and 1 dollar.[52]

The Negro Division of the Screen Actors Guild participated in the 1938 Los Angeles Labor Day parade, for which F. Paul Sylas of Talisman Studios built a float. Jesse Graves was chair of the committee and Hattie McDaniel—a perennial film star in black mammy roles—and Theresa Harris helped finance the project. The committee members were Edward Boyd, Anna Mabry, Caldwell Clinton Rosamond, Clarence Muse, David Horton, and Mae Turner—all important community and Hollywood activists. The float had a rural cabin mounted upon it with Aunt Jemima flapping pancakes at the door and a few other black women in the front and rear.[53] The Cotton Club in New York had featured this scenario in *Cabin in the Cotton Club* in 1933 in which Ethel Waters starred. Its popularity resulted in a successful Broadway run in 1940, then a film in 1943.[54]

*Dixie Goes Hi-Hat* was a popular theme in black entertainment culture because it reflected the transition from rural crudeness to urbane sophistication. "Hi-Hat" meant high class, formality, and was derived from formal dress, the tuxedo and silk high hat. For many blacks, the shift from rural overalls dress to urbane fashions symbolized the release from rural poverty, shame, and white brutality to a new sense of race pride, energy, and joy fostered in big Northern or Western cities that offered better jobs. This, in turn, made possible a more vigorous, stimulating, and glamorous social and nightlife culture. Harlem in New York, Central Avenue in black Los Angeles, and "Harlem in Hollywood" culture were celebrations of this transition. What is more, fame and fabulous fortunes, at least by black standards of wealth at the time, could be won literally for a song and dance in Harlem and Hollywood. The Labor Day parade featuring a cabin with black mammies, however, indicated ambivalence and retention of rural customs and comedy. Indeed, the persistence of black stereotypes indicated their hold on both whites and blacks.

Blacks jubilantly celebrated their urbane sophistication. In September of 1938, the *California Eagle* reported that "Stars and Movie Fans Turn Out for Dedication of Bill Robinson Theatre" in the Central Avenue district "at 43rd and Central Avenue." The Tivoli Theatre was renamed the Bill Robinson Theatre. "All the glamour, crowds, confusion and grazed chins, typical of a Hollywood opening were present as the Tivoli—oops—Bill Robinson went to town." A new film, *The Duke Is Tops,* featuring Ralph Cooper and Lena Horne, was shown. The opening was attended "by the most outstanding of Legion big-wigs." What is more, the "most famous visitor of all was the Grand Duke of Dance, the Maharajah of Rhythm, His Highness of Tap—Bill 'Bojangles' Robinson." Nina Mae McKinney, Louise Beavers and Ralph Cooper, the Snowden Brothers (Al and Ruben), who owned the theater, and many others attended.[55] The new theater added prestige and helped institutionalize the "Harlem in Hollywood" movement in Los Angeles. An advertisement boasted: "Bill Robinson Theatre, 4319 So. Central, telephone AD-7367" and "(formerly Tivoli), The Show Place of Holly-Harlem-Wood."[56] Another ad ran, "Savoy Theatre, 54th and Central" with Herbert Jeffries (who won a reputation as Duke Ellington's vocalist on the song "Flamingo") and Mantan Moreland in *Harlem on the Prairie*.[57] Its namesake was the famous Savoy Ballroom in Harlem.

Another Harlem Cotton Club luminary, Duke Ellington, went to Los Angeles and added to this movement. Ellington over the years had made trips to Los Angeles to play in Hollywood films and for musical performances. His was the main house band for years at the Cotton Club in Harlem. He performed live on radio from the Cotton Club. From 1929 to 1931 he recorded such tunes as "Wall Street Wail" (in recognition of the Wall Street stock market crash of 1929), "Cotton Club Stomp," "Runnin' Wild," "Mood Indigo" (a very popular hit and landmark tune), "Rockin' in Rhythm," and "Double Check Stomp." This resulted in his first film performance with the popular comics "Amos 'n' Andy" in the film *Check and Double Check* in 1930. He also recorded such tunes as "Harlem Speaks," "Caravan," "The Gal from Joe's," and many other songs in recognition of Harlem and its black culture.[58] Ellington epitomized success and sophistication within the highly competitive Harlem cabaret culture.

In 1940 Ellington went to perform at the Culver City Casa Ma ana near the M-G-M film studios. He stayed at the Dunbar Hotel on 42nd and Central Avenue, in the heart of the black entertainment district. Segregation of the races prevented him from staying elsewhere. Sid Kuller, a Hollywood screenwriter who lived in Studio City, a Los Angeles suburb, saw Ellington and his band and was captivated. Kuller objected to the Jim Crow restrictions that kept Ellington out of the best white hotels. When Kuller saw the conditions of the Dunbar, where the walls were still cracked from the 1933 earthquake, he invited Ellington to stay at his home. They had nightly house parties while Ellington stayed there which were attended at various times by Tony Martin, Lana Turner, Jackie Cooper, Mickey Rooney, W.R. Burnett, John Garfield, Dan Daily, Bonita Granville, and many other Hollywood stars.[59] Thus some Hollywood whites practiced racial integration and democracy at a time when it was not popular and legally prohibited. Kuller, for the moment at least, played a role well established in New York by Carl Van Vechten of promoting interracial house parties as a means of breaking down race barriers with the hope that the pattern would spread throughout society. Another Harlem Renaissance tradition became part of Hollywood and the impact was obvious.

At one of these parties people pledged $20,000 toward a musical called *Jump for Joy* under Ellington's direction. Hal Borne, a Hollywood studio musician, and Ellington, as well as Mickey Rooney and Mercer Ellington, Duke's son, wrote sixteen songs for the show. Paul Francis Webster, a lyricist, and Hollywood sketch writer Hal Fimberg worked on the musical. Borne worked for the RKO film studio on dance and orchestra, and had arranged the Fred Astaire/Ginger Rogers masterpieces *Flying Down to Rio, The Gay Divorcee, Top Hat,* and *The Story of Vernon and Irene Castle.* In short, many of Hollywood's top artists supported and worked on *Jump for Joy.*[60]

The Hollywood film colony had always contained a group of radicals. They supported *Jump for Joy.* "Now you have to remember that all of them, including the Duke himself, wanted to do more than put together a jazz musical. They also wanted to make a social and political statement. They wanted to strike a blow for racial equality. And so, in various sketches and in some of the song lyrics, racial stereotypes were ridiculed and satirical broadsides were launched against the continuing injustices still being practiced against black people," Maurice Zolotow wrote.[61] One proposed sketch had an Uncle Tom on his deathbed with a chorus dancing about to send him on his way while Hollywood and Broadway producers desperately tried to pump adrenaline into his veins to keep him alive. It was a telling critique of Hollywood film stereotypes. Also featured was the number "I've Got a Passport from Georgia (and I'm Going to the USA)." Poet Langston Hughes also wrote for the musical. The final act featured "Uncle Tom's Cabin Is a Drive-in Now" with the verse: "There used to be a chicken shack in Caroline,/But now they've moved it up to Hollywood and Vine;/They paid off the mortgage—nobody knows how/—And Uncle Tom's Cabin is a drive-in now!" The show lasted three months in 1941 and prepared for a new season in Chicago, then Broadway, but folded in Los Angeles. Ellington said the loss of personnel to the draft caused it to collapse, but others said it was too far ahead of its time, according to Almena Davis.[62]

Ellington, well respected in white and black circles, was not without critics, however. John Hammond, a famous talent scout and descendant of the Vanderbilt family, became enchanted with black jazz and jazzmen in New York in the 1920s. He charged that Duke Ellington had played only at the most exclusive white clubs and for white patrons in the 1920s and 1930s. Ellington's band was one of the first large black bands to perform on film—*Check and Double Check* (1930). "Duke had, I felt, an old-line point of view of the Negro's ability to survive in a white commercial world," said Hammond. He compromised to achieve success and recognition, charged Hammond, a fervent and chauvinistic supporter of black culture, especially jazz and spirituals, in the service of civil rights for blacks. Hammond also was a member of the board of directors of the NAACP and was well aware of the Harlem Renaissance faction which had sought to use arts for civil rights for blacks. Ellington had rejected Hammond's solicitation to create racially mixed bands. Hammond said Ellington gave him the impression, "why help the white bands by filling them with black players, thereby threatening the survival of the Negro bands?" Hammond rejected the notion that jazz was exclusively black. His view was: "I feel that jazz always has had a duty to promote racial understanding and interracial cooperation." He promoted the arts, as had Carl Van Vechten, in quest of cultural pluralism and racial democracy. On the other hand, "most Negro band leaders were discouraged, if not defeated, by the Depression," said Hammond.[63]

Hammond got involved with the NAACP and civil rights because "my dedication to their cause, growing out of my love for their music, made it seem essential to understand as much as I could about their problems, the solutions they proposed, and the men who were undertaking to lead American blacks in their long fight for equal justice."[64] He epitomized the Harlem Renaissance man who sought to use art for civil rights.

Hammond, however, partially represented the Du Boisian view that art should be used for propaganda. But he apparently did not agree that only black conservative images were valid while all others were suspect or stereotypes. Hammond tried to prod Ellington into a more direct propa-ganda role, which Ellington resisted. Hammond was quick to add, "None of this is to suggest that Duke was not proud of his own people. In his way he fought the battle for equal rights as effectively as any other Negro leader. Duke loved the highest of societies, white and black. He sought the best locations, both because he enjoyed mingling with the cream of any social circle and because the money was better."[65] Ellington replied to his critics: "All round the world I've had to answer questions about the race situation in my country, often hostile ones. People asking why Negro artists haven't done more for the cause, that kind of thing. It makes me very angry, and I say that people wouldn't ask questions like that if they knew what they were talking about. But then usually I cool down and tell them of the things since the 1930s, all the shows and concerts and benefits the band has done."[66] Ellington thought he had demonstrated his race pride and commitment.

A biographer of Ellington noted that he boasted with pride that he and his band did their own freedom marching in the 1930s throughout the South. "We went down in the South without federal troops." He recorded many famous black tunes such as "Black Beauty" and "Deep South Suite." He preferred to make his statements musically and rejected propaganda on stage: "Screaming about it onstage don't make a show."[67] Ellington epitomized the Harlem Renaissance man who thought that direct racial propaganda was harmful—a position with which many black and white Harlem Renaissance men and women agreed.

The Harlem Renaissance ideological battles brought the jazz world the same divisions between the art for propaganda faction and the pure art school which believed that subtlety and merit would break down racial stereotypes and thereby undermine Jim Crow. Ellington's appearance in Los Angeles must have electrified the local party-goers and the radicals struggling against Hollywood stereotypes. Apparently, they thought that due to Ellington's fame, the *Jump for Joy* musical was a vehicle for their radical ideas. Although the show was short-lived its impact was not necessarily negligible.

A series of Hollywood films in the early 1940s resulted in the continuation of the Harlem Renaissance controversy between those who differed over the nature of urban jive and rural simplicity of blacks as either negative stereotypes or worthy portrayals of black folk culture. The film *Tales of Manhattan* in 1942 caused ambivalence and controversy among blacks and some white critics. The blacks in the film were Ethel Waters, Paul Robe-

PERFORMING ARTS

son, and Eddie Anderson.[68] The plot of the film was based around six episodes—five with an all-white cast with such stars as Ginger Rogers, Henry Fonda, and Charles Laughton, and the sixth with an all-black one—in which a coat brings bad or good luck to its owner according to his own character. In the fifth episode, a shootout aboard an airplane leads the owner to discard the coat, which falls to earth and winds up in the hands of Paul Robeson and Ethel Waters—two poor black sharecroppers.[69] Robeson and Waters and the Hall Choir singers find the coat with $50,000 in one pocket. They sing and praise the finding as manna from heaven. The coat finally winds up on the back of a scarecrow.

One reviewer said the sixth episode was "the most completely artificial" because of its stereotype ". . . with its comedy-relief treatment of Negroes." Another said the coat "is alternatively a jinx or joy to its successive owners, until it comes to rest as a raffish example of what the well-dressed scarecrow will wear in a Negro sharecropper's cotton field."[70] Another critic called the film "a socially conscious minstrel show in which Paul Robeson and Ethel Waters find $50,000 in the tail coat, and with the help of Jack Benny's Rochester (Eddie Anderson, who starred with Benny as his foil) divided it with the Hall Johnson Choir and other Hollywood sharecroppers." Moreover, he noted, "each actor was permitted to make changes in the script, but the only one who bothered much was Paul Robeson. He piously refused to have any religious words put in his mouth."[71]

Manny Farber, a constant critic of Hollywood's stereotypes of blacks, called *Tales of Manhattan* "the romantic distortion of Negro life" that "is a discrimination as old as Hollywood." He complained of the six Jim Crow episodes: "If the movies want to give a Negro front billing, it has to be an all-Negro picture or nothing." Moreover, "the segregation in 'Tales of Manhattan' is complete" because black and white performers were shown only in all-black or all-white casts in each episode. Farber added bitterly, "After segregating them, the movie shows the Negro his place in the social scale." The whites were professionals, and blacks were "either sharecroppers or nothing." Finally, noted Farber, "once the Negro recognizes his place in movies, he is treated with a great love."[72] These white critics did not approve of the stereotype roles assigned to blacks, and neither did some blacks.

Paul Robeson especially criticized the film and refused to act in any more Hollywood films as a result of *Tales of Manhattan*. As noted in a headline, he bitterly complained, "Hollywood's 'Old Plantation Tradition' Is Offensive to My People." He noted that Hollywood producers insisted on making the usual "plantation hallelujah shouters" and despite his objections and changes made in the film, "in the end it turned out to be the same old thing—the Negro solving his problems by singing his way to glory. This is very offensive to my people. It makes the Negro child-like and innocent and is in the old plantation tradition. But Hollywood says you can't make the Negro in any other role because it won't be box office in the South. The South wants its Negroes in the old style."[73] Robeson was determined to destroy these stereotypes which, in his view, injured the reputation of blacks and helped to justify Jim Crow practices.

Robeson called for a nationwide boycott of Hollywood films. The *Chicago Defender* endorsed the boycott. It added that Hollywood was "fascist-minded." It noted Robeson's views on Hollywood: "He has found it one of the foremost builders of a stereotype" that promoted a "'hat-in-hand,' 'me-too-boss' Negro." The *Defender* charged that "the presentation of Negro life on the screen is pure, unadulterated Hitlerism." Moreover, "it is un-American and subversive. It is treasonable." The *Defender* encouraged its readers to flood Hollywood with letters of protest and to send delegations to picket theaters showing films stereotyping blacks.[74]

Lawrence LaMar (or Lamar) disagreed with the criticism that *Tales of Manhattan* slandered blacks by portraying them as superstitious country bumpkins. He noted the "theatre management" and distributors arranged to show the Twentieth Century-Fox film at a "press preview" at the Lincoln Theatre (one of the Harlem in Hollywood institutions of film and entertainment for blacks) in the Central Avenue district of Los Angeles, where most blacks resided. They wanted to "feel out the public on some of the so-called objectionable scenes" because of black protest and threats of a boycott. Lamar said he had "failed to see anything in the film but good entertainment." He noted that in the scene featuring blacks they "are depicted as superstitiously religious."[75] Ethel Waters, who starred in the film, noted that "when Tales of Manhattan was released various Negro organizations picketed the theaters showing it. Their placards protested picturing us colored people as wretched, dirty, and poorly clad." She added, "I didn't understand that. These same organizations were forever complaining that we Negroes in America are under-privileged. So why did they object to anyone showing us that way on the screen?"[76] Black and white critics thought that black poverty and superstition were featured to ridicule black folk culture and promote contempt for blacks.

The film *Star Spangled Rhythm* epitomized the extreme of the black G.I. Jive movement. It was a wartime patriotic entertainment film capitalizing on the *Star-Spangled Banner*. It was designed to appeal to war fever and patriotism. A galaxy of Harlem and Hollywood black entertainers paraded across the screen. It featured "Slim" Gaillard and "Slam" Brown, who were masters of comedy, jazz, and Harlem Jive language; Katherine Dunham, a scholar trained in African and Afro-Caribbean dances; Eddie "Rochester" Anderson, of Jack Benny fame; and dance director Danny Dare. Twenty-four top black male and female dancers from the Pacific Coast, largely black Los Angeles, were featured as well.

One tune from the movie "Belt in the Back" was written by Harold Arlen of Cotton Club fame and Johnny Mercer, a leading figure in the recording industry. Both built careers as well in Hollywood. Arlen had long been associated with the Cotton Club in Harlem. He was embraced by blacks as one of their own. He had mastered Harlem culture and wrote such torch tunes as "Harlem Holiday," "Pool Room Papa," "My Military Man," and "High Flyin' Man." He and Ted Koehler produced the Cotton Club shows called "Cotton Club Parades." Arlen was noted for his "inside look" at Harlem life which fascinated many white Americans and Europeans who came to the Cotton Club to revel in Harlem jazz and jive.[77]

Film critic Philip T. Hartung noted that *Star Spangled Rhythm* (1942) "is a sprightly film; it glitters almost as much as its name—but not quite." He noted that Paramount paraded its stars, who drifted in and out doing specialty dance and song numbers. "The two best numbers of this de luxe potpourri are: a song and dance item with Eddie 'Rochester' Anderson and Katherine Dunham (proving the advantages of a soldier's uniform over a Zoot suit); and Bing Crosby's singing the big patriotic finale: 'Old Glory.'"[78] *Time* magazine noted that the parade of top stars of Paramount Pictures made the film expensive: it cost $1,500,000, of which a third went for "its high-priced performers' salaries." *Time* added that Eddie "Rochester" Anderson "in a Zoot-suit," checkered, with a wide-brimmed white hat, and black-and-white spats" performed "with a strutting" wild jitterbug dance with Katherine Dunham to the song "Sharp as a Tack."[79] Hartung thought it simply harmless flashy high-priced entertainment. Anderson ended his routine by entering double doors in the background props in his Zoot suit and emerging in an Army khaki brown uniform to impress upon black Zooters who might view the film that it was cool to join the military.[80]

Hartung was impressed, but not so Manny Farber, who perpetually criticized what he judged to be stereotyped or allblack segregated films. He charged that there was a rush to produce segregated or all-black movies that were "obscene." He noted, "Now we are going to be democratic; it's the fashion. This is not in any way to say the movies have changed their attitude toward Negroes; there is just more of it." He charged in regard to *Star Spangled Rhythm*: "Witness the wholly objectionable caricature of Negro dress and dancing in the Zoot-suit number, in which Rochester and Katherine Dunham sing and dance something you could spend all your life in Harlem and never see the like of." He appreciated the Golden Gate Quartet in the film, but their "talent for rhythmic singing" was cancelled "by making the men clown."[81]

Farber was a diehard Du Boisian in his perspective that any depictions of blacks other than "normal" or middle-class were caricatures. Blacks should be integrated with whites rather than Jim Crowed into typical black stereotype menial and comedy relief roles. He believed that such roles helped to perpetuate the negative public opinion about blacks which undergirded the whole Jim Crow system of inequality. Billy Rowe and John T. McManus also followed this Du Boisian line.

Billy Rowe agreed with John T. McManus, writing for the newspaper *PM*, who charged that Hollywood had not kept its promise to NAACP president Walter White to halt stereotypes. *Star Spangled Rhythm*, in their view, reflected stereotypes. McManus noted that Hollywood films with more blacks were designed "simply to exploit more colossally than ever the reservoir of Negro talent." What is more, "no attempt has been made to purge films of the false but enduring Negro stereotypes—the eye-rollers, the Uncle Toms, the white ghost shiverers. To those have been added the Zoot-suits and the Afro-maniacs, as well as a variety of ingratiating new talents and faces, all ironically helping to perpetuate the concept that the Negro is still just a happy-go-lucky ward of democracy." McManus said *Star Spangled Rhythm*'s "Zoot-suit sequence proved that Negroes can be made their worst caricatures."[82] Black actors, he thought, should object to playing such roles and obviously thought Zoot suits were clownish and demeaning.

The black and white actors in the film, and many viewers, had a completely different perception of the roles they played. Many whites had starred in *Star Spangled Rhythm,* including Bing Crosby, Alan Ladd, Fred MacMurray, Vera Zorina, and Bob Hope, who was master of ceremonies. The film was a model "patriotic variety form" that became a norm for many similar films which soon followed, such as *Stormy Weather* (the film as a biography of Bill Robinson begins with a military parade of the New York 369th Regiment's return from Europe, a march down Broadway, and the grand party that followed) and *Stage Door Canteen.* These films merged jazz, jive, and jitterbug dancing into what became a popular and "patriotic" formula: G.I. Jive. Among performers, especially in Hollywood, where contributing to the war effort was a hot topic, it became hep to lift the morale of soldiers and war workers with highly entertaining musicals containing lively dance routines, flashy wardrobes—Zoot suit uniforms—and jive language and jazz.[83] Universal Studios signed Elyse Knox and Robert Paige to star in the romantic leads in the film *Oh, Say Can You Swing* to cash in on popular musicals which mixed escapism and patriotic fervor. It formerly had been titled *School for Jive!*[84]

In 1933 Ethel Waters performed in the Cotton Club "Stormy Weather Show" and was asked to do a dozen encores. It turned out to be one of the most successful shows in Cotton Club history. In the Cotton Club's "Stormy Weather Show" Waters sang "Cabin in the Cotton Club" while standing by a lamppost with a cabin in the background. Duke Ellington's band dramatized the show with musical sounds resembling a storm. In 1940 *Cabin in the Sky* was performed as a musical on Broadway, starring Ethel Waters with jazz pianist Eubie Blake.[85]

The film version was made in 1942 and played through the end of 1943. The plot was an allegory about good versus evil. Eddie "Rochester" Anderson played Little Joe Jackson, a gambler and hustler, whose wife Petunia (Ethel Waters) battles for his soul by pleading for his reform so they can go to heaven together. Meanwhile, Lucifer uses Georgia Brown (Lena Horne) to entice Little Joe back into his evil ways. In a dream, Little Joe and Petunia are shot and killed in a gunfight at Jim Henry's Cafe. Petunia pleads with the Lord to save Joe and let them go to heaven together. Her wish is granted. Little Joe Jackson wakes up from his dream and reforms himself. Louis Armstrong and Buck and Bubbles (Ford Washington and John Sublett), a dance team, and Duke Ellington and his band were featured in the nightclub scene. The Cotton Club's Harold Arlen and lyricist Yip Harburg produced the show and wrote the famous movie score, "Happiness Is Just a Thing Called Joe" sung by Ethel Waters.[86]

During the filming of *Cabin in the Sky,* Waters was bitterly resentful of Horne who kept her distance. Horne hurt her ankle while filming, and cast and crew rushed to Horne's side to assist her, offering a pillow to rest her ankle on. Waters blew up with jealousy and envy. They did not speak again.[87] Waters said during the film, "I objected violently to the way religion was being treated in the screen play." She felt the plea to save Little Joe undermined her role as a woman. She added, "I rejected the part because it seemed to me a man's play rather than a woman's. Petunia, in the original script, was no more than a punching bag for Little Joe." As a result of her protest, she noted, "some of the changes I demanded had been made [and] I accepted the role, largely because the music was so pretty." It was six years before she got another film role.[88]

Lena Horne had established a reputation as a "lady" and had joined with NAACP president Walter White to repudiate negative racial stereotypes. Ethel Waters often played stereotype roles, as in *Tales of Manhattan,* and she had protested pickets and critics of the film. Each actress symbolized a type in bitter contention for recognition and respectability. Apparently, it became very personal.

The critics, too, divided over the merits of *Cabin in the Sky. Time* magazine noted that despite their talent, blacks were portrayed "as picturesque, Sambo-style entertainers." It added, "This tendency, not confined to Hollywood, old in American life, is encouraged by a plot which has a flavoring of The Green Pastures fantasy. . . ." The dance routines were fantastic. "The best things in the picture are a rebuke to all kinds of pretentiousness."[89] Philip T. Hartung thought the black actors and the new songs by Harold Arlen and E. Yip Harburg of the Cotton Club were superb. He noted, "Since 'Cabin in the Sky' is a Negro fantasy, Hollywood might be excused for portraying Negroes as theatrical, crap-shootin', buck-and-wing darkies."[90]

*Newsweek,* too, was impressed with the black actors, music, and song and dance routines. *Cabin in the Sky* reflected the new policy worked out between Walter White and Wendell Willkie and the Hollywood moguls with the support given by the Office of War Information (OWI), which was concerned with building black morale in support of the country and the war. The OWI sought to undergird black G.I. Jive with its Harlem roots and traditions, and press it into the service of Uncle Sam. But the film fell short of those expectations. *Newsweek* noted that the understanding was a reaction to "plain-spoken hints last summer from Wendell Willkie, Lowell Mellett of the Office of War Information, and others, that now was the time to give the Negro his place as a dignified, responsible citizen." Marc Connelly, the author of *Green Pastures,* which was well received in earlier years, backed out of the film and refused to allow his name to be associated with it. He and *Newsweek* felt *Cabin in the Sky* perpetuated stereotypes and was not a New Deal for blacks.[91]

Manny Farber claimed that *Cabin in the Sky* was "Hollywood's latest example of segregation" and "is the usual religious-comic handout that is given the Negro by a white studio whose last thought is to make a movie that is actually about Negroes." He added that *Cabin in the Sky* was a Jim Crow [all-black] film that constructs "a nigger-town—out of jimcrack architecture, stage grass and magnolia trees—to look like paradise." He lamented, "The tragic fact is that the Negro artists are in no position to bargain with Hollywood. . . ." He praised the black actors: "The one value of all-Negro films lies in giving Negro artists an outlet for their talents. And the one value of 'Cabin in the Sky' is the talent of Rochester, Lena Horne and Louis Armstrong, irrespective of anything in the movie script." The larger question, in Farber's view, and the damage of such a film was that "Hollywood, in its position of greatest public influence, solidifies racial prejudice to an enormous degree by its 'Cabin in the Sky,' which is an insidious way of showing the Negro his place."[92] Once again, Farber militantly restated the Du Boisian interpretation of what constituted stereotype characterizations.

The black press criticized *Cabin in the Sky.* Joseph D. Bibb suggested in his headline that "The Riff Raff: Unthinking Majority of Bad Actors Are Always in the Focus of Publicity." Bibb thought it was a "rancid movie." He bitterly charged that only "the riff raff of the colored American people" would patronize such a movie. Moreover, these black patrons were "the very characters, who in everyday life, are hanging like millstones around the necks of thirteen million dark people." This type was epitomized, in his view, by the film characters Domino Johnson, a "strutting, swaggering, amorous killer," and Mose Henry, "vice lord, gambler, cafe owner and evil spirit of the sordid community."[93] Bibb's bitter denunciation was a restatement of the Du Boisian attack on Carl Van Vechten's novel *Nigger Heaven* (1926), which, according to Du Bois, viewed black life in Harlem as one giant cabaret and vice orgy.

*Los Angeles Sentinel* editor Leon Washington objected to *Cabin in the Sky* because it was advertised with a drawing of a "Zoot-suited . . . couple doing a jitterbug dance while a longheaded, big, red lipped boy looks on grinningly." In Los Angeles, it was due to open in May of 1943 at Grauman's Chinese in Hollywood and Loew's State and the Rivoli on Western Avenue.[94] Leon Washington threatened to picket the theaters. The *New York Amsterdam News* noted a *Cabin in the Sky* appearance on Broadway at the Criterion Theatre. The film was the first big all-black movie since *Hallelujah* in 1929. The *News* thought that *Cabin in the Sky* was "an insult masking behind the label of folklore. It isn't folklore." What is more, "it pictures Negroes, heads tied up, with crap shooting inclinations and prayer meeting propensities at a time when Negroes are daily proving their heroic mettle in battle and defense plant. This is the sort of thing that keeps alive misconceptions of the Negro." It noted, however, the film was very popular and broke the house attendance record at the Criterion Theatre. The "excellent cast" was praised for its swell performance.[95]

Arthur Freed produced and Vincente Minnelli directed *Cabin in the Sky* and were very proud of it as the best black musical ever. Philip Carter, a native of Pasadena, California, who had been working in New York as a journalist for ten years, was hired by M-G-M and given an office on the company's lot to provide special publicity for the film to reduce the growing number of black critics.[96] Noble Sissle of Cotton Club and Broadway fame praised *Cabin in the Sky.* He said the film was "as powerful in fostering Americanism and tolerance as Harriet Beecher Stowe's 'Uncle Tom's Cabin.'" What is more, he said in defense of M-G-M, producing the film "promoted racial goodwill."[97] Many artists wanted to work and rejected the notion that jazz, jive, jitterbugging, all-black films, or certain roles were demeaning to blacks as a group.

Racists objected. A white mob in Mount Pleasant, Tennessee, raided a theater and halted the showing of *Cabin in the Sky* because of fear that the spread of black culture would break down the Jim Crow system as it was doing in New York and Harlem cabarets, on Broadway and in Hollywood films.[98] They did not want whites to patronize or appreciate black culture for fear whites would attempt to participate in local black entertainment and thereby integrate the races.

Sissle's defense of *Cabin in the Sky* was an understandable position from artist like himself, who had won fame and fortune in the highly prestigious Harlem cabarets, especially the Cotton Club, and Broadway entertainment culture. Moreover, he was part of the school of thought in the Harlem Renaissance that Carl Van Vechten, Langston Hughes, Claude McKay, Walter White, and many others were part of—they advocated cultural pluralism, even within black society and culture. They respected the black rural folk and urban jive cultures as exotic, beautiful, and unique. They had long ago rejected social Victorianism and the values and codes of conduct that placed their entertainment culture and behavior patterns out of bounds. Their success in Hollywood and at the box office had confirmed their views and behavior.

Amid the bitterness of Ethel Waters toward Lena Horne, who was hurt and distraught by the bickering among blacks and objections to her push for "better roles" for blacks, the filming of *Cabin in the Sky* almost came to a halt. During the filming Horne left for New York and jazz pianist Count Basie had to use some strong persuasion to get her to return. Lena told him, "I'm back where I belong. I'm never going to leave New York again." She felt comfortable in the Harlem and Broadway entertainment world, where Cotton Club culture was supreme. Harlem entertainment culture in Hollywood films resulted in bitter criticism of the films and, often in some quarters, the entertainers as well. Then, too, critics of black entertainers and some entertainers themselves were becoming bitterly divided over the images projected by the roles they played. Count Basie told Horne, "They chose you; we don't get the chance. You've got to go, and you've got to stay there, and you've got to be good, and you've got to be right and do whatever they want you to do and make us proud of you."[99] Blacks in the arts respected their own pioneers who opened doors and expanded the work, roles, and dignity of the race.

Lena Horne had become the symbol of genteel Harlem Jive. Harlem entertainers looked to her to keep Hollywood open for them and to broaden the forum for their talents. Just as important, Noble Sissle, Lena Horne, and Walter White wanted to duplicate in Hollywood the Harlem entertainment cultural experience, by which black entertainers and their culture had broken down a substantial amount of Jim Crow practices and contempt of blacks because of the respect and appreciation they had achieved among white patrons who came from every quarter of the nation and the world to share the Harlem experience and culture. Moreover, Sissle insisted that *Cabin in the Sky* would boost blacks' standing during World War II just as Stowe's *Uncle Tom's Cabin* had helped to develop pro-black sentiment prior to the Civil War. He thought the film was a great black G.I. Jive movie that met the OWI standards.

Blacks were featured in the summer of 1943 in the film *This Is the Army*. Written by Irving Berlin during World War I, it was redone by him in the summer of 1942 on Broadway and was a huge success. The next summer it was made into a film.[100] Jack T. Warner pledged about fifty percent of the money raised by the film to the Army Emergency Relief Fund. Nearly $2 million was raised. The film was a G.I. Jive musical designed to raise "morale through putting on theatricals." It was a two-hour movie packed with first-rate entertainment. Irving Berlin provided four songs for the film: "This Is the Army, Mr. Jones," "I'm Getting Tired So I Can Sleep," "I Left My Heart at the Stage Door Canteen," and "Oh, How I Hate to Get up in the Morning." Other songs and acts were contemporary with World War II. Boxer Joe Louis led a group of black soldiers dressed in brown khaki in a skit to the song "What the Well Dressed Man in Harlem Will Wear," which critic Philip T. Hartung thought "almost steals the show—and this is something in a show that is full of outstanding entertainment."[101]

Joe Louis gave his now famous pro-war speech claiming America was "on God's side." Kate Smith performed her patriotic song, "God Bless America."[102] *Time* magazine noted that "the all-Negro 'What the Well-Dressed Man in Harlem Will Wear', vividly sung, scatted and danced, and abetted by some punching-bag polyrhythms from Sergeant Joe Louis and by his startling stage presence" was a work of art. The film stage had a large billboard backdrop with three huge black Harlem Zoot suiters in high step with bulging and surprised eyes, wide-brimmed flat topped hats and bow-ties and facial expressions suggesting that they were outdone by the black G.I. Jive routine of Sergeant Joe Louis and his soldiers dressed in khaki brown military uniforms with ties and wave hats. Both groups of men were sandwiched between buildings with one sign reading "Dixie's Beau Shoppe" and the other "Sporting Goods." Another read "Orchestra Club" and the street sign says "Lennox [sic] Avenue."[103] The unmistakable message intended for blacks in Harlem and throughout the nation was "Look at this black G.I. Jive" and if you really want to be hep, join the Army. Zoot suits must be exchanged for Army uniforms and jazz and jive must be pressed into service for the country's good in the war. The song, the dance routine, and Joe Louis's message epitomized the black G.I. Jive movement (well under way by 1943) which was undergirded by Harlem heroes and entertainers who were bringing the "Cotton Club Parades" cabaret culture into the civilian and military spheres to mobilize the nation—both its black and white citizens.

Another important G.I. Jive favorite was the film Stage Door Canteen of the summer of 1943. The American Theater Wing, which operated canteens in six cities, sponsored it. United Artists produced it and Sol Lesser directed. The film featured about 100 entertainers and "at least 48 are guaranteed, gilt-edged stars," noted one reviewer. It showed "six of jivedom's hottest swing bands" (Count Basie, Xavier Cugat, Benny Goodman, Kay Kyser, Guy Lombardo, and Freddy Martin). The picture "celebrates the well-known Forty-Fourth Street home-away-from-home for enlisted men" or the Manhattan Stage Door Canteen. Uniformed soldiers danced to the exciting swing music in the film.[104] It was an impressive musical.

Blacks performed in the film. Ethel Waters was "syncopating with Count Basie's Afric jazz band," noted Time magazine, and "the film's patriotism is as torrential as its talent." War songs like "Marching through Berlin" and "The Machine-Gun Song" were performed. Film critic James Agee thought it was an excellent period film because it "carries a saturation of the mannerisms of fourth-decade entertainment, patriotism, and sub-idealized lovemaking. . . ." He thought, however, that "the entertainment is best" in the film. Film critic Manny Farber agreed and predicted that "the jazz band will replace the movie player and the jazz singer the jazz band." Surprisingly, he had none of the usual objections to portrayals of blacks, apparently because they were integrated into the cast and performed classical jazz songs and music.[105]

Walter White was so impressed with Stage Door Canteen that he gave it the "unqualified endorsement of the National Association for the Advancement of Colored People" in appreciation of the integrated and dignified roles accorded blacks. Herman Hill wrote for the Pittsburgh Courier, "Stage Door Canteen is [a] Great Film." The film reflected the racial makeup of the United States and was clearly a response to black protest. It was made "for the soldiers of all the United States," including blacks.[106] These shows and films were Hollywood's and Broadway's salute to the armed forces and war workers. Their contributions were "a solid sender" (a jive language phrase used in the 1940s) to soldiers headed for overseas war theaters to face an uncertain and fearful destiny. Stage Door Canteen reflected an integration trend advocated by critics who rejected all-black movies as racist.

The film Stormy Weather (1943), an all-black musical, had its origins in the Cotton Club in 1933 as one of the shows written by Harold Arlen and Ted Koehler in the "Cotton Club Parades" series. The Cotton Club "Stormy Weather Show" featured Ethel Waters. "Singing 'Stormy Weather' proved a turning point in my life," said Waters, and it "became the talk of New York." She added, "Stormy Weather, which might have been the theme song of my life, was proving to be the first dramatic hit out of a night club."[107] Stormy Weather featured the who's who of the Cotton Club: Lena Horne, Bill "Bojangles" Robinson, Cab Calloway, Katherine Dunham and her dancers, Ada Brown, Zutty Singleton, Mae Johnston, Dooley Wilson, Harold and Fayard Nicholas, Flournoy Miller, and the comedian Nickademus.[108] M-G-M studios noted that musicals were more successful than heavy dramas because of the pressure to escape and be happy during the war. "This concentration upon musicals in particular, has meant a greater and more constant employment of Negro talent," reported the Pittsburgh Courier. As a result, M-G-M planned three more musicals. It produced Girl Crazy with Mickey Rooney, Judy Garland, and black dancers Buck and Bubbles, I Dood It with Red Skelton and Buck and Bubbles, and Kay Kyser and Lena Horne in Right about Face.[109]

The black press stirred up passionate interest in the new surge of blacks in film, especially Stormy Weather because it featured the best black talent in the country. Its filming resulted in an overflow crowd of observers. "Stormy Weather Gets Grandstand for Fans," noted the Pittsburgh Courier, because the "Galaxy of Stars Drew Such Hordes that Extra Seating Arrangements Were Supplied for the First Time in History." The crowds grew so large that the director put up "No Visitors Allowed" signs to halt the influx of onlookers.[110] Bill "Bojangles" Robinson was admired in Hollywood and thought blacks now had a bright future in films.[111] He and the other actors took time out and made trips to perform in California and nearby states.

Songs from *Stormy Weather* were played over the radio at home and abroad. At least four million people had heard or seen parts of *Stormy Weather* in personal performances or shortwave radio programming. Servicemen flooded the studio with fan mail: "A wave of fan mail from the servicemen has borne postmarks from Africa, Austria, Iceland and every military zone on the globe where U.S. men are stationed," reported the *Pittsburgh Courier*.[112] Lena Horne paid her own fare to Fort Huachuca, Arizona, to perform before the "Bronzed Yanks." The appreciative black troops dubbed her "Sergeant Lena Horne." Ernie Fields, also in *Stormy Weather,* and his orchestra performed at the Army Air Force Technical Training Base at Lincoln, Nebraska, to "boost servicemen's morale."[113] In the film he portrayed Lt. James Reese Europe, who led New York's 369th Regimental Marching Jazz Band to Europe and won international acclaim, and helped launch the jazz dance craze of the 1920s in association with Irene and Vernon Castle, who got Americans to dance to big bands. *Stormy Weather* opened with the New York 369th Colored Regimental Marching Jazz Band returning from Europe and parading through Harlem. This aspect of the film, contrary to the opinions of some film critics who considered it strictly an escapist film, put it in the musical and G.I. Jive genre of films designed to build morale among the soldiers and civilians.

The *Pittsburgh Courier* noted that *Stormy Weather* "Finish[ed] . . . Amid Fanfare, Color in Film Colony." The film featured impressive stage costumes and action "with Cab Calloway in a super 'Zoot suit.' It added, "many in Hollywood predict that 'Stormy Weather' will be one of the greatest box-office attractions of the year."[114] Billy Rowe, theatrical editor for the *Pittsburgh Courier,* campaigned to have black film stars "listed as essential" for building up morale at home in order to be excused from the draft. He noted that the Office of War Information (OWI) and a few other government agencies supported the view that actors and musicians could better serve at home by building up patriotism and participation in the war effort through entertainment. England and the Soviet Union deferred actors and musicians. In the United States only two blacks, boxer Joe Louis and John Kirby, were given any rank. Many whites, however, received officer rank in ex-

change for their services. Big band leader Kay Kyser had worked for the OWI's radio staff since the bombing of Pearl Harbor selling war bonds—$95 million worth. Nevertheless, he was classified as A-1 (immediately eligible for the draft).[115]

Kyser was drafted by his Rocky Mount, North Carolina, draft board, an action upheld by the Presidential Appeal Board despite the fact he was nearly 38, practically blind without his glasses and "stumbles from a trick knee," and had made 1,000 appearances in 300 camps to entertain the troops.[116] As a result, Rowe finally conceded that there was "little hope for listing of entertainers as essentials."[117] He saw *Stormy Weather* as a powerful G.I. Jive film which won acclaim from servicemen, white and black. He thought it a vehicle to promote black stars and entertainers, and win recognition for blacks in the war effort.

Critics had mixed reactions to *Stormy Weather*. Philip T. Hartung noted the fine black talent and performances but said the film was "such a fizzle." He added, "The film's weakness is its routine plot. . . ." The film's story line was based on the life of Bill "Bojangles" Robinson. He admitted that "Ain't Misbehavin'," "Diga, Diga Do," "I Can't Give You Anything but Love, Baby," and "Stormy Weather" "are first-rate songs." Moreover, "the film does not treat the Negroes as children even though it does little to boost their position as our most gifted entertainers."[118]

*Newsweek* thought *Stormy Weather* was an improvement for blacks. It noted, however, that *Casablanca* portrayed Dooley Wilson, the only black in the film, in a much better light.[119] Wilson met some critics' standards because he was portrayed as a normal human being and acted in an integrated setting. *Time* magazine best summarized the white magazines' views: "*Stormy Weather* is an all-Negro musical which packs enough talent and enough plain friendliness, if only they were used well to temper even the contemporary weather of U.S. race relations. Unfortunately, not much comes off as it might have."[120] Critics, black and white, had higher expectations for *Stormy Weather*.

Black critics had a mixed reaction to *Stormy Weather*. They praised the black actors but bitterly resented the showcasing of the Zoot suit in film. Billy Rowe complained to Twentieth Century-Fox officials "pointing out that the Zoot Suit isn't funny to clear-thinking theatre-goers, but is accepted as synonymous with crime and the illiterate . . ." and Rowe "asked Will Hays' office to start a vigorous censorship of such costumes on the screen."[121] Cab Calloway wore an all-white Zoot suit in the extreme of the fashion in *Stormy Weather.* He "parades" a new "take-off in the latest thing in Zoot Suits," noted the *Pittsburgh Courier.* Moreover, "The 'High Highness of Hi-De Ho' gets 'hep' and he's still 'groovy' in the 'Zooty' spell." Calloway added that his Zoot suit was "the Zoot Suit to end all Zoot Suits."[122] Malcolm Little (later known as Malcolm X) wore a Zoot suit during the war and was impressed by the film and Calloway's Zoot suit.

Herman Hill, writing for the *Pittsburgh Courier,* applauded the Zoot suit and Cab Calloway. He noted, "Cab Calloway, King of hi-de-ho, makes a spectacular entrance attired in a Zoot-Suit designed to end all Zoot-Suits."[123] Billy Rowe on the other hand thought Calloway's showcasing the Zoot suit was "An Ode to Crime." He noted that since the federal government and the police were then involved in "an extensive effort to suppress Zoot Suits, it's about time that the screen called a halt to its exploitation of the garb of the criminals." He thought that Cab Calloway, Eddie "Rochester" Anderson (who wore the suit in the film *Star Spangled Rhythm*), and other famous artists should stop wearing it. Rowe charged that film producers were "aiding an evil that will eventually destroy the minds of our youth. . . ."[124]

Harry Levette, a newspaper columnist, and Charles Butler, a black Hollywood talent recruiter, were disturbed because Levette revealed "Puzzled Hollywood Asks 'What Kind of Films [Do] Negroes Want?'" Militant letters were pouring into Hollywood film studios protesting black stereotypes despite a number of solid roles for blacks in recent films. Levette lamented, "in fact, they are wondering if when the script calls for a colored servant, if they should not make it Irish, Swedish, English, or any other nationality but Negro." He charged that the letters pouring in were uninformed and needed clarity. Butler feared that blacks were threatened with losing jobs and might get pushed out of Hollywood altogether.[125] Levette said Hollywood was discovering black skin color conflicts and "that there is a world of jealousy, and successful figures become the target for attacks for no other reason; that some will sell out the race for a 'mess of pottage.' . . ." What is more, blacks did not even support black film makers and some blacks threatened by their protest to ruin those blacks working in Hollywood. He concluded, "This new type of letters that are going to drive our famous established artists out of work, unless the complainants write again [and] explain themselves more clearly about the servant angle."[126] Le-

vette was worried that blacks might get fewer jobs if they kept up what he obviously regarded as mixed signals to Hollywood producers based on petty critiques.

Lena Horne became the center of controversy among blacks and Hollywood producers over stereotyped roles. Walter White, executive secretary of the NAACP, courted and cultivated Horne. Both he and Horne feared that Hollywood "would force me [Horne] to play roles as a maid or maybe even as some jungle type." She felt that "it would be essential for me to try to establish a different kind of image for Negro women." She noted that Hollywood used white women in more respectable roles by using "Light Egyptian" skin cream in order not to use black women.[127] Other black actors met and protested Horne's and White's activities because blacks were threatened with losing their acting jobs and careers if so-called stereotype roles were reduced or cut out altogether. Horne recalled at a black protest meeting directed at her that "I was called 'an Eastern upstart' and a tool of the NAACP and I was forced to get up and try to explain that I was not trying to start a revolt or steal work from anyone and that the NAACP was not using me for any ulterior purpose." She lamented that "in a large part of the Hollywood Negro community I was never warmly received." She noted, however, that Eddie "Rochester" Anderson and Hattie McDaniel, two preeminent blacks who played so-called stereotype roles regularly, never attacked her and treated her with kindness.[128]

The old Harlem Renaissance ideological struggles reached a renewed intensity with the G.I. Jive films—especially *Stormy Weather* which included the best black actors and actresses of both schools of thought: those for roles of respectability and those for roles judged as stereotypes either for employment or who defended such roles as legitimate characterizations of blacks and art forms. Despite the internal bickering and hurt feelings among blacks, *Stormy Weather* was a superb G.I. Jive film which reached millions over the radio and screen or in live performances on military bases. It was part of a series of well-received films by both white and black G.I.'s and civilian jitterbuggers committed to jive and jazz.

New York blacks like Lena Horne, Cab Calloway, and Bill "Bojangles" Robinson were the star performers in *Stormy Weather* and they brought hallowed Cotton Club traditions in jazz, jive, and Harlem Zoot suit culture to Hollywood. The black New Yorkers often became the preeminent stars of black Hollywood. This generated resentment among some Los Angeles blacks. Black and white genteel factions that had emerged with the Harlem Renaissance had never achieved a consensus on how blacks should be portrayed in literature, in film, and on stage. The Harlem in Hollywood movement carried the seeds of the same conflicts which black and white Harlem Renaissance men and women had failed to resolve in the 1920s.

## Notes

1. Quoted in Nathan I. Huggins, *Harlem Renaissance* (Oxford: Oxford University Press, 1973), p. 30.

2. Howard Swan, *Music in the Southwest* (New York: Da Capo Press, 1977), pp. 225-226.

3. *Ibid.*, pp. 225-226.

4. *Ibid.*, p. 231.

5. *Ibid.*, pp. 249, 254, 257-258.

6. *Ibid.*

7. *Ibid.*, pp. 258-260.

8. Judge Earl C. Broady Sr., Beverly Hills, California, telephone interview, 15 August 1988; Mrs. Mae Alice Harvey, Los Angeles, telephone interview, 24 December 1988; "Death Takes Aunt of Earl Dancer," *California Eagle*, 11 August 1938, p. 2-A, col. 5.

9. "Hollywood Movie Colony Studios Resembles League of Nations: Cosmopolitan Air Vogue at Smart Film Colony; Race Actors Are Plentiful; 'Thunderbolt,' New Bancroft Vehicle Has 75 Colored Actors in Cast," *Pittsburgh Courier*, 15 June 1929, p. 3, sec. 2, col. 1.

10. Emory J. Tolbert, *The UNIA and Black Los Angeles* (Los Angeles: Center for Afro-American Studies, University of California, Los Angeles, 1980), pp. 66, 71-72.

11. "West Coast Jazz—Volume 1," Arcadia 2001, record album (n.d.), liner notes by Dick Raichelson; Judge Earl C. Broady, Beverly Hills, California, telephone interview, 16 August 1988.

12. Judge Broady telephone interview, 16 August 1988.

13. Ruby Berkley Goodwin, "From 'Blackbird' Chorine to 'Talkin' Star: At Last!" *Pittsburgh Courier*, 8 June 1929, sec. 1, p. 12, sec. 2, p. 7.

14. *Ibid.*

15. *Ibid.*; "'Hallelujah' at Regal for Entire Week of January 25," *Chicago Defender*, 25 January 1930, p. 10, col. 1.

16. "Many Find Steady Work in Hollywood," *Chicago Defender*, 22 March 1930, p. 11, col. 7.

17. "'Hallelujah' at Regal for Entire Week of January 25," *Chicago Defender*, p. 10, col. 1; Bruce M. Tyler's review of the film.

18. Judge Broady telephone interview, 16 August 1988; "West Coast Jazz—Volume 1," liner notes by Dick Raichelson; Frank Driggs and Harris Lewine, *Black Beauty, White Heat: A Pictorial History of Classic Jazz* (New York: William Morrow and Company, Inc., 1982), p. 186.

19. Driggs and Lewine, p. 175.

20. *Ibid.*, pp. 181, 184.

21. *Ibid.*, p. 187; Judge Earl C. Broady telephone interview, 16 August 1988; Louis Armstrong, *Swing That Music* (New York: Longmans, Green and Company, 1936), p. 95.

22. John Hammond with Irving Townsend, *John Hammond on Record: An Autobiography* (New York: Summit Books, Bridge Press, 1977), p. 106.

23. Driggs and Lewine, p. 189; "Les Hite's Famous Orchestra," *Pittsburgh Courier*, 1 May 1937, p. 18, col. 1; "Maestro Les Hite's Cuties Swing in Downtown Theatre," *California Eagle*, 11 August 1938, p. 3-B, col. 3.

24. Driggs and Lewine, p. 191.

25. *Ibid.*, p. 170.

26. Gardner Bradford, "Our Gay Black Way: Central Avenue," *Los Angeles Times*, Sunday Magazine, 18 June 1933, pp. 5, 10.

27. Hazel Augustine Washington, Los Angeles, telephone interview, 23 December 1988.

28. *Fifteenth Census of the United States, 1930, Population, Vol. IV, Occupation by States, Report by States Giving Statistics for Cities of 25,000 or More*, United States Department of Commerce, Bureau of the Census, 1933, pp. 200-202.

29. *Sixteenth Census of the United States: 1940, Population, Vol. III, The Labor Force, Occupation, Industry, Employment, and Income, Part 2: Alabama-Indiana*, United States Department of Commerce, Bureau of the Census (Washington: United States Government Printing Office, 1943), pp. 244, 246, 248-249.

30. Driggs and Lewine, p. 180.

31. "1,500 Extras Auditioned," *Pittsburgh Courier*, 20 February 1937, p. 19, col. 8.

32. "Greatest Number Ever Used in One Day in Hollywood," *Pittsburgh Courier*, 20 March 1937, p. 13, col. 2.

33. Thomas Cripps, ed., *The Green Pastures* (Madison: The University of Wisconsin, 1979), pp. 204-205; Alfred LeGon, Los Angeles, telephone interview, 9 August 1988.

34. Sharon Kane, "'Green Pastures' Termed Biggest Hit of the Season," *Chicago Defender*, 22 March 1930, p. 11, col. 5.

35. "Green Pastures Renews Interest in Racial Dramatics," *Chicago Defender*, 10 May 1930, p. 11, col. 4.

36. Salem Tutt Whitney, "Timely Topics," *Chicago Defender*, 22 March 1930, p. 11, col. 4.

37. *Ibid.*

38. "Author of 'Green Pastures' Is Guest of N.A.A.C.P.," *Chicago Defender*, 19 April 1930, p. 11, col. 3.

39. "Harrison of 'The Green Pastures,'" *The Literary Digest*, 4 April 1931, p. 19.

40. Victor Daly, "Green Pastures and Black Washington," *The Crisis*, 30, No. 5 (May 1933), 106.

41. *Ibid.*

42. "The New Pictures: 'Harlem on the Prairie,'" *Time*, XXX, No. 24 (13 December 1937), 24.

43. *Ibid.*

44. Earl J. Morris, "Maxine Wows 'Em on L.A.'s Central Avenue; Bojangles Puts on One of His Famous Shoes at Club Alabam—Sends Police Escort for Jeni LeGon's Shoes," *Pittsburgh Courier,* 13 August 1938, p. 21, col. 4; Earl J. Morris, "Grandtown Day and Night: Happy New Year, Folks," *Pittsburgh Courier,* 31 December 1938, p. 17, col. 1.

45. Earl J. Morris, "Grandtown: Don't Kick a Guy When He Is Down—He May Get Up. . . and . . .," *Pittsburgh Courier,* 20 August 1938, p. 20, col. 1.

46. Roscoe Washington (retired L.A.P.D. officer), Los Angeles, telephone interview, 7 August 1988; Alfred LeGon telephone interview, 9 August 1988; Ethel Waters with Charles Samuels, *His Eye Is on the Sparrow: An Autobiography* (Garden City: Doubleday & Company, Inc., 1951), p. 173.

47. "South East Harlem Aristocrat of Night Spots . . .," *California Eagle,* 25 August 1938, p. A-7, col. 5; "Dunbar Cocktail Lounge, Host Harry Spates . . .," *California Eagle,* 25 August 1938, p. 7-A, col. 4; "Summer Visitors!" *California Eagle,* 30 June 1938, p. 3-B, col. 5; Helen Oakley Dance, *Stormy Monday: The T-Bone Walker Story* (Baton Rouge: Louisiana State University Press, 1987), p. 50.

48. "Hollywood Meets Harlem," *California Eagle,* 14 July 1938, p. B-4, col. 5.

49. "Hollywood to Meet Harlem," *California Eagle,* 21 July 1938, p. 3-B, col. 7; "Complete Plans for Funfest at Warner Bros. Tonight," *California Eagle,* 21 July 1938, p. A-8, col. 6; Helen F. Chappell, "Society Editor": "Chatter and . . . Some News," *California Eagle,* 30 June 1938, p. 9-A, col. 1.

50. "Clarence Muse to Stage Gala Movie Ball at Warner's," *California Eagle,* 30 June 1938, p. 3-B, col. 2.

51. Ray Smith, Los Angeles, telephone interview, 23 December 1988.

52. "Dixie Goes Hi-Hat," *California Eagle,* 14 July 1938, p. 4-B, col. 1.

53. "As Thousands Cheered . . . The Winner!" *California Eagle,* 15 September 1938, p. 2-B, col. 3.

54. James Haskins, *The Cotton Club* (New York: Random House, 1977); Ethel Waters with Charles Samuels, pp. 254, 258.

55. "Stars and Movie Fans Turn Out for Dedication of Bill Robinson Theatre," *California Eagle,* 22 September 1938, p. 2-B, col. 4.

56. "Bill Robinson Theatre," *California Eagle,* 22 September 1938, p. 2-B, col. 7.

57. "Savoy Theatre," *California Eagle,* 22 September 1938, p. 2-B, col. 4.

58. Duke Ellington and the Jungle Band, "Duke Ellington 'Rockin' in Rhythm," Jazz Heritage Series, MCA Records, 2077 (formerly DL7-9247), Vol. 3 (1929-1931), notes by Stanley Dance, 1977; "Duke Ellington," Up Front Records, UPF-144 (no date given).

59. Maurine Zolotow, "The Duke's 'Forgotten' L.A. Musical," *Los Angeles,* 27, No. 2 (February 1982), 170-173, 223-224; Lena Horne and Richard Shickel, *Lena* (Garden City: Doubleday, 1965), pp. 122-124.

60. Zolotow, p. 172.

61. *Ibid.,* p. 173; Derek Jewell, *Duke: A Portrait of Duke Ellington* (New York: W.W. Norton & Co., Inc., 1977), p. 76.

62. Jewell, pp. 78-79; Zolotow, pp. 173, 223; Al Monroe, "Jump for Joy, Duke Ellington Will Stage the Show Here Soon," *Chicago Defender,* 22 August 1942, p. 11, col. 3; Almena Davis, "Jump for Joy Closes in L.A.," *Pittsburgh Courier,* 4 October 1941, p. 21, col. 2.

63. Hammond, pp. 136-137, 89, 91.

64. *Ibid.,* pp. 81, 158, 91.

65. *Ibid.,* p. 137.

66. Jewell, pp. 77-78.

67. *Ibid.,* pp. 77-78.

68. "Tales of Manhattan; Cast Has Many Stars: Ethel Waters, Paul Robeson and Eddie Anderson in Film," *Pittsburgh Courier,* 11 October 1941, p. 20, col. 1; "Screen News Here and in Hollywood," *New York Times,* 24 September 1942, p. 23, col. 17, col. 5 for ad.

69. David Lardner, "The Current Cinema: Actors Rampant," *The New Yorker,* 26 September 1942, pp. 53-54; "Make-Believe," *Commonweal,* XXVI, No. 22 (18 September 1942), 518.

70. "Make-Believe," p. 518; "'Tales of Manhattan' Is the Tricky Star-Studded Adventure of a Tailcoat,'" *Life,* 13, No. 4, (27 July 1942), 44 ff.; "Movies: Coat's Coterie," *Newsweek,* XX, No. 13 (9 September 1942), pp. 62-63.

71. "The New Pictures: 'Tales of Manhattan' (20th Century-Fox)," *Time,* XL, No. 12 (21 September 1942), p. 69.

72. Manny Farber, "Black Tails and White Lies," *The New Republic,* 107, No. 15 (12 October 1942), 466.

73. Philip S. Foner, ed., *Paul Robeson Speaks: Writings, Speeches, Interviews, 1918-1974* (New York: Brunner/Mazel Publishers, 1978), 142.

74. "Paul Robeson and Hollywood," *Chicago Defender,* 3 October 1942, p. 16, col. 2.

75. Lawrence F. LaMar (or Lamar), "Here's Tales of Manhattan; See If You Think It Objectionable," *Chicago Defender,* 31 October 1942, p. 14, col. 4.

76. Waters, p. 257.

77. "'Slim' and 'Slam' Join Rochester and Katherine Dunham in Picture," *Chicago Defender,* 4 July 1942, p. 12, col. 1; James Haskins, *The Cotton Club,* pp. 77-78; Richard Buckle, *Katherine Dunham: Her Dancers, Singers, Musicians* (London: Ballet Publications, Ltd., 1978), pp. vii-ix.

78. Philip T. Hartung, "Star Spangled Rhythm," *Commonweal,* XXXVII, No. 13 (15 January 1943), 328.

79. "'Star Spangled Rhythm,' by Paramount," *Time,* XLI, No. 3 (18 January 1943), 8.

80. This writer reviewed the film.

81. Manny Farber, "To What Base Uses," *The New Republic,* 108, No. 9 (1 March 1943), 283-284.

82. Billy Rowe, "Says Hollywood Made a Promise It Hasn't Kept," *Pittsburgh Courier,* 6 March 1943, p. 21, col. 4.

83. William Robert Faith, *Bob Hope: A Life in Comedy* (New York: G.P. Putnam's Sons, 1982), p. 170.

84. "Screen News Here and in Hollywood," *New York Times,* 18 February 1943, p. 19, col. 1.

85. James Haskins, *The Cotton Club,* pp. 84-89; Al Rose, *Eubie Blake* (New York: Schirmer Books, 1979), p. 121.

86. James Haskins and Kathleen Benson, *Lena: A Personal and Professional Biography of Lena Horne* (New York: Stein and Day Publishers, 1984), pp. 75-76.

87. *Ibid.,* p. 77.

88. Waters, pp. 254-255.

89. "Cabin in the Sky," *Time,* XLI, No. 15 (12 April 1943), 96.

90. Philip T. Hartung, "Lighter Side," *Commonweal,* XXX-VIII, No. 9 (18 June 1943), 225-226.

91. "Hollywood Cabin," *Newsweek,* XXI, No. 17 (26 April 1943), 88.

92. Manny Farber, "The Great White Way," *The New Republic,* 109, No. 1 (5 July 1943), 20.

93. Joseph D. Bibb, "The Riff Raff: Unthinking Majority of Bad Actors Are Always in the Focus of Publicity," *Pittsburgh Courier,* 29 May 1943, p. 13, col. 1.

94. "Cabin Film Draws Fire," *Pittsburgh Courier,* 8 May 1943, p. 20, col. 5.

95. "Cabin Picture Called Insult: Despite Excellent Cast of 'Cabin in the Sky'; The Negro Is Belittled," *New York Amsterdam News,* 12 June 1943, p. 17, col. 2.

96. Haskins, *Lena,* pp. 73-74; "Scribe, In Film Job," *Chicago Defender,* 31 October 1942, p. 13, col. 2.

97. "Noble Sissle Previews 'Cabin in the Sky': Lauds Performance," *Pittsburgh Courier,* 23 January 1943, p. 21, col. 2.

98. Leonard Feather, *The Book of Jazz; From Then till Now* (New York: Horizon Press, 1965 [1957]), p. 39.

99. Haskins, *Lena,* p. 74.

100. "'This Is the Army': Sgt. Berlin and His Men Fight Battle of Broadway with Huge Success," *Newsweek,* XX, No. 2 (13 July 1942), 52, 54.

101. Philip T. Hartung, "The Screen: Is This the Army?," *Commonweal,* XXXVIII, No. 19 (27 August 1943), 466-467.

102. "Hollywood's Army," *Newsweek,* XXII, No. 6 (9 August 1943), 84.

103. "New Picture: This Is the Army," *Time,* XLII, No. 7 (16 August 1943), 93-94.

104. "Entertainment: Canteenful of Stars," *Newsweek,* XXI, No. 25 (21 June 1943), 100-101; David Lardner, "The Current Cinema," *The New Yorker,* XIX, No. 19 (26 June 1943), 43-44; Philip T. Hartung, "Three Ring Movie," *Commonweal,* XXXVIII, No. 11 (2 July 1943), 275-276.

105. "Cinema: New Picture," *Time,* XLI, No. 24 (14 June 1943), 94; James Agee, "Films," *The Nation,* 156, No. 24 (12 June 1943), 844; Manny Farber, "When the Pie Was Opened," *The New Republic,* 109, No. 4 (26 July 1943), 110.

106. Herman Hill, "Stage Door Canteen Is Great Film," *Pittsburgh Courier,* 26 January 1943, p. 20, col. 6

107. Waters, pp. 220-221; Cab Calloway and Bryant Rollins, *Of Minnie the Moocher & Me* (New York: Thomas Y. Crowell Company, 1976), p. 178.

108. Waters, p. 178; "Stormy Weather Features Kay Dunham-Dooley Wilson," *Pittsburgh Courier,* 6 February 1943, p. 21, col. 2.

109. "Metro-Goldwyn-Mayer Features Sepia Artists in Musicals," *Pittsburgh Courier,* 6 February 1943, p. 21, col. 2.

110. *Pittsburgh Courier,* 13 February 1943, p. 21, col. 2.

111. Herman Hill, "Hollywood Likes Clarence Robinson," *Pittsburgh Courier,* 13 March 1943, p. 20, col. 3.

112. "Servicemen Up on 'Stormy Weather,'" *Pittsburgh Courier,* 13 March 1943, p. 20, col. 4.

113. "Ernie Fields Boosts Servicemen's Morale," *Pittsburgh Courier,* 13 February 1943, p. 21, col. 4.

114. "Finish 'Stormy Weather' Amid Fanfare, Color in Film Colony," *Pittsburgh Courier,* 20 March 1943, p. 20, col. 2.

115. Billy Rowe, "Feels Performers Should Be Listed as Essentials," *Pittsburgh Courier,* 20 March 1943, p. 20, col. 4.

116. "The Draft: Nonessential Band Leader," *Time,* XLI, No. 14 (5 April 1943), 75.

117. Billy Rowe, "See Little Hope for Listing of Entertainers as Essentials," *Pittsburgh Courier,* 27 March 1943, p. 21, col. 1.

118. Philip T. Hartung, "The Screen: Rain! No Game!," *Commonweal,* XXXVIII, No. 14 (23 July 1943), 344-345.

119. "Hollywood Cabin," *Newsweek,* XXI, No. 17 (26 April 1943), 88.

120. "Stormy Weather," *Time,* XLII, No. 2 (12 July 1943), 94, 96.

121. Charlotte Charity, "Billy Rowe Told Film Producers Willing to Help," *Pittsburgh Courier,* 3 April 1943, p. 25, col. 5.

122. "Hollywood May Censor Screen 'Zoot Suits,'" *Pittsburgh Courier,* 3 April 1943, p. 25, col. 2.

123. Herman Hill, "Coast Fans Applaud Lena Horne at 'Stormy Weather' Opening," *Pittsburgh Courier,* 7 August 1943, p. 20, col. 1.

124. Charlotte Charity, p. 25, col. 5.

125. Harry Levette, "Puzzled Hollywood Asks 'What Kind of Films [Do] Negroes Want?'" *Pittsburgh Courier,* 1 May 1943, pp. 20-21.

126. *Ibid.*

127. Horne, *Lena,* pp. 120-121, 134, 136-137.

128. *Ibid.,* pp. 120-121, 134, 136.

# ROBERT LANG (ESSAY DATE 1994)

**SOURCE:** Lang, Robert. "*The Birth of a Nation*: History, Ideology, Narrative Form." In *The Birth of a Nation: D. W. Griffith, director,* edited by Robert Lang, pp. 3-24. New Brunswick, N.J.: Rutgers University Press, 1994.

*In the following essay, Lang explains historical, ideological, and narrative influences on the production of* The

Birth of a Nation, *characterizing the film as a melodramatic representation of the historical viewpoint held by its director.*

In filming *The Birth of a Nation,* I gave to my best knowledge the proven facts, and presented the known truth, about the Reconstruction period in the American South. These facts are based on an overwhelming compilation of authentic evidence and testimony. My picturisation of history as it happens requires, therefore, no apology, no defence, no "explanations."
—D. W. Griffith, in a letter to *Sight & Sound,* 1947

Shortly after the Civil War, Robert E. Lee noted the importance of "the opinion which posterity may form of the motives which governed the South in their late struggle for the maintenance of the principles of the Constitution," adding that he hoped, "therefore, a true history [would] be written, and justice done them."[1] Nearly a hundred years later, Robert Penn Warren wrote that "the Civil War is, for the American imagination, the great single event of our history. Without too much wrenching, it may, in fact, be said to *be* American history."[2] In America, however, the Civil War is remembered not as history but as legend. The process of turning the bloody, traumatic reality into a Victorian melodrama began shortly after the fighting ceased. For Southerners and Northerners alike, it was a psychological necessity to make a legend out of the chaos and contradiction of the experience. In *The Birth of a Nation,* Griffith gave plastic reality to many of the images that dominated the historiographic Imaginary of the Civil War and its aftermath, and Griffith's narrative organization of history—his attempt to identify the causes of the Civil War and to explain Reconstruction to a people who needed romance, not realism—can perhaps be best described in terms of melodrama.

Griffith's grasp of historiography was astonishingly naïve. In an article he wrote for a magazine called *The Editor* in 1915, he had this to say about the teaching of history:

The time will come, and in less than ten years . . . when the children in the public schools will be taught practically everything by moving pictures. Certainly they will never be obliged to read history again.

Imagine a public library of the near future, for instance. There will be long rows of boxes or pillars, properly classified and indexed, of course. At each box a push button and before each box a seat. Suppose you wish to "read up" on a certain episode in Napoleon's life. Instead of consulting all the authorities, wading laboriously through a host of books, and ending bewildered, without a clear idea of what exactly did happen and confused at every point by conflicting opinions about what did happen, you will merely seat yourself as

a properly adjusted window, in a scientifically prepared room, press the button, and actually see what happened.

There will be no opinions expressed. You will merely be present at the making of history. All the work of writing, revising, collating, and reproducing will have been carefully attended to by a corps of recognized experts, and you will have received a vivid and complete expression.[3]

From this quotation it is easy to see Griffith's inability to perceive the ideological encodings of the "natural." To "actually see what happened" is, of course, to actually see a construction; and the ideological underpinnings of Griffith's library of the future are implicit in his remark that "you will merely be present at the making of history." Griffith's complacent belief in "recognized experts" ignores the fact that experts have their own perspective on history.

In Andrew Sarris's words, "The best that could be said for Griffith was that he was not fully conscious of all the issues involved in his treatment of Reconstruction after the Civil War," and that "unlike Gance and Eisenstein, Griffith relied more on a theory of character than a theory of history."[4] The melodramatic move is toward character, and an example of how this process of characterization works is offered in Alan T. Nolan's observation that the Civil War "is defined in our consciousness by the clichés with which historians and the purveyors of popular culture have surrounded it: the troublesome abolitionists, the brothers' war, Scarlett and Tara, the faithful slave, the forlorn Confederate soldier, the brooding Lincoln, High Tide at Gettysburg, the bloody Grant, the Lost Cause, and the peerless Robert E. Lee. These images, each laden with emotion, are in our bones."[5]

Melodrama certainly cannot conceive of storytelling in anything other than these clichés that Nolan, the historian, deplores. However, my point here is not to establish where Griffith was inaccurate, or how he misplaced his emphases or distorted "the facts." What interests me here is Griffith's historiography as ideological practice, his shaping of history as fact and how that shaping itself is ideologically informed.

Since 1915, and certainly since the Civil War itself, much has changed in the historical landscape. Not only is the Civil War now remote in time, but there is a sense in which—thanks, partly, to the influences of film and television—we share a national culture. Some of the more extreme racial attitudes that underlie the clichés that dominated the discourse on the Civil War and Reconstruction have been dismantled or modified. But although these changes might shape our contemporary perspective, we need to understand that the Civil War was "the obsessive trauma of American politics and historiography of [Griffith]'s generation,"[6] and as a Southerner, Griffith presents a "Southern" point of view.

Historically, as Nolan points out, the South's contribution to the way in which the War and Reconstruction period were understood and represented had two elements: "The first concerned the role of slavery; the second involved the changing image of the slave and the freedman."[7] As in Griffith's film, it was not slavery but "liberty, independence, and especially states' rights [that] were advanced by countless southern spokesmen as the hallowed principles of the Lost Cause."[8] (Cf. intertitles 107, 146, and 507.)

Griffith was concerned to make sense of the defeat of the South by justifying the Southern effort and reclaiming its dignity. This discourse has come to be known as the Southern Legend, or Lost Cause. Although Russell Merritt has noted that "by 1914 most Southern writers considered the job finished and the legend dried up,"[9] Griffith was still greatly attracted to it. Like his Southern compatriot Thomas Dixon, upon whose book and play *The Clansman* much of *The Birth of a Nation* is based, he obviously still felt the need to redeem the defeat of the South. As we know, the result, in Everett Carter's words, is a record of a cultural illusion that is without equal.

Carter gives the essentials of this image of the South shared by Dixon and Griffith when he writes that the film became "a visualization of the whole set of irrational cultural assumptions which may be termed the 'Plantation Illusion.' The Illusion has many elements, but it is based primarily upon a belief in a golden age of the antebellum South, an age in which feudal agrarianism provided the good life for wealthy, leisured, kindly, aristocratic owner and loyal, happy, obedient slave."[10]

More importantly for some, Carter has noted how "the violation of the Southern illusion by the North" is translated by the film into sexual terms. Griffith's film, like Dixon's book, "incorporates one of the most vital of the forces underlying the illusion—the obscure, bewildering complex of sexual guilt and fear which the ideal never overtly admits, but which are . . . deeply interwoven into the Southern sensibility."[11] Crises of narrative and sexuality—the mainstays of melodrama—become intertwined with Griffith's reconstruction of historical fact. It is precisely on the terrain of sexuality that history becomes legend and melodramatic myth.

### Thomas Dixon's Historical Romance, The Clansman

In her autobiography, Lillian Gish insists that "Mr. Griffith didn't need the Dixon book. His intention was to tell his version of the War between the States. But he evidently lacked the confidence to start production on a twelve-reel film without an established book as a basis for his story."[12] Although this may have been so, a great deal of *The Birth of a Nation* (most of the second part, which deals with Reconstruction) closely follows Dixon's *The Clansman* and his play of the same title. While Dixon is remembered as an obsessed racist, and Griffith is not, both Dixon's novel and Griffith's film clearly share a narrative mode, and their subject matter bears the same distinctive relationship to history.[13]

The full title of Thomas Dixon's book is: *The Clansman: An Historical Romance of the Ku Klux Klan.*[14] In a preface, Dixon informs the reader that "*The Clansman* is the second book of a series of historical novels planned on the Race Conflict," and it "develops the true story of the 'Ku Klux Klan Conspiracy,' which overturned the Reconstruction régime." In a style that matches his measure of the events of the era, Dixon writes that "the chaos of blind passion that followed Lincoln's assassination is inconceivable to-day. The revolution it produced in our Government, and the bold attempt of Thaddeus Stevens to Africanize ten great States of the American Union, read now like tales from 'The Arabian Nights.'"

The term "historical romance" is something of an oxymoron—at least, as it can be used to describe *The Clansman*—despite Dixon's insistence that he has "sought to preserve in this romance both the letter and the spirit of this remarkable period." Dixon states that "the men who enact the drama of fierce revenge into which I have woven a double love story are historical figures. I have merely changed their names without taking a liberty with any essential historic fact."

More remarkable, surely, than anything that could be called "historical," is Dixon's description of the defeated South and the rise of the Ku Klux Klan:

> In the darkest hour of the life of the South, when her wounded people lay helpless amid rags and

ashes under the beak and talon of the Vulture, suddenly from the mists of the mountains appeared a white cloud the size of a man's hand. It grew until its mantle of mystery enfolded the stricken earth and sky. An "Invisible Empire" had risen from the field of Death and challenged the Visible to mortal combat.

How the young South, led by the reincarnated souls of the Clansmen of Old Scotland, went forth under this cover and against overwhelming odds, daring exile, imprisonment, and a felon's death, and saved the life of a people, forms one of the most dramatic chapters in the history of the Aryan race.[15]

Griffith emphatically claimed, as Dixon did with regard to his book, that he had not in his film taken a liberty with any essential historic fact. Yet what are we to make of such florid prose? Or of its "picturisation" in Griffith's film?

The historical romance—still popular in the early years of this century—is grounded in realism; but its highly charged emotionalism, driven by desire, pushes the form to the very limits of the plausible. Certainly, it feels no special allegiance to fact, and it freely modifies aspects of the past in accordance with current desires. The historical film melodrama works the same way. In Philip Rosen's words, Griffith's methods of narrative organization "involve a balance . . . between individual motives and traits on the one hand and general truths on the other. The balance is achieved through the mediation of family romance situations in historically significant settings. This method remained a staple of classical cinema."[16]

## Melodrama

*The Birth of a Nation* announces the themes of its melodrama with its first title: "If in this work we have conveyed to the mind the ravages of war to the end that *war may be held in abhorrence,* this effort will not have been in vain." The kind of cinema that Griffith pioneered and consolidated, with its immediate origins in nineteenth-century stage melodrama, has always been concerned with articulating a moral ideology and demonstrating that the world is, finally, a coherent (and potentially benevolent) place. If human suffering is not to go unredeemed, the drama must, at the very least, offer a lesson, especially if the misfortunes represented have been brought about by human folly. *The Birth of a Nation,* like all melodramas, is a film with a message. But just what is that message?

Griffith told a reporter, nearly thirty years after the release of *The Birth of a Nation,* that a good picture is "one that makes the public forget its troubles. Also, a good picture tends to make folks think a little, without letting them suspect that they are being inspired to think. In one respect, nearly all pictures are good in that they frequently show the triumph of good over evil."[17] These admirable sentiments continue to inform the American film melodrama to this day, giving it shape and ideological purpose—but the film melodrama is frequently unclear, and sometimes plainly wrong, about who or what the villain is. Human suffering is described and attempts are made to name causes, but more often than not the film melodrama as a form is inadequate to the business of figuring out why people suffer. For our purposes, it is equally inadequate to the task of analyzing why, for example, the American Civil War took place, or why, as Griffith understood it, the South had to suffer "degradation and ruin" (shot 913).

The second intertitle of *The Birth of a Nation* declares that "the bringing of the African to America planted the first seed of disunion." Already, even before the film's first image, Griffith attempts to identify evil with "the African" by implying that an America without Africans was a harmonious Eden. Although nowhere in the film does Griffith explicitly identify the institution of slavery as the root cause of the Civil War, the suggestion is insinuated immediately in this intertitle. It should be noted that Thomas Dixon was quite clear, but also irrational, about who the villains were. In 1905, he wrote that the South before the Civil War was ruled by an "aristocracy founded on brains, culture, and blood," the "old fashioned dream of the South" which "but for the Black curse . . . could be today the garden of the world."[18]

But Griffith was not the fanatic Dixon was, and his attitudes are not so stark, or so easy to dismiss. With his "spotty knowledge of history, his literary eccentricities, [and] his 'petit-bourgeois' morality,"[19] Griffith presents, paradoxically, a more insidious case than Dixon, who has been described as an "unasylumed maniac."[20] Like Lincoln (the historical figure, not the character portrayed by Joseph Henabery in the film), Griffith accepts the institution of slavery,[21] and with the third intertitle launches the notion that those who sought to end slavery, not the Africans themselves, were to blame for the troubles his film treats: "The Abolitionists of the Nineteenth Century demanding the freeing of the slaves" (shot 9). (In the second part of the film dealing with Reconstruction, Griffith is content to blame everything on scalawags and carpetbaggers.)

Griffith's attitude toward slavery can perhaps be clarified by briefly considering Robert E. Lee's position on the subject. Although Lee's role as a character in *Birth* is small and almost entirely iconic, he was, for Griffith, and appears to have remained for most Southern partisans, "the embodiment of all that was good and noble in the Old South . . . the foremost Southern hero."[22] Lee's position on slavery more or less corresponds to Griffith's, as it can be inferred from *The Birth of a Nation.* As summed up by Nolan in *Lee Considered:*

1. Northerners' opposition to slavery, or to its expansion into the territories, was an "interference" with "the domestic institutions of the South," with which they had no appropriate concern.

2. In opposing slavery, Northerners were intolerant of the "Spiritual liberty" of the Southerners who supported slavery.

3. Although Northerners opposed to slavery had the right to proceed by "moral means and suasion," their opposition was somehow "unlawful," violated their duty as citizens, and predicted civil war.[23]

While the viewer's belief that war, as stated in the film's first title, should be "held in abhorrence" may or may not be reinforced by Griffith's film, this, surely, is not quite the point.[24] As a melodrama, the film is ostensibly committed to clarifying how to prevent future wars—not to persuading viewers that war is bad. The narrative enigma launched by the film's second intertitle— "The bringing of the African to America planted the first seed of disunion"—is resolved near the end of the film by asserting a way of eliminating the African threat: images of an election in which we see black voters intimidated by mounted Clansmen (1594-1599). This image of blacks being intimidated is the true *telos* of Griffith's vision—not the images of Margaret and Phil, and Ben and Elsie on their respective honeymoons, or the muddled intertitle that follows: "Dare we dream of a golden day when the bestial War shall rule no more. But instead—the gentle Prince in the Hall of Brotherly Love in the City of Peace" (1603). The very last intertitle reads: "*Liberty and union,* one and inseparable, *now and forever!*" (1609). Rather than offer a discourse against war, Griffith proposes the idea that the unity of the country is the most important thing, and this is to be bought at the price of subordinating the blacks.

A synopsis of the film submitted to the U.S. Copyright Office on February 8, 1915, describes the end of the film this way: "To Ben and Elsie, to Phil and Margaret, the sequel is a beautiful double honeymoon by the sea. To the American people, the outcome of four years of fratricidal strife, the nightmare of Reconstruction, and the establishment of the South in its rightful place, is the birth of a new nation."[25] That the film ends on images of the double honeymoon reveals not so much the melodrama's inability to come to grips with the real causes of the conflicts that structure the film, but Griffith's preference for the familial dimension of it, and perhaps, more importantly, his unwillingness to examine his own racism.

A profound ambivalence underlies every aspect of the narrative characterized by a hypocritical stance of outward benevolence toward blacks and an underlying corrosive fear. An intertitle that appears late in the film succinctly expresses the controlling logic of the numerous oppositions in the narrative: "The former enemies of North and South are united in common defense of their Aryan birthright," and it is duplicated in the mise-en-scène of the besieged cabin in which Dr. and Mrs. Cameron, their daughter Margaret, her suitor Phil Stoneman, and the Camerons' faithful servants Jake and Mammy are given refuge by two Union veterans. (The cabin is surrounded by black troops sent by Lynch to capture the elder Cameron.) The strand of the narrative involving the blacks does not end on shots of slaves being returned to Africa, as it is sometimes claimed was originally the case,[26] but on an image of their subordination. As the second of the two synopses submitted to the U.S. Copyright Office puts it, "At the next election the negroes dare not vote and the threat of a black empire is dissolved."[27] To the extent that the film tries to be plausible, this is realistic, for historically the war was lost over slavery and independence, but peace was waged— and won—for states' rights, white supremacy, and honor.

Griffith's feeling about the new relationship between whites and blacks in the South after the war—ambivalent, hypocritical—appears to be similar to Lee's; and as Nolan notes, Lee's public and private assertions regarding the freedman were in conflict:

Publicly, [Lee] was protective and benign. Everything would be all right if the North did not "stir up" the blacks. Dependent on their labor, the South would, of course, employ them. Privately, he was bitter toward the freedman and intervened personally to their detriment. In truth, Lee and his fellow Southerners were groping for a new method of white supremacy and exploitation of the blacks. With Northern complicity, the South-

A scene from the film *The Birth of a Nation*.

ern effort was eventually to succeed; the outcome was a hundred years of near-slavery: disenfranchisement, Black Codes, Jim Crow, and suppression.[28]

If Griffith was at all ambivalent, confused, hypocritical, or self-deluding about what the "message" of his film was, Dixon was not. Rolfe Cobleigh, a newspaper editor who gained an interview with Thomas Dixon, wrote in a sworn deposition:

> I asked Mr. Dixon what his real purpose was in having *The Birth of a Nation* produced, what he hoped to accomplish by it. . . . [Dixon replied] that one purpose of his play was to create a feeling of abhorrence in white people, especially white women against colored men. Mr. Dixon said that his desire was to prevent the mixing of white and Negro blood by intermarriage. [. . .] Mr. Dixon said that the Ku Klux Klan was formed to protect the white women from Negro men, to restore order and to reclaim political control for the white people of the South. He said that the Ku Klux Klan was not only engaged in restoring law and order, but was of a religious nature.[29]

It is particularly important to note that Dixon's reference to the protection of white women is precisely what gets narrativized in the film, in accordance with melodramatic principles. It is, in fact, the film's core. Dixon's statements surely say it all—for the second part of Griffith's film bears out this ideological position with shocking conviction. Indeed, the "abhorrence in white people, especially white women against colored men" that Dixon speaks of exemplifies with more truth and force the film's real message than that other "abhorrence" for war that Griffith attempts to persuade us is his reason for making the film.

We are given to understand that, before the "seed of disunion" referred to in the film's second intertitle grows to disruptive proportions, there is a state of harmony and union in America—which is offered in the image of the Cameron family on their front porch at Cameron Hall (46). Every melodrama, as we have said, shows, or refers to, such an image—of the world before the villain enters it. As one intertitle puts it, with rather self-conscious simplicity and more than a little nostalgia, this is "the Southland. Piedmont, South Carolina, the home of the Camerons, where life runs in a quaintly way that is to be no more" (33). This image of course will be shattered, and the whole effort of the film will be to restore it. Griffith's aim above all is to offer a "picturisation" of the Civil War and Reconstruction that will honor the Southern Legend, and its imagery necessarily lies in the iconography of melodrama.

Griffith prefigures the nature of the conflict that will be the motor of his narrative when he disrupts this tableau of the idealized and sentimentalized family by showing a kitten being dropped onto the puppy at Dr. Cameron's feet. "Hostilities" (53), announces the intertitle that follows; and the kitten and puppy start to fight. Griffith the narrator organizes his fictional world into binary oppositions (one puppy is white, and the other black), and puts them into conflict. We should perhaps not read too much into this little scene—by suggesting, for example, that the kitten be associated with the abolitionists, or with the scalawags and carpetbaggers who disrupt the happy relationship between Southern whites and blacks—but the scene makes it clear that Griffith is less concerned with analyzing *why* there is conflict, or with being (from our point of view) ideologically responsible, than with telling a good story and successfully controlling the dramatic rhythms of his narrative. The scene is also typical of Griffith's method of giving symbolic resonance to people, objects, and places, thus lending an allegorical dimension to his "history."

It is with considerable irony, but not surprising, that we discover that Woodrow Wilson—who was President of the United States when *The Birth of a Nation* was made, and from whose *History of the American People* Griffith quotes in *Birth* to help persuade us of the film's historical accuracy—was himself more concerned with impressing audiences with his style than with his ideas. While in the history department at The John Hopkins University in Baltimore, pursuing the doctorate he never completed, Wilson confessed to his fiancée:

> Style is not much studied here; *ideas* are supposed to be everything—their vehicle comparatively nothing. But you and I know that there can be no greater mistake; that, both in its amount and in its length of life, an author's influence depends upon the power and the beauty of his style; upon the flawless mirror he holds up to nature; upon his facility in catching and holding, because he pleases, the attention.[30]

It is worth noting—for the obvious reason that there are parallels between Griffith and the President; and because, in Lillian Gish's words, "Mr. Griffith had great respect for [Wilson's] erudition"[31]—that, when Wilson was a young professor, he wrote "a prodigious amount, almost all of it frankly inspirational and aimed at the widest

public. His five-volume *History of the American People* was composed in the 1890s in the form of lavishly illustrated articles for *Harper's*. He was paid $1,000 for each article, an unheard-of price at the time."[32]

In the writing of history, striking a proper balance between searching for what we call "truth" and reaching a popular audience is far from being a satisfactorily resolved matter. Consider the following remark made in 1991 by Simon Schama (author of *Citizens,* a best-selling [but antirevolutionary] book about the French Revolution): The "pressing task," he writes, is to restore history "to the forms by which it can catch the public imagination. That form, as Ken Burns's stunning PBS series on the Civil War demonstrated, ought to be narrative; not to discard argument and analysis, but to lend it proper dramatic and poetic power."[33]

But the PBS series on the Civil War is not a commercial film (a Hollywood movie),[34] and it does not in the same way have the "dramatic and poetic power" of Griffith's film. Perhaps Edward Jay Epstein's remark about Oliver Stone's film, *JFK*—"When you mix fact and fiction you get fiction"[35]—is another way of saying: when you attempt a "picturisation of history," you get melodrama.

### The Besieged House

Like Woodrow Wilson, Griffith understood that "an author's influence depends upon the power and the beauty of his style,"[36] and, like Abraham Lincoln before him, Griffith appealed to an audience with an essentially emotional solution. In 1861, Lincoln told an Indiana audience: "To the salvation of this Union, there needs but one single thing, the hearts of a people like yours."[37] Lincoln understood that the American people had to be emotionally involved if the Union were to be preserved, and his chosen metaphor of the besieged house was a conventional (but, as he knew, powerful) way of "figuratively expressing the Union." He called slavery "an element of division in the house."[38]

Before the war, Lincoln was not alone among American politicians who "increasingly tended verbally to structure the crisis according to the conventions of melodrama. Indeed, it is only a slight exaggeration to say that by the end of the 1850s, the crisis of the Union not only imitated, but had become, a work of art, with the paradoxical result that as the crisis grew more serious its seriousness grew more difficult to measure."[39]

Fifty years later, Griffith's problem was one of organizing the war and the Reconstruction period into a commercially viable dramatic narrative; and according to the conventions of melodrama and his own definition of a "good picture," Griffith must attempt to "show the triumph of good over evil" in a way that is not simplistically reductive.

In the melodramatic tradition that figures evil as a rapist and virtue as a threatened virgin, Griffith organizes most of his narrative around images of women under threat.[40] Indeed, Lillian Gish writes in her autobiography about the audition that won her the part of Elsie Stoneman: "During the hysterical chase around the room, the hairpins flew out of my hair, which tumbled below my waist as Lynch held my fainting body in his arms. I was very blonde and fragile-looking. The contrast with the dark man evidently pleased Mr. Griffith."[41]

Such a scene, which of course appears in the film (1323 passim), describes very well the nature of Griffith's melodramatic imagination. The scene is emblematic of the sorts of contrasts that define melodrama and that give Griffith's films their undercurrents of perversity. Furthermore, it can be argued that such scenes of sexual aggression structure the narrative itself, rendering all discourses on history and politis somewhat ancillary. In Nick Browne's words,

> If there is a fantasy animating Griffith's narrative project, which cross-cutting and rape come to symbolize, it has to do, I think, with the seduction and at the same time the defense of the woman by his symbolic possession of her through his art. This scenario of rescue is essentially a chivalrous project couched in a kind of medieval and allegorical idiom, that has as its end the stabilization of the place and integrity of the bourgeois family against the threat of abandonment, dismemberment, homelessness or worse, that constitutes the clear and present danger in his films. It is in this role that the moralism of Griffith's vision as a director lies. The Griffith fantasy . . . is the protection or restoration of the holiness of the American family. It is the prerequisite of this vision that it be achieved in the mode of nostalgia.[42]

One of Griffith's nostalgic images of the ideal relationship between white Southerners and their slaves (who have their place in a *familial* sense on the plantation) is offered early in *The Birth of a Nation*. Shortly after the Stoneman brothers arrive at Cameron Hall to visit their Southern friends, Ben, Margaret, Flora, and Phil take a walk "over the plantation to the cotton fields" (78). The scene describes the very conditions of property ownership in the South and the way in which the familial and romantic strands of Griffith's narrative are subtly intertwined with the economic discourse to suggest a "natural" order of things. As Margaret and Phil chat intimately, almost oblivious to their surroundings, Ben picks a cotton blossom and turns to beckon Phil. As the friends contemplate the blossom, two slaves can be seen in the background, industriously picking cotton. Ben and Phil are wearing top hats, and Margaret is twirling a parasol. Young Flora scampers about as if the field were a playground, and Margaret glances complacently at the slaves, confirming their status as scenery. When Ben notices the cameo in Phil's hand, he takes it from him and Phil explains that it is a likeness of his sister, Elsie. Ben smiles as he studies the portrait and in a playful gesture takes off his hat and bows to it.

Griffith thus effects a transfer of metaphors, or symbolisms—from the cotton blossom as "flower" of the South (shown in extreme close-up), to a close-up of the cameo of Elsie (the very flower of femininity; the linchpin of the chivalric code by which Southern gentlemen live). The close-up of the cotton blossom functions like a cameo. It is an overdetermined image which refers to the foundations of the economic system of the South—although, ironically, Ben contemplates it as an object of beauty, free of ideology. There is a sense in which we are being asked to see a natural connection or parallel in this visual zeugma. Ben dashes off, clutching the portrait of Elsie in which, an intertitle tells us, "he finds the ideal of his dreams" (93), thus condensing the pastoral, nostalgic scene in an image of love for the idealized woman. As Phil and Margaret depart, Phil (the Northerner) gives the slaves in the field a quick— perhaps self-conscious—wave. The scene is extended by shots 101-106, in which slaves are seen dancing to entertain the visitors. When the dancing comes to an end and Ben brings up the rear of the departing group, two old slaves approach Ben, who pauses to shake hands with one of them and put his hand paternalistically on the other slave's shoulder.

This extended image of the hierarchies of the Old South—so necessary to melodrama's method of showing, or referring to, a stable order that will be disrupted and then restored—is immediately followed by an intertitle that introduces the "historical" threat to this order: "The gathering storm. The power of the sovereign states, established when Lord Cornwallis surrendered to the individual colonies in 1781, is threatened by the new administration" (107); just as the earlier intertitle, "Hostilities" (53), announced the threat to the harmonious image of the two puppies playing at Dr. Cameron's feet. Later in the film, when the fortunes of the South are approaching their nadir, Flora will adorn her shabby dress with cotton wool, described in an intertitle as "Southern ermine" (515); and Ben will refuse the hand proffered by a black man (716). The order of things has been reversed; the "element of division in the house" has brought the house down. In this way, Griffith creates the symmetries on which his melodramatic vision is founded.

As a form, melodrama turns on the central need to keep alive the notions of symmetry and difference; and in this film, Griffith resolves the North-South opposition in the birth of a new nation, and the male-female difference in the marriages of Ben and Elsie, Phil and Margaret. But the film clearly has trouble with the difference between blacks and whites, and this is expressed in the figure of the mulatto.

### Virtue and Villainy

The North-South opposition in *The Birth of a Nation* is expressed by the fact of the Civil War—two sides in opposition. Griffith tries to state this opposition in clear, melodramatic terms—indeed, before he shifts the focus of his film away from the war altogether, he attempts to propose it as a stark and Manichaean conflict—and he includes a shot of Ben showing Flora their state flag, on which we see the motto: "Conquer We Must—Victory or Death—For Our Cause is Just" (198).

But the animating concern of the film is not really this conflict at all. As Dixon told Rolfe Cobleigh, one of the main reasons for making the film was to help "prevent the mixing of white and Negro blood by intermarriage." The film's obsession with miscegenation is the key to its structure and meaning as a melodrama. Throughout its history, the melodrama as a form has favored the image of the virgin as the representative of virtue—the principle around which the whole drama as a moral ordering turns[43]—and in *The Birth of a Nation,* it is above all Flora's death and Elsie's danger that symbolize the South's unhappy fate ("To escape with honor intact, [Flora] leaps . . . from a high cliff"[44]). Flora's death and Elsie's imperilment also provide the narrative with the revenge formula that is so serviceable to melodrama's requirement of an unassailably clear and simple logic: outrage begetting outrage. Flora's brother Ben, leading the Klan, vows to avenge her death: "Brethren, this flag bears the red stain of the life of a Southern woman, a priceless sacrifice on the altar of an outraged civilization" (1172). In 1913,

only months before Griffith began shooting *The Birth of a Nation,* Pitchfork Ben Tillman, governor of South Carolina (the home state of Griffith's fictitious Camerons), publicly supported the lynching of [black] rapists, claiming that "forty to a hundred Southern maidens were annually offered as a sacrifice to the African Minotaur, and no Theseus had arisen to rid the land of this terror."[45]

The villain who stands in opposition to Flora as a figure of virtue is, of course, Gus. While the threat of rape is repeatedly the melodramatic hook in the film's articulation of villainy, it is important to observe that Gus's villainy does not derive simply from his apparently rapacious intentions. Nor does it derive ultimately from the stark fact of his obvious *difference* from Flora—that is, his blackness, or his maleness—but rather from the fact that he has compromised his identity as a loyal slave. He is called a "renegade" because, after the Civil War, he betrays his white masters.

For a proper understanding of villainy as it functions in *The Birth of a Nation* as a melodrama, it must be observed that every villain in the film is in some way a *traitor,* confusing the clarity of a binary order in which identity is conceived of as being decisively one thing or another. Indeed, the war itself, as James Baldwin has observed, is represented as a "great betrayal by the Northern brethren" of "the gallant South."[46]

Silas Lynch is described as "a traitor to his white patron and a greater traitor to his own people" because he "plans to lead [his people] by an evil way to build himself a throne of vaulting power" (720). He also wants to marry Elsie, thus violating the taboo in the film on miscegenation. But his villainy originates in the fact that he is neither white nor black—that is, he is worse than black. Some of the complex and contradictory meanings of Lynch's character are suggested by Dixon's description of him, which Lillian Gish quotes in her autobiography: "A Negro of perhaps forty years, a man of charming features for a mulatto, who had evidently inherited the full physical characteristics of the Aryan, while his dark yellowish eyes beneath his heavy brows glowed with the brightness of the African jungle."[47]

The film's point is that if Gus had not become a traitor to his white masters and had remained true to his identity as a Southern black, he would be like Jake and Mammy, the "faithful souls" of the Cameron household. According to the dire logic of melodramatic symmetry, Gus is lynched for his ostensible intention to rape Flora.[48] Lynch, however, is one of the film's essentially villainous figures—as a mulatto he is cast as a villain from birth, a demonized product of miscegenation—long before Stoneman turns him into a "Frankenstein" (*sic*).[49]

By similar logic, when the blacks who raid Piedmont in the film's first scenes of the town "scarred by war" break into Cameron Hall, they are led by a "scalawag white captain [who] influences the negro militia to follow his orders" (249). The raid is understood to be an aberration, a consequence of a betrayal—by a white man whose first allegiance should be to his whiteness (his "Aryan birthright").

The same goes for all carpetbaggers, white people who are so much motivated by profit that they become "as much enemies of the one race as of the other" (622). And the introductory intertitle of the second part of the film, "The blight of war does not end when hostilities cease" (620), is an echo of an earlier intertitle about Stoneman's desire for his mulatto housekeeper, Lydia Brown—described as "the great leader's weakness that is to blight a nation" (133). James Baldwin notes the false logic of the meanings Griffith attempts to assign to the figure of the mulatto when he writes that "the baleful effect of this carnal creature on the eminent Southern politician helps bring about the ruin of the South. I cannot tell you exactly *how* she brings about so devastating a fate, and I defy anyone to tell *me:* but she does."[50] Sex returns over treachery, and the consistent theme is of pure entities marred, compromised, misled, sullied—above all, betrayed—which results in evil.

Baldwin precisely identifies the film's logic of origins and causes, even as the film attempts to disguise the truth of its own logic. As he puts it, "*The Birth of a Nation* is really an elaborate justification of mass murder. The film cannot possibly admit this, which is why we are immediately placed at the mercy of a plot [that] is labyrinthine and preposterous."[51] The logic at the heart of the film's baroque structure is this:

> For the sake of the dignity of this temporarily defeated people [the Southern whites], and out of a vivid and loving concern for their betrayed and endangered slaves, the violated social order must, at all costs, be re-established. And it *is* re-established by the vision and heroism of the noblest among these noble. The disaster which they must overcome (and, in future, avert) has been brought about, not through any fault of their

own, and not because of any defection among their slaves, but by the weak and misguided among them who have given the mulattoes ideas above their station.[52]

Baldwin goes on to ask, "But how did so ungodly a creature as the mulatto enter this Eden, and where did he come from? The film cannot concern itself with this inconvenient and impertinent question."[53] At any rate, the South is "shamefully defeated—or, not so much defeated, it would appear, as betrayed: by the influence of the mulattoes."[54]

> The plot is entirely controlled by the image of the mulatto, and there are two of them, one male and one female. All of the energy of the film is siphoned off into these two dreadful and improbable creatures. It might have made sense . . . if these two mulattoes had been related to each other, or to the renegade politician, whose wards they are: but . . . they are related to each other only by their envy of white people.[55]

Neither white nor black, the mulatto is a living embodiment of a disturbance in the melodramatic field, in which one is *either* white *or* black. The order of things is confused by this merging of opposites, and *The Birth of a Nation* finds it convenient and logical to designate the mulatto as the villainous consequence of "the bringing of the African to America."

### Lincoln, the "Great Heart"

While the Civil War made some sense of the political confusions of the 1850s, the war and Reconstruction in turn were structured by the simplifying terms of the melodrama, which characteristically converts complex problems into a struggle between virtue and vice. In the figure of Abraham Lincoln, however, Griffith achieves an extraordinary synthesis of potential incompatibilities. Lincoln's status in the film is unique. He is portrayed as an infinitely thoughtful and suffering man, rather in the manner of a father who must make unpopular decisions for the good of the entire family. Griffith aims for a proper solemnity in representing one of the first of those decisions Lincoln makes that will so affect the destinies of the Camerons and Stonemans: "Abraham Lincoln uses the Presidential office for the first time in history to call for volunteers to enforce the rule of the coming nation over the individual states" (146). When he has finished signing the proclamation, he is left alone in his office. He takes a handkerchief from his hat on the table and dabs his eyes with it, leans forward on the desk, and clasps his hands in prayer (147).

After the South has been defeated, Stoneman visits Lincoln to "protest against [his] policy of clemency for the South" (529). Lincoln responds to Stoneman's impassioned demand that the Southern leaders "be hanged and their states treated as conquered provinces" (531) by replying calmly: "I shall deal with them as though they had never been away" (533). Lincoln is thus also claimed by the South as a hero, and an intertitle announces that "the South under Lincoln's fostering hand goes to work to rebuild itself" (535).

Griffith offers only one brief and unconvincing image of the South rebuilding itself: Ben, rolling up his shirtsleeves, appears to be readying himself to direct Jake in some work in the garden, as Mrs. Cameron and Margaret attach a sign to one of the porch columns of Cameron Hall advertising that they will take in boarders (536). The melodramatic structure of the film, and the logic of Lincoln as a figure worthy of Southern hero-worship, depends entirely on the premise that if Lincoln had not been assassinated on "the fated night of April 14, 1865" (537), all the horrors of Reconstruction that we see in the second part of the film would never have occurred. Part One ends on Dr. Cameron's anguished cry: "Our best friend is gone. What is to become of us now!" (617).

Lincoln's untimely death provides the South with a convenient explanation for the failure of Reconstruction, and it establishes Lincoln's mythic status, which was historically—and in the film—so necessary to the South's attempt to find some dignity for themselves in their defeat. The Southern cause was not after all a dignified one, which explains why a mystique had to form around the idea of the "Lost Cause." The historical Lincoln understood, or was able to convey that he understood, that "the essence of what we call the crisis of the Union was not a conflict between one group that wanted to preserve a particular way of life or value and another group who wanted to destroy it. The conflict was one in which many groups competed—all of them conservatives who sought to preserve cherished values and traditions that had come into conflict with other cherished values and traditions."[56] This explains why even Dixon could be a "passionate admirer" of Lincoln, and in 1920, in a play called *A Man of the People,* could describe Lincoln as "the savior, if not the real creator, of the American Union of free Democratic states."[57] Richard Hofstadter has described the way in which

Lincoln was able simultaneously to appeal to people who were hostile to slavery (he said it was wrong and must someday die) and to people who were hostile to blacks (he said he was opposed to their becoming socially or politically equal to whites) by insisting with regard to slavery and implying with regard to blacks that the territories not be ruined by either. Lincoln was similarly able to appeal to Young America types who wanted action and manhood, and to sentimentalists who wanted the restoration of, and regression to, a supposedly more secure past.[58]

With quintessentially melodramatic logic, Griffith portrays Lincoln as "the Great Heart." The intertitle that tells us Ben is to be hanged as a guerilla (476) is not necessary to the plot, but it reminds us that Ben is his "mother's gift to the cause" (201) and provides a scene in which Mrs. Cameron "will ask mercy from the Great Heart" (478)—described as "The mother's appeal" (480). We see a shot of Lincoln angrily denying the request of a demonstrative petitioner, who has to be led away by a White House official (483), and at first the President refuses Mrs. Cameron's plea that he intervene to save her son from hanging (487). But Elsie encourages Mrs. Cameron to appeal again, and the camera irises in on a shot of Ben in his hospital bed, demonstrating Lincoln's empathetic power to imagine the scene she has just described. Of course, he pardons her boy, as a father would pardon a son, and Mrs. Cameron is so moved with gratitude that, on a familial impulse, she nearly embraces the President (495). When she returns to the make-shift hospital, she tells Ben that "Mr. Lincoln has given back your life to me" (497), thus connecting in a single remark the apex of the public realm (the President of the United States) and the defining center of the personal realm (herself/the mother's bond with her child). Then, "Her son convalescent, Mrs. Cameron starts back for Piedmont to attend the failing father" (499). Thus, even politics becomes "familialized" in melodrama.

It is no coincidence that Dr. Cameron's health declines during the war in a direct correspondence to the deteriorating fortunes of the South. He is sickest when Ben is in the hospital, during the last days before "the surrender of Gen. Robt. E. Lee, C.S.A., to Gen. U. S. Grant, U.S.A." at Appomattox Courthouse (505). The film can be seen as an attempt by Griffith to resolve his own Oedipal conflicts;[59] and just as we can see Lincoln historically as having had a filial, or Oedipal, relation to George Washington and the "founding fathers," it can be said that Griffith, in turn, saw a parental figure in Lincoln.

In Part Two, the film's central metaphor—the birth of a nation-as-a-family—undergoes a troubled response to Lincoln's assassination. There are several vengeful assaults on actual or figurative fathers in the second part of the film: Dr. Cameron's humiliation and imprisonment by former slaves; the disenfranchisement of Piedmont's white-bearded city fathers; Lynch's manhandling of Stoneman—to list only a few of the film's coded enactments of filial hostility.

As a symbolic parricide, Lincoln's assassination in Ford's Theatre is the film's Oedipal climax. We see the father figure cut down by a son of the South, John Wilkes Booth, who shouts, "Sic semper tyrannis!" (literally: "thus always to tyrants"); and when Booth leaps from the Presidential box to the stage, he breaks his leg, in what can only be described as an example of life imitating Freud. When Baldwin writes that he cannot tell us exactly how Lydia Brown's "baleful effect" on Stoneman "helps bring about the ruin of the South," he is only half serious, for the Oedipal logic becomes clear when the mulatto housekeeper informs Stoneman of the assassination and proclaims gleefully, "You are now the greatest power in America" (611). There are shades of *Macbeth* in her exultation, for there is a sense in which Stoneman himself, who is later described as the "uncrowned king" (625) of the Reconstruction state, is the author of this regicide/parricide.

Griffith's attempt to recuperate his drama in the mainstream terms of Oedipal logic shows some strain, for he represents Lincoln as an androgynous figure—a Northern *and* a Southern hero, the "Great Heart" that understands all Americans—and ends the film on an image of Jesus Christ. In the moment before Lincoln is shot, the President draws his shawl about his shoulders, as though in response to the chill of approaching death. It is a gesture coded culturally as feminine. Like Washington before him, the historical Lincoln also combined in his character and person both masculine and distinctively feminine qualities. "[Lincoln] was the masculine, rugged rail-splitter of the West and (to some people) he would become the bearded patriarch. But the beard was offset by the shawl, and [the] picture of Lincoln going to market wearing that garment, carrying a basket and with children in tow, casts up a domesticated image indeed."[60]

With the death of Lincoln, in the film, the nation/family loses both a mother and a father, resulting in "a veritable overthrow of civilization in the South" (623). The white South, impoverished by cynical carpetbaggers, mocked by buffoonish politicians, and threatened by the frenzy of unleashed black sexuality, resorts to violent repression in a desperate attempt to restore order. Historically, the Klan "sought to take the place of both the departed personal authority of the master and the labor control function the Reconstruction state had abandoned."[61] In *The Birth of a Nation,* the Klan is described as "the organization that saved the South from the anarchy of black rule" (925). In the end, however, neither the triumph of the Ku Klux Klan nor the couplings of the Stoneman and Cameron children is enough to achieve satisfactory closure.

Without a patriarch of Lincoln's stature to preside over the new nation, Griffith feels impelled to invoke the image of Jesus Christ himself. As Freud notes, regarding Christian doctrine, "In the same deed which offers the greatest possible expiation to the father, the son also attains the goal of his wishes against the father. He becomes a god himself beside or rather in place of his father."[62] This explains the logic of ending this melodrama as Oedipal drama on an image of Jesus: the contradictions of Oedipal desire are resolved in a figure who is both son and father.

While the apocalyptic style of the ending of *The Birth of a Nation* is a closing device used frequently by Griffith during this period, it signals nothing less than a tremendous, hysterical effort to assert that, though a great deal has been lost, something even greater has been gained. The nostalgic register of the film, which began with the intertitle that introduced an image of "the Southland . . . where life runs in a quaintly way that is to be no more" (33), produces this intolerable fact: all that has been lost cannot be regained. The Oedipal tensions of *The Birth of a Nation,* also originating in a sense of something having been lost, are resolved, *après coup,* in the figure of Lincoln as a fantasy of the ideal father/mother/son— the "Great Heart." The resolution of *The Birth of a Nation*'s inherent narrative contradictions can only be achieved, therefore, in a fantasy of apocalypse and utopia.

## Notes

1. Quoted by Edmund Jenings Lee, M.D., "The Character of General Lee," in *Gen. Robert Edward Lee: Soldier, Citizen, and Christian Patriot,* ed. R. A. Brock (Richmond: Royal Publishing Co., 1897), 405.

2. Robert Penn Warren, *The Legacy of the Civil War: Meditations on the Centennial* (New York: Random House, 1961), 1.

3. D. W. Griffith, "Five Dollar 'Movies' Prophesied," *The Editor,* April 24, 1915. Reprinted in *Focus on D. W. Griffith,* ed. Harry M. Geduld (Englewood Cliffs, N.J.: Prentice-Hall, 1971), 34-35.

4. Andrew Sarris, "*Birth of a Nation,* or White Power Back When," *The Village Voice,* July 17 and July 24, 1969. Reprinted in *Focus on "The Birth of a Nation,"* ed. Fred

Silva (Englewood Cliffs, N.J.: Prentice-Hall, 1971), 107-108. Gance, incidentally, described *The Birth of a Nation* as a *chanson de geste.* This is an apt description, considering the historical discrepancy in the earliest extant and most famous *chanson* of the Charlemagne cycle, *La Chanson de Roland,* which has Roland fighting the Muslim Saracens at Roncevaux, when in reality, Charlemagne and the Saracens were allies at Roncevaux, fighting against the Christian Basques. As in Griffith's film, legend rewrites history to conform to ideological imperatives.

5. Alan T. Nolan, *Lee Considered: General Robert E. Lee and Civil War History* (Chapel Hill: University of North Carolina Press, 1991), 3.

6. Philip Rosen, "Securing the Historical: Historiography and the Classical Cinema," in *Cinema Histories, Cinema Practices,* ed. Patricia Mellencamp and Philip Rosen, American Film Institute Monograph Series, vol. 4 (Frederick, Md.: University Publications of America, 1984), 23.

7. Nolan, *Lee Considered,* 164.

8. Robert F. Durden, quoted by Nolan, *Lee Considered,* 164.

9. Russell Merritt, "Dixon, Griffith, and the Southern Legend: A Cultural Analysis of *The Birth of a Nation,*" in *Cinema Examined,* ed. Richard Dyer MacCann and Jack C. Ellis (New York: E. P. Dutton, 1982), 169.

10. Everett Carter, "Cultural History Written with Lightning: The Significance of *The Birth of a Nation,*" *American Quarterly* 12 (Fall 1960). Reprinted in Silva, *Focus on "Birth,"* 136.

11. Ibid., 138.

12. Lillian Gish, with Ann Pinchot, *Lillian Gish: The Movies, Mr. Griffith, and Me* (Englewood Cliffs, N.J.: Prentice-Hall, 1969), 132.

13. James Chandler discusses the influence of the historical romance as a literary form on Griffith in "The Historical Novel Goes to Hollywood: Scott, Griffith, and the Film Epic Today," reprinted in this volume, 225-249.

14. Thomas Dixon, *The Clansman: An Historical Romance of the Ku Klux Klan* (New York: Grosset & Dunlap Publishers, 1905).

15. The Nazi period in Germany is an even sadder and more gruesome chapter in "the history of the Aryan race"; and it is not surprising that members of the modern Ku Klux Klan have appropriated the specific ideological formulations and symbology of Hitler's fascism.

16. Rosen, "Securing the Historical," 23.

17. Quoted by Sergei Eisenstein, *Film Form,* ed. and trans. Jay Leyda (New York: Harcourt Brace, 1949), 206.

18. Quoted by Carter, "Cultural History Written with Lightning," 136.

19. Richard Griffith, "Foreword," *D. W. Griffith: American Film Master* by Iris Barry, rev. Eileen Bowser (New York: The Museum of Modern Art/Doubleday, 1965), 5.

20. William Monroe Trotter, quoted by Richard Schickel, *D. W. Griffith: An American Life* (New York: Simon and Schuster, 1984), 299.

21. Frequently after 1854 Lincoln insisted that "all I have asked or desired anywhere is that [slavery] should be placed back again upon the basis that the fathers of our government originally placed it upon." By this, Lincoln meant that "as those fathers marked [slavery], so let it be again marked, as an evil not to be extended, but to be tolerated and protected only because of and only so far as its actual presence among us makes that toleration and protection a necessity." (Quoted by George B. Forgie, *Patricide in the House Divided: A Psychological Interpretation of Lincoln and His Age* [New York: Norton, 1979], 276.)

22. Rod Gragg, *The Illustrated Confederate Reader* (New York: Harper & Row, 1989), 224.

23. Nolan, *Lee Considered,* 14.

24. Griffith articulated his melodramatic method by indicating his attitude toward war as a moral problem in relation to its value as spectacle when he remarked: "War is hideous, but it can be made the background for beauty, beauty of idea." (Quoted by Schickel, *D. W. Griffith,* 290.)

25. Reprinted in full in John Cuniberti, *"The Birth of a Nation": A Formal Shot-by-Shot Analysis Together with Microfiche* (Woodbridge, Conn.: Research Publications, 1979), 196-198.

26. There is no hard evidence that the film ever actually included shots of a wholesale deportation of American blacks to Africa, although there is some indication that there may have been an intertitle referring to "Lincoln's solution," "Back to Liberia!" (see Cuniberti, *"The Birth of a Nation,"* 166-167). If this intertitle had once been in the film, there may have been an image to support it, as Seymour Stern claims to remember having seen. The synopsis submitted to the U.S. Copyright Office on February 8, 1915, includes the comment, "Lincoln's plan of restoring the negroes to Africa was dreamed of only, never carried out," which lends credence to the hypothesis that the film once included at least an intertitle to this effect.

27. This synopsis was printed in Clune's Program, 1915, and submitted to the U.S. Copyright Office, February 13, 1915. (Reprinted in Cuniberti, *"The Birth of a Nation,"* 180.)

28. Nolan, *Lee Considered,* 147.

29. Geduld, *Focus on D. W. Griffith,* 98-99.

30. Quoted by Garry Wills, "The Presbyterian Nietzsche," *The New York Review of Books,* January 16, 1992, 3.

31. Gish, *Lillian Gish,* 136.

32. Wills, "The Presbyterian Nietzsche," 3.

33. Simon Schama, "Clio Has a Problem," *The New York Times Magazine,* September 8, 1991, 32.

34. *The Civil War.* A film by Ken Burns. Produced by Ken Burns and Ric Burns/Florentine Films and WETA-TV. Written by Geoffrey C. Ward, Ric Burns, and Ken Burns. Narrated by David McCullough. Edited by Paul Barnes, Bruce Shaw, and Tricia Reidy.

35. Quoted by Georgia Brown, "Patsies," *The Village Voice,* March 31, 1992, 58. Brown's article is mostly about a debate sponsored by *The Nation* at Town Hall (New York City) about Oliver Stone's film *JFK.*

36. Wilson, quoted by Wills, "The Presbyterian Nietzsche," 3.

37. Quoted by Forgie, *Patricide in the House Divided,* 271.

38. Quoted in ibid., 271.

39. Ibid., 268.

40. Cf. the following: Rick Altman, "*The Lonely Villa* and Griffith's Paradigmatic Style," *Quarterly Review of Film Studies* 6, no. 2 (Spring 1981): 123-134; Nick Browne, "Griffith's Family Discourse: Griffith and Freud," *Quarterly Review of Film Studies* 6, no. 1 (Winter 1981): 67-80; Russell Merritt, "D. W. Griffith's *The Birth of a Nation:* Going After Little Sister," in *Close Viewings: An Anthology of New Film Criticism,* ed. Peter Lehman (Tallahassee: The Florida State University Press, 1990), 215-237.

41. Gish, *Lillian Gish,* 133.

42. Nick Browne, "Griffith's Family Discourse," 79.

43. "Virtue is almost inevitably represented by a young heroine, though in classical French melodrama (unlike later American melodrama) she need not be a virgin, for it is moral sentiment more than technical chastity that is at issue." (Peter Brooks, *The Melodramatic Imagination: Balzac, Henry James, Melodrama, and the Mode of Excess* [New Haven: Yale University Press, 1976], 32.)

44. Synopsis submitted to the U.S. Copyright Office, February 13, 1915. (Reprinted in Cuniberti, "*The Birth of a Nation,*" 180.)

45. Thomas F. Gossett, *Race: The History of an Idea in America* (New York: Schocken Books, 1965), 271.

46. James Baldwin, *The Devil Finds Work* (New York: The Dial Press, 1976), 45.

47. Gish, *Lillian Gish,* 134.

48. The essential elements of the film's ideological underpinnings are made starkly clear by Susan Brownmiller's observation that, "Rape is to women as lynching was to blacks: the ultimate physical threat by which all men keep all women in a state of psychological intimidation." (*Against Our Will: Men, Women, and Rape* [New York: Bantam Books, 1975], 281.)

49. The synopsis printed in Clune's Program, 1915, and submitted to the U.S. Copyright Office, February 13, 1915, adverts to Lynch's supposedly *unnatural* character in this compressed description of the context of Lynch's supreme villainy: "In the meantime, Stoneman returns and Lynch tells him he is to marry Elsie. Stoneman now realizes the Frankenstein [*sic*] he has himself created, but is helpless until the Klan arrives, disarms all the negroes and rescues Elsie." (Reprinted in Cuniberti, "*The Birth of a Nation,*" 180.)

50. Baldwin, *The Devil Finds Work,* 45.

51. Ibid.

52. Ibid., 48.

53. Ibid., 48-49.

54. Ibid., 45.

55. Ibid., 47.

56. Forgie, *Patricide in the House Divided,* 184-185.

57. Edward Wagenknecht and Anthony Slide, *The Films of D. W. Griffith* (New York: Crown Publishers, 1975), 60.

58. Cited by Forgie, *Patricide in the House Divided,* 253-254.

59. See Michael Rogin's "'The Sword Became a Flashing Vision': D. W. Griffith's *The Birth of a Nation,*" reprinted in this volume, 250-293.

60. Forgie, *Patricide in the House Divided,* 254-255.

61. Eric Foner, *Reconstruction: America's Unfinished Revolution, 1863-1877* (New York: Harper & Row, 1988), 428.

62. Sigmund Freud, *Totem and Taboo* [1913], trans. A. A. Brill (New York: Vintage Books, 1946), 199.

## JEFFREY C. STEWART (ESSAY DATE 1997)

**SOURCE:** Stewart, Jeffrey C. "Paul Robeson and the Problem of Modernism." In *Rhapsodies in Black: Art of the Harlem Renaissance,* pp. 92-101. Berkeley: University of California Press, the Hayward Gallery, and the Institute of International Visual Arts, 1997.

*In the following essay, Stewart chronicles the career of Paul Robeson in the context of the Harlem Renaissance, citing the actor as an example of the struggle faced by African Americans in their efforts to fit into white modernistic culture of that time.*

Modernism is a tricky word when used in association with the Harlem Renaissance. Modernism most often refers to the rebellious artistic and literary movements of the late-nineteenth and early-twentieth-century Europeans and white Americans, whose sense of alienation from the rise of the corporate industrialized state was reflected in the breakdown of the representational and the familiar in literature and art.[1] But modernism is also linked to more sociological processes, usually termed modernity: social forces such as industrialization, urbanization, secularization and commodification, and technological innovations such as photography and film that reflect the rise of the machine age in Western Europe and America.[2] It is because of these social forces and technological innovations that America is usually thought to have reached modernity in the 1920s—the Model A, the rise of motion pictures, the radio, etc.—but it is because of modernism that the Harlem Renaissance, according to many commentators, emerged as a distinctive African-American literary and artistic movement in the 1920s.[3] This argument is made rather explicitly in George Hutchinson's recent book, *The Harlem Renaissance in Black and White.*[4] When we add to this Houston Baker's argument, in *Modernism and the Harlem Renaissance,* that modernism in African-American culture is voiced by an imagined community or nationalism in turn-of-the-century literary forms, the scope for what is and is not modernism widens considerably.[5] Yet several factors have prevented the African-American from fitting neatly into the white American narrative of modernism or modernity in American life, and a brief look at the Harlem Renaissance and the career of Paul Robeson, one of its most talented prodigies, may help to explain why.

My impression of the limitations of the usual sense of modernism comes from Raymond Williams's posthumously published book, *The Politics of Modernism,* in which he shows how modernism has been a way of elevating one part of an enormously complex and varied constellation of social forces and movements around the turn of the century.[6] By privileging the artistic and literary rebellions of the late nineteenth and early twentieth century, modernist theorists usually validate the primacy of the art object as the center of any aesthetic interpretation and consider the social, political and economic underpinnings of cultural productions as marginal. For black intellectuals what that has meant is that one is forced to look at African or African-American art in these terms; and if it is not spare, pristine, highly formalized and elitist—then it is not modern, not important, and not to be valued. This is essentially Houston A. Baker's point. But Baker constructs a competing modernism, one that redefines, again, what is important and thereby marginalizes that which is not in an effort to recapture for the Harlem Renaissance the prestige associated with the term. In other words, the real modernism must be black and must be a nationalist discourse. Challenging this view in his book *The Harlem Renaissance in Black and White,* George Hutchinson argues that the Harlem Renaissance was modernist and laudably redefines the original notion of modernism to include not only the literary but also the broader philosophical and anthropological writings of William James, John Dewey, Franz Boas and Horace Kallen, which launched cultural pluralism and made it the reigning ideology of twentieth-century liberalism. Here, at least, in Hutchinson's reformulation, the really distinctive characteristic of Harlem Renaissance modernism was that it was an *interracial* cultural strategy for transforming America into an ethnic 'pluriverse'—an argument that surfaces more in the writings of W.E.B. Du Bois, Alain Locke and Charles S. Johnson than in the writings of their mentors, James, Boas and Robert Park. But Hutchinson's formulation ignores those black cultural formations of the 1920s that are not interracial, that were developed solely for a black audience and linked directly to a segregated social formation lived by the majority of African-Americans during that period. Even more importantly, such a definition of Harlem Renaissance modernism

ignores the issues of control over the ownership and production of knowledge and culture in the 1920s. Du Bois and Johnson, for example, edited the magazines *The Crisis* and *Opportunity,* respectively, which published most of Harlem's poetry, fiction and visual illustration, but they operated at the behest of largely white organizations with whom both editors had problematic relationships. More broadly, black intellectuals such as Du Bois and Locke did not interact with James and Boas as cultural or social equals; and neither did Paul Robeson, despite his sometimes affectionate collaborations with Eugene O'Neill and Carl Van Vechten. A system of white vetting of black intellectuals and artists ensured that when the writers or actors veered too far outside of the parameters of white modernist enthusiasm, the black recipients of white patronage often found themselves abandoned. That experience spawned what I would call the 'double consciousness' of Harlem Renaissance modernism, that is the experience of feeling oneself at one moment an artist, qua artist, à la modernism, with considerable inflated social status, and then a Negro, to paraphrase Du Bois.[7] The lived experience of modernism for many African-American intellectuals and artists in the 1920s included the sense that if one violated the prescriptions of modernist discourse, if one dared to foreground the historical and contemporary oppression of peoples of color in one's notion of culture, then one fell out of the loop. Paul Robeson's struggle to create a career reveals much about the problem of modernism facing a black artist and about why, in the 1930s, he broke with the modernist notion of culture to begin an analysis of the global reach of racism and imperialism.

Let us start with a film, *Body and Soul* (1924), made by the independent black film-maker Oscar Micheaux, and the first film that Robeson appeared in.[8] Developed for, and marketed to, an all-black audience, this film tells the story of a black criminal, played by Robeson, who escapes from jail, poses as a minister and takes advantage of a black community, especially a young woman, whose God-fearing mother cannot accept her daughter's assertions that 'Reverend Jenkins' is a drunk, a faker and a rapist. This film is modern because it breaks with the 'Black Victorian' expectation that black people always present a positive image of themselves in their art—a position in the 1920s best expressed by Du Bois that 'all art is propaganda for or against the race'—and instead provides a searing self-critique of the folly of the black community, especially its over-confidence in black ministers, whom Micheaux was known

Paul Robeson in a scene from the 1933 film adaptation of *The Emperor Jones.*

to dislike.[9] The film is modern in a formal sense: it uses dream sequences and flashbacks, and it cuts between scenes to create not only movement in the story but also the sense that one is part of the community portrayed. The film is also modern for what it takes on: it is one of the first (if not *the* first) films to contain an African-American rape scene (a black man violating a black woman); it powerfully portrays the intergenerational conflict between old and 'New Negroes', the principal conflict of the Harlem Renaissance; and it deconstructs the black self-help ideology with a deep and unrelenting irony. For example, a portrait of Booker T. Washington hangs on the mother's wall, but the film shows how feeble Washington's vision of the black independent businessman has become when the 'black businessman' (so captioned in the film) is a crooked liquor salesman and gambling-parlor owner. Another scene reveals the irony of the 'hooping and howling' preaching of the black ministry; Jerkins's exuberant preaching is fueled by alcohol, which he drinks secretly under the podium. Even though Jenkins is an escaped criminal, it is astonishing that Micheaux was able to get

away with such a devastating critique of the ministry. The viewer needs little imagination to grasp the movie's not too subtle point—that most ministers are exploiters of their communities. But what is exceptional is Micheaux's casting of Robeson in a double role as two brothers—Jenkins, the criminal masquerading as a minister, and Sylvester, the budding inventor—for it stresses the point, absent from the more celebrated Eugene O'Neill play, *The Emperor Jones,* that not all black men are evil.[10] As Sylvester, Robeson steps forward to ask for the daughter's hand in marriage when she has become pregnant by Jenkins. Even here, Micheaux uses the model of the good black man to make another critique of the black community. When Sylvester makes his offer, he is rejected by the mother because he does not have enough money; while there are good Negro men, their ultimate valuation by the community is based on materialism rather than character.

This film does not even appear in George Hutchinson's index to his book because it does not conform to Hutchinson's thesis that what was important about the Harlem Renaissance was that it was interracial. The omission of the film rein-scribes a familiar narrative in the history of black culture in America—that nothing existed prior to the discovery of black themes by Columbus-like whites—but, more seriously, the conceptualiza-tion that Harlem Renaissance modernism was interracial implies that there was not an indig-enous modernist movement within the black community. *Body and Soul* interrupts that narra-tive by showing that the modernism within the black community was a movement committed to breaking with the tradition of respectability,—of always 'putting the best foot forward' in the arts to convince whites that blacks were equal—and, instead, uses the arts as a self-critical mirror on the black community. Nor does the film fit easily in the frame that Houston Baker constructs in *Mod-ernism and the Black Renaissance*. Here Baker ana-lyzes the literature leading up to and including Alain Locke's *The New Negro: An Interpretation* to argue that the modernism of the black renais-sance consists of the literary 'sounds' of an 'imag-ined community' or nationalism among African-Americans in the 1920s.[11] *Body and Soul* is certainly a film about an autonomous black community and yet the film goes beyond nationalistic con-sciousness to expose, as Frantz Fanon would put it, the 'pitfalls of national consciousness' for the black community.[12] In a way, *Body and Soul* is a narrative on race as false consciousness: skin color is not a reliable barometer of character or moral-ity. In this sense, *Body and Soul* moves beyond the concerns of race and nation to address a com-munity that listens to its youth, listens closely to the 'sounds' of malignancy even among its own.

The reality, however, is that Robeson could never have been a star of the Harlem Renaissance if he had relied exclusively on parts in plays and films written by poorly financed African-American producers like Micheaux. As with many other successful 'New Negroes' of the 1920s, Robe-son had to practice another brand of double con-sciousness—to keep one foot in black modernism until he could gain enough support from the white modernists to lever himself into a career as a crossover artist. And to enter that world the talented black performer had to be 'discovered' or vetted by white playwrights and artists, and act or otherwise participate in Negro productions writ-ten or created by artists that were not really mod-ernist in the radical aesthetic sense of late-nineteenth and early-twentieth-century modernism in Europe and America. Why?

The reason is not hard to find for the Negro was never considered part of the machine age: indeed, in the popular myth of John Henry, the Negro is eulogized precisely because he resists mo-dernity.[13] In order to enter modernist discourse the African-American had to do so as the primi-tive. In Robeson's first major play, for example, *Taboo* (written by the white woman, Mary Wiborg), he plays first a lazy African-American from Louisiana and then an African king, honored by his regal robes in the American production, demeaned and humiliated by his tawdry garb in the London version.[14] A noble savage in New York and then a savage buffoon in London. In both cases the Negro becomes interesting to moderns only through a maneuver that imprisons him in his primitive past. When Eugene O'Neill cast Robeson in the play *All God's Chillun Got Wings,* a modern love story between a black man and a white woman, the poster for the production de-picted an African mask. In the title role of the 1924 production of The *Emperor Jones* (O'Neill decided to stop using Charles Gilpin, the origina-tor of the role, because he had become too uppity), Robeson, though initially an assimilated African-American, succumbs to a primitive fear of witch doctors.[15] Robeson's other major acting role of the 1920s, as Jim singing 'Old Man River' in *Show Boat,* casts him as a lazy southern darkie, whose resis-tance to work is part of his charisma as a preindus-trial figure.[16] That role, and others such as John Henry in the 1940 play of that name by Roark Bradford (Bradford stated that Paul Robeson *was* John Henry) suggests that romanticism is a far more accurate genre for the literature of the move-ment than modernism.[17] For what distinguished white usages of Robeson's talents in the 1920s and 1930s was a symbolic return to the past, a past in which the pre-industrial, pre-modern qualities of the Negro were both romanticized and envied by the white author or viewer.

Romanticism also characterizes the frame in which much of the 'New Negro' literary and dra-matic efforts of the 1920s most easily fits: films, unlike Micheaux's, that were intended primarily for a white or educated African-American audi-ence. The dominant narrative of the Harlem Re-naissance was nostalgia, especially for those, like Robeson's father, who had participated in the Great Migration that brought hundreds of thou-sands of African-Americans out of the South into northern cities during the 1910s and 1920s. In that move north, the dominant refrain was a long-ing for the South, a note that is overwhelming in

Jean Toomer's *Cane,* the short fiction of Rudolph Fisher, and in the short stories and novels of Zora Neale Hurston.[18] Much of this writing is pre-realism rather than post-realism, as in the literary modernism of the late nineteenth century that is so often regarded as the model for the black movement of the 1920s. What is at issue here is nothing less than what W.B. Yeats and others searched for in the Irish Renaissance—a romantic re-engagement with a folk tradition that is still within reach historically and emotionally for an educated generation of cosmopolitans.[19] Here Robeson uniquely embodies the dominant note of the Harlem Renaissance, for his enormous success in the 1920s comes as a concert singer of the spirituals, music of the nineteenth century, rather than as a singer of the blues or jazz of the 1920s.[20] White and black romantic constructions of the Negro's cultural identity dominated in the Harlem Renaissance, and those forms that were most successful were those that blended both.

And this is not surprising. The 1920s was a transitional period in American history for African-Americans socially, economically and politically, one in which the locus of black presence is shifting northward and urbanward, thereby remapping the African-American landscape and the American perception of what blackness means in American culture.[21] Negro history inevitably remains in the subconscious of America's most creative white people and the South remains in the subconscious of the recent black migrant.

Of course for Hutchinson and other critics of the Harlem Renaissance the exploration of a deeply malignant persona is what makes Eugene O'Neill's *The Emperor Jones* the archetypal modernist drama of the 1920s.[22] The play narrates the story of how an African-American Pullman porter gains control of the indigenous population of a Caribbean island (one 'that has not yet been self-determined by white Marines') through brutality and terror, but plagued by voodoo spells, dreams and hallucinations, he is eventually assassinated by the island's witch doctor for his crimes against the people.[23] *The Emperor Jones* has been and can be read many ways—as a narrative on what Marcus Garvey's rule in a mythical little Africa would really come to; as a critique of Americanism imported into the Caribbean; and as a commentary on the 'Black As Other', not only in America but also in adopted homelands like Haiti. But many black intellectuals, both in the 1920s and later in histories of the Harlem Renaissance, have criticized the play, although as Hutchinson argues

persuasively, some African-American intellectuals such as Alain Locke and Montgomery Gregory, the organizer of the Howard Players, loved the play, especially with Gilpin in the lead role.[24] But when the play was presented on stage in Harlem during the 1930s and Emperor Jones became fearful of the 'ha'nts' in the forest, Langston Hughes recalled that those in the Lafayette Theatre audience laughed and screamed to the actor: 'Them ain't no ghosts, fool! . . . Why don't you come on out o' the jungle—back to Harlem where you belong?'[25] That was, in fact, a message that could have been delivered directly to the playwright. For *The Emperor Jones* was directed towards a white audience or at least an audience that thought about African-American identity in Victorian and primitivist categories.

*The Emperor Jones* was certainly modernist in terms of its complex approach to its central character, Jones, who is driven by complicated impulses—conscious desires to be free, to rise above his station, to be respected, but also unconscious needs to control, abuse, and perhaps be loved by, others. But the play remains problematical in that it maps this identity with a Haitian primitivism that replicates the same Victorian racial dichotomies of white man/rational, black man/irrational that are endemic to nineteenth-century colonialism. That Jones, a conniving, coldly calculating, supremely rationalist and rationalizing ruler would suddenly become paralyzed by superstition and fear of ghosts at the end of the play is preposterous simply from the standpoint of plausible character development and is believable only if the audience draws upon its Victorian notions of black people as ultimately superstitious and irrational, no matter how sophisticated they may appear to be. Without such primitivist notions of blackness, the Harlem audience just laughed. Like many other modernist projects of the 1920s, *The Emperor Jones* inevitably fell back into portraying black people within the Victorian categories that post-modernism would challenge.

Why were such modernist liberals as Eugene O'Neill unable to break with the Victorian racial construction of black identity? In part it was related to the fact that another modernist, Sigmund Freud, had also reified primitivist categories when he argued in *Totem and Taboo* (published in English in 1918) that primitive peoples had preserved a connection with unconscious and spiritual impulses in their daily lives. Literary modernists of the 1920s who wished to portray such 'deep' feelings naturally turned to Africa and African-Americans as part of modernism's romantic attempt at recovering a kind of consciousness—seeing spirits and ghosts, for example—that had been lost by most civilized men.[26] In Jones, O'Neill fused what would normally be considered two separate identities—that of a white conqueror and a black primitive—in one character, and by having the character succumb to self-destruction, O'Neill suggested his critique of Western mentality. But O'Neill narrated his critique only through a kind of blackface: he projected the drama of self-destruction on to the black man who adopts the values, ironically, of Western capitalism—greed, ruthless individualism, unrelenting self-promotion, to the detriment of the larger community, the Caribbean black people on the Emperor's island. It does not take much imagination to realize that Eric Lott's analysis of the motivation behind nineteenth-century blackface (which O'Neill donned for one play)—that the white actor in blackface, here a white writer for our purposes, could act out as a black person those qualities or issues he could not take responsibility for as a white man—applies to O'Neill's play.[27] The play narrates the history of exploitation in the Caribbean, but without any reference to the history of colonialism that engendered that exploitation. Modernism tended to silence the historical and social context of the conflicts in modernity, and announce the central drama of the twentieth century as essentially an internal psychological conflict, in which whiteness was not implicated. But imagine, for a moment, that the character of Emperor Jones had been written as a white man: that would have made a revolutionary and more psychologically provocative play!

To do so, however, would mean to repudiate the privilege that O'Neill and other so-called modernists of the Harlem Renaissance were not ready to relinquish. We see a similar pattern in Carl Van Vechten, Robeson's other patron of the mid-1920s, who was the single most important figure in publicizing Robeson as a singer of the spirituals, a man who gave white people tours of Harlem, who wrote one of the best novels of the period, *Nigger Heaven,* and who epitomized in his personality, at least, a modernist boulevardian.[28] Van Vechten not only encouraged Robeson in his study of the spirituals but also in his discovery of Africa. But rather than a modernist, Van Vechten was a romanticist with an Oscar Wildean aestheticism: in his photographs he would pose African-Americans with African artifacts—an African mask, for example, in his photograph of Billie Holiday—as if the viewer could tease out the transatlantic connections. As long as Robeson was content to play the primitive for European and American romantics, he could enjoy social freedom, associate with whites in conditions of relative social equality and was an appropriate subject for Van Vechten. But when Robeson began to question the imperialistic and capitalistic roots of racism, when he became associated with Communism and anti-racist activism, and when he began to commit himself to creating an alternative to the exploitative system of labor and race that existed in mid-twentieth-century America, Van Vechten, for one, dropped him.[29]

Finally, it is worth looking at what happened when black and white romanticism came together, rather disastrously, in the film *Sanders of the River*. As Martin Duberman, Robeson's biographer, writes: 'early in the summer of 1934, the Korda [Alexander and Zoltan] brothers offered him the role of the African chief Bosambo in a film they were planning based on Edgar Wallace's book *Sanders of the River*.'[30] Robeson jumped at the chance because of his increasing interest in the study of Africa and in identifying himself as an African. He thought he had found a dignified African role to play, in part because of the willingness of the Kordas to include footage collected in Africa that showcased African folkways. As in *Body and Soul* Robeson's character, Bosambo, is an escaped criminal, but this time a good-hearted one who becomes the benevolent chief of his tribe under the tutelage of Sanders, an English commissioner. Bosambo approaches 'Sandy' to get his help against his enemy, King Mofolaba, the 'Bad African King', a slave trader who wants to drive the British out of Africa. Sanders takes on Bosambo as a collaborator through whom 'Sandy' can more easily collect taxes for the British. The two African kings maintain an uneasy peace until Sandy decides to return to England and two unscrupulous British traders spread the rumor 'Sandy is dead. There is no law any more.' In the scenes that follow, the natives become 'restless', war dances erupt, even the elephants, hyenas and giraffes become distraught, simply because an English commissioner has left. When the inevitable showdown comes between Bosambo and Mofolaba, it is Sandy who must rescue Bosambo from death at the hands of his adversary and re-establish peace among the Africans. Although the Kordas must have thought of their film as modern—it portrays a close relationship between a white man and an African; contains a scene where one Englishman defends the Africans against charges that they are 'savages'; and shows Africans willing to adopt English ways in their march towards peace and prosperity—there are images of African women dancing bare-breasted, witch doctors whipping up the natives into a fever pitch and African men climbing trees like monkeys. It reads as a stereotype today, and apparently did so in 1935. When Robeson saw the edited film he was aghast at how completely the film reified the notion that English colonialism was good because it brought peace to warring African tribes. Robeson stated afterwards that the film had been recut to glorify imperialism, suggesting that there were no such elements in the scenes in which he acted.[31] But there are too many scenes in which Robeson participates to make that explanation completely satisfactory. One of the most embarrassing episodes takes place near the end of the film. Sandy is about to leave and one of the African kings states, 'We love one another now, and you know why, Lord Sandy? Because we know that if we don't, you will punish us,' to which Sandy replies, 'That's right.' Robeson is standing right next to him when the king articulates the ideology of African dependency.

There could be several explanations for Robeson's naivety in this instance. He wanted the film to be different and to rise above the cheap characterizations of Africa and African folkways in popular media, and he believed that the Kordas, who shot footage on location in Africa, had been true to his vision. In addition, I believe that Robeson's enthusiasm for a film that would show African dances, dress and social practices eclipsed the film's narrative, particularly the ways in which the Kordas reworked Edgar Wallace's story so that it ultimately glorified British colonial administration.[32] This interest in the anthropological was part of the black romanticism of the Harlem Renaissance and after the filming Robeson began to realize how inadequate that Harlem Renaissance ideology—whether we call it modernism or romanticism—was for him, as a black man, self-conscious about the influence his cultural productions would have. Modernism as it had germinated in the 1920s and in regard to the African-American had failed to destroy white privilege or European colonialism, and it had not created the social formation in which cultural productions funded by white capital could imagine an alternative post-colonial world for people of African descent. Robeson realized that simply pursuing his art and displaying his talent—and trusting white American and British directors because they treated him nicely—would not result in movies and performances that would honor the black experience. He learned that he could not escape the reality of race distinction by going abroad or confining himself to his art. Precisely at the moment in his life when he benefited the most from the commodification of the primitive on stage and in film, his frustration with the limits of his role as an actor in modernist projects grew.

In the 1930s Paul Robeson moved out of the black modernist nationalism of the 1920s and the white primitivist modernism of Greenwich Village to fashion a new identity for himself as a black artist who was an activist leader of a global cultural and political movement. It was partly because Robeson was a performing artist that his struggle and failure to craft what he saw as authentic representations of the black experience forced him into a confrontation with the economics of cultural production that radicalized him. That struggle pointed up his own dependency on romantic white patronage and opened his eyes to the ways in which he and his art were used to advance the racial propaganda he rejected. Yes, interracial modernist artistic productions made it possible for a small segment of the black middle class to live more integrated and aesthetically rich lives; but the structures of racism and colonialism remained, and their power was veiled by the illusion that creating works of art transformed the economic and social conditions that underlay them. Try as he might, Robeson's collaborations with white modernists ended up reproducing the very structures of domination that he wished to overthrow. Disillusioned with the limits of the modernist artistic space, Robeson moved out into a political space in which he could challenge the social formations of racism and colonialism. He would later argue that a fundamental transformation of American society and international capitalism was necessary if the world was to be made safe for democracy. His contribution would be to extend the notion of culture beyond the modernist frame and, in so doing, point the way towards the Direct Action Movement of the 1950s and the Black Arts Movement of the 1960s.

## Notes

I wish to thank Gilbert Morris for conversations on this subject and Fath Davis Ruffins for reading and making comments on an early draft of this essay. I also wish to thank Marta Reid Stewart for her support during the writing of this essay.

1. Although there are exceptions, most of the theorizing in relation to the Harlem Renaissance has borrowed more from literary than visual art notions of modernism. Two early and remarkably clear articles on the subject are Harry Levin 'What Was Modernism?', *Mas-*

sachusetts *Review* I, August 1960, pp. 609-30, and Robert Martin Adams 'What Was Modernism?', *Hudson Review* 31, Spring 1978, pp. 19-38. A veritable 'renaissance' of scholarly writing on modernism seems to be occurring. Consider Frederick Jameson, *Theory of Culture,* Y. Hameda, Tokyo, 1994; Bonnie Kime Scott, *Refiguring Modernism,* Indiana University Press, Bloomington, 1995; Joseph N. Riddel, *The Turning Word: American Literary Modernism and Continental Theory,* University of Pennsylvania Press, Philadelphia, 1996; Carola M. Kaplan and Anne B. Simpson, eds., *Seeing Double: Revisioning Edwardian and Modernist Literature,* St. Martin's Press, New York, 1996; Andrew Hewitt, *Political Inversions: Homosexuality, Fascism, & the Modernist Imaginary,* Stanford University Press, Stanford, 1996; Jack Selzer, *Kenneth Burke in Greenwich Village: Conversing with the Moderns, 1915-1931,* University of Wisconsin Press, Madison, 1996; Terri A. Mester, *Movement and Modernism: Yeats, Eliot, Lawrence, Williams, and Early Twentieth-Century Dance,* University of Arkansas Press, Fayetteville, 1997; Daniel R. Schwartz, *Reconfiguring Modernism: Explorations in the Relationships between Modern Art and Modern Literature,* St. Martin's Press, New York, 1997; David Weir, *Anarchy and Culture: the Aesthetic Politics of Modernism,* University of Massachusetts Press, Amherst, 1997; and Joyce Piell Wexler, *Who Paid for Modernism: Art, Money, and the Fiction of Conrad, Joyce, and Lawrence,* University of Arkansas Press, Fayetteville, 1997, among many others. For recent investigations of modernism in the visual arts and the Harlem Renaissance, see Richard J. Powell, *The Blues Aesthetic: Black Culture and Modernism,* Washington Project for the Arts, Washington, 1989, and Amy Helene Kirsche, *Aaron Douglas: Art, Race, and the Harlem Renaissance,* University Press of Mississippi, Jackson, 1995.

2. Raymond A. Williams, ed., *The Politics of Modernism: Against the New Conformists,* with an introduction by Tony Pinkney, Verso, London, 1989, and Peter Wagner, *A Sociology of Modernity: Liberty and Discipline,* Routledge, London & New York, 1994.

3. For a discussion of modernity in relation to the United States, see Alan Trachtenberg, *The Incorporation of America: Culture and Society in the Gilded Age,* Hill & Wang, New York, 1982, especially pp. 38-69, 182-234; Robert Sklar, *Movie-Made America: A Cultural History of American Movies,* Random House, New York, 1975.

4. George Hutchinson, *The Harlem Renaissance in Black and White,* Oxford University Press, London and New York, 1996. Nathan Irvin Huggins's *Harlem Renaissance* (Oxford University Press, New York, 1971) is the classic comparative analysis of the Harlem Renaissance in relation to American and European modernism.

5. Houston A. Baker, *Modernism and the Harlem Renaissance,* University of Chicago Press, Chicago, 1987.

6. Raymond A. Williams, op. cit.

7. W.E.B. Du Bois, 'Of Our Spiritual Strivings', *The Souls of Black Folk* (1903) in *W.E.B. Du Bois Writings,* The Library Press of America, New York, 1986, p. 364.

8. Martin Bauml Duberman, *Paul Robeson,* Alfred A. Knopf, New York, 1988, p. 77. See also Donald Bogle, *Blacks in American Films and Television: An Encyclopedia,* Garland Publishing, Inc., New York & London, 1988, pp. 32-33.

9. For discussion of Black Victorianism, see Jeffrey C. Stewart, 'Alain Locke and Georgia Douglas Johnson: Washington Patrons of Afro-American Modernism', in David McAleavey, ed., *Washington and Washington Writing,* Center for Washington Area Studies, George Washington University, Washington, 1986; and Fath Davis Ruffins, 'Mythos, Memory, and History: African American Preservation Efforts, 1820-1990', in Ivan Karp, Christine Mullen Kreamer and Steven D. Lavine, eds, *Museums and Communities: The Politics of Public Culture,* Smithsonian Institution, Washington and London, 1992, pp. 513-21. For Du Bois's discussion of art and propaganda, see 'The Criteria of Negro Art', *Crisis* 32, October 1926, pp. 290-97. Micheaux's attitude towards ministers is noted in Donald Bogle, op. cit. p. 33.

10. Eugene O'Neill, *The Emperor Jones, 'Anna Christie'. The Hairy Ape,* Vintage Books, New York, 1995, pp. 3-41.

11. Alain Locke, *The New Negro: An Interpretation,* Albert and Charles Boni, New York, 1925. For discussion of 'imagined community', see Benedict Anderson, *Imagined Communities: Reflections on the Origins and Spread of Nationalism,* Verso, London and New York, 1996.

12. Frantz Fanon, *The Wretched of the Earth,* translated by Constance Farrington and with a preface by Jean-Paul Sartre, Grove Press, New York, 1963, pp. 148-205.

13. Guy B. Johnson, *John Henry: Tracking Down a Negro Legend,* AMS Press, New York, 1969.

14. Program for *Taboo,* 1922, Theatre Collection, New York Public Library for the Performing Arts.

15. Joel Pfister, *Staging Depth: Eugene O'Neill and the Politics of Psychological Discourse,* University of North Carolina Press, Chapel Hill, 1995, p. 134.

16. Martin Bauml Duberman, op. cit., p. 114. Duberman quotes J.A. Rogers, a correspondent for the *Amsterdam News,* as repelled by 'the character of Joe's being simply another instance of the "lazy, good-natured, lolling darkey" stereotype "that exists more in white men's fancy than in reality."'

17. Roark Bradford, 'Paul Robeson is John Henry', *Collier's Magazine,* 13 January 1940. Frank Kermode offers another interpretation of the relation of primitivism to modernism in 'Modernism, Postmodernism, and Explanation', in Elazar Barkan and Ronald Bush, eds, *Prehistories of the Future: The Primitivist Project and the Culture of Modernism,* Stanford University Press, Stanford, C.A., 1995, pp. 357-72. I agree with Kermode's identification of modernism with dissociation of sensibility and disillusion with explanation in modern literature, and a resultant preference for descriptive forms of writing. But I also see modernism as implying a recognition of the constructed nature of human experience, without any explanatory givens such as God, nature, etc., to relieve man and woman of the terrible responsibility to create his or her world, as Jean-Paul Sartre argued in *Being and Nothingness* (Grammercy Books, New York, 1994). As such, to embrace the primitive is not so much a part of modernism as a reaction to modernist consciousness and thus a desire to return to or bond with that which is perceived as wholly given, i.e. the primitive as a creature of instinct, nature, spiritual forces, indeed any givenness that precludes the awareness of the constructed nature of all human essence and agency. This maneuver is romantic not only in that it longs for a past that can never be returned to, but also because,

as James Clifford suggests (in *The Predicament of Culture: Twentieth Century Ethnography, Literature, and Art,* Harvard University Press, Cambridge, 1988), such 'primitivism' is largely imagined, a mapping of premodern mentality that is misrepresentative and misperceived.

18. Jean Toomer, *Cane,* with an introduction by Darwin T. Turner, Liveright, New York, 1975; Rudolph Fisher, 'Vestiges: Harlem Sketches', in Alain Locke's *The New Negro: Voices of the Harlem Renaissance,* with an introduction by Arnold Rampersad (1925), Atheneum, New York, 1992 edition, pp. 75-84; Zora Neale Hurston, 'Spunk', in Alain Locke, op. cit. pp. 105-11.

19. I am indebted to Gilbert Morris, with whom I have had several conversations this year, for this observation. For more on Yeats, see Uta von Rienersdorf-Paczensky und Tenczin, *W.B. Yeats's Poetry and Drama Between Late Romanticism and Modernism: an Analysis of Yeats's Poetry and Drama,* P. Lang, New York, 1997.

20. Martin Bauml Duberman, op. cit., pp. 77-82.

21. For the Great Migration and its interpretation, see Jeffrey C. Stewart, *1001 Things Everyone Should Know About African American History,* Doubleday, New York, 1996, pp. 52-60 and '(Un)Locke(ing) Jacob Lawrence's Migration Series' in *Jacob Lawrence: The Migration Series,* with an introduction by Elizabeth Hutton Turner, The Phillips Collection and the Rappanhannock Press, Washington, D.C., 1993, pp. 41-51.

22. George Hutchinson, op. cit., pp. 194, 309.

23. Joel Pfister, op. cit., pp. 129-32.

24. George Hutchinson, op. cit., pp. 193-94.

25. Langston Hughes, *The Big Sea,* 1940, quoted in Joel Pfister, op. cit., pp. 131-32.

26. Joel Pfister, op. cit., *passim.*

27. Eric Lott, *Blackface Minstrelsy in the American Working Class,* Oxford University Press, New York, 1993.

28. Jervis Anderson, *This Was Harlem: A Cultural Portrait, 1900-1950,* Farrar, Straus, Giroux, New York, 1982, pp. 212-20.

29. Martin Bauml Duberman, op. cit., p. 235.

30. *Ibid.,* p. 178.

31. *Ibid.,* p. 179.

32. *Ibid.,* p. 180. Robeson's interest in Africa in the 1930s is chronicled on pages 173 to 178.

# INFLUENCE OF MUSIC ON HARLEM RENAISSANCE WRITING

## CHERYL A. WALL (ESSAY DATE 1995)

**SOURCE:** Wall, Cheryl A. "Whose Sweet Angel Child? Blues Women, Langston Hughes, and Writing during the Harlem Renaissance." In *Langston Hughes: The Man, His Art, and His Continuing Influence,* edited by C. James Trotman, pp. 37-50. New York: Garland Publishing, 1995.

*In the following essay, Wall recounts the influence of blues singers, including Bessie Smith, on the cultural and literary history of the Harlem Renaissance.*

RECKLESS BLUES
When I was young, nothing but a child,
When I was young, nothing but a child,
All you men tried to drive me wild.

Now I'm growing old,
Now I'm growing old,
And I got what it takes to get all you men's soul.

My mama says I'm reckless, my daddy says I'm
  wild,
My mama says I'm reckless, my daddy says I'm
  wild,
I ain't good lookin', but I'm somebody's angel
  child.

Daddy, Mama wants some loving; Daddy, mama
  wants
  some hugging
Honey, Pretty Poppa, Mama wants some loving,
  I vow.
Honey, Pretty Poppa, Mama wants some loving
  right
  now.[1]

Recorded by Bessie Smith in 1925, "Reckless Blues" is a statement of self-validation in the face of social rejection, sexual exploitation, and personal alienation. In her maturity the speaker has seized control of her sexuality—autonomy compensates for aging—and relishes the pleasures that autonomy affords. The lyric dissolves the proverbial dichotomy between the good woman and the bad woman. Despite her inability to conform to the accepted standards of female beauty and her refusal to conform to the acceptable standards of female behavior, Smith's persona insists that she is *somebody's* angel child.

Smith's two accompanists on the record are Fred Longshaw, who gets composer credit for this version of a folk blues, and Louis Armstrong. Longshaw plays the harmonium; its organlike timbre complements the poignancy of the lyric and Smith's mournful contralto. But Armstrong's cornet provides the emotional counterpoint. His response to Bessie's call confirms that life's challenges can be and have been met. The last verse particularizes Smith's version of the song; it makes the point explicitly that while a woman's sexuality makes her vulnerable to male exploitation, it is the key to survival. The mood of the lyric and the music meet. Smith's increasingly assertive tone and Armstrong's increasingly intricate ob-

Bessie Smith.

bligatos culminate in the final verse to convey the persona's mastery of her life and situation. The recording documents Smith's mastery of her art.

Today, scholars recognize Bessie Smith and the so-called classic blues singers as major figures in the cultural history of the 1920s and 1930s.[2] For many writers, particularly black women writers, the blues woman is a symbol of black female creativity and autonomy whose art informs and empowers their own. That was surely not true in the blues women's time. Generally even those black intellectuals who, like W.E.B. Du Bois and Alain Locke, wrote of the profound beauty and meaning of the spirituals, were deaf to the same qualities in the blues. Blues women were even less likely than their male counterparts to have their music acknowledged as art. (Sterling Brown's poetic portrait of Ma Rainey is the most notable exception.) Among other reasons, their propensity for flamboyant dress and reckless behavior dismayed and embarrassed their more decorous brothers and sisters.

Langston Hughes was, characteristically, prescient in his understanding of the blues women's significance. As one imperative of his artistic manifesto, "The Negro Artist and the Racial Mountain," declared: "Let the blare of Negro jazz bands and the bellowing voice of Bessie Smith singing Blues penetrate the closed ears of the colored near-intellectuals until they listen and perhaps understand" (309). Not only was Hughes drawn to the compressed poetry of the blues, he aspired to a cultural role analogous to the blues troubadour. Fittingly, he was a student and admirer of the blues woman's art.

In 1926 Hughes made his pilgrimage to the Empress's domain. Bessie Smith was appearing at the Regent Theater in Baltimore when the author of the just published *The Weary Blues* made his way backstage to pay his respects. Doubtless he knew her recording "Mama's Got the Blues," which began "Some people say the weary blues ain't bad." Perhaps he hoped for recognition as a fellow blues artist. According to Hughes's biographer, Arnold Rampersad, whatever such aspirations he held were dashed. Miss Smith was not impressed. Hughes was disappointed in turn when he asked whether she had a theory about blues as Art: "Naw, she didn't know nothing about no art. All she knew was that blues had put her 'in de money'" (Rampersad, 123).

Whether she chose to theorize about it or not, Hughes understood that Bessie Smith knew a great deal about art. He understood as well that her life, and the lives of the other blues queens, could be the stuff of fiction. In his 1930 novel, *Not Without Laughter,* Hughes became the first writer to represent the figure of the blues woman in literature. His character Harriett Williams should be considered a precursor to the memorable blues women invented by Alice Walker in *The Color Purple,* Toni Cade Bambara in "Medley," and Sherley Anne Williams in *Someone Sweet Angel Child.* I want to analyze Hughes's representation and to speculate briefly about the reasons no comparable representation would appear in the fiction of black women for decades to come.

Hughes knew the folk blues from childhood. As an adult, he came to admire the so-called "classic blues" as well. Scholar Steven Tracy, whose authoritative study, *Langston Hughes & the Blues,* reconstructs the blues influences which shape and inform Hughes's poetry, notes the writer's "preference for the city, and especially vaudeville blues singers." Bessie, Mamie, Clara, and Trixie Smith, along with Ma Rainey, were among his personal favorites (Tracy, 117-119).

Their interest in the blues was something Hughes and Carl Van Vechten (novelist, music critic, and bon vivant) shared. Hughes offered his assistance to Van Vechten when the latter wrote several pioneering articles on the blues, particularly women's blues, for the magazine *Vanity Fair.*

Van Vechten was persuaded that the blues were at least equal to the spirituals as music and superior to them as poetry. Blues were "eloquent with rich idioms, metaphoric phrases, and striking word combinations" (Kellner, 44). To support his premise, Van Vechten quoted "Gulf Coast Blues," as recorded by Bessie Smith, and evoked the authority of "the young Negro poet, Langston Hughes," whose career he had begun to promote.

In a letter from which Van Vechten quotes at length, Hughes glossed the blues lyric and praised the vividness of its imagery.[3] Recounting his own visit to West Africa, he suggested a link between the blues ethos and African musical traditions. In the most incisive comment, Hughes drew his own contrast between the spirituals and the blues: "The blues always impressed me as being very sad, sadder even than the Spirituals, because their sadness is not softened with tears, but hardened with laughter. The absurd, incongruous laughter of a sadness without even a god to appeal to" (Kellner, 46). It is this laughter which his novel seeks to inscribe.

Two women embody the conflict between the spirituals and the blues in *Not Without Laughter*. Hager Williams and her youngest daughter Harriett are locked in a battle that is both philosophical and generational. Initially, Harriett appears to be her mother's opposite. Angry and rebellious, she refuses to accept the place society assigns her. She is highly intelligent but drops out of school after her seemingly liberal teacher and classmates fail to intervene when she is Jim-Crowed on a class trip. With each racist incident, Harriett's hatred of whites intensifies. In vain Hager urges her daughter to transcend bitterness. As an ex-slave, Hager recognizes the evil whites have done, yet she refuses to view them *as* evil. Instead, she grants whites a humanity equal to hers. She explains that whites are good as far as they can see, but when it comes to blacks, they cannot see far. Harriett is not moved.

No passage exemplifies Sterling Brown's description of the novel as "poetic realism" better than the prose poem recounting Hager Williams's forty years as a washerwoman: "Bought this house washin,' and made as many payments as Cudge [her husband] come near; an' raised ma chillen washin'; an' when Cudge taken sick an' laid on his back for mo'n a year I taken care o' him washin' . . . an' here I is with ma arms still in de tub!" (135-136).[4] Harriett, by contrast, refuses the domestic's role. Disgusted by the low pay, insults,

and sexual harassment, she quits her job at a country club. There is no poetry in her catalog of the menial tasks required to earn a weekly wage of five dollars.

Most tellingly, Harriett rejects her mother's religion. Christianity is the bedrock out of which Hager derives her beliefs and behavioral codes. She is shocked to hear Harriett declare that the church has made "you old Negroes act like Salvation Army people . . . afraid to even laugh on Sundays, afraid for a girl and boy to look at one another, or for people to go to dances. Your old Jesus is white, I guess that's why! He's white and stiff and don't like niggers" (42). Harriett's words, like her music, are blasphemous to her mother, whose response to this particular outburst is to begin a fervent prayer.

A cultural rebel, Harriett enacts the role blues scholar William Barlow attributes to blues men: "They acted as proselytizers of a gospel of secularization in which the belief in freedom became associated with personal mobility—freedom of movement in this world here and now, rather than salvation later on in the next" (5). In Harriett's view, Hager's faith has no utility. It transforms neither Hager's material condition—the family remains poor and is occasionally destitute—nor her social status. Whites call on her to nurse their sick and comfort their bereaved, but they deny her even the respect a proper name and title confer. She is "Aunt" Hager. Bound by her work and religion, Hager is locked in place. Harriett's disavowal of Christianity enables her to imagine alternative sites.

Harriett's secular temple is the cabaret; the priests are jazz musicians.[5] In one of the novel's most extended scenes and through some of its most evocative language, Hughes depicts BENBOW'S FAMOUS KANSAS CITY BAND in performance. The typography stresses the brashness of the commercial enterprise. The text experiments further with its transliteration of musical sounds ("Whaw-whaw . . . whaw-whaw-whaw"), as it represents the phases of performance from the "hip-rocking notes" of *Easy Rider* to the *Lazy River One-Step* to the urbane rhythms of *St. Louis Blues*.

Tellingly, the music that produces catharsis is the band's improvised rendition of a folk blues, a "plain old familiar blues, heart-breaking and extravagant, ma-baby's-gone-from-me blues." Like the other congregants, Harriett is transported. "It was true that men and women were dancing together, but their feet had gone down through the floor into the earth, each dancer's alone—down into the center of things" (93). They go to the point, perhaps, where one experiences the existential validation that one is, indeed, somebody's angel child.

However cleansing spiritually, in the social world of the novel, Harriett's behavior is irresponsible. Lost in the music, she has stayed out all night herself, and worse, she has kept her young nephew Sandy out all night as well. Awaiting Harriett's return, her mother sits "with the open Bible on her lap . . . and a bundle of switches on the floor at her feet" (98).

Clearly, Harriett is destined to leave home. Hughes constructs the narrative of her leave-taking out of the myths and legends that surrounded the blues queens. Gertrude Rainey left home at fourteen to join a vaudeville act; only after serving a long apprenticeship working tent shows did she emerge in the 1920s as the Mother of the Blues. Although Bessie Smith began her career as a professional in a traveling show in 1912 when she was eighteen, she had been singing for nickels and dimes in her hometown of Chattanooga since age nine. After leaving home and marrying at fifteen, Sippie Wallace returned and left home a second time to work as a maid and stage assistant to a snake dancer, Madame Dante, who performed in Phillips Reptile Show.[6] In like fashion, Harriett, unable to make peace with her mother or to make a life for herself, joins a carnival and hits the road.

Schooled by her brother-in-law Jimboy, an itinerant blues man, Harriett has already honed her art. Jimboy anticipates Harriett's rebelliousness when he refuses to work under demeaning conditions. He is equally unwilling to be tied down by his family. His frequent and prolonged absences make the lines from "Gulf Coast Blues," an apt leitmotif for the character of his wife Annjee: "The mailman passed but he didn't leave no news/I'll tell the world he left me with those Gulf Coast blues."

Appropriately, too, the chapter that introduces Jimboy is called "Guitar"; he is less a fully formed character than an aesthetic principle. "Guitar" opens with a twelve-bar blues:

Throw yo' arms around me, baby,
Like de circle round de sun!
Baby, throw yo' arms around me
Like de circle round de sun,
An' tell yo' pretty papa
How you want yo' lovin' done.

(46)

The lines function in the novel less as a sexual boast than as a celebration of the blues man's art.

The blues, as Sterling Brown observed, represents collective yearnings and feelings, but, unlike the earlier musical forms of the work songs and spirituals, the life of the artist becomes the prototype of the collective. Harriett, as a member of the collective, can appropriate Jimboy's songs.

He teaches her the full range of the rural blues man's repertoire: traditional folk seculars and ballads, popular ragtime tunes, and the floating lines of the blues. The latter constitute the storehouse of blues lyrics which can be repeated and varied in limitless combinations. Jimboy is also Harriett's dance instructor; he teaches her the *parse me la,* the buck and wing, and the fundamentals of tap. In the novel's romantic representation, the blues man's art compensates for his marital infidelity and his dereliction of paternal responsibility. When Jimboy plays, "the singing notes of the guitar became a plaintive hum, like a breeze in the grove of palmettos; became a low moan, like the wind in a forest of live-oaks strung with long strands of hanging moss" (51). His talent is admirable both for the beauty it creates and for the generosity with which he shares it.

On one level, the novel encapsulates the history of the blues—representing its development from the folk blues Jimboy sings in the yard of Aunt Hager's home to the blues Harriett, now Harrietta Williams, Princess of the Blues, performs on stage at Chicago's Monogram Theater at the novel's conclusion. The schematic design of the novel reinforces the link between the two song forms. In one of her stage numbers, Harriett, dressed in a blue calico apron with a bandanna handkerchief knotted about her head, sings a blues she has learned from Jimboy. The lyrics are traditional:

It's a mighty blue mornin' when yo' daddy
    leaves yo' bed.
I says a blue, blue mornin' when yo' daddy
    leaves yo'
        bed—
'Cause if you lose yo' man, you'd just as well be
    dead!

(298)

It moves many in the audience, including Sandy's mother, to tears. But neither its style nor its substance define Harriett.

While the blues women did demonstrate "a common bond" with rural southern blacks, as scholar Daphne Harrison affirms, the connection was highly mediated. Consider, for example, the complaint of blues queen Alberta Hunter. Hunter, whose stage persona exemplified sophistication and glamour, resented theater owners' requirement that black entertainers conform to plantation stereotypes. "They wouldn't accept us Negro girls in smart clothes," she complained. They insisted instead that black women perform "wearing bandannas, Aunt Jemima dresses, and gingham aprons; the men wore overalls" (Quoted in Taylor, 68). For reasons of profit and prejudice, theater owners sought to sustain the illusion of a fundamental identity between performer and audience through costumes, stage sets, and advertisements. They wished to increase the entertainers' appeal to a mass audience whose background was predominantly southern and rural, and they were loath to grant complex identities to either their employees or their customers.

*Not Without Laughter* highlights the shifting personas that blues women assumed on stage and off. For her initial entrance, Harriett is dressed in "glowing orange, flame-like against the ebony of her skin" (297). The effect is to evoke the image of a jungle princess and to enforce the myth of exotic primitivism that was pervasive during the 1920s. The description of the song she sings, "a popular version of an old Negro melody, refashioned with words from Broadway," helps the reader deconstruct the image as commercial and counterfeit. After singing the folk blues, Harriett reappears: "Her final number was a dance-song which she sang in a sparkling dress of white sequins, ending the act with a mad collection of steps and a swift sudden whirl across the whole stage as the orchestra joined Billy's piano in a triumphant arch of jazz" (298). Its placement at the end of her performance suggests that this is the persona which embodies Harriett's greatest achievement as an artist. The triumph inheres as well in Harriett's successful invention of a life which she can lead without denying her self.

But the price is high. *Not Without Laughter* is honest enough in its depiction of Harriett's life to show her broke and stranded in Memphis—she has quit the carnival because she was not being paid—and to allude to the prostitution which she practices when she has no other way to earn a living.[7] It notes the latter by interpolating a news clipping headlined NEGRESSES ARRESTED, which both provides the information and comments on the dominant society's refusal to recognize the individual humanity of black people. In addition to countering such stereotyped racial and gender representations, the novel refuses to reinscribe the good woman/bad woman dichotomy. Indeed it subverts that dichotomy in the same way "The Reckless Blues" does. Harriett, a scarlet woman—in one of the novel's many allusions to

Hughes's poetry, she wears red silk stockings—is also the guardian angel who enables Sandy to fulfill Hager's dream for him.

Harriett and Sandy are reunited when he and Annjee attend her performance. Harriett castigates her sister for requiring Sandy to quit school and take a job running an elevator. She promises to give him the money he would have earned. The words that accompany her gesture strain credulity. Harriett says to her sister that "you and me was foolish, all right, breaking mama's heart, leaving school, but Sandy can't do like us. He's gotta be what his grandma Hager wanted him to be—able to help the black race, Annjee! You hear me? Help the whole race!" (303). The gesture itself does not.

Although the story emphasizes Harriett's estrangement from her mother, the discourse of the novel inscribes a common bond. One key imagistic link is the figure "whirl."[8] It is first associated with Harriett at the moment that Sandy discovers her performing at the carnival. Then in a passage that begins by identifying Harriett, Jimboy, Hager, and Afro-Americans generally as "a band of dancers," the figure is applied to Hager. "Sandy remembered his grandmother whirling around in front of the altar at revival meetings in the midst of the other sisters, her face shining with light, arms outstretched as though all the cares of the world had been cast away" (293). Finally, at the culmination of her performance as the Princess of the Blues, Harriett performs "a swift sudden whirl across the whole stage." In each instance, whirling becomes a sign of spiritual release. Following a pattern characteristic of African religious practices, spiritual ecstasy is manifested in sudden, intense physical movement.[9] Whirling signals the momentary freedom from the oppression and sadness which define much of these characters' lives. Truly Hager's daughter, Harriett finds in Afro-American secular music the joy her mother found in the Christian God.

Hughes's representation of the blues woman invests her with moral and spiritual power. She is an artist who, despite her professional success, bespeaks the aspirations and desires of the masses. The novel draws a sharp distinction between Harriett, as the avatar of a new generation, and her snobbish sister, Tempy. Tempy mouths the rhetoric of the New Negro and reads *The Crisis,* the journal of the National Association for the Advancement of Colored People edited by Du Bois, while acting out an extreme form of racial self-hatred. By contrast, Harriett's militancy grows out of a hard-won self love, that is uncountenanced

# ON THE SUBJECT OF...

## BESSIE SMITH

Known as the "Empress of the Blues," Bessie Smith (April 15, 1894-September 26, 1937) is considered the greatest female singer of urban blues and, to many, the greatest of all blues singers. White record companies found Smith's brand of blues too unrefined for mass appeal; her performances were often laced with vulgarities and sexual innuendo. As a result, Smith was not recorded until 1923, when the Black buying public had already demonstrated that there was a market for blues songs and the companies became eager to exploit it.

Smith was recorded by the Columbia Gramophone Company. Columbia touted itself in Black newspapers as having more "race" artists than other companies. Smith recordings like "Down Hearted Blues" and "Gulf Coast Blues" saw massive sales. By 1924, she was the highest-paid African American in the country. Smith sang about everyday problems, abuse and violence, unfaithful lovers, and the longing for love. She performed these songs with a conviction and dramatic style that reflected the memory of her own suffering, captured the mood of black people who had experienced pain and anguish, and drew listeners to her with empathy and intimacy.

Smith recorded regularly for Columbia until 1929, producing 150 selections, of which at least two dozen were her own compositions. By the end of the 1920s, women blues singers were fading in popularity, largely because urban audiences were becoming more sophisticated. Her single film, *St. Louis Blues* (1929), immortalized her, although by this time, rough living had taken a toll on her voice and appearance. Because of the Great Depression, the recording industry was in disarray by 1931. Columbia dismantled its race catalog and dropped Smith. She altered her act and costumes in an attempt to appeal to club patrons, but she did not live to fulfill her hope of a new success with the emerging swing ensembles. Smith died in 1937 in an automobile accident while on a tour of southern towns.

by social or divine authority. Harriett follows her own path to self validation. Yet, as a model for the women in her audience, she charts the way for others to identify themselves as "somebody's angel child."

Given the role the blues woman played in Afro-American culture during the 1920s, her total absence from the work of contemporary black women writers is striking. None of the Harlem Renaissance women writers, including Jessie Fauset, Nella Larsen, Martia Bonner, Gwendolyn Bennett, and Georgia Douglas Johnson fashioned a character after the blues queens.[10] Few of them even acknowledged the existence of the blues. The blues woman, whose penchant for wild and reckless living was well known even to those who never deigned to listen to her music, could not be embraced by her literary sisters until the impulse toward conformity, decorousness, and the staider forms of uplift was spent. Only when black women writers ceased to valorize "the careful development of thrift, patience, high morals, and good manners" to the exclusion of the "dreadful funkiness of passion, the funkiness of nature, the funkiness of the wide range of human emotions," as Toni Morrison phrases it in *The Bluest Eye* (64), was the blues woman welcomed in her sisters' fiction.

Even Zora Neale Hurston, the one literary woman who embraced the cultural legacy that was the blues and who had little patience with any kind of racial uplift, did not represent a blues woman in her prose. When, for example, in *Their Eyes Were Watching God* she sought to give her heroine Janie Crawford access to the liberating and self-affirming ethic of the blues, she invented a male character, Tea Cake, to be Janie's mentor. If she did not create a fictional blues woman—though one could argue contrarily that the character Janie is informed by the blues ethos and floating blues lines recur throughout the novel—Hurston did pay her personal homage to Bessie Smith. She met her in the company of Langston Hughes.

During the summer of 1927, Hurston and Hughes crossed paths unexpectedly in New Orleans. She was beginning her field work; he was visiting the South for the first time. When they met, he had already listened both to records and street singers in Baton Rouge and New Orleans and "heard many of the blues verses [he] used later in [his] short stories and [his] novel" (*The Big Sea*, 290). Earlier that year he had drawn on similar models to write the poems in the landmark volume, *Fine Clothes to the Jew,* his "most radical achievement in language" (Rampersad, 141). Still, despite the great bravado with which he had renounced the impulse toward propriety in "The Negro Artist and the Racial Mountain," he had limited firsthand knowledge of the lives of the "low-down" folk he celebrated. He knew that in Hurston he would have the ideal tutor to instruct him in southern black culture and folkways. "Blind guitar players, conjur (sic) men, and former slaves were her quarry, small town jooks and plantation churches, her haunts" (*The Big Sea*, 296). He expected that it would be fun traveling with Hurston, and it was.

In Macon, Georgia, they heard Bessie Smith sing in a small theater. Of course, as Hughes jested, one did not have to go near the theater to hear Bessie sing; she could be heard from blocks away. Due doubtless to the exigencies of segregation, the Empress and the two writers were staying at the same hotel. There they heard Smith practice every morning; they met and "got to know her pretty well" (296). "With Hurston taking the lead," Rampersad concludes, "Smith was warmer this time to the Bard of the Blues" (153). Hughes reciprocated the gesture in his representation of Harriett Williams, a portrait of the blues woman as artist and hero.[11] Perhaps in their shared encounter, Zora Neale Hurston helped Langston Hughes gain possession of his own sweet angel child.

## Notes

1. "Reckless Blues," Columbia 14056-D.

2. See, for example, Hazel Carby, "It Jus Be's Dat Way Sometime: The Sexual Politics of Women's Blues," and Cheryl A. Wall, "Poets and Versifiers, Singers and Signifiers: The Women of the Harlem Renaissance."

3. Clarence Williams was the composer credited with "Gulf Coast Blues," which Bessie Smith recorded on February 16, 1923 (Columbia A3844); it was the "B" side of her first Columbia Records release, "Down Hearted Blues."

4. Sterling Brown referred to the novel's "poetic realism" in his review in *Opportunity*, 8 (September 1930), and in *The Negro in American Fiction*, where he called the novel "one of the best by a Negro author" (155).

5. The representation of jazz musicians as priestly figures anticipates James Baldwin's more elaborate representation in "Sonny's Blues" and *Another Country*. So, too, does Harriett prefigure the representation of Ida Scott, the blues woman who is sister to the novel's protagonist.

6. For further biographical information, see Sandra Lieb, Mother of the Blues: A Study of Ma Rainey; Chris Albertson, Bessie; and Daphne Duval Harrison, Black Pearls: Blues Queens of the 1920s.

7. At other points, particularly in the description of life in "the Bottoms," the novel does romanticize the lives of the poor. Describing the neighborhood as "a gay place," the narrator asserts that "in the Bottoms folks ceased to struggle against the boundaries between good and bad, or white and black, and surrendered amiably to immorality" (216).

8. Hughes employed the figure most famously in the poem "Dream Variation," which begins "To fling my arms wide/In some place of the sun,/To whirl and to dance/Till the white day is done." Selected Poems (14).

9. Albert Raboteau asserts that despite the discontinuities in the tenets of belief, "it is in the context of action, the patterns of motor behavior preceding and following the ecstatic experience, that there may be a continuity between African and American forms of spirit possession" (64-65).

10. Jessie Fauset comes closest with Marise Davies, a character in Comedy: American Style (1933), whose career seems inspired by Josephine Baker's.

11. By the time Not Without Laughter was published, Hughes and Hurston were no longer friends. Thereafter, they rarely spoke about, let alone to, each other. Accounts of their friendship, artistic collaboration, and disaffection are collected in Langston Hughes and Zora Neale Hurston, Mule Bone, edited by George Houston Bass and Henry Louis Gates Jr. (New York: Harper Perennial, 1991).

## Works Cited

Albertson, Chris. *Bessie*. New York: Stein and Day, 1972.

Barlow, William. *Looking Up at Down: The Emergence of Blues Culture*. Philadelphia: Temple University Press, 1989.

Brown, Sterling. "The Blues." *Phylon* 13 (Autumn 1952): 286-292.

———. *Negro Poetry and Drama and The Negro in American Fiction*. 1937. Rpt. New York: Atheneum, 1969.

———. Review of *Not Without Laughter*. *Opportunity* 8 (September 1930): 279-280.

Carby, Hazel. "It Jus Be's Dat Way Sometime: The Sexual Politics of Women's Blues." *Radical America* 20.4 (1986): 9-22.

Harrison, Daphne Duval. *Black Pearls: Blues Queens of the 1920s*. New Brunswick, NJ: Rutgers University Press, 1988.

Hughes, Langston. *The Big Sea*. 1940. Rpt. New York: Hill & Wang, 1963.

———. "The Negro Artist and the Racial Mountain." 1926. Rpt. in Nathan Huggins, ed. *Voices from the Harlem Renaissance*. New York: Oxford University Press, 1976.

———. *Not Without Laughter*. 1930. Rpt. New York: Macmillan, Collier Books Edition, 1969.

———. *Selected Poems*. 1959. New York: Vintage, 1974.

———, and Zora Neale Hurston. *Mule Bone*. Edited with Introductions by George Houston Bass and Henry Louis Gates, Jr. New York: Harper Perennial, 1991.

Kellner, Bruce, ed. *Keep a Inchin' Along: Selected Writings of Carl Van Vechten about Black Art and Letters*. Westport, CT: Greenwood Press, 1979.

Lieb, Sandra. *Mother of the Blues: A Study of Ma Rainey*. Amherst: University of Massachusetts Press, 1981.

Morrison, Toni. *The Bluest Eye.* New York: Holt, Rinehart and Winston, 1970.

Raboteau, Albert. *Slave Religion.* New York: Oxford University Press, 1978.

Rampersad, Arnold. *The Life of Langston Hughes: Vol. I: I, Too, Sing America.* New York: Oxford University Press, 1986.

Taylor, Frank. *Alberta Hunter: A Celebration in Blues.* New York: McGraw-Hill, 1987.

Tracy, Steven C. *Langston Hughes & the Blues.* Urbana: University of Illinois Press, 1988.

Wall, Cheryl A. "Poets and Versifiers, Singers and Signifiers: the Women of the Harlem Renaissance." Virginia Lussier and Kenneth Wheeler, eds. *Women, the Arts, and the 1920s in Paris and New York.* New Brunswick, NJ: Transaction Books, 1982.

## TOM LUTZ (ESSAY DATE 2000)

**SOURCE:** Lutz, Tom. "Claude McKay: Music, Sexuality, and Literary Cosmopolitanism." In *Black Orpheus: Music in African American Fiction from the Harlem Renaissance to Toni Morrison,* edited by Saadi A. Simawe, pp. 41-64. New York: Garland Publishing, 2000.

*In the following essay, Lutz studies the representation of music in McKay's writings, noting that the author perceived music as a key factor in understanding the African American heritage.*

To talk about music in the novels of Claude McKay might seem like an exercise in paraphrase, since his novels so straightforwardly present an argument about Black music. The eponymous hero of the novel *Banjo* (1929/1957), for instance, plays the prototypical African American instrument that gives him his name, and his musical career illustrates the cultural arguments McKay sets out to make. The music Banjo plays, like that Crazy Bow plays in *Banana Bottom* (1933), or that Jake enjoys in *Home to Harlem* (1928/1987), and the vernacular culture these three characters represent, are contrasted quite explicitly to the deadening crush of Euro-American civilization, "the ever tightening mechanical organization of modern life" (McKay 1929/1957, 324). A typical passage is this on Banjo:

> That this primitive child, this kinky-headed, big-laughing black boy of the world, did not go down and disappear under the serried crush of trampling white feet; that he managed to remain on the scene, not worldly-wise, not "getting there," yet not machine-made, nor poor-in-spirit like the regimented creatures of civilization, was baffling to civilized understanding. Before the grim, pale rider-down of souls he went his careless way with a primitive hoofing and a grin.
>
> (314)

And although Banjo hits on the idea of starting an orchestra in order to make money in the first few pages of the novel, he doesn't just play

for the money, like White musicians: "They played in a hard unsmiling way, and only for sous. Which was doubtless why their playing in general was so execrable. When Banjo turned himself loose and wild playing, he never remembered sous" (40). The careless, big-laughing, grinning primitive is his own antidote, or at least analgesic, to overcivilization and wage slavery.

His music is similarly antitoxic to those around him. Ray, the character who represents, among other things, the overcivilized Negro (even to himself), is a "book fellah" who provides the other half of McKay's argument in *Banjo* (and in *Home to Harlem*). Banjo has his banjo, and Ray has his pen, and while Ray's educated alienation is contrasted to Banjo's natural integrity, Ray also provides a road map to Banjo's sensibility for McKay's educated readers. Ray finds that music is the quickest and surest route to understanding Banjo's primitive sensibility. "But you're interested in race—I mean race advancement, aren't you?" an activist character asks Ray midway through the novel. "Sure," answers Ray, "but right now there's nothing in the world so interesting to me as Banjo and his orchestra" (92). Ray is interested in the problems of civilization, which he has thought about quite seriously, but more interested in the rewards of primitivism, which he knows less well, and to which he finds an introduction in Banjo's world and music.

I was once scolded by my students in a graduate seminar for using the word *primitive* in reference to McKay and other writers associated with the Harlem Renaissance, but the word is one McKay used proudly, and he used it in a particular sense grounded in the discourses of his time. Influenced by D. H. Lawrence, whom he considered "a spiritual brother" (Cooper 1987, xiii), McKay believed, along with Sherwood Anderson, H. L. Mencken, and a host of others in the 1910s and 1920s, that the deadening weight of civilization was choking off people's primitive, vital life force. McKay argued, in his fiction and criticism, that African American performative culture escaped this particular noose. In his fictional arguments the more "primitive" option tends to win, whether it is all-night dancing versus civilized bedtimes, the "colorful" speech of the uneducated versus the anglicized speech of the overcivilized Negroes, or the banjo and the fiddle versus the player piano and the symphony. McKay does not deny the value of European forms, either musical, linguistic, or social, but he firmly tips the balance toward the "earthy people," whose continued existence, and continued expression, he represents as heroic and salutary.

The argument is not one of respecting difference, as our own multi-cultural pieties would have it, but of evaluation. African diasporic art is not just different than much Western art, McKay argued, it is better, and it is therefore the wave of the future. Joyce Hope Scott (1992) has written that with his trickster characters McKay shows that the African American artist must embrace "his cultural heritage" (133). But McKay is not just making an argument about African American artists, he is making one about art itself. "Our age is the age of Negro art," McKay wrote in *The Negroes in America* (1923/1979). "The slogan of the aesthetic world is 'Return to the Primitive.' The Futurists and Impressionists are agreed in turning everything upside-down in an attempt to achieve the wisdom of the primitive Negro" (63). McKay represents the primitive as a progressive future, not as a past to which we might return. In this he is taking a position contrary to the critique of African American folk forms made by such old school critics as Jessie Fauset and W. E. B. Du Bois, those who saw all primitivist culture as a rejection and refutation of progress. In McKay's review of the first all-black Broadway musical *Shuffle Along* (1921), he rails against conservative critics who declare that

> Negro art . . . must be dignified and respectable like the Anglo-Saxon's before it can be good. The Negro must get the warmth, color, and laughter out of his blood, else the white man will sneer at him and treat him with contumely. Happily the Negro retains his joy of living in the teeth of such criticism; and in Harlem, along Fifth and Lenox avenues, in Marcus Garvey's hall with its extravagant paraphernalia, in his churches and cabarets, he expresses himself with a zest that is yet to be depicted by a true artist.
>
> (63)

McKay in the years after this review himself became the "true artist" representing that joyful expressiveness, and one of the main shapes this took was the representation of Black music.

None of this is news for those who have studied McKay's fiction or other writings. Scholars of the Harlem Renaissance from Nathan Huggins to David Levering Lewis have noted the disdain the old school and many in the new had for jazz and blues, but all note that among the New Negroes Langston Hughes took these forms seriously and used them as a basis for an African American aesthetic, and those few who mention McKay note that he did as well. Sherley Anne Williams (1972) discussed the way McKay used Black music as "a symbol of liberation from a stifling respectability and materialistic conventionality which have an odor of decay about them," but found—wrongly, in my opinion—that McKay "is content with implying this conflict through the use of the jazz life as a framework" (137). Kathy J. Ogren (1789) has discussed, more aptly, albeit briefly, McKay's use of jazz clubs in *Home to Harlem* to "establish an open, emotional, and participatory ambiance" (170) and help create "an Afro-American aesthetic based on folk and working-class culture" (179). Wayne F. Cooper has noted that McKay's representations of music are important sites for his arguments about the value of African diaspora culture and his critique of civilization. In this chapter I want to add just a few related points to the discussion. First, while it is true that McKay argues for the progressive force of primitivism, he also argues for the value of Tolstoy and any number of other European artists, expressive and intellectual forms, and cultural values. McKay's argument is not Afrocentric, in other words; it is, I want to show, cosmopolitan. That is, he exercises a kind of connoisseurship of cultural value, picking through the best that the world has thought, written, composed, and improvised, and he champions African diaspora culture from the standpoint of such cosmopolitan connoisseurship. Second, by examining McKay's representation of music in relation to the Orpheus myth, a slightly more complicated picture emerges, in which McKay's representation of music is also used to make arguments about sexuality. And, third, McKay's argument for African diasporic culture is also an argument for a certain kind of subjectivity, one that we might call a selfhood of cosmopolitan integrity.

Banjo is Orpheus. His songs, like those of Orpheus, overcome all resistance and charm all who hear them. Like Orpheus, Banjo's career takes him to hell and back. Like Orpheus after losing Eurydice, Banjo is finally less interested in female companionship than male. And like Orpheus, Banjo returns to the civilized world, but not entirely. McKay followed a similar route. He produced fiction that approached the condition of music and is meant to charm a particular, yet wide, audience: one that has left or is attempting to leave conventional civilization behind or to one side in favor of a cosmopolitan subjectivity made possible through exactly the kind of literary vagabondage McKay and the other literary writers of his day were providing.

## Blues, Jazz, and the Primitivist Critique of Civilization

In the opening chapter of *Banjo* (1929/1957), Banjo both declares his intention to start an orchestra as a way to make a living and announces his aesthetics: "I *is* an artist" (8) he says, and McKay agrees. Banjo has arrived in Marseilles, and is one among the "great vagabond host of jungle-like Negroes trying to scrape a temporary existence from the macadamized surface of this great Provençal port" (68). Banjo assumes (as does McKay) that "the American darky is the performing fool of the world today"; this is true at least in part because of a lack of true economic opportunity, that whatever work is available is hard, unremunerative, and deadening. "We kain't afford to choose," Banjo tells his educated friend Ray, "because we ain't born and growed up like the choosing people" (319). Unlike most of those who can't afford to choose, Banjo has an avocation he recognizes can earn him a living, which is more than just coincidence. McKay argues that African American performance is in demand the world over because it expresses the "irrepressible exuberance and legendary vitality of the black race," and that exuberance and vitality are at least in part due to the fact that the black race has not been fully deadened by civilized living. (For a discussion of the relation of race, civilization, and physical energy see Lutz, *American Nervousness* (1991), 3-13, 244-275, and "Curing the Blues" (1991).)

In the 1920s, the questioning of civilization was reaching a fever pitch. The publication of Harold Stearns's *Civilization in the United States* (1922), with contributions from many of the best known young turk intellectuals and literati, was seen as a battle cry on the part of those who, like McKay, found American civilization at once both too much and too little. Stearns's contributors damned American civilization for its deadening and leveling propensities, for its overdevelopment as a system of social control, and for its lack of sophistication, its underdevelopment as an accumulation of art and thought.

These cultural critics had been influenced by Freud and others to see civilization as the curbing of instinct, and therefore the limiting of human possibility, to see social proprieties as restraints, containments. They had been taught by a tradition culminating in Henry James and T. S. Eliot that American civilization was impossibly rudimentary and unformed compared to British civilization. They had learned from the anthropologists to see a broader array of cultural possibilities and to understand their own culture as fundamentally artificial. And they knew that knowledge was being produced so rapidly, in so many specialized fields, that a true understanding of their own culture, however undeveloped and constrained it might be, was now impossible for any one thinker. As I have argued elsewhere, in the context of this world of rapidly expanding, highly specialized knowledges, literary writers offered readers a cosmopolitan overview none of the specialists could offer (Lutz 1998). Literary writers could not pretend to know human sexuality in the precise way a physiologist or psychologist did, or understand economics the way an economist might. But they did suggest that they understood the significance of the full range of knowledges being produced better than the overspecialized professionals in other fields. McKay's aesthetic is fully in line with this cosmopolitan mainstream of American literature. He demonstrates that he knows both Tolstoy and the blues, both White and Black culture, both American and European, both upper and lower classes. He shows that he knows what the race scientists, the anthropologists, the sociologists, and so on are saying, and thus offers a synthetic overview of the Black man's relation to civilization.

Several of McKay's poems that were published in Alain Locke's *The New Negro* (1925/1992)—without McKay's permission—express his aesthetic at the time he was writing his first novels:

> Like a strong tree that reaches down, deep, deep,
> For sunken water, fluid underground,
> Where the great-ringed unsightly blind worms
>     creep,
> And queer things of the nether world abound:
> So I would live in imperial growth,
> Touching the surface and the depth of things,
> Instinctively responsive unto both.
>
> (134)

As Melvin Dixon (1987) has pointed out (46ff), this poem, titled "Like a Strong Tree," states McKay's artistic credo and Ray's struggle, in *Home to Harlem* and *Banjo,* to negotiate the high and the low, cultivation and spontaneity, intellect and instinct. Blues and jazz, as Dixon also notes, regularly denote low, spontaneous, instinctual pleasure, and Ray finally learns, haltingly and partially, to embrace both, to create stories out of "the fertile reality around him" (McKay 1928/ 1987, 228). Dixon is right in seeing in this McKay's "critique of the cultural misdirection of the Harlem Renaissance, which favors portrayals of bourgeois respectability and assimilation" (49), and right that the music in these texts are both proof and harbinger of a common base for Black art. But the poem goes further than this as well, as does another poem in the Locke collection, "Baptism," to which I'll return in a moment. These poems embrace "the queer things of the nether world" and the surface, both.

McKay examines the high and the low, the cultivated and the instinctual, not just in music, but in speech patterns, eating practices, sexual mores, and ways of understanding Black experience. The different views of racial possibility are somewhat schematically personified in the first two novels. In each novel two main characters and their different views take center stage. In *Home to Harlem,* it is Ray and Jake who are contrasted; in *Banjo* it is Banjo and Ray, but in both cases it is the educated versus the uneducated, the happy primitive versus the anxious bourgeois. We are also given a series of minor characters representing other possibilities. Some of these (and they never fare very well) are shown to be completely unconscious, unthinkingly bouncing against racism, economic hardship, and crime, unable or unwilling to think about the nature of the social world into which they have been born and through which they move. Bugsy in *Banjo* and Zeddy in *Home to Harlem,* for instance, are shown to be primitive and instinctual enough, but tainted, corrupted by civilized values, by the desire for money, prestige, luxury, leisure. "Primitive peoples could be crude and coarse, but never vulgar," McKay writes in *Banjo,* and Bugsy and Zeddy are vulgar. "Vulgarity was altogether a scab of civilization" (192). Other characters stand in for forms of Black radicalism and Black conservatism, representatives of the parties of race pride, race uplift, radical individualism, and the like.

But the main argument takes place in the relation to Ray and his opposite number. We are encouraged, in the first instance, to read in sympathy with the seeming protagonist, and so Jake and Banjo, with whom the novels open, are our first frames of reference. Readers are asked to enter into their enjoyment of their low life. They are, after all, "handsome, happy brutes" (McKay 1929/1957, 48), and the narrator imperatively enjoins us to shake our things to the music they make and dance to:

> Shake to the loud music of life playing to the primeval round of life. Rough rhythm of darkly-carnal life. Strong surging flux of profound currents forced into narrow channels. Play that thing! . . . Sweet dancing thing of primitive joy, perverse pleasure, prostitute ways, many-colored

variations of the rhythm, savage, barbaric, refined—eternal rhythm of the mysterious, magical, magnificent. . . . Oh, Shake That Thing!

(57-58)

The language here mimics not just the tempo and syncopation of the music, but its disregard for civilized conventions. It revels in its primitivisms—"savage, barbaric"—yet it is ferociously modern stylistically. Formally, more than anywhere else in McKay's poetry or fiction, these passages about music announce their own modernism in their abandonment of syntax, neologizing freedom, and combination of vernacular and literary diction. McKay rejected the most modern innovations in poetic form in his own poetry; according to Wayne Cooper (1987), he believed that "'real' poetry adhered to Victorian poetic conventions, and that the modernists substituted novelty for discipline and incomprehensibility for beauty" (153). But in those sections of his novels in which he describes music, he grants himself the modernists' freedoms from formal convention. In *Home to Harlem,* Readers are offered a verbal representation of the freedom from "civilized" constraints that makes for and is made by jazz and blues:

> Oh, "blues," "blues," "blues." Red moods, black moods, golden moods. Curious syncopated, slipping-over into one mood, back-sliding back to the first mood. Humming in harmony, barbaric harmony, joy-drunk, chasing out the shadow of the moment before.

(54)

Such passages are supposed to give readers some taste of the "joy-drunk" response to music the characters feel; the more primitive those characters are, the less trammeled the appreciation.

With the entrance of Ray, we are asked to rethink our sympathies, since Ray seems so clearly to be an authorial stand-in. He has the education that most of McKay's readers would have had, and he has the diction, seriousness of purpose, and relation to meaning-making associated with literary communities. Here, just a few pages later, is a bit of free indirect discourse representing Ray's thoughts:

> But it was not by Tolstoy's doctrines that he was touched. It was depressing to him that the energy of so many great intellects of the modern world had been, like Tolstoy's, vitiated in the futile endeavor to make the mysticism of Jesus serve the spiritual needs of a world-conquering and leveling machine civilization.

(66)

At first, this remarkable difference in mood makes us confront the difference in value that the vagabonds and primitives represent, and they can appear frivolous and, in fact, somewhat unsatisfied with the vicissitudes of their lives. Then Ray, enamored of the freedom and vitality of Banjo or Jake, sings their praises and abandons his own beliefs, and we are asked to reevaluate them once more. Whatever our first relation to the primitivist characters might have been—slumming, escapism, vicarious experience—after we reapproach these characters through Ray's emulative desire, we are asked to realize that the debate is being staged not so that we might take sides, but that we might comprehend the debate. Ray, as our guide, moves back and forth and among the various possibilities: respect for an "African" mode of existence, envy of its carefree vitality, exultation at his own brief experiences of it, distress at the impossibility of its existing in the context of corrupt civilization, distaste for the ignorance that seems to be a prerequisite for it, irritation at its headlong refusal to contemplate tomorrow. These perspectives on the "joy-drunk" mode of existence are all represented as valid, and their orchestration for our benefit is not meant to resolve into a vote for or against a particular cultural style. "Dance down the Death of these days, the Death of these ways in shaking that thing," the "Shake that thing!" passage in Banjo continues. "Jungle jazzing, Orient wriggling, civilized stepping. Shake that thing!" Jungle jazzing and civilized stepping, together, with a little Oriental wriggling thrown in for good measure—a cosmopolitan inclusiveness is at the heart of the ethos.

This does not mean that anything goes. Banjo's music, Ray's angst, and Malty's shiftlessness at one level come to the same thing, after all—they all serve to condemn "leveling machine civilization." We are asked not to approve Banjo's lackadaisical energy over and above Ray's literary desires, anymore than we are asked to condemn the various pimps or Marxists who make their appearances. We are asked to acquire, and the novel provides precisely this for us, a cosmopolitan overview of the positions offered by the text. That cosmopolitan overview is sanctioned by its literary genealogy. Literary art, in fact, especially in the genres McKay's novels participate in—realism, regionalism, the picaresque, the novel of ideas—takes such cosmopolitanism as the highest value. And, as critics have long noted, McKay's primary affiliation was with the literary life rather than to a specific racial program.

Toward the end of Banjo, Banjo pronounces a version of the cosmopolitan perspective in a speech about the war. The world went crazy, he says,

> and one half of it done murdered the other half to death. But the wul' ain't gone a-mourning forevah because a that. Nosah. The wul' is jazzing to fohgit. . . . The wul' is just keeping right on with that nacheral sweet jazzing of life. And Ise jest gwine on right along jazzing with the wul'. The wul' goes round and round and I keeps right on gwine around with it.

Banjo sees the great whirl of life transcending the lines of national difference, and the job of individuals to comprehend and live the fullness of life. That Banjo's notion of that comprehension is one of "jazzing" is significant (as is his idea that jazzing is a mode of forgetfulness, more on which in a moment), because it is the music of primitive enjoyment. Banjo's diction and predilections are primitive, but his sentiment is cosmopolitan.

In fact, McKay's interest in the question of the primitive is itself literary and cosmopolitan. The argument about primitivism and civilization is at the heart of the cosmopolitan novel of the 1920s, which can be seen in a quick roster of the writers who took it as an important subject in their fiction: Hemingway, Fitzgerald, Faulkner, Cather, Eliot, Wharton, the entire Harlem Renaissance, and so on. Take this well-known passage from Lawrence's Women in Love (1920/1992), in which Birkin contemplates a statue of an African woman:

> She knew what he himself did not know. She had thousands of years of purely sensual, purely unspiritual knowledge behind her. . . . Thousands of years ago, that which was imminent in himself must have taken place in these Africans; the goodness, the holiness, the desire for creation must have lapsed. . . . Is our day of creative life finished? Does there remain to us only the strange awful afterwards of the knowledge in dissolution, the African knowledge, but different in us, who are blond and blue-eyed from the North?
>
> (330-31)

In Sherwood Anderson's Poor White (1920/1969), black dock workers throw parcels and words around, feeling their bodies and work and words all in harmony and "unconscious love of inanimate things lost to whites" (106). In Dark Laughter (1925), Anderson, himself influenced by Lawrence, uses the free laughter of the uncivilized Negro soul to provide ethical commentary on the ridiculousness of civilized morality. Both of these writers were in turn important influences on McKay, as was, for that matter, the writer who set off the sharpest debates on the subject among African American literati with his novel *Nigger Heaven* (1926), Carl Van Vechten.

For Lawrence and Anderson, primitive vitality and primitive wisdom had been lost, and theirs was a primitivism drenched in nostalgia. For Van Vechten and McKay, the cultural worlds of the primitive and the civilized coexisted, mingled, created hybrids, and would continue to do so. McKay loved Lawrence, he said, because he represented "all of the ferment and torment and turmoil, the hesitation and hate and alarm, the sexual inquietude and the incertitude of this age, and the psychic and romantic groping for a way out" (McKay 1970/1985, 247). McKay works in his fiction to the same effect, multiplying the ambiguities and incertitudes of contemporary civilization. At one point in *Banjo*, Ray grins to himself "at the civilized world of nations, all keeping their tiger's claws sharp and strong under the thin cloak of international amity and awaiting the first favorable opportunity to spring" (135), thus showing civilization itself to be savage. The average White man, he muses, can be violently seized at any moment by his "guarded, ancient treasure of national hates" (135), and revert to savagery. "He hated civilization," McKay tells us later in the novel. "Once in a moment of bitterness he had said in Harlem, 'Civilization is rotten.' And the more he traveled and knew of it, the more he felt the truth of that bitter outburst" (163). Yet the carefree, laughing primitives, at the same time, lived in a "slimy garbage-strewn little space of hopeless hags, hussies, touts, and cats and dogs forever chasing one another about in nasty imitation of the residents," their vaunted sensuality simply "low-down proletarian love, stinking, hard, cruel" (87). Even the music that so liberates Ray's senses and sense of human possibility can, as in the parties at Gin-head Suzy's apartment in Brooklyn, make for brawls and ugliness. Civilization is rotten, but so is primitive life. And just as primitive life is full of benefits, so is civilized life: "The whites have done the blacks some great wrongs," McKay wrote in *A Long Way from Home* (1970/1985), "but they also have done some good. They have brought to them the benefits of modern civilization" (349).

These multiple valuations point to the real moral of the story, which is that the truly educated person is one with an aesthetic cosmopolitan openness to difference, someone with a broad enough purview to comprehend the myriad cultural forms that make up the world in which Ray and Banjo, McKay and his readers all live. Sometimes the arguments between characters are resolved in favor of a broader overview quite explicitly. In *Banjo*, for instance, a French bartender and a Senegalese student argue about the fate of Negroes in America, the bartender saying that the African Americans are the most privileged and progressive in the world, the student saying that they are lynched and Jim Crowed into submission. Ray, expressing the literary cosmopolitan point of view, takes the overview: "You are both right," he says, and goes on to explain that both the facts of oppression as the student understands them and the facts of progress as the bartender understands them are true. This scene is followed by one in which Ray argues with his friend Goosey about the meaning of interracial marriage, and there Goosey is given the chance to up the cosmopolitan ante. Ray gives Goosey the cosmopolitan Marxist argument about class, to which Goosey replies:

> To me the most precious thing about human life is difference. Like flowers in a garden, different kinds for different people to love. I am not against miscegenation. It produces splendid and interesting types. But I should not crusade for it because I should hate to think of a future in which the identity of the black race in the Western World should be lost in miscegenation.
>
> (208)

The point is not to acquire some kind of predetermined cosmopolitan correctness, but to develop a habit of cosmopolitan perspectivalism.

The musical passages, with their undifferentiation, mimic the cosmopolitan argument: they erase differences by incorporating them. Blues is not just blue; it incorporates "red moods, black moods, golden moods . . . slipping-over into one mood, back-sliding back to the first mood." (*Home to Harlem*, 54) The musical passages are also all parts of the "nether" life of the characters—blues and jazz are played in the brothels, at the wild house parties, in the bars of the "ditch"—and so they are part of the process by which the reader's difference from the low-class characters is erased in aesthetic appreciation. The musical passages mimic the argument syntactically as well, with moods following moods in apposition, adjectives spouted in succession without commas separating them, and the sentences composed of dependent clauses with no independent clause to support. Kimberly W. Benston (1979) has argued, also with reference to the myth of Orpheus, that jazz is able to undermine rigid ideologies, and thus free the imagination, and McKay is clearly arguing something similar. For Benston, as it has been for many commentators on music through the years, the myth is one about the power of music to obliterate socially constructed boundaries—Houston Baker's (1984) trope of the blues detective is one such incarnation. In *Home to Harlem,* at the end of a chapter about labor unrest, police beatings, and their relation to gambling-incited violence, the proprietress of a buffet flat orders the piano to play a blues after Zeddy and Jake almost end up in a knife fight with a loan shark. "Oh, 'blues,' 'blues,' 'blues.' Black-framed white grinning. Finger-snapping. Undertone singing. . . . Zeddy's gorilla feet dancing down the dark death lurking in his heart" (54). In McKay's fiction, too, then, the blues can erase, at least temporarily, social unrest at both the micro- and macroeconomic level.

In another scene, though, we see that McKay does not believe that this deconstruction of ideology is the whole story. At Madame Suarez's one night, a prostitute is singing a jazz song at the piano, and even the other prostitutes "carried away by the sheer rhythm of delight, had risen above their commercial instincts . . . and abandoned themselves to pure voluptuous jazzing" (108). The breakdown of social order is more marked in this scene because there are five White men in the room as well. But, and here is McKay's argument, "then the five young white men unmasked themselves as the Vice Squad and killed the thing."

Later in the novel a similar scene occurs, this time with an added twist. I quote it at length because the movement of ideas takes some time to develop. Again, in his description of the music, McKay becomes most modernist in syntax as he describes the most primitive aesthetics, and again the police intervene (the ellipses are in the original):

> The piano-player had wandered off into some dim, far-away, ancestral source of music. Far, far away from music-hall syncopation and jazz, he was lost in some sensual dream of his own. No tortures, banal shrieks and agonies. Tum-tum . . . tum-tum . . . tum-tum . . . tum-tum. . . . The notes were naked acute alert. Like black youth burning naked in the bush. Love deep in the heart of the jungle. . . . The sharp spring of a leopard from a leafy limb, the snarl of a jackal, green lizards in amorous play, the flight of a plumed bird, and the sudden laughter of mischievous monkeys in their green homes. Tum-tum . . . tum-tum . . .

> tum-tum . . . tum-tum. . . . Simple-clear and quivering. Like a primitive dance of war or of love . . . the marshaling of spears or the sacred frenzy of a phallic celebration.

> Black lovers of life caught up in their own free native rhythm, threaded to a remote scarce-remembered past, celebrating the mid-night hour in themselves, for themselves, of themselves, in a house in Fifteenth Street in Philadelphia. . . .

> "Raided!" A voice screamed. Standing in the rear door, a policeman, white, in full uniform, smilingly contemplated the spectacle.
>
> (196-97)

This passage moves from the immersed undifferentiation of the "jungle" music, to a formulaic invocation of primitivist aesthetic theory ("free native . . . scarce-remembered past"), to an invocation of political theory with the echoes of the declaration of independence, to an invocation of social reality in the street address, to the arrival of the police. The policeman in this passage turns out to be a customer, and there is no raid, but his appearance reminds us that the moment of erasure is an aesthetic rather than a social fact. The point is not to live in the "nether world," as McKay calls it in "Like a Strong Tree," but to visit the netherworld and come back.

Just as the music is the orphic mark of and entryway to the "queer things of the nether world" for the characters in the book, these musical passages also represent the counterperspective to machine civilization. The fact that jazz is a music whose primary form of diffusion is the phonograph, and thus that its very existence is the result of machine civilization, is not so much a contradiction as an added level of cosmopolitan complexity. The mechanical reproduction of jazz comes in for some criticism, since the parties at which fights break out are more often those at which a phonograph rather than live music is being played. But it nonetheless accompanies our readerly descent into regions we, the text suggests, have never before seen. Just as the jazz clubs of Harlem were an important site of White American exposure to African American culture, so, in McKay's novels, music is the characters', and in turn the readers', ticket to the wider, deeper world, an entree to African American perspectives for their largely White readership, and to the lower classes for the Black bourgeoisie.

The banjo, in the 1920s, was an apt symbol of such cross-cultural exchange. Developed from African instruments, the banjo was a distinctly African American instrument in the late 19th century. By the 1920s, however, it had crossed over, and there were banjo clubs at most universities, with large groups of elite White young men strumming on their old banjos, and fancy "presentation" banjos were available by mail order for the price of a fairly good piano. Some African American leaders looked down on the banjo as a symbol of plantation culture, while for many people it signified the most modern, "jazzy" music. There is some argument between the musicians in *Banjo* at one point about whether banjo music is, like the "coon song," a mark of subjection, or whether it is a pure form of expression of the Negro spirit. The fact is, though, that the most innovative jazz bands in the 1920s were dropping their banjo players in favor of pianos. *Banjo*'s banjo is thus a symbol that bridges many of the dichotomies from which the novel is built—modern-traditional, traditional music-jazz, White-Black, low class-high class, primitive-civilized, and, of course, the path toward understanding through rational thought versus that through emotional engagement. And, finally, as Banjo says, his banjo is "moh than a gal, moh than a pal, it's mah-self" (6). Ray envies and tries to imitate his friend's natural ease with his world, his self, and his music, and we as readers are asked to consider whether we can descend into the nether regions of our own self-hood by listening to the music that McKay is making for us.

### *Orpheus and Dangerous Sexuality*

Orpheus plays the lyre, like the classic banjo a four-stringed instrument that is picked or strummed. Orpheus's music gives him access to the "queer things of the nether world" as well. The son of the god Apollo and Calliope, the muse of epic poetry, Orpheus could charm not only gods, mortals, and animals with his songs, but stones and trees as well. He marries the beautiful nymph Eurydice, but on their wedding day she is bitten by a poisonous snake and dies. He then journeys to the underworld and tries to free her. He melts the cold hearts of the lords of the underworld with his music, and they give him permission to take Eurydice back, with one condition—that he not turn to look at her as they ascend. Orpheus, of course, does, and she is swallowed up again by Hades. Back in this world, Orpheus's music becomes even more moving in his renewed grief.

Ovid is one of many who tells the story:

> His eyes th' impatient lover backward threw:
> When she, back-sliding presently with-drew.
> He catches at her, in his wits distraught;
> And yeelding ayre for her (unhappy!) caught.
> Nor did she; dying twice, her spouse reprove:
> For what could she complaine of, but his love?
> *(The Tenth Booke, 61-66)*

Orpheus represents the bard, and thereby the artist in general. He can, with his songs, bring the dead back to life as Homer, in a sense, did for Odysseus, giving him another life in epic form; if one looks too hard at such representations, however, if one looks at them in a distrustful way, they die or disappear. Orpheus is also a mythic transgressor of the law—like Eve with the apple, Orpheus perversely does the only thing that he has been asked not to. In attempting to ensure the satisfaction of his desire he kills his own love. "Too well he loved," perhaps, but also too poorly.

The fact Eurydice was killed by a "snake" on her wedding night suggests a myth of the dangers of sexuality as well. When Orpheus returns from the underworld, he wanders and refuses the love of other women. He prefers, instead, the company of young men. Some classic Greek sources, in fact, credit Orpheus with introducing the practice of men having sex with men to the region. Orpheus's disdain for the charms of the local women so angers them that they tear Orpheus to pieces. In one version of the myth, after he is torn to pieces, his head is thrown into a river but continues to sing. Heterosexual desire is represented in the myth as deadly, homosexual as perhaps the preferable option, although this, too, in effect, kills him.

McKay himself was bisexual. He had sexual relations with women and with men, according to Cooper (1987), who cites the testimony of many people who, he suggests, were in a position to know. Although, as Cooper says, McKay "never openly explored or publicly acknowledged homosexuality as an aspect of his personal life" (74), he did write about his homosexual encounters in a number of ways. In his autobiography, *A Long Way from Home* (1937), McKay never directly discusses sex, but he gives readers, especially his more cosmopolitan readers, plenty of information. McKay lived in Morocco in the late 1920s, attracted, as Cooper suggests, by its tolerance of homosexuality, and in describing Fez in his autobiography he writes, that "that antique African city was the unaware keeper of the cup of Eros containing a little of the perfume of the flower of the passion of ancient Greece" (299). Later in the autobiography he reacts against what he hears as a "desecration of the great glamorous name of Sappho" (310).

More significantly, he tells a number of stories in *A Long Way from Home* that have as a subtext a homosexual encounter. For instance, he tells a story about meeting a young man in a diner. The man is running from the police. He is a pickpocket, he tells McKay, "and he was refreshingly frank about it. He was a little pickpocket and did his tricks most of the time . . . while [his victims] were asleep or by getting friendly with them" (45-46). He had almost been busted in the men's room in the subway before coming into the diner. McKay not only befriends him but takes him home for the night. When his girlfriend comes in the next morning to find this man in McKay's apartment, she reacts with horror. "Foh the land's sake!" McKay recounts her saying, "I wonder what will happen next!" (46). His girlfriend was hostile to "poor white trash," McKay explains, but he also says that he lied to her, saying that the man was an old friend. "There was always a certain strangeness between Manda and me," he adds (46). This is a story that no one familiar with gay life in the 1920s could mistake for anything but a sexual encounter. McKay tells another story of being "often in the company of a dancer." Once, while they were in McKay's apartment, his ex-wife unexpectedly drops in. "The dancer exclaimed in a shocked tone, 'Why, I never knew that you were *married!*'" McKay writes, "As if that should have made any difference to *him*" (149).

One of the big complaints that the Old Crowd had against McKay's fiction was that it portrayed African Americans as sexually promiscuous, thus feeding debilitating stereotypes of Black sexuality and depravity. But McKay does not represent homosexuality directly. He relies, in such stories, on a cosmopolitan audience that will understand the stories he is telling, and perhaps as well a somewhat more provincial audience which will not. He tells of a White man in Paris who says, "*J'ai le béguin pour toi*" (328), a French phrase meaning "I have a crush on you," but which McKay leaves untranslated. McKay replies, "*Merci, mais je n'ai pas.*" But he is not rejecting the man because he is a man: "[H]is bloodless white skin was nauseating. He had no color" (329). McKay sometimes admits and denies at the same time—"as if that should have made any difference to *him*," he says of the dancer, but is this because McKay is not interested in him as a sexual partner, or because it was just a woman? In the last chapter of the autobiography, discussing his time in Morocco, he says that the most interesting European visitor he had was a young man named Charles Henri Ford, "who published a queer book of adolescence in Paris under the rather Puritan title of *The Young and the Evil*" (337). Ford published the "queer book" about young gay artists in Greenwich Village in 1933. Louis Kronenberger, in the *New Republic,* called it "the first candid, gloves-off account of more or

less professional young homosexuals," and the book was banned for a time in the United States. McKay doesn't mention the novel's contents (which hadn't yet been published when Ford visited Morocco), but he does say that Ford "was like a rare lily squatting in among the bearded and bournoused natives, and he enjoyed it." His Moroccan friends "all rather liked him. They said he looked wonderfully like the cinema portraits of Marlene Dietrich." The point of these references is obvious, and one even wonders if double entendres were intended when McKay describes his own hospitality—"When he left [the first] evening I gave him a chunk of meat from what had been given to me" (337)—or when McKay reports that Ford "came again and again" (338).

In the novels, similar double readings are available. When Jake and Ray meet, in *Home to Harlem,* Ray is reading a novel titled *Sappho* and explains to Jake that the real Sappho gave the words *sapphic* and *lesbian* to the language, and that they are "beautiful words." Jake sings a popular blues lyric ("And there is two things in Harlem I don't understan' / It is a bulldyking woman and a faggoty man"), but Ray scolds him for being childish and savage. "Bumbole!" says Jake. We then get a quick dissertation on this latest slang appropriation of his:

> "Bumbole" was now a popular expletive for Jake, replacing such expressions as "Bull," "bawls," "walnuts," and "blimey." Ever since the night at the Congo when he had heard the fighting West Indian girl cry, "I'll slap you bumbole," he had always used the word. When his friends asked him what it meant, he grinned and said, "Ask the monks."

To understand the passage from *balls* to *bum hole,* McKay and Jake suggest, just ask the monks, the male society that kept cosmopolitan culture alive in the Dark Ages. For the next several pages, Ray tells Banjo about the history of Haiti, about Wordsworth's sonnet to Toussaint L'Ouverture, about Liberia, about Abyssinia and Egypt, about Daudet and the intellectual life. Cosmopolitan literary knowledge, homosexuality, and homosociality are the intertwined themes, then, of the meeting of our twinned protagonists.

Once Ray is on the scene, both Banjo and Jake often decide to spend time with him instead of their women and make various protestations about the relative importance of male over female companionship. Just as Ray learns about the joys of vernacular music from Banjo, so he learns about the joys of camaraderie as well. The rough boys of the ditch, Ray discovers, "possessed more potential power for racial salvation than the Negro literati, whose poverty of mind and purpose showed never any signs of enrichment, even though inflated above the common level and given an appearance of superiority" (322). This power is directly linked to their disregard for civilized morality. "From these boys he could learn how to live—how to exist as a black boy in a white world and rid his conscience of the used-up hussy of white morality" (322). One could trace a whole series of homosocial and veiled homosexual comments in the novels, but I will just give one more here, since it functions as such a summation for McKay as well. At the very end of *Banjo* we find Banjo asking Ray if he will go away with him. Ray then spends several pages musing about the relative value of Banjo's life and his own, about machine civilization and primitive spontaneity, and about happiness ("the highest good" [325]) and difference ("the greatest charm" [325]). "What you say, pardner?" Banjo asks. "You gwine with a man or you ain't?" (325). Ray hesitates, then says that it would have been great if they could take Latnah, a woman Banjo had been living with, along with them. Banjo says no, and explains in these, the last words of the novel:

> Don't get soft ovah any one wimmens, pardner. Tha's you' big weakness. A woman is a conjunction. Gawd fixed her different from us in moh ways than one. And theah's things we can git away with all the time and she just kain't. Come on pardner. Wese got enough between us to beat it a long ways from here.

Any student of American literature will recognize in this ending the recurrence of a theme Leslie Fiedler described, beginning with his article "Come Back to the Raft Ag'in, Huck, Honey" and culminating in *Love and Death in the American Novel* (1960), a theme central to classic American literature. For Fiedler, Huck Finn lighting out for the territories before Aunt Polly civilizes him and Natty Bumppo and Chingachgook heading into the woods to avoid encroaching civilization represent the typical American novelistic ending: two men bond and go off into the wilderness together, leaving women and civilization behind. Instead of a resolution in marriage, as in the classic British novel, American novels end in isolation and flight, or buddying up and flight. Fielder analyzed this flight from civilization as a form of immaturity, among other things. But it is clear that in many of these early formations, the primitive alternative to civilization is also racialized, and as Fiedler makes clear, it confronts normative heterosexuality as well.

## Vagabondage and Cosmopolitanism

McKay announces, in this poem from the mid-1920s, that he will go to hell and back for his poetry:

> In the furnace let me go alone;
> Stay you without in terror of the heat.
> I will go naked in—for thus 'tis sweet—
> Into the weird depths of the hottest zone.
> I will not quiver in the frailest bone,
> You will not note a flicker of defeat;
> My heart shall not tremble its fate to meet,
> Nor mouth give utterance to any moan.
> The yawning oven spits forth fiery spears;
> Red aspish tongues shout wordlessly my name.
> Desire destroys, consumes my mortal fears,
> Transforming me into a shape of flame.
> I will come out, back to your world of tears,
> A stronger soul within a finer frame.
> (Locke 1925/1992, 134)

That this verse equates hell and desire, sex and removal from the world, is not surprising, given McKay's backhanded defenses of homosexuality. McKay, like many other writers of fiction at the time, adopted the necessary role of one who comprehends the social proprieties and the advance of civilization, but who understands them as contingent rather than natural, and who can survey all the realms, including the hells, that propriety tries to keep at bay.

The only thing natural in this world of constructed relations and identities, many of the writers of the 1920s agreed, is the human animal in all its pleasure-seeking glory. Whites, with more developed "sex-complexes," attributed "oversexed emotions" to Blacks, but this was simply a mark of their greater distance, McKay (1929/1957) argued, from a natural relation to their own bodies:

> Even among rough proletarians Ray never noticed in black men those expressions of vicious contempt for sex that generally came from the mouths of white workers. It was as if the white man considered sex a nasty, irritating thing, while a Negro accepted it with primitive joy. And maybe that vastly big difference of attitude was a fundamental, unconscious cause of the antagonism between white and black brought together by civilization.
> (253)

At the same time, the figure of Jake or Banjo or any other Mr. Natural is not the model to be followed. The end of *Home to Harlem* shows Jake envious of the kind of woman Ray has—educated, accomplished, professional, cosmopolitan—and desiring to be more like Ray. Just before the Fiedleresque moment at the end of *Banjo*, Ray expresses his impatience with the boys of the ditch, finding it "dismaying" that they can "in a moment become forgetful of everything serious in a drunken-like abandon of jazzing" (316). Earlier, Ray considered how Anglo-Saxons had been shaming people from other cultures, especially those with "strong appetites" (164), and he decides, "No being ashamed for Ray. Rather than lose his soul, let intellect go to hell and live instinct!" (165) But that is only if he had to choose between intellect and instinct. The preferable option is to have both.

McKay includes his own performance in this double analysis: just as Banjo plays dance music that induces ecstasy in the players and the audience, so jazz provokes McKay's most ecstatic, stylistically innovative, vernacular-tinged, modernistic prose in both *Banjo* and *Home to Harlem*. In both cases the music, in all its primitiveness, can be a force for social progress, as J. A. Rogers, in his article on jazz in *The New Negro* (1925), also argued. Rogers wrote that jazz was "recharging the batteries of civilization with a primitive new vigor" that will drive the "needless artificiality" out of American life, and that therefore jazz is a democratizing "assimilator" (224). Rogers had a very different conception of the blues than McKay, though they had similar positions on jazz. For Rogers, the blues was humorless, irony-free, and therefore simply depressive. For McKay, as for Langston Hughes, the blues were full of ambivalence and ambiguity. As James de Jongh (1990) has written, Hughes identified Harlem with "the duality, paradox, and irony of jazz and blues" (24), as did McKay. But if McKay agreed with Rogers's belief in jazz's virtues, he is less sanguine about its political effects. Just as pure bodily sensation is not enough to found a culture on, neither is jazz; in either case, one must still deal with the police.

But even the police are understandable from a fully cosmopolitan perspective, McKay suggests. The stylistic innovations McKay uses to represent jazz within the confines of a traditional picaresque novel suggest the cultural model McKay has in mind, one in which either-or questions are always given the answer of both. The model is much closer to someone like Ray is in the process of becoming than someone like Banjo, of course. The model is someone like the readers of these texts after reading them, someone, indeed, like McKay, who knows, appreciates, and can experience the primitive and the civilized, the hetero and the homo, the licit and the illicit, someone who has the cosmopolitan chops to hang with the band and to assess novelistic representations of hanging with the band. "Ray had found that to be

educated, black, and his instinctive self was something of a job to put over," (*Banjo*, 323) McKay writes, and that is the chore he sets for his readers as well. Civilization is hell, the ditch is hell, Harlem is hell, and all three are "glory," as McKay suggests (with a dose of irony) in his last novel, *Harlem Glory*, written in the late 1940s, and first published in 1990.

Ray, Jake, and Banjo represent what James Clifford (1997) has called "discrepant cosmopolitanisms" (36), in that they all have a cosmopolitan view of the world, made up in each case of a variety of perspectives, positions, and experiences. McKay's *Banana Bottom* (1933) is full of discrepant cosmopolitanisms: Crazy Bow plays classical European music, American Negro spirituals, New World dance music, and West Indian folk music. Squire Gensir is a British aristocrat who knows all of these musics as well, and also collects Anancy stories, puts together dictionaries of slang, attends native religious observances, and collects the "songs, jammas, shey-sheys, and breakdowns," and any other peasant music he can find: the "songs of the fields, the draymen's songs, love songs, satiric ditties of rustic victims of elemental passions" (71). Gensir is not the ultimate cosmopolitan, though. "Being an enthusiast of the simple life, he was like many enthusiasts, apt to underestimate the underlying contradictions that may inhere in his more preferable way of life" (176). Gensir mentors the protagonist Bita as she comes to terms with the relation of her British musical training to her life in the Jamaican countryside, as well as her series of sexual injuries and irregularities. In the end she decides, however, that "love and music were divine things, but none so rare as the pure flight of the mind into the upper realms of thought" (314).

McKay suggests that we, as the literary community, in our pure flights of mind, can be the true cosmopolitans, the ones who empathize with all of these characters and understand their hell and their glory. For those who would complain that such Enlightenment-sounding cosmopolitanism is itself ideologically saturated, indeed imperialistic, McKay might have responded, in the words of his poem "Like a Strong Tree," quoted earlier, "So I would live in imperial growth, / Touching the surface and the depth of things, / Instinctively responsive unto both" (Locke 1925/1992, 134). McKay touched on these surfaces and depths in his life and work, and given his youth in Jamaica, young adulthood in the United States, and extensive travels and stays in Europe and North Africa. Addison Gayle, Jr.

(1972) is right to say that his "wandering from one city to another" brought to his work "a cosmopolitan perspective that few of his contemporaries possessed" (17). McKay, who cites not just the instinctive primitivist Lawrence but Whitman, the great encompasser of multitudes, as a formative influence, sees vagabonding through "the weird depths of the hottest zone" and back into the "world of tears" as the basis of literary representation. And he sees literature as the music, the great song of himself, that can introduce his readers to the fullness of the world and the self made possible through such imperial, cosmopolitan literary vagabondage. McKay is his own Orpheus, and wants to be his reader's.

## Works Cited

Anderson, Sherwood. *Poor White* (1920). New York: Viking, 1969.

———. *Dark Laughter.* New York: Boni and Liveright, 1925.

Baker, Houston. *Blues, Ideology, and Afro-American Literature: A Vernacular Theory.* Chicago: University of Chicago Press, 1984.

Benston, Kimberly W. "Late Coltrane: A Re-Membering of Orpheus." In *Chant of Saints: A Gathering of Afro-American Literature, Art, and Scholarship,* edited by Michael S. Harper and Robert B. Stepto. Urbana: University of Illinois Press, 1979.

Clifford, James. *Routes: Travel and Translation in the Late Twentieth Century.* Cambridge, MA: Harvard University Press, 1997.

Cooper, Wayne F. Foreword to *Home to Harlem,* by Claude McKay. Boston: Northeastern University Press, 1987.

———. *Claude McKay: Rebel Sojourner in the Harlem Renaissance: A Biography.* Baton Rouge: Louisiana State University Press, 1987.

———, ed. *The Passion of Claude McKay: Selected Poetry and Prose, 1912-1948.* New York: Schocken, 1973.

de Jongh, James. *Vicious Modernism: Black Harlem and the Literary Imagination.* Cambridge, MA: Harvard University Press, 1990.

Dixon, Melvin. *Ride Out the Wilderness: Geography and Identity in Afro-American Literature.* Urbana: University of Illinois Press, 1987.

Fiedler, Leslie A. *Love and Death in the American Novel.* New York: Criterion, 1960.

Fiedler, Leslie. "Come Back to the Raft Ag'in, Huck Honey!" In *The Adventures of Huckleberry Finn: A Case Study in Critical Controversy.* Edited by Gerald Graff and James Phelan, 528-34. Boston: Bedford/St. Martins, 1995.

Gayle, Addison, Jr. *Claude McKay: The Black Poet at War.* Detroit: Broadside Press, 1972.

Hutchinson, George. *The Harlem Renaissance in Black and White.* Cambridge, MA: Harvard University Press, 1995.

Lawrence, D. H. *Women in Love* (1920). Baltimore: Penguin, 1992.

Locke, Alain. *The New Negro: An Interpretation* (1925). New York: Athenaeum, 1992.

Lutz, Tom. *American Nervousness, 1903: An Anecdotal History.* Ithaca, NY: Cornell University Press, 1991.

———. "Curing the Blues: W. E. B. Du Bois, Fashionable Diseases, and Degraded Music in 1903." *Black Music Research Journal* 11 (1991), 137-56.

———. "Cosmopolitan Vistas: Willa Cather, Regionalism, and the Location of Literary Value." In *To Recover a Continent,* edited by Robert Sayre, 86-106. Madison: University of Wisconsin Press, 1998.

McKay, Claude. *Banana Bottom.* New York: Harper & Row, 1933.

———. *Banjo: A Story without a Plot* (1929). Harcourt, Brace, 1957.

———. *The Negroes in America* (*Negry v. Amerike,* 1923). Translated by Robert J. Winter. Port Washington, NY: Kennicat Press, 1979.

———. *A Long Way from Home* (1937). London: Pluto, 1985.

———. *Home to Harlem* (1928). Boston: Northeastern University Press, 1987.

———. *Harlem Glory.* Chicago: Kerr, 1990.

———. Review of *Shuffle Along. Liberator* 4 (December 1921): 24-26.

McLeod, A. L., ed. *Claude McKay: Centennial Studies.* New Delhi, India: Sterling Publishers, 1992.

Ogren, Kathy J. "Controversial Sounds: Jazz Performance as Theme and Language in the Harlem Renaissance." In *The Harlem Renaissance: Revaluations,* edited by Amritjit Singh, William S. Shiver, and Stanley Brodwin, 159-84. New York: Garland, 1989.

Ovid. *Ovid's Metamorphosis: Englished, Mythologized, and Represented in Figures* by George Sandys. Edited by Karl K. Hulley and Stanley T. Vandersall. Lincoln, Nebraska: University of Nebraska Press, 1970.

Rogers, J. A. "Jazz at Home." In *The New Negro: An Interpretation.* Edited by Alain Locke, 216-224. New York: Athenaeum, 1992.

Scott, Joyce Hope. "Black Folk Ritual in *Home to Harlem* and *Black Thunder.*" In *Claude McKay: Centennial Studies,* edited by A. L. McLeod, 123-34. New Delhi, India: Sterling Publishers, 1992.

Stearns, Harold. *Civilization in the United States.* New York: Harcourt, Brace & Co., 1992.

Williams, Sherley Anne. *Give Birth to Brightness: A Thematic Study in Neo-Black Literature.* New York: Dial, 1972.

## PAUL A. ANDERSON (ESSAY DATE 2000)

**SOURCE:** Anderson, Paul A. "'My Lord, What a Morning': The 'Sorrow Songs' in Harlem Renaissance Thought." In *Symbolic Loss: The Ambiguity of Mourning and Memory at Century's End,* edited by Peter Homans, pp. 83-102. Charlottesville: University Press of Virginia, 2000.

*In the following essay, Anderson investigates the use of slave spirituals in the poetry of early-twentieth-century Black writers, focusing on the writings of W. E. B. Du Bois, Jean Toomer, and Zora Neale Hurston.*

In the preface to her collection of poetry, *A Woman's Mourning Song,* bell hooks recalls the black community she was a part of as a working-class girl in rural Kentucky. It was a tightly knit world where the ritual of "passing on," the natural death of the elderly and infirm, followed a lively public spirit that blended grief with celebration. Individual and communal assumptions of spiritual continuity lessened the immobilizing sense of grief among survivors. "One celebrates the passing of life," hooks writes, "not only to ease the transition of the dead but to make it known that the moment is also a time of reunion, when those who have been long separated come together."[1] Where ascension into the ancestral spirit-world is assumed, the threshold between the natural and supernatural worlds can be approached as a benign passageway rather than as a site of horror.

*A Woman's Mourning Song,* with its attentiveness to folk responses to death in the black diaspora, brings to mind the ritualized "tame death" that Phillipe Ariès attributed to traditional European culture before the medical privatization of death and the tidal wave of cultural modernization.[2] Sigmund Freud represented a new wave of modernization when he formulated his psychoanalytic models of mourning and melancholia under the assumption that mourning had become a secular and largely individualized process. He wrote of mourning as a kind of work undertaken by an individual's psychic economy; it was a difficult but usually successful process, combining grief, memorialization, reality testing, and decathexis or disattachment. According to Freud's definition in "Mourning and Melancholia," mourning "is regularly the reaction to the loss of a loved person, or to the loss of some abstraction which has taken the place of one, such as one's country, liberty, an ideal, and so on."[3] Although the lost object being mourned might be a collective identification, the real work of mourning still took place on an individual level. If an individual's mourning process lost its progressive thrust and became stalled or ensnared, the psychoanalyst could offer clinical assistance by probing for the pathologies blocking forward movement. The pathological melancholic, for example, suffered in remaining affectively fixated on a desire for some known or unknown lost object. Thus, Freud interpreted melancholia as an ultimately regressive and narcissistic identification. He left to later generations the task of exploring how collective processes of mourning could be set in motion by the shared loss of an abstract ideal, collective practice, or identification.

One might map an arc or spectrum for the varieties of mourning summoned in *A Woman's Mourning Song.* At one point of the spectrum there is a gentle acceptance of death fueled by a community's assurance of sacred restitution. In her poetry and prose, hooks stages a personal scene of mourning over her weakened ties to these older traditions. In the book's cover photograph, Billie Holiday (1915-59) stands before a stage microphone singing with arms crossed and eyes closed. Holiday was raised Catholic, an outsider to the full-throated gospel shouts and dramatic catharses of the black evangelical church. Holiday's mature singing voice often evoked an affective world far removed from the sacred mourning practices hooks remembers from her childhood community and longs to incorporate into the work of what she calls black "self-recovery."[4] Today, forty years after her death, Holiday's reputation as an unparalleled jazz vocal artist is especially linked to her balladry and its demanding testimonies about romantic love and loss. In her later years, Holiday often entranced audiences with theatrical renderings of popular songs that approached sorrowful inconsolability. Holiday's greatest music, fans concur, has the potential to light the path out of bleak solipsism and despair even as it illuminates the darkest corners of heartbreak. "Lady Day," Leon Forrest wrote, "prophetically read out the terrorized terms of the heart, more than any other national black female artist in American culture."[5]

As a public intellectual, hooks asks how black diasporic practices for the overcoming of loss and grief can be nurtured under present historical conditions. She has written that traditional and "healthy approaches to death and dying made it possible for black people to confront and cope with loss." Although hooks perceives a weakening of these traditions, she asserts that "Many southern black people have held to the belief that a human being possesses body, soul, and spirit—that death may take one part even as the others remain."[6] *A Woman's Mourning Song* uses images of music as sites of mourning that speak to hopes for black "self-recovery" through reattachment and reconnection rather than through a Freudian decathexis and disconnection from highly energized sites of loss and identification. With its deep traditions and long memory—and because it is varied enough to appeal to so many needs and constituencies—music may be the most intensely developed of all sites of black diasporic memory.[7]

The slave spirituals have long occupied sacred ground as a place of memory among African Americans. The writer and activist W. E. B. Du

Bois articulated an especially resonant image of the spirituals as "sorrow songs" a century ago. Through his influential writings, Du Bois hoped to manage and reframe this site of memory according to his own very ambitious agenda for social transformation. A long debate over the inheritance of the spirituals took on a particular urgency in the 1920s context of the "New Negro" Renaissance or Harlem Renaissance. This essay contrasts Du Bois's image of the "sorrow songs" as a site of memory with the responses of Jean Toomer, Alain Locke, and Zora Neale Hurston, three prominent voices of the Harlem Renaissance era. Toomer, an avant-garde writer, and Locke, a philosopher and cultural critic, responded to Du Bois's paradigm by encouraging modernist postures of mourning toward black folk culture. Locke's sponsorship of "New Negro" art as, in part, a commemorative project resembled Du Bois's dialectic of black continuity in cosmopolitan development. Toomer, on the other hand, gestures toward a more radical and post-racial view of mourning. Zora Neale Hurston, an ethnographer and novelist, refused the "New Negro" rhetoric of mourning the loss of immanent obsolescence of black folk culture and offered an alternative conception of black cultural continuity.

In his 1888 valedictory address at Fisk University in Nashville, the graduating college senior William Edward Burghardt Du Bois celebrated Otto von Bismarck, the long-time chancellor to Wilhelm I and the political architect of a newly united German nation. Bismarck's glory was in making a nation "out of bickering peoples." "The life of this powerful Chancellor illustrates the power and purpose, the force of an idea," the young Du Bois explained.[8] The great idea that so gripped Du Bois's imagination was modern nationhood, though he would later repudiate Bismarck's imperialism. After receiving a doctorate in sociology from Harvard and publishing several important scholarly studies, including *The Philadelphia Negro* (1899), Du Bois fashioned a more personal voice in *The Souls of Black Folk* (1903). The book, an autobiographically influenced account of "the problem of the color line," described the struggle for racial equality and the recognition of black contributions to America's growth. Du Bois took hold of the "sorrow songs" in order to dig deep into the southern past and the legacy of slavery. His goal was to distill the power of the most solemn spirituals and capture that power in his own intensely lyrical prose. He would then wield a transformed fragment of the black past as

a tool for social transformation. One might view his strategy of redemptive recontextualization in the light of a later messianic formulation from Walter Benjamin: "Only that historian will have the gift of fanning the spark of hope in the past who is convinced that *even the dead* will not be safe from the enemy if he wins."[9] To fan the embers of "hope in the past" Du Bois had to evoke the traumatic wounds of displacement and subjugation that first inspired black slaves in America to express their grievances, joys, and dreams in collective song.

Du Bois explained in the "Sorrow Songs" chapter of *The Souls of Black Folk* that he first heard some of the old slave spirituals during his western Massachusetts childhood. He had always been moved by them but only came to grasp their meaning in the southern black world of Fisk. "Then in after years when I came to Nashville," he wrote, "I saw the great temple builded of these songs towering over the pale city. To me Jubilee Hall seemed ever made of the songs themselves, and its bricks were red with the blood and dust of toil." In the 1870s, the Fisk Jubilee Singers took "those weird old songs in which the soul of the black slave spoke to men" to the wider world and raised funds for the school.[10] The singing group of black college students presented an arranged and somewhat Europeanized version of the folk music to concert hall and church audiences in the United States, the British Isles, and Western Europe. Their tours' unexpected success funded, among other things, the construction of Jubilee Hall on the Fisk campus. Other black colleges soon followed suit and pursued this unique fund-raising opportunity. "Making black expressiveness a commodity . . . is not simply a gesture in a bourgeois economics of art," the literary critic Houston A. Baker has noted, but "is a crucial move in a repertoire of black survival motions in the United States." "Afro-America's exchange power," Baker concludes," has always been coextensive with its stock of expressive resources."[11] Du Bois's reflection on the "sorrow songs" emphasized the uplifting commemorative work of the Fisk Jubilee Singers as a repudiation of minstrelsy.

The spirituals inspired minstrel parodies and crude imitations both before and after the Fisk Jubilee Singers' vogue in the twilight of Reconstruction. Du Bois distinguished the real "sorrow songs" from variations that ridiculed or improperly memorialized the slaves' millennial hopes and collective sorrow. "Caricature," he exclaimed, "has sought to spoil the quaint beauty of the music, and has filled the air with many debased melodies which vulgar ears scarce know from the real." Du Bois held up the "sorrow song" legacy as proof that African Americans were not bereft of collective memory or valuable folk cultural traditions. His childhood memory of an ancestral African lullaby, passed on for generations, demonstrated that the "sorrow songs" bound Americans to a barely known African past. A mixture of African and diasporic memories had congealed into musical form, as the haunting music of the "sorrow songs" was "far more ancient than the words."[12]

The double meanings of spirituals like "My Lord, What a Morning," "Go Down, Moses," "Swing Low, Sweet Chariot," "Deep River," and "Were You There (When They Crucified My Lord)?" were not to be forgotten. To mask the dangerous messages from the ears of whites, song lyrics wove together motifs of spiritual and secular liberation through frequent identification of the tribulations of American slaves with the sacred trials of earlier "suffering servants," whether Christ or the Israelites in bondage. The songs' most rebellious strains—"naturally veiled and half articulate," Du Bois noted—remained obscure to outsiders. Du Bois usually concentrated on the worldliness of the "sorrow songs" and referred to Christianity as a "dimly understood theology" among the slaves. Moreover, he expressed no great sympathy for religious emotionalism and "frenzy," whether in animistic spirit-worship or evangelical enthusiasm.[13] His understanding of the "sorrow songs" beckoned instead toward a social and political transformation of this world:

> Through all the sorrow of the Sorrow Songs there breathes a hope—a faith in the ultimate justice of things. The minor cadences of despair change often to triumph and calm confidence. Sometimes it is faith in life, sometimes a faith in death, sometimes assurance of boundless justice in some fair world beyond. But whichever it is, the meaning is always clear; that sometime, somewhere, men will judge men by their souls and not by their skins. Is such a hope justified? Do the Sorrow Songs ring true?[14]

Du Bois wanted readers to apprehend a chain of logic linking his sense of the Fisk Jubilee Singers as placeholders for the "sorrow songs" to his demands for a new paradigm in civil rights agitation and black nationalist consciousness. The success of the Fisk Jubilee Singers, like the adaptation of motifs from the spirituals in Antonin Dvorak's symphony *From the New World* (No. 9 in E minor) of 1893, called for a new aesthetic of cultural nationalism.

For Du Bois, the "sorrow songs" crystallized the deepest collective longings of the African American slaves. "They are the music of an unhappy people," he wrote, "of the children of disappointment; they tell of death and suffering and unvoiced longing toward a truer world, of misty wanderings and hidden ways." Du Bois's emphasis on "sadness, disappointment . . . [and] unvoiced longing" invites us to revisit Freud's "Mourning and Melancholia." For Freud, melancholic grief is usually incapable of fully identifying its own cause; with no clear origin for the pain, the sufferer can find no path away from it and toward reparation. Instead, the horizon is bereft and emptied of worthy new love objects or ideals. "The complex of melancholia," Freud argued, "behaves like an open wound, drawing to itself cathectic energies . . . from all directions, and emptying the ego until it is totally impoverished."[15] The Du Boisian image of the "sorrow song" differs in important ways from Freud's depiction of the melancholic's "open wound." Although Du Bois's "sorrow songs" constitute a perennial site of loss and memory, they do not emphasize self-directed aggression or a static repetition of ego impoverishment. When performed, the songs can instead address "open wounds" and memories of subjugation through a more subtle dynamic of repetition, artifice, and mournful reparation. Sacred and secular hopes for deliverance, along with the ritualized demonstration of communal support, can counteract a vertiginous fall into inconsolable melancholia at the traumatic site of a collective "open wound." Du Bois's image of the "sorrow songs" represented something more than a melancholy inducing memorial to undifferentiated trauma. His reparative and forward-looking model of black cultural development insisted that the pull of despair could be met and intertwined with restitutive memories and an idealism that began to articulate the spirituals' "unvoiced longing toward a truer world." Freud's avowedly secular ideal of successful mourning meant coming to terms with or "working-through" the loss of the beloved person, object, or ideal through a gradual and ultimately complete decathexis of libidinal investment. Public performances of the "sorrow songs" respectfully staged and remembered the sadness addressed in the original songs; these same performances could recuperate the slaves' millennial hopes as contexts for new collective ideals in the post-slavery era.

It should be noted that the cultural logic of mourning in Du Bois's "sorrow song" ideal appears only implicitly in his writings.[16] As a historical frame for the present interpretation, one might consider the general predicament of folkloric cultural nationalism.[17] Countless varieties of romantic nationalism in the modern era have presented idealized and lyrical images of the rural folk. Often distinctly pastoral, these images serve as abstract love objects for bourgeois audiences dissociated from the texture of everyday rural life and alienated from, if not outrightly critical of, the urban "masses." The ideal of the national folk allows for a mythic reconciliation between the urban bourgeoisie and the peasantry qua specters of "pre-modernity" and insurers of the nation's archaic authenticity.[18] The cosmopolitan Du Bois urged the preservation of some elements of the black folk inheritance for the sake of a black nationalist wing in the "kingdom of culture." His famous notion of black "double-consciousness" depicted a racialized form of psychic alienation among African Americans that was felt most acutely by highly assimilated intellectuals like himself. "One ever feels his two-ness," Du Bois wrote, "—an American, a Negro; two souls, two thoughts, two unreconciled strivings, two warring ideals in one dark body, whose dogged strength alone keeps it from being torn asunder. . . . The history of the American Negro is the history of this strife,—this longing to attain self-conscious manhood, to merge his double self into a better and truer self. In this merging he wishes neither of the old selves to be lost."[19] Du Bois's vision of black liberation, influenced by Hegelian idealism and Herderian nationalism, took shape as a dialectical conception of individual and collective self-consciousness and disalienation. Moreover, the logic of *Aufhebung* or dialectical sublation (the intertwined developmental work of cancellation, preservation, and elevation) might be likened to Freud's normative vision of successful mourning. Mitchell Breitwieser argues in *American Puritanism and the Defense of Mourning* that Freud's model of ideal mourning "may be dialectic's purest case."[20] Apropos of critical theory in the wake of deconstruction, Breitwieser illuminates a relationship between the evasion of the unsublated remainder in Hegelian dialectics and the disavowal or repression of the leftover of melancholic identification in Freud's model of ideal mourning.

Du Bois crafted a usable past out of idealized images of the black folk and the "sorrow songs" even as he de-emphasized the songs' role in a living religious tradition. He believed that the songs'

innermost nugget of folk authenticity and moral seriousness could be preserved while their musical forms were dialectically lifted into more refined concert idioms appropriate to the cosmopolitan "kingdom of culture." The dialectical aspects of both Du Bois's "sorrow song" ideal and his implicit cultural logic of mourning assumed an abstract negation or casting off of those aspects he considered vulgar, counterprogressive, or simply backward in black culture. "As a highly educated Western black intellectual," the philosopher Cornel West has noted, "Du Bois himself often scorns the 'barbarisms' (sometimes confused with Africanisms) shot through Afro-American culture." A mixture of folk romanticism and bourgeois self-righteousness courses through *The Souls of Black Folk.* West counts "eighteen allusions to the 'backwardness' of black folk."[21] The "talented tenth," as Du Bois referred to the prospective race leaders, was to reach backward and capture the heroic memories crystallized in the expressive products of black slave culture. Throughout his very long and active life, Du Bois (1868-1963) sternly evaluated African American art and cultural thought in terms of services or disservices to the long campaign for black liberation, as he understood it. During the 1920s Harlem Renaissance, younger African American writers (including Zora Neale Hurston, Langston Hughes, and Sterling Brown) came to the defense of the dialectical residue within black vernacular culture that Du Bois judged backward or counterprogressive. Before we move to Hurston's particular critique of Du Bois's "sorrow song" ideal, it is instructive to sketch two 1920s variations on the spirituals offered by Jean Toomer and Alain Locke.[22]

James Weldon Johnson, field secretary of the NAACP, looked back on *The Souls of Black Folk* as "a work which, I think, has had a greater effect upon and within the Negro race in America than any other single book published in this country since *Uncle Tom's Cabin.*"[23] For an example of Du Bois's influence upon black modernist writing, one might look to Jean Toomer's poem "Song of the Son." Toomer (1894-1967) first published the poem in *The Crisis* (the NAACP monthly under Du Bois's editorial leadership) in June of 1922. "Song of the Son" appeared the next year in Toomer's book *Cane* and then again in *The New Negro* (1925), a landmark anthology of fiction, poetry, and nonfiction edited by Alain Locke. "Song of the Son," like other stories and poems with rural settings in *Cane,* mimics the plaintive tone and unrushed tempo of the most mournful spirituals:

Pour O pour that parting soul in song,
O pour it in the sawdust glow of night
Into the velvet pine-smoke air to-night,
And let the valley carry it along.
And let the valley carry it along.

O land and soil, red soil and sweet-gum tree,
So scant of grass, so profligate of pines,
Now just before an epoch's sun declines
Thy son, in time, I have returned to thee,
Thy son, I have in time returned to thee.

In time, for though the sun is setting on
A song-lit race of slaves, it has not set;
Though late, O soil, it is not too late yet
To catch thy plaintive soul, leaving soon gone,
Leaving, to catch thy plaintive soul soon gone.

O Negro slaves, dark purple ripened plums,
Squeezed, and bursting in the pine-wood air,
Passing, before they stripped the old tree bare
One plum was saved for me, one seed becomes

An everlasting song, a singing tree,
Caroling softly souls of slavery,
What they were, and what they are to me,
Caroling softly souls of slavery.[24]

The elegiac poem evokes the "sorrow songs" as a haunting music that reaches out from the past to confront and challenge the present. The exhausted culture of a "song-lit race of slaves" slowly winds down as an "epoch's sun declines." "Caroling softly souls of slavery," the apparitional song echoes through the rural Georgia valley. The eulogizing son, poised to receive his ancestral heritage at a tragic site of memory, responds by catching and rehearsing the song's cadence as if it may be his only inheritance. Within the broader context of *Cane*, the speaker who has "in time returned to thee" also represents the vast distance between urban modernity and a rural black folk culture forged in slavery.[25] A posture of nostalgic identification with that past world is not available. The collapsing epoch of a "song-lit race of slaves" is rendered as raw and brutal rather than pastoral: "O Negro slaves, dark purple ripened plums, / Squeezed, and bursting in the pine-wood air[.]"

The process of mourning becomes pathological, according to Freud, when the identification with the lost object is excessively prolonged, thus leading to heightened feelings of ego impoverishment and dejection. "In mourning," Freud contended, "it is the world which has become poor and empty; in melancholia it is the ego itself. The [melancholic] patient represents his ego to us as worthless, incapable of any achievement and morally despicable."[26] "Song of the Son," a black modernist elegy directed at a fading folk culture, suggests a logic of mourning that parts ways with Freud's ideals for "working-through" profound losses. The wind "Caroling softly songs of slavery" through the rural Georgia valley passes along memories of racial terror in slavery as well as the restitutive spiritual resources of the black folk community. Traumatic legacies, according to Du Bois's cultural logic of mourning, would be commemorated in music and other rituals and sublimated into refined expressive forms. Such commemorative mourning-work would also enable present collective solidarity and anti-racist activism. When the speaker laments the folk culture's fragile and eroding beauty in "Song of the Son," the old folk culture extends a precious remnant to him: "Passing, before they stripped the old tree bare / One plum was saved for me, one seed becomes / An ever-lasting song, a singing tree[.]" "Song of the Son" dramatizes the last-minute rescue of a restitutive and "everlasting song."

A two-month stay in Sparta, Georgia, first inspired the young Toomer, a native of the black bourgeoisie of Washington, D.C., to write *Cane*. In contrast to the hopeful implications of the above poem's "everlasting song," Toomer's correspondences and unpublished writings recorded a different perspective on African American folk culture's powers of endurance. He wrote the following about how the "folk-songs and spirituals" first captured his imagination:

> The setting was crude in a way, but strangely rich and beautiful. . . . A family of back-country Negroes had only recently moved into a shack not too far away. They sang. And this was the first time I'd ever heard the folk-songs and spirituals. They were very rich and sad and joyous and beautiful. But I learned that the Negroes of the town objected to them. They called them "shouting." They had victrolas and player-pianos. So, I realized with deep regret, that the spirituals, meeting ridicule, would be certain to die out. With Negroes also the trend was towards the small town and then towards the city—and industry and commerce and machines. The folk-spirit was walking in to die on the modern desert. That spirit was so beautiful. Its death was so tragic. Just this seemed to sum life for me. And this was the feeling I put into *Cane*. *Cane* was a swan-song. It was a song of an end. And why no one has seen and felt that, why people have expected me to write a second and third and a fourth book like "*Cane*," is one of the queer misunderstandings of my life.[27]

Toomer's "swan-song" commentary followed a broader meta-narrative of modernization as cultural disenchantment. The meta-narrative of modernity as entropic decline casts an elegiac expectation over the eradication of spiritually integrated folk and indigenous cultures in the face of the ever-advancing monolith of cultural and economic modernization. Toomer sounded another note of modernist despair when he announced the pervasiveness of cultural fragmentation and discontinuity: "The modern world was uprooted, the modern world was breaking down, but we couldn't go back. There was nothing to go back to. Besides, in our hasty leaps into the future we had burned our bridges."[28] The cultural anthropologist James Clifford has written effectively about the modern "entropologist" who mourns the "vanishing 'loop-holes' or 'escapes' from a one-dimensional fate" in the face of the "prophetic disintegration of all real cultural differences."[29] The "salvage paradigm," a perennial accompaniment to the entropic narrative of modernity, reflects a "desire to rescue 'authenticity' out of destructive historical chance." Present "in a range of familiar nostalgias," the "salvage paradigm" is "a pervasive ideological complex" that reproduces distorted images of history and cultural difference "that need to be cleared away if we are to account for the multiple *histories* and *inventions* at work in the late 20th century."[30]

Toomer was more eager to build a new and discontinuous personal identity in the context of modernist disintegration than to salvage black folk "'authenticity' out of destructive historical chance." He explained his position in a letter to Waldo Frank:

> But the fact is, that if anything comes up now, pure Negro, it will be a swan-song. Don't let us fool ourselves, brother: the Negro of the folk-song has all but passed away. . . . The supreme fact of mechanical civilization is that you become part of it, or get sloughed off (under). Negroes have no culture to resist it with (and if they had, their position would be identical to the Indians), hence industrialism the more readily transforms them. . . . In those pieces [of *Cane*] that come nearest to the old Negro, there is nothing of the buoyant expression of a new race.[31]

A sense of deep discontinuity between the folk culture of the "Old Negro" and contemporary modernity emerged from Toomer's assumption that the "Negroes have no culture to resist it [mechanical civilization] with." In the end, he chose not to sustain the "everlasting song" of "Song of the Son" as a homeopathic balm and marker of black ancestralism and cultural continuity. For Du Bois, the "sorrow songs" and the utopian "spark of hope in the past" would never be abandoned. Toomer, by contrast, came to terms with the African American past and its consequences for his sense of selfhood by imagining a "new race": mystically constituted, radically modern, and ethnically unmarked. His personal situation enabled this new perspective. With his light skin color, straight hair, and Caucasian features, he easily "passed" as racially white. Having completed his "swan-song" to the rural "Old Negro," Toomer felt no strong artistic or personal attachment to what he apprehended as an altogether new urban black culture.[32] Not long after the publication of *Cane,* he chose to no longer identify himself as black and parted ways with the "New Negro" movement and the ascending Harlem Renaissance. Toomer instead welcomed the opportunity for modernist re-enchantment through a mystical passage into a "new race."

Toomer interpreted his new identification not as "passing" for white but as a refusal of dominant regimes of racialization. His next major work, *Essentials* (1931), clustered together philosophical aphorisms emblematic of his discipleship of the spiritual master Gurdjieff. All distinctions of racial identity, along with other fixed and local forms of identity, were no longer relevant: these distinctions were, more precisely, inessential. The literary critic Henry Louis Gates has described Toomer's project as an attempt to invent "an entirely new discourse, an almost mythic discourse . . . in which irreconcilable opposites, sexual and racial differences were not so much reconciled as absent, unutterable, unthinkable, and hence unpresentable."[33] Moreover, Toomer effectively hollowed out each moment of the hybridizing process outlined in Du Bois's dialectic of black "double-consciousness." Toomer left the hope of ancestralist continuity and cosmopolitan hybridization to other modernists of the "New Negro" Renaissance.

Alain Locke (1885-1954) was among those charting a cosmopolitan vision of "New Negro" artistic development in the inter-war years. Armed with a doctorate in philosophy from Harvard, the Howard University professor felt confident in his self-assigned leadership responsibilities. Locke hoped to ensure the continuous development of African American expressive traditions while also shepherding them into more classicized forms. While Toomer mourned over the passing of black folk culture as an irreparable rupture and a "death [that] was so tragic," Locke saw stronger signs of continuity between particular folk forms and black achievements in modern concert music and other arts. It was inevitable, Locke held, for some residual "premodern" aspects of rural black culture to dissipate under the force of migration and industrial opportunity. His somewhat urgent tone suggested less regret about folk cultural disintegration than an eager desire to salvage the past and publicize the necessity of mourning. The Fisk Jubilee Singers "only anticipated the inevitable by a generation—for the folk that produced them is rapidly vanishing," Locke wrote.[34] The great achievement of the black college singing groups that circulated the spirituals outside the church was that the songs "were saved during that critical period in which any folk product is likely to be snuffed out by the false pride of the second generation."[35]

Locke saw it as a proper aspiration for concert music to represent a national culture. Like Du Bois and others, he looked to the "sorrow songs" as universally appealing, but nationally specific, folk ballads. The concert spiritual was fit to play an equal role in recitals of European art songs.[36] A steady evolution from folk spirituals to art songs and symphonies based on folk sources, Locke contended, demanded the presence of black artists in the most advanced circles of cosmopolitan achievement. At the same time, he approached many developments in black popular music with grave concerns about the exoticizing appeals of primitivism and neo-minstrelsy. His program for "New Negro" art shared many themes with Du Bois's more politicized dialectic of "double-consciousness," mourning, and hybridic reconstitution. The "rapidly vanishing" folk culture would be memorialized as a lost object and divided into its perceived contingent and essential characteristics. Splitting the lost object allowed for a deliberate and permanent incorporation of its most treasured characteristics; artists and critics did not always agree about which of the folk object's characteristics were indispensable. A rebirthing of "the Negro" as an idealized "New Negro," as Locke read the situation, would sublimate a traumatic legacy through sophisticated modes of artifice and stylized expressivity and thereby evade a counterprogressive melancholic position.

Alternative voices took aim at the developmental priorities of Du Bois and Locke and their domesticated idealizations of black folk culture. The intellectual counteroffensive, a discursive "return of the repressed," challenged what is being described here as a "New Negro" cultural logic of mourning. If one might characterize Toomer's avant-garde post-racialism and Locke's "New Negro" aesthetic in terms of a deliberate desire to mourn, then Zora Neale Hurston's contrasting perspective might be read as a principled refusal to mourn. Although Locke was an early supporter of Hurston's fiction and ethnographic work, she refused to join the "swan song" chorus that regarded black folk culture as a world in inevitable

decline. Instead, she critiqued "New Negro" evolutionism as hopelessly assimilationist, Eurocentric, and tone-deaf to the full richness of black folk culture. On the matter of real folk spirituals, Hurston rejected Du Bois's emphasis on slavery as the definitive context of the songs' creation: "Their creation is not confined to the slavery period. Like the folk tales, the spirituals are being made and forgotten every day." Hurston contributed the short essay "Spirituals and Neo-Spirituals" to Nancy Cunard's *Negro* (1934) anthology. The essay distinguished between the authentic black folk spirituals (with their African-derived traits of communal improvisation, "jagged harmony," and intentionally "rough" tonality) and the fully scored, more Europeanized "neo-spiritual" compositions and arrangements made popular by college singing troupes and "New Negro" concert artists like Roland Hayes and Marian Anderson. "There never has been a presentation of genuine Negro spirituals to any audience anywhere," Hurston declared. "What is being sung by the concert artists and glee clubs are the works of Negro composers or adaptors *based* on the spirituals."[37]

Most importantly, Hurston moved to invalidate the claims of developmental necessity made in support of arranged spirituals and art music "based on the spirituals." Du Bois, Locke, and like-minded "New Negro" spokesmen held that such formal compositions were often genuinely uplifting memorials to a fading folk culture. Hurston preferred to locate the "genuine Negro spirituals" and their function within a resilient, living continuum of Afro-Christian worship. Among the Harlem Renaissance figures discussed in the present essay, only Hurston (1891-1960) was a native of the deep South. Her fond memories of growing up in the all-black rural town of Eatonville, Florida, left her eager to prove that the difference between folk and elite culture was not a distinction between the raw, untutored expressivity of the "Old Negro" and the cosmopolitan sophistication of the "New Negro." Therefore, she took pains in "Spirituals and Neo-Spirituals" to distinguish between the primitivist myth of raw and unmediated folk expressivity and the reality of carefully crafted vernacular practices in the black church. Hurston's essay values "training," "sound effects," and formal rules not only as markers of European-style concert music but as essential characteristics of vernacular "Negro expression" as well. Far from the anarchy of "every man for himself," the folk church service involved numerous formalities that helped shape a highly stylized and aesthetically impressive event. Especially in the service's most spontaneous and improvised moments, Hurston insisted, "ability is recognized as definitely as in any other art." She explained the dynamic interplay between individual and group spontaneity and preexisting formalized constraints: the "individual may hang as many new ornaments upon the traditional forms as he likes, but the audience would be disagreeably surprised if the form were abandoned." In short, elite "New Negro" assumptions that rural folk lacked rigorous aesthetic criteria were simply mistaken. "The truth is," Hurston asserted, "that the religious service is a conscious art expression. The artist is consciously creating—carefully choosing every syllable and every breath."[38]

Hurston's argument in "Spirituals and Neo-Spirituals" also disrupted the logic of continuity underwriting Du Bois's inheritance claims to the "sorrow songs" as a self-styled patriarch of early-twentieth-century black nationalism. As a student of folk culture, she insisted that any "idea that [the] whole body of spirituals are 'sorrow songs' is ridiculous. They cover a wide range of subjects from a peeve at gossipers to Death and the Judgment."[39] Du Bois's "sorrow song" concept, in other words, struck Hurston as vastly misleading about most spirituals and their ritual functions. She especially disliked seeing the spirituals understood only according to their "minor cadences of despair." In contrast to the stress put on alienation and dialectical progress in Du Bois's sense of "double-consciousness," Hurston preferred to celebrate the humor, playfulness, and immanent pleasures of black folk traditions. She argued that black folk culture's many positive traits, including the skill of cultivating joy through ritualized vernacular practices, needed to emerge from beneath the ultimately counterproductive anti-racist imagery of black alienation, sorrow, and victimization under segregation. Reclaiming the joyful folk spiritual and religious "shout" as a celebratory rather than mournful site of memory was one strategy in Hurston's iconoclastic campaign to repeal the anti-racist rhetoric of black suffering and damage. She explained in the essay "How It Feels to Be Colored Me" (1928) that "I am not tragically colored. There is no great sorrow dammed up in my soul, nor lurking behind my eyes. I do not mind at all. I do not belong to the sobbing school of Negrohood. . . . No, I do not weep at the world—I am too busy sharpening my oyster knife."[40] Hurston's literary virtuosity in capturing the oral dimensions of black folk culture was widely applauded. Nevertheless, many black intellectuals complained in the 1930s that

her rejection of a radicalized social realism left too little room in her art for the indictment of segregation and white racism as barriers to black opportunity. Hurston lost the support of the black literary establishment. The full scope of her achievement was recognized only posthumously after her "rediscovery" in the 1970s.

Hurston criticized those who sought to formalize black music according to what she considered an inevitably Eurocentric conceit of cosmopolitan development. She countered that the folkloric and ethnographic study of black vernacular culture was itself at a crude stage and that the "New Negro" concert spiritual was "some more passing for white."[41] Her protectiveness about folk culture was, perhaps, an element of a more personal campaign of mournful recuperation and ancestral commemoration; Hurston's work, as a mournful song of the daughter, placed a limit on her willingness to appreciate a process she termed the hybridic "exchange and re-exchange of ideas between groups."[42] The literary critic Hazel Carby has argued that Hurston's ethnographies and novels idealized a particular folk subculture as the repository of authentic African American culture. Hurston may have reconstituted her memories and her rural ethnographies into an ahistorical refuge from pressing issues of migration, urban industrialization, and proletarianization. Idealized images of folk cultures as refuges from modernity threaten to harden, of course, into static visions of "otherness." Carby argues that "On the one hand, [Hurston] could argue that forms of folk culture were constantly reworked and remade when she stated that 'the folk tales' like 'the spirituals are being made and forgotten every day.' But, on the other hand, Hurston did not take seriously the possibility that African American culture was being transformed as African American peoples migrated from rural to urban areas."[43] Nevertheless, Hurston's public refusal of Du Bois's "sorrow song" model and Locke's "New Negro" agenda also highlighted the regional, class, and masculinist limitations of her interlocutors. Indeed, despite her claim that there was "no great sorrow dammed up in my soul," many readers have located powerful countercurrents of mournful commemoration in Hurston's writing, including her masterpiece, the novel *Their Eyes Were Watching God* (1937). Hurston's autobiography, *Dust Tracks on a Road* (1942), includes a piercing description of her mother's death and the confession that "I was old before my time with grief of loss, of failure, and of remorse."[44] Hurston's writings have become con-

PERFORMING ARTS

stant companions in many recent reflections on memory and the folk inheritance, especially in the work of black feminist artists and critics. Her readers have been keen to uncover alternate vernacular paths for mourning the dead and coming to terms with private and public losses.

Hurston's insights struck the black intelligentsia of her own day as unassimilable to dialectical formulations about black progress, but they might now lend valuable sources of energy and possibility to that same dialectic. A rapprochement with the politically progressive, indeed utopian, strains of the Du Boisian tradition may no longer be out of the question. Hurston argued that black folk culture, including its religious dimensions, amounted to more than a raw resource for cosmopolitan refinement or a "premodern" specter or unassimilable remainder from the past. The sublimation of sorrow and joy and the elucidation of memory have, of course, taken on innumerable styles in black diasporic music. Among these sites of cultural memory, the "sorrow song" tradition does not glorify the "open wounds" of collective and personal memory. The tradition seeks instead to cultivate and pass on a practice of compassion rich enough to illuminate the most guarded places of memory and soften the most bitter moments of loss. It is a practice of mourning and restitution that retains deep connections to long-standing traditions within the black diaspora. Whether through a cosmopolitan work of concert art, a blues-tinged jazz ballad, an elegant soul anthem, or a "down-home" spiritual, the "everlasting song" remains a highly energized tool of memory.

## Notes

1. bell hooks, *A Woman's Mourning Song* (New York: Harlem River Press, 1993), 3.

2. Phillipe Ariès, *The Hour of Our Death* (New York: Knopf, 1981). See also Pierre Nora's essay, "Between Memory and History: Les Lieux de Memoire," in *History and Memory in African-American Culture,* ed. Genevieve Fabre and Robert O'Meally (New York: Oxford University Press, 1994), 284-300.

3. Sigmund Freud, "Mourning and Melancholia," in *The Standard Edition of the Complete Psychological Works of Sigmund Freud,* ed. James Strachey (London: Hogarth Press, 1953-74), 14:243.

4. For Holiday's distance from the gospel tradition, see Leon Forrest, "A Solo Long-Song: For Lady Day," in *The Furious Voice for Freedom* (Wakefield RI: Asphodel Press, 1994), 344-95. On black "self-recovery," see bell hooks, *Sisters of the Yam: Black Women and Self-Recovery* (Boston: South End Press, 1993).

5. Forrest, "Solo Long-Song," 377.

6. bell hooks, *Sisters of the Yam* (Boston: South End Press, 1993), 100-101, 102.

7. This essay has been strongly influenced by the analyses of music and cultural memory in Paul Gilroy, *The Black Atlantic: Modernity and Double Consciousness* (Cambridge: Harvard University Press, 1993).

8. Du Bois quoted in David Levering Lewis, *W. E. B. Du Bois: Biography of a Race, 1868-1919* (New York: Henry Holt, 1993), 77.

9. Walter Benjamin, "Theses on the Philosophy of History," in *Illuminations,* ed. Hannah Arendt, trans. Harry Zohn (New York: Schocken Books, 1969), 255.

10. W. E. B. Du Bois, *The Souls of Black Folk* (New York: Vintage, 1990), 180.

11. Houston A. Baker Jr., *Blues, Ideology, and Afro-American Literature* (Chicago: University of Chicago Press, 1984), 194, 196.

12. Du Bois, *Souls of Black Folk,* 182.

13. Ibid., 182, 185. For Du Bois's views on religion, see Wilson Jeremiah Moses, *Afrotopia: The Roots of African American Popular History* (Cambridge: Cambridge University Press, 1998), 136-68.

14. Du Bois, *Souls of Black Folk,* 188.

15. Freud, "Mourning and Melancholia," 253.

16. For another perspective on Du Bois and mourning, see Claudia Tate, *Psychoanalysis and Black Novels: Desire and the Protocols of Race* (New York: Oxford University Press, 1998), esp. 47-85.

17. See Roger Abrahams, "Phantoms of Romantic Nationalism in Folkloristics," *Journal of American Folklore* 106, issue 419 (winter 1993), 3-37.

18. See Slavoj Žižek, *For They Know Not What They Do* (London: Verso, 1991), 20.

19. Du Bois, *Souls of Black Folk,* 8-9. For a contrasting interpretation of Du Bois and dialectical thought, see Shamoon Zamir, *Dark Voices: W. E. B. Du Bois and American Thought, 1888-1903* (Chicago: University of Chicago Press, 1995).

20. Mitchell Robert Breitwieser, *American Puritanism and the Defense of Mourning: Religion, Grief, and Ethnology in Mary White Rowlandson's Captivity Narrative* (Madison: University of Wisconsin Press, 1990), 42.

21. Cornel West, *The American Evasion of Philosophy* (Madison: University of Wisconsin Press, 1989), 143.

22. For a fuller discussion of the spirituals debate, see Paul A. Anderson, *Deep River: Music and Memory in Harlem Renaissance Thought* (Duke University Press, forthcoming).

23. James Weldon Johnson, *Along This Way* (New York: Penguin Books, 1990), 203.

24. Jean Toomer, *Cane,* ed. Darwin T. Turner (New York: W. W. Norton, 1988), 14.

25. For the elegiac mode in modern poetry, see Jahan Ramazani, *Poetry of Mourning: The Modern Elegy from Hardy to Heaney* (Chicago: University of Chicago Press, 1994).

26. Freud, "Mourning and Melancholia," 246.

27. Jean Toomer, "On Being an American," from "Outline of an Autobiography" (ca. 1931-32), in *The Wayward and the Seeking: A Collection of Writings by Jean Toomer,* ed. Darwin T. Turner (Washington DC: Howard University Press, 1980), 123.

28. Ibid., 129.

29. James Clifford, *The Predicament of Culture: Twentieth-Century Ethnography, Literature, and Art* (Cambridge: Harvard University Press, 1988), 244, 241.

30. James Clifford, "Of Other Peoples: Beyond the 'Salvage' Paradigm," in *Discussions in Contemporary Culture,* ed. Hal Foster (Seattle: Bay Press, 1987), 121.

31. Jean Toomer to Waldo Frank, [n.d., late 1922 or early 1923], in *A Jean Toomer Reader: Selected Unpublished Writings,* ed. Frederick L. Rusch (New York: Oxford University Press, 1991), 24.

32. Although the folk Negro lamented in *Cane* had "all but passed away," Toomer nevertheless felt that "when I come up to Seventh Street and Theatre, a wholly new life confronts me. A life, I am afraid, that Sherwood Anderson would not get his beauty from. From it is jazzed, strident, modern. Seventh Street is the song of crude new life. Of a new people. Negro? Only in the *boldness* of its expression. In its healthy freedom. American." Toomer quoted in Michael North, *The Dialect of Modernism: Race, Language, and Twentieth-Century Literature* (New York: Oxford University Press, 1994), 167.

33. Henry Louis Gates Jr., "The Same Difference: Reading Jean Toomer, 1923-1982," in *Figures in Black: Words, Signs, and the "Racial Self"* (New York: Oxford University Press, 1994), 167.

34. Alain Locke, "The Negro Spirituals," in *The New Negro,* ed. Alain Locke (New York: Atheneum, 1968), 201.

35. Alain Locke, *The Negro and His Music* (Port Washington NY: Kennikat Press, 1968), 19.

36. For a critique of "New Negro" music leaders, see Michael Harris, *The Rise of Gospel Blues: The Music of Thomas Andrew Dorsey in the Urban Church* (New York: Oxford University Press, 1992). For a defense, see Jon Michael Spencer, *The New Negroes and Their Music: The Success of the Harlem Renaissance* (Knoxville: University of Tennessee Press, 1997).

37. Zora Neale Hurston, "Spirituals and Neo-Spirituals," in *Negro: An Anthology,* ed. Hugh Ford (New York: Frederick Ungar, 1970), 223, 224.

38. Ibid., 225, 224.

39. Ibid., 224.

40. Zora Neale Hurston, "How It Feels to Be Colored Me" [1928], *I Love Myself When I Am Laughing . . . And Then Again When I Am Looking Mean and Impressive: A Zora Neale Hurston Reader,* ed. Alice Walker (New York: Feminist Press, 1979), 153.

41. Zora Neale Hurston, "Concert" [c. 1942], unpublished appendix to *Dust Tracks on a Road,* in *Zora Neale Hurston: Folklore, Memoirs, and Other Writings,* ed. Cheryl A. Wall (New York: Library of America, 1995), 805.

42. Zora Neale Hurston, "Characteristics of Negro Expression," in *Negro: An Anthology,* ed. Hugh Ford, 28.

43. Hazel V. Carby, "The Politics of Fiction, Anthropology, and the Folk: Zora Neale Hurston," in *New Essays on Their Eyes Were Watching God,* ed. Michael Awkward (Cambridge: Cambridge University Press, 1990), 75, 76.

44. Zora Neale Hurston, *Dust Tracks on a Road* (New York: Harper Perennial, 1991), 64. For a brilliant reading of unconscious and preconscious desire and the work of mourning in Hurston's novels, especially *Seraph on the Suwanee* (1948), see Claudia Tate, *Psychoanalysis and Black Novels* (New York: Oxford University Press, 1998), 148-77. Tate argues that Hurston took up folklore collecting as a way to "work through the trauma of her mother's death" and that this "professional devotion would be more than a vocation; it would be a means of mourning and reparation" (160). I agree but emphasize in this essay how Hurston's critique of the "school of sobbing Negrohood" was a repudiation of the "New Negro" logic of mourning and cultural evolution propagated by Du Bois and Locke.

## Further Reading

Breitwieser, Mitchell Robert. *American Puritanism and the Defense of Mourning: Religion, Grief, and Ethnology in Mary White Rowlandson's Captivity Narrative.* Madison: University of Wisconsin Press, 1990.

A textually sensitive and theoretically audacious reading of a classic early American text that features a powerful interrogation of psychoanalytic models of mourning and melancholia and their applicability to cultural analysis.

Cavell, Stanley. *This New Yet Unapproachable America.* Albuquerque: Living Batch Press, 1989.

A brief but philosophically powerful meditation on the theme of epistemological skepticism and responses made to it in the work of Wittgenstein, Heidegger, and Emerson that deftly argues for the place of Freud's "Mourning and Melancholia" in the tradition of modern philosophy.

Santner, Eric. *Stranded Objects: Mourning, Memory, and Film in Post-war Germany.* Ithaca: Cornell University Press, 1990.

Along with a set of elegant psychoanalytically informed interrogations of representations of the Holocaust in German film, this book offers a deep challenge to some basic assumptions in postmodern thought and, particularly, the deconstructivist interpretive models of Paul de Man and Jacques Derrida.

Schiesari, Juliana. *The Gendering of Melancholia: Feminism, Psychoanalysis, and the Symbolics of Loss in Renaissance Literature.* Ithaca: Cornell University Press, 1992.

A useful overview and powerful feminist critique of patriarchal thinking within psychoanalytic depictions of mourning and melancholia that confronts and finds wanting the work of Freud, Kristeva, Lacan, and others.

# FURTHER READING

## Criticism

Avery, Laurence G. "Introduction." In *A Paul Green Reader,* edited by Laurence G. Avery, pp. 1-14. Chapel Hill: University of North Carolina Press, 1998.

*Overview of Green's writing career, focusing on his major theatrical themes.*

Butcher, Margaret Just. "The Negro in American Drama." In *The Negro in American Culture,* based on materials left by Alain Locke, pp. 187-206. New York: Knopf, 1969.

*A detailed analysis of the evolution of African American drama, tracing its evolution from the late 1800s to the mid-1950s.*

Carter, Everett. "Cultural History Written with Lightning: The Significance of *The Birth of a Nation* (1915)." In *Hollywood as Historian: American Film in a Cultural Context*, edited by Peter C. Rollins, pp. 9-19. Lexington: University Press of Kentucky, 1983.

*Discusses the historical and cultural significance of* The Birth of a Nation.

Dyer, Richard. "Into the Light: The Whiteness of the South in *The Birth of a Nation*." In *Dixie Debates: Perspectives on Southern Cultures*, pp. 165-76, edited by Richard H. King and Helen Taylor. New York: New York University Press, 1996.

*Overview of characterization and racial contrasts in* The Birth of a Nation.

Fox, Ted. "Harlem's Early Years—The Apollo's Heritage." *Showtime at the Apollo*, pp. 39-66. New York: Holt, Rinehart, and Winston, 1983.

*Provides a history of the Apollo Theatre during its early years.*

Frank, Rusty E., editor. *Tap! The Greatest Tap Dance Stars and Their Stories, 1900-1955*. New York: William Morrow and Company, 1990, 330 p.

*Essays by various tap dancers, including Willie Covan, Ruby Keeler, and Fayard Nicholas.*

Gill, Glenda E. "*White Dresses, Sweet Chariots, In Abraham's Bosom, The No 'Count Boy* and *A Hymn*: Paul Green's Vehicles for the Black Actor." *Southern Literary Journal* 22, no. 2 (spring 1990): 90-97.

*Maintains that among white American playwrights, Green was one of the first to carve out a niche for the Black actor.*

Grandel, Hartmut. "The Role of Music in the Self-Reflexive Poetry of the Harlem Renaissance." In *Poetics in the Poem: Critical Essays on American Self-Reflexive Poetry*, edited by Dorothy Z. Baker, pp. 119-31. New York: P. Lang, 1997.

*Recounts the influence of Black music in the poetry of such authors as W.E.B. Du Bois, James Weldon Johnson, Langston Hughes, and Sterling A. Brown.*

Haskins, Jim. *The Cotton Club*. New York: Random House, 1977, 169 p.

*A history of the Cotton Club, one of the most prominent nightclubs in Harlem during the early 1920s.*

Hill, Errol, editor. *The Theater of Black Americans, Vol. 1* Englewood Cliffs, N.J.: Practice Hall, Inc., 1980, 221p.

*Critical essays on early twentieth-century drama by African Americans.*

Hokanson, Robert O'Brien. "Jazzing It Up: The Be-Bop Modernism of Langston Hughes." *Mosaic* 31, no. 4 (December 1998): 61-82.

*Discusses Hughes's use of bebop in "Montage of a Dream Deferred."*

Holton, Deborah Wood. "Revealing Blindness, Revealing Vision: Interpreting O'Neill's Black Female Characters in *Moon of the Caribbees, The Dreamy Kid* and *All God's Chillun Got Wings*." *The Eugene O'Neill Review* 19, nos. 1 & 2 (spring/fall 1995): 30-44.

*Discussion of O'Neill's representation of the Black experience as mostly stereotypical, focusing on his treatment of Black female characters.*

Huggins, Nathan Irvin. "Personae: White/Black Faces—Black Masks." In *Harlem Renaissance*, pp. 244-301. London: Oxford University Press, 1971.

*Proposes that the theatrical stage has provided a mirror for race relations in the United States, including a history of theater development as it relates to Black actors and playwrights.*

Kornweibel, Theodore, Jr. "Theophilus Lewis and the Theater of the Harlem Renaissance." In *The Harlem Renaissance Remembered: Essays Edited with a Memoir*, edited by Arna Bontemps, pp. 171-89.

*Overview of Lewis's career and his philosophy regarding Black theater.*

Krasner, David. "Whose Role Is It Anyway? Charles Gilpin and the Harlem Renaissance." *African American Review* 29, no. 3 (fall 1995): 483-96.

*A history of Gilpin's acting career in the context of the Harlem Renaissance, noting his attempts to modify dialogue that appeared excessively offensive towards Blacks.*

Mandl, Bette. "Theatricality and Otherness in *All God's Chillun Got Wings*." In *Feminist Rereadings of Modern American Drama*, edited by June Schlueter, pp. 48-56.

*Discusses the treatment of race in O'Neill's play.*

Scott, Freda L. "Black Drama and the Harlem Renaissance." *Theatre Journal* (December 1985): 426-39.

*An overview of Black dramatists during the Harlem Renaissance, including insight into difficulties faced by African American theater.*

Spencer, Jon Michael. *The New Negroes and Their Music: The Success of the Harlem Renaissance*. Knoxville: University of Tennessee Press, 1997, 171p.

*Detailed study of Black music during the Harlem Renaissance.*

Tracy, Stephen C. "Folklore and the Harlem Renaissance." In *Langston Hughes and the Blues*, pp. 11-57. Urbana: University of Illinois Press, 2001.

*Study of the influence of blues music and Black folklore on the writings of Langston Hughes.*

Turner, Darwin. "Introduction." In *Black Drama in America: An Anthology*, pp. 1–24. Greenwich, Conn.: Fawcett Publications, Inc., 1971.

*Introduction to a collection of Black drama that includes works by Willis Richardson, Langston Hughes, and others.*

Welsch, Tricia. "Killing Them with Tap Shoes: Violent Performance in *The Cotton Club*." *Journal of Popular Film and Television* 24, no. 4 (winter 1998): 162-71.

*Review of Coppola's production of* The Cotton Club, *focusing on the racial separatism highlighted in the film.*

Williams, Ned E. In *Hear Me Talkin' to Ya,* by Nat Shapiro and Nar Hentoff. New York: Rhinehart and Co., 1955, 432 p.

*Relates his experiences of playing with Duke Ellington's orchestra at the Cotton Club.*

# VISUAL ARTS DURING THE HARLEM RENAISSANCE

Although the Harlem Renaissance was largely a literary movement, the visual artists who flocked to Harlem during the early decades of the twentieth century also played a role in shaping this revolutionary period in African American cultural history. A number of important painters, sculptors, and photographers came into prominence during this period. Before the Harlem Renaissance, African Americans did not have the option of becoming professional artists. Most Blacks lived in the South, and racism, Jim Crow laws, and limited access to education prevented them from producing fine art. The racial oppression faced by Blacks, however, did not prevent the flourishing of a rich folk culture. After the first World War, Blacks moved en masse from the South to northern cities, seeking better lives; with the migration came a new sense of opportunity, hope, and cultural identity. In Harlem and other urban centers of the North, gifted and educated Blacks finally had the opportunity to develop their talents as artists. They also were able, for the first time, to work not in isolation, as they had been forced to in the past, but to be connected to and inspired by other artists with similar interests and backgrounds. Like their fellow writers, visual artists of the era drew upon their rich folk heritage, African roots, and racial identity to impart a radical new aesthetic. There was a sense that art, as the greatest achievement of civilized human beings, could build a bridge between the races in the United States, alleviate racial prejudice, disprove the myth of racial inferiority, and prove that Blacks had something positive to contribute to American cultural life. Some of the themes explored in the works of artists of the era included Africa as a source of inspiration, African American history, folk idioms, music and religion of the South, and social injustice.

The direction in which young Black artists should take their work was a subject of discussion among intellectuals of the movement. Because Black artists had no formal or mature tradition to draw upon, they were, in a sense, unconstrained in their ability to develop a new African American aesthetic in the fine arts. Some critics, including the highly influential scholar and philosopher Alain Locke, argued that the true heritage of African American artists was African art. In his famous 1925 essay, "The Legacy of the Ancestral Arts," Locke maintained that Blacks ought to lay claim to the African sculptural tradition rather than seek inspiration from Western models. African art, he noted, had influenced such European movements as Cubism, and by embracing its techniques and combining it with his own experience, the Black artist could decrease his feelings of inferiority and produce truly authentic and inspired art. Other critics, such as George Schuyler, rejected the concept of "racial art," arguing that African Americans were Americans and had been influenced by European traditions just as white Americans had been. Some Black artists had been schooled in traditional techniques, and practicing these became important for gaining professional acceptance in a society where Art had been determined by the white majority. It was also a tool for disrupting the stereotypes that Blacks could not be "true" artists. Many artists did, however, turn to Africa as a source of inspiration. While the use of African themes and techniques enriched the work of many of them, the emphasis on African-inspired art created a sense, especially among white critics and patrons, that African Americans ought to concentrate on primitive art, using crude techniques, bold colors, sensuous themes, and depictions of the unfettered and "natural" African. On the other hand, the work of the two most famous photographers of the period, James VanDerZee and Gordon Parks, was very much concerned with realism and the setting of Harlem itself. VanDerZee, a commercial photographer who came to prominence during the years of the Harlem Renaissance, photographed domestic and street scenes and is now credited with having preserved through his work the emergence of a Black middle and upper class. In 1924, he also became the official photographer for Marcus Garvey and his Universal Negro Improvement Association, during which time his photographs gained international exposure. Gordon Parks worked mainly as a documentary and fashion photographer, although he was also a composer, poet, novelist, and film director. His camera captured the images of many of the famous personages of the Harlem Renaissance and the art world at large, including writers, performers, and musicians.

Locke was influential not only because of his role as a critic of Black art but also because of his work in promoting the work of artists. One of the most important events of the Harlem Renaissance was the publication in 1924 of the "Harlem" issue of the journal *Survey Graphic,* which he edited. The issue, which contained the work of the era's best writers and intellectuals, was subsequently reprinted as a book called *The New Negro* (1925), illustrated with six African-inspired illustrations by the young artist Aaron Douglas. The book illustrations were Douglas's introduction to the elite society of the Harlem Renaissance, and he subsequently became the "official" artist of the movement and the era's most prominent visual artist. In addition to producing paintings and murals, Douglas illustrated books by a number of prominent Harlem Renaissance authors. Locke also had a hand in convincing the wealthy real estate developer William E. Harmon, under the auspices of his Harmon Foundation, to sponsor an annual national competition, exhibition, and awards program for Black artists. The Harmon Foundation thereafter became an anchor for promoting the works of African American artists. However, some critics viewed the Harmon Foundation as promoting stereotypes of Blacks and further segregating African American artists from their white counterparts. Its exhibits emphasized works incorporating African and primitive subjects and techniques, and promoted the idea that there were "inherent" Black traits that were revealed in the often crude, simple, and colorful paintings that were exhibited.

While art patrons often embraced cultural stereotypes and critics debated theories of art, most artists themselves did not subscribe to any particular aesthetic point of view. A number of artists—including Douglas and the sculptors Augusta Savage and Richmond Barthé—celebrated their African ancestry, and the noted painter William H. Johnson embraced primitivism after producing skillful, realistic tableaux in his early years. But while the number of Black artists in Harlem and around the country grew, they were not sufficiently connected to constitute a formal movement. They were, however, inspired by the creative energy of the New Negro movement and the Harlem Renaissance, and the notions of pride in the Black racial heritage, freedom to depict racial themes, and the importance of Black history are certainly reflected in their work. Because of their backgrounds as migrants facing a new life in an urban landscape, the themes of rural life, Black folk idioms, city life, poverty, racial oppression, and the fight for social justice also figure prominently in their works. Critics speculate that it is probably because of this lack of a unified aesthetic that the visual artists of the Harlem Renaissance, unlike the writers of the period, remain virtually unknown—even among art historians. However, several exhibitions in recent years have aimed at calling attention to the work of this unique group—the first professional African American painters, sculptors, and photographers—whose innovative images paved the way for subsequent generations of Black artists.

# REPRESENTATIVE WORKS

### Richmond Barthé
*West Indian Girl* (sculpture) 1930

*African Dancer* (sculpture) 1932

*Life Mask of Rose McClendon* (sculpture) 1932

*Blackberry Woman* (sculpture) 1933

*Shilluk Warrior* (sculpture) 1934

## Arna Alexander Bontemps
*Forever Free: Art by African-American Women 1862-1980* (exhibit catalog) 1980

## Aaron Douglas
*The Creation* (illustration) 1925

*From the New World* (illustration) 1925

*Invincible Music, the Spirit of Africa* (illustration) 1925

*Meditation* (illustration) 1925

*The Poet* (illustration) 1925

*Rebirth* (illustration) 1925

*The Crucifixion* (illustration/painting) 1925–27

*Go down Death* (illustration/painting) 1925–27

*Judgment Day* (illustration/painting) 1925–27

*Let My People Go* (illustration/painting) 1925–27

*Listen Lord a Prayer* (illustration/painting) 1925–27

*The Negro in an African Setting* (mural) 1933

*Song of Towers* (mural) 1933

*Aspects of Negro Life: From Slavery through Reconstruction* (murals) 1934

*Triborough Bridge* (painting) 1935

*Building More Stately Mansions* (painting) 1944

## Meta Vaux Warrick Fuller
*Ethiopia Awakening* (sculpture) 1914

*Henry Gilbert* (sculpture) 1928

*Talking Skull* (sculpture) 1937

## Palmer C. Hayden
*Dove of God* (painting) 1930

*Midsummer Night in Harlem* (painting) 1930

*Fétiche et Fleurs* (painting) 1932-33

*Just back from Washington* (painting) 1938

*The John Henry Series* (paintings) 1944-47

## Malvin Gray Johnson
*Negro Masks* (painting) 1932

*Marching Elks* (painting) ca. 1933

*Southern Landscape* (painting) 1933

## William H. Johnson
*Landscape, Cagnes-sur-Mer* (painting) 1928-29

*Evisa* (painting) 1929

*Jacobia Hotel* (painting) 1930

*Minnie* (painting) 1930

*City Gates, Kairouan* (painting) 1932

*Street Musicians* (painting) ca. 1940

*Going to Church* (painting) 1940-41

## Archibald J. Motley, Jr.
*Dans la Rue* (painting) 1927

*Kikuyu God of Fire* (painting) 1927

*Jockey Club, Paris* (painting) 1929

*Black Belt* (painting) 1934

*Saturday Night* (painting) 1935

## Augusta Savage
*Gamin* (sculpture) 1929

*Marcus Garvey* (sculpture) 1930

*Gwendolyn Knight* (sculpture) 1934

*Lift Every Voice and Sing* (sculpture) 1939

*The Pugilist* (sculpture) 1943

## Allon Schoener
*Harlem on My Mind: Cultural Capital of Black America, 1900-1968* (New York Metropolitan Museum of Art exhibit catalog) 1969

## James VanDerZee
*Mamie Smith* (photograph) ca. 1923

*Nude Study* (photograph) 1923

*The Funeral of Blanche Powell* (photograph) 1926

*Future Expectations (Wedding Day)* (photograph) 1926

*Woman in Fur-Trimmed Coat* (photograph) 1928

*Man with Cane* (photograph) 1930

## Hale A. Woodruff
*Two Old Women* (painting) 1926

*Medieval Chartres* (painting) 1927-29

*Tornado* (painting) ca. 1933

*Poor Man's Cotton* (painting) 1934

*Returning Home* (painting) 1935

## Exhibition Catalogs
*Exhibition of the Works of Negro Artists* (Harmon Foundation exhibit catalog) 1933

*Negro Artists: An Illustrated Review of Their Achievements* (Harmon Foundation exhibit catalog) 1935

*Exhibition of the Art of the American Negro* (Tanner Galleries exhibit catalog) 1940

*Hale Woodruff: An Exhibition of Selected Paintings and Drawings, 1927–1967* (New York University exhibit catalog) 1967

*Hale Woodruff: Fifty Years of His Art* (Studio Museum in Harlem exhibit catalog) 1979

*Augusta Savage and the Art Schools of Harlem* (The Schomburg Center for Research in Black Culture of the New York Public Library exhibit catalog) 1988

"The Harmon Foundation in Context" in *Against the Odds: African American Artists and the Harmon Foundation* (Newark Museum exhibit catalog) 1989

## PRIMARY SOURCES

### ALAIN LOCKE (ESSAY DATE 1933)

**SOURCE:** Locke, Alain. "The Negro Takes His Place in American Art." In *The Portable Harlem Renaissance Reader,* edited by David Levering Lewis, pp. 134-37. New York: Viking, 1994.

*In the following essay, originally published in 1933 in the Harmon Foundation catalog titled* Exhibition of the Works of Negro Artists, *which presented pictures and descriptions of works by Harlem Renaissance artists, Locke describes the objectives of the movement in African American art: the encouragement of Black artists, the development of a distinctively African American art, and the promotion of Black themes and subjects as an important aspect of American life.*

There are, I take it, three objectives to the movement in Negro art of which this fifth Harmon Exhibition of the Work of Negro Artists is an integral part, and to which, in the years of its activity, it has made and is making a formative and important contribution. One is the encouragement of the Negro artist; another, the development of Negro art; and a third is the promotion of the Negro theme and subject as a vital phase of the artistic expression of American life. Six years ago the share of Negro subject material in the field of American fine art was negligible; little, if anything, was being done for the encouragement of the Negro artist as such, and many thought that there was some implied restriction and arbitrary limitation of the Negro artist in the program of Negro art as "racial self-expression." Yet in the short intervening space of time, practically each of these situations has been reversed in a spurt of accumulative and perfectly compatible development.

As a net result not only is the Negro and his art more definitely upon the artistic map, but the Negro theme and subject is coming increasingly to the fore in the general field of art interest, as any analysis of today's art exhibitions will show if compared with similar exhibitions of even five years ago. Some day, it is to be hoped, an exhibition of contemporary American art dealing with the Negro theme and subject, irrespective of the racial affiliation of the artists, will be sponsored and that it will show a remarkable development in increased emphasis, deepened interest, and reveal mature mastery and understanding of the general handling of the Negro theme in painting, sculpture and the graphic arts—a development parallel to the remarkable growth of the Negro artist which these Harmon exhibits have so unmistakably shown.

We may well pause for a moment to consider the causes of this advance and to estimate briefly its gains. A few years back there were Negro artists, but little or no Negro art. Most of our artists subscribed to the creed that racialism in art was an unwarranted restriction, but they either avoided racial subjects or treated them gingerly in what I used to call "Nordic transcriptions." As a result, contrasted with the vital self-expression in poetry, fiction, drama and music, there was almost nothing representative or racial in the field of the fine arts. While the poets, playwrights, writers and musicians were in the sunlight and warmth of a proud and positive race-consciousness, our artists were still for the most part in an eclipse of chilly doubt and disparagement.

Why? I think mainly because social prejudice had seized on the stigma of color and racial feature, and the Negro artist was a sensitive victim of this negative color-consciousness and its inhibitions. Sad as was the plight of Negro art in his hands, as long as the Negro artist was in this general frame of mind, his whole expression was to some extent weak and apologetic in conception and spirit, because it was bound to be derivative, indirect and falsely sophisticated.

As the Negro subject has become more popular with the Negro artist, a steadily maturing firmness and originality in the handling of non-racial subjects have been a noteworthy and, I think, a not unconnected accompaniment. In 1929 a young Negro painter, with a creditable prize record at one of the great national schools of art, refused an invitation to exhibit in a special showing of Negro artists. He very seriously, and at that time perhaps pardonably, preferred to try for recognition "as a painter, not as a Negro painter." After an award of a fellowship for foreign study on his technical merits and promise, he was in two years' time exhibiting in the successor of the show he first refused to join, six paintings—five of them studies of race types, and one perhaps the most striking color study of a pure blood type that I have ever seen from the brush of an American artist, black or white.

It is of still greater significance that this artist's conversion of attitude seems to have occurred primarily or entirely on artistic and technical rather than sentimental or sociological grounds. Welcome as is the very real and vital racialism that is now stirring in the world of the Negro artist, it is artistically important as a sign of aesthetic objectivity and independence, and thus a double emancipation from apologetic timidity and academic imitation. We are now able to see that Negro art does not restrict the Negro artist to growth in his own soil exclusively, but only to express himself in originality and unhampered sincerity.

In fact, the relation of the Negro artist to his subject matter is not so very different from the relation of his white fellow artist to the same material, with the possible exception and advantage of closer psychological contact and understanding. It is important local color material, or provincial or national subject matter to both, and the development of the theme in contemporary American art is more and more demonstrating this.

We must soon begin, now, the frank and objective comparison of the work of the outstanding Negro artists with that of men like William Benton, James Chapin, Julius Bloch, Covarrubias, Orozco, Maurice Sterne, William McFee—to name some of the outstanding few who have notably touched the Negro subject in their art—no matter how bold or temporarily disparaging the contrast. The rapid mastery of his provincial handicaps by the Negro artist makes parity hopeful and eventually certain. There was a time, and not so far back, that the white American artist was in a no better relative position when compared with the more mature schools and traditions of European art. Every successive showing of Negro artists seems to bring Negro and white American artists closer together in this common interest in the promotion of Negro art and over the common denominator of contemporary American art expression.

One other denominator suggested by the inclusion of a Negro artist from Cuba in this exhibition is that of an interest, far from academic, in uniting for purposes of comparison the work of Negroes separated by differences of cultural background and artistic tradition. The inclusion of the interesting sculpture of Teodoro Ramos Blanco makes another interesting beginning in the stimulating influence that has emanated from these shows. Its logical extension will certainly bring together the little known but increasing contemporary art work of the native African. I have no doubt that each segment of Negro expression will show more in common with its own immediate art background; but the question of distinctive racial idiom or aptitude is purely theoretical and academic until such broad scale comparisons can actually be made.

In last analysis we should not expect art to answer or solve our sociological or anthropological questions. We must judge, create and consume it largely in terms of its universal values. But no art idiom, however universal, grows in a cultural vacuum; each, however great, always has some rootage and flavor of a particular soil and personality. And just as it has been a critical necessity to foster the development of a national character in the American art of our time, by the very same logic and often by the very same means, it has been reasonable and necessary to promote and quicken the racial motive and inspiration of the hitherto isolated and disparaged Negro artist. The day may soon come, however, when he will need no special encouragement and no particular apologetic brief. It is good both for him and for American art that he is so rapidly reaching maturity.

# OVERVIEWS

## DAVID DRISKELL (ESSAY DATE 1987)

**SOURCE:** Driskell, David. "The Flowering of the Harlem Renaissance: The Art of Aaron Douglas, Meta Warrick Fuller, Palmer Hayden, and William H. Johnson." In *Harlem Renaissance: Art of Black America*, pp. 105-54. New York: Harry N. Abrams, Inc., 1987.

*In the following excerpt, Driskell discusses the work of four artists—Aaron Douglas, Meta Warrick Fuller, Palmer Hayden, and William H. Johnson—all of whom, he notes, helped to establish a new tradition among Black artists, affirmed their individual and racial identities, and helped nurture other Harlem Renaissance artists.*

Harlem, the cultural capital of Black America, has for many decades provided enlightened leadership in the arts, unmatched by other urban communities. Significantly situated in the center of New York City, on the island of Manhattan, Harlem has attracted persons from all walks of life striving to become entertainers in the music, theater, and film worlds. Black poets and novelists have idealized Harlem and implanted its ethos in the soul of every Black American since the 1920s, when the community became a mecca for the exploration of all the arts. Prior to that time, little was known of Black visual artists, other than those who managed to make their reputations in Europe. Few, indeed, were the aspiring artists fortunate enough to be well financed themselves or to be sponsored for a sojourn in Europe, particularly in Paris, then the capital of art in the Western world. For most Black artists who dreamed of practicing their craft in a supportive environment, Harlem seemed a likely place to call home.

As early as 1905, the rush to own property in Harlem began among well-heeled Blacks. Their arrival brought stability to the community and the interest required to create a support system that would sustain Harlem's intellectual and artistic movement in the early 1920s. Yet, the climate the community needed to prove itself worthy of the New Negro's cultural regeneration was the result of forces within and outside Harlem. Before World War I, Black intellectuals were already migrating to Harlem from Philadelphia, Washington, D.C., Chicago, Los Angeles, and the principal cities of the South. They swelled the ranks of Harlem's cultural activists and championed the call for a rebirth of the artistry Black people once had in their native Africa. Simultaneously, the art of Black Africa was beginning to enter American museums and was accessible through the collections of prominent avant-garde art dealers Alfred Stieglitz and J. B. Naumann, and the renowned patron of modern art Albert Barnes. The impact of African designs could also be seen in the art of the premier modernists, including Picasso, Modigliani, and Brancusi. In response to these events, a renaissance of ideas and artistic expressions manifested itself in Harlem by the 1920s. Thereafter, American culture experienced an infusion of Black creativity in the arts unknown since the age of artistic genius in the homelands of Black Africa prior to European colonization.

Most historians accept 1925 as the established date of the New Negro Movement's flowering of artistic expression, later called the Harlem Renaissance. Yet, as early as 1919, when Black soldiers returned from the war in Europe, signs of a changing cultural order appeared in Harlem. There was a proliferation of literary clubs, private and public art exhibitions, and evenings of music, poetry, and dance that existed for the sole purpose of "uplifting the arts within the race." The year 1919 was also the year in which an unusually sagacious, socially determined mind-set developed among the Black intellectuals assembled in Harlem. They espoused political philosophies that interested those Black artists who showed allegiance to their race and who felt the need to participate in the founding of a national movement to enlighten the arts of Black America. The voices that gave direction to the artists, who like their intellectual counterparts came to Harlem from across the nation, represented the best minds that Black America had to offer. Those who encouraged the visual artists to join ideological ranks with their literary counterparts were the leaders of the Harlem Renaissance: eminent philosophers and sociologists, seasoned critics, gallery dealers, and patrons of the arts.

Perhaps no voice was heard and heeded more often than that of Alain Locke. America's first Black Rhodes Scholar, Locke carried the twin banners of aesthetician-philosopher and historian-critic for the New Negro Movement. His dream was to found a "Negro School of Art" in Harlem, which made him the ideal catalyst for the entire Black arts movement. Locke cautioned Black artists against joining the avant-garde circles of New York and Paris and warned them away from modernist trends. He directed them instead to African art as an important source of aesthetics and iconography that would be meaningful for their race. He called for all Black visual artists "to return to the ancestral arts of Africa for inspiration" and instructed painters and sculptors working in Harlem to seek out important art collections that highlighted African art. In this ancestral heritage, Locke saw a new and viable art capable of sustaining the creativity of Black artists and fulfilling the needs of thousands of Black constituents.

Among those who responded to Locke's vision of African visual culture reawakening in America were four Black artists, each of whom, like so many of the Renaissance's leading participants, had either joined the migration to Harlem or were actively engaged in the Harlem art world. Aaron Douglas had come to Harlem from Topeka, Kansas. He chose to observe aspects of African rituals expressed in dance and everyday life and incorporated the iconography into his own work. He selected design elements, particularly from the masks and figural sculptures of West Africa, to serve as visual signposts in the new art he was creating for Black America.

Meta Fuller's art came to the attention of the leaders of the Harlem Renaissance after she had spent several years working in Paris. As early as 1902, African-inspired themes were evident in the sculpture of Meta Warrick, whose marriage in

472

1909 to Dr. Solomon Fuller from Liberia, West Africa, was an important event in Black America both socially and culturally. She inventively interpreted African folktales in her sculptures, bringing new insights to the portrayal of neo-African themes in American art.

Palmer Hayden came to Harlem from Wide Water, Virginia, after World War I. He became the principal artist to communicate Black folklore from the South through his paintings and to express visually the native customs of Southern Blacks. He introduced the magic of Black American legends and myths to the Harlem scene and brought them to life with narrative scenes of musicians and dancers colorfully reminiscent of the stories told by his ancestors in ancient Africa.

William H. Johnson migrated to Harlem in the 1920s and gradually established himself as a special interpreter of the culture of Black people in the South and of the primitive peoples of several European countries that he was to visit between the years 1929 and 1938. His self-imposed aesthetic rules and restrictions, relating to what he called "primitive painting," freed him from academic traditions and permitted a lyrical artistry to flow from his brush.

The wisdom, insightful artistry, and creative will of these four artists helped establish a new tradition among Black American artists that affirmed both their individual and racial identities. Each made vital contributions to the development of American art. During the flowering years of the Renaissance the work of these four individuals helped to direct the artistic genius of a people whose place was Harlem.

### Meta Vaux Warrick Fuller (1877-1968)

Celebrated as a sculptor whose artistic perception and understanding of the Black experience was well ahead of her contemporaries', Meta Fuller was the first Black American artist to draw heavily on African themes and folktales for her subject matter. She was a native of Philadelphia and the product of Black middle-class rearing. She attended the Pennsylvania Museum and School for Industrial Arts (now the Philadelphia College of Art) from 1894 to 1899 and continued her studies at the Pennsylvania Academy of The Fine Arts in Philadelphia from 1903 to 1907. By 1902, however, Fuller was already an established artist in Paris, where her work had been exhibited at S. Bing's famous gallery for modern art and design, l'Art Nouveau. Her art reflects the strong influence of Auguste Rodin, with whom she studied while in Paris, but is free from the Impressionist

*Ethiopia Awakening,* by Meta Vaux Warrick Fuller.

formulas and preoccupation with visual sensations that informed the work of so many of her contemporaries. In choosing her subject matter, she looked to the songs of Black Americans and to African folktales for inspirational themes that focused on pathos and joy in the human condition.

Fuller's style echoes the romantic realism commonly seen in French sculpture of the late nineteenth century, but her figures are also imbued with powerful Expressionist characteristics.

By modeling in a manner which often permitted the clay to distribute light evenly over the entire surface of a sculpture, she created strong statements in plaster and clay—many of which were later cast in bronze—that implied form rather than delivering total realism.

Fuller introduced America to the power of Black American and African subjects long before the Harlem Renaissance was under way. Until Fuller, the aesthetics of the Black visual artist seemed inextricably tied to the taste of White America; more particularly, perhaps, to subject matter and definitions of form derived from European art. The occasional portrait of a Black subject was painted or carved by an aspiring Black artist, but apart from Edmonia Lewis's *Forever Free* (1867) and Henry O. Tanner's two masterpieces of Black genre, *Banjo Lesson* (1893) and *The Thankful Poor* (1894), few visual statements with a pronounced Black program were created in the nineteenth century.

In 1914, Fuller created a sculpture which anticipated the spirit and style of the Harlem Renaissance. Entitled *Ethiopia Awakening,* it symbolized the emergence of the New Negro—whom Alain Locke was not to acclaim as an established member of Black American society until 1925. The composition reveals a partially wrapped mummy, bound from the waist down but with the hair and shoulders of a beautiful African woman. The suggestion of death, a theme frequently explored by the artist from as early as 1902, is evident in the lower half of the figure, while the upper part of the torso is alive and expressive, evoking the emotions of motherhood, the rebirth of womanhood, and the emergence of nationhood. The woman wears the headdress of an ancient Egyptian queen. She may be derived from a portrait of Queen Tye, the mother of Akhenaton, or perhaps the Queen Mother of the sixteenth-century kings of Benin. But in title and spirit she is unquestionably the image of Ethiopia, mythical symbol of Black Africa.

*Ethiopia Awakening* was a truly Pan-Africanist work of art. At a time when Picasso and followers of the modernist tradition gleaned design elements from the art of non-Western societies without being responsible for the cultural context out of which the work came, Fuller's art evidenced a hereditary union between Black Africa and Black America. Her desire to awaken Black people to the consciousness of nationhood and anticolonialism is evident in her choice of the African motif: Africa is on the brink of self-propulsion and self-fulfillment in *Ethiopia Awakening.* Fuller's work

was precocious, communicating a message of hope in what seemed like a hopeless world beset with war and famine which made a travesty of the edict of peace purported to exist among the nations of the Western world. Fuller may well have been articulating in plastic form the biblical prophecy of the psalmist who proclaimed: "Princes shall come out of Egypt. Ethiopia shall soon stretch out her hands unto God" (a theme also illustrated by Aaron Douglas). The symbol of Africa who reaches forth from bondage to freedom connotes the awakening of the forces of good, truth, and beauty in rebellion against colonialism and European exploitation of African peoples and resources.

Fuller met W. E. B. Du Bois in early 1900 in Paris, and their association revealed her devotion to understanding the full range of race relations at home and abroad. The astuteness of her inquiry into African and Black American politics, to which she was introduced by Du Bois as well as other Black American visitors to Paris during her stay there, is reflected in the artistic subjects she used, like *Ethiopia Awakening,* to comment on the Black experience. Beyond her preoccupation with Black themes, however, arose the somber specter of death and sorrow, both of which were themes that often appeared in her work. Her art was so concerned with subjects of the afterlife that critics often referred to her sculptures as macabre and highly emotional. Yet Fuller was also capable of endowing her figures with gracefulness, as she revealed in *Danseuse, Primitive Man,* and *Oriental Dancer,* which were among many of her sculptures that graced the rooms of S. Bing's gallery. Her works also included images of intimate emotional relationships, including the tenderness of a mother's love for her infant child, portrayed in a bronze composition she began in 1914.

The culminating statement of the artist's career is found in her celebrated work *Talking Skull,* executed in 1937. An African male kneels gently in front of a skull silently communicating his thoughts, undisturbed by the gulf which separates life from death. Dramatic in its appeal to have us reason with ourselves to see our final end, the work, like *Go Down Death* by Aaron Douglas, executed about ten years earlier, is convincing in its symbolic, traditional means of communicating the mysteries of life and death.

Best remembered for compositions that represented a macabre and shocking use of Black subject matter, Fuller's art demonstrates her astute observance of history and her insightful understanding that Black subject matter could be meaningful in the work of Black artists. Paris was Fuller's courtly city, Rodin her friend, and she lauded the polite manners of the French. Framingham, Massachusetts, and the city of Boston represented for her the partial fulfillment of the European ideal in America. Indeed, Harlem itself was never home for Meta Warrick Fuller, but the ideals of the Harlem Renaissance were hers in form and spirit. She exhibited in Washington, D.C., with The Harmon Foundation exhibitions of the 1930s and later traveled to New York to serve as a juror for their exhibitions, which presented the most outstanding examples of art by Black Americans at that time. Her early Pan-Africanist approach to art, which she realized in the plasticity of sculpture, provided Alain Locke and the followers of the New Negro Movement with important ingredients for the making of an internationally significant Black statement in the visual arts.

## Aaron Douglas (1899-1979)

Aaron Douglas arrived in Harlem in 1924, armed with a bachelor's degree from the University of Nebraska in Lincoln which certified him to teach art. A year of teaching on the high school level in Kansas City had quickly convinced him, however, that there was a higher calling in art for his services. Soon after arriving in New York, Douglas made the acquaintance of the German artist Winold Reiss, who questioned Douglas's untiring devotion to academic painting and suggested that instead of joining the ranks of realist painters he look to African art for design elements that would express racial commitment in his art.

Douglas closely followed the teachings of Reiss. His exploration of African aesthetics and use of Black subject matter in his work brought him to the attention of the leading Black scholars and activists, including W. E. B. Du Bois and Alain Locke. Du Bois invited Douglas to become a frequent contributor to *The Crisis* magazine, furthering his career as an important illustrator for periodicals, including *Opportunity, Vanity Fair,* and *Theater Arts Monthly* magazines. Locke, who was already deeply committed to encouraging the establishment of a "Negro School of Art" in Harlem, whose artists would draw heavily on design elements from African sculpture, used illustrations by Douglas between chapters of *The New Negro,* his famous anthology of Black writers published in 1925. Locke labeled Douglas a "pioneering Africanist," the first such praise given to a visual artist and a stamp of approval that influenced future historians to consider him "the father of Black American art." Douglas's reputation quickly reached beyond Harlem. He was sought after by patrons in Chicago and Nashville—among the many places his art was exhibited—to paint murals and historical narratives relating to Black history and racial pride.

One of Douglas's most celebrated series of paintings was executed at the wishes of poet James Weldon Johnson for his book of poems *God's Trombones: Seven Negro Sermons in Verse.* He created images for Johnson's book inspired by stories from the Bible, Negro spirituals, recent Black history, and the customs of Africans and Black Americans. The original series was completed in 1927 and included the illustrations *Judgment Day, Let My People Go, Go Down Death, Noah's Ark,* and *The Crucifixion.* Each work was executed in a flatly painted, hard-edge style that defined figures with the language of Synthetic Cubism and borrowed heavily from the lyrical style of Reiss and the forms of African sculpture. He employed a syncopated flow of circular lines amidst smoothly painted surfaces in each work, and by following this formula he was able to move closer to a personal interpretation of his Black subjects. In fact, Douglas came close to inventing his own painting style by this eclectic combination of elements in his work. As a result of the success of the *God's Trombones'* illustrations, he was invited frequently by other authors to illustrate their literary works. The most notable invitation came from Paul Morand, who requested illustrations by the young artist for his book *Black Magic.*

Douglas's academic training and painterly ambition came through clearly in his Precisionist-style drawings for *God's Trombones.* While his images visually describe particular themes in the text, they also stand as individual statements and indeed are legitimately fine paintings. Special design concepts are observed, however, for Douglas's works in *God's Trombones* complement the gospel-inspired, poetic sermons that Johnson borrowed from the mouths of illiterate Black poets and preachers and gracefully transformed into his sophisticated prose. His colorful writing captures the spirit and flavor of thousands of unschooled Black voices.

It was Douglas's desire as well to capture the essence of Black expression in a painterly formula. By closely observing the crowds of Black bodies swaying back and forth at the Savoy Ballroom, The Dark Tower, and the many clubs where Black social climbers gathered nightly to see and be seen, the prowling artist began to find the images, if not the subject matter, he needed. The sounds of music were heard everywhere, according to

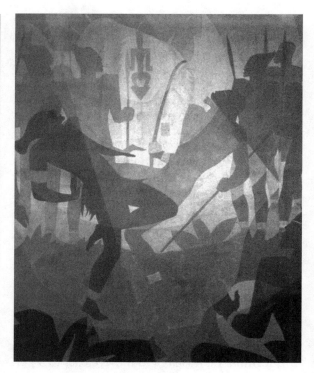

*Aspects of Negro Life: The Negro in an African Setting,* by Aaron Douglas.

Douglas. The spoken word flared through colorful poetic expressions from the pens of the well-trained writers who now saw Harlem as the most soulful city in the world. Indeed, all of the activities of the White observers and Black participants in the Harlem Renaissance eventually got translated into some form of artistry. Yet, the themes that recurred over a period of years in Douglas's work were not based on Harlem nightlife and Black entertainment. Instead, he chose to review Black history, religion, and myth for the substantive sources that were at the core of the stylized subjects he created during the Harlem Renaissance.

Critics looked upon Douglas's art as a breath of fresh air in what had been a rather stagnant climate. Black imagery in the academic tradition of painting had existed predominantly with paintings that pointed to "African types" as "good" subject matter. There were the almost anthropological studies of Blacks by Cyrus Baldridge, created at the behest of Mrs. John D. Rockefeller. Winold Reiss, too, had done similar paintings of Georgia Sea Island subjects. Forsaking the realism of these interpretations of Blacks and any established forms of iconography associated with persons of African descent, Douglas instead chose to use geometric formulas, creating synthesized

compositions. Circles, triangles, rectangles, and squares became the dominant design motifs of Douglas's compositions. Figures were prominently displayed so as to fulfill his principles of highly designed, "meaningful spatial relations." Design concepts were at the core of his art, and the importance of the composition was a lesson Douglas spoke of hearing Mary Beattie Brady, director of The Harmon Foundation, preach over and over again when she saw works by artists she described as "persons of African descent." (Douglas believed it was Miss Brady who made the latter phrase fashionable, as she despised references to "colored" and seldom used the word "Negro.")

Miss Brady, along with the patrons Charlotte Mason and Carl Van Vechten, cheered the stylistic accomplishments of Douglas. They were among the small number of Whites who believed that there was something innate about the way Black artists responded to auditory and visual phenomena. They did not see themselves as patronizing by encouraging Black artists to "be primitive." Douglas, however, spoke often of his concern that Charlotte Mason, whom he never described as an intellectual, was causing undue harm to the artistry of literary figures such as Langston Hughes and Zora Neale Hurston by her efforts to encourage the primitive elements in their writing. He maintained a close but guarded friendship with Carl Van Vechten throughout Van Vechten's lifetime. With Georgia O'Keeffe and Charles S. Johnson, he was influential in having the art gallery at Fisk University named for Van Vechten in 1946. O'Keeffe donated a sizable part of the Alfred Stieglitz Collection to Fisk University, and The Carl Van Vechten Gallery opened in 1949 on the premier Black campus for the arts. The gallery also housed a large selection of photographs by Van Vechten, including numerous portraits of the Black intelligentsia and key participants in the Harlem Renaissance.

Van Vechten saw himself as a patron and critic of all the arts of the Renaissance. He advised Douglas on the salability of his work to writers and publishing houses. But it was Douglas's own strength of character and inventive artistry that enabled him to have a lasting impact on the future course of Black expression in art. And it was in the series of paintings for *God's Trombones* that Douglas first expressed his commitment to creating a language for Black artists. He adhered closely to the salient principles of design he had learned from Reiss, boldly defining his figures within decisive geometric boundaries. Faces and limbs, however, were carefully drawn to reveal African features and recognizable Black poses.

Nowhere in Douglas's entire oeuvre is the concept of Black humanism more personally and successfully displayed than in *The Crucifixion*. James Weldon Johnson's intonement "Jesus, my gentle Jesus, Walking in the dark of the Garden" poignantly reveals the agony of the Savior suffering for all mankind as He walks quietly through Gethsemane. Douglas sought to reinforce the literary message by painting the gentle figure of Jesus walking in the shadow of a towering Black crossbearer. Jesus the Savior is also Jesus the bearer of everyman's burden, particularly the Black man's burden. The central figure in the composition is a Black male, who towers above the crowd, which includes a Roman sentinel representing the White guardianship of Black affairs in America and Africa. The Black man carries a cross much larger than he is, and the strain and agony of his travail is keenly accented on his face. The weight of the world rests also on the shoulders of this Black crossbearer: he is the worker among men, the builder of cities that circumscribe his access. Indeed, he is the legendary Simon, a Black man who took upon himself the yoke of Jesus' cross in order to relieve him of one last earthly misery. It is Simon who received the threats of the Roman soldiers.

*The Crucifixion* breaks with traditional Christian iconography. A Black subject dominates the Christian theme. Man's inhumanity to man, as seen through Black eyes, is poignantly revealed through cultural disguises. Like the Negro spiritual, which made much of satire and cultural subservience by rewording Christian dogma through alliterations that spoke to the tragic conditions of Black slavery and human deprivation, Douglas's message comes alive in a visual accord that strikes out at the core of American racism and the denial of the Black man's humanity. The sorrowing, blameless, and lonesome Jesus, about whom Johnson wrote in his poem "The Crucifixion," becomes every Black American of the 1920s.

In *God's Trombones,* Douglas also achieved his early mastery of hard-edge painting (as it is now called). With an agility of line and an economic use of recognizable symbolic features, Douglas was able to bring to life his stiffly painted figures, which he designed to some degree after the prevailing stylistic features of Art Deco. However, unlike the decorative programs of Art Deco, he capitalized on the possibilities of movement—perhaps influenced by the rhythms of Art Nouveau. Each of the paintings executed by Douglas for *God's Trombones* expressed his humanist concerns. In *Judgment Day,* the iconography is again politically divorced from traditional paintings by White artists. A supreme Black figure stands above land and sea and announces the call to Judgment. In the provenance of traditional Christian art, Blacks were omitted completely from God's Creation except as servants, according to Douglas. For this reason he was determined to show Blacks as part and parcel of biblical events. He noted that Johnson had unerringly captured the essence of the Black man's religious ascendancy in his poem "The Creation." And it was his sense of "the spirit made flesh"—specifically the Black man's flesh—that Douglas wanted to present in *God's Trombones.*

In *Judgment Day,* Douglas planned to emphasize the positive appearance of Black power. Gabriel, the archangel, sounds the trumpet to awaken the dead from their spiritual and physical slumber. He is a lean Black man from whom the last earthly vocal sound is heard. The sound, which travels across the world, is the inventive music of the Black man. In his poem "The Last Judgment," Johnson's Gabriel talks with God:

> And Gabriel's going to ask him: Lord,
> How long must I blow it?
> And God's a-going to tell him: Gabriel,
> Blow it calm and easy.
> Then putting one foot on the mountain top,
> And the other in the middle of the sea,
> Gabriel's going to stand and blow his horn,
> To wake the living nations.

The music which awakens all nations, in the words of Johnson, is the song of a bluesman or a famous trumpet player. He is a timeless echo in the universe: the Louis (Satchmo) Armstrong, Miles Davis, or Wynton Marsalis of our time. The musician, consequently the artist, stands majestically in the center of the universe sounding the loud clarion of Judgment Day. He is at once a musician of earthly note and at the same time a biblical character, the Angel Gabriel.

In *Judgment Day,* Douglas followed Johnson's chronicle and used simplified figures and forms to permit his interpretation of the Black man's place in the Creation and the destiny of the world to dominate the iconographic meaning of a well-known Christian theme. As in *The Crucifixion,* a Black subject is central to God's divinity. Gabriel, who sounds the last trumpet, is already safely called to God and looks down on all others who shall be summoned to submit to a final, irrevocable assembly before God's throne. (Gabriel's

# ON THE SUBJECT OF...

## AARON DOUGLAS

In 1925, Aaron Douglas earned three important distinctions that launched his career: first prize for a front cover illustration of *Opportunity,* first prize in drawing (for *The African Chieftain*) from *Crisis,* and a commission to illustrate Alain Locke's anthology *The New Negro.* Over the next decade, Douglas would illustrate books by Charles S. Johnson, Claude McKay, Paul Morand, and Andre Salmon, as well as numerous magazine covers and articles. In the 1930s, Douglas based himself in New York as an arts leader and muralist. The year after he was elected president of the Harlem Artists' Guild (1935), he addressed the First American Artists Congress. With sponsorship from New Deal art programs and various grants, Douglas completed several murals, most notably *Aspects of Negro Life,* at the 135th Street Harlem Branch of the New York Public Library (1934); those for the Hall of Negro Life exhibited at the Texas Centennial Exposition (1936); and *Education of the Colored Man,* at the Atlanta City Housing Project (1938). In 1938, Douglas received a travel fellowship to the American South and Haiti from the Julius Rosenwald Fund. He exhibited his paintings of Haitian life at the American Contemporary Art Gallery in New York the following year.

stance is repeated in the postures of the blues musician and migrant worker who occupy the central positions in the fourth panel of *Aspects of Negro Life,* a mural Douglas painted for the 135th Street branch of The New York Public Library in 1934.) It is the Black trumpeter in Douglas's painting who is charged by God to sound the colorless requiem to end all earthly acts. Douglas commented that few people knew the "power invested in these Black paintings."

An equally startling message is revealed in *Go Down Death,* another painting executed for *God's Trombones.* The message is one of deliverance, as well as one in which the awesome sight of death is softened—indeed it is welcomed by the Black participants who wait for God's call. The work responds to the imagery of James Weldon Johnson's poetry and his account of Death's call on Sister Caroline, who is on her sickbed in wretched pain. When Death comes for Sister Caroline, she welcomes him and gladly goes home to Jesus in the arms of the angels. Douglas reacted against traditional depictions of death, so often portrayed hastening to snuff out the candle of life. In *Go Down Death,* his figure of Death appears astride a swiftly moving horse racing out of the picture plane. Douglas referred to the speed of Death aboard the horse as the "unknown dimension of life." The time to face mortality and reality was meant to be communicated. A large star is within reach of the rider, whose journey is hastened by wings borrowed from Gabriel. Rushing into an exosphere unknown, Death, who makes equals of us all, seems so far away and yet so near.

The language of form Douglas sought to implement in *Go Down Death* was commensurate in spirit with the verbal language of the Negro spiritual, one of the most popular musical forms in the Black community at the time he painted the series of illustrations for *God's Trombones.* It was the Negro spiritual which had retained the vivid language of enslavement, while at the same time providing all of the psychological escape mechanisms needed to affirm Black consciousness. The transfer of this dynamic from verbal to visual expression permitted Douglas to exercise his keen imagination in extending the iconography of death to earthly society. He reasoned that death was to be embraced as relief from the troubles of a segregated and racist world. Death is therefore rendered neutral and colorless in its judgment, but is still a passionate and urgent moment. The awesome sight of Death is softened by earthly tranquillity and the pleasurable experiences of the world. The swiftly moving horse that rushes through time to call on Sister Caroline helps to make Death acceptable and an ordinary occurrence.

When Douglas executed his mural painting series for the 135th Street branch of The New York Public Library in 1934, he had already begun to reconsider the use of realism in his work, responding to the art community's growing interest in portraiture and genre scenes. He roamed New York by day looking for views to paint. The Triborough Bridge, a park in Harlem, even a power plant, all served to kindle the growing interest he felt toward the ordinary aspects of city life. Later in his career, after completing a series of murals for the second floor of the Erasto Milo Cravath Library at Fisk University, Douglas responded positively to the plea of his longtime friend Charles S. Johnson—one of the "midwives" of the Harlem Renaissance who became president of Fisk University in the 1940s—to join the faculty at Fisk. He taught painting there from 1937 until his retirement in 1966.

The attempts by Douglas to combine modernist aesthetics with African ancestral imagery afforded him a chance to stylize his art in a manner which had not been achieved by Black American artists before him. Black heritage and racial themes were the subjects he attempted to paint when he became aware of the interest Black people were developing in their own history and destiny. He was, on one occasion, severely criticized by James A. Porter, the leading Black art historian and critic of the 1940s, for borrowing too often from African art without properly applying these themes to the Black American condition. But had Douglas not led the way in using African-oriented imagery during the Harlem Renaissance, Alain Locke's brief to visual artists to "return to the ancestral arts of Africa for inspiration" would have taken even longer to be realized on the canvases of Black painters. It was Douglas who effected the crucial move toward affirming the validity of the Black experience and thereby made one of America's most worthy contributions to art.

Although Douglas returned from time to time to portrait and landscape painting, his lasting impact on the arts of Black America was his inventive approach to painting themes that related in form and style to the Black experience and consciousness. His death, in 1979, at his beloved Fisk University in Nashville, brought to an end the career of "a pioneering Africanist," whose artistic insight reached far beyond the walls of Harlem.

### Palmer Hayden (1890-1973)

Palmer Hayden, a name given to the World War I veteran by his White commanding sergeant who could not pronounce his real name (Peyton Hedgeman), was born in Wide Water, Virginia. He is often referred to as a self-trained artist. However, the record reveals he was a student at Cooper Union in New York and pursued independent studies at Boothbay Art Colony in Maine. He studied and painted independently in France, where he lived from 1927 to 1932. Hayden's reputation emanates from his realistic depictions of folklore and Black historical events. He, like Douglas, was also among the first Black American artists to use African subjects and designs in his painting

(which helped, in fact, to distinguish between certain ethnic stylistic differences in the art of Black Africa). His *Fétiche et Fleurs,* a composition of 1926, highlights a Fang mask from Gabon and Bakuba raffia cloth from the Congo (now Zaire), which have been placed in a traditional still-life setting. Locke praised the artist for his modernist approach to painting. But Hayden was not a modernist in his stylistic approach. Instead, he broke with tradition by depicting African art in his paintings.

Hayden spent many years at work for The Harmon Foundation and maintained his loyalty to the ideals of the foundation and a strong friendship with its founding director, Mary Brady. He exhibited in the Harmon exhibitions beginning in 1926. Most of his works depict Black people comfortably situated in the humble surroundings in which they lived. Other images extol the work ethic and Black devotion to public service. He also painted numerous watercolors in the 1930s which are remembrances of Black nurses in the Red Cross and Black soldiers marching to reveille during World War I.

While most critics and art analysts, including James A. Porter, saw Hayden as a naive painter producing racial images that were almost grotesque, some saw him as an original interpreter of Black themes who highlighted Black folklore and certain aspects of the ancestral legacy. Locke specifically praised the pictorial attempts by Hayden to relate to his African past and did not agree with Porter's analysis of how far Hayden had strayed from the ideal, healthy approach to making Black images. In his interpretations of the Black legacy, Hayden saw no reason to refrain from borrowing from the popular images of Blacks by White artists. He often exaggerated Black features, stylizing eyes, noses, lips, and ears, and making the heads of many of his subjects look bald and rounded in form. But he insisted that he was not poking fun at Black people. Some people living in the better sections of Harlem found it hard to believe that Hayden was not being satirical when they saw *Dove of God* (1930) and *The Janitor Who Paints. Dove of God,* a watercolor executed in a free-flowing style, depicts the spiritual uplift Black people receive in fundamentalist church services. The preacher is shown dramatizing his sermon to the point where the attentive audience demonstrates its empathy with what is being said by an outpouring of emotions. So moved is the spellbound audience by the words of the preacher, who no doubt describes the biblical passage "This is my beloved son in whom I am well pleased" (at which point the dove of God descends from the sky), that little attention is paid to the half-hidden figure of a man who releases the bird from the ceiling. Such scenes were common in Hayden's oeuvre and were derived from a previous era in Black American painting. They recalled the traditional affinity Black artists had with the art of the American mainstream before the Harlem Renaissance. Indeed, it was this affinity which Locke sought to abolish when he encouraged Black artists to look to Africa for inspiration in their work. However, Locke saw positive elements in Hayden's work that the general public did not see.

In an interview at Fisk University, where his John Henry series of paintings was exhibited in February 1970, Hayden recounted to me the experience of trying to explain to an often critical Black public what the subjects were about. Too often, they were classified as Black stereotypes. He spoke of the folk tradition and of its heroes, such as John Henry. He spoke also of the autobiographical *The Janitor Who Paints*. But Hayden's audience was critical of both his subject matter and the stylistic manner in which he worked. Some were so personal in their criticism as to argue that although Hayden served as janitor and handyman at the offices of The Harmon Foundation, he did not return home to a Black family with humble surroundings. But Hayden insisted that he was painting an era, and his works symbolically made reference to the comedy, tragedy, and pleasures of a Black life-style.

In a celebrated composition entitled *When Tricky Sam Shot Father Lamb* (1940), Hayden directs our attention to an act of violence in the Black community. The title suggests "Black on Black" crime—as it is called today—but crime is not the intended emphasis of the painting. Instead, the artist dramatically portrays a concerned crowd: the same type of people who were seen sitting around, strolling along the street, and parading their latest fashions in *Midsummer Night in Harlem* (1936). He offered a smaller, similar audience gazing down at the dead body of John Henry in *He Died with the Hammer in His Hand* (from the John Henry series). The crowd in the street, watching evening events, marching in parades, and experiencing the everyday occurrences of everyday life, were an important part of Hayden's work.

The fashions and manners of the people he painted are important elements in the appeal of Hayden's art. *Just Back from Washington,* shows a young, cigar-smoking Black man, majestically posed in a super-dapper outfit, sporting patent-leather shoes, striped pants, Palm Beach hat, white vest, white driver's gloves, silk coat, and bamboo strolling cane. He represents the "city-dude," who was a perennial presence at the night spots of Harlem. A young boy kneels, as if in submission, before the well-groomed man, shining his already polished shoes to a spit-shine quality. Hayden's paintings of the 1930s and 1940s chronicle the various manners of dress found in the Black rural South and Northern urban communities. They are culturally telling depictions of print designs, hairstyles of women, and the flamboyant dress often associated with Northern Black males. Yet the fear of pejorative imagery by a Black artist made some Blacks uneasy. They felt that Hayden's caricature-like images were what White Americans welcomed. He did not, they claimed, define Black imagery that was positive. However critical Hayden's audience was of his interpretation of the Black experience, his lasting impact on Black American painting cannot be denied. His art is positive, born of a true affection for the quality of Black life Hayden knew, believed existed, and dreamed about.

His paintings depicting African themes were not always geographically accurate, but this was not his intention. *Blue Nile* and *African Dancers* (1932) conjure up the prevailing visual attitude of how Africans—without national distinction—live in their native land. Here, again, dress and common customs associated with African peoples are derived from the usual formulas European artists had applied to the subject. Indeed, some of these subjects were based on themes Hayden had developed while living in Paris in the early 1930s.

Hayden's art cannot be defined as a systematic approach to painting. While he seldom paid strict attention to the rules of academic painting, Hayden never thought of himself as a primitive artist, a label often associated with his work. Instead, he saw himself as an artist whose themes and style of painting were consistent with the time in which he lived. These works he regarded as symbols of the changing order of contemporary American life. Folklore was at the core of many of his compositions, but he was also keenly aware of the plight of rural Blacks making their way to the industrial North in search of a more humane life-style. Industrial America is symbolically dependent on the hands of Black workers in many of his compositions, an observation Hayden frequently made in paintings, such as the John Henry series.

Hayden's love of life and people is paramount in all of his art. His keen observation of nature, the land, and sea is outstandingly represented in oil and watercolor compositions, including many of

Boothbay Harbor, Maine. His paintings, which chronicled the Black experience, are often without particular reference to a specific time. But one is seldom left wondering from what community Hayden derives his themes of urban life. The place is Harlem, spiritual home of the Black Renaissance.

### William H. Johnson (1901-1970)

William H. Johnson arrived in Harlem when the Renaissance was in the making. He had come to New York in 1918 from Florence, South Carolina, and became a student at the National Academy of Design. He remained there for five years, absorbing the teachings of George Luks and Charles Hawthorne, and readying himself for a career in art that would take him to places in North Africa and Europe in search of a permanent residence. It was through the influence of Hawthorne that Johnson traveled first to Paris in 1926, where he settled, painted, and studied the works of modern European masters.

Johnson's introduction to art had come through the cartoons he saw in a local newspaper in Florence. Little did he dream that one day he would become a seasoned traveler, whose art interests would take him from Tunisia to Norway. But the skills he had acquired in painting at the National Academy of Design stood him in good company with sympathetic European artists, who encouraged him to remain abroad and devote his life to art. By 1929, Johnson's carefully developed style of painting, which borrowed heavily from both realism and Impressionism, was beginning to show signs of change. He had come in contact with the work of Paul Cézanne, Georges Rouault, and Chaim Soutine. He admired the rugged and direct style of painting associated with Vincent van Gogh's work. His mind and eyes were wide open to change as he embraced one style of painting after another in search of a permanent way to express himself through art. By 1930, Johnson began to develop a stable stylistic consciousness. He became increasingly attracted to the work of Soutine. In Soutine's work, he found a way of removing himself stylistically from the smooth painterly style he had developed under Hawthorne. His compositions became somewhat cumbersome, with emotional displays of elongated, curving forms. Academic realism would no longer play an important role in Johnson's work, as he moved his art closer to the style of painting recently made famous by the German Expressionists.

Johnson settled in Denmark in the spring of 1930. He had married Holcha Krake, a local potter, and they made Kerteminde, a small fishing village, their home for the next few years. It was in Kerteminde and its vicinity that many of the landscapes Johnson praised as his best works were painted. He expressed feeling a close kinship with the life-style of the Danish villagers, often describing his own way of living in the rural South as closely related to that of his adopted countrymen. By 1932, he and his wife headed south to explore North Africa and to study the art of the region. Their stays in Tunis, Tangiers, and outlying villages permitted them to learn from local artists about African pottery and the arts and crafts of the region. Johnson continued to formulate his expressive style during his entire stay in North Africa. He was devoted to seeing what he described as the primitive ways of people and once spoke of having learned more from the fishermen of Kerteminde and the Arabs of North Africa than he had in his entire academic career.

Johnson's strong interest in what he described as the primitive life-style of the people inspired him to experiment with his painting, attempting to make his philosophy of art commensurate with his adopted philosophy of life. He wanted to rid himself of the attributes of the trained academic painter and revert to a style of painting that he later referred to as primitive. When asked why he had forsaken the academic style he had mastered in earlier paintings, he responded, "My aim is to express in a natural way what I feel both rhythmically and spiritually, all that has been saved up in my family of primitiveness and tradition." The primitive style to which Johnson referred should not be confused with the more naive form of painting developed upon his return to Harlem in 1938. Instead, the "primitiveness" of Johnson was to manifest itself in his work in ways which celebrated the Expressionism of Edvard Munch, Soutine, and van Gogh. But, by 1938, Johnson had forsaken the Expressionist painting associated with his European sojourn and was concentrating on subjects and themes that celebrated the Black experience.

Johnson's return to America in 1938 provided him with the subjects he needed to make the crossover from Expressionism to a style of painting that bordered on primitivism. It was a difficult task for an artist so well trained in the academic process to forsake all that he had learned and to turn "primitive" overnight. But Johnson was not one to give up easily on his goals. When he re-

*Ezekiel Saw the Wheel,* by William H. Johnson.

turned to Harlem, the cabaret and nightlife scenes so enthralled him that he began working endlessly to capture the spirit and flavor of what he was experiencing in postwar America. For the next six years, he devoted an enormous amount of energy creating hundreds of compositions that expressed various aspects of the Black experience in the United States. Harlem became the central theme of many works that emanated from his new way of painting.

The style of this new work has often been described as naive, primitive, and folk-oriented. His formula was simple and direct. He applied flat paint to geometrically drawn forms, which were still somewhat dependent on the elements of Expressionism that had dominated his work over the previous ten years. By the late 1930s, Johnson's style had moved permanently in the direction of naive painting, and he had reduced his palette to four or five colors. He became increasingly interested in Black subjects that emphasized Christian themes. Compositions such as *Nativity* (c. 1939), *Descent from the Cross* (c. 1939), and *Mount Calvary* presented an all-Black cast as the family of Jesus.

Aaron Douglas had introduced Black religious subjects into his work in the 1920s. Malvin Gray Johnson had painted Black religious themes based on Negro spirituals, as had Alan Rohan Crite. But none of these artists had celebrated the theme of Black Christianity with the depth of Johnson's presentations. Douglas's introduction of Black Christian themes came through literary formats acceptable to the Renaissance audience. James Weldon Johnson's poetry, which echoed the voices of untutored Black preachers, seemed a fitting place for Douglas to begin. Malvin Gray Johnson had limited his interpretation of the Christian theme to spirituals. Alan Rohan Crite drew heavily on the iconography of the Italian Renaissance for his interpretation of the Negro spiritual in a series of drawings he completed in 1938.

But William H. Johnson changed the course of artistic interpretations of Black American themes in Christianity. He undertook reinterpretations of many of the familiar subjects by European artists on the life and death of Jesus. *Jesus and the Three Marys*—a theme also painted by Henry O. Tanner—shows the crucified body of a Black Christ before three Black women. The Virgin Mary is shown bent with emotion at the foot of the cross. Interestingly, the scene of the Crucifixion differs little in formal structure from another Johnson painting, of about the same date, in which similar female figures are seen next to the body of a lynching victim.

Johnson always showed great devotion to painting themes that celebrated Black Christianity. *Climbing Jacob's Ladder* (c. 1939) and *Swing Low, Sweet Chariot* are paintings based on a literal interpretation of spiritual occasions. In the former, four female figures are shown in the company of two males, struggling to climb a pyramid-shaped ladder that rises to a sky in which the sun, the moon, and stars are seen. All of the figures are nude and one of the male figures lies sprawled on the ground in front of the ladder. It becomes quite clear to the observer that Johnson was integrating religious and social messages in this painting, a practice he shared with Aaron Douglas. In *Swing Low, Sweet Chariot,* Johnson shows the lyrical finesse of his work and his narrative skill. A chorus of Black angels, who resemble the women seen frequently in Johnson's paintings of everyday scenes, are lined up in midair waiting, with white horse and chariot, to carry home an aging Black male, modestly clothed in short pants, who is about to receive the rewards for his good life. In *Mount Calvary,* Mary, the mother of Jesus, is joined by three women dressed in contemporary prints. The figure of Christ is placed slightly above the center of the composition, balanced by the two thieves who receive no attention from the women. Johnson has introduced contemporary human suffering into his story, a way of saying to the observer that Mount Calvary is the legacy of all who live in the contemporary world. The figure of Mary is in the foreground and is separated by the presence of the cross from the other women in attendance. The formula of aligning figures side by side appealed greatly to Johnson. Not only did he look closely at the religious compositions of the Italian Renaissance before painting the series, but he was equally drawn to the study of Byzantine art. The results are evident in the positioning of the figures and their static depiction.

Before Johnson returned to Denmark in 1946, he created a number of paintings that dealt with political and social Harlem. *Café, Chain Gang,* and several works that center around the theme of the Black dancer were executed while Johnson lived in Harlem. He began recounting his experiences of growing up in the South and recorded impressions of families going to church on Sunday mornings in their wagons, farm workers sowing and reaping crops, as well as members of his own family, often referring to them by titles such as *Li'l Sis, Little Sweet* (1944), and *Mom and Dad* (1944). In *Mom and Dad,* the artist's aging Black mother is seen sitting in a rocking chair in front of a portrait of Johnson's White father on the wall. The artist no doubt meant to make a social statement about the circumstances of his illegitimate birth, the father he was never allowed to know, and the knowledge he had of his family roots.

Johnson also painted subjects that commented on political issues in Harlem. In *Moon over Harlem* (1944), community violence is depicted in a bloody scene which involves policemen and citizens in a night brawl. During the same period, Johnson turned his attention to the depiction of Black heroes, abolitionist figures, and world leaders. He painted George Washington Carver in several poses—accepting awards from dignitaries, working in the laboratory, and displaying the numerous products that he created from peanuts and sweet potatoes. In another work, Chiang Kai-shek, Franklin D. Roosevelt, and Winston Churchill are shown meeting in Cairo, Egypt, on Thanksgiving Day, 1943. Johnson added notes to give historical summations of the people in his late paintings, most of whom could be recognized from the modified portraits from which they were taken. But, by 1945, Johnson's work had begun to lose its ethnic and formal vitality. An unfinished,

disorderly feeling was evident in his art. The paintings seldom attained the power and appeal of earlier works such as *Chain Gang* and *Going to Church.* But Johnson insisted on continuing to document historical and social issues in his paintings. Most of these works had but one showing in the United States before the artist packed them up and sailed again for Denmark in 1946. Thereafter, he became ill and was not able to paint. He returned to America and was confined to a hospital on Long Island until his death in 1970.

Johnson's work represented an important break with tradition. It signaled the beginning of the acceptance of Black subjects as part and parcel of the Christian experience in Western art. Moreover, Johnson did not share the view that art was a gift to be enjoyed only by polite society. He chose to rid himself of elitist views about art. He had worked hard upon his return to postwar America to develop an awareness of the social plight of Black people in America. Harlem was the place for such information, and the Renaissance enlivened his sensitivity to the racial problems of America. His last years of painting in Harlem centered around a plan to bring peace of mind to himself through his art and the creation of works that served to enlighten the Black community about their own history and heritage.

## Conclusion

Lauded as the most glorious period in the history of Black American culture, the Harlem Renaissance represented the will of a select number of people who felt the time was right for the promotion of the arts of persons of African ancestry. The four visual artists . . . left a lasting impression on Black artists of the following generations. Their influence should not be diminished in the art world and there is growing interest in defining the roles they played in the broader context of American art.

Meta Fuller's art bridged the gap between a well established Black presence in European art circles and the gradual acceptance of the Black artists' work at home. She labored to uplift the level of visual literacy among her own people to direct their artistic taste to important forms of creative expression within Black culture. Aaron Douglas, Palmer Hayden, and William H. Johnson continued Fuller's legacy. Each of these artists responded favorably to the call by Alain Locke and the founders of the Harlem Renaissance to look among themselves and to the art of Africa for the inspiration needed to create a world-class movement in art that would be lasting in its appeal and interest within the Black community. Harlem, the place, provided the necessary ingredients for such a cultural revolution.

## ROMARE BEARDEN AND HARRY HENDERSON (ESSAY DATE 1993)

**SOURCE:** Bearden, Romare and Harry Henderson. "The Twenties and the Black Renaissance." In *A History of African-American Artists from 1792 to the Present,* pp. 115-25. New York: Pantheon Books, 1993.

*In the following excerpt, the authors provide a history of the origins of the Harlem Renaissance and the cultural life of the period.*

World War I made it clear that the United States had emerged as a world power. Yet, except for overly idealized "patriotic" versions, American history was neither widely known nor understood. In fact, many European-oriented academicians still argued that America had no history—paralleling what they said about Africans. The idea that there was an American literature, music, theater, or art was not widely recognized either in this country or abroad.

This historical situation opened the way for development of an American cultural identity that was not dominated by European concepts. As a writer in *The Freeman,* one of the leading intellectual magazines of the day, put it: "The great hope of culture in America lies in the fact that we in this country have not yet agreed upon a definition of 'American culture.' The greatness of our opportunity consists in the very fact that thus far we have set up no definite boundaries of nationality where culture is concerned."[1]

From the perspective of today, it would seem that African-Americans recognized this situation as their opportunity to participate in the evolving American culture and way of life. In contrast to the many young writers and artists who felt disillusioned and alienated by World War I and who went to Paris in search of an acceptable identity as Americans, most black people had a proud sense of being Americans. And they strongly felt it was time to shuck off the stereotyped limitations imposed on them historically, including the old denial of their artistic ability. The emergence of a number of young black artists reflected this profound change among African-Americans. They knew that spirituals had won worldwide respect, and they saw that jazz had America up and dancing. They believed, as one analyst of the period, Nathan Irvin Huggins, has put it, that they "were on the threshold of a new day."[2]

Three major factors had given rise to this new attitude among African-Americans. First, some 200,000 black men had served in the savagery of World War I, and the black 369th Infantry from New York, alone among United States troops, had been decorated en masse by the French government with the Croix de Guerre for its heroism. The old ways were gone forever for these men, their families, their friends, black leaders, and intellectuals.

Second, millions of poor black people had silently, both individually and in family groups, left the South in a determined effort to improve their lot in northern cities. In 1910 eight of ten black Americans had resided in the eleven former Confederate states, with 90 percent living in rural areas with almost no schools. Jobs in northern factories, mills, and mines during World War I started this great migration, but it continued between 1920 and 1925, when some two million African-Americans left the South. The black population of Chicago rose from 44,102 persons in 1910 to 233,903 by 1930. New York, with 91,709 black persons in 1910, had 327,706 by 1930. Harlemites proudly called it "the black capital of the world."[3]

This major change in their economic and cultural circumstances, from rural to urban, contributed to African-Americans' general feeling that, despite difficulties, they were not helpless, that they were moving ahead. The mass migration helped provide a psychological basis for the optimistic feeling of "renaissance," the rebirth of black people as effective participants in American life. Leaving the South prompted individual and collective examinations by African-Americans of who they were, of their own thoughts and feelings, as well as their rights as Americans and the complexity of their abilities and aspirations.

Without this migration, the development of a significant group of African-American artists in the 1920s could not have occurred. In earlier periods, there had been only a few, isolated black artists. As long as the overwhelming majority of African-Americans lived in the impoverished rural South, there could not be a substantial number of black artists. Most of the African-American artists who developed in the 1920s—Palmer Hayden, Malvin Gray Johnson, Richmond Barthé, James Lesesne Wells, Ellis Wilson, and Augusta Savage, to mention a few—were born in small southern towns.

Pride in African-American soldiers, whose frontline courage had been expected to end the denial of full citizenship rights for all black people, and the mass migration, in which nearly every African-American family participated in some way, contributed to the third factor—the great outpouring of creative energy by many talented African-Americans in all the arts, most noticeably in music and the theater. While it may be seen as an aspect of the fundamental change in African-Americans' attitudes toward themselves and their participation in American life, this creative activity had a synergistic effect, particularly on the demand for better conditions, education, and the encouragement of talented individuals. Even a poor, uneducated migrant could see that some African-Americans were now musical and theatrical "stars." To African-Americans as a group, this development meant great heights could be scaled. Intellectuals optimistically believed that discrimination and prejudice could be ended by demonstrating that African-Americans were capable doctors, judges, lawyers, writers, and artists. Their work, creating a bridge across ignorance and prejudice, was expected to win respect and full rights for black people.

Although this creative period has been generally called the "Harlem Renaissance," the term is a misnomer. Harlem's creativity was simply the most publicized and most diverse. The same kind of activity went on in Philadelphia, Chicago, Boston, Baltimore, and San Francisco, where the sculpture of Sargent Johnson was winning prizes. These efforts made many influential Americans aware of African-American poets, writers, musicians, artists, and theatrical stars. It was something new and disturbing to old ideas about the role of African-Americans in American life.

Although northern cities gave these aspiring artists some opportunities to see works of art, to visit museums and libraries, prejudice still kept them from receiving technical training at many art schools. The Art Students League, the National Academy of Design, and Cooper Union in New York and the Art Institute of Chicago were among the few schools that accepted black students. African-Americans were made to feel unwelcome at many art galleries and some libraries.

However, the artists' first concern was survival, not art. Hard work, long hours, and poor pay left little time for museums. W. H. Johnson labored as a longshoreman on the docks; Augusta Savage was a laundress. Cloyd L. Boykin worked as a janitor, and Palmer C. Hayden did odd jobs and cleaned apartments. All were constantly advised by people of both races to give up their hopes of becoming artists. Many were forced to do so. Carleton Thorpe, for example, exhibited paintings in a 1921 Harlem library show but was told he had no chance of becoming an artist because he was black. He took a darkroom job with Peter A. Juley, a specialist in photographing art, and gave up painting.[4]

A handful of older black artists encouraged and sometimes taught younger ones. Among them were William E. Braxton, a skilled and much-published Chicago illustrator; William McKnight Farrow, originally from Ohio, who acquired his own training while a curator's assistant at the Art Institute of Chicago, became an expert etcher, and taught etching there;[5] William Edouard Scott, who had studied with Henry Ossawa Tanner in France and become an illustrator and muralist; Laura Wheeler Waring, originally from Hartford, Connecticut, who trained at the Pennsylvania Academy of Fine Arts, studied in Rome and in Paris with Auguste Rodin, and taught at the Cheyney Training School for Teachers near Philadelphia. Having achieved some recognition, these older artists were admired by younger ones and served as their guides.

African-American identity was enhanced by the recognition that jazz was changing the nation's music—was indeed becoming its music. This was something very different from the sympathetic appreciation of religious spirituals. The rhythms of jazz set people to dancing; "we're living," people said, "in the Jazz Age." A new, fascinated awareness of black people, their spirit, and their capacity to live spread across America.

This helped to stimulate interest in the visual arts created by black artists. Between August 1 and September 30, 1921, the first large exhibition of work by African-American artists was displayed in the Harlem branch of the New York Public Library.[6] Nearly 200 paintings and sculptures, including some from Boston and Washington, D.C., had been assembled by an enthusiastic Harvard graduate, Augustus Granville Dill, whose Harlem bookstore became a mecca for young black writers. Tanner sent a painting to encourage younger artists. Five engravings by Patrick Reason, a lithographer during the 1830s, gave many New Yorkers their first inkling that there had been black artists in America long before the Civil War.

Other exhibits followed, such as the 1921 Tanner Art League show at the Dunbar High School in Washington, D.C., and the 1922 Wabash YMCA show in Chicago, which included the work of Farrow, Charles C Dawson, Arthur Wilson, and Ellis Wilson, who later made Haitian landscapes and people his central themes. In 1927 a major show was held at the Art Institute of Chicago under the sponsorship of the Chicago Women's Club. Called "The Negro in Art Week," it included African art as well as that of contemporary Chicago artists, work by Tanner, Edward M. Bannister, and Edmonia Lewis.[7] At this show Richmond Barthé was so successful with his clay portraits that he turned from painting to sculpture. Other exhibitors included Farrow, Scott, William A. Harper, Arthur Diggs, Aaron Douglas, John Hardrick, Hale A. Woodruff, Edwin A. Harleston, Leslie Rogers (the *Chicago Defender* cartoonist), and photographer King Ganaway. An unusual aspect of this show was its wide community sponsorship. In addition to the Chicago Women's Club, it was supported by other women's groups of both races, religious groups, the National Association of Advancement for Colored People, and the Urban League. Among its patrons were nationally known Chicagoans, including attorney Clarence Darrow, sculptor Lorado Taft, attorney Harold Ickes, poet Carl Sandburg, and social worker Jane Addams. This sponsorship guaranteed wide publicity.

Long before this, W. E. B. Du Bois, who had known Tanner in Philadelphia, had begun publishing African-American artists' work on the cover of the NAACP magazine, *The Crisis.* The weekly *New York Age* and the Urban League's publication, *Opportunity,* also reproduced their work. Citing the example of Tanner, Du Bois particularly championed the development of artists.

Until these publications and exhibits appeared, few Americans had any idea that black artists existed. For the African-American artists, the exhibition provided direct encouragement, and they demonstrated another aspect of the renaissance to African-Americans in general.

In New York the exciting spurt of self-discovery in this period was heightened by the concentration of the African-American community. It then occupied a narrow section of Manhattan, less than a fourth of Harlem today. This narrow strip—then a Jim Crow street, where many restaurants barred black people—provided a physical intimacy and identification with people and events. A newcomer from Georgia or the Carolinas might find himself walking side by side with the dignified Du Bois, the vivacious Florence Mills, or Noble Sissle and Eubie Blake, whose all-black musical *Shuffle Along* was making Broadway history. At the 135th Street branch of the public library one might find a display of paintings by black artists or see Arthur A. Schomburg arranging a display of African masks. Or one might glimpse James Weldon Johnson, the NAACP

leader who had dramatized the need for a federal antilynching law, talking with Godfrey Nurse, one of the cities leading African-American physicians.

On most evenings the newcomer could hear street speakers, including Marcus Garvey calling for self-help and militant self-assertion in establishing an African nation. At the Gray Shop, Wallace Thurman, a novelist and managing editor of the labor-oriented *Messenger,* ran an almost continuous forum for writers and artists. Outside the Lafayette Theater, one might see famous performers like Bill "Bojangles" Robinson.

On 138th and 139th streets, between Seventh and Eighth avenues, many black professionals in handsome homes, some of which were designed by Stanford White. Off Lenox, in a block-size lot, Colonel Hubert Fauntleroy Julian was preparing a plane for a transatlantic flight; when he tested the engine, all Harlem heard it. On 137th Street one could dance at the Renaissance Casino and sometimes see the "Renaissance Five," whose ball handling dazzled the leading basketball teams of the era.

To many Harlemites, the renaissance meant the rebirth of a great black culture that had once created golden kingdoms in Africa. And just about everybody was participating in it. There were frequent parades by fraternal groups, such as Masons, Elks, Odd Fellows, and Moose, as well as religious and political organizations, with their members resplendent in uniforms, swinging down Seventh Avenue behind marching bands. In the evening thousands enlivened their social lives by strolling along Harlem's main streets. "This is not simply going out for a walk," wrote James Weldon Johnson, "it is more like going out for an adventure."[8]

Artists like W. H. Johnson and Augusta Savage, who came from small southern towns, were greatly nourished and stimulated by what they found in Harlem—by a new sense of black identity and importance, of community, of power and talent. When she had tried to get portrait commissions among middle-class black people in Florida, Savage had been turned down. But in New York she did busts of both Du Bois and Garvey, the outstanding black leaders of the day, with critically divergent views, enormously different backgrounds, and sharply contrasting personalities. Each offered ideas and programs that appealed to tens of thousands, providing a cultural richness in the bitter rivalry unknown to African-American artists only a few years earlier. That both men considered artists important and arranged time to sit for an unknown young black woman artist gave all of Harlem's black artists a sense of pride and of their importance in the development of their own people's influence on American history.

The cities' greater social and personal freedom and the resultant spiritual and artistic freedom and sense of initiative also contributed to individual development, according to Hale Woodruff, a newcomer to New York whose drawing of young black artists at their easels appeared on the August 1928 cover of *The Crisis*. "I can't tell you how free I felt just being in the city," he said.[9]

Yet Woodruff also pointed out that, unlike the jazz musicians they were constantly advised to emulate, young black artists did not have opportunities to get together for regular exchanges, to give each other the support, response, and stimulation that foster a sense of artistic group identity. According to Woodruff, the young artists' work schedules as they struggled to earn a living, usually at menial jobs, and their differing levels of aesthetic experience worked against such exchanges.

In 1924 the editors of *Survey Graphic* magazine asked Alain L. Locke, the first African-American Rhodes scholar and head of the philosophy department at Howard University, to prepare a "Harlem" issue of their magazine. Drawing upon the work of many African-American writers, artists, and critics, Locke assembled a wide range of material that included poetry, drama, music, fiction, black history, folklore, literary criticism, discussion of the problems of black women, Du Bois's vision of the relationship of the colored peoples of the world, and other historical, sociological, and educational studies. In this way African-Americans themselves imaginatively and aesthetically presented what is now called "the black experience."[10]

The impact of this issue was far-reaching. Within a year, *The Crisis* published a symposium on "the criteria of Negro art," with many African-American writers and leaders presenting their views.[11] *The Nation* extended this discussion. William E. Harmon, a wealthy real estate developer, set up the Harmon Foundation to provide "Negro Achievement Awards," including one for art, and a group of New York black writers and artists attempted to organize their own avant-garde magazine, *Fire!!* But nothing more objectively conveys the impact of the "Harlem" issue of *Survey Graphic*, published in March 1925, than the reprinting of

its nucleus as a book in November because the demand for it was so great. Titled *The New Negro*, the book was enhanced by six distinctive African-based design panels by Aaron Douglas, representing his first efforts to create lyric, silhouette-style black figures in action. Their vitality immediately demonstrated how different the "new Negro" was. "The day of the 'aunties,' 'uncles,' and 'mammies' is done. Uncle Tom and Sambo have passed on," Locke wrote in his introduction.[12] For many influential Americans, *The New Negro* was the first demonstration of the rich cultural capabilities of African-Americans in fields other than music and the theater.

Two articles in *The New Negro* dealt specifically with black artists. One was written by Albert C. Barnes, one of the book's few white contributors, who had assembled a great collection of modern and African art on his estate outside Philadelphia. As proof of the creativeness of the African-American, Barnes cited songs and poetry as "the true infallible record of what the struggle [against oppression] has meant to his inner life. . . . This mystic, whom we have treated as a vagrant, has proved his possession of a power to create, out of his own soul and our own America, moving beauty of an individual character whose existence we never knew."[13]

The second article was Locke's essay on "the legacy of the ancestral arts," which strove to influence the direction of African-American artists. Locke was one of the relatively few Americans at the time who were aware that Pablo Picasso and Georges Braque had utilized African sculpture in developing Cubism in 1909. By illustrating his essay with photographs of African art, he hoped to stimulate a link between this ancient art and the development of African-American artists. While debatable in many respects, Locke's essay touched on vital, complex issues confronting the black American artist, and it remains a primary document in their history.

"The characteristic African art expressions are rigid, controlled, disciplined, abstract, conventionalized," Locke wrote. In contrast, he saw the work of black American artists as "free, exuberant, emotional, sentimental, human." He stressed that the "spirit of African expression, by and large, is disciplined, sophisticated, laconic, and fatalistic. The emotional temper of the American Negro is exactly the opposite. What we have thought primitive in the American Negro—his naiveté, his sentimentalism, his exuberance, and his improvising spontaneity—are then neither characteristically African nor to be explained as an ancestral heritage. They are the result of his peculiar experience in America and the emotional upheaval of its trials and ordeals," essentially derived from environmental influences rather than "original artistic temperament."[14]

Locke knew that the African-American artist at that time felt no connection with African art. But because African art had influenced modern European art, he suggested,

> there is the possibility that the sensitive artistic mind of the American Negro, stimulated by a cultural pride and interest, will receive from African art a profound and galvanizing influence . . . the valuable and stimulating realization that the Negro is not a cultural foundling without his own inheritance. Our timid and apologetic imitativeness and overburdening sense of cultural indebtedness have, let us hope, their natural end in such knowledge and realization. . . . If the forefathers could so adroitly master these mediums . . . why not we?[15]

In addition to decreasing feelings of inferiority, what could be gained from African art was, Locke said, "the lesson of a classic background, the lesson of discipline and style of technical control pushed to the limits of technical mastery. A more highly stylized art does not exist than the African. If after absorbing the new content of American life and experience, and after assimilating new patterns of art, the original artistic endowment can be sufficiently augmented to express itself with equal power in more complex patterns and substance, the Negro may well become what some have predicted, the artist of American life."[16]

Through his optimistic essay and his personal access to patrons, important foundation heads, and educators, Locke shaped attitudes that influenced the development of African-American artists. At many levels, from art teachers to artists and philanthropists, he made many distinguished Americans aware of the emergence of African-American artists as a group. He also deepened the artists' own awareness of their cultural heritage. Visiting New York, Philadelphia, Chicago, and other cities, Locke often met with African-American artists. He provided them with an orientation and sense of direction in their relationships with one another and their own people, increasing their confidence in their potential to sound a new note in American art.

Although some of the concepts presented by Barnes and Locke lay beyond their technical skills, for most African-American artists *The New Negro* was a landmark. That black people had a history as artists and that their ancestors' art influenced

modern art were facts of enormous psychological importance in erasing negative images of themselves and in shaping their own positive identity. Years later Hale Woodruff recalled his excitement as an isolated young art student when, in 1924, a sympathetic Indianapolis book dealer gave him a German book on African art. Until then Woodruff had not known, beyond his own inner feelings, that any black person could create anything of artistic value.

One idea that flowered during the Black Renaissance was that racial prejudice could be greatly reduced and alleviated by art, that the artist could refute the myth of racial inferiority. This idea, derived from the widespread acceptance of spirituals, was particularly advocated by James Weldon Johnson. He asserted that "through his artistic efforts the Negro is smashing [an] immemorial stereotype faster than he has ever done . . . impressing upon the national mind the conviction that he is a creator as well as a creature . . . helping to form American civilization."[17]

On an individual level, talent did seem to mitigate the painful sore of prejudice. The idea of the artist as a level for achieving interracial socializing became very popular in some New York circles in the mid-1920s. Interracial socializing soon became the most publicized aspect of the Renaissance. At A'Leila Walker's salon, "The Dark Tower," white intellectuals, publishers, producers, and rich socialites could meet talented black writers.

However, few young African-American visual artists took on this role. Except for Aaron Douglas and Bruce Nugent, who was both a writer and an artist, they were infrequent visitors at "The Dark Tower." Some, like W. H. Johnson and Augusta Savage, never came, for they were too busy working to survive and trying to learn how to solve technical problems. Their working hours already limited their visits to museums, galleries, and libraries.

While James Weldon Johnson's concept had some validity, it applied to relatively few individuals. Most young black artists and writers were concerned with the fundamental problem of being black in white America and the need for broader economic and social changes than Johnson's concept promised. Meeting in Douglas's apartment one night in 1926, a group of seven, including Nugent, Langston Hughes, Wallace Thurman, Zora Neale Hurston, Gwendolyn

Bennett, and John P. Davis, decided to publish a quarterly magazine "devoted to the Younger Negro Artists" and entitled *Fire!!*

Hughes outlined their goal: "We young Negro artists who create now intend to express our individual dark-skinned selves without fear or shame. If white people are pleased, we are glad. If they are not, it doesn't matter. If colored people are pleased, we are glad. If they are not, their displeasure doesn't matter either."[18]

Few people, however, saw the one issue of *Fire!!* that was published. In it, contradicting Johnson's concept, the young artists and writers expressed their belief that the barrier of racial prejudice had to be overcome by economic, social, and political pressure—it could not be overcome by art alone. As Hughes's statement makes clear, the creators of *Fire!!* were struggling with their dependency on both black and white audiences. This complex, biracial dependency was at the core of the struggle to establish an African-American identity.

While Johnson's goal was the admission of African-Americans to American life, Du Bois offered a more complex view. He suggested that the unique understanding and insight gained by black experience could change the qualities of American life. Addressing the NAACP convention, Du Bois asserted that it was not only civil rights that "we are after. . . . We want to be Americans, full-fledged Americans, with all the rights of other American citizens. But is that all? Do we simply want to be Americans? Once in a while through all of us flashes some clairvoyance, some clear idea of what America really is. We who are dark can see America in a way that white Americans cannot. And seeing our country thus, are we satisfied with its present goals and ideals?"[19]

For young black artists, Johnson's and Du Bois's ideas raised disturbing questions about their feelings and identity as African-Americans, their African heritage, and their role in American life. In addition to coming up with the rent and acquiring technical know-how, they had to confront the controversial question of how their people should be portrayed.

Debate about how African-Americans should be depicted arose in many quarters and took many forms after publication of *The New Negro*. Centuries of abuse had made many African-Americans extremely self-conscious and suspicious about portrayals of their lives. A novel, play, or painting that depicted black people gambling, dancing, drinking, loitering, sloppily dressed—anything that seemed to support the stereotypes applied to black people—was certain to be attacked regardless of aesthetic truth. In their search for an acceptable identity as Americans, some black people wanted to see their lives glorified. A similar phenomenon can be found in some Irish people's reaction to their portrayal by Sean O'Casey and James Joyce, who illuminated their weaknesses as fallible human beings as well as their strengths.

Du Bois particularly concerned himself with this question, writing in 1920:

> It is not that we are ashamed of our color and blood. We are instinctively and almost unconsciously ashamed of the caricatures done of our darker shades. Black in caricature is our half-conscious thought and we shun in print and paint that which we love in life. . . . We remain afraid of black pictures because they are cruel reminders of the crimes of the Sunday "comics" and "Nigger" minstrels. Off with these thought chains and inchoate soul-shrinkings, and let us train ourselves to see beauty in "black."[20]

Du Bois was not alone in raising the question of how African-Americans should be portrayed. During the twenties, many intellectuals, writers, and artists of both races debated this issue and whether African-American artists were under any obligation to portray black people in a positive way—a question that came sharply into focus with Archibald J. Motley, Jr.'s portrayal of night life in what he called "Bronzeville."

Du Bois formalized this debate by publishing a long series of responses to this question in *The Crisis*, beginning in March 1926.[21] The poet Countee Cullen believed that black artists did have such an obligation, but that each artist had to "find his treasure where his heart lies."[22] Vachel Lindsay, who had attempted to capture the speech rhythms of black people in his poetry, felt what mattered most was the artist's "own experience and his inmost perceptions of truth and beauty, in its severest interpretation, should be his only criteria."[23]

H. L. Mencken, the twenties' most influential critic, who had published many articles and stories favorable to black people in *Smart Set* and the *American Mercury*, felt this was not the time to worry about how black people were presented. He urged a satiric attack on the racial foolishness and inconsistencies of the majority. He asserted that "the remedy of the Negro is not to bellow for justice—that is, not to try and apply scientific criteria to works of art. His remedy is to make works of art that pay the white man off in his own coin. The white man, it seems to me, is extremely ridiculous. He looks ridiculous to me, a white man myself. To the Negro, he must be a hilarious spectacle indeed. Why isn't the spectacle better described? Let the Negro sculptors spit on their hands. What a chance!"[24]

Related to the question of how African-Americans should be portrayed was the question of a distinct racial style urged by Locke. In *The New Negro* he had argued that the contemporary black artist lacked a mature tradition to follow and appealed for a consideration of African art as the real heritage of African-American artists. He wrote:

> There is a real and vital connection between this new artistic respect for African idiom [in "modern art"] and the natural ambition of Negro artists for a racial idiom in their art expression. . . . Only the most reactionary conventions of art, then, stand between the Negro artist and the frank experimental development of those fresh idioms. This movement would, we think, be well under way . . . but for the conventionalism which racial disparagement has forced upon the Negro mind in America. . . . The Negro physiognomy must be freshly and objectively conceived on its own patterns if it is ever to be seriously and importantly interpreted. . . . We ought and must have a school of Negro art, a local and racially representative tradition.[25]

Although he never precisely defined a "school of Negro art," Locke wrote many essays reiterating his plea, and he exhibited art from the Congo to stimulate awareness of the "legacy of the ancestral arts." He was supported by others, such as Arthur A. Schomburg, curator of the 135th Street branch of the New York Public Library and founder of the great collection of African-American history that bears his name. Schomburg argued: "History must restore what slavery took away."[26]

A different perspective on the nature of African-American art was expressed in *The Nation* by the conservative black journalist George S. Schuyler:

> The Aframerican is merely a lampblacked Anglo-Saxon. If the European immigrant after two or three generations of exposure to our schools, politics, advertising, moral crusades, and restaurants becomes indistinguishable from the mass of Americans of older stock (despite the influence of the foreign language press), how much truer must it be of the sons of Ham who have been subjected to what the uplifters call Americanism for the last 300 years. . . . As for the literature, painting, and sculpture of Aframericans, such as there is, it is identical in kind with the literature, painting, and sculpture of white Americans; that is, it shows more or less evidence of European influence.[27]

Schuyler, who modeled his literary style on that of H. L. Mencken, was attacking Locke's concept of a "racial school of art" and the idea that African-American artists could produce an art that differed from that of other American artists. There was some truth in what he said. What was considered art in America had been determined by the white majority. Young black artists, struggling to learn their craft, unable to obtain formal training, scrambling to exist, were simply trying to gain some acceptance as artists by doing traditional work. In a day when white-sheeted Klansmen were marching in many parts of the country, they were challenging the prevailing stereotype which denied that African-Americans could be artists. Most of them exhibited in churches and at state fairs, where their work was often displayed with the needlework of the "handicapped." This in some ways was a recognition of the deprivations suffered by African-Americans, and in other ways an insulting continuation of the racial stereotype.

Schuyler did not deal with the fact that the more talented the artists were, the more they were subjected to pressure to paint in ways that the majority perceived as "primitive." That perception required—indeed, demanded—a degree of awkwardness or crudity, violent color, and sensuality. Catering to that idea became the easiest way for an African-American artist or writer to gain attention from dealers, influential collectors, and publishers—the gatekeepers of recognition and acceptance.

Pressure on African-American artists to work in a "primitive" style was intensified by social and cultural factors, specifically by the presentation of warped, sensationalized black characters in novels and plays such as Julia Peterkin's novel *Scarlet Sister Mary,* Dorothy and DuBose Heyward's *Porgy,* and Eugene O'Neill's *Emperor Jones.* Their emotionally distorted black characters derived from—and fostered—the stereotype that African-Americans were unschooled, ignorant, superstitiously religious, immoral, incapable of forethought or intelligence, and controlled by sensuality and fear. These characters were, in varying degrees, racist caricatures, not based on objective observation or insight into the African-American character.

Because these novels and plays were successful, African-American writers and artists were expected to follow such models—and to be even more "primitive."

Fortunately, there were other models. The translations in the mid-1920s of René Maran's *Batouala,* an absorbing story of African village life, deeply impressed many black artists and intellectuals. Maran was a Frenchman of African descent. Winning the Goncourt prize in 1921, his book was, in some respects, a forerunner of Zora Neale Hurston's authentic and penetrating presentation of African-American folkways.

In addition, the naturalism that characterized the writings of Theodore Dreiser, Frank Norris, and Upton Sinclair, as well as the art of John Sloan, George Luks, and others, was a rapidly growing force. A tenet of naturalism was that artists should represent people and events with objectivity, without preconceptions, and this viewpoint increasingly began to inform African-American critical writing.

Rebelling against prevailing preconceptions, Langston Hughes refused the demand of a patron who had rejected his poem satirizing the idle rich, saying, "It's not you," and had asked him to write something different. As Hughes explained: "She wanted me to be primitive and know and feel the intuitions of the primitive. But, unfortunately, I did not feel the primitive surging within me, and so I could not live and write as though I did. I was only an American Negro—who had loved the surface of Africa and the rhythms of Africa—but I was not Africa. I was Chicago and Kansas City and Broadway and Harlem."[28]

Similarly, Aaron Douglas and other artists who had patrons were sometimes told their work was "not you." Some patrons looked upon the education and professional training of black artists as destructive to their "natural" abilities.

The demand for the African-American artist to be "primitive" has persisted to this day, and it has been the source of much misunderstanding and confusion. In the 1920s, the word *primitive* tended to isolate black artists from other American artists, and yet it became, in the 1920s, what was expected of them.

Because the term *primitive* continues to be used inappropriately, clarification of its meaning in relation to African-American artists is essential. The word, which is derived from the Latin *primus,* meaning "first," came to be used in reference to archaeology and anthropology. In brief, these disciplines applied the term to early, original, and basic forms of societal and cultural organizations as well as to housing and craft products. Then ethnologists, describing the cultural artifacts of past societies, applied the term to objects fashioned with crude tools and, ultimately, to peasant handicraft work. Initially such objects, including religious and symbolic statues and pictorial representations, were preserved for their ethnological interest. However, after the discovery of the ancient African, Aztec, and Inca cultures, which were demonstrably advanced and had developed sophisticated ceramic, mineral, and metallurgical technology, it was gradually recognized that these objects were not "primitive" but based on disciplined artistic and cultural concepts and traditions, and required aesthetic consideration.

By the 1920s, the word *primitive* in relation to the arts meant to be unschooled and indifferent to moral and legal codes, without thought or intellectual substance. Freudian concepts of the repression of an individual's natural sexual instincts by "civilization" were popular in American intellectual circles at the time, and an oversimplification of these concepts contributed to the demand for "primitive" expression by African-American artists, with particular emphasis on violent color and sensuous expression. To many white intellectuals and artists, the black American was the opposite of dehumanizing industrialization—a natural man, unfettered by the customs, morals, and character of the organization of modern society. In works like *Emperor Jones,* when a black man goes against his "primitive" nature, he meets with disaster.

Generally, to whites, the term came to mean a style that was crude and unschooled in the "stilted affectations of the more cultured styles and conceptions," as V. F. Calverton phrased it in the thirties.[29] This misuse of the term arose from a distorted perception of black people, dating back to the days of slavery.

Today, similar misuses continue and the term *primitive* has lost any clear meaning.[30] What does it mean, for example, to refer to African sculpture, a highly sophisticated art form, as "primitive art," and then use the same term for the work of Grandma Moses and other folk artists? In this and other contexts the term carries a note of disparagement—implying that this is not "real" art.

African-American artists were continually confronted with the question: Who would buy their work? Directing their work to either a black or a white audience carried severe limitations. In seeking appreciation from a white audience, they faced possible suppression of their inner feelings and convictions. On the other hand, the black audience had its own particular taboos about subject matter. It also offered considerably fewer opportunities for support.

Artists' responses to this situation varied. Some, notably Sargent Johnson, Aaron Douglas, Richmond Barthé, and James Lesesne Wells, experimented with African styles. James A. Porter and others felt that the "self-conscious pursuit of the primitive" would further separate Negro art and artists from American art and artists. They "insisted that the Negro [artist] should encompass all experience, not attempting to suppress non-Negro influence, for such suppression meant intellectual and aesthetic negativism."[31]

Hughes rejected any denial of racial experience, recalling a young man who said to him, "'I want to be a poet—not a Negro poet.' . . . And I was sorry the young man said that, for no great poet has been afraid of being himself. And I doubted that, with his desire to run away spiritually from his race, this would ever be a great poet. But this is the mountain standing in the way of any true Negro art in America—this urge within the race toward whiteness, the desire to pour racial identity into the mold of American standardization, and to be as little Negro and as much American as possible."[32]

None of the spokesmen for these varying views ever abandoned his point. Locke continued to be a persistent, important influence, and his endorsement often meant a foundation grant. He jabbed, goaded, and held up the popularity of jazz as an inspiration. Jazz musicians were basking "in the sunlight and warmth of a proud and positive race-consciousness" while "our artists were still for the most part in an eclipse of chilly doubt and disparagement."[33] However, Locke's plea for a return to "the legacy of the ancestral arts" was challenged in 1927 by the African-American sociologist E. Franklin Frazier. He pointed out that developing group experiences and traditions and utilizing such experiences in artistic creativity "is entirely different from seeking in the biological inheritance of the race for new values, attitudes and a different order of mentality." Biological inheritance could not provide a "unique culture."[34]

African-American artists' difficult struggle to achieve identity was evident in exhibitions by the Harmon Foundation between 1928 and 1935.[35] Although it presented achievement awards to African-Americans in nine areas of endeavor, including religion and business, the Harmon Foundation is remembered today only for its rec-

ognition of African-American artists. An expression of the idea that art could help break down racial prejudice, the foundation's touring shows frankly accepted segregation in the South in trying to win recognition for black talent. The exhibitions helped African-American artists become aware of one another, and to gain some public attention. By 1935 some 400 black artists from all over the nation were "in regular touch with the foundation."[36]

The Harmon exhibitions accepted all kinds of work—traditional, naive, academic, abstract, and experimental. Porter, who exhibited, later remarked that the jury's selections for prizes showed "too liberal taste in subject matter and too little concern for execution."[37] Although disclaiming any point of view, the foundation's catalogs urged black artists "to create a genuine interpretation of racial background" and published Locke's exhortations on the "ancestral arts." Each successive show exhibited not only more work than earlier exhibitions, but also more black subject matter—a significant, if oversimplified, indication of growing self-acceptance.

The Harmon exhibitions were the largest and most publicized effort at the time to encourage African-American artists and show what they were doing. What was confusing, both aesthetically and in terms of black identity, was the assembling of very different types of work at all levels of achievement—bringing together a Cubist, a Romantic, an illustrator, and a naive—and calling them all representative of "Negro art" simply because the artists were black.

This situation drew criticism from African-American artists with the first public exhibition in 1928 (earlier competitions were not public). The artist-poet Gwendolyn Bennett, later a leader of the Harlem Artists Guild, complained that the works shown "lack the essence of artistic permanency. . . . There can be no cultural contribution unless something distinctive is given, something heightened and developed within the whole form that did not exist before the artist's hand took part in its molding. But where in this exhibition is there any such deftness of hand?"[38]

A few years later, in 1934, Mary Beattie Brady, the director of the Harmon Foundation and selector of its juries, was stung when Romare Bearden, a young Harlem artist, severely criticized its exhibitions as misguided, however well intentioned, because they lacked artistic standards and no unified aesthetic or social philosophy existed among African-American artists. Under the title "The

Negro Artist and Modern Art," he argued for abandoning the "outmoded academic practices of the past," which most black artists were following in seeking acceptance as artists, and for the creation of an art that genuinely reflected the black artist's life and character. He condemned the Harmon Foundation:

> Its attitude from the beginning has been of a coddling and patronizing nature. It has encouraged the artist to exhibit long before he has mastered the technical equipment of his medium. By its choice of the type of work it favors, it has allowed the Negro artist to accept standards that are both artificial and corrupt.
>
> It is time for the Negro artist to stop making excuses for his work. If he must exhibit, let it be in exhibitions of the caliber of "The Carnegie Exposition." Here among the best artists of the world his work will stand or fall according to its merits. A concrete example of the accepted attitude towards the Negro artist recently occurred in California where an exhibition coupled the work of Negro artists with that of the blind. It is obvious that in this case there is definitely a dual standard of appraisal.[39]

Yet whatever its faults aesthetically and from an African-American viewpoint, the Harmon Foundation brought encouraging public attention to the development of African-American artists in a critical period.[40] Without its activities, exhibitions, and publicity, many artists would not have survived as artists, and its awards often identified important leaders among them. It particularly stimulated the formation of art departments in African-American colleges through its traveling shows, which generally had a higher artistic level than the exhibitions themselves.

The Harmon shows demonstrated that there were many African-American artists and that black subject matter—the lives, activities, and portraits of African-Americans—was a legitimate, valuable, and unique part of American life, worthy of artistic expression and the unique province of black artists. How some of the significant black artists of the twenties developed—their problems, what they created, what influenced them, how individual they each were, and how they survived—provides insight into many aspects of American cultural life in that period.

## Notes

1. G. T. Robinson, *The Freeman Book* (New York: B. W. Huebsch, 1924), p. 97.

2. Nathan Irvin Huggins, *Harlem Renaissance* (New York: Oxford University Press, 1971), p. 5.

3. For migration's impact on Chicago, see St. Clair Drake and Horace R. Cayton, *Black Metropolis* (New York: Harper & Row, 1962), p. 52. For its impact on New York, see Gilbert Osofsky, *Harlem: The Making of a Ghetto* (New York: Harper & Row, 1968), p. 128.

4. Thorpe, who was listed in the catalog of the 1921 exhibition at the 135th Street branch of the New York Public Library, told this to the authors in 1967, when they were searching Juley's files for photographs of Tanner's work.

5. For background on Farrow, see *The Negro in Chicago, 1779-1927*, vol. 1 (Chicago: Washington Intercollegiate Club, 1927), p. 96. Also, Theresa Dickson Cederholm, ed., *Afro-American Artists* (Boston: Trustees of the Boston Public Library, 1973).

6. There were much earlier shows. In October 1905 the Colored Men's Branch of the Brooklyn YMCA on Carleton Avenue exhibited forty-five paintings by William E. Braxton, Samuel O. Collins, W. O. Thompson, and Clinton DeVillis. Another exhibition was held there in 1913 and the NAACP held an exhibition in its New York offices that year in conjunction with its annual meeting. In 1917 the Arts and Letters Society of Chicago exhibited paintings and drawings by Charles Dawson, William M. Farrow, William Harper, and Archibald J. Motley, Jr. In August 1918 the Negro Library Association exhibited work by Braxton, Collins, DeVillis, Thompson, Robert H. Lewis, Robert H. Hampton, Albert A. Smith, Ella Spencer, Laura Wheeler Waring, Richard Lonsdale Brown, and William Edouard Scott. This exhibition also included books, manuscripts, and twenty-one African sculptures from the Modern Art Gallery of Marius de Zaya. In 1919 the Tanner Art Students Society at Dunbar High School in Washington, D.C., exhibited some thirty paintings and six sculptures by Scott, Waring, Julien Abele, Meta Vaux Warrick Fuller, May Howard Jackson, and John E. Washington. See Beryl J. Wright, "The Harmon Foundation in Context," in *Against the Odds: African-American Artists and the Harmon Foundation* (Newark, N.J.: Newark Museum, exhibition catalog, 1989), pp. 13-25.

7. "The Negro in Art Week" was suggested by Alain L. Locke to Zonia Baber of the University of Chicago and Chicago Women's Club. It was scheduled from November 16 to 27, 1927. When attendance averaged 800 a day, the institute extended the show to December 4 (*The Negro in Chicago*, vol. 1-2, p. 27).

8. James Weldon Johnson, *Black Manhattan* (New York: Atheneum, 1968), p. 163.

9. Hale A. Woodruff, undated letter to authors, c. 1971.

10. W. E. B. Du Bois, "The Criteria of Negro Art," *The Crisis* 32 (Oct. 1926), p. 290. This was his speech at the NAACP convention. It followed a questionnaire (*The Crisis* [Feb. 1926], p. 165) on "how to treat the Negro in art," which was sent to leading publishers, writers, and artists of both races who responded in subsequent issues. Among them were Sherwood Anderson, Benjamin Brawley, Charles W. Chesnutt, Countee Cullen, J. Herbert Engbeck, Jessie Fauset, DuBose Heyward, Langston Hughes, Georgia Douglas Johnson, Robert T. Kerlin, A. A. Knopf, Sinclair Lewis, Vachel Lindsay, Otto F. Mack, Haldane McFall, H. L. Mencken, Mary W. Ovington, Julia Peterkin, William Lyon Phelps, Joel E. Spingarn, Walter White, and Carl Van Vechten.

11. Alain L. Locke, ed., *The New Negro* (New York: Albert & Charles Boni, 1925; reprint, New York: Atheneum, 1968).

12. Ibid., p. 5.

13. Ibid., pp. 21, 24.

14. Ibid., p. 254.

15. Ibid., p. 256.

16. Ibid., p. 258.

17. Johnson, *Black Manhattan*, pp. 283-84.

18. Langston Hughes, in *Fire!!*, vol. 1, no. 1; quoted in his reminiscing account, "The Twenties: Harlem and Its Negritude," *African Forum* 1 (Spring 1966), pp. 11-20.

19. Du Bois, "Criteria," p. 290.

20. W. E. B. Du Bois, "Opinions of W. E. B. Du Bois: In Black," *The Crisis* 20 (Oct. 1920), pp. 263-64.

21. W. E. B. Du Bois, "The Negro in Art," *The Crisis* 32 (March 1926), p. 219.

22. Countee Cullen, in *The Crisis* 32 (Aug. 1926), p. 193.

23. Vachel Lindsay, in *The Crisis* 32 (May 1926), pp. 35-36.

24. H. L. Mencken, in *The Crisis* 32 (March 1926), p. 220. Although Mencken used racist terms at times, he was sympathetic to African-Americans in the 1920s and corresponded with Du Bois, George S. Schuyler, and James Weldon Johnson. In 1922 he suggested to Johnson "a history of ragtime, establish names and dates accurately. . . . It ought to be done. Then you might do similar essays on negro poets, and negro painters and sculptors, and so have a second book on the negro as an artist." (See Charles Scruggs, *The Sage in Harlem: H. L. Mencken and the Black Writers of the 1920s* [Baltimore: Johns Hopkins University Press, 1984], p. 191, n. 16.)

25. Locke, *The New Negro*, pp. 262-66.

26. In ibid., p. 231.

27. George S. Schuyler, "The Negro Art-Hokum," *The Nation* 122 (June 16, 1926), pp. 663-64.

28. Langston Hughes, *The Big Sea* (New York: A. A. Knopf, 1945; reprint, New York: Hill & Wang, 1968), pp. 312-30.

29. V. F. Calverton, in *America Now: Civilization in the United States*, ed. H. E. Stearns (New York: Scribner's, 1938), p. 496.

30. For example, Peter and Linda Murray, eds., *Penguin Dictionary of Art and Artists* (Harmondsworth, England: Penguin Books, 1978), describe *primitive* as "a word that is now almost meaningless," noting that it originally applied to Netherlandish and Italian artists before 1500, and all Italian painters between Giotto and Raphael, although these artists have "no obvious connection with the naive, unsophisticated, unspoilt vision consistent with amateur, or 'Sunday' painter status." They cite Edward Hicks, Jean-Jacques Rousseau, and Grandma Moses as examples of how the definition has blurred.

31. James A. Porter, *Modern Negro Art* (New York: Dryden Press, 1943), p. 100.

32. Langston Hughes, "The Negro Artist and the Racial Mountain," *The Nation* 122 (June 23, 1926), pp. 662-64.

33. Alain Locke, *Negro Art: Past and Present* (Washington, D.C.: Associates in Negro Education, 1936; reprint, New York: Arno Press and *The New York Times*, 1969), p. 119.

34. E. Franklin Frazier, "Racial Self-Expression," in *Ebony and Topaz*, ed. C. S. Johnson (New York: Opportunity, 1927; reprint, Freeport, N.Y.: Books for Libraries Press, Black Heritage Library Collection, 1971), p. 119.

35. The Harmon exhibitions were not yearly and initially not public, although there were juries and awards in 1926 and 1927. The first public exhibition was in 1928, followed by exhibitions in 1929, 1930, 1931, and 1933. The 1935 exhibition was limited to the work of three artists—Richmond Barthé, Malvin Gray Johnson, and Sargent Johnson.

36. *Negro Artists: An Illustrated Review of Their Achievements* (New York: Harmon Foundation, exhibition catalog, 1935), p. 5.

37. Porter, *Modern Negro Art*, p. 107.

38. Gwendolyn Bennett, in *The Southern Workman* 57 (March 1928), pp. 111-12.

39. Romare H. Bearden, "The Negro and Modern Art," *Opportunity* 12 (Dec. 1934), pp. 371-73.

40. See David Driskell, "Mary Beattie Brady and the Administration of the Harmon Foundation," in *Against the Odds* (Newark Museum), pp. 59-69.

## MARY ANN CALO (ESSAY DATE 1999)

**SOURCE:** Calo, Mary Ann. "African American Art and the Critical Discourse between World Wars." *American Quarterly* 51, no. 3 (1999): 580-621.

*In the following essay, Calo examines the critical reception of African American artists during the interwar decades and maintains that the fact that their art was understood in terms of constructs of racial identity created a foundation for the marginalization of Black artists.*

[F]or African American artists, their struggle for inclusion has often been met with various strategies to justify their continuing marginalization.

Lowery Sims

The lovely thing about art criticism, perhaps its only redeeming virtue and its best shot at historical transcendence, is that it offers lubricated penetration of the unconscious of the cultural mainstream, of the mechanisms that produce, perpetuate, and render invisible the maintenance of privilege.

Catherine Lord

In *The New Negro*, his celebrated anthology published in 1925, cultural critic and philosopher Alain Locke marshalled impressive evidence that America was on the threshold of a black artistic coming of age.[1] With the subsequent emergence of an African American cultural intelligentsia, and the flurry of artistic activity we have come to know as the Harlem Renaissance, it seemed an opportune moment to consider the possibility that a characteristically "Negro" art had developed in America and to speculate on its contribution (past, present, future) to the formation of national culture. During the interwar decades, this emphasis on racial distinctiveness created an audience for visual art made by Americans of African descent. However, as an invention of the 1920s, the category "American Negro artist" soon found itself suspended between the rhetoric of cultural nationalism and the reality of a segregated society as yet ill-equipped to fulfill its democratic promise.

Within the black community during these years, lively exchanges on the nature of black creativity were consistently framed in terms of a dynamic interaction of race and nationality. But critics writing for mainstream publications underscored the separateness of "Negro art" from the over-arching category "American art." As exposure to so-called "Negro art" grew, alongside it there emerged a set of critical constructs, rooted in the discourse of racial difference, that collectively functioned to isolate black artistic production from mainstream cultural practice. This article will argue that the critical reception of African American artists during the interwar decades created a foundation for what Charles Gaines has called the "theater of refusal," a discursive space wherein the marginalization of black artists is enforced through art criticism. As Gaines suggests, African American art understood largely in terms of constructs of racial identity remains fairly resistant to alternate narratives and models of historical analysis, resulting in a critical practice that "punishes the work of black artists by making it immune to history and by immunizing history against it."[2]

## I

The artistic production of the "New Negro," as described by Locke, sought both to affirm a positive racial identity and to claim a place for black artists in American culture. African American writers such as Locke and W. E. B. Du Bois argued that the creation of great art was a mark of racial maturity; they proposed that the black population would gain greater respect because of the demonstrated talent of its artists. In its headier moments, the leaders of this so-called Negro or Harlem Renaissance believed in the capacity of artistic expression to alter deeply ingrained as-

sumptions of black inferiority and eliminate prejudice, a phenomenon scholar David Levering Lewis has referred to subsequently as "civil rights by copyright."[3]

Paralleling the Harlem Renaissance and its aftermath was the forecast of a renaissance on a national level that would eventuate in the creation of an authentic American art. Apologists for the Harlem Renaissance and the American Renaissance alike called for the development of unique artistic idioms that would reflect specific cultural identities. In the context of both movements, the interwar decades were characterized repeatedly as periods plagued by confusion and uncertainty as American artists struggled towards mature expression. Claims were made on both fronts for the eventual emergence of a coherent culture that would embody individual expression as well as collective racial/national identity.[4]

Historians of the Harlem Renaissance have long recognized the interdependence of these respective phenomena. For example, Nathan Huggins, in his seminal history of the Harlem Renaissance, understood the creative dilemma of the African American as a variation on the larger problem of American creativity.[5] At the root of intense cultural self-consciousness, Huggins argued, both in the black American community and the majority population, were lingering self-doubt and defensiveness about the presumed inadequacy of the peoples in question. Just as America hoped to overcome its sense of cultural inferiority in relation to Europe, black America hoped to do the same in relation to white America. These sentiments echoed through the writings of Alain Locke, who consistently positioned the creative efforts of black Americans within this program of national self-discovery and self-definition.

More recently, George Hutchinson argues that the goals of the Harlem Renaissance, as they were articulated by Locke and others, must be understood in the context of heated battles over the relationship between race, nation and culture which dominated the intellectual landscape of the early twentieth century.[6] His thesis, that African American writers and artists recognized and indeed negotiated their strategic relationship to the discourses of cultural nationalism, augments Huggins's observations. While Huggins located the Harlem Renaissance within the climate of pervasive anxiety about America's cultural provincialism, Hutchinson stresses its seminal role in the systematic program to define the spirit of the nation and control its public meanings, a program that was, in part, directed towards alleviating this anxiety.[7]

Despite these obvious affinities, African American art of the interwar decades has remained largely invisible in mainstream histories of the period. In her catalog essay for the 1987 exhibition, *The Harlem Renaissance: Art of Black America,* Mary Schmidt Campbell noted that the historical legacy of the Harlem Renaissance has been contained within the limiting conditions of cultural separatism, a byproduct of legal segregation that has been sustained by ignorance, neglect and critical distortion.[8] Although these artists emerged during a time of intense interest in the creation of an authentic American culture, and were in fact deeply embedded in the struggle for power to articulate its essence, their artistic production remained outside of mainstream discourse. Campbell's observation is echoed by Hutchinson who affirms that studies of American cultural nationalism have ignored black expression, resulting in "the exclusion of blackness from definitions of Americanness."[9]

As figurative artists whose modernity often presented itself in sociopolitical rather than formal terms, African Americans have certainly been casualties of the widespread critical neglect experienced by many artists of the interwar decades. But neither the limitations of modernist thinking nor its hegemony adequately explain the scant representation of black expression in mainstream histories, which persists even in the face of revisionist scholarship.[10] The theoretical coherence of modernism is largely a construction of the post-World War II era; in the early twentieth century any form of expression not obviously conventional or academic was likely to be described as modern. But critics with only vague ideas about modernity felt more secure in their conceptions of national identity; and in the historiography of American art, issues of nationalism are as pressing as issues of modernity.[11] If African American art has disappeared from the cultural history of the early twentieth century, it is due to a refusal of its essential modernity and its claim to occupy a vital place in the process of national self-definition, a priority shared by the majority of American artists working during these years.[12]

## II

Prior to the 1920s, there had been little need for white critics to examine their assumptions about black culture. This was altered dramatically by the ascendance, in the American imagination, of exotic notions of blackness that emerged in the early twentieth century, casting the sensuous, intuitive, natural black as the opposite of the calculating, pragmatic and deeply repressed Caucasian. Much has been written on the extent to which this construction of black identity served the needs of white intellectuals seeking an escape from boredom or an antidote to the soulless materialistic culture of their age. For a brief period, this critical literature suggests, white Americans thought they had discovered in Harlem what they lacked in themselves.

To a certain extent, this perception of black difference was encouraged by African American critics such as Alain Locke. Locke's writings made frequent reference to racially specific dimensions of experience and culture which, in America, he maintained, existed as fortunate compliments to one another. For example, in a lecture on "The Negro and Art," drafted for a symposium at Mt. Holyoke College in 1931, he stated:

> In white America, the Negro finds the pattern of practical endeavor and discipline, and the mastery of physical and scientific civilization, both for his own good and for the sake of his handicapped brother in Africa, to whom he is a possible missioner of civilization. In black America, the white man has either a base or a noble antidote to Puritanism and its emotional sterility, depending on whether he contacts with the Negro spirit on the low level of primitive animalism or on the high level of fine artistic expression.[13]

Furthermore, Locke urged black artists to express themselves in characteristically racial terms by drawing on the uniqueness of their experience and on their position as heirs to both an authentic American folk culture and the artistic traditions of ancestral Africa.

Paradigms for the development of a black aesthetic during the interwar decades were not unlike paradigms for the development of an American aesthetic. Locke's ideas about racial expression were, for the most part, consistent with theories of modern American expression advanced by cultural nationalists, a connection he clearly understood and even encouraged.[14] In the foreword to *The New Negro,* he wrote:

> America seeking a new spiritual expansion and artistic maturity, trying to found an American literature, a national art, and national music implies a Negro-American culture seeking the same satisfactions and objectives. Separate as it may be in color and substance, the culture of the Negro is of a pattern integral with the times and with its cultural setting.[15]

Artistic expression was understood by cultural critics of this generation as a function of individual temperament negotiating the context of a specific (national/racial) environment. Significant artistic content could not be prescribed but rather emerged from both personal and communal experience, with the presumption that the artist's unique psyche would necessarily be mediated by broader societal concerns.[16]

Also, like other critic-advocates of his generation, Locke was a kind of cultural entrepreneur and as such was able to capture the attention of the African American intelligentsia as well as institutions and individuals interested in fostering black artistic creativity. He was close to white art patrons such as Charlotte Mason and Albert Barnes, and had strong ties to the Harmon Foundation, a philanthropic organization that devoted itself to rewarding artistic achievement among African Americans and to the promotion of black artists.[17] More than any other single individual—with the possible exception of James Porter, whose influence will be felt somewhat later—Locke was responsible for shaping the historical understanding and critical appraisal of African American art in the imagination of the interested public.

Locke's critical position combined American theories of art as expression with turn of the century aestheticism and belief in the civilizing power of culture. (It is worth noting here that Locke's dissertation advisor at Harvard, Ralph Barton Perry, was Bernard Berenson's brother-in-law.)[18] The most progressive artistic theorists in early twentieth-century America were Alfred Stieglitz and Robert Henri, both of whose ideas are evident in Locke's thinking. To an extent, Locke's perception of black art as uniquely endowed within American culture, because of its resonant spirituality and the broad scope of human experience it embodies, can be understood as the productive fusion of their respective critical positions.[19]

Henri, with his more obvious concern that human experience and the social realities of American life act as catalyst and raw material of national cultural expression, is traditionally positioned in opposition to Stieglitz. An archetypical modernist, Stieglitz was committed to the importance of formal innovation and aesthetic transcendence, and understood the artist as a vital spiritual force in an increasingly materialistic world. The accentuation of these differences has encouraged a convenient, if somewhat distorted, historical narrative wherein Henri plays champion of American realism to Stieglitz's advocacy of international modernism. But, for all this presumption of disagreement, Henri and Stieglitz held many similar ideas about the origins of artistic expression. Both preached the importance of modernity, urging artists to resist the pull of the moribund genteel tradition. Each placed great emphasis on individual artistic freedom and the authenticity of artistic emotion; and both were responsive to a cultural climate in which modernism was not incompatible with nationalism.[20]

To this foundation of American aesthetic and cultural theory, Locke contributed his own emphasis on African ancestral roots as an important stimulus in the formation of black cultural identity.[21] Locke's promotion of African art, both as a valuable form of expression in its own right and as an inspiration for modern black artists, was intended to instill pride in the racial past and encourage black artists to learn from the technical mastery and expressive power of African sculpture.[22] But the naming of ancestral Africa as a vital dimension of black American cultural identity can also be understood in terms of Van Wyck Brooks's concept of the "usable past." The search for a cultural legacy to displace Puritan and frontier values as the formative elements of American experience was a central theme of cultural nationalist thinking in the 1920s.

### III

Before examining the nature of critical discourse brought to bear on African American artists during the interwar decades, a distinction must be made between art criticism and what is more properly regarded as art journalism. By differentiating one from the other, I do not intend to suggest anything about their respective merits, but merely to establish the important fact that they constituted very different vehicles for conveying information about African American art and artists. The vast majority of critical opinion on black art falls into the category of art journalism. Complex issues surrounding race, culture, identity and nationalism in these years were addressed by critics, historians, and artists such as Locke, James Porter, Meyer Schapiro, Stuart Davis, and Thomas Craven, individuals variously grounded in social theory, anthropology, aesthetic philosophy and art history. But journalists writing for the popular press rarely progressed beyond such basic questions s "what is Negro art and why should anyone be interested in seeing it?"

To an extent, this situation reflects the general state of American art criticism during the early twentieth century. With some notable exceptions, a good deal of art writing in American before World War II was a mixed bag of journalism and editorial commentary. Art criticism was not highly professionalized in the United States and American critics with a consistent, recognizable methodology were rare. Essays on art and culture, featured regularly in literary magazines and the popular press, were often written by individuals with very little background in the visual arts. Furthermore, when appraising African American visual art, these critics often leaned on typologies structured around the musical and literary expression with which they were more familiar. Thus they tended to raise general issues rather than engage in complex critical analysis of specific objects or artists.[23]

Another impediment to the development of coherent critical dialog about African American art was the involvement of the Harmon Foundation in its promotion. Widely recognized for its tireless and sorely-needed efforts on behalf of black artists, the Harmon Foundation was significant not only because of the scope and duration of its activities, but also insofar as it acted as a powerful determinant of viewer response to their work. The Harmon Foundation group shows premiered in New York and travelled throughout the country, where they were often seen in non-art contexts. Exhibitions were typically sponsored by regional inter-racial councils and race relations committees and displayed in black churches, in libraries and public schools, or in local branches of the YWCA. These circumstances tended to encourage a sociological, rather than aesthetic, way of thinking about the work of black artists.

Also, the aggressive public relations strategies employed by the Harmon Foundation often overwhelmed the art itself, closing down interpretation and constricting the critical frame. Newspaper coverage of the Harmon awards for Negro achievement in the visual arts, and of their annual exhibitions of Negro art, was shaped largely by press releases from the Foundation, preempting the need for further inquiry and analysis. A good deal of writing about African American art during the interwar period was simply Harmon Foundation publicity posing as art criticism.

## IV

In spite of, and to an extent in response to, these conditions, a set of issues did emerge from the context of the Harlem Renaissance that provided mainstream critics with a fairly consistent focus when considering the works of African American artists.[24] The notions that emerged in the late 1920s were remarkably resilient: Negro art was consistently evaluated during the interwar decades in terms of *a priori* assumptions about amateurism, primitivism, authenticity and racial uniqueness. Often these qualities were fused into simplistic ideals that then functioned to delimit the expressive field of black artists by creating a concrete set of expectations: authentic Negro art will be primitive because it is the product of amateurs or individuals predisposed to the primitive by virtue of their unique racial heritage; such authenticity and uniqueness should be manifest in both the form and content of Negro art. Ultimately, these expectations will prompt critics to express displeasure when the work of African American artists presented itself as similar to, or derivative of, mainstream artistic practices. Even when such practices reflected mutual admiration for many of the same general principles, racial difference was expected to override shared national cultural ideals.

The presumption of amateurism hung like a cloud over the 1920s and 1930s, causing enormous frustration among black artists who strove to demonstrate their technical mastery (and eventually hoped to qualify for the federal assistance that became available to "professional" artists during the Depression). In a well-known 1934 essay, "The Negro Artist and Modern Art," Romare Bearden blamed the Harmon Foundation for fostering a patronizing attitude towards black artists by encouraging them to exhibit prematurely.[25] This accusation may seem unduly harsh given that the Foundation was also instrumental in establishing the professional credentials of black artists seeking employment on the projects. Nevertheless, the condescension Bearden described was a conspicuous dimension of press coverage of the Harmon Foundation Awards for Distinguished Achievement in the Visual Arts, as well as that directed towards the traveling exhibitions.

The recipient of the first gold medal in 1926, Palmer Hayden, achieved instant notoriety as the "Janitor Who Paints," an image supplied to journalists by Harmon Foundation press releases. Although Hayden had already exhibited his work in group shows sponsored by the Harlem branch of the New York Public Library, he was characterized as a remarkable discovery. Articles on Hayden served as opportunities to indulge in sentimental and often florid prose, creating an aura around him that made the nature or quality of his work seem beside the point. The following account, which appeared in one of the New York papers, typifies this kind of coverage:

You wouldn't notice anything particular about 29 Greenwich Ave. . . . But behind those dull brick walls and up three flights of creaking stairs, hollowed out by the footsteps of hundreds of tired feet, lives Palmer C. Hayden. And in a tiny six by six cubicle, lit by a minute dust-covered skylight, there is a dramatic struggle going on. As the one-burner kerosene stove sputters in the corner, the soul of a negro burns higher as he dips his brushes into the lurid paint and transfers it to the clean canvas.[26]

The subsequent departures of Hayden and bronze-medal winner Hale Woodruff for Paris in 1927 were treated as Cinderella stories, even though Woodruff had attended art school and was by no means an amateur. More importantly, their aspirations to study in Europe were touted as evidence that the Foundation's program to foster black creative achievement was working, as their trips were made possible, at least in part, by the cash and recognition afforded by the awards.[27] Benjamin Brawley's refusal of the Harmon medal for education in the same year served to dramatize further the humble status of these artists. Brawley, a well-known educator and writer, declined the second place award because he said he had never done anything but first class work, thus casting in high relief the seeming immaturity of these artists in relation to accomplishments by African Americans in other fields.[28]

The fascination with Hayden's story had as much to do with the myth of the romantic artist as it did with beliefs about disadvantaged blacks. But it was a compelling image and in the ensuing years newspapers covering the Harmon awards were rife with hard luck stories about aspiring black artists who supported themselves through manual labor, and who showed remarkable creative ability in spite of their lack of experience. Press releases on current award winners always included biographical information or what the Foundation called "human interest" material. Sometimes this was repeated verbatim, but often the information was used selectively, with the emphasis typically falling on the humble circumstances of the artist rather than training or experience.[29]

In 1928, the Harmon Foundation sponsored the first of what would be a series of exhibitions devoted to Negro art. These shows, which originated in New York in conjunction with the Harmon wards, and then travelled throughout the United States, became the primary venue for the exhibition and sale of art made by African Americans in the 1920s and 1930s. Although Harmon Foundation press releases continued to shape public discourse about Negro art during these years, especially in more provincial locations, a greater effort was made by the New York critics in response to these shows to evaluate the work in terms of larger debates about the nature of black creativity which were of central concern to the Harlem Renaissance.

The 1928 show stimulated a fair amount of speculation about the future direction of African American art. Informing these discussions are the same issues that occupied critics in literary circles, where they were clearly articulated and hotly contested. Questions were raised about the relationship between contemporary black expression and black folk culture, about the meaning of Africa to modern American blacks, and about the transmission of racial characteristics across time and place. With very few exceptions, critics writing for mainstream publications expected to see racial qualities in black art and were disappointed when they didn't. Rehearsing the arguments advanced by literary critics involved with Harlem Renaissance writers, they noted with surprise the technical proficiency of many African American artists, but complained when the work was derivative or lacked what they regarded as pronounced racialism.[30]

Concerns about the proper representation of African Americans ran high in these early exchanges, especially in literary circles, as African American writers came to terms with the sudden fascination with black life in the 1920s. The respective merits of depicting professional blacks with identifiably bourgeois values, versus the decadence of Harlem or what Du Bois had called the "black peasantry," figured prominently in these debates. Interest in this question was stimulated by the wave of literature written in the 1920s taking as its subject certain controversial aspects of African American life. In February of 1926, *Crisis* published a series of questions regarding the portrayal of blacks in art and solicited the opinions of its readers as to the responsibilities of artists for whom the representation of African Americans is a primary theme.[31] The questionnaire was aimed primarily at authors, but Locke's writing raised the issues of stereotype and caricature in the visual arts as well. This interest in representation was coupled with an ongoing discussion about the nature of black creativity.

In the literary arena, these concerns came to a head in the dramatic confrontation of 1926 between poet Langston Hughes and writer George Schuyler on the pages of *The Nation*. Schuyler argued against the interpretation of black art as expressive of a Negro soul or essence. He referred to the African American as a "lamp blacked Anglo Saxon," who is more American than Negro. Hughes response, entitled "The Negro Artist and the Racial Mountain," became one of the central documents of the period; he located such thinking about racial expression in the regrettable desire on the part of black writers to be white and to write like whites.[32] An occasional reviewer of the early Harmon shows shared Schuyler's skepticism, and was thus unsympathetic to the expectation that black art be performative of racial essence:

This demand on the Negro artist and writer is yet another kind of exploitation; certainly it is absurd to expect Negroes brought up in an American world, in all sections of the world, young—the prize winners, for instance, are all in their thirties—taught in white schools and academies, to make a unique contribution as a matter of course. The night life of Harlem as seen by Winold Reiss and Covarrubias enters their lives no more than does Broadway the lives of white artists; slavery is as remote as the European experiences of the grandparents of most of us.[33]

However, this reviewer ultimately concurs with Locke's position that a distinctively racial art will emerge as support for its development grows within both the black community and the majority culture.

When these issues were brought to bear on discussions of visual art, the artists' individual life experiences mediated by the circumstances of their training were presumed to determine the expressive parameters of black art. The 1928 Harmon exhibition occasioned an interesting showdown on the value of artistic training for black artists between George E. Haynes of the Harmon Foundation and the Federal Council of Churches, and Fred Gardner who was Vice-President of the Society of Independent Artists. Gardner registered the familiar lament about the lack of racial qualities in the works exhibited, which he blamed on the artists' regrettable desire to follow established standards of European culture. Urging black artists to "let their innermost feelings prompt their efforts" he added:

The colored race must possess a vast amount of unrecognized talent which will never be found in the art schools but must be sought for through open non-jury exhibitions in which production is encouraged by hanging all work that is submitted regardless of skill according to technical standards. . . . It is altogether likely that from the lat-

ter class a powerful school will eventually develop that will enrich the whole world by its existence as the literature and music of the Negro has already done.[34]

Haynes defended the Foundation's policy of enlisting members of the professional art world as jurors for the awards and exhibitions, so as to insure that the work selected would measure up to "universal standards of artistic value."

Representing the position of the Harmon Foundation, Haynes responded that:

Mr. Gardner seems to be laboring under a common misapprehension about the peculiar talents of the Negro, and seems to be expecting that they are spontaneous gifts of God and need no guidance for development, and that Negroes should avoid education and the standards of universal values of beauty and in order to have spontaneity in original creation.[35]

Gary Reynolds pointed out that Haynes's belief in the existence of universal standards was fundamentally incompatible with the concept of the nonjuried exhibition advocated by the progressive Society of Independent Artists.[36] What is also at stake here, however, is the doctrine of racial uplift which echoes through a good deal of Harlem Renaissance criticism, especially within the black community. Haynes clearly reacted to these remarks as an assault on the value of educational opportunity for African Americans, sensing in them an insinuation that black artists could not be improved and thus should not waste their time in trying.[37]

Underlying Gardner's comments was the Society's historic commitment to the non-juried exhibition, which had it origins in the views of Robert Henri who promoted the idea of direct, authentic artistic expression unmediated by academic conventions. Gardner's dismissal of technical standards also echoes the sentiments of the Stieglitz group, and its romantic glorification of the artistic primitive who exists outside of established culture. But this collision of views on the respective merits of professional art education testifies to the impossibility of the black artist's position during these years, one often exacerbated by the well-intentioned remarks of progressive art critics.

African Americans seeking recognition in mainstream terms, and counting on their work to serve as entry into the domain of high culture, could ill-afford the kind of anti-establishment, outsider position extolled by Gardner. As Houston Baker has explained, the rejection of traditional values so emblematic of western modernism can be located in a specific matrix of race, gender and class privilege, one from which most black Americans were philosophically and practically alienated.[38] Yet, black artists were often most encouraged in progressive circles quite self-conscious and strident in their contempt for formal mastery and bourgeois values. To Gardner, non-professionalism was a creative advantage; to Haynes it was a regrettable result of circumstance to be overcome.[39]

The exchange also reveals the extent to which the efforts of the Harmon Foundation, however commendable, contributed to the critical confusion surrounding African American Art. Their official promotional literature insisted that the artists who entered their competitions were judged solely on the technical or aesthetic merits of their works; but it simultaneously stressed conspicuous racial identity as a criterion of value. Similarly, while Haynes rejected the call for a naïve, unschooled expression among black artists, the Foundation continued to make an issue of the fact that many of their exhibiting artists were in actuality non-professionals.[40]

Deliberate contrast between the outlook of the amateur and that of the trained professional was not restricted to critical discourse on black artists; it also figured prominently in the cultural nationalist discourse of the era. For example, books such as R. L. Duffus's *The American Renaissance* (1928) attempted to explain the growth of popular interest in the arts as a function of grass roots support for the community arts center. This was the domain of the amateur whose primary function was to encourage people in artistic pursuits who gain immense satisfaction from them in spite of their questionable talents. The underlying philosophy here, that art becomes important to a culture only when interest in it is cultivated among ordinary people, was also a motivating force behind the establishment of similar art centers in African American and other communities throughout the 1930s.[41]

In critical discourse about African American art, the concept of primitivism often served to amplify the creative advantage of the amateur and to underscore the notion of authenticity. Recent scholarship on the cult of the primitive in early twentieth century western culture and art has demonstrated the extent to which the conceptual formation known as primitivism functioned as an effective agent of consolidation in the construction of black difference. In the context of American art criticism, this process was complicated by wide-spread confusion in the understanding and use of terminology, as the word "primitive" came to signify a vast array of artistic qualities and possibilities, some of which had little to do with African American art.[42]

Regionalist critic Thomas Craven, for example, promoted the idea of a modern Midwestern primitivism linked to the glorification of the American frontier. For Holger Cahill, a collector and early scholar of American folk art, the primitive suggested a genuine "American" character embodied in the work of so-called naïve artists of the premodern period, by which he meant artists who worked outside the boundaries of the professional art world, or without the benefit of formal training. Albert Barnes, who collected European modern art and African sculpture, understood the primitive in terms of delivery from the pragmatic and materialistic impulses of the postindustrial age through accentuation of the emotional and the natural, qualities he associated with tribal culture. In art historical discourse, the word primitive was used to describe an artistic phase at its early stage of development. Thus, the concept of the primitive served simultaneously to promote fourteenth century Italian painting, American Regionalism, and European modernism; in discussions of African American art it summoned images of artistic immaturity, black folk culture and African tribal art.

Press coverage of African American art furnishes ample evidence that the ideology of racial primitivism, which often collapsed beliefs about authenticity, amateurism and atavism into a single construct, resulted in a clear preference among mainstream critics for black artistic expression that manifest racial qualities in these terms. Although the fascination with tribal art will, in the populist climate of the 1930s, be displaced by the idealization of folk art, insofar as Africa and rural black culture were understood as authentic subject matter for African American artists, they were welcomed. The popularity in the late 1920s of the painters Archibald Motley and Malvin Gray Johnson can, in part, be explained by this enthusiasm for art which confirmed such *a priori* notions of racial primitivism.

In March 1928, shortly after the exchange of views between Gardner and Haynes, a lengthy article on Motley written by critic Edward Alden Jewell appeared in *The New York Times Magazine*. Motley was from Chicago, but became well known to the New York art press after his one-man show at the New Gallery, which provided the focus for Jewell's remarks and no doubt contributed to Motley's subsequent fame. Although specifically concerned with Motley, at the core of this essay was a theme that remained constant in Jewell's criticism of African American art: his desire to see black artists place their uniqueness and racial heritage, their "difference," at the center of their artistic expression.[43]

Employing evocative prose, Jewell immediately drew attention to the pictures' racial themes, especially those on Africa which Motley had made expressly for this show at the urging of the New Gallery director:

> Here are steaming jungles that drip and sigh and ooze . . . devil-devils watching in the solemn night or poised to swoop on hapless human prey. . . . Myriad age-old racial memories drift up from Africa and glowing islands of the sea to color more recent ghostly memories of plantation days . . . and these memories sift, finally, through negro life in Northern cities of the present, leaving everywhere their imprint and merging with a rich blur of tribal echoes.[44]

Jewell characterized Motley as an "important link in the chain of Negro culture in this country" whose work demands to be taken seriously, both as self-expression and as an expression of race psychology, wherein "The same fundamental rhythms are found, whether the setting is the jungle presided over by witchcraft or a cabaret rocking to the syncopation of jazz."[45]

Jewell obviously exploited the primitive vogue to stimulate interest in the show and the artist; but this article is nonetheless distinctive for the extent to which it represents a serious piece of critical writing on a black artist in a mainstream publication. In addition to this predictable focus on exotic racialism, and the recounting of "hard luck and hard work" anecdotes that were ubiquitous in critical notices on black artists, Jewell also discussed the quality and emotional range of Motley's work, his artistic philosophy, and his influences. Through a skillful weaving of Motley's own pronouncements on what he hoped to accomplish as an artist for himself and for his race, with statements on the nature of Negro genius quoted from the authoritative texts of Benjamin Brawley, Jewell made a thoughtful attempt to address the complexity of Motley's position as a black artist working in modern America. Notwithstanding his unmistakable readiness to lapse into unimaginative racial stereotyping, Jewell's sincere admiration for the artist is evident as he concludes that "in all his work Motley shows an alert mind that draws its material from a sound esthetic fount."

Mainstream critics looking for racial primitivism in the work of African American artists were especially pleased when they discovered evidence of an emotional sensibility rooted in the southern black folk culture and religion. They were in fact looking for the visual equivalents of the Negro spiritual. Emanating from the widespread belief that cultural sophistication would be the ruination of the "real American Negro," this sentiment was nearly universal among critics who followed developments in African American art and literature. For many white Americans, the so-called "sorrow songs" were the most familiar, and therefore most representative, form of black expression.

This position accounts for both the cynicism and profound sense of loss with which Locke's *New Negro* was sometimes received in critical circles. Describing the anthology in 1926, Leon Whipple called it "an encyclopedia of the Negro as an artist and as a living member of American society," and expressed admiration for the quality and range of expression it contained. Whipple supported the creative initiatives of black artists, but he was suspicious of the exploitive attention they received from "profiteers and parasites" for whom the New Negro was a fad, the source of commercial gain or social thrills.[46] And while he applauded black artists' desire to speak in their own voice, Whipple worried about the preservation of the "Negro soul" in the wake of such modern artistic accomplishments:

> [The New Negro] presents its inheritance of which it is so proud as a credential that it may join a tradition and share a mode of life that will deflower and murder that inheritance with the noiseless efficiency of its own machines. The very articulateness of the Negro at the moment in the white medium seems token enough that he is loosing his African soul.[47]

Whipple assumes an almost wistful tone as he describes the drastic transformation of modern urban black Americans who have completely abandoned the soil (soul) of Africa and its extension in the rural South, lamenting the fact that one does not hear Negroes singing spirituals in the streets of New York.

The yearning for contact with "authentic" racial experience of this sort in visual art was satisfied by a series of works based on the sorrow songs undertaken by Malvin Gray Johnson. "Swing Slow, Sweet Chariot," was awarded the 1929 exhibition prize for best picture in the second Harmon group show and was widely celebrated as evidence of the black artist's potential to make a distinctive contribution to American culture. Critics were near ecstatic in their praise for Johnson. Assertions that he had captured the true spirit of the

American Negro were supported by artist's own description of his intended sentiment, as quoted in the Foundation press release:

> I have tried to show the escape of emotions which the plantation slaves felt after being held down all day by the grind of labor and the consciousness of being bound out. Set free from their tasks by the end of the day and the darkness, they have gone from their cabin to the river's edge and are calling upon their God for the freedom for which they long.[48]

A lengthy notice in *Art Digest* referred to the painting as a "significant art world event . . . worthy of the highest traditions in American painting." The latter claim was reinforced by a favorable (and most unusual) comparison of Johnson's painting to the work of a well-known American artist, one who was himself thoroughly encapsulated in romantic mythology: "This painting, with its group of old plantation Negroes, beholding their vision in the sky, is on as mystic and spiritual plane as one of the master works of Albert P. Ryder."[49]

## V

The Harmon Foundation did not begin organizing group shows until 1928 and enjoyed its greatest period of success in the early 1930s. Even though the fascination with primitivism and black culture generated by the climate of the Harlem Renaissance was by then in decline, notices on the Harmon Foundation shows from 1930 to 1933 rehashed many of the same issues that had emerged in the early reviews. In the face of persistent disappointment with the evident lack of authentic racial expression, reviewers continued to regard increased technical skill and the mastery of existing conventions as symptomatic of black artists' regrettable eagerness to imitate mainstream traditions rather than forging their own. Jewell's comments in *The New York Times* exemplify this position. In 1930, he wrote: "Instead of devoting themselves to material of true racial significance, so many of these artists waste their time over art school formulae."[50]

The 1930 exhibition showcased the work of prize winners William H. Johnson and Sargent Johnson, thus prompting speculation about the characteristics of an emergent black modernism. William Johnson had just returned from several years abroad and responses to his work can often be read as measures of the reviewer's sympathy (or antipathy) towards European ideas. Jewell's review of the 1930 Harmon show suggested that artists such as Johnson were staying abroad too long. Several years later, in 1934, he complained that:

Such racial aspect as may once have figured has virtually disappeared, so far as most of the work is concerned. Some of the artists, accomplished technicians, seem to have slipped into grooves of one sort or another. There is the painter of Cezannesque still-life; there is the painter of Gauguinesque nudes; and there are those who have learned various "dated" modernist tricks.[51]

These sentiments were echoed by Stanley Olsmtead of the *Washington Herald,* who cautioned "Paris is a proverbial danger for the racial instinct."[52]

Critics of these later shows consistently remarked on the extent to which the works produced by black artists resembled the efforts of their white counterparts, modern or otherwise. Although Johnson's work was frequently cited as the best in this show, it also prompted (along with the work of Hale Woodruff) the common observation that the Harmon collection did not differ significantly from that of any other modern art exhibition coming out of New York. This observation was typically intended as a pejorative, but it formed an important component of discussions which foregrounded the recognition of technical parity and an obvious similarity of interests among artists of both racial groups. In their straining after distinctive racial qualities, mainstream critics resorted to cliches about Negro rhythm, spontaneity of emotion, and affinity for bright color. But more often than not, writers concluded that, were in not for the ubiquity of black subjects, the work might "pass" for that of any group of contemporary artists.

Albert Cochrane of the *Boston Evening Transcript* offered this reproach in 1930 directed at viewers who blamed black artists when their work is too suggestive of their white contemporaries:

> It seems a bit unfair, and not a little stupid, to demand that they shall be characteristically racial in their paintings, when we ourselves, regardless of native origins, are eagerly taking orders from Paris and when success is measured by the degree of exactitude with which we can ape her greatest masters.[53]

Remarks such as these suggest that criticism of African American artists in these years is best understood in the context of shifting interests and priorities among art critics increasingly drawn to cultural nationalist ideals, especially after the onset of the Depression.

In the wake of the crash of 1929, and throughout the decade of the 1930s, American critical discourse was saturated with nationalistic rhetoric. A fusion of ideas from the left and right, sharing the vaguely articulated goal that American art

Self-portrait by William H. Johnson.

of the century; these were mediated by a populist, egalitarian spirit that was at once anti-elitist and anti-modernist. By the middle of the decade, the American Scene Movement had become a quasi-official national style. It was the preferred idiom of the federal art projects and was promoted by a number of influential critics and publications.

Although artists within the American Scene Movement were extremely diverse in their thematic and stylistic interests, those associated with rural Midwestern life, the so-called Regionalists, enjoyed greater prominence and thus exercised considerable influence on the artistic formations of the decade. By 1935, Regionalism represented a clearly articulated point of view, with representative artists (Thomas Hart Benton, Grant Wood and John Steuart Curry) and a critic (Thomas Craven) who polemicised on their behalf. The popularity of Regionalism owed much, as Baigell and others have noted, to Craven's strategic appropriation of the American Scene Movement on behalf of the Midwest, thus acquiring privilege of place in cultural nationalist discourse for rural values and frontier mythology. Although in retrospect the agrarian interests of the central Regionalist painters seem to have been exaggerated and even distorted, both by contemporary critics and by subsequent historians, the fact remains that through a series of key works and publications, they captured the imagination and sympathy of the majority culture with greater success than any of their contemporaries within the American Scene Movement.[56]

For African American artists the ascendance of Regionalism on the cultural landscape, and its increasing influence on Americanist ideology, had important consequences. In theory, the American Scene Movement encouraged artists to share their individual sentiments as Americans hailing from a diversity of backgrounds and locales, and in so doing collectively define what it meant to be an American. Within this model African American artists could continue to pursue the cultural agenda set in the previous decade, weighing personal experience against the particulars of a distinctive cultural environment. In practice, however, Regionalism thrived on the popular belief in agrarianism as the "true" source of American character and virtue, and on its identification with the Midwest as the most "authentic" area of the country. Democratic populism and anti-modernism were cornerstones of American Scene thinking; increasingly these signified a mentality

and culture should manifest some organic connection to American life, these multiple nationalisms have come to define the decade. Although in the early years of the Depression, they were more clearly and identifiably partisan, after 1935 cultural nationalism increasingly took the form of an uncritical and even celebratory Americanism, encompassing a wide range of seemingly incompatible political, social and aesthetic ideologies. Extremes on the left and right continued to heard, but Americanist discourse held the center, encouraged by the rhetoric and cultural politics of the Popular Front and the New Deal.[54]

Cultural nationalism in the visual arts during the 1930s was linked to the so-called American Scene Movement, an expression used to identify artists who consistently explored subject matter and themes drawn from everyday American life. Historian Matthew Baigell has explained the American Scene Movement as an attempt to "develop a democratic art easily accessible to the ordinary person, capable of moving him along nostalgically, politically, and aesthetically, by means of commonly recognizable images presented in easily understood styles."[55] To a large extent, the American Scene Movement represented a consolidation of romantic cultural nationalism and environmental theories of artistic expression that had been in place since the turn that was pro-rural and anti-foreign, thus altering the discursive field of Americanism in the direction of a nativism more narrowly conceived.

The 1920s had forecast the coming of an invigorated American culture that would be expansive and replete with possibilities.[57] Artistic explorations of national experience in the 1920s emanated from complex understandings of American identity, and it was in this context that black artists made their claims as important contributors to American national culture. The call for a national art during the following decade will, however, be drastically altered by the shrill nativist propaganda of critics such as Thomas Craven. Matthew Baigell has described the process whereby a genuine, and sometimes ambivalent, search for national identity characteristic of the 1920s was transformed in the 1930s into the hardening of a particular kind of identity.[58] African Americans who participated in the Harmon Exhibitions of the early 1930s were thus seeking entry into the American art world as a critical mass during a period of increasingly nativist sentiments. Tribal Africa was very distant from the mythologies of historic America which, in the popular imagination, comprised the nation's official heritage.

This situation was further exacerbated by the growing antipathy towards European modernism in the 1930s. The issue of aesthetic modernity and its relationship to traditional African art is a recurrent theme in much of the writing about black art in the interwar decades. Remarks on a Harmon exhibition of 1931 by African American artist Selma Day typify the kind of critical confusion which existed in minds of the general public with respect to their understanding of black modernism:

> A few of the artists are producing what is called modern art by some, Negro art by others, and still another group will name the same paintings primitive art. I imagine that one often wonders where one style ends and the other begins, and more often questions whether or not any such thing as modern art or Negro art or primitive art really exists.[59]

In *The New Negro,* Locke had underscored the extent to which African tribal art had invigorated European painting and sculpture, helping free it of academic practices, and he claimed that it could be an even more potent stimulant for the African American artist.

While this connection between Africanism and European modernism may have been profitable in the more experimental and aesthetically inclusive 1920s, it could only serve to further marginalize black art in an increasingly xenophobic climate wherein American artists were being advised by critics at every turn to discard European influences as antithetical to their mission of cultural self-definition. An important distinction involving the repudiation of modernism was made by mainstream critics of the era: American artists were urged to purge themselves of foreign influence to cultivate their national identity; black artists were admonished to do so in order to protect their racial uniqueness. In other words, they were instructed to reject European (though not necessarily African) artistic prototypes in order to preserve blackness, not to affirm Americanness.

Locke reiterated his faith in (and preference for) the Africanist tendencies of contemporary black artists in an article published for the *American Magazine of Art* in 1931. Although this essay contains ideas which Locke had advanced throughout the 1920s, their appearance in a mainstream art publication at a critical moment in the ascendance of the American Scene Movement is significant. Locke classified modern black artists as traditionalists, modernists and what he called "neo-primitives or Africanists." The construction of these categories was symptomatic of his struggle to reconcile issues of form and content, a problem that plagued cultural nationalist discourse as well as efforts to define a racial aesthetic in American art.[60]

African American traditionalists, as Locke described them, were artists who dealt with racial themes without altering stylistic conventions. He then speculates that such academicism is bound to be eclipsed by the efforts of younger artists open to experimentation with more recent (foreign) models:

> But conservatism on this point seems doomed, since the young Negro artist has a double chance of being influenced by Negro idioms, if not as a deliberate racialist or conscious "Africanist," then at least at second-hand through the reflected influence of Negro idioms on general modernist style.[61]

There is a sense of inevitability in his words which weds the future vitality of Negro art to precisely the kind of art many Americans were being encouraged to repudiate. Partly in response to the increasingly nativist climate within the American Scene Movement, and also in keeping with the widespread admiration for American folk art throughout the decade, Locke's writing in the 1930s demonstrates a shift of emphasis from the tribal antecedents of African American expression to native black folk culture, but he never abandoned his belief that African art could function as powerful catalyst for black expression.

In the years prior to and immediately following the crash of 1929, the most important challenge to the hegemony of cultural expression linked to the American scene came from the left, which concerned itself with the development of a proletarian culture in America that would further the interests of international communism. By 1935, however, the fusion of progressive impulses under the collective platform known as the Popular Front enacted a crucial transformation of American cultural politics and created a climate in which the triumph of Americanism was insured. A great deal has been written about the absorption into the Popular Front of ideals that had been the mainstay of cultural nationalist thinking since the onset of the Depression. Among the most important was the adaptation of a strategic populism that recast the partisan image of the worker into a more generic configuration loosely recognized as the "people" or the "folk. The ideology of the Popular Front became increasingly flexible as the decade progressed, aligning itself more closely with the rhetoric and spirit of the New Deal, and accommodating a wide variety of its cultural initiatives, from interest in documenting the lives and experiences of ordinary Americans to the recovery and revival of American historical myths and heroes.[62]

It is generally agreed that the cultural politics of the Popular Front ultimately served to consolidate and advance the interests of American nationalists, especially in their ardent defense of democracy as the protector of individual liberty and enemy of (fascist) political oppression. But it was also in this climate that Locke encountered the most serious opposition to his advocacy of racial artistic expression as a manifestation of cultural nationalism. Popular Front rhetoric tended to de-emphasize racial and ethnic alignments in the interest not only of celebrating the collective identity of the American "people," but also of ensuring strong opposition to the threat of fascism through national unity. Also, the shift of emphasis from antiforeign to antifascist rhetoric encouraged resistance to Locke's advocacy of racialism among artists and intellectuals associated with the Popular Front for whom any reference to racial identity was suspect as fascist and reactionary.

In the African American community, Locke's promotion of Africanism had already been challenged by historian and artist James Porter, who questioned the wisdom of encouraging black artists in America to express themselves in terms of an African past so remote from their actual experience. Reviewing a 1934 exhibition of African American art at the Smithsonian for the *American Magazine of Art,* he noted the stylistic diversity of black artists in these terms:

> One finds among them excursions into mysticism, cubism, expressionism, Africanism, and the like; but those that merit the closest attention are, of course, the forthright productions founded on the real experience of the artist rather than on foreign modes of expression.[63]

Porter counted tribal Africa among the foreign influences on the black American artist, a position perfectly consistent with the values of the American Scene Movement, although one not widespread among mainstream critics with a vested interest in the preservation of racial difference.

Porter continued to take issue with the advocacy of racialism in art on political, aesthetic and historical grounds. These views were also shared by mainstream art historians such as Meyer Schapiro, who, at the peak of the cultural nationalist debates in the middle of the decade, identified what he thought to be the fallacy and dangers of insisting that art embodies some kind of racial or national character. On the pages of *Art Front,* Schapiro along with the artist Stuart Davis, launched a scathing critique of Regionalist art and politics, including accusations that the aesthetic agenda of American nationalists such as Craven was similar to that being advanced in Nazi Germany. This situation caused them to question not only nativist sentiments in the American Scene movement, but also the call for racial qualities in the works of black artists. In a 1936 essay for *Art Front* entitled "Race, Nationality and Art," Schapiro argued that appeals to race mask the political realities of class division, transforming minority peoples into "victims for the blind rage of economically frustrated citizens."[64]

On the subject of African American art, Schapiro cautioned against the assertion of racial identity through the cultivation of African models, insisting that its end result will be "the segregation of the Negro from modern culture."[65] These concerns were amplified by Porter who, in a 1937 review Locke's *Negro Art: Past and Present* for *Art Front,* referred to Locke as a "segregationist."[66] Schapiro, Porter, and Locke all embraced environmental theories of culture that disallowed the notion of racial determinism in artistic creativity; but while Locke stressed the value of reclaiming a distant racial past, Schapiro and Porter emphasized instead the matrix of socio-cultural and historical conditions of production as the primary determinants of expression. Furthermore, Schapiro identified the nativist position of the Regionalist with a clear rejection of certain individuals who wished to be recognized as legitimate Americans and even the justification of their oppression.[67]

## VI

Despite its increasingly pronounced chauvinism and the growing hostility on the cultural left towards what was perceived to be the reactionary politics of the Regionalists, Locke himself continued to believe that the American Scene Movement would actually help black artists enter the mainstream. Schapiro and Davis represented an internationalist position in American cultural politics, which decried provincialism and minimized antiforeign rhetoric. But the widespread support for Americanism within both the Popular Front and the New Deal made this majority position far more compelling for Locke. Also, African Americans figured only tangentially in these debates about race, nationalism and culture, which, as the decade advanced, were more specifically concerned with combating European fascism than American racism. From Locke's point of view, the greater visibility of African American subjects in the work of mainstream artists such as Thomas Hart Benton and John Steuart Curry was evidence of a more appreciative understanding of black culture and its vital contribution to American life[68]

It was in the context of his attempt to situate black artists within the American Scene Movement that Locke most effectively articulated his vision of a black aesthetic mediated by cultural nationalism. As historian Jeffrey Stewart explains, Locke was not always consistent in his efforts to locate black culture in relation to American culture as a whole.[69] Stewart characterizes Locke as a critic with acute sensitivity to the constant mutations of cultural discourse, a quality which has led to the not infrequent (but somewhat misleading) observation that the conditions of the 1930s brought about a fundamental change in Locke's thinking. The catalog essays for the Harmon shows of the early 1930s reveal, rather, a subtle but very strategic shift of emphasis as Locke worked towards the integration of black artists into a cultural mainstream preoccupied with "Americanism."

Prior to 1931, the Harmon catalogs had been essentially illustrated checklists, but in 1931 and again in 1933 Locke contributed substantial essays which sought to position the works in an explicit critical and historical frame. The essay of 1931, entitled "The African Legacy and the Negro Artist," rehearses arguments that formed the cornerstone of Locke's criticism in the 1920s, and that had been repeated in his article on African American art for the *American Magazine of Art* during the same year. He emphasizes the importance of African art as an inspiration and instructive model for contemporary black artists who sought to avoid the sterility of academic art and create something unique and characteristic:

> African art, therefore, presents to the Negro artist in the New World a challenge to recapture this heritage of creative originality, and to carry it to distinctive new achievement in a vital, new, racially expressive art. . . . In this downfall of classic models and Caucasian idols, one may see the passing of the childhood period of Negro art, and with the growing maturity of the Negro artist, the advent of a truly racial school of expression.[70]

As has been demonstrated, in the spiteful climate of the 1930s, Locke's support for such expression struggled against strident demands for a unified national culture increasingly inhospitable to the protection of ethnic or racial autonomy, as well as insinuations that racialism in art was tantamount to fascism. Thus, his writing for the remainder of the decade often shows considerable caution in its assertions of racial difference.

For example, Locke's essay for the 1933 Harmon catalog, "The Negro Takes His Place in American Art," emphasizes instead the collective purpose that unifies all American artists. Given the universal call for an American art embodying American experience, artists of both races, he reasoned, now had a vested interest in the thoughtful and accurate portrayal of African Americans.[71] The common ground over which the races meet is that of the Negro theme, and Locke contends that the black artist's relation to his subject does not differ greatly from the relation of his white fellow artist to the same material. In this essay, Locke also submits that the time has come for "frank and objective comparison" between artists of both races who have taken up this theme, boldly suggesting that the most effective way to measure the progress of the black artists, or properly evaluate the handling of Negro themes, is through exhibitions organized irrespective of race.[72]

Locke's call for integrated exhibitions, repeated throughout the 1930s, went largely unheeded.[73] Notwithstanding the insistently inclusive rhetoric introduced by the federal relief programs in the arts, separate exhibitions remained the norm and, with a few notable exceptions, black artists were poorly represented in the sweeping surveys of contemporary American art organized at the end of the decade.[74] In contrast, historically black institutions, such as the Howard University Art Gallery, began in the 1930s to create inclusive contexts for African American artists by exhibiting their work along side that of the majority culture.[75]

For the remainder of the decade critics sympathetic to the goals of cultural nationalism continued to seek *a priori* notions of racial difference in black art while simultaneously calling for a distinctive national art liberated from its dependence on foreign models. While regional differences were considered inevitable and even desirable in this paradigm of American culture, within mainstream criticism the discourses of manifest racialism and national identity remained clearly separate. The emergence of African American artists as a collective presence was virtually ignored in the numerous publications advocating cultural nationalism throughout the 1930s, even by writers such as Edwin Alden Jewell who had demonstrated a sustained interest in, and familiarity with, the development of African American art.

In his 1939 book, *Have We An American Art,* Jewell used the critical reception of recent exhibitions held in Paris and London as a means to explore the progress of cultural nationalism in American art.[76] To answer the questions that embarrass us today but which defined the decade for several generations of historians—Do we have an American art? Should we want one? What is it?—Jewell turned to the reactions of British and French critics who reviewed these shows. These critics, he reported, found American art in the main derivative, warming only to those works which seemed to them embodiments of authentic American life.

The rhetoric Jewell employed to register the disappointment of Europeans with these shows was nearly identical to that which pervades his recurrent complaints about the invariable failings of African American art. He reported that European critics seeking a sense of American difference went away unrewarded, an observation often rendered with respect to viewers of the Harmon shows. Jewell proposed in this essay that a true

American art cannot be forced but will emerge as America's artists develop the courage to be themselves. This is an interesting comment coming from a critic for whom the ideal of racial expression in African American art was found in paintings of tribal Africa made to order by Archibald Motley, a Roman Catholic artist who grew up in Chicago.

In sharp contrast to mainstream critics who clearly seemed to lose interest in issues of race as they shifted their focus to patriotic nationalism and the celebration of American culture, Locke's writing at the end of the decade keeps before the interested public an understanding of black art as racially influenced yet still bound to American art. He did this chiefly by framing his discussions of African American art in terms of the artistic interests of the majority culture. Locke's catalog essay for the exhibition, "Contemporary Negro Art," organized for the Baltimore Museum of Art, is a case in point. Published in the same year as Jewell's *Have We An American Art,* and no doubt mindful of its almost certain failings with respect to the recognition of African American contributions to the project of national self-definition, Locke used this exhibition as an opportunity to position the work of black artists within the "generally accepted objective to have American art fully document American life and experience, and thus more adequately reflect America."[77]

The essay begins with the kind of declaration that became commonplace in writing about American art at the end of decade: "Art in a democracy should above all else be democratic, which is to say that it must be truly representative." As populist sentiments and support for the arts are encouraged, he claims, there is greater hope that this mandate might be fulfilled. In this frame of reference the Negro art exhibition takes on new meaning:

> it serves as a declaration of principles as to what art should and must be in a democracy and as a gauge of how far in this particular province we have gone and may need to go in the direction of representative native art.[78]

Locke then goes on to mention artists of both races who have explored aspects of black culture as part of their mutual immersion in the task of documenting the American scene. This roster includes well-known painters from the early American realist tradition such as Winslow Homer, Robert Henri, and George Bellows, as well as artists associated with the American Scene Movement, inclusive of both Regionalist and Social Realists. Among African Americans, he draws special attention to the work of Archibald Motley and Malvin Gray Johnson, artists whose popularity and "authenticity" had been established in the late 1920s. The primary significance of the Baltimore exhibition, Locke concludes, is to illuminate the future prospects of the black artists and to demonstrate unequivocally the "complete compatibility between the interests of contemporary Negro and contemporary American art."

## VII

Implicit in all Locke's writing was an unrelenting conviction that black Americans, by virtue of their distinctive racial heritage and singular experience, were destined to make a unique contribution to national culture at a critical moment in its development. However, because they were more inclined to deal with the artist of African descent in the United States as an "American Negro," rather than a "Negro American," mainstream art critics typically did not acknowledge African American art as a vital manifestation of cultural nationalism. During the interwar period, at a time when black expression, especially in music, was a powerful signifier of American culture in Europe, racism and segregation made it improbable that the visual art of African Americans would be so recognized at home.

Although visual representations of American blacks were considered authentic American subject matter, the discussions of democracy and culture that dominated the American art world during the Depression rarely extended to the work of black artists. Instead, African American artists, constantly accused of sacrificing their birthright, were entreated to articulate their difference through archetypal images of suffering, naïveté, or racial primitivism. In an age that merged nationalistic and aesthetic issues, and in which critical discourse about art often lacked sophistication and focus, race seems to have remained the only relevant issue in considerations of African American art.

The failure to recognize black expression as the fulfillment of cultural nationalist ideals during the interwar decades is, of course, in part a function of widespread confusion in these years about the very concepts of culture and nationhood. Such debates were plagued by disagreements about the nature of high art versus mass culture, as well as by the competing claims of particularism versus universalism in the establishment of American identity, that is, the challenge to reconcile regional and ethnic uniqueness with the striving towards a unified nationalistic consciousness. Furthermore, interest in black subjectivity and cultural expression which emerged in the hot-house intellectual climate of the 1920s could not escape the transformation of cultural nationalist discourse enacted by the economic and political pressures of the 1930s. To assert that the realities of the Depression brought an end to the spiritual yearnings and searching critique of American culture that characterized the decade after World War I has become an historical commonplace. But it is worth recalling here that theorizing about American culture in the 1920s, marked by a romantic cultural nationalism cultivated in the wake of the Progressive movement, often took the form of apolitical intellectual abstractions that favored the inclusion (even celebration) of marginalized peoples.

As Richards Pells has explained in his discussion of the crisis of identity among many American intellectuals after the war:

To have abandoned social action in the traditional sense did not mean that they were surrendering hope for a genuine transformation of American life. Many writers saw artistic experimentation and cultural analysis as preludes to a more fundamental change in the social order. . . . From this perspective, the world of culture was itself a model community of men sharing the same values, the same feelings of comradeship, the same dedication to the rejuvenation of America through painting, poetry and prose.[79]

The process of reconceptualizing this "model community" was the task of the 1930s and in this context African American cultural promise will be reconfigured: first by demands for the radical transformation of American society and the creation of a proletarian culture which, though instrumental in encouraging black social activism, also privileged class identity over racial, later by the rhetoric of Americanism and its various mutations, from Regionalist agrarianism to the New Deal and the Popular Front.

In *Negro Art: Past and Present* Locke wrote "everything that Mr. [Holger] Cahill advocates for a program of contemporary American art can be underscored for the advance program of contemporary Negro art." He maintained that Cahill's prescriptive for an "imaginative realism" rooted in social reality and modern American experience "might profitably be adapted as today's creed and gospel for the younger progressive Negro artist."[80] But critical reaction to emergent racial expression in the Harlem Renaissance and its aftermath cast in sharp relief the persistent status of the African American as a political, social and artistic outsider, whose official role in the national project of cultural and spiritual renewal would remain narrowly conceived. During the interwar decades, by positioning the artistic production of African Americans within a carefully controlled and delimited discursive frame, American art criticism acted as an effective agent of exclusion. The failure to fundamentally alter this frame has resulted in the continued neglect and distortion of African American artists in both American art history and in contemporary art, wherein their work is rarely understood in complex terms that would affirm, to use Locke's words, "how naturally and effectively the Negro artist can range through all the media, provinces and various styles of a common human art."[81]

## Notes

1. This article was developed from papers presented at the Reynolda House Museum of American Art (1994), the College Art Association (1996), and the Corcoran Museum (1998). Alain Locke, ed., *The New Negro* (1925, rpt. New York, 1992).

2. Charles Gaines, Maurice Berger, and Catherine Lord, *Theater of Refusal: Black Art and Mainstream Criticism* (Irvine, Calif., 1993). The marginalization of black artists through various forms of critical and historical discourse is a subject of continuing interest in the consideration of African American art. In an earlier discussion about the wisdom of continuing to organize all-black exhibitions, Joseph Jacobs wrote:

   > The fact that a large number of black artists function within both a white and a black world presents a problem for the white-dominated art establishment, for scholars and critics have difficulty putting the work into proper perspective. More often than not, one aspect of the work is emphasized at the expense of the other, and generally it is the black component that is stressed, with the result that the artist is often divorced completely from the other activities of contemporary art and in effect is eliminated from the history of American art.
   > (Joseph Jacobs, *Since the Harlem Renaissance: 50 Years of African-American Art* [Lewisburg, Penn., 1984], 5)

   For analysis of this process and its effects on contemporary African American art and artists see, in addition to Gaines and Jacobs, David Driskell et al., *African American Visual Aesthetics: A Postmodernist View*; Kinshasha Holman Conwill, "In Search of an 'Authentic' Vision: Decoding the Appeal of the Self-Taught African-American Artist," *American Art* 5 (fall 1991): 2-9; Lowry Stokes Sims, "Subject/Subjectivity and Agency in the Art of African Americans," *Art Bulletin* 76 (Dec. 1994): 587-590; Richard J. Powell, Letter to the Editor and Lowry Stokes Sims, Reply, *Art Bulletin* 77 (Sept. 1995): 514-16; Judith Wilson, "Shades of Grey in the Black Aesthetic, Part One, The Myth of the Black Aesthetic," in *Next Generation: Southern Black Aesthetic* (Winston-Salem, N.C., 1990).

3. David Levering Lewis, *When Harlem Was in Vogue* (1979; New York, 1989), xvi.

4. For insight into manifestations of American cultural nationalism in the visual arts during the interwar decades, I am indebted to the work of historians Wanda Corn and Matthew Baigell. See especially Corn, "Identity, Modernism, and the American Artist after World War I: Gerald Murphy and Americanism," *Studies in the History of Art* 29 (1991), 148-69; and *Grant Wood: The Regionalist Vision* (New Haven, Conn., 1983); Baigell, "The Beginnings of 'The American Wave' and the Depression," *Art Journal* 27 (summer 1968), 387-396, 398; "American Art and National Identity: The 1920s," *Arts* 6 (Feb. 1987): 48-55; and *The American Scene: American Painting of the 1930s* (New York, 1974).

5. Nathan Irvin Huggins, *Harlem Renaissance* (New York, 1971).

6. George Hutchinson, *The Harlem Renaissance in Black and White* (Cambridge, Mass., 1995).

7. Huggins, *Harlem Renaissance,* 8; and Hutchinson, *The Harlem Renaissance in Black and White,* 12.

8. Mary Schmidt Campbell, Introduction, *The Harlem Renaissance: Art of Black America* (New York, 1987), 14 and 25.

9. Hutchinson, *The Harlem Renaissance in Black and White,* 14. It is worth noting here that, in separate histories of African American art, discussions of this period typically consider racially specific expressive idioms in the context of mainstream discourse and artistic practice. This precedent was established in the groundbreaking early histories written by Alain Locke and James Porter, and continues to characterize more recent scholarship. I am especially indebted to the work of David Driskell, Romare Bearden and Harry Henderson for thoughtful presentation of the issues and challenges facing African American artists during the interwar decades. David C. Driskell, *Two Centuries of Black American Art* (New York: Alfred A. Knopf for the Los Angeles County Museum of Art, 1976) and Romare Bearden and Harry Henderson, *A History of African-American Artists From 1792 to the Present* (New York, 1993). See also Richard J. Powell, *Black Art and Culture in the Twentieth Century* (London, 1997); Samella Lewis, *African American Art and Artists* (1978; Berkeley, Calif., 1990); and Elsa Honig Fine, *The Afro-American Artist: A Search For Identity* (1973; New York, 1982).

10. The hegemony of modernism, for example, does not explain why, in 1968, when the Whitney Museum organized an exhibition of American Art in the 1930s it neglected the work of black artists. (In protest, the Studio Museum of Harlem mounted an exhibition called "Invisible Americans: Black Artists of the 1930s.")

    The analysis of theoretical modernism as an instrument of exclusion in canonical histories and mainstream criticism has become a major trope in contemporary critical discourse about African American art. See, for example, David C. Driskell, ed. *African American Visual Aesthetics: A Postmodernist View* (Washington, D.C., 1995); and Eloise E. Johnson, *Rediscovering the Harlem Renaissance: The Politics of Exclusion* (New York, 1997).

    Johnson's study departs from postmodern critiques of modernism as a universalizing discourse which is inherently exclusionary, and more specifically, from the work of Houston Baker, who reconsiders the "failed" modernity of the Harlem Renaissance in light of the realities of black experience. See Houston A. Baker, Jr., *Modernism and the Harlem Renaissance* (Chicago, 1987). It should be noted that the 1999 Whitney exhibition "The American Century: Art and Culture 1900-1950" presented a more balanced and inclusive history of early twentieth-century American art than past general surveys, in both print and exhibition form.

11. On the theoretical instability and uncertainty which plagued early conceptions of modernity in American art criticism, see Susan Noyes Platt, *Modernism in the 1920s: Interpretations of Modern Art in New York from Expressionism to Constructivism* (Ann Arbor, Mich., 1985). For a discussion of nationalism as it has been manifest in the historiography of American art, see Wanda Corn, "Coming of Age: Historical Scholarship in American Art," *Art Bulletin* 70 (June 1988): 188-207, repr. in Mary Ann Calo, ed. *Critical Issues in American Art: A Book of Readings* (New York, 1998), 1-34.

12. Although interest in African American culture has grown during the last two decades, this lack of visibility within the historical mainstream, and the failure of art criticism to come to terms with the complexity and range of black visual art, continues to vex artists and critics, as well as historians who seek a more representative history of American art. To a degree, this problem can be understood as a function of neglect, but it also unmistakably reflects the priorities and interests of scholars working in the field of early twentieth-century American art and culture. For example, while there is a fair amount of literature on the history of American art criticism and theory, it rarely addresses art or criticism produced by African Americans. Thus the issues which preoccupied American critics and artists during these years have been clearly identified, but these have not been brought to bear on the analysis of African American art.

Also, while scholarship on the Harlem Renaissance is plentiful, it often does not draw large distinctions between artistic activity in different media. Accomplishments in poetry and music tend to be centralized as the most representative forms of artistic expression during the Harlem Renaissance; production in the visual arts has been overlooked until quite recently. A similar condition exists in studies of American culture in the interwar decades, which deal extensively with cultural nationalism but tend to privilege written expression and popular culture, while the visual artists receive only cursory attention.

This is certainly evident in the recent works on the culture of the 1920s and 1930s by Ann Douglas (*Terrible Honesty* [New York, 1995]), Lynn Dumenil (*Modern Temper* [New York, 1995]), Warren Sussman (*Culture as History* [New York, 1984]), Terry Cooney (*Balancing Acts* [New York, 1995]), Michael Denning (*Cultural Front* [London, 1996]), and Richard Pells (*Radical Visions and American Dreams* [New York, 1973]) to mention only a few. All of these authors provide rich and provocative analysis of the period, but their discussions of expression in the visual arts are far less comprehensive than those devoted to literature and music. Growing interest in mass culture has resulted in a fair amount of attention to photography, film and modern design in these sweeping cultural studies, while painting and sculpture, in the main, receive only minor consideration. The seminal work of Charles Alexander (*Nationalism in American Thought* [Chicago, 1969]; and *Here This Country Lies* [Bloomington, Ind., 1980]) is an exception insofar as it does pay considerable attention to visual artists, but, regrettably not to African Americans.

13. Locke, "The Negro and Art," address delivered at the International Student Service Convention, Mt. Holyoke College, Sept., 1931. Typescript in the Harmon Foundation Papers, Box 66, Library of Congress, Manuscript Division.

14. For a provocative analysis of Locke's thinking as it relates to cultural nationalist practice see Hutchinson, *The Harlem Renaissance in Black and White,* esp. 90-93, 182-186, 400-403 and 424-428.

15. Locke, *The New Negro,* xxvi.

16. For a discussion of theories of modern American realism in the interwar decades and their formation, see Platt, *Modernism in the 1920s*; Wayne Lloyd Roosa, "American Art Theory and Criticism During the 1930s; Thomas Craven, George L. K. Morris, Stuart Davis," (Ph.D. diss., Rutgers State University, 1989); and Peninah Y. Petruck, "American Art Criticism: 1910-1939," (Ph.D. diss., New York University, 1979).

17. Locke's interaction with white patrons is discussed extensively in the literature on the Harlem Renaissance. See also Jeffrey C. Stewart, "Black Modernism and White Patronage," *International Review of African American Art* 11 (1994): 43-55. On Locke and Barnes see Mark Helbling, "African Art: Albert C. Barnes and Alain Locke," *Phylon* 44 (Mar. 1982): 57-67. The definitive source on the Harmon Foundation is Gary A. Reynolds and Beryl I. Wright, *Against the Odds: African-American Artists and the Harmon Foundation* (Newark, N.J., 1989).

In her study of American art criticism of the 1920s, Susan Noyes Platt described the institutional context in which modernist values and paradigms were articulated as "the interlacing of commercial, philanthropic, and philosophical motives." Due to the lack of curatorial expertise and theoretical sophistication among mainstream museums and critics in America, dealers such as Stieglitz and Marius de Zayas both sold modern art and positioned themselves as authoritative critical voices on its behalf. Platt, *Modernism in the 1920s,* 33.

A similar climate of trade stimulated by advocacy surrounded the promotion of African American art. Although the Harmon Foundation was not a commercial operation, one of its stated goals was the achievement of financial self-sufficiency among black artists, and works in the traveling shows were offered for sale. The Foundation nominally committed itself simply to excellence of expression and the cultivation of black creative ability, but the purity of these goals was bound to be undermined by its multiple roles. It functioned as both museum and agent, as benefactor and critical authority. Opponents of the Harmon Foundation then and since have regarded such conflicts of interest in a white agency occupied with the promotion of African American art as a hindrance to the artists' subsequent growth and development.

18. For a discussion of Berenson's influence on modern critical traditions see Mary Ann Calo, *Bernard Berenson and the Twentieth Century* (Philadelphia, 1994).

19. On the differences and similarities between the aesthetic philosophies of Stieglitz and Henri, and their respective influence on American art criticism, see Petruck, "American Art Criticism: 1910-1939."

More recently, George Hutchinson and Mark Helbling have noted the impact of American pragmatist aesthetics and cultural anthropology on Locke's thinking. See Hutchinson, *The Harlem Renaissance in Black and White*, Part I "American Modernism, Race, and National Culture," esp. 42-50 and 62-77; and Mark Helbling "Feeling Universality and Thinking Particularistically: Alain Locke, Franz Boas, Melville Herskovits, and the Harlem Renaissance," *Prospects* 19 (1994): 289-314.

Henri was one of the few American artists (along with Winslow Homer) praised by Locke in his later writing for their serious portrayals of African American subjects. Hutchinson notes that Locke initially considered including Henri's sketches of black subjects as illustrations for the *Survey Graphic* issue on Harlem that formed the basis of *The New Negro* anthology. See Hutchinson, *The Harlem Renaissance in Black and White*, 254.

20. Charles C. Alexander, *Here This Country Lies: Nationalism and the Arts in Twentieth Century America* (Bloomington, Ind., 1980), xii.

21. See esp. "The Legacy of the Ancestral Arts," in *The New Negro*. Locke's promotion of an African ancestral legacy in black American culture is one of the most important, and controversial, ideas to emerge from the Harlem Renaissance. For an extensive consideration of this legacy in the visual arts, see David Driskell, et al., *Black Art—Ancestral Legacy: The African Impulse in African-American Art* (Dallas, 1989).

22. While this initiative has proven to be enormously important in the subsequent development of African American art and culture, it was a radical strategy fraught with risk in the interwar decades, especially given the presumption of concrete social and political gains emanating from the Harlem Renaissance climate of cultural renewal. Huggins pointed out that many black Americans were ambivalent and uncertain about the question of what Africa should mean to them; "nor was it easy for some to understand how identification with Africa would win them acceptance as full American citizens." Huggins, *Harlem Renaissance*, 80-81 and 41.

Hutchinson, on the other hand, does not consider this process of identification as incompatible with the values of cultural nationalism: "The desire to 'recapture' the African heritage and promote pan-African consciousness coexists with pride in African American culture as both 'mixed' and uniquely 'American.'" Hutchinson, *The Harlem Renaissance in Black and White*, 184.

23. See Platt, *Modernism in the 1920s*; Petruck, "American Art Criticism: 1910-1939"; and Roosa, "American Art Theory and Criticism During the 1930s."

24. Gary Reynolds's essay "The American Critics and the Harmon Foundation Exhibitions," is an excellent introduction to the critical issues which surrounded art made by African Americans as they were manifest in reviews of the Harmon Foundation Shows. See Reynolds, in *Against the Odds*, 107-119.

Erma Meadows Malloy's dissertation, "African-American Visual Artists and the Harmon Founda-

tion," (New York, 1991), which covers much of the same material, contains useful insights into Harmon's motivation for supporting black achievement, as well as into the consequences of the Foundation's activities. Malloy examines Harmon's ideological stance (developed in conjunction with the Charity Organization Society Movement) as a philanthropist associated with a particular vision of social improvement enacted through the rewarding of individual achievement among disadvantaged peoples (rather than the encouragement of structural change). Her conclusions, that the Harmon Foundation reinforced traditional inequalities of race, wealth and power by constructing the black artist as a distinct category, and then marginalizing his/her work through the promotion of racial themes and a separate black aesthetic, echoes the concerns of contemporary writers such as Wilson, Sims, Conwill and Gaines.

Both Reynolds and Malloy drew extensively on the large collection of press clippings contained in the Harmon Foundation Papers, which also served as the basis for my research. My understanding of the critical reception of African American art has been greatly enriched by their work.

25. Romare Bearden, "The Negro Artist and Modern Art," *Opportunity* (Dec. 1934): 371-372.

26. Lois M. Bull, *New York Evening Graphic*, 15 Dec. 1926, Harmon Foundation Papers, Box 109.

One article on Hayden begins with an admission that the writer knew nothing of the artist's work but presumed that, as a Harmon award winner, it must by worthwhile. The news was clearly the artist's story. "Up From the Depths," *Troy* [New York] *Record*, 9 Dec. 1926, Harmon Foundation Papers, Box 113.

27. Stories about Hayden's and Woodruff's departures for Europe were used as opportunities to plug the awards program, thus creating anticipation for the following year.

Woodruff, winner of the second place award in 1926, set sail for Europe in September 1927. Descriptions of his trip were more specific to his artistic goals, such as his desire to study the old masters and attend the Academy Julien in Paris. Although he too had worked as a janitor, Woodruff's formal training diminished the potential to exploit his story for a human interest angle. Also, his trip was partly financed by the sale of his own pictures, in combination with outside support from the Harmon Foundation award and Otto Kahn.

See especially the *New York Sun*, 3 Sept. 1927, Harmon Foundation Papers, Box 109.

28. Brawley's action received extensive press coverage in reports on the Harmon Awards for 1927. See Harmon Foundation Papers, Box 110.

29. In 1928, John T. Hailstalk emerged as another popular amateur. Hailstalk's "discovery" by a New York dealer was widely publicized in articles with headlines such as "Negro Novice Wins Over Noted Artists; Elevator Man's Painting First Sold."

The papers recounted an exchange between dealer Thomas Russel and Hailstalk who, in his capacity as handyman, had on occasion carried paintings from the elevator into the gallery where Russel worked. Having seen some of the modernist works exhibited in the gallery, Hailstalk allegedly claimed he could do better, even though he had never picked up a brush. Russel challenged him to make good on this claim, and Hailstalk proceeded to paint a country landscape in what Russel later described as a "primitive" style. Russel stated that Hailstalk had "out-moderned the moderns;" he placed the painting on display in the gallery with works by John Singer Sargent and other well known professional artists, then sold it to a collector interested in children's art.

This exchange capitalized on the common conflation of the primitive with the modern, and the philistine view of modern art as a hoax. But the end result was condescension to Hailstalk as an "un-schooled" amateur, who, although preferred to the professional, is of interest largely as a curiosity.

30. For articles from the mainstream press which contain fairly extensive discussions of the nature and promise of emergent African American art in response to the Harmon show of 1928, often seemingly informed directly by Locke's ideas, see esp. Ivy Achoy, "International House Gives Modern Negro Artist a Stage Upon Which to Display His Craft," *New York World,* 15 Jan. 1928, Harmon Foundation Papers, Box 110; Edward Allen Jewell, "A Negro Artist Plumbs the Negro Soul: Motley's Vivid Paintings are Weirdly Influenced by Racial Tradition," *New York Times Magazine,* 25 Mar. 1928, 8+; Worth Tuttle, "Negro Artists are Developing True Racial Art," *New York Times,* 9 Sep. 1928, 10.

These issues were also addressed by writers for the black press who followed the Harmon shows. See esp. Gwendolyn B. Bennett, "The American Negro Paints," *Southern Workman,* March 1928, Harmon Foundation Papers, Box 110.

31. Many of the respondents were prominent literary figures such as Langston Hughes, Countee Cullen, Walter White, Jessie Faucet, Sherwood Anderson, Sinclair Lewis and Carl Van Vechten.

32. George Schuyler, "The Negro Art Hokum," *The Nation* 122 (16 June 1926), 662-663 and Langston Hughes, "The Negro Artist and the Racial Mountain," *The Nation* 122 (28 June 1926), 692-694.

33. F. L. K., "American Negroes as Artists," Survey 60 (1 Sept. 1928), 548-549.

34. Fred Gardner, "Negro Art at International House," *New York Amsterdam News,* 29 Feb. 1928, Harmon Foundation Papers, Box 64.

35. George P. Haynes, "Negro Art at International House," *New York Amsterdam News,* 14 Mar. 1928, quoted from a typescript of Haynes reply, Harmon Foundation Papers, Box 64.

36. Reynolds, "American Critics and the Harmon Foundation," 108.

37. Coverage in the black press of the successful sculptors Elizabeth Prophet and Augusta Savage, both of whom struggled against overt racism in their efforts to obtain artistic training, exemplifies this outlook. In an article entitled "Can I become a Sculptor? The Story of Elizabeth Prophet," the author describes the artist's triumph over adversity and concludes:

> Miss Prophet has not finished her work. She has scarcely begun it: but she stands today as one of the most promising figures in American sculpture without regard to color or race,

and as such she should be an inspiration to every American artist, who handicapped by color, is turned aside by poverty and prejudice. Only remember this thing. Elizabeth Prophet never whined or made excuses for herself. She worked. She never submitted to patronage, cringed to the great, or begged of the small. She worked. She is still working.

(Crisis 39 [Oct. 1932], p. 315)

38. Baker, *Modernism and the Harlem Renaissance.*

39. This remains one of the most troubling issues in terms of mainstream considerations of black artists. See, for example, Conwill, "In Search of an 'Authentic' Vision: Decoding the Appeal of the Self-Taught African American Artist," and Cornel West, "Horace Pippin's Challenge to Art Criticism," in *Keeping Faith: Philosophy and Race in America* (New York, 1993)

40. Scholarly opinion as to whether or not the Harmon Foundation deliberately promoted essentialist notions of a black aesthetic is by no means uniform. Reynolds stressed Haynes' belief in the universality of artistic standards, embodied in the make up of the juries for the awards. But the Foundation literature sent mixed and even conflicting messages. They were concerned about the technical proficiency of African American artists but also aware that their greatest potential for stimulating interest in "Negro art" was to identify it as distinctive.

Molloy states unequivocally that the Foundation actively encouraged its exhibiting artists to make characteristically racial art and certainly Locke's close association with the Foundation supports this. However, Harmon Foundation catalogs and publicity materials represented both the universalist and essentialist positions, and sometimes placed them in conversation. Press packets for the traveling shows, for example, included quotes from reviews of past exhibitions in which both the affirmation of characteristically racial artistic qualities and the mastery of prevailing conventions are mutually acknowledged.

41. R. L. Duffus, *The American Renaissance* (New York, 1928). African American artists seem to have sought a compromise position in this debate about the value of training. In an interview with the Boston press on the occasion of an exhibition of her work at Vose Gallery, Elizabeth Prophet affirmed her belief in the eventual triumph of innate ability, but also stressed the importance of sound training: "It is foolish to talk of the danger of destroying talent by training." "Sculpture That Has Something To Say," *Boston Sunday Herald,* 6 Nov. 1932, Harmon Foundation Papers, Box 119.

Augusta Savage, who was noted for her work as an art educator in the context of her own studio and the Harlem Community Art Center, stressed the need to teach young art students the essentials without allowing academic conventions to rob their work of its freshness. "Exhibition of Negro Art at Adult Education Project in Harlem YWCA," *New York Herald Tribune,* 15 Feb. 1935, Harmon Foundation Papers, Box 120.

Although the programs of the Harlem Community Art Center were very successful and have been widely acknowledged for their contribution to the development of modern African American art, in press coverage of community art centers established to nurture black artistic talent, racial difference tended to be both essentialized and celebrated, as well-meaning teachers described their efforts to cultivate "native" sensibilities. This was especially true when (unlike in Harlem) the art centers were staffed primarily by white instructors. The object was to rid students of reliance on established convention and thus work which displayed pronounced racial qualities generated great satisfaction among instructors who professed that:

> These people have as distinctive an art-taste as the Egyptians and Greeks. It is our belief they can express it in other arts as beautifully as they have in their music. We believe they can develop it best unhindered by the formalities of technique. If they were taught to paint according to rules, the important thing, the representation of an object as viewed emotionally, would be thwarted and eventually would be become impossible. Hence, except for basic points, we do not advise them about their drawings.
> Richard Amerycke, "Art on Plain Paper," *Richmond-Times Dispatch,* Sunday Magazine Section, 6 Mar. 1938, Harmon Foundation Papers, Box 105.

42. The bibliography of primitivism is vast. For a discussion of the intersection in the early twentieth century of the ideologies of the primitive and the folk as they were brought to bear on African American art, see esp. Eugene Metcalf, "Black Art, Folk Art and Social Control," *Winterthur Portfolio* 18 (winter 1983): 271-289

43. One exception to Jewell's typical remonstrations of black artists for failing to cultivate their uniqueness was his admiration for the work of Albert Alexander Smith. In a 1929 review, he referred to Smith alternately as an "American painter" and a "Negro painter" of extraordinary talent, who has been influenced by Velasquez without sacrificing his originality. Although some of Smith's best work dealt with racial themes, Jewell remarked that he did not restrict himself to such themes for "he is first an artist" and "the wide earth is his theater." "To Suit Many Tastes," *The New York Times,* 6 Jan. 1929, Harmon Foundation Papers, Box 121.

44. Jewell, "An Artist Plumbs the Negro Soul: Motley's Vivid Paintings are Weirdly Influenced by Racial Tradition," 8.

45. Ibid., 22. Jontyle Robinson has noted that Jewell was alone among New York critics in appreciating the artist's desire to forge cultural links between African ancestral heritage and modern black culture, a major theme of the Harlem Renaissance. Jontyle Theresa Robinson, "The Life of Archibald J. Motley, Jr.," in *The Art of Archibald J. Motley, Jr.* (Chicago, 1991), 12-13.

46. Leon Whipple, "Letters and Life," *Survey* 56 (1 Aug. 1926): 517-519. *Survey* had close ties to the New Negro movement; Locke's anthology grew out of a special issue on African Americans which had originally appeared in the journal.

47. Ibid., 518. Not surprisingly, this nostalgia for the "old Negro" was especially pronounced in the south. A writer for an Alabama paper offered the following commentary on "The Old Servant" by Edwin Harleston:

> such an old figure upon which we gaze with dimming eyes because we know she is a remnant of a by-gone era—loyal, gentle, faithful—toil-warn hands lying in her lap— hands that have gentle in many ministrations—and an old bosom on which perhaps little white heads have lain. As we look we can almost hear a quavering sweet voice which may have sung to the slow rock of a chair, 'Go to Sleep, Mammy's Lil Baby Boy.
> (Emma L. Roche, "Negro Painters' Work Shown in Mobile Exhibit," *Mobile Register,* 26 July 1931, Harmon Foundation Papers, Box 118)

48. Press release dated 7 Jan. 1929, Harmon Foundation Papers, Box 66.

49. "'Swing Low, Sweet Chariot' Will Be Popular," *Art Digest* 3 (Jan. 1929): 5-6.

50. *The New York Times,* 12 Jan. 1930, Harmon Foundation Papers, Box 116.

51. *The New York Times,* 6 May 1934, sec. 9, p. 7. These sentiments were shared by William Auerbach-Levy, who wrote:

> If not a great artist by a standard which does not take account of the temperamental differences of race, then one may at least hope for signs of greatness, of originality and strong feelings in Negro terms. But, with one exception, the work is disappointingly like canvases at any ordinary art show. There is the same imitation of this or that school.
> ("Negro Painters Imitate Whites," *New York World,* 5 Jan. 1930, Harmon Foundation Papers, Box 116)

On occasion such comments functioned as a springboard for editorializing on race relations. A writer for the *Oakland Tribune* observed that it was still too dangerous for African Americans to be unguarded in their self-expression:

> Some who have viewed the exhibit have expressed disappointment that a distinct Negro school of art was not represented instead of simply universal art. In answer to this question, the writer will state that when the American public will begin to treat the American Negro citizens everywhere as human beings, and will cease to lynch either his body or spirit and cease to treat or speak of the Negro as a joke, then the unfettered soul of the Negro will unloose itself and give to the world a masterpiece of art and music.
> (*Oakland Tribune,* 23 Nov. 1930, Harmon Foundation Papers, Box 116)

52. Jewell, *The New York Times,* 12 Jan. 1930, Harmon Foundation Papers, Box 116; Stanley Olrnsted, "Student Art Exhibit to be Continued," *Washington Herald,* 8 June 1930, Harmon Foundation Papers, Box 116.

53. Albert Franz Cochrane, "Art of American Negro at Library," *Boston Evening Transcript,* 9 Apr. 1930, Harmon Foundation Papers, Box 116.

54. Terry Cooney's characterization of the ideological contradictions of the decade as a "balancing act" is especially apt here:

> The image of the 1930s as a decade when writers and artists turned toward politics and the people draws attention to a number of

important strains in the cultural life of the period. . . . Especially during the second half of the thirties, strains of radicalism, documentary recording, and nationalistic feeling became intertwined in sometimes improbable ways, helping to mold and to confuse lingering impressions of the decade.

(Terry A. Cooney, *Balancing Acts: American Thought and Culture in the 1930s* [New York: 1995], 130)

55. Baigell, *The American Scene Movement,* 18.

56. For a discussion of the chronic impulse to simplify Regionalist art and politics, see esp. James M. Dennis, *Renegade Regionalist* (Madison, Wisc., 1998); Erica Doss, *Benton, Pollock and the Politics of Modernism* (Chicago, 1991), and Cecile Whiting, *Antifascism in American Art* (New Haven, Conn., 1989).

57. As Charles Alexander explains:

In retrospect what seems most striking about the intellectual-artistic 1920s is not a general disinterest in politics and ideology but an enormous diversity and fecundity, an intense occupation with the full realization of the creative potential of both individuals and the whole society. The post-World War I decade, it now becomes clear, featured a continuing ardent quest for a rich and recognizable American culture.

(Alexander, *Here This Country Lies,* p. 153)

58. Baigell, "American Art and National Identity: The 1920s," 48.

59. Selma Day, "Harmon Art Exhibit in New York High Class," *Pittsburgh Courier,* 7 Mar. 31, Harmon Foundation Papers, Box 118.

60. Susan Noyes Platt observes that as a critic, Thomas Craven, for example, was less preoccupied with broad theorizing about American culture than with the reconciliation of an American artistic form and content. This was also true of Locke, whose theorizing about emergent Negro art, or what he called a "racial idiom of expression," addresses (but does not effect) such a reconciliation. Although he defined Negro art as "the proper development of the Negro subject as an artistic theme," the terms of classification he employs are largely stylistic. See Locke, *Negro Art: Past and Present* (Washington, D.C., 1936), 12. I am grateful to Susan Noyes Platt for making available to me in manuscript form portions of her book on American art criticism in the 1930s, *Art and Politics in the 1930s: Modernism, Marxism and Americanism: A History of Cultural Activism During the Depression Years* (New York, 1999). In this work, Locke's cultural criticism receives careful consideration as both participant in, and distinct from, the dominant discourses of the period.

Most of the cultural movements of the interwar decades suffered from this chronic failure to make coherent connections between form and content. In this intensified political climate, proletarian art, Regionalism, Social Realism, Negro art, Popular Front art and the New Deal, were united in what they opposed but too woefully divided by conflicting priorities and agendas to arrive at a reasonably concise vision of what form the most desirable or representative art should take.

61. Locke, "The American Negro as Artist," *American Magazine of Art* 23 (Sept. 1931): 210-220, quote 215.

62. Michael Denning has challenged conventional wisdom that the romantic populism of the Popular Front represented a capitulation to majority sentiments that brought about the eventual collapse of radical politics in the United States. To embrace this view, Denning argues, is to confuse populist rhetoric with populist politics: "There was not a radical break between the 'proletarian movement' of the early 1930s and the Popular Front; the politics of the Popular Front was not populist, but remained a class-based labor politics." By linking his analysis to the labor movement rather than nationalism, Denning credits the Popular Front with an enduring legacy that most historians have denied. Michael Denning, *Cultural Front: The Laboring of American Culture in the Twentieth Century* (London, 1996), 124-125.

63. James, Porter, "Negro Art on Review," *American Magazine of Art* 27 (Jan. 1934): 33-38. In the ensuing years, Porter will become one of the most vocal critics of Locke's Africanist position. For a discussion of Porter's distinguished career as a painter, teacher and pioneer historian of African American art, see Starmanda Bullock Featherstone, et al., *James A. Porter, Artist and Art Historian: The Memory of the Legacy* (Washington, D.C., 1992).

64. Meyer Schapiro, "Race, Nationality and Art," *Art Front* 2 (Mar. 1936): 10-12. For further analysis of the *Art Front* assault on Regionalism see Dennis, Baigell, and Whitting.

65. Ibid., 10. For further discussion of Schapiro's contributions to *Art Front* see Patricia Hills, "1936: Meyer Schapiro, Art Front and the Popular Front," *The Oxford Art Journal* 17 (winter 1994): 30-31.

66. James A. Porter, "The Negro Artist and Racial Bias," *Art Front* 3 (June-July 1937): 8-9. For Locke's response to these comments see his letter to the editor, *Art Front* 3 (Oct. 1937): 19-20.

For further discussion of these exchanges in *Art Front* and their importance in terms of familiarizing Americans interested in the visual arts with issues of central concern to African American artists, see Bearden and Henderson, *A History of African American Artists,* 232-234.

67. In *Negro Art: Past and Present,* Locke also emphasized the importance of acquiring a historical perspective before judging the accomplishments of black artists in terms of an ancestral legacy which had been virtually destroyed by slavery. The African American artist seeks to recapture his ancestral gifts "in the medium and manner of his adopted civilization and the modern techniques of painting, sculpture and the craft arts. But when this development finally matures, it may be expected to reflect something of the original endowment, if not as a carry-over of instinct then at least as a formal revival of historical memory and the proud inspiration of the reconstructed past" (*Negro Art: Past and Present,* 5).

Debates about the existence of a "black aesthetic," which often turn on the presumption or disavowal of an African cultural legacy, are deeply embedded with racial politics. As Lowery Sims points out: "Within the African American community itself the acceptance or denial of distinct aesthetic values and canons based on race or national origin correlated with long-standing debates over assimilationist or separatist stances with regard to American society as a whole" (Sims, "Subject/Subjectivity and Agency in the Art of African Americans," 588).

68. Locke was very aware of the fact that while African Americans had played a relatively prominent role in the cultural politics of the 1920s, their position in the 1930s ran the risk of becoming less central as the grounds shifted first to revolutionary politics and later to celebrations of generic Americanism. He was convinced that blacks would have their greatest chance to stake a cultural claim within the latter. Looking back on the dual tendencies throughout the decade towards Regionalism and what he called "Proletarian realism," Locke wrote:

> The former of course is more congenial to the retention of the notion of racial idioms; the latter, over-simplifying the situation in my judgement, discounts and ignores almost completely in its emphasis on class status and class psychology, the idioms of race.
> (Locke, "The Negro's Contribution to American Culture," *Journal of Negro Education* 8 [July 1939]: 521-529, quoted from Jeffrey C. Stewart, ed., *The Critical Temper of Alain Locke* [New York, 1983], 454)

69. Jeffrey C. Stewart, *The Critical Temper of Alain Locke: A Selection of His Essays on Art and Culture,* xix.

70. Locke, "The African Legacy and the Negro Artist," in *Exhibition of the Work of Negro Artists* (New York, 1931), 12.

71. Locke, "The Negro Takes His Place in American Art," in *Exhibition of Productions by Negro Artists* (New York, 1933). Bearden and Henderson explain the changes in these Harmon catalog essays as a response to anxiety, on the part of Foundation administrators, that advocacy of Africanism would be perceived as tantamount to black nationalism. They also claim that Locke wanted to reassure black artists that his argument need not be understood as a restrictive mandate. Bearden and Henderson, *A History of African American Artists,* 245.

In *Negro Art: Past and Present,* published in 1936, Locke's Africanist and Americanist arguments are given equal weight in an extensive chronicle of black art which also includes discussion of African tribal art and European modernism.

72. "[T]he question of distinctive racial idiom or aptitude is purely theoretical and academic until such broad scale comparisons can actually be made."

In 1939 Locke reiterated these sentiments when he wrote: "In art it is color not the color line that counts; and that not so much the hue of the author as the complexion of the idiom." Locke also makes reference in this essay to an emerging model of African American cultural hybridity that is expanding the study of racial expression to include a greater diversity of influences from within the black diaspora. Locke, "The Negro's Contribution to American Culture," quoted from Stewart, *The Critical Temper of Alain Locke,* 454.

The recent work of historian Richard J. Powell manifests a similar vision in its emphasis on racial expression in twentieth-century art that has arisen from a constellation of individuals who are neither exclusively black nor American. See esp. Powell, *Black Art*

*and Culture in the Twentieth Century* (London, 1997); *Rhapsodies in Black: Art of the Harlem Renaissance* (Los Angeles, 1997); and *The Blues Aesthetic: Black Culture and Modernism* (Washington, D.C., 1989).

73. Locke would have preferred integrated exhibitions, but he continued to believe that all-black shows were important until such things could be realized. He was involved in the organization of a number of important Negro art exhibitions at the end of the decade and complained when the large expositions in New York and San Francisco did not have them.

74. One such exception was the exhibition of 1935 "An Art Commentary on Lynching." For a discussion of this exhibition and the attending political context see Marlene Park, "Lynching and Antilynching: Art and Politics in the 1930s," *Prospects* 18 (1993): 311-365.

The inconsistencies of promise and practice with respect to racial inclusiveness in the federal art programs have remained largely unexamined in the art historical literature on the New Deal era. Jonathan Harris, for example, asserts that in project discourse "'Negro,' 'citizen,' and 'artist' were terms of equivalence." In the interest of sustaining the ideological hegemony of New Deal reform and populist nationalism, a conciliatory rhetoric of "difference without antagonism" prevailed in discussion of race. Jonathan Harris, *Federal Art and National Culture: The Politics of Identity in New Deal America* (New York, 1995), 51

But in practical reality, antagonism did exist between the interests of black participants in these programs and those responsible for administering them. While historians of African American art tend to agree on the positive outcome of the projects from the standpoint of providing encouragement and financial support for black artists, Rena Fraden argues that presumptions of equality guaranteed by their democratic spirit and anti-discriminatory policies were by no means taken for granted. Rena Fraden, "Feels Good, Can't Hurt: Black Representation on the Federal Arts Projects," *Journal of American Culture* 10 (winter 1987), 21-29.

On black artists and the federal art projects see Ruth Ann Stewart, *New York/Chicago: WPA and the Black Artist* (New York, 1977), *Black Artists in the WPA, 1933-1943* (Brooklyn, N.Y., 1976); Leslie King-Hammond, *Black Printmakers and the WPA* (New York, 1989), *Alone in a Crowd: Prints of the 1930s-1940s by African Americans From the Collection of Reba and Dave Williams* (New York, 1993), and David R. Brigham, "Bridging Identities: Dox Thrash as an African American and Artist," *Smithsonian Studies in American Art* 4 (spring 1990): 27-39.

For insight into myths of objectivity and egalitarianism in New Deal art, see also Karal Ann Marling, *Wall-to-Wall: A Cultural History of Post-Office Murals in the Great Depression* (Minneapolis, Minn., 1982); Helen Langa, "Egalitarian Vision, Gendered Experience: Women Printmakers and the WPA/FAP Graphic Arts Project," in *The Expanding Discourse: Feminism and Art History,* eds. Norma Broude and Mary Garrard (New York, 1992); and Barbara Melosh, *Manhood and Womanhood in New Deal Art and Theater* (Washington, D.C., 1991).

75. On the role of historically black colleges in the exhibition and development of modern African American art see Keith Morrison, *Art in Washington and Its Afro-*

*American Presence: 1940-1970* (Washington, D.C., 1985); and Floyd Coleman, "Black Colleges and the Development of an African American Visual Arts Tradition," *International Review of African American Art* 11 (fall 1994): 31-38.

76. Edward Alden Jewell, *Have We An American Art* (New York, 1939).

77. Locke, foreword, *Contemporary Negro Art* (Baltimore, Md., 1939), n.p.

78. Ibid.

79. Richard H. Pells, *Radical Visions and American Dreams: Culture and Social Thought in the Depression Years* (New York, 1973), 38.

80. *Negro Art: Past and Present*, 120. Locke's remarks were made in reference to Cahill's introduction to *New Horizons in American Art* (New York, 1936).

81. Locke, foreword, *Contemporary Negro Art*.

## PAINTERS

### AARON DOUGLAS WITH L. M. COLLINS (INTERVIEW DATE 1971)

**SOURCE:** Douglas, Aaron with L. M. Collins. "Aaron Douglas Chats about the Harlem Renaissance." In *The Portable Harlem Renaissance Reader,* edited by David Levering Lewis, pp. 118-27. New York: Viking, 1994.

*In the following interview, originally conducted in 1971 and published in* Black Oral Histories, *Douglas remembers the Harlem Renaissance, discussing his thoughts about the movement's publications, personalities, and aims, as well as about the composition of some of his own art works.*

*Aaron Douglas's career was a classic illustration of the meld of civil rights and the arts. Charles S. Johnson, editor of* Opportunity, *recruited Douglas from a Kansas City high-school teaching position to serve as the painter of the movement. After a period of tutelage under Winold Reiss, Douglas produced for books and magazines canvases, murals, and illustrations distinguished by geometrical motifs depicting the progress from antiquity to modern times of African peoples. Like Hughes, Douglas was drawn into the patronage empire of "Godmother," the formidable Charlotte Osgood Mason. His close association with the hugely influential Johnson, as well as his considerable talent, enabled him to obtain a fellowship at the Barnes Foundation, another for study in Paris, and eventually the chairmanship of the art department of Fisk University. Douglas and his wife, Alta, knew everyone involved in the Harlem Renaissance, black and white, interesting and influential, destitute and deviant. Their Harlem apartment was one of the principal gathering spots. "Aaron Douglas Chats about the Harlem Renaissance," excerpted from a tape-recorded interview with Leslie Collins, professor of English at Fisk, is a memoir both analytically and anecdotally rich—a candid assessment of the era by the distinguished artist at the end of his career.*

Self-portrait by Aaron Douglas.

[Leslie Collins]: *Mr. Douglas, as a participant in the Harlem Renaissance, what would you say was the best moment of the times, the most memorable?*

[Aaron Douglas]: Well, that isn't easy to say. There are *so many* things that I had seen for the first time, so many impressions I was getting. One was that of seeing a big city that was entirely black, from beginning to end you were impressed by the fact that black people were in charge of things and here was a black city and here was a situation that was eventually to be the center for the great in American Culture.

*What was the Renaissance to you? How would you define it?*

It was a cultural experience; in a sense, a sort of spiritual experience. Actually it was difficult to put your hands on it, because it wasn't something that the people actually understood as *really* a thing of great importance; they had the feeling that something was going on and we acknowledged that this perhaps was something unique and destined in American black-white relationships, this touched upon the experience of black people in America, but to get hold of anything particular is difficult to realize—to achieve. So, it was only later that you had the feeling that here was something of importance to us and something that had the possibility of being a base for greater development in the future.

*What of the man on the streets? Was he aware of anything on the way, any spiritual value being pursued by a person such as yourself, Arna Bontemps, and, earlier, James Weldon Johnson and in the Renaissance through his* God's Trombones? *Did he feel that all of you were part of a literary scheme or literary mood?*

I doubt that that is true. My feeling is that the man in the street actually had no thoughts upon this thing as being a matter of importance to black and white, that it was a matter of cultural importance. As a matter of fact, if you had asked him about culture, he would have been hard-put to explain it at all, certainly to explain the black man's part in it. But he was a part of it, although he didn't understand this thing—he did not actually, consciously make a contribution; he made his contribution in an unconscious way. He was the thing on which and around which this whole idea was developed. And from that standpoint it seems to me his contribution is greater than if he had attempted consciously to make a contribution. The inner thing that came from him that some were able to understand and some of us, I believe, consciously understood (we who understand that sort of thing)—and that's the thing that made it unique, in my estimation.

*Then the Harlemite, the man on the street, was an unconscious participant, was he not?*

Yes, he was a participant. He didn't put his hands on anything. He didn't mold anything, excepting the thing was being emitted, something was coming out of him which the various artists responded to, could get hold of and make something that was later known as the Harlem Renaissance.

*What, then, is your response to those critics who from the long view of the 60's and 70's say that those blacks who participated in the Harlem Renaissance were special beings enjoying white patronage, doll-like creatures who were manipulated and maneuvered?*

To the contrary. Participants never felt like that, I do not think. Of course, I personally never felt that was true. One aspect is certain and I think we might as well acknowledge it that there were certain white people at that time that came in contact with blacks and helped make it possible for them to reach a level from which they could create, but it was *not* something dictated by white culture. It stemmed from Black culture. We were constantly working on this innate blackness at that time that made this whole thing important and unique. And in no way do I think that we should have any feeling of being talked down to

or talked into things that they had no share in, that is to say, were given certain things and were simply manipulated and so on. I think that there's no reason that idea should be maintained.

*In your estimation, how did* The Crisis *differ from* Opportunity *as a medium for the expression of younger Black authors and artists such as yourself? You were an active participant in the Renaissance with your sketches, with your illustrations for a number of dramatic moments such as James Weldon Johnson's* The Creation, *which through the years has been a beloved piece of literature both for its verse and illustrations. What, first of all, is your feeling about* The Crisis? *Did it make a different kind of offer to you as an artist than* Opportunity *did? I'm thinking now that* The Crisis *was under the aegis of Du Bois and* Opportunity *under the editorship of Charles S. Johnson.*

Well, this idea might have emerged in other fields of art, but the field of plastic art was in a unique position in that there was almost no background; we had no tradition. Everything was done . . . almost for the first time, let us say, and we were so hungry at that time for something that was specifically black that they were perfectly willing to accept almost anything. I say that because as I look back at the things that I produced, it was so readily received and cheerfully received. You wonder how they could have done it! I look at it and wonder how I could have done it. And next, could there have been a group to receive it, who were willing to receive it? And although the illustrations were definitely very primitive, very unskillful, the certain drawings that I did at that time were received and I was encouraged and I went on from that to other things.

*Then* The Crisis *as the official journal of the NAACP was no different to you than* Opportunity *magazine was as the official organ of the Urban League?*

Not really . . . They never refused anything that I did. They accepted it; they put it forward. As a matter of fact, Du Bois once carried my name on *The Crisis* as the art editor. I'm sure he had his tongue in his cheek, but he was willing to do that, you see. And I've always been grateful to him for it, because it increased my motivation. I was encouraged to go on feeling that I should some day really become *worthy* of that sort of thing. My feeling was that I should go on and be worthy of the distinction that Dr. Du Bois conferred upon me.

*Then you are saying that Dr. Du Bois did exert an influence on you?*

In sponsorship, yes. If he hadn't done anything else, even that, what he had meant to me, for a young person reading his editorials way back when I was at an early age in the beginning of high school—beautiful things . . . the inspiration from those things was enough to make me realize the importance of any kind of association with this man.

*Was he ever critical of you as an artist? Did he ever suggest a political angle that you might have emphasized graphically?*

Yes.

*At the beginning point of your career and earlier as a young boy spiritually and philosophically?*

Yes. Yes. Tremendously.

*Now, what about Charles S. Johnson, as editor of* Opportunity? . . . *Do you suppose he was endowed especially to help in a first step or that he was just singularly endowed with a certain kind of intuitive ingenuity to spot talent?*

I suppose the both. I suppose he was, of course, a man of broad vision. But specifically, he understood how to make the way, how to indicate the next step for many of these young people at that time and make it possible for them to go on to other things.

*In other words, he established contacts?*

Yes, that's it. For instance, I met Carl Van Vechten through Charles Johnson. I met Dorothy Barnes and I went on to the Barnes Foundation through Dr. Johnson. As a matter of fact, many years passed before I was out of the real influence of Dr. Johnson. . . .

*What are your recollections of James Weldon Johnson at this time? So many of the analysts and the critics refer to him as an "elder statesman" of the Renaissance. Were you aware very deeply of his presence as an associate or as an acquaintance in this period?*

Yes, naturally you knew his earlier life and his association with the stage and that sort of thing and you've read about his work with the NAACP and he had done marvelous work and was a national figure in that respect. But then this artistic aspect of it is something that was coming on. He was a man of great culture and one that was quite capable of inspiring younger men to go on in this field and to attempt to do something *worthy* of the opportunities and worthy of those who had gone before them or those who are actively engaged in this work.

*Were you conscious of his seeming lifetime creed that the Negro had a genius, that the Black man in America possessed a genius and that he had been and was responding to that genius?*

Unconsciously, I must have been. Unconsciously. I don't remember now that attitude, that idea in respect to Johnson as I was in respect to Du Bois. Yet, Johnson had been actively working in the field much more so that Du Bois, because Du Bois was a scientist. His work was in sociology, history, and so on and so on, but Johnson had been actively engaged in the creative side of Negro life in the theater, in music, and so. And when he met me in the hall one day and asked me if I would . . . like to undertake some illustrations for [Johnson's book of poems *God's Trombones*], I was, of course, totally pleased. . . . And so I accepted the challenge and went on to do the sort of thing that we see, which didn't please me at the *time*. It was the best that I could do, I suppose, with the time I had, with the development I had. But I had the feeling that eventually I would be able to do something much more adequate with the material because I was and I am very much impressed with the enormous power, spiritual power that's behind Negro life and it's . . . if it can be mined, it's a gold mine if you can write or draw it. . . .

*What was his response to your illustrations?*

He was very enthusiastic about them. Apparently, it was just the sort of thing he wanted. He urged me to go on with the rest of them when I finished one of them and I went on to finish the work.

*Well, you created a graphic phasing of the black man, did you not, that became rather a signature of yours?*

Yes. There's a certain artistic pattern that I follow . . . I used the Egyptian form, that is to say, the head was in perspective in a profile flat view, the body, shoulders down to the waist turned half way, the legs were done also from the side and the feet were also done in a broad perspective. . . . The only thing that I did that was not specifically taken from the Egyptians was an eye . . . so you saw it in three dimensions. I avoided the three dimension and that's another thing that made it sort of unique artistically. . . .

*One of the interpreters of the new impulse of the time was Dr. Alain Locke, who, it is said, phased the period the Negro Renaissance or Harlem Renaissance. . . . I was wondering if you as a young artist had come in contact with Dr. Locke and if you were aware of his being cognizant of your own contributions?*

Well, I think so very much. I was sort of the fair-headed boy for this reason, not because the work was, I suppose, so important (they couldn't have known that), but I was the first one to give this thing something of a Negro content. They had the feeling this isn't something that was done by a caucasian person. This is a black person. Here at last it is a black person doing this thing. He isn't criticizing his people; he isn't placing them in a situation that they would not normally *have*; he isn't trying to exalt them and you would see that in many of these things. I was very careful to associate my figures so that they looked like the working people, see. You would not confuse them with the aspiring middle-upper-class, not that I had any antagonism, but that I felt that here is the essence of this Negro thing, here among these people. So I tried to keep it there with simple devices, such as giving the clothing, any clothing, giving—sometimes giving it ragged edges, you know, so as to keep the thing realistic. . . .

*How did Wallace Thurman organize you and Langston Hughes and Zora Neale Hurston? What did he say to you about* Fire!! *in order to get it started, in order to get you writing and drawing to produce this magazine? Both of you had no money and you knew it to be rather an adventure that in a measure became a misadventure, but did anything deter you at all? Were you always this enthusiastic?*

Oh, yes. Oh certainly. We were so enthusiastic that we forgot that there was such a thing as . . . these things were run with money. And that we knew what we wanted. We wanted a magazine to express our ideas, to set forth our ideas. . . . Putting out a magazine was, well, just *fantastic,* I mean fantastic that we could only put out the whole of Negro life. We could only put out two magazines that I know of. Two or three. The *Messenger,* of course, the labor was so definitely behind the *Messenger.* I suppose the money that went into that was so definitely *there.* That, everybody could see. And *The Crisis, Opportunity,* but that's for the whole of Negro life,—two or three little magazines. And we, just a little bunch of us, were daring enough to come forth with a thing like that. It was outrageous, outlandish and everything else for us to do that.

*But nevertheless stimulating.*

Oh, well, certainly we thought that was the greatest thing.

*Why* Fire!!*?*

Well, I guess it was the uninhibited spirit that is behind life. I suppose that is what we meant by

that. I don't remember it ever being *spelled out!* But certainly that must have been the feeling behind it. . . .

*And that experience was one of the memorable moments for you in the Harlem Renaissance?*

Oh, yes. Of course, I had previously seen these things done in *Opportunity* magazine. In *The Crisis* magazine which I had been with almost a year or more. These things had come out. Some good, some serviceable, and some of them never should have been produced, but they grabbed them up and published them. As I say, I look at these things and wonder if they could have been any use to anybody, but I wasn't their editor then. They were happy to have these things. Sure, there were other artists. There were plenty good artists, but they didn't have this feeling. . . .

*Today, the black college student is extraordinarily fascinated by the Renaissance and its people, its time. . . . Have you any explanation for their excitement by the period?*

I think so. I think they were excited because they found that at that time almost fifty years ago here were some people doing the things that they were interested in doing. That as a matter of fact their function was to pick this thing up and go on with it. We only got it started. We only lit the flame. We only set fire to this thing. But it's their business to take it, magnify it and to carry it on. I think that's the thing that excited them. And the thing that I've always tried to talk to them to infuse in them the feeling not that they were second in this thing, but it was their responsibility first to understand it—and then to take it all. The need is *greater* for them almost than it was for us in the very beginning. Their struggle and their work and their work and their achievement—it *can* be greater as we (struggle through the years) up till now. Here we are, fifty years after—being remembered is something! How many others have been remembered? But here we are. If they take this thing and go on with it, they can be *far* more . . . have a greater place in this thing than what ours was at the very beginning. That's the thing that I'll always try to make them conscious of.

*One of the most pleasant aspects of these extraordinary times of Black assertion is the evident joy that these students take in the Douglas Murals in the Old Fisk Library. . . . Won't you review the story of how the University entered into the contract with you to decorate the walls of the Library with murals?*

It was in 1929 and my wife and I were on our way to Kansas. I was going back after about ten or twelve years away from home. I considered myself sort of a success at that time. I had a contract in my pocket for the book illustrations for Van Vechten's book *Nigger Heaven,* and I was doing a number of jackets. I think I was doing book-jackets for Claude McKay at that time, which was about to be published and I was sort of walking on air. Before I got to Topeka, I got a telegram from Dr. Charles S. Johnson, saying that Dr. [Thomas Elsa] Jones was interested in some murals for Fisk University. . . . Well, to make a long story short, I talked with Dr. Jones. We got the idea. . . . After we drew up a contract, I asked for a certain amount. They couldn't quite see that amount, but we finally ended upon a price that was considerably lower, but it was considerably higher than anything I had ever dreamed of. We went on with that. The contract was signed. When school was out, Dr. Jones said to me, "Look, Mr. Douglas, we have a place up in Canada and I'm going up there with my family for the summer. Now, if you and Mrs. Douglas want to stay here at the Heritage House for the summer, you can have the whole run of the place. And you don't have to pay any rent." It worked out *beautifully.*

Well, anyway, I had my cartoons all ready for the commencement of the work, when everyone was interested, you see. The builders, the people who had to do with the inner part of the Library, the architect and so on, they were all interested in what I was going to do. So some of them, of course, thought I was going to fall on my face and I was too, but I went right on. I was fortunate enough that summer to get some graduates . . . and I had Mr. Edward Harleston who was really our finest portrait painter. He trained under Van Voston and had done a picture of DuPont for the Wilmington people and is now in the state capitol down there, but he was more or less free for that summer. I wrote him and asked if he'd come over and help me. He's the only trained person I had to work with. The other fellows were just fellows who'd never had a brush in their hands. I said, well, you don't have to know anything, just go on and I'll show you. So with these five people we started. . . .

As I said, they expected me to fall on my face, but I had this one single artist and he took charge of the work. I said Mr. Harleston, you just sort of guide this thing. That left me free again. I would come in the mornings, go over and get things started. I had to show Mr. Harleston what I wanted him to do and the whole thing just went along like clockwork. . . .

*Then Charles S. Johnson was instrumental in your getting the commission?*

Oh, definitely so.

*And the murals were completed in what year?*

The summer of 1930 and then up till October 1. Finished in October.

*What was in your mind as you formulated thematic plans for the murals, arriving at the mythological motif in several spots and the African element in others?*

Well, the main part of it was designed as a sort of panorama of the development of Black people in this hemisphere, in the new world. I began in Africa. On the one wall I began with the African life, the animal life and so on, the pyramids in Egypt, and so on, and so on. Then picking it up over on the other side, I have the slave situation and then the emancipation and freedom, and so on. Then I used Fisk as the model or the pattern of the Fisk University as represented by Jubilee Hall. I put in the sun, the rising sun and across that I had a series of graduates from the various facilities of the various sciences and literature and so on as they moved across the walls. But that was the idea from Africa to America to the slave situation, freedom and so on. Now on the other side, on the other walls I used two things: one, the Spiritual as being important or relevant to Negro life and on the other side, the south wall, I used laboring aspects of work. I was thinking of labor has been one of the most important aspects of our development. . . . It isn't grand, but it is important and it is a thing that we should be proud of, because we have that part of our life that has gone into the building of America. Not only of ourselves, but in the building of American life. And it's very worthy. We should always keep that in mind.

## ROMARE BEARDEN AND HARRY HENDERSON (ESSAY DATE 1993)

**SOURCE:** Bearden, Romare and Harry Henderson. "Archibald J. Motley, Jr." In *A History of African American Artists from 1792 to the Present,* pp. 147-56. New York: Pantheon Books, 1993.

*In the following excerpt, Bearden and Henderson describe painter Archibald Motley's work as a "superb, joyous celebration of the vitality of African American life."*

A member of a talented, closely knit African-American family with high aspirations, Archibald J. Motley, Jr., emerged as an artist at a time when Henry Ossawa Tanner was the only widely recognized American artist of African descent. Very different in their techniques and fundamental aesthetic and philosophical concepts, Tanner and Motley demonstrated the range of ability of black artists and the significant change in the attitudes of black Americans that took place between the early 1900s and the 1920s. While Tanner was a more fluent technician, Motley was the first artist to establish the social life of African-Americans in cities as memorable subject matter. Where Tanner turned to mystic religious symbolism to express his feelings, Motley sought to portray the spirit of urban black neighborhoods, usually in a twilight or evening atmosphere.

Today Motley's work is recognized as a superb, joyous celebration of the vitality of urban African-Americans as well as an unparalleled picture of their social activities in the 1920s and early 1930s. His paintings reflect the experiences of a man sensitive to social forces, who turned to the life he knew best for his subject matter. Motley dealt cogently with subject matter that not only most African-American artists during the early 1920s, but most white artists as well, considered undignified for high artistic expression. It was the work of artists such as George Bellows, Glenn Coleman, George Luks, and John Sloan, together with the novels of Upton Sinclair, Theodore Dreiser, and Frank Norris, that turned attention to the world of the American city.

In Motley's paintings there is an intense personal urgency based on his complete conviction of the importance of what he saw. "It is my earnest desire and ambition to express the American Negro honestly and sincerely, neither to add nor detract. . . . [I] believe Negro art is someday going to contribute to our culture, our civilization," Motley said.[1] This belief, making up for some shortcomings in technique, holds one fascinated with his teeming world. The people he portrayed are hurrying, gesturing, going someplace—and rushing to get there. And in this activity his paintings assert something that goes beyond black neighborhood life: it is both a self-respect—a liking of one's self—and a promise of something interesting and good, a promise that ignores the roles to which American society then restricted its black people. In these early paintings Motley directly expressed the deep feelings that underlay the concept of the "New Negro" and made the onlooker wonder how the inherent drama would unfold. In this sense, his work differed profoundly from that of Tanner, whose religious painting had moved Paris a quarter of a century earlier. Motley's characters played jazz, not hymns. "I feel my work is peculiarly American, a sincere personal expression of the age, and I hope a contribution to soci-

ety. . . . [It] is, indeed, a racial expression and one making use of great opportunities which have long been neglected in America. The Negro is part of America and the Negro is part of our great American art," Motley asserted.[2]

Archibald Motley, Sr., and his wife, Mary Huff, became the parents of Archibald, Jr., on October 7, 1891, in New Orleans, where the senior Motley operated a general merchandise store. But eighteen months later threats from white competitors forced his father to abandon his store and the family to begin a search for a new home. They tried Buffalo and St. Louis before settling in Chicago, where his father became a Pullman porter and the family moved into a quiet neighborhood on the West Side. . . .

Young Archibald discovered at an early age that he had an unusual gift for drawing. He compulsively filled his school tablets with sketches. By the time he reached high school, he had become convinced that he could do nothing else and told his father to give up ideas of his becoming a doctor. He resolutely pursued his goal of becoming an artist. . . .

His father, who was in charge of a buffet Pullman car on a famous train, the Wolverine, considered art "risky" and suggested architecture to Archibald as a field that was more "practical." One of his father's frequent Wolverine guests was Dr. Frank Gunsaulus, then head of the Armour Institute (now the Illinois Institute of Technology). On learning of Archibald's interests, Gunsaulus offered him a four-year scholarship in architecture at the Armour Institute. Years later Motley recalled, "I told him no, that I'd never make an architect. I said, 'I want to do something completely out of my soul, out of my mind.'" Appreciating such determination, Gunsaulus agreed to pay for Archibald's first year at the Art Institute of Chicago.

Motley began his formal training at the Art Institute of Chicago before World War I. After the first year he gained a tuition-paying job—dusting statuary; moving chairs, podiums, and easels; and doing other tasks. This work and other odd jobs, plus twenty-five cents a day from his father, enabled him to stay for four years. At the institute Motley formed a close, lifelong friendship with two other young aspiring artists, Joseph Tonanek and William Schwartz, later well-known Chicago artists.

Motley encountered none of the prejudice at the institute that plagued many young black artists. As he recalled later: "I was treated with the greatest respect, not only by the faculty but by the students as well." There were a few other African-American students at the institute at the time, including Charles C. Dawson, William McKnight Farrow, and William Edouard Scott. . . .

Motley's education was considerably broadened during the summer vacation of 1917, when his father got him a job as a porter on trains that his father worked. "We traveled all over the country, from Hoboken to Los Angeles, north and south," Motley recollected. He found the travel stimulating and educational. Not only did he see a great deal of the country's varying landscape and major cities, with their diverse social conditions, but the porter's job enabled him to sketch between stops.

During that summer Motley began to paint. Lacking money for canvas, he used old railroad laundry bags. One of his best works, a portrait of his grandmother titled *Mending Socks,* was painted on this material.

After completing his Art Institute studies in 1918, Motley frequently painted with his friends Schwartz and Tonanek at Schwartz's studio in suburban Berwyn. Turned down every time he applied for commercial art jobs,[3] he supported himself by working as a laborer, coal heaver, steamfitter's helper, and plumber.

In 1919 he returned to the Art Institute to audit a series of lectures by George Bellows, who presented a robust and democratic view of city life in realistic paintings that teem with action in their brilliant colors and slashing wet brushwork. . . .

[A]t this time Motley was terrified of failure. Fear of rejection kept him from submitting work to the institute's annual show. "In school you always depend upon that instructor to straighten you out," he later said. "When you are alone, a lot of people lose their confidence. I lost a lot of confidence."

Finally, in 1921, Tonanek insisted that Motley submit a recently completed portrait of his mother. When that painting was well received, Motley rapidly gained confidence. In 1923 he showed several other portraits and his first major composition, *Black and Tan Cabaret,* depicting an interracial nightclub and reflecting some of his own experiences with Edith Granzo, whom he married in 1924. While the institute jury accepted this painting, it was not mentioned by reviewers.

Then, in 1925, Motley's work won high praise. The portrait of his grandmother, *Mending Socks,* was very popular. His striking portrait of the wife of a Chicago physician, titled *A Mulatress* in line with the racial terminology of the day, won the $200 Frank G. Logan Prize. Another painting, *Syncopation,* received the $200 Joseph Eisendrath Award.[4] These paintings have not been located.

Motley had been advised by Farrow, who was then president of the African-American Chicago Art League and had long been employed by the Art Institute, not to submit *Syncopation* because, in his opinion, this dance hall scene reiterated racist stereotypes of black "low life," dwelling on jazz and sexuality. Farrow warned that the painting would not be accepted. Motley later told Elaine D. Woodall, "The [black artists] were awfully afraid, years ago, of sending anything that was Negroid to any of the exhibitions. Well, I, myself, felt they belonged. . . . I said [to Farrow], 'I'm going to send this painting in.' Not only was the painting awarded a prize, but reviewers praised it."[5] Even Farrow commented favorably.

Motley had exhibited his work earlier at the Municipal Pier, where it attracted a French critic, Count Chabrier. Just as French critics had recognized the musical merits of jazz before it was taken seriously in the United States, Count Chabrier saw in Motley's tender portraits and vital depictions of African-American social life something very new and different in American art. He corresponded with Motley and, in 1925, published two articles about him in *Revue du Vrai et du Beau,* a Paris art magazine.[6] This recognition encouraged Motley and impressed art circles in Chicago and New York.

Recognition also came from Chicago artists, who elected him director of the Chicago No-Jury Society of Art, making him the first African-American artist to be named to this post.[7] The exhibition put together by this group of independent artists was an important way for young, non-academic, and abstract artists to win attention. . . .

Edward Alden Jewell, the *New York Times* art critic and one of the nation's most influential art writers, devoted a major magazine article to Motley and his work—"A Negro Artist Plumbs the Negro Soul."[8] Visually, the article contrasted *Waganda* [Uganda] *Charm-makers,* a fantasy of African dance rituals now lost, with his prize-winning African-American dance hall scene, *Syncopation.*[9]

In a sense, Motley seems to have been trying in these African fantasies to connect Alain Locke's "ancestral legacy" with contemporary African-American city life. This is hinted at by Jewell, who cited Motley's pioneer effort to forge "a substantial link in the chain of Negro culture in this country." Jewell described Motley's paintings in this way:

> Glistening dusky bodies, stamping or gliding, shouting or silent, are silhouetted against hot ritual fires. Myriad age-old racial memories drift up from Africa and glowing islands of the sea to color more recent ghostly memories of plantation days when black was black and slaves were slaves; and these memories sift, finally, through Negro life in northern cities of the present, leaving everywhere their imprint and merging with a rich blur of tribal echoes. Such are the themes and the material that enter into this artist's work. . . .[10]

Praising Motley's eloquence, Jewell said that "he has caught the spirit of life at moments both high and deep; and it is doubtless the underlying seriousness in his work that forces the spectator to pause and try to understand what he had done, what it is his steady aim to accomplish." Noting that Motley's road had been difficult because of prejudice, Jewell quoted him as saying, "'I believe, deep in my heart, that the dark tinge of my skin is the thing that has been my making. For, you see, I have had to work 100 per cent harder to realize my ambition.'" Jewell also quoted an unnamed critic, who defined Motley's ambition in this way: "'It is to arouse in his own people a love of art, and he feels that his goal can be reached most effectively if his people see themselves as the center of some artistic expression.'"[11]

Jewell's review had a direct impact. Twenty-two of the twenty-six paintings in Motley's show immediately sold, netting him between $6,000 and $7,000.[12] Before this he had not sold a painting in Chicago, but now collectors and dealers sought his work. After surviving on part-time jobs as a plumber or laborer for years, Motley, at the age of thirty-seven, was at last able to devote himself entirely to his painting. The Jewell review, Motley said when he was eighty years old, "changed my life."[13] Although some African-American leaders continued to object to his scenes of dancing, gambling, and nightlife because of the stereotypes of sensuous black women and sporty males, Motley had succeeded in establishing the artistic validity of black city life. He had also shown that the Black Renaissance was not just a Harlem phenomenon.

Considering the liveliness of the people in his paintings and the realism of the record he created of black city life in the 1920s and early 1930s, it is interesting that Motley worked in an abstract manner in the initial compositional phases. After visualizing the painting for "weeks, sometimes months," he began with numerous abstract pencil sketches, then moved to geometrical forms, and finally worked on color and spatial relations. What absorbed him most was the interaction of colors when two lights of a different character oppose one another; this concern is often an identifying characteristic of his work. As he said in an essay on his methods written after he won the Harmon gold medal:

> I have always possessed a sincere love for the play of light in painting, and especially the combination of moonlight and artificial light. *Black Belt* [his prize-winning work] was born of that desire, and secondly, to depict street scenes wherein I could produce a great variety of Negro characters. This painting was built first in the stem shape, the round or oval next, the square or oblong shape, and finally the triangular shape [all common compositional concepts].

> The color problem was this—"an arrangement of light and color." Early moonlight and shadows not too dark (out of doors). First, harmonize the color of the moonlight and the artificial light. In the background, plain sky, walls. A window of a house [with] artificial light shining through the windows and curtains or houses in the background. Let the illuminated shadow of artificial light remain to show the two effects of light, moonlight, and artificial light. Keep one of the two lights showing through the other.[14]

The combination of artificial and natural light and a concentration on the colors created within their shadows continued to preoccupy Motley throughout his life. His essay, which reveals his thoroughly professional approach, goes on to discuss in detail some of the major concepts of American painting of the 1920s. It also presents Motley's ideas about portraying black people, a subject that many African-American and white intellectuals were then discussing:

> For many years artists have depicted the Negro as the ignorant, southern "darky," to be portrayed on canvas as something humorous; an old southern black Negro gulping a large piece of watermelon; one with a banjo on his knee, possibly a "crapshooter" or a cotton-picker or a chicken thief. This material is obsolete and I sincerely hope that with the progress the Negro has made, he deserves to be represented in his true perspective, with dignity, honesty, integrity, intelligence and understanding. Progress is not going to be made by going backward. The Negro is no more the lazy, happy-go-lucky shiftless person he was shortly after the Civil War. Progress has changed all this. In my painting I have tried to paint the Negro as I have seen him and as I feel him, in myself without adding or detracting, just being frankly honest.[15]

Although reflecting some stereotyped myths about black history, Motley's 1929 statement was significant historically. He articulated what many African-American artists were trying to express. While Tanner had felt that he had to demonstrate that an African-American artist could successfully compete in the leading European art circles, those of the 1920s turned to portraying their own people in a very direct way. For Motley, who lived and had his studio in a white neighborhood, this meant he had to travel to Chicago's South Side. Despite his focus on African-American life and dedication to its authentic portrayal, he was a detached observer. . . .

During this period Motley taught a Sunday drawing class for young artists with advanced skills, one of whom was Richmond Barthé. He was also in touch with a small group of older black artists in Chicago. . . .

In 1929, after winning the Harmon gold medal, Motley received a Guggenheim Fellowship for a year's study in Europe, where lack of prejudice about interracial marriages made life easier for him and his wife. Alone among the black artists who went to Europe, he made no effort to contact Tanner. In fact, he isolated himself from fellow Americans altogether and never met the other black artists, such as Hale Woodruff, Palmer Hayden, Augusta Savage, and W. H. Johnson, who were living there at the time. He ignored invitations, he later said, because "I think when you go to a foreign country, you don't go there to see Americans." Talking over these and other views with a Russian-born sculptor, Benny Greenstein, eventually led to their sharing a Montmartre studio. There Motley did two of his most famous paintings, *Jockey Club, Paris,* which reflects his interest in the color effects of different kinds of light at night, and *Blues,* a lively interracial nightclub scene. Aesthetically, however, Europe did not change Motley's work.

When he returned to the United States, the Depression had already begun. On a trip to Pine Bluff, Arkansas, he painted *Holy Rollers* and several portraits, including his mother's brother, *Uncle Bob,* "an old lumberjack, short but tough," who kept a Bible on the table and "cussed every minute." This portrait won a prize the following year in a show of Guggenheim Fellows in New York. His work was exhibited at the Whitney Museum of American Art in New York and the Toledo Museum of Art in Ohio.

On returning to Chicago, Motley was employed by one of the first federal art programs, the Public Works of Art Project; fourteen of his paintings were placed in public buildings in Chicago. Later, Motley was made a supervisor on the Works Progress Administration art project.

In 1935 Motley left the WPA project because, after competing with 220 artists in a U.S. Treasury contest, he was chosen to do a mural for one of fourteen Illinois post offices. Motley's assignment for the mural—really a panel painting—was Wood River, a small town near Alton in southern Illinois. When he visited the site, Motley was astonished to see people parting window curtains to look at him. Men even climbed out of barber chairs to stare as he passed. The genial postmaster, who invited Motley to dinner, explained that because no black people lived there, everyone was fascinated by the presence of a black artist. After completing the mural, *U.S. Mail,* a "closeup" of a stagecoach pulling uphill, Motley returned to the WPA project in Chicago. . . .

Motley painted steadily in the early 1940s, but in 1945 he suffered a severe depression when his wife died after refusing a relatively simple surgical procedure that would have saved her life. Their only child, Archie, was then only fourteen years old.[16]

Motley became so depressed that he was unable to paint. Several months after his wife's death, in an effort to overcome his depression, he went to work in a large studio factory that employed 125 artists in decorating plastic shower curtains. This mechanical work was a far cry from the aesthetic problems that had absorbed him for years. In the factory the design was laid down in heavy black lines on a large table. The transparent plastic was placed on top of it, and the artist directly transferred the design to the plastic curtain.[17]

Motley found the work relaxing. He rejoiced to find "that I was in the midst of wonderful people. You could make good money but the important thing was the relationship with the people. They were wonderful, lovely people from all over the world—Finland, Germany, Italy, America, Russia. All very interesting and helpful. It was wonderful therapy for me. It pulled me out of the depths of my sorrow."

But the healing process was not rapid. Motley continued this factory work for eight years and only very gradually resumed painting, largely as a result of his nephew's efforts. In the 1930s, when

Archibald Motley was in his prime as a painter, his nephew Willard, twenty years younger, was just beginning to become a writer. Willard greatly admired his uncle and through him met a number of young black artists who revered Archibald for his achievements. Archibald's efforts had helped direct their attention to black people, their activities, and their neighborhoods as subjects. In 1940, when these talented young artists exhibited at Hull House, Willard described the studios and work of Eldzier Cortor, Charles Davis, Ramon Gabriel, Charles Sebree, and Charles White in detail in *Opportunity*.[18]

By the early 1950s Willard Motley had achieved national recognition with his first novel, *Knock on Any Door* (a best-seller in 1947-48), and other writings.[19] In 1953 he established a home in Cuernavaca, Mexico, and insisted that Archibald come for a prolonged visit. There Archibald found himself renewed as an artist. In the Mexican people and that country's bright, mountainous landscape, he discovered fresh and very different subject matter. Moreover, Mexico's lack of virulent racial prejudice made it a haven from the harsh intolerance in the United States. In his first six months in Mexico, Motley completed twelve canvases, which he sold soon after his return to Chicago.

When interest in the cultural contributions of black Americans developed in the 1960s, the demand for Motley's work increased. What became clear to art historians was that Motley was the first significant African-American artist to devote himself to the life of urban black people. A city dweller all his life, he was not drawn to rural scenes, as were such contemporaries as W. H. Johnson and Malvin Gray Johnson. . . .

Reviewing his life's work, Motley said that it did not pass through different phases of development: "I think it has basically remained the same. It has been in a steady direction, and I believe it has improved—at least I hope it has."

If Motley did not change, the world around him did, moving in on him both literally and symbolically. In the late 1960s the city life of African-Americans, with its bad housing, poor schools, and unemployment, became a major theme of young black artists in works that contrasted to Motley's celebration of black life. These artists criticized Motley for not portraying such victimizations. Motley, whose dignified portraits of his grandmother and other black people represented his concern and sincere appreciation of them, was deeply hurt. "I don't know why they

feel that way," he said, "but I know they criticize me, that they say a lot of these things are sort of Uncle Tomish and all that stuff. . . . They want something a little more militant. . . . I have never hated a man in my life, regardless of race or color or creed, and I hope to God I never shall. Personally, I think I have been a much happier man for it. I think when a person hates he only makes himself miserable. And the guy they're hating, he doesn't know anything about it, so he doesn't give a damn."

By the early 1970s, however, conditions in his old neighborhood had reached a point where Motley made up his mind to move. "People here no longer know who I am or what I have done," he remarked. In a televised WMAQ-NBC interview in 1972, which displayed his work to millions, Motley denounced racial prejudice as he discussed his work.[20] On April 14 of that year, some of the pain he felt from criticism by the militants was eased when the National Conference of Artists (an organization of African-American artists, teachers, and administrators) honored him with a dinner, a gift of money, and a plaque recognizing his historical role in the development of America's black artists.

At the time Motley was still working on a large painting he had begun in 1963 to celebrate the 100th anniversary of the Emancipation Proclamation—"the Centennial, we call it," he said. He expected it to be finished that year. But instead of a parade of progress, it became a haunted history of violence as Motley's despair deepened over the explosive struggle for civil rights. The painting became a religious allegory, including many portraits and historical scenes, such as the assassinations of President John F. Kennedy and the Reverend Martin Luther King, Jr., the killing of black children in the bombing of an Alabama black church, and the revival of the Klan. In 1972, nearly ten years after he began, Motley was still working on this painting, of which he said, "I have in it this very deep feeling—that's why I used a lot of blues in it. I have got that blue feeling."

Originally titled *1963—The First 100 Years— 1863,* it acquired an inscription as part of its composition that reflected Motley's deep religiosity: *He Amongst You Who Is Without Sin Shall Cast the First Stone—Forgive Them, Father, For They Know Not What They Do.* This large canvas, so different from his paintings of the 1920s, remained a work that Motley never felt was finished, although he stopped work on it when he left his old neighborhood in the late 1970s.

Despite the recognition he received in the late 1920s, Motley and his work have been shockingly neglected and omitted from American art histories. In 1977 Elaine D. Woodall listed 105 Motley paintings out of an estimated lifetime production of 400 to 500, but she was able to locate only 31, most of which were held by the Motley family and a few African-American colleges.[21] Our efforts to locate Motley murals in three Chicago-area schools failed. In two, there was no record or even memory of them. In the third, the principal reported he had been told the music room had once had three Motley panels—one was a dance scene, the second showed black children, and the third portrayed "black musicians in a parade similar to the type one sees in pictures of New Orleans."[22] A former band director had felt Motley's musicians were not holding their instruments "properly," and this may have been the rationale for the mural's destruction. Undoubtedly, the mural was Motley's depiction of the funeral bands that originated jazz in New Orleans, his birthplace. As *Stomp* and other paintings reveal, Motley loved jazz.

Motley died on January 16, 1981, at his Chicago home. The year before he was one of ten African-American artists honored by President Jimmy Carter, and some of his paintings were exhibited at the Corcoran Gallery of Art in Washington as part of a group show of the work of these artists, held at the suggestion of the National Conference of Negro Artists. This was followed in 1988 by an exhibition of more of his work, together with that of Eldzier Cortor and Hughie Lee-Smith, in New York at Kenkeleba House.[23] This art center on the Lower East Side seeks to nurture young minority artists by alternating exhibitions of their work with work by significant minority artists of the past, such as Motley.

Motley's importance lies in his recognition that African-American city life, its energy and optimism, can be the subject of art. That he had the courage to focus on this subject matter at a time when it was frowned upon, and even denounced, makes him a key figure in the history of African-American artists and American art.

## Notes

*Unless otherwise indicated all quotations attributed to Archibald J. Motley, Jr., are from two interviews with him, May 6 and June 6, 1972, which are the basis of much of this chapter. We have also drawn upon the work of Elaine D. Woodall, "Archibald J. Motley, Jr.: American Artist of the Afro-American People, 1891-1928" (M.A. thesis, Pennsylvania State University, 1977), and her article "Archibald Motley and the Art Institute of Chicago: 1914-30," Chicago History 9 (Spring 1979), pp. 53-57. In addition, we have utilized the research of*

*Jontyle T. Robinson, who located more than 100 "lost" Motley paintings, including many portraits of now unknown women and fantasies of African scenes and gods. See Carroll Greene, Jr., Afro-American Art 1986 (Washington, D.C.: Visions Foundation, 1987), pp. 28-34, and Robinson's essay in the exhibition catalog Three Masters: Cortor, Lee-Smith, and Motley (New York: Kenkeleba Gallery, 1988), pp. 42-45.*

1. Jacob Z. Jacobson, ed., *Art of Today: Chicago, 1933* (Chicago: L. M. Stein, 1933), p. 93. Motley was the only African-American artist asked to make a statement for this book. His friend William Schwartz also made a statement.

2. Ibid.; quoted by Woodall, in *Chicago History*, p. 9.

3. Ibid., p. 54.

4. *Bulletin of the Art Institute of Chicago*, March 1925, p. 36.

5. Woodall, in *Chicago History*, p. 55.

6. Count Chabrier, in *Revue du Vrai et du Beau*, Feb. 16 and July 10, 1925.

7. Woodall, in *Chicago History*, p. 56.

8. Edward Alden Jewell, "A Negro Artist Plumbs the Negro Soul," *New York Times Magazine*, March 25, 1928, pp. 8, 22.

9. Jontyle T. Robinson and Wendy Greenhouse believe that Motley's African scenes were suggested by his New York dealer, George Hellman, who, in a letter, urged the exhibition contain "some paintings showing various phases of negro life in its more dramatic aspects—scenes, perhaps, in which the voodoo element as well as the cabaret element, but especially the latter—enter." The letter says nothing of Africa. Robinson and Greenhouse believe Motley drew upon his grandmother's stories of East Africa for his fantasies. He himself was never in Africa (Jontyle T. Robinson and Wendy Greenhouse, *The Art of Archibald J. Motley, Jr.* [Chicago: Chicago Historical Society, exhibition catalog, 1991], p. 11).

10. Jewell, "A Negro Artist."

11. Ibid.

12. Woodall, in *Chicago History*, p. 56.

13. Ibid.

14. Archibald J. Motley, Jr., "How I Solve My Painting Problems," 1929 (Harmon Foundation Collection, Library of Congress, Washington, D.C.).

15. Ibid.

16. Archie Motley is now curator of manuscripts, Chicago Historical Society.

17. "Shower Curtain Artists," *Ebony* (Feb. 1953), pp. 85-86, describes this factory but does not mention Motley; see also "Top Negro Artist Works in Factory Job," *Chicago Sunday Tribune*, Dec. 2, 1956, p. 3, and *Chicago Sun-Times*, Dec. 2, 1956, p. 3.

18. Willard Motley, "Negro Art in Chicago," *Opportunity* 18 (June 1940), p. 19-22, 28.

19. Willard Motley also wrote *We Fished All Night* (1951), *Let No Man Write My Epitaph* (1958), and *Let Noon Be Fair* (1966).

20. "The Last Leaf," interview by Warren Saunder, produced by William Heit; another interview in this period was by critic Harold Hayden, *Chicago Sun-Times*, Showcase sec., Aug. 29, 1971.

21. Woodall, "Motley: American Artist," appendix A.

22. Claude Mazzocco, principal of Nichols Middle School, Evanston, Ill., letter to authors, July 16, 1980.

23. Robinson and Greenhouse, *Art of Motley.*

24. Ibid.

## ROMARE BEARDEN AND HARRY HENDERSON (ESSAY DATE 1993)

**SOURCE:** Bearden, Romare and Harry Henderson. "Malvin Gray Johnson." In *A History of African American Artists from 1792 to the Present,* pp. 181-84. New York: Pantheon Books, 1993.

*In the following excerpt, Bearden and Henderson review the life of painter Malvin Johnson, citing him as a "highly individual modern painter" whose life and work ended too early.*

"Prefers Negro subject matter" is how the 1933 Harmon Foundation catalog characterized Malvin Gray Johnson, an inspired and innovative artist who died unexpectedly a year later, on the eve of his full development of a highly individualized modern style. The 1935 Harmon exhibition was dedicated to him, featuring thirty-five oils and eighteen watercolors. Today, except for a few paintings in the Schomburg Center for Research in Black Culture in New York and the National Museum of American Art in Washington, D.C., Johnson's work is scattered and there is very little information about him.[1]

Johnson, who was called "Gray" by his friends, was born in Greensboro, North Carolina, in the heart of tobacco-raising country, on January 28, 1896. His family moved to New York when he was a boy. Although he discovered his artistic talent at an early age and decided to become an artist, he could not afford to enter the National Academy of Design until he was twenty-five years old. He studied there with well-known academicians Ivan Olinsky, Charles Curran, and H. Bolton Jones in 1921, 1926, and 1927. The five-year gap in his studies was necessitated by his need to earn tuition at menial jobs.[2] Eventually he supported himself as a commercial artist while painting at night and on weekends.

Johnson's first recognition came in early 1928, when he won the $250 Otto H. Kahn prize at the Harmon exhibition for a painting titled *Swing Low, Sweet Chariot,* an attempt to express the theme of that famous spiritual. The award stimulated him to further efforts in interpreting the spirituals. For example, in the 1930 Harmon show, he exhibited *Mighty Day, I Know the Lord Laid His Hands on Me,* and *Climbing Up the Mountain.* In 1931 he exhibited *Roll, Jordan, Roll,* as well as a sympathetic portrait of an African-American

woman, which he titled *Meditation,* and *Water Boy.* Johnson also exhibited at the Anderson Galleries in 1931 and in the Depression-born Washington Square Outdoor show in 1932. One of his paintings, *Negress,* was purchased by the Whitney Museum of American Art.

His studies of Impressionism and awareness of the individuality of some innovative American painters "lifted him out of his earlier scholastic manner," according to James A. Porter, a teacher at Howard University.[3] "He became an experimentalist, first with color, solving problems of reflected light and of direct light with glasses of water and other still-life objects," Porter noted. "Subsequently there was a turning from these essays to deeper problems of form," based on his study of African sculpture and its influence on modern European painting. When Johnson painted a self-portrait, he made African masks a part of the background.

Beginning with his paintings of African-American city life in 1931, Johnson gradually abandoned academic concepts to apply Paul Cézanne's dictum that all objects could essentially be reduced to a cone, a cylinder, and a square. His reductionistic efforts linked him to such American artists as Arthur Dove and Charles Demuth. Johnson may also have been aware of the Chinese masters of reduction, who are said to have studied an object for years, absorbing every detail into their very being before making a single brushstroke. In a few lines they were able to delineate mountains, trees, and rocks—a distillation of long analytical observation and reflection on the nature of these elements.

This was the direction that Johnson took when in 1933, fulfilling a promise to himself to paint southern black people, he went to Brightwood, Virginia. There he made a series of watercolors from which he later made oil paintings of African-Americans—thinning corn, picking beans, washing clothes, raking hay, picnicking, in old age, at revival meetings, and in chain gangs, as well as in their southern landscapes.[4]

Porter, who was fascinated by Johnson's swift transition from a traditional academic style to a modern one, remembered: "Artistic or creative fervor was of the essence of this man. . . . I shall never forget my first meeting with him, when his apparent relaxation and poise of mind masked for a while his more electric quality, with which I became more impressed at subsequent meetings."[5] Johnson alternated between incisive speech and quick sardonic humor, Porter said, and "one could trace in it a slight tinge of bitterness and exasperation. No doubt he felt the pressures that everywhere have forced apart the modern artist and the society of which he could be the interpreter."

As already noted, one of Johnson's major inspirations was his study of African sculpture, which expresses an object's spiritual and psychological essence in simple forms. Johnson increasingly sought to convey the fundamental structure of a figure or object. In his Brightwood watercolors, his reductionist approach brought him close to a Cubist style in his treatment of simplified masses.

His development as a highly individual modern painter prompted Delphic Studios in New York to plan a one-man show. This was regarded by African-American artists, and by Mary Beattie Brady of the Harmon Foundation, as a real breakthrough because galleries at that time were not exhibiting the work of black artists. However, before that could take place, he died suddenly on October 4, 1934.[6]

. . . While some of Johnson's work was preserved by the Harmon Foundation and some of it found its way to the Schomburg Center as gifts, most of it was scattered after his death. Records and data about him are sparse. His widow remarried, and efforts to locate her have failed.

The significance of Johnson lies in the fact that in the space of a few years he challenged the academic traditionalism that then dominated American art and that held most African-American artists in its grip in their efforts to win acceptance as artists. This is why Porter eulogized him in an essay in *Opportunity,* and why this essay was reprinted in the catalog for the 1935 Harmon show, where he was the only painter of the three artists exhibited.

## Notes

1. The Harmon Foundation exhibition catalogs are a primary source of information. Johnson exhibited in these shows in 1928, 1929, 1930, 1931, 1933, and 1935.

2. Records of the National Academy of Design, New York.

3. James A. Porter, "Malvin Gray Johnson," *Opportunity* 13 (Oct. 1935), p. 117.

4. Mary Beattie Brady showed these watercolors to one of the authors during a visit to her office in August 1966.

5. Porter, "Malvin Gray Johnson."

6. Brady, author interview.

# ROMARE BEARDEN AND HARRY HENDERSON (ESSAY DATE 1993)

SOURCE: Bearden, Romare and Harry Henderson. "Hale Woodruff." In *A History of African American Artists from 1792 to the Present,* pp. 200-15. New York: Pantheon Books, 1993.

*In the following excerpt, the authors review the life and work of painter Hale Woodruff, whom they consider a seminal figure who influenced hundreds of other artists.*

In the 1960s several black artists in New York formed Spiral, a group that met regularly to discuss the relationship of their art and their lives with African-Americans' efforts in the South to win full civil rights. One artist who constantly added depth and wisdom to these exchanges was Hale A. Woodruff. His voice had the authority of true experience. As a young painter in the Midwest in the 1920s, Woodruff had been moved by the same influences—Paul Cézanne and the Cubist movement—that prompted Stuart Davis and Alfred Maurer, and he had liberated himself from the restraining traditionalist concepts then dominating American art. Despite poverty, he pushed his way through to Paris and maintained his Cézanne-stimulated studies in France for four years. Unlike some of his fellow expatriates, he went to great lengths to meet Henry Ossawa Tanner and talk to him about his ideas on art. Admiring African art and understanding its relationship to Cubism and Pablo Picasso's work, he began to collect it.

When he returned to the United States in 1931, the misery of the Depression gave Woodruff a new perception of his own people and modern art. He began teaching black students in the Deep South to draw and paint what they saw and what they experienced. He also went to Mexico to study with Diego Rivera, an exponent of the mural as a method of teaching oppressed people their history. At Talladega College in Alabama, he then created his strong, linear *Amistad* murals, a brilliant portrayal of the slaves who mutinied and were freed when tried in the United States. At Atlanta University he initiated the annual exhibitions of the work of black artists that for more than a quarter-century provided a powerful stimulus for black artists all over the United States. In 1966, at New York University, where he taught from 1946 until 1967, students elected him "Great Teacher," a singular annual honor reflecting their appreciation of his efforts to teach and, in Woodruff's case, to learn from them.

Woodruff's was never the pessimistic voice of the past. Optimism expressed itself in everything he said; his next painting would be better. He laughed over the past, although he told stories of personal experiences that revealed its pain and the depths of prejudice he had encountered. He focused on the new generation of unknown African-American artists and their concern for their own people and their history. Working with them gave him a sense of commitment re-warded—and renewed. "A great teacher learns from students how to be a great teacher," he said.

Woodruff was on the cutting edge of American art for over fifty years. He never lost his interest in murals and their role in defining the relationship of the artist to his people. Yet his own work became increasingly nonrepresentational after World War II, making him a precursor of the Abstract Expressionist movement. What was unique and special in his abstract work was its African imagery. He found African design an aid to achieving a deeper, more satisfying expression of his own artistic vision. Honored by prizes and fellowships, Woodruff was a seminal figure, influencing hundreds of artists and art educators, until his death in his eightieth year in 1980. His friends included such leading artists as Jack Tworkov and Willem de Kooning.

Hale Aspacio Woodruff was born in Cairo, Illinois, on August 26, 1900. His father, George Woodruff, died soon after his birth. His young mother, Augusta Bell Woodruff, moved to Nashville, Tennessee, to become a domestic. Her work often necessitated leaving young Hale for hours. An only child, he found activities he could enjoy doing alone. His mother was skillful enough with a pencil to show Hale the rudiments of drawing. To her delight, he began to draw at an early age and was soon copying newspaper cartoons and engravings in the family Bible. "Years later I found out that they were by Gustave Doré," he said. He also drew from "the excellent Greek and Roman statues from my ancient history textbooks. I learned wherever I could." At Pearl High School he was the school paper's cartoonist.

On graduating in 1918, he and his closest friend, George Gore, got summer jobs in Indianapolis "as house-boys in a big hotel, scrubbing carpets, and anything else they gave us to do. We talked a lot about what we were going to be. George wanted to be a journalist and I said I only wanted to be an artist," Woodruff remembered.

That fall Gore, later president of Florida Agricultural and Mechanical College, entered DePauw University and Hale began his art studies at the John Herron Art Institute in Indianapolis. The "colored" YMCA gave him a room in return for his services as a desk clerk. He got five dollars a week

for a cartoon dealing with political and racial problems from a local black newspaper. He also lettered sales-counter posters for local stores. These efforts, and his mother's help, enabled him to attend the only art school in Indianapolis.

The Herron Art Institute, located in a small brick building, had about forty students, including one other black student, William Holloway, who later left to become the *Pittsburgh Courier* cartoonist. Woodruff's instructor was William Forsythe, who had studied in Munich and was a friend of the well-known American artist William Merritt Chase. Forsythe, like Chase, believed in the "juicy brush" technique—loading a brush with pigment and working quickly with great facility. "Forsythe was a very good teacher," Woodruff said fifty years later, when he himself was considered an excellent teacher. Herron instructors concentrated on the human figure, and Woodruff became a superb draftsman. In his seventies, he rated drawing his greatest skill. . . .

Eventually, unable to pay the year's full tuition in advance, Woodruff was forced to give up his Herron studies. He went to Chicago, hoping better job opportunities there would permit him to study part-time at the Art Institute. However, after a few sessions at the institute, he felt that he could do as well on his own. He returned to Indianapolis and his old "Y" job. Through its lecture series he had already met a number of outstanding African-American leaders, among them William Pickens, Sr.,[1] whose portrait he later painted; W. E. B. Du Bois; John S. Hope of Morehouse College (who was later to play an important role in his life); Walter White of the National Association for the Advancement of Colored People; and many others. Those who excited him most were the poet Countee Cullen[2] and the painter William Edouard Scott, who discussed studying with Tanner in France. Woodruff had learned of Tanner through *The Crisis,* and Scott's stories gave him hope that he could study abroad. . . .

While still at Herron, Woodruff became friendly with German-born Herman Lieber, who ran an art supply store. In 1923 Lieber gave him a book titled *Afrikanische Plastik* by Carl Einstein, published by Ernst Wasmuth in Berlin, and said he should learn something of the art of his own people. Recalling this incident, Woodruff commented:

> You can't imagine the effect that book had on me. Part of the effect was due to the fact that as a black artist I felt very much alone there in Indianapolis. I had heard of Tanner, but I had never heard of the significance of the impact of African art. Yet here

it was! And all written up in German, a language I didn't understand! Yet published with beautiful photographs and treated with great seriousness and respect! Plainly sculptures of black people, my people, they were considered very beautiful by these German art experts! The whole idea that this could be so was like an explosion. It was a real turning point for me. I was just astonished at this enormous discovery.

Woodruff wanted very much to study abroad. Learning from "Y" publications of the new Harmon competition for black artists in 1926, he painted a large canvas depicting two alert, dignified older black women standing together. He won second prize, a bronze medal, and $100 in the first of these competitions.[3]

This success changed Woodruff's life. Mary Beattie Brady, the Harmon director, was trained as a journalist at Columbia University. She wired Indianapolis newspapers that an unknown black artist in the local "colored" YMCA had won an important national art contest. Not only did the local press "jump on it," Woodruff recalled, "but Governor [Ed] Jackson called up and asked if he could have the honor of coming to the YMCA to present the medal to me. We black people just did not get this kind of attention in Indianapolis in those days."

When the press reported Woodruff hoped to study abroad, a ladies' literary club in nearby Franklin invited him to exhibit his paintings and have supper with them. Woodruff recalled: "This was supposedly Klan country! Yet here they were giving me $150 along with praise. Knowing the history and reality of the way we were treated day in and day out, it was virtually unbelievable!"

The *Indianapolis Star* offered Woodruff $10 for each Parisian scene he illustrated and wrote about,[4] and his old friend Herman Lieber offered to try to sell his paintings. In New York Walter White obtained a $250 gift from philanthropist Otto H. Kahn for him, and Du Bois put one of Woodruff's sketches showing young black artists at their easels on the cover of *The Crisis* and paid him $25.[5] With that, Woodruff was off to Paris, third class, on September 3, 1927.

In Paris his fellow Harmon Prize-winner, Palmer Hayden, found him a room and Woodruff enrolled at the Académie Moderne and the Académie Scandinave. However, excited by the work of Claude Monet, whose memorial exhibition at the Jeu de Paume museum had recently opened, Woodruff decided he could learn more in museums than in school. In the Luxembourg Museum he found Tanner's *Raising of Lazarus*. The more he studied this 1897 prize-winner, the more he felt

he had to see Tanner, talk to him, and show him his own work. Tanner was, for young African-American artists, a great hero. Yet his letters asking Tanner for an appointment went unanswered.

Hearing Tanner was at his studio-home in Etaples, on the Channel coast, Woodruff decided to seek him out. Late in 1927, on a cold, rainy day, he reached Tanner's home, carrying a portfolio of his work. Recognizing the portfolio as part of the attire of a young art student rather than a tourist, Tanner invited him in. That afternoon Woodruff had an extraordinary discussion with Tanner, who encouraged him but also suggested that he consider man and his humanity in a historical sense as a subject.

Because Woodruff's work showed him to be a serious artist, Tanner went on to discuss Peter Paul Rubens, Jan Vermeer, El Greco, and many other artists. He reflected on his own work in relationship to Rembrandt and the Dutch school and their use of light. He also revealed his own efforts to achieve pervasive luminosity through new glazing methods.

At one point Tanner asked a few penetrating questions about young black artists and racial prejudice in the United States, but he did not pursue the matter. At another point he discussed some of the work Woodruff was seeing in Paris. He felt that Monet, whom Woodruff admired, risked the loss of "a sense of form and structure." Then Tanner asked: "Who is your real artist-god?"

"Cézanne," replied Woodruff. Reflecting a moment, Tanner said: "All right! A real master—space, color, light, form—all of it. He is in the tradition yet is a real innovator. You have made a good choice!"

That Tanner had accepted him as an artist and shared his views and problems encouraged Woodruff. So did the fact that, contrary to rumor, Tanner showed a genuine interest in young black artists and racial problems in America. Although he never adopted Tanner's artistic concepts, the impact of this visit on Woodruff was lasting, and his recollections of this talk became the most authentic record of Tanner's artistic concerns.[6] Many years later Woodruff concluded that Tanner was more than the leading black painter of the turn of the century: "He was one of the truly great painters, regardless of race, to come out of America.". . .

Circumstances prevented Woodruff and Hayden from sharing a studio, although they saw one another often and Woodruff used Hayden's hands for a model in one painting.[7] Early in 1928 Woodruff left the city of Paris for a suburb to live— mostly on rice pudding—with three other American artists, Forrest Wiggins, Charles Law, and Robert Miller; his share of the rent was eight dollars a month. When his friends had to leave, Woodruff was without food for several days. Finally he borrowed trolley fare from the landlady to go to Paris, where he found a $200 check from a sale of a painting by the Harmon Foundation. . . .

Economically, however, Woodruff was in dire straits. When Walter White informed him that Otto H. Kahn was in Paris, Woodruff hastened there to show his work. Kahn gave him another $250. Eventually Woodruff survived as a road-gang laborer, his dark skin fooling French authorities into thinking he was a Moroccan French citizen and therefore eligible for work.

After four years abroad, Woodruff returned to the United States. John Hope, president of the newly formed Atlanta University, who was keenly aware of the work of Edward M. Bannister and Tanner and who had met Woodruff in Indianapolis, offered him an art instructorship. Thus in 1931 Woodruff became the first African-American artist with extensive training and experience abroad to teach art in a southern black university.

Woodruff's aesthetic ideas changed swiftly under the impact of the Depression and the problems of trying to teach art to black young people in two basement rooms in Spelman College (part of Atlanta University) in the segregated South. Seeing the struggles of African-Americans to obtain relief allocations or jobs in the cities or to eke out a miserable existence in the South's one-crop economy led him to question the value of much that he had learned abroad. Cubism and modern art did not say anything meaningful to most Americans, he concluded, and they did not seem appropriate for teaching drawing and painting to beginners. Faced with eager students, but almost no art resources, he tried to be realistic and helpful. "He was down to earth. . . . He did not use fancy aesthetic language that had no meaning to us," Wilmer Jennings remembered.[8] One of his two rooms was both his office and his studio. He urged students to come at any hour, letting them see that he was constantly working on his own to encourage them.

Woodruff used the college library for a continuous display of work by black artists. Sometimes he could put up only photographs of work in previous Harmon shows, but sometimes he held one-man shows of artists such as Palmer Hayden, Allan Freelon, and William Edouard Scott.

Woodruff made student exhibitions a feature of commencement week. He secured a Carnegie Corporation gift of 5,000 photographic slides of paintings, sculpture, and architecture. Later, he obtained a traveling exhibition from the Whitney Museum of American Art of the work of George Bellows, Leon Kroll, Eugene Speicher, Reginald Marsh, and Georgia O'Keeffe. He set up a show of Bannisters and Tanners owned by Hope and J. J. Haverty, an Atlanta businessman and collector, as well as an exhibition demonstrating the art of printmaking. . . .

Woodruff was determined to open all channels of art to his students and the African-American community. Soon after he arrived he took the trolley to the High Museum of Art and walked past an astonished black man sweeping its steps. Inside he insisted on seeing the director. Identifying his own background in art and his role as a teacher at Atlanta University, he gained permission to bring his student classes to the museum. When he came out, the man sweeping the steps told him he was the first black man he had ever seen go into the museum. "Well, I won't be the last," said Woodruff.[9]

Initially Woodruff's relations with the museum were uncertain and uneasy. When he appeared, for instance, for a lecture by Grant Wood, whose paintings *American Gothic* and *Daughters of Revolution* had provoked much controversy, Woodruff was denied admission. The next day Wood learned of this. In a rebuff to the museum officials, Wood called Woodruff and asked if he could visit him at Spelman. The two artists had an enjoyable day together.[10] This incident helped break down residual prejudice among museum officials.

Woodruff first brought his class to the museum in the early 1930s. The precise date is forgotten, but not the experience. Entering this once-forbidden place made more of an impression on the students than any of the paintings they saw. One student recalled: ". . . it was a very big thing when Woodruff took us to the High Museum. He had to get special permission because blacks didn't go in there at all unless they worked there, for they were not welcome to any of the shows. You couldn't just walk in there as a viewer. . . . I remember his taking his class to the gallery, but there really wasn't much there. Yet it was really wonderful since it was our first contact with a museum.[11] Another said: "Woodruff took you into the community, to the High Museum of Art— these were first steps for blacks. . . . We saw his work hang there. In other words, Mr. Woodruff was very much like Fred Douglass. Although segregation was in Atlanta, Woodruff was such a powerful person, such an articulate man, we had a chance to see something there. . . . We were all proud of him."[12]

As a result of Woodruff's initiative, the color bar at the High Museum began to erode long before the sit-ins of the 1960s. Now considered one of the outstanding museums in the South, it has presented many one-person shows of significant black artists as well as large group shows. By linking art with democratic progress, Woodruff gave art a meaning in Atlanta's African-American community it never had before. By regularly bringing the traveling Harmon exhibitions to Spelman he connected the students as well as the local community to the world of art outside Atlanta. In 1933 the Harmon show included his work as well as that of one of his best students, Wilmer Jennings, which gave the entire university and the community a new appreciation of what was being achieved in their midst.

By that time, in order to create in his advanced students a sense of identity and purpose, Woodruff had organized them into a "Painters' Guild." Regionalism had replaced traditionalism in American art, and Woodruff led his "Guild" out of the studio to paint their region—Georgia's red-clay hills, piney woods, and scrawny barnyards. These expeditions made them part of the latest movement in American art. "We are interested in expressing the South as a field, as a territory; its peculiar rundown landscapes, its social and economic problems, and Negro people," Woodruff told *Time.* "The students and I . . . used to talk about these problems. Not only talked about them, we experienced them. . . . You'll see their work reflects our interest in the Negro sociological theme or scene."[13]

*Time,* although recognizing that Atlanta University was becoming an outstanding art center in the South, sneered at these efforts, calling the work "Outhouse Art" because some students included privies in their Georgia landscapes. "It hurt," Woodruff recalled. "It made it seem that we were concerned with getting a two-seater into every painting. It hurt the students more than it bothered me, for it made it seem that whatever efforts we made, such publications would ridicule us."

A more difficult problem was what Woodruff called the "absence" of black artists on the national scene. Segregation and prejudice effectively blocked recognition of black artists in museums,

art magazines, and the academic world everywhere, not only in the South. After its 1935 show the Harmon Foundation ended its New York exhibitions. "This situation led me to the idea of an all-Negro annual for the purpose of (1) offering a place to show, (2) providing an opportunity to earn a little money through purchase prizes, and (3) establishing a collection of art by Negroes at Atlanta University, which would be available to students, schools, and other institutions," Woodruff later explained.[14] . . .

During the 1930s Woodruff increasingly saw art as a way of meeting the needs of the African-American community as a whole. Like many other American artists during the Depression, he was attracted to the Mexican muralists—Diego Rivera, José Orozco, David Siqueiros, and others—who used their work to increase the self-esteem of their poor fellow-countrymen as well as their knowledge of their own history. To Woodruff, this seemed an ideal way to relate African-American and African history to black people in the United States. He also felt that learning how to paint murals would enhance his own development as an artist.

Gaining a grant to study Mexican art in July 1934, Woodruff disregarded the indignities that tormented African-Americans trying to travel into Mexico and found Rivera painting his famous Hotel Reforma mural in Mexico City. He introduced himself to this master muralist, explaining his desire to work with him. Rivera said that as long as Woodruff did not expect to be paid, he could join the crew preparing the walls and mixing the paint. . . .

On returning to Atlanta, Woodruff did two murals under the Works Progress Administration art projects. He was assisted by an outstanding student, Wilmer Jennings. One mural was a bland pictorialization of black people that he later disliked. The second, in the Atlanta School of Social Work, consisted of two panels, *Shantytown* and *Mudhill.* Ralph McGill, later the editor of the *Atlanta Constitution,* called these the works of a "modern master." He wrote: "They are worth more, they say more, than all the studies on economics and the need for slum clearance and better housing."[15]

This experience prepared Woodruff to paint a mural series at Talladega College, a small African-American institution in Alabama, not far from Atlanta, which had no art department. Its president, Buell M. Gallagher, later the head of City College of New York, was determined to break down the self-demeaning attitude toward African-Americans that then pervaded many black colleges. He told Woodruff the college would like him to paint a series of murals about the *Amistad* mutiny in its new library to show students that their people were not willingly made slaves.

Woodruff himself had not heard of the 1839 *Amistad* mutiny, but he began intensive research. He learned that the revolt of the slaves aboard the Spanish slave ship *Amistad* had been led by the African prince Cinque. Tried on charges of murder and mutiny in a United States court, Cinque and his fellow Africans were acquitted and returned to their homeland. The legal process took three years. One of the chief defense lawyers was former president John Quincy Adams, who came out of retirement to argue the right of free men to revolt with arms against slavery. . . .

In these murals, notable for their linear composition and brilliant color as well as their historical accuracy, Woodruff made a unique contribution to African-American history and demonstrated a role for artists that was generally unknown in this country. Du Bois paid for color reproductions of the mural to accompany his own historical article on the *Amistad* mutiny in the African-American literary journal *Phylon*.[16]

The Talladega murals convinced Atlanta University officials to agree to Woodruff's repeated requests to create murals on "the art of the Negro" for its Trevor Arnett Library. However, a satisfactory teaching-painting schedule could not be immediately worked out. Meanwhile, Woodruff was awarded a Rosenwald Fellowship in 1943, and it was renewed in 1944, enabling him to study and paint in New York for two years. . . .

Woodruff impressed New York's art circles. Few American artists had his firsthand knowledge of the art centers of France, Parisian artists, Rivera's work in Mexico, and the traditions and problems of American art. Woodruff's own work was admired, and he had achieved national recognition for his teaching in the Deep South.

Not surprisingly, just a year after he returned to Atlanta, Woodruff was appointed an associate professor of art at New York University, so he came back to New York. Although teaching cut heavily into his energy, Woodruff felt it helped him as an artist. "You can learn from a good student or a bad one," he liked to say. "I have never taught how to do something. I have tried to recognize what the students are trying to do—and let

them do it. I just try to light a fire under their coat-tails. No two students are alike—and that helps make teaching interesting, really absorbing." . . .

Woodruff always felt that his teaching and counseling schedule did not allow him sufficient time for painting. Yet this situation did not preclude other projects. In 1948 Woodruff and Charles Alston, who had won considerable recognition as a WPA muralist, were commissioned to paint two large murals on black history in California for the Golden State Mutual Life Insurance Company in Los Angeles. That summer they toured California to dig up historical material.

The murals were for a building designed by Paul Williams, an African-American architect. They were painted separately by the two artists but in the same studio. Alston painted the early colonial period, while Woodruff covered California history after the 1849 discovery of gold. Each panel, nine by sixteen feet, was painted on canvas in New York, then shipped to California for wall mounting.

The California experience led directly to a resumption of Woodruff's efforts to paint the six panels of *The Art of the Negro* for Atlanta University. Woodruff offered to paint the murals in New York if he was given a free hand, for in both the Talladega and California murals the subject had been dictated. "In the Talladega murals I was able to employ a linear style. In the California murals, since Alston and I worked together, I tended to abandon my style so that the panels would be compatible," Woodruff said. "But in the Atlanta murals I could select the subject and paint as I wanted."

The Atlanta University murals were completed in New York in 1951. The first panel concerns the styles and forms of African art; the second, the influence of the art of black Africa on the cultures of ancient Greece, Rome, and Egypt. The third depicts the destruction of African culture, symbolized by the looting and burning of Benin. The fourth panel shows parallels between African and pre-Columbian, Native American, and Oceanic art forms, considering all of them basic forms of human aesthetic expression. The fifth panel demonstrates the influence of African art on modern painting and sculpture, as reflected in the art of Modigliani, Picasso, Lipchitz, Henry Moore, and others. The sixth portrays the important black artists of history, starting with the cave artists of Africa and including older African-American artists, such as Tanner, Bannister, and Robert S. Duncanson, as well as such contemporaries as Alston, Jacob Lawrence, and Richmond Barthé.

Woodruff's style varies with each panel to accommodate the subject matter. At times it becomes abstract in its treatment of African imagery. Both emotionally and aesthetically, the *Art of the Negro* murals synthesize many elements in Woodruff's background with the emerging abstract movement of the early 1950s in New York. He considered these murals to be one of his major achievements.

By 1955 Woodruff's work had become completely abstract, although based on the African motifs and forms that had first appeared in his woodcuts in Atlanta. He particularly regretted not knowing in his childhood that Africans produced great art, saying:

> We were told that we were only slaves and savages and not shown this art. I feel that if the great Greek and Roman antique sculpture can inspire a white artist, certainly the work of my ancestors in Africa can inspire me. I don't say this on a tit-for-tat basis, but simply because it compares favorably with the great art of Europe, the art of Asia, with pre-Columbian and [American] Indian art.
>
> I have tried to study African art in order to assimilate it into my being, not to copy but to seek the essence of it, its spirit and quality as art. There are many mistakes made in talking and writing about the influence of African art, it seems to me. It is a great pity that while people generally credit African art with having set off Cubism, they do not understand how superficially some artists, whatever their intent, used African art.
>
> I have never taught African art to my students or pushed it in any way. It is a kind of personal interest and feeling that you can't impose on others. If students seek it out, that is fine, that is something they do then for themselves, and I am delighted to offer them the benefit of my experiences. I have consistently advised students that blackness alone will not imbue their works with greatness or immortality. Whatever the source or theme of their expression, the answer to that question will rest finally in their attaining the highest possible level of achievement and transcendence in their work as art. . . .
>
> The greatness of African art, while admittedly a source of inspiration and interest to the twentieth-century artist, does not lie in this fact alone. African art possesses those basic and inherent qualities of all great art. It is in this sense that it should be judged. . . .

In 1966, two years before Woodruff retired from New York University, its students elected him "Great Teacher," reflecting his wide influence. His students included several generations of artists and art teachers, among them the painters Larry Rivers and Robert Goodnough, the watercolorist Erwin Greenberg, the jewelry designer Wilmer Jennings, Eugene Grigsby of the University of Arizona, Vernon Winslow, head of the art department of Dillard University in New Orleans, Augustus Freundlich, chairman of the art department of Syracuse University, John Howard of the University of Arkansas, and Edward Colker, dean at the State University of New York at Purchase.[17]

In 1966 Woodruff showed slides of his *Amistad* murals in Sierra Leone to descendants of the mutineers who made African and American history. This experience sharpened his awareness of the cultural diversity of African peoples, evoking a wish for their unity. In his *Celestial Gate* series, an abstracted Dogon granary door is decorated, not with Dogon symbols, but with Woodruff's symbols of Ashanti gold weights—a deliberate combining of different tribal cultures in an aesthetic unity. His *Ancestral Memory* also represents an aesthetic unity, with its large red mask forming an iconographic symbol of the continent. This work was intended for the First World Festival of Black Art at Dakar, but Woodruff withdrew from the exhibition to protest its politicalization. Nevertheless, his wish for unity remains expressed.

Woodruff's concern with African imagery did not eliminate other observations. At times he painted landscapes in brilliant slashing colors in an Expressionist manner. He also created a series on children playing in which he emphasized action, depicting a girl skipping rope, for example.

Howard Conat, head of New York University's creative division, has noted that Woodruff's evolving style over the years came from "the deepening urgency of his determination to strive for the highest possible level of qualitative excellence in the mode of expression that he, rather than other artists, critics, or dealers, felt most appropriate. Woodruff calls his shots, and his aim is correctly high."[18]

Almost every day, for more than a decade after his university retirement, Woodruff drew sculpturally conceived torso figures inspired by Shango, the thunder god of the Yoruba people in Nigeria. He chose the torso for his studies, he said, because "while the head and limbs control the torso's action and animation, its bulk carries their weight and properties. This is why *Winged Victory* lives today." Such studies, he felt, brought him close to what he called his own particular vision and its own unity. This unity was apparent when a major retrospective exhibition of Woodruff's work was organized in 1979 at the Studio Museum in Harlem by its director, Mary Schmidt-Campbell. By this time his work was in the collections of the Metropolitan Museum of Art, the Detroit Institute of Arts, the Newark Museum, and many black colleges and universities.

Woodruff continued to work into his eightieth year. He died in New York on September 26, 1980. Several years before his death, talking to the novelist Albert Murray, Woodruff said: ". . . any black artist who claims that he is creating black art must begin with some black image. The black image can be the environment, it can be the look on a man's face. It can be anything. It's got to have this kind of pin-pointed point of departure. But if it's worth its while, it's also got to be universal in its broader impact and its presence."[19] It is this universality that Woodruff sought, and it is what makes him a seminal figure, whose importance has only begun to be recognized.

Woodruff created an imagery that, as Mary Schmidt-Campbell put it in summing up his fifty years of painting, "is not intrusive or protesting, but one which quietly celebrates the beauty and strength of Afro-Americans and their rich cultural heritage."[20]

### Notes

*This chapter, including biographical information and all quotations attributed to Hale A. Woodruff, unless otherwise indicated, is based on interviews with him April 16, 1967, April 27, 1972, and June 2, 1973, as well as letters April 14 and June 3, 1974, supplemented by many informal conversations and discussions in New York and one at Dillard University, New Orleans, where Woodruff was a guest lecturer in 1978. Additional material is drawn from* Hale Woodruff: Fifty Years of His Art *(New York: Studio Museum in Harlem, exhibition catalog, April 29-June 24, 1979).*

1. William Pickens, Sr., helped Du Bois organize the "Niagara movement" that led to the formation of the NAACP.

2. Countee Cullen became Woodruff's friend, bought his work, and often played cards with him and Palmer Hayden in France, inspiring Woodruff's *Cardplayers.*

3. Woodruff submitted five paintings; four were landscapes.

4. Arranged by Lucille Morehouse, art editor of the *Indianapolis Star.* Woodruff's illustrated articles started in January 1928 and continued bimonthly for fourteen months (Winifred Stoelting, "From Indianapolis to France," *Woodruff* (Studio Museum), p. 13.

5. *The Crisis* 35 (Aug. 1928), cover.

6. *The Crisis* (Jan. 1970), pp. 7-12.

7. The painting was *Old Woman Peeling Apples,* 1927, reproduced in *Woodruff* (Studio Museum), p. 11.

8. Wilmer Jennings quoted in ibid., p. 18.

9. Albert Murray interview in ibid., p. 80.

10. Winifred Stoelting, "Teaching at Atlanta," ibid., p. 18.

11. Jenelsie Walden Holloway, professor of art, Spelman College, Atlanta University, quoted in ibid., p. 20.

12. Hayward Oubre of Alabama State College quoted in ibid., p. 20.

13. *Time,* Sept. 21, 1942, p. 74.

14. Stoelting, "Teaching," *Woodruff* (Studio Museum), p. 21.

15. *Atlanta Constitution,* Dec. 18, 1935; reprinted *Opportunity* (Jan. 1936).

16. *Phylon 2* (First quarter, 1941), p. 4; in an accompanying note, Du Bois wrote: "Woodruff of Atlanta dropped his wet brushes, packed the rainbow into his knapsack and rode post-haste and Jim Crow into Alabama. There he dreamed upon the walls of Savery Library the thing of color and beauty portrayed on the opposite page, to keep the memory of Cinque, of the friendship, and the day when he and his men, with their staunch white friends, struck a blow for the freedom of mankind."

17. Woodruff's distinguished former students also included Howard Fussiner, painter and professor of art at Yale University, and Hans Peter Kahn, a painter who formerly taught at Cornell University. Some students have developed a new generation of black artists and educators. For example, Jeff Donaldson, teaching at Howard University, was a student of John Howard.

18. Foreword, *Hale Woodruff: An Exhibition of Selected Paintings and Drawings, 1927-1967,* (New York: Loeb Student Center, New York University, exhibition catalog, May 15-June 8, 1967).

19. Albert Murray interview in *Woodruff* (Studio Museum), p. 85.

20. Mary Schmidt-Campbell, "Hale Woodruff: Fifty Years of His Art," in ibid., p. 57. In 1979 New York Public School No. 224 in Brooklyn was named for him. In April 1981, Atlanta University paid tribute to Woodruff's initiation of its art collections and to his mural *The Art of the Negro* with a major exhibition, "Homage to Hale Woodruff."

# SCULPTORS

## ROMARE BEARDEN AND HARRY HENDERSON (ESSAY DATE 1993)

**SOURCE:** Bearden, Romare and Henderson, Harry. "Richmond Barthé." In *A History of African American Artists from 1792 to the Present,* pp. 136-46. New York: Pantheon Books, 1993.

*In the excerpt below, Bearden and Henderson discuss the work of the sculptor Richmond Barthé, focusing on his lyrical portrayal of Blacks and praising the beauty of the human form evident in his works of the Harlem Renaissance period.*

The black figures that Richmond Barthé modeled in a lyric, romantic, and often monumental style expressed the aspirations of a community that was almost immediately drawn to his imagery. Whether his subjects were such nationally known African-American leaders as Booker T. Washington or simply people to whom he was artistically attracted, Barthé's work of the 1920s and 1930s is clearly that of an artist who empathized with his people.

Barthé "has come to us at a time when we are sadly in need of real inspiration—of that spiritual food that heartens and strengthens . . . hopes that embody the willingness to do the larger and truer things in life," said William H. A. Moore in *Opportunity* in November 1928.[1]

In focusing on black people as his subjects, Barthé joined a few other pioneers. Where Palmer Hayden turned to memories of his life in the South and Archibald J. Motley, Jr., was drawn to the surging vitality of black social life after dark in the city, Barthé sought delineation of character through the marks of physiognomy and stance. Aesthetically, he brought a new insight to the individuality and physical grace of all types of black people.

A handsome and gracious man, who took a traditionally based approach to art, Barthé very early found his milieu. Once out of art school, he worked steadily as a professional artist, becoming one of the first contemporary black artists to support himself in this way. Never caught up in social movements, he was fascinated with portrait sculpture. He was able to move socially among those persons who wanted portrait sculpture and could afford it. Indeed, his poise made him sought after in wealthy and fashionably elite circles and undoubtedly helped to win commissions. His concern with personalities and with dancing led him into theatrical circles, where he came to know people intimately, from the stars to the chorus dancers. In work other than portraiture, Barthé often attempted to capture some action at a dramatic peak, giving his art a livelier quality than the work of many contemporaries.

That his work was instantly accessible to the public, never baffling with symbolism or abstract forms, contributed to Barthé's popularity. Often reproduced in the press, his statues helped to establish the image of the "New Negro."

His work also won praise from academicians, from whose traditions his art emerged. James A. Porter, for example, referring to three small bronzes (*The Harmonica Player, Shoe-shine Boy,* and *The Boxer*), called them "so close to perfection . . . that their effect upon the spectator is transporting."[2]

Yet despite the universal appeal of his work, critical attention to the work of such abstract sculptors as Constantin Brancusi and Henry Moore after World War II made much of Barthé's work seem peculiarly dated and limited. Moreover, as a sensitive and complex man, he increasingly suffered from internal conflicts that made his life in Manhattan stressful. Finally, in the late forties, Barthé left the United States for Jamaica, where initially he found life less trying. Many of his British friends, like Noël Coward, as well as wealthy British aristocrats, came there to escape England's harsh winters. Still later, he settled in Florence, Italy, and he spent his final years in California.

Today, Barthé's sculpture is in the Whitney Museum of American Art, the Metropolitan Museum of Art, the Schomburg Center for Research in Black Culture, and many private collections all over the world. The only sculptor with two portrait busts—of Booker T. Washington and George Washington Carver—in the serpentine portico of the Hall of Fame in New York, Barthé asserted that being black was a help rather than a hindrance to his being an artist.

Barthé was born on January 28, 1901, in Bay St. Louis, Mississippi, a Gulf Coast summer retreat for wealthy New Orleans families that was famous for its beaches and one of the largest Catholic parishes in the South. His parents were of African, French, and Native American descent. His father, Richmond Barthé, Sr., died at the age of twenty-two, when his son was only a few months old. His mother, Marie Clementine Robateau, whose people had been free blacks in St. Martinsville, Louisiana, supported the family through her sewing for six years. She then married William Franklin, Richmond's godfather, a working man who also played the cornet in a band.

Barthé's drawing ability was discovered very early. "When I was crawling on the floor, my mother gave me paper and pencil to play with," he later recalled. "It kept me quiet while she did her errands. At six years old I started painting. A lady my mother sewed for gave me a set of watercolors. By that time, I could draw very well." His drawings won family admiration: "My mother and I would give names to the people I drew and make up stories about them. My stepfather admired them."

As a boy, Barthé helped his stepfather deliver ice during the summer. A Mrs. Lorenzen from New Orleans "didn't like my working on the ice truck. She said that carrying ice on my shoulder

# ON THE SUBJECT OF...

## RICHMOND BARTHÉ

Richmond Barthé (January 28, 1901-March 6, 1989) came to New York in February 1929, following his graduation from the Art Institute of Chicago. The following two decades saw him build a reputation that would be the envy of many of his peers. The 1930s and 1940s would see him rise to great prominence and gain high praise for his work from both critics and collectors. By 1934, Barthé was granted his first solo show at the Caz Delbo Galleries in New York City. Numerous other exhibitions and important commissions followed thereafter. His works were added to important collections such as the Whitney Museum of American Art (*African Dancer*), the Metropolitan Museum of Art, the Pennsylvania Museum of Art, the Virginia Museum of Fine Arts, and the Museum of the Art Institute of Chicago (*The Boxer*).

Barthé's commissions included a bas relief of Arthur Brisbane for New York's Central Park and an eight-by-eighty-foot frieze, *Green Pastures: The Walls of Jericho,* for the Harlem River Housing Project. Other commissions included two portrait busts and a garden sculpture for the Edgar Kaufman house (*Falling Water*), designed by architect Frank Lloyd Wright; a Booker T. Washington portrait bust for the Hall of Fame of New York University; an Othello modeled after Paul Robeson for Actor's Equity; and the General Toussaint Louverture Monument, Port-au-Prince, Haiti.

would give me rheumatism. She bought my first pair of long pants and sent me with a letter to see her friend, Mrs. [Harry] Pond, asking her to give me a job. Mrs. Pond took me to New Orleans to work and live with them and I stayed there until I was sent to Chicago to study art at the age of twenty-three."

During his years of employment in the various homes of the wealthy Pond family, helped by the considerateness of his employers, Barthé developed a natural poise and graciousness. His social ease is one of the first characteristics that his friends recall about him.

Through the Pond family, Barthé met Leslie Ducros, a *New Orleans Times-Picayune* writer. She introduced him to Lyle Saxon, the paper's critic, who posed for Barthé and criticized his work. "We used to plan that some day he would give up his job on the paper and write his first book and I would leave the Ponds, become an artist and have my first exhibition. Both our dreams came true," Barthé recalled. Later a novelist, Saxon died in 1946.[3]

Impressed by a painting of Christ that Barthé had done for a church festival, the Reverend Jack Kane, pastor of the Catholic Blessed Sacrament Church, inquired into Barthé's background and problems. Finding no local art school would accept black students, Father Kane paid "with his own money," according to Barthé, for him to attend the Art Institute of Chicago. Barthé partially supported himself for these four years, from 1924 to 1928, as a waiter in a French restaurant.

In Chicago Barthé met a number of black artists at the Art Institute. One was Archibald J. Motley, Jr., who was beginning to achieve some recognition at the institute and who held a Sunday drawing class for other black artists in his studio, which Barthé attended. Most of these students could not attend the institute for lack of funds or because of their work schedules.

The greatest influence on Barthé's development was a painter, Charles Schroeder, who taught summer and Saturday classes at the Art Institute for more than thirty years. Under his guidance, Barthé studied anatomy and figure construction, both at the institute and privately. It was Schroeder's suggestion that ultimately made Barthé turn to sculpture. As Barthé explained it:

One day, during the last year I was with him, he asked me to do a couple of heads in clay, saying that they would give me a feeling for a third dimension in my painting. He said not to bother casting them—just throw them back into the clay box. I did heads of two classmates, one male and one female. They turned out so well, I cast and patined them and they were shown during "The Negro in Art Week" [at the Art Institute, sponsored by the Chicago Women's Club].[4] The critics praised them and I was asked to do busts of Henry O. Tanner and Toussaint L'Ouverture for the Lake County Children's Home in Gary, Indiana.

At the opening of this exhibition . . . four Jubilee Singers sang. I went home and from memory did a small head of one of them— *The Jubilee Singer.* A photo of it was used on the cover of *Crisis.* I sold many copies of it. I showed this and photographs of other first attempts to Jo Davidson and Lorado Taft [prominent American sculptors of the time], and they both advised that I keep away from instructors, that I had something in my work, a spiritual quality, that I could lose if I was influenced by an instructor. Since I knew anatomy, I did not need anyone to help me with proportions.

Thus began Barthé's career as a sculptor. His particular gift was in modeling a figure or face with a certain elegance and sensitivity. In contrast to many present-day sculptors, Barthé had little feeling for carving and very rarely did it. Clay was undoubtedly a medium more congenial to Barthé's talent; most American sculptors then followed the tradition of Augustus Saint-Gaudens of modeling figures in clay for later casting.

At times, particularly early in his career, Barthé's work reflected the racial conflicts of the United States. One such work is *Head of a Tortured Negro.* Later, at the 1939 New York World's Fair, Barthé exhibited *Mother and Son,* an eloquent depiction of a black mother mourning over her dead son, whose neck shows rope marks.[5] These themes of protest had a genuine and deep reality to Barthé, who had come from Mississippi, where lynchings were common in his boyhood.

Soon after his work appeared in *The Crisis,* Barthé was offered a one-man show in New York. Feeling he was not ready for it, he declined and spent 1929 studying at the Art Students League in New York. On returning to Chicago in 1930, he exhibited forty pieces at the Women's City Club. Fortunately for his continued development, he was awarded, on the strength of his first exhibition, a Julius Rosenwald Fund fellowship.

Barthé's work won an honorable mention in the 1929 Harmon exhibition, and his first one-man show in New York at the Caz-Delbo Gallery in 1931 won high critical praise. Edward Alden Jewell, the influential *New York Times* critic, characterized Barthé as "a sculptor of unmistakable promise," noting that his "modeling is most sensitive, communicating at once the spirit of the subject and the spirit that distinguishes all of this young sculptor's aspirations. Richmond Barthé penetrates far beneath the surface, honestly seeking essentials, and never . . . stooping to polish off an interpretation with superficial allure. There is no cleverness, no damaging slickness in this sculpture. Some of the readings deserve, indeed, to be called profound."[6]

Jewell reported that an interviewer (who may have been Jewell) had asked Barthé about his response to Alain Locke's call for a racial art. Barthé responded, "I don't think art is racial, but I do feel that a Negro can portray the inner feelings of the Negro people better than a white man can."[7]

Barthé's New York success brought him permanently to New York, and his Rosenwald grant was renewed. The esteem with which he was held by his gallery was reflected in 1933 when, on moving to Rockefeller Center, the Caz-Delbo Gallery opened with an exhibition of Barthé's work surrounded by old master drawings.

Barthé also exhibited at the 1933 Chicago World's Fair with Tanner and Motley. Copies of his portrait of a leading African educator, James Aggrey, commissioned by the Phelps-Stokes Fund, were distributed in many African countries. In 1934 Xavier University, a prominent Catholic institution in New Orleans and now one of the few institutions in the South to provide training for sculptors in casting, awarded him an honorary master of arts degree.

Much interested in Barthé's work, Gertrude V. Whitney, herself a sculptor, and Juliana Force, then director of the Whitney Museum of American Art in New York, arranged another exhibition of his sculpture. The museum bought three statues from the show: *Blackberry Woman, African Dancer,* and *The Comedian.*

Recognition from all these sources, particularly the Whitney, prompted other museums and collectors to seek his work. Although Barthé worked briefly as a "duster" in an admirer's antique shop,[8] his work was soon in such demand that he was able to devote himself entirely to his art. His success was such that, late in 1934, he was able to go to Europe. This tour of European museums and galleries, in his words, "opened up a new world" and led to exhibitions abroad. Today his work is in private collections in many countries.

During the 1930s, like many other African-American artists, Barthé was fascinated by dance. To deepen his own feeling and understanding of the body's musculature, Barthé joined a modern dance group under Mary Radin at Martha Graham's studio. His figures of dancers, lyric portrayals of the body in motion, are among his best works, achieving their effects through linear qualities rather than volume and mass. His dance experiences were of considerable help to Barthé when, in 1937, he was commissioned by the Treasury Public Works of Art Project to create two eight-by-forty-foot bas-relief panels for the Harlem River Housing Project amphitheater. In one panel he depicted black dancers, and in the other, the "Exodus" scene from the 1930 Pulitzer Prize winner, *The Green Pastures.*

In March 1939 Barthé's largest exhibition, with eighteen bronzes, opened at the Arden Galleries in New York. Critically acclaimed, it helped him gain a Guggenheim fellowship in 1940 and again in 1941.

When the United States entered World War II, circumstances combined to place Barthé under severe strain. In his absorption with his art and his social success, Barthé somehow remained fixed in attitudes characteristic of the Harlem Renaissance. For most black artists those attitudes had vanished with the Depression, when, as Langston Hughes put it, they discovered black people "were no longer in vogue."[9] But Barthé had never experienced this change in the social tides, and with the coming of the war he found himself in demand for political and social functions related to the war. He became the most highly publicized black artist in the country.

What underlay the publicizing of Barthé was the need to mobilize black manpower for the war effort and to convince both black and white citizens, as well as the Allies, that the United States was, despite segregation and discrimination, democratic. Barthé was included in programs of all kinds. The New York City radio station WNYC dramatized his life. The Office of War Information filmed Barthé at work and displayed much of his work; the film was shown in the United States and abroad. . . .

Barthé's work in this period included a bust of the Hearst journalist Arthur Brisbane, an eighty-foot frieze for the Kingsborough Housing Project in Brooklyn, and sculpture for the Social Security Board Building in Washington, D.C. He also turned out three Christ figures for Catholic churches and institutions, which, as a devout Catholic, meant a great deal to him. He wanted to emphasize Christ's humanity, personal charm, and popularity, he said, adding, "Jesus was always being asked out to dinner. People were crazy about him."[10]

During these war years, Barthé created heroic statues of black generals of the past, including Toussaint L'Ouverture and General Jean Jacques Dessalines, the first important black military leaders in the Western Hemisphere.[11] These monumental works stand in Port au Prince, Haiti, and his portrait of Toussaint L'Ouverture appears on Haitian coins.

Profound changes in aesthetic values and concepts following World War II tended to cut Barthé off from the most dynamic currents in sculpture. Aesthetic interest moved in the direction of Abstract Expressionism, stimulating acceptance and enthusiasm for the symbolic imagery of Brancusi, the eloquent forms of Henry Moore, and ultimately for the welded-steel abstractions of David Smith. In this ground swell even the status of Jo Davidson and Jacob Epstein, the foremost modeling portraitist of America and England, sagged. In contrast, the work of Jacques Lipchitz, who had come to the United States during the war as a refugee, gained favor with expressionistic dramatizations of ancient myths.

All of this tended to push Barthé into the backwaters of public interest, for he was neither an innovator nor an experimentalist, but very much a traditionalist. Always absorbed in how emotional and spiritual feelings express themselves in physiognomy, movement, stance, and gesture, he was not drawn to symbolism or mythology. New materials did not attract him nor did the work of Elie Nadelman, whose concern with social types offered a new concept in American sculpture. If Barthé admired anyone, it was Auguste Rodin. However, Barthé's work moved toward the lyrical rather than the intense dramatizations that Rodin created.

That Barthé had not been on the WPA separated him from most artists, and that he rarely got to Harlem isolated him from African-American artists. Being highly publicized during the war had further distanced him.

Previously interested in a wide range of black personalities and types, he now turned almost exclusively to portraiture of wealthy people and particularly of theatrical stars. From his first arrival in New York he was attracted to theatrical people and increasingly traveled in their circles. In these postwar years Barthé turned to an extraordinarily difficult type of portraiture, one which in itself is a severely demanding and restrictive art form. Barthé's first attempt at such portraiture was a head, *The Comedian,* which was purchased by the Whitney Museum. His interest—indeed, his fascination—in stage stars was reinforced by an early success. In 1930 an African-American folk drama about getting into heaven written by Marc Connelly, *The Green Pastures,* had become a memorable hit, running for years. Its star was the brilliant African-American actor Richard B. Harrison, who had earlier gained a national reputation with dramatic readings and interpretations of Shakespearean roles. In *The Green Pastures* he appeared as "de Lawd" in the plain black suit of a black preacher who is confronted with the perplexing life problems of various sinners. Harrison won the Spingarn medal of the National Association for the Advancement of Colored People for his performance, which he played over 1,600 times. Barthé, intrigued by the theater and deeply religious, made a portrait bust of "de Lawd" as he appeared in the play.[12] His portrait was acclaimed by theater critics.

This success, and the popular response to his mask of Rose McClendon, the star of *Deep River, Abraham's Bosom,* and *Mulatto,* led Barthé to embark on a series of portraits of stars in their favorite or current roles. In 1942, at the Arden Galleries, he exhibited portraits of Maurice Evans as Richard II and John Gielgud as Hamlet. Such sculpture was an exceedingly ambitious effort, requiring interpretation of the dramatic character as well as the personality and likeness of the star. Moreover, the series was uncommissioned yet inevitably highly publicized. Once Barthé started on this project, he had to "capture" stars whom he initially did not know well in order to have enough portraits for a full exhibition, creating greater tension for himself. Economically, the series required an enormous investment of time and energy. Eventually he added Laurence Olivier as Hotspur, Katharine Cornell as Candida, Judith Anderson as Mary, and others. While the stars were not collectors, there was always the chance that they or some admirer might purchase the work. To complete this series, Barthé was kept in a state of feverish anxiety and activity. He also was winning new honors—an award of $500 and recognition from the National Institute of Arts and Letters in 1946.

When his theater portraits were exhibited at Grand Central Art Galleries in the spring of 1947, the critical response was favorable but bland. Emily Genauer, then the *New York World-Telegram* critic, more perceptive than others, applauded the "excellent likenesses," but recognized that something else was happening: "In their over-elaboration of meaningless details of costume and feature, they are made commonplace and quite empty of inner meaning."[13] In short, the very quality that had made his earlier portraits of black working people so perceptive and meaningful was missing from his portraits of the famous actors. Barthé sought, in an ambitious way, to portray both the role, for which the actor was famous, and the actor as a serious artist. Although he worked hard, these portraits were somehow caught up in superficial theatrical pretense, with costumes and likenesses, but not the force of the actor's personality.

In this situation the internal and external pressures of Barthé's life brought him to a crisis. He was dissatisfied with himself and his work and without friends. Old English friends, like Noël Coward, had gone back to England. Both Harrison and McClendon had died. The theater he felt a part of was gone. So was the prewar Harlem he had occasionally visited; its artists were scattered. And the critical excitement over abstract sculpture left him feeling estranged and abandoned. In a certain sense his whole milieu had vanished.

Depressed and anxious, he reached a state of nervous exhaustion. "My nerve ends were sick and the doctor ordered me to leave New York," Barthé recalled. "He said there was too much tension for me. A friend bought a home in Jamaica and invited me down—and I went and fell in love with the beauty of the island. I built a home there and was very happy in it." By 1950 many of his old friends, including English theatrical stars, were visiting him there.

On the Caribbean island Barthé gradually resumed work, turning out many portraits and small figures with a steady flow of commissions from wealthy American and British tourists. In March 1966, he wrote to a friend: "Tourists come here to see paintings, sculpture, my seashell collection, old Jamaican furniture. . . . I raise my own coffee, chocolate, breadfruits, bananas, and plantain. . . . I enjoy the easy life with the rolling hills, pure air, and beautiful flowers. . . . I don't think I shall ever want to live any place else. I don't like cities and rushing anymore."[14]

However, in the mid-1960s, when the civil rights movement was stirring the nation, Barthé's work was remembered by those seeking to change the image of the black American. Responding to an invitation to return to his birthplace, Barthé was delighted when the mayor of Bay St. Louis held a reception and presented him with the key to the city. Another reception was held at St. Augustine's Seminary, a Catholic school for black priests. There was also a reception at Tulane University, giving New Orleans artists and students a chance to meet Barthé, who had once been barred from study in that city. Still later, in 1971, a street in Bay St. Louis was named for him. These events were heavily covered by the press and television.

Barthé's triumphal visit to the South further stimulated tourist visits to his Jamaican home, a two-acre plot he called "Ioalus." As the home and studio of Jamaica's only internationally known artist, it became a tourist showplace. The pattern of hectic social activity that had driven Barthé from New York now reappeared. In the same letter in which he rejoiced over his pleasures in Jamaica, he also revealed things were getting out of control. He wrote: "I have been so busy with unfinished work, unanswered letters, and tourists. . . . Since the first of January I have had 118 tourists sign my guest book. I am trying to get enough work finished for a one-man show in New York."[15]

Almost twenty years had lapsed since Barthé had had a show, but, as the pace on the island became faster, it became apparent to him that he could not put together an exhibition, that he had to get off the island to escape its pressures. "With the coming of all the hotels, the people and the atmosphere of the islands changed," he later said. "So in 1969 I decided to leave. I spent the winter in Switzerland and in April 1970 I came down to Florence and decided this is where I shall stay. I love it here, surrounded by the great art of the Renaissance, where buildings never change."[16]. . .

Barthé died March 5, 1989.[17] He had willed his work to [James] Garner, who, feeling he knew nothing about art, turned it over, as Barthé had suggested in his will, to Samella Lewis, an art historian and founding director of the Museum of African American Art in Los Angeles.[18] Those Barthé sculptures previously on loan to the Schomburg Center in New York were given to it, and Lewis has planned a major memorial exhibition of Barthé's work.

Barthé emerged as the outstanding academic sculptor of the Black Renaissance, and his work continued to demonstrate a compelling unity in theme and style over a period of more than sixty years. This unity is all the more striking because of the changes not only in the social milieu but also in the concepts of art during this period; Abstract Expressionism, for example, soon became outmoded. What Barthé's life and work make clear is the individuality of African-American artists. Although they share a racial identity and, especially in the 1920s, certain common experiences, each works out of his or her own experience and vision of the world.

A sensitive, creative man, and the least parochial of the black artists of the 1920s, Barthé at times offered contradictory accounts of his past. Although he himself was not allowed to study in New Orleans, he later recalled no difficulties, claiming, "While I was there I met no problems because of color. From the very beginning of my career I exhibited along with white artists and I was invited to join their groups. I was a member of the Sculptors Guild, the Audubon Artists—a director for one year—and the National Sculpture Society. I found that being a Negro was an asset, not a hindrance."

Barthé desired to be identified as a black artist. In the late 1960s he was deeply hurt when an exhibition committee selecting work that demonstrated the contribution of African-American artists to American art omitted his work. With works in public and private collections all over the world, he felt he deserved more than this, saying, "I don't know any Negro, living or dead, who has done more than I have in sculpture."

Asked what he considered his most significant work, Barthé responded, "I don't know. My favorites are—the *Mother,* with her lynched son; *Come Unto Me,* a six-foot figure of Jesus;[19] and *The Awakening of Africa.*" Interestingly, these works express a social and racial consciousness not generally associated with Barthé. . . .

During his initial and most productive period, Barthé portrayed black Americans and their spirit in a lyric way—a view that was new to most Americans. His outlook throughout his work was based on his observance of universal human qualities and was not restricted to black subject matter. No matter how or where he has lived, his work possesses a marked thematic and stylistic unity.

In his best work, done mostly in the 1930s and 1940s, Barthé created a tension between the repose and supple action of his figures. In his full figures, the movements flow upward and outward with an expressive intensity that derives from a deep appreciation of human vitality. The genuine movement in his work frees it from the frozen world of Neoclassical sculpture. Barthé was always aware that as a sculptor he was, in his art, singing in praise of the beauty of the body. In this, he did not overlook the passions, the sadnesses and felicities, of life. Within the traditions of his period, Barthé must be considered one of the most distinguished contributors to American sculpture.

## Notes

*Unless otherwise noted, quotations from Richmond Barthé and most of the biographical material in this chapter are based on his responses from Florence, Italy, to questions from the authors, August 26, 1972. Conversations with his brother, Louis J. Franklin (Dec. 18 and 29, 1989), Kathy Register of the Pasadena Star-News (March 16, 1989), Esther Jones (Dec. 18, 1989), Samella Lewis (Jan. 2 and March 13, 1990), and Mary Ann Rey (James Garner's assistant), magazine writer Nanette Turner, and Frances White (all June 1-3, 1992) clarified the events of Barthé's last days.*

1. William H. A. Moore, in *Opportunity* 19 (Nov. 1928), p. 334.

2. James A. Porter, *Modern Negro Art* (New York: Dryden Press, 1943), p. 137.

3. Saxon wrote *Father Mississippi* (1927), *Children of Strangers* (1937), and other books about southern life, and directed the WPA Louisiana Federal Writers Project.

4. See *The Negro in Chicago, 1779-1927* (Chicago: Washington Intercollegiate Club, 1927), p. 223. Barthé is listed as a member of the African-American Art League of Chicago (p. 83).

5. Only photographs of this work remain. It was accidentally destroyed in transit after being exhibited at the American Negro Exposition in Chicago in 1940.

6. *New York Times,* Dec. 18, 1931, p. 28.

7. Ibid.

8. *Negro Artists: An Illustrated Review of Their Achievements* (New York: Harmon Foundation, exhibition catalog, 1935). This exhibition displayed the work of only three artists: Barthé, Malvin Gray Johnson, and Sargent Johnson.

9. Langston Hughes, *The Big Sea* (New York: A. A. Knopf, 1945; reprint, New York: Hill & Wang, 1968), pp. 223-28.

10. *Current Biography,* 1940, p. 57.

11. Barthé was reportedly commissioned to create a heroic military figure for the U.S. Military Academy, but M. J. McAfee, West Point Museum curator, wrote the authors on August 26, 1976, that it could not be located and that many files on both completed and suspended projects had been destroyed.

12. Meta Vaux Warrick Fuller also portrayed Harrison as "de Lawd," seated on a bench as in the play in 1935. Her sculpture is reproduced in Porter, *Modern Negro Art,* unpaged section.

13. Reviews summarized in *Art News,* April 1947, p. 48.

14. Barthé to Henry Ghent, March 21, 1966.

15. Ibid.

16. Ibid.

17. Kathy Register, obituary, *Pasadena Star-News,* March 7, 1989; *New York Times,* March 16, 1989.

18. According to Mary Ann Rey, Garner's assistant.

19. Deeply religious, Barthé did three portraits of Christ. *The Angry Christ* is in the Schomburg Center; the six-foot bronze, *"Come Unto Me," Christ,* is in the Church of St. Jude in Montgomery, Alabama; the third portrait is in the Clark-Atlanta University collection.

## ROMARE BEARDEN AND HARRY HENDERSON (ESSAY DATE 1993)

**SOURCE:** Bearden, Romare and Henderson, Harry. "Augusta Savage." In *A History of African American Artists from 1792 to the Present,* pp. 168-80. New York: Pantheon Books, 1993.

*In the excerpt below, the authors review the life and works of Augusta Savage, who overcame prejudice against her as a Black and as a woman and dedicated her life to art and to nurturing young artists.*

The most popular work in a huge New York exhibition of African-American artists in 1967 was a plaster head of an attractive boy modeled almost forty years earlier. *Gamin,* which has

moved people ever since Augusta Savage created it, is one of the few fully realized works of an artist whose total output was small and uneven.

Brilliant, friendly, fierce, and difficult at times even for her friends, Augusta Christine Savage had to overcome prejudice against her as a black and as a woman, in a period of history when women had only just won the right to vote. When her efforts to become an important sculptor were overwhelmed by the Depression, she turned to nurturing young black artists in New York. For a generation of such artists, her influence was critical. She did more than teach in an academic sense. She sought talent. She found jobs for young artists and helped them focus on their own experiences and values. She fought political battles that helped hundreds of Works Progress Administration artists regardless of race. In these struggles her resources, emotional and aesthetic, were depleted. More than a decade before she died in 1962, she abandoned all efforts to create and isolated herself.

Yet her talent and her responses to the problems she faced made Savage one of the most significant leaders of black artists to emerge in the 1920s. She was perhaps the first who could be identified as a black nationalist.

Augusta Fells (Savage) was born, she always said, "at the dark of the moon," on February 29, 1892, in Green Cove Springs, near Jacksonville, Florida.[1] She was the seventh child of a very poor fundamentalist preacher, the Reverend Edward Fells, and his wife, Cornelia. They had seven more children after Augusta; only nine of the fourteen reached adulthood.

Green Cove Springs was a brick-making town, abounding in clay, and Augusta discovered her skill in modeling ducks, pigs, and chickens at an early age. She was so drawn to the clay pits that she became a truant. Her father feared she was "fashioning graven images in a Godly house" and beat her. "My father licked me five or six times a week and almost whipped all the art out of me," she said later.[2]

When she was about fifteen years old, her father became the minister of a West Palm Beach congregation, which improved the family's circumstances. At her new school Augusta's sensitive poetry won her teachers' admiration and her truancy ended. When a local potter gave her clay, she modeled an eighteen-inch Virgin Mary that made her father regret his earlier harshness. With the potter donating the clay, the school board accepted the principal's recommendation that Augusta, though still a student, be paid a dollar a day for every day she taught modeling in the last six months of her senior year.[3] This satisfying experience gave her a lifelong interest in teaching.

During this period, in 1907, Augusta Fells married John T. Moore and they had a daughter. Soon after, Moore died and Augusta returned with her child to her parents.

Knowing Palm Beach's main business was catering to tourists, Augusta showed the country fair superintendent, George Graham Currie, an array of amusing farm animals. He gave her a booth, and her ducks and other animals became a major attraction. The delighted fair officials, initially apprehensive about a black girl having a booth, voted her a $25 prize and special ribbon for the most original exhibit. When the fair ended, Augusta had earned $175—a fantastic sum for a poor black girl in Florida at the time.[4]

Currie came to believe deeply in Augusta's talent and commissioned a portrait of himself.[5] This stimulated her to seek similar commissions among well-to-do black people of Jacksonville. They were unwilling, however, to become the paying sitters of an unknown young sculptor. Then Currie, who had once met Solon Borglum (the sculptor father of Gutzon Borglum, who carved the presidential heads on Mount Rushmore), wrote him about Augusta and urged her to go to New York to study art.

On the eve of her departure, Augusta expressed her gratitude to Currie in verse:

"MY SOUL'S GETHSEMANE"
At the forks of life's high road
    alone I stand,
And the hour of my temptation
    is at hand,
In my soul's Gethsemane
    I still have your faith in me,
And it strengthens me
    to know you understand.[6]

Arriving in New York with $4.60, Augusta Savage went to see Solon Borglum. He pointed out that the young ladies who "study with me are the children of the rich and pay immense fees."[7] He suggested she study instead at Cooper Union because it charged no tuition, and he wrote a letter urging her admission to its registrar, Kate Reynolds.

At Cooper Union an unknown young black man persuaded Reynolds to see Savage's work. Overnight, she modeled the head of a Harlem minister, and this work, along with Borglum's letter, won her immediate admission in October 1921. During this time she also met and married James Savage, a carpenter, but divorced him within a few months. Her name on Cooper Union records, however, was Savage, and she left it that way.

The sculpture course was a four-year program. Her instructors passed Savage through the first year's work in two weeks and through the second year's in a month. She then was admitted to a life class taught by George T. Brewster, a well-known portrait sculptor. However, a few months later, by February 1922, she had exhausted her funds. Impressed by Savage's talent, Reynolds, the registrar, immediately got her a temporary job and called an emergency meeting of the Cooper Union Advisory Council. For the first time in the school's history, the council voted to supply funds for a student, covering room, board, and carfare.[8]

Long after she was doing notable portraits herself, Savage continued in Brewster's classes. Years later, when she had more confidence, she said: "I didn't know how good I was."[9]

Early in 1923 Savage sought admission to a summer art school sponsored by the French government in Fontainebleau, outside Paris. One hundred young American women were to be selected for it by a committee of eminent American artists and architects. Tuition would be free, but the fare to France and living expenses, estimated at $500, would have to be borne by those accepted. Savage paid a $35 application fee when friends promised the needed $500. She was then informed she had to supply two references, but before she could send the references, her $35 was returned. The committee, "with regret," rejected her.

Knowing she was more qualified than some who were accepted, Savage was disappointed and enraged. She decided to fight her rejection by exposing the committee's bias. When the Ethical Culture Society leader Alfred W. Martin learned of Savage's rejection, he promised to fight it if the story was true. He asked Ernest Peixotto, the internationally known artist heading the Fontainebleau committee, for an explanation. Peixotto replied that Savage's application was not accompanied by two references, but he also "frankly" added that the committee felt this avoided a difficult situation for the accepted "southern" girls. They would all have to travel on the same ship, eat together, work in the same classes, and this would have been "embarrassing" to Savage.[10]

Martin, denouncing such flagrant racial discrimination, called for reconsideration by the committee, which included the president of the National Academy of Design, Edwin Blashfield; the president of the Society of Beaux-Arts Architecture, James Gamble Rogers; and Hermon A. MacNeil, a leader of the National Sculpture Society. That "intelligent" and "liberal" artists practiced racial discrimination made first page news in New York and stimulated a *Nation* editorial on May 9, 1923. Harlem ministers and leading scholars, such as the Columbia University anthropologist Franz Boas, assailed the committee.[11] In the *New York World* of May 20, 1923, Augusta Savage gave her own point of view:

> I don't care much for myself because I will get along all right here, but other and better colored students might wish to apply sometime. This is the first year the school is open and I am the first colored girl to apply. I don't like to see them establish a precedent. . . . Democracy is a strange thing. My brother was good enough to be accepted in one of the regiments that saw service in France during the war, but it seems his sister is not good enough to be a guest of the country for which he fought. . . . How am I to compete with other American artists if I am not to be given the same opportunity?

The uproar continued. Martin sailed to France to protest in person to French authorities. Emmett J. Scott of Howard University compared the committee's action to a recent Missouri lynching. Boas, in an open letter to Peixotto, ridiculed the committee's "narrow racial prejudice."

The committee avoided the press, but one member concluded it had been wrong. He was sculptor Hermon A. MacNeil, who many years earlier had briefly shared a Paris studio with Henry Ossawa Tanner and knew that he had been driven abroad by prejudice. A sensitive portrayer of Native Americans, he tried to make amends by inviting Savage to study with him. She accepted and in later years cited him as one of her teachers.[12]

This struggle brought Savage, then thirty-one years old, national attention. But even more important was that, as a result, she became an experienced fighter in the struggle for equal rights. She not only made many Americans aware of unknown black artists in their midst, but in the character of her fight she expressed the existence of the "new Negro."

Savage paid a heavy price for taking the lead in this fight. She was one of the first black American artists to challenge the art establishment head-on and, due to circumstances beyond her control, that struggle—rather than her art—came

to be where she spent much of her life's energies. Throughout the rest of her life she was considered a troublemaker by those whose racial prejudice she exposed—a group that included influential artists, museum curators and directors, dealers, foundation personnel, critics, and government officials. No one knows how many times she was excluded from exhibits, galleries, and museums because of this confrontation.

Working in Manhattan steam laundries to earn money needed by her family, Savage was sustained by knowing that an earlier black woman sculptor, Meta Vaux Warrick Fuller, had studied at the Colarossi Academy in Rome in 1899 and later with Auguste Rodin.[13] Gradually Savage realized that the black artist was caught in the economic plight of African-Americans as a whole and that she could not escape their struggles. When her father was paralyzed by a stroke, she brought her parents north to live with her, and when a hurricane destroyed their home and killed her brother, the rest of the family came too. For a while she had nine people in her three-room apartment on West 137th Street.[14]

Yet she did not stop her studies. A librarian, Sadie Peterson, was impressed by Savage's persistent study of art history in the Harlem branch library and quietly arranged for the Friends of the Library to commission her to create a portrait bust of W. E. B. Du Bois. Considered the finest portrait ever made of Du Bois, the bust was formally presented to the library in 1923. "Militancy, intelligence, and resolve are present in every plane," Elton C. Fax, a painter and writer, wrote of this bust in 1962.[15]

This success brought more commissions, the most important of which was a portrait of Du Bois's bitter enemy Marcus Garvey, the black nationalist who, through his Universal Negro Improvement Association, urged black people to develop self-reliance and to take pride in their African heritage. With his massive head and small alert eyes, Garvey was not an easy subject. Yet Savage captured his intelligence, his thrusting determination, and his self-dramatizing, insistent pride. Unlike the Du Bois portrait, which was displayed in the Harlem branch library for over twenty-five years, the Garvey portrait was seen only in a few black newspapers on completion. Today it is in his widow's home in Jamaica.[16]

Through the Garvey commission, Savage came to know one of his most trusted assistants, Robert L. Poston, secretary general of the Universal Negro Improvement Association. Soon after completing the bust, she married Poston. But whatever happiness Augusta found was soon shattered when Poston, sent to Liberia to set up a Garvey colony, died on a steamship on his way home.[17] This was another blow to an already embittered young woman.

Her contact with Du Bois, Garvey, and Poston deepened Savage's loving identification with black people. It also gave her a sense of the need for black leadership and the qualities required for it. Although Du Bois and Garvey were enemies, both were able, profoundly influential, and deeply concerned with redefining relations between the white and black races. From this time onward, Savage became consciously absorbed in trying to fight for and lead black people, an effort that had many ramifications for her as an artist. . . .

In 1925 Du Bois secured a scholarship for Savage at the Royal Academy of Fine Arts in Rome.[18] It provided both tuition and working materials, always a financial burden for sculptors. However, the fare and living expenses, estimated to total $1,500, were not included, and she was not able to raise this sum. Once again, it seemed to her that her aesthetic development was frustrated by economic circumstances arising from discrimination.

Yet Savage never stopped modeling. Resilient and determined, she made many small clay portraits of ordinary people or types, such as the *Young Boxer,* which became part of her "permanent" exhibition at the Harlem branch library. She also had the satisfaction of having her work accepted at the Sesquicentennial Exposition in Philadelphia.

One day Savage coaxed an attractive boy she met near her studio into posing for her. Casually questioning and joking with him as she worked, she created a portrait representative of thousands of young black boys who lived on the streets and whose knowledge of life and people far exceeded their years. Her portrait caught the liveliness, the tenderness, and the sly wisdom of such boys. She titled it *Gamin.*

Immediately recognized as outstanding, *Gamin* moved everyone who saw it. Two prominent Harlem businessmen, Eugene Kinckle Jones, of the National Urban League, and John E. Nail, a real estate operator and father-in-law of James Weldon Johnson, agreed that funds had to be raised for Savage to study abroad; they knew the Fontainebleau story. Jones turned to the Julius Rosenwald Fund, established by the president of

Sears Roebuck to aid minority groups. An art expert, assigned by the foundation to evaluate her work, was so enthusiastic that Savage was immediately awarded two successive fellowships.[19] In addition, each award was increased from $1,500 to $1,800 per year in special recognition of her merit and her problems in supporting herself.

Knowledge of Savage's Fontainebleau troubles was, in fact, so widespread among black Americans that when her fellowships were announced, many wanted to help pay for her travel and wardrobe so that her funds could go entirely for study, sculpture tools and materials, and living expenses. Fund-raising parties were held in Harlem and Greenwich Village. Many black women's groups sent money. Black teachers at Florida A & M collected fifty dollars for her. Few artists have ever received this kind of support from ordinary people. Augusta Savage was their artist. They also knew the pain of discrimination and wanted to help someone with talent overcome it.

In September 1929 Savage enrolled in a leading Paris art school, the Académie de la Grande Chaumière. She also began studies with Félix Benneteau-Desgrois, a winner of the Grand Prix of Rome in 1909 and the portraitist of many well-known French actors and political figures. To Eugene Kinckle Jones, she soon wrote of Benneteau: "Although he does not speak English, we manage to understand each other. He is very strict but patient with me. I am very sure that I shall be able to make great progress under his instruction. He promises to enter my work in the Salon in May if I work hard."[20]

The next year Savage's work won citations in the fall and spring Salons. An African figure she created was selected for medallion reproduction at the French Colonial Exposition.[21]

In Paris, Savage studied briefly with Charles Despiau, one of the great modern portraitists. Despiau emphasized expressive modeling and sensitivity to the emotional outlook of the subject, something Savage had demonstrated in *Gamin.* At the time Despiau had turned from the flowing movements of Rodin to the severe and formal figures of archaic sculpture in his search for simplicity. When Savage continued her studies by traveling through France, Belgium, and Germany, she sought out archaic sculpture in cathedrals, churches, and museums.

In Europe Savage evolved a personal viewpoint that allowed her to consider anything potential subject matter, whether a panther chasing a gazelle, a gesture, or an emotion. But however "free," her efforts tended to be more decorative than innovative in terms of concept, material, and treatment. Leading modern sculptors such as Constantin Brancusi or Jacob Epstein apparently did not interest her. Nor did any relationship between Cubism and African art.

Later, referring in a distorted way to Locke's plea for African-American artists to study the "ancestral arts of Africa" for the psychological benefits, Savage asserted she was "opposed to the theory of critics that the American Negro should produce African art." Instead, she emphasized the culture black and white Americans share. "For the last 300 years we have had the same cultural background, the same system, the same standard of beauty as white Americans. In art schools we draw from Greek casts. We study the small mouth, the proportions of the features and limbs. It is impossible to go back to primitive art for our models." However, she added, "there are certain traits and inherent racial characteristics which occur frequently in Negro artists' work which may approach the primitive." As examples, she cited "the sense of rhythm and spontaneous imagination."[22]

By the end of 1931, when Savage had exhausted her Rosenwald funds, the Depression had overtaken the world, virtually ending art sales. Savage, however, was not daunted. Economic depression had been the permanent state of her world for many years, and she had managed to survive in spite of it. Returning to America, she had spirit, strength, and a new confidence born of her studies abroad.

In New York Savage's work was accepted at the innovative Argent Gallery and at the Art Anderson Galleries, which exhibited such well-known artists as Max Weber and sculptor Robert Laurent. But her immediate survival depended on commissioned portraits of such prominent black leaders as James Weldon Johnson and the surgeon Dr. Walter L. Gray Crump. She also did a portrait of Major Edward Bowes, whose radio "Amateur Hour" then enthralled America. Her sensitive 1934 bust of Ted Upshure, a handicapped Greenwich Village musician and entertainer, so impressed other artists that she became the first black artist to be elected to the National Association of Women Painters and Sculptors.

As the Depression deepened, Savage began teaching in the Savage Studio of Arts and Crafts, located in a basement apartment on West 143rd Street.[23] She had a way of making friends and immediately becoming part of the neighborhood. Soon young people interested in art began to

gather there, and she obtained a $1,500 grant from the Carnegie Foundation to teach children. If a boy or girl stopped before the window in which she displayed work, she was at the door, crying, "Come on in! Come on in!" She insisted her librarian friend Anne Judge Bennis bring delinquent boys to her studio "because they ought to know there are black artists."[24]

She attracted the gifted like the Pied Piper. Her students included Norman Lewis, whose paintings are now in many museums; the developing sculptor and potter William Artis, who later became an art teacher; the painter and illustrator Ernest Crichlow; and Elton C. Fax. What gave Savage special stature among Harlem's young artists was that although she had achieved important recognition and studied abroad, she had settled in their midst instead of disappearing "downtown." She opened her studio to anyone who wanted to paint, draw, carve, or model.

Former students describe Savage as an inspiring teacher. Yet words generally fail them when asked to describe what was so different in her approach. The clearest account of her teaching comes from a nonartist, the well-known black social psychologist Kenneth B. Clark, whose research was the basis of the 1954 U.S. Supreme Court decision outlawing school segregation. In the early 1930s Clark, attracted to art and preferring clay modeling to painting, enrolled in Savage's class. "Once I was doing this nude," he told Jervis Anderson, "and was having trouble with the breasts. Gwendolyn Knight [who developed into a fine artist] was sitting next to me, and I kept looking at her, to see whether I could make a breast that looked like a breast. Gwen knew what I was doing, but she would not help me. Augusta came along and said, 'Kenneth, you're having trouble with that breast.' I said, 'Yes, I am.' And she simply opened her blouse and showed me her breast."[25]

This incident provides insight into her grasp of her students' needs and her readiness to dramatize that art must ignore social convention in seeking reality. Although Clark decided he had only mediocre talent and presently gave up art, he had learned that artists "communicate something about the human predicament with a reality and depth that are beyond words. It was Augusta Savage who implanted in me the respect and envy I feel for artists, and I thank her for lighting that spark."[26]

"Augusta had a way with people" is how she was most frequently described by the Harlem artists who knew her.[27] Yet no one was close to her. However brilliant and striking, warm and friendly she was, she could also be moody and distant at times. While she could cajole, coax, humor, and laugh, most artists also remember that she could at times be very stern, sharp, demanding, capable of attacking with rage, especially if she felt she was not taken seriously. Her moods were not to be trifled with.

Savage strongly believed that everyone possesses some artistic ability, and as the WPA federal art projects developed, her studio school evolved into the Harlem Community Art Center. Under her direction some 1,500 people of all ages participated in its workshops, which ranged from fine arts to weaving, pottery, photography, sewing, and quilting. Its interracial staff included Vacla Vytlacil, later an important abstract artist. The art center was the largest in the nation, and its students' work was exhibited in special shows at the Metropolitan Museum of Art, New York University, and the Harlem YWCA.[28]

The WPA revived old but acute problems in new forms for Savage. Initially ignorant of African-American artists, WPA administrators refused to hire them until overwhelming evidence from the Harmon files, universities, colleges, galleries, and leading white artists demonstrated their existence. The deeper struggle with racism was whether a black artist could supervise white artists.

Whether Savage could direct the Harlem Community Art Center was one aspect of this struggle—which she won hands down. But the WPA supervisory question revived her own deep, bitter feelings of having been cheated years earlier by the Fontainebleau committee. It galled her to have bureaucrats—all of whom were white—making decisions about African-Americans' opportunities and activities. She could not stand the fact that people without art experience made decisions that were critical for black artists. As a result, she clashed repeatedly with Mary Beattie Brady, director of the Harmon Foundation, who controlled its exhibitions of black artists' work and selected its juries, but at the same time readily admitted knowing nothing about art and spoke condescendingly about what African-Americans needed.

Ultimately, the struggle over WPA supervisory jobs resulted in the organizing of the Harlem Artists Guild, in which Savage played a major role, becoming its first vice president and later president. She emerged as a strong leader. Her prestige as an accomplished artist was one element in her authority. Her personality was another. . . .

Her personal contact with the three most influential black leaders of the time—Du Bois, Garvey, and James Weldon Johnson, with their very different styles, philosophies, and aims—gave Savage a perceptive grasp of the roots of power and what leadership requires. Through her teaching and by personal demonstration, she tried to develop racial consciousness and pride along with artistic talent. To deepen Guild members' understanding of their difficulties—artistic, social, and political—she organized the Vanguard Club, which met weekly to discuss the issues in black artists' work and lives. These discussions sharpened the demands of both the WPA artists' union and the Harlem Artists Guild for more jobs. The group also strengthened its political clout in the community through exhibitions in churches and schools. Soon, however, various people began to charge that the Vanguard group was "Communist."[29]

In 1935 Savage resigned from the Vanguard leadership, claiming that it had been taken over by Communists—a course she doubtless considered political self-preservation.[30] These repeated attacks contributed to the end of the busy Harlem Community Art Center and its constructive role in Harlem lives. Richard D. McKinzie, in his history of the WPA art projects, *The New Deal for Artists,* points out that the congressional opponents of Franklin D. Roosevelt's social programs, many of whom were racist southern politicians, forced major WPA cutbacks and launched a massive assault in 1938. "The cultural projects were to be their first targets. They could charge radicalism and corruption, and by exploiting the peculiarities of the projects in New York City [with such "frills" as large numbers of WPA actors, dancers, artists, writers; the large Harlem Community Art Center; and the demand of the Harlem Artists Guild for exemptions from cutbacks], they would win their point with a majority of legislators."[31] By 1939 the WPA art projects were reduced to virtually nothing.

At times friends told Savage that she was wasting her talent on teaching and political struggles, but she rarely revealed any feelings of conflict. Once, when Bennis came into her apartment full of excitement about having just heard Marian Anderson sing, Savage said, "I'm just as important, just as much an artist as Marian Anderson, and you don't act like that after being with me." She "was really hurt," Bennis remembered.[32]

On another occasion, however, Savage said, "I have created nothing really beautiful, really lasting. But if I can inspire one of these youngsters to develop the talent I know they possess, then my monument will be their work. No one could ask for more than that."[33] In this sense Savage succeeded, even if one counts only the work of Norman Lewis and Jacob Lawrence, both of whom were significantly helped by her. At the same time her statement reflects an inner demoralization concerning her own artistic development.

One cannot be certain about the factors, subjective and external, that cause changes in an artist's work; even the artist may not be fully aware of the pressures to which she or he is responding. But in the case of Savage, a profound change took place that was apparent by the mid-1930s. Instead of continuing to do sensitive portraits, such as that of Du Bois and *Gamin,* she turned to other subject matter. James A. Porter attributed this shift to the influence of her European studies. As he saw it, they caused "the setting aside of her convictions [in order] to learn techniques and to communicate a certain *joie de vivre*—but [one] which happened to be trivial."[34]

Savage's actual production dwindled by the mid-1930s. Many of the pieces she exhibited were done in Europe. Her new work lacked the significance that many had come to expect. In the late 1930s she modeled a sleek, semiclad girl with a hairdo suggesting a cat's ears and called it *The Cat.* She created a small dancing girl, *Suzie Q,* and a male companion, *Truckin'.* Another work, *Green Apples,* portrayed a small boy holding his stomach in distress. Although her friends defended her, some African-American artists were openly critical of the way she was using her talents. Locke complained she was attempting to go beyond her technical competence.[35]

The major factor in producing these changes may well have been the prolonged Depression. As Savage's understanding of the depth of the Depression grew, as she fought social and political battles every day over a period of years—first to gain WPA work-relief projects, then to preserve them—she inevitably came to a new assessment of what she personally, as an artist, was up against. The problem of trying to feed a family on $4.29 a week was overwhelming.

At the 1931 Salons of America exhibition, Savage and other artists, including Reginald Marsh, Max Weber, and Robert Laurent, agreed to set a price on their work and to refuse to cut that price regardless of how desperate their need might be. During the Depression, despite such interracial unity, hundreds of artists were driven from the field. In such a situation the expectation of creating monumental and memorable sculpture seemed ridiculous.

In 1935 Savage created a life-size group—with a pensive young black woman sitting on a rock and looking at what a Chicago critic called "an uncertain future."[36] Beside her, crouching in a frightened way, is a black man. She called this work *Realization.* Some thirty Harlem citizens contributed funds to have this statue, which reflected their appreciation of such situations, cast in bronze. Such casting was something Savage had never been able to afford.

Encouraged, she created a larger-than-life-size antiwar memorial, *After the Glory,* the following year. It depicted an African-American grandmother, a mother, and a child gazing into space in search of the missing son, husband, and father. Funds for casting this work could not be raised. Her inability to get support from conventional sources and the inability of black people to fund her work as a result of their poverty often left Savage feeling bitter. Yet she kept trying.

Nevertheless, Savage seemed to have come to the conclusion that her opportunity for creating memorable sculpture—and the chance of a poor black woman becoming a great sculptor—had disappeared forever, destroyed by the Depression. Her art became wholly secondary to her work as an encouraging teacher and a determined organizer.

Savage was therefore astonished in early December 1937, when the World's Fair Corporation announced that it was commissioning her to create a large statue reflecting "the American Negro's contribution to music, especially to song."[37] Three other leading women sculptors—Gertrude V. Whitney, Malvina Hoffman, and Brenda Putnam—were also commissioned to do sculptures. Eventually Savage took as her theme *Lift Every Voice and Sing,* "the Negro national anthem" composed by James Weldon and Rosamond Johnson, and announced she was taking a year's leave of absence from her directorship of the Harlem Community Art Center to do the statue.

After months of preparation, working from a small clay model in the backyard of the building in which another African-American artist, Louise Jefferson, had her studio, Savage created a huge harp—sixteen feet tall—whose strings were a line of singing black children. A huge forearm and hand with the fingers curving upward, symbolizing God's gift, formed the base of the harp in the foreground, where a kneeling young black man symbolically offered a plaque with musical notes on it to represent the musical gifts of black people. Cast in plaster, *Lift Every Voice and Sing* was blackened with paint to give it a basaltlike finish.

Of the four commissioned statues, *Lift Every Voice and Sing* was the most popular, most photographed, and most publicized. Because it was linked to the spirituals, and people rarely saw black faces in sculpture, its deficiencies as a work of art were overlooked. People liked it and sent postcard pictures of it from the fair, and it brought Savage national attention from the mass media. Yet, as a work of art, many artists thought that it was a superficial mixture of fantasy and realism, and poorly composed.[38] After the fair, Savage did not have funds to cast or store it, so it was smashed by bulldozers demolishing the fair's buildings—an event that went unnoticed in the press.

Months before the destruction of her statue, Savage discovered to her consternation that her leave of absence would not be accepted by the WPA administration. In its view Savage was now privately employed—the goal of the WPA. Savage had helped her friend Gwendolyn Bennett, an able, well-trained artist and teacher, take over the position of director of the Harlem Community Art Center on what she assumed was a temporary basis. In the end Savage was left a famous but poor, unemployed black artist. The politicians and bureaucrats who had found her a jabbing thorn in their sides were finally rid of her as director of the center. It is even possible that her World's Fair Commission was arranged with this outcome in mind. Finally, in February 1938, she was made a consultant to the project at $1,800 a year and in July a project supervisor at $1,750 yearly.[39] Although better known than ever, she no longer had the authority and platform she once had and she resigned in mid-April 1939.

Savage had already decided to renew her struggle to establish herself as an important artist and an authority on African-American art on different planes. To take advantage of the still-booming World's Fair publicity, she planned an exhibition of her own work. She had never had a one-woman show and had neither critical en-dorsements nor museum credits. She felt keenly that she had never won a Harmon award.

And she had another plan—to open her own art gallery on Harlem's 125th Street. She was encouraged to think along these lines by the past support she had had from Harlem people even when she was unknown. And she had created the largest community art center in the nation there. She hoped the exhibition would bring critical honors and reinforce the attractiveness and status of her Harlem gallery.

Her exhibition opened at the Argent Gallery soon after she left the WPA. However, most of the work exhibited was not new, some dating back to her European days (for she had not had time to create while fighting for WPA jobs).

Unfortunately, her exhibition did not win high praise. The *Art News* of May 27, 1939, in one of the most favorable notices, said her work revealed "if not a startlingly original artist, an accomplished practitioner. In addition to an assortment of lively heads, of which the shining black Belgium marble *Woman of Martinique* is probably the finest, there are such figure pieces as the lithe *Terpischore at Rest,* and a feline female entitled *The Cat.* The Rodin-inspired *Creation* was perhaps a mistake. Miss Savage seemed to be at her best in such expressions of personal humor as the small group of nuns, *Sisters in the Rain,* and in her strong portraits."

Savage was deeply hurt. Just when her name was best known, she felt destroyed by a combination of factors: her political activism had not only alienated the politicians and WPA administrators, but also diverted her energies from her art. In addition, she recognized that the coming of World War II would wipe out the WPA art projects she had struggled to establish and preserve as a means of training young black artists.

Despite her disappointments, Savage rallied by going ahead with her private art gallery, the Salon of Contemporary Negro Art, on the third floor of a building on 125th Street. Some 500 people of both races turned up for its opening on June 8, 1939. She exhibited the work of many African-American artists including that of Richmond Barthé, Gwendolyn Knight, Ronald Joseph, Norman Lewis, Beauford Delaney, Ernest Crichlow, James Lesesne Wells, Elba Lightfoot, and Ellis Wilson. However, the people of Harlem had no money for art and the people who had money for art were not inclined to look for it in Harlem. She was soon forced to close the gallery.

Amid the ruins of her plans, Savage remained determined to gain a place for herself. Her situation was much like the one she faced when she first came to New York. The difference was that she was now nationally known, experienced in dealing with organizations and political struggles. Gaining the sponsorship of the now-defunct Architectural League of Washington, she planned a nine-city Midwestern tour with her work to conclude with the opening of the American Negro Exposition in Chicago in July 1940.[40] Early in May she came to Chicago from Gary, Indiana, and set up an exhibition in Perrin Hall, adjacent to the Chicago Auditorium. Her statues included *Gamin,* a garden fountain figure, *The Cat,* her portrait of James Weldon Johnson, a teak carving titled *Envy, Realization,* and other works.[41]

To mark the opening of her exhibition, she presented a provocative and highly personal history of art, "Crisis: Past and Present," in the Chicago Auditorium recital hall.[42] Introduced by Edward R. Embree, head of the Rosenwald Fund, she held an audience, which included many prominent social figures, spellbound with her stories of her own struggles to become an artist. To reach Chicago African-Americans, she set up a three-day exhibition, May 6-9, at the Southside YWCA, appearing three times a day, from nine o'clock in the morning until nine at night, to discuss her work.[43] Thousands of African-American schoolchildren came to see and hear her.[44]

Yet this intensive effort did not result in significant sales or commissions. Socialites did not know what to do about her sculptures of black people. And Chicago's African-Americans, like those in New York, did not have the money to buy her work. In her remarks Savage lamented that only two of many African-American homes that she visited had works by African-American artists. Such artists should not have to depend on WPA projects, she said.[45]

This grim situation forced her to abandon her tour, although the details are unclear (records of the Architectural League of Washington no longer exist). The heavy cost of moving her large works to New York makes it uncertain that they were returned. *Realization* and other works were apparently either destroyed or abandoned. They cannot be found today.

In any case, when the art exhibition of the American Negro Exposition opened on July 4 at the Tanner Galleries in Chicago, Savage was represented only by *Prima Donna,* a carved hardwood statue, perhaps inspired by the rise of Marian Anderson.[46] Simplified in its handling of masses and seemingly influenced by Elie Nadelman, it departed from her usually detailed realism in portraying a type. Certainly Savage hoped for honors and positive critical attention. However, young Elizabeth Catlett's *Mother and Child* won first prize and Barthé's *Shoe-shine Boy* second prize. No honorable mention came her way, and today *Prima Donna* cannot be located.

Undoubtedly Savage felt rejected by her own people. She may have even abandoned or destroyed her work.

Returning to New York, depressed and embittered, Savage gave up. She saw only a few old personal friends, like Bennis, who had nothing to do with art.[47] In the early 1940s she moved to an old chicken farm in Saugerties, New York, near the Woodstock art colony. Yet she made no effort to meet Woodstock artists and instead worked as an assistant for a commercial mushroom grower. Nor did she attempt any art. What she wanted, she told friends, was complete isolation. She told Bennis that she was disgusted and sick of New York.

A neighboring farm family, discovering who she was, set up a place for her to work on sculpture in one of their buildings, but she apparently never used it. Yet, "in a sense Augusta couldn't stop working," Bennis said later. "If you sat down on the grass with her, she'd pick up a twig, or grass, or dirt, or anything, and start shaping it, trying to do something with it." According to Bennis, Savage kept only one piece of sculpture at the farm: "It was something I always called 'Aspiration,' although I don't know what Augusta called it. It was wood—and like a long flame shooting up from two entwined hands, and very beautiful."[48]

In the late 1950s her health deteriorated, and in 1961 her daughter, Irene Allen, convinced her to return to Allen's home in the city, where she could be cared for. Eventually hospitalized, she died on March 27, 1962. Fax, one of the few artists to visit her in Saugerties, pointed out that "during the seventeen years preceding her death . . . Augusta Savage lived in virtual professional exile."[49]

Today, much of Savage's work cannot be located. There are not even photographs of many statues. Fax believed that her best works never returned from Chicago. In October 1988 Deirdre L. Bibby, the Schomburg Center's art curator, organized an exhibition of Savage's work under the title "Augusta Savage and the Art Schools of Harlem" at the center.[50] . . .

Some of her work disappeared under curious circumstances, the most mysterious being the theft of her magnificent bust of Du Bois from the Harlem branch of the New York Public Library. Known to generations of library users, it sat undisturbed in the 135th Street library from 1923 until 1960. According to Jean Blackwell Hutson, then head of the Schomburg collection, an unknown African-American man tried to take the statue one evening, saying that Savage had requested him to do so.[51] When librarians insisted that it belonged to the library, he surrendered it willingly. The incident was forgotten. But on October 26, 1960, the bust was discovered to be missing and has never been found. Some librarians believe that Savage did indeed send someone to get it and that she destroyed it, possibly because she no longer admired Du Bois.

Fax has said that, "like most American Negroes, her awareness of race was made to supersede her awareness of what she, a gifted, trained human being, was prepared to offer society."[52] Despite her enormous talent and drive, Savage's creative efforts were first cruelly frustrated by discrimination and then crushed by the Depression and the struggles in which she found herself. Her importance lies not so much in her own work as it does in her heroic efforts to aid the development of subsequent generations of African-American artists. Her hope of nurturing young black artists—"My monument will be in their work"—has been fully realized. At the same time her sharp self-assessment—"I have created nothing really beautiful, really lasting"—is not exactly true, as *Gamin* testifies more than half a century later.

## Notes

1. Savage's death certificate gives this date. See sketch by Dewitt S. Dykes, Jr., in *Notable American Women: The Modern Period* (Cambridge, Mass.: Belknap Press of Harvard University Press, 1980), pp. 627-29. Confusion has arisen because she gave her birth date as 1901 on a passport (Deirdre L. Bibby, *Augusta Savage and the Art Schools of Harlem* [New York: Schomburg Center for Research in Black Culture, New York Public Library, exhibition catalog, 1988], p. 27). See also *Pittsburgh Courier,* May 5, 1934.

2. Unidentified newspaper clipping in Augusta Savage file, Schomburg Center, 1969; missing in 1983. Elton C. Fax referred to it (*AMSAC* [American Society of African Culture] *Newsletter,* Suppl. Oct. 1962) and he said to the authors: "Augusta Savage herself told me that" (Oct. 27, 1983).

3. From an unidentified, undated, but apparently late 1923 article by Eric Walrond (Savage file, Schomburg Center).

4. Ibid.

5. Currie dedicated a poem to Savage in his book *Songs of Florida,* quoted by Walrond.

6. Walrond.

7. Ibid.

8. Ibid. Walrond interviewed Kate Reynolds.

9. *New York Times,* Dec. 9, 1937.

10. *New York World,* April 5 and April 30, 1923; *Baltimore Afro-American,* April 27, 1923; *New York Times,* May 3, 1923.

11. *New York World,* May 10, 1923; among the protesters were Rev. Thomas M. O'Keefe, Rev. J. W. Brown, and Dr. Emmett J. Scott.

12. *Exhibition of the Work of Negro Artists* (New York: Harmon Foundation, exhibition catalog, 1931), p. 46.

13. Savage apparently had no contact with Meta Vaux Warrick, who was older but still her contemporary. Born in Philadelphia, June 9, 1877, Warrick studied first at the Pennsylvania School of Industrial Art, where she won a prize for a crucifix showing Christ in agony, and later in Rome and Paris with Rodin. Her early work, preoccupied with pain, suffering, and despair, disturbed many people. A 1910 studio fire destroyed nearly all of it, but some works have been described by Benjamin Brawley, who characterized them as grim but "vital . . . from them speaks the very tragedy of the Negro race in the New World" (*The Negro Genius* [New York: Dodd, Mead & Co, 1937], pp. 134-39). In 1909 Warrick married Dr. Solomon Fuller, the first African-American psychiatrist, and afterward turned to portraits and social themes, such as the black migration to the North (*Exodus*). See Rayford W. Logan and Michael R. Winston, eds., *Dictionary of American Negro Biography* (New York: W. W. Norton, 1982), pp. 245-47. Also James A. Porter, *Modern Negro Art* (New York: Dryden Press, 1943), pp. 86-94; Alain L. Locke, *Negro Art: Past and Present* (Washington, D.C.: Associates in Negro Folk Education, 1936; reprint, New York: Arno Press/New York Times, 1968), pp. 28-30; Theresa O. Cederholm, *Afro-American Artists* (Boston: Trustees of the Boston Public Library, 1973).

14. *Norfolk* [Virginia] *Journal & Guide,* Oct. 19, 1929.

15. Fax, in *AMSAC Newsletter.*

16. Amy Jacques Garvey, the widow of Marcus Garvey, recalled Savage coming Sunday mornings to make studies (letter to authors, Oct. 1, 1970).

17. Amy Jacques Garvey described Poston's mission in *Garvey and Garveyism* (New York: Macmillan-Collier Books, 1970), p. 149.

18. Savage's brief autobiographical sketch in *The Crisis* (Aug. 1929), p. 269.

19. The expert was Professor Charles F. Richards, the art director of the General Education Board of New York (*Norfolk Journal & Guide,* Oct. 19, 1929).

20. *Amsterdam News* (New York), Nov. 6, 1929.

21. *Chicago Whip,* Aug. 15, 1931.

22. *Pittsburgh Courier,* Aug. 29, 1936.

23. *Negro Artists: An Illustrated Review of Their Achievements* (New York: Harmon Foundation, exhibition catalog, 1935) described the studio; a Dutch-born illustrator, Angela Straeter, was Savage's assistant.

24. Anne Judge Bennis, author interview, March 28, 1972.

25. Jervis Anderson, *This Was Harlem: A Cultural Portrait, 1900-1950* (New York: Farrar, Straus, & Giroux, 1982), pp. 273-74.

26. Ibid.

27. Norman Lewis, Ernest Crichlow, and Elton C. Fax were among the former students interviewed about Savage.

28. James H. Baker, "Art Comes to People of Harlem," *The Crisis* 46 (March 1939), pp. 78-80; Sophia Steinbach, "Harlem Goes in for Art," *Opportunity* 14 (April 1936), p. 114; "1600 Study Art in Harlem," *Art Digest* 13 (April 15, 1939), p. 15.

29. Mary Beattie Brady was one who charged this; author interview, Oct. 8, 1969.

30. Reported by her brother-in-law, Ted Poston, in *Metropolitan,* Jan. 1935, pp. 28, 51, 66.

31. Richard D. McKinzie, *The New Deal for Artists* (Princeton, N.J.: Princeton University Press, 1973), pp. 101-2.

32. Bennis, interview.

33. Poston, in *Metropolitan.*

34. Porter, *Modern Negro Art,* p. 138

35. Locke, *Negro Art,* p. 77.

36. In "The Art Notebook," a column the *Chicago Bee,* May 10, 1940, William Carter called *Realization* Savage's "most ambitious piece and surely one of her masterpieces." He described the man as crouched beside the woman "as a child would crouch beside its mother—afraid" (Savage file, Schomburg Center). Contributors to casting *Realization* were listed by the *Amsterdam News,* March 7, 1936.

37. World's Fair press release (Savage file, Schomburg Center); *New York Times,* Dec. 9, 1937.

38. "There was sculptural inconsistency, however, in the realistic treatment of the heads and in the handling of the compositionally unrelated kneeling figure holding a plaque. Enlarged to near-heroic size, those errors became more glaring and less complimentary to an otherwise original and distinctive design," wrote Fax in the *AMSAC Newsletter.*

39. WPA Records of Employment (Francis V. O'Connor papers, Archives of American Art, Smithsonian Institution, Washington, D.C., microfilm roll 1090, frame 0906).

40. An unidentified Chicago newspaper article, undated but apparently late April or early May, described her tour, her lecture in the Chicago Auditorium recital hall, and her exhibition at Perrin Hall; the previous six cities on the tour were not named. It reported a committee of 100 was sponsoring her Chicago visit; Frances Taylor Moseley was general chairman of the Chicago arrangements (Savage file, Schomburg Center).

41. Ibid. An undated *Chicago Bee* clipping shows a photograph of Savage at work on the full-scale model for *After the Glory,* her antiwar memorial statue (Savage file, Schomburg Center). This statue was apparently destroyed when Savage could not obtain funds for its casting. The photo was part of the publicity that preceded her Chicago visit. Although an unidentified newspaper clipping suggests *Realization* was to be exhibited at the Art Institute of Chicago, this did not happen (John W. Smith, Art Institute archivist, author interview, July 6, 1992).

42. An undated, unidentified Chicago African-American newspaper clipping of a column titled "Typovision" by Elizabeth Galbreath reported the Savage lecture included references to "four whippings a day" and family disasters (Savage file, Schomburg Center).

43. An unidentified newspaper clipping, May 4, 1940, describes her YMCA appearances and social events linked to her visit (Savage file, Schomburg Center).

44. The *Chicago Herald-American,* May 9, 1940, describes visits of "more than ten thousand Negro students of Chicago schools" to Savage's exhibit at the YWCA and includes a photograph of *Gamin.* The "Art and Artists" column by Ernest Heitkamp, *Chicago Herald-American,* May 12, 1940, also describes her YWCA exhibit.

45. Carter, "The Art Notebook," *Chicago Bee,* May 11, 1940 (Savage file, Schomburg Center). William Carter won first prize in oils at the first Atlanta University exhibition in 1942 and became a well-known African-American artist in Chicago.

46. *Exhibition of the Art of the American Negro* (Chicago: Tanner Galleries, catalog of the American Negro Exposition, July 4-Sept. 2, 1940).

47. Bennis, interview.

48. Ibid.

49. Elton C. Fax, author interview, April 23, 1978.

50. Bibby, *Savage and Art Schools of Harlem.*

51. Jean Blackwell Hutson, author interview, April 20, 1970; letter to authors, July 5, 1974.

52. Fax, in *AMSAC Newsletter.*

# ROMARE BEARDEN AND HARRY HENDERSON (ESSAY DATE 1993)

**SOURCE:** Bearden, Romare and Henderson, Harry. "Sargent Johnson." In *A History of African American Artists from 1792 to the Present,* pp. 216-25. New York: Pantheon Books, 1993.

*In the following excerpt, Bearden and Henderson discuss the work of Sargent Johnson, whom the authors consider one of the most versatile Black artists in America.*

"It is the pure American Negro I am concerned with, aiming to show the natural beauty and dignity in that characteristic lip and that characteristic hair, bearing, and manner; and I wish to show that beauty not so much to the white man as to the Negro himself. Unless I can interest my race, I am sunk."[1]

With these words, Sargent Claude Johnson, one of America's most versatile black artists, described his goals in 1935. Although he won many honors, particularly in San Francisco, Johnson has been largely omitted from accounts of American art in the 1920s and 1930s. One reason may be that, ignoring contemporary Western aesthetics, he persistently used color in his statues. He was also a daring innovator, creating huge murals on enameled porcelain steel panels. Today's increasing awareness of the world's pluralism, of the cultures of Africa, pre-Columbian, America, and Asia, may stimulate a new appreciation of Johnson, for he turned to these cultures, rather than traditional Western art, for inspiration and ideas.

A short, cheerful man, Johnson's personality reflected his confidence. Consuelo Kanaga, whose photography recorded much of the history of the period and who knew him well, said: "He was beautiful in his spirit, the way he talked, the way he thought, the way he worked, the way he felt. I don't mean he didn't have problems. He did—terrible problems—but he was still beautiful. It was his spirit, the way he looked at everything."[2] Clay Spohn, a painter friend since the 1930s, called him "one of the few persons I have ever known who seemed perennially happy, joyous, exuberant in living. . . . For he really had the love of life and was always willing to share his enthusiasm."[3]

Johnson's works "have a gentleness, an inner fire, and a great spiritual calm," emphasized Evangeline J. Montgomery in her monograph accompanying the Oakland Museum's 1971 retrospective exhibition. She related his work to West African tribal art as well as to Mexican, Art Deco, and Cubist art.[4] She might well have added classical Egyptian and early Greek sculpture.

Born in Boston on October 7, 1887, Johnson was the third of six children. His father, Anderson Johnson, was of Swedish descent, and his mother, Lizzie Jackson Johnson, had African-American and Cherokee ancestors. The serious illnesses of his parents combined with the stressful problems that beset interracial marriages at the time (including social ostracism and the inability to find work and decent housing) made his early life turbulent. In 1897, when young Sargent was ten years old, his father died. His mother, ill with tuberculosis, lived another five years but was increasingly incapacitated.

After their father's death, the six Johnson children were temporarily taken in by their mother's brother, Sherman William Jackson, a high school principal in Washington, D.C., and his wife, May Howard Jackson, a recognized sculptor. Born in 1877 in Philadelphia and trained at the Pennsylvania Academy of Fine Arts, she was an expert modeler, although her concepts were not original. Her work, shown in major museums, included portraits of African-American leaders. She also taught art to black children in Washington.[5]

Observing his aunt as she modeled, Sargent Johnson began his first attempts at sculpture. His aunt's efforts made a lasting impression and, in a sense, established a goal that did not seem impossible. When the Johnson children were presently sent to their mother's parents in Alexandria, Virginia, young Sargent continued his efforts at modeling clay, trying to copy lambs and angels in a nearby tombstone cutter's shed.

However, the care of the children proved too much for the aging grandparents. In 1902, when their mother died, the children were separated. The boys were sent to the Sisters of Charity Orphanage in Worcester, Massachusetts, while the girls went to a Catholic school for African-American and Native American girls in Pennsylvania. This was the last time the girls saw Sargent. According to Montgomery, some Johnson children had difficulty in identifying with their African-American heritage and lived as Caucasians or Native Americans, but Sargent Johnson chose to be considered black and lived his life as an African-American.

As an adolescent in the orphanage, Johnson attended public school and worked in the Sisters of Charity Hospital. While convalescing after a long illness, he began painting. At one point he copied pictures chosen by the nuns onto the greenhouse wall with whatever paint he could find in the workshop. Interested in singing because he had a pleasant voice, he was later sent to a Boston music school, but he soon abandoned it for a night-school course in drawing and painting.

Johnson's transition from boy to man, from student to artist, is largely undocumented. He reportedly left Boston and lived for a while with relatives in Chicago, who considered his desire to become an artist unrealistic for an orphaned black boy. At some point Johnson determined to go to California. When he arrived in San Francisco, where he first worked, and what he did are unknown.[6] Apparently he arrived some time before the great Oakland fair of 1915, the Panama-Pacific International Exposition, which exhibited the work of West Coast artists and greatly stimulated the art community. Soon after his arrival he studied drawing and painting at the avant-garde A. W. Best School of Art, according to Montgomery.[7]

Johnson was twenty-eight years old in 1915, the year he married Pearl Lawson, an attractive woman from Georgia of African-American, English, and French Creole descent. He worked as a fitter for Schlusser and Brothers in 1917, but three years later he was tinting photographs and the next year he became a framer in the city's busiest frame shop, Valdespino Framers.

This was a critical period for Johnson. Nourished by San Francisco's cosmopolitan atmosphere, its relative social freedom and its casual acceptance of racial differences and the aesthetic values of different cultures, Johnson determined shortly after he married that he must now make a major effort to become a sculptor. At the mature age of thirty-two years, he began studying at the California School of Fine Arts with two of the best-known sculptors on the West Coast. He worked for two years with Ralph Stackpole and for one year with Beniamino Bufano. Twice he won student prizes.[8] On leaving school, he worked as a framer to survive, but he also continued to work with Bufano as an assistant. Traces of Bufano's influence can still be seen in Johnson's later work.

In San Francisco Johnson's development was influenced by factors that differed from the experience of black artists on the East Coast. West Coast artists were relatively isolated from the influence of European art trends, but at the same time they were continually exposed to Asian art. Both sailors and millionaires brought back art from every Asian country. The art of Asia, exhibited everywhere from museums to curio shops, was widely admired and collected. People were also aware of the work of the Native Americans of British Columbia, whose totem poles represented some of the most original and distinctive art on the continent. California artists, and particularly Johnson, were also strongly influenced by the art of Aztec and Mayan cultures in Mexico and Central America.

As a result of all these influences, California or Pacific sculpture differed from the "mainstream" contemporary sculpture of the time in several ways. First, the sculpture tended to be treated as a precious *object d'art,* highly polished and worked over in a craft sense. At the same time the work had an underlying conceptual simplicity, so that when it was polished, it tended to have a static and decorative appearance rather than a dynamic one. In addition, the sculpture was at times derived from natural objects, ranging from driftwood to peculiarly shaped stones, rather than being a design wholly imposed by the sculptor on

the material. Both Bufano and Johnson adopted the Asian and Northwest Native American practice of coloring their sculpture—and they knew that ancient Egyptian and Greek sculptors had painted and gilded their work.

In this period Johnson was becoming increasingly aware of his African heritage through discussions about Alain Locke's book *The New Negro,* the Harlem Renaissance, and reports of eastern exhibitions of Congo and other African art. In the midst of all the other influences, Johnson sought to establish his identity as a black American artist. Years later he said: "I had a tough time in the early days. They didn't give me much of a chance. They didn't know who I was, but I had made up my mind that I was going to be an artist."[9] Although never identified, "they" apparently refers to early San Francisco employers and acquaintances who tried to discourage his artistic ambitions.

Artistically, Johnson was fascinated by new techniques and was constantly experimenting, especially with the use of glazes on porcelain figures. His constant experiments may have seemed to indicate a lack of focus and resolution in direction, but were a process of learning that aided his later innovating.

The birth of his daughter, Pearl Adele, in 1923 helped Johnson gain a specific focus. She awoke in him a delight in children, and he made many studies of her and other cherubic infants, usually in glazed terra-cotta. Seemingly simple and straightforward in line, these portraits express an appealing innocence and beauty. Never sentimental nor caught up in excessive detail, their buoyancy conveys the spiritual essence of new life.

One of these statues was a ceramic bust, glazed in color, of a Chinese neighbor's child, *Elizabeth Gee.* It was Johnson's first work to win newspaper attention. In the same year, 1925, Johnson's study *Pearl* received a medal at the San Francisco Art Exhibition. As a result, when the Harmon Foundation exhibitions began in 1926, Johnson was invited to show his work. In the 1928 Harmon show he won the Otto H. Kahn prize with *Sammy,* a portrait of a black youth. In 1929 he won the Harmon bronze award, and his work became part of the Harmon traveling exhibits. Thousands came to see these exhibitions at the Oakland Municipal Art Gallery in 1930 and 1931.[10] Johnson, already well known in the Bay area, was the only Californian in these shows. Several copies of a terra-cotta portrait of a young boy, *Chester,* were sold, including one to the German minister to Italy, a casual visitor. The San Diego Fine Arts Gallery purchased *Esther,* and *Sammy* was also sold.

In the 1933 Harmon show Johnson exhibited an unusual study of his daughter that combined bronze with blue-green in a porcelain glaze. He also exhibited a drawing of a mother and child and a striking drawing titled *Defiant,* depicting a mother holding a small girl and boy close to her. These works won the $150 Ogden prize for the most outstanding combination of materials.

Some eastern commentators, however, considered Johnson's work superficial and decorative, primarily because glazing was associated with lamp bases and pottery in their minds. For example, James A. Porter, although conceding Johnson was "diverting" and "lively," cast him aside as a serious artist: "His work leans more to the decorative side, and his talent is more precisely that of a ceramic artist."[11] Yet Johnson was able to impose, as all significant artists do, his own vision and meaning on his work. . . .

In his own people Johnson found much that was inspiring. He often made masks, usually in copper, in African styles, some of which were idealized portraits, such as *Negro Mother.* Frequently he turned to the classic mother-child theme in his drawings, lithographs, paintings, and sculpture. (Albert M. Bender purchased and gave many of these works to the San Francisco Museum of Art.) Johnson also created several murals for black congregations in the Oakland area in this period.

In a backyard studio on Park Street in Berkeley in 1935, Johnson created what many consider his greatest work, *Forever Free.* Based on his earlier drawing *Defiant,* this polychrome wood sculpture depicts in a highly stylized way a black mother with her two children gathered close to her side by her protecting arms. Johnson began by carving the piece in redwood; then he sanded and covered it with coats of gesso and fine linen, sanding it again after each layer. Finally, he painted it, coloring the skirt black, the blouse white, and the flesh areas a rich copper brown. The whole statue is polished to a very high luster. Simple but dramatic, it resembles African sculpture in its stylistic severity and spiritual strength. Indeed, in creating it, Johnson made use of techniques from Egypt, Asia, and Africa.

*Forever Free* won the 1935 San Francisco Art Association medal for sculpture.[12] Impressive in its aesthetic simplicity, it was widely reproduced

and influenced many artists, including the photographer Consuelo Kanaga and the composer William Grant Still, whose music Johnson had always liked because of its African-American themes. After *Forever Free* achieved national recognition, it was purchased and given to the San Francisco Museum of Modern Art by Albert M. Bender. . . .

The instant success of *Forever Free* prompted the *San Francisco Chronicle* to interview Johnson at length on October 6, 1935. Observing that he worked with equal facility in wood, ceramics, oils, watercolors, and graphics, the *Chronicle* quoted Johnson as saying:

> I am producing strictly a Negro art, studying not the culturally mixed Negro of the cities, but the more primitive slave type as existed in this country during the period of slave importation. Very few artists have gone into the history of the Negro in America, cutting back to the sources and origins of the life of the race in this country. . . .
>
> The slogan for the Negro artist should be "Go South, young man!" Too many Negro artists go to Europe and come back imitators of Cézanne, Matisse, or Picasso, and this attitude is not only a weakness of the artists, but of their racial public. In all artistic circles I hear too much talking and too much theorizing. All their theories do not help me any, and I have but one technical hobby to ride: I am interested in applying color to sculpture as the Egyptian, Greek, and other ancient people did. I try to apply color without destroying the natural expression of sculpture, putting it on pure and in large masses without breaking up the surfaces of the form and respecting the planes and contours of sculpturesque expression. I am concerned with color, not solely as a technical problem, but also as a means of heightening the racial character of my work. The Negroes are a colorful race; they call for an art as colorful as they can be made. . . .

When the Works Progress Administration art project began in California in 1936, Johnson was one of the first artists hired. He began in the position of a senior sculptor, because of his thorough knowledge. Soon he was promoted to assistant supervisor, then assistant state supervisor, and finally unit supervisor—without the struggle required in the East and elsewhere to win such posts for African-American artists.

The cost of materials is often a deterrent to the development of sculptors. The WPA program provided Johnson with his first opportunity to work on a large scale. In the well-equipped WPA studios, he could use any technique and tackle massive projects. One of the first of these was a twenty-two-foot-long organ screen for the California School for the Blind in Berkeley. Carved in redwood, the screen was a celebration of music. In its center panel, Johnson featured singers, whose faces resembled the masks of African-Americans he had created earlier. In other panels he carved birds and forest animals as well as a harp.

Two years later, for the Golden Gate International Exhibition, Johnson created massive cast-stone Inca riders astride llamas. He also designed low-relief sculptures for San Francisco's Aquatic Park. These sculptures, incised in green Vermont slate, were installed in what is now the exhibition hall of the Museum of the Golden Gate National Park. The entrance panels depict men of the sea and marine life. The promenade panel, facing the Bay, is a mosaic mural in varying shades of green, black, and white. These diverse public projects established Johnson as a sculptor with a range of abilities. . . .

Johnson longed to study abroad—not in Europe, but in Mexico and Asia. Awarded the Abraham Rosenberg Scholarship in 1944 and again in 1949, he made extended trips to Mexico and continued to travel there for twenty years. He was particularly attracted to southern Mexico, near Oaxaca, where archaeologists were looking for pre-Columbian pottery and sculpture. He was often invited to join American archaeologists at their excavation sites. He also visited Chichén Itzá in the Yucatn to study the decorative patterns on ancient buildings and the polychrome Chelula pottery, which featured mythological animals, flowers, and heroes. . . .

In 1947 Johnson advanced in a new direction when he met Mr. Mahoney, a partner in the Paine-Mahoney Company, which produced enameled signs on steel plates. He invited Johnson to use their shop to create aesthetic porcelain panels on steel. Working with brilliant colors, Johnson produced approximately 100 panels over the next twenty years on a great variety of themes—religious, mother-and-child, multiracial, and anti-war. He also did abstract designs. Often he painted his design on a white ground coat that had been previously fired. At times he worked with porcelain enamels that were fired every few minutes at 1,500 degrees Fahrenheit. Some panels were done in relief. Others ranged from small trivets to huge decorative works.

Ultimately this work led to commissions for large enameled panels. One of the first was a brilliant abstract mural of pots and pans that was mounted over a store entrance in San Francisco.[13] The Paine-Mahoney Company then employed Johnson to create several huge enameled murals. . . . In these large works, Johnson created the most important figures and directed other artists, who worked on the backgrounds. . . .

Johnson strongly opposed the contemporary view that color "contaminated" sculptural materials. "Sculpture was never meant to be colorless," he asserted. "There is no reason why it should be; most ancient sculpture, with the exception of the late Greek, was polychrome." He continued to create polychrome wood figures expressing universal themes.

A readiness to experiment was one of Johnson's outstanding characteristics. After studying metal sculpture techniques with Clair Van Falkenstein, he created welded sculpture that combined wire forms with enameled steel. . . .

Johnson died of a heart attack in San Francisco on October 10, 1967, at the age of eighty. A few years later, in 1971, Montgomery, with Marjorie Arkelian and others, organized a major retrospective show of his work at the Oakland Museum. It was his first one-man exhibition.

Throughout the years Johnson's work was singularly consistent. Strongly influenced by African and pre-Columbian sculpture, it was eminently suited to architectural use. His clean, direct shapes create handsome volumes in three-dimensional space. The forms are never accidental and express his motifs clearly. Even when massive, his sculpture never seems heavy. His fine portrait heads, use of polychrome techniques on simple, chaste volumes, and ongoing experimentation establish Sargent Johnson as one of the most unusual and versatile African-American artists to emerge in the 1920s.

### Notes

1. Interview in *San Francisco Chronicle,* Oct. 6, 1935.

2. Consuelo Kanaga, author interview, March 12, 1971. Her photograph of a black mother and children in Edward Steichen's *Family of Man* (New York: Museum of Modern Art, 1953) was inspired by Johnson's *Forever Free.*

3. Quoted by Evangeline J. Montgomery, *Sargent Johnson* (Oakland, Calif.: Oakland Museum, exhibition catalog, 1971), p. 30. This monograph is a basic informational source on Johnson. As the museum's consultant on African-American artists, Montgomery interviewed Johnson, his family members, and his friends, and prepared its retrospective Johnson exhibition (Feb. 23-March 21, 1971) with the assistance of Marjorie Arkelian, the museum's art historian, and others.

4. Ibid., p. 31.

5. May Howard Jackson (1877-1931) exhibited at the Corcoran Gallery, Washington, D.C., and the Na-

tional Academy of Design, New York. James A. Porter was one of her students (see his *Modern Negro Art* [New York: Dryden Press, 1943], pp. 92-93).

6. Johnson's obituary (*Oakland Tribune,* Oct. 12, 1967) reported he arrived in the Bay area when he was twenty-one years old, in 1909. However, Montgomery gives his arrival as 1915 (*Johnson,* p. 10).

7. Montgomery, *Johnson,* p. 10.

8. Ibid. He studied at the California School of Fine Arts from 1919 to 1923, and from 1940 to 1942.

9. Ibid., p. 9.

10. Ibid., p. 12. Montgomery attributes these figures to Delilah L. Beasley, in *Oakland Tribune,* Oct. 12, 1967.

11. Porter, *Modern Negro Art,* p. 139.

12. The 1935 Harmon exhibition featured Johnson, along with Malvin Gray Johnson and Richmond Barthé. It carried a brief sketch and picture of Sargent Johnson.

13. This panel, for the Nathan Dohrmann store, was destroyed with the building. Johnson also created a decorative map in enameled porcelain steel of Richmond, California, for its city hall.

James VanDerZee.

# PHOTOGRAPHERS

## DEBORAH WILLIS-BRAITHWAITE (ESSAY DATE 1987)

**SOURCE:** Willis-Braithwaite, Deborah. "They Knew Their Names." In *James VanDerZee: Photographer 1886-1983,* pp. 9-25. New York: Harry N. Abrams, Inc., 1987.

*In the following essay, Willis-Braithwaite offers an overview of the themes, techniques, and subjects of VanDerZee's photography, which she says is about the connection between self and family and self and community.*

Since the rediscovery of James VanDerZee's photographic archives in 1969, when his photographs were included in the Metropolitan Museum of Art's controversial exhibition "Harlem On My Mind," VanDerZee's images of the people of Harlem have been celebrated as an important and beautiful historic document. If, in the years since, critics and historians have come to value them primarily as a visual record of the emergence in America of the African American middle and upper classes, we should not be surprised, but we should not let this judgment limit our responses to the photographs themselves. It is ironic that this photographer, whose style it was to be extremely directorial, should be esteemed as a neutral observer of his times.

During the 1920s and 1930s, VanDerZee—a commercial portrait and street photographer—was indeed the photographer of choice for Harlem's most distinguished residents. Included in

his archives, for example, among hundreds of prints and negatives of African Americans of comfortable means dating from the years between the wars, are photographs of World War I heroes Henry Johnson and Needham Roberts; singers Mamie Smith, Hazel Scott, and Florence Mills; poet Countee Cullen; and heavyweight boxing champions Jack Johnson, Harry Wills, Sam Langford, and Joe Louis. He was hired to photograph the major political and religious leaders of the period, such as Adam Clayton Powell, Sr., Adam Clayton Powell, Jr., Father Divine, Daddy Grace, George Becton, Rabbi Matthew, and the Barefoot Prophet. In 1924 he was made the official photographer for Marcus Garvey and the Universal Negro Improvement Association, in which capacity he created the most comprehensive visual record of that organization's activities in photographs that were published internationally in *The Negro World,* the UNIA newspaper.

Yet, to consider James VanDerZee's photographs primarily as historical documents—which is what the organizers of "Harlem On My Mind" did, inciting many in the Harlem community to protest that a museum ostensibly dedicated to art suddenly adopted a documentary stance when confronted with the visual presence of the "other" within its walls—is to overlook his contribution to photography as a form of expression. As critic

A. D. Coleman had already observed in 1971, commenting on this ostensibly conventional commercial photographer's elaborate and handsome prints, some of which combined images from several negatives, VanDerZee "goes beyond mere professional expertise, suggesting a concern with the aesthetic impact of his images which is significant in our evaluation of his work." Accepting at face value the photographer's own assertion that he "was both self-taught and, by his own admission, entirely out of touch with the aesthetic movements of his day in the photographic world," Coleman professed to be astonished by VanDerZee's high level of aesthetic sophistication.

VanDerZee's photographs are widely known through numerous exhibitions and through three published monographs. While they have been acknowledged as a sweeping survey of the most vital pre-World War II African American community existing in the United States, VanDerZee has never been seen as the innovative photographic artist that he was. There has been virtually no critical analysis that describes the ideals that VanDerZee brought to and was able to express within his photography. This omission is, in part, due to the fact that viewers are often challenged, engaged, and overwhelmed by VanDerZee's subject matter, for his photographs are an overt celebration of black middle-class life, and particularly family life.

It is this picturing of middle-class life that gives VanDerZee's images much of their power to enchant and engage the viewer. Many of VanDerZee's portraits utilized the conventions and forms of studio portrait photography as they evolved in the second half of the nineteenth century in thousands of small photography businesses, a style created for clients who valued their dignity, independence, and comfort: they were formal and carefully composed works, and like the bourgeois and the celebrities in the photographs of the French photographer Nadar (1820-1910), their subjects are often made to appear both heroic and self-aware.

Yet, given the violent and tragic history of African Americans in the United States, this sense of self and self-worth, so apparent in VanDerZee's portraits, has a wholly other meaning than it does for the subjects of Nadar's photographs. VanDerZee's photographs—like the majority of photographic works associated with European and American modernism, with which they otherwise have little in common—were responses to the political and social upheavals of the early twentieth century. Like August Sander's massive photographic survey of pre-World War II Germans, VanDerZee's images define a people in the process of transformation and a culture in transition. Unlike Sander, who was obsessed with the representation of class structure and so-called "types," VanDerZee presented in visual terms the growing sense of personal, and national, identity of his sitters. Underpinning this is the thoroughly modern sensibility with which he confronted the issue of race. The conventional ideals of the bourgeois portrait studio served him well as a means to capture the culturally integrationist aspirations of his black clients. We might be tempted to call VanDerZee's work "radical" in the sense that the cultural critic and scholar bell hooks intends when she writes, regarding the representations of blacks in American culture, "Unless we transform images of blackness, of black people, our ways of looking and our ways of being seen, we cannot make radical interventions that will fundamentally alter our situation." VanDerZee's photography wrought one transformation on the image of blackness in America, and it is indeed possible to believe that for many, to be the subject of a VanDerZee photograph might be to experience a radical intervention in one's life, just as the rediscovery of his work in the late 1960s led many in the African American community to feel that a radical intervention had taken place in the historical record. It is this transformative power in his work that made VanDerZee a model of the visionary and optimistic early-twentieth-century American photographer.

In VanDerZee's work, this transformation takes the form of depicting people with a cosmopolitan style that, in the words of Mary Schmidt Campbell, was "partially real pride and partially carefully constructed artifice." The sitter provided the pride, and VanDerZee provided the artifice. VanDerZee's photographs suggest that the waves of African American immigration from the Caribbean and the migration from the rural South to the cities of the North forever changed the visual self-image of the people who made the journey: they have been metamorphosed into suave and aware big-city dwellers; the degradations of the past have been seemingly eliminated from their present lives. In one striking photograph that could stand for all the rest, an attractive couple dressed in matching raccoon coats poses with a beautiful Cadillac roadster. The passenger door is open, the man is half in the car itself, and the woman is standing next to it on the street, as if they are waiting patiently for the photographer to finish his work before they depart. But the man is not quite ready to leave: literally at the center of the image, framed by the luxurious automobile, he has turned his eyes directly into the lens, inviting the viewer to join them for a moment in their world. And this photograph, it is worth remarking, was made in 1932, fully three years after the stock market crash that signaled the beginning of the depression. In viewing VanDerZee's photographs taken in Harlem between the wars, one receives a sense of well-being and a feeling that the African American community is healthy, diverse, spiritual, prosperous, and productive.

We tend to think of VanDerZee as an observer, as a recorder, of the drama that we call the Harlem Renaissance, the decade-long (1919-29) flowering of African American art and culture in Harlem, but it might be more faithful to his role in it to think of him as one of its creators. His portraits of handsome men and beautiful women can be viewed as the visual embodiment of the racial ideals promoted by such leading African American intellectuals and writers of the era as W. E. B. DuBois, Claude McKay, Alain Locke, Langston Hughes, and Zora Neale Hurston in Locke's noted 1925 book *The New Negro.* There is a powerful connection between the literary works of the Harlem Renaissance writers, which demanded full democratic participation for African Americans in American life, and VanDerZee's photographs.

VanDerZee himself never doubted his creative role, and he had an artist's investment in his own photographs: "Sometimes they seemed to be more valuable to me than they did to the people I was photographing because I put my heart and soul into them. I was never satisfied with the ways things looked. I liked working with a big portrait camera so I could make changes." The changes that VanDerZee literally made—retouching away evidence of poor health and dental care or old, well-worn clothes—posed a challenge to popular cultural myths about African Americans. We need only remember that the bulk of his photographs were created during an era when the overwhelming majority of postcards, greeting cards, comic strips, and other popular cultural artifacts made with images of African Americans consisted of crude, degrading racial caricatures. In the face of this barrage of images, VanDerZee was tireless in devising ways to use composition, image manipulation, props, and staged studio setups to establish a space in which his subjects could expand spiritually, emotionally, and symbolically.

VanDerZee had a deft feeling for the power of everyday objects as symbols in popular culture. He occasionally created humorous photographs that used them to poke fun at stereotypical domestic situations—sitcoms before their time. An example is *Just Before the Battle,* with its irons, bottles, china, and a rolling pin, all of which constituted a wife's ammunition in the unceasing war of the sexes. A more serious use of such icons can be found among his enormously powerful images of African American soldiers, from returning World War I veterans to servicemen in World War II, that position African American men firmly in the forefront of the struggle for democratic ideals. In one studio portrait made in about 1923, a young man in uniform sits cross-legged, gazing down at a small dog at his feet. Standing on the floor next to him is an American flag. Through the use of simple props, VanDerZee suggests how important the patriotic notions of home, country, and family were to this African American soldier.

For VanDerZee, the loving family is central to the life of the African American community, and he never tired of exploring it as a subject, from his earliest photographs of his family, through his countless wedding portraits, to his poignant and moving photographs of parents holding their dead children. In his strangely beautiful mortuary photographs, VanDerZee not only used familiar biblical figures as simple symbols of comfort and eternal life, but he even made symbolic use of portraits of the dead when they were still alive, to express their continuing presence in the lives of their loved ones. In the 1926 photograph of the funeral of Blanche Powell, the daughter of Adam Clayton Powell, Sr., a smiling image of the deceased girl hovers above the congregation of the Abyssinian Baptist Church in a manner that suggests that the spirit lives on after the body is broken. We know of no one else who photographed the rites of the dead so imaginatively, although postmortem photography has been widely practiced throughout American history. Such photographs must have had a special resonance in a Harlem where Victorian spiritual sentiment still found many eager adherents.

The main technique VanDerZee used in his mortuary photographs was photomontage, which involved using more than one negative to make a single photograph. The practice—called "combination printing"—was already established in art photography of the late nineteenth century. VanDerZee, as we have seen, always claimed to have had no exposure to mainstream art photography, but by World War I, photomontage was being used in the mass media, particularly in movies and advertising, and he would certainly have been aware of the convention of using ghostly images of loved ones in photographs to evoke spirits of the dead communicating with the living. His explanation of why he used the convention was characteristically expressive of his need to push the medium beyond the limitations inherent in straight photography: "I guess it was just a matter of not being satisfied with what the camera was doing. I wanted to make the camera take what I thought should be there, too." A 1927 mortuary portrait of singer and comedienne Florence Mills reveals his working methods and his sense of photographic construction: in a work print, Mills's portrait is first placed in the upper right of the photograph above her coffin; in the final version of the photograph, Mills looks through the window of the chapel at her own corpse, in a way that suggests both the liberation of the soul and the contemplation of mortality.

The foregoing examples show VanDerZee manipulating symbols to establish a set of associations or ideas in the viewer's mind and to get at some essential truth about his subject. For VanDerZee, who had considerable early training in art and music, studio photography seems to have been a form of theater; an opportunity to "tell a story" with deliberately fictionalized elements. This led him to the exploration of startling and slightly surrealistic avenues that only opened up for mainstream "art photographers" in the 1980s. In one 1925 photograph, a father and son bundled up in winter clothes are posed in front of a backdrop painted with a snowy landscape, a rather unusual choice of setting given that most photographers using a backdrop of an outdoor scene would probably opt for something a little less ordinary and more exotic. More curious still is the well-known nude study—made for one of the calendars that VanDerZee published over the years—showing a young woman looking pensively into a fireplace, the very picture of a domesticized sensuality. That her skin glows in the warm light of the fire is a tribute to VanDerZee's subtle control of studio lighting, for the fireplace with its cheery blaze is nothing more than a backdrop—visible in the photograph *Future Expectations* as well—painted by VanDerZee and Eddie Elcha, a fellow Harlem photographer. The convention of using painted backdrops was a staple of turn-of-the-century portrait-studio pho-

tography, but we would have to look far and wide for a photographer who pushed it so far as to have a model warming herself before a picture of a fire. . . .

VanDerZee's photographs are about the connection between self and family and self and community. James Baldwin, writing about the residents of Harlem in his memoir *Nobody Knows My Name,* suggested that "They struggle to instill in their children some sense of dignity which will help the child to survive. This means, of course, that they must struggle, solidly, incessantly to keep this sense alive in themselves." The fruits of this struggle are missing from most documentary imagery of African American life in the 1930s and 1940s; they can be found, for obvious reasons, in the photographs of the civil rights movement.

Because VanDerZee's work was largely absent from public view for several decades, it was not known to the generations of photographers that came of age after the 1940s, for whom it might have made a difference. His secure, middle-class upbringing gave him an invaluable perspective on African American life and culture, enabling him to make photographs that were removed from what came to be, by the depression, the predominant and accepted way of depicting the African American experience in photographs. What has always distinguished the middle classes is a strong, autonomous sense of self, and this VanDerZee both had for himself and was able to recognize in his subjects.

Nor was the photographic establishment particularly sympathetic to VanDerZee's aesthetic approach to the medium of photography, nurtured as it was by his artistic temperament and early training in art and music, when the work was first presented to a wide public in the 1970s. Today, however, that establishment has arrived at a view of photography that is far more inclusive of different modes of expression, and many of the techniques that VanDerZee used—the *mise-en-scène,* photomontage, the manipulation of the image through retouching—have gained wide acceptance.

VanDerZee's photographs can be considered the foundation for much of the subjective and self-referential work currently being produced by African American photographers like Dawoud Bey, Jeffrey Scales, Roland Freeman, Roland Charles, and Coreen Simpson, to name a few. The spiritual link between VanDerZee and contemporary artists has at its core the creation of a revision-

# ON THE SUBJECT OF...

### James VanDerZee

James VanDerZee (June 29, 1886-May 15, 1983) was born in Lenox, Massachusetts, where he grew up and attended public schools. In 1900, he won a small camera for selling packets of sachet powder. Shortly afterward he purchased a larger camera and began photographing family members, friends, and residents in Lenox. In 1908, he moved to Phoebus, Virginia. While there, VanDerZee continued photographing and made some of his most notable early images: photographs of the faculty and students of the Whittier School, a preparatory academy for Hampton Institute. Later that same year, VanDerZee and his family returned to New York. For a brief period he commuted to Newark, New Jersey, where he operated the camera in a department-store portrait studio. Following some personal setbacks, VanDerZee opened his first photography portrait studio in 1916 in Harlem. The studio became one of Harlem's most prominent photographic operations. He specialized in portraits and wedding photographs but also took on assignments away from the studio. Among these assignments was his work for Marcus Garvey in 1924. It was also during these years that VanDerZee began his experimental photomontage assemblages.

VanDerZee purchased the building he had been renting at 272 Lenox Avenue. However, a decline in business began and several financial setbacks led to a prolonged period of hardship for the photographer and his family, and by 1969 they had been evicted from their building. Ironically, VanDerZee's greatest fame and success as a photographer were yet to come. VanDerZee's fame grew when, in 1969, Reginald McGhee and other young black photographers formed the James VanDerZee Institute, which showed his work in the United States and abroad. By 1976, VanDerZee had become a symbol of artistry and courage to the Harlem community.

ist history of the African American experience that emphasizes family, community, and per-

sonal identity. In James VanDerZee's photographs the elusive and essential nature of the selfhood of African Americans is defined and contained.

## *LEGENDS ONLINE* (ESSAY DATE 2001)

**SOURCE:** http://www.pdnonline.com/legends/parks/intro_set.shtml. "Gordon Parks: 'Photography Is My Choice of Weapons.'" Retrieved May 31, 2002.

*The following anonymous essay provides a brief overview of the life and career of Parks, an important Harlem Renaissance figure, who continues to produce films, books, and photographs today.*

Don't call Gordon Parks a Renaissance Man to his face. This incredibly talented American icon who's also a composer, poet, novelist, film director, and extraordinary documentary and fashion photographer, laughs at the comparison. "I haven't even learned how to spell Renaissance yet," he modestly jokes as he sits in his Manhattan apartment overlooking the East River. "There's really no genius attached to what I've done in my life," he further explains with more seriousness. All I've really done is try to survive, more than anything else. Studying my favorite writers, my favorite composers, whether it be Rachmaninoff or Duke Ellington, and whether it's Satie or Debussy . . . I never closed myself off from any possibility."

To paint a picture of the artist, then, one must use broad strokes and not forget to mention Parks's parents', and particularly his mother's influence on the course of his life. Born on November 30, 1912, in Fort Scott, Kansas, Parks was the youngest of 15 children, all of whom grew up in extreme poverty. He says his mother wanted him taken out of Kansas right after she died (when Parks was 15), away from the racism and bigotry that he experienced as a child. "I realized early on," says Parks, "that my father and his little farm would never be able to give me the inspiration I needed for the bigger world out there. I welcomed the move to my sister's home in St. Paul, Minnesota." That move took Parks to an integrated high school where black and white kids took classes together, something unheard of back in Fort Scott. Nevertheless, racism eventually reared its ugly head. Parks can still recall a white teacher, Miss McClintock, advising the black students not to go to college and spend their families' money because they were going to "all wind up as porters and maids regardless of their education." "She actually told us this," Parks exclaims. "Her statement killed some kids, and some kids, it jolted them into action. She said 'Just finish high school, you'll be all right.' She wasn't an evil person, she really believed what she was saying. So when I recently got my 45th doctorate at Princeton University, I wished Miss McClintock was there so I could hand it to her. Because I didn't finish high school," he laughs.

At 16, Parks found himself homeless and did everything he could do to make money, from waiting tables to playing piano in a brothel to mopping floors. As Parks tells it, his first foray into photography came after he found a magazine left behind by a passenger on a train. A portfolio inside the magazine, documenting the terrible living conditions of migrant workers inspired Parks to buy his first camera, a Voightlander Brilliant, at a pawnshop in Seattle. "I bought what was to become my weapon against poverty and racism," he says.

And what a weapon it became. In 1941 Parks became the first photographer to receive a fellowship from the Julius Rosenwald Foundation and chose to work with Roy Stryker at the photography section of the Farm Security Administration (FSA), a government agency set up to call attention to the plight of the needy during the Depression. It was at the FSA in Washington, D.C., where Parks took his first professional photograph and signature image: "American Gothic." Recalls Parks: "It happened in one of the government's most sacred strongholds. I set up my camera for my first professional photograph and asked Ella [Watson] to stand before the American flag hanging from floor to ceiling, placed the mop in her one hand, a broom in the other, then instructed her to look into the lens."

From that point on, Parks was destined to do great things and take great photographs. He worked tirelessly and single-mindedly, and from the Forties through the Seventies he covered the major themes of each decade for *Life* magazine: social injustice, overwhelming poverty in the U.S. as well as in Brazil and Portugal, gang violence, the civil rights movement, and segregation in the Deep South. Though Parks's awareness of race, racism and hatred is a constant thread found through much of his work, this theme was juxtaposed early on with his expanding talent as a fashion photographer for *Vogue,* where he covered the Paris shows for several years. "The camera is not meant to just show misery," Parks says. "You can show beauty with it; you can do a lot of things. You can show things you like about the universe, things you hate about the universe. It's capable of doing both." And so was Parks.

## ON THE SUBJECT OF...

**GORDON PARKS ON SUCCESS**
Success can be wracking and reproachful, to you and those close to you. It can entangle you with legends that are consuming and all but impossible to live up to.

**SOURCE:** Gordon Parks, excerpt from his autobiography *Voices in the Mirror,* Doubleday, 1990.

In portraiture he captured several of the leading figures of the day: boxing champ Muhammad Ali, writer Langston Hughes, jazz great Duke Ellington, actress Ingrid Bergman. . . . Never one to pigeonhole himself into one concentration, Parks eventually expanded into film and became a pioneer African-American film director. His first film, *The Learning Tree,* was based on his autobiographical novel of the same name and focused on his childhood in Kansas. In 1971 he directed the "blaxploitation" movie *Shaft,* which Parks says was an attempt to give black people a positive role model. In this case it came in the form of a strong, studly "black private dick," the likes of whom audiences had never encountered before. (Parks recently made a cameo appearance in director John Singleton's modern-day remake of the movie.)

In addition to venturing into the motion picture industry, Parks has delved into the written word, writing over 14 books, including *Arias in Silence* and *Glimpses Toward Infinity,* his most recent books on color photographs and poetry. *A Star For Noon,* coming out in September from Bulfinch Press, is Parks's book of nudes and will be accompanied by a CD of his own musical compositions. "After working so hard at showing the desolation and the poverty, I have a right to show something beautiful as well," Parks explains. "It's all there, and you've done only half the job if you don't do that." Gordon Parks certainly need not worry about only doing half the job.

## FURTHER READING

### Bibliography

Igoe, Lynn Moody and James Igoe. *250 Years of Afro-American Art: An Annotated Bibliography*. New York: R. R. Bowker, 1987, 1291 p.

Comprehensive bibliography of more than 25,000 citations on the art history, work, and artists, with entries on prominent Harlem Renaissance figures.

## Criticism

Brawley, Benjamin. "Meta Warrick Fuller." In *The Negro in Literature and Art in the United States*, pp. 149-61. New York: Duffield and Company, 1930.

Discusses Fuller's life and work; views her sculpture as belonging in two categories—the romantic and the social.

Butcher, Margaret Just. "The Negro as Artist in American Art." In *The Negro in American Culture*, pp. 207-40. New York: Alfred A. Knopf, 1964.

Study based on materials left by Alain Locke; traces in historical sequence the folk and formal contributions of African Americans to American art.

Fine, Elsa Honig. *The Afro-American Artist: A Search for Identity*. New York: Holt, Rinehart, and Winston, 1973, 310 p.

Chronologically arranged work, focusing on African American artists' search for identity; views the Harlem Renaissance artists as interpreters of life.

Galassi, Peter. "Introduction." In *Roy DeCarava: A Retrospective*, pp. 11–39. New York: Museum of Modern Art, 1996.

Originally written as an introduction to a book of photographs accompanying an exhibition of DeCarava's work; Galassi provides biographical and critical information about DeCarava's life and career.

Hedgepeth, Chester. *Twentieth-Century African-American Writers and Artists*. Chicago: American Library Association, 1991, 336 p.

Profiles of 250 African American artists, including Aaron Douglas, Richmond Barthé, Augusta Savage, and Henry Tanner.

Huggins, Nathan Irvin. "Art: The Black Identity." In *Harlem Renaissance*. Oxford: Oxford University Press, 1971, 343 p.

Discusses the attempt by writers and visual artists to forge a uniquely Black identity, which prompted their interest in primitivism and African themes.

Johnson, Eloise. *Rediscovering the Harlem Renaissance: The Politics of Exclusion*. New York: Garland Publishing, Inc., 1997, 169 p.

Uses postmodern theories to understand the movement and to ask why Black artists are left out of mainstream histories.

Kirschke, Amy Helene. "The Depression Murals of Aaron Douglas: Radical Politics and African-American Art." In *International Review of African American Art* 4 (1995): 18-29.

Explores the art and experiences of Douglas to argue against the view held by some critics that the Harlem Renaissance was an inauthentic movement that relied on white patronage.

———. *Aaron Douglas: Art, Race, and the Harlem Renaissance*. New York: Pantheon Books, 1995, 172 p.

Comprehensive study of Douglas's life and work, touching on his early years in Topeka, his move to New York City, his experience with patronage, his intellectualism, his style, and his racial consciousness.

Porter, James. *Modern Negro Art*. Washington, D.C.: Howard University Press, 1992, 276 p.

Overview of African American art, originally published in 1943, with a chapter covering the period of the Harlem Renaissance.

Powell, Richard J. *Homecoming: The Art and Life of William H. Johnson*. New York: National Museum of American Art and Rizzoli, 1993, 255 p.

Study that focuses on Johnson's work, which is reproduced; includes two chapters relating to Johnson's experiences during the period of the Harlem Renaissance.

———. *Rhapsodies in Black: Art of the Harlem Renaissance*. London: Hayward Gallery Institute of International Visual Arts and the University of California Press, 1997, 182 p.

Views the Harlem Renaissance as an extended cultural moment that cut across geographic boundaries within the United States and the Black diaspora; includes discussions of and works by Black and white artists who worked in New York and elsewhere.

VanDerZee, James, with Candice Van Ellison. "Interview with James VanDerZee." In *The World of James VanDerZee: A Visual Record of Black Americans*, compiled and with an introduction by Reginald McGhee. New York: Grove Press, 1969.

Interview in which VanDerZee reflects on his early life, his beginnings as a photographer, and his years in Harlem.

Washington, Johnny. "African Arts and Culture." In *Alain Locke and Philosophy: A Quest for Cultural Pluralism*. Westport, Conn.: Greenwood Press, 1986, 242 p.

Washington examines the philosopher and critic Locke's view of the cultural similarities and differences between Africans, African Americans, and Europeans before discussing his views on African art.

Yearwood, Gladstone L. "Expressive Traditions in Afro-American Visual Arts." In *Expressively Black: The Cultural Basis of Ethic Identity*, edited by Geneva Gray and Willie L. Baber. New York: Praeger: 1987, 372 p.

Discusses the social realist, modernist, and social protest movements in Black art; touches on various artists of the Harlem Renaissance.

# INDEXES

## The main reference

Hughes, (James) Langston (1902-1967) **1:** 24, 82, 87, 91–92, 94, 124, 176, 191, 215, 253, 257, 279, 281–282, 284–285, 288, 307, 321–325, 348–363, 438–443, 442–443; **2:** 69, 171, 373, 413, **595–646,** 652; **3:** 5, 39, 144, 199, 281, 282, 290, 296, 299, 315, 347–348, 390–391, 413, 482, 593–594

*lists the featured author's entry in either volume 2 or 3 of* Harlem Renaissance; *it also lists commentary on the featured author in other author entries and in volume 1, which includes topics associated with the Harlem Renaissance. Page references to substantial discussions of the author appear in boldface.*

## The cross-references

*See also* AAYA 12; AFAW 1, 2; AMWR 1; AMWS 1; BLC 2; BW 1, 3; CA 1-4R; 25-28R; CANR 1, 34, 82; CDALB 1929-1941; CLC 1, 5, 10, 15, 35, 44, 108; CLR 17; DA; DA3; DAB; DAC; DAM DRAM, MST, MULT, POET; DC 3; DLB 4, 7, 48, 51, 86, 228; EXPP; EXPS; JRDA; LAIT 3; MAICYA 1, 2; MTCW 1, 2; PAB; PC 1; PFS 1, 3, 6, 10; RGAL 4; RGSF 2; SATA 4, 33; SSC 6; SSFS 4, 7; WCH; WLC; WP; YAW

*list entries on the author in the following Gale biographical and literary sources:*

*AAL:* Asian American Literature

*AAYA:* Authors & Artists for Young Adults

*AFAW:* African American Writers

*AFW:* African Writers

*AITN:* Authors in the News

*AMW:* American Writers

*AMWR:* American Writers Retrospective Supplement

*AMWS:* American Writers Supplement

*ANW:* American Nature Writers

*AW:* Ancient Writers

*BEST:* Bestsellers (quarterly, citations appear as Year: Issue number)

*BLC:* Black Literature Criticism

*BLCS:* Black Literature Criticism Supplement

*BPFB:* Beacham's Encyclopedia of Popular Fiction: Biography and Resources

*BRW:* British Writers

*BRWS:* British Writers Supplement

*BW:* Black Writers

*BYA:* Beacham's Guide to Literature for Young Adults

*CA:* Contemporary Authors

*CAAS:* Contemporary Authors Autobiography Series

*CABS:* Contemporary Authors Bibliographical Series

*CAD:* Contemporary American Dramatists

*CANR:* Contemporary Authors New Revision Series

*CAP:* Contemporary Authors Permanent Series

*CBD:* Contemporary British Dramatists

*CCA:* Contemporary Canadian Authors

*CD:* Contemporary Dramatists

*CDALB:* Concise Dictionary of American Literary Biography

*CDALBS:* Concise Dictionary of American Literary Biography Supplement

*CDBLB:* Concise Dictionary of British Literary Biography

*CLC:* Contemporary Literary Criticism

*CLR:* Children's Literature Review

*CMLC:* Classical and Medieval Literature Criticism

*CMW:* St. James Guide to Crime & Mystery Writers

*CN:* Contemporary Novelists

*CP:* Contemporary Poets

*CPW:* Contemporary Popular Writers

*CSW:* Contemporary Southern Writers

*CWD:* Contemporary Women Dramatists

*CWP:* Contemporary Women Poets

*CWRI:* St. James Guide to Children's Writers

*CWW:* Contemporary World Writers

*DA:* DISCovering Authors

*DA3:* DISCovering Authors 3.0

*DAB:* DISCovering Authors: British Edition

*DAC:* DISCovering Authors: Canadian Edition

*DAM:* DISCovering Authors: Modules

> *DRAM:* Dramatists Module; *MST:* Most-Studied Authors Module;
>
> *MULT:* Multicultural Authors Module; *NOV:* Novelists Module;
>
> *POET:* Poets Module; *POP:* Popular Fiction and Genre Authors Module

*DC:* Drama Criticism

*DFS:* Drama for Students

*DLB:* Dictionary of Literary Biography

*DLBD:* Dictionary of Literary Biography Documentary Series

*DLBY:* Dictionary of Literary Biography Yearbook

*DNFS:* Literature of Developing Nations for Students

*EFS:* Epics for Students

*EXPN:* Exploring Novels

HOW TO USE THE AUTHOR INDEX

246; EXPP; LAIT 2; MTCW 1,
2; NCFS 1; PFS 13; RGAL 4;
SATA 42; WLC

Dunbar-Nelson, Alice (Ruth
Moore) (1875-1935) **2:** 17,
**323–361; 3:** 52, 71
*See also* BW 1, 3; CA 122, 124;
CANR 82; DLB 50; FW; MTCW
1

# F

Fauset, Jessie Redmon (1882-1961)
**1:** 86, 160–161, 257–258,
293–294; **2:** 18–19, 235,
**363–393,** 619
*See also* AFAW 2; BLC 2; BW 1;
CA 109; CANR 83; CLC 19, 54;
DAM MULT; DLB 51; FW;
MAWW

Fisher, Rudolph (John Chauncey)
(1897-1934) **1:** 58, 132, 176,
198–199, 203–204, 207–208, 292;
**2: 395–449; 3:** 587, 592
*See also* BLC 2; BW 1, 3; CA 107;
124; CANR 80; DAM MULT;
DLB 51, 102; SSC 25; TCLC 11

# G

Garvey, Marcus (Moziah, Jr.)
(1887-1940) **1:** 11, 18, 42–43,
106, 107, 140, 159–160, 184,
217–228, 239, 297–298, 337–338,
395, 545–546; **2: 451–505; 3:** 5,
103, 104, 343–344, 521–522, 529
*See also* BLC 2; BW 1; CA 120;
124; CANR 79; DAM MULT;
TCLC 41

Grimké, Angelina Ward
(1880-1958) **2: 507–538**
*See also* BW 1; CA 124; DAM
POET; DLB 50, 54

# H

Heyward, (Edwin) DuBose
(1885-1940) **1:** 257; **2: 539–586**
*See also* CA 108; 157; DLB 7, 9,
45, 249; SATA 21; TCLC 59

Horne, Frank Smith (1899-1974) **2:**
**587–594; 3:** 17
*See also* BW 1; CA 125; CA 53–
56; DLB 51; WP

Hughes, (James) Langston
(1902-1967) **1:** 24, 82, 87, 91–92,
94, 124, 176, 191, 215, 253, 257,
279, 281–282, 284–285, 288, 307,
321–325, 348–363, 438–443,
442–443; **2:** 69, 171, 373, 413,
**595–646,** 652; **3:** 5, 39, 144, 199,
281, 282, 290, 296, 299, 315,
347–348, 390–391, 413, 482,
593–594
*See also* AAYA 12; AFAW 1, 2;
AMWR 1; AMWS 1; BLC 2; BW
1, 3; CA 1-4R; 25-28R; CANR
1, 34, 82; CDALB 1929-1941;
CLC 1, 5, 10, 15, 35, 44, 108;
CLR 17; DA; DA3; DAB; DAC;
DAM DRAM, MST, MULT,
POET; DC 3; DLB 4, 7, 48, 51,
86, 228; EXPP; EXPS; JRDA;
LAIT 3; MAICYA 1, 2; MTCW
1, 2; PAB; PC 1; PFS 1, 3, 6, 10;
RGAL 4; RGSF 2; SATA 4, 33;
SSC 6; SSFS 4, 7; WCH; WLC;
WP; YAW

Hurston, Zora Neale (1891-1960)
**1:** 35–36, 92, 94, 125, 130–133,
220–221, 269–272, 283–284, 292,
317, 325, 442–443, 462–464; **2:**
**647–706; 3:** 58, 77, 78–79, 508
*See also* AAYA 15; AFAW 1, 2;
AMWS 6; BLC 2; BW 1, 3; BYA
12; CA 85-88; CANR 61;
CDALBS; CLC 7, 30, 61; DA;
DA3; DAC; DAM MST, MULT,
NOV; DC 12; DFS 6; DLB 51,
86; EXPN; EXPS; FW; LAIT 3;
MAWW; MTCW 1, 2; NFS 3;
RGAL 4; RGSF 2; SSC 4; SSFS 1,
6, 11; TCLC 121; WLCS; YAW

# I

Isaac, Jane
*See* West, Dorothy

# J

Johnson, Charles Spurgeon
(1893-1956) **1:** 1–2, 70–74, 83,
87–88, 102, 187–188, 190, 192,
318, 320, 330–334, 519, 521; **2:**
467; **3: 1–21**
*See also* BW 1, 3; CA 125; CANR
82; DLB 51, 91

Johnson, Georgia (Blanche)
Douglas (Camp) (1887?-1966 ) **1:**
127, 258; **2:** 333; **3: 23–66,**
71–72, 588
*See also* BW 1; CA 125; DLB 51,
249; WP

Johnson, Helene (1907-1995) **1:**
130; **2:** 19–21, 22–24, 28–32; **3:**
16, **67–84**
*See also* CA 181; DLB 51; WP

Johnson, James Weldon
(1871-1938) **1:** 144, 176–177,
200–201, 273, 277, 279–280, 288,
311, 475, 488–489; **2:** 138, 171,
193, 421, 609; **3:** 3–4, **85–137,**
235, 361–362, 371–372, 377–378,
381–382, 383–384, 488, 503–505,
523
*See also* AFAW 1, 2; BLC 2; BW
1, 3; CA 104; 125; CANR 82;
CDALB 1917-1929; CLR 32;
DA3; DAM MULT, POET; DLB
51; EXPP; MTCW 1, 2; PC 24;
PFS 1; RGAL 4; SATA 31; TCLC
3, 19

# L

Larsen, Nella (1891-1964) **1:** 23,
86–87; **2:** 167–171, 172–177; **3:**
**139–180,** 274, 588
*See also* AFAW 1, 2; BLC 2; BW
1; CA 125; CANR 83; CLC 37;
DAM MULT; DLB 51; FW

Locke, Alain (LeRoy) (1885-1954)
**1:** 5–11, 29, 35, 62–63, 75–76,
78–79, 85, 86, 94–95, 98,
122–123, 126, 162–163, 183–184,
206–207, 227–228, 230, 246–248,
294, 304–306, 305–306, 317, 318,
324, 325–326, 342, 388–392,
461–462, 467, 471–472, 487–488,
490, 492, 496–497, 505–510,
519–520; **2:** 154, 199, 200–203,
231–233, 274, 635–636; **3:** 3, 6–8,
14, 18–19, 35, 36–37, 39, 49,
51–52, 82–83, 143, 144–145,
**181–223,** 284–285, 414,
453–456, 488, 489, 537, 538, 594
*See also* BLCS; BW 1, 3; CA 106;
124; CANR 79; RGAL 4; TCLC
43

Locke, Arthur LeRoy
*See* Locke, Alain

# M

Mandrake, Ethel Belle
*See* Thurman, Wallace

McKay, Claude (1889?-1948) **1:** 16,
23, 43–44, 49, 86, 93, 94,
103–106, 159, 196–197, 215, 222,
280–281, 283, 286–287, 444–455,
477; **2:** 113, 139, 278, 372, 467,
611–612; **3:** 4, 146, **225–278,**
530, 531, 586–587, 594–596
*See also* AFAW 1, 2; AMWS 10;
BLC 3; DAB; DLB 4, 45, 51,

The Title Index alphabetically lists the titles of works written by the authors featured in volumes 2 and 3 of Harlem Renaissance and provides page numbers or page ranges where commentary on these titles can be found. English translations of foreign titles and variations of titles are cross referenced to the title under which a work was originally published. Titles of novels, dramas, nonfiction books, and poetry, short story, or essay collections are printed in italics; individual poems, short stories, and essays are printed in body type within quotation marks.

## A

"African Art: Classic Style" (Locke) **3:** 211

"African Fundamentalism" (Garvey) **2:** 452, 483–484

"After Winter" (Brown) **2:** 161

"Alain Locke's Relationship to the Negro in American Literature" (Braithwaite) **3:** 187–191

*Along This Way* (Johnson, James Weldon) **3:** 118–130, 133–137

"Amateur Night in Harlem" (West) **1:** 344–347

"America" (McKay) **3:** 227–228

"The American Composer" (Van Vechten) **3:** 490

"American Fundamentalism" (Garvey) **2:** 461

"American Literary Tradition and the Negro" (Locke) **1:** 305–306

"Anarchy Alley" (Dunbar-Nelson) **2:** 357–358

"And the Walls Came Tumblin' Down" (Cullen) **3:** 130–133

*And Yet They Paused* (Johnson, Georgia D.) **3:** 63–65

"Any Wife to Any Husband: A Derived Poem" (Spencer) **3:** 369

"Art Lessons from the Congo" (Locke) **3:** 211

"Art or Propaganda?" (Locke) **3:** 183

"As I Grew Older" (Hughes) **2:** 604

"As We Have Sowed" (Grimké) **2:** 513

"At the Carnival" (Spencer) **1:** 128, **3:** 365–366, 368

*The Autobiography of an Ex-Coloured Man* (Johnson, James Weldon) **1:** 277; **2:** 311–313; **3:** 87–91, 101, 111–130

*An Autumn Love Cycle* (Johnson, Georgia D.) **3:** 24, 51–53

## B

"Backslider" (Fisher) **2:** 409

"A Bad, Bad Man" (Brown) **2:** 157–158

"The Ballad of Joe Meek" (Brown) **2:** 191–192

"Ballad of Negro Artists" (Schuyler) **1:** 260

*Banana Bottom* (McKay) **3:** 244, 249–251, 260–261

*Banjo* (McKay) **1:** 43–44, 86, 444–455, **3:** 236–239, 247–249, 258–260

"A Banjo Song" (Johnson, James Weldon) **3:** 93–94

"Baptism" (McKay) **3:** 255

"Beauty Instead of Ashes" (Locke) **1:** 246–248

"Before the Feast at Shushan" (Spencer) **3:** 72, 367–368, 381–382

"Beggar Boy" (Hughes) **2:** 605

"Behold de Rib" (Hurston) **2:** 682

"Beware Lest He Awakes" (Grimké) **2:** 514

*The Big Sea* (Hughes) **3:** 144, 392, 490

*A Bill to be Passed* (Johnson, Georgia D.) **3:** 63–65

"Birth" (Hughes) **2:** 605

*Black and Conservative* (Schuyler) **3:** 332–334, 335–336

"The Black Child" (Grimké) **2:** 512

*The Black Christ and Other Poems* (Cullen) **2:** 224, 246–247

"The Black Christ" (Cullen) **2:** 212–213, 226–227, 230, 245–247

"The Black Finger" (Grimké) **2:** 514

*The Black Flame* (Du Bois) **2:** 294–296

# E

"Early Evening Quarrel" (Hughes) **2:** 628

"Eatonville Anthology" (Hurston) **2:** 656–657

*Ebony and Topaz: A Collectanea* (Johnson, Charles S.) **1:** 102

"The Ebony Flute" (Bennett) **2:** 25

"Editing *The Crisis*" (Du Bois) **1:** 249–252

*Education and the Cultural Crisis* (Johnson, Charles S.) **3:** 10–11

*Eight-Day World* (Toomer) **3:** 429

*Ellen and William Craft* (Johnson, Georgia D.) **3:** 32

"Ellen Fenton" (Dunbar-Nelson) **2:** 343–347

"The Enemies at Work" (Garvey) **2:** 456–458

"Enslaved" (McKay) **3:** 229

"Envoy" (Johnson, James Weldon) **3:** 110–111

*Essentials* (Toomer) **3:** 469

*Exit, An Illusion* (Bonner) **2:** 58

"Ezekiel" (Fisher) **2:** 411

"Ezekiel Learns" (Fisher) **2:** 411

# F

"Failure" (Spencer) **3:** 372–373

"Fantasy" (Bennett) **2:** 22

"Father and Son" (Hughes) **2:** 619–620

*Fields of Wonder* (Hughes) **2:** 605–607

*Fifty Years and Other Poems* (Johnson, James Weldon) **3:** 93–95, 106–108, 110

"Fifty Years" (Johnson, James Weldon) **3:** 108

*Fine Clothes to the Jew* (Hughes) **2:** 616, 636–644, **3:** 593

"Fire Burns" (Thurman) **1:** 263

*The Fire in the Flint* (White) **1:** 83, 274–275, **3:** 605–610

*The Flight of the Natives* (Richardson) **3:** 311–312

*Flight* (White) **3:** 405, 613–617

"Flower of Love" (McKay) **3:** 239

*A Fond Farewell to Carlo* (Schuyler) **3:** 485

"For Jim, Easter Eve" (Spencer) **3:** 72, 379, 383–384

"Forethought" (Du Bois) **2:** 265–266

Foreward to *Caroling Dusk: An Anthology of Verse by Negro Poets* (Cullen) **1:** 295–297

Foreword to *The New Negro* (Locke) **2:** 217

"Forty-five Lines of Actual Poetry in the Magazines of 1906" (Braithwaite) **2:** 135

"Frankie and Johnny" (Brown) **2:** 156–157

*Frederick Douglass* (Johnson, Georgia D.) **3:** 24, 32

"Free" (Johnson, Georgia D.) **3:** 55–56

"Freedom" (Larsen) **3:** 156

"The Friends" (Bonner) **2:** 38

"From the Dark Tower" (Cullen) **2:** 208

*Frye Street & Environs: The Collected Works of Marita Bonner* (Bonner) **2:** 37–43

"Fulfillment" (Johnson, Helene) **2:** 23–24

"Futility" (Johnson, Helene) **3:** 80

# G

"The Garden Seat" (Grimké) **2:** 511

*Gentleman Jigger* (Nugent) **3:** 287–288, 289, 291

"Gesture" (Johnson, Georgia D.) **3:** 56

*Gingertown* (McKay) **3:** 239–240

*Give Us Each Day: The Diary of Alice Dunbar-Nelson* (Dunbar-Nelson) **2:** 328–339

"Go Down Death" (Johnson, James Weldon) **3:** 95, 132

"Go Down Moses" (Johnson, James Weldon) **3:** 96

*God Send Sunday* (Bontemps) **2:** 62, 84–85

*God's Trombones: Seven Negro Sermons in Verse* (Johnson, James Weldon) **1:** 475–478, **3:** 95–97, 108–110, 130–133

"Goldie" (Grimké) **2:** 515, 525–526

"Governing the Ideal State" (Garvey) **2:** 484–485

"A Grave Wrong to the Negro" (Braithwaite) **2:** 115

*Growing Up in the Black Belt* (Johnson, Charles S.) **3:** 10

"Guardian of the Law" (Fisher) **2:** 406, 411

# H

"Harlem: The 'Beautiful' Years" (Bontemps) **2:** 64–67

"Harlem Facets" (Thurman) **3:** 415

"Harlem" (Horne) **2:** 591, 593

"Harlem Literati" (Hughes) **2:** 652, **3:** 390–391

*Harlem Shadows* (McKay) **3:** 222–230

"Harlem Shadows" (McKay) **3:** 229–230, 254–255

"Harvest Song" (Toomer) **3:** 425, 463–464, 466

*Haverstraw* (Horne) **2:** 593–594

"He Was a Man" (Brown) **2:** 188–189

*The Heart of a Woman and Other Poems* (Johnson, Georgia D.) **3:** 24, 26, 49–50, 71–72

"The Heart of a Woman" (Johnson, Georgia D.) **3:** 49–50

"Heritage" (Cullen) **2:** 225–226, 235–236

*Herod the Great* (Hurston) **2:** 652–653

"High Stepper" (Bonner) **2:** 49–51

"High Valley" (Fisher) **2:** 403

"High Yaller" (Fisher) **2:** 409, 422–423, **3:** 592

"Holly Berry and Mistletoe" (Braithwaite) **2:** 108

"*Home to Harlem*: An Insult to the Race" (Garvey) **1:** 11

*Home to Harlem* (McKay) **1:** 11, 105, 215, 217–218, 447–455; **2:** 278, **3:** 234, 245–247, 257–258, 269–270, 274–277, 595

"Hope Deferred" (Dunbar-Nelson) **2:** 324–328

"The Hope of a Negro Drama" (Richardson) **3:** 316–317

*The House of Falling Leaves* (Braithwaite) **2:** 108–109

"How It Feels to be Colored Me" (Hurston) **1:** 130–133; **2:** 656, 679

# I

"I Have a Friend" (Spencer) **3:** 374

"I Sit and Sew" (Dunbar-Nelson) **2:** 346; **3:** 71

*The Idle Head* (Richardson) **3:** 312

"If We Must Die" (McKay) **1:** 49, 159; **2:** 611; **3:** 4, 228, 232, 252, 267–268, 269–270, 271–274

"Impressions of the Second Pan-African Congress" (Fauset) **2:** 369

"In Bondage" (McKay) **3:** 253

*Infants of the Spring* (Thurman) **1:** 26, 328, **3:** 78–79, 191, 283, 298, 404, 406–407, 410–411, 420–421

*Intelligentsia* (Fauset) **1:** 262–263

*The Interne* (Thurman) **3:** 402

SUBJECT INDEX

*The Subject Index includes the authors and titles that appear in the Author Index and the Title Index as well as the names of other authors and figures that are discussed in the* Harlem Renaissance *set. The Subject Index also lists literary terms and topics covered in the criticism. The index provides page numbers or page ranges where subjects are discussed and is fully cross referenced. Page references to significant discussions of authors, titles, or subjects appear in boldface; page references to illustrations appear in italic.*

A

"Aaron Douglas Chats about the Harlem Renaissance" (Douglas and Collins)**1:** 517–521
ABB
  *See* African Blood Brotherhood
Abbott, Craig S. **2:** 123–130
Abyssinian Baptist Church **1:** *101*
Accommodationists **1:** 157–158, 234–238
"The Achievement and Failure of *Nigger Heaven*" (Perkins, M.)**3:** 505–515

Actors and actresses, black **1:** 399
Adams, Brooks **3:** 349
Adelman, Lynn **3:** 97–106
Adler, Felix **3:** 298
Advertising, in black press **1:** 251, 268
Aesthetic, Black
  *See* Black aesthetic
Africa
  in African American drama, **1:** 389
  common race ancestry,**1:** 10, 63, 75; **3:** 253–254
  Du Bois, W.E.B. on, **2:** 318–319
  in early black histories, **1:** 232, 238
  emigration to, **1:** 42–43, 159–160, 184, 222–223, 338; **3:** 5
  folk tradition of, **1:** 63, 209
  in *The New Negro*, **1:** 298
  in poetry of Cullen, Countee, **2:** 211
  portrayal in "A Day in Africa," **2:** 293–294
  portrayal in "Heritage," **2:** 235–236
    *See also* African art; Garvey, Marcus
"African-American Aesthetics and the Short Fiction of Eric Walrond" (Wade)**3:** 536–546
African American art
  *See* Visual arts
"African American Art and the Critical Discourse between World Wars" (Calo)**1:** 494–517

African Americans in literature **1:** 271–272, 305–306; **2:** 118–119
  Heyword, DuBose, **2:** 543–546, 549, 553–572
  O'Neill, Eugene, **1:** 80–81, 343–344, 432–434; **3:** 201
  *Opportunity* contests and, **1:** 330–332
  in plays, **1:** 386
  Torrence, Ridgely,**1:** 364–372
African Americans in movies **1:** 392–414, 419–427
African art
  of Berkeley, Mae, **1:** 11–12
  of Fuller, Meta Warrick, **1:** 473–475
  of Hayden, Palmer, **1:** 479–480
  Johnson, Charles S. on, **3:** 12
  Johnson, Sargent and, **1:** 555
  Locke, Alain on, **1:** 75–76, 467–468, 472, 487–488, 490, 492, 505–507; **3:** 204–205, 211
  Woodruff, Hale on, **1:** 535
"African Art: Classic Style" (Locke)**3:** 211
African Blood Brotherhood (ABB)**1:** 42
"African Fundamentalism" (Garvey)**2:** 452, 483–484
*Afro-American* (newspaper)**1:** 383
Afro-American Realty Company **1:** 181–182
Afrocentric feminism
  *See* Black feminism
*After the Glory* (Savage)**1:** 549
"After Winter" (Brown)**2:** 161

HARLEM RENAISSANCE: A GALE CRITICAL COMPANION, VOL. 1

581

SUBJECT INDEX

contributions of, **3:** 4–5
Du Bois, W.E.B. on, **2:** 238
on *Fire!!,* **1:** 324
forward to *Caroling Dusk,* **1:** 295–297
Harper and, **1:** 276–277, 280
Horne, Frank on, **2:** 589–590
on Johnson, James Weldon, **3:** 130–133
in *Palms* magazine, **1:** 277–278
principal works, **2:** 207, 208
relationship with father, **2:** 221–222
Root, E. Merrill on, **1:** 77–78
standard literary forms and, **1:** 67
as undergraduate, **2:** 214–218
use of Christian imagery, **2:** 225–228
Walrond, Eric and, **3:** 528
on "The Weary Blues," **2:** 633–634
White, Walter and, **3:** 585–586, 596–598
Cultural anthropology **2:** 654–655, 657–660, 679–680
Cultural integration **3:** 8, 17, 18
*vs.* black separatism, **1:** 218
Calverton, V.F. on, **1:** 306–309
Genteel school, **3:** 27, 28
Johnson, Charles S. on, **1:** 73
Johnson, James Weldon on, **1:** 488–489; **3:** 128–130
Locke, Alain on, **1:** 8–9, 206–207, 247–248, 496–497; **3:** 37, 209
McLaren, Joseph on, **1:** 348–353
National Urban League on, **1:** 68–70
in *Plum Bun,* **2:** 377–378, 381–391
in poetry, **1:** 296–297
remapping, **3:** 612–617
Schuyler, George Samuel on, **3:** 333–336, 339–340, 345–356
Talented Tenth and, **1:** 18–21, 160–161
Thurman, Wallace and, **3:** 392–394, 397–398, 409–410, 416–417, 418–420
use of standard literary forms, **1:** 66–67
Van Vechten, Carl on, **1:** 164–165
in visual arts, **1:** 507–510
writing contests and, **3:** 6–7
young Turks and, **3:** 37–39
Cultural pluralism **1:** 34–36, 57–58; **3:** 216–221
black art and, **1:** 494–510
Bonner, Marita and, **2:** 39
Du Bois, W.E.B. on, **1:** 489
movie industry and, **1:** 393, 397–398

"Cultural Relativism" (Locke)**3:** 207
Cunard, Nancy **1:** 286–287
Cuney, Waring **3:** 16
"The Cup-Bearer: William Stanley Braithwaite of Boston" (Clairmonte)**2:** 109–113
Current, Gloster B.**3:** 580–584

# D

"Dad" (Cullen)**2:** 221
*The Daily American* (newspaper)**3:** 98–99
Dance **1:** 141–142, 149, 150–151
Dancer, Earl **1:** 395, 402–403
Daniel, Walter C.**1:** 311–315
*Dark Princess* (Du Bois)**2:** 294–296
"The Dark Tower" (Cullen)**2:** 25, 219
Darwinism **2:** 483–484
Davis, Thadious M. **3:** 143–147
*A Day at the Races* (film)**1:** 399
Day, Billie **1:** 347
"A Day in Africa" (Du Bois)**2:** 293–294
De Armond, Fred **1:** 143–146
"De Little Pickaninny" (Johnson, James Weldon)**3:** 95
*The Deacon's Awakening* (Richardson)**3:** 309–310, 317
Death, in sculpture of Fuller, Meta Warrick **1:** 474–475
"Death of an Old Seaman" (Hughes)**2:** 605
"Dedication" (Walker)**2:** 676–678
*Democracy and Race Friction* (Mecklin)**3:** 350–351
Democracy, multicultural **1:** 57
Department of Labor, role in migration from South **1:** 4–5
Desmond, John **3:** 618–619
Detective fiction
*The Conjure-Man Dies,* **2:** 412, 417–419
"John Archer's Nose," **2:** 419–420
Deutsch, Leonard J.**2:** 406–414
Dewey, John **2:** 301–302
D'Haen, Theo **1:** 153–169
Diagne, Blaise **1:** 250–251
Dialect
Bontemps, Arna and, **2:** 70
Brown, Sterling Allen and, **2:** 163, 169–176, 193, 196
Cullen, Countee on, **1:** 297
Dunbar, Paul Laurence and, **1:** 50–51
Johnson, James Weldon and, **2:** 421; **3:** 93–97, 100, 104–105, 106–107, 109, 131
McKay, Claude and, **3:** 229

Richardson, Willis and, **3:** 318, 325
in *Tropic Death,* **3:** 525
*The Dialect of Modernism* (North)**2:** 170
Diaspora, black
*See* Emigration, to Africa
*The Dictionary Catalog of the Schomburg Collection of Negro Literature and History,* **1:** 119
*Die Nigger Die* (Brown, H.)**3:** 333
"The Dilemma of the Double Audience" (Johnson, James Weldon)**3:** 315
Diop, David **2:** 254
Discrimination
*See* Racial discrimination
Disenfranchisement **1:** 170–171
Disillusionment, after Harlem Renaissance **1:** 28–29
"Disrupted Motherlines: Mothers and Daughters in a Genderized, Sexualized, and Racialized World" (Brown-Guillory)**2:** 535–537
Diversity
*See* Cultural pluralism
"Dixie Flyer Blues" (Smith)**1:** 130, 131
*Dixie Goes Hi-Hat* (film)**1:** 403
*Dixie to Broadway* (Mills)**3:** 591
Dixon, Thomas **1:** 342, 418–419
"Do Negroes Want to be White?" (Schuyler)**3:** 340
Dodson, Owen **3:** 45
Domestic drama **3:** 311, 323
Domestic help **1:** 142
"Dorothy Grumpet" (Heyword)**2:** 551
"Dorothy West (1907-1998)" (Champion)**3:** 554–558
"Dorothy West (1907-1998)" (Yemisijimoh)**3:** 550–554
Double consciousness
in African American art, **1:** 76
Bontemps, Arna and, **2:** 68
in *The Conjure-Man Dies,* **2:** 444–446
Du Bois, W.E.B. on, **1:** 459; **2:** 290–291, 299–308, 315, 316–317, 319, 444–445; **3:** 254, 341–345
Gaines, Kevin on, **2:** 445
in Harlem culture, **1:** 356–359
of Harlem Renaissance modernism, **1:** 430
Locke, Alain on, **1:** 8–11; **3:** 206–215
"'Double-Consciousness': Locating the Self" (Zamir)**2:** 297–311
"A Double Standard" (Harper)**3:** 70
Douglas, Aaron **1:** 94–95, 468, 475–479, *476,* 517–521; **2:** 168, 169

in *Fire!!,* **1:** 208–210
in *The New Negro,* **1:** 209–210
Douglass, Frederick
abolition of slavery,**3:** 4
education and, **1:** 143
political protest and, **1:** 233
*Dove of God* (Hayden)**1:** 479–480
*Down Home* (Bone)**1:** 28–29
Doyle, Don H. **2:** 578–585
"Drab Rambles" (Bonner)**2:** 40
Drama **1: 364–392**
audience and, **3:** 315
black identity in, **3:** 313–323
Bonner, Marita and, **2:** 40–43,
54–59
*Carolina Magazine* and, **1:** 320–
321
children's, **3:** 309, 312, 313
comedy,**3:** 319–320
domestic, **3:** 311, 323
Du Bois, W.E.B. on, **1:** 388–392
intraracial prejudice in, **3:** 287–
288, 322–328
Locke, Alain on, **1:** 342, 388–
392; **3:** 199, 200–203
lynching, **3:** 29–32, 63–66, 64
in *Opportunity,* **1:** 78–82
protest, **2:** 508; **3:** 28–33, 200
purpose of, **3:** 200–203, 310,
322, 324
realism in, **2:** 149
Richardson, Willis and, **3:** 307–
328
scientific racism in, **3:** 53–54,
317, 322–323
underrepresentation of, **3:** 313–
321
Van Vechten, Carl on, **1:** 294
by white playwrights, **1:** 79–81,
364–372, 373–384
*See also* Black theater;
specific types of drama
"A Dream of John Brown"
(Spencer)**3:** 370, 384
"Dream Variations" (Hughes)**2:**
603
"The Dreams of the Dreamer"
(Johnson, Georgia D.)**3:** 50
"Drenched in Light" (Hurston)**2:**
655–656
Driskell, David **1:** 471–484
"Drought" (Walrond)**3:** 525,
540–541
Du Bois, W.E.B.**2:** *259,* **259–321**
on black nationalism, **1:** 67–68;
**2:** 281–288
on black theater and drama, **1:**
388–392
bust of, **1:** 545–546, 552
Calverton, V.F. and, **1:** 305
on changing focus of Harlem
Renaissance, **1:** 22
*Crisis* magazine and, **1:** 192,
249–252, 335–336
on Cullen, Countee, **2:** 238

on double-consciousness, **2:**
290–291, 299–308, 315, 316–
317, 319, 445; **3:** 254, 341–345
Douglas, Aaron on, **1:** 518–519
ethics of, **2:** 266
on *Fire!!, 1:* 324
on Garvey, Marcus, **1:** 220
on *God Sends Sunday,* **2:**84–85
Hegelianism and, **2:** 297–307
on Johnson, Georgia Douglas,
**3:** 26
journalistic biography of, **1:**
335–336
on Larsen, Nella, **3:** 274
on literary contests, **1:** 330–334
Marxism and, **2:** 260, 261, 300–
301, 313–314, 317, 319
on McKay, Claude, **3:** 257, 274
modernism and, **2:** 609
*Negro World* on, **2:** 472–473
on *New Era,* **1:**316–317
on *The New Negro,* **1:**163
New York Public Library and, **1:**
119
on *Nigger Heaven,* **3:**409, 482,
488, 509
*Palms* and, **1:** 319
politics of, **2:** 311–319
principal works, **2:** 260–261,
261–262
on propaganda as art, **2:** 83,
268–269, 270–280; **3:** 19, 38,
414, 522
on racism, **3:** 4
Richardson, Willis and, **3:** 324
on slave spirituals, **1:** 456–459
on *Stylus,* **1:**317
*Survey Graphic* and, **1:** 317–318,
319
on transnationalism, **1:** 45
*vs.* Washington, Booker T., *1:*
157–158, 182, 236–238, 337
on women's suffrage, **2:** 266–
267
*See also* Black identity
Drugs and alcohol, jazz and **1:**
397–398
"DuBose Heyward: Memorialist
and Realist" (Heyward)**2:**
541–546
"DuBose Heyward's 'Lost' Short
Stories" (Heyword)**2:** 549–552
Duke Ellington
*See* Ellington, Edward Kennedy
Dunbar-Nelson, Alice **2:** 17, *323,*
**323–361**
Callis, Arthur and, **2:** 334
diary of, **2:** 328–339
friendships of, **2:** 333
gender identity and, **2:** 333
health of, **2:** 336–337
on Johnson, Georgia Douglas,
**3:** 52
lesbianism of, **2:** 334–335
local color and, **2:** 350–358

Nelson, Robert J. and, **2:** 330,
334
principal works, **2:** 324
Robinson, Fay Jackson and, **2:**
334–335
as social activist, **2:** 330, 335–
336
use of romance, **2:** 342–343
Dunbar, Paul Laurence **1:** 50–51,
52
Dunbar-Nelson, Alice and, **2:**
329–330, 332
Johnson, James Weldon and, **3:**
93–97, 106
portraits of southern blacks, **3:**
4
"Dunbar" (Spencer)**3:** 382
DuPlessis, Rachel **2:** 342
Durham, Frank **2:** 546–552,
574–578
*Dusk of Dawn* (Du Bois)**2:** 280,
313–315
"Dust" (Fisher)**2:** 406, 410
*Dust Tracks on a Road* (Hurston)**2:**
671
Dyer Anti-Lynching Bill **3:** 104,
135, 581

# E

"Early Evening Quarrel"
(Hughes)**2:** 628
Early, Gerald **2:** 218–229
"Early Recognitions: Duke
Ellington and Langston Hughes
in New York: 1920-1930"
(McLaren)**1:** 348–354
Eastman, Max **3:** 265–268
"Eatonville Anthology"
(Hurston)**2:** 656–657
Eatonville, Florida **2:** 648,
654–661, 679–680
*Ebony and Topaz: A Collectanea*
(Johnson, Charles S.)**1:** 102
"The Ebony Flute" (Bennett)**2:** *18,*
25
Economics **1: 139–241**
civil rights and, **1:** 230–234
migration and, **1:** 155, 173–
174, 182
of publishing, **1:** 286
Edankraal **3:** 377, 379
"Editing *The Crisis*" (Du Bois)**1:**
249–252
Editors, mainstream, relationships
with black authors **1:** 279–282
Education
Garvey, Marcus *vs.* Talented
Tenth, **1:** 218–219
industrial *vs.* liberal arts, **1:**
157–158, 182, 232–233, 237

## H

"Harlem Personalities: Cliff Webb and Billie Day" (Byrd)**1:** 347

Harlem Renaissance
background and sources of, **1: 38–56**
beginnings of, **1:** 14–15
Black arts movement and, **3:** 37
decline of, **1:** 193
distorted Harlem views and, **1:** 213–217
emergence of black history,**2:** 67–72
*vs.* Garvey, Marcus, **1:** 217–228
gender issues, **1:** 2; **3:** 46–51, 57, 73
history of, **1:** 180–186, 187–193
Huggins, Nathan Irvin on, **2:** 67
Hughes, Langston on, **3:** 144
Locke, Alain on, **3:** 143, 144–145, 198–200, 203–205
McKay, Claude on, **3:** 146
origins and significance of, **3:** 3–8
overviews and general studies, **1: 1–138**
performing arts in, **1: 341–466**
representative works, **1:** 2–3
social, economic and political factors influencing, **1: 139–241**
Thurman, Wallace on, **3:** 290
visual arts in, **1: 467–564**
White, Walter on, **3:** 146

*Harlem Renaissance* (Huggins)**1:** 28; **2:** 67, 426; **3:** 161–162

*The Harlem Renaissance in Black and White* (Hutchinson)**1:** 33–35, 68–91, 303–309, 360, 429–430

*The Harlem Renaissance Remembered* (Sato)**2:** 368

*The Harlem Renaissance: The One and the Many* (Helbling)**1:** 27–38

"Harlem Rent Parties" (Byrd)**1:** 146–150

"The Harlem School: Jean Toomer" (Bone)**3:** 456–460

*Harlem Shadows* (McKay)**3:** 222–230

"Harlem Shadows" (McKay)**3:** 229–230, 254–255

"The Harlem Swing Club" (Morris)**1:** 150–151

"Harlem: The 'Beautiful' Years" (Bontemps)**2:** 64–67

*Harlem, the Making of a Ghetto* (Osofsky)**3:** 18

"Harlem's Bohemia" (New York Times)**3:** 420–421

Harmon Foundation **1:** 24, 185–186, 468, 471–472
art criticism and, **1:** 498–499
exhibitions of, **1:** 492–493, 498, 503, 555–556
Hayden, Palmer at, **1:** 479–480

Harper, Frances **3:** 70, 148

Harper (publishers)**1:** 275–276, 280

Harrigan, Anthony **2:** 541–546

Harris, Leonard **3:** 216–222

Harris, Trudier **1:** 19

Harris, Violet J.**2:** 74

Harris, William Torrey **2:** 307

Harrison, Richard B.**1:** 540–541

Hartung, Philip T. **1:** 407

"Harvest Song" (Toomer)**3:** 425, 463–464, 466

Haslam, Gerald **3:** 391–394

Hauke, Kathleen A.**3:** 2

*Have We An American Art* (Jewell)**1:** 508

*Haverstraw* (Horne)**2:** 593–594

Hay, Samuel A.**3:** 200–203

Hayden, Palmer **1:** 473, 479–481, 498–499

Hayden, Robert **1:** 297–299

Haynes, George E.**1:** 500–501

"He Was a Man" (Brown)**2:** 188–189

"Healing Songs: Secular Music in the Short Fiction of Rudolph Fisher" (McCluskey)**2:** 421–426

*The Heart of a Woman and Other Poems* (Johnson, Georgia D.)**3:** 24, 26, 49–50, 71–72

"The Heart of a Woman" (Johnson, Georgia D.)**3:** 49–50

Hedgeman, Peyton
See Hayden, Palmer

Hedonism **2:** 691–692

Hegelianism
Dewey, John and, **2:** 301–302
Du Bois, W.E.B. and, **2:** 297–307
Locke, Alain and, **3:** 208
Marx, Karl on, **2:** 307
Royce, Josiah and, **2:** 305
St. Louis Hegelians, **2:** 302–304

*Hegel's Logic* (Harris, W.)**2:** 307

Heglar, Charles J.**3:** 269–271

Helbling, Mark **1:** 27–38; **3:** 488–498

*Hell's Half Acre* (Hill)**3:** 29

Hemenway, Robert E.**2:** 652–661

Henderson, Harry **1:** 484–494
on Barthé, Richmond, **1:** 536–543
on Johnson, Malvin Gray,**1:** 528–529
on Johnson, Sargent, **1:** 553–558
on Motley, Archibald, **1:** 521–528
on Savage, Augusta, **1:** 543–553
on Woodruff, Hale, **1:** 529–536

Henderson, Mae Gwendolyn **3:** 394–404, 412

Henderson, Stephen E.**1:** 32

Henri, Robert **1:** 497

Henry, Oliver Louis **2:** 402–406

*Her* (Spence)**3:** 319

"Heritage" (Cullen)**2:** 225–226, 235–236

Herndon, Angelo **1:** 150–151

*Herod the Great* (Hurston)**2:** 652–653

Heroism
in *The Collected Poems of Sterling A. Brown,* **2:** 198–202
in *The Last Ride of Wild Bill and Eleven Narrative Poems,* **2:** 185–192
male *vs.* female, **2:** 703–704

Herron, Carolivia **2:** 509–515

Herskotvits, Melvin J.**3:** 617–618

Heyward, DuBose **2:** *539,* **539–586**, **3:** 292–293
on blacks in literature, **1:** 257
principal works, **2:** 540–541
short stories, **2:** 549–552

Hicks, Granville **3:** 292

"High Stepper" (Bonner)**2:** 49–51

"High Valley" (Fisher)**2:** 403

"High Yaller" (Fisher)**2:** 409, 422–423; **3:** 592

Hill, Abram **3:** 29

Hill, Adelaide Cromwell **3:** 162

Hill, Robert A.**2:** 475–486

Hirsch, David A. Hedrich **2:** 515–527

Historical romances **1:** 418–419

History, black
See Black history

*History of the Negro Race in America, from 1619 to 1880* (Williams)**1:** 232

Hite, Les **1:** 398

Holiday, Billie **1:** 456

*Holiday* (Frank)**1:** 83

"Holly Berry and Mistletoe" (Braithwaite)**2:** 108

Hollywood, blacks and **1:** 392–414

Hollywood Blue Devils **1:** 397

Holmes, Eugene C.**3:** 184–187

Holstein, Casper **1:** 253–254, 332, 333

Home, Harlem as **1:** 194–201

"Home in Harlem, New York: Lessons from the Harlem Renaissance Writers" (Bremer)**1:** 194–203

*"Home to Harlem:* An Insult to the Race" (Garvey)**1:** 11

*Home to Harlem* (McKay)**1:** 447–455; **3:** 234
class consciousness in, **3:** 245–247, 257–258
Du Bois, W.E.B. on, **2:** 278
Garvey, Marcus on, **1:** 11, 217–218
*Nigger Heaven* and, **1:** 215
publishing history of, **3:** 595
Schomburg, Arthur on, **1:** 105
symbolism and irony in, **3:** 274–277
trope in, **3:** 269–270

SUBJECT INDEX

Politics **1: 139–241**
  early black participation in, **1:** 170–171
  ideologies, **1:** 15–16, 25
  overviews, **1: 153–187**
  transnationalism and, **1:** 40–41
  in *Tropic Death,* **3:** 539–545
    *See also* National Association for the Advancement of Colored People; specific ideologies
"The Politics of Fiction, Anthropology and the Folk: Zora Neale Hurston" (Carby)**1:** 35–36
Popular Front **1:** 506
Populist modernism **1:** 355–363
*Porgy* (Heyward)**2:** 539–540, 543–549, 556–557, 559–566, 570–572, 573–574, 574–576; **3:** 292–294
*Porgy and Bess* **2:** 547, *561,* 566, 574–578
"Porgy Comes Home–At Last!" (Durham)**2:** 574–578
*The Portable Harlem Renaissance Reader* (Lewis)**1:** 12–27
Porter, James **1:** 506–507
"Portrait of Wallace Thurman" (Henderson)**3:** 394–404
Portraiture **1:** 540–541, 563
"A Possible Triad on Black Notes" (Bonner)**2:** 37, 55
Postmortem photographs **1:** 559–560
*The Pot Maker* (Bonner)**2:** 56–57
Potter, Vilma **2:** 239–243
Pragmatism **1:** 35–36
*Prancing Nigger* (Firbank)**1:** 83
"Prayer Meeting" (Hughes)**2:** 638
*The Predicament of Culture: Twentieth-Century Ethnography, Literature, and Art* (Clifford)**1:** 32
Preface to *The Book of American Negro Poetry* (Johnson, James Weldon)**2:** 97
Preface to *The New Negro,* edited by Alain Locke (Hayden)**1:** 297–299
Prejudice
  *See* Racism
"Prescription for the Negro Theater" (Van Vechten)**3:** 491
Price, Richard **1:** 64
Pride
  *See* Black identity
Priebe, Richard **3:** 243–252
*Prima Donna* (Savage)**1:** 551
Primitivism
  African art and, **1:** 75–76
  in black art, **1:** 481–482, 490–492, 501–503
  Bontemps, Arna on, **2:** 83
  Calverton, V.F. on, **1:** 306–309
  in *The Conjure-Man Dies,* **2:** 442–443, 446
  Cullen, Countee and, **2:** 211

  defined, **1:** 491, 501
  in *The Emperor Jones,* **1:** 433–434
  Heyword, DuBose on, **2:** 558–559, 562–563, 568
  Huggins, Nathan Irvin on, **2:** 446
  Hughes, Langston on, **3:** 482
  Hurston, Zora Neale on, **2:** 691–692
  McKay, Claude on, **1:** 444–455; **3:** 255–263
  McLaren, Joseph on, **1:** 350–353
  in *Nigger Heaven,* **3:** 500–501, 510–511
  Savage, Augusta on, **1:** 547
  Van Vechten, Carl and, **3:** 482–483, 495–496
  white patrons and, **1:** 2, 29, 92, 359
"The Problem of Classification in Theory of Value" (Locke)**3:** 203–205
"The Prodigal Son" (Johnson, James Weldon)**3:** 132
Proletarian literature
  *See* Class consciousness; Propaganda
"The Promethean Self and Community in the Philosophy of William James" (McDermott)**1:** 34
"The Promised Land" (Fisher)**2:** 404–405, 409, 423
Promised Land project **2:** 493–494
Propaganda
  as art, **1:** 388–389; **2:** 83–84, 267–269; **3:** 19–20, 183, 201–203, 209–214, 411, 413–415, 522
  Garvey, Marcus and, **1:** 226–227
  Hammond, John on, **1:** 405
  Hughes, Langston and, **1:** 281–282
  Johnson, James Weldon and, **3:** 106–108
  proletarian literature and, **3:** 213–214
    *See also* Du Bois, W. E. B.
"Propaganda in the Theater" (Richardson)**3:** 324
"Propaganda–Or Poetry?" (Locke)**3:** 213
Prosser, Gabriel **2:** 70, 90–92
Protest literature
  abolition, **3:** 69–70
  in *Challenge,* **1:** 312–315
  Johnson, Charles Spurgeon, **3:** 4
  Johnson, Georgia Douglas, **3:** 25, 28–33
  Johnson, James Weldon, **3:** 101–102, 107–108

McKay, Claude, **3:** 4, 226–227, 228–230
  in *New Era,* **1:** 315–316
  New Poetry Movement, **3:** 27
  *Rachel* as, **2:** 508
  Spencer, Anne, **3:** 363, 382
  style *vs.* subject, **1:** 51–52
Provincialism, in black identity **1:** 28
Provisional Republic of Africa, parade of **1:** *232*
Psychology, of African Americans **1:** 8–9
Publishing **1: 243–340**
  mainstream, **1:** 11, 243–244, 268–291, 352–353
  overviews, **1:** 252–268
    *See also* Periodicals
"Purgation" (Bennett)**2:** 21
Purnell, Idella **1:** 277–278, 280; **2:** 239–243
*The Purple Flower* (Bonner)**2:** 40–41, 57–58
"The Purple Flower" (Bonner)**2:** 55

## Q

Quakerism **3:** 444
Quality Serenaders **1:** 397
Quarles, Benjamin **3:** 326
*The Quest of the Silver Fleece* (Du Bois)**2:** 283–284, 294–296
"Questing" (Spencer)**3:** 366, 373
*Quicksand* (Larsen)**1:** 23, 86; **3:** 143–147, 148–153, 155, 156–158, 159–166
"Quicksands of Representation: Rethinking Black Cultural Politics" (Carby)**1:** 35–36

## R

Race consciousness
  *See* Black identity
"Race Consciousness in Countee Cullen's Poetry" (Reimherr)**2:** 208–213
"Race Contacts and Interracial Relations: A Study of the Theory and Practice of Race" (Locke)**3:** 219–220
"The Race Problem: Schuyler's Major Essays" (Peplow)**3:** 336–341
Race purity **2:** 488–489
Race relations
  affect of Harlem Renaissance on, **1:** 374–375

Locke, Alain on, **2:** 635–636
"The Weary Blues" (Hughes)**1:** 253, 254; **2:** 603, 625
"W.E.B. Du Bois and the Theory of a Black Aesthetic" (Turner, D.)**2:** 269–281
"W.E.B. Du Bois as a Man of Literature" (Rampersad)**2:** 288–297
Webb, Cliff **1:** 347
Webb, Lawrence "Speed" **1:** 397
"Wedding Day" (Bennett)**1:** 262; **2:** 5–6
*The Wedding* (West)**3:** 549, 553, 560–571
*Weekly Review* (periodical)**2:** 469
Weil, Dorothy **2:** 93
Wendell, Barrett **3:** 204–205**3:** 204–205 **3:** 206
West, Dorothy **1:** 311–315, 344–347; **3:** *547,* **547–573**
   Johnson, Helene and, **3:** 67, 77, 78–79
   principal works, **3:** 548
   Thompson, Louise and, **3:** 298–299
   Thurman, Wallace and, **3:** 294, 298–300, 399, 415
West Indian Americans
   Césaire, Aimé on, **1:** 32–33
   immigration of, **3:** 520, 527–528, 530–531
   *Opportunity* issue on, **1:** 101–102
   prejudices against, **1:** 223–224; **3:** 519–520
"A Westerner in Search of 'Negro-ness:' Region and Race in the Writing of Arna Bontemps" (Flamming)**2:** 78–89
"The Wharf Rats" (Walrond)**3:** 542
"What Do I Care for Morning?" (Johnson, Helene)**2:** 20–21
"What Is Your Brain Power?" (Johnson, James Weldon)**2:** 119; **3:** 92–93
Wheatley, Phyllis **3:** 69
"When Harlem Was in Vogue: History of the Harlem Renaissance" (Johnson)**1:** 180–188
*When Harlem Was in Vogue* (Lewis)**1:** 29
*When Peoples Meet* (Locke)**3:** 196–197
"When the Bayou Overflows" (Dunbar-Nelson)**2:** 356–357
*When Tricky Sam Shot Father Lamb* (Hayden)**1:** 480
Whipple, Leon **1:** 333
"White Man, What Now?" (Walrond)**3:** 520

"The White Man's Game, His Vanity Fair"
   *See The Tragedy of White Injustice*
"White Man's Solution for the Negro Problem in America" (Garvey)**2:** 459–460
White population
   expectations of, **1:** 214–215
   films on African Americans by,**1:** 432–435
   Harlem nightlife and, **1:** 59–60, 131–132, 191–192
   literature on African Americans by,**1:** 17, 246–247
   *See also* Literary race relations; Patronage and promotion; Race relations
"White Things" (Spencer)**3:** 363, 382
White, Walter **1:** 83; **3:** 405, 575, **575–620**
   on black aestheticism, **3:** 590–591, 597
   on blacks in literature, **1:** 257
   Cullen, Countee and, **3:** 585–586, 596–598
   Fisher, Rudolph and, **3:** 587, 592
   Frissell, A.S. and, **3:** 607–608
   George Doran Company and, **3:** 609
   on Harlem Renaissance, **3:** 146
   Hughes, Langston and, **3:** 593–594
   Johnson, Georgia Douglas and, **3:** 588
   Larsen, Nella and, **3:** 588
   McKay, Claude and, **3:** 586–587, 594–596
   as mentor, **3:** 584–598
   on passing, **3:** 578–579
   principal works, **3:** 576
   Van Vechten, Carl and, **3:** 489–490, 499–500
   on voting, **1:** 326
   white publishers and, **1:** 274–275
Whitman, Walt **2:** 609
"Widow with a Moral Obligation" (Johnson, Helene)**3:** 80–81
"The Wife-Woman" (Spencer)**3:** 369–371
Wiggam, Albert **3:** 350
*William and Ellen Craft* (Johnson, Georgia D.)**3:** 24
"William James and Twentieth Century Ethnic Thought" (Miller)**1:** 34
"William Stanley Beaumont Braithwaite" (Robinson)**2:** 113–123
"William Stanley Braithwaite" (Brawley)**2:** 107–109

Williams, Bettye J.**3:** 147–153
Williams, Dorothy **1:** 118
Williams, George Washington **1:** 232
Willis-Braithwaite, Deborah **1:** 558–562
"Willis Richardson and Eulalie Spence: Dramatic Voices of the Harlem Renaissance" (Giles)**3:** 313–321
"Willis Richardson" (Perry)**3:** 308–313
Wilson, Woodrow **1:** 41–42, 422
"Wind" (Bennett)**2:** 22
*"Winds Can Wake up the Dead": An Eric Walrond Reader* **3:** 518–531
"The Winning Loser" (Heyword)**2:** 550
Wintz, Cary D.**1:** 170–180, 230–241, 272–291; **3:** 509
Wirth, Thomas H.**3:** 280–282, 293
"Wishes" (Johnson, Georgia D.)**1:** 127
"Witness for the Defense" (Dunbar-Nelson)**2:** 357
Woerner, John Gabriel **2:** 305
Wolseley, Roland E.**1:** 335–339
"Woman" (Johnson, Georgia D.)**3:** 45–46
*A Woman's Mourning Song* (hooks)**1:** 456
Women
   as autobiographers, **2:** 329
   blues music and, **1:** 437–443
   in *Cane,* **3:** 457–458, 471
   in *Fine Clothes to the Jew,* **2:** 641–642
   of Harlem Renaissance, **1: 121–137**
   in the Peace Mission movement, **2:** 488, 491–495
   in the UNIA, **2:** 488–491, 495
Women's suffrage **2:** 266–267; **3:** 309–310
Wood, Clement **1:** 83; **2:** 234
Woodruff, Hale **1:** 529–536
Woodson, Carter **1:** 106–107
Woodson, Jon **2:** 426–438
Woodward, C. Vann **1:** 64
Workers' Party of America
   *See* Communist Party of the U.S.A.
Working class **1:** 314–315; **3:** 103–104
   *See also* Class consciousness
*Workings of the Spirit: The Poetics of Afro-American Women's Writing* (Baker)**2:** 16–17
Works Progress Administration (WPA)**1:** 27
   Johnson, Sargent and, **1:** 556–557
   libraries and, **1:** 117